ENCYCLOPEDIA OF WORLD RELIGIONS

ENCYCLOPEDIA OF
Judaism

Sara E. Karesh and Mitchell M. Hurvitz

J. Gordon Melton, Series Editor

ברכה וברכה

Rabbi Mitch

Checkmark Books
An imprint of Infobase Publishing

Encyclopedia of Judaism

Checkmark Books
An imprint of Infobase Publishing
132 West 31st Street
New York NY 10001

ISBN-10: 0-8160-7337-6
ISBN-13: 978-0-8160-7337-5

Library of Congress Cataloging-in-Publication Data
Karesh, Sara E.
  Encyclopedia of Judaism / Sara E. Karesh and Mitchell M. Hurvitz.
    p. cm. — (Encyclopedia of world religions)
  Includes bibliographical references and index.
  ISBN 0-8160-5457-6 (hc)—ISBN 0-8160-7337-6 (pbk)
  1. Judaism—Encyclopedias. I. Hurvitz, Mitchell M. II. Title. III. Series.
  BM50.K37 2005
  296′.03—dc22   2004026537

Checkmark Books are available at special discounts when purchased in bulk quantities for businesses, associations, institutions, or sales promotions. Please call our Special Sales Department in New York at (212) 967-8800 or (800) 322-8755.

You can find Facts On File on the World Wide Web at http://www.factsonfile.com

Text design by Erika Arroyo
Cover design by Joo Young An

Printed in the United States of America

VB Hermitage 10 9 8 7 6 5 4 3 2 1

This book is printed on acid-free paper.

"... WHEREVER YOU GO, I WILL GO ..." RUTH 1:16

FOR DAVID, ROSEANNE, SIMON, NAOMI, EZRA, AND FAITH

WE DEDICATE THIS VOLUME TO YOU,
FOR IF YOU HAD NOT BEEN WITH US ON OUR JOURNEY TO CREATE THIS BOOK,
WE WOULD NOT HAVE HAD THE RESOLVE TO REACH OUR GOAL.

CONTENTS

ABOUT THE EDITOR

Series editor J. Gordon Melton is the director of the Institute for the Study of American Religion in Santa Barbara, California. He holds an M.Div. from the Garrett Theological Seminary and a Ph.D. from Northwestern University. Melton is the author of *American Religions: An Illustrated History, The Encyclopedia of American Religions, Religious Leaders of America,* and several comprehensive works on Islamic culture, African-American religion, cults, and alternative religions. He has written or edited more than three dozen books and anthologies as well as numerous papers and articles for scholarly journals. He is the series editor for Religious Information Systems, which supplies data and information in religious studies and related fields. Melton is a member of the American Academy of Religion, the Society for the Scientific Study of Religion, the American Society of Church History, the Communal Studies Association, and the Society for the Study of Metaphysical Religion.

LIST OF ILLUSTRATIONS

PREFACE

The Encyclopedia of World Religions series has been designed to provide comprehensive coverage of six major global religious traditions—Buddhism, Hinduism, Islam, Judaism, Roman Catholicism, and Protestant Christianity. The volumes have been constructed in an A-to-Z format to provide a handy guide to the major terms, concepts, people, events, and organizations that have, in each case, transformed the religion from its usually modest beginnings to the global force that it has become.

Each of these religions began as the faith of a relatively small group of closely related ethnic peoples. Each has, in the modern world, become a global community, and, with one notable exception, each has transcended its beginning to become an international multiethnic community. Judaism, of course, largely defines itself by its common heritage and ancestry and has an alternative but equally fascinating story. Surviving long after most similar cultures from the ancient past have turned to dust, Judaism has, within the last century, regathered its scattered people into a homeland while simultaneously watching a new diaspora carry Jews into most of the contemporary world's countries.

Each of the major traditions has also, in the modern world, become amazingly diverse. Buddhism, for example, spread from its original home in India across southern Asia and then through Tibet and China to Korea and Japan. Each time it crossed a language barrier, something was lost, but something seemed equally to be gained, and an array of forms of Buddhism emerged. In Japan alone, Buddhism exists in hundreds of different sect groupings. Protestantism, the newest of the six traditions, began with at least four different and competing forms of the religious life and has since splintered into thousands of denominations.

At the beginning of the 19th century, the six religious traditions selected for coverage in this series were largely confined to a relatively small part of the world. Since that time, the world has changed dramatically, with each of the traditions moving from its geographical center to become a global tradition. While the traditional religions of many countries retain the allegiance of a majority of the population, they do so in the presence of the other traditions as growing minorities. Other countries—China being a prominent example—have no religious majority, only a number of minorities that must periodically interface with one another.

The religiously pluralistic world created by the global diffusion of the world's religions has made knowledge of religions, especially religions practiced by one's neighbors, a vital resource in the continuing task of building a good society, a world in which all may live freely and pursue visions of the highest values the cosmos provides.

In creating these encyclopedias, the attempt has been made to be comprehensive if not exhaustive. As space allows, in approximately 800 entries, each author has attempted to define and explain the basic terms used in talking about the religion, make note of definitive events, introduce the most prominent figures, and highlight the major organizations. The coverage is designed to result in both a handy reference tool for the religious scholar/specialist and an understandable work that can be used fruitfully by anyone—a student, an informed lay person, or a reader simply wanting to look up a particular person or idea.

Each volume includes several features. They begin with an essay that introduces the particular tradition and provides a quick overview of its historical development, the major events and trends that have pushed it toward its present state, and the mega-problems that have shaped it in the contemporary world.

A chronology lists the major events that have punctuated the religion's history from its origin to the present. The chronologies differ somewhat in emphasis, given that they treat two very ancient faiths that both originated in prehistoric time, several more recent faiths that emerged during the last few millennia, and the most recent, Protestantism, that has yet to celebrate its 500-year anniversary.

The main body of each encyclopedia is constituted of the approximately 800 entries, arranged alphabetically. These entries include some 200 biographical entries covering religious figures of note in the tradition, with a distinct bias to the 19th and 20th centuries and some emphasis on leaders from different parts of the world. Special attention has been given to highlighting female contributions to the tradition, a factor often overlooked, as religion in all traditions has until recently been largely a male-dominated affair.

Geographical entries cover the development of the movement in those countries and parts of the world where the tradition has come to dominate or form an important minority voice, where it has developed a particularly distinct style (often signaled by doctrinal differences), or where it has a unique cultural or social presence. While religious statistics are amazingly difficult to assemble and evaluate, some attempt has been made to estimate the effect of the tradition on the selected countries.

In some cases, particular events have had a determining effect on the development of the different religious traditions. Entries on events such as the St. Bartholomew's Day Massacre (for Protestantism) or the conversion of King Asoka (for Buddhism) place the spotlight on the factors precipitating the event and the consequences flowing from it.

The various traditions have taken form as communities of believers have organized structures to promote their particular way of belief and practice within the tradition. Each tradition has a different way of organizing and recognizing the distinct groups within it. Buddhism, for example, has organized around national subtraditions. The encyclopedias give coverage to the major groupings within each tradition.

Each tradition has developed a way of encountering and introducing individuals to spiritual reality as well as a vocabulary for it. It has also developed a set of concepts and a language to discuss the spiritual world and humanity's place within it. In each volume, the largest number of entries explore the concepts, the beliefs that flow from them, and the practices that they have engendered. The authors have attempted to explain these key religious concepts in a nontechnical language and to communicate their meaning and logic to a person otherwise unfamiliar with the religion as a whole.

Finally, each volume is thoroughly cross-indexed using small caps to guide the reader to related entries. A bibliography and comprehensive index round out each volume.

—J. Gordon Melton

ACKNOWLEDGMENTS

This volume could not have been completed without the support of many. Our families and friends lived through month after month of hearing about nothing but "the encyclopedia," yet they stood by us through it all. We would especially like to thank Kathryn McClymond, Ellen Posman, Tatyana Leifman, and Noah Hurvitz for contributing to the initial draft of the volume. Their contributions to the breadth of the volume were crucial to its success. We would also like to thank Susan Shapiro, the librarian at the Charles E. Smith Jewish Day School, for her research assistance. Finally, the infinite patience of Claudia Schaab at Facts On File and J. Gordon Melton is much appreciated and made the completion of this project possible.

NOTE ON TRANSLITERATION

The Chicago Manual of Style suggests that authors and editors make distinct decisions about Hebrew transliterations when writing and editing a particular work. While we loosely followed the suggestions articulated in *Chicago,* we often chose to transliterate a term based on its common appearance in other texts. Thus, we have followed the following format: the Hebrew letter *chet* (ח) generally has been represented by the letters *ch* instead of *h* with a dot underneath it. The Hebrew letter *chaf* (כ) generally has been represented by the letters *kh*. Generally when a word ends with the Hebrew letter *hey* (ה), we have used the letter *h* at the end of the word. However, several exceptions to these guidelines occur when a word is commonly recognized with a different transliteration, such as the *H* instead of *Ch* for *Hasidism* and *Rosh Hodesh,* the *ch* instead of *kh* for the word *bracha.* In addition, we used the letters *tz* to represent the Hebrew letter *tzadi* in words such as *tzaddik, tzedakah,* and *tzitzit.*

INTRODUCTION

JUDAISM

Defining the Subject Matter

Encyclopedia of Judaism illustrates the history and civilization of the Jews across the millennia, and presents Judaism as a singular yet multifaceted religion.

The Patriarchs, Matriarchs, and the other Israelites who people the Hebrew Bible, called the Tanakh, are considered to be the ancestors of the Jews, and the biblical Moses is considered the religion's lawgiver. Jews today still identify so strongly with this heritage and history that most of them think of Abraham, Moses, and the rest as practicing Jews. However, Judaism in the modern world falls into the category of rabbinic Judaism, which evolved from biblical religion but is based on the traditions of the ancient rabbis of some 2,000 years ago.

Beginning as a small people following a local sacrificial cult, Jews and Judaism began spreading through the world from the time of the first Exile in 586 B.C.E. The first Diaspora community began to develop institutions and sacred texts that eventually would carry Jewish traditions around the world. Later, the Jewish people built distinct communities in all corners of the globe. As Judaism grew and adapted, these communities borrowed customs and culture from the surrounding non-Jewish societies while maintaining common traditions based on the sacred texts.

Covering the full 3,000 years of Judaism, this volume highlights the excitement, the joy, the innovations, the sorrows, and the pain that have made Judaism a living, vibrant tradition. Using an A to Z format, these entries provide coverage of the individuals, places, events, theologies, ideologies, organizations, movements, and denominations that have contributed to the development of the multifaceted Judaism that exists today.

In constructing this volume, the authors have encountered the ambiguity of terms such as *liberal, progressive, traditional,* and *normative.* The terms *liberal* and *progressive* stand in opposition to the term *traditional,* and denote innovation and change from what tradition claims "has always been." The term *normative* has been defined in its own entry, as has *traditional,* in order to clearly delineate the boundaries of Jewish communities as commonly accepted. In other words, the authors have attempted to explain how world Jewry has defined itself through the inclusion of groups such as Ethiopian Jews and the exclusion of other groups such as Messianic Jews.

The authors have used the notations of C.E., or Common Era, and B.C.E., or Before the Common Era, instead of A.D. and B.C. to indicate dates before and during the present age in an attempt to secularize the Christian calendar.

Sacred Texts, Commentaries, and Codes

Judaism's birth can be traced back approximately 4,000 years to one man's belief in a single God. The events in the life of that man, Abraham, and the lives of the other Patriarchs and Matriarchs and their descendants over some 1,500 years, are found in the Bible. Jews do not refer to their Bible as the Old Testament because they recognize no other testament as their own; there can be no *Old* testament when there is no *New* one. Jews call their Bible the Tanakh, an acronym that stands for *Torah* (the Five Books of Moses), *Nevi'im* (Prophets), and *Ketuvim* (Writings).

According to the Jewish tradition, the Tanakh is the primary source for Jewish belief and practice. The Torah is considered the most holy or sacred set of books within the Hebrew Bible. Traditional dogma asserts that Moses received the Torah from God on Mount Sinai, and that the text we have today is unchanged from then, having been passed down from Moses to the Judges to the biblical prophets and then to the Pharisaic sages, or rabbis. Not only did Moses receive the Written Torah, or Written Law, from God, but he also received the Oral Torah, or Oral Law. Tradition teaches that God provided the Oral Law because the written text is often ambiguous. The Written Torah is preserved in scroll form, and read as part of the regular Jewish liturgical cycle in the synagogue at designated times. The Oral Torah is the commentary on the written text; it was eventually committed to writing, in the form of the Mishnah, the Talmud, and other rabbinic texts.

When seeking a biblical proof text to answer a religious question, the Torah is considered the most authoritative place to look. However, the remainder of the Tanakh is also considered holy. Each of the Torah's five books is equal in authority to the others. The teachings of the various books in Nevi'im, while not as authoritative as those of the Torah, are also equal in weight to each other. The last section of the Tanakh, Ketuvim, is the least authoritative, though still important. A traditional Jew studies the entire Tanakh to develop and maintain a firm grasp on the foundations of Judaism, but Torah study takes priority in allocating a student's biblical study time.

The word *Torah* (Hebrew for "teaching" or "law") is related to the Hebrew word meaning "to shoot." The rabbis explained that God gave the Israelites the Written and Oral Law so that they and their descendants would properly shoot at and hit the divine target. One who goes beyond the intended target is committing an *aveirah,* literally "overshooting" but metaphorically a transgression of the law. The word *Torah,* apart from referring to the five books of Moses, is also commonly used for the entire collective of Jewish laws, traditions, legends, commentaries, and customs.

Around the year 220 C.E., the Oral Torah was written down in the form of the Mishnah. The Mishnah codified many standard Jewish traditions, practices, and ideas. It articulated a complete religious system, which replaced the ancient centralized sacrificial cult and was even considered superior to it. The Mishnah highlighted the key categories of Jewish law and preserved legal opinions and narrative interpretations of the law. It became an authoritative text that in many practical ways became as important to Judaism as the Torah itself. Commentaries and debates among the ancient rabbis concerning the contents of the Mishnah were compiled to create the Gemara. The Mishnah and the Gemara appear together as the Talmud, which was redacted in two versions around the years 400 and 550 C.E. Scholars often refer to the Talmud as the "Sea of the Talmud," so vast and complicated were these records of rabbinic debates and discussions on the Mishnah. In traditional Judaism, all of rabbinic law is considered grounded upon the Torah, but explicated by the Talmud. In most traditional Jewish circles, Talmudic study is emphasized over biblical study.

It is the Talmud that ultimately framed rabbinic Judaism.

There are two primary components to the Talmud, *halakhah* and *aggadah*. *Halakhah* denotes Jewish law. The verb root literally means "pathway." Halakhah implies how one is to walk on God's path. Jewish law is the social contract of the Jewish people. Stamped by the traditional authority of God and the Torah, *halakhah* defines how the Jew is supposed to live, wherever he or she may be. The genius of the Jews is that they created a portable constitution at a time when it was not an easy feat. Though they lacked political sovereignty over a piece of land, they were able to take their law with them wherever they went. With the law always in their midst, they reconstituted their Jewish communities over and over again. While *halakhah* governed the Jews, *aggadah* taught the narratives of the Jewish people. *Aggadah* consisted of ethical teachings and stories, which framed the purpose of Jewish law. *Halakhah* and *aggadah* went hand in hand, one unable to exist without the other. In the modern setting, within all Jewish religious movements, Jewish law, traditions, and customs are always balanced by the narrative or the ethics behind the law itself.

Once the Talmud, both the Mishnah and the Gemara, was in place, rabbis began analyzing and commenting on them. Rashi's 11th-century commentaries on Tanakh and Talmud are the first studied by any young student. They are written in a special "Rashi" script; and a common method of study is to ask, "What was Rashi's problem [with this text]?" Rashi identified the questions that any student of the primary text of the Talmud would have, and he provides his answers, usually derived from standard rabbinic tradition. After Rashi's lifetime, his school continued his studies, producing further commentaries called Tosafot. Several of the Tosafists, writers of Tosafot, were Rashi's grandchildren, and they commented on Rashi and on the Talmud itself. A typical page of Talmud contains the Mishnah and Gemara in the center, with Rashi, Tosafot, and other commentary surrounding it. The Talmud represents the world's first hypertext, as many indicators are used to refer the student to other parts of the Talmud for further edification.

In the 12th century, Maimonides wrote the *Mishneh Torah,* which was the first systematic Jewish code of law based on the Mishnah. In this text, Maimonides articulated his own occasional disagreements with Talmud interpretations, but he consistently stated that the Talmudic teaching was nonetheless binding upon the Jews. In this way, Maimonides demonstrated freedom to interpret while at the same time accepting the rule of well-established Talmudic law. Maimonides' *Mishneh Torah* does not list the references that support his interpretations. This is one reason that it did not become the standard authority. Instead most traditional Jews follow the *Shulchan Arukh,* penned by Joseph Caro in the 16th century, and the *Mapah,* added to the *Shulchan Arukh* by Moses Isserles not long after.

The mystical text called the *Zohar* appeared in the early 14th century and became the key book for the Kabbalists, who ascribed authorship to the ancient sage Rabbi Shimon bar Yochai; scholars believe it was actually composed by the Spanish scholar Moses de León. Kabbalah is still studied in Hasidic, ultra-Orthodox Jewish circles, but Jewish custom requires a strong grounding in all traditional texts before beginning a study of Kabbalah.

The Tanakh, Mishnah, Talmud, and codes represent text and commentaries that are still studied by Jews in the contemporary world. In addition to these texts, compendiums of responsa also exist. While the codes provide general rules and regulations for everyday life, responsa provide specific answers to the problems of real individuals and communities. Since the early Diaspora, Jews have had questions about Judaism; if there was no rabbi around to answer they would write to one of the rabbinic academies or a respected rabbi in another community. The written answers to these Jewish questions form collections of responsa. Some responsa appear in the Talmud, but there are also separate compilations of responsa. Such collections provide insight into the world of historical

Jewish communities. In modern times, the responsa format was used for practical questions when Jews were faced with new situations. Contemporary rabbis, both traditional and liberal, still use this format today to publish answers to questions regarding modern Jewish life and action.

A Historical Perspective

While contemporary Judaism is technically rabbinic Judaism, the religion established by biblical history was not. Judaism as practiced today was developed by the ancient rabbis after the destruction of the second Temple in the year 70 C.E. Thus, much of the Jewish religion as practiced since the first century of the Common Era cannot be explicitly found in the Tanakh.

Three distinct religious traditions are depicted in the Tanakh. First, there is the category of non-Israelite religions, including paganism, idolatry, and polytheism. Second, there is the religion that the biblical prophets wanted the Israelites to practice. Finally, there is the religion that was actually practiced by the Israelites. It is important to note this distinction because the sociological reality is that the Israelites struggled to balance their own distinctive practices with those that their religious leaders demanded that they practice.

Israelite transgression is a repeated topic in the Bible. Moses often reprimanded, coerced, prodded, and pleaded in his efforts to get the Israelites to observe God's law. He was not alone in Israelite history. The Prophets eventually took on the same role, often without success. The Israelites often wandered from the will of God; their subsequent punishments were cited as evidence of their evil ways. The Prophets created the parameters for what would ultimately evolve into rabbinic Judaism.

Over the centuries, Israelite religion evolved. The core was always the same—the belief in one God, or monotheism. Biblical monotheism perceived God as creator, redeemer, lawgiver, and sovereign of the natural world. Biblical monothe-

ism was at its core ethical; in other words, it taught that right and wrong existed and it showed people how to distinguish one from the other. Ethical behavior even impacted the natural world: if the Israelites remained true to ethical monotheism, God promised to reward them with nature's bounty. If they strayed from that path, God promised to keep nature from being productive. This simple biblical theology was very powerful in an agrarian society, and it laid a firm foundation for the later Jewish belief in ethical monotheism.

Judaism underwent multiple periods of theological, ideological, and sociological evolution. After the Israelites settled in Eretz Yisrael, the land of Israel, they were led by the Judges. Periodic upheavals followed and at the conclusion of the time of the Judges, the prophet Samuel emerged to lead the Israelites into a period of stability. According to the Hebrew Bible, the tribes of Israel wanted to be like other nations and asked Samuel to appoint a king over the nation even though God had not done so originally. Samuel resisted, warning of the terrible things a king can do to a people. Yet they insisted, and with God's begrudging permission, Samuel anointed Saul as the first King of Israel in approximately 1020 B.C.E. At first Saul was a successful king and a good religious leader. However, he ultimately disobeyed the will of God, and his descendents did not succeed him as rulers. Instead, he was succeeded by David, also anointed by the prophet Samuel.

David is considered to be the greatest king of Israel. Under his leadership, the Israelites took full control of all the land promised them by God; he captured Jerusalem, which was named the eternal capital of the Israelite nation, and he brought the Ark of the Covenant to Jerusalem. However, David was perceived in the Tanakh as a flawed leader. Despite God's favor he was a sinner. God at times abandoned him, and he suffered the loss of children, several of whom rebelled against him. Because of his sins, David was not permitted to build the Temple, which was meant to be the site of the Israelite sacrificial cult and the place where God's presence was most felt. Upon his death,

David was succeeded by his son Solomon, who led from a position of strength in the early years of his tenure. He reinforced his father's successes and built the Temple. Biblical tradition teaches that King David's influence was the apex of Israelite success. For this reason, messianic motifs in later biblical and rabbinic literature depend on the propagation of David's seed.

The apex of Davidic rule, however, ended halfway through Solomon's reign. He began to sin and tolerate idolatrous activities. His vast construction activities led to a heavy tax and labor burden on the Israelite nation. After Solomon's death, the Israelite kingdom split. The Northern Kingdom called itself Israel and established its own Temple; it consisted of 10 of the original tribes of Israel. Jerusalem remained the capital of the Southern Kingdom of Judea. Ultimately, the Northern Kingdom was conquered by Assyria in the early eighth century B.C.E.; its people were exiled and disappeared from history, except in legends and historical speculations about the Ten Lost Tribes.

Sixty years after the conquest of the Northern Kingdom, Judea went through an intensive series of religious reforms, directed by King Josiah, which expanded on earlier reforms initiated by King Hezekiah. These reforms were the first steps toward rabbinic Judaism. The Bible relates that Josiah rediscovered the fifth book of the Torah, Deuteronomy, which had been lost by the Israelites. Critical scholars maintain that the book was new, and that it signaled a new Israelite theology they call the Deuteronomic school. Its adherents wrote the new book and edited the first four books of the Torah from the standpoint of Deuteronomic theology. The Deuteronomic school introduced a perspective that rejected any anthropomorphism. They discouraged belief in a God with a physical essence. Rather, God was without physical being, but omnipotent, omniscient, and all-good. The Deuteronomic school also strongly emphasized the role of central cultic worship and the preeminence of the Temple and Jerusalem in religious life.

Some 50 years later, in 586 B.C.E., the Babylonians conquered Judea. They destroyed Jerusalem and the Temple, eradicating the Israelite aristocracy and relocating the religious leaders to Babylonia. The need to rebuild the Temple and restore central cultic worship remained paramount for the Israelite religious leadership, but Ezra the Scribe instituted additional religious reforms to guarantee cultural continuity even in the absence of a temple.

Ezra replaced the ancient Hebrew letters of the Torah scroll with the more familiar Aramaic letters to allow widespread access to the sacred text. He instituted regular public Torah readings, so that the entire Torah was read to the people over the course of the year. Ezra's reforms laid the foundation for the future institution of the synagogue; they gradually led to daily worship and study, which eventually replaced the cultic sacrificial worship system. Ezra also implemented a xenophobic agenda, although converts determined to become part of the people of Israel were always welcomed into the community. He urged the Israelites to cast out foreign spouses and not to intermarry. Ezra's xenophobia would also take root in future rabbinic Judaism, which maintained a high degree of tension between the desire to remain separate from the non-Jewish world and the appeal of secular knowledge and the advantages it can bring.

The Babylonian exile was short-lived. The Persians who conquered Babylonia allowed the Israelites, now also referred to as Jews, to return to Judea and rebuild the Temple. Sacrifices resumed, but it is believed that Ezra's worship and study innovations survived intact and continued in parallel with the cultic system. Besides, Temple worship faced many crises over the centuries, most notably under the Hellenistic Syrians, who defiled the Temple and provoked the Maccabee revolt. The successful national-religious revolt and the rededication of the Temple are celebrated in the holiday of Chanukah.

The early rabbis resisted this holiday, as being a secular celebration of a military victory. They also objected to the glorification of the Maccabees, whose descendants were extremely corrupt. Yet the holiday survived, in a classic case of rabbinic acceptance of the desires of the people. The common Jews did not care about the later corruption; they wanted to maintain their nationalistic celebration in an era of oppression, this time by the Romans. The rabbis, according to critical scholarship, invented a religious reason for Chanukah—the miracle of the oil—and transformed the nationalistic holiday into a religious holiday. Even so, Chanukah remains a minor festival and the book of Maccabees was not included in the canon of the Tanakh.

Deep sectarian divisions emerged among the Jews during the first century of the Common Era. The Essenes are now widely known through their theorized role in creating or preserving the Dead Sea Scrolls. They were ascetics who kept themselves apart from other Jews, although periodic social intercourse did take place; they preached an apocalyptic, messianic faith.

Unlike the Essenes, the Pharisees and Sadducees interacted with each other, but as opponents. The two sects competed for the support and fidelity of the Jews. The Sadducees primarily consisted of the old Israelite aristocracy; they were the priests who ran the sacrificial Temple cult. Their interpretations of the Oral Torah, or Oral Law, were often unsympathetic towards the concern of the commoners. The Pharisees primarily represented the common Israelites, though they boasted a few aristocrats among their ranks. Their leaders were the ancient sages and rabbis who ultimately solidified rabbinic Judaism.

Hillel and Shammai were perhaps the most important of the sages at the end of the second Temple era. Each developed his own school of disciples. In almost all cases in rabbinic law, Hillel's teachings are followed over the teachings of Shammai. Shammai is often the more conservative of the two, and least sympathetic to the commoner's plight. It has been speculated that the school of Shammai became the origin for the Sadducean split from the Pharisees.

In the first century of the Common Era, another new sect emerged, the Nazareth cult, which followed the teacher Jesus of Nazareth. According to some scholars, Jesus was a Jew born into the Pharisaic tradition. However, he preached his own more liberal interpretation of the law, emphasizing the Jewish teachings of love and compassion. Most of the early followers of Jesus were Jews, and they were traditionally observant. Jesus apparently raised the ire of some members of the established Pharisaic leadership and most likely was not well liked by the Jewish "establishment." However, his preaching was even more unacceptable to the Roman rulers of Judea, who opposed new religious movements and feared the Jewish tendency toward rebellion. They decided to execute Jesus. While it is historically plausible that some Jewish leaders endorsed this execution, the murder of Jesus was probably seen by most Jews as just one of the many Roman injustices inflicted upon their fellow Jews.

After Jesus's death, his followers claimed that he was resurrected. Under the leadership of Paul, himself a convert from Judaism, and the other apostles, all of them born Jewish, early Christianity evolved. Paul allowed non-Jews to become Christians without obliging them to observe Jewish law, even though Jewish Christians were committed to the observance of Jewish law. Gentile influences quickly came to predominate, and the two religions parted company.

The turning point in the development of rabbinic Judaism was the Roman destruction of the second Temple in the year 70 C.E. The Jews of Judea, at least those who escaped the widespread killing and starvation, lamented this second destruction of their beloved city and the violent suspension of their sacrificial cult. Until the modern period, the destruction of the Temple was the most cataclysmic moment in the history of the Jewish people. Without the Temple, the Sadducees no longer had any claim to authority, and they faded away. The sage Yochanan ben Zakkai, with permission from Rome, set up the outpost of Yavneh to continue to develop Pharisaic, or rabbinic, Judaism.

By the time of the Bar Kokhba revolt in 132 C.E., both rabbinic Judaism and Christianity had evolved in different directions, and the distinction between the two hardened. Many Jewish Christians joined in the Bar Kokhba revolt, but gentile Christians did not. This choice cemented the final separation of Christianity from Judaism. Those Jewish Christians who survived the revolt were reassimilated into Pharisaic Judaism. Two centuries later, Christianity, once also oppressed by Rome, became the official religion of the Roman Empire and the new persecutors of the Jewish people.

After the Bar Kokhba revolt failed, the Roman Empire embarked on a firm plan to destroy any potential Jewish revolt. Having already destroyed the Temple, the Romans purposefully turned Jerusalem into a pagan city. They outlawed many of the practices of Judaism, murdered many of the Jewish sages, and exiled the majority of the Jews from Judea, which they renamed Palestine. The Pharisees represented the surviving Jewish leadership, and their traditions prevailed in the new world order. Under the leadership of Judah the Prince, head of the Sanhedrin, the Oral Torah, as interpreted by the Pharisaic tradition, was committed to writing in 220 C.E. in the Mishnah, to ensure its survival in those terrible times of persecution. These early codifiers of the law were called the *tannaim*.

Over the next several centuries new generations of rabbis, called the *amoraim*, developed vast commentaries on the Mishnah. Two authoritative collections of these commentaries were eventually compiled—one developed in Palestine and was called the Palestinian or Jerusalem Talmud, and the other developed in Babylonia and was called the Babylonian Talmud. Ultimately, the Babylonian Talmud came to be accepted as the most authoritative.

After the completion of the Babylonian Talmud, the Jews were led by rabbinic authorities in Babylon called the *geonim* from the sixth to the 11th centuries. They were accepted by most Jews as the authentic interpreters of Jewish law, although they faced their own rebels. The Karaite

school of Judaism rose to challenge the rabbinic leadership and their interpretation of the Written Law. The Karaites rejected the Talmud, and took a more literal view of biblical teachings. In response to the Karaite rebellion, the following Geonic teaching was clearly articulated: "The Talmud is the final word accepted by the collective of the Jewish people. From the Talmud nothing can be diminished, and nothing can be added." The Karaite movement faded during the medieval period, and Talmudic authority was not rigorously opposed until the rise of Reform Judaism at the end of the 18th century.

After the *geonim*, new rabbinical schools emerged in different countries to build on the Talmudic foundation, and no central authority ever again emerged in the rabbinic world. Before the 16th century, the most notable rabbinic academies were found in France, Germany, Italy, North Africa, and Spain. These included the school of Rashi, the famous 11th-century commentator. Many Jewish texts were written and codified during the Middle Ages, such as the *Mishneh Torah,* the *Zohar,* and the *Shulchan Arukh.*

In 16th-century Safed, Israel, a center for Jewish mysticism, Moses Cordovero and Isaac Luria developed what became the standard system of Kabbalah or Jewish mysticism, known for centuries as the Lurianic Kabbalah. Kabbalah was resisted by many rabbis, some of whom claimed it taught a dualistic notion of God. On the other hand, Kabbalah was studied by many other rabbis, and it remains a strong influence within most Hasidic groups today. The Kabbalah also influenced certain more widely held Jewish notions of God and Torah, and has had a significant influence on the liturgy of the traditional prayer book.

Life for Jews and Jewish communities in the Middle Ages was unpredictable. In most countries of the world, east and west, Jews had few rights. They were not allowed to own land, and they were usually restricted from craft guilds. In some eras, in some lands, such as in Spain and Persia, the Jews attained high degrees of economic prosperity and professional acumen, in such fields as medicine, politics, or commerce, only to see the good times disappear as new rulers restricted their ability to maintain their livelihood and often exiled them from their lands. Many Jews in the Middle Ages practiced moneylending, as this profession was often the only one open to them. Such practices, however, brought antagonism among both the nobility and the peasants, and Jewish communities often suffered great persecution and violence. On a positive note, as the Middle Ages waned, many Jewish communities won high levels of communal autonomy. While the Jews were ill equipped to defend themselves, they often were allowed to run their own internal affairs without interference from the ruler of the land, as long as taxes were paid.

Despite uncertainty, Jewish life continued to develop, and after the 16th century, important rabbinic academies were established in Lithuania, Palestine, and Poland. These schools continued to churn out commentaries to the Tanakh and the Talmud. Over the course of the centuries many false messiahs appeared, offering hope to a people who had little aside from their eternal dream to return to Eretz Yisrael. In the 17th century one such false messiah was Shabbatai Zvi. His conversion to Islam marked one of the greatest disappointments in medieval Jewish history.

In the early 18th century a new Jewish movement called Hasidism emerged to offer hope. Its founder was Rabbi Israel ben Eliezer, known as the Baal Shem Tov. The Hasidic movement taught two primary ideas. The first, that one must become attached to God, was not controversial within the Jewish world. The second, loyalty to a new type of Jewish leader called the *tzaddik* (righteous one) or rebbe, created significant controversy in Jewish life. The rebbe's authority came from his spiritual leadership, not so much from knowledge of rabbinic law and literature. The Hasidim were opposed by the Mitnagdim (opponents). Led by the Vilna Gaon in Lithuania, the Mitnagdim believed that the notion of the rebbe as a conduit to God violated the primary teachings of Judaism; no human beings should need an intermediary between themselves and God. The

Hasidic tendency to glorify the rebbe struck the Mitnagdim as a form of idolatry. The Mitnagdim were also suspicious of leniency in Jewish ritual observance among the Hasidim, who tended to value emotional religiosity over intellectual study of the texts. Yet when the two groups were faced with the challenges of Enlightenment thought and Jewish religious reform, their differences seemed far less significant. The Hasidim became more stringent in their personal observance, and while non-Hasidic Orthodox Jews still dislike the emphasis on the rebbe, tension between the two groups has declined.

The next key transition in the Jewish world came with the Haskalah, the Jewish Enlightenment movement that began late in the 18th century. The maskilim, the enlighteners, first emerged in Berlin. They were led by Moses Mendelssohn, who preached the need to embrace the ideals of Western society and modernity. The maskilim wanted to leave the autonomous Jewish community and became full participants in general society. Many of those who embraced the Enlightenment came to reject traditional Judaism; they were fiercely opposed by both the Hasidim and the Mitnagdim.

After the Napoleonic emancipation of the Jews, many Jews fled the ghettoes to fully embrace the Enlightenment and completely reject their Judaism. The Reform movement emerged in Germany to combat this trend. Led by Abraham Geiger and Samuel Holdheim, Jewish reformers believed it was necessary to reform Judaism to keep it relevant for the modern Jew. Ritual that did not have intrinsic value was eliminated, and ethics became paramount.

These ritual reforms were rejected by the traditionalists, but they did provoke the creation of Neo-Orthodoxy (Modern Orthodoxy) in Germany, originally led by Samson Raphael Hirsch. He maintained that a Jew could live within modern society and still observe the laws of God. The Positive-Historical School also emerged, aiming to provide a middle ground between Reform and Orthodoxy. Led by Zachariah Frankel, this movement taught that traditional Judaism had always been an evolving religion; a critical study of Judaism would demonstrate how organic changes have occurred in the past, and how, by extension, they could still occur.

Frankel's views took root in the United States with the emergence of Conservative Judaism. Reform Judaism also matured in the United States, along with several other movements that first saw the light of day in the new world. These included the 20th-century movements of Reconstructionism and Jewish Renewal. Reconstructionist Judaism was a small movement that began as an outgrowth of Conservative Judaism. The movement has had minimal success in terms of numbers, but its ideas, as taught by Jewish thinker and leader Mordecai Kaplan, significantly impacted American Jewish life.

In the middle and end of the 19th century huge numbers of Jews emigrated from Europe to the United States. The German Jews arrived first in midcentury, recognizing the potential of religious pluralism. More than 2 million eastern European Jews immigrated as the 19th century turned into the 20th, fleeing the violence and poverty of their native lands. The story of Jewish life in America has been far less violent than that of the Jews of Europe, despite surges of anti-semitic activity and sentiment. In the new world, Jewish culture and religion flourished and continue to do so. The three dominant Jewish religious movements of 20th- and early 21st-century America are the Orthodox, Conservative, and Reform Movements.

Zionism, the Jewish nationalistic movement, emerged in the late 19th century. Catalyzed into the modern world by Theodor Herzl, Zionism sought to secure a new Jewish homeland in Palestine. Concerned for the physical safety of Jews in eastern Europe and aware of rising antisemitism in the west, the Zionist Organization worked with Jewish pioneers in Palestine to settle the land. Initially, the concept of Zionism was rejected by most ultra-Orthodox and Reform Jews. The ultra-Orthodox believed that Israel could be re-created only after the messianic era arrived, while Reform preferred to view Judaism as devoid of national identity. Conservative Jewish leaders, and some individuals from within Orthodoxy and Reform, joined mostly secular Jews in participating in the Zionist mission. However, as the horrors of the Holocaust became clear to the world, most mainstream Jews ceased to criticize the Zionist dream.

As the Jewish pioneers struggled to settle in Palestine, the greatest tragedy of modern Jewish history occurred, the rise of the Third Reich and the Holocaust from 1933 to 1945. Six million European Jews, one-third of world Jewry, were exterminated by the German Nazis. This horror was a culmination of centuries of religious, nationalistic, political, and ultimately racial anti-Judaism, or antisemitism. The Holocaust proved to the world that Jews needed a land of their own, and for a brief period, international sympathy led the United Nations to support a partition of Palestine into two states, one for the Jews and the other for the Arabs. The Jews reluctantly accepted the plan; the Arabs rejected it and, after Israel declared its independence, declared war. Israel managed to persevere, and stave off several decades of Arab aggression.

In 1967, waging the pre-emptive Six-Day War, Israel won significant additional territory and reunited Jerusalem. The triumph inspired world Jewry, and for a brief period made Jews feel as though they had gone from being the conquered to the conquerors. This feeling of elation dissipated, as Israel had to face the task of ruling an Arab majority in occupied lands. In 1973, Egypt and Syria launched a surprise military attack on Yom Kippur, the holiest day in the Jewish calendar, and Israel at first suffered terrible losses. Ultimately the Arab attack was repelled, but Jewish pride was severely damaged. Six years later, Egypt accepted a peace treaty in exchange for the return of Egyptian land. In the 1980s Israel invaded Lebanon to remove terrorists who threatened Israel's northern border. The war was the first military maneuver in Israel's history that did not receive the full support of Israel's citizens. In 1993, a peace accord was reached with the Palestinian leadership, which resulted in a peace treaty between Israel and Jordan. Unfortunately, the Palestinian leadership and Israeli leadership have not reached a comprehensive peace agreement, and violence and terrorism continues to haunt Israel.

Jews and Jewish communities continue to develop around the world. The decimation of Jewish life in Europe, however, eradicated hundreds of centers of Jewish life and growth. Today, the United States and Israel maintain the largest and most productive Jewish communities in the world. These two centers provide leadership for all Jews and Jewish communities.

An Encyclopedic Approach

This volume seeks to be comprehensive. However, not everything that exists in Judaism and the history of the Jewish people, nor every person or place, is given space. Choices had to be made. For example, although the important Jewish community of Lithuania does not receive its own entry, the Vilna Gaon, its revered leader, does. In addition, it was decided to include biographical profiles of some Jews who have shown few, if any, ties to the Jewish community. The success of unaffiliated Jews is a double-edged sword, revealing a dangerous degree of assimilation, yet highlighting the freedom of Jews to blend completely into non-Jewish society. Regardless, it is clear that many Jews have impacted the world around them outside the Jewish community itself. As often as possible, the authors discovered links between these secular Jews and the Jewish community.

The authors have made a special effort to include topics that are difficult for the non-Jew to research in libraries. Many of these constitute the vernacular of religious Jews, such as *sheitel* and *shuckling*. Others include common terms that are difficult to discover, such as the word and symbol *chai* and the Lion of Judah. Finally, an effort has been made to include descriptions under the most commonly used phrase, whether it be Hebrew or English.

In the pages that follow, the *Encyclopedia of Judaism*, in approximately 800 entries, presents the world of Judaism from its origins to the present. The entries highlight the significant people, places, institutions, texts, and beliefs that have constituted Judaism since its inception. In an effort to provide context to Jewish life in the arena of religious studies, the authors have included entries such as secularization, modernity, syncretism, sacred time, and sacred space.

Judaism and its people are highly diversified in almost every aspect. While it was not possible to include every important concept, this volume provides numerous points of entry for the student to begin a comprehensive inquiry into the forces that shaped contemporary Judaism.

—Sara E. Karesh and Mitchell M. Hurvitz

CHRONOLOGY

c. 2000–1700 B.C.E.

* The Patriarchs and Matriarchs of the Jewish people—Abraham, Sarah, Isaac, Rebecca, Jacob, Rachel, and Leah—settle in the land of Israel.

c. 1700–1300

* Joseph becomes prime minister of Egypt. After Joseph dies, Israelites become slaves to Pharaoh.

c. 1300–1260

* Exodus from Egypt led by Moses. Israelites receive Torah at Mt. Sinai, followed by 40 years of wandering in the wilderness.

c. 1260

* Conquest of Canaan led by Joshua.

c. 1200–1050

* Period of the Judges.

c. 1050–1020

* Philistines threaten Israelites, seize Ark of the Covenant. Samuel preserves Israelite confederation.

c. 1020

* Saul becomes first Israelite king.

c. 1000

* David succeeds Saul as king.

c. 990

* David conquers Jerusalem and makes city his capital. Ark of the Covenant retrieved.

c. 960

* Solomon succeeds David as king.

c. 950

* Solomon builds first Temple in Jerusalem.

c. 930

* Israelites divide into Northern (Israel) and Southern (Judah) Kingdoms.

722–720

* Northern Kingdom conquered by Assyrians; 10 Israelite tribes lost to history.

715

◆ Judah undergoes Hezekiah's religious reforms.

704

◆ Hezekiah revolts against Assyria despite Isaiah's warnings.

701

◆ Assyrian invasion. Northern Judah devastated.

c. 640

◆ Judah undergoes Josianic religious reforms, religious centralization. Pagan influences uprooted. Deuteronomic editing of the Bible.

604

◆ Judah becomes vassal of Babylon.

601

◆ Judah revolts against Babylon.

597

◆ Israelite rebellion defeated. First exile of Judean leadership to Babylon.

589

◆ Judah revolts against Babylon again, despite Jeremiah's warning.

586

◆ Judah falls, first Temple destroyed.

586–538

◆ Babylonian Exile. Ezra the Scribe implements religious reforms to strengthen community in exile. Exile ends with Cyrus's edict to return to Judah.

515

◆ Second Temple completed under Persian rule.

445

◆ Nehemiah comes to Jerusalem under Persian authority; rebuilds walls and initiates religious reforms to strengthen and unify Israelites.

332

◆ Alexander the Great conquers Judea. Hellenistic rule begins.

323

◆ Alexander dies, Ptolemy takes control of Judea.

c. 200

◆ Antiochus III of Syria seizes Judea.

c. 175

◆ Antiochus IV of Syria tries to Hellenize the Jews.

c. 167–165

◆ Maccabees, or Hasmoneans, lead successful uprising against religious repression and desecration of the Temple.

165

◆ Rededication of the Temple by the Hasmoneans (holiday of Chanukah).

161

◆ Judah Maccabee killed, succeeded by brother Jonathan

152

◆ Jonathan makes himself high priest. Beginning of sectarian period.

140

◆ Jonathan killed and replaced by brother Simon, who also takes title of high priest.

134–104

 * Son of Simon, John Hyrcanus becomes ruler of Judea. Forced conversions of conquered peoples.

104

 * Hasmoneans proclaim themselves kings of Judea.

80

 * Romans oversee Hasmonean rule.

67–63

 * Civil war for throne of Judea.

63

 * Rome supports Hyrcanus, who becomes high priest. Antipater becomes Roman administrator over Judea; Jews lose independence.

40

 * Herod, son of Antipater, recognized by Rome as king of Judea; he refurbishes the Temple.

4 B.C.E.

 * Herod's kingdom divided among three sons.

6 C.E.

 * Rome assumes direct control of Judea.

26–36

 * Pontius Pilate becomes procurator of Judea.

30

 * Jewish preacher Jesus of Nazareth put to death by Romans. After his death some Jews join Gentiles in early Christianity.

66–72

 * Jewish revolt against Romans ends in defeat.

70

 * Jerusalem and second Temple destroyed. Second great exile of the Jews; Yochanan ben Zakkai establishes Sanhedrin in Yavneh.

73

 * Siege of Masada.

115–117

 * Three Jewish revolts against Rome defeated. Increased persecutions of Jews and repression of Judaism.

130–132

 * Hadrianic persecution of Jews.

132–135

 * Bar Kokhba revolt. Many Jewish Christians participate, reassimilated into rabbinic Judaism. After defeat, Christianity distanced from Judaism. Hundreds of thousands of Jews die.

135

 * Jewish sages tortured and executed by Romans. Jerusalem transformed into a pagan city, Aelius Hadrianus.

c. 140

 * Office of Exilarch created in Babylon; significant autonomy won.

195

 * Judah HaNasi extends power of Sanhedrin in Palestine, restores productive relations with Rome, firmly establishes rabbinic dominance within Judaism.

c. 200–220

 * Mishnah compiled by Judah HaNasi.

212

♦ Some Jews granted citizenship rights by Rome.

c. 219

♦ Sura Academy created in Babylon.

259

♦ Pumbeditha Academy created in Babylon.

c. 300

♦ El Vira church council in Spain passes anti-Jewish legislation.

c. 313–315

♦ Church aggression toward Judaism increases under Constantine, setting precedent for entire Christian medieval world.

351

♦ Jewish revolt against Rome in land of Israel. Many Jewish towns decimated as rebellion defeated.

359

♦ Jewish lunar calendar begun, replaces monthly witnesses in deciding dates; still in use today.

360

♦ Roman emperor Julian promises to rebuild Jewish Temple in Jerusalem. Many Jews return to Israel. Julian dies and Temple plans are stopped; Christian aggression returns.

c. 385

♦ Renewed anti-Jewish activity and laws implemented throughout Roman Empire. Forced conversions increase; synagogues burned, Jews expelled.

c. 400

♦ Palestinian Gemara completed.

419–422

♦ Anti-Jewish riots and synagogue destruction in Palestine, led by monk Bar Sauma.

c. 429

♦ Emperor of Rome abolishes post of *nasi* as head of the Jews. Sanhedrin power reduced; Jewish intellectual life in land of Israel greatly curtailed.

450–470

♦ Persecution of Jews in Babylon led by the Sassanids. Position of exilarch abolished for a short period.

513–520

♦ Autonomous Jewish state in Babylon; crushed, Mar Zutra crucified.

520

♦ Resumption of Jewish communal institutions and traditions in Babylon.

c. 550

♦ Babylonian Gemara completed.

576

♦ Forced conversions of Jews in France; those who refuse are exiled.

580

♦ Renewed persecutions against Jews in Babylon. Pumbeditha Academy forced to relocate.

581–582

♦ Frankish (German) persecution of the Jews.

600

♦ Pope Gregory sets official church policy toward Jews: Jews should convert to Christianity, but not by force or violence. Restrictions on Jewish activity permitted, as well as inducements for converts.

613

⬧ Jews of Spain told to convert or be expelled.

614–630

⬧ Persians gain temporary control of Palestine and Jews return to Jerusalem.

622–628

⬧ Muhammad forces Jews to leave Arabia.

628

⬧ Byzantine emperor Heraclius demands all Jews convert to Christianity.

636

⬧ Muslims conquer Palestine; allow Jews to return.

691

⬧ Caliph Abd el-Malik builds Dome of the Rock on site of first and second Temples in Jerusalem.

711

⬧ Muslims conquer Spain. Allow greater freedom for Jews and attract more Jews to the country.

717

⬧ Muslims oppress Jews in Babylon.

c. 765

⬧ Karaite schism from rabbinic Judaism.

c. 780–965

⬧ Conversion to Judaism of Khazar kingdom; remains Jewish until Russian conquest.

c. 800

⬧ Jews move to Rhine area.

808

⬧ Jews admitted to Fez, Morocco.

820–830

⬧ Agobard, bishop of Lyons, attacks Western European Jewry.

839

⬧ Bodo, a high churchman at the court of Frankish emperor Louis, converts to Judaism, which leads to heightened church tensions against Jews.

c. 940

⬧ High Jewish courtiers join Muslim court in Spain.

c. 970

⬧ First Spanish yeshiva created in Córdoba, Spain.

c. 1013

⬧ Start of Jewish golden age in Spain.

c. 1020

⬧ Egyptian Jews persecuted. Many flee to Byzantine Empire or Yemen.

c. 1050

⬧ Birth of the Yiddish language.

1066

⬧ Jews allowed into England.

1070

⬧ School of Rashi takes root in northern France.

c. 1080

◆ Christians expand rule in Spain and outlaw Judaism.

1095–1096

◆ First Crusade. Numerous Jews massacred in Europe.

1099

◆ Crusaders capture Jerusalem, massacre Muslim and Jewish residents.

1144

◆ First recorded blood libel, in Norwich, England.

1147–1149

◆ Second Crusade. Renewed violence targeting Jews.

c. 1150

◆ Rabbenu Tam and Rashbam initiate first rabbinical synod in Ashkenaz (France and Germany).

1163

◆ Jews establish a synagogue in Kai-feng, China.

1165

◆ Shi'ite Muslims force Jews to convert in Yemen.

c. 1175–1250

◆ Hasidei Ashkenaz established; a Jewish movement for inner piety.

1185

◆ Moses Maimonides completes the *Mishneh Torah*.

1187–1192

◆ Muslims reconquer Jerusalem. Jews invited to return.

1190

◆ Jews facing death by angry mobs during Third Crusade take their own lives in York, England.

1211

◆ 300 Western European rabbis answer Saladin's call to return to Jerusalem.

1213

◆ First Jewish community in Switzerland established in Basel.

1215

◆ Fourth church Lateran Council promotes more intense anti-Jewish legislation.

1232

◆ A French rabbi bans Maimonides' *Guide to the Perplexed* (1190).

1236

◆ Pope Frederick II proclaims blood libel to be baseless.

1239

◆ The Christian king of Aragon grants a charter of rights for the Jews.

1240

◆ Paris disputation, followed by burnings of the Talmud.

1250

◆ First blood libel in Spain.

1263

◆ The Barcelona Disputation, Nachmanides vs. Pablo Christiani.

1264

- Polish Jewish community inaugurated with first charter of rights, expanded in 1333.

1288

- Jews expelled from Naples kingdom and southern Italy.

1290

- England expels its Jews.

1291

- Muslims drive crusaders out of the land of Israel.

1298

- Rindfleisch massacres of Jews in Germany.

1305

- Rabbi Shlomo Ben Aderet of Spain bans all Jewish study of philosophy and science for anyone under the age of 25.

1306

- Jews of France expelled.

1348–1349

- "Black Death" plague strikes Europe; Jews accused of poisoning wells.

1349–1360

- Jews expelled from Hungarian communities.

1391–1492

- Inquisition, forced conversions of Jews, and final expulsion of the Jews from Spain.

c. 1475

- First Hebrew printing press, in Italian and Iberian peninsula.

1497

- Expulsion of Jews from Portugal.

c. 1500

- Development of the Ladino language.

c. 1500

- First appearance of Conversos in the "New World."

1510–1516

- Jewish expulsion from Naples.

1516

- First Jewish ghetto established, in Venice.

1517

- Turkish Ottoman Empire conquers land of Israel. Jews return in large numbers to Palestine. New Jewish mystical center arises in Safed.

1528

- Two suspected Conversos burned at the stake in the New World.

1543

- Martin Luther attacks the Jews.

1551

- Polish and Lithuanian Jews appoint their first chief rabbi.

1554

- Pope Paul IV strengthens anti-Jewish legislation, promotes ghettoization of Jews.

1555

- Joseph Caro completes his *Shulchan Arukh*.

1579

♦ Rabbi Isaac Luria relocates to Safed.

1581

♦ Council of the Four Lands established in eastern Europe; Jews become semiautonomous.

1585

♦ Amsterdam emerges as a major center for Conversos.

1593

♦ Leghorn (Livorno), Italy, develops into major Jewish center.

c. 1600

♦ Prague develops into major Jewish center.

c. 1600–1625

♦ Northern European ports develop major Jewish communities.

1603

♦ Council of German Jewry created in Frankfurt.

1630–1654

♦ Jewish settlement in Brazil.

1648–1649

♦ Chmielnicki Massacres in the Ukraine.

1654

♦ First Jews in North America arrive in New Amsterdam.

1655

♦ Rabbi Menashe Ben Israel petitions for Jews to be allowed to return to England.

1656

♦ Rabbis excommunicate Baruch Spinoza in Amsterdam.

1657

♦ Jews allowed to settle in Denmark.

1665

♦ False messiah Shabbatai Zvi flourishes.

1676

♦ Jews expelled from Yemen.

1723

♦ Sephardic Jewish community in Bordeaux, France, officially recognized.

1730

♦ First synagogue in America, Shearit Israel, established in New York.

c. 1740

♦ Baal Shem Tov begins Hasidic movement.

1764

♦ Poland abolishes the council of the four lands, ending two centuries of Jewish semiautonomy.

1768

♦ Haidamack attacks against Jews in Poland.

1770–1780

♦ Haskalah movement in Europe begins.

1772

♦ Vilna Gaon orders excommunication of any Jews who embrace Hasidism.

1778

◆ First modern Jewish school opens in Berlin, Germany.

1783

◆ Moses Mendelssohn translates the Torah into German.

1789

◆ First debate on Jewish emancipation in France.

1790

◆ American president George Washington pledges religious liberty to Jews.

1791

◆ Jews granted French citizenship. Pale of Settlement created in Russia.

1794

◆ Jewish Legion formed in Poland.

1796

◆ Italian Jews emancipated by Napoleon.

1802

◆ First chief rabbi of England appointed. Volozhin Yeshiva established in the Pale.

1804

◆ Czar Alexander I implements new anti-Jewish legislation.

1805

◆ Jewish massacre in Algeria.

1806

◆ Yeshiva established in Pressburg, Hungary, to lead opposition to reform within Judaism.

1812

◆ Semi-emancipation of Jews in Prussia.

1819

◆ Riots directed against Jews in Denmark and Germany.
◆ Rebecca Gratz establishes first independent Jewish women's charitable society in Philadelphia.

1820

◆ Beginning of Reform Judaism and Neo-Orthodoxy in Germany.

1821

◆ Jewish massacre in Greece.

1824

◆ First Reform Jewish group in America formed in Charleston, South Carolina.

1830

◆ Large immigration of German Jews to United States begins.

1836

◆ Russian government begins censorship of Jewish books and closes down Jewish printing presses.

1837

◆ Major earthquake in Safed kills thousands of Jews.

1839

◆ Forced conversions of Jews in northern Persia.

1840

◆ Damascus blood libel.

1841

♦ David Levy Yulee elected first Jew in U.S. Congress, as senator from Florida territory.

1842

♦ Musar movement begins in Lithuania.

1843

♦ B'nai B'rith founded; first secular Jewish organization in the United States.

1844

♦ Russia abolishes the *kahal,* the community organization of the Jews.
♦ First Reform rabbinical meeting, in Brunswick, Germany.

1846

♦ New anti-Jewish legislation in Yemen.

1850

♦ Jews travel to California to sell to gold rush miners; 6 percent of San Francisco population is Jewish, two synagogues created.

1854

♦ Zachariah Frankel opens the Jewish Theological Seminary in Breslau, Germany.

1858

♦ Edgardo Mortara, Jewish child, kidnapped by church in Italy; causes international furor.
♦ First Jew sits in British Parliament.

1860

♦ First modern Jewish neighborhood, Mishkenot Shaananim, built outside Jerusalem's walls.
♦ Alliance Israelite Universelle founded, first modern international Jewish organization.

1861

♦ Jews of Baden, Germany, granted full civil rights.

1862

♦ Judah Benjamin appointed secretary of state of American Confederacy.
♦ U.S. Army appoints first Jewish chaplain.

1863

♦ Montefiore petitions sultan of Morocco to improve living conditions for Jews.

1867–1870

♦ Jews granted full emancipation in Austria, Germany, and Italy.

1873

♦ Union of American Hebrew Congregations (Reform) founded.

1875

♦ Isaac Mayer Wise founds Hebrew Union College, first rabbinical seminary.

1879

♦ New Jewish agricultural settlement in Palestine, Petach Tikvah.

1881

♦ Pogroms in southern Russia in aftermath of czar's assassination.

1881–1924

♦ More than 2 million eastern European Jews immigrate to America.

1882–1903

♦ First Aliya: large-scale Jewish immigration to Palestine, mainly from Russia. Four more waves of immigration to follow.

1885

◆ Pittsburgh Platform issued by U.S. Reform Jews.

1886

◆ Conservative Judaism takes hold in America. Jewish Theological Seminary founded in New York.

1891

◆ Jews expelled from Moscow.

1892

◆ Workmen's Circle established, promotes Yiddishist and socialist ideas among Jewish laborers.
◆ American Jewish Historical Society established.

1894

◆ Dreyfus Affair in France.

1895

◆ First Jewish federation organized in Boston.

1896

◆ Cairo Genizah discovered by Solomon Schechter.

1897

◆ First Zionist Congress convened by Theodor Herzl in Basel, Switzerland; founds Zionist Organization.
◆ Founding of the Bund in Russia.
◆ Rabbi Isaac Elchanan Theological Seminary trains Orthodox rabbis; later becomes part of Yeshiva University.
◆ *Jewish Daily Forward* founded.

1898

◆ Union of Orthodox Congregations founded in United States.

1901

◆ Industrial Removal Office operates in United States.

1902

◆ Mizrahi movement created.
◆ Solomon Schechter arrives in New York to head Jewish Theological Seminary.

1903

◆ Herzl backs Uganda as temporary Jewish home.
◆ Kishinev pogrom.

1909

◆ First kibbutz, Degania, and first modern Jewish city, Tel Aviv, founded in Palestine.

1911–1913

◆ Kiev blood libel trial of Mendel Beilis.
◆ Triangle Shirtwaist Factory fire kills 146 women workers, most of them Jewish.

1912

◆ Agudath Israel movement founded.
◆ Henrietta Szold founds Hadassah, the Women's Zionist Organization of America.

1913

◆ Leo Frank accused of murdering girl in Atlanta, Georgia; sentenced to life in prison.
◆ Anti-Defamation League formed by B'nai B'rith.

1915

◆ Leo Frank lynched.

1916

◆ Louis Brandeis becomes first Jewish justice of the Supreme Court of the United States.
◆ HaShomer Hatzair movement created.

1917

♦ British end 400 years of Ottoman rule over Palestine. Balfour Declaration proclaims British support for Jewish home in Palestine.

1920

♦ Henry Ford publishes *Protocols of the Elders of Zion* in the *Dearborn Independent*.
♦ Histadrut (Jewish labor federation) and Haganah (Jewish defense organization) founded in Palestine. Vaad Leumi (National Council) set up by Jewish community (yishuv) to conduct its affairs.

1921

♦ New United States immigration quotas limit Jewish immigration.
♦ First moshav, Nahalal, founded in Palestine.

1922

♦ Britain granted Mandate for Palestine by League of Nations; Transjordan set up on 75 percent of area. Jewish Agency for Palestine created.
♦ Mordecai Kaplan establishes Society for the Advancement of Judaism.

1924

♦ Technion, first Palestine technical institute, founded in Haifa.

1925

♦ Hebrew University of Jerusalem opened on Mt. Scopus

1928

♦ Soviet Union creates autonomous area for Jews in Birobidzhan.

1929

♦ Hebron Jews massacred by Arab militants.

1930–1940

♦ Stalin government actively attempts to destroy Jewish culture in Soviet Union.

1933

♦ Rise of the Third Reich.
♦ Albert Einstein flees Germany; finds refuge in United States.

1936–1939

♦ Anti-Jewish riots in Palestine by Arab militants.

1938

♦ Kristallnacht, Night of Broken Glass, in Germany.

1939

♦ Jewish immigration to Palestine severely limited by British White Paper.
♦ SS *St. Louis* denied permission to dock at a U.S. port; returns to Europe, most passengers later murdered in the Holocaust.
♦ Irving Berlin writes *God Bless America*.

1939–1945

♦ World War II and the Holocaust. Murder of 6 million European Jews by German Nazis.

1945

♦ Yeshiva University founded in New York.

1946

♦ Irgun blows up British headquarters at King David Hotel.

1947

♦ United Nations proposes establishment of Arab and Jewish states in Palestine, via Partition Plan.

1948

♦ State of Israel declares independence, defeats Arab invaders.

- Brandeis University founded; first secular Jewish university in United States.

1949

- Israel signs armistice with Egypt, Jordan, Syria, and Lebanon. Jerusalem divided under Israeli and Jordanian rule. First Israeli Knesset (parliament) elected.

1949–1952

- Mass Jewish immigration from European and Arab countries to Israel.

1952

- Germany agrees to pay reparations to Israel.

1955

- Jonas Salk develops polio vaccine.

1956

- Sinai War in Israel.

1962

- Adolf Eichmann tried and executed in Israel for his role in the Holocaust.

1967

- Six-Day War. Jerusalem reunited under Jewish control.

1972

- Sally Priesand ordained first woman rabbi.

1973

- Yom Kippur War.

1977

- Labor party loses Knesset to Likud for first time.
- Anwar Sadat visits Jerusalem.

1979

- Camp David Accords between Egypt and Israel; Menachem Begin and Anwar Sadat awarded Nobel Peace Prize.

1981

- Israel Air Force destroys Iraqi nuclear reactor.

1982

- Israel completes withdrawal from Sinai. Lebanon/Israeli War drives PLO terrorist leadership to Tunisia.

1983

- Jewish Theological Seminary decides to accept women to rabbinical school.

1985–1991

- Israel rescues Ethiopian Jewry.

1986

- Anatoly Sharansky, a Russian refusenik, released by Soviet Union.

1987

- First Intifada begins against Israel.

1989

- Massive Jewish aliyah from former Soviet Union begins.

1991

- Israel attacked by Iraqi scud missiles during Gulf War. Middle East peace conference convened in Madrid.

1993

- Oslo Peace Accords between Israel and PLO.
- U.S. Holocaust Memorial Museum opens in Washington, D.C.

1994

- Implementation of Palestinian self-government in Gaza Strip and Jericho.
- Peace treaty between Israel and Jordan.

1995

- Broadened Palestinian self-government in West Bank and Gaza Strip; Palestinian Council elected. Prime Minister Yitzhak Rabin assassinated at peace rally by Jewish extremist.

1996

- Arab terrorist attacks grow, targeting civilians on buses and at social gatherings.
- University of Judaism Ziegler Rabbinical School breaks from Jewish Theological Seminary.

1998

- Israel and PLO sign Wye River Memorandum to facilitate implementation of an interim peace agreement.

1999

- In the United States, Council of Jewish Federations, United Jewish Appeal, and United Israel Appeal merge to form United Jewish Communities.

2000

- Palestinian Authority and Israel fail to conclude a comprehensive peace agreement at Camp David.
- Joseph Lieberman named Al Gore's running mate for the Democratic presidential ticket.
- Pope John Paul II visits Israel.
- Al-Aksa (Second) Intifada begins.

2001

- Sbarro Pizza massacre in Jerusalem. Israeli government suspends dialogue with Arafat until Palestinian violence ends.

2002

- Israel captures a ship smuggling 50 tons of illegally procured weapons for the Palestinian Authority. Netanya Passover massacre kills 28 and injures 134.

2003

- Israel begins to build security fence; fence reduces terror attacks in Israel by 90 percent. Prime Minister Sharon plans unilateral Gaza withdrawal.
- Reform Judaism changes the name of umbrella organization from Union of American Hebrew Congregations (UAHC) to Union for Reform Judaism (URJ).

2004

- The Israeli Knesset passes Prime Minister Ariel Sharon's proposal to withdraw unilaterally Israeli troops from Gaza Strip.
- Yasser Arafat, leader of Palestine Liberation Organization and president of Palestinian Authority, dies in a Paris hospital.

2005

- Mahmond Abbas is elected president of Palestinian Authority.
- First national Holocaust memorial is completed in Berlin, Germany, after 15 years of controversy and debate. It is called the Memorial to the Murdered Jews of Europe.

ENTRIES A TO Z

A

Aaron (c. 13th century B.C.E.) *brother of Moses and first high priest of the Israelites*
Aaron was born in Egypt to Amram and Jochebed (Ex 6:20), and was the older brother of MOSES. Both were members of the tribe of Levi, which thanks to them became the tribe of priests and LEVITES (assistants to the priests). According to the book of EXODUS, Aaron accompanied Moses to beseech the PHARAOH to free the Israelite slaves. Aaron acted as the spokesperson for Moses, who was "slow of speech" (Ex 4:10). Aaron's rod, like Moses', became a conduit of miracles and plagues, and God, who usually spoke only to Moses, sometimes spoke to Aaron as well. Each of the two thus meets the definition of a prophet.

Once freed from slavery, Aaron played a fundamental role in the life of the Israelites in the desert. On the one hand, God consecrated Aaron and his sons as the priests of ISRAEL. On the other hand, Aaron agreed to build the GOLDEN CALF for the people of Israel when they become frightened while Moses was up on the mountain for 40 days, supposedly receiving the law from God. Despite this lapse, God retained Aaron as HIGH PRIEST, and his male descendants are KOHANIM, or the priestly class. Aaron's right to be high priest was confirmed in the story of Korach in the book of Numbers. Korach led a rebellion against Aaron, but the rebels were swallowed up by the earth, demonstrating the family of Aaron were the only legitimate high priests (Ex 16:25–35).

The ancient rabbis seemed to place Moses and Aaron on an equal footing, sometimes even giving Aaron a higher status than Moses. According to rabbinic thought, Moses represents a strict political leader, while Aaron represents a gentler priest of the people.

Further reading: Moshe Greenberg, *Studies in the Bible and Jewish Thought* (Philadelphia: Jewish Publication Society, 1995); Ronald H. Isaacs, *Legends of Biblical Heroes: A Sourcebook* (Northvale, N.J.: Jason Aronson, 2002); *Tanakh: The Holy Scriptures* (Philadelphia and Jerusalem: The Jewish Publication Society, 1985).

abortion
Traditional interpretation of HALAKHAH, Jewish law, allows abortion if the fetus presents a serious physical threat to the mother, but authorities differ about its permissibility in other cases. *Halakhah* defines full human life as existing only when the head of an infant emerges from the womb. The fetus is considered "potential life" and has sacred value, but complete human status begins only with actual birth.

RASHI, the great 12th-century commentator on the Hebrew Bible (see TORAH) and TALMUD, states clearly that the fetus is not a person. The Talmud contains the expression "ubar yerech imo—the fetus is as the thigh of its mother." In other words, the fetus is deemed to be part and parcel of the pregnant woman's body. Therefore, abortion is permitted if the fetus creates a direct threat to the life of the mother.

While there is a rabbinic consensus that permits abortion if the fetus presents a physical threat to the mother, there are differing Jewish opinions about whether the psychological health of the mother takes precedence over the pregnancy. Because the Talmud (Yevamot 69b) states that "the embryo is considered to be mere water until the 40th day," after which the embryo is considered partially human until it is born, many traditional Jews will consider an abortion to be a greater option prior to the 41st day. Few rabbinic scholars would accept the notion that abortion may be utilized merely as a form of birth control.

Further reading: David M. Feldman, *Birth Control in Jewish Law: Marital Relations, Contraception, and Abortion As Set Forth in the Classic Texts of Jewish Law* (Lanham, Md.: Jason Aronson Publishers, 1998); Isaac Klein, *A Guide to Jewish Religious Practice* (New York: Jewish Theological Seminary of America, 1988); Daniel Schiff, *Abortion and Judaism* (Cambridge: Cambridge University Press, 2002).

Abravanel, Isaac ben Judah (1437–1508)
medieval scholar and public figure

Isaac ben Judah Abravanel was born in Lisbon, PORTUGAL in 1437. He was an accomplished scholar of the Hebrew Bible (see TORAH), TALMUD, and philosophy. Abravanel also established a reputation as a scholar of secular studies while remaining a devoted Jew, even when faced with expulsion; he is recognized as an exegete, philosopher, historian, and mystic. Influenced by the great Renaissance writers of his time, Abravanel's commentary to the prophets (see NEVI'IM) yields rich insights into 15th-century European society because of his comparisons between I Samuel and the monarchies of his day. In his biblical commentaries, Abravanel interpreted the texts with attention to society and history, using in this endeavor many Christian sources. He also analyzed messianic texts, maintaining a belief in a future messianic age when Jews would once again dwell in ERETZ YISRAEL.

Although Abravanel was dedicated to Judaism and spent much energy on the pursuit of Jewish knowledge, he also understood the practical importance of finance and diplomacy; he is best known for his genius in these fields. Abravanel also understood the role a diplomatic position could play in mitigating the living conditions and political situations of his fellow Jews. While serving as the personal assistant to King Alfonso V in Portugal, he was able to raise the ransom to redeem 250 Jews held captive by the king. Despite his influence among wealthy Christians, however, Abravanel had to flee Portugal in 1483 when life for Jews became more difficult under Pope John II.

When Abravanel arrived in bordering SPAIN, he had not intended to resume his former position in another ruler's court, but when King Ferdinand requested his services, he did not refuse, taking the position in 1484 even though it was illegal for a Jew to assume such a high position in the land. Thus, Abravanel became one of the most recognized COURT JEWS in history. Even so, his position and wealth did not make it possible for Abravanel to convince or bribe King Ferdinand and Queen Isabella to rescind their decision to expel all Jews from Spain in 1492. Choosing not to convert, Abravanel fled from Spain with his son, first to Naples and finally to Venice, where he died five years after he arrived.

Further reading: Joseph Dan, ed., *Studies in Jewish History* (New York: Praeger Publishers, 1989); Benzion Netanyahu, *Don Isaac Abravanel: Statesman and Philosopher* (Philadelphia: Jewish Publication Society, 1972).

accommodation (acculturation)

The term *accommodation* is used by some scholars to refer to the practice of many modern Jews of adapting Jewish tradition, culture, and rituals to the non-Jewish cultures of the modern world. Some scholars prefer to use the term ASSIMILATION to refer to the same practice, which they believe has led to the loss of Jewish culture as Jews became secularized and more like non-Jews. However, the first group claims that Jews have not assimilated to modern Western culture, but have transformed within it, or accommodated to it.

The years surrounding World War II saw an increase in ANTISEMITISM in the UNITED STATES, and during this time some American Jews made an effort to fit into Christian America. They downplayed their success in all arenas, Anglicized their names for both economic and social reasons, and shirked all traditions that might separate them from American society. However, in the 1960s Americans began to value ethnicity on a large scale and the American Jewish community began to feel comfortable enough to display their Jewishness.

American Jews began to feel pride in their Jewish names, to express Jewish characteristics and customs such as wearing a KIPPAH, and to look for ways in which they could be Jewish and American without conflict between the two. In fact, it had become clear that a Jewish person could choose to be Jewish or not to be, but either way he or she had to make a conscious decision.

Scholars who support the idea that individuals in the Jewish community have accommodated to American culture rather than simply assimilated into it point to evidence that most Jews continued to live near other Jews, join professions and businesses with a large Jewish presence, and celebrate holidays such as PASSOVER and CHANUKAH, which have become part of the American consciousness. Ultimately the American example of accommodation includes a continuing similarity among many Jews, as compared with non-Jews, in occupation, lifestyle, residence, values, schooling, family, and economic and political interests.

Since the exile in the early first century, Jews have lived in a variety of host societies. In some they have been forced to convert or die, to flee, or to hide their JEWISH IDENTITY. However, there have been others where the Jewish community was free, at least for a time, to be a Jewish community. These instances include medieval SPAIN, Hellenistic EGYPT, America, and even to a degree the Roman Empire and czarist RUSSIA. In many situations, Jewish communities have chosen to adapt to their environment, maintaining core identity while including customs and observances of their host society. To the extent that this has happened in contemporary America, it can be called accommodation.

Further reading: Calvin Goldscheider, *Jewish Continuity and Change: Emerging Patterns in America* (Bloomington: Indiana University Press, 1986); Calvin Goldscheider and Alan D. Zuckerman, *The Transformation of the Jews* (Chicago and London: The University of Chicago Press, 1984); Charles S. Liebman and Bernard Susser, *Choosing Survival: Strategies for a Jewish Future* (New York: Oxford University Press, 1999); Charles E. Silberman, *A Certain People: American Jews and Their Lives Today* (New York: Summit Books, 1985).

Adler, Cyrus (1863–1940) *rabbi and educator*

Cyrus Adler was an educator, scholar, rabbi, and leader in the American Jewish community at the end of the 19th century and the beginning of the 20th. He was born in Van Buren, Arkansas, in 1863 and raised in Philadelphia from the age of four, when his father died. Living with his mother and her brother's family, he grew up learning the culture of German Jews, many of whom had emigrated from GERMANY with his own father in the 1840s. In his early years Adler attended a Jewish day school (*see* JEWISH DAY SCHOOL MOVEMENT), but he later attended public school, receiving Jewish learning through private tutors. Adler's interest in libraries began while he was still a high school student; he developed a catalog of authors of books donated by Isaac LEESER to the library of the

Philadelphia Young Men's Hebrew Association (YMHA).

Having already begun to favor a life of scholarship, Adler attended the University of Pennsylvania, receiving his B.A. in 1883 and his M.A. in 1886. He earned his Ph.D. from Johns Hopkins University in 1887, marking the first degree in Semitics granted at an American university. At Johns Hopkins from 1884 to 1893 he taught courses in HEBREW, Assyrian, Ethiopic, Arabic, biblical archaeology, and history of the ancient Near East. Throughout his life Adler produced more than 600 writings, including articles, reports, notes, catalogs, bibliographies, translations, and book reviews. These are currently housed in the AMERICAN JEWISH HISTORICAL SOCIETY, of which he was the founder. Adler also published books, including *Told in the Coffee House* (with Allen Ramsey, 1898), *International Catalogue of Scientific Literature* (1905), *Jews in the Diplomatic Correspondence of the United States* (1906), *Jacob H. Schiff: His Life and Letters* (1928), and *I Have Considered the Days* (1941), his autobiography.

Adler was known for his incredible ability to multitask, and this trait is obvious when one looks at the contributions he made to the American Jewish community at the turn of the 20th century. Beyond his work with the historical society, he was also a founding member of the AMERICAN JEWISH COMMITTEE, the National Jewish Welfare Board, the United Synagogue of America (*see* CONSERVATIVE JUDAISM), and the JEWISH PUBLICATION SOCIETY. Adler remained active in all of these organizations, taking leadership positions. He was cochairman of the International Jewish Agency for Palestine, even though, like many of his fellow German-American Jews, he was not a supporter of ZIONISM. He attended the 1919 Paris Peace Conference following World War I and fought for the rights of Jews in European countries ravaged by war.

Adler's achievements are not limited to the world of Jewish welfare; he contributed to the world of academics as well. From 1889 to 1908 he served as the curator of historic archaeology and historic religions at the United States National Museum of the Smithsonian Institution in Washington, D.C. He was the Smithsonian Institute's librarian from 1892 to 1905, and its assistant secretary from 1905 to 1908. In his lifetime, Adler edited several publications, including the *Jewish Encyclopedia, The Jewish Quarterly Review,* and the *American Jewish Year Book* after 1899. From 1908 to 1940, Adler was the president of Dropsie College. In 1916 he became acting president of the JEWISH THEOLOGICAL SEMINARY following the death of Solomon SCHECHTER, and in 1924 he assumed the position permanently.

Adler's impact on the American Jewish community cannot be overstated. He influenced Jewish and secular academics and led the community in developing organizations and associations that cemented the power of the American Jewish community well into the future. Adler did not marry until he was 42, and he and his wife had one child, a girl. He did not slow down his academic and communal activities until his faltering health demanded it, spending his last years with his family until his death in 1940.

Further reading: Cyrus Adler, *I Have Considered the Days* (New York: Burning Bush Press, 1969); Moshe Davis, *The Emergence of Conservative Judaism: The Historical School in 19th Century America* (Philadelphia: Jewish Publication Society, 1963); A. Neuman, *Cyrus Adler: A Biographical Sketch* (New York: American Jewish Committee, 1942).

afikomen

The *afikomen,* a piece of MATZAH (unleavened bread), is the final food eaten at the SEDER on PASSOVER. The word is a loan from Greek, where it meant "that which is coming," or, in the case of a meal, dessert.

During the seder, the afikomen serves several purposes. First, it is a symbol of the Paschal Lamb, the lamb that was ritually sacrificed on the holiday of Passover during the time of the TEMPLE in JERUSALEM and eaten as the last part of the festive meal. Since the destruction of the Temple in the year 70 C.E., Jewish tradition discontinued the practice of animal SACRIFICE and the afikomen has come to represent the sacrifice that no longer takes place.

During the first section of the seder the middle of the three ritual matzah loaves is broken in two. The larger portion is wrapped and stored away to be the afikomen. There are different traditions surrounding this piece of matzah. Some contemporary Jewish families hide the matzah and reward the child who finds it at the end of the meal. Others encourage the children to take the matzah and hold it for ransom, since the meal cannot end without it. Either way the purpose of this game is to retain the attention of the children throughout the seder. The ritual of hiding the afikomen appears in Jewish history only a couple of centuries ago, based on a Talmudic passage (Talmud Pesachim 109a) (*see* TALMUD) that describes a children's game surrounding the matzah to keep them awake.

Further reading: Irving Greenberg, *The Jewish Way: Living the Holidays* (New York: Touchstone, 1988); Dalia Hardof Renberg, *The Complete Family Guide to Jewish Holidays* (New York: Adama Books, 1985).

aggadah

Aggadah is one of the two main types of interpretive commentary found in the TALMUD and other ancient Jewish texts. It is based on parable, legend, and other nonlegal ways of thinking.

To a large degree the Talmud and other texts from the Talmudic era consist of midrashic attempts (*see* MIDRASH) to interpret and understand the TANAKH, the Hebrew Bible. The ancient rabbis who speak in the Talmud sought to explain any difficulties in understanding, or anomalies that appear in, the text. They used many different techniques to accomplish that task.

Of the two major forms of commentary, midrash HALAKHAH is primarily concerned with finding legal remedies to particular issues—in other words, defining what exactly is the law. In the context of legal or judicial debates, midrash *halakhah* will locate relevant biblical texts and then derive laws from them, often based on fine grammatical and lexical distinctions; it may include majority and minority opinions.

Midrash *aggadah,* by contrast, is a more playful style of interpretation. It uses parable, legend, or other creative methods. In this method, the rabbis answer questions about the text by telling a story that explains why it is so.

The midrash *aggadah* so influenced normative Jewish biblical perspectives that many Jews view parts of midrash *aggadah* as actual stories in the Hebrew Bible. The most common aggadic story mistaken for being part of the Hebrew Bible is the story of Abraham destroying the idols in his father's idol shop. In other words, this story is not part of the Bible but instead a part of midrash *aggadah.*

Aggadah helps to bring the biblical text alive. These "stories of the rabbis" inspire the reader or listener to imagine how the heroes of the Hebrew Bible felt or suggest reasons for their behavior. While the *aggadah* does not give authoritative answers, it enables the reader to more deeply engage the text. The modern writer Chaim Nachman BIALIK, in recording the *aggadah* for modern Jews, described midrash *halakhah,* "interpreting the law," as the Jewish body, but midrash *aggadah,* as the Jewish soul.

See also HAGGADAH.

Further reading: Hayyim Nahman Bialik, Yehoshua Hana Rawnitzki, and William G. Braude, eds., *The Book of Legends: Sefer Ha-Aggadah: Legends from the Talmud and Midrash* (New York: Schocken Books, 1992); Louis Ginzberg, *Legends of the Bible* (Philadelphia: The Jewish Publication Society of America, 1956); Reuven Hammer and Judah Goldin, *The Classic Midrash: Tannaitic Commentaries on the Bible* (Mahwah, N.J.: Paulist Press, 1995).

agunah

An *agunah* (literally, a "chained" woman) is one whose husband is unwilling or unable to give her a religious divorce, or GET, even though the couple underwent a civil divorce and/or the husband has abandoned her. She is recognized as divorced by the civil authorities, but she is not able to marry again in a Jewish religious ceremony, according to ORTHODOX JUDAISM and CONSERVATIVE JUDAISM.

If a husband is missing in action while at war, his wife is considered an agunah until his body is found; she remains in a state of limbo, unable to remarry. In the past, married couples often went through divorce proceedings to protect the wife against such an eventuality.

Many women and courts have attempted to solve this legal dilemma, but there are few solutions for women today who are considered agunahs. If a husband refuses to give a get to his wife, a BET DIN, or rabbinic court, is religiously empowered to fine and/or excommunicate him. Excommunication was a far more powerful tool in earlier historical periods when a man depended almost exclusively on the Jewish community for his livelihood and ability to pray to God. In more ancient times a man who refused the bet din's order to grant a divorce would be flogged until he relented. In Israel today, some men are imprisoned if they do not provide their ex-wife with a get. Yet, there are still many women who live in our modern world as agunahs.

In Orthodox Judaism rabbis try to procure a get whenever possible. Rabbi Moshe FEINSTEIN, one of the most respected Orthodox rabbis of the postwar era, permitted agunahs to remarry if the rabbi who originally married them belonged to either the Conservative or Reform (see REFORM JUDAISM) movements. As those rabbis were not considered valid, the original marriage was invalid too, and no get was required. This solved the problem for Jewish women who were not originally Orthodox but wanted to marry an Orthodox man. While the other movements did not welcome this invalidation of their Jewish legal authority, Rabbi Feinstein's action shows how Orthodox rabbis often create legal loopholes to mitigate an agunah's plight.

Conservative rabbis have found more flexibility in providing creative solutions to the problem of the agunah. The Conservative solutions include both preventive measures before a marriage and curative measures when facing the agunah scenario. The primary preventive solution is to create a separate document, not part of the traditional KETUBAH, or wedding contract, which authorizes a get to be delivered if a civil divorce were to take place. Another solution, called the "Lieberman Clause," penned by a leading 20th-century Conservative rabbi, Saul LIEBERMAN (1898–1983), is a prenuptial agreement included within the actual ketubah that grants a get if there is a civil divorce.

If these preventive measures are not taken, some Conservative rabbis (and a handful of Orthodox ones) are willing to annul marriages. In doing so, Conservative rabbis rely on a Talmud dictate that "all betrothals receive the approval of the rabbis, and therefore the rabbis have the power to rescind their approval."

Further reading: E. Berkovits, *Jewish women in Time and Torah* (Hoboken, N.J.: KTAV Publishing House, 1990); R. Biale, *Women and Jewish Law: An Exploration of Women's Issues in Halakhic Sources* (New York: Schocken Books, 1984); L. M. Epstein, *The Jewish Marriage Contract: A Study in the Status of the Woman in Jewish Law* (New York: Arno Press, 1973).

Ahad Ha'am (1856–1927) *writer and proponent of cultural Zionism*

Born Asher Ginsberg in 1856, Ahad Ha'am was one of the most influential early literary supporters of ZIONISM. He began life in the town of Skvira in the Ukraine. He came from a prominent and well-to-do family, and as a child he formally studied only Jewish texts and thought. He became an accomplished TALMUD scholar and student of the devotional literature of HASIDISM. Although his teachers were forbidden to teach him the Russian alphabet, for fear that this would lead to secular studies and heresy, Ginsberg taught himself to read Russian when he was eight years old, beginning his journey into the secular world. Eventually he would be known as the agnostic rabbi.

In 1868, at the age of 12, Ginsberg moved with his family to a leased estate. He studied constantly, delving into the works of MAIMONIDES and then into the MASKILIM, the Jewish Enlightenment (see HASKALAH) thinkers. Eventually he turned to German and Russian philosophy, and abandoned his religious roots entirely to seek a secular path to Jewish identity, with an emphasis on cultural Judaism. He made several attempts to pursue his studies in larger cities such as Vienna, Berlin, Breslau, and Leipzig, but always returned to his family and sickly wife.

In 1886 a new Russian law forbidding Jews to lease land forced the Ginsberg family to relocate to Odessa. In this center of Zionist thought, Ginsberg was able to pursue his own philosophical ideas.

At the age of 33 he published his first and now-classic essay entitled "This Is Not the Way." The essay outlined the recent political and national attempts of European Jews to settle in PALESTINE; the author concluded that nationalistic energy was waning, and that a spiritual and cultural renewal of Judaism within the hearts of the Jewish people was the correct path to the survival of Judaism itself. The article was published under the name Ahad Ha'am, meaning "one of the people," illustrating Ginsberg's humility and tendency to downplay his own influence. In 1897, after two visits to Palestine (1891 and 1892), Ahad Ha'am published "Jewish State and Jewish Problem," reinforcing his earlier opinion that massive settlement of Jews in Palestine was not the answer to the Jewish problem. He discussed such obstacles as difficulties in developing the land, the opposition of the ruling Turks, and the protests of Arab communities.

Ahad Ha'am lived and wrote during the early Zionist years, which were influenced by the rise of violent POGROMS in Russia. Jewish societies such as Hovevei Zion, also called HIBBAT ZION, developed political and nationalistic platforms based on settlement in Palestine, ERETZ YISRAEL, as the answer to the alienation of Jews in the world. Ahad Ha'am, however, saw this rush to settle Palestine as a hasty method toward Jewish renewal, and he cautioned that it should be done with great care.

Inspired by Ahad Ha'am's essay "This Is Not the Way," a group of young Zionists founded an organization called Bnei Moshe that emphasized the regeneration of Jewish thought, culture, and modern HEBREW as the first step toward rejuvenating Judaism itself. They believed that settlement of Palestine without cultural renewal was pointless and destined to failure and disaster. The intention of this originally secret society was to redirect Hovevei Zion to accept the ideas of cultural Zionism and deemphasize political Zionism and the call for the reestablishment of the Jewish state.

Ultimately, Ahad Ha'am wished to see a select few settle in Palestine and create a center that all Jews in the DIASPORA could depend upon for the spiritual and cultural renewal of Judaism. He believed that there would always be Jews living in the diaspora and that the answer to Jewish alienation would come from his idea of a cultural renewal. Ahad Ha'am attended the first Zionist Congress but none of the subsequent meetings. However, Zionist leaders such as Chaim WEIZMANN and Chaim Nachman BIALIK used many of Ahad Ha'am's ideas in their pursuit of the Zionist dream.

As influential as Ahad Ha'am's writings were, he did not consider himself to be a writer or a leader. From 1896 to 1902 he supported his family as the editor of a monthly Jewish newsletter entitled *Ha-Shiloah*, which developed as a forum for discussion of contemporary Jewish issues. He resigned that post and left his public career behind to pursue business interests as an official of the Wissotzky Tea Company, traveling across Europe and settling in London with his family in 1907. In 1921 Ahad Ha'am left London to live in Tel Aviv. The street he lived on was named after him, and he died there in 1927.

Further reading: "Essential Texts of Zionism" Web site URL: www.geocities.com/Vienna/6640/zion/essential. html, accessed on May 10, 2004; Arthur Hertzberg, ed., *The Zionist Idea: A Historical Analysis and Reader*

(Philadelphia: Jewish Publication Society, 1997); David H. Weinberg, *Between Tradition and Modernity: Haim Zhitlowski, Simon Dubnow, Ahad Ha-Am, and the Shaping of Modern Jewish Identity* (New York: Holmes & Meier, 1996); Steven J. Zipperstein, *Elusive Prophet: Ahad Ha'am and the Origins of Zionism* (Berkeley: University of California Press, 1993).

Akedah

The Akedah ("the binding") is the Hebrew term that refers to the Genesis story (22:1–19) in which Abraham (*see* PATRIARCHS) ties his son Isaac to an altar in preparation for his SACRIFICE. Traditionally, the story is understood as a test of Abraham's faith in God. So strong is this faith paradigm that the narrative is highlighted every year by a reading during the service of ROSH HASHANAH, the Jewish New Year.

In the biblical narrative, God tells Abraham to offer up his "one and only son." Abraham obeys this seemingly unreasonable command to kill the very son who God has promised will inherit his estate and mission. It is only at the last possible moment that God stays Abraham's hand, praises his obedience, and promises him and his offspring great blessings for the future.

Traditional sources interpret the Akedah as a celebration of Abraham's immense devotion to God. Abraham has to be tested, because God must be sure that he is fully devoted. Rabbinic literature imagines that God had been challenged by the prosecuting angel (SATAN) who questioned Abraham's devotion.

Yehudah HALEVI (1075–1141) and NACHMONIDES (1194–1270) assert that Abraham had to be tested by God in order to justify the future blessings that were promised to him and his descendants. Since the death of Isaac would bring the line of Abraham and Sarah (*see* MATRIARCHS) to an end, Abraham's willingness to perform this sacrifice demonstrated a willingness to give up all that he was and all that his tradition would be.

Some rabbinic commentators are uncomfortable with God commanding Abraham to sacrifice his son. They instead assert that Abraham misunderstood what was being asked of him. While God did call upon him to take Isaac up to the mountain, according to these interpreters, God never asked him to slaughter Isaac, only to prepare him as a burnt offering (*veha'alehu le'olah*). Presumably, God wanted to see how Abraham would interpret the request, and what he would do in response to his interpretation. This interpretation pictures Abraham as confused and frustrated when he is told not to sacrifice his son. The MIDRASH says that God told Abraham: "I did not tell you to slaughter him but rather to take him up to the top of the mountain. You have indeed taken him up. Now take him down again." The point of this interpretation is that the biblical reader must learn how to interpret carefully what God wants, without ever doing harm in the process of learning from the TANAKH, the Hebrew Bible.

Some modern interpreters of the Akedah perceive the narrative as an example of a moral lapse, even a sign of mental derangement. Michael Lerner, a leader of the JEWISH RENEWAL movement, writes that "Abraham is victimizing Isaac because of an unconscious compulsion on Abraham's part to repeat in reverse his own earlier experience of victimization. Moreover, the voice that told Abraham to offer Isaac as a sacrifice was not really the voice of God but a projection of his own mind." Burton Visotzky, a scholar of CONSERVATIVE JUDAISM, also stresses the psychological dimensions of the Akedah story.

No matter the interpretation, the Akedah story remains a key lesson in how one should observe faith. Whether one interprets the narrative as a warning to beware of voices that seem to be God or as an example of supreme faith in God, one can derive rich meanings from it.

Further reading: Avrohom Davis, *Metsudah Chumash/ Rashi: A New Linear Translation* (Jersey City, N.J.: Ktav Publishing House, 1999); Isidore Epstein, ed., *Soncino Hebrew/English Babylonian Talmud* (Brooklyn, N.Y.: Soncino Press Ltd., 1990); H. Freedman and Maurice Simon, eds., *Soncino Midrash Rabbah* (CD-ROM), 3rd ed. (Brooklyn, N.Y.: Soncino Press, 1983); Michael

Lerner, *Jewish Renewal: A Path to Healing and Transformation* (New York: G. P. Putnam's Sons, 1994); Burton Visotzky, *The Genesis of Ethics: How the Tormented Family of Genesis Leads Us to Moral Development* (New York: Three Rivers Press, 1996).

Akiva ben Yoseph (50 C.E.–132 C.E.) *ancient rabbinic leader*

Akiva ben Yoseph was one of the most important TANNAIM (teachers of the MISHNAH), and the greatest of the early rabbinic leaders. A primary force in the early development of rabbinic law and a strong nationalist leader, Akiva died a martyr's death at the hands of the Romans (*see* ROME).

There are many legends about Akiva's life. He was born to humble parents, but according to the TALMUD he fell in love with Rachel, daughter of a great landowner, while he was still an illiterate peasant. Against Rachel's father's wishes, they married, and she was disowned. But Rachel encouraged her husband, at the age of 40, to attend school. Akiva excelled in his studies, and he became the preeminent sage of his time. The Talmud, tractate Nedarim 50a, records that at one point Akiva had 48,000 disciples.

Legend further teaches that Akiva, with his students, joined in the failed revolt against Rome in 132–135 C.E., led by Shimon BAR-KOKHBA. Sentenced to death by torture, Akiva is said to have ignored the pain and uttered the sacred words of the SHEMA, "Hear O Israel, the Lord our God, the Lord is One." When his torturers asked him how he managed to ignore the pain, he patiently told them that as he lived his life for God, now he was privileged to give his life for God.

Akiva is held as a primary role model for modern day rabbinic leadership, thanks to his willingness to learn at an advanced age, his charisma, intellect, and leadership qualities. Akiva's greatest attributes were his "benevolence and kindness toward the sick and needy" (Nedarim 40a). Akiva represents these universal characteristics, and so he remains a positive example even in the contemporary world.

Further reading: Louis Finkelstein, *Akiba: Scholar, Saint and Martyr* (Northvale, N.J.: Jason Aronson Press, 1990); H. Freedman and Maurice Simon, eds., *Soncino Midrash Rabbah* (CD-ROM), 3rd ed. (Brooklyn, N.Y.: Soncino Press, 1983); Judah Nadich, *Rabbi Akiba and His Contemporaries* (Northvale, N.J.: Jason Aronson Press, 1990).

Akkadian

Akkadian is the oldest member of the family of Semitic languages to be recorded in writing. It was the primary language of ancient Mesopotamia for well over 2,000 years; the languages of BABYLONIA and Assyria (*see* ASSYRIANS) were dialects of Akkadian. The TANAKH, or Hebrew Bible, contains traces of the Akkadian language, and some of the stories in the Hebrew Bible reflect the influence of Akkadian literature, which was cherished by many of the cultures surrounding the territory of the ancient ISRAELITES.

Akkadian was written in the cuneiform script originally developed for the earlier Sumerian language. Modern scholars first deciphered this script in the mid-19th century. Today, scholars possess primary Akkadian documents covering the period 2350 B.C.E. to the first century C.E.

The Epic of Gilgamesh is probably the best-known Akkadian literary document. Considered the first extant heroic epic, copies have been found that predate the Hebrew Bible by centuries. The Epic of Gilgamesh includes an episode about a massive flood, which has some parallels to the biblical flood story of NOAH.

Further reading: Robert M. Best, *Noah's Ark and the Ziusudra Epic: Sumerian Origins of the Flood Myth* (Fort Myers, Fla.: Enlil Press, 1999); S. Dalley, *Myths from Mesopotamia: Creation, The Flood, Gilgamesh and Others* (Oxford and New York: Oxford University Press, 1989); Norman K. Gottwald, *The Hebrew Bible: A Socio-Literary Introduction* (Philadelphia: Fortress Press, 1985); Hans J. Nissen, *The Early History of the Ancient Near East: 9000–2000 B.C.* (Chicago: University of Chicago Press, 1988).

Alexander II (1818–1881) *progressive Russian czar*

Russian czar Alexander II played a significant role in Jewish history. He sought to modernize Russia, and his reforms and concessions improved living conditions for many Jews as well as other minority and poor groups living under his rule. His assassination by political radicals brought about a fierce reactionary backlash that proved to be a catastrophe for the Jewish communities of eastern Europe.

Alexander II was crowned in September of 1856, and he instituted many reforms throughout Russia. At the time of his coronation, Alexander announced in his Coronation Manifesto that he planned changes in law and customs that went beyond what most new rulers dared to seek. Many poor people in Russia benefited: back taxes were cancelled, tax exemptions granted, better distribution of the poll-tax announced, military recruitment was suspended for three years, and many soldiers returned to their families. Specifically for the Jews, special Jewish taxes were annulled. In 1861, Alexander freed the serfs.

The promises of Alexander II's reign included the end of juvenile conscription, which had been set at an earlier age (12) for Jews than for Christians. In addition, a larger number of Jews were allowed to live outside the PALE OF SETTLEMENT, where they were previously forced to live; exemptions were granted to merchants, graduates of universities, mechanics, or artisans. Those few Jews already living in the larger cities of St. Petersburg, Odessa, and Moscow were joined by many more. Alexander's plans to "Russify" the Jewish populations allowed Jews to participate in the intellectual, social, and economic life of Russia. Mostly wealthier Jews were able to take advantage of new areas of settlement, while the masses remained in their villages in the Pale of Settlement.

Life was improving for the Jews of Russia, but this was not without its repercussions. The Jewish communities had to face the dangers of ASSIMILATION, and as their prominence in Russian society grew so too did ANTISEMITISM. The old myth of BLOOD LIBEL reappeared in Russian society. Yet life was generally better than it had been for the Jews before the rule of Alexander II.

In 1881, Alexander II was assassinated, and life for the Jewish communities in Russia grew worse. Some claimed that a Jewish woman had been involved in the plot to kill the czar, and POGROMS ignited throughout the country, decimating many Jewish communities. In May of 1882, the Temporary Laws were passed, preventing Jews from living in Russian villages or from trading on Sundays and Christian holidays, and denied them jobs in the civil service. The Pale of Settlement was reduced by 10 percent, forcing tens of thousands of Jews from their homes and livelihoods. Thus, Russian Jews found themselves in physical and economic danger as a direct result of the death of Alexander II. This set the stage for massive emigration from Russia for those who were able to flee, and the emergence of large Jewish communities in western Europe and the United States.

Further reading: W. E. Mosse, *Alexander II and the Modernization of Russia* (London: English Universities Press, Ltd., 1958); Gabriella Safran, *Rewriting the Jew: Assimilation Narratives in the Russian Empire* (Stanford, Calif.: Stanford University Press, 2000).

aliyah (pl.: aliyot)

The word *aliyah* in HEBREW literally means "going up." Within Jewish tradition, the word is used in two specific ways: aliyah is the act of going up to the elevated platform (bima) where the TORAH is being read during a worship service in order to participate in the rituals; it is also the act of immigrating to ISRAEL.

The Torah is divided into 54 portions—which are read in rotation during SHABBAT and holiday worship services over the course of the year—and each portion is divided into seven aliyot. In other words, during most Shabbat morning worship services, seven people are individually called up to the Torah scroll, which is spread out for reading, and each says a blessing before and after the section is read. After the seven regular aliyot, an additional aliyah is given, called the *maftir*, which is a repetition of the last few verses. The person who has the honor of this aliyah often goes on to chant the day's selection from the NEVI'IM; this selection is known as the HAFTARAH.

When attending a Jewish worship service it is considered a great honor to receive an aliyah. In some congregations the honor is purchased by a promise of charity, or TZEDAKAH. In some of those congregations the purchaser then gives the aliyah to an honored worshipper other than himself. The tradition of purchasing aliyot is no longer widespread in American SYNAGOGUES. In recent decades, both CONSERVATIVE JUDAISM and REFORM JUDAISM have decided to give aliyot to women as well as men, a practice that may have existed in ancient times.

The second utilization of the term *aliyah* applies to Jews who immigrate to Israel. Leaving the DIASPORA to return to the Promised Land is perceived as "ascending" to Israel. Moving to Israel is perceived by many rabbis as its own MITZ-VAH, a fulfillment of God's will. While the immigrant to Israel is considered praiseworthy, the emigrant from Israel is often perceived as "going down" (*yored*), although some consider this term to be pejorative.

Historians label the waves of immigration to PALESTINE as a succession of mass aliyot. They number each aliyah for easy reference to critical time periods when many people immigrated. These stages are First Aliyah, 1882–1902; Second Aliyah, 1904–14; Third Aliyah, 1919–23; Fourth Aliyah, 1924–28; and Fifth Aliyah, 1932–39. Each aliyah was characterized by different countries of origin and/or political or religious affiliation.

The First Aliyah consisted mostly of Jews from RUSSIA and ROMANIA who organized agricultural settlements in an attempt to resurrect large-scale Jewish life in the land of Israel. The Second Aliyah also consisted of eastern European Jews, this time with socialist ideas and a dedication to the revival of HEBREW as a modern language. The Third Aliyah

consisted of young eastern European Jews, who built roads and towns, drained marshes, built industry, organized government, and instituted a nascent defense force. The Fourth Aliyah brought middle-class Polish Jews who built business and expanded the cities and towns, and the Fifth Aliyah brought professional Germans, who were fleeing HITLER, and more eastern Europeans. Following the Fifth Aliyah, waves of immigration were no longer numbered, but often referred to by the types of Jews who arrived: Ethiopian, Iraqi, Soviet.

Further reading: Hayim Halevy Donin, *To Pray as a Jew: A Guide to the Prayer Book and the Synagogue Service* (New York: Basic Books, 1980); David Maisel, *The Founding Myths of Israel: Nationalism, Socialism, and the Making of the Jewish State* (Princeton, N.J.: Princeton University Press, 1998); Howard Morley Sachar, *Aliyah: The People of Israel* (Cleveland, Ohio: World Publishing Company, 1961).

Alliance Israelite Universelle

The Alliance Israelite Universelle was founded in Paris in 1860 as the first Jewish defense organization in the modern world. The organizers were prodded into action by the Mortara Affair, in which an Italian Jewish child was taken from his parents to be raised by Christians after his nurse secretly baptized him as a baby.

The Alliance aimed to defend the civil and religious rights and freedoms of Jews around the world, to help those Jews who desired to emigrate from their homes, and to promote education among Jewish youth. By helping Jews achieve political and economic success, the Alliance hoped to show that they were productive members of society, worthy and capable of EMANCIPATION. The Alliance had considerable success with its schools in the Middle East. Many Jews in Iraq and Iran attended them; in 1882 the Bilu pioneers (*see* ZIONISM) learned agricultural techniques at an Alliance training center in Palestine called Mikveh Israel.

The Alliance Israelite Universelle remains active from its Paris headquarters. It continues to be involved in Jewish defense, and it has developed programs that encourage interreligious dialogue. It maintains divisions in countries around the world such as Canada, Israel, Morocco, and Spain.

Further reading: Ben Halpern and Jehuda Reinharz, *Zionism and the Creation of a New Society* (New York: Oxford University Press, 1998); Michael Laskier, *The Alliance Israelite Universelle and the Jewish Communities of Morocco, 1862–1962* (Albany: State University of New York Press, 1983); Aron Rodrigue, *French Jews, Turkish Jews: The Alliance Israelite Universelle and the Politics of Jewish Schooling in Turkey, 1860–1925* (Bloomington: Indiana University Press, 1990); ———, *Images of Sephardi and Eastern Jewries: The Teachers of the Alliance Israelite Universelle, 1860–1939* (Seattle: University of Washington, 1993).

Amalek

The Amalekites were a nomadic nation that lived south of ISRAEL; they attacked the children of Israel after the EXODUS, and became the archetypical enemy in Jewish tradition.

In the genealogy citation of Genesis (36:12), Amalek is cited as the grandson of Esau (*see* PATRIARCHS), and he is the presumed father of the Amalekite nation. In Deuteronomy (25:17–19), God tells the Israelites, "Remember what Amalek did to you on your journey, after you left Egypt, how, undeterred by fear of God, he surprised you on the march, when you were famished and weary, and cut down all the stragglers in your rear. Therefore . . . you shall blot out the memory of Amalek from under heaven. Do not forget!" The nation of Amalek is especially evil because they attacked the weak in particular.

On the Jewish Sabbath (*see* SHABBAT) prior to the holiday PURIM, the biblical verses on Amalek are read in the SYNAGOGUE as a reminder to the congregation to blot out the metaphoric, and sometimes literal, evil that confronts the Jews. Rabbinic tradition teaches that the villain of the story of Purim, Haman, is also a descendent of Amalek.

Within Jewish literature, the term *Amalek* came to represent all the enemies of Israel, those who are bent on her destruction or the destruction of the Jewish people. These evildoers are never to be forgotten, and one has a religious imperative to remove the evil from one's midst. *Amalek* thus became a metaphor supporting the idea that enemies in the midst of the community needed to be dealt with and not forgotten. For example, some right-wing Israelis today cite the case of Amalek to argue in favor of expelling all Arabs from Israel and/or from all territories under Israeli control.

Further reading: H. Freedman and Maurice Simon, eds., *Soncino Midrash Rabbah* (CD-ROM), 3rd ed. (Brooklyn, N.Y.: Soncino Press, 1983); Norman K. Gottwald, *The Hebrew Bible: A Socio-Literary Introduction* (Philadelphia: Fortress Press, 1985); Cristiano Grottanelli, *Kings and Prophets: Monarchic Power, Inspired Leadership, and Sacred Text in Biblical Narrative* (Oxford and New York: Oxford University Press, 1999); *Tanakh: The Holy Scriptures* (Philadelphia and Jerusalem: The Jewish Publication Society, 1985).

amen

The Hebrew interjection *amen* is translated as "so be it," "it is true," or "certain." It is derived from the root *aman,* which means to be permanent. The word has been adopted into multiple languages, including Greek, Latin, English, and Spanish. In the English language, it may be the root of the word "amenable."

Multiple examples of the use of the word *amen* can be found in Deuteronomy, Chapter 27. One example: "Cursed be the man that makes any graven or molten image, an abomination unto the LORD . . . *And all the people shall answer and say, amen.*" In utilizing the term here, the ISRAELITES are affirming their faithful embrace of God's instructions.

Within Jewish liturgy, Jews answer "amen" to the prescribed prayers recited by others. They are affirming that the statements they hear others utter are "truthful declarations." The TALMUD teaches that even if a Jew cannot recite his or her own blessing, he or she may answer "amen" to the blessing of another, and thus fulfill the liturgical ritual requirement. The recitation of the word "amen" can also signify the end of a particular prayer or prayer service.

Further reading: Ismar Elbogen, *Jewish Liturgy: A Comprehensive History* (Philadelphia and Jerusalem: The Jewish Publication Society, 1993); H. Freedman and Maurice Simon, eds., *Soncino Midrash Rabbah* (CD-ROM), 3rd ed. (Brooklyn, N.Y.: Soncino Press, 1983); Rabbi Jules Harlow, ed., *Siddur Sim Shalom: A Prayerbook for Shabbat, Festivals, and Weekdays* (New York: The Rabbinical Assembly, United Synagogue of America, 1989); Abraham Millgram, *Jewish Worship* (Philadelphia and Jerusalem: The Jewish Publication Society, 1975); *Tanakh: The Holy Scriptures* (Philadelphia and Jerusalem: The Jewish Publication Society, 1985).

American Israel Public Affairs Committee (AIPAC)

The American Israel Public Affairs Committee (AIPAC) is a lobbying group of Americans supporting an American foreign policy favorable to Israel. Formed in the 1950s, it now has more than 65,000 members. It operates in the political arena in Washington, D.C., and in communities throughout the country.

Fortune magazine lists AIPAC as one of the most effective political action committees in the UNITED STATES. AIPAC generates support across the country through regional offices that make contact with activists through meetings in people's homes, gala events, or encouragement to participate in AIPAC conferences in Washington, D.C. Individuals interested in AIPAC's work can also access information about its activities and information about the situation in the Middle East through their newsletter called *The Near East Report,* published quarterly.

AIPAC's primary mission is to help ensure the security of the State of Israel. They formally lobby American leaders to address the perceived chal-

lenges facing Israel. These challenges include the need for economic and military aid and strong American cooperation in fighting the threat of terrorism aimed at Israel.

Mainstream political experts and media sources recognize AIPAC to be the most important nongovernmental organization affecting America's relationship with Israel. AIPAC activists help generate within Congress more than 100 pro-Israel legislative initiatives a year, and its lobbyists are well received within Congress. The committee carefully covers every hearing on Capitol Hill that touches on the U.S.-Israel relationship. AIPAC has developed a political leadership program, which educates and trains many young leaders in pro-Israel advocacy, and it also coordinates an active college campus program, which encourages students to be politically active and learn how to effectively advocate for a strong U.S.-Israel relationship.

AIPAC has identified specific actions that the United States government can take to create a more secure Middle East for Israel. These activities would include countering terrorism aimed at the United States and Israel, pressuring Arab leaders to make peace with Israel, enhancing U.S.-Israel strategic cooperation, delaying nuclear weapons programs among hostile countries, broadening the U.S.-Israel relationship, protecting Jerusalem as the capital of Israel, and ending Israel's isolation in world bodies, such as the European Union and the United Nations.

Further reading: J. J. Goldberg, *Jewish Power: Inside the American Jewish Establishment* (Reading, Mass.: Perseus Publishing, 1996); I. L. Kenen, *Israel's Defense Line: Her Friends and Foes in Washington* (Buffalo, N.Y.: Prometheus Books, 1981); official Web site for AIPAC, URL: www.aipac.com, accessed April 13, 2004.

Americanization

The process in which immigrants to the United States gradually adopt American culture and values is often called Americanization. The different waves of Jewish immigration, starting with

SEPHARDIM from the Latin world in the colonial era, moving to German Jews in the 1840s, and culminating in the massive migrations from eastern Europe in the late 19th and early 20th centuries, all came to adopt American culture, in differing degrees.

Some Jews chose to adopt American customs entirely, leaving behind their own. This is called ASSIMILATION. Others chose to synthesize their customs and culture with the American culture they encountered. This is often called ACCOMMODATION or acculturation. Finally, some Jewish immigrants chose to adopt as few American customs as possible in an attempt to safeguard and pass on their own religious and cultural traditions. While this final group attempted to maintain European Jewish culture in America, even they became Americanized in ways that could not be avoided; for example, changes in cuisine were unavoidable due to differences in the available food supply.

The process of Americanization included learning to eat and enjoy American foods, sometimes modified in accordance with KASHRUT (kosher food requirements), dressing in American fashions, celebrating American holidays such as the Fourth of July, and speaking English. Immigrants adapted at different rates to different customs; often the adoption of English did not occur until a generation was born on American soil. The development of the public school system speeded the process for many children.

Further reading: Daniel J. Elazar, *The Organizational Dynamics of American Jewry* (Philadelphia: Jewish Publication Society, 1995); Gerald Sorin, *A Time for Building: The Third Migration, 1880–1920* (Baltimore and London: Johns Hopkins University Press, 1992).

American Jewish Committee (AJC)

The American Jewish Committee is a voluntary organization of American Jews that pursues educational and political activities in support of religious freedom and human rights for Jews and others.

The committee was founded in 1906 by a number of wealthy and influential members of the German-Jewish community in the United States who controlled the group, though it was set up as a representative body made up of 14 districts throughout the United States. Concerned for the well-being of Jews all over the world, this group of men, including Cyrus ADLER, Jacob SCHIFF, Oscar Straus, Cyrus Sulzberger, and Louis MARSHALL, took it upon themselves to organize an institution that would be able to address ANTISEMITISM and Jewish needs worldwide. They were particularly responding to continued reports of violent POGROMS against Jews in RUSSIA, and they sought to create an organization that could counteract persecution and provide relief.

The early leadership used their personal authority to influence lawmakers and political leaders to maintain the American dream of religious freedom and equality not only for Jews but for all individuals and communities. The committee also operated with an eye toward relief. For example, it opposed immigration quotas, but supported the GALVESTON PLAN, an attempt to direct ships bringing new immigrants to Galveston, Texas, instead of to ELLIS ISLAND and New York, where high numbers of immigrants were believed to be creating vast social problems. It also influenced officials responsible for drafting the Treaty of Versailles to include protections for Jews and other minorities in Europe. Its efforts on behalf of the League of Nations were less successful.

In later years, the committee walked a tightrope between Jewish and American identities. It supported open immigration to PALESTINE, but its ties to ZIONISM were somewhat weak because of fear of alienating the many Jewish-American opponents of Zionism before World War II.

Today the American Jewish Committee has 33 regional offices, or chapters, across the United States and headquarters in New York City. The committee continues to address issues of religious freedom and human rights. The stated mission of the organization is: "To safeguard the welfare and security of Jews in the United States, in Israel, and throughout the world. To strengthen the basic principles of pluralism around the world, as the best defense against anti-Semitism and other forms of bigotry. To enhance the quality of American Jewish life by helping to ensure Jewish continuity and deepen ties between American and Israeli Jews."

The committee pursues this mission by transmitting its ideals in a variety of settings, including schools and synagogues, churches and community centers, city and state legislatures, businesses and civic associations. The committee addresses major world issues such as religious liberty and church-state relations, antisemitism and racism, immigration policies, education, and energy resources. The committee believes that education is one route to better understanding among people, but it also pursues its goals through economic, political, and social channels. It sponsors the intellectual magazine *Commentary.*

Further reading: Naomi W. Cohen, *Not Free to Desist: The American Jewish Committee, 1906–1966* (Philadelphia: Jewish Publication Society of America, 1972); Michael N. Dobkowski, *Jewish American Voluntary Organizations* (Westport, Conn.: Greenwood Press, 1986); *Toward Peace and Equity: Recommendations of the American Jewish Committee* (New York: The American Jewish Committee, 1946); Web site URL: http://www.ajc.org, accessed May 13, 2004.

American Jewish Congress (AJC)

The American Jewish Congress was founded in 1918 as a political action group to defend religious and human rights for Jews and others. Its founders were eastern European immigrants who felt unrepresented by the German-Jewish Americans who founded and led the AMERICAN JEWISH COMMITTEE and other communal or charitable groups.

These eastern European Jews wanted to assume a leadership role in the wider community, but they perceived that their wealthier and more assimilated coreligionists treated them in a condescending and humiliating manner. As World War

I drew to a close, rising ANTISEMITISM and violence in Europe was a catalyst for them to form a Jewish defense vehicle of their own.

After much debate within the Jewish community, including opposition from the American Jewish Committee, the congress held its first meeting in 1918. The original focus was on rising violence toward Jews in Europe following World War I; the congress saw itself as vital to the survival of Jews around the world. Largely Zionist (*see* ZIONISM) in orientation, the American Jewish Congress began with the following stipulations: that it convene after the war concluded, that national Jewish organizations elect 25 percent of the delegates to the congress, that the remaining 75 percent be nominated at regional conventions through direct elections, and that the organization disband once it had accomplished its goals of rehabilitating Jewish communities in Europe and obtaining basic human rights for those Jews living there.

The congress sent a group of representatives to the Paris Peace Conference following the war. This delegation helped obtain clauses and promises in peace treaties that established and protected the rights of European Jews; however, the delegation felt that since these decisions were not made by the people of their countries but by politicians, they did not ensure security on the local level. The congress reconvened in 1922, establishing itself as a watchdog organization with an eye toward protecting the human rights of Jews in Europe and around the world.

The American Jewish Congress never garnered the power needed to prevent the decimation of European Jewry during the HOLOCAUST. Stephen WISE, one of its foremost leaders, was thought to have influence with President Roosevelt, but it proved to be too little. Once World War II ended, the American Jewish Congress saw the importance of defending all peoples, Jews and non-Jews, from bigotry, prejudice, and discrimination. It focused its resources on constitutional law and fought many battles in the courts to preserve the human rights of all minorities.

Today the congress national headquarters is in New York City. There is a second national office in Washington, D.C., and nine regional offices throughout the United States. The organization is run by a lay president, who serves a two-year term, and an executive director. Its 50,000 members are invited to participate in biennial meetings, and the operations of the organization are established by an 80-member governing council.

The American Jewish Congress defines its objectives as follows: "to protect fundamental constitutional freedoms and American democratic institutions, particularly the civil and religious rights and liberties of all Americans and the separation of church and state; advance the security and prosperity of the state of Israel and its democratic institutions, and to support Israel's search for peaceful relations with its neighbors in the region; advance social and economic justice, women's equality, and human rights at home and abroad; remain vigilant against anti-Semitism, racism, and other forms of bigotry, and to celebrate cultural diversity and promote unity in American life; and invigorate and enhance Jewish religious, institutional, communal and cultural life at home and abroad, and seek creative ways to express Jewish identity, ethics and values."

Further reading: Morris Frommer, "The American Jewish Congress: A History, 1914–1950" (Ph.D. diss., Ohio State University, 1978); Stephen S. Wise, *Challenging Years: The Autobiography of Stephen S. Wise* (New York: Putnam's Press, 1949); Web site: http://www.ajcongress. org, accessed May 14, 2004.

American Jewish Historical Society (AJHS)

The American Jewish Historical Society is a research and educational organization that gathers and disseminates information about the history of Jews in America.

In the late decades of the 19th century, Cyrus ADLER, one of the foremost American Jewish leaders of his time, recognized a need for a formal organization devoted to gathering information about Jews in America. Some sources claim that Adler was in part motivated by antisemitic comments from prominent non-Jewish historians (*see* ANTISEMITISM). Adler felt that the Jewish community needed a repository of information about their lives and roles in the history of the UNITED STATES. Throughout its life the society has been funded by generous philanthropists and members.

In 1892, the American Jewish Historical Society was formally created by a group of men gathered at the JEWISH THEOLOGICAL SEMINARY in New York City. Their initial activities included publishing papers about Jews in the United States, primarily in a yearly journal called *Publications*, which became a quarterly in 1948. In 1961, the title of the journal changed to the *American Jewish Historical Quarterly* and then to *American Jewish History* in 1978. The society also gathered materials and collections pertaining to American Jewish history, housing them first in a reading room and then transferring them to the Jewish Theological Seminary in 1903.

After World War II, the society's leadership decided to focus on the history of eastern European Jewish immigrants and on Jews living in the western and southern regions of the United States. The collections, manuscripts, and materials accumulated, creating a need for a larger space. In 1968 the society relocated to its own building on the campus of BRANDEIS UNIVERSITY in Waltham, Massachusetts. In 2002, the organization moved its headquarters to New York City, where it became one of the founding institutions in the Center for Jewish History. Some facilities remain at Brandeis.

The society sponsors lectures, conferences, and fellowships that encourage the study of American Jewry and American Judaism. The collection, which is open to scholars, includes a variety of resources, including the papers of the Baron de Hirsch Fund (*see* HIRSCH, BARON MAURICE DE), the Council of Jewish Federations (now called the UNITED JEWISH COMMUNITIES), the Galveston

Movement (*see* GALVESTON PLAN) and the INDUSTRIAL REMOVAL OFFICE, Shearith Israel Congregation of New York, the Synagogue Council of America, and the American Jewish Congress. The society also houses the Rutenberg and Everett Yiddish Film Library. The society is fully modernized and holds traditional media such as pamphlets, periodicals, newspapers, and annual reports as well as audio, visual and computer resources.

According to the society itself, its mission today is: "to foster awareness and appreciation of the American Jewish heritage and to serve as a national scholarly resource for research through the collection, preservation and dissemination of materials relating to American Jewish history."

Further reading: John J. Appel, "Immigrant Historical Societies in the United States, 1880–1950" (Ph.D. diss., University of Pennsylvania, 1960); Web site URL: http://www.ajhs.org, accessed on May 14, 2004.

American Jewish Joint Distribution Committee (JDC; "The Joint")

The American Jewish Joint Distribution Committee, a cooperative venture among a number of Jewish communal organizations, is devoted to providing relief and rehabilitation for Jews and other victims of political persecution and other disasters.

In response to a plea for help from Jews living in PALESTINE as World War I began, the Union of Orthodox Jewish Congregations (UOJC) (*see* ORTHODOX JUDAISM) organized a group called the Central Committee for the Relief of Jews (CCRJ) in early October 1914. At the same time, the AMERICAN JEWISH COMMITTEE (AJC) also began to contribute funds to aid Jewish war victims. In an attempt to avoid duplicating their efforts, representatives from 40 Jewish agencies came together to form another organization in November of 1914, which they called the Joint Distribution Committee of American Funds for the Relief of Jewish War Sufferers (JDC). The main mission was to raise money to send abroad to Jews who

were suffering from dislocation or privation during the war. Although it was meant to represent the whole spectrum of Jewish communities, the JDC was controlled mainly by the Reform Jews, mostly of German descent (*see* REFORM JUDAISM). Even in its infancy, the organization raised $1.5 million and sent 900 tons of food to Jews in Palestine, then controlled by Turkey. In 1917, with the help of the Red Cross and the influence of President Woodrow Wilson, the JDC raised $4.75 million to provide relief to Jewish war sufferers.

By 1919, a year after World War I ended, the JDC had shifted its focus to reconstruction. It began to develop more comprehensive programs to help Jews in need abroad. It sent trained emissaries to Europe to assess living conditions and needs, to help local communities improve sanitation and child care, and to provide more economic choices. Ultimately, the JDC set up local social service agencies in European cities and towns and funded them until they could become independent, sustainable organizations. The work of the JDC extended into Bolshevik RUSSIA. "The Joint" became a familiar name in many European countries, especially POLAND, with its huge Jewish community.

Although its leaders had seen the JDC as a temporary relief organization, all thoughts of dissolving it disappeared as the organization gained in sophistication in the 1920s, and especially after Hitler rose to power in Germany and ANTISEMITISM gained strength throughout Europe in the 1930s. During World War II, the JDC rescued children and adults from Europe, organized social service agencies in GHETTOS, provided relief to the Warsaw ghetto, and aided the Jewish underground. JDC workers were the first to arrive at the displaced persons camps following the conclusion of World War II. Though it had remained neutral toward the idea of ZIONISM prior to the onset of World War II, the JDC began encouraging and aiding in the migration of Jews to Palestine. After the State of ISRAEL became a reality, the JDC operated a number of programs to help Jews immigrate to Israel. For example, in 1945–50, the organization ran Operation Magic Carpet, relocating a large group of

Yemenite Jews to Israel. And in 1991, the JDC contributed to Operation Solomon, the airlifting of 15,000 starving Ethiopian Jews to Israel.

Today the American Jewish Joint Distribution Committee remains one of the most efficient and successful worldwide Jewish social service agencies. Their current mission includes rescue, relief, renewal, Israel, and nonsectarian emergency needs. JDC is dedicated to the relief of suffering throughout the world based on the Jewish principle of TIKKUN OLAM, the Jewish responsibility of repairing the world.

Further reading: Yehuda Bauer, *My Brother's Keeper: A History of the American Jewish Joint Distribution Committee, 1929–1939* (Philadelphia: Jewish Publication Society of America, 1974); Oscar Handlin, *A Continuing Task: The American Jewish Joint Distribution Committee, 1914–1964* (New York: Random House, 1964); Web site URL: http://www.jdc.org, accessed on May 17, 2004.

am ha-aretz

Am ha-aretz is an ancient and a contemporary term, usually pejorative, for a person lacking education, whether general or in Jewish topics. The opposite term is *talmid hacham,* a scholar.

The term appears in Genesis (23:12–13) (*see* TORAH), where it apparently retains its literal Hebrew meaning of "the people of the land," or the ordinary citizens. In the period of the TALMUD, the term *am ha-aretz* referred to the Jewish peasants, who were poorly educated and, perhaps out of ignorance, did not scrupulously observe Jewish law. The Talmud records certain scholars as being dismissive of these people. However, many rabbis were embarrassed by this rhetoric against the uneducated; they decreed that everyone has sufficient learning, whether from books or life experience, to exempt them from the category of am ha-aretz.

The term survived in Yiddish (usually as *amoretz,* pl. *amoratzim*). In contemporary Jewish polemics (in Hebrew or other languages), the term is once more used in a derogatory fashion.

Further reading: Isidore Epstein, ed., *Soncino Hebrew/English Babylonian Talmud* (Brooklyn, N.Y.: Soncino Press Ltd., 1990); Marcus Jastrow, *Dictionary of the Targunim, Talmud Babli, Yerushalmi, and Midrashic Literature* (Brooklyn, N.Y.: Judaica Press, 1989).

Amichai, Yehuda (1924–2000) *modern Israeli poet*

Yehuda Amichai was one of ISRAEL's most important 20th-century HEBREW poets. He influenced the direction of modern Israeli poetry and attained wide popularity.

Amichai was born in Bavaria in 1924 to a family steeped in ORTHODOX JUDAISM, and he received a traditional Jewish education. In 1935 the family fled HITLER and immigrated to PALESTINE, finding a home in JERUSALEM. During World War II, Amichai fought with the Jewish Brigade of the British army. After his honorable discharge in 1946, he joined the PALMACH, and fought in the ISRAELI WAR OF INDEPENDENCE. Later, he also participated in the 1956 Suez War and the YOM KIPPUR WAR.

After the war, Amichai attended HEBREW UNIVERSITY, specializing in the study of biblical texts and Hebrew literature. Amichai's first volume of poetry, *Now and in Other Days,* was published in 1955 and prompted significant interest among both readers and literary critics. This collection, and subsequent volumes of poetry, demonstrated Amichai's devotion in both content and language to a modern literary approach and subject matter. He addressed what had previously been ignored—the realities of the modern day, things such as tanks, airplanes, fuel, war, and bureaucracy. Amichai strongly believed that the modern poet must confront the pressing issues of the times.

Thus, Amichai was innovative in his use of the Hebrew language. He drew from the entire linguistic history of the Hebrew language, including classical biblical Hebrew and Hebrew spoken in the streets. Amichai became known for changing the language of poetry, creating new Hebrew idioms and slang. His linguistic versatility reflected his interest in the contemporary, as opposed to a strict grounding in classical genres. Yet he also wrote about his childhood, emphasizing the peace and innocence he remembered before Hitler.

In 1982 Amichai was awarded the Israel Prize for his unique contribution to the field of poetry. Robert Alter, literary scholar, wrote in the *New York Times Magazine*, "For sheer energy of imagination, for the constantly renewed sense of poetry's ability to engage reality, Amichai has no close competitors on the Israeli scene, and perhaps only a few worldwide."

Amichai's poetry covered all the human emotions, but his emphasis was on the individual as part of the collective. His works often included biting criticism of Israel's contemporary political realities. Eventually he published many books of poetry as well as short stories, two novels, radio sketches, and children's literature. Although the themes in Amichai's work are generally highlighted by the Hebrew language, many of his works have been translated into other languages.

Further reading: Glenda Abramson, *The Experience Soul: Studies in Amichai* (Boulder, Colo.: Westview Press, 1997); Yehudah Amichai, *The Selected Poetry of Yehudah Amichai* (Berkeley: University of California Press, 1996); Yehuda Amichai, Benjamin Harshaw, and Barbara Harshaw, *Yehuda Amichai: A Life of Poetry, 1948–1994* (New York: HarperCollins, 1994); Haim Chertok, *Stealing Home: Israel Bound and Rebound* (New York: Fordham University Press, 1988); John Piling, *A Reader's Guide to Fifty Modern European Poets* (London: Heinemann US, 1982).

Amidah

The Amidah (literally the "standing," for the position in which it is recited) is the central prayer sequence of every Jewish worship service. As such it is recited three times a day by every observant Jew, and four or five times on SHABBAT (the Sabbath) and holidays (in a somewhat different format). It is often called the Shemoneh-Esrei, the "Eighteen," for the number of blessings or benedictions it originally contained, or simply Ha-T'filah, "the Prayer." Unlike nearly all other Jewish prayers, it is recited silently or in a very low voice.

The Amidah was composed as a vehicle to teach the basic dogmas of rabbinic Jewish belief. Written 2,000 years ago by the rabbis of the SANHEDRIN, it retained its central status through every historical period and in every Jewish community. It is one of the primary sacred texts taught to Jewish children today. The prayer was considered so important that it was ruled long ago that the CANTOR or prayer leader must repeat it out loud at most services, for the sake of those who were illiterate or unable to pray, and the custom continues to this day among most congregations.

The prayer consists of three principal sections: praise, supplication and thanksgiving. The first and third sections comprise three blessings each; they are said in every Amidah every day of the year. The number of blessings in the second section varies between ordinary and special days in the calendar.

The first three blessings speak of the eternal bond between God and the Jewish people; God's awesome might, including the power to revive the dead; and God's holiness. The middle 13 blessings in the weekday Amidah (one was added to the original 12) ask for wisdom, repentance, forgiveness, redemption from suffering and exile, good health for all, bountiful harvest, the ingathering of the exiles to Israel, justice, the downfall of the renegades (heretics or informers), reward for the righteous, the rebuilding of Jerusalem, the restoration of the Davidic kingship (presumably via the MESSIAH), and acceptance of prayer. The final three blessings, in the third section, are a request for the reestablishment of the TEMPLE service, an acknowledgement of God's compassion, and a prayer for peace.

Over the centuries, certain phases and passages were inserted into the Amidah, such as the request for rain in the winter and dew in the summer, as were prayers that recognize specific Jewish holidays, when appropriate to recite.

Every Amidah concludes with a private meditation: "that God help us refrain from talebearing, slander, and deceit, and that He protect us against the evil intention of others and strengthen us to observe the Torah." Jewish liturgical tradition also encourages the worshipper to use the time during the Amidah to add private prayer and thought to the required benedictions.

Further reading: Ismar Elbogen, *Jewish Liturgy: A Comprehensive History* (Philadelphia and Jerusalem: Jewish Publication Society, 1993); Rabbi Jules Harlow, ed., *Siddur Sim Shalom: A Prayerbook for Shabbat, Festivals, and Weekdays* (New York: Rabbinical Assembly, United Synagogue of America, 1989); Abraham Millgram, *Jewish Worship* (Philadelphia and Jerusalem: Jewish Publication Society, 1975); *Tanakh: The Holy Scriptures* (Philadelphia and Jerusalem: Jewish Publication Society, 1985).

amoraim (sing.: *amora*)

The *amoraim* (literally "interpreters") were the rabbis of the academies in BABYLONIA and PALESTINE who interpreted and expanded upon the MISHNAH; their discussions and rulings were compiled in the GEMARA. The Mishnah and Gemara together constitute the TALMUD, the basic repository of rabbinic Jewish law and ethics. The Amoraic period lasted from 219 C.E. to 500 C.E.

JUDAH HA-NASI completed the redaction (editing) of the Mishnah around 219 C.E. The Mishnah then served as the basis for discussion by the *amoraim*. Among the best-known *amoraim* were Abaye and Rava. Their debates appear frequently in the Babylonian Talmud. Moses MAIMONIDES in his MISHNEH TORAH (4:3) declared that the legal debates of these great *amoraim* were the foundation for practical Jewish law.

Further reading: Richard Lee Kalmin, *Sages, Stories, Authors and Editors in Rabbinic Babylonia* (Providence, R.I.: Brown Judaic Studies, 1994); Alfred J. Kolatch, *Masters of the Talmud: Their Lives and Views* (Middle Village, N.Y.: Jonathan David Publishers, 2002); Moses Maimonides, *Mishne Torah: Hilchot Yesodei Hatorah: The Laws, Which Are the Foundations of the Torah, Mishne Torah Series* (New York: Moznaim Publishing Corporation, 1989); Adin Steinsaltz, *The Essential Talmud* (New York: Basic Books, 1976); H. L. Strack and G. Stemberger, *Introduction to the Talmud and Midrash* (Minneapolis: Fortress Press, 1992).

ancient synagogues

Most scholars trace the origins of the SYNAGOGUE back to local gatherings by Jews in BABYLONIA during the first EXILE (586–538 B.C.E.). Before the exile, the religion of the ISRAELITES mainly revolved around the TEMPLE in JERUSALEM, the site for communal gatherings and ritual sacrifice. Upon the destruction of this central location, the exiled Jewish communities would meet in small assemblies (Greek *synagog*, Aramaic *knishtu*), which gradually developed into worship services.

The habit of meeting weekly for worship, TORAH teaching, and cultural life was brought into JUDEA with the return of the exiles. It has been argued that the development of the synagogue with its threefold purpose of study, prayer, and communal gathering is the single most important reason that Judaism was able to survive and flourish during historic periods of exile.

Further reading: Howard Clark Kee and Lynn Cohick, *Evolution of the Synagogue: Problems and Progress* (Harrisburg, Pa.: Trinity Press International, 1999); Lee I. Levine, *The Ancient Synagogue: The First Thousand Years* (New Haven, Conn.: Yale Books, 2000).

angels *See* MALAKHIM.

Anti-Defamation League (ADL)

The Anti-Defamation League is an independent voluntary organization dedicated to opposing prejudice and discrimination against minority groups, especially Jews in the UNITED STATES and ISRAEL.

In 1913 the leaders of B'NAI B'RITH, already established as a fraternal order and benevolent society, decided to launch an organized struggle against a wave of ANTISEMITISM, which included the incendiary campaigns surrounding LEO FRANK, who was later lynched. They established the ADL with a mission to fight discrimination and prejudice against Jews.

According to its leader, Sigmund Livingston, a lawyer living in Chicago, Illinois, the ADL aimed "to stop, by appeals to reason and conscience, and if necessary, by appeals to law, the defamation of the Jewish people . . . to secure justice and fair treatment to all citizens alike . . . [and to] put an end forever to unjust and unfair discrimination against and ridicule of any sect or body of citizens." While Livingston's vision has not rid the world of antisemitism, racial hate, bigotry, or prejudice, the ADL has made great strides in ridding the public arena of expressions of prejudice. The group has helped pass state and federal laws protecting religious, racial, and other minority groups from discrimination in hiring, housing, immigration, and college admissions, and has made the media more alert to harmful negative portrayals of these groups.

In one of its early and most striking successes, after auto magnate Henry Ford published and promoted books based on the fraudulent document, the PROTOCOLS OF THE ELDERS OF ZION, which outlined a supposed Jewish conspiracy to take over the world, the ADL demanded and eventually secured a public apology by Ford, who published evidence refuting the *Protocols*. In the 1930s, the ADL began to gather data on people and organizations designed to promote hate, such as the Ku Klux Klan (KKK). Information leads to power, and the ADL has used its stores of information to bring dangerous groups motivated by hate to public attention in order to break their power, as they did when they successfully "unmasked" the KKK by law in the 1950s. The ADL was active in the Civil Rights movement of the 1960s and became instrumental in the passing of laws that prevented outright discrimination.

By the second half of the 20th century it became clear that the ADL needed to attend to issues of hate, bigotry, and prejudice on a global scale. The ADL does not, therefore, limit its activities to the United States, but watches for evidence of prejudice and discrimination to the world's minorities in all areas of the globe, including unfair representations of Israel around the world. The ADL promotes a variety of educational programs as well, to combat racism, prejudice, and discrimination. The group has also utilized the horrors of the HOLOCAUST to teach the serious ramifications of hate to children and adults. In addition, the ADL has monitored issues of church-state separation in the United States, encouraged the peace process in the Middle East, and fought defaming images of Jews in the context of the ongoing crisis in that region.

With a sophisticated approach to education, and a vigilant concern with the image of Jews and other minority groups in the media, the ADL has become a successful monitoring force in the fight against hate worldwide. The organization boasts 30 regional and satellite offices.

Further reading: Daniel J. Elazar, *The Organizational Dynamics of American Jewry* (Philadelphia: Jewish Publication Society, 1995); *Extremism in America: A Guide*, (CD-ROM), 2002 edition, published by the Anti-Defamation League; Web site URL: http://www.adl.org, accessed on May 17, 2004.

anti-Judaism

The term *anti-Judaism* is often used in historical works to refer to a dislike or hatred of the Jews because of their religious beliefs or opinions, or, in the ancient context, because of their political actions and their threat to the ruling power, such as the Jewish rebellions against ROME that led to the destruction of the second TEMPLE.

It is important for the student of Judaism to distinguish between anti-Judaism and the more familiar term ANTISEMITISM, which is more properly used in the context of the modern era. Antisemitism is a product of the rise of nationalism and racism in the last two centuries, and depends on constructs or concepts of nations and ethnic groups. It promotes negative feelings and hatred of the Jews based on their lack of a nation (before 1948) and their alleged nature as foreigners in other nations. It uses misconceived negative stereotypes and images of Jews, and myths such as the BLOOD LIBEL.

Judaism first developed as the national religion of a fairly isolated people. Once it evolved into a more international religion in the context of other cultures and belief systems, anti-Judaism became a factor as other religions struggled against it. Anti-Judaism did not necessarily reflect any dislike or hatred of Jews as a people or race or any perceived negative stereotypes. For example, from the start of Christianity until the present there have been Christians who felt and expressed dislike for Jews because they did not accept JESUS OF NAZARETH as the messiah. Those who espoused this form of anti-Judaism would often welcome any Jewish person who converted to CHRISTIANITY and thus accepted Christ as the MESSIAH; their hatred was not based on a perceived Jewish racial characteristic that cannot be removed even by conversion. However, a Christian who continued to hate a Jew on national grounds even after he or she converted can fairly be called antisemitic.

In the modern democratic tradition most people reject the view that religious differences, heresy, or error justify hatred for the people who hold those different views, and many Christian clergy, for example, would condemn anti-Judaism just as they would condemn antisemitism. However, anti-Judaism is no different in essence from anti-Catholicism or even anticapitalism. It is important to recognize this difference from antisemitism, which has its own connotations and unique historic characteristics.

Further reading: David Berger, *History and Hate: The Dimensions of Anti-Semitism* (Philadelphia: Jewish Publication Society, 1986); Jeremy Cohen, *The Friars and the Jews: The Evolution of Medieval Anti-Judaism* (Ithaca, N.Y.: Cornell University Press, 1982); Judith M. Leiu, *Anti-Judaism and the Fourth Gospel* (Louisville, Ky.: Westminster John Knox Press, 2001); Marvin Perry, ed., *Jewish-Christian Encounters over the Centuries: Symbiosis, Prejudice, Holocaust, Dialogue* (New York: Peter Lang, 1994).

Antiochus (Antiochus Epiphanes)
(215–164 B.C.E.) *Seleucid king*

Antiochus Epiphanes was the Hellenistic ruler who, in the second century B.C.E., provoked a Jewish revolt led by the Maccabee family, which reestablished Jewish independence and which is celebrated in the holiday of CHANUKAH.

A member of the Seleucid dynasty, which inherited one-third of the empire built by Alexander the Great, Antiochus came to power around 175 B.C.E. He tried to impose Hellenistic culture on the Jewish people in Judea, at the time a Seleucid province, and outlawed many Jewish religious practices. His actions culminated in the defilement of the Second TEMPLE in December 167 B.C.E. He or his agents offered unclean animals (such as a pig) on the altar, dedicated the Temple to the Greek deity Zeus, erected a statue of Zeus within the Temple, and plundered the Temple of valuable ritual objects.

According to the book of MACCABEES in the APOCRYPHA, Antiochus's actions prompted the Maccabean revolt, leading to the reclamation of the Temple and its rededication in 164 B.C.E. During Chanukah, Jews light candles to memorialize the miracle of the oil lamp in the rededicated Temple that burned for eight days, though it contained only sufficient oil for one.

Some historians conjecture that Antiochus became involved in conflicts between priests in the Temple; in this view, he entered into a series of bribe negotiations that resulting in the installation of Menelaus into the office of HIGH PRIEST, thus interrupting the traditional succession to that position through the Zadokite family lineage, and setting the stage for a Jewish civil war.

Further reading: Norman Bentwich, *Hellenism* (New York: The Jewish Publication Society of America, 1920); Shaye J. D. Cohen, *From the Maccabees to the Mishnah* (New York: Westminster Press, 1987).

antisemitism

Antisemitism is a modern term denoting hatred against Jews or the Jewish people, quite apart from any rejection of the Jewish religion (*see* ANTI-JUDAISM).

The term *antisemitism* does not have a single meaning. It can refer to a general hostility without any claimed justification, or it can refer to a hatred based on false beliefs about the behavior or characteristics of individual Jews or the Jewish people as a group, such as brutal religious rituals (*see* BLOOD LIBEL), unethical business behavior, or dangerous political activity. It often involves conspiracy theories about supposed Jewish desires to dominate non-Jews economically or politically.

Antisemitism often relies on negative stereotypes concerning the physical appearance or health of Jews, with little or no basis in reality. In fact, the concept, no matter how it is defined, generally involves the idea that the Jewish person is fundamentally different from or inferior to other humans in a way that cannot be changed. It is similar to concepts such as racism and sexism. Racism, sexism, and antisemitism all include the notion that the people thus described are "other," they are unlike the person perpetuating the dislike, and they are thus less than human and do not deserve sympathy or rights as other humans do.

The term was coined in 1879 by the German writer Wilhelm Marr to categorize the anti-Jewish sentiment then increasing in Europe; he first used it in a pamphlet entitled "The Victory of Judaism over Germanism." Marr based the term on a linguistic category: the Semitic languages, which include Hebrew as well as many ancient languages like AKKADIAN and various languages spoken today in the Middle East and North Africa by people of many different races and origins.

Since that time, it has become common to use the term *antisemitism* to refer to any activity in the past or present that exhibits hatred or animosity toward someone of Jewish descent, or toward the modern state of ISRAEL. Nevertheless, historians prefer to restrict its use to the context of modern social and political behavior, and to the history of nationalism and racism, primarily in the European and Middle Eastern world.

There are several problems with the term *antisemitism*. In a sense it was always a misnomer, as there is no such thing as a "Semite" or Semitic individual, only a Semitic language. The category of Semitic language includes Arabic. Thus, it seems silly to call an Arab antisemitic, since he or she speaks a Semitic language; nevertheless, the modern behavior and belief system known as antisemitism is present in the Arab world, where the products of European antisemitism such as the *PROTOCOLS OF THE ELDERS OF ZION* have been widely distributed. This oddity causes one to look at the term more closely.

Scholars agree that the term *antisemitism* has often been used in an anachronistic fashion—projecting our modern notions of race and peoplehood to time periods where people did not organize themselves into nations and races. For example, during the height of the Roman Empire, the Romans did not hate the Jews any more or less than any other non-Roman people, all of whom they considered to be barbarians. The Romans destroyed the TEMPLE in 70 C.E. because the Jews were rebelling against them, not because of any ideas of race or irrational categorical hatred. Christians living in the early centuries of the first millennium may have hated the Jews either because they did not accept Jesus of Nazareth as the MESSIAH or because the Christians held the Jews responsible for his death. This dislike, however, is an extension of a belief system about the world in general, not a result of an irrational hatred toward the Jews as a group. The Romans and the Christians, therefore, could be seen as exhibiting anti-Jewish sentiment, but not antisemitism in the narrow sense of the term.

Adolf HITLER, on the other hand, perpetuated a systematic hatred against the Jews based on their very existence, an irrational categorical condemnation of a group of people, whether or not they ascribed to any Jewish beliefs. Hitler's antisemitism is often called political antisemitism. Cultural and religious forms of antisemitism also exist.

The reasons for the existence of antisemitism around the globe are difficult to identify. It cannot be traced to one culture or exclusively identified as social, economic, political, or psychological. One reason that goes across cultures is that the Jews, since Roman days, have lived as a minority group in many different countries, and were often regarded as strangers in their host lands, an existence made even more dangerous with the rise of nationalism and a growing intolerance of minorities among majority cultures.

Another aspect of Jews that some cultures found intimidating is their tendency to live in urban areas and their disproportionate presence in commerce and finance. There are historic reasons for this presence, including Christian laws that prohibited Jews from owning land, working in agriculture, or practicing crafts, and other laws that prohibited Christians from charging interest on loans or making a profit. In addition, Jews maintained contact across political boundaries for religious reasons, which facilitated commerce.

This created a negative stereotype of Jews as money-hungry and exploitative, ultimately resulting in the ideas summarized in the *Protocols,* which claimed that wealthy Jews were conspiring to take over the world. Economic antisemitism developed to the point that extremist or cynical political leaders have often used the Jews as scapegoats for all a nation's economic ills, such as in RUSSIA at the end of the 19th century and in GERMANY after World War I.

The UNITED STATES has often been viewed as an exception among host countries in its attitude toward the Jews. It is possible to attribute a higher degree of acceptance to the general multicultural nature of the country and its democratic and egalitarian principles. However, America also has a history of antisemitism and anti-Judaism, seen most clearly in Henry Ford's publication of the *Protocols* or in the anti-Jewish radio speeches of the wildly popular priest Father Charles Coughlin before World War II. Today, the ANTI-DEFAMATION LEAGUE and the AMERICAN JEWISH COMMITTEE express concern over rising antisemitism. Often in the contemporary world, political beliefs about the State of Israel are connected with preexisting antisemitic sentiment.

Further reading: Yehuda Bauer, series editor, *Studies in Antisemitism* (Chur, Switz.: Harwood Academic Publishers, 1994); David Berger, *History and Hate: The Dimensions of Anti-Semitism* (Philadelphia: Jewish Publication Society, 1986); Stephen Eric Bronner, *A Rumor about the Jews: Reflections on Anti-Semitism and "The Protocols of the Learned Elders of Zion"* (Houndmills, Basingstoke, Hamps., U.K.: Palgrave McMillan, 2000); Leonard Dinnerstein, *Anti-Semitism in America* (New York and Oxford: Oxford University Press, 1994); Arnold Forster and Benjamin R. Epstein, *The New Anti-Semitism* (New York: McGraw-Hill Book Company, 1974).

Apocrypha (Deuterocanon)

Literally "hidden writings," the Apocrypha is a collection of ancient Jewish religious books that are included in many Christian Bibles but were not included by the rabbis when they compiled the TANAKH or Hebrew Bible. Several of the books do appear in most manuscripts of the SEPTUAGINT, so scholars believe they were probably accepted as Scripture by many Jewish communities in the early rabbinic period.

The Apocrypha includes historical material such as First and Second MACCABEES; moral tales such as Tobit, Judith, and Susanna; wisdom literature such as Ecclesasticus; letters such as the Letter of Jeremiah; and poetry such as the Prayer of Manasseh. Material from the Apocrypha was eventually accepted as canonical within the Roman Catholic community, but it was excluded from the Tanakh and Protestant Christian Bibles (*see* CHRISTIANITY).

Further reading: Bruce M. Metzger and Roland E. Murphy, eds., *The New Oxford Annotated Bible with the Apocrypha* (New York: Oxford University Press, 1994); J. R. Porter, *The Lost Bible: Forgotten Scriptures Revealed* (Chicago: University of Chicago Press, 2001).

Arab-Israeli conflict

The conflict between Arabs, particularly Palestinian Arabs, and Jews is a modern phenomenon. While the struggle is certainly affected by religious and cultural differences, the driving issue is a dispute over territory in the Middle East that Jews wish to possess as their own Jewish state.

The land known as PALESTINE is claimed by both Arabs and Jews. After the end of the ISRAELI WAR OF INDEPENDENCE in 1949, the territory that formerly comprised the BRITISH MANDATE of Palestine was divided into three parts: the State of Israel, the West Bank (*see* JUDEA and SAMARIA) of the Jordan River, and the Gaza Strip. These three parts together cover about 10,000 square miles, roughly the size of Belgium or Maryland. The Jewish claim and Arab claim to be legitimate governors of these lands is irreconcilable unless significant compromise can be made by both sides.

Jews claim ownership rights to the land variously called CANAAN, ERETZ YISRAEL, Judea, and Palestine, based on several arguments: they believe they have a biblical title to the land; their religious and national ancestors occupied the land for 1,500 years and developed ethical MONOTHEISM there; no other nation, religion, or language was ever exclusively identified with that land; and there is an imperative need for a Jewish state to ensure the safety of world Jewry, while dozens of Arab countries already exist, some of which share the culture, dialect, and history of the Palestinian Arabs.

Arabs claim the land of Palestine belongs to them because Arabs were the majority of the population there for more than a thousand years (although the land was ruled by Turkish Muslims or western European Christians for most of that period). They reject Jewish history as a claim for land, and they believe that the Koran interprets the words of the Hebrew Bible to indicate that the Arabs are the correct heirs to the land. They also do not believe a safe haven for world Jewry should be created in a country where the Arabs were the majority when European Jews began to return and settle the land.

ZIONISM emerged as a political movement in the 19th century at the same time that many nationalist movements began, including Arab nationalism. The Zionist movement demanded the right of self-determination and sovereignty in the land of Israel. In 1882, Zionist Jewish immigration to Palestine began. At this time, the land in question was governed by the Muslim Turkish Ottoman Empire. By the time World War I began in 1914, the population of Jews in Palestine was between 60,000 and 85,000, while the non-Jews (mostly Arabs) numbered 683,000. Initially, most Arab landowners welcomed Jewish settlers, actively wishing to profit on the purchase of land. Many poor Arabs benefited from the modern economy built by the immigrants, and Arab immigrants flocked from neighboring countries.

The Zionist Organization (*see* WORLD ZIONIST CONGRESS) was established by Theodor HERZL in 1897, and it subsequently led the movement to secure a national home for the Jews in Palestine. At the conclusion of World War I, the British Empire took control of Palestine and vast other territories in the Middle East. They needed to balance the competing interests and desires of both Jews and Arabs. In 1917, the British foreign secretary, Lord Arthur Balfour, issued the BALFOUR DECLARATION announcing British support for the establishment of a Jewish national home in Palestine. The British helped set up several independent Arab states after World War I, including Iraq, Transjordan, and Saudi Arabia, but the Arabs believed Britain had promised them Palestine as part of Syria, as well, and were angry about the Balfour Declaration. The Arabs' concern grew stronger in the 1920s as Jewish immigration to Palestine continued unchecked. Beginning in 1920 the Jewish National Fund began to purchase large areas of land in Palestine from absentee Arab landowners. Violent clashes between Arab and Jewish residents in Palestine began at that time; they continued intermittently throughout the British Mandate period, and still continue.

With the rise of Adolph HITLER in GERMANY, Jewish immigration to Palestine soared, and land purchases accelerated. This resulted in an Arab revolt that lasted from 1936 to 1939, which was suppressed by a British-Zionist alliance. The British issued the 1939 WHITE PAPER, which laid down a new British policy that limited Jewish immigration and land purchases. The Zionists believed this to be a violation of the Balfour Declaration, and a major threat to the safety of world Jewry as Hitler's power increased and the persecution and discrimination against Jews in Europe spread.

By the end of 1946, 608,000 Jews and 1,269,000 Arabs resided in Palestine. The Jews had purchased approximately 7 percent of the total land in Palestine from Arab landowners, comprising 20 percent of available arable land. The British turned to the UNITED NATIONS to resolve the competing claims of the Arabs and Jews. In response, the United Nations approved a PARTITION PLAN, which the Zionist leadership reluctantly accepted and the Arab leadership completely rejected. When Israel declared its independence on May 15, 1948, it was immediately attacked by its Arab neighbors. The war ended in 1949, when armistice agreements were signed between the Arab countries and Israel based on the "green line" of disengagement, which remained the practical border for 18 years.

The Jewish State of Israel encompassed approximately 77 percent of what had been Palestine. Approximately 700,000 Palestinian Arabs became refugees following the Israeli War of Independence. Today there are approximately 3 million Arab Palestinians living within the areas of Israel, the West Bank, and Gaza, and 700,000 of them are citizens of Israel. Outside Israel's official border, 1.3 million Palestinians live in the West Bank and 1 million in the Gaza Strip. It is estimated that another 3 million Palestinians live outside these three contested areas, of whom 1.3

million reside in Jordan (which before 1922 was a part of Palestine). Some 70 percent of the land assigned to Britain in its Mandate is now Jordan, 85 percent of whose population can be considered Palestinian.

In June 1967, the SIX-DAY WAR resulted in Israel taking possession of both the West Bank and the Gaza Strip. The occupation of these territories restored JERUSALEM to Jewish control, and the Israelis now claim the entire city as their eternal capital. The war placed a significant number of Palestinians under Israeli military rule. The Palestinian national cause reached its own crescendo, led by the PALESTINE LIBERATION ORGANIZATION (PLO), a collection of political, military, and terrorist factions.

In 1973 the Arab nations launched a surprise attack against Israel on the Jewish holy day of YOM KIPPUR. After initial military success, the Arab nations were defeated, marking the last formal aggression by Arab states against Israel. Several years later Egyptian President Anwar SADAT initiated a peace agreement with Israel, which won back the Sinai Peninsula for Egypt and secured Israel's southern border.

Since 1967, Israel has developed Jewish settlements in the West Bank and Gaza. While concentrated in specific areas, this is a source of further stress between the Jews and the Arabs. The PLO was endorsed and supported by the Arab League, by the Communist bloc, and eventually by most countries in the world. With the Arab defeat of 1967, the group pursued both legal and illegal means to achieve their goal of securing a Palestinian state. Led by their chairman, Yasser Arafat, they rejected the right of Israel to exist as a Jewish state, calling for its destruction and organizing violence against it. At the same time, they lobbied the world for support of their Palestinian cause. When Jordan no longer wished to serve as an operations base for Palestinian aggression against Israel in 1970, the Palestinians relocated to Lebanon. Their attacks against Israel from that country eventually sparked the LEBANON WAR in the 1980s. Israel succeeded in removing the

Palestinian military groups from Lebanon, but the war had long-term consequences for both Lebanon and the Israeli conscience.

In December 1987, the PLO helped organize the first INTIFADA, or uprising against Israel by Palestinians residing in the West Bank and Gaza. The intifada utilized both civil disobedience and violence directed toward Israeli Jews. Israel managed to suppress the rebellion, and after the first Gulf War in 1991, negotiations between the two sides formally began. In 1993, an agreement was reached in which both the Israelis and the Palestinians mutually recognized each other's national claims. As a result, they set forth parameters by which both a Palestinian and a Jewish state could live side by side.

In 1994 the PLO became the core of the PALESTINIAN AUTHORITY (PA), a semiautonomous government in the West Bank and Gaza. In January 1996, elections were held for a Palestinian legislative council, and Arafat became the president of the PA. In July 2000, UNITED STATES president Bill Clinton invited Israeli prime minister Ehud BARAK and Arafat to CAMP DAVID ACCORDS to negotiate a final comprehensive agreement. Israel agreed to significant withdrawal from Palestinian land areas, awarding the PA approximately 97 percent of the land they asked for (plus transfers of Israeli land to make up the difference) and allowing for the creation of a Palestinian capital in East Jerusalem. However, the Israelis agreed to allow only limited numbers of Palestinians to return to Israel proper. Whether for those reasons, or because he was not interested in a peace agreement, Arafat rejected the proposal. In the meantime, PA-sponsored groups embarked on a second Intifada, called the al-Aksa Intifada, which focused on suicide bombings of civilian facilities in Israel. Arafat's terrorist groups were joined by Hamas, an Islamic Arab extremist group which continues to explicitly reject Israel's right to exist.

Israel, unable to reach an agreement with the Palestinians, has embarked on the controversial project of building a security fence to cut off Jewish territories from Palestinian territories. Prime Minister Ariel SHARON announced a plan in 2004 to withdraw all Israeli settlements from Gaza, and several from the West Bank, as a unilateral interim solution to the conflict. The United States had declared that since Arafat was unwilling to renounce the use of terrorism, they no longer accepted him as a representative of the Palestinian people. It seemed that the Arab-Israeli conflict would remain at the same point of irreconcilable differences as existed in 1920. However, following Arafat's death in November 2004, the Palestinian people elected Mahmoud Abbas (b. 1935), also known as Abu Mazen, to be their president. Both Israelis and Palestinians hope for peace, as new leadership brings the promise of new possibilities.

Further reading: Mitchell G. Bard, *Myths and Facts: A Guide to the Arab-Israeli Conflict* (Chevy Chase, Md.: American-Israeli Cooperative Enterprise, 2001); Robert O. Freedman, *World Politics and the Arab-Israeli Conflict* (New York: Pergamon Press, 1979); Walter Laqueur, *The Israel-Arab Reader: A Documentary History of the Middle East Conflict* (New York: Penguin Books, 2001); Benny Morris, *Righteous Victims: A History of the Zionist-Arab Conflict, 1881–2001* (New York: Vintage Books, 2001).

Aramaic

Aramaic was a widely spoken language in the Middle East for 2,000 years before and after the start of the Common Era; it was the primary language of Jews during the early rabbinic period (70 C.E.–640 C.E.).

The GEMARA, the largest component of the TALMUD and the major source of Jewish rabbinic law, was written down in Aramaic. In addition, about 200 verses of the TANAKH, the Hebrew Bible, are written in the language, including a large part of the book of Daniel. It is also the language of a few important HEBREW prayers to this day.

The rabbis in the TALMUD discussed the surprising fact that many Jewish sacred texts were written in the Aramaic vernacular of their time, though Hebrew was the language of nearly all the

Tanakh and most prayers. In the Talmud, the rabbis claimed that even Adam, the first human being, spoke Aramaic (SANHEDRIN 38b). This explanation justifies for the ancient rabbis the extensive use of Aramaic in rabbinic and biblical literature.

Aramaic was originally written in cuneiform, the writing system developed for Sumerian and AKKADIAN, but was later written in its own version of the alphabet. The Aramaic alphabet eventually replaced the ancient Hebrew alphabet. The prophet NEHEMIAH was apparently the first to use the Aramaic alphabet for the books of the Tanakh, when he saw that the Israelite people were no longer familiar with the ancient Hebrew letters.

JESUS OF NAZARETH probably spoke Aramaic as his mother tongue, since it was the common language spoken in Judea 2,000 years ago. Some words in the NEW TESTAMENT are also in Aramaic. Some of the first widely used translations of the Hebrew Bible were into Aramaic. These versions, known as the Targums, have been used for centuries by scholars seeking to understand how the ancient rabbis interpreted the Hebrew Scriptures.

Further reading: John Bowker, *The Targums and Rabbinic Literature: An Introduction to Jewish Interpretation of Scripture* (Cambridge: Cambridge University Press, 1969); Norman K. Gottwald, *The Hebrew Bible: A Socio-Literary Introduction* (Philadelphia: Fortress Press, 1985); Marcus Jastrow, ed., *Hebrew Aramaic English Dictionary* (New York: Shalom Publications, 1967).

Arendt, Hannah (1906–1975) *political philosopher and writer*

Trained as a political scientist in GERMANY before World War II, Hannah Arendt was a rising student of philosophy as the war commenced. She is credited with establishing the concept of totalitarianism and its negative relationship with the nation-state, and she is also known for her theory of "the banality of evil" in the 20th-century bureaucratic state, which she developed in her reporting on the EICHMANN TRIAL. Arendt's writings are universal in scope, although she never denied or specifically ignored her Jewish heritage or experiences.

Born in Hanover, Germany, on October 14, 1906, Arendt was an only child. Both her parents were raised in homes of Russian-Jewish businessmen. Arendt's father died of a syphilis-related disease when she was seven. She grew up in the city of Konigsberg, which witnessed extensive fighting between RUSSIA and Germany during World War I. War was not a foreign concept to Arendt as she grew from childhood to adulthood.

In 1924 Arendt graduated from high school and began her university studies with Rudolf Bultmann at the University of Marburg. There she met Martin Heidegger, who was also on staff at the university. They both explored and wrote about the philosophical schools of existentialism and phenomenology. Arendt and Heidegger had a romantic affair, but she soon relocated her studies to the University of Heidelberg to study with Karl Jaspers. Ironically, Heidegger was to become an ardent antisemite (*see* ANTISEMITISM) and proponent of the Nazi worldview. At the age of 22, Arendt received her doctorate from the University of Heidelberg.

Escaping Germany and the Nazis in 1933, Arendt fled to FRANCE, where she was involved with a Zionist group called Youth Aliyah, which sent young European Jews to PALESTINE (*see* ALIYAH, ZIONISM). Arendt served as director of the group from 1935 to 1938, and she even had the opportunity to go with some of the young people to Palestine. However, in 1940, Arendt became an inmate in the Gurs concentration camp in France. Along with a group of 100 intellectuals, Arendt, her husband Henrich Blucher, and her mother were allowed to immigrate to the UNITED STATES as part of a political agreement made with President Roosevelt.

Arendt arrived in the United States in 1941 and became a U.S. citizen 10 years later. In the United States she fashioned a successful career as a scholar, editor, and research director. She continued to move in prominent intellectual circles in the United States, forging a strong relationship with the

Twentieth-century philosopher Hannah Arendt, on the left, proposed the theory of the banality of evil after reporting on the Eichmann trial in Jerusalem in 1961. *(Library of Congress)*

historian Salo Baron and his wife, Jeanette. She was research director for the Conference on Jewish Relations (1944–46), chief editor of Schocken Books (1946–48), and executive secretary of Jewish Cultural Reconstruction (1949–52). Arendt was the first woman to become a full professor at Princeton University, and she also taught at the University of Chicago, Wesleyan University, and the New School for Social Research. She was the author of many works that discuss the political aspects of human behavior, including *Origins of Totalitarianism* (1951), *The Human Condition* (1958), *On Revolution* (1963), *Eichmann in Jerusalem* (1963, first appearing in a series of articles in the *New Yorker* magazine), and *On Violence* (1970).

Arendt's career was not without struggle. The publication of *Eichmann in Jerusalem* met with opposition from the Jewish community. Arendt argued that Eichmann's actions were not those of an evil villain, but simply of a cog in the Nazi machine. She suggested that Eichmann was guilty more of thoughtlessness in pursuing his duties as a Nazi than as an evil leader who masterminded the murder of millions. Arendt received even more criticism for her comments suggesting that fewer Jews would have died in the HOLOCAUST if the Jewish councils, the JUDENRAT, had been less helpful to the Nazis. While Arendt did see herself as a Jew, she did not connect with the Jewish community beyond her early activities as a Zionist and her belief in a binational state in Palestine. Arendt's ideas of the banality of evil and its connection to the modern state remain vital parts of Holocaust study today despite the initial rejection of many of her ideas. In recent decades, she has been criticized for defending Heidegger after World War II despite his Nazi activities.

Further reading: Hannah Arendt, *Eichmann in Jerusalem: A Report on the Banality of Evil* (New York: Penguin Books, 1977); Lewis P. Hinchman, and Sandra K. Hinchman, eds., *Hannah Arendt: Critical Essays* (Albany: State University of New York Press, 1994); Dana R. Villa, *Politics, Philosophy, Terror: Essays on the Thought of Hannah Arendt* (Princeton, N.J.: Princeton University Press, 1999).

Argentina

The story of Jewish life in Argentina, Latin America's third-largest country and the one with the largest Jewish community, can be defined by immigration patterns not unlike that of the UNITED STATES. Waves of Jewish immigration occurred after 1492, in the middle of the 19th century, and around the turn of the 20th century. The Jews who immigrated to Argentina and the communities that they formed experienced times of peace along with instances of ANTISEMITISM. During the middle of the 20th century, Argentina became home to many Nazis (*see* GERMANY), including war criminals fleeing justice.

The first wave of Jewish immigration to Argentina occurred after the expulsion of Jews from SPAIN in 1492. These Jewish immigrants are called CONVERSOS, as they had openly converted to CHRISTIANITY to avoid the Inquisition but secretly retained Jewish practices behind closed doors. Most of the Jews of the first wave of immigration probably assimilated into Argentinean society (*see* ASSIMILATION) because of the tolerant atmosphere in the early 19th century created by the first president of independent Argentina, Bernardino Rivadavia.

Rivadavia's policies also opened Argentina's doors to the second wave of Jewish immigration in the mid-19th century. During this period, Ashkenazic Jews from western Europe arrived on Argentinean soil where they were encouraged to farm the land. The first recorded MINYAN came together in 1862, and the first Argentinean Jewish SYNAGOGUE was established a few years later; it was called the Congregación Israelita de la República Argentina. Scholars estimate the number of Jews living in Argentina in 1870 at 300 to 500. Though a small community, the Jewish settlers in Argentina enjoyed many civil rights, including the ability to marry in both the legal and religious realms. They were subject to some discrimination, mostly due to the personal actions of immigration officers rather than codified and encouraged by the government.

In the late 19th century Jewish immigrants from RUSSIA began to arrive in Argentina, encouraged by the loose immigration laws and by philanthropist Baron de HIRSCH. Hirsch viewed Jewish immigration to Argentina as a viable option for those young Zionists (*see* ZIONISM) who were unable to immigrate into PALESTINE because of Turkish restrictions. The Russian immigrants were called "Rusos," and they were to become part of Argentinean society, taking on roles as farmers, peddlers, artisans, and shopkeepers. At least one group of Jewish immigrants, those who arrived on the SS *Weser* in 1889, became gauchos, or Argentinean cowboys, working the land with the financial backing of Hirsch, who founded the Jewish Colonization Association. Today many Jews still manage these properties, although many are now owned by non-Jews.

By the year 1920, more than 150,000 Jews had made Argentina their home. Jewish immigration had remained steady between 1906 and 1912, resulting in approximately 13,000 Jewish immigrants each year. Most of the immigrants from this period were ASHKENAZIM from Europe, but some were SEPHARDIM from Morocco and the Ottoman Empire. They settled in a country mostly free of antisemitism, which did not appear in Argentina in force until after World War I. The Russian Revolution (1918–30) sparked POGROMS aimed at the Rusos in Buenos Aires in January of 1919, but it was the rise of Juan Perón to power in 1946 that marked the beginning of ongoing antisemitic sentiment in Argentina. Perón closed Argentina's doors to Jewish immigrants, and he allowed Nazis to settle there without recrimination. At the same time, he recognized the existence of the State of ISRAEL in 1949. Perón was removed from power in 1955, but more instances of antisemitism dotted Argentina's history as Adolf EICHMANN was abducted in Argentina by Israeli agents and put on trial in Israel for war crimes in 1960. The Argentinean Jewish community would suffer further when the country fell under military rule between the years 1976 and 1983. Of the 9,000 people who disappeared off the streets of Argentina for political "crimes," it is estimated that around 1,000 of them were Jewish.

Antisemitism has decreased in Argentina, though there were two major terrorist attacks in the 1990s, one at the Israeli embassy in 1992 and the other at the Jewish community headquarters in 1994. Carlos Saúl Menem, elected president in 1989, has been a friend to the Jewish community in Argentina despite his Arab origins, although he has recently been accused of complicity or negligence regarding the 1994 attack.

The recent economic crisis of Argentina's middle class has reduced many Jewish families to poverty levels, causing Jewish communities around the world to rally to their support. The AMERICAN JEWISH JOINT DISTRIBUTION COMMITTEE and the JEWISH AGENCY played a role in training young Argentinean Jews to rebuild the Jewish community and its institutions. Many young Jews have emigrated from Argentina in the last half of the 20th century and the beginning of the 21st.

The contemporary Jewish community in Argentina numbers at most a quarter of a million, most of whom live in Buenos Aires. About 60 percent of Jewish children attend some form of Jewish educational institution. There are many Jewish aid societies in Argentina, including the political Delegación de Asociaciones Israelitas Argentinas (DIAI), the Ashkenazic Mutual Aid Society (AMIA), and the Vaad HaKehilot, the federation of Jewish communities. While most of Argentina's synagogues are traditional, the Conservative movement has been a strong influence. The JEWISH THEOLOGICAL SEMINARY established a branch in Argentina in 1962, and Rabbi Marshall Meyer was influential within the Jewish community and with the Argentinean government until his departure in 1984. The seminary continues to provide rabbis for Latin America, and the Jewish community of Argentina is beginning to find its voice as an energetic expression of contemporary Judaism, including a more open Sephardic culture and the appearance of ultra-Orthodox Jews (*see* ORTHODOX JUDAISM) on the scene.

Further reading: Haim Avni, *Argentina and the Jews: A History of Jewish Immigration* (Tuscaloosa: University of Alabama, 1991); Martin A. Cohen, ed., *The Jewish Experience in Latin America* (Waltham, Mass.: American Jewish Historical Society, 1971); Daniel Judah Elazar and Peter Medding, *Jewish Communities in Frontier Societies—Argentina, Australia and South Africa* (New York: Holmes & Meier, 1983); Eugene F. Sofer, *From Pale to Pampa: A Social History of the Jews of Buenos Aires* (New York: Holmes & Meier, 1982); Robert Weisbrot and Robert Murciano, *Jews of Argentina: From the Inquisition to Peron* (Philadelphia: Jewish Publication Society, 1989).

ark

The English word *ark* evokes several images from Jewish history and civilization. In chronological order, the most popular images of an ark are the ark of NOAH, the Ark of the COVENANT, and the Holy Ark that is the most important fixture in every SYNAGOGUE.

In the book of Genesis in the TORAH, God commands Noah to build an ark (*Teivah*), a very large boat, of gopher wood (Gn 6:14–16). God warns Noah that there is going to be a global flood, and that the animals and people who are allowed onto the ark will be saved from death. Thus, the ark in Jewish lore may often refer to the boat that Noah built to save each species of animal as well as his own family from drowning during the flood. There are many legends about Noah's ark; occasionally a modern archaeologist will claim to know where it rests, although no convincing evidence has yet been uncovered. The Hebrew word for the ark of Noah is not related to that of the Ark of the Covenant or the Holy Ark.

The Ark of the Covenant (Aron HaBrit) is first mentioned in the book of Exodus in the TANAKH. This time God commands MOSES to build a wooden box to house the tablets of the law, or the Ten Commandments (*see* DECALOGUE) that God gave to Moses and the ISRAELITES at MOUNT SINAI (Ex 25:10–22). The ark was known to encase the tablets of the law, but it was also known to be in a sense a dwelling place for God. The box was made from acacia wood and was four feet long, two and one-half feet wide and two and one-half feet high. It was lined with gold and had rings of gold through which poles could be inserted to carry it. There was another plate of gold the size of the box on the top, and two cherubim, or angels, who protected the ark with their wings.

The ark was carried by the LEVITES, the priestly class, as the Israelites wandered through the desert, and sometimes it was brought into battle. Aside from times of war, the ark rested inside the Tabernacle (*see* MISHKAN) and was approached only by the HIGH PRIEST on YOM KIPPUR, the Day of Atonement. After the Israelites settled in CANAAN,

in ERETZ YISRAEL, the ark rested in the Holy of Holies in a sanctuary in Shiloh. The Bible states that it was once captured by the Philistines, but it was returned after a series of misfortunes befell them. King DAVID transferred the ark to JERUSALEM, and when King SOLOMON built the first TEMPLE, it was housed there. No one knows where the ark may be today.

However, every Jewish sanctuary contains a different kind of ark, the Holy Ark that holds Torah scrolls (Aron Ha-Kodesh). The ark in a modern sanctuary is a sort of closet that houses the Torah, usually positioned at the front, toward Jerusalem in the east, or in the very center of the room. Either way, the ark is the focal point of any Jewish sanctuary, and when it is opened to reveal the Torah scrolls inside, the congregation rises with respect.

While Noah's ark led to a covenant, or agreement, between God and all humans to repopulate the earth with animals and people, the Ark of the Covenant represented God's covenant with the Jewish people to be their God. The Holy Ark carries forth the promise to modern times. As the Ark of the Covenant was believed to be a vessel for God's presence, so too does the Holy Ark contain the promise between God and the Jews to protect them and to provide law for them.

Further reading: Hayim Halevy Donin, *To Pray as a Jew: A Guide to the Prayer Book and Synagogue Service* (New York: Basic Books, 1980); Louis Ginzberg, *Legends of the Bible* (Philadelphia: Jewish Publication Society of America, 1956); Avram Kampf, *Contemporary Synagogue Art: Developments in the United States, 1945–1965* (Philadelphia: The Jewish Publication Society of America, 1966); Patrick D. Miller, *The Religion of Ancient Israel* (London: SPCK, 2000).

Ashkenazim

World Jewry includes two significant cultural groups. One group is called the SEPHARDIM, and the other is called the Ashkenazim. Both groups emerged during the early Middle Ages—the

Believed to be a representation of the portable Ark of the Covenant, this relief was found by archaeologists in the Capernaum synagogue located on the northern shore of the Sea of Galilee. Mention of the Ark of the Covenant first appears in the biblical book of Exodus. It was made of wood and housed the tablets of the Ten Commandments. The Holy Ark was considered to be a dwelling place for God. *(Library of Congress)*

Sephardim in the Iberian Peninsula, the Ashkenazim in central Europe. The first Ashkenazi communities were founded in the Rhineland in what is now western GERMANY, probably by Jews migrating north from Italy, where they had been exiled following the destruction of the TEMPLE.

The term Ashkenazim comes from a HEBREW name for a particular people mentioned in the Hebrew Bible (*see* TORAH). Beginning in the ninth century the term Ashkenaz was applied to Germany, and German Jews began to be called Ashke-

nazim to distinguish them from the Sephardim. When the Crusades concluded, Ashkenazim began to relocate to eastern European countries. Therefore, when one refers to the Ashkenazim today, eastern European Jews are included in that category. Eventually, Ashkenazim settled in western Europe and in America.

Ashkenazim pronounce Hebrew differently than Sephardim do, their liturgies are slightly different, and some of their ritual practices differ as well, such as the types of food permitted to be eaten during the holiday of PASSOVER. Until the beginning of the 20th century, most Ashkenazim spoke YIDDISH, a blend of Hebrew and German. However, Hebrew remained the language of religious scholarship among Ashkenazim.

The Ashkenazim lived under the Christian rulers of Europe. By the 11th century, they had organized themselves into *kehillot* and *kahals* (*see* KAHAL, KEHILLAH), autonomous communities formally recognized by the feudal rulers. The kehillot and kahals developed their own administrative, judicial, educational, medical, and social support systems. The Ashkenazim paid the feudal rulers their taxes and enjoyed their insular existence. Almost all legal matters were taken care of in the kehillot and kahals, with the local Jewish authorities maintaining their own systems of justice.

Ashkenazim, unlike Sephardim, did not embrace the study of secular philosophy and science, concentrating their intellectual resources on the oral study of Jewish law and religion. The spread of printing in Europe greatly assisted the mass distribution of religious scholarship written by Ashkenazi RABBIS, such as the scholar RASHI in 11th-century France. The primary goal of the Ashkenazi Jew before the enlightenment of the 18th century was to lead a devout religious life devoted to traditional Jewish textual study.

The HOLOCAUST that occurred in Europe during World War II destroyed 6 million of the 18 million Jews who once populated the world. The majority of those murdered were Ashkenazim. In the UNITED STATES, the significant majority of the Jewish community is of Ashkenazi decent. In

ISRAEL, the Jewish population is split more or less in half between Ashkenazim and Sephardim.

Further reading: David Biale, *Cultures of the Jews: A New History* (New York: Schocken Books, 2002); Jacob Rader Marcus, *The Jew in the Medieval World: A Source Book, 315–1791* (Cincinnati: Hebrew Union College Press, 1999); Stephen Sharot, *Judaism: A Sociology* (New York: Holmes & Meier Publishers, 1976); H. J. Zimmels, *Ashkenazim and Sephardim, Their Relation, Differences, and Problems as Related in the Rabbinical Responsa* (London: Marla, 1976).

assimilation

Assimilation is the process by which a minority group adapts to a surrounding culture, usually at the expense of part or all of its own original culture. It has been a major issue in Jewish history, especially since the EMANCIPATION of the Jews in Europe beginning in the 1800s. Even in ancient times, Jews were faced with assimilation. When Jews lived under Greek rule, for example, from 333–174 B.C.E., they were influenced by the prevailing HELLENISM, often adopting Greek names and participating in aspects of Greek culture such as the gymnasium. In modern times, assimilation is rampant among American Jewry and some believe it to be a threat to the survival of Judaism.

Of course, there are varying degrees of assimilation. Jews can accept partial AMERICANIZATION by eating pizza or hot dogs but only at kosher fast-food restaurants, work with and go to school with non-Jews but only date fellow Jews, and take off work or school on Christmas while avoiding any possible religious participation in the holiday. Such a degree of assimilation is often termed ACCOMMODATION—one keeps one's JEWISH IDENTITY and practices but also enjoys the amenities of American culture. A further level of assimilation may include shopping on Shabbat (after all, Saturday is the major shopping day in America), eating a McDonald's cheeseburger (a particularly nonkosher item), intermarrying with non-Jews, and having a Christmas tree in one's home. In this case, as one assimilates more into American culture, one becomes in danger of losing one's Jewish identity and practices.

Further reading: Steven M. Cohen, *American Assimilation or Jewish Revival* (Bloomington: Indiana University Press, 1988); Alan M. Dershowitz, *The Vanishing American Jew: In Search of Jewish Identity for the Next Century* (New York: Simon & Schuster, 1998); Gerhard Falk, *American Judaism in Transition: The Secularization of a Religious Community* (Lanham, Md.: University Press of America, 1995); Calvin Goldscheider and Alan S. Zuckerman, *The Transformation of the Jews,* (Chicago: University of Chicago Press, 1986); Arthur Hertzberg, *A Jew in America: My Life and A People's Struggle for Identity* (San Francisco: HarperSanFrancisco, 2002); Menachem Mor, ed., *Jewish Assimilation, Acculturation, and Accommodation: Past Traditions, Current Issues, and Future Prospects* (Lanham, Md.: University Press of America, 1992); Charles E. Silberman, *A Certain People: American Jews and their Lives Today* (New York: Summit Books, 1986).

Association of Jewish Family and Children's Agencies (AJFCA)

The American Jewish community has a long history of social service, on behalf of both Jews and non-Jews. The Association of Jewish Family and Children's Agencies is an umbrella agency attesting to the breadth and depth of Jewish social service agencies across the UNITED STATES.

The AJFCA traces its roots back to the 19th century, when the needs of new immigrants made specifically Jewish social services essential. The group is not itself a service-providing agency, but a membership organization that provides support to other agencies that do provide direct services to those in need.

The mission of the AJFCA is to provide support to the more than 145 preventive and social service agencies that look to it for support of their programs. Among its many goals, AJFCA advocates for safety nets for the poor and other families with special needs, assists member agencies with management, capacity building, strategic planning, and personnel development, educates lay and professional leaders, improves program quality by highlighting and publicizing programs that work, engages in public policy development and legislative monitoring, establishes standards of practice to increase the professionalism of the field of social service, and encourages member agencies to share and communicate with one another.

Further reading: Jerome A. Chanes, Norman Linzer, and David J. Schnall, *A Portrait of the American Jewish Community* (Westport, Conn.: Praeger Publishers, 1998); Web site URL: http://www.ajfca.org, accessed June 9, 2004.

Assyrians

In biblical times, the Assyrian state often bordered ISRAEL, and there were numerous battles between the ISRAELITES and the Assyrians. Assyria, like EGYPT and BABYLONIA, was a major empire during biblical times; it was at its peak from approximately 1100 to 645 B.C.E., ruling extensive territories from its capital of Nineveh. From biblical sources as well as from the extensive royal library that archaeologists have uncovered at Nineveh, we know a significant amount about the kingdom of Assyria and its relationship to ancient Israel.

In the year 722 B.C.E., the Assyrians conquered the northern kingdom of Israel, known as Samaria, leaving the southern kingdom of Judea intact but under Assyrian domination (*see* JUDEA AND SAMARIA). The citizens of the northern kingdom assimilated (*see* ASSIMILATION) into Assyrian culture and have never been heard from again. Many legends have arisen about these people, who are often referred to as the TEN LOST TRIBES of Israel. The Assyrians were eventually conquered by the revived Babylonian Empire, and disappeared from history.

Further reading: Norman K. Gottwald, *The Hebrew Bible: A Socio-Literary Introduction* (Philadelphia: Fortress Press, 1985); H. J. Zimmels, *Peoples of the Old Testament World,* ed. Alfred J. Hoerth, Gerald L. Mattingly & Edwin M. Yamauchi (Grand Rapids, Mich.: Baker Books, 1998).

aufruf

Aufruf is a YIDDISH term that means "calling up." It originated as a European Jewish custom, still practiced, in which a groom (or both bride and groom in egalitarian congregations) is called up to the TORAH during a worship service, in order to receive a special pre-wedding blessing, called a MI SHEBERAKH. The congregation asks God to bless the bride and groom on their forthcoming marriage and their life together as husband and wife. The *aufruf* traditionally occurs on the SHABBAT morning before the wedding.

Further reading: Rita Milos Brownstein, *Jewish Weddings: A Beautiful Guide to Creating the Wedding of Your Dreams* (New York: Simon and Schuster, 2003); Anita Diamant, *The New Jewish Wedding* (New York: Charles Scribner's Sons, 2001).

Auschwitz (Oswiecim)

Auschwitz was the largest CONCENTRATION AND DEATH CAMP, called by the German name of the nearby Polish city Oswiecim; apart from its vast slave labor facilities, it was known as the largest death camp, where vast numbers of Jews and a smaller number of non-Jews were murdered by the Nazis during World War II.

Most Jews arrived at the camp by train and were immediately divided into two lines. Those in one line—the elderly, weak, and most children—were immediately gassed. Others were set to work in appalling conditions until they died or became too weak to work, at which point they were sent to the gas chambers. More than 1.5 million Jews were gassed to death in this camp alone during the HOLOCAUST. In addition, hundreds of inmates were forced into medical experiments supervised by Dr. Josef MENGELE, the chief physician at Auschwitz.

The phrase *arbeit macht frei* ("work makes free") greeted inmates as they entered the camp; the sign has become a well-known image, representing the hellacious experience of the Holocaust, comprising both life in unbearable conditions and the massacre of innocents. In addition to Jews, many Gypsies, Poles, and others deemed subhuman by the Nazis were murdered in Auschwitz. Auschwitz was liberated on January 27, 1945. Soldiers were so appalled by the skeletal figures they saw that many of them were physically sickened.

Auschwitz came to represent the failure of the world community to recognize and respond to Jewish persecution. The proximity of the camp to the town makes it virtually impossible for the city's residents not to have had some idea of what was going on inside the camp, but no one in the city spoke out. Allied war leaders have also been criticized for failing to bomb the camp

This is an aerial photograph of Auschwitz, World War II's most notorious concentration and death camp. The highly organized layout of the camp reveals how the Nazis murdered 1.5 million Jews in an extremely efficient manner. *(U.S. National Archives)*

or the rail lines leading to it to slow the Nazi death machine.

Further reading: Peter Cunningham, "Bearing Witness: Notes from Auschwitz," *Tricycle* 6, 3 (Spring 1997): 35–39; Michael R. Marrus, *Auschwitz: New Perspectives on the Final Solution* (New York: Oxford University Press, 1997); Terence Des Pres, *The Survivor: An Anatomy of Life in the Death Camps* (New York: Oxford University Press, 1976); John K. Roth and Richard L. Rubenstein, *Approaches to Auschwitz: The Holocaust and its Legacy* (New York: John Knox Press, 1987).

Austria

Jews have lived in Austria since the time of the Romans. The first written record of a Jewish presence in the country dates from the years 903–906. The oldest Jewish tombstone in Austria bears the date 1130, and the earliest evidence of a Jewish settlement dates to 1194. The first SYNAGOGUE appears to have stood in Vienna in 1204. In fact, most of the Jews who have lived in Austria since the late medieval period resided in that city. By the 13th century, the Jewish community had established Vienna as a center of Jewish learning. In addition, many Jews had become involved in Viennese commerce, holding important positions in tax collection and trade.

Even though the Jews had established a place for themselves in Vienna and Austria, they were not free from discrimination and prejudice. Frederick II of Hohenstaufen granted the Jews of Vienna a charter in 1238, followed by another charter for all of Austria in 1244. Such charters granted minorities certain rights, although not full membership in society, and the number of Jews immigrating to Austria from GERMANY increased. However, by the end of the same century, the Jews saw increasing discrimination and anti-Jewish sentiment, much of it emanating from the Catholic Church, especially after the ecclesiastical Council of Vienna in 1267. Four instances of BLOOD LIBEL can be found in the records from this era, in addition to massacres, mercantile restric-

tions, and the random cancellation of debts owed to Jews.

By the end of the 18th century, Austria was developing into a centralized modern state, and the Jewish population was encouraged to become more integrated into Austrian society. The Jews no longer were required to wear the yellow badge (*see* YELLOW STAR) identifying them as Jews, and they were encouraged to teach their children to speak German and to send them to German-speaking schools. In 1784 the judicial autonomy of the Jewish community was dissolved; instead, the Jewish population was required to use the Austrian court system and to join the army. Joseph II of the Hapsburg Empire made these sweeping changes; after his death life for the Jews declined in quality, as various restrictive laws were passed, ranging from a quota on marriages to a requirement that Jewish children attend Christian schools. Yet the Jews were not stripped of all rights, and the late 19th century brought another upswing in the status of Jews, especially during the reign of Franz Josef.

In 1867 Austria-Hungary (*see* HUNGARY) adopted a new constitution that guaranteed religious freedoms, officially granting equality within the law to peoples of different religious traditions. ASSIMILATION among the Jews of Vienna had already begun to take hold, and by the end of the 19th century, the upper and middle economic classes of Jews identified strongly with German culture. Even so, more instances of blood libel accusations were to develop, and strains of modern ANTISEMITISM appeared in Austrian society. The city of Vienna at the turn of the 20th century was governed by a mayor elected on an explicitly anti-semitic platform, yet Jews participated fully in economic, cultural, and political life without much encumbrance, even from the mayor.

Movements to combat antisemitic trends appeared in Austrian society, especially ZIONISM, which attracted wide support in the country thanks to the writings and activities of THEODOR HERZL (1860–1904), a Viennese journalist. The Zionist influence increased during and after

World War I, as 36,000 mostly poor refugees arrived in Vienna from eastern Europe; this was not the first time eastern European Jews had migrated to Austria. By 1918 300,000 Jews lived in the newly created Austrian Republic, two-thirds of them residing in Vienna. Despite instances of antisemitism and civil rights that changed by the year, the Jewish community thrived.

By the 1930s, a very large number of Jews were prominent in the Austrian economy, in industries ranging from scrap iron, which was traded exclusively by Jews, to advertising, furniture, banking, and textiles, where the proportion of Jews was at least 75 percent. By this time, the Austrian Jewish community had created several Jewish schools, a teacher's seminary, Zionist organizations, youth organizations, and Jewish political parties. There was open debate in the community about the benefits and dangers of assimilation. On the part of the German Austrian community, however, there was a vast different between the government's attitude toward the Jews, which was positive, and the public's attitude toward the Jews, which was still heavily influenced by antisemitic ideologies. Austrian-born Adolf HITLER is believed to have been strongly influenced by antisemitic writings and organizations he encountered while living for several years in Vienna.

On March 13, 1938, Germany annexed Austria, an event called the Anschluss. At the time there were between 180,000 and 220,000 Jews living in Austria, 90 percent of them in Vienna. The Nazis immediately removed all civil rights from Jews, fined the community, incited POGROMS, seized property, desecrated synagogues, and imprisoned the leaders and intelligentsia of the Jewish community at the Dachau CONCENTRATION CAMP. Sigmund FREUD (1856–1939) was among the first of thousands of Austrian Jews forced to flee their homeland to save their lives. In the next few years, the majority of the Jewish population emigrated from Austria with the help of Zionist groups and even the German authorities. By the time of World War II, well over 100,000 had left,

leaving around 66,000 living in Vienna. Nearly all these remaining Jews were either murdered in concentration camps, sent to GHETTOS in POLAND or RUSSIA, killed on the road, or finally sent to the concentration camp called Theresienstadt to die. By the time the Jewish community of Vienna was officially dissolved, there were only 7,000 Jews living there, most of them married to non-Jews. By 1943 there were only 800 Jews left in Vienna, and these were secretly helped by some in the non-Jewish community and by the Budapest Jewish rescue committee. Some of the 800 survived World War II.

Most Jewish communities in Austria were never rebuilt, but the Viennese community, today called the Israelitische Kultusgemeinde, did reconstitute and begin to resurrect Jewish communal institutions, among them the Jewish Labor Federation and the Zionist Federation. The AMERICAN JEWISH JOINT DISTRIBUTION COMMITTEE funded half the Viennese Jewish community's budget until the 1950s, when the financial situation began to improve.

Despite the continued vibrancy of anti-semitism in Austria, relations between ISRAEL and Austria have been decent. Bruno Kreisky, a Christian whose parents had been born Jewish, was elected federal chancellor (prime minister) in 1970, though critics decried his decision to end the prosecution of Nazi war criminals in Austria, which had provided a disproportionate number of high functionaries in the HOLOCAUST, including Adolf EICHMANN. Even before, Austria was notorious for its leniency toward Nazi war criminals, and the country never fully participated in the search for lost property or in the payment of war reparations or restitution, though belated attempts were carried out in the late 1990s and afterward. Before World War II there were 97 synagogues in Austria; only six have been rebuilt.

Further reading: George E. Berkley, *Vienna and Its Jews: The Tragedy of Success, 1880–1980s* (Cambridge, Mass.: Abt Books, Inc., 1988); Gordon Brook-Shepherd, *The Austrians: A Thousand-Year Odyssey* (New York: Carroll

& Graf Publishers, 1996); David W. Weiss, *Reluctant Return: a Survivor's Journey to an Austrian Town* (Bloomington & Indianapolis: Indiana University Press, 1999).

Auto-Emancipation *See* PINSKER, YEHUDAH LEV.

Azazel, goat of

The concept of a "scapegoat," often used in modern Western society, has a very literal meaning in the TANAKH, the Hebrew Bible—the goat of Azazel. In chapter 16 of the book of Leviticus, God tells AARON the HIGH PRIEST to present a sin offering on the altar, in order to make "expiation for himself and for his household." Aaron was to bring two rams "before the Lord at the entrance of the Tent of Meeting; and he shall place lots upon the two goats, one marked for the Lord and the other marked for Azazel. . . . the goat designated by lot for Azazel shall be left standing alive before the Lord, to make expiation with it and to send it off to the wilderness for Azazel" (Leviticus 16).

The high priest, in the original instance Aaron but later the priests of the TEMPLE in Jerusalem, would symbolically lay his hands upon the head of the goat marked for Azazel and confess over it the sins of the people; he would then send the goat out into the wilderness. In English translation, the goat of Azazel became commonly known as the "scapegoat" (the goat that escapes).

The medieval rabbinic commentator NACHMANIDES taught that Azazel was a goatlike demon to which the ISRAELITES sometimes offered sacrifices (*see* SACRIFICE). He further taught that sending the goat to the wilderness was a symbolic expression of the idea that the people's sins, such as worshipping a foreign demon, and the punishment for those sins, were to be sent back to their original source—the spirit of desolation and ruin beyond the sphere of law and true religion.

This Azazel cultic practice ceased when prayer replaced sacrifice, after the destruction of the Second Temple in JERUSALEM in 70 C.E. However, the model of symbolically ridding oneself of sin remains in place today in the traditional Day of Atonement liturgy. On the day of YOM KIPPUR, Jews gather in public worship, confess their sins, ask God for forgiveness, and hope that if they are sincere, God will forgive the sins committed against God. Sins against other people must be addressed directly with the wronged individuals before they can be forgiven by God.

Some European Jews perform a ritual recalling the goat of Azazel in the days before Yom Kippur. A live chicken is waved over the head of each member of the family to absorb his or her sins; the chicken is then slaughtered and given to poor people.

The notion of a scapegoat became significant in the history of medieval and modern ANTISEMITISM. When Jews were blamed for epidemics, economic crises, and other disasters, it was said that they were being "scapegoated." It is a historical irony that the concept of "scapegoat" itself originates with the ritual of the high priest in the ancient Temple.

Further reading: Ralph D. Levy, *The Symbolism of the Azazel Goat* (San Francisco, Calif.: International Scholars Publication, 1998); Patrick D. Miller, *The Religion of Ancient Israel* (Louisville, Ky.: Westminster/John Knox Press, 2000); *Tanakh: The Holy Scriptures* (Philadelphia and Jerusalem: The Jewish Publication Society, 1985).

B

Baal

The term *baal* has multiple connotations within the Jewish religion. The Hebrew root of the word translates as "possess"; in combination with other words, it usually means "possessor of" or "characterized by." By itself, it can mean "lord" in all its secular contexts. Most often, in the TANAKH, the Hebrew Bible, it refers to one of the ancient pagan deities of the Semitic cultures neighboring the ISRAELITES.

Baal worship is commonly referred to in the Tanakh as the illicit religious behavior of the Israelites when they joined in the practices of their pagan neighbors. Baal worship represented the immoral or cruel behavior that people can indulge in, especially as typified by pagan hedonism.

The Book of 1 Kings (16:31) records that a king of Israel, Ahab, "took as a wife Jezebel, daughter of Ethbaal, king of the Sidonians," and he went and served Baal. Elijah the Tishbite, a great Jewish prophet, battles Ahab, Jezebel, and the Baal worshippers. Jezebel assists in a campaign to wipe out the "prophets of the Lord," but when Elijah is the only prophet left, he has a final confrontation with the Baal worshippers, and with God's help, destroys them all.

Further reading: Norman K. Gottwald, *The Hebrew Bible: A Socio-Literary Introduction* (Philadelphia: Fortress Press, 1985); Hershel Shanks, ed., *Ancient Israel* (Englewood Cliffs, N.J.: Prentice Hall, 1988); *Tanakh: The Holy Scriptures* (Philadelphia and Jerusalem: Jewish Publication Society, 1985).

Baal Shem Tov (the Besht) (1700–1760)
founder of modern Hasidism

Originally named Rabbi Israel ben Eliezer, the Baal Shem Tov ("Master of the Good Name") is considered the founder of the modern movement of HASIDISM (which literally means "piety"). Though an attested historic figure, he has become the subject of many legends and morality tales.

The Baal Shem Tov is said to have been born to poor elderly parents and orphaned while still young. He worked at various jobs; he was an assistant in a Hebrew religious school, quarry laborer, and innkeeper. Legends abound about him, all emphasizing his piety, his simple life, and his skill as a healer and teacher.

In 1740 the Besht (an acronym for Baal Shem Tov) moved to Meziboz, and he began to attract students through his focus on individual piety and joyfulness rather than on rigorous TALMUD study and ascetic practices, which were then commonly deemed the highest goals of religious life. He established the basic elements of Hasidism, including the focus on developing a religious spirit and closeness to God, appreciation of physical pleasures as creations of God, and respect for every Jew. He emphasized that individuals worship God in many ways, not just in formal religious observances.

Most significantly, the Besht taught that the true spiritual leader (the TZADDIK) should not only have deep knowledge of the TORAH, but should also be a model of religious piety. Later leaders in Hasidism would expand the importance of the tzaddik, but its roots were in the Besht's teachings. His teachings put him at odds with the MITNAGDIM, the religious conservatives of the time. All contemporary Hasidic movements trace their roots back to the Besht.

Further reading: D. Ben Amos and J. R. Mintz, eds. *In Praise of the Baal Shem Tov* (Lanham, Md.: Jason Aronson, 1994); Martin Buber, *Hasidism* (New York: Philosophical Library, 1948); Martin Buber and Maurice Friedman, *The Origin and Meaning of Hasidism* (New York: Horizon Press, 1960).

baal teshuvah

A *baal teshuvah* ("master of return" or repentance) is a formerly nonobservant Jew who has returned to a traditional observant Jewish lifestyle. Within today's ORTHODOX JUDAISM there is an informal *baal teshuvah* movement. Many Jewish people seeking a greater sense of spirituality, or who have found life in the secular world to be unsatisfactory, choose to become *baal teshuvahs*, sometimes jocularly called B.T.s. A return to tradition can provide a structure and belief system that seems to make sense to some modern individuals.

Many organizations are active in the baal teshuvah movement, including CHABAD and Aish HaTorah, Ohr Sameach, and other YESHIVAS dedicated to the training of nonobservant Jews. It is not uncommon for baal teshuvahs to become religious zealots, intolerant of Jews who are less observant or who identify with liberal Judaism. *Baal teshuvahs* often have problems relating to

non-Orthodox family members; a whole literature has arisen to advise both children and parents on both sides of the divide.

Most *baal teshuvahs* are welcomed in the Orthodox world, but some are considered to be a poor reflection on orthodoxy. Some Orthodox Jews distinguish themselves from *baal teshuvahs* by referring to themselves as *frum* (pious) from birth, or F.F.B.

Further reading: Agi L. Bauer, *Black Becomes a Rainbow: The Mother of a Baal Teshuvah Tells Her Story* (Nanuet, N.Y.: Feldheim Publishers, 1991); Jack Wertheimer, *A People Divided: Judaism in Contemporary America* (New York: Basic Books, 1993).

Babylonia

The ancient land of Babylonia, comprising most of present-day Iraq, played a central role in the development of Judaism. After the destruction of both the first and the second TEMPLES in JERUSALEM (in 586 B.C.E. and 70 C.E., respectively), strong Jewish communities emerged in Babylonia that were able to adapt Judaism and Jewish culture creatively to the new realities.

The Babylonian Empire, centered on the vast and wealthy capital city of Babylon, annexed the territory of Judea (*see* JUDEA AND SAMARIA) in 586 B.C.E. The Hebrew Bible, the TANAKH, is itself a source of information about Babylon; the prophet Jeremiah mentions its walls and the prophet ISAIAH remarks on its greatness.

After the Babylonians destroyed the first Temple in Jerusalem in 586 B.C.E. they exiled many of the Jews, including the leadership classes. The exiles headed for Babylonia and settled there along the canals at Babylon, a city located on the eastern bank of the Euphrates River. Psalm 137 (*see* TEHILLIM) records their cries of woe: "By the waters of Babylon, there we sat down, and we wept when we remembered Zion." Even though the Persian CYRUS the Great, who conquered Babylon, allowed the Jews to return to Judea 70 years later, many Jews remained in Babylonia, having established their own autonomous communities governed by Jewish officials known as the EXILARCH and the NASI. Some scholars believe that Babylonian culture absorbed by the first exiles strongly influenced the final shape of biblical Judaism.

When the Romans defeated the rebellions in Judea in 70 C.E. (when they destroyed the second Temple) and again in 132, they laid waste to the entire country, and a large part of the surviving population left. The Jewish community in Babylonia grew in strength, both economically and, more important, culturally, especially in the field of RABBINIC LAW and literature.

Around the year 220 the TANNAIM in Palestine completed their redaction of the MISHNAH, the authoritative compilation of the ORAL LAW ultimately derived from the Torah. Over the next 300 years, the Babylonian and Palestinian Jewish communities each developed a body of commentary on the Mishnah which was eventually compiled into the GEMARA. The combination of Mishnah and Gemara is called the TALMUD. One Talmud came to be known as the Babylonian Talmud, completed around 550 B.C.E., the other the Palestinian or Jerusalem Talmud, completed around 400 B.C.E. Over the years, the authority of the Babylonian Talmud came to be accepted over that of the Palestinian Talmud. Most references to the Talmud today are understood to imply the Babylonian version.

One reason historians propose for the greater authority of the Babylonian Talmud is that the Babylonian scholars tended to address issues of the DIASPORA in greater detail, since they themselves lived outside of ISRAEL. In doing so, they spoke directly to the broader Jewish community as it spread around the world. In addition, the Palestinian community suffered severe repression under Byzantine rule, while the Babylonian Jewish community remained strong for many more centuries, even well after the emergence of the Muslim Caliphate at Baghdad, near Babylon.

Babylonia was to become the home of the greatest rabbinic academies, places of study that would produce a gigantic collection of rabbinic commentary, legal and religious opinions, and liturgy, and would provide leadership to Jewish communities around the world through the Middle Ages. The chief academies were located in the cities of SURA and PUMBEDITA. The exile of the Jews to Babylonia did not technically end until 1948, when most of the 200,000-strong Jewish community of Iraq immigrated to the new state of Israel.

Further reading: Shaye J. D. Cohen, *From the Maccabees to the Mishnah* (Philadelphia: Westminster Press, 1987); Jacob Neusner, *There We Sat Down: Talmudic Judaism in the Making* (New York: Ktav Publishing House, Inc., 1978); *Tanakh: The Holy Scriptures* (Philadelphia and Jerusalem: The Jewish Publication Society, 1985).

Baeck, Leo (1873–1956) *modern German rabbi*
Leo Baeck was born in what is now Lezno, POLAND, and raised in a family loyal to ORTHODOX JUDAISM, but he was also educated in classical and German secular philosophy. He received his rabbinical ordination in 1897. Beginning in 1912, Baeck served as a rabbi in Berlin, where he also lectured on the literature of the MIDRASH. As a rabbi, Baeck is best known for his contributions to the liberal stream of Judaism. Within that tradition, which tended to focus on ethical behavior, he insisted on the need for mystery, spirituality, and the divine.

Early in his rabbinic career, Baeck became the recognized spiritual leader for German REFORM JUDAISM, serving as the chairman of the Union of Rabbis. Most of his philosophical positions are captured in his book, *The Essence of Judaism*. Baeck's ideas were grounded upon the teachings of Hermann COHEN (1842–1919). Both Baeck and Cohen believed that the fundamental essence of Judaism was ethical MONOTHEISM. After the universalistic embrace of God came the religion's ethical emphasis, which was expressed within the context of particularistic religious teachings.

In Baeck's theological system Jewish particularism represented how the Jew understood and practiced holiness. Ultimately, Baeck moved beyond

Cohen's idea that the belief in God was sufficient. He urged individual Jews to cultivate an emotional awareness of God in everyday life. Baeck asserted that such a state would eventually result in proper ethical behavior in accordance with God's ethical commandments, or mitzvot (*see* MITZVAH). Baeck also laid great emphasis on the concept of Jewish PEOPLEHOOD, believing that the Jews had a historical role to play in Western civilization.

Baeck believed that the Jewish system of ritual enabled Jews to solidify their relationships with God. While Baeck, like most other Reform Jews, did not believe Jewish rituals were obligatory, he abandoned the anti-ritual perspective of many of the earlier German reformers.

Baeck, unlike Cohen, believed in a real supernatural God, and helped to move Reform Judaism away from Cohen's idea of a religion grounded solely on reason. Baeck's emphasis on universal ethical ideas as mandated by a supernatural God created a bridge between Jewish philosophical rationalists and modern Jewish existentialists.

Baeck's personal life experiences became an important model for Jewish leadership. When the Nazis took power in Germany in 1933, Baeck, as head of the Jewish community, was given the opportunity to flee the country. He explained that he would remain in Germany as long as there was a MINYAN of 10 men. Thus, in 1943 he was sent to the TEREZÍN concentration camp. There he continued to preserve his own personal dignity by helping and teaching others, acts of spiritual resistance. While witnessing Nazi barbarism, he refused to abandon his notion of God or the ethical mandates that God teaches. He taught that Nazi evil was a result of human free will, and that the Nazis had chosen to darken God's presence within the world.

Baeck survived the HOLOCAUST, and in 1946 resettled in London. There he organized the World Union of Progressive Judaism and served as its first president. He frequently visited America, serving as a visiting professor at the HEBREW UNION COLLEGE in Cincinnati, the rabbinical school of the American Reform movement.

Further reading: Leo Baeck, *The Essence of Judaism* (New York: Schocken Books, 1948); ———, *Judaism and Christianity: Essays* (Philadelphia: Jewish Publication Society of America, 1958); Leonard Baker, *Days of Sorrow and Pain: Leo Baeck and the Berlin Jews* (New York: Macmillan Publishing Company, 1978); Anne E. Neimark, *One Man's Valor: Leo Baeck and the Holocaust* (New York: Penguin USA: 1986).

Balfour Declaration

The Balfour Declaration was an official statement of the British government in 1917 calling for a Jewish homeland in PALESTINE. It represented the first time any government had openly supported ZIONISM, and became a call to Jews around the world to immigrate to Palestine.

On November 2, 1917, in an attempt to win international support for Britain during World War I (*see* ENGLAND), British foreign secretary Lord Arthur James Balfour publicized a letter to Lord Rothschild that became known as the Balfour Declaration. He wrote: "His Majesty's Government view with favour the establishment in Palestine of a national home for the Jewish people, and will use their best endeavors to facilitate the achievement of this object, it being clearly understood that nothing shall be done which may prejudice the civil and religious rights of existing non-Jewish communities in Palestine or the rights and political status enjoyed by Jews in any other country." Balfour had acted with the endorsement of the British cabinet and after consultations with Jewish leaders, such as Chaim WEIZMANN.

After the war, during which Britain seized Palestine from the Ottoman Turks, the 52 governments of the League of Nations on July 24, 1922, formally recognized a British mandate over Palestine to pursue the objectives of the Balfour Declaration. Though the UNITED STATES did not belong to the League of Nations, Congress endorsed the Mandate on September 21, 1922. Congress resolved: "That the United States of America favors the establishment in Palestine of a national home for the Jewish people, it being clearly understood that nothing shall be done which will prejudice the civil and religious rights of Christian and all other non-Jewish communities in Palestine, and that the holy places and religious buildings and sites in Palestine shall be adequately protected" (Public Resolution No. 73, 67th Congress, Second Session).

Further reading: Ismar Elbogen and Moses Hadas, *A Century of Jewish Life* (Philadelphia: Jewish Publication Society of America, 1946); Nahum Sokolow, *History of Zionism 1600–1918: Two Volumes in One* (Brooklyn, N.Y.: Ktav Publishing House, 1969).

baraita (pl.: baraitot)

A *baraita* (Aramaic for "external") is any rabbinic teaching or ruling from the generation of the TAN-NAIM (between the years 10 and 220 C.E.) that was not included in the MISHNAH, the earliest authoritative written collection of previously oral rabbinic teachings, when it was redacted in 220.

Though they were left out of the Mishnah, many of these *baraitot* found their way into the TALMUD when they were cited by the AMORAIM (the rabbis who developed the GEMARA between 220 and 550 C.E.). An *amora* would quote a *baraita* he had learned orally in order to bolster his argument or to clarify an otherwise obscure or contradictory Mishnah. When a sage could corroborate his legal view with a baraita, his opinion would often hold more authority. *Baraitot* do have legal standing in Talmudic discussions.

Many ancient collections of *baraitot* exist, such as the TOSEFTA and various books of MIDRASH. Others are known only from citations in the Gemara and others, presumably, have been lost.

Further reading: Jacob Neusner, *Sources and Traditions: Types of Compositions in the Talmud of Babylonia* (Lanham, Md.: National Book Network, 1992); ———, *The Talmud of Babylonia* (Lanham, Md.: University Press of America, 1984); H. L. Strack and G. Stemberger, *Introduction to the Talmud and Midrash* (Minneapolis: Fortress Press, 1992).

Ehud Barak was prime minister of Israel from 1999 to 2001. He is a member of the Labor Party, which is aligned with Israel's political left wing. *(Ya'acov Sa'ar, Government Press Office, The State of Israel)*

Barak, Ehud (b. 1942) *Israeli political leader*

Ehud Barak was prime minister of Israel from 1999–2001. Born in 1942 in KIBBUTZ Mishmar Hasharon, he joined the ISRAEL DEFENSE FORCES (IDF) in 1959. Serving as a soldier and commander of an elite unit, he received numerous medals and promotions during his military career. Barak attended the HEBREW UNIVERSITY OF JERUSALEM, graduating with a B.Sc. in 1976, and Stanford University in Palo Alto, California, earning an M.Sc. in Engineering–Economic Systems in 1978. In April 1991, he became the chief of the General Staff and was promoted to the highest rank of lieutenant general.

In 1996, after his retirement from a full-time military career, Barak was elected to the KNESSET, where he served as a member of the Foreign Affairs and Defense Committee. In 1996 he was elected chairman of the LABOR PARTY and in 1999 he formed the One Israel Party, from the Labor, Gesher and Meimad Parties. On May 17, 1999, Ehud Barak was elected prime minister of Israel. He is best remembered for pulling Israel out of Lebanon after two decades of occupation and reigniting peace talks that had stalled under the former prime minister, Benjamin NETANYAHU (b. 1949). After the outbreak of the second INTIFADA and the collapse of the peace talks, Barak lost a reelection bid to Ariel SHARON (b. 1928) in 2001.

Further reading: Adam Garfinkle, *Politics and Society in Modern Israel: Myths and Realities* (Armonk, N.Y.: M. E. Sharpe, 2000); Colbert C. Held and Mildred McDonald Held, *Middle East Patterns: Places, Peoples, and Politics* (Boulder, Colo.: Westview Press, 1989); *The Middle East* (Washington, D.C.: Congressional Quarterly Press, 2000).

bar/bat mitzvah

At the age of 13 for boys and 12 or 13 for girls, Jewish children undergo a rite of passage and enter the Jewish community as formal adults who are then considered members of the COVENANT and bound by that covenant to observe HALAKHAH, Jewish law. This rite of passage is known as a bar mitzvah (son of the commandment) for boys and a bat mitzvah (daughter of the commandment) for girls.

The exact rituals of a bar mitzvah or bat mitzvah vary considerably depending on the denomination, the SYNAGOGUE, or the family. It is traditional for the child to act as TORAH reader during a worship service, generally on SHABBAT. To prepare for a bar or bat mitzvah, the child often learns the TROPE (melodies) for leyning (chanting) Torah. At the Shabbat service the bar or bat mitzvah child may read as much of the week's Torah PARSHA (portion) as he or she has mastered, rang-

ing from just the *maftir*, the last few lines of the portion, to the entire *parsha*. Alternatively, or in addition, one may also read the week's HAFTARAH or prophetic reading, which has a different trope, deliver a *DVAR TORAH*, a commentary on the week's Torah portion, or lead prayers for a section of the Shabbat service or the whole service.

In ORTHODOX JUDAISM a bar mitzvah boy often performs all of the above responsibilities, while an Orthodox bat mitzvah generally consists of only a *dvar Torah* given on a Sunday or a Friday evening. Within other denominations, the individual boy

This boy is reading from the Torah as he becomes a bar mitzvah. This is the central activity at the bar mitzvah of both boys and girls among many contemporary Jews. (© *Claudia Kunin/Corbis*)

or girl and his or her parents often choose how many of the above tasks to accomplish. In recent years, some Orthodox bat mitzvah girls also read from the Torah, but in a separate service at which only women are present.

In modern America, the highlight of the event is often the reception, which can draw friends and family from around the country. There has been a tendency for the receptions to become more and more elaborate; critics have raised concerns that the ceremonial aspects as well as the religious meaning are becoming marginalized.

Further reading: Harvey E. Goldberg, *Jewish Passages: Cycles of Jewish Life* (Berkeley: University of California Press, 2003); Ronald H. Isaacs, *Rites of Passage: A Guide to the Jewish Life Cycle* (Hoboken, N.J.: Ktav Publishing House, 1992); Cantor Helen Leneman, ed., *Bar/Bat Mitzvah Basics: A Practical Family Guide to Coming of Age Together* (Woodstock, Vt.: Jewish Lights Publishers, 2001).

Bar Ilan University

Bar Ilan is a religiously oriented university that also offers a full range of degrees in secular subjects.

Located east of Ramat Gan in the suburbs of TEL AVIV, Israel's most metropolitan city, Bar Ilan University was established in 1955 in honor of Rabbi Meir Bar-Ilan, who was committed to the survival of TRADITIONAL JUDAISM after the HOLOCAUST. The school is unique in its attempts to merge traditional Jewish thought, belief, and practice with the technology and scholarship of the modern world. Though considered to be a religious university, Bar Ilan seeks to create a bridge between secular and religious Israelis by offering a curriculum that includes study of Jewish ethics and heritage and a highly ranked academic program. In the mid-1990s Bar Ilan was the third-largest university in Israel, and it had five satellite campuses throughout the small country.

Further reading: Walter Ackerman, "The Americanization of Israeli Education" *Israel Studies* 5:1 (2000):

228; Web site URL: http://www.biu.ac.il, accessed on July 5, 2004.

Bar-Kokhba, Shimon (d. 135 c.e.) *leader of anti-Roman rebellion*

Shimon Bar-Kokhba, born Bar Kasivah, was the chief military leader in the Jewish revolt against ROME that lasted from 132 to 135 c.e. He was a self-proclaimed MESSIAH, who took the messianic name Bar-Kokhba, which translates as "son of the star." Bar-Kokhba succeeded in recapturing JERUSALEM from the Romans, but his troops could not withstand the counterattack in 133 by 35,000 Roman troops under the command of Emperor Hadrian and General Julius Severus. Bar-Kokhba and his troops fled to Betar, in the Judean Hills, where they came under siege in 134 and were annihilated in battle the following year.

There are few literary sources on Bar-Kokhba or the revolt. Rabbinic literature such as the TALMUD and MIDRASH contain some legendary material on the era, as do the writings of the Church Father Eusebius, who describes the failed revolt and characterizes Bar-Kokhba himself as a "bloodthirsty bandit." Ancient coins impressed with variations of the name Bar-Kokhba and letters written by Bar-Kokhba have been discovered dating from the time of the Bar Kokhba Revolt.

According to tradition, Bar-Kokhba was a ruthless leader who held his troops together by strength of personality and threats. He is also described as a diligent follower of Jewish tradition. Under his military leadership, Jewish troops retook more than 50 Roman strongholds in PALESTINE. It is said that Jews from outside the land of ISRAEL returned to join in the revolt, and even some non-Jews joined in the battle against the Romans.

When Hadrian appointed General Julius Severus to lead his troops it marked a turning point in the war. Severus used the effective technique of laying siege and starving out the enemy. The final battle of the war took place in Betar; after the walls were pierced, the Romans killed every

Jewish soldier. The Romans devastated the Jewish communities of Palestine to retaliate against the Bar Kokhba Revolt. The land was ruined, many Jews were sold into slavery, and Jerusalem was turned into a pagan city called Aelius Hadrianus. Hadrian implemented intense anti-Jewish (*see* ANTI-JUDAISM) legislation and persecution.

Jewish tradition maintains that during and after the Bar Kokhba Revolt many RABBIS were tortured to death, most notably Rabbi Akiva (*see* AKIVA BEN YOSEPH). The failure of the Bar Kokhba Revolt, and the subsequent devastation and persecution, threatened the ability of the Jewish people and Judaism to survive. This dire situation convinced the rabbis to begin the process of putting the ORAL LAW into final written form.

Further reading: Peter Schafer, *Bar Kokhba War Reconsidered: New Perspectives on the Second Jewish Revolt Against Rome* (Philadelphia: Coronet Books, 2003); Yigael Yadin, *Bar-Kokhba: The Rediscovery of the Legendary Hero of the Last Jewish Revolt Against Imperial Rome* (London: Weidenfeld and Nicolson, 1971); Yigael Yadin, ed., *The Documents from the Bar Kokhba Period in the Cave of Letters: Hebrew, Aramaic, and Nabatean-Aramaic Papyri*.(Jerusalem, Shrine of the Book, 2002).

Beame, Abraham (1906–2001) *mayor of New York City*

Abraham Beame was the first Jewish mayor of New York City, elected in 1974. He was born in London, ENGLAND, in 1906. His parents had left Warsaw, POLAND, when it became clear that his father, a known Socialist and revolutionary, was in danger of arrest by the police. Far along in her pregnancy, Beame's mother remained in England to wait for the birth before joining her husband in New York City, via ELLIS ISLAND. Abe Beame's life was to be an example of the saga of the hard-working immigrant who accepts the challenge of American opportunity.

Once in the United States, the Beames made their home on the LOWER EAST SIDE of Manhattan. Beame's father continued to pursue his interest in socialism, and Abe too attended many Socialist Party meetings. He was also the recipient of immigrant aid and frequented the University Settlement House for checkers and sports. Although Abe did not follow in his father's footsteps to become a full-fledged Socialist, he was certainly influenced by popular socialist speakers such as union leader Eugene V. Debs. He grew up with the belief that government should maintain an interest in the well-being of its citizens.

As a young adult, Beame did not intend to enter politics. In fact, he graduated with honors from the highly competitive and tuition-free City College in 1928 with a degree in business accounting. Acquiring an accounting license after graduation, Beame and several friends set up an accounting firm, but its success was truncated by the Great Depression of the 1930s. While practicing accounting in his own firm, Beame taught the subject at Richmond Hill High School in Queens after marrying his high school sweetheart, Mary Ingerman. He taught for 15 years, and his family grew with the addition of sons Edmund and Bernard. During World War II, Beame also taught accounting at Rutgers University.

Beame became involved in politics in 1946, when he accepted a position as New York City's assistant budget director, the start of a 31-year career in public service. This first appointment came as a reward for his work for the Democratic Party and in recognition of his financial expertise. It led to his election to the city comptroller's office in 1961, and eventually to the mayor's office in 1974. Known to be down-to-earth, and respected for his simple middle-class background, Beame defeated Republican candidate John V. Lindsay, an attorney and former congressman who represented a very different social and economic background.

Beame entered office with wide support from Jewish voters, who then constituted the largest ethnic group in the city. He inherited a debilitating deficit and worked laboriously to correct the gap. By the time Beame left office in 1978, with the election of Ed Koch, New York City's budget enjoyed a surplus of $200 million. Beame's mayoral term was marked by the "Son of Sam" serial killings, the New York City financial crisis, and both the Bicentennial celebration and the hosting of the Democratic National Convention in 1976.

Further reading: Abraham Beame Collection, LaGuardia and Wagner Archives, Web site URL: http://www.abrahambeame.lagcc.cuny.edu/beame/, accessed June 17, 2004; Charles Brecher, Robert A. Cropf, Raymond D. Horton, and Michael Mead, *Power Failure: New York City Politics and Policy Since 1960* (New York: Oxford University Press, 1993).

Begin, Menachem (1913–1992) *Israeli political leader*

Menachem Begin was prime minister of ISRAEL from 1977 to 1983, after first rising from underground commander to become a political leader, member of the KNESSET (the Israeli parliament), and cabinet minister.

Born in Brest Litovsk, POLAND, in 1913, Begin was a passionate supporter of ZIONISM from an early age, joining the Betar youth movement (*see* ZIONIST YOUTH MOVEMENTS) at the age of 16.

In 1938 Begin became head of Betar Poland, a 70,000-member organization that formed part of the Jewish nationalist movement founded by Ze'ev JABOTINSKY (1880–1940). Begin concentrated on military training, foreseeing the need to defend Polish Jewry in the atmosphere of violence before World War II. Following the outbreak of World War II, he made his way to PALESTINE after a period of internment in RUSSIA. There he revitalized the IRGUN TZEVA'I LE'UMI (Etzel), a militant defense force for Jews.

In 1944, when the magnitude of the HOLOCAUST became evident, Etzel broke away from the HAGANAH and aggressively challenged British rule in Palestine. Etzel most notably led the Akko prison breakout and destroyed the British administration's central offices located at the King David Hotel in JERUSALEM.

The growing militancy of Etzel's operations brought Begin into conflict with the mainstream

Menachem Begin, pictured here, was the first prime minister elected from the Likud Party, which is aligned with Israel's political right wing. *(Ya'acov Sa'ar, Government Press Office, The State of Israel)*

Zionist strategy of David BEN-GURION, and these two great leaders would be political adversaries throughout their lives. With the creation of Israel, the Haganah and Etzel joined together once again to become the ISRAEL DEFENSE FORCES (IDF).

Menachem Begin founded the Herut Party, based on the political ideology of his mentor Jabotinsky. Its ideology combined economic liberalism with a hard-line stance toward the country's enemies. As a member of the Knesset, he dominated the political opposition to the ruling Labor Party's rule for the first three decades of Israel's independence. Begin was known for his fiery eloquence and his modest lifestyle.

In the 1977 elections, Begin's LIKUD party won 43 Knesset seats, and he became prime minister. His most outstanding achievement was the signing of the peace treaty with EGYPT. In November 1977, six months after Begin became prime minister, President Anwar SADAT of Egypt came to JERUSALEM. This visit inaugurated two years of negotiations that culminated in the CAMP DAVID ACCORDS, which called for Israel's withdrawal from Sinai and the establishment of Palestinian autonomy in exchange for peace and normal relations with Egypt. A treaty of peace terminating the state of war between the two countries was signed in 1979. Prime Minister Begin and President Sadat were awarded the 1978 Nobel Peace Prize for this achievement.

During the early 1980s, Begin led Israel to war in Lebanon. After the death of his wife, Aliza, in November 1982 and the continuation of the controversial LEBANON WAR, Begin resigned from the position of prime minister at the age of 69 on August 30, 1983. He lived the remaining years of his life in isolation and was buried in Jerusalem.

Further reading: Jacob Abadi, *Israel's Leadership: From Utopia to Crisis* (Westport, Conn.: Greenwood Press, 1993); Thomas L. Friedman, *From Beirut to Jerusalem* (New York: Farrar, Straus, Giroux, 1990); Gershon R. Kieval and Bernard Reich, *Israel, Land of Tradition and Conflict* (Boulder, Colo.: Westview Press, 1993); Amos Perlmutter, *The Life and Times of Menachem Begin* (Garden City, N.Y.: Doubleday, 1987); Ned Temko, *To Win or to Die* (New York: Morrow, 1987).

Bellow, Saul (1915–2005) *American Jewish writer*

Saul Bellow was born in Lachine, Quebec, in 1915, to Russian immigrants. His family moved to Chicago when he was nine. He attended the University of Chicago, and received his bachelor's degree from Northwestern University in sociology and anthropology. He did some graduate work at the University of Wisconsin but joined the merchant marines during World War II.

Bellow is considered by many to be the greatest Jewish fiction writer of contemporary times. Within the Jewish community, Bellow received the B'NAI B'RITH Jewish Heritage Award (1968) for "excellence in Jewish literature," and he was awarded the America's Democratic Legacy Award (1976) of the ANTI-DEFAMATION LEAGUE, the first time the award was made to a writer.

In addition to Jewish communal recognition, he was awarded a Guggenheim Fellowship, the National Book Award, and the Pulitzer Prize. In 1965 Bellow was awarded the International Literary Prize for his work *Herzog,* becoming the first American to receive the prize. In 1968 FRANCE awarded him the Croix de Chevalier des Arts et Lettres, the highest literary distinction awarded by that nation to noncitizens. His greatest recognition came on December 10, 1976, when King Carl XVI Gustaf of Sweden presented him with the Nobel Prize for Literature. The Swedish Academy's presentation emphasized Bellow's contribution to the field of fiction and writing.

Bellow's writings reflect a humanistic concern combined with a clear-sighted analysis of contemporary society with all its foibles and conflicts. His characters struggle with themselves and their social environment. Bellow's writings include novels, short stories and plays, but he was also noted as a nonfiction writer. During the 1967 Arab-Israeli war, he served as a war correspondent for *Newsday.* He taught at Bard College, Princeton University, and the University of Minnesota, and he was a member of the Committee on Social Thought at the University of Chicago.

Among Bellow's works are *Dangling Man,* 1944; *The Victim,* 1947; *The Adventures of Augie March,* 1953; *Seize the Day,* 1956; *Henderson the Rain King,* 1959; *Herzog,* 1964; *Mr. Sammler's Planet,* 1970; *Humboldt's Gift,* 1975; *The Dean's December,* 1982; *More Die of Heartbreak,* 1987; *Mosby's Memoirs and Other Stories,* 1968; *A Wen,* 1965; *The Wrecker,* 1944 (teleplay); *The Future of* the Moon, 1970: *To Jerusalem and Back: A Personal Account,* 1976 (nonfiction).

Further reading: Saul Bellow, *Saul Bellow: Novels 1944–1953: Dangling Man, The Victim, and The Adventures of Augie March* (New York: Library of America, 2003); Jeanne Braham, *A Sort of Columbus: The American Voyages of Saul Bellow's Fiction* (Athens: University of Georgia Press, 1984); Robert R. Dutton, *Saul Bellow* (Boston: Twayne, 1982); Ellen Pifer, *Saul Bellow Against the Grain* (Philadelphia: University of Pennsylvania, 1990).

ben Abuya, Elisha (first century C.E.)
controversial rabbi and scholar

Very little is known about the historical figure Elisha ben Abuya, but he was derided in the TAL-MUD as an apostate and heretic. He was one of the TANNAIM who lived during the first century of the common era, born sometime before 70 C.E. A couple of sayings are attributed to him in the MISHNAH and TALMUD. However, he is most famous for his HERESY and apostasy. He renounced the traditions of the PHARISEES, and may have been either a SADDUCEE or an Epicurean. In Talmudic sources Elisha is always represented as a traitor to the Jewish people, but there is internal evidence that he only rejected the Pharisaic community, not the Jewish community as a whole.

The Jerusalem Talmud asserts that Elisha kept forbidden books, such as volumes of Greek philosophy, and attempted to lead students away from the study of TORAH. It is said that he went so far as to betray the Pharisees by telling the Romans when Jews disobeyed their orders to violate the Torah by working on the Sabbath. Both Talmuds note that he did not believe in life after death and that he rode through town on the Day of Atonement: in other words, he flouted the Torah in both word and deed. For this reason, he is generally referred to in the Talmud as "the other" (i.e., the heretic).

The most famous legend concerning Elisha ben Abuya is the Talmudic story of the four sages who entered paradise (or the orchard): Ben Azzai, Ben Zoma, "The Other" (Elisha ben Abuya), and Rabbi AKIVA. Ben Azzai died, Ben Zoma went mad, Elisha ben Abuya became a heretic (literally, he "destroyed the plants"), and only Rabbi Akiva survived and attained wisdom. A modern work of fiction, *As a Driven Leaf* by Milton STEINBERG (1903–50), tells the story of Elisha ben Abuya and his path away from rabbinic Judaism.

Further reading: Jeffrey L. Rubenstein, *Talmudic Stories: Narrative Art, Composition, and Culture* (Baltimore: Johns Hopkins University Press, 1999); Milton Steinberg, *As A Driven Leaf* (New York: Behrman House, 1996); Alon Goshen-Gottstein, *The Sinner and the Amnesiac: The Rabbinic Invention of Elisha ben Abuya and Eleazar ben Arach* (Stanford, Calif.: Stanford University Press, 2000).

Ben-Gurion, David (1886–1973) *Israeli political leader*

David Ben-Gurion was for many years the leader of the Zionist movement (*see* ZIONISM); he became Israel's first and longest-serving prime minister.

Ben-Gurion was born David Green in Plonsk, POLAND, in 1886. In 1906 he immigrated to PALESTINE, where he became immersed in Zionist politics and helped to establish the Jewish self-defense group Ha-Shomer.

In the 1920s, Ben-Gurion was elected secretary-general of the HISTADRUT, the General Federation of Labor. The position provided the base for his political power and for the realization of his goal of founding a Jewish state. By 1935, Labor Zionism, Ben-Gurion's movement, had become the most important faction in the Zionist movement.

In many ways Ben-Gurion set the course of Zionist history and molded the character of the Jewish state. His political platform blended vision with pragmatism. After World War II, Ben-Gurion challenged British authority by organizing mass "illegal" immigration; he created de facto boundaries for a Jewish state by establishing Jewish settlements in all parts of the country. He developed the Jewish defense capability, and organized the procurement of heavy armaments.

In 1948, as head of the provisional government, David Ben-Gurion proclaimed the establishment of the State of Israel and the beginning of the "ingathering of the exiles." In the first five years of statehood, Ben-Gurion's forceful and charismatic leadership as prime minister facilitated the waves of mass immigration that doubled the country's population. He directed absorption endeavors, investing the majority of the new nation's limited resources in integrating the immigrants; secured outlying areas by building settlements on the periphery; and instituted universal education in a nonpartisan public school system (in place of the earlier partisan movement schools).

As minister of defense, Ben-Gurion masterminded and carried out the tense transition from underground units to a regular army. He helped mold the character as well as the structure of the ISRAEL DEFENSE FORCES (IDF).

David Ben-Gurion held the position of prime minister twice, from 1948–53 and then again from 1955–63. In 1970 Ben-Gurion concluded his political career. He is recognized as one of the most influential figures in the course of modern Zionism.

Further reading: David Ben-Gurion, *Rebirth and Destiny of Israel* (New York: Philosophical Library, 1954); Zeev Sternell, *The Founding Myths of Israel: Nationalism, Socialism, and the Making of the Jewish State* (Princeton, N.J.: Princeton University Press, 1998).

Benjamin, Judah P. (1811–1884)
Confederate American political leader

Judah P. Benjamin was one of the most important figures in the Confederate government during the American Civil War, serving in a variety of formal and informal posts throughout the conflict.

Born in the Danish West Indies (now the U.S. Virgin Islands) on August 6, 1811, Benjamin grew up in Georgia and North Carolina, attended Yale University, studied law in Louisiana and became a politician. He served as a senator for Louisiana as a member of the Whig Party, and later as a Demo-

crat. When Louisiana seceded from the Union, Benjamin first served as attorney general for the Confederacy. President Jefferson Davis later appointed him secretary of war, and then secretary of state. Thus, Judah P. Benjamin became the first Jew to serve in the cabinet of a North American president.

Benjamin did not become involved with his local Jewish community, nor did he identify with Jewish causes. Nevertheless he was often attacked for being a Jew, and Davis was criticized for appointing him to his cabinet. When the economic and political situation of the Confederacy turned for the worse, critics often held "the Jew" Benjamin responsible for the ills of the administration and the country. Thus, Benjamin's experience presents a solid example of the strength of prejudice and ANTISEMITISM even in regard to an individual who did not strongly identify with Judaism or the Jewish people. Benjamin died in Paris on May 6, 1884.

Further reading: Seymour Brody, *Jewish Heroes and Heroines of America: 150 True Stories of American Jewish Heroism* (Hollywood, Fla.: Lifetime Books, 1996); Leanard Dinnerstein and Mary Dale Palsson, *Jews in the South* (Baton Rouge: Louisiana State University Press, 1973); Eli N. Evans, *Judah P. Benjamin: The Jewish Confederate* (New York: Free Press, 1988); Robert Douthat Meade, *Judah P. Benjamin: Confederate Statesman* (Baton Rouge: Louisiana State University Press, 2001).

Benjamin, Walter (1892–1940) *philosopher*

Walter Benjamin was born on July 15, 1892, in Berlin, GERMANY. He became a philosopher and is today considered one of the founders of the field of cultural criticism. Cultural criticism is the process of stepping back from one's own culture in order to analyze its assumptions and question its commonly held opinions such as, in Benjamin's case, the beneficial nature of capitalism. In addition, Benjamin's writings help to make popular culture acceptable to intellectuals as a legitimate form of social expression; he articulated standards by which popular culture and art could be judged on their own terms.

After the Nazis forced him into EXILE in 1933, Benjamin moved to FRANCE, where he stayed until 1940. His literary-philosophical style tended to express itself in short prose forms, such as essays, letters, and reviews. Benjamin's philosophy owes much to both MARXISM and Jewish mysticism (see KABBALAH), which many assume are due respectively to the influence of two of his closest friends, Bertolt Brecht and Gerschom SCHOLEM. In flight from the Gestapo, Benjamin took his own life in 1940 while trying to cross the Pyrenees into SPAIN.

Further reading: Walter Benjamin, *Reflections: Essays, Aphorisms, Autobiographical Writing* (New York: Schocken Books, 1986); Robin Ridless and Peter Lang, *Ideology and Art: Theories of Mass Culture from Walter Benjamin to Umberto Eco* (New York: Peter Lang Publishing, Inc., 1984); Bernd Witte, *Walter Benjamin: An Intellectual Biography* (Detroit: Wayne State University Press, 1991).

Ben-Yehudah, Eliezer (1858–1922) *early Zionist leader and founder of Modern Hebrew*

Born in the Lithuanian town of Luzhky on January 7, 1858, Eliezer Ben-Yehudah's original name was Eliezer Yitzhak Perelman. Ben-Yehudah began learning HEBREW at a young age as part of his scrupulous religious upbringing, like all the local Jewish children of his time. He proved to be an excellent student, and was sent by his family to a YESHIVA in order to become a RABBI. Ben-Yehudah, however, also like many other young Jews of his time, became interested in the secular world, trading the yeshiva for a modern secular school setting.

In 1877, when RUSSIA proclaimed war on the Ottoman Empire in support of the Bulgarian quest to regain independence, Ben-Yehudah became enthralled with the notion of Bulgaria as a modern independent nation. Knowing that several European nations had been revived in his own century, Ben-Yehudah came to believe that the Jewish people could also revive the Jewish nation on its ancient national soil.

Fervently embracing ZIONISM, Ben-Yehudah believed that in addition to reacquiring Jewish sovereignty in ISRAEL, the Jews needed to revitalize their language, Hebrew. Since the Jewish exile began in 70 C.E., Hebrew had become a "dead language," utilized only in written form and no longer spoken.

Ben-Yehudah set out to revive the spoken Hebrew language. In 1881, in very poor health, he relocated to PALESTINE, embarking on the mission to bring about the "renaissance of the Jewish people, their land, and their language." Ben-Yehudah's approach to ubiquitous Jewish usage of Hebrew was "Hebrew in the home," "Hebrew in the school," and "words, words, words." He himself set the example, deciding with his wife to speak only Hebrew and raising their son as a native Hebrew speaker. Ben-Yehudah's son, Ben-Zion, also known as Itamar, became the first all-Hebrew speaking child in modern Jewish history, and the Ben-Yehudah family proved that the complete revival of the Hebrew language was possible. They also abandoned the ASHKENAZI pronunciation of Hebrew in favor of a new pronunciation heavily influenced by the patterns of the SEPHARDIM and by spoken Arabic.

Ben-Yehudah coined many new words and wrote the first modern Hebrew dictionary. He also urged to the world Jewish community that Hebrew should become the sole language of instruction in Jewish schools, both religious and secular, in place of Yiddish or non-Jewish languages. Hebrew could become once again the unifying language of the Jewish people.

Ben-Yehudah wrote in 1886 in his Hebrew newspaper, *Hatzvi:* "The Hebrew language will go from the synagogue to the house of study, and from the house of study to the school, and from the school it will come into the home and . . . become a living language." With time this is in fact what occurred. A young all-Hebrew-speaking generation emerged and developed.

Ben-Yehudah became a scientific lexicographer, and his works culminated in his 17-volume

Complete Dictionary of Ancient and Modern Hebrew. In order to confront issues of terminology, pronunciation, spelling, and punctuation, in 1890 Ben-Yehudah created the Hebrew Language Council. This council exists today as Israel's Hebrew Language Academy, the official authority on all matters pertaining to the Hebrew language.

Ben-Yehudah implemented and developed the dream to revive the original language of the Jews, and ultimately Jewish society followed his dream. Today, Hebrew is the living language of Israel, spoken by 6.5 million Israelis, and studied by much of world Jewry. A popular street in Jerusalem is named BEN YEHUDAH STREET to commemorate the life and work of Eliezer Ben-Yehudah.

Further reading: Jack Fellman, *Revival of a Classical Tongue: Eliezer Ben Yehuda and the Modern Hebrew Language.* (The Hague, Marton, 1973); Arthur Hertzberg, *The Zionist Idea: A Historical Analysis and Reader* (Philadelphia: Jewish Publication Society, 1997); Kenneth Katzner, *The Languages of the World* (New York: Taylor & Francis Group, 2002); Robert St. John, *Tongue of the Prophets: The Fascinating Biography of Eliezer Ben-Yehudah, the Father of Modern Hebrew* (Beverly Hills, Calif.: Wilshire Book Company, 1972).

Ben Yehudah Street

Ben Yehudah Street is an outdoor pedestrian mall in modern JERUSALEM; before it became a mall, for many years it was a central thoroughfare in the New City or West Jerusalem. Popular with tourists and young Israelis, the street is filled with souvenir, jewelry, and Judaica shops, as well as restaurants and cafes. In more relaxed times, the street is abuzz with vendors and customers during the day and in the evening. However, Ben Yehudah Street and nearby commercial areas have become targets of suicide bombers; the decreased number of people visiting the mall can be seen as a sign of the current state of political tension.

Further reading: *Let's Go Israel and the Palestinian Territories 2002* (New York: St. Martin's Press, 2002);

Robert Ullian, *Frommer's Israel* (Foster City, Calif.: IDG Books Worldwide, 2000).

ben Zakkai, Yochanan (first century C.E.)
rabbinic scholar and leader of the Pharisees

Yochanan ben Zakkai is considered to be the most significant disciple of the great sage HILLEL, and one of the giants of rabbinic Judaism. He is often referred to as the "father of wisdom and the father of generations." He obtained this high praise because he made possible the continuation of

Ben Yehudah Street became a center of gathering and tourism. Because of suicide bombing in the early 21st century the vibrant social and commercial center now is more subdued. *(Zolton Kluger, Government Press Office, The State of Israel)*

Jewish scholarship after JERUSALEM fell to the Romans in 70 C.E.

According to rabbinic tradition, ben Zakkai lived in Jerusalem in the year 68 C.E. while the Holy City was under siege by General Vespasian. At this juncture the militant ZEALOTS controlled Jerusalem; their fellow Zealots were among those who would commit mass suicide rather than surrender at MASADA. Ben Zakkai promoted conditional surrender to the Romans, but the Zealots completely rejected his calls for negotiation.

As a result, legend has it that ben Zakkai faked his own death and had his disciples smuggle him out of Jerusalem in a coffin. According to the MIDRASH, his coffin was carried to General Vespasian's tent, where ben Zakkai emerged and negotiated a political arrangement. The scholar promised his political loyalty, and the loyalty of his followers, if he could be granted a new location in which Jewish study and leadership could continue outside Jerusalem. Vespasian, soon to be Roman emperor, agreed, and the new rabbinic government was set up at YAVNEH, near modern-day Rehovot.

The school at Yavneh became the center of Jewish learning for centuries, and ultimately replaced Jerusalem as the location for the SANHEDRIN, the rabbinic council that governed the Jewish people. Ben Zakkai's willingness to compromise in the face of the enemy is understood as a vitally significant step that saved the Jewish people and culture from being extinguished by Roman oppression.

Further reading: Jacob Neusner, *A Life of Yohanan Ben Zakkai, ca.1–80 C.E.* (Leiden, The Netherlands: E. J. Brill, 1970); Solomon Zeitlin, *The Rise and Fall of the Judaean State: A Political, Social and Religious History of the Second Commonwealth,* vol. 3 (Philadelphia: Jewish Publication Society of America, 1962).

Berlin, Irving (1888–1989) *American songwriter*

Irving Berlin was one of the most successful songwriters in American history. His story is a rags-to-riches celebration of the American immigrant.

Irving Berlin composed more than 1,500 songs in his lifetime. These included American favorites "Blue Skies," "White Christmas," and "God Bless America." *(Library of Congress)*

Berlin was born Israel Baline in Mohilev, RUSSIA, in 1888, the youngest child in a large family. His father was a *shochet* (ritual slaughterer; *see* KASHRUT) and a CANTOR. The family immigrated to the UNITED STATES in 1893, pushed out by violence and discrimination against Russian Jews (*see* POGROMS). They settled in the LOWER EAST SIDE of New York City.

When Berlin's father died, he set out to bring in income for his family. He took different types of jobs, sang for pennies, and even became a singing waiter in Chinatown. In 1907 he published his first song, "Marie from Sunny Italy." That same year, he officially changed his name from Israel Baline to Irving Berlin. In 1909, Berlin worked as a staff lyricist in Tin Pan Alley, and by 1911 he had his first hit, "Alexander's Ragtime Band," which became a sensation around the world.

Although he never learned to play a piano properly or read music, Berlin composed 1,500 songs in his lifetime, including "Blue Skies," "White Christmas," "Anything You Can Do, I Can Do Better," "There's No Business Like Show Business," "Puttin' on the Ritz," and "God Bless America;" he penned the lyrics to several hit shows and movies, including *Annie Get Your Gun*. In 1942, Berlin won the Academy Award for "White Christmas" in the category of original song. "God Bless America" represents Berlin's strong patriotism and appreciation for the freedom he found in his new country.

Berlin was an intuitive businessman. He successfully opened his own Broadway theater in 1921, called The Magic Box. He established several charitable foundations to express his love for America, including the God Bless America Fund and This Is The Army. He donated millions of dollars to Army Emergency Relief and to the Boy and the Girl Scouts.

Berlin's personal life held tragedy and success. His life exhibits the immigrant's ability to make it in America, but also highlights the hardships of immigrant life. His first wife, Dorothy Goetz, died of typhoid fever after their marriage in 1912. Berlin was not to marry again until 1926, when he scandalously (for both families) married a 22-year-old Catholic socialite. They remained married until her death in 1988.

After decades at the center of American music, Berlin became reclusive, making it difficult for biographers to learn of his life directly from the source. Yet, in 1988 his centennial was celebrated in an all-star tribute at Carnegie Hall, featuring luminaries of the music world like Frank Sinatra, Leonard Bernstein, Natalie Cole, and Willie Nelson. Berlin died in his sleep in New York City at the age of 101.

Further reading: Laurence Bergreen, *As Thousands Cheer: The Life of Irving Berlin* (New York: Viking,

1991); Charles Hamm, *Irving Berlin: Songs from the Melting Pot: the Formative Years, 1907–1914* (New York: Oxford University Press, 1997); Ian Whitcomb, *Irving Berlin and Ragtime America* (New York: Limelight Editions, 1988).

Bernstein, Leonard (1918–1990) *composer and conductor*

In the history of American music, Leonard Bernstein holds many firsts. In a field dominated by European artists, Bernstein was the first American to conduct the Berlin Philharmonic, the London Symphony Orchestra, and the Royal Concertgebouw. His influence on American music stretched from Broadway to the classical world. It would not be an overstatement to say that Bernstein was the most famous conductor who ever lived.

Bernstein was born in Lawrence, Massachusetts, to middle-class parents in 1918. His musical talent became apparent in childhood, although his parents were concerned that his interest would not yield a stable income through adulthood. Still, he persevered, studying piano as a child and transforming his talent into the professional realm while a student at Harvard. In 1940 Bernstein became involved with Tanglewood, the Boston Symphony Orchestra's new summer festival, and eventually taught master classes there.

At the age of 25, Bernstein, then conducting assistant at the New York Philharmonic at Carnegie Hall, took his first turn as conductor of the orchestra when Bruno Walter was unable to perform. Bernstein was an immediate success; he gained a reputation overnight and was soon offered conducting opportunities all over the world. In his lifetime, he would conduct in such cities as London, Moscow, and Vienna, among many others.

Bernstein's career as a composer took off around the same time as his popularity as a conductor. In 1943 he wrote his Symphony No. 1: *Jeremiah*, which won him the New York Music Critics Award. In 1944 Bernstein collaborated with his friend Jerome Robbins to produce a new ballet, called *Fancy Free,* which was later transformed into the Broadway hit *On The Town.* In the 1950s, 1960s, and 1970s, Bernstein added television work and numerous recordings to make his impact on American music last. Bernstein managed what many thought was impossible—he brought classical music to the popular ear, making it fun and interesting to all types of people with his award-winning television series *Young People's Concerts.*

While building his career and becoming a worldwide celebrity, Bernstein did not forget his Jewish roots. In the mid-1940s he conducted in TEL AVIV, establishing a lasting relationship with the new state of ISRAEL and her people. The Israel Philharmonic honored Bernstein with a festival in 1978 to acknowledge his years of dedication to the country. In 1988 he was given the permanent title of Laureate Conductor for the Israel Philharmonic. In 1963, after the assassination of President John F. Kennedy, he dedicated a symphony to the president's memory, and called it Symphony No. 3: *Kaddish* (the name of the Jewish prayer for the dead; *see* KADDISH). He conducted its premiere with the Israel Philharmonic Orchestra. In addition, Bernstein taught classes at BRANDEIS UNIVERSITY.

Bernstein received hundreds of awards, and dozens of festivals were produced in his honor. In 1981, he was awarded the Gold Medal of the American Academy of Arts and Letters and simultaneously elected a member. His lifelong support of humanitarian causes brought him the National Fellowship Award in 1985. Bernstein received a variety of other honors throughout his career, including gold medals, keys to cities, honorary degrees, and festivals in countries including AUSTRIA, DENMARK, Finland, FRANCE, GERMANY, Israel, Italy, JAPAN, and Mexico. In 1980 he received the Kennedy Center Honors, and in 1985 he was honored by the National Academy of Recording Arts and Sciences with a Lifetime Achievement Grammy award.

Bernstein and wife Felicia Montealegre, a Chilean actress and pianist, had three children together, Jamie, Alexander, and Nina. More than a decade after Bernstein's death in 1990, the Leonard Bernstein Center for Learning was funded by the Grammy Foundation. It is dedicated to music education for children of all ages. Even after death, Bernstein continues to bring classical music to everyone.

Further reading: Leonard Bernstein, *Joy of Music* (New York: Simon & Schuster, 1978); Irene Heskes, *Passport to Jewish Music: Its History, Traditions, and Culture* (Westport, Conn.: Greenwood, 1994); Johanna Hurwitz, *Leonard Bernstein: A Passion for Music* (Philadelphia: Jewish Publication Society, 1993).

Beruriah (second century C.E.) *woman scholar cited in the Talmud*

Beruriah is the most notable woman in early rabbinic Judaism. She was the daughter of Rabbi Hananyah ben Teradyon and the wife of Rabbi Meir, a primary disciple of the great Rabbi AKIVA. In early rabbinic literary sources Beruriah is cited as residing in the town of Usha in the Galilee. She is the only woman scholar quoted in the TALMUD. Though her name appears only seven times there, she has in modern times become a model for pioneer women scholars in what was once the exclusively male preserve of Talmud study. Beruriah's opinions on HALAKHAH, Jewish law, appear in the text, although she was never seen as an authority, probably because of her status as a woman.

There is significant folklore surrounding Beruriah. Rabbinic tradition depicts her as a sensitive but strong individual. She is praised for her piety, compassion, and wit. In one MIDRASH, Beruriah rebukes her husband, Rabbi Meir, telling him not to be angry with his enemies, and not to pray for their death. She suggests that instead he pray that their sins cease and that they repent (B'rachot 10a). When Beruriah's two sons die, the midrash reports that she cleverly manages to break the news to her husband in a way that will not crush his spirit. Her father is said to have been martyred in the rebellion led by BAR-KOKHBA, her two sons died, her sister was taken prisoner by the

Romans (*see* ROME), and her brother was murdered. Yet, in the face of these great tragedies, she retained her internal strength and faith.

During the Middle Ages, misogynistic rabbis uncomfortable with Beruriah's role as an independent woman role model created stories to defame her character. Her husband is said to have deceived her in a test of her fidelity, and she is said to have subsequently committed suicide after participating in this adulterous scenario. Modern rabbinic critics recognize these stories to be slander; they instead emphasize Beruriah's original thought and leadership. The best-known contemporary portrayal of Beruriah's character was in Rabbi Milton STEINBERG's popular novel, *As a Driven Leaf.*

Further reading: Rachel Adler, "The Virgin in the Brothel: The Legend of Beruriah," *Tikkun* 3 (1998): 28–31; Daniel Boyarin, *Carnal Israel: Reading Sex in Talmudic Culture* (Berkeley: University of California Press, 1993); Leila Leah Bronner, *Rabbinic Reconstructions of Biblical Women* (Louisville, Ky.: Westminster/John Knox Press, 1994); Isidore Epstein, ed., *Soncino Hebrew/English Babylonian Talmud* (Brooklyn, N.Y.: Soncino Press Ltd., 1990); H. Freedman and Maurice Simon, eds., *Soncino Midrash Rabbah* (CD-ROM), 3rd ed. (Brooklyn, N.Y.: Soncino Press, 1983); David Goodblatt, "The Beruriah Traditions," in *Persons and Institutions in Early Rabbinic Judaism,* ed. William Scott Green (Missoula, Mont.: Scholars Press, 1977).

Betar *See* ZIONIST YOUTH MOVEMENTS.

bet din

A *bet din* ("house of judgment") is a rabbinic court that adjudicates disputes between traditional Jews based on Talmudic law and Jewish traditions.

According to the GEMARA, the rabbinic compendium that set down much of practical Jewish law, a *bet din* must be composed of three learned ordained rabbis. Because *smicha,* the act of ordination, had been reserved only for scholars living in the land of ISRAEL, the courts outside PALESTINE created the means to appoint their own rabbis as judges. Over time the term *rabbi* began to refer to scholars who lived outside the land of Israel as well as those who lived in the Holy Land.

Historically, the primary functions of the bet din were to decide matters of civil law and to enforce ritual conformity within a Jewish community. Jews in many countries were often granted autonomy to administer their own local affairs, from ancient times up to, in a few cases, the 20th century. Marriage, divorce, and conversions were processed via the *bet din,* which also reconciled Jews involved in business and other disputes.

Today, a *bet din* often acts as a supervising agent for Jewish communities in regard to ritual matters such as the laws of KASHRUT (kosher food). A letter from a recognized *bet din* is recognized as authoritative by Jewish communities. *Bet dins* continue to supervise divorce, child custody, and conversion ceremonies. Some modern Jews choose to use a *bet din* as a form of binding arbitration in financial and personal matters with other Jews. By avoiding the government's civil courts, they keep the disputes within the community, reduce legal expenses, and resolve the dispute according to Jewish values rather than by legal technicalities.

ORTHODOX JUDAISM allows only men to serve on *bet dins,* but CONSERVATIVE JUDAISM and REFORM JUDAISM accept women as judges—both movements ordain women rabbis. There is also a Jewish legal tradition that one rabbi may serve on a *bet din* and appoint two knowledgeable Jewish lay people as accompanying members. This is especially done in relation to divorce and conversion ceremonies.

A *bet din* does not convene on SHABBAT or major festivals, and it meets only during daylight hours. On the eve of YOM KIPPUR (Day of Atonement), Jewish communities gather prior to sunset to create a symbolic *bet din.* The TORAH is removed from the ARK as a sign of the court's legitimacy; the court then pronounces a formula permitting everyone to pray in the company of sinners. The congregation then begins the KOL NIDRE prayer, which declares that all vows made to God are legally cancelled, the first step in the daylong process of personal and communal repentance.

Further reading: Isadore Epstein, ed., *Soncino Hebrew/English Babylonian Talmud,* 30 vols. (Brooklyn, N.Y.: Soncino Press, 1990); Isaac Klein, *A Guide to Jewish Religious Practice* (New York: Jewish Theological Seminary of America, 1988).

Bialik, Chaim Nachman (1873–1934)
Zionist writer

Born in southern RUSSIA, Chaim Nachman Bialik lost his father as a child and was raised by his grandfather in a traditional Jewish household. He was strongly influenced by traditional Jewish literature as well as contemporary Russian writers. As a young man he moved to Odessa, an early center of ZIONISM. His first poem, "El ha-Zippor" (To the bird), published in 1892, included themes he would address throughout his life: the difficulty of Jewish life in eastern Europe and the need for a Jewish homeland. One of his most important poems, "Be-Ir ha-Haregah" ("In the City of Slaughter") describes Odessa after a severe POGROM, and calls upon Jews to defend themselves.

Bialik wrote in both HEBREW and YIDDISH, working as a writer, translator, and publisher in Berlin and TEL AVIV. He is best known for his success in shaping Hebrew into a vibrant language for a modern Jewish society. He did this in part by translating classical works such as *Julius Caesar, Don Quixote,* and *Wilhelm Tell,* and in part by writing modern versions of traditional biblical and Talmudic works. His Hebrew poetry, for adults and children, has had a strong influence on all subsequent Hebrew literature and poetry. His work has been widely translated, including three English poetry collections in 1924, 1926, and 1948.

Further reading: Hillel Barzel, "The Last Prophet—The Biblical Ground of Bialik's Poetry," in *Biblical Patterns in Modern Literature* (Chicago: University of Chicago,

1984); Hayyim Nahman Bialik, *Random Harvest: The Novellas of Bialik,* eds. David Patterson and Ezra Spicehandler (New York: Westview Press, 1999); Mordecai Ovadyahu, *Bialik Speaks: Words from the Poet's Lips, Clues to the Man,* trans. A. El-Dror (New York: Herzl Press, 1969).

biblical Hebrew

Biblical Hebrew is classified together with Phoenician and Moabite in the Canaanite subgroup of the Semitic languages; it is believed to have become an independent language by the 12th century B.C.E., though it retained strong similarities to the neighboring tongues. The name *Hebrew* may well derive from the Egyptian term *apiru,* referring to a laboring class within Egyptian society. The Hebrew alphabet, which has always been read from right to left across a page, includes 22 letters, all of which were originally consonants, though some of them are now pronounced as vowels. Vowel markings were not included in manuscripts of the TANAKH, the Hebrew Bible, until the masorete scribes of the sixth century C.E. included the vowels to ensure that the text would continue to be read according to the oral tradition (*see* ORAL LAW).

Hebrew is considered a sacred language, the language with which God brought forth CREATION. Judaism, unlike some other world religions, encourages all adherents to learn Hebrew rather than to depend on translations for worship and study.

See also HEBREW, MODERN.

Further reading: Thomas O. Lambdin, *Introduction to Biblical Hebrew* (New York: Charles Scribner's Sons, 1971); Zohar Livnat, "WLY from Biblical to Modern Hebrew: A Semantic-Textual Approach," *Hebrew Studies* 42 (2001): 81–104.

Birkat Ha-Mazon

Birkat Ha-Mazon ("blessing of the food") is the Hebrew name for the collection of prayers and blessings (*see* BRACHA) recited by men and women after a meal in which bread has been eaten (which is considered a proper meal).

Deuteronomy 8:10 (*see* TORAH) declares: "When you have eaten your fill, give thanks to the Lord your God for the good land that God has given you." In satisfaction of this commandment, Jewish tradition has evolved a liturgy after a meal that emphasizes thanksgiving for all good things, not just for food. This tradition expresses the understanding that when one lives in prosperity, one should remember the divine source of that prosperity, namely God. NACH-MONIDES, a medieval sage, taught that the Birkat Ha-Mazon was the rabbi's antidote to the arrogance that naturally arises when someone enjoys a life of abundance. Birkat Ha-Mazon became the shield that guards against self-satisfaction and haughtiness.

The structure of the Birkat Ha-Mazon is specified in the TALMUD. It consists of four blessings: the first blesses God for providing food to all living things; the second speaks about ERETZ YISRAEL, the Torah, REDEMPTION, and the COVENANT; the third used to give thanks for JERUSALEM and the TEMPLE, but later became a prayer for God to rebuild Jerusalem and restore the dynasty of DAVID; and the fourth asks for prosperity, redemption, and blessings on all those present while expressing gratitude for God's goodness (Talmud B'rachot 48b).

HALAKHAH, Jewish law, dictates that Birkat Ha-Mazon is to be recited at the table where one ate any meal that included as little as a morsel of bread. The ability to perform this ritual was paramount, and therefore the Jew was permitted to recite the Birkat Ha-Mazon in the vernacular, if unable to do so in Hebrew.

While the Torah required an acknowledgement of satiation and gratitude after eating, the rabbis created the rituals of blessings prior to eating as well. Sociologically, many more Jews are familiar with the prayer over bread, the Motzi, than the Birkat Ha-Mazon. This is probably due to the brevity of the former prayer in comparison to the longer prayer of Birkat Ha-Mazon.

Further reading: Rabbi Hayim Halevy Donin, *To Pray as a Jew: A Guide to the Prayer Book and the Synagogue Service* (New York: Basic Books, 1980); Ismar Elbogen, *Jewish Liturgy: A Comprehensive History* (Philadelphia and Jerusalem: The Jewish Publication Society, 1993); Isidore Epstein, ed., *Soncino Hebrew/English Babylonian Talmud* (Brooklyn, N.Y.: Soncino Press Ltd., 1990); Moses Maimonides, *Mishne Torah, Hilchot Yesodei Hatorah: The Laws, Which Are the Foundations of the Torah* (Mishe Torah Series) (Brooklyn, N.Y.: Moznaim Publishing Corporation, 1989).

black-Jewish relations

The history of the relationship between the American Jewish community and the African-American community is varied. It begins with a memory of slavery, continues through the Civil Rights movement of the 1960s, and passes through some struggles toward the end of the 20th and start of the 21st century. Some scholars question whether blacks and Jews will ever be able to mesh their shared minority status into a relationship that could benefit both communities, while others insist that the intensity of the Civil Rights movement created the perfect conditions for such a union.

It is true that some individual Jews were involved in the African slave trade of the 17th century and some Jews owned slaves, as did some blacks; however, the percentage of Jews who participated in the trade of human beings was proportionately minuscule, and today's American Jews mostly descend from poor eastern Europeans who arrived in America long after slavery was formally abolished. It was not until the early 20th century that a relationship between the Jewish and African-American communities developed, centered around problems in the northern urban environment that African-American migrants from the South shared with eastern European Jewish immigrants.

Conscious of similar histories of oppression "back home," many Jews and blacks living in the growing cities sought social justice in common or faced related struggles in the areas of labor, education, and employment. Jewish support for ZIONISM helped inspire black dreams of a return to Africa and influenced black leaders such as Marcus Garvey and W. E. B. Du Bois. During the Civil Rights movement of the 1960s, a bond existed between the organized black and Jewish communities on the value of civil rights for minorities, nondiscrimination, and larger issues of social justice, where Jewish values seemed to mesh with black needs. Jews were generous with their financial support of the movement, and prominent rabbis voiced their support. Abraham Joshua HESCHEL, having escaped Nazi Europe and pursued study and teaching at the JEWISH THEOLOGICAL SEMINARY, joined Martin Luther King, Jr., in his struggle for civil rights in the UNITED STATES.

Scholars do not agree on how strong the tie between blacks and Jews in the United States has ever been. However, by the 1970s it became clear that issues involving ISRAEL and the rising leader of the Nation of Islam, Louis Farrakhan, would impede further cooperation and positive relations between the black and Jewish communities. In addition, African-American neighborhoods in the Northeast share space with ultra-Orthodox communities (*see* ORTHODOX JUDAISM), and there were a number of clashes between them during the last decade of the 20th century. Accusations of Jewish racism and black ANTISEMITISM have weakened any links that blacks and Jews shared in the 1960s. Increasingly, black spokespeople such as Farrakhan accuse the Jews of masterminding the slave trade itself and Jews accuse the blacks of spewing antisemitism that rivals the *PROTOCOLS OF THE ELDERS OF ZION*. Urban clashes and cultural differences seem to have erased the hope that King and Heschel shared for both their communities.

Further reading: Mark K. Bauman and Berkley Kalin, eds., *The Quiet Voices: Southern Rabbis and Black Civil Rights, 1880s to 1990s* (Tuscaloosa: University of Alabama Press, 1997); Jack Salzman and Cornel West, eds., *Struggles in the Promised Land: Towards a History of Black-Jewish Relations in the United States* (New York: Oxford University Press, 1997); Benjamin Sevitch, "W. E. B. Du Bois and Jews: A Lifetime of Opposing Antisemitism," *The Journal of African American History* (June 2002); Micheal E. Staub, *Torn at the Roots: The Crisis of Jewish Liberalism in Postwar America* (New York: Columbia University Press, 2002).

blood libel

Blood libel, also known as the accusation of ritual murder, is the false charge that Jews kill Christians, especially children, during Easter week in a ritual reenactment of the Crucifixion. Though the details have evolved over the centuries, the most common and persistent reason given for the supposed murders is that Jews use the victim's blood in baking MATZAH, the unleavened bread used in the PASSOVER SEDER. The origins of the ritual murder accusation can be traced to pre-Christian times, at least to the second century before the Common Era, when Hellenistic writers accused Jews of sacrificing non-Jews in the TEMPLE. Ironically, early Christians were also accused of ritual murder by the Romans.

The first well-documented blood libel took place in 1144 in Norwich, ENGLAND, where a boy named William disappeared shortly before Easter. A convert from Judaism charged that every year Jews kidnapped or bought a Christian child and killed him in a reenactment of the Crucifixion in order to mock CHRISTIANITY. Though no Jews were tried or punished for the crime since there was no evidence of murder, William was later declared a martyr and beatified by the church. A lack of evidence, however, did not stop authorities from pressing charges against Jews in 1168 in Gloucester, England, when a boy was found dead there. The first case of the blood libel in continental Europe occurred in 1171 in Blois, FRANCE, where Jews were burned at the stake as the result of the accusation. From France, the accusation spread to GERMANY, where it became particularly prominent, reaching its peak in the 15th and 16th centuries. The libel reached POLAND in the 17th century and later appeared in RUSSIA. Often, a blood libel accusation was followed by the burning of individual Jews, expelling an entire community, or mob violence.

Though individual clergymen were often involved in the various blood libels, the Catholic Church as a whole condemned them. Already in 1245 Pope Innocent IV forbade Christians from bringing the accusation. This prohibition was reiterated by many succeeding popes. Martin Luther declared the charge ridiculous, as it went against fundamental teachings of the Jewish religion, and wicked. And yet at one time or another ritual murder accusations have been made in every country where Jews have resided. Two of the most famous cases were the DAMASCUS AFFAIR (1840) and the Beilis case in Russia. There, in 1911, a Jewish factory foreman was put on trial, accused of murdering a 13-year-old Christian boy so he could use his blood in baking matzah. The Beilis case attracted an international outcry, but the Russian government was determined to proceed with the case. Beilis was defended by a team of leading liberal Russian lawyers and professors. The evidence of a frame-up was so clear that Beilis was acquitted in 1913 by a jury of 12 peasants, the majority of whom were actually members of the notorious right-wing Black Hundreds society. Beilis later immigrated to the UNITED STATES.

In modern times the blood libel was a popular motif in Nazi antisemitic propaganda (see ANTISEMITISM). Most recently it has appeared in Muslim countries. The Syrian minister of defense repeated it in a book he published in 1983, and in 2003 a Saudi Arabian newspaper published an article accusing Jews of using Muslim children's blood in the making of pastry for the holiday of Purim. In addition, the Syrian ambassador to the UNITED NATIONS repeated the Damascus Affair (1840) blood libel accusation in 1991; only pressure from the UNITED STATES challenged this entry in the records of the United Nations.

Further reading: R. Po-chia Hsia, *The Myth of Ritual Murder: Jews and Magic in Reformation Germany* (New Haven, Conn.: Yale University Press, 1988); Gavin Langmuir, "Thomas of Monmouth: Detector of Ritual Murder," *Speculum* 59, 4 (October 1984); Maurice Samuel, *Blood Accusations: The Strange History of the Beilis Case* (Philadelphia and Jerusalem: Jewish Publication Society, 1966); Joshua Trachtenberg, *The Devil and the Jews: The Medieval Conception of the Jew and Its Relation to Modern Anti-Semitism* (Philadelphia and Jerusalem: Jewish Publication Society, 1983).

Bnai Akiva *See* ZIONIST YOUTH MOVEMENTS.

B'nai B'rith International

B'nai B'rith ("Sons of the COVENANT") is one of the world's oldest and largest Jewish fraternal organizations. It was founded by Henry Jones and 11 other German-speaking Jews in New York City on October 13, 1843. It was originally named Bundes Brüder (League of Brothers), and was modeled after other secret brotherhoods of the time, such as the Freemasons. The first English-speaking lodge was established in Cincinnati, Ohio, in 1850. At first the members of B'nai B'rith were exclusively men, but in 1920 the organization added "ladies auxiliaries," today called B'nai B'rith Women. The structure of B'nai B'rith includes local lodges and regional and international offices.

B'nai B'rith developed and grew as both a fraternal organization and a benevolent society. It established multiple community service and welfare activities, beginning with a mandatory donation to a fund to aid WIDOWS AND ORPHANS. Branches were founded in other countries, and B'nai B'rith eventually became engaged in promoting human rights around the world, assisting hospitals, and helping to rescue victims of natural disasters. Over the years B'nai B'rith has participated in drug-abuse education, volunteer services, aid to the disabled, prisoner rehabilitation, assistance to new immigrants, refugee and rescue during the HOLOCAUST, and aid to the elderly. B'nai B'rith also played an important role in the AMERICANIZATION of new Jewish immigrants to America's shores.

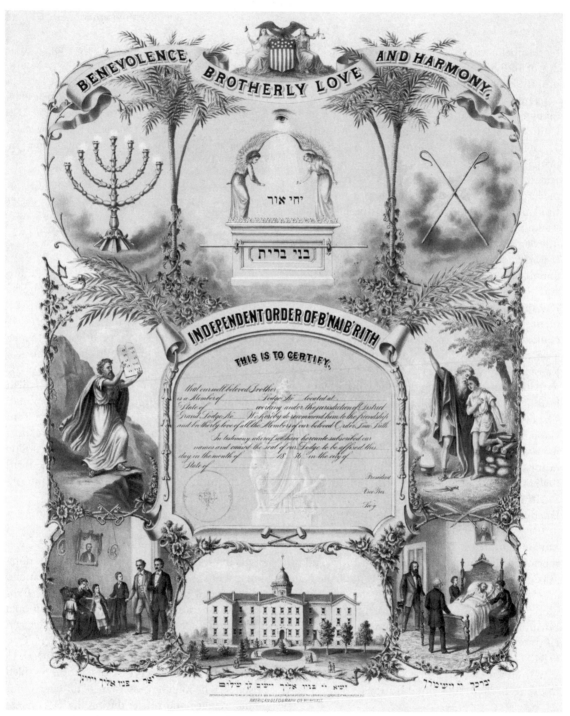

B'nai B'rith is both a fraternal organization and a benevolent society. Pictured here is a membership certificate. Note the image in the bottom right corner of an ailing person receiving care and on the left center of Moses and the Decalogue, representing God's covenant with the Jewish people. *(Library of Congress)*

The group provides scholarships to Jewish college students. In 1923 it created the B'nai B'rith HILLEL Foundation, which is the primary college campus resource in the UNITED STATES for Jewish student activism and religious services. Until 2001, B'nai B'rith sponsored the B'nai B'rith Youth Organization (*see* JEWISH YOUTH GROUPS), which is now BBYO. Among many other subsidiary institutions, B'nai B'rith maintains the B'nai B'rith Center for Human Rights and Public Policy. This organization focuses on concerns for the security of ISRAEL, rising Islamic militancy, Jewish renewal in eastern Europe, and new evidence of ANTISEMITISM. Fighting to protect Jews around the world has always been a major activity of B'nai B'rith. Through the establishment of the ANTI-DEFAMATION LEAGUE (now independent), the organization was a pioneer in combating antisemitism and all forms of racism.

B'nai B'rith has offices and lodges all over the world and it contributes to the unity of world Jewry. It remains a membership organization with members in more than 50 countries around the world.

Further reading: Daniel J. Elazar, *Community and Polity: The Organizational Dynamics of American Jewry* (Philadelphia: Jewish Publication Society, 1995); J. J. Goldberg, *Jewish Power: Inside the American Jewish Establishment* (Boston, Mass.: Addison Wesley Publishing Company, 1997); Deborah Dash Moore, *B'nai B'rith and the Challenge of Ethnic Leadership* (Albany: State University of New York Press, 1981); Web site URL: http://www.bnaibrith.org, accessed June 26, 2004.

B'nai B'rith Youth Organization *See*
JEWISH YOUTH GROUPS.

Bolshevik Revolution
The Bolshevik Revolution in RUSSIA in 1918 began with the violent overthrow of the democratically elected Constituent Assembly, which had been elected after the overthrow of Czar Nicholas II of RUSSIA a few months before. The Bolsheviks had originally begun as a faction of the Russian socialist movement, which was guided largely by the teachings of the German Jewish philosopher Karl MARX. Although Jews constituted less than 5 percent of the Russian population, Jewish individuals played a prominent, visible role in the early Bolshevik regime, though the large majority of Bolsheviks and their leaders were non-Jewish and most Jews actually supported democratic parties. The primary Bolshevik leader was Lenin (Vladimir Ulyanov), who was mostly of Russian ancestry, but whose maternal grandfather, Israel (Alexander) Blank, was possibly a Ukrainian Jew who was later baptized into the Russian Orthodox Church.

Taking firm control of Russia by 1920, Lenin was supported by several Jewish colleagues: Leon TROTSKY (Lev Bronstein), who headed the Red Army, Yakov Sverdlov (Solomon), who was the Bolshevik Party's executive secretary, Grigori Zinovyev (Ovaal Radomyslsky), who headed the central agency for spreading revolution in foreign countries, Karl Radek (Sobelsohn), who was the press commissar, and Maksim Litvinov (Meir Walach), who was the foreign affairs commissar.

Many Russian Jews had been attracted to the cause of revolution because of the prevailing ANTI-JUDAISM of the czarist regime. Most notorious was the czarist creation of the PALE OF SETTLEMENT. Thereafter, Jews were forbidden to reside outside this specifically defined area of Russia; also, it was probably czarist officials who created the infamous antisemitic tract, the *PROTOCOLS OF THE ELDERS OF ZION*. Bolshevik idealism, by contrast, imagined a world without ethnic or cultural divisions between human beings. The utopian dream had drawn Jews because it was a secular vision of what had previously been the religious vision for a messianic era.

When Lenin died in 1924, an internal power struggle ultimately led to the victory of Joseph Stalin over his political rivals. Subsequently, Stalin succeeded in putting to death nearly every one of the most prominent early Bolshevik leaders. A rabid supporter of ANTISEMITISM, Stalin eliminated most Jews from the leadership of the Soviet state and the Communist Party by 1928. Unfortunately, the impression had already been created among millions of people around the world that Bolshevism was "Jewish," which enabled legitimate anti-Communist views to be channeled into brutal antisemitism.

The Bolshevik utopian dream turned out to be a lie. Stalinism quickly perverted the initial Marxist idealism. The Communist Soviet Union continued the Russian history of antisemitic actions; Jewish religion and culture was suppressed more thoroughly than they had been under the czars, and the Jews suffered greatly until the overthrow of the Soviet regime in the late 20th century.

Further reading: Richard Pipes, *The Russian Revolution* (New York: Alfred A. Knopf, 1990); Edvard Radzinksy, *The Last Czar* (Garden City, N.Y.: Doubleday & Company, 1992); Louis Rapoport, *Stalin's War Against the Jews* (New York: Free Press, 1990).

Book of Life

According to Jewish tradition, God keeps track of everyone's deeds and records them in the Book of Life. Every year on ROSH HASHANAH, the Jewish New Year, Jews pray to be written into the Book of Life for a good year. The prayers say, "On Rosh Hashanah it is written, and on YOM KIPPUR [the Day of Atonement 10 days later] it is sealed." Jews are supposed to be on their best behavior during the Days of Awe, between Rosh HaShanah and Yom Kippur, focusing on TESHUVAH (repentence), PRAYER, and TZEDAKAH (charity) to ensure a positive judgment.

The concept of the Book of Life existed in ancient times and is most likely of BABYLONIAN origin. References to a record, a book of life, or a book of remembrance can be found in the TANAKH, the Hebrew Bible, particularly in EXODUS, Psalms (*see* TEHILLIM), ISAIAH, Malachi, and Daniel. To have one's name blotted out from the book was equivalent to death. By the time of the

PHARISEES, the concept had emerged of an annual verdict on Rosh HaShanah that was inscribed in such a book; and by the time of the MISHNAH, the RABBIS maintained that all of an individual's deeds are recorded therein.

Further reading: Shmuel Yosef Agnon, *Days of Awe: Being a Treasury of Traditions, Legends and Learned Commentaries Concerning Rosh ha-Shanah, Yom Kippur and the Days Between, Culled from Three Hundred Volumes, Ancient and New* (New York: Schocken Books, 1965); Irving Greenberg, *The Jewish Way: Living the Holidays* (New York: Summit Books, 1988).

Borscht Belt

The Catskill Mountains of upstate New York once contained a large number of hotels that catered to the American Jewish community. Since these hotels often served the eastern European cold beet soup called borscht, the area was often referred to as "the Borscht Belt"; the term was also used to describe an era in American entertainment history centered on the region's hotels.

The history of the area begins with the Jewish philanthropist Baron de HIRSCH, who promoted Jewish farming in many areas such as ARGENTINA, South Dakota, and the Catskills. What began as a Jewish farming experiment developed into a popular vacation spot for New York Jews who wanted to escape the oppressive city summers.

The heyday of the Jewish resort culture was the 1950s, when more than 1 million people would visit the Catskills bungalow colonies, summer camps, and small hotels every year. There they partook of sports, leisure, and entertainment. Many famous Jewish comedians, musicians, and performers such as Milton Berle and Henny Youngman honed their craft in the Borscht Belt. Even more numerous were the thousands of college students who funded their studies working in the resorts as busboys, waiters, and performers. The popular 1987 Hollywood movie *Dirty Dancing* illustrated the culture of these resorts. The film also took note of the end of the era as characters talked about the new trend of vacations to Florida.

Although the mid-20th century Borscht Belt provided a way for mainstream Jewish Americans to acculturate (*see* ACCOMMODATION), the area is now largely abandoned, with only a few larger hotels remaining. Many Jewish religious institutions use the facilities for retreats, and the Orthodox community (*see* ORTHODOX JUDAISM) frequents the area's resorts and colonies that still observe KASHRUT (kosher food laws).

Further reading: Joey Adams and Henry Tobias, *The Borscht Belt* (New York: Bobbs-Merrill, 1966); Phil Brown, ed., *In the Catskills: A Century of Jewish Experience in "The Mountains"* (New York: Columbia University Press, 2002); Myrna Katz Frommer and Harvey Frommer, *It Happened in the Catskills: An Oral History in the Words of Busboys, Bellhops, Guests, Proprietors, Comedians, Agents, and Others Who Lived It* (New York: Harcourt Brace, 1991); Stefan Kanfer, *A Summer World: The Attempt to Build a Jewish Eden in the Catskills, from the Days of the Ghetto to the Rise and Decline of the Borscht Belt* (New York: Farrar Straus Giroux, 1992).

bracha (pl.: *brachot*)

The Hebrew word *bracha* is commonly translated as blessing, but the original meaning is far more specific. For a prayer or blessing to qualify as a *bracha*, it must follow a legal rabbinic formula that begins with the three words "Baruch Atah Adonai," which is commonly translated as "Blessed (or Praised) are You, My Lord."

The origin of the *bracha* goes back to the period of the MISHNAH. After the destruction of the second TEMPLE of Jerusalem in the year 70 C.E., prayer and study in Jewish tradition replaced SACRIFICE as the primary means of communion with God. Initially prayer used simple quotes from the TANAKH, or Hebrew Bible, but eventually the TANNAIM, ancient rabbis, determined to write new prayers as a way to proclaim their theological consensus, and to have Jews affirm the principles of Jewish belief.

The first major prayer they wrote was a collection of 18 *brachot* that became known as the Shemoneh Esrei, "the 18"; Ha-Tefillah, "the Prayer"; or AMIDAH, "the Standing." These *brachot* constituted a theological list of God's characteristics and involvement with the world, and included language asking for Divine intervention.

HALAKHAH, Jewish law, teaches that an individual who hears a *bracha* should answer AMEN, "it is true," in response to the dogmatic statement of belief. For example, the *bracha* prior to eating a meal is "Baruch Atah Adonai Eloheinu Melech Ha-Olam Hamotzi Lechem Min Ha-Aretz," which means "Blessed/Praised are You, O Lord, our God, ruler of the universe, Who causes bread to come forth from the land." This *bracha* signifies God's role as Creator, and God's power is affirmed by the listener to this prayer.

Scholars have asserted that the Semitic origin of the word *bracha* comes from the verb root BRK, which means power. In that view a *bracha* is more than just a statement of appreciation or hope; it may have originally involved a dogmatic statement of belief: "The Power that is You, O Lord. . . ."

Because *brachot* were the carefully worded products of dogmatic consensus among the ancient rabbis, it is traditionally forbidden for Jews to write *brachot* today. New prayers are allowed, and they may use the word *baruch,* but traditional Jews refrain from writing a prayer that begins with Baruch Atah Adonai. Some more liberal Jews have, however, written original *brachot* that relate closely to the concerns of modern life.

Jewish tradition prescribes that a Jew should recite 100 *brachot* per day. Because the daily liturgy contains hundreds of *brachot*, Jews who pray at the commanded times easily fulfill this commandment.

Further reading: Ismar Elbogen, *Jewish Liturgy: A Comprehensive History* (Philadelphia and Jerusalem: The Jewish Publication Society, 1993); Abraham Millgram, *Jewish Worship* (Philadelphia: The Jewish Publication Society of America, 1971).

Brandeis, Louis Dembitz (1856–1941)

U.S. Supreme Court justice

Louis Brandeis was born in Louisville, Kentucky, to immigrant parents from Prague. His parents were proponents of European liberalism, and his career represented the politically liberal atmosphere in which he grew up. Although Brandeis did not become a Zionist himself until after his career was well under way, he had been influenced at a young age by an uncle who had been a Zionist.

Brandeis studied in Dresden, GERMANY, from 1873–75, returning to the UNITED STATES to study law at Harvard University. Upon graduation he remained in Boston and became a successful lawyer, involving himself especially in legal cases

Louis Brandeis was the first Jewish U.S. Supreme Court justice. He was also an American Zionist who encouraged the development of Palestine as a refuge for Jews in need while at the same time voicing his own commitment to his birthplace, the United States. (*Library of Congress*)

that had a political agenda. Following in his parents' footsteps, Brandeis supported the rights of the people in business affairs and was known as "the people's attorney." He had a particular interest in representing smaller companies against giant corporations, and he led the fight for the universal implementation of a minimum wage for all American laborers. In addition, through frugal living and good investments, Brandeis became financially independent, enabling him to serve those he thought needed his expertise and to pursue ideas that might not be popular with his peers.

Just five years before he would be nominated to the U.S. Supreme Court, Brandeis acted as a mediator in the New York garment workers' strike in 1911. Impressed with the intelligence of the eastern European Jewish immigrants he encountered, Brandeis became more interested in his Jewish heritage. When he met Jacob De Haas, former secretary to Theodor HERZL, the father of ZIONISM, he became excited by the Zionist writing De Haas made available to him. Thus, when the beginning of World War I brought European Zionists to the United States, Brandeis accepted the role of chairperson of the Provisional Executive Committee for General Zionist Affairs, an American Zionist organization. Brandeis significantly impacted the American branch of the Zionist movement both philosophically and practically. He attracted numerous followers and sympathizers, and he helped improve the organizational structure and overall finances.

In 1912 soon-to-be president Woodrow Wilson sought Brandeis's advice on issues of political and social reform, and after he was elected to the presidency, he nominated Brandeis to the U.S. Supreme Court. After months of discussion in the Senate, in 1916 Brandeis took his seat as the first Jewish U.S. Supreme Court justice. Following his appointment, Brandeis continued to support the Zionist cause, working to secure support from President Wilson for both the BALFOUR DECLARATION and the BRITISH MANDATE in PALESTINE.

After World War I, Brandeis took a trip to Paris, London, and then to Palestine, where he was impressed with the spirit of the settlers and distressed by their living conditions. In London he met Zionist leader Chaim WEIZMANN, a meeting with great potential, as both were committed to the future of Zionism and a homeland for Jews in Palestine. However, a meeting of these great minds was not to be. In 1920 Brandeis and Weizmann parted ways over disagreements concerning the financial portfolio of the Zionist Organization, and Brandeis withdrew from formal Zionist activities, though he continued to help the Jewish community in Palestine lay the economic foundation for the hoped-for Jewish state there.

Brandeis helped create a special American brand of Zionism. He encouraged his compatriots to embrace Zionism out of their own American identity. He wrote that "Zionism finds in it, for the Jews, a reason to raise their heads, and, taking their stand upon the past, to gaze straightforwardly into the future." While European Zionists saw the end result of Zionism to be the ingathering of world Jewry to the land of ISRAEL, Brandeis and most American Jews supported the idea of a Jewish state for those Jews in need, while remaining committed to their American home.

Brandeis retired from the Supreme Court in 1939, and he died in Washington, D.C., in 1941.

Further reading: Alberta Eiseman, *Biographies of Four Jewish Americans: Uriah Phillips Levy, Ernestine L. Rose, Louis D. Brandeis, Lillian D. Wald* (Garden City, N.Y.: Doubleday & Company, 1976); Arthur Hertzberg, *The Jews in America* (New York: Columbia University Press, 1998); Melvin I. Urofsky and David W. Levy, eds., *Half Brother, Half Son: The Letters of Louis D. Brandeis to Felix Frankfurter* (Norman: University of Oklahoma Press, 1991).

Brandeis University

Brandeis University was founded in 1948 as a secular university with a Jewish religious and cultural affiliation.

The university was named for the first Jewish Supreme Court justice, Louis Dembitz BRANDEIS,

The Berlin Chapel at Brandeis University is one of three chapels on the campus. Its curving walls allow many students to gather together for study, prayer, or celebrations. Brandeis also houses the Bethlehem Chapel for its Catholic students, the Harlan Chapel for its Protestant students, and a Muslim Prayer Room and Resource Center. *(Verner Reed/Getty Images)*

and was intended to reflect his ideals of academic excellence and social justice. The Jewish leaders who established Brandeis University hoped to offer admission to students of all creeds without discrimination, and to offer posts to qualified professors and teachers based solely on merit. During that era many universities maintained numeric quotas to limit the number of Jewish students and professors.

Coeducational classes began in Waltham, Massachusetts, with 107 students and 13 faculty members. The university was led for its first 20 years by its founding president, Abram L. Sachar. During this time it quickly became an important national and international center for teaching and research. In 1985 Brandeis University was elected to membership in the Association of American Universities, which represents the 59 leading research universities in the UNITED STATES and Canada. As of 2003, the university had approximately 3,000 undergraduates, 1,300 graduate students, and 500 faculty members.

Brandeis University is the only secular Jewish-sponsored college or university in the United States. The university seal contains the Hebrew motto *Emet* (truth).

Further reading: Israel Goldstein, *Brandeis University, Chapter of Its Founding* (New York: Bloch Publishing, 1951); Susan Pasternack, ed., *From the Beginning: A Picture History of the First Four Decades of Brandeis University* (Waltham, Mass.: Brandeis University, 1988); Abram Sachar, *Brandeis University: A Host at Last* (Lebanon, N.H.: University Press of New England, 1995); Web site URL: http://www.brandeis.edu/overview/index.html, accessed June 26, 2004.

Brazil

Brazil is the largest and most populous country in South America. Like its neighbors, it is predominantly Roman Catholic, and its official language is Portuguese. The language was not the only gift PORTUGAL gave to Brazil. The first Jews who arrived in the country in the 16th century were CONVERSOS, secret Jews fleeing the Portuguese Inquisition. They found it possible to become active in Brazil's early economic endeavors.

When the Dutch ruled Brazil from 1631 to 1654, Jews were able to practice their traditions openly and the community thrived. The Kahal Zur synagogue was built in the capital city of Recife in 1636. During this time, Jews earned their livelihood from a variety of occupations including importing/exporting, teaching, and writing. They also traded in sugar and slaves, and ran sugar plantations that depended on slave labor. Although the slaves were often sold for profit, it has been said that they preferred Jewish owner-ship, as this allotted them an extra day off on SHABBAT, the Jewish Sabbath. When the Portuguese conquered the territory, their intolerance of Judaism followed them. A large portion of the Jewish community migrated to the West Indies, back to Europe, or to New Amsterdam.

In the 18th century diamond mines were discovered in Brazil, providing an opportunity for Jewish merchants to export Brazilian diamonds to the European marketplace; poor Moroccan Jewish emigrants helped create an Amazon rubber boom in the mid 19th century, centered on the city of Manaus.

In the late 19th and early 20th centuries, various Jewish leaders and philanthropists tried to encourage eastern European Jews to immigrate to agricultural colonies, an occupation they thought would appeal to those fleeing persecution. In 1902 the Jewish Colonization Association (JCA), funded by Baron de HIRSCH, bought land in southern Brazil, but few Jews wanted to settle there. In 1904 the crop failed and by 1907 only 17 of the original 122 Jewish families remained. The JCA continued to purchase land, but every attempt to maintain successful farms failed, and in 1935, finally beaten by new Brazilian immigration restrictions, the JCA sold the land and abandoned the plan. The Jewish agricultural colonists moved into the cities and by the beginning of World War I, around 7,000 Jews lived in Brazil. The community in Porto Alegre established a Jewish school in 1910 and a YIDDISH newspaper in 1915. The Jews of São Paolo organized philanthropic, cultural, and mutual aid societies in 1916. They were prepared when World War I refugees began to arrive.

Following World War I about 30,000 SEPHARDIM arrived in Brazil from the Near East and North Africa, building a vibrant Jewish community. The growth of the Jewish community in Brazil was complex, and it proved difficult for Jewish immigrants from different cultures to merge. This process became even more complicated with the arrival of German Jewish refugees after HITLER became chancellor of GERMANY in 1933. Central and western European Jewish immigrants grew in number as the war progressed and after it ended. Even though Brazil had restricted immigration in 1938, almost 17,500 Jews were able to make Brazil their new home.

Brazil was looking for particular types of immigrants during this period, namely skilled workers and farmers. Their reticence to accept many Jewish immigrants derived at first from a belief that Jews would not "Brazilianize," but as Nazi Germany worked to incite ANTISEMITISM around the world, including among the large émigré German community in Brazil, prejudice against the Jews increased, and several editions of the *PROTOCOLS OF THE ELDERS OF ZION* were disseminated. In 1938 the Brazilian government began a program to assimilate its immigrants (*see* ASSIMILATION), a process not restricted to the Jewish community. All Yiddish newspapers and Jewish organizations were closed. Jewish communal culture did not revive until a new democratic government came into power in Brazil in 1945.

Brazil supported the creation of a Jewish state and the PARTITION PLAN in PALESTINE in 1947. In 1949 Brazil recognized the State of ISRAEL and established an embassy there three years later. By this time, there were approximately 100,000 Jews living in the country, as Jewish immigration continued from North Africa in the 1950s. By the 1960s, the community in Brazil had gained considerable strength; Jews began to be well represented in government and commerce, and communal institutions thrived. In 1971 the Jewish population of Brazil was 150,000, where it has stabilized. Most Jewish merchants, manufacturers, and professionals live in the largest cities in Brazil, including Rio de Janeiro, São Paulo, Pôrto Alegre, Belo Horizonte, Recife, and Belém.

Antisemitism is not a widespread problem in Brazil, although Jews there have occasionally experienced harassment, threats, and desecration of property. The Brazilian Jewish community is on the alert because of more intense antisemitism in neighboring ARGENTINA. The community has developed a medley of institutions not unlike those in most Jewish communities around the world; 200 of these are represented by an umbrella organization called the Confederacão Israelita do Brasil (CONIB), founded in 1951. Jewish institutions include a variety of Sephardic and Ashkenazic (*see* ASHKENAZIM) synagogues, from liberal to Orthodox, secular and religious Jewish schools, the Center for Jewish Studies of the University of São Paulo, the Marc CHAGALL Institute in Pôrto Alegre, HADASSAH International, B'NAI B'RITH, Jewish and Israeli film festivals, CHABAD, several Jewish publications, and a weekly television program, *Mosaico*. The Jewish community continues to contribute to the economy of Brazil, taking an active part in publishing, banking, the jewelry industry, and politics. In 1994 Jaime Lerner became Brazil's first Jewish governor and in 1998 distinguished professor Dr. Eva Alterman Bay became the first Jewish woman to become a member of Brazil's senate.

The challenges of Brazilian Jewry today include the slowing economy and the high rate of assimilation. The organized Jewish community works to ameliorate these conditions, and as a strong symbol of their dedication has reopened the first Jewish synagogue in Recife, closed by the Portuguese more than 300 years ago.

Further reading: Avi Beker, ed., *Jewish Communities of the World* (Minneapolis, Minn.: Lerner Publication Co., 1998); Jeff H. Lesser, "Continuity and Change Within an Immigrant Community: The Jews of São Paulo, 1924–1945," *Luso-Brazilian Review* 25, 2 (Winter 1988): 45–58; Jeffrey Lesser, *Negotiating National Identity: Immigrants, Minorities, and the Struggle for Ethnicity in Brazil* (Durham, N.C.: Duke University Press, 1999); Jeffrey Lesser, *Welcoming the Undesirables: Brazil and the Jewish Question* (Berkeley: University of California Press, 1995); Harold M. Midkiff, Royce A. Wight, and George Wythe, *Brazil, An Expanding Economy* (New York: Twentieth Century Fund, 1949).

British Mandate

In July 1922, the League of Nations assigned Great Britain (*see* ENGLAND) a "mandate" or protectorate for PALESTINE or ERETZ YISRAEL, which specifically recognized "the historical connection of the Jewish people with Palestine." Great Britain, which had conquered the area from the Ottoman Turks in 1917, was charged with helping to establish a Jewish national state in the country.

In September 1922, the League and Great Britain decided that the Jewish national home would not include the areas east of the Jordan River, which constituted three-fourths of the geographic area known as Palestine. This portion of Palestine became the Emirate of Transjordan, a British protectorate.

Under the British Mandate, both the Jewish and Arab communities were given the right to run their own internal affairs, although it was the British who built the foundation of a modern capitalist economy. The Jews continued to develop their internal community, called the YISHUV, and established an elected assembly and national council. The yishuv oversaw the development of the Jewish economy, established a HEBREW-based school network, encouraged cultural activities, and laid the foundation for an independent governmental system. Lacking experience with European styles of government, Palestine's Arab population did not develop these types of governing and organizational bodies.

While the British Mandate allowed the Jewish community to thus sow the seeds for a future state, the British failed to live up to the terms of the League of Nations mandate. Arab political and economic pressure led Great Britain to withdraw its support for an independent Jewish state. Great Britain severely restricted immigration of desperate refugees trying to flee Europe in the 1930s and stopped Jewish land purchases.

On November 29, 1947, the United Nations General Assembly resolved to end the British Mandate over Palestine and to partition the country into two independent states. Great Britain announced it would terminate control on May 15, 1948. Israel published a declaration of independence on May 14, knowing that without British military protection, the Arab nations would immediately declare war against the new Jewish state.

Further reading: Amir Ben-Porat, *Between Class and Nation: The Formation of the Jewish Working Class in the Period before Israel's Statehood* (New York: Greenwood Press, 1986); Judith M. Brown, *The Oxford History of the British Empire: The Twentieth Century* (Oxford: Oxford University Press, 2001); Michael Dumper, *The Politics of Jerusalem since 1967* (New York: Columbia University Press, 1997); Walter Laqueur, *A History of Zionism* (New York: MJF Books, 1996).

Brit Milah

Brit Milah, the "covenant of circumcision," can be traced back to Abraham, the PATRIARCH of the Jewish people. According to Genesis (17:9–14), Abraham circumcised himself and all males in his household as a sign of his COVENANT with God. In this covenant, God promised land and progeny to Abraham in exchange for a vow to be faithful and obedient. Circumcision of males at the age of eight days was to be the sign of God's covenant with Abraham's descendants throughout the generations. Other ancient peoples performed male circumcisions, but generally at puberty.

To this day, Jewish male infants have the foreskin of their penis removed in a ritual ceremony eight days after their birth, bringing them into the covenant of Abraham. While many non-Jews are circumcised in modern America, circumcision in the past often served as a physical sign distinguishing Jewish men from non-Jews. The practice is so ingrained in Jewish tradition that when ANTIOCHUS tried to impose Hellenism on the Jews, his prohibition of circumcision was considered a key step.

Traditionally circumcision (*milah*) is performed by a mohel (from the same Hebrew root as *milah*), someone specially trained in circumcision, often as part of a family tradition. In the presence of extended family and friends, the child's godfather holds him while the mohel circumcises him and he is given his HEBREW name. It is considered a festive occasion and a reception is often held.

Over the centuries, circumcision has in some Diaspora communities been the one practice that designated Jews as Jews; as a result, the misconception has arisen that an uncircumcised male cannot be Jewish. However, circumcision is not sacramental in Judaism; if a male has a Jewish mother, he is Jewish whether he is circumcised or not.

Males who undergo conversion to Judaism are also required to be circumcised. If the man has already been circumcised medically, then a symbolic drop of blood is drawn from the penis. In the 19th century, some leaders of Reform Judaism began to call for the elimination of circumcision, arguing that it was a "barbaric bloody rite." Likened to sacrifice, it was viewed as an element from Judaism's primitive past that was best set aside. This position never took strong hold, however, and to this day circumcision continues to be performed on most Jewish boys.

Further reading: Hayim Halevy Donin, *To Be a Jew: A Guide to Jewish Observance in Contemporary Life* (New York: Basic Books, 1972); Harvey E. Goldberg, *Jewish Passages: Cycles of Jewish Life* (Berkeley: University of California Press, 2003); Ronald H. Isaacs, *Rites of Passage: A Guide to the Jewish Life Cycle* (Hoboken, N.J.: Ktav Publishing, 1992); P. C. Remondino, *History of Circumcision, from the Earliest Times to the Present: Moral and Physical Reasons for Its Performance* (New York: AMS Press, 1974); *Tanakh: The Holy Scriptures* (Philadelphia and Jerusalem: The Jewish Publication Society, 1985), Genesis 17:10–14, 23–27.

Bronfman Foundation

Active in Montreal, home of Canada's largest Jewish community, the Bronfman family is one of the major sources of Jewish philanthropy in the contemporary world. They have been referred to as today's version of the Rothschilds, and they have contributed to causes from medicine to Zionism.

The parents of Samuel Bronfman (1891–1971) immigrated to Canada in the late 19th century, opening a hotel there. Samuel worked for his father in the hotel business, but then became

involved in the mail-order liquor trade. Once he acquired Seagram's, his fortune was secured. He became an active philanthropist, funding universities, hospitals, charities, and museums, and donating his time and talents. He pioneered efforts in Jewish fund-raising and was president of the Canadian Jewish Congress for 23 years, including the World War II years. He was active in the United Jewish Appeal (*see* United Jewish Communities).

Samuel and Saidye Bronfman had four children, Minda, Phyllis, Edgar, and Charles, all of whom are active in the Jewish community. The family and its foundation seek to illustrate the belief that serving the community is instrumental in creating a well-developed society. The Bronfmans contribute to Jewish and non-Jewish social, cultural, and educational causes.

The family's Zionist leanings have led to such projects as Birthright Israel, which provides free trips to Israel for Jewish young adults from around the world, the Bronfman Youth Fellowships in Israel, and the Partnership for Excellence in Jewish Education. Edgar Bronfman served as president of the World Jewish Congress for more than 20 years.

Further reading: Michael R. Marrus, *Samuel Bronfman: The Life and Times of Seagram's Mr. Sam* (Hanover, N.H.: University Press of New England, 1991); Ronald Weir, *The History of the Distillers Company, 1877–1939: Diversification and Growth in Whisky and Chemicals* (Oxford: Oxford University Press, 1995).

Buber, Martin (1878-1965) *scholar and mystic*

Martin Buber was a philosopher and student of Jewish mysticism who became one of the most influential Jewish thinkers of the 20th century.

Martin Buber was born on February 8, 1878, in Vienna, Austria. He received a traditional Jewish education from his grandfather and went on to pursue secular studies in philosophy and art history at the Universities of Vienna and Berlin. He worked as a professor of Judaism and then of the history of religions at the University of Frankfurt in GERMANY, but he resigned in 1933 when HITLER came to power. Before his emigration to ISRAEL in 1938, Buber coauthored a new translation of the Hebrew Bible (*see* TANAKH) and created the Lehrhaus, a Jewish academy, in Frankfurt with his colleague Franz ROSENZWEIG. After moving to Israel, he became a professor of social philosophy at the HEBREW UNIVERSITY in Jerusalem. His participation in developing ZIONISM, his writings on the lives of the masters of HASIDISM, and his existential philosophy combined to make Buber a remarkably popular intellectual figure in his lifetime.

In his twenties Buber joined the Zionist movement, identifying himself as a cultural rather than a political Zionist. Buber maintained that Jewish culture needed to experience a renaissance in the modern world. He identified several areas that the Jewish community needed to explore to improve its self-awareness—art, literature, theater, and education. Only as the Jewish community became aware of its history and culture would it be possible for the Jews to become a secure nation in the world.

Buber encouraged participation in Jewish MYSTICISM, and supported the development of the modern HEBREW language. He also emphasized the need to develop feelings for the land, ERETZ YISRAEL. He envisioned Israel as a land built on the prophetic vision of righteousness and peace, and he was adamant about fairness toward Arabs in the process of developing the State of Israel.

Meanwhile, Buber expressed his literary genius through his retelling of the legends of Hasidic masters, in works such as the *Legend of the Baal-Shem* (*see* BAAL SHEM TOV) and his *Tales of the Hasidim.* Buber's interest in the Hasidic movement and its emphasis on mysticism, joy, and love greatly affected his own philosophy. He believed that Hasidism had succeeded in inserting spirituality into everyday life, rather than separating spirituality and mysticism from the mundane. Hasidism made everyday life sacred, rather than consecrating sacred time and space only outside one's daily tasks. Buber was instrumental in familiarizing modern Jews with the lifestyles, point of view, and stories of the Hasidic masters.

Buber is perhaps most famous for his book *I and Thou,* which he considered the most successful presentation of his philosophy. In it, Buber develops his philosophy of dialogue. In an "I-It" relationship, one party is utilizing the other, whereas in an "I-Thou" relationship each party wholly values the other, opening a space for true dialogue and a true relationship. An I-Thou relationship opens the I up to the wholeness of the other. The ultimate I-Thou relationship, which human relationships can only approximate, is the one between the individual and God. Buber believed that the world of the I-It relationship was a necessary part of life, but he encouraged his readers to strive to achieve relationships that could be described as I-Thou, however elusive they might be.

Buber died on June 13, 1965, at his home in JERUSALEM.

Further reading: Asher D. Biemann, *The Martin Buber Reader: Essential Writings* (New York: Palgrave Macmillan, 2002); Martin Buber, *Hasidism and Modern Man* (New York: Horizon Press, 1958); Martin Buber, *I and Thou* (New York: Scribner, 1970); ———, *Tales of the Hasidim* (New York: Schocken Books, 1991); ———, *The Writings of Martin Buber,* with an introduction by Will Herberg (New York: Meridian Books, 1956); Maurice S. Friedman, *Martin Buber's Life and Work* (Detroit: Wayne State University Press, 1988); Donald J. Moore, *Martin Buber: Prophet of Religious Secularism* (New York: Fordham University Press, 1996); Stephen M. Panko, *Martin Buber* (Peabody, Mass.: Hendrickson Publishers, 1991); Gerda Gilya Schmidt, *Martin Buber's Formative Years: From German Culture to Jewish Renewal* (Tuscaloosa: University of Alabama Press, 1995).

Bund

The General Jewish Worker's Union in Lithuania, POLAND, and RUSSIA, commonly known as the Bund (Yiddish for "union"), was born in the

Lithuanian town of Vilna in 1897 (*see* VILNA GAON). Thirteen Jewish men and women met to consolidate the socialist efforts of Jews across Russia and Poland. Within two years, the group had become the largest worker's socialist party in czarist Russia, drawing thousands of workers and intellectuals to its cause, and contributing greatly to the formation of the Russian Social Democratic Labor Party in 1898.

In a time when nationalism was on the rise and ZIONISM became solidified as a Jewish movement, members of the Bund provided a counterpoint to such trends. The Bund was devoted to YIDDISH culture (and not the Hebrew language), the idea of Jewish autonomy, and secular Jewish nationalism. The Bundists were openly anti-Zionist. Rather than fostering hope for a Jewish homeland elsewhere, they believed it was possible to achieve equal status in eastern Europe based on the egalitarian ideas of socialism. As did all Jews at the time, the Bundists sought relief from antisemitic (*see* ANTISEMITISM) persecution.

The Jewish labor movement received support from three groups of people in 19th-century eastern Europe: the working class, the radical intelligentsia influenced by MARX as well as their own Jewish roots, and the semi-intelligentsia, who had little secular schooling but sought a safe haven for their Jewish communities. In the early years of the 20th century, the Bund had between 25,000 and 35,000 members. On a political level, the Bund sought equal political and civil rights for Jews in eastern Europe. It also organized defense measures to combat the increasing number of POGROMS in eastern Europe in the late 19th and early 20th centuries. The Russian government considered many Bundists enemies of the state, and approximately 4,500 became political prisoners.

The Bund's influence peaked in 1905, and it began to abandon positions that no longer seemed practical. For example, recognizing the increased power of nationalism around the world, the Bund no longer advocated Jewish autonomy within a larger Russian nation, and it recognized that it would be unable to reduce the violence and dan-

ger that Jews faced in eastern Europe. Their socialist dreams of equality were not to become reality. After 1905, the Bund began to focus on a cultural rather than a political agenda, turning its attentions to the development of literature, music, and drama. The political aspirations of the Bund were transferred across the Atlantic Ocean. By 1912 the Bundist philosophy had reached American shores, and the Jewish Socialist Federation of America was formed.

In the 1920s the Bund in eastern Europe was swallowed by the Communist Party, but a small fraction of its supporters in the region left to form the independent Socialist Democratic Party. Jewish activists in both groups were persecuted by the rising Communist government in Russia. Some Polish Bundists did escape to the UNITED STATES as World War II began, and helped organize the International Jewish Labor Bund. However, by then the Bund has lost its relevance, and none of its branches ever progressed beyond immigrant organizations. It would seem that the Zionist platform held a more realistic answer to the Jewish problem in eastern Europe.

Further reading: Abraham Brumberg, "Anniversaries in Conflict: On the Centenary of the Jewish Socialist Labor Bund," *Jewish Social Studies* 5 (1999): 3; Emanuel S. Goldsmith, *Modern Yiddish Culture: The Story of the Yiddish Language Movement* (New York: Fordham University Press, 1997); J. L. H. Keep, *The Rise of Social Democracy in Russia* (Oxford: Clarendon Press, 1963); Henry J. Tobias, *The Jewish Bund in Russia from Its Origins to 1905* (Stanford, Calif.: Stanford University Press, 1972).

burning bush

The burning bush, which served as a vehicle through which God first spoke to MOSES in the book of Exodus, later became a potent symbol of Jewish resilience and survival.

In the second book of the TANAKH, the Hebrew Bible, Moses flees EGYPT and eventually becomes a shepherd to the Midianite priest Yitro. While pasturing his flock, Moses sees an angel of God appear in the guise of a bush that was "burning but not consumed" (Ex 3:2).

Through the symbolism of the miracle, God demonstrates that while the idol worshippers of the time worshipped nature, the "True God" rules over nature. This demonstration ensures that God will be able to command Moses' ultimate obedience. God then commands Moses to return to Egypt along with his older brother AARON, and tell Pharaoh to "Let my people go."

While standing before the burning bush, Moses asks God's name. God at first responds with the name "the God of your fathers," but then utilizes the divine title "I am that I am" (Ex 3:13–14). This name/description of God (see GOD, NAMES OF) became a fundamental Jewish theological understanding. God's essential nature is "oneness," which is the fundamental tenet of Jewish ethical MONOTHEISM.

The image of the burning bush that is not consumed remains a powerful one in the post-HOLOCAUST world. The JEWISH THEOLOGICAL SEMINARY uses the symbol as its logo, along with the words ". . . and the bush was not consumed."

Further reading: Martin Buber, *Moses* (Oxford: East and West Library, 1946); *Tanakh: The Holy Scriptures* (Philadelphia and Jerusalem: The Jewish Publication Society, 1985).

C

calendar

The Jewish year follows a modified lunar calendar with 12 months. The months, whose names come from ancient BABYLONIA, have 29 or 30 days each, totaling 354 days. As the years pass, the Jewish calendar begins to diverge from the solar year (and thus from the modern Gregorian calendar used around the world). In order to keep the spring and fall holidays in their proper seasons as prescribed by the TORAH, the RABBIS added seven "leap years" in every 19-year cycle; in these years an extra month is added.

The Jewish calendar has several different "new years." In the TANAKH, the Hebrew Bible, the "first month" is Nisan in the spring, which commemorates the EXODUS from EGYPT; but a new *calendar* year takes effect on ROSH HASHANAH, the first day of the month of Tishri in the fall. This date commemorates the CREATION of the world and initiates the High Holidays. Thus, the first day of the Jewish year 5765 was Tishri 1, which began on the evening of September 15, 2004.

In the Jewish calendar, days begin at sundown and continue until the following sundown. This is particularly important in observance of SHABBAT, the final day of the week, which begins at sundown on Friday and ends at sundown on Saturday.

Further reading: Nathan Bushwick, *Understanding the Jewish Calendar* (New York: Moznaim Publishing, 1989); Uwe Glessmer, "Calendars in the Qumran Scrolls" in *Dead Sea Scrolls After Fifty Years,* vol. 2 (Leiden, Netherlands: E. J. Brill, 1999); Adin Steinsaltz, *The Essential Talmud* (New York: Basic Books, 1976).

Camp David accords (framework for peace in the Middle East)

Camp David, a well-utilized American presidential retreat in Maryland, was the site of two major peace negotiations between Israel and Arab powers, in 1978 and 2000.

On September 10, 1978, Anwar SADAT, president of EGYPT, and Menachem BEGIN, prime minister of Israel, met with President Jimmy Carter and agreed on a framework for peace in the Middle East, inviting the other Arab nations to adhere to the agreement. The preamble of the Camp David accords declared that after "four wars during thirty years, despite intensive human efforts, the Middle East, which is the cradle of civilization and the birthplace of three great religions, does not yet enjoy the blessings of peace. The people of the Middle East yearn for peace so that the vast human and natural resources of the region can be turned to the pursuits of peace and so that this area can become a model for coexistence and cooperation among nations."

These Camp David accords resulted from the historic visits of President Sadat to JERUSALEM and Prime Minister Begin to Ismailia. Egypt and Israel signed a treaty, still honored today, in which they agreed "not to resort to the threat or use of force or military blockade against each other."

Over the next several decades only Jordan among the Arab nations has followed the example of Egypt. However, in July 2000, President Clinton invited Israeli prime minister Ehud BARAK and Palestinian Authority chairman Yasser Arafat (*see* PALESTINE LIBERATION ORGANIZATION), to return to Camp David and continue negotiations for a comprehensive agreement for peace in the Middle East.

With significant concessions being offered by Israel, there was great optimism for a final resolution, but ultimately this Camp David experience resulted in the Palestinian rejection of an agreement, and a new war has been waged against Israel.

Further reading: *21st Century Complete Guide to the Carter Presidential Archives: President Jimmy Carter, Carter Administration, Iran Hostage Crisis, Camp David Accords between Egypt and Israel, Speeches, Daily Diary, Documents, Presidential Library Material* (CD-ROM) (Washington, D.C.: Progressive Management, 2003); Ziva Flamhaft, *Israel on the Road to Peace: Accepting the Unacceptable* (Boulder, Colo.: Westview Press, 1996); Clyde Prestowitz, *Rogue Nation: American Unilateralism and the Failure of Good Intentions* (New York: Basic Books, 2003); Richard C. Thornton, *The Carter Years: Toward a New Global Order* (New York: Paragon House, 1991); Web site, Israel Ministry of Foreign Affairs, URL: http://www.mfa.gov.il/, accessed June 26, 2004.

Canaan

Canaan is the term applied to the land, flanked by the Mediterranean Sea and the Arabian Desert, occupied by the ISRAELITES after the EXODUS from EGYPT. This land was extremely fertile, and its location in the Fertile Crescent made it an important political and commercial region. When the Israelites began to occupy Canaan, it was populated by several tribal communities. Over several hundred years, the Israelite military leaders and kings established, to varying degrees, political cohesion and a sense of Israelite and then Jewish national identity in the country. At the same time, Canaan's abundant natural resources and strategic political and commercial location continued to make it a prime target for other empires, leading to successive invasions over the centuries.

Further reading: Meir Ben-Dov, *Historical Atlas of Jerusalem* (New York: Continuum, 2002); Suzanne Boorer, "The Earth/Lan ('RS) in the Priestly Manual: The Preservation of the 'Good' Earth and the Promised Land of Canaan Throughout the Generations," in *Australian Biblical Review* 49 (2001): 19–33; Martin Gilbert, *The Atlas of Jewish History* (New York: William Morrow and Company, 1993).

Canada

The story of the Jews in Canada does not drastically differ from that of the Jews in the UNITED STATES, although it has a somewhat different start: SEPHARDIM did not put down lasting roots in the early years in Canada, and a sizable Jewish community of any kind did not emerge until somewhat later than in the neighbor to the south.

Although there is a record of Jews living in Halifax in 1750 under British rule, the first permanent community in Canada did not emerge until 1759. The early Jews lived mostly in Montreal, where the first synagogue was established in 1768. Interestingly, Shearith Israel was a congregation of ASHKENAZIM from ENGLAND, the NETHERLANDS, and GERMANY who adopted the Sephardic liturgy. Montreal Jews built a second synagogue called Sha'ar Hashomayim in 1846. Its members hailed from England, Germany and POLAND.

In 1807 a Jew by the name of Ezekiel Hart was elected to the Legislative Assembly for Lower Canada (now Quebec), but he was unable to take office after he refused to be sworn in as a Christian. Canada granted full civil rights to its Jews in

1832, considerably earlier than many European countries where EMANCIPATION was still in progress. Thus, Jews had full rights to take part in Canada's parliamentary government, including the ability to sit in Parliament and hold public office, by the time the assassination of Czar Alexander II, which provoked POGROMS that sent large numbers of Jewish refugees to Canadian shores. Many synagogues sprung up in the eastern cities of Canada, and Toronto's rich Jewish history commenced. In 1883 the Goel Tzedec Congregation was established in Toronto and Beth Hamidrash Hagadol Chevrah, mostly composed of Russian members, opened its doors in 1887. The majority of 19th-century Jewish synagogues in Canada eventually affiliated with CONSERVATIVE JUDAISM.

The Jewish population at first grew slowly. In 1891 there were only around 6,400 Jews in Canada, but the number swelled to 125,000 between 1900 and 1920. Jewish immigration in the 1930s was severely limited by the government, because of both anti-immigrant and anti-Jewish sentiment. In addition, Canadian policy only encouraged the immigration of farmers. Canadian Jewish communal organizations such as the Jewish Immigrant Aid Society and the Canadian Jewish Congress (CJC) worked to open Canada to war refugees, but with little success. It was not until 1947, after the end of World War II, that immigration laws changed in Canada. Initially, the CJC focused on bringing refugees from European displaced persons camps to Canada. Between 1945 and 1960, 40,000 Jews immigrated to Canada, including groups from HUNGARY, Morocco, North Africa, and the Middle East, further diversifying Canada's Jewish community.

As in ARGENTINA and BRAZIL, Jewish philanthropists helped to settle Jewish immigrants in farming colonies in the western province of Saskatchewan. They thought that the cold winters in Saskatchewan would be not unlike those in RUSSIA, making it a viable location for new Jewish communities. Herman Landau, an English Jew who had made his fortune in the London Stock Exchange, advocated for the idea; his support,

with some modest help from the Jewish Colonization Association, funded by Baron de HIRSCH, resulted in the establishment of a series of Jewish farming communities in the region from 1886 to 1921, when the movement reached its peak of approximately 2,500 Jewish farmers. The experiment did not survive the drought and depression of the 1930s. Most of the Jews who had owned farms moved to urban areas.

Canada has a somewhat unique history of ANTISEMITISM. No organized antisemitism existed until the rise of Nazism in the 1930s, when Adrien Arcand attempted to exploit the xenophobic nature of French Canadians in that direction. In the late 20th century, several men were tried and convicted of teaching or disseminating antisemitic ideas and literature, including HOLOCAUST denial and conspiracy theories. James Keegstra, Ernst Zundel, and Malcolm Ross, in three separate cases, were convicted with the help of Canadian authorities and Jewish communal organizations such as B'NAI B'RITH and the CJC. The effort to expel Nazi war criminals living in Canada has had mixed success; some were extradited while others have been acquitted.

The Canadian Jewish community supports Jewish social service agencies, synagogues, newspapers, and a Jewish education system. Synagogue schools (*see* SUPPLEMENTARY SCHOOL) are popular in Canada, but the JEWISH DAY SCHOOL MOVEMENT has been widespread too, even in the smaller cities of Ottawa, Windsor, Hamilton, Calgary, and Edmonton. The Canadian Jewish Congress, established in 1919, represents the Canadian Jewish community. B'nai B'rith has lodges in Canada, although those in western Canada are affiliated with their closest geographical district in the United States. Many Zionist organizations are active in the country as well, including HADASSAH and the Zionist Organization of Canada (ZOC). Canadian Jewry has consistently held a positive and supportive attitude toward Zionism and the State of ISRAEL.

At present the Canadian Jewish community stands as the sixth-largest DIASPORA community in the world. Almost 30 percent of Canada's 356,000

Jews live in the province of Quebec; Toronto is also a thriving center of Jewish life.

Further reading: Irving M. Abella, *A Coat of Many Colours: Two Centuries of Jewish Life in Canada* (Toronto: Lester & Orpen Dennys, 1990); Michael Greenstein, et al., *Contemporary Jewish Writing in Canada; An Anthology* (Lincoln: University of Nebraska Press, 2004); Gerald J. J. Tulchinsky, *Taking Root: The Origins of the Canadian Jewish Community* (Hanover, N.H.: University Press of New England, 1993).

candles

Candles have played a significant role in Jewish ritual life from earliest times. Lighting candles dates back to the TEMPLE when the priests would light a seven-candle candelabra called the MENORAH every day. It is said that this menorah symbolized the mission of ISRAEL to be a light unto the nations (Is 42:6). In modern times, Jews light candles for a variety of reasons: to celebrate holidays, to mark the difference between holy times and secular times, to remember those who have died, and to preserve the Jewish way of worship.

The ritual lighting of SHABBAT and holiday candles, traditionally the domain of women, is often practiced by men as well today, in a nod to EGALITARIANISM. The Shabbat candles are lit before sunset on Friday to mark the beginning of the Sabbath with all its joys and restrictions. A MIDRASH teaches that when the first human being, Adam, opened his eyes on the eve of Shabbat and found himself in the dark shadows of the GARDEN OF EDEN, he was very afraid. However, he stumbled upon two stones, picked them up and struck them, starting a fire. He felt that the light and the warmth created by the fire was a gift from God, and he then pronounced the very first blessing: "Praised are You, God, Sovereign of the Universe, who creates the light of the fire."

At the conclusion of Shabbat, Jews ritually mark the end of the day by lighting the HAVDALAH candle. *Havdalah* means "separation," and this is the ceremony that marks the line between the Sabbath and the working week. The havdalah candle is specially braided with at least two wicks. The blessing over the candle is to remind oneself of God's first creation of light.

Lighting CHANUKAH candles is a well-known Jewish ritual practice. The TALMUD teaches that to commemorate Chanukah, a candle should be lit for each day observed. There was a debate as to procedure. The school of SHAMMAI taught: "On the first day eight lights are lit and thereafter they are gradually reduced"; but the school of HILLEL says: "On the first day one is lit and thereafter they are progressively increased." The views of the school of Hillel were accepted as common practice because one should desire increase in matters of sanctity and not decrease. The Chanukah lights are intended to be a reminder of the miracle of oil. When the MACCABEES rededicated the TEMPLE they found only enough sanctified oil for one day, but miraculously the oil lasted eight days. Light from the Chanukah candles is a metaphor for God's divine light in the world.

Candles in the Jewish tradition are not reserved only for times of celebration; they are also used to commemorate the life of one who has passed away. Each year on the date that a person died, his or her immediate family members light a YAHRZEIT (anniversary) candle, which is specially designed in a glass to burn safely for 24 hours. Often *yahrzeit* candles are also used in remembrance ceremonies for the 6 million Jews who died in the HOLOCAUST.

Further reading: Isadore Epstein, ed., *Soncino Hebrew/English Babylonian Talmud* (Brooklyn, N.Y.: Soncino Press, 1990); Irving Greenberg, *The Jewish Way: Living the Holidays* (New York: Simon & Schuster, 1988); Ronald H. Isaacs and Kerry M. Olitzky, *A Jewish Holiday Handbook* (Hoboken, N.J.: Ktav Publishing House, 1994).

cantillation *See* TROPE.

cantor

A cantor (*hazzan* in HEBREW) is a Jewish clergy person specifically trained as a vocalist. The primary responsibility of the cantor is to lead the congregation in singing the prayers.

The Babylonian TALMUD seems to use the term *hazzan* differently; there the *hazzan's* duties in the SYNAGOGUE included bringing out the scrolls of the TORAH, opening them to the appointed readings for the week, and putting them away. The Jerusalem Talmud, however, records that the *hazzan* led the prayers in the synagogue.

During the early medieval era, reading from the Torah, reciting (not necessarily singing) the prayers, and blowing the SHOFAR became the primary functions of the cantor. Soloists or choirs would sometimes accompany the cantor as he led the prayers.

Over the centuries the role of the cantor increased in importance. Public worship began to develop extensively during the era of the GEONIM, and as Jews' knowledge of HEBREW declined, the cantor had to carry more of the burden for the congregation. By this time a cantor had to be knowledgeable in biblical and liturgical literature, have a pleasant voice, and be a righteous individual.

To a degree, the profession of cantor is a modern creation. Traditionally only a man was a cantor, but REFORM and CONSERVATIVE JUDAISM train both men and women for the role. When a lay person leads public prayer, which is permissible in all streams of Judaism, he or she is called the *shaliach tzibbur,* or emissary (to God) of the congregation. Cantors have their own organizations through which they protect their interests, learn from one another, and continue their education.

Further reading: Reuven Hammer, *Entering Jewish Prayer: A Guide to Personal Devotion and the Worship Service* (New York: Schocken Books, 1995); Stefan C. Reif, *Judaism and Hebrew Prayer: New Perspectives on Jewish Liturgical History* (Cambridge: Cambridge University Press, 1995).

Cardozo, Benjamin (1870–1938)
U.S. Supreme Court justice
Benjamin Cardozo, the second Jewish U.S. Supreme Court Justice, was known as an active member of the Jewish community and acclaimed for his emphasis on the influence of law to support social change.

Cardozo was born in 1870, the son of Judge Albert Cardozo and Rebecca Nathan. A member of a distinguished Sephardic Jewish family in New York, Cardozo's father resigned in disgrace from his judgeship because of an impending impeachment against him due to acts of nepotism. In the wake of his father's professional disgrace, Benjamin studied law, and excelled both in his studies and later as a litigator. Cardozo was known for superlative speaking skills and impeccable integrity. In 1932, President Herbert Hoover appointed him to the Supreme Court of the UNITED STATES. He thus became the second Jew, after Louis D. BRANDEIS, to serve on the nation's highest court.

In his personal life, Cardozo maintained many Jewish traditions, including, to a degree, KASHRUT. Cardozo was also active as a trustee of Columbia University and with various organizations in the Jewish community. He served on the board of the AMERICAN JEWISH COMMITTEE and embraced the Zionist Organization of America (*see* WORLD ZIONIST CONGRESS). Considered to have been one of the great legal minds in American history, Cardozo was honored by YESHIVA UNIVERSITY in 1976 when it established the Benjamin N. Cardozo School of Law.

Further reading: Benjamin N. Cardozo, *The Nature of the Judicial Process* (New Haven, Conn.: Yale University Press, 1946); Andrew L. Kaufman, *Cardozo* (Cambridge, Mass., and London: Harvard University Press, 1997); Richard Polenberg, *The World of Benjamin Cardozo: Personal Values and the Judicial Process* (Cambridge, Mass.: Harvard University Press, 1997).

Caro, Joseph ben-Ephraim (Joseph ben-Ephraim Karo) (1488–1575) *medieval mystic and legal scholar*
Joseph Caro is best known as the author of the SHULCHAN ARUKH, the "Prepared Table," the 16th work still regarded as the standard legal code of Judaism.

Born into a rabbinical family, Caro began life in Toledo, SPAIN. He left as a child when Jews were expelled from the country in 1492, and his family moved to PORTUGAL. Eventually he settled in SAFED, PALESTINE.

Caro was part of a group of Jewish scholars in Safed who claimed to have experienced mystical events frequently, often in dreams. These men reinstituted the practice of SEMIKHA, or ordination of RABBIS. They hoped that this step would attract many scholarly Jews to return to ERETZ YISRAEL, making the land once more an intellectual center for Jews. Caro himself was ordained by Rabbi Jacob Berab in 1538. Their hopes for a new intellectual center were not fulfilled, but Caro saw his own ordination as a genuine source of personal authority.

Caro came to believe that a *maggid,* or spiritual guide, was giving him instructions on HALAKHAH in his dreams, which he then compiled into an extensive legal compendium called *Bet Joseph* (House of Joseph). However, this work, not unlike MAIMONIDES' legal tome, MISHNEH TORAH, was too long for everyday use. Caro himself published an abbreviated version called the *Shulchan Arukh,* which quickly became popular. Since the work is largely based upon the customs of SEPHARDIM, Rabbi Moses Isserles, an Ashkenazi Jew (*see* ASHKENAZIM), wrote a supplement called the *MAPAH,* or tablecloth, which included the customs of his own community. The two works often appear together in the same volume.

Like many of his contemporaries, Caro believed that there was no conflict between close legal study and mystical experience. He recorded a number of his mystical experiences in a diary, which was eventually edited and published in 1646 under the title *Maggid Mesharim.*

Caro was the leading scholar and mystical figure in Safed until eclipsed by Isaac LURIA, but the *Shulchan Arukh* firmly established his reputation as a legal authority. The work, in various editions, remains the most important one-volume legal reference work in ORTHODOX JUDAISM.

Further reading: Joseph Dan, *Intellectual History in the Middle Ages* (New York: Praeger, 1994); Yehiel Michel Ha-Levi Epstein, *Arukh Ha-Shulhan* (New York: Ktav Publishing House, 1992); Abraham A. Glicksberg, *Educational Values in the Shulchan Aruch* (New York: Shengold Publishing, 1984); Joseph Karo, *The Traditional Law of Sale: Shulhan Arukh, Hosehn Mishpat, chapters 189–240,* trans. Stephen M. Passamaneck (Cincinnati, Ohio: Hebrew Union College Press, 1983).

cave of Machpelah

The cave of Machpelah, located in Hebron, is the burial site for the PATRIARCHS and MATRIARCHS of the Jewish people. It is thus the second holiest site for Jews, after the KOTEL.

According to Genesis, Abraham bought the cave as a burial site for Sarah and insisted on paying for it. Jewish tradition holds that he refused to accept the property as a gift or take it in conquest so that its ownership would never come into question. Three pairs of foremothers and forefathers are believed to be buried in the cave: Abraham and Sarah, Isaac and Rebecca, and Jacob and Leah. Rachel is buried separately. Some legends claim that Adam and Eve are buried there as well.

The site is holy to Judaism, CHRISTIANITY and ISLAM, all of which revere Abraham as their progenitor. Over the centuries, the site has changed hands, alternately serving as a church or a mosque. At times access to the site has been limited, while at other times it has been open to all pilgrims.

Currently the site is a mosque, known as the mosque of Abraham, though Jews also have access to pray at the cave. Because of its holy status for both Jews and Muslims, as well as its location in Hebron in the West Bank (*see* JUDEA AND SAMARIA; SIX-DAY WAR), the site has been a hotbed of religious violence between Palestinians and Israelis in recent years.

Further reading: Louis Ginzberg, *Legends of the Bible* (New York: Jewish Publication Society of America, 1956); *Let's Go. Israel and the Palestinian Territories 2002* (New York: St. Martin's Press, 2002); Joan E. Taylor, *Christians and the Holy Places: The Myth of Jewish-Christian Origins* (London: Clarendon Press, 1993).

Central Conference of American Rabbis

See UNION FOR REFORM JUDAISM.

Chabad

Chabad, or Chabad Lubavitch, is a movement within ORTHODOX JUDAISM that adheres to the practices of HASIDISM but emphasizes outreach to the non-Hasidic Jewish world.

Until the death of the last rebbe (spiritual leader), Rabbi Menachem SCHNEERSON (1902–94), the group was led by a succession of leaders descended from its founder, Rebbe Shneur Zalman of Liadi (1745–1812). Since the last rebbe's death Chabad has been led by the spirit of previous teachings; individual rabbis provide leadership within the internal organizational structure.

The name Chabad, a HEBREW acronym for *chochma* (wisdom), *bina* (understanding), and *da'at* (knowledge), was chosen by Shneur Zalman to reflect the group's emphasis on studying KABBALAH or mystical teachings (the words represent aspects of the divine in Kabbalistic teaching). Lubavitch is a small town in RUSSIA where the movement first took root—Hasidic dynasties of rebbes are typically named after the town the founders lived in. The followers of Lubavitch ("town of love" in Russian) believe their name accurately represents their inclusive attitude toward all Jews.

It was Schneerson who initiated the movement's proactive missionary work within world Jewry. Today Chabad sends rabbinic leaders throughout the world to assist Jews in need and to teach them to embrace their heritage through traditional Judaism. Chabad helped to create the BAAL TESHUVAH movement, the goal of which is to bring non-Orthodox Jews into the spiritual, ideological, and theological camp of Orthodoxy. Some followers of Lubavitch believe that the last rebbe was the Messiah, a position that has been sharply criticized by others both within and outside the movement.

Chabad houses can be found on many college campuses and in many cities throughout the United States. Chabad Lubavitch runs 3,300 institutions around the world, employing tens of thousands of people in their cause to bring secular Jews back to Judaism. The worldwide headquarters of the Chabad movement is 770 Eastern Parkway in Brooklyn.

Further reading: Sue Fishkoff, *The Rebbe's Army: Inside the World of Chabad-Lubavitch* (New York: Schocken Books, 2003); Zalman I. Posner, *Think Jewish: A Contemporary View of Judaism, A Jewish View of Today's World* (Brooklyn, N.Y.: Merkos L'Inyonei Chinuch, 2002); Menachem M. Schneerson, *The Unbreakable Soul: A Discourse by Rabbi Menachem M. Schneerson of Chabad-Lubavitch* (Brooklyn, N.Y.: Kehot Publication Society, 2003); Web site URL: http://www.chabad.org, accessed on June 27, 2004.

Chafetz Chaim (Rabbi Yisroel Meir HaKohen or Kagan) (1838–1933) *revered 19th-century rabbi and leader*

Rabbi Yisroel Meir HaKohen is considered one of the great rabbis of modern times. He was known for his brilliant scholarship, but more important, he is revered as an extraordinarily righteous individual. He is called the Chafetz Chaim after the title of his most popular book about the importance of avoiding gossip. The phrase *Chafetz Chaim* literally translates as "he who wants to live."

The Chafetz Chaim was born in Zhetl, POLAND, on February 6, 1838. Even after he was recognized as a leading rabbinic figure, he refused to accept a salaried rabbinic position. Instead, he chose to support himself through a small grocery run by his wife in the town of Radin, Poland. This business allowed him the time to pursue his study and teaching of TORAH. In fact, his home soon became a popular place to study Torah, eventually becoming known as the Radin YESHIVA. In addition to teaching those who appeared on his doorstep, the Chafetz Chaim traveled extensively, spreading his love of Torah and his desire to increase the observance of mitzvot (*see* MITZVAH) among the Jews of Europe. He traveled even into his 90s, and died at the age of 95.

The Chafetz Chaim's most notable teaching was how to avoid the sin of LASHON HARA, or evil language. It was the subject of his first book in 1873; the title *Chafetz Chaim* was derived from the 34th Psalm: "Who is the man who desires life (chafetz chaim)? . . . keep your tongue from evil." He later published two more books on the subject and, as was the custom with many great rabbis, he became known by the name of his most famous book.

The Chafetz Chaim eventually wrote on many other subjects in more than 20 books. His most important scholarly work is considered to be the *Mishneh Berurah,* a six-volume commentary dealing with the laws of daily life and holidays.

Further reading: Hayim Halevy Donin, *To Be a Jew: A Guide to Jewish Observance in Contemporary Life* (New York: Basic Books, 1972); Israel Meir, Chafetz Chaim, and Charles Wengrov, *Concise Book of Mitzvoth: The Commandments Which Can Be Observed Today* (Nanuet, N.Y.: Feldheim Publications, 1990); Moses M. Yoshor, *Chafetz Chaim, The Life Works of Rabbi Yisrael Meir Kagan of Radin* (Brooklyn, N.Y.: Mesorah Publications, 1986).

Chagall, Marc (1887–1985) *Russian-French modern artist*

Born with the family name Segal in Vitebsk, Byelorussia, in 1887, Marc Chagall was the eldest of nine children. Chagall's family was Hasidic (*see* HASIDISM), and so he spent his childhood in a heder (children's religious school). When he began attending a secular Russian school, he discovered his artistic talent. While Chagall's father

Marc Chagall is one of the most renowned Jewish artists of the modern era. He is pictured here accepting an honorary doctorate at a ceremony held at the Weizmann Institute in Rehovot, Israel. *(Moshe Milner, Government Press Office, The State of Israel)*

was disappointed, his mother supported his efforts in the field of art. Yet the religious nature of Chagall's family would come through in Chagall's art; his familiarity with Jewish customs, stories, and way of life appear often in his work.

Chagall moved to St. Petersburg in 1907 to study art with Leon Bakst. He developed a distinctive childlike style that reflected his exposure to contemporary Russian painting, and his art often centered on images of his childhood, using the Jewish quarter of Vitebsk, the city of his birth, as a common theme. From 1910 to 1914, Chagall received an allowance from a lawyer who admired his talent, and he was able to live in Paris to continue developing his artistic style. During these years, Chagall produced some of his most famous paintings of the Jewish SHTETL, having studied cubism and realism, and adopting a semi-cubist quality in his work.

During World War I Chagall remained in RUSSIA, where in 1917 he endorsed the BOLSHEVIK REVOLUTION. He was appointed commissar for fine arts in Vitebsk, and then director of the Free Academy of Art. However, the Bolshevik authorities soon came to disapprove of Chagall's artistic style as too modern, and in 1922 Chagall left Russia for FRANCE. He stayed in France permanently, leaving only during World War II, when he was given safe harbor in the UNITED STATES. Chagall was horrified by the Nazi's rise to power and their evil acts. His works during this time period expressed the plight of the Jewish martyrs.

Chagall's work blends fantasy and religion, using strong, bright colors and a dreamlike representation of the world; his works were replete with animals, workmen, lovers, and musicians. He actually created nostalgia; SHOLOM ALEICHEM's "Fiddler on the Roof" as a recurring motif recalled Jewish life in eastern Europe. Chagall worked in multiple mediums, using oils, watercolors, ceramics, mosaics, and stained glass. Chagall was often inspired by themes from the Bible (*see* TORAH). He created more than 100 works illustrating Bible stories, many of which incorporated elements from Jewish folklore and his own religious childhood. Some of Chagall's most famous works can be found on the ceiling of the Paris Opera House, the murals at the New York Metropolitan Opera, a glass window at the UNITED NATIONS, and decorations at the Vatican. Chagall also endowed ISRAEL with many of his works; the most famous on display are the 12 stained glass windows at HADASSAH Hospital and his wall decorations at the KNESSET.

Further reading: Marc Chagall, *My Life* (Cambridge, Mass.: Da Capo Press, 1994); Jean-Michel Foray and Jakov Bruk, *Marc Chagall* (New York: Harry N. Abrams, 2003); Guggenheim Museum Web site URL: http://www.guggenheimcollection.org, accessed June 30, 2004.

chai

The Hebrew word *chai* means "life." Since each Hebrew letter has a numerical value, and the letters of *chai* total 18 (8 for *chet,* the first letter in the word, and 10 for *yud,* the second and last), the number 18 has acquired symbolic meaning in Judaism.

The system of assigning numerical values to letters led to the creation of an entire discipline of Jewish mysticism known as GEMATRIA, devoted to finding hidden meanings in the numerical values of words. The number 18 has consequently become very popular among Jews. In modern times, it has become a common tradition to make monetary donations to charity in multiples of 18 to invoke *chai* and its meaning, life. The commonly used phrase *"L'chaim"* also shares its root with the Hebrew word *chai.*

Further reading: Harold S. Kushner, *To Life: A Celebration of Jewish Being and Thinking* (New York: Warner Books, 1994).

chametz

The TORAH prohibits Jews from eating or possessing *chametz* (leaven or leavened food products including derivatives of wheat, barley, rye, oats, or spelt) on PASSOVER (Ex 12:39). Jews are obligated to eat MATZAH, unleavened bread, at their Passover SEDERS as a reminder of the Jews' quick flight from PHARAOH'S EGYPT. The ISRAELITES fled so quickly they did not even have time for the bread to rise. In memory of this, Jews do not eat leavened bread during the holiday of Passover.

The prohibition of *chametz* serves two purposes: first, it highlights the importance of matzah; in addition, tradition teaches that *chametz* is a metaphor for the human being's evil inclination, which can easily rise like leaven. One must be careful to resist this inclination and instead emphasize the inclination to do good.

Prior to Passover, homes are meticulously cleaned, and all *chametz* is removed or destroyed. Many Jewish communities use this as an opportunity to engage in "spring cleaning." One makes a ritual announcement after the final search, the night before Passover: "All *chametz,* leaven and leavened bread, that is in my possession which I have not seen, removed or is unknown to me, should be annulled and considered ownerless like the dust of the earth."

The final search, as in ancient times, is conducted by the light of a candle. There is a custom to place 10 pieces of *chametz* in the room so that they can be found as a reminder of the TEN PLAGUES.

Further reading: Irving Greenberg, *The Jewish Way: Living the Holidays* (New York and London: Simon and Schuster, 1988); *Passover Haggadah,* Deluxe Edition (Northfield, Ill.: Kraft General Foods, 1994); *Tanakh: The Holy Scriptures* (Philadelphia and Jerusalem: The Jewish Publication Society, 1985).

Chanukah

Chanukah is the Jewish holiday that celebrates the victory of the MACCABEES early in the second century B.C.E. The word *Chanukah* means "dedication"; it refers to the rededication of the TEMPLE in JERUSALEM after it was recaptured from the Seleucid Greeks, who allegedly profaned it through idolatry.

The holiday lasts for eight days, beginning on the 25th day of the month of Kislev, which usually

This kindergartener is lighting a *hanukkiyah,* the special eight-branched candelabra used to commemorate the holiday of Chanukah. The hanukkiyah is often called a menorah, but a menorah has only seven branches and is not connected to a Jewish holiday. *(Ya'acov Sa'ar, Government Press Office, The State of Israel)*

falls in December. Jews celebrate by lighting an eight-candle Chanukah lamp or MENORAH, called a *HANUKKIYAH,* adding one candle each successive night. It is also customary to give money (gelt) or gifts, to eat oily foods, especially potato pancakes and doughnuts, and to play the game of DREIDEL.

According to the book of Maccabees in the APOCRYPHA, the era was filled with political turmoil in Judea. When ANTIOCHUS IV first ascended to the throne of the Seleucid monarchy (one of the successor states to the empire of Alexander the Great), a conflict arose over whom he should appoint as HIGH PRIEST of ISRAEL, one of his territories. Civil war erupted between the pietists, who supported the rightful hereditary high priest, and the Jewish leaders who had assimilated into Hellenistic culture (*see* HELLENISM). Antiochus IV backed the Hellenized Jews and issued edicts prohibiting Jewish practices and mandating sacrifices to Zeus in the Temple.

Many pietists died as martyrs under Seleucid persecution, but others, led by the Maccabees, revolted and won independence. At the end of the revolt, which lasted from 167–164 B.C.E., the Jews purified and rededicated the Temple on the 25th of Kislev, inaugurating the first festival of Chanukah.

Chanukah is marked by prayers that thank God for miracles, but the exact miracle being celebrated is unclear. Some maintain that the miracle was that the small Maccabean army defeated the larger Seleucid army, but the TALMUD recounts another miracle. When the Temple was rededicated, the priests could find only one small cruse of sanctified oil, with enough oil to keep the ETERNAL LIGHT lit for one night. Miraculously, the oil lasted eight nights, just enough time to obtain more oil. Eating fried food commemorates this miracle of the oil.

The rabbis gave an additional explanation for the eight-day duration of Chanukah. The Jews had been unable to celebrate their harvest festival SUKKOT (which lasts for eight days) in the defiled Temple. Once the Temple was rededicated, they decided to hold a late Sukkot on the eight days beginning on 25 Kislev, and they continued the tradition of an eight-day midwinter holiday ever since.

Although it is a post-biblical holiday, Chanukah has gained in importance both inside and outside the land of Israel. In Israel, the struggle of the Maccabees is honored as a model for the country's own battle for independence in 1948. In the UNITED STATES, Chanukah has gained prominence because it falls during the Christmas season, and Jewish communities have taken the opportunity to teach and gather together. In this way emphasis on a previously minor holiday has enhanced the Jewish lives of many American Jews. Some criticize that the holiday has become commercialized as gift giving has become central to Chanukah, as it is to Christmas.

Further reading: Shaye J. D. Cohen, *From the Maccabees to the Mishnah* (Philadelphia: Westminster Press, 1987); Irving Greenberg, *The Jewish Way: Living the Holidays* (New York: Touchstone, 1988); Moses Hadas, ed. and trans., *The Third and Fourth Books of Maccabees* (New York: Ktav Publishing House, [1976] c1953); Martin Schoenberg, *The First and Second Books of Maccabees* (Collegeville, Minn.: The Liturgical Press, 1966).

chavurah

A *chavurah* is a small group that meets for prayers and religious activities. It is less organized than a SYNAGOGUE in that prayers are usually run by the members of the *chavurah* rather than by a RABBI or CANTOR. Also, the services generally take place in a home instead of an official synagogue, and so there is usually no official membership or dues structure. Originating in the 1960s, in an era of antiestablishment sentiments, *chavurah*s sought to provide a larger role to the participant in seeking spirituality by emphasizing the participation of its members in the absence of clergy.

The word *chavurah* derives from the HEBREW word for "friend," and the groups tend to have an informal character, while the services tend to be more spiritual or emotional than in more routine synagogues. In 1970, Rabbi Harold SCHULWEIS brought the idea of the *chavurah* into the synagogue. In this way, smaller groups formed within a larger institution based on commonalities among members. The goal is to create bonds and meaning in Jewish life.

Further reading: Riv-Ellen Prell, *Prayer and Community: The Havurah in American Judaism* (Detroit: Wayne State University Press, 1989); Bernard Reisman, *The Chavurah: Contemporary Jewish Experience* (New York: Union of American Hebrew Congregations, c1977); Chava Weissler, *Making Judaism Meaningful:*

Ambivalence and Tradition in a Havurah Community (New York: AMS Press, 1989).

cherubim

The term *cherubim* (*chruvim* in Hebrew), refers to various spirits or beings mentioned in the TANAKH, the Hebrew Bible that live in God's presence or perform divine tasks.

The word itself may come from the ASSYRIAN term *kirubu*, meaning "to be near," a reference to those who are near to God in the heavenly court, busy praising and worshipping God's holiness.

References to cherubim occur throughout sacred literature. They are first mentioned in Genesis (3:24). Later, in accordance with God's instructions, images of cherubim were placed on the cover of the ARK of the Covenant in the HOLY OF HOLIES, representing nearness to God's presence. In the TALMUD, cherubim are associated with the "order of wheels" (*ophanim*). In the Middle Ages, they were thought to be the guardians of the heavens.

Further reading: Robert Critney, and Robert Critney, Jr. *The Cherubim of the Ark* (New York: Morris Publishing, 2002); *Tanakh: The Holy Scriptures* (Philadelphia and Jerusalem: Jewish Publication Society, 1985).

China

Since the ninth century there have been Jews living in China. Historians believe that the early Chinese Jews arrived in caravans from PERSIA, searching for a new place to settle. The best-known Chinese Jewish community started in the 10th century in Kaifeng and participated in the silk trade. This community, however, assimilated into mainstream Chinese culture and completely disappeared by the 19th century.

In the late 19th century a new Jewish community appeared in China, SEPHARDIM from Baghdad, Bombay, and Hong Kong who settled in Shanghai, Harbin, and Tianjin. Notable Jewish families such as the Sassoons, the Hardoons, and the Kadoories

had significant success in import and export trade, assisted by their close connections in British-occupied territories throughout the world. The Sassoons and the Kadoories settled in Hong Kong in the mid-1800s. The Shanghai community built a synagogue, a school, and a hospital, but they were Westernized people and did not become integrated into Chinese culture.

The 1917 BOLSHEVIK REVOLUTION pushed another group of Jews to seek haven in China. This group of Russian Jews did not have the same international business connections as the Sephardic community. They came with little money, opened small businesses, and eventually entered the mid-

Note the Asian influence in the architecture of this synagogue in Hong Kong. Today almost all Jews who live in China reside in Hong Kong. *(Courtesy J. Gordon Melton)*

dle class. Unlike the Sephardic Jews, this group became more involved in the social life of Harbin, the city they had adopted.

World War II brought a great number of Jewish refugees to Shanghai and China. The wealthy Sephardic community provided financial support, as did American Jewish organizations such as the AMERICAN JEWISH JOINT DISTRIBUTION COMMITTEE. During the war the Jewish population swelled to between 25,000 and 35,000. Thousands arrived in Shanghai through the aid of Dr. Feng Shan Ho, the Chinese consul general to Austria from 1937–41. Ho authorized visas to all who applied, even reopening the consulate with his own funds after a reprimand from the Chinese authorities. He issued more than 12,000 visas; but most of the Jews he helped used Shanghai as a means of escape from AUSTRIA rather than as a final destination. Ho is listed as one of the "Righteous among the Nations," a non-Jew who altruistically saved Jewish lives during the HOLOCAUST (*see* YAD VASHEM).

The Chinese Jewish community at the end of the 1930s, the largest in the Far East, set up all the basic Jewish communal structures. These included service agencies, schools, cemeteries, synagogues, hospitals, newspapers, and Zionist organizations. A few Jews participated in the Chinese fight against the Japanese, such as Hans Shippe, a writer and reporter from GERMANY who died fighting the Japanese, and Dr. Jacob Rosenfeld, who served in the Communist-led army for 10 years, achieving the rank of commander of the Medical Corps. In 1939 Japan occupied Shanghai, putting the Jewish community behind ghetto walls in unsanitary conditions. Immigration ended completely in 1941. The Jewish community of Shanghai lost its economic and property base during this time, and most of its members left for such countries as the UNITED STATES, ENGLAND, ISRAEL, and Australia after the war ended.

Even though Israel was one of the first non-Communist countries to recognize the People's Republic of China in 1949, thereby damaging its relationship to Taiwan, China eventually established ties with the Arab world and became hostile toward the Jewish state, condemning its Westernizing influences. Relations improved in the last decade of the 20th century, and formal ties were established in 1992.

Hong Kong, now officially part of the Chinese nation, is home to approximately 3,000 Jews. The community is known as one of the world's wealthiest Jewish communities, a mark of success for a community that expanded on the efforts of refugees from Hitler's Holocaust. The Jewish community in Hong Kong grew in the 1960s, 1970s, and 1980s to include bankers, lawyers, computer experts, and Israeli academics and scientists. The community has built synagogues, a Jewish Community Center, kosher restaurants, and a Jewish school. Even though the community seems rooted in Hong Kong, all of its Jewish residents hold passports from another nation, such as the United States, Britain, or Israel.

It is possible to learn about Jewish culture in China firsthand. In Kaifeng there is a small Jewish museum, and in Shanghai one can visit the Jewish Refugee Hall of Shanghai, located in the Ohel Moishe Synagogue. While there are several thousand Jews living in Hong Kong, only 200 Jews live permanently in the rest of China today, mostly in Shanghai.

Further reading: Avi Beker, ed., *Jewish Communities of the World.* 1998–1999 Edition (Jerusalem: Institute of the World Jewish Congress, 1998); Benjamin I. Schwartz, *The Jews of China* (Armonk, N.Y.: M. E. Sharpe, 1999).

Chmielnicki Massacres

Many Jews in 17th-century Ukraine occupied an unusual social niche, serving as tax collectors for the Polish Catholic landowners, creating a belief among the Ukrainian Orthodox peasants that the Jews were responsible for their poverty and for religious oppression. The landowners, recognizing their need for the Jews, protected the Jewish communities from the resulting animosity among Cossacks, soldiers, and peasants. In 1648, the Thirty Years' War ended, leaving the Cossacks with a new enemy, the Polish nobles. When Bogdan Chmielnicki led the Cossacks in their quest for an autonomous Ukraine, Polish Jewish communities were caught in the middle of the violence, without the resources to flee or defend themselves. The Chmielnicki Massacres were the result.

Between 40,000 and 100,000 Jews were massacred in the years 1648 and 1649, more than a quarter of all the Jews living in Poland. A few were converted to CHRISTIANITY and some were sold into slavery to the Tatars. Most of the killing was carried out between May and November of 1648. Jewish communal institutions were incapable of dealing with the massive destruction and social dislocation. Some scholars believe that the subsequent rise of the false messiah, SHABBATAI ZVI, was a direct result of the psychological depression that pervaded the survivors of the Chmielnicki Massacres.

Elie Wiesel's novel *The Trial of God* is set in a Ukrainian town after all but two of the Jewish inhabitants have been butchered. While Wiesel's book is set in the 17th century, he based it on a scene he witnessed while in AUSCHWITZ. The death and destruction experienced by the Jews of Poland at the hands of the Cossacks was the worst example of violence against Jews until the rise of the Nazis.

Further reading: Nathan Hanover and Abraham J. Mesch, *Abyss of Despair/Yeven Metzulah: The Famous 17th Century Chronicle Depicting Jewish Life in Russia and Poland During the Chmielnicki Massacres* (Brunswick, N.J.: Transaction Publishers, 1983); Bernard D. Weinryb, *The Jews of Poland: A Social and Economic History of the Jewish Community in Poland from 1100 to 1800* (Philadelphia: Jewish Publication Society of America, 1973); Elie Wiesel, *The Trial of God* (New York: Schocken Books, 1995).

Chosen People

Judaism teaches the historically important notion that the Jews are God's "Chosen People." Many see this concept as illustrating a privileged relationship with God. However, tradition posits that God "chose the Jews" as a means to become known to the world. Historically, this can be seen as a reflection of the actual path along which MONOTHEISM spread.

The ISRAELITES introduced Western civilization to the idea of ethical monotheism. CHRISTIANITY and ISLAM first arose under the direct influence of Judaism, and through them the Israelite notion of God became pervasive.

Judaism does not teach that being chosen bestows any special status beyond the obligation to serve the historical mission of God. Nor does it bestow any special rights or power over other human beings. Furthermore, Judaism teaches that non-Jews can find their own unique pathway to God. Being chosen does mean that God holds Jews to the highest standard. In the Book of Amos (3:2) God tells the people of Israel: "You alone have I singled out of all the families of the earth. That is why I call you to account for all your iniquities."

The status of being chosen can be voluntarily adopted by any individual of any group, simply by embracing Jewish beliefs and undergoing conversion. Such an act mirrors the decisions of biblical Jewish figures to accept God's yoke, which is why some Jews refer to themselves as the "Choosing People."

The first one to choose God was Abraham (*see* PATRIARCHS), whom God in turn chose to engage in a special COVENANT (Hebrew *brit*) (*see* BRIT MILAH). Abraham had a specific role to play in bringing God into the world, which was passed along to Isaac, Jacob, and Jacob's sons, who became the fathers of the 12 tribes of Israel, and thus ultimately of the Jewish people.

The 12 tribes were enslaved in EGYPT, but upon gaining their freedom, they made their way to MOUNT SINAI where they collectively experienced God's REVELATION. MIDRASH teaches that God asked the Israelites if they wished to be God's People, and they collectively responded: "We will do, and we will hear." Deuteronomy (7:7) specifically acknowledges that God chose the Israelites not because they were numerous, but because they were "the smallest of people." There are other stories in the midrash that describe the Israelites as reluctant recipients of the covenant, but at the end of each story, the people accept God's sovereignty and the idea that they were chosen to participate in the covenant.

Because Jews have never been more than a tiny proportion of the world's population, Judaism teaches that their success in spreading the knowledge of God is a sign of the truth and power of the monotheistic idea of a caring God. If the Jews had been numerous, then the spread of the knowledge of God could have been attributed to might alone.

The Chosen People idea is powerful. Christianity has adopted the language to describe its own relationship to God. Nearly all Christians always agreed that God initially chose the Jewish people, but they have argued that 2,000 years ago a new covenant was made with those who accepted Christ. During most of Christian history, Christian chosenness meant that Christians alone would be saved and go to heaven. Islam also embraced the notion of chosenness, but declared that the covenant was passed not through Isaac, but rather through Ishmael, Isaac's half brother. Jews believe chosenness is about living according to God's will and setting an example for others to follow, and is not a testament to special status or privilege.

As Judaism has become more diverse in the modern world, some reformers have had difficulty explaining the Jewish concept of chosenness, and some theologians and philosophers, such as Mordecai KAPLAN, rejected the idea completely.

Further reading: Daniel H. Frank, *A People Apart: Chosenness and Ritual in Jewish Philosophical Thought* (Albany: State University of New York Press, 1993); Irving Greenberg, "Covenantal Pluralism," *Journal of Ecumenical Studies* 34, 3 (Summer 1997): 425–436; Jeffrey S. Gurock and Jacob J. Schacter, *A Modern Heretic and a Traditional Community: Mordecai M. Kaplan, Orthodoxy, and American Judaism* (New York: Columbia University Press, 1997); Ruth Langer, "Jewish Understandings of

the Religious Other," *Theological Studies* 64, 2 (2003); *Tanakh: The Holy Scriptures* (Philadelphia and Jerusalem: The Jewish Publication Society, 1985).

Christianity

Christianity traces its roots to JESUS OF NAZARETH, an itinerant healer and teacher in the early first century C.E. According to the Gospels Jesus was crucified by the Romans around 30 C.E., and a small sect of his followers, mostly Jews, began to teach that he had been resurrected and was the promised MESSIAH foretold by the prophets (*see* NEVI'IM). Christianity quickly developed into a religious tradition separate from Judaism, for theological and political reasons.

Theologically, Christianity developed certain views that were unacceptable to mainstream JUDAISM. Beginning with PAUL (Saul of Tarsus), Christianity taught that every person was separated from God by original sin (*see* SIN AND REPENTANCE), and that the only means of reconciliation was atonement through the blood of Jesus Christ. Individuals were exhorted to recognize Jesus as the true son of God.

Traditional Judaism rejects the doctrine of original sin. It also rejects the doctrine that Jesus was the promised Messiah, let alone that he was fully human and fully divine, another fundamental doctrine of mainstream Christianity. The rabbinic tradition developed very different interpretations for the passages in the TANAKH, the Hebrew Bible, that Christians see as clear prophecies of Jesus.

In addition to theological differences, Christianity and Judaism have enjoyed dramatically different histories as civic communities, leading to political tensions over the centuries. Constantine in the early fourth century, Christianity became the official religion of which effectively marginalized Judaism while elevating Christianity.

In the centuries that followed, Jews experienced severe persecution at the hands of Christians, as for example during the

POGROMS were a frequent occurrence in Europe during the Middle Ages, decimating whole communities of Jews. In modern times, Christians responded slowly and in small numbers to protest the persecution of Jews under HITLER, leading many Jewish leaders to conclude that Jews needed their own homeland.

At present, Jewish and Christian communities coexist in many countries with varying degrees of cordiality, ranging from individual episodes of hate crimes at one extreme, to sustained efforts at inter-religious cooperation in many democratic countries.

Further reading: Henry Chadwick, *The Early Church* (New York: Oxford University Press, 2001); Jacob Katz, *Exclusiveness and Tolerance: Studies in Jewish-Gentile Relations in Medieval and Modern Times* (Springfield, N.J.: Behrman House, 1983); Jacob Neusner, Bruce Chilton, and William Graham, *Three Faiths, One God: The Formative Faith and Practice of Judaism, Christianity, and Islam* (Boston: Brill Academic Publishers, 2002).

ristian-Jewish relations

early 2,000 years most Jews have lived as a
'y people amid a majority professing
religion. Although there are exceptions,
usually lived in Muslim or Christian
s. The experiences of Jews in Christ-
ave ranged from peaceful and pros-
rtain and violent, but genuine
occurred recently, when Jews
Christians at the highest lev-
urch and the World Council

developed in the early
Era, so too did CHRIS-
ckly throughout the
stantine made it the
mpire (*see* ROME).
ly emerged from
wish ethnicity
church mem-
ed far from

their Jewish beginnings, especially concerning the divinity of Jesus and the Triune nature of God.

Once in power, Christianity suppressed pagan worship completely, but Judaism was allowed to exist. However, a pattern of persecution soon emerged that would last for centuries.

In the post-Constantine era, Roman persecution of Christianity ceased, but Roman strictures against Judaism remained in force. Christianity soon became the dominant religion throughout the Roman Empire and adjacent areas. The early Christians defined themselves in part by their difference from Jews. Based on the New Testament they considered themselves the new elect of God, in place of the Jews, who, they believed, had rejected JESUS OF NAZARETH, their savior and the son of God, and contributed to his crucifixion and death. Prior to Vatican II in the 20th century, most Christian churches did not discourage the belief that the Jews had killed Jesus, and were adamant in stating that unconverted Jews could not be saved.

This ANTI-JUDAISM bred violent, dangerous emotions from the start. Living as a minority religion in a Christian world, Jewish communities accepted their fate as part of the consequence of EXILE.

Periods of Christian religious enthusiasm have often proved difficult for Jews. In the 11th century Christians on their way to the Crusades and back attacked and destroyed many defenseless Jewish communities in their path. In the 13th and again in the 15th century Jews were required to formally defend the TALMUD against Christian scholars in widely publicized DISPUTATIONS, which were accompanied by rioting and anti-Jewish violence.

On the other hand, periods of peace for Jews living under Christian rule often depended on the benevolence of a particular king or bishop. When the Christians recaptured much of SPAIN from the Muslims in the 13th century, for example, the Jews were welcomed and encouraged to help rebuild commerce and industry. Sometimes a king would even be admonished by a pope for allowing Jews to exercise power over Christians, such as in the case of Alfonso VI in 1081. Years later, Alfonso X incorporated this idea into his law code, declaring that "No Jew may ever hold an esteemed position or public office so as to be able to oppress any Christian in any way whatsoever." Even so, Jews did hold some positions of authority right up until the EXPULSION in 1492, but the legal ambiguity always cast a shadow on their status.

After a while, a frighteningly consistent pattern emerged in Jewish life. Jews would be asked to settle in a Christian land in order to bring commerce or other needed skills, then expelled at a later date, and then asked back again (see ENGLAND; FRANCE; GERMANY; PORTUGAL).

Jews were often forced to live in walled enclaves called GHETTOS. In RUSSIA, this took the form of a geographic area called the PALE OF SETTLEMENT. The Jews there did not interact with Russian culture nor learn the Russian language, instead speaking their own tongue, YIDDISH. Even this bleak picture did have some beneficial elements. The Jews were often left alone to govern themselves in a semiautonomous system, as long as they continued to pay taxes to their host society. The community was called a *kahal* or *kehillah* (see *KAHAL, KEHILLAH*), and it often allowed for a rich cultural and religious life.

The modern period created an interesting dilemma for the Jewish communities of Europe. With the rise of nationalism and the development of the idea of equality, many Jews left their isolated communities and actively sought EMANCIPATION, using the ideals of the ENLIGHTENMENT to make their case. They did win a degree of equality in most European countries, sometimes at the price of ASSIMILATION. Nevertheless, ANTISEMITISM steadily increased, culminating in the HOLOCAUST, which decimated the European Jewish population, assimilated or not. Neither the Catholic nor the Protestant communities as a whole assisted the Jews during the Holocaust, and relations between Christians and Jews have been somewhat strained under the pressure of this reality.

The Vatican II church council in 1965 drastically changed the perspective of the Catholic Church toward the Jews, and the church has continued to work toward reconciliation and better ties. In 1970 the Catholic-Jewish Liaison Committee was established to encourage mutual understanding and cooperation on common issues, such as social justice. In 1986, Pope John Paul II visited a synagogue in Rome, the first such visit in the history of the papacy. There the pope condemned antisemitism and spoke about respect between Catholics and Jews.

Jewish groups also began dialogue with Protestant churches, especially those affiliated with the World Council of Churches (WCC). Progress here was slower, as the Protestant movement is divided into hundreds of separate denominations, many of which have a commitment to evangelism toward all non-Christians, including Jews. One landmark in that ongoing process of dialogue occurred at a meeting of the WCC's Committee on the Church and the Jewish People in Sweden in November of 1988. A document was formulated that agreed on the following principles: (1) The covenant of God with the Jewish people remains valid; (2) antisemitism and all forms of contempt for Judaism are to be repudiated; (3) the living tradition of Judaism is a gift of God; (4) coercive proselytism directed toward Jews is incompatible with Christian faith; and (5) Jews and Christians bear a common responsibility as witnesses to God's righteousness and peace in the world. The committee also recognized the State of ISRAEL, acknowledged spiritual concepts shared by Christians and Jews, clarified that the Jews should not be held responsible for the death of Jesus, and expressed sadness at Christian participation in Jewish suffering. In July 2004, however, the mainline Presbyterian Church (USA) endorsed a proposed divestment of companies that operate in Israel, marking a severe rupture in the relationship between Presbyterian Protestants and world Jewry.

Dialogue with evangelical Christians, those represented by the World Evangelical Alliance, has been much slower, as their dedication to world evangelism has included ministries focused primarily on the Jewish community. At the same time, some dialogue has been possible, building on the evangelical community's strong support for Israel.

Many societies dedicated to dialogue between Jews and Christians exist in Europe, such as the German Council for Jewish-Christian Cooperation and the Jewish-Christian Brotherhood in France. In Israel there are many groups that focus on Jewish-Christian dialogue, including the Interfaith Committee, the AMERICAN JEWISH COMMITTEE office in JERUSALEM, the Ecumenical Institute, the Ecumenical Discussion Center for Students in Jerusalem, and the Inter-religious Group in TEL AVIV.

The situation of Jews in America has always been vastly different from that in Europe. While suffering some discrimination in the early colonies, Jews soon found their niche in a pluralistic American society. Although there are strains of antisemitism among individuals in the UNITED STATES, it is not inherent in American Christian religious institutions. The United States is host to a vast number of organizations dedicated to improving the relationship between Christians and Jews, such as the National Conference of Community and Justice (formerly the National Conference of Christians and Jews), and the Center for Christian-Jewish Understanding at Sacred Heart University, which has many sister organizations in other Catholic schools such as Boston College.

American Jews are still a minority in a larger consciously Christian culture, but that culture is far more pluralistic and secular than it has been in Europe in the past. Most Jews feel comfortable in the United States; sociologist Will Herberg published a volume entitled *Protestant-Catholic-Jew* in the 1950s, suggesting that Jews had become part of mainstream America. At that time, the idea of a "Judeo-Christian heritage" became popular in the United States. This idea has opened doors to discussions and dialogue between Christians and Jews that is unique to the contemporary period. Many urban and suburban American communities have active fellowships of clergy, whereby rabbis, priests, and ministers share in fellowship and cooperative values.

Further reading: Jack Bemporad and Michael Shevack, *Our Age: The Historic New Era of Christian-Jewish Understanding* (Hyde Park, N.Y.: New City Press, 1996); Jeremy Cohen, ed., *Essential Papers on Judaism and Christianity in Conflict: From Late Antiquity to the Reformation* (New York: New York University Press, 1991); Andrew Greeley and Jacob Neusner, *Common Ground: A Priest and a Rabbi Read Scripture Together* (Cleveland: Pilgrim Press, 1996); Jacob Katz, *Exclusiveness and Tolerance: Studies in Jewish-Gentile Relations in Medieval and Modern Times* (London: Oxford University Press, 1961); Ellis Rivkin, *What Crucified Jesus? Messianism, Pharisaism and the Development of Christianity* (New York: UAHC Press, 1997).

chuppah

Jewish couples are required to get married under a wedding canopy called the chuppah. Traditionally, the chuppah is made from a *TALLIT,* or prayer shawl. However, in modern times, the chuppah is often a beautifully decorated piece of cloth held up by four poles. The chuppah may be free-standing or held by attendants above the bride and groom. Tradition teaches that the chuppah is a symbol of the home the new married couple will be creating. As it is open on all four sides but covered on the top, it provides shelter while at the same time remaining open to visitors. This vision is reminiscent of Abraham and Sarah and their value of round-the-clock hospitality illustrated in the TORAH in Genesis 18. The chuppah also metaphorically represents God's "Tabernacle of Peace."

Further reading: Rita Milos Brownstein, *Jewish Weddings: A Beautiful Guide to Creating the Wedding of Your Dreams* (New York: Simon and Schuster, 2003); Anita Diamant, *The New Jewish Wedding* (New York: Charles Scribner's Sons, 2001); *Tanakh: The Holy Scriptures* (Philadelphia and Jerusalem: The Jewish Publication Society, 1985).

chutzpah

Chutzpah is the Yiddish term for "nerve" and is used to describe someone with the courage to say or do something that will not be well received. Depending on its use, it can have either a positive or a negative connotation. As with many Yiddish words, no English equivalent has the same meaning or emotional import. Thus, the word *chutzpah* has entered into the English language and can be found in English-language dictionaries, in mainstream television programs, and on the streets of New York City.

Further reading: Gene Bluestein, *Anglish/Yinglish: Yiddish in American Life and Literature* (Lincoln: University of Nebraska Press, 1998); Fred Kogos, *The Dictionary of Popular Yiddish Words, Phrases, and Proverbs* (New York: Citadel Trade, 2000); Jackie Mason, *How to Talk Jewish* (New York: St. Martin's Press, 1991).

circumcision *See* BRIT MILAH.

CLAL—The National Jewish Center for Learning and Leadership

CLAL was founded in 1974 as a Jewish think tank, aiming to provide religious training and resources to Jewish leaders from across the spectrum of the community. The organization describes itself as "dedicated to building a Jewish life that is spiritually vibrant and engaged with the intellectual and ethical challenges of the wider world."

CLAL was founded by Orthodox Rabbi Irving "Yitz" GREENBERG (*see* ORTHODOX JUDAISM). He envisioned CLAL as a model of Jewish pluralism, and a way to overcome the growing divisions among Orthodox, CONSERVATIVE, REFORM, and RECONSTRUCTIONIST JUDAISM. CLAL seeks to allow pluralism to help create a vibrant new Jewish culture.

CLAL works closely with American Jewish federations (*see* UNITED JEWISH COMMUNITIES) in an attempt to infuse federation philanthropic activities with a more religious character. Because CLAL is not synagogue-based, and has specifically aligned itself with the primary American Jewish fund-raising organization, there have been periodic tensions between pulpit rabbis and the organizational leadership of CLAL. CLAL has been accused of diminishing Jewishness to "shallow behavior" in their efforts to reach Jews at all levels of observance and identity. CLAL has become increasingly sensitive to these charges, and has redoubled its efforts to reach out to synagogues and pulpit rabbis in addition to Jewish communal organizations.

Further reading: Daniel J. Elazar, *Community and Polity: The Organization Dynamics of American Jewry* (Philadelphia: Jewish Publication Society, 1995); Irving Greenberg, "Seeking the Religious Roots of Pluralism: In the Image of God and Covenant," *Journal of Ecumenical Studies* 34, 3 (1997); Web site URL: http://www.clal.org, accessed on June 26, 2004.

Code of Hammurabi

The legal code of the early Babylonian emperor Hammurabi (1728–1686 B.C.E.) was the first ancient legal code to become known to modern scholars. Like other ancient codes subsequently unearthed, the Code of Hammurabi included ritual guidelines and rules for maintaining purity, a value during ancient times, along with what modern people would consider legal clauses. This is one of the parallels with the legal codes found in the TORAH. One striking difference, however, is that Hammurabi gives great weight to social stratification; certain punishments vary according to the offender's social standing, a concept that is completely absent from Jewish law.

Further reading: S. G. Lambert, "The Laws of Hammurabi in the First Millennium" in *Reflets des deux fleuves* (Louvain, Belgium: Peeters, 1989); Zer-Kavod Mordecai, "The Code of Hammurabi and the Laws of the Torah," *Jewish Bible Quarterly* 26 (April–June 1998): 107–110.

codes of law

Jewish rabbis and scholars have written many law codes over the centuries, systematic compilations of rules and customs governing the full range of religious and secular behavior by individuals and communities. They were written to make the HALAKHAH (Jewish law) accessible to the wider Jewish community, and not just to the relatively few scholars who were skilled enough to interpret the TORAH and TALMUD.

The most significant medieval codes are the *Sefer ha-Halakhot* (Book of the Laws) edited in the 11th century C.E., and the MISHNEH TORAH, written by MAIMONIDES a century later. The *Mishneh Torah* is an exhaustive compilation ranging over a wide variety of subjects. Two centuries later Jacob ben Asher compiled his own code, the *Arba'ah Turim* (Four Rows), commonly called the *Tur.* In the 16th century Rabbi Joseph CARO produced the *SHULCHAN ARUKH* (Prepared Table), based largely on the *Tur.* R. Moses ISSERLES produced a companion for Caro's code, which attempted to balance Caro's Sephardic interpretive slant with an Ashkenazic approach (*see* ASHKENAZIM; SEPHARDIM). These two works remain the most authoritative codes in the world of ORTHODOX JUDAISM today. Several other codes have been produced more recently, such as Abraham Danziger's *Hayye Adam,* and the *Mishneh Berurah* by the CHAFETZ CHAIM, but none surpasses the authority of the codes developed in the 11th through 16th centuries.

The phrase "codes of law" can also be understood to refer to hidden meanings buried in texts. This type of secret code is found mostly in mystical literature, such as the KABBALAH. It often involves using one letter of the alphabet in place of another, so the reader must determine the substitution rule to decipher the code.

Further reading: Anne Fitzpatrick-McKinley, *The Transformation of Torah from Scribal Advice to Law* (Sheffield, U.K.: Sheffield Academic Press, 2001); Steven F. Friedell, *Introduction to Jewish Law in Talmudic Times* (Ramat Gan: Bar-Ilan University Press, 1999); N. S. Hecht, *An Introduction to the History and Sources of Jewish Law* (New York: Oxford University Press, 1996).

Cohen, Hermann (1842–1918) *philosopher*

Hermann Cohen is considered the greatest Jewish philosopher of the 19th century. He is best known for coining the idea of ethical MONOTHEISM.

Born the son of a CANTOR in Coswig, GERMANY, Cohen began his post-secondary studies at the Jewish Theological Seminary at Breslau. He originally had planned to become a rabbi, but turned instead to a lifetime study of philosophy, studying at the University of Breslau and then at the University of Berlin. In 1865 Cohen received his doctorate from the University of Halle, and in 1873 he began lecturing in philosophy at the University of Marburg, where he taught until 1912. Cohen spent the last years of his life in Berlin studying and teaching at the Hochschule für die WISSENSCHAFT DES JUDENTUMS, a school that focused on the study of Judaism using literary criticism and modern methods of research.

While he often wrote about Judaism, Cohen's philosophical works were grounded in secular philosophy. His primary agenda was to build upon the genius of Immanuel Kant. Kant had posited that all humanity is obligated to live lives according to universal ethical imperatives that are clearly defined and easily understandable to any reasonable person. Cohen agreed with Kant's philosophic embrace of universal ethics, and further stated that all ethical behavior must be defined as that which most greatly helps the broader society. Cohen asserted that humanity must infinitely strive for total social justice.

While the natural world worked according to a fixed order, the human realm of ethical behavior could change. Nature worked in defined cycles, regardless of human intervention, but the individual could choose to act ethically or not, according to whim. The only choice a reasonable human being had was to impose order on the ethical realm, and the existential means to achieve this was the individual's embrace of God. God became the philosophic idea by which human beings could pursue their ultimate goal of a world of complete social justice. Cohen called this philosophic and rational embrace of God the "religion of reason."

After creating the philosophic paradigm for the "religion of reason," Cohen highlighted Judaism's belief in the uniqueness of God and the idea that God compels individual ethical behavior. Cohen, in the philosophic realm, defined the universal mission of ethical monotheism for all of humanity.

Cohen's philosophy greatly influenced German Jews of his era. His emphasis on Judaism's universal ethics and its drive to make the world better helped encourage Jews to become involved in and influence the secular world. Jewish ASSIMILATION, Cohen believed, was acceptable when the Jew's intention was to further develop society's ethics and sense of justice. Thus, Cohen maintained that it was important to keep those Jewish rituals that emphasized ethics.

The term *ethical monotheism* eventually became accepted by all streams of Judaism to describe the basic belief in one God who distinguishes right from wrong. Cohen's ideas laid the philosophical foundation for what would later become the theology of Reform Judaism.

Further reading: Samuel Hugo Bergman, *Faith and Reason: An Introduction to Modern Jewish Thought* (Washington, D.C.: Schocken Books, 1961); Eugene B. Borowitz, *Renewing the Covenant: A Theology for the Postmodern Jew* (Philadelphia: Jewish Publication Society, 1991); William Kluback, *Hermann Cohen, The Challenge of a Religion of Reason* (Providence, R.I.: Brown Judaic Studies, 1984); Jehudah Melber and Emanuel S. Goldsmith, *Judaism: A Religion of Reason* (Middle Village, N.Y.: Jonathan David Publishers, 2003); Michael Zank, *The Idea of Atonement in the Philosophy of Hermann Cohen* (Providence, R.I.: Brown Judaic Studies, 2000).

commandment *See* MITZVAH.

Commentary

Commentary is a Jewish monthly magazine established in 1945 by the AMERICAN JEWISH COMMITTEE. The magazine flourished under the leadership of its first editor, Elliot Cohen. Half its articles covered specifically Jewish material, leaving the other half for topics of general and political interest. *Commentary* attempted to maintain diversity, but remained mostly liberal. On domestic issues, the magazine was more conservative, and until the establishment of the State of ISRAEL, it did not take a hard Zionist stance, in order not to alienate those Jews who had yet to endorse ZIONISM.

The magazine, at first a mouthpiece for American Jewish liberalism, took a more conservative stand starting in the late 1960s under the long editorship of Norman Podhoretz (1960–95). It eventually became a home for Jewish neoconservatives who had abandoned their earlier liberalism in response to domestic and international developments they considered inimical to Jews.

Commentary has a circulation of around 27,000. Like other intellectual magazines, it is not for profit; it covers such topics as national security, education, religion, and art. Prominent intellectuals from the Jewish community have been represented in the magazine, including Isaac Bashevis SINGER, Primo Levi, Cynthia OZICK, Hannah ARENDT, and Robert Alter. Podhoretz was awarded the Presidential Medal of Freedom in 2004, the highest civilian honor in the United States, for his 35 years as editor of *Commentary* and his contribution to the country's intellectual life.

Further reading: J. J. Goldberg, *Jewish Power: Inside the American Jewish Establishment* (Reading, Mass.: Perseus Publishing, 1996); Web site URL: www.commentary-magazine.com, accessed on July 5, 2004.

communism

Communism is a political and economic belief system that emerged in the early 20th century. The German Jewish social philosopher Karl MARX first developed the theory of communism. Marx's ideas were further developed by V. I. Lenin, who led the BOLSHEVIK REVOLUTION in Russia in 1917. The primary appeal of communism was its claim that it could create equal economic security for all.

From a Jewish perspective, the theory of communism had great philosophical and practical influence on the Jewish people, although most rejected the communist governments and parties that emerged after Lenin's takeover of Russia in 1917. Marxist and communist beliefs initially appealed to many Jews because they offered a worldview that posited equality for all peoples. While Marx believed that religion was an "opiate of the masses," Marxist communism imagined a world where the Jew could be freed from ethnic, cultural, or religious bias. In addition, the economic social justice of communism appealed to Jewish messianic idealism.

Early pioneers in PALESTINE attempted to live the dream of communism through the establishment of the KIBBUTZ, or collective farm, a community where members participated equally in labor and profit in the attempt to maintain economic equality among all members. The first chief rabbi of Palestine, Rabbi A. I. KOOK, while dismissing communism's antireligious stance, legitimized its dream of a world of economic and social equality as an authentic Jewish desire.

Communism never succeeded in its idealism. The Soviet Union, shortly after the Bolshevik Revolution, corrupted the notion of communism, reserving power and money for the political elite, and eventually reviving official ANTISEMITISM and discrimination against the Jews. In Israel, kibbutzim failed to succeed within a pure communist environment and transformed themselves into socialist communities that had both collective and private ownership. Today the kibbutz movement has greatly declined in Israel.

Further reading: Dennis K. Fischman, *Political Discourse in Exile: Karl Marx and the Jewish Question* (Amherst: University of Massachusetts Press, 1991); Karl Marx, *Capital: The Communist Manifesto and Other Writings* (New York: Modern Library, 1959).

community *See* KAHAL, KEHILLAH.

concentration and death camps

Soon after Adolf HITLER rose to power in Germany, he began setting up concentration camps. The first such camp was established in Dachau, GERMANY, in March 1933. The term "concentration camp" had been used before; the British had set up "concentration camps" for Afrikaner opponents in South Africa. The Nazi camps, however, were far more brutal, as their inmates were considered enemies of the "true German" people. These prisoners included Jews, Gypsies (Roma), Communists, political prisoners, homosexuals, and anti-Nazi priests and ministers, along with many other groups.

After World War II began in September 1939, the Nazis utilized camp inmates for slave labor. Arriving prisoners were immediately subjected to a selection process that determined whether the person would be killed immediately or kept alive for hard labor. Conditions were intolerable. Barracks were crammed with three or four times the number of people their builders intended. Food and water were scarce, and the lack of any hygiene facilities led to the spread of diseases such as typhus and spotted fever. Prison guards killed victims who spoke out; inmates lived in terror and sought only to survive. Medical experiments were carried out by German doctors (*see* Joseph MENGELE) and unspeakable horrors occurred on a daily basis. All of these elements combined to dehumanize the inmates of the camps in the eyes of guards and commanders, which made it psychologically easier for them to continue with killing, experimentation, and terror.

During World War II, the Nazis decided to physically exterminate world Jewry. To achieve this goal, they transformed some concentration camps into death camps and built new camps with the express purpose of systematically murdering Jews. By the end of 1942, the Nazis had created six death camps, all in Nazi-occupied POLAND: AUSCHWITZ, Belzec, Chelmno, Majdanek, Sobibor, and Treblinka. The massacres at these death camps were carried out with assembly-line efficiency. Sometimes Jews on the workforce were given the responsibility of taking the dead bodies from the "showers" to the crematoriums. These squads were killed on a rotating basis so that word of what was happening would be less likely to reach the outside world. The most infamous concentration and death camp was Auschwitz. During World War II, the Nazis murdered more than 1.5 million people there. The victims of Auschwitz were primarily Jews, but many Poles, Gypsies, and Soviet prisoners of war were exterminated as well.

Further reading: Eugene Aroneanu, ed., *Inside the Concentration Camps: Eyewitness Accounts of Life in Hitler's Death Camps* (Westport, Conn.: Praeger, 1996); Terrence Des Pres, *The Survivor: An Anatomy of Life in the Death Camps* (Oxford: Oxford University Press, 1980); Martin Gilbert, *The Holocaust* (New York: Holt, Rinehart & Winston, 1985); Hermann Langbein, *Against all Hope: Resistance in the Nazi Concentration Camps, 1938–1945* (New York: Paragon House, 1994).

confession

Judaism provides its followers with a formal method of confessing sin, expressing regret, and obtaining forgiveness.

In general, sinners are required to express their regret verbally, asking forgiveness from God and the person they harmed. During the High Holy Days there is an even more formal confession of sins, called the *vidui,* which is recited by all worshippers several times during the YOM KIPPUR service. The vidui includes two types of confessions: general trespasses and specific types of sins such as gossip and robbery. The sins are listed in the plural, using the formula "for the sins *we* have committed . . . ," so that each individual includes himself in the community's wrongdoing. Usually, penitent worshippers beat their chests with each mentioned sin.

Unlike the familiar Catholic practice, the sin is confessed directly to God or the victim of the sin, and not to a priest or leader. If the sin is merely against God (for example, if a person violated SHABBAT, the Sabbath), then if the sinner confesses

honestly and regretfully, and promises to refrain in the future, Judaism presumes that God will grant forgiveness. If the sin is against another human being, then the sinner must confess to the victim as well, ask forgiveness, and provide proper reparations, before God will wipe the slate clean. The person wronged must be approached at least three times before the sinner can begin to turn the issue over to God.

When the victim cannot be located, or in the case of murder, cannot be confessed to, this sin cannot be forgiven, even if confessed out loud. Even in these cases, Jews are expected to cultivate a confessional spirit. The confessional liturgy of Yom Kippur is familiar to nearly all Jews, but even the daily liturgy recited by traditional Jews includes prayers of confession. The ideal forum for confession is considered to be a MINYAN, a public quorum of at least 10 Jews. The minyan provides a context for public admission to sin, and also lets the sinners know that they are not alone in their transgressions.

While a Jew is still alive, his or her sins cannot be forgiven without following the proper process of *TESHUVAH,* or repentance. However, Jewish tradition states that one's own death can be an offering to help cancel out one's lifetime of sins. Judaism provides this deathbed confessional: "If my death be fully determined by Thee, I will in love accept it at Thy hand. O may my death be atonement for all the sins, iniquities and transgressions of which I have been guilty against Thee."

Further reading: Ismar Elobgen, *Jewish Liturgy: A Comprehensive History* (Philadelphia and Jerusalem: The Jewish Publication Society, 1993); Abraham Millgram, *Jewish Worship* (Philadelphia: The Jewish Publication Society of America, 1971); N. Scherman, *The Complete Artscroll Siddur* (Brooklyn, N.Y.: Artscroll, 1989).

confirmation

One of the innovations advocated by early proponents of REFORM JUDAISM was to replace bar mitzvah (*see* BAR/BAT MITZVAH), the rite of passage for

13-year-old males, with a confirmation ceremony for children between the ages of 16 and 18. The attempt to do away with bar mitzvah was ultimately rejected in Reform Judaism, but both Reform and CONSERVATIVE JUDAISM have instituted a confirmation ritual as a way to encourage teens to continue their Jewish studies past the age of 13. Many Reform and Conservative rabbis perform confirmation ceremonies for teens who continue Jewish studies classes through at least the 10th grade. The ceremony is usually performed on SHAVUOT, a festival that falls in late spring near the end of the academic year and commemorates the granting of the TORAH to the Jews at Sinai—an appropriate time to encourage continued study and participation in Jewish life.

Further reading: John D. Rayner, *A Jewish Understanding of the World* (Providence, R.I.: Berghahn Books, 1998); Joseph Reimer, *Succeeding at Jewish Education: How One Synagogue Made It Work* (Philadelphia: Jewish Publication Society, 1998); Jack Wertheimer, ed., *The American Synagogue: A Sanctuary Transformed* (Hanover, N.H.: University Press of New England, 1987).

consecration

Jews are instructed by the TORAH to bring holiness into their lives by various acts of consecration. Jewish liturgy frequently declares that God has commanded Jews to make their actions sacred or holy. For example, eating, which is a mundane activity, should be preceded by an act of consecration; the Jew makes a BRACHA, or blessing, over the food, declaring that it is holy to accept God's bounty with gratitude. The challenge within religious Judaism is to leave sin for holiness and depart from the mundane for the sacred.

The term *consecration* is commonly utilized within liberal Judaism for a ceremony recognizing the completion of the first full year of religious study by students. In REFORM and CONSERVATIVE JUDAISM, many synagogues expect students to begin intensive after-school religious study in third grade; this is commonly the grade that includes a consecration ceremony. The occasion can be marked by giving students their own siddurim, or prayer books (*see* SIDDUR), or by ceremonially giving them their Hebrew name.

Further reading: Barbara Binder Kadden, *Teaching Jewish Life Cycle* (Denver, Colo.: A.R.E. Publishers, 1997).

Conservative Judaism

As the movement in the ideological center of American Judaism, Conservative Judaism seeks to "conserve" Jewish traditions while living within the modern world. Rabbi Mordecai Waxman captured the challenge of Conservative Judaism in the title of his book *Tradition and Change*—the Conservative Jew tries to balance the demands of modern times with a commitment to Jewish observance. Conservative Judaism also embraces the critical study of Jewish and secular texts along with traditional methods of study. The underlying assumption is that all resources are permitted in the pursuit of "truth."

Conservative Judaism finds its roots in 19th-century GERMANY. Zachariah FRANKEL, once a more traditional voice within REFORM JUDAISM, became the leader of what would one day become the Conservative movement. He felt that the Reform movement was pushing change too fast, without reference to the community or to historical precedent. In 1854 he became the head of the first Conservative rabbinical school, The Jewish Theological Seminary of Breslau. The Seminary taught and lived according to what became known as the POSITIVE-HISTORICAL SCHOOL of Judaism; the idea was to pay close attention to historical precedent and to the hearts and minds of the community whenever considering any proposed reform.

By 1887 the American Conservative movement had also set up a seminary—the JEWISH THEOLOGICAL SEMINARY OF AMERICA (JTS) in New York. The school began with eight students under the leadership of Rabbis Alexander Kohut and Sabato MORAIS. Neither the seminary nor the Conservative movement flourished until a group of Reform Jews, including Cyrus ADLER, Jacob SCHIFF, and Louis MARSHALL, came on board; they wanted to create a middle ground between Reform and ORTHODOX JUDAISM that might appeal to the millions of eastern European Jewish immigrants arriving on American shores. They believed the seminary could help in the AMERICANIZATION of the new immigrants, allowing them to find a comfortable place within American Judaism while shedding their old-country customs, which embarrassed the already acculturated German Jews in the Reform world. The JTS was able to create role models for eastern European Jews that allowed them to preserve much of their traditional Jewish lifestyle and still become part of American society. In 1902 the widely respected Solomon SCHECHTER, reader in rabbinics at Cambridge University in ENGLAND, arrived at the seminary, and the success of Conservative Judaism was assured.

Conservative Jews stress that Judaism has evolved historically to meet the changing needs of the Jewish people in various eras and circumstances. They believe that Jewish law should continue to evolve in the present and future. Nevertheless, Conservative Judaism maintains the traditional view that Jews must obey and observe the will of God through the commandments. The movement also puts great emphasis on the Jewish people—Klal Yisrael, the totality of Israel. Schechter, who helped to firmly establish the JTS as the predominant school for Conservative rabbis, was well known for his teachings on this concept. He posited that Jewish legal decisions are largely grounded on the common practice of observant Jews of the time.

To ensure conformity to these practices, the Conservatives set up a central authority for HALAKHAH, Jewish law, called the Committee on Jewish Law and Standards (CJLS). It consists of scholars appointed by the JTS, the Rabbinical Assembly (RA, consisting of all affiliated Conservative rabbis), and the United Synagogue of Conservative Judaism (USCJ, made up of lay representatives of all Conservative synagogues). The CJLS often publishes both majority and minority positions on controversial matters of Jewish law. Individual rabbis serve as the *mara d'atra* (Aramaic for "master of the law") for their own communities, and are free to follow the legal rulings as they see fit.

Nevertheless, Conservative rabbis are expected to support certain declared standards of the movement. These standards have been approved by votes of at least 80 percent of the membership of the CJLS, and a majority of Rabbinical Assembly members. At present, there are four standards: 1) Rabbis and cantors are prohibited from officiating at intermarriages in any way; 2) rabbis may not perform remarriages if the previous partner is alive without an acceptable GET (Jewish divorce) or *haf'kaat kidushin* (annulment); 3) Jewish lineage is determined by matrilineal descent only; and 4) conversions to Judaism require both circumcision (*see* BRIT MILAH) and MIKVAH immersion for males and *mikvah* immersion for females. A Conservative rabbi who willfully violates these standards may be forced to resign or be expelled by the Rabbinical Assembly.

Conservative Judaism maintains that the TORAH is of divine origin; however, there is debate within the movement as to how it was authored. Some Conservative rabbis assert that God directly wrote the Torah, some that the Torah was divinely inspired, and yet others that human beings wrote the Torah based on their understanding of God's will, and that their writings were accepted as the social contract for the Jewish people. In any case, the Conservative movement has always in principle believed that *halakhah,* though open to scholarly interpretation, is binding on every Jew.

Many American Jews affiliate with Conservative Judaism because they desire a satisfactory home "in between" Orthodox and Reform. Often Conservative Rabbis find themselves in the distinct minority in their own congregations regarding their level of Jewish observance. Conservative rabbis, and Conservative Judaism at large, are constantly working to raise the level of Jewish education and observance among their lay membership.

Conservative Judaism supports many institutions. Synagogues that affiliate with the movement become members of an umbrella organization called United Synagogue of Conservative Judaism (for many years known as the United Synagogue of America). The group offers guidelines and instructions to member synagogues. Rabbis who graduate from the Jewish Theological Seminary of America, which has branches in New York and ARGENTINA, may join a professional group called the Rabbinical Assembly, which serves as both a professional union and a forum for study.

Further reading: Daniel J. Elazar, and Rela Mintz Geffen, *The Conservative Movement in Judaism: Dilemmas and Opportunities* (Albany, N.Y.: State University of New York Press, 2000); Neil Gillman, *Conservative Judaism: The New Century* (Springfield, N.J.: Behrman House Publishing, 1993); Robert Gordis, *Emet Ve-Emunah: Statement of Principles of Conservative Judaism* (New York: United Synagogue Book Service, 1988); Mordecai Waxman, ed., *Tradition and Change* (New York: Burning Bush Press, 1958); Jack Wertheimer, *Jews in the Center: Conservative Synagogues and Their Members* (New Brunswick, N.J.: Rutgers University Press, 2002).

conversion

Conversion to Judaism, which is open to people of any religious or ethnic background, means that the convert adopts the religious faith of Abraham and Sarah (*see* MATRIARCHS; PATRIARCHS) and becomes a full-fledged member of the Jewish people. Converts are called *gerim*, which is a biblical word that means "sojourners," but their status in Jewish law is no different from that of any other Jew (although they can never be KOHANIM or LEVITES).

Jews who convert to other faiths are called *meshumadim,* or "destroyers," implying that they have destroyed their faith, and that their actions, if imitated, would destroy Judaism.

Historically, Judaism since biblical days encouraged conversion to the Jewish faith, especially by people who had previously been idol-worshippers. The biblical paradigm for conversion was RUTH, the Moabite woman whose story is recorded in the Book of Ruth in the TANAKH, the Hebrew Bible. Ruth has remained celebrated for her declaration to her widowed ISRAELITE mother-in-law: "Do not urge me to leave you, to turn back and not follow you, for wherever you go, I will go; wherever you lodge, I will lodge; your people shall be my people, and your God my God" (Ru 1:16). This utterance is considered to have been her act of conversion to Judaism.

Ruth demonstrates the foreigner's ability to adopt the Jewish God, Jewish laws, and the Jewish people. Her embrace of Judaism is recounted on SHAVUOT, the holiday celebrating the moment that the Jews received the TORAH from God. The Bible also states that Ruth's merit in converting to the Jewish faith would be rewarded. She would become the great grandmother to King DAVID, from whose seed the Messiah will come, according to Jewish tradition.

While Ruth has always been beloved by Jews as the exemplar of conversion, Judaism has had an ambivalent attitude toward actively pursuing converts ever since the rise of CHRISTIANITY. Jews, often themselves victims of aggressive and sometimes violent proselytizing by other faiths, created legal provisions that discouraged non-Jews from rapid conversions. They are expected first to study their own faith, then the faith of others, and only after that to study for Jewish conversion. After this, a non-Jew who still insists of his or her own free will on becoming Jewish is accepted for Torah training and converted by a rabbinical court, after undergoing immersion in a MIKVAH, or ritual bath, and, in the case of men, BRIT MILAH, or ritual circumcision.

Judaism teaches that a convert's status is equal to one born Jewish, and in fact a Jew is forbidden to refer to another Jew as a convert. ORTHODOX JUDAISM demands that potential converts strictly observe all laws and undergo serious learning about religious practices before the conversion can take place. CONSERVATIVE JUDAISM insists on the same training and conversion rituals, but it requires only a general commitment to Jewish traditional observance. REFORM JUDAISM varies among rabbis and congregations in their educational and ritual demands on converts; as a result, many non-Reform Jews question the Jewish status of Reform converts. The status of non-Orthodox converts has sparked an ongoing debate in the State of ISRAEL, and the Orthodox political parties have tried to change Israeli law to recognize only Orthodox converts in Israel or abroad as Jews.

American rabbis do not actively recruit candidates for conversion; however, when faced with a Jew who is determined to marry a non-Jew, most will agree to prepare the potential spouse to embrace Judaism to ensure that the new home remains attached to the Jewish faith.

Jews who convert to another faith are still recognized as part of the Jewish people, but are considered apostates in a state of semi-excommunication from the community, and they cannot be counted in a MINYAN (prayer quorum). However, if they later reject their apostasy they resume their legal status as full Jews.

Further reading: Allan L. Berkowitz and Patti Moskovitz, *Embracing the Covenant: Converts to Judaism Talk About Why & How* (Woodstock, Vt.: Jewish Lights Publishing, 1996); Lydia Kukoff, *Choosing Judaism* (Cincinnati, Ohio: UAHC Press, 1981); Julius Lester, *Lovesong: Becoming a Jew* (New York: Arcade Publishing, 1988).

Conversos

Conversos were Jews (mostly Spanish or Portuguese) who had converted to CHRISTIANITY under threat of death, confiscation of property, or expulsion, but who privately still considered themselves Jews and practiced some Jewish rituals in secret.

The Roman Catholic Church under Pope Innocent III (1198–1216) launched the Inquisition to fight against perceived heretics within the church. The Inquisition authorities would use any means to elicit confessions from suspected heretics; those

who recanted might be welcomed back to the church; others were turned over to the civil authorities for punishment, often execution. By 1255 the Inquisition had spread to most of central and Western Europe with the exception of ENGLAND. While the Inquisition did not technically have legal authority to persecute Judaism itself, any Jew who had converted came under their purview and could be investigated on suspicion of practicing Judaism, and any Jews who had not converted could be investigated for undermining the Christian faith of converts.

The church called the secret Jews Conversos. In Spain they were popularly referred to as Marranos, or "swine." This pejorative was used by Catholics as well as by those Jews who had refused to convert. Historians today often use a third term, Crypto-Jews.

A significant Converso population lived in SPAIN. Beginning in 1481 Spain targeted both Jews and Conversos with an intense series of Inquisitions led by Tomás de Torquemada, the inquisitor-general. In Seville, approximately 700 Conversos were burned at the stake, though another 5,000 were allowed to openly repent and embrace the church. Additional burnings of Conversos took place in Aragon, Catalonia, Ciudad Real, Toledo, and ultimately Barcelona, which had the largest number of Conversos. More than 13,000 Conversos were tried during the Spanish Inquisition. In 1492 all Jews and Conversos were expelled from Spain. By that time, the majority of Conversos had either assimilated into the Christian communities or had returned to normative Jewish practices, usually in countries of refuge like Turkey or the Netherlands. It is not uncommon for a modern family of Spanish or Portuguese heritage in those countries or in the Americas to discover their Jewish roots after generations of practicing Christianity.

Further reading: Jane S. Gerber, *The Jews of Spain: A History of the Sephardic Experience* (New York: Free Press, 1992); David M. Gitlitz, *Secrecy and Deceit: The Religion of the Crypto-Jews* (Philadelphia: Jewish Publication

Society, 1996); B. Netanyahu, *The Origins of the Inquisition in Fifteenth-Century Spain* (New York: New York Review of Books, 2001); Norman Roth, *Conversos, Inquisition, and the Expulsion of the Jews from Spain* (Madison: University of Wisconsin Press, 1995).

Cordovero, Moses (1522–1570) *mystic*

Moses (in HEBREW, Moshe) Cordovero was a renowned practitioner of KABBALAH, Jewish MYSTICISM. He headed the Portuguese YESHIVA in SAFED, the center of Jewish mysticism in ISRAEL during his lifetime. Cordovero's philosophical works created the primary models for later Kabbalism and HASIDISM.

Cordovero was apparently born in Safed to a family of Spanish origin. He is believed to have studied with the legalist Joseph CARO. His most important work was *Pardes Rimmonim* (Krakow, 1592), which discusses the divine nature, theodicy, the cosmos, humanity, and the worship of God. It also illuminates the parable of fire and the spheres, later treated in his great work *Or Yaqur.* The primary Kabbalistic topics, such as the Ein Sof and the SEFIROT, aspects of the divine, are well detailed in Cordovero's books. He also wrote commentaries on Jewish liturgy and a final book on his personal mystical endeavors.

Cordovero believed that the study and practice of Jewish mysticism would help to speed up God's REDEMPTION of the Jewish people. To that end, he emphasized that a Jew was to pray daily with KAVANAH, or devotion. Cordovero was ultimately concerned with how the human soul related to God; his works were all aimed at building and improving that relationship. Cordovero and his peers were probably responsible for the implementation of the *Kabbalat Shabbat* liturgy, which welcomes the SHABBAT queen and is still recited in most synagogues at Friday evening services.

Further reading: Moses Cordovero, *The Palm Tree of Deborah* (New York: Hermon Press, 1974); Lawrence Fine, *Safed Spirituality: Rules of Mystical Piety, the Beginning of Wisdom* (New York: Paulist Press, 1984).

Council of Jewish Federations *See* UNITED JEWISH COMMUNITIES.

court Jews

In the 17th and 18th centuries it became common for rulers and powerful nobles in central and eastern European states to utilize the services of Jews for administration and finance; such Jews were often referred to as *court Jews.*

Jewish communities all across Europe and beyond often remained in contact with one another, and rulers were eager to exploit this network to obtain financing. Apart from their international trade connections, court Jews tended to have high levels of education and commercial skills, and were often personally wealthy. Thanks to these factors they tended to be good financial managers for the nobility. They would help rulers set up centralized systems to manage their property; their tasks often included administering lands, organizing agricultural production, provisioning armies, and obtaining needed grain, timber, cattle, precious metal for the mint, and luxury items. Often the court Jews would lend money to the nobility, and they were able to use their credit among other Jews to move goods and services across state boundaries with little difficulty.

Many states had expelled their Jewish communities in the late Middle Ages, but exceptions were made for court Jews. The position entailed other privileges, which varied under different rulers. They could include official status, a salary, access to the ruler, freedom to travel and live anywhere, and exemption from rabbinic jurisdiction. Court Jews often chose the route of ASSIMILATION, though they often sought to marry into the families of other court Jews in an attempt to secure employment for their descendants. Court Jews generally did try to help other Jews gain settlement privileges; thus they helped prepare a path for eventual EMANCIPATION.

While Isaac ben Judah ABRAVANEL was probably Europe's most famous court Jew before the modern era, the biblical figure of JOSEPH appears to have been an even earlier example of the role. Some say that Judah P. BENJAMIN, the American Confederacy's vice president, took on this role, and former U.S. secretary of state Henry KISSINGER has been accused of playing the part, though he personally rejects the label. The term can sometimes take on a pejorative tone bordering on ANTISEMITISM.

Further reading: Simon Noveck, *Great Jewish Personalities in Modern Times* (Washington, D.C.: B'nai B'rith Department of Adult Jewish Education, 1960); Selma Stern, *The Court Jew* (Philadelphia: The Jewish Publication Society of America, 1950).

covenant

A covenant is an agreement between two parties; in the case of Judaism, the two parties tend to be humans and God. Jews regard the most important covenants to be those between God and Abraham (*see* PATRIARCHS), which was reaffirmed by Isaac and Jacob, and between God and the people of ISRAEL at MOUNT SINAI.

The first covenant to appear in the TANAKH, the Hebrew Bible, was between God and NOAH (Gn 9:8–13). God promises Noah never to destroy all of humankind, as nearly happened during the flood, and Noah in return commits to keeping seven commandments that forbid idolatry, incest, bloodshed, profaning God's name, injustice, robbery, and cutting flesh from a living animal. The RAINBOW, God explains, will be an eternal reminder of this covenant.

The covenant between God and Abraham is first referenced in Genesis (15:17). God promises to give Abraham progeny, and to give them possession of the holy land (converts are considered to be children of Abraham and Sarah and are thus included in the covenant). In turn, Abraham and his descendants must agree to serve only the one God, and must symbolize that promise by observing BRIT MILAH, the covenant of circumcision. The covenant of land in exchange for faithful service is reaffirmed with Isaac (Gn 26) and Jacob (Gn 28:35).

The second covenant (Ex 19) provides that God will make the ISRAELITES a prosperous and holy people if they will follow his commandments (*see* MITZVAH). The first 10, known as the DECALOGUE, are explicitly part of the covenant, but the rabbis list a total of 613 TORAH commandments that must be observed.

These covenants were part of what modern critics have called DEUTERONOMIC HISTORY, named for the Book of Deuteronomy. According to this worldview, when Jews obey the commandments, they prosper and are able to dwell in ERETZ YISRAEL, the land of Israel. However, when they disobey the commandments, they are punished and/or sent into EXILE. The Jewish people are never disowned by God, whose love is eternal, but they will be punished if they fail to keep their commitment as promised in the covenant. While many Jews still hold this understanding of the covenant and history, others believe that the HOLOCAUST—a severe punishment of the Jews with no apparent provocation—nullifies Deuteronomic history and makes the idea of a covenant with God problematic.

Further reading: Dan Cohn-Sherbok and Lavinia Cohn-Sherbok, *A Short Introduction to Judaism* (Oxford, U.K., and Rockport, Mass.: Oneword Publications, 1997); Arthur Hertzberg, *Judaism: The Classic Introduction to One of the Great Religions of the Modern World* (New York: Simon and Schuster, 1991); Peter Ochs, ed., with Eugene B. Borowitz, *Reviewing the Covenant: Eugene B. Borowitz and the Postmodern Revival of Jewish Theology* (Albany: State University of New York Press, 2000).

Creation

Creation is one of the three central concepts in Judaism, along with REVELATION and REDEMPTION. "In the beginning, God created the heavens and the earth," reads the King James Version of Genesis 1:1, the first line of the TORAH. Like Christians, Jews tend to believe in Creation *ex nihilo*, meaning Creation from nothing. However, some scholars believe the HEBREW should be translated somewhat differently; as in the following quote: "When God began to create heaven and earth—the earth being unformed and void, with darkness over the surface of the deep and a wind from God sweeping over the water—God said 'Let there be light'; and there was light." (Gn 1:1–3) Such a translation suggests that something already existed and God gave it definite form.

According to the Genesis account God created the universe in six days. Creation occurred in this order: on the first day, God created darkness and light; on the second, water and sky; on the third, land, seas, and vegetation; on the fourth, the sun, moon, and stars; on the fifth, insects, fish, and birds; and on the sixth, animals and humans. In this account, God creates the human male and female together (Gn 1:27), and grants them dominion over all the animals and vegetation. God rests on the seventh day, which Jews commemorate with SHABBAT.

The second chapter of Genesis presents a somewhat different account of Creation. In this account, God creates the human male before animals and vegetation. He places the man in the Garden of Eden, and creates all sorts of vegetation for him to eat. God then creates all the types of animals and birds, which the man names, but as none can serve as a good helper, God creates a woman from the man's rib to fill the job.

Many scholars attribute the varying accounts to different strands of oral tradition, one known as the J strand, and one as the E strand. Jewish tradition, on the other hand, holds both versions to be true and reconciles them in various ways. For example, some rabbis theorized that the woman in the first version, whom they named LILITH, turned out to be too independent to be an appropriate helper to Adam, the man, and was banished; God then created Eve from Adam's rib. Alternately, some rabbis hold that God first created a hermaphrodite, who was then split into Adam and Eve.

Further reading: Jacob Neusner, *Confronting Creation: How Judaism Reads Genesis: An Anthology of Genesis*

Rabbah (Columbia, S.C.: University of South Carolina Press, 1991); Raphael Posner, ed., *The Creation according to the Midrash Rabbah* (Jerusalem and New York: Devora Publishing, 2002); *Tanakh: The Holy Scriptures* (Philadelphia and Jerusalem: Jewish Publication Society, 1985).

Cresques, Abraham and Judah (c. 14th century) *cartographers*

Abraham Cresques was a 14th-century cartographer in southern Europe. Although historians believe that the Cresques family had been living in Majorca, an island off of present-day SPAIN, for several generations, whether they originally came from Catalonia or North Africa is uncertain.

Abraham constructed maps and compasses for Pedro IV of Aragon and his son John. His map of the world was sent as a gift to Charles VI of France in 1381. It is believed that he prepared the Catalan atlas, possibly with the help of his son Judah. The atlas, currently held by the Bibliothèque Nationale in Paris, is the most famous extant example of medieval cartography.

Abraham's talents won him special privileges. Both he and Judah were granted royal protection in 1381 and were exempted from wearing the Jewish badge. After the death of his father, Judah continued as a cartographer for John I and Martin of Aragon. During the anti-Jewish violence in Spain in 1391, Judah chose to convert to CHRISTIANITY. He settled in Barcelona in 1394 with the new name Jaime Ribes. Under the name Mestre Jacome de Mallorca he worked as cartographer for Prince Henry the Navigator in Portugal in the 1420s.

Further reading: Abraham Cresques, *Mapamundi, the Catalan Atlas of the Year 1375* (New York: Abaris Books, 1978); G. R. Crone, *Maps and Their Makers: An Introduction to the History of Cartography* (London: Hutchinson's University Library, 1953).

customs See MINHAG.

Cyrus (d. 529 B.C.E.) *Persian king*

Cyrus the Great, emperor of PERSIA in the sixth century B.C.E., rescued the Jews from Babylonian exile, and was instrumental in the survival of Judaism past the biblical era.

In 586 B.C.E., the territory of Judea (*see* JUDEA AND SAMARIA) was conquered by BABYLONIA. The conquerors destroyed the first TEMPLE and exiled many Jews, including the leaders, to Babylonia. After Cyrus conquered Babylonia, he allowed the Jews to return to JERUSALEM and to rebuild the Temple in the year 538 B.C.E., inaugurating the second Temple period. Traditional Judaism interprets Cyrus's victory as an act of God ending the period of punishment as foretold by the NEVI'IM, the Prophets. The book of ISAIAH calls the emperor "Cyrus, His anointed one—whose right hand He was grasped, Treading down nations before him, Ungirding the loins of kings" (Is 45:1). Cyrus was a master propagandist, and legend has it that he conquered Babylon "without firing a shot." The British Museum holds an example of his propaganda in the "Cyrus Cylinder," which states that the emperor would restore correct religious order wherever he rules, which confirms in its way the biblical account.

Further reading: Andrew Robert Burn, *Persia and the Greeks: The Defense of the West, c. 546–478 B.C.* (New York: St. Martin's Press, 1962).

D

Damascus Affair

The 1840 Damascus Affair, which involved BLOOD LIBEL accusations and the torture of innocent Jews, represented one of the first times that human rights abuses rose to the attention of an international public, and marked the start of organized efforts by modern Jews to help their coreligionists in other countries.

The event was sparked by the disappearance of a monk, but it was based upon centuries of myths that accused Jews of using the blood of Christians to make Passover MATZAH. Such accusations are historically known as the blood libel, and they caused many massacres of Jews in Europe throughout the Middle Ages, often in conjunction with Christian celebrations of Easter. The Damascus Affair is but one example of how modern ANTISEMITISM thrived on these ancient lies.

The Damascus Affair began when the elderly monk Tomaso de Camangiano disappeared along with his servant. A story began to spread that the monk had been murdered by Jews for his blood. Subsequently, a Jewish barber, Solomon Negrin, was arrested and tortured to induce him to confess to the crime and implicate Jewish communal leaders. These leaders were arrested, tortured until they too confessed to the crime that they did not commit, and imprisoned.

Word of the torture leaked out into the world, and Moses MONTEFIORE, Isaac-Adolphe Cremieux, and James de Rothschild tried to intervene with the French government, which occupied Syria at the time. When the French government refused to act, Rothschild released the report to the European press, and the Damascus Affair became public knowledge. Both Jews and Gentiles throughout Europe were horrified by the tales of torture and the revival of a deadly medieval myth.

On July 8, 1840, a meeting took place in London at which members of Parliament and Christian clergy protested the blood libel and the torture of the accused Jews. UNITED STATES president Martin Van Buren ordered the American consul in Syria to help the Jews of Damascus. After prolonged negotiations, those who had survived the torture were freed.

The Damascus Affair became a major turning point in Jewish history. World Jewry had awakened to antisemitism within the Catholic Church, and they worked together with enlightened Gentiles. Together Jews and Christians began to formally organize to combat worldwide antisemitism. Even more important, the affair resulted in increased solidarity among the Jewish communities of Europe as they began to understand the importance of acting together to combat this revitalized threat to their lives and their hopes for EMANCIPATION.

Further reading: Esther Benbassa, *The Jews of France: A History from Antiquity to the Present* (Princeton, N.J.: Princeton University Press, 1999); Norman A. Stillman, *The Jews of Arab Lands: A History and Source Book* (Philadelphia: The Jewish Publication Society of America, 1979).

Daughters of Zelophehad

In the Book of Numbers in the TANAKH, the Hebrew Bible, the five daughters of Zelophehad stand out as defenders of equal property rights for women, at least in certain circumstances.

According to the story (Nm 27:1–4), Mahlah, Noa, Hoglah, Milcah, and Tirzah come before an assembly of MOSES, Eleazar, the chieftains, and the entire ISRAELITE community to protest that no land would be given to their family, since their father had died without leaving any sons. God tells Moses that the daughters' plea is just and that they should be given land. Thus the Hebrew Bible provided some rights of inheritance for women, a revolutionary concept for its time and for many centuries thereafter.

Within rabbinic literature the daughters of Zelophehad are praised for their courage and leadership. The sages, all of them males, asserted that God treats males and females alike, quoting Psalms (145:9), "Adonai is good to all, and God's tender mercies are over all God's works." While traditional Judaism remains male-centered, many feminist Bible critics cite the narrative of the daughters of Zelophehad as a seminal narrative. It represents the biblical cornerstone for a feminist embrace of equality between the genders.

Further reading: David L. Lieber, *Etz Hayim: Torah and Commentary* (New York: The Rabbinical Assembly, United Synagogue of Conservative Judaism, Jewish Publication Society, 2001); *Tanakh: The Holy Scriptures* (Philadelphia and Jerusalem: Jewish Publication Society, 1985).

David (d. 962 B.C.E.) *second biblical king of Israel*
King David is the Jewish prototype of the benevolent and legitimate monarch. Though a flawed human being, his model of leadership and piety have fed a tradition that the MESSIAH will come from his line.

The story of King David is found in the books of 1 and 2 Samuel in the TANAKH, the Hebrew Bible. David, from the tribe of Judah and a great-grandson of NAOMI the Moabite, is still a young shepherd when God tells the prophet Samuel to anoint him as the chosen one. David proves his worth by winning a battle against Goliath, the Philistine, and wins the support and love of King Saul's son Jonathan as well as of the general population. Sensing a threat, King Saul persecutes David, but David survives and becomes king of ISRAEL.

As king, David moves the capital to JERUSALEM and brings the ARK of the Covenant there, thereby unifying the northern and southern tribes into one kingdom. According to tradition, David was exceedingly devout; he is credited with writing the Psalms, and legends say his last days were consumed with TORAH study.

However, David angered God by sending Uriah the Hittite to the front lines of battle so that he would be killed, freeing David to marry Uriah's wife, Bathsheba. David's punishment was the death of his and Bathsheba's infant child. In addition, he was deemed unworthy to build the grand TEMPLE, the house of God, because he had Uriah's blood on his hands. The honor of building the Temple passed to David and Bathsheba's son, SOLOMON. David also suffered strife within his own family, when his son Absalom attempted to seize the throne from him.

Despite ambiguities in David's character, Jews have revered him as a great king and his rule as a model for a strong sovereign Jewish state. Additionally, it is believed that the messiah will be a member of the Davidic line, that is, a direct descendant of King David.

Further reading: Robert Alter, *The David Story: A Translation with Commentary of 1 and 2 Samuel* (New York:

W. W. Norton, 1999); Ronald H. Isaacs, *Legends of Biblical Heroes: A Sourcebook* (Northvale, N.J.: Jason Aronson, 2002); Jonathan Kirsch, *King David: The Real Life of the Man Who Ruled Israel* (New York: Ballantine Books, 2001); *Tanakh: The Holy Scriptures According to the Traditional Hebrew Text* (Philadelphia and Jerusalem: Jewish Publication Society, 1985).

Dayan, Moshe (1915–1981) *Israeli military and political leader*

Moshe Dayan was a world-famous military and political leader, credited with some of the most impressive Israeli accomplishments in both fields.

Dayan was born on May 20, 1915 on the Deganya Alef KIBBUTZ by the Sea of Galilee. At the age of 14 Dayan joined the HAGANAH, an underground Jewish defense force dedicated to protecting Jewish settlements from Arab attacks. Dayan acquired valuable experience in how to combat guerrilla warfare both as a member of a police force in Galilee and as a member of the Haganah.

In 1939 the British outlawed the Haganah, and Dayan was sentenced to 10 years' imprisonment, although he only served two. Released in 1941, he was allowed to join the British army in order to fight the Nazis. Dayan was wounded in battle in Lebanon and lost his left eye. This injury prompted Dayan to wear a black eye patch, which makes him easily identifiable. He continued to assist British intelligence in PALESTINE until the conclusion of the war, after which he rejoined the Haganah.

In 1948, during the ISRAELI WAR OF INDEPENDENCE, Dayan commanded the defense of Jewish settlements in the Jordan Valley. He led an attack on the city of Lydda that stopped the Egyptian forces on the southern front. Promoted to chief of staff for the Israeli armed forces in 1953, he was in charge of the successful October 1956 campaign that captured the Sinai peninsula from EGYPT.

Dayan left the military in 1958 to enter the Israeli political arena as a member of the KNESSET for Mapai, the Labor Party. He served as minister of agriculture and later minister of defense, where he served during the astonishing Israeli military successes of the 1967 SIX-DAY WAR. Dayan kept his position as defense minister under Golda MEIR. On October 6, 1973, Israel was taken by surprise when Egypt and Syria attacked on the Jews' holiest day of the year, YOM KIPPUR. Israel pushed back the Arab enemies, but Dayan resigned from office in public disgrace for allowing the surprise attack, which resulted in heavy casualties.

In 1977, Dayan's political opponent, Likud Party prime minister Menachem BEGIN, offered Dayan a chance at a new political life by becoming Begin's minister of foreign affairs. Dayan, still a member of the Labor Party, was eager to accept the appointment and assist with Israel's attempt to reach a comprehensive peace with the Arab states. Dayan became Begin's lead negotiator with the Egyptians, and he led the brokering of a peace agreement, consecrated by the CAMP DAVID ACCORDS of 1978.

In 1979, Dayan had a falling out with Begin over the building of settlements in the West Bank (*see* JUDEA AND SAMARIA) and the lack of continued peace talks with the Palestinians, and he resigned his position. Shortly thereafter, he was diagnosed with colon cancer, and he died on October 16, 1981. Moshe Dayan is recognized as one of the great modern-day Jewish warriors, who ultimately became a crusader for Israeli/Arab peace.

Further reading: Moshe Dayan, *Moshe Dayan: Story of My Life* (New York: Morrow, 1976); Robert Slater, *Warrior Statesman: The Life of Moshe Dayan* (New York: St. Martin's Press, 1991).

Day of Atonement *See* YOM KIPPUR.

Dead Sea Scrolls

The Dead Sea Scrolls comprise a set of ancient HEBREW manuscripts and fragments discovered in the 1940s, including the oldest surviving copies of nearly every book in the TANAKH, the Hebrew Bible.

Today one can see the actual Dead Sea Scrolls on display. Many of the scrolls are housed in the Shrine of the Book in the Israel Museum in Jerusalem. *(Avi Ohayon, Government Press Office, The State of Israel)*

The scrolls were found in clay pots in caves along the shore of the DEAD SEA. The manuscripts have been dated to the period from 200 B.C.E. to around 100 C.E., and are thus 1,000 years older than the earliest previously known biblical texts. They include portions of every book of the Tanakh except for ESTHER.

Perhaps most important, the Dead Sea Scrolls helped prove that the 1,000-year-old Masoretic text of the Bible, considered authoritative by Jews, does indeed accurately preserve far more ancient versions of the Hebrew books, thus underscoring its reliability. The scrolls also include selections from the APOCRYPHA literature, as well as pseudepigraphical writings (books written in the name of biblical figures). There are also several previously unknown

books associated with the Qumran community, a radical group of pietists living in the desert near the Dead Sea. The scrolls contributed greatly to historians' understanding of the context in which rabbinic Judaism and early CHRISTIANITY developed.

A controversy has developed around the scrolls because much of the material discovered in Cave IV, the largest collection of scrolls, was unpublished and inaccessible for many years. Recently the Huntington Library in California has published a complete photographic facsimile of the scrolls, and a new editorial team has been organized to supervise full publication of all the fragments.

Further reading: Frank Moore Cross, Jr., *The Ancient Library of Qumran and Modern Biblical Studies* (Garden

City, N.Y.: Doubleday, 1958); A. Dupont-Sommer and E. Margaret Rowley, *The Dead Sea Scrolls, a Preliminary Survey* (Oxford, U.K.: Blackwell, 1952); Lawrence H. Schiffman, *Reclaiming the Dead Sea Scrolls: The History of Judaism, the Background of Christianity, the Lost Library of Qumran* (Philadelphia: Jewish Publication Society, 1994).

death camp *See* CONCENTRATION AND DEATH CAMPS.

Deborah (12th century B.C.E.) *biblical leader and prophet*
Deborah's story is found in the book of Judges (4:4) in the TANAKH, the Hebrew Bible. She was the only female among the judges who led the ISRAELITES in the era before the monarchy emerged.

Deborah was a prophet, a leader, a warrior, and a judge. The biblical text describes her sitting beneath a palm tree while the Israelites brought questions and problems to her for decision. Deborah, following God's will, orders Barak to attack Sisera, an enemy commander. Deborah accompanies Barak into battle, the battle is successful, and a woman named Yael slays the fleeing Sisera. The song of Deborah follows: it is a beautiful piece of poetry that praises both God and Deborah. Following the battle, led and successfully completed by a woman, the land is said to be at peace for 40 years. Biblical scholars compare Deborah to MOSES as a leader, prophet, and judge.

Further reading: Cheryl Anne Brown, *No Longer Be Silent: First Century Jewish Portraits of Biblical Women* (Philadelphia, Pa.: Westminster Press, 1992); Naomi M. Hyman, ed., *Biblical Women in the Midrash: A Sourcebook* (Northvale, N.J.: Jason Aronson, 1997); Ronald H. Isaacs, *Legends of Biblical Heroes: A Sourcebook* (Northvale, N.J.: Jason Aronson, 2002); *Tanakh: The Holy Scriptures According to the Traditional Hebrew Text* (Philadelphia and Jerusalem: Jewish Publication Society, 1985).

Decalogue

While Judaism counts 613 total commandments (*see* MITZVAH), only 10 were given directly by God to the people of ISRAEL. The rest MOSES obtained from God and brought back to the people at MOUNT SINAI.

The Decalogue (Greek for "10 words," an accurate translation of the traditional Hebrew phrase *asseret ha-dvarim*) is usually known in English as the Ten Commandments. They are recorded twice in the TORAH, once in the book of EXODUS (20:1–17) and once in Deuteronomy (5:1–21; *see* TORAH).

Many synagogues display the Decalogue, or Ten Commandments, in their sanctuaries. This example shows how the Decalogue is abbreviated to artistically recreate the tablets that Moses brought down from Mount Sinai. *(Getty Images)*

According to the Jewish interpretation of the text (which does not clearly delineate where each commandment begins and ends), the commandments are as follows: 1) I am the Lord your God, and you shall have no other gods besides me; 2) you shall not make for yourself a sculptured image and shall not bow down to or serve idols; 3) you shall not take in vain the name of the Lord; 4) remember the Sabbath day and keep it holy; 5) honor your father and your mother; 6) you shall not murder; 7) you shall not commit adultery; 8) you shall not steal; 9) you shall not bear false witness against your neighbor; and 10) you shall not covet your neighbor's wife or possessions. Interestingly, Catholics and Protestants (*see* CHRISTIANITY), using the same ancient text, have a slightly different set of commandments.

The lists of commandments in the two books are almost identical; however, the rationale for observing SHABBAT, the Sabbath, differs. While the Exodus version says to remember the Sabbath day because God rested on the seventh day of CREATION, the Deuteronomy version says to remember the Sabbath day because God freed the ISRAELITES from SLAVERY in EGYPT. Some point to a third rendition of the Ten Commandments in Exodus 34, when Moses returns from Mount Sinai with a second set of tablets after smashing the first. This list, however, varies significantly from the other two; for example, it includes the commandment not to boil a kid in its mother's milk, which many interpret to mean, according to the laws of KASHRUT, not to eat meat together with any dairy food.

Although Judaism holds that all 613 commandments are important, the Ten Commandments hold special significance because of their REVELATION at Sinai to the entire Jewish community. This revelation is reenacted each year on the festival of SHAVUOT. The rabbis decided that Shavuot, the Feast of Weeks established in the Torah, is intended to commemorate receiving the Ten Commandments. Traditionally, Jews stay up all night on Shavuot studying Torah and recreating the anticipation of receiving the Ten Commandments; in the morning prayer service, the Commandments are read before the standing congregation with a special musical TROPE.

In modern times, some people have argued that the Ten Commandments represent universal ethical norms and that they underpin the laws of the UNITED STATES; therefore, these people argue, they should be displayed in public places, such as courthouses and schools, to encourage society to follow biblical standards of morality. Others point out, however, that though secular law may be partly based on the Ten Commandments, the latter remains by definition a religious document; in addition, some of the commandments are specific to certain religions and thus not universal, such as the prohibition of idols and the commandment to keep the Sabbath.

Further reading: Abraham Chill, *The Mitzvot: The Commandments and Their Rationale* (New York: Bloch, 1974); J. H. Hertz, *The Pentateuch and Haftarahs: Hebrew Text, English Translation and Commentary* (Brooklyn, N.Y.: Soncino Press, Ltd., 1997); Jacob Neusner, ed., *How Judaism Reads the Torah* (New York: P. Lang, 1993); Anthony Phillips, *Ancient Israel's Criminal Law; a New Approach to the Decalogue* (Oxford: Blackwell, 1970); *Tanakh: The Holy Scriptures* (Philadelphia and Jerusalem: The Jewish Publication Society, 1985).

Denmark

King Christian IV invited the first Jewish community to Denmark in 1622. He offered religious freedom and commercial privileges to SEPHARDIM from Amsterdam and Hamburg. Most of the Jews who came were financiers involved in trading or manufacturing. By 1782 there were 1,830 Jews living in Denmark, most of them in Copenhagen.

In 1814 Danish Jews received citizenship, and in 1849 the Danish constitution removed the last remaining law that stood in the way of Jews participating in any element of economic, social, or political life. By the beginning of the 20th century most Jews living in Denmark were members of the middle and upper classes. The Jewish population of 4,200 had begun to decline because of

In keeping with the good relations between Denmark and its Jewish citizens, the nation of Denmark has always had a strong relationship with the State of Israel. President Herzog (1981–83) (far left) stands here with his wife (second from right), the Prince Consort, and Queen Margrethe II of Denmark on the steps of the Fredensborg Palace in Denmark. *(Ya'acov Sa'ar, Government Press Office, The State of Israel)*

from POLAND arrived in Denmark, fleeing an antisemitic purge. While Danish Jews actively participated in helping Soviet Jews, especially by providing educational materials, fewer than 100 Jewish immigrants from the former Soviet Union have been allowed to settle in Denmark.

By the mid-1990s there were 8,000 people in the Danish Jewish community. The population has remained steady, with neither natural increase nor immigration.

The Jewish community in Denmark primarily adheres to ORTHODOX JUDAISM. REFORM JUDAISM has had a steady influence, but it remains in the minority. The Jewish community is recognized by the state. It has the power to levy taxes, and its rabbis have the authority to perform marriages and register births and deaths. There is at least one Jewish Day School in Denmark as well as an active Zionist Federation, youth organizations, a B'NAI B'RITH lodge, and two-old age homes for the Jewish elderly. The community is active in international organizations such as the World Jewish Congress and the World Zionist Organization. Denmark's Jews show a vital interest in ISRAEL and have an active B'nai Akiba youth group (*see* ZIONIST YOUTH MOVEMENTS). The government of Denmark has always had a friendly and warm relationship with ISRAEL, beginning with its vote for the PARTITION PLAN in 1947 and its recognition of the Jewish state on November 29, 1947. The Danish Jewish community encourages a strong relationship with Israel and the Israeli people, believing that this tie may strengthen their community and negate the effects of ASSIMILATION.

Historically the Danish people have embraced the country's Jewish community, and the Nazi occupiers in World War II were unable to instill ANTISEMITISM. GERMANY did not seek to molest the Jews of Denmark until 1943 when relations between Germany and occupied Denmark deteriorated. In September that year it became clear that the Jewish community was no longer safe; a rescue operation was launched, involving a broad range of people, from politicians to fisherman. In three weeks' time, almost the entire Jewish community of Denmark, including approximately 1,400 refugees

INTERMARRIAGE and a low birthrate. In 1903 the community was augmented by immigrants fleeing POGROMS in RUSSIA; the new immigrants were able to integrate smoothly into the established Danish-Jewish society. By 1921, the population had increased to 6,000 Jewish people.

Jews in Denmark participated in all spheres of life, as sculptors, literary critics, botanists, physicians, scientists, politicians, bankers, and poets. After 1969 a significant number of immigrants from Germany, AUSTRIA, and Czechoslovakia, were ferried to Sweden in safety. The operation cost 12 million Danish crowns, and the price was split between the Jewish community and private and public Danish contributions. By the time the Germans came for the Danish Jews in October of 1943, they found fewer than 500 victims. These were transferred to the CONCENTRATION CAMP of Theresienstadt, where some 50 of them later died. After the successful escape, Danish and Swedish Jews organized a flow of illegal traffic between the two countries, keeping Denmark in touch with the Allies as the war drew to a close. The Jewish community returned to Denmark after the war ended, where they found most of their property intact. Only about 120 Danish Jews died in the Holocaust, less than 2 percent of Denmark's Jewish population.

Denmark's positive relationship with its Jewish community remained intact even during an outburst of Danish nationalist feeling against immigrants in the 1980s; the Jews were not seen as strangers but countrymen. Many of the newcomers are Muslims. An office of the PALESTINE LIBERATION ORGANIZATION (PLO) was opened in Denmark, but when plans were uncovered to assassinate Danish Jews visiting Israel, as well as the chief rabbi of the country, the office lost its support. Denmark continues to celebrate its successful rescue of the Danish Jewish community, and the community remains an integrated part of Danish society.

Further reading: Herbert Pundik, *In Denmark It Could Not Happen: The Flight of the Jews to Sweden in 1943* (Jerusalem: Gefen Publishing House, Ltd., 1998); Emmy E. Werner, *A Conspiracy of Decency: The Rescue of the Danish Jews During World War II* (Boulder, Colo.: Westview Press, 2002); Nechama Tec, *When Light Pierced the Darkness: Christian Rescue of Jews in Nazi-Occupied Poland* (New York: Oxford University Press, 1986).

Dershowitz, Alan M. (b. 1938) *legal scholar, defense attorney, and human rights advocate*

Born in Brooklyn, New York, Alan M. Dershowitz attended YESHIVA UNIVERSITY high school and gradu-

ated from Brooklyn College. He received his law degree from Yale University, where he was the editor-in-chief of the *Yale Law Journal*. After becoming a member of the Harvard University Law faculty at the age of 25, Dershowitz achieved the rank of full professor three years later at the age of 28, the youngest person to do so at Harvard Law School.

Dershowitz has won wide acclaim, and some notoriety, as a lecturer, newspaper columnist, author of several books, and, especially, criminal defense attorney. Among his controversial clients have been Patty Hearst, Michael Milken, Jimmy Bakker, O. J. Simpson, and Claus von Bulow, whose murder trial Dershowitz chronicled in *Reversal of Fortune*, later made into a successful movie. His wide interests are reflected in the courses he has taught, which include criminal law, psychiatry and law, constitutional litigation, civil liberties and violence, comparative criminal law, legal ethics, and human rights.

Dershowitz has been a vocal defender of Jewish interests. He authored the best seller *Chutzpah: Candid Reflections on Being Jewish in America* (1992). In another book, *The Vanishing American Jew: In Search of Jewish Identity for the Next Century* (1997), he makes the controversial argument that mainstream American Jews are in danger of disappearing through INTERMARRIAGE, ASSIMILATION, and a relatively low birthrate.

Dershowitz's commitment to civil rights has earned him recognition by several national oraganizations. In 1983 the ANTI-DEFAMATION LEAGUE honored him with its William O. Douglas First Amendment Award for his "compassionate eloquent leadership and persistent advocacy in the struggle for civil and human rights." He has received honorary doctorates of law from Yeshiva University, the HEBREW UNION COLLEGE, Monmouth College, and HAIFA UNIVERSITY. Throughout his career, Dershowitz has exhibited commitment both to the practice and teaching of law and to the worldwide Jewish community.

Further reading: Alan M. Dershowitz, *The Case for Israel* (New York: John Wiley & Sons, 2003); ———,

Chutzpah (Little Brown, 1991); ———, *The Vanishing American Jew: In Search of Jewish Identity for the Next Century* (New York: Touchstone, 1997).

Dessler, Elijah Eliezer (1891–1954)
Talmudic scholar

E. E. Dessler was an important religious thinker and leader in the Musar movement. He was a great-grandson of Israel SALANTER, the founder of the Musar movement, which encouraged study of ethics and right conduct as a necessary companion to TALMUD study. Like his great-grandfather, Dessler became a renowned Talmud scholar.

Born and raised in Homel, RUSSIA, Dessler received a traditional Jewish education and eventually became a RABBI. After an early attempt in the business world failed, Dessler sought a rabbinic appointment in the East End of London. He went on to establish the first formal YESHIVA in ENGLAND, the Gateshead Kollel near Newcastle, where Jewish men can study Talmud full time.

Later in his life, Dessler became the head of the yeshiva of Ponivezh in ISRAEL. Among the thousands of students Dressler influenced at both schools were L. Carmel and A. Halpern, who eventually published their rabbi's discourses in the four-volume *Mikhtav me-Eliyahu,* or Writing of Elijah, which has become a standard text for those who study in the Musar tradition.

Dessler, while devoted to Musar, was also an expert in KABBALAH and HASIDISM, as well as in modern psychological theories. His secular knowledge won him high regard among a nontraditional Jewish audience, although he remained devoted to ORTHODOX JUDAISM his entire life.

Dessler believed that the primary purpose of Judaism was to help the Jew come closer to God in this world and the next. The only way to do this was through complete dedication to the study of TORAH. Dessler lectured on the subconscious mind, and taught that only the Torah can prevent the human being from becoming completely self-serving and destructive.

Unique within his movement, Dessler tried to combine the austere milieu of Musar with the more joyful celebration of Hasidic masters. In fact, Dessler's special contributions to Jewish thought stemmed from his thought-provoking combination of rabbinic texts, Musar, Hasidic thought, and Freudian analysis.

Further reading: Eliyahu Dessler, *Strive for Truth* (New York: Feldheim, 1988); Lewis Glinert, *The Joys of Hebrew* (New York: Oxford University Press, 1993); Yonason Rosenblum, *Rav Dessler: The Life and Impact of Rabbi Eliyahu Eliezer Dessler, the Michtav m'Eliyahu* (Brooklyn, N.Y.: Mesorah, 2000).

Deuteronomic history

Modern historians have coined the term *Deuteronomic history* to describe the point of view expressed in Deuteronomy, the fifth book of the TORAH, and other parts of the TANAKH, the Hebrew Bible, concerning the covenantal relationship between God and the Jewish people.

In 2 Kings (22:3–8) the HIGH PRIEST Hilkiah discovers a lost scroll written by MOSES. The scroll records Moses' final speeches to the ISRAELITES prior to his death and their own entry into the Promised Land. King Josiah is overwhelmed by the discovery, and decides to enforce the scroll's commandments. He institutes what historians call the "Josianic religious reforms," extinguishing all idolatrous influences within the Israelite community. These events have been dated to 622 B.C.E.

Both traditional and critical scholars agree that the "newfound scroll" was the book of Deuteronomy, or the Deuteronomic Code. The book consists primarily of Moses' reminders to the people of Israel of their special COVENANT with God, and their responsibility to live up to its demands. Moses spells out the rewards or punishments that await Israel, depending upon their actions once they enter the land.

ORTHODOX JUDAISM accepts the narrative of 2 Kings literally, and teaches that Deuteronomy was part of the five books authored by Moses himself. Many modern biblical scholars believe that the Deuteronomic Code was actually newly written in Josiah's day by the "Deuteronomists" as a reinterpretation of the existing biblical narrative, to provide textual support for Josiah's religious reforms. In any case, the reforms took hold and became the cornerstone for future rabbinic Judaism.

The presumed writers or editors are often referred to as Deuteronomic Historians; their initial intention was most likely to depict Josiah as the MESSIAH, the king who would restore the glory to Israel that had once existed in the time of King David. Such glory was only possible if Israel was united in religious piety. When Josiah died unexpectedly in battle, the messianic movement lost momentum, but the new Deuteronomic Code continued to inspire the future religious leaders of Israel.

Several generations of Deuteronomists, it is believed, continued to refine the book in light of new circumstances. They also edited the previous four books of the Torah to reflect the new theological perspective, and may have influenced some of NEVI'IM (Prophets) as well. The 20th-century German scholar Martin Noth (1902–68) is credited with uncovering the Deuteronomic strand of the Bible and the methods with which the Deuteronomic historians edited the Tanakh.

Noth recognized the common language and ideology reflected in Deuteronomy and the subsequent historical books through 2 Kings. His basic thesis has been adopted by almost all critical biblical scholars today. Many scholars, continuing the work of Noth, have found Deuteronomic language throughout the Tanakh, in original and edited sections.

A primary theological agenda of the Deuteronomic editors was to shift Israelite theology from a physical to a nonphysical understanding of God. They rewrote earlier texts to downplay or replace anthropomorphic descriptions of God. This theological understanding became a core belief within Judaism, and explains Jewish resistance to any notion that God can assume a physical form.

Further reading: Robert Alter and Frank Kermode, *The Literary Guide to the Bible* (Cambridge, Mass.: Harvard University Press, 1987); Lawrence Boadt, *Reading the Old Testament: An Introduction* (Ramsey, N.J.: Paulist Press, 1985); Richard E. Friedman, *Who Wrote the Bible?* (San Francisco: HarperSanFrancisco, 1997); *Tanakh: The Holy Scriptures* (Philadelphia and Jerusalem: The Jewish Publication Society, 1985).

Diaspora

For Jews, to live in the Diaspora means to live outside ISRAEL. The word *diaspora* (from Greek) literally means to scatter or spread out.

The first large spreading out occurred with the EXILE of the Jews from Israel to BABYLONIA in 586 B.C.E. after the destruction of the TEMPLE by the Babylonians. While many of the exiles returned to Israel in 539 B.C.E., others stayed behind. Eventually this Diaspora spread throughout the region, although most Jews outside Israel remained concentrated in Babylonia or EGYPT.

After the second Exile in 70 C.E., when the second Temple was destroyed, the Diaspora continued to grow, and Jewish communities sprang up throughout the known world. Large communities existed in western Europe, especially the Iberian Peninsula, eastern Europe, the Middle East, and North Africa. Some Jews even settled as far away as INDIA and CHINA.

With the discovery of the New World, many Jews left Europe and settled in North and South America, beginning with Spanish Jews banished from SPAIN by Ferdinand and Isabella in 1492. Central and eastern European Jews moved to the New World (including Australia and SOUTH AFRICA) in two waves of emigration in the 1840s and from 1881 to 1914 (*see* RUSSIA). Thus, Jews came to live in hundreds of countries and thousands of cities and towns in every part of the world.

In all of these communities, the Jews adapted to the culture and law of the land in which they lived. Today it is often said that the success of the Jews is a result of their ability to take from the surrounding culture while retaining Jewish customs, traditions, and memories. Religious Jews in the medieval world interpreted the continuing Jewish Diaspora in two very different ways: 1) The Diaspora and exile from the Land of Israel was a punishment from God for not following God's law, and 2) the Diaspora was God's way of scattering the Jews so that they would spread the divine light to cultures and peoples around the world (see KABBALAH; LURIA, ISAAC).

In present times, the number of Jews in the Diaspora still exceeds the number of Jews in Israel, though the gap has been narrowing. There are some differences between Diaspora Jews and Israeli Jews in terms of religious practices as well as Jewish identity. For example, Jews in Israel celebrate many of the Jewish holidays for one day, while Diaspora Jews celebrate two-day holidays. The original reason was probably to ensure that Jews abroad were marking the correct day, as determined by sightings of the new moon in Jerusalem. The holiday of CHANUKAH has taken on added importance among American Jews, while SUKKOT, because of its agricultural roots, is celebrated in Israel even among many secular Jews.

Moreover, in Israel there has been a conscious effort to interpret Judaism from a nationalist perspective, as the faith of a people with a strong history of sovereignty and military prowess dating back to biblical times. Thus Israelis may admire the image of strong, militarily efficient Jews. In the Diaspora, however, where concerns about ANTISEMITISM still persist, some teachers of Jewish history and identity continue to present the Jews as a victimized, persecuted people.

Further reading: Frédéric Brenner, Diaspora: Homelands in Exile (New York: HarperCollins, 2003); Allan Levine, Scattered Among the Peoples: The Jewish Diaspora in Twelve Portraits (Woodstock, N.Y.: Overlook Duckworth, 2003); Charles Liebman and Steven M. Cohen, Two Worlds of Judaism: The Israeli and American Experiences (New Haven and London: Yale University Press, 1990); Howard Morley Sachar, Diaspora: An Inquiry into the Contemporary Jewish World (New York: Harper &

Row, 1985); Howard Wettstein, ed., Diasporas and Exiles: Varieties of Jewish Identity (Berkeley: University of California Press, 2002).

Diaspora Museum

The Diaspora Museum, or Beth Ha-Tefutsoth, opened in TEL AVIV in 1978. Its exhibits tell the story of the Jews of the DIASPORA from the first EXILE up to the present day, highlighting various communities from different regions and eras. The museum spans 2,500 years of Jewish history, with a focus on both the unity and the diversity of the Jewish people.

The museum strives to emphasize the idea of continuity even in the face of the vast distances that sometimes existed between Jewish communities. The museum has succeeded in attracting visitors from across the spectrum: young, old, religious, secular, Israelis, and tourists. Many visit the museum online, where they can research a variety of topics. The hope of the curators is that new generations may learn from the success of Diaspora communities in preserving Jewish continuity

The museum includes permanent, temporary, and traveling exhibitions, a database of Jewish family names, a Jewish genealogy center, a music center and collection, a visual documentation (photographs) center, and a database of Jewish communities. The museum also produces a variety of educational programs. Membership is available to the general public, and there is a rich schedule of events and programs offered at the museum each month.

Further reading: Beth Ha-Tefutsoth Web site URL: http://www.bh.org.il; Nahum Goldmann, Beth Hatefutsoth: The First Ten Years (Tel Aviv: Beth Hatefutsoth, the Nahum Goldmann Museum of the Jewish Diaspora, 1988); Let's Go Israel and the Palestinian Territories (New York: St. Martin's Press, 2002).

dietary laws See KASHRUT.

Dinah *biblical daughter of Jacob*

According to Genesis (32–36) Dinah was the only daughter among Jacob's 13 offspring (*see* PATRIARCHS). After her birth, the text does not mention her until she has sexual relations with Shechem, a prince of CANAAN, after going out to the fields alone. Shechem takes her to his city and asks Jacob for her hand in marriage. Many commentators insist she was raped, while others maintain that the relations were consensual. In either case, Shechem's behavior was wrong in contemporary eyes, and Dinah's brothers consider their family dishonored.

The brothers decide to take revenge. They convince Shechem and his townsmen to become circumcised as a condition of marriage (*see* BRIT MILAH). While the men are recuperating, Dinah's brothers Simeon and Levi slaughter Shechem and his followers and despoil the town. Jewish tradition generally considers the brothers' violent behavior problematic; the fact that an entire community received severe punishment for the sin of one individual is also disturbing to many biblical commentators.

Dinah's own silence throughout her ordeal has been highlighted by modern commentators. A literature has appeared expressing the story from her perspective, to better understand how she may have felt after being raped. One novel, *The Red Tent* by Anita Diamant, fleshes out the suggestion that Dinah had consented to relations with Shechem and wished to marry him. The novel gives voice to Dinah and her mother and aunts; it is a story about the MATRIARCHS that provides a good example of modern MIDRASH.

Rape, although treated somewhat differently in biblical times, remains an unacceptable violent crime. Many modern Jews use the story of Dinah as a means to teach against rape, date rape, and abusive relationships.

Further reading: Anita Diamant, *The Red Tent* (New York: Picador, U.S.A., 1998); Ellen Frankel, *Five Books of Miriam: A Woman's Commentary on the Torah* (San Francisco: HarperSanFrancisco, 1998); Judith Plaskow, *Standing Again at Sinai: Judaism From A Feminist Per-* *spective* (San Francisco: HarperSanFrancisco, 1990); *Tanakh: The Holy Scriptures* (Philadelphia and Jerusalem: The Jewish Publication Society, 1985).

disputations

Disputations were public debates between Christian and Jewish scholars in the Middle Ages. The Jews were always coerced to participate in these debates, which were aimed at demonstrating that Christianity was the "true religion."

Three famous disputations recorded by the church each pitted a Jewish convert to CHRISTIANITY against a Jewish scholar, who had to demonstrate why a Jew should not depart from his faith. In effect, the Jewish participant had no choice but to endanger his own life by philosophically attacking Christianity.

The first of these three disputations occurred in Paris, FRANCE, in 1240. Rabbi Jehiel of Paris and other rabbis defended the TALMUD against the accusations of Nicholas Donin, who asserted that the work denigrated the character of JESUS OF NAZARETH. Rabbi Jehiel, while defending the authenticity of Judaism, was not able to cast Jesus in a positive light. As a result 24 cartloads of Talmud scrolls were burned, resulting in a severe shortage of Talmudic texts in Europe.

The second disputation took place in Barcelona in 1263, between Pablo Christiani and the Talmudic scholar NACHMONIDES. King James I of Aragon oversaw this debate and ensured that Nachmonides received fair treatment, so he could fully express the Jewish perspective. The debate focused on the Christian assertion that Jesus was divine and was the MESSIAH predicted in the TANAKH, the Hebrew Bible. Nachmonides was able to control the conflict by showing that Judaism placed significantly less emphasis on the messianic notion. He later wrote that King James rewarded him with 300 gold coins for his debating skill; nevertheless, he was pressured to leave SPAIN for PALESTINE soon after the disputation concluded.

The third disputation was held in Tortosa from 1413 to 1415. This time the disputants were the

Christian Gerónimo de Santa Fe and Rabbi Astruk Halevi, Rabbi Joseph Albo, and other Jewish scholars, including a descendant of Nachmonides. Rabbi Albo's views on Christianity became the foundation for his later work *Sefer Ha-Ikkarim.* The Tortosa disputations lasted 20 months, fanning anti-Jewish sentiment that forced many Jews to convert (*see* ANTI-JUDAISM).

Further reading: Jane S. Gerber, *The Jews of Spain: A History of the Sephardic Experience* (New York: The Free Press, 1992); Hyam Maccoby, ed. *Judaism on Trial: Jewish Christian Disputations in the Middle Ages* (Portland, Ore.: Vallentine Mitchell, 1993).

Disraeli, Benjamin (1804–1881) *British prime minister*

Born in London on December 21, 1804, Benjamin Disraeli was the son of a scholar of history and literature. His father, Isaac Disraeli, had his son privately educated and then trained as a solicitor. Born Jewish, Benjamin Disraeli is considered to be Britain's first Jewish prime minister, although he was a practicing Anglican, having been baptized by his father at age 13 following the death of Isaac Disraeli's father. Isaac had never been attached to Judaism, and Benjamin himself viewed Christianity as the highest development of Judaism. His baptism allowed him to serve in the British parliament early in his career, though practicing Jews were forbidden to do so until 1858. In 1839 he married Wyndham Lewis, a wealthy widow. Though never a practicing Jew, Disraeli's membership in an often despised minority group influenced his politics throughout his life. He occasionally acknowledged his membership among the Jewish people, especially in response to antisemitic taunts.

Disraeli, like his father, was a scholar of literature, and he published several novels: *Vivian Grey* (1826), *The Young Duke* (1831), *Contarini Fleming* (1832), *Alroy* (1833), *Henrietta Temple* (1837), and *Venetia* (1837). These novels reflect Disraeli's personal ambition and his desire to be a "great man." In the early 1830s Disraeli took an interest in pol-

itics, and in 1837 he was elected to the House of Commons. Disraeli became a progressive Tory, very sympathetic to the rights of laborers. In 1842 Disraeli helped to create the Young England group, which held the political aim of aligning the aristocracy and the working class. He wanted the aristocracy to use its economic and political power to help protect the poor; his novels *Coningsby* (1844), *Sybil* (1845), and *Tancred* (1847) reflected this consistent Disraeli theme.

Disraeli continued to climb in stature and position in Parliament. In 1867 he proposed and managed to pass a new Reform Act that gave the right to vote to all male adult householders living in a borough constituency. This politically empowered 1.5 million new voters. The Reform Act also redrew the constituencies and boroughs, in a way that helped Disraeli become prime minister for a brief period in 1868, until the liberals regained control after a new general election. Disraeli led the Conservative Party in opposition for six years. In 1874 he led the Tories to their first General Election victory in over 36 years.

During his tenure as prime minister, Disraeli managed to pass many social reforms, including the Artisans Dwellings Act (1875), the Public Health Act (1875), the Pure Food and Drugs Act (1875), the Climbing Boys Act (1875), and the Education Act (1876). He also succeeded in passing measures to protect workers and improve the legal status of trade unions.

When the Liberals defeated the Conservatives in 1880, Disraeli was replaced as prime minister by William Gladstone. Disraeli retired to continue publishing novels, but after *Endymion* appeared in 1880, he took ill, dying on April 19, 1881.

Further reading: Bernard Glassman, *Benjamin Disraeli: The Fabricated Jew in Myth and Memory* (Lanham, Md.: Rowman & Littlefield, 2003); B. R. Jerman, *The Young Disraeli* (Princeton, N.J.: Princeton University Press, 1960); Paul Smith, *Disraeli: A Brief Life* (Cambridge: Cambridge University Press, 1999); M. G. Wiebe, Mary S. Millar, and Ann P. Robson, *Benjamin Disraeli Letters: 1852–1856* (Toronto: University of Toronto Press, 1998).

divination

The word *divination* means the attempt to predict, or divine, the future by consulting spirits or the souls of departed people, or by any other occult means. The practice is explicitly prohibited in the TORAH and RABBINIC LAW. Deuteronomy reads (18:10–12): "There shall not be found among you one that uses divination, a soothsayer, or an enchanter, or a sorcerer, or a charmer, or one that consults a ghost or a familiar spirit, or a necromancer. For whosoever does these things is an abomination unto God." Several different pagan methods for divining are mentioned in the TANAKH, the Hebrew Bible. These include using a goblet, using arrows, inspection of a liver, and astrology.

MAIMONIDES lists the prohibition against divination as the 31st negative commandment in his work *The 613 Commandments* (see MITZVAH). Rabbinic dogma prohibits divination, in the belief that the false actions of those who practice divination may lead the religious person away from God. However, even Maimonides permits the use of the Hebrew Bible to predict the future, a practice that seems to fall into the category of divination.

Further reading: Cristiano Grottanelli, *Kings & Prophets: Monarchic Power, Inspired Leadership, & Sacred Text in Biblical Narrative* (New York: Oxford University Press, 1999); Ronald H. Isaacs, *Divination, Magic, and Healing: The Book of Jewish Folklore* (Northvale, N.J.: Jason Aronson, 1998); Michael D. Swartz, *Scholastic Magic* (Princeton, N.J.: Princeton University Press, 1996); Joshua Trachtenberg, *Jewish Magic and Superstition: A Study in Folk Religion* (Philadelphia: University of Pennsylvania Press, 2004).

divorce

Judaism has recognized the concept of divorce for thousands of years. While considering divorce a disappointment, the ancient RABBIS maintained that it was better for a couple to divorce than to remain together in a state of constant bitterness and strife.

While divorce is an acceptable way to end a MARRIAGE, Jewish law discourages it through numerous and complex procedural details, as well as financial burdens in the form of alimony and child support. On the other hand, there are cases where divorce is ritually required, as when there has been a violation of marital fidelity.

Under traditional Jewish law, a man need not provide a reason to divorce his wife. However, Jewish society frowned upon divorces executed without merit. According to the TORAH, divorce is accomplished simply by writing a bill of divorce called a GET, handing it to the wife, and sending her away. The rabbis instituted rules regarding the process: writing the document, delivery, and obtaining the wife's acceptance. An entire tractate of the TALMUD is dedicated to this subject.

Civil divorce is not sufficient to dissolve a Jewish marriage. The husband must also give his ex-wife a *get*. If a husband refuses to give a get to his wife, the BET DIN (rabbinic court) is empowered to fine him and/or excommunicate him. Excommunication was a far more powerful tool in earlier historical periods, when a man depended almost exclusively on the Jewish community for his livelihood and his ability to pray to God, than it is now. In ancient times a man who refused the *bet din's* order to grant a divorce would be flogged until he relented. In Israel today, men are sometimes imprisoned if they do not provide their ex-wife with a *get*.

Yet there are still many women who live in our modern world as AGUNAHs, or "chained women." A woman finds herself in that status if she has obtained a civil divorce or her husband has left her, but her husband is either unwilling or unable to give her a *get* to complete the religious divorce. She is recognized as divorced by the civil authorities, but she is not able to marry again in a religious ceremony.

In the case of a husband missing in action during a war, a woman is considered an *agunah* until his body is found. Many women and Jewish courts have tried to find ways of helping to free *agunahs*, but there is still no overall solution. However, sometimes men going to war may leave a *get* for use if they do not return.

In liberal Judaism, rabbis may sometimes annul a marriage if the husband refuses to give his wife a *get*. They often use what is known as the "Lieberman Clause" in the KETUBAH (wedding contract), a prenuptial agreement that grants a *get* automatically if there is a civil divorce. Those who do not subscribe to the use of 20th-century conservative rabbi Saul LIEBERMAN's (1898–1983) solution rely on a Talmudic dictate that "all betrothals receive the approval of the rabbis, and therefore the rabbis have the power to rescind their approval."

Further reading: Irving A. Breitowitz, *The Plight of the Agunah in American Society* (Westport, Conn.: Greenwood Press, 1993); *Celebration & Renewal: Rites of Passage in Judaism* (Philadelphia: Jewish Publication Society, 1993); Blu Greenberg, *On Women and Judaism: A View from Tradition* (Philadelphia: Jewish Publication Society, 1998).

Doctorow, E. L. (b. 1931) *novelist*

Edgar Laurence Doctorow was born in New York City on January 6, 1931, to Russian-Jewish parents who were liberal intellectuals and political idealists. He was named after the renowned American writer Edgar Allan Poe.

Doctorow attended the Bronx High School of Science and Kenyon College. He did graduate work at Columbia University before joining the U.S. Army and serving in GERMANY. Doctorow holds the Glucksman Chair in American Letters at New York University. He has taught at the Yale University Drama School, Princeton University, Sarah Lawrence College, and the University of California, Irvine.

During his career he has held many positions, including editor-in-chief of a newspaper, but he is best known for his forte—historical novels, which blend historical fact with fictional characters. His first novel, *Welcome to Hard Times* (1960), was set in the 19th century. One of his best-known works, *The Book of Daniel* (1971) was based on the Rosenbergs, who conveyed American nuclear secrets to the Soviet Union during the cold war. The couple was tried, found guilty, and executed. Doctorow portrays an America gripped with cold war hysteria, and highlights latent, but sometimes blatant, anti-Jewish and anti-black attitudes that sometimes complicated American fears about communism. *The Book of Daniel* was turned into a movie called *Daniel* nearly a decade after publication.

Doctorow's other novels include *Ragtime* (1975), set in pre–World War I America and later transformed into a hit Broadway musical and movie; *Loon Lake* (1980), set during the Great Depression; *World's Fair* (1985), a semiautobiographical work set in the Bronx, New York, of the 1930s; *Billy Bathgate* (1989), about the gangsters of the Prohibition era; *The Waterworks* (1994), set in 1870s New York; and *City of God* (2000), which explored ideas about faith at the end of the 20th century. Doctorow has also published nonfiction essays, collected in *Reporting the Universe* (2003).

Doctorow has received many awards for his work, including the National Book Award, two National Book Critics Circle Awards, the PEN/Faulkner Award, the Edith Wharton Citation for Fiction, the William Dean Howell Medal of the American Academy of Arts and Letters, and the presidentially conferred National Humanities Medal. Doctorow and his wife have three children.

Further reading: E. L. Doctorow, *Ragtime* (New York: Plume Books, 1997); Desmond F. McCarthy, *Reconstructing the Family in Contemporary American Fiction* (New York: Peter Lang Publishing, 1997); John Williams, *Fiction as False Document: The Reception of E. L. Doctorow in the Postmodern Age* (Rochester, N.Y.: Camden House, 1996).

Dov Baer of Lubavitch (1773–1827)
Hasidic rebbe

Rebbe Dov Baer of Lubavitch was the successor to his father, Shneur Zalman of Liady, one of the founders of HASIDISM. His leadership helped to establish the CHABAD stream, perhaps the most influential group within Hasidim. He gave the movement its more familiar name, Lubavitch, by settling in that town in RUSSIA.

Dov Baer was a mystic, but also a very strong organizer, who successfully encouraged his followers to engage in farming while saving enough time for proper TORAH study. Dov Baer expanded upon his father's intellectual work, writing the well-known tracts *On Contemplation* and *On Ecstasy.* The latter is held in especially high regard. In it, Dov Baer explores the history of Jewish spirituality, and creates a template by which to mystically but rationally pursue God. He also warns against charlatans who joined the Hasidic movement for mere pleasure and as an excuse to drink alcoholic beverages, which Lubavitch Hasidim used to help enhance spirituality.

Dov Baer embraced the teachings of the KABBALAH, but tried to approach them through rational study. Many other Hasidic groups ridiculed this approach; they approached mysticism as a belief and practice, not as an intellectual exercise.

Upon his death, the leadership of Chabad passed to Dov Baer's son-in-law and nephew, Manachem Mendel of Lubavitch (1787–1866).

Further reading: Karen Armstrong, *A History of God: The 4,000-Year Quest of Judaism, Christianity and Islam* (New York: Ballantine Books, 1994); Naftali Lowenthal, *Communicating the Infinite: The Emergence of the Habad School* (Chicago: University of Chicago Press, 1990); Zalman Schachter Shalomi and Nataniel M. Miles-Yepez, eds., *Wrapped in a Holy Flame: Teachings and Tales of the Hasidic Masters* (San Francisco: Jossey-Bass, 2003); Dov Baer, Schneersohn, *On Ecstasy: A Tract,* trans. by Louis Jacobs (Chappagua, N.Y.: Rossel Books, 1983).

drash

Rabbinic tradition provides for several different ways of interpreting the text of the TORAH and the ancient commentaries. Rabbi Bachya ben Asher (1255–1340) popularized a fourfold categorization of these methods, which he called by the Hebrew word *pardes* ("orchard"). The word is an acronym for PSHAT, the simple, direct meaning of the text;

remez, philosophical interpretation; *drash,* homiletical treatment; and *sod,* mystical probing.

While *pshat* is relatively straightforward, *drash* requires more of an interpretative perspective. The reader must ask: what was the meaning the rabbis derived from the text over time? What is the deeper meaning of the text? What practical or moral lessons can we derive from it? *Drash* was of paramount importance in the rabbinic study of the Torah and its implications for Jewish life. The ORAL LAW, comprising the MISHNAH and the TALMUD, is grounded on the method of drash.

One can "do *drash*" by explaining inconsistencies or blanks in the text, thereby creating MIDRASH, detailed stories or interpretations of biblical texts. Thus the term *drash* serves as a verb to the noun *midrash* (they come from the same Hebrew root).

Most midrash is rabbinic by nature; the ancient rabbis spent their lives providing explanations for questions, practical or not, that might arise from the study of the TANAKH, the Hebrew Bible. Some of their explanations became so widely known that amateur Bible scholars often take *midrashim* to be quotes from the Torah itself.

For example, Genesis, the first book of the Tanakh, says little about Terach, Abraham's father, or about Abraham's path toward MONOTHEISM. The rabbis fill in the details. They tell us that Terach owned an idol shop; one day the child Abraham smashed most of the idols and mischievously placed a big stick in the hands of the largest one. When told that one idol had destroyed the others, Terach angrily denied that idols could move, thereby confirming his son's growing skepticism and undermining idol worship for all time.

Further reading: Bachya Asher and Eliyahu Munk, *Torah Commentary: Midrash Rabbeinu Bachya* (Philadelphia: Coronet Books, 2003); H. Freedman and Maurice Simon, eds., *Soncino Midrash Rabbah* (CD-ROM), 3rd ed. (Brooklyn, N.Y.: Soncino Press, 1983); David F. Sandmel, *Irreconcilable Differences?: A Learning Resource for Jews and Christians* (Boulder, Colo.: Westview Press, 2001); Howard Schwartz, *Reimagining the Bible: The Storytelling of the Rabbis* (New York: Oxford University Press, 1998).

This wooden spinning top is called a dreidel. Each of its four sides is inscribed with a Hebrew letter that begins one of the Hebrew words in the saying "A great miracle happened there." In Israel, the saying is "A great miracle happened here." The game is played during the festival of Chanukah, and the miracle refers to the last bit of oil found in the desecrated Temple when the ancient Maccabees took it back in battle. The oil was only enough to last one day, but it lasted eight. Thus, the dreidel reminds us of the miracle of Chanukah. *(Getty Images)*

dreidel

A dreidel is a spinning top used to play a children's game during the festival of CHANUKAH. Each of its four sides contains a HEBREW letter. In ISRAEL, the four letters are nun, gimel, he, and pe, standing for the four words *nes gadol haya poh,* or "A great miracle happened here." Outside Israel, the fourth letter is a shin for *sham,* "there," meaning ERETZ YISRAEL. The miracle of Chanukah is variously interpreted as the military victory of a small band of Jewish pietists against a large Seleucid army, and/or that a small cruse with only enough oil to last one night lasted eight nights.

According to legend, during the Hellenistic persecutions of the Jews that led to the revolt commemorated by Chanukah, Jews were not allowed to study TORAH. When a raid would occur, the Jews would pretend to be gambling—another fact relating the game of dreidel to Chanukah.

The rules of the most traditional dreidel game played today are as follows: each participant antes a set number of coins, usually chocolate gelt (money). If the dreidel lands on nun, nothing happens; if it lands on gimel, the player takes the whole pot of coins; if it lands on he, the player receives half the pot; and if it lands on shin, the player adds a set number of coins to the pot. The varying rules are limited only by imagination.

Further reading: Ronald H. Isaacs, *Every Person's Guide to Hanukkah* (Northvale, N.J.: Jason Aronson, 2000); Jeffrey A. O'Hare, *Hanukkah, Festival of Lights: Celebrate with Songs, Decorations, Food Games, Prayers, and Traditions* (Honesdale, Pa.: Boyds Mills Press, 2000); Noam Zion and Barbara Spectre, *A Different Light: The Hanukkah Book of Celebration* (New York: Pitspopany Press, 2000).

Dreyfus Affair

In 1894, after FRANCE's defeat at the hands of Prussia, Alfred Dreyfus (1859–1935), an assimilated Jewish captain in the French military, was tried for selling military secrets to GERMANY. Found guilty based on forged evidence, he was sentenced to imprisonment at Devil's Island, a French penal colony off the coast of Guiana. An 1899 retrial freed Dreyfus with a pardon, and he was completely exonerated in 1906. However, the prolonged case provoked bitter political struggles in France, and fed both ANTISEMITISM and Jewish support for ZIONISM as the only hope for European Jewry.

During the trial antisemitic riots broke out in many French cities. French leaders knew that Dreyfus was innocent; he was being used as a scapegoat for France's military defeat.

The Dreyfus Affair shocked the world Jewish community. Modern Jews could hardly believe that France, the home of the ENLIGHTENMENT, would act in such an obviously antisemitic manner. Many Jews realized that even assimilation would not make them immune from latent antisemitic attitudes. French Jews even began to question their security, prompting some to turn toward the nascent Zionist movement, and others to push toward further ASSIMILATION into non-Jewish French culture. Theodor HERZL covered the trial as a newspaper reporter. The blatant antisemitism unveiled during the trial prompted the previously assimilationist Jew to become the founder of the modern political Zionist movement, and thereby the prophet of the State of ISRAEL.

Further reading: Guy Chapman, *The Dreyfus Case: A Reassessment* (New York: Reynal, 1955); Michael A. Meyer, *Response to Modernity: A History of the Reform Movement in Judaism* (New York and Oxford: Oxford University Press, 1988); Jeremy D. Popkin, *A History of Modern France* (Upper Saddle River, N.J.: Prentice Hall, 2001 (1994).

Dubinsky, David (1892–1982) *union leader*

David Dubinsky was born in 1892 in Brest-Litovsk, RUSSIA the sixth and youngest child of a poor Jewish family. As a 14-year-old working in his father's bakery, Dubinsky joined a union of bakers affiliated with the General Jewish Workers' Union, the BUND. His labor activism led to several years in jail while the Russians waited for him to be old enough to do hard labor in Siberia. A few years later, when the authorities began the process, he charmed his way out of jail and in 1911 made his way to the UNITED STATES. There he became a cloak cutter and joined the International Ladies Garment Workers Union (ILGWU). Some of Dubinsky's relatives urged him to go into medicine and become a doctor, but he felt his calling to change the world. And change it he did.

Dubinsky rose through the union ranks, serving as president from 1932 until his retirement in 1966. Early in his presidency he oversaw a significant increase in membership for his union. Dubinsky

wanted younger people in leadership in order to attract younger American-born workers. He considered foreign-born organizers and leaders to be dinosaurs, and he ousted many notable labor leaders, like Fania Cohn. Dubinsky became a major leader in the American Federation of Labor (AFL) and the Congress of Industrial Organizations (CIO), both as separate entities and after they merged in 1955.

Dubinsky was effective at ridding the unions of corrupt leaders, and he helped to draw up the anti-racket codes adopted by the AFL-CIO in 1957. He was anticommunist, and he led the unions to a moderate political position, supportive of the labor policies of President Franklin Delano Roosevelt. After Dubinsky's retirement, a $1 million Dubinsky Foundation was established in his honor by the labor unions he had worked with. Dubinsky himself sums up his contribution to the world: "Yes, we were dreamers when we advocated legislation for unemployment insurance, for social security, for minimum wages. They laughed at our crazy ideas. Although we have not reached perfection, many of our 'wild dreams' have now become realities of everyday life."

Further reading: Max Danish, *The World of David Dubinsky* (Cleveland and New York: World Publishing Co., 1957); David Dubinsky and A. H. Raskin, *David Dubinsky: A Life with Labor* (New York: Simon and Schuster, 1997); Gus Tyler, *Look for the Union Label: A History of the International Ladies' Garment Workers' Union* (Armonk, N.Y.: M. E. Sharpe, 1995); Gus Tyler, "David Dubinsky: A Life with Social Signficance," *Monthly Labor Review* 117, 10 (1994).

Dubnow, Simon (1860–1941) *historian*

Simon Dubnow, a self-taught scholar, was one of the founders of modern Jewish history.

Dubnow's Jewish heritage made it impossible for him to obtain a teaching position in a university in RUSSIA, so he dedicated his life to independent scholar ship and teaching. He wrote several studies of Jewish life in Russia and

POLAND, but his greatest achievement was a 10-volume work on the entirety of Jewish history. This monumental opus was published first in German, and then in Russian and HEBREW. Dubnow's work is considered seminal to the contemporary study of Jewish history.

Dubnow was concerned with the future of the Jewish people. He maintained that the Jews had survived as a people by establishing a system of law and a way of life that allowed them to keep themselves apart while living in foreign lands. They could only continue to survive, he believed, if they developed new centers of spiritual strength. He disagreed with the view of contemporary ZIONISM that Jewish life could only endure in a Jewish homeland.

Dubnow preached "Jewish autonomism": A viable Jewish life was still possible in the DIASPORA if Jews continued to maintain a measure of self-rule through community organization, and kept up support for educational and mutual-assistance institutions. In other words, the Jews could thrive in the Diaspora so long as they sustained the "spiritual nationhood" of Jewry.

Dubnow's ideas for a flourishing Diaspora Jewish community were borne out in North America; however, his ideas of autonomism could not survive in Russia after the rise of the Soviet Union, or anywhere in Europe with the advent of Nazism and the massive slaughter of European Jewry during the HOLOCAUST. On December 8, 1941, the Nazis murdered the 81-year-old scholar for being a Jew.

Further reading: Sophie Dubnov-Erlich, *Life and Work of S. M. Dubnov: Diaspora Nationalism and Jewish History*, ed. Jeffrey Shandler (Bloomington: Indiana University Press, 1991); Simon M. Dubnow, *History of the Jews in Russia and Poland, from the Earliest Times until the Present Day*, vols. 1–3 (Philadelphia: Jewish Publication Society of America, 1916); David H. Weinberg, *Between Tradition and Modernity: Haim Zhitlowski, Simon Dubnow, Ahad HaAm, and the Shaping of Modern Jewish Identity* (New York: Holmes & Meier Publishers, 1996).

dvar Torah (pl.: *divrei Torah*)

Dvar Torah, literally "TORAH word or matter," is the common term used for any discourse on a Torah topic, from a brief comment to an extended sermon.

Any individual who has studied a particular Jewish text may share a *dvar Torah* with others in order to further everyone's learning of the TANAKH, the Hebrew bible. To deliver *divrei Torah* is considered one of the most important functions of rabbis. They are carefully trained as to how to study and explicate the text on a scholarly level, and how to explain it at whatever level a particular student or group might best understand.

Any Jew, student or adult, can and often does give *divrei Torah*, in schools, SYNAGOGUES, or other Jewish settings, in part as a way to motivate them to learn more. It is commonplace at meals or gatherings in more observant communities for the host to ask a guest to enrich the event with words of Torah. JEWISH YOUTH GROUPS also use this technique to empower their members, as does the JEWISH DAY SCHOOL MOVEMENT. The fact that any Jew is entitled to read the text and derive meanings from it makes the *dvar Torah* an important feature of Jewish life.

Further reading: Irving Greenberg, *The Jewish Way: Living the Holidays* (New York and London: Simon & Schuster, 1988); Daniel B. Kohn, *Practical Pedagogy for the Jewish Classroom: Classroom Management, Instruction, and Curriculum Development* (Westport, Conn.: Greenwood Press, 1999).

dybbuk

In Jewish lore a dybbuk is an evil spirit. Such spirits were commonly referred to in early Jewish literature, but among 17th-century Polish and German Jews the word acquired a more specific meaning; a dybbuk was an evil spirit who possessed an individual's body. Jewish literature of the period also contains many stories of people possessed by the spirit of a dead person, the spirit being the dybbuk.

The word *dybbuk* comes from the HEBREW root *davak,* which means "to cleave." The dybbuk or evil spirit would cleave to the body. The mystical literature of the KABBALAH describes how evil spirits can make the possessed individual commit sins. The dybbuk originally gained entry through illness, or because of a secret sin the possessed person committed. Some stories portray dybbuks as souls with unfinished business in this world.

The mystics created an exorcism ceremony by means of which a holy man could order a dybbuk to leave the body it was possessing. In more modern times, the term *dybbuk* is often used ironically, for instance to describe a child's poor behavior.

The subject of dybbuks was popularized once again in the 20th century, thanks to S. Ansky's play, *The Dybbuk.* Written in Yiddish in 1912–19, it was originally called *Tsvishn Tsvey Veltn* (Between two worlds) and performed by the Vilna troupe in 1920. The play was translated into Russian, and then into modern HEBREW by the great poet Chaim Nachman BIALIK. Bialik combined elements of the different Yiddish and Russian versions, and incorporated echoes and idiomatic expressions from his own Hebrew poetry. Many credit Bialik with significantly improving the play; it became a standard in the Israeli theater repertoire, the celebrated classic of the Habimah theater company of Israel.

The play has been performed in numerous productions in several languages. A movie version filmed in Poland in the 1930s is considered one of the finest Yiddish films ever made.

Further reading: Howard Schwartz, *Reimagining the Bible: The Storytelling of the Rabbis* (New York: Oxford University Press, 1998); Shmuel Werses, "S. An-ski's 'Between Two Worlds' (The Dybbuk): A Textual History," in *Studies in Yiddish Literature and Folklore* (Jerusalem: Hebrew University of Jerusalem, 1986); Gershon Winkler, *Dybbuk* (Brooklyn, N.Y.: Judaica Press, 1981).

E

Eban, Abba (1915–2002) *Israeli political leader*

Abba Eban was born in Cape Town, SOUTH AFRICA in 1915 to Lithuanian Jewish parents. Born as Aubrey Eban, he was raised in London, receiving a classical education at St. Olave's School while obtaining his Jewish education from his grandfather on the weekends. Eban became a world-renowned diplomat, who was able to balance his fervent love for ISRAEL with an ability to see the need for compromise with his country's Arab neighbors, specifically with the Palestinians (*see* ARAB-ISRAELI CONFLICT; PALESTINE).

Eban's personal history was eclectic, though most of his life was consistently dedicated to ZIONISM. He worked with Chaim WEIZMANN at the Zionist headquarters in London before joining the British military as an intelligence officer. After the birth of the State of Israel in 1948, Eban became active in Israeli politics, serving in a variety of national posts in the government, including representative to the UNITED NATIONS in the crucial year 1949. He was foreign minister from 1966–74, serving during both the SIX-DAY WAR (1967) and the YOM KIPPUR WAR (1973). He was forced to resign as foreign minister in 1974 when Yitzhak RABIN became prime minister, but he continued to serve as a member of the KNESSET until 1988. As a

politician Eban worked to secure relations with the United States and the European countries.

Eban wrote several books, including *Personal Witness: Israel Through My Eyes* (1992). He also authored a popular history of the Jews for schoolchildren, often utilized in supplementary religious schools across the UNITED STATES, entitled *My People*. Eban's collections of books and other media have been made available to the public at the Abba Eban Centre for Israeli Diplomacy, housed within the Truman Institute in Jerusalem, Israel. This center speaks to Eban's belief that diplomacy was the way to ensure the survival of the State of Israel.

Further reading: David Bamberger and Abba Eban, *My People: Abba Eban's History of the Jews* (Springfield, N.J.: Behrman House, 1996); Abba Eban, *Abba Eban: An Autobiography* (New York: Random House, 1977); ———, *Personal Witness: Israel Through My Eyes* (Putnam, 1992); ———, *Diplomacy for the Next Century* (New Haven, Conn.: Yale University Press, 1998); Rafael Medoff, *Abba Eban Reconsidered* (Montreal: Dawn Publishing Company Ltd., 1985).

egalitarianism

In the Jewish context, especially in liberal Judaism, egalitarianism usually implies the active removal of ritual inequalities between men and women. Egalitarianism can also refer to the inclusion of traditionally marginalized groups, such as women and homosexuals, in ritual practice. It also reflects equality among all members of a community.

Reform Judaism quickly embraced egalitarianism in the late 1960s and early 1970s. In 1972 HEBREW UNION COLLEGE (HUC) ordained Sally PRIESAND as its first female RABBI, removing the last important gender difference between Reform Jewish men and women.

The Reconstructionist Rabbinical College in Philadelphia (*see* RECONSTRUCTIONIST JUDAISM) soon followed the example of HUC, but CONSERVATIVE JUDAISM did not ordain a woman rabbi until 1983. The decision was highly controversial; it provoked some of the more conservative leaders of the movement to leave Conservative Judaism for a MODERN ORTHODOX setting.

Today, half of the students being trained for the clergy in the seminaries of liberal Judaism are women. Outside of Orthodox Judaism, synagogues in the UNITED STATES provide full opportunities for women to participate equally in all aspects of ritual, religious, and educational programming, and to take leadership roles in the community. Women read TORAH and *HAFTARAH* portions, receive aliyot (*see* ALIYAH), lead public PRAYER, can be counted as one of the 10 people required for a MINYAN, and serve as *gabbai*, the person who ensures the correct chanting of the texts during services.

This equal access did not come overnight. For many years, some synagogues allowed women to chant Torah and *haftarah* but did not count them in a minyan or allow them to lead prayer services. Such congregations sometimes called themselves Torah Egalitarian, since they were egalitarian during the Torah service only.

Some liberal synagogues practice what they call Traditional Egalitarianism. Men in these congregations are required to observe all ritual requirements, while women have the option to assume the rituals they wish to perform. This may include wearing a *KIPPAH* (head covering) or *TALLIT*

(prayer shawl), ritual garments usually worn by men. Many liberal rabbis consider this policy to be a concession to those who did not grow up with egalitarian practices and to women who simply do not feel comfortable with the new roles. They may require children to follow these egalitarian practices, in order to acculturate them to these egalitarian norms.

Jewish egalitarianism has also extended to the liturgy in many liberal synagogues. English-language prayers that use masculine pronouns to refer to God are almost always modified to be gender-neutral. In HEBREW, the AMIDAH prayer is altered to include the MATRIARCHS as well as the PATRIARCHS.

Liberal synagogues often make a conscious effort to engage both male and female scholars and teachers, to accustom children to see adults of both sexes in a variety of nurturing and leadership roles.

Further reading: Rachel Adler, *Engendering Judaism: An Inclusive Theology and Ethics* (Philadelphia: Jewish Publication Society, 1998); Beryl Lieff Benderly and Hasia R. Diner, *Her Worlds Praise Her: A History of Jewish Women in America from Colonial Times to the Present* (New York: Basic Books, 2002); Jack Wertheimer, *A People Divided: Judaism in Contemporary America* (New York: Basic Books, 1993).

Egypt

A country in Northeast Africa bordering the Mediterranean Sea. Some of the most important events in ancient Jewish history took place in Egypt.

Many scholars believe that the EXODUS of the ISRAELITES from Egypt described in the TANAKH, the Hebrew Bible, took place during the reign of Ramses II, sometime between 1290 and 1223 B.C.E. Though the liberation from Egyptian SLAVERY was a key factor in the self-definition of the Jews, the subsequent relationship between ISRAEL and Egypt was not entirely negative. It is said that King SOLOMON married a princess of Egypt. During the first EXILE, a DIASPORA community emerged there, and the remains of a Jewish military colony have been uncovered in ELEPHANTINE in the south. After Alexander the Great conquered Egypt in 333 B.C.E. many Jews migrated to Alexandria, the new capital, and a strong Hellenistic Jewish community grew up there (*see* HELLENISM). Evidence of ancient Jewish synagogues in Egypt has been found dating back to the third century B.C.E. The Jewish population may have reached 1 million. The huge size of the community sometimes provoked a certain amount of violent ANTI-JUDAISM. Yet conditions for the Jews in Egypt were relatively good, at least until the rise to power of CHRISTIANITY in the Roman Empire, when strong anti-Jewish sentiments made Jewish life more precarious.

Under early Muslim rule the Jewish community, centered in Cairo, began to accommodate to its Arab surroundings. Apart from a period of persecution under Caliph Hakim between 996 and 1021 C.E., conditions for the Egyptian Jewish community were generally favorable. The Jews maintained ties with the rabbinic academies in Babylonia, and the sage Saadiah Gaon received much of his rich Jewish education in Egypt. When the Fatimid dynasty took power in 969, the situation of the Jews improved even more. The Fatimids were liberal toward religious minority groups. Egyptian Jews prospered as new opportunities for industry and commerce emerged, thanks to the unification of almost all of North Africa, Syria, and Palestine. The Fatimid rulers allowed

Ezer Weizman (center), seventh president of Israel (1993–2000), makes an official visit to Egypt. To his right is Egyptian president Hosni Mubarak. Weizman was known for his charm and dedication to the peace process. *(Avi Ohayan, Government Press Office, The State of Israel)*

the Jews to rebuild some of their synagogues as well. Even after the Fatimid dynasty was replaced, the Egyptian Jewish community prospered. Fleeing persecution in SPAIN, for example, Moses MAIMONIDES settled in Egypt around 1165 C.E. It was not until the middle of the 13th century, when the Mamluks came to power, that the Egyptian Jewish community experienced significant persecution, though such persecution was not limited to Jews.

In 1517 Egypt was conquered by the Ottoman Turks and the condition of the Egyptian Jewish community improved dramatically for a while, although in 1545 the central synagogue in Cairo was closed by order of the governor, remaining closed until 1584. Many Jews held important positions as financial administrators under the Ottomans. However, as the Ottoman Empire declined, so too did the status of Egyptian Jewry. Its members became impoverished, victims of the high levels of corruption that were endemic in a declining power.

During this time, the Jews of Cairo and Alexandria fell into three different groups: Arabic-speaking Jews, Spanish immigrants, and settlers from other areas of North Africa. The Turkish government became tyrannical during the 17th and 18th centuries; wealthier Jews suffered the most, as they were employed and exploited by governors and ministers. The rich, long-established Jewish culture declined as well.

The fate of the Egyptian Jewish community paralleled the social and economic conditions of the country as a whole. When Egypt became an autonomous state in the 19th century, the Jews at first felt some pains of transition, but prosperity and commerce returned with the opening of the Suez Canal. Jews from Europe settled in Cairo and Alexandria, opening modern schools and maintaining good relations with their Arab neighbors, apart from a few cases of BLOOD LIBEL in Cairo in 1844, 1881, 1901, and 1902. Some SEPHARDIM from elsewhere in the Middle East migrated to Egypt after World War I.

There were approximately 60,000 Jews in Egypt in 1917, half of them in Cairo, and 64,000 by 1937, split between Cairo and Alexandria. In 1915 a Jew became a member of Egypt's parliament, and another was a member of the Senate in the 1930s. Zionist organizations appeared in Egypt in the late 19th century, and the Egyptian Jewish community developed ties with the large number of Palestinian Jews who fled to Egypt during World War I.

The first anti-Jewish disturbance in modern Egypt occurred in 1945, when a synagogue, a hospital, and an old-age home were burned down by the "Young Egypt" group led by Ahmad Husayn. Intermittent violence directed at the Jewish quarters was an ominous sign for the future. In 1947 Egypt instituted the Companies' Law, stating that at least 75 percent of a company's employees must be Egyptian citizens. Since only 20 percent of the Egyptian Jews were citizens, the law marked the end of prosperity for the Egyptian Jews. Persecution began in earnest after the birth of the state of ISRAEL in 1948. Hundreds of Jews were arrested, property was confiscated, bombs were planted in Jewish neighborhoods, and Jewish businesses were looted. Conditions improved slightly with a change in government in 1950, but when dictator Gamal Nasser seized power, conditions once more worsened.

Many Jews left Egypt after each of the wars with Israel, in 1948, 1956, and 1967. Some were encouraged to emigrate after being imprisoned. Some 35,000 immigrated to Israel, 10,000 to FRANCE, 9,000 to the UNITED STATES, 9,000 to ARGENTINA, and 4,000 to ENGLAND. Approximately 400 Jews, mostly elderly, remained in Egypt after 1967, served by only one synagogue in Cairo and one in Alexandria.

It was not until 1979 that the remnant of a once vibrant Egyptian Jewish community was able to reestablish ties with Israel and world Jewry. In 1978 Egyptian president Anwar SADAT and Israeli prime minister Menachem BEGIN signed a peace treaty establishing peaceful relations between their two countries. Israel returned the Sinai peninsula, and the two countries have not been at war since. Israel maintains an embassy in Cairo and a consulate general in Alexandria. The small Jewish community is allowed to practice Judaism freely. In more recent years, however, ANTISEMITISM has become common in the government-controlled press, especially after the start of the two INTIFADAS and the continuing violence between Israelis and Palestinians. There have not been any reports of antisemitic incidents against the 100 Jews remaining in Egypt.

Further reading: Elias J. Bickerman, *The Jews in the Greek Age* (Cambridge, Mass., and London: Harvard University Press, 1988); Benjamin Braude and Bernard Lewis, eds., *Christians and Jews in the Ottoman Empire: The Functioning of a Plural Society* (New York: Homes & Meier Publishers, 1982); Joseph Meleze Modrzeiewski, *From Rameses II to Emperor Hadrian* (Philadelphia: Jewish Publication Society, 1995); Norman A. Stillman, *The Jews of Arab Lands: A History and Source Book* (Philadelphia: The Jewish Publication Society of America, 1979).

Eichmann, Adolf (1906–1962) *Nazi leader in charge of the Holocaust*

Adolf Eichmann was the architect responsible for planning and implementing the HOLOCAUST, the Nazi "FINAL SOLUTION" that tried to exterminate all of European Jewry. Eichmann was executed in Israel in 1962, after having been prosecuted and found guilty of war crimes in an Israeli court.

Adolf Eichmann was born in Solingen, GERMANY on March 19, 1906, but he grew up in AUSTRIA. Before joining the Austrian Nazi Party in 1932, Eichmann studied engineering. Instead of completing the engineering program, Eichmann attempted to work for his father's mining company and then as a salesman. But only after joining the Nazis did he find success.

In September 1934, Eichmann took a position in Himmler's Security Service (SD), and he demonstrated a keen ability at managing the organizational needs of the growing SS bureaucracy. In 1935, Eichmann became responsible for the Jewish section of the SD, and he subsequently studied both HEBREW and YIDDISH. He visited PALESTINE to

discuss the idea of large-scale Jewish emigration with Arabs leaders in the region. From August 1938, he was given responsibility for the forced emigration of Jews from Nazi-controlled land. In 18 months, he expelled about 150,000 of them. His expertise in Jewish relocation provided the template for the assembly and deportation of Jews to the Nazi death camps (*see* CONCENTRATION AND DEATH CAMPS).

In December 1939, Eichmann took over the SS office responsible for all Jewish affairs, and it was in this role that he directed the implementation of the "Final Solution," which began in the summer of 1941. Eichmann's office built the death camps and developed the gas chambers for the efficient extermination of the Jews. Eichmann also organized the transportation system that made the Holocaust possible. For his efforts, he was promoted to SS lieutenant-colonel in 1941. By the time of the WANNSEE CONFERENCE of January 20, 1942, which made the final decision to kill all of European Jewry, the infrastructure was already in place. Eichmann was the Nazi "Jewish specialist," enjoying the full faith of his Nazi superiors in his work to ensure the success of the Final Solution. Though he claimed to harbor no fanatical ANTISEMITISM, he was a zealot to succeed in his mission with factory-like efficiency. Even when in 1944 his SS boss, Himmler, became less passionate in his pursuit of the war against the Jews, Eichmann refused to slow the murder down. In August that year, he reported with pride that he had led the successful extermination of approximately 4 million Jews in the death camps and another 1.5 million by the EINSATZGRUPPEN, mobile extermination units.

Eichmann was arrested at the end of the war, but his name was not recognized and he escaped from an American internment camp in 1946. He moved to ARGENTINA, where he lived with a new identity. Israeli secret agents located him there on May 2, 1960. Nine days later they captured him, brought him to ISRAEL, and he stood trial in the spring of 1961. The EICHMANN TRIAL generated intense international interest and helped educate many people about the horrors of the Holocaust.

In addition, it awakened many Israelis who had tried to ignore the pain of the Holocaust, and was instrumental in incorporating this piece of the Jewish past into the culture of the new state.

On December 2, 1961, Adolf Eichmann was sentenced to death for crimes against the Jewish people and crimes against humanity. On May 31, 1962, he became the only person ever executed in Israel.

Further reading: Zvi Aharoni and Wilhelm Dietl, *Operation Eichmann: The Truth about the Pursuit, Capture and Trial* (New York: John Wiley, 1997); Robert P. Archer, et al., *The Quest for the Nazi Personality: A Psychological Investigation of Nazi War Criminals* (Hillsdale, N.J.: Lawrence Erlbaum Associates, 1995); Hannah Arendt, *Eichmann in Jerusalem: A Report on the Banality of Evil* (New York: Penguin Books, 1977).

Eichmann trial

Adolf EICHMANN (1906–62) was the SS lieutenant-colonel in charge of the Gestapo's "Jewish section," and as such was a chief architect for the Nazi "FINAL SOLUTION." He participated at the WANNSEE CONFERENCE (January 20, 1942), which concretized the Nazi plan to eliminate world Jewry, and went on to organize the systematic transportation of Jews from all over Europe to their murder in the CONCENTRATION AND DEATH CAMPS.

At the conclusion of World War II Eichmann was arrested in the American zone of occupied Germany, but he managed to escape to ARGENTINA. Ultimately the Israeli Secret Service (MOSSAD) found him, and on May 11, 1960, smuggled him to ISRAEL to stand trial for his crimes.

The Eichmann trial took place in JERUSALEM from April until December 1961. Eichmann was convicted and sentenced to death. He was executed on May 31, 1962, the only individual ever executed by the Israeli judicial system.

The significance of the Eichmann trial goes far beyond justice for an individual. The trial was televised around the world, bringing the brutal truth about the HOLOCAUST to the attention of millions of people, including Israelis. The details revealed at the trial about the factory-like workings of the Final Solution reminded the world of the evil potential that lies within ordinary people, and reinforced the sense among Jews around the world of the importance of a Jewish state. Israelis had previously worked hard to build a sense of strength and heroism to counter the historical reality of Jewish victimization and weakness, but as a result of the Eichmann trial, a full discussion of the horrifying events and circumstances of the Holocaust could no longer be avoided. The trial and execution of Eichmann signified the end of Israeli avoidance of the Holocaust and allowed for a period of mourning and integration of the tragedy into Israeli culture.

Further reading: Hannah Arendt, *Eichmann in Jerusalem: A Report on the Banality of Evil* (New York: Penguin, 1994); Raul Hilberg, *The Destruction of the European Jews* (New York: Holmes & Meier, 1985); Anita Shapira, "The Holocaust: Private Memories, Public Memory," in *Jewish Social Studies*, 4, 2 (1998).

Eighteen Benedictions *See* AMIDAH.

Einhorn, David (1809–1879) *German and American Reform rabbi*

Born in Bavaria, GERMANY in 1809, David Einhorn was a rabbi and leader in the German movement to reform and modernize Judaism (*see* REFORM JUDAISM).

Einhorn was raised in a household committed to ORTHODOX JUDAISM, and he was given a strong background in Jewish learning. At the age of 17 he was ordained as a RABBI, but his education did not end there. He studied secular philosophy and classics at German universities in Erlagen, Wurzburg, and Munich. His Judaica background coupled with his classical education made Einhorn the consummate reformer for Judaism. He took a radical view of the process of reform, and helped change the face of Jewish life irrevocably.

The path to reform was not easy. Not only did Einhorn have to work against more traditional-minded Jews, but he also had to struggle against governments uncomfortable with any type of radical change. In 1838 he was asked to become rabbi of a community in Wellhausen, but confirmation of his appointment by the Bavarian government never came because of his liberal views on Judaism. The Bavarian government allowed the Reform Jews to worship, but they were fickle concerning the amount of reform they would allow.

Supporting the positions of his mentors Abraham GEIGER (1810–74) and Samuel HOLDHEIM (1806–60), Einhorn rejected the authority of the TALMUD and advocated the right to alter or drop Jewish rituals. He expressed his own beliefs quite clearly; at the Frankfurt Rabbinical Conference of 1845, he supported introduction of the vernacular into the prayer service and he favored the elimination of prayers that sought restoration of sacrifice and longings for a Jewish state.

Einhorn finally received an official rabbinical appointment in 1847 when he succeeded Samuel Holdheim as chief rabbi of Mecklenburg-Schwerin. Again, the government's fluctuating attitude about Jewish reform made it difficult for him to preach and teach his views, and he became involved in several controversies. One time, for example, he was reprimanded for giving a blessing to an uncircumcised child in the synagogue. Finally, Einhorn realized that the future of Jewish reform and his own rabbinical career lay across the ocean in the UNITED STATES.

Accepting a position with the Har Sinai Congregation of Baltimore in 1855, Einhorn arrived in the United States in time for the Cleveland Rabbinical Conference, where he immediately entered into a bitter feud with Isaac Mayer WISE (1819–1900), whose perspective on Reform Judaism included compromise in order to preserve unity with the rest of the Jewish community. Einhorn felt that such compromises would endanger the efforts of reformers, and he began to publish a monthly magazine called *Sinai* (1856–62) to promote his views. Einhorn also wrote his own

prayer book, *Olat Tamid* in 1856. Unlike Wise's *Minhag America*, *Olat Tamid* was not merely a shorter version of a more conservative prayer book, but a wholly new service that removed references to a personal messiah, a return to Israel, and the renewal of the sacrificial cult. It did not include blessings for the SHOFAR or the CHANUKAH lights, and it deemphasized the idea of the CHOSEN PEOPLE. *Olat Tamid* expressed Einhorn's beliefs in Judaism as a universal tradition, without the particularistic strains that seemed antiquated to Einhorn in the new world, but it did include some Sephardic religious poetry. *Olat Tamid* eventually became the model for the first official Reform prayer book (*see* SIDDUR), the *Union Prayer Book*.

Einhorn's perspective was not confined to the Jewish community. Finding his place within American culture, Einhorn did not hesitate to speak about political and social issues such as SLAVERY. He spoke out against slavery from the pulpit and in the pages of *Sinai*. He explained that the TANAKH, the Hebrew Bible, had to be read with a modern perspective. He claimed that the spirit of Judaism required the abolition of slavery, and explained that the TORAH laws on slavery were only meant to control the institution, not to make it eternal.

Einhorn's writings were published in several New York newspapers, and he and his family were clearly in danger from Baltimore mobs who disagreed with his views. In 1861 the Einhorn family fled to Philadelphia. When the pro-slavery rioting ended in Baltimore, Har Sinai sent him a message asking for his return. However, when Einhorn inquired about his right to express his views on the pulpit, the congregation cautioned against it, asking him to avoid the more "exciting" topics of the day. Einhorn did not return to Baltimore.

Remaining in Philadelphia, Einhorn became rabbi of Congregation Kenesseth Israel; he later took a pulpit at Congregation Adath Israel in New York, later known as Temple Beth El. In 1869 Einhorn continued his quest for a radical Reform platform, leaving his mark at the Philadelphia Rabbinical Conference, where his views alienated the more traditional attendants. While it did not become clear for many years, David Einhorn's theology and thought influenced the development of Reform Judaism and its rabbinical school, HEBREW UNION COLLEGE. It was Einhorn's son-in-law and student Kaufman Kohler who formulated the PITTSBURGH PLATFORM of 1885, laying the foundation for American Reform Judaism.

Further reading: Isaac M. Fein, *The Making of an American Jewish Community: The History of Baltimore Jewry from 1773 to 1920* (Philadelphia: Jewish Publication Society, 1971); Norman H. Finkelstein, *Heeding the Call: Jewish Voices in America's Civil Rights Struggle* (Philadelphia: Jewish Publication Society, 1997); Michael A. Meyer, *Response to Modernity: A History of the Reform Movement in Judaism* (New York and Oxford: Oxford University Press, 1988); Aaron M. Petuchowski, Elizabeth R. Petuchowski, and Jakob J. Petuchowski, eds., *Studies in Modern Theology and Prayer* (Philadelphia: Jewish Publication Society, 1998).

Einsatzgruppen

On June 22, 1941, Nazi GERMANY invaded the Soviet Union. This marked a significant turning point in Nazi policy towards the Jews. Prior to this date the Nazis had already murdered some 30,000 Jews, but they had mostly focused on expelling or confining those Jews who fell under their control. With the occupation of eastern Europe, with its millions of Jews, Nazi ANTISEMITISM reached its logical conclusion—extermination.

As the German armies moved toward the east, SS (Schutzstaffel, the Nazi elite guard) leader Heinrich Himmler organized special mobile killing units called Einsatzgruppen, whose sole purpose was to massacre Jewish communities. These units, under the overall command of Reinhard Heydrich, and with the cooperation of local antisemitic forces in the Ukraine and POLAND, went from town to town, rounding up Jewish men, women, and children. They would force their captives to dig mass graves in the fields and forests, and then shoot them all. In 1942, some

Einstazgruppen switched to using vans that asphyxiated their victims as they were driven along. In all, the Einsatzgruppen were responsible for the murder of more than 1.5 million Jews between 1941 and 1944.

Further reading: Christopher R. Browning, *Fateful Months: Essays on the Emergence of the Final Solution* (New York: Holmes & Meier, 1991); Lucy S. Dawidowicz, *The War against the Jews, 1933–1945* (Garden City, N.Y.: Doubleday, 1991).

Einstein, Albert (1879-1955) *noted physicist*

Albert Einstein was born in Ulm, GERMANY, in 1879 and raised in Munich. A poor student in his younger years, he failed his first entrance exam to the Swiss Federal Institute of Technology in Zurich. He was eventually admitted in 1896, graduated, and became a technical assistant at a Swiss patent office in Bern.

In 1905 he published an article, "A New Determination of Molecular Dimensions," which earned him a doctorate from the University of Zurich, where he went on to teach. He published his most famous work, on the special theory of relativity, that same year. It won him instant acclaim among physicists, as it seemed to revolutionize the field. Research conducted at the Royal Society of London later confirmed his theories, and brought him international attention, though not all physicists accepted his views; his name became a household word and a symbol of genius. In 1921 Einstein was awarded the Nobel Prize in physics. Notably, this award focused on his research in theoretical physics—not his still-controversial work with relativity.

While continuing to defend and develop his theories, Einstein became involved in social issues. As a pacifist, he opposed World War I; following the war, he publicly endorsed ZIONISM. His first tour of the UNITED STATES was in 1921 to raise funds for the PALESTINE Foundation Fund. He became increasingly distressed over events in Europe, and in 1933, just after HITLER became

Famous Jewish scientist Albert Einstein was a supporter of Zionism. In addition, he recognized the danger Hitler posed to the Jews early and immigrated to the United States to continue his career in science. *(Government Press Office, The State of Israel)*

chancellor of Germany, he renounced his German citizenship and immigrated to the United States. There he became a member of the Institute for Advanced Study at Princeton University. Despite his commitment to pacifism, Einstein became convinced that Hitler had to be stopped, and he encouraged President Roosevelt to develop research on nuclear fission, thus indirectly contributing to the use of the atomic bomb in 1945. His earlier work relating mass and energy (with the famous formula $E = mc^2$) laid the theoretical groundwork for the effort.

Einstein is remembered primarily for this research and for his connection with the development of atomic power in the modern age.

Further reading: Albert Einstein, *Autobiographical Notes,* trans. Paul Arthur Schlipp (La Salle, Ill.: Open Court, 1979); ———, *Relativity, the Special and the General Theory: A Popular Exposition by Albert Einstein,* trans. Robert W. Lawson (New York: Crown Publishers, c1961); ———, *The World as I See It* (Secaucus, N.J.: Citadel Trade, 1993); Don Howard and John Stachel, eds. *Einstein: The Formative Years, 1879–1909* (Boston: Birkhauser, 2000); Paul Arthur Schilpp, *Albert Einstein: Philosopher-Scientist* (La Salle, Ill.: Open Court, 1970); Carl Seelig, ed., *Ideas and Opinions,* trans. Sonja Bargmann (New York: Crown Publishers, 1982).

Elephantine

Elephantine was a small military community established in southern EGYPT in the sixth century B.C.E. Papyri and scrolls found there, dating from the fifth and early fourth centuries, indicate that a "Jewish Force" was settled there, which included families organized into military units. The community had a temple similar to the TEMPLE in JERUSALEM, where they offered sacrifices to "Yahu," the God of ISRAEL. The community deferred to the Jerusalem Temple on matters of religious practice. The regular communication between the two communities has been seen as evidence of ongoing connections between Jerusalem and the DIASPORA as far back as the Persian Empire.

Further reading: E. C. B. MacLaurin, "Date of the Foundation of the Jewish Colony at Elephantine," in *Journal of Near Eastern Studies* 27, 2 (April 1968): 89–96; Joseph Meleze Modrzejewski, *The Jews of Egypt: From Rameses II to Emperor Hadrian,* trans. Robert Cornman (Philadelphia and Jerusalem: Jewish Publication Society, 1995); Michael H. Silverman, "The Religion of the Elephantine Jews: A New Approach," in *Proceedings of the Sixth World Congress of Jewish Studies,* vol. 1, Hebrew University of

Jerusalem, 1973 (Jerusalem: World Union of Jewish Studies, 1977): 377–388.

Elijah (ninth century B.C.E.) *biblical prophet*

An important biblical figure, Elijah has also been a familiar figure in Jewish folklore throughout the ages, a symbol of human charity and divine salvation.

Elijah's career is chronicled in 1 and 2 Kings (*see* TANAKH). He appears as a prophet of the God of Israel who sternly denounces IDOLATRY and its supporters, especially the wicked King Ahab and his wife, Jezebel. In the end, he defeats and annihilates the prophets of BAAL with divine help. After appointing the prophet Elisha as his successor, Elijah is carried up to heaven by a fiery chariot; he apparently never physically dies.

Because of this special distinction, numerous legends grew up about Elijah. He is said to reside in heaven, where he records everyone's deeds and guides the dead to paradise. He also ventures down to earth periodically, in disguise, as God's messenger to help the needy, as attested in many tales from the rabbinic and medieval eras. Children are told to give help to beggars, any one of whom might be the prophet Elijah.

To this day, a chair is set aside at every BRIT MILAH (circumcision ceremony) so that Elijah may attend, and a cup of wine is placed on every SEDER table at PASSOVER so that Elijah may stop by and take a sip. Elijah's cup is the fifth cup of wine at the seder; it is not consumed by the guests but saved for Elijah. At a certain point in the seder, the door is opened and Elijah is welcomed in, amid song and prayers for REDEMPTION.

According to Jewish tradition, Elijah will announce the coming of the MESSIAH. He will blow the SHOFAR and inaugurate the ingathering of the exiles as well as the resurrection of the dead.

Further reading: Robert B. Coote, ed., *Elijah and Elisha in Socioliterary Perspective* (Atlanta, Ga.: Scholars Press, 1992); Ronald H. Isaacs, *Messengers of God: A Jewish Prophets Who's Who* (Northvale, N.J.: Jason Aronson, 1998); *Tanakh: The Holy Scriptures According to the Traditional Hebrew Text* (Philadelphia and Jerusalem: Jewish Publication Society, 1985).

Ellis Island

For centuries the port of New York was the primary portal for immigrants entering the British colonies and later the UNITED STATES. It is estimated that more than 100 million Americans, including the majority of American Jews, are directly related to immigrants who passed through Ellis Island in New York harbor during its tenure as a federal immigration station.

The Ellis Island Immigration Center was opened on January 1, 1892. More than 17 million immigrants passed through its rooms between that year and 1924. Some 2.5 million Jews immigrated to the United States between 1881 and 1924; most of those who arrived after 1892 did so through Ellis Island.

When immigrants arrived in the Great Hall of Ellis Island they were exhausted from their journey, but nevertheless they were immediately led to governmental inspections. In order to gain access to the United States, immigrants needed to be free of disease, and they had to demonstrate that they could make a living in America or had family who would sponsor them. About 2 percent of would-be immigrants were returned to their home country. Ellis Island came to be known as the "Island of Hope, Island of Tears."

Those who passed inspection were released, and no records were kept of their arrivals. While government authorities did not create and maintain lists of the millions of immigrants who passed through Ellis Island, the ship companies who brought the passengers did. Today one can electronically search for names of Ellis Island arrivals at the site itself or on the Internet.

The National Origins Act of 1924 severely reduced immigration, especially from southern and eastern Europe. All immigrants had to obtain visas before leaving their country of origin; quotas for each country were established based on the

Exhausted from their journey, these immigrants wait to have their physical examination before they will be allowed to enter the United States. The exams were very important, for those who did not pass, about 2 percent, were sent back to their country of origin. *(Library of Congress)*

ethnic makeup of the United States *before* the era of mass immigration. The quota restrictions became even more severe with the National Origins Act in 1929.

The Ellis Island Immigration Center closed in 1954 after millions of immigrants had entered America through its doors. In 1982, the Statue of Liberty–Ellis Island Foundation was founded to raise money to restore and preserve both sites as national landmarks. In 1986 the foundation restored the main building at Ellis Island, in what was the largest historic restoration project in the United States. The Ellis Island Immigration Museum was opened in September 1990, and a project was created to document an American Immigrant Wall of Honor to list the names of all family members who passed through Ellis Island.

Further reading: Edward Corsi, *In the Shadow of Liberty: The Chronicle of Ellis Island* (New York: Macmillan Company, 1935); Irving Howe, *How We Lived: A Documentary History of Immigrant Jews in America, 1880–1930* (New York: R. Marek, 1979); ———, *World of Our Fathers: The Journey of the East European Jews to America and the Life They Found and Made* (New York: Random House, 1997).

emancipation

Emancipation was the process by which European Jews emerged from their status as an isolated and oppressed minority community and became equal citizens of the various modern states.

In the Middle Ages, Jewish communities in Europe and the Middle East existed as autonomous self-governing entities within their host lands. Most Jews lived in GHETTOS and SHTETLS. The Jews as a community were granted certain privileges by the ruling powers, and as individuals they enjoyed the protection of Jewish law as administered by rabbis and elders within their own community. But they were not considered citizens of the wider community, where they suffered from many more restrictions than rights.

This situation ended with the birth of the concept of nationhood and the spread of the ENLIGHTENMENT, which upheld a belief in the equality of all people. Gradually, Jews were granted full rights as citizens, which included the eligibility for public office and the right to vote.

Sometimes the emancipation of the Jews came with a sudden proclamation, as in 1787 when the UNITED STATES Constitution guaranteed the rights of citizenship in the new country irrespective of religion or national origin (though slaves were excluded). In FRANCE, Jewish emancipation began with the French Revolution and the Declaration of the Rights of Man in 1787, although with the rise of Napoleon, the Jews had to once again prove their worth and loyalty as citizens (*see* NAPOLEON'S SANHEDRIN). ENGLAND emancipated its Jews in 1858 by an act of Parliament, although Jews had already achieved partial emancipation and were allowed to serve in municipal offices starting in the 1830s. In GERMANY the emancipation of the Jews was a gradual process that was finally completed in 1870, only to be revoked in 1933 by the Nazis and reinstated after World War II in 1945. In Austria-Hungary (*see* AUSTRIA) emancipation came in 1867 and in SWITZERLAND in 1877. Emancipation did not reach Eastern Europe until after World War I. Thus eastern European Jews remained in their autonomous communities far longer than those living in Western Europe and the United States.

While emancipation has been a positive experience for the Jews, it also has had negative results. Once Jews were emancipated by a nation, and could participate fully in public and secular society, in many cases the preexisting Jewish communal structures were weakened. After emancipation, individual Jews could more easily than ever before choose to leave the Jewish community. In addition, Judaism could now be interpreted in a variety of ways, and in Europe it became more secularized, allowing Jews to abandon religious

practice and traditional customs and still retain a Jewish identity. This led to considerable ACCOMMODATION, and even ASSIMILATION, within the various Jewish communities. Eventually this helped lead to the development of REFORM JUDAISM, which stripped Judaism of its national character and its hopes to return to the land of Israel. In the early Reform view, Judaism became more an enlightened ethical system within European and American culture than a culture unto itself.

Further reading: Jacob Katz, *Jewish Emancipation and Self-Emancipation* (Philadelphia: Jewish Publication Society, 1986); ———, *Out of the Ghetto: The Social Background of Jewish Emancipation, 1770–1870* (Syracuse, N.Y.: Syracuse University Press, 1998); Michael A. Meyer, *Response to Modernity: A History of the Reform Movement in Judaism* (Detroit: Wayne State University Press, 1995); David Weinberg, *The Challenge of Modern Jewish Emancipation* (St. Louis: Forum Press, 1979).

England

Individual Jews may have lived in England from the Roman conquest, but it was the Norman Conquest of William the Conqueror in 1066 C.E. that brought the first notable Jewish community to the island. A significant number of Jews migrated from FRANCE, along with smaller numbers from GERMANY, Italy, SPAIN, RUSSIA, and Muslim areas. They built a Jewish community that by the mid 12th century had spread throughout England's cities, including York, Lincoln, Oxford, Winchester, Norwich, Bristol, and most important, London, which had the only Jewish cemetery. A larger Jewish population brought with it unprecedented levels of anti-Jewish sentiment (*see* ANTI-JUDAISM). Violent incidents of BLOOD LIBEL, in which Jews were accused of using the blood of Christians to bake their MATZAH for PASSOVER, cropped up in Norwich in 1144, Gloucester in 1168, Bury St. Edmunds in 1181, Bristol in 1183, and Winchester in 1192. English Jewry also suffered violence at the hands of the crusaders. Many survived only by the protection of the Crown, conversion, or good luck.

The Jews prospered when the ruler at any given time was friendly to them, and they suffered when the political situation shifted. By 1253, the Jews of England were restricted to towns that already had organized Jewish communities. They were allowed to trade, but could not charge interest on loans. They were not allowed to own land.

By 1272, the Jews of England had become so impoverished that they could no longer function as moneylenders. Since they were no longer useful to the Crown, Edward I had no problem expelling every Jew from England in 1290. They were given until November 1 to leave the country, and they did so, moving to France, Flanders, and Germany.

The Jews did not return until the 16th century, when the expulsion from Spain in 1492 and the Inquisition ignited new waves of Jewish migration throughout Europe. Isolated communities of CONVERSOS settled in England, but they had no charter and thus no protection from the rulers themselves. In the 17th century, an Amsterdam rabbi, Manasseh ben Israel, began negotiations with Oliver Cromwell to admit the Jews into England officially. No official proclamation was issued, but Cromwell provided an oral guarantee in 1656; thereafter the Conversos were able to practice Judaism openly.

Once the door was open, Jewish immigrants arrived from the NETHERLANDS, Spain, and PORTUGAL, opening a synagogue in 1657. Charles II officially sanctioned the existence of the English Jewish community in 1664 with a written promise of protection. A group of German Jews established a synagogue in 1690, bringing the total number of Jews in England to 400 souls. The Act for Suppressing Blasphemy recognized the legality of practicing Judaism in England in 1698, and in 1700, William III knighted the first Jew, a man named Solomon de Medina.

The community grew. By 1734, there were 6,000 Jews living in England. Jews entered all spheres of English life, although the Jewish upper class maintained their classic interests in banking and foreign trade. While the first Jewish settlers were SEPHARDIM, ASHKENAZIM soon established synagogues and communities throughout the country.

In England, the process of EMANCIPATION of the Jews began early and ended late. The Jewish Naturalization Bill, also referred to as the Jew Bill, was issued in 1753, finally giving foreign-born Jews the privileges of Jews born in England, but it had to be rescinded because of anti-Jewish tension. Although the Jewish community was not politically emancipated until 1858, individual Jews found their way into English politics and high society. The first Jew was admitted to the bar in 1833, and the first Jewish sheriff was appointed in 1835. Queen Victoria knighted Moses MONTEFIORE in 1837, and in 1841, the first Jew in history was given a hereditary title. In 1855 the first Jewish lord mayor of London took office, and in 1858 the Jewish baron Lionel de Rothschild was able to take his seat in the House of Commons after the removal of the obligatory Christian oath of office. In 1871 Jews were granted the right to receive degrees in English universities.

In 1874 Benjamin DISRAELI, a practicing Christian of Jewish birth, became England's first and only Jewish prime minister. Parliament has had Jewish members ever since 1858; and in recent years that number has reached more than 40.

As Jews fled the POGROMS of eastern Europe, many settled in England's urban areas; they recreated the clothing industry in England. Immigrants set up a multitude of organizations and associations to support Jewish interests and culture. Eventually the new immigrants successfully integrated into English society. There were approximately 250,000 Jews living in England in 1914. Some 50,000 of them fought in World War I, 10,000 dying for the freedom they had so recently won. World War I ended further immigration until the onset of World War II; some antisemitism did appear, but it never reached politically significant levels.

In the 1920s, at a time when Britain was supporting ZIONISM through the BRITISH MANDATE of 1922, many English Jews found their place in professional society, taking positions as doctors, lawyers, and accountants. They entered the universities and moved to the suburbs. When World War II began, Jewish refugees came to England, fleeing the Nazi threat. Many of them left when the war ended, but approximately 50,000 remained and integrated into British REFORM JUDAISM or ORTHODOX JUDAISM.

Before the war the English Jewish community supported a variety of different Jewish causes, including the settlement of Jews in Palestine, although the community was split over the issue of a possible state of Israel, especially whenever Jewish forces in Palestine fought against British soldiers, which caused a short-term increase in antisemitism. However, when Britain issued the WHITE PAPER of 1939, which sharply restricted Jewish immigration to Palestine on the eve of the HOLOCAUST, the entire community united against the measure. Once the State of Israel was declared in 1948, tensions eased. With the establishment of diplomatic relations with Israel, English Jewry no longer had to look for ways to reconcile their Jewish heritage with their English citizenship.

England is rich with Jewish organizations, such as the United Synagogue, which unifies nearly all the Ashkenazi synagogues in the country. There are numerous Zionist organizations as well. There are Jewish schools, associations, organizations, and social service agencies. One can walk through downtown London and see evidence of medieval English Jewry before the expulsion in the street name "Old Jewry."

The Jewish community in England is organized through the Board of Deputies of British Jews, which has 500 members representing synagogues throughout the country. This organization has successfully monitored antisemitism in England for years, and it also serves to safeguard minority rights. The religious life of English Jews is split between the Orthodox and the Reform movements. Each group has schools to train rabbis. The Reform rabbinical seminary, the Leo Baeck College, attracts students from all over Europe. The Central Synagogue on Great Portland Street is a modern building that complements the other older synagogues in London. England has truly welcomed its Jews, and the variety of Jewish museums, schools, synagogues, and active Jewish cultural life represent the freedom that contemporary Jews have, to worship and live their lives as both Jews and English citizens.

Further reading: Leonard B. Glick, *Abraham's Heirs: Jews and Christians in Medieval Europe* (Syracuse, N.Y.: Syracuse University Press, 1999); Albert M. Hyamson, *A History of the Jews in England* (London: Published for the Jewish Historical Society of England by Chatto & Windus, 1908); Robin R. Mundill, et al. *England's Jewish Solution: Experiment and Expulsion, 1262–1290* (Cambridge: Cambridge University Press, 1998); Cecil Roth, *A History of Jews in England* (Oxford, U.K.: Clarendon Press, 1941); Goldwin Smith, *A History of England* (New York: Charles Scribner's Sons, 1957).

This street sign in London, England, marks the area where medieval Jews lived before they were expelled in 1290. The street is called Old Jewry. *(Courtesy J. Gordon Melton)*

Enlightenment

The Enlightenment was an intellectual and political movement in Europe that took place during the 17th and 18th centuries, and that eventually exercised a powerful influence on European Jews.

Taking their cue from the humanist movement of the Renaissance, thinkers such as Voltaire, Rousseau, and Kant assigned greater value to human reason than to traditional beliefs and practices. They used logic and analysis to develop treatises on ethics, political systems, and individual rights. The Western world had entered an era when empiricism, science, reason, liberty, and equality dominated intellectual thought, which trickled down to the middle and lower classes as well.

The Enlightenment in Europe contributed to the EMANCIPATION of the Jews. It also sparked a specifically Jewish enlightenment, known as the HASKALAH, in which Jewish philosophers developed new and more liberal interpretations of Judaism and Jewish tradition. The writers of the Haskalah also emphasized reason and history over faith and tradition. Ultimately these new ideas led to the emergence of REFORM JUDAISM. This represented a radical break from Jewish tradition, which had always expected individual submission to tradition and rabbinical leadership.

An important aspect of the Enlightenment that had a big impact on Jewish life was its emphasis on the individual's ability to make choices based on conscience. If individuals were equal and each capable of using reason and logic, then they were also capable of thinking through their actions and activities, including religious ones. The issue of authority rose to the fore, where it has remained throughout the contemporary period.

The most famous example of Jewish Enlightenment thought appears in Moses MENDELSSOHN's (1729–86) work *Jerusalem*. In this volume, Mendelssohn, the first *Maskil,* or practitioner of the Haskalah, explains that there are two paths to understanding Torah and Judaism: one is faith and the other is reason. Mendelssohn tailored his work to the modern reader, combining religious thought with contemporary Enlightenment ideas.

Further reading: Allan Arkush, *Moses Mendelssohn and the Enlightenment* (Albany: State University of New York Press, 1994); Shmuel Feiner, *Haskalah and History: The Emergence of a Modern Jewish Historical Consciousness* (Portland, Oreg.: Littman Library of Jewish Civilization, 2002); ———, *The Jewish Enlightenment* (Philadelphia: University of Pennsylvania Press, 2003); Moses Mendelssohn, *Jerusalem* (Hanover, N.H.: Brandeis University Press, 1983); Michael A. Meyer, *Response to Modernity: A History of the Reform Movement in Judaism* (Detroit: Wayne State University Press, 1995).

Entebbe

On June 27, 1976, anti-Israel terrorists hijacked an Air France airplane and forced it to land at Entebbe in UGANDA. The terrorists demanded that ISRAEL release 53 convicted terrorists in exchange for their hostages. To demonstrate their intentions, they freed the French crew and non-Jewish passengers, but held the 105 Jewish and Israeli hostages. The terrorists gave Israel a 48-hour deadline to meet their demands, after which the Jewish hostages would be executed.

The Israeli government entered negotiations to stall for time, while it arranged a seemingly impossible military mission. Before the final deadline was reached, on Sunday, July 4, the ISRAEL DEFENSE FORCES (IDF) managed to dispatch 200 of their best soldiers to raid the airport of Entebbe and secure the safety of the Jewish hostages. Under Lt. Col. Yonatan Netanyahu, the soldiers freed the hostages in a lightning attack, killing all eight terrorists in the process. Unfortunately, two hostages died and Netanyahu was killed while leading the hostages toward safety.

The incredible success of this mission demonstrated to the world the powerful military remedy of counterterrorism when facing senseless terror. It garnered worldwide respect for Israeli skill in the fields of intelligence and defense.

After the Jewish hostages held by terrorists at Entebbe airport were freed by Israeli soldiers, they were reunited with their families. *(Ya'acov Sa'ar Government Press Office, The State of Israel)*

Further reading: Francis Anthony Boyle, *World Politics and International Law* (Durham, N.C.: Duke University Press, 1985); Iddo Netanyahu, *Yoni's Last Battle: The Rescue at Entebbe, 1976* (Jerusalem: Gefen Books, 2001).

entertainment

In the years around the start of the 20th century, a large number of Jews in several different countries used the entertainment industry to rise from immigrant poverty and achieve the fame and fortune that the new countries had promised.

In America, from VAUDEVILLE and the BORSHT BELT, and from Times Square to Hollywood, Jews have participated in America's developing enter-

tainment industries as performers and business pioneers. In the process, they have left a special Jewish imprint on their fields, and helped win acceptance for Jews as an integral part of American life.

Many of the theaters in New York City's theater district were built by Oscar Hammerstein (1847–1919), a German Jew who began by building opera houses but is now known as the "Father of Times Square." Included on the long list of famous Jewish actors, singers, and comedians that have graced the stage, screen, and television are Tony Martin, Danny Kaye, Eddie Fisher, Milton Berle, Molly Berg, Sid Caesar, Jerry Lewis, Jackie Mason, Buddy Hackett, George Burns, Fanny

Brice, Woody Allen, Barbara STREISAND, Sophie Tucker, and Gilda Radner. Many Jews also became famous playwrights and composers in the Broadway theater, including Leonard BERNSTEIN, Richard Rodgers, Jerome Kern, Oscar Hammerstein II, Stephen Sondheim, George S. Kaufman, Lillian Hellman, and ARTHUR MILLER.

Jewish entrepreneurs left an indelible mark on the motion picture industry. Most of Hollywood's first generation of studio executives were Jews: William Fox, Samuel Goldwyn, Carl Laemmle, Jesse Lasky, Marcus Loew, Louis B. Mayer, and Adolph Zukor. The next generation of moviemakers was also mostly Jewish, including men such as Jack and Harry Warner, Harry Cohn, Irving Thalberg, and David Selznick. These men had seen the popularity of the nickelodeon and were ready to take full advantage of such a business opportunity. From the early 1920s to the present day, it is not uncommon to hear spectators remark on the ruthless ambition and shrewd business sense of these men, which often, surprisingly, went along with a keen judgment about art and entertainment.

Jewish influence in America continued to be felt through the end of the 20th century. During the 1990s network television shows boasted an unprecedented number of Jewish actors, especially comedians, such as Jerry SEINFELD. The hit sitcom *Seinfeld* represents the Jewish move into the American mainstream. His Jewishness was subtly layered into the life of a New Yorker and his friends. Other situation comedies with clearly Jewish characters were *Mad About You, The Nanny, Friends,* and *Will and Grace.*

The disproportional success of Jewish people in show business, on the stage, on the small screen, and on the silver screen has produced positive and negative attention toward the Jewish community. While some antisemites (*see* ANTISEMITISM) have suggested that the power of many Jews in Hollywood is part of a larger Jewish conspiracy (*see* PROTOCOLS OF THE ELDERS OF ZION), the presence of Jewish performers in all mediums of entertainment shows that Jewish life has found a place in the fabric of American life. Whether this fact can be attributed mostly to ASSIMILATION or ACCOMMODATION remains to be seen.

However, at least one Jewish moviemaker has used his success to bring important Jewish issues to the general public. Steven Spielberg, one of the most successful moviemakers in American history, used his position in Hollywood to produce an unflinching movie about the HOLOCAUST called *Schindler's List;* without downplaying its horrific setting, the film highlights the altruistic acts of one man who saved many Jewish lives. In this way, perhaps the film reflects Jewish and American values of faith and optimism that have informed so many Hollywood movies and made them successful around the world.

Further reading: Vincent Brook, *Something Ain't Kosher Here* (New Brunswick, N.J.: Rutgers University Press, 2003); Neal Gabler, *An Empire of Their Own: How the Jews Invented Hollywood* (Garden City, N.Y.: Anchor, 1989); J. Hoberman and Jeffrey Shandler, *Entertaining America: Jews, Movies, and Broadcasting* (Princeton, N.J.: Princeton University Press, 2003).

epikoris

An *epikoris* (derived from Epicurus, the Greek philospher's name) is a heretic, someone who deliberately rejects or rebels against God's commandments (*see* MITZVAH).

In Jewish tradition, an ignorant person cannot be an *epikoris*, since he or she may not be fully aware of God's teachings. Traditionally, an *epikoris* was to be shunned or even, theoretically, executed. Milton STEINBERG's widely read novel *As a Driven Leaf* tells the story of an *epikoris* named Elisha BEN ABAYA, an ancient rabbi mentioned in the TALMUD who rejected Judaism for the study of Greek thought and mathematics, only to find that what he sought was within Jewish tradition all along.

Further reading: David Biale, "Historical Heresies and Modern Jewish Identity" in *Jewish Social Studies* 8: 2/3 (Winter/Spring 2002): 112–133; Todd M. Endelman, *Jewish Apostasy in the Modern World* (New York: Holmes

& Meier, 1987); Milton Steinberg, *As a Driven Leaf.* (Springfield, N.J.: Behrman House, 1996).

Eretz Yisrael

Eretz Yisrael is literally the land of ISRAEL, but symbolically it denotes more than a parcel of land. Eretz Yisrael is the Promised Land, the fulfillment of the COVENANT between God and the PATRIARCHS. The TANAKH, the Hebrew Bible describes it as a land flowing with milk and honey, a fertile earthly paradise.

After the TEMPLE was built in JERUSALEM, the land became further sanctified as the dwelling place of God. In the future, it was believed, the land of Israel, also known as Zion, will expand its borders to accommodate the returning Jews who will dwell there in the MESSIANIC AGE.

The ancient rabbis glorified the land of Israel, declaring it the navel of the universe, insisting that those who live there must lead a sinless life, and maintaining that any life inside Eretz Yisrael is holier than a life outside it. Through the Middle Ages poems and prayers yearned for the land and extolled its virtues. In modern times ZIONISM has pushed for a return of the Jews to Eretz Yisrael. The dreams of a Jewish state within the land of Israel were realized in 1948.

Further reading: Jean-Christophe Attias and Esther Benbassa, *Israel: The Impossible Land* (Stanford, Calif.: Stanford University Press, 2003); Martin Buber, *On Zion: The History of an Idea* (Syracuse, N.Y.: Syracuse University Press, 1997); Lawrence A. Hoffman, ed., *The Land of Israel: Jewish Perspectives* (Notre Dame, Ind.: University of Notre Dame Press, 1986); Tzvia Ehrlich-Klein, *To Dwell in the Palace* (Jerusalem and New York: Feldheim Publishers, 1991).

eruv

An *eruv* is a ritual enclosure around a town or neighborhood that creates a common area, within which observant Jews may carry objects on SHAB-BAT, the Sabbath day. Talmudic law prohibits Jews from carrying items on Shabbat outside the area of their home or yard. According to the ancient RAB-BIS, one cannot carry any object more than is useful, such as two sips of milk, because any amounts more than these would be functional and thus constitute melachah (work).

This prohibition can cause great inconvenience to observant Jews. For example, religious Jews, who do not ride in vehicles on the Sabbath and therefore walk to SYNAGOGUE, at times need to carry items such as keys or a baby stroller. To get around the prohibition, rabbis permit carrying within an area enclosed by an eruv.

Technically, an eruv can be set by stringing nearly invisible wire between poles or buildings. It creates an invisible shield within which one's "home" boundaries are extended and one is permitted to carry items. The area may enclose a few homes, or a few streets, an entire neighborhood, or even a city. It can also be an island, as long as its population does not exceed a certain number of people.

Further reading: Yosef Gavriel Bechhofer, *The Contemporary Eruv: Eruvin in Modern Metropolitan Areas* (Jerusalem and New York: Feldheim, 1998); Herbert Danby, ed., *The Mishnah: Translated from the Hebrew with an Introduction and Brief Explanatory Notes* (Oxford: Clarendon Press, 1933, 1977); Alan Dundes, *The Shabbat Elevator and other Sabbath Subterfuges: An Unorthodox Essay on Circumventing Custom and Jewish Character* (Lanham, Md.: Rowman & Littlefield Publishers, 2002); Isaac Klein, *A Guide to Jewish Religious Practice* (Philadelphia and Jerusalem: Jewish Theological Seminary of America, 1988).

eschatology

The term *eschatology* refers to the study of the end times as predicted in various religions, and derives from the Greek word *eschaton,* meaning "last" or "final." The term itself is found in Christian rather than Jewish texts, but the questions addressed in eschatological writings have been explored extensively by Jewish thinkers as well.

Scholars of eschatology often ask questions concerning the sequence of events and the nature of the MESSIANIC AGE to come, and often try to find answers by exploring the symbolism used in eschatological texts. For Jews, the best example of eschatological literature is found in the biblical book of Daniel, although certain passages in ISAIAH and EZEKIEL are important as well.

Eschatological views vary within Judaism. The most common understanding is that wars and catastrophes will precede the coming of the MESSIAH, who will be announced by the prophet ELIJAH. The Messiah will rebuild JERUSALEM, and the sacrificial system will be reinstituted in the TEMPLE. Suffering will cease and all humanity will acknowledge that the God of Abraham, Isaac, and Jacob (see PATRIARCHS) is the one true god. After the Messianic Age ends, the Day of Judgment will occurs, during which the righteous will be rewarded with everlasting life and joy, while the wicked will be punished.

Further reading: Abraham Cohen, *Everyman's Talmud.* (London: J. M. Dent, 1949); David Novak, "Law and Eschatology: A Jewish-Christian Intersection" in *Last Things* (Grand Rapids, Mich.: Eerdmans, 2002).

Eshkol, Levi (1895–1969) *Zionist leader*

Levi Eshkol was a Labor Zionist leader and the third prime minister of the State of ISRAEL.

Eshkol was born Levi Shkolnik in the Ukraine in 1895. He received a traditional Jewish education, as he was part of a wealthy Hasidic (see HASIDISM) family. In 1914 he immigrated to PALESTINE. He volunteered for the Jewish Legion of the British Army during World War I, founded the agricultural community Detah Tikvah, and then became a founding member of KIBBUTZ Degania Bet. Eshkol combined manual labor with political activism. He was among the founders of the HISTADRUT (General Federation of Labor), where he became involved in labor issues and later in the promotion of cooperative agricultural development.

In 1937 Levi Eshkol played a central role in the establishment of the Mekorot Water Company.

Eshkol served as Mekorot's managing director until 1951, introducing a system of countrywide water management that made intensive irrigated farming possible, and turned the desert into an oasis. On the political front, he was able to persuade the German government to allow Jews immigrating to Palestine to take some of their assets with them.

Like most Israelis Eshkol also participated in the defense of the state. He served in the HAGANAH high command. As director-general of the Ministry of Defense in 1950–51 he helped lay the foundation for Israel's defense industries. From 1951 to 1963 Eshkol was minister of agriculture and development, while also serving as head of the settlement division of the JEWISH AGENCY.

In 1963, Levi Eshkol became prime minister of Israel, the highest office in the state. In 1964, he made the first state visit of an Israeli prime minister to Washington, D.C., laying the foundation for the close rapport that has existed between the two countries ever since.

And in 1965, Eshkol oversaw the establishment of formal relations between West Germany and Israel. As a conciliatory gesture to the political opposition, he ordered that the remains of Labor's fiercest political rival, Ze'ev JABOTINSKY, founder and ideological leader of the Revisionist movement, be brought to Israel and reinterred in a state funeral on Mount HERZL in JERUSALEM. Thus, Eshkol honored Jabotinsky's last will, written in 1935, requesting that his remains be transferred to Israel "only on the instruction of a future Jewish government."

Levi Eshkol died in office in February 1969 of a heart attack at the age of 73. Though his establishment of good relations with the UNITED STATES was important, the 1967 SIX-DAY WAR, with its stunning military victory, was undoubtedly the highlight of Eshkol's six years as prime minister.

Further reading: Theodore Draper, *Israel and World Politics: Roots of the Third Arab-Israeli War* (New York: Viking Press, 1968); Adam Garfinkle, *Politics and Society in Modern Israel: Myths and Realities* (Armonk, N.Y.:

M. E. Sharpe, 2000); Colbert C. Held and Mildred McDonald Held, *Middle East Patterns: Places, Peoples, and Politics* (Boulder, Colo.: Westview Press, 1989).

Essenes

The Essenes were one of the three primary sects or religious factions within Judaism during the late second TEMPLE period (150 B.C.E–70 C.E.), alongside the PHARISEES and the SADDUCEES.

While the Jewish philosopher PHILO JUDAEUS and the Roman Jewish historian JOSEPHUS both mention the Essenes, there is no direct reference to them in the TALMUD. However, many scholars believe that Talmudic passages about the Hasidim ha-rishonim, "the first pious ones," may have been referring to the Essenes.

According to Philo and Josephus, the Essenes numbered approximately 4,000 followers, most of them living in secluded areas within Judea (*see* JUDEA AND SAMARIA). The sect arose in about 150 B.C.E. and disappeared some 250 years later.

The Essenes adhered to MONOTHEISM, stressing the omnipotence and omniscience of the One God. They were extremely concerned with ritual purity, and had a heightened awareness of the need for a virtuous lifestyle, including truthfulness and obedience to God's will. They led a monastic, ascetic lifestyle and many chose to remain unmarried or to become celibate after having children. The Essenes emphasized the rituals of daily immersion in water and eating meals communally. They had a socialist economy, interpreted the Bible allegorically, stringently observed SHABBAT, the Sabbath, and believed that an individual's destiny could not be changed.

Many modern scholars consider the DEAD SEA SCROLLS to have been the property of the Essenes, although this has not been proven beyond a doubt. However, unlike the Pharisees, the Essenes had little impact on the development of NORMATIVE JUDAISM.

Further reading: Gabriele Boccaccini, *Beyond the Essene Hypothesis: The Parting of the Ways Between Qumran and*

Enochic Judaism (Grand Rapids, Mich.: Wm. B. Eerdmans, 1998); Lawrence H. Schiffman, *From Text to Tradition: A History of Second Temple and Rabbinic Judaism* (Hoboken, N.J.: Ktav Publishing House, 1991); James C. Vanderkam, *An Introduction to Early Judaism* (Grand Rapids, Mich.: Wm. B. Eerdmans, 2000).

Esther (fifth century B.C.E.) *biblical figure, Jewish queen of Persia*

Esther is one of only two women to have a book of the TANAKH, the Hebrew Bible, named for her (RUTH is the other). She remains one of the great heroes of Jewish history.

Esther, in the biblical account, was an orphaned Jewish girl raised by her uncle and foster father Mordechai. When Persian king Ahashverous banishes his queen, Mordechai enters Esther in a beauty contest to win the king's favor, but directs her not to reveal her identity as a Jew. The king then chooses Esther as his new queen.

Meanwhile, the king's minister Haman issues a decree that everyone in the kingdom should bow down to him. Mordechai refuses to do so because he is Jewish and will only bow down before God. Angered, Haman asks the king to issue a decree ordering the death of all the Jews in the kingdom, and the king agrees. In the end, Esther successfully beseeches the king to spare her life and the life of her people and thus saves the Jews. The events are commemorated in the holiday of PURIM, which is specifically established in the book of Esther.

The book is written with literary flair, and has attributes of hyperbole, satire, and farce. Thus, scholars question the accuracy of the details, although the character of King Ahashverous may be accurately based on an actual Persian ruler, one of the emperors named Xerxes, and the story may very well represent incidents that occurred to Jewish communities in the ancient DIASPORA.

The ancient rabbis debated whether to include the Book of Esther in the Tanakh, because of its questionable religious status. There is no mention of God, and the Jewish people seem to be saved entirely by human actions, although a period of fasting indicates that prayer is involved. Moreover, when Esther conceals her Jewish identity, she presumably did not observe KASHRUT, the laws of kosher food, nor SHABBAT; heralding her as a true heroine is therefore problematic.

Nevertheless, Esther has become one of the most popular books of the Tanakh; it is read in the synagogue twice during Purim, when congregants are permitted to try to drown out every mention of Haman's name. *Purimspiels,* or dramatic reenactments of the story, became very widespread from the medieval period; they were often improved with topical additions relating to the issues facing particular Jewish communities, especially from their local "Hamans."

Finally, the story of Esther provides a model for managing dual loyalties and the pressures of ASSIMILATION and ACCOMMODATION on minority Jewish communities in the Diaspora.

Further reading: Leila Leah Bronner, *From Eve to Esther: Rabbinic Reconstructions of Biblical Women* (Louisville, Ky.: Westminster/John Knox Press, 1994); Naomi M. Hyman, ed., *Biblical Women in the Midrash: A Sourcebook* (Northvale, N.J.: Jason Aronson, 1997); Ronald H. Isaacs, *Legends of Biblical Heroes: A Sourcebook* (Northvale, N.J.: Jason Aronson, 2002); *Tanakh: The Holy Scriptures According to the Traditional Hebrew Text* (Philadelphia and Jerusalem: Jewish Publication Society, 1985).

eternal light

The eternal light, or *ner tamid*, is a standard fixture in SYNAGOGUES; it is the lamp that hangs above the ARK where the TORAH scrolls are kept.

Several traditions have helped continue this custom into modern times. In ancient days, such a lamp stood in the tabernacle (*see* MISHKAN) in the desert, remaining lit at all times (Ex 27:20–21). The TEMPLE in Jerusalem also contained a MENORAH with seven branches; according to tradition, one of the seven lamps was always lit,

even when the others were being cleaned. Finally, a flame burned above the sacrificial altar in the Temple that was never extinguished (Lv 6:6).

Today, synagogues keep the eternal light lit even when the synagogue is closed. The light represents the idea that God is always present in the world.

Further reading: Rudolph Brasch, *The Unknown Sanctuary: The Story of Judaism, Its Teachings, Philosophy and Symbols* (Sydney: Angus and Robertson, 1969); Hayim Halevy Donin, *To Pray as a Jew: A Guide to the Prayer Book and the Synagogue Service* (New York: Basic Books, 1980); Irving Greenberg, *The Jewish Way: Living the Holidays* (New York: Touchstone, 1988).

Ethics of the Fathers (Pirkei Avot)

Of the 63 books of the MISHNAH, all except one deal primarily with HALAKHAH, or legal matters. The one exception is Pirkei Avot, or Ethics of the Fathers, which deals primarily with ethical behavior. It is a collection of philosophical and ethical sayings of the TANNAIM, the first generation of ancient rabbis whose discussions and rulings are still considered authoritative. Jewish tradition dictates that SHABBAT (Sabbath) afternoons during spring and summer be spent reviewing this work, which has remained immensely popular, as one of the most accessible volumes in the Talmudic literature.

Some of the more famous aphorisms from this work include, "Say little and do much"; "Who is rich? He who is happy with what he has"; and "If I am not for myself, who will be for me? But if I am only for myself, then what am I? And if not now, when?"

Further reading: Herbert Danby, ed., *The Mishnah: Translated from the Hebrew with an Introduction and Brief Explanatory Notes* (Oxford: Clarendon Press, 1933, 1977); Leonard Kravitz and Kerry M. Olitzky, *Pirke Avot: A Modern Commentary on Jewish Ethics* (New York: Union of American Hebrew Congregations, 1993); Morris Schatz, *Ethics of the Fathers in the Light of Jewish History* (New York: Bloch Publishing, 1971).

Ethiopia

The northeast African nation of Ethiopia is referenced several times in the Hebrew Bible (*see* TORAH), for example, when the prophet ISAIAH warns of its doom alongside that of EGYPT. In the second century B.C.E., Ethiopia was ruled by an Arabian dynasty that traced its heritage back to King SOLOMON and Queen Sheba. Some stories in Ethiopian lore explain that the son of Solomon and Sheba brought Judaic customs to the land. Other stories blend together Christian lore and Jewish legends. Around the fifth century C.E., Ethiopia became a Christian nation, but it retained some Jewish traits, such as identification with the LION OF JUDAH, the symbol of the emperor of Ethiopia down to the 20th century.

Scholars estimate that the Ethiopian Jewish community has existed since the second and third centuries. The name of the community was Beta Israel. In modern times, Ethiopian Jews have been called Falashas, meaning strangers or immigrants in the language of the land. The term *falasha* took on a pejorative tone in the late 20th century.

There are four main theories concerning the origins of the Ethiopian Jewish community. Some argue that the Beta Israel are the descendants of the lost Israelite tribe of Dan, exiled from Israel after the destruction of the first Temple in 586 B.C.E. (*see* TEN LOST TRIBES); some say they may be the descendents of Menelik I, who is claimed to be a son of King Solomon and Queen Sheba; others propose that they may be descendants of Ethiopian Christians and pagans who converted to Judaism long ago; and still others theorize that they may be descendants of the Jewish tribes who lived in nearby Yemen since ancient times. Ethiopian Jewish tradition differs significantly from the rabbinic Judaism practiced in most Jewish communities in the modern world. Its laws were based on Torah, rather than on the rabbinic law of the TALMUD, which was not part of their heritage. In that way, they are similar to the KARAITES; the latter were familiar with rabbinic law, but rejected it. In the 16th century an Egyptian rabbi recognized the Ethiopian community as genuine Jews.

Diplomatic relations between Ethiopia and Israel were relatively positive until 1973, when 28 African nations, Ethiopia included, broke diplomatic ties with Israel under the threat of an Arab oil embargo. Soon after, the situation of Ethiopian Jewry became critical. Civil war brought death to 2,500 Ethiopian Jews and left another 7,000 homeless. The new government forced the Jewish community to share its farms with non-Jews, and instigated ANTISEMITISM. By the early 1980s, the Jews were no longer allowed to practice Jewish rituals or to teach the HEBREW language.

Various Israeli and Jewish organizations had consistently provided education and welfare to the Ethiopian Jewish community for many years, and small numbers of Ethiopian Jews were brought to live in Israel, some to be trained as teachers for their community. For many years the groups waged a campaign to win Ethiopian Jews the right to immigrate to Israel, despite lack of support from either the Ethiopian or the Israeli government. In 1975, the official Israeli rabbinate approved the legitimate Jewish status of Ethiopian Jews. This opened the door for them to enter Israel under the LAW OF RETURN, which grants Israeli citizenship to any person with at least one Jewish grandparent. However, the Ethiopian government did not allow significant emigration until 1984, when civil war raged in Ethiopia. Israel was allowed to airlift the Ethiopian Jews to Israel via Sudan.

Approximately 10,000 Ethiopian Jews were airlifted to Israel, in a program called Operation Moses. The Sudanese withdrew their cooperation earlier than was expected, leaving another 15,000 Ethiopian Jews stranded. In 1991, the remaining Ethiopian Jews were airlifted to Israel during Operation Solomon. The Ethiopians were taken in by Israeli absorption centers, where they were taught Hebrew and other skills useful in the modern world. Many Ethiopian Jews have successfully integrated into Israeli society, joining the army and participating in Israeli culture; they have also created organizations that advocate for the remaining Jews in Ethiopia.

Further reading: Esther Hertzog, *Immigrants and Bureaucrats: Ethiopians in an Israeli Absorption Center* (New York: Berghahn Books, 1999); David Kessler, *The Falashas: A Short History of the Ethiopian Jews* (London and Portland, Oreg.: Frank Cass Publishers, 1996); I. M. Lews, "The Hyena People: Ethiopian Jews in Christian Ethiopia," *Journal of the Royal Anthropological Institute* 9, 2 (2003); Asher Naim, *Saving the Lost Tribe: The Rescue and Redemption of the Ethiopian Jews* (New York: Ballantine Books, 2003).

evil eye

The concept of the evil eye does not appear in Jewish literature until the third century C.E. The belief was strongest in Babylonia, whose culture contained many similar images and concepts. By the Middle Ages, when many Jews were living in Europe, Christian conceptions of the evil eye found their way into Jewish custom and thought as well.

Many thought a person could cast an evil glance at someone, calling upon a malicious force that some associate with a bad angel. Therefore, it was considered unwise to call attention to oneself, especially by being ostentatious or behaving in a way that might arouse jealousy in others. Healthy or good-looking children were considered magnets for the evil eye, and were often shielded from the view of strangers as a protective measure. A demon named LILITH, referred to in MIDRASH as Adam's first wife, was commonly thought to cast the evil eye upon newborn babies in her bitterness about losing her place in the Garden of Eden. The evil eye could manifest itself as an illness, and Jewish children sometimes wore amulets and charms to ward it off. Amulets were often hung above newborn babies to achieve the same goal, sometimes in the form of a hand. Wearing TALLIT or TZITZIT can protect a person, according to some traditions, as can wearing red, or carrying salt. To remove the evil eye after it has taken effect, one can recite special verses and spit three times.

Further reading: Brenda Z. Rosenbaum and Stuart Copans, *How to Avoid the Evil Eye* (New York: St. Martin's Press, 1985); Hayim Shoys, *The Lifetime of a Jew throughout the Ages of Jewish History* (New York: Union of American Hebrew Congregations, 1998); Rivka Ulmer, *The Evil Eye in the Bible and in Rabbinic Literature* (Hoboken, N.J.: Ktav Publishing House, 1994).

exegesis

In the Jewish context, exegesis is the process of explaining or interpreting texts, especially from the TANAKH, the Hebrew Bible. The ancient rabbis were experts in exegesis; much of the MISHNAH and TALMUD consists of exegesis, as does a great deal of rabbinic MIDRASH.

Midrash can be divided into two categories: homiletical and exegetical (*see* HOMILETICS). Homiletical midrash are essentially sermons deriving lessons from the actions described in the text, while exegetical midrash, such as in Genesis Rabbah or Exodus Rabbah, proceed line by line through the biblical text to elucidate every word or concept. Numerous rules were followed to determine the authoritative interpretation of each verse.

In later times, many philosophers were known for their allegorical interpretations of Scripture, while scholars of the KABBALAH favored more mystical or obscure exegesis. In all, tradition talks of four styles of exegesis, whose initials make up the word *pardes* ("orchard" or "paradise"): PSHAT (literal meaning), *remez* (allegorical meaning), DRASH (interpretative meaning), and *sod* (secret meaning).

Further reading: Michael A. Fishbane, *The Garments of Torah: Essays in Biblical Hermeneutics* (Bloomington: Indiana University Press, 1992); Jacob Neusner, *Introduction to Rabbinic Literature* (Garden City, N.Y.: Doubleday, 1999); Nahum M. Sarna, *Studies in Biblical Interpretation* (Philadelphia: Jewish Publication Society, 2000); H. L. Strack and G. Stemberger, *Introduction to the Talmud and Midreash* (Minneapolis: Fortress Press, 1992).

exilarch

During the early rabbinic period after the loss of Jewish independence, the political leader of the

Jews in PALESTINE was known as the NASI, while the political leader of the Jews in BABYLONIA was known as the exilarch. The exilarch was a hereditary position; the family was commonly thought to be descended from King David. Just as the *gaon* (*see* GEONIM) was the religious authority of the Jewish community in Babylonia, the exilarch wielded the political power.

After the redaction of the two TALMUDS and the decline of the Palestinian community, the exilarch was recognized as the political leader of all the Jews in the DIASPORA. For centuries he was in effect the royalty within the Jewish world. He lived and was treated like a prince, supported by taxes. As long as Babylonian Jews exercised self-government, the exilarch supervised criminal law, collected taxes, and appointed officers and judges. The post of exilarch existed from the first to the 12th centuries C.E.

Further reading: Jacob Neusner, *A History of the Jews in Babylonia* (Leiden: Brill Academic Publishers, 1997); Jacob Neusner, *Talmudic Judaism in Sasnian Babylonia: Essays and Studies* (Leiden: Brill Academic Publishers, 1976); Heinrich Graetz, *History of the Jews,* vol. 3 (Philadelphia: Jewish Publication Society, 1949).

exile *(galut)*

Exile, or *galut* in Hebrew, can refer to the act of expulsion from ERETZ YISRAEL, or to the life the Jews lived after being exiled from their sacred homeland.

The first Exile occurred in 586 B.C.E. when the Babylonians destroyed the TEMPLE, conquered JERUSALEM, and removed its inhabitants to BABYLONIA. The second or Great Exile occurred in 70 C.E. when the Romans destroyed the second Temple, laid waste to the land and took many prisoners into foreign slavery. While the first Exile lasted only until the Jews' return in 539 B.C.E., the second is considered to have lasted almost 2,000 years, ending only when ISRAEL emerged as a Jewish state in 1948.

Numerous theological approaches have been taken toward exile. The earliest traditions suggested that exile is the result of the behavior of the Jews: God sent the Babylonians and Romans to punish the Jews and exile them for their sins. As the second Exile grew longer, new theories emerged. In response to early Christian accusations blaming the Exile on the Jews' rejection of CHRISTIANITY, some Jewish theologians countered that Jews had been exiled to atone for the sins of the entire world. Meanwhile, rabbis of the KABBALAH maintained that the Exile provided an opportunity for Jews living all over the world to "gather divine sparks" and repair the world; they believe that God went into exile along with the Jews.

There is a group of ultra-Orthodox Jews who do not recognize 1948 as the end of the Exile. They maintain that only God can end the Exile, while the creation of the State of Israel in 1948 was a human event, not a divine one. Thus, this group believes the Great Exile has not yet come to an end.

Further reading: Yitzhak Baer, *Galut* (Lanham, Md.: University Press of America, 1988); David Biale, *Power and Powerlessness in Jewish History* (New York: Schocken Books, 1986); Franz Kobler, ed., *A Treasury of Jewish Letters: Letters from the Famous and the Humble,* vol. 1 (Philadelphia: Jewish Publication Society of America, 1953); "Lamentations," in *Tanakh: The Holy Scriptures* (Philadelphia and Jerusalem: The Jewish Publication Society, 1985); Etan Levine, ed., *Diaspora: Exile and the Contemporary Jewish Condition* (New York: Steimatzky/Shapolsky, 1986).

Exodus

The term *exodus* refers to the mass liberation of ISRAELITES from slavery in Egypt as recorded in the TORAH and commemorated in the PASSOVER celebration. Exodus is also the title of the second book of the TANAKH, the Hebrew Bible, which describes this event.

According to the biblical story, God called upon MOSES (Ex 3), an Israelite who had been raised in PHARAOH'S court, to return to Egypt and demand that Pharaoh let the Israelite slaves go. After suffering through TEN PLAGUES, culminating in the death of every Egyptian first-born male, Pharaoh finally relented and released the Israelite slaves to freedom (Ex 7–12). The slaves left hurriedly, but were soon pursued by Pharaoh's army when the ruler changed his mind. In a miraculous event, God parted the waters of the Red Sea to allow the slaves to pass through, and then closed the waters upon the Egyptian army, drowning them (Ex 14). The Exodus of Israelite slaves to freedom has come to be a symbol for spiritual liberation as well as political and historical liberation for peoples of many religions and nationalities around the world.

In modern time, the *Exodus* was the name of a boat carrying 4,500 Jewish refugees from FRANCE to PALESTINE in 1947. The boat was seized by six British destroyers who fired on the ship, killing several passengers. The British foreign minister, Ernest Bevin, decided to make an example of the ship once it had docked in HAIFA, and he sent the passengers back to Europe. Refusing to disembark in France, they were sent on to GERMANY, where British troops forced the people to disembark. The story spread like wildfire around the world, and prompted the UNITED NATIONS committee responsible for considering a Jewish homeland to approve the establishment of the nation of ISRAEL. Eleven years later, Leon URIS published a fictional version of the story in his novel *Exodus*, which became a powerful force creating pro-Israel sentiment among Jews and gentiles alike, and helped spark a revival of Jewish identity among SOVIET JEWRY.

Further reading: Bruce M. Metzger and Roland E. Murphy, eds., "Exodus" in *The New Oxford Annotated Bible with the Apocrypha* (New York: Oxford University Press, 1991); Ronald S. Hendel, "The Exodus in Biblical Memory" in *Journal of Biblical Literature* 120, 4 (Winter 2001): 601–622; Leon Uris, *Exodus* (Garden City, N.Y., Doubleday, 1958).

expulsion

Jewish communities have suffered many expulsions over the centuries, in particular from various Christian lands during the Middle Ages. Often, a ruler would expel the Jews to gain favor from the general population, and then invite them to return some years later when it was economically, politically, or socially advantageous to do so.

The first official expulsion occurred in Mainz, GERMANY, in 1012. In 1290, ENGLAND expelled its Jews, and FRANCE followed suit in 1306. The year 1483 saw a multiplicity of expulsions, in Warsaw, Sicily, Lithuania, and PORTUGAL. The most famous, and probably the largest, such expulsion took place in SPAIN in 1492, at the instigation of the Inquisition. In 1510 another Jewish community in Germany was expelled, this time in Brandenburg, and in 1593 both Italy and Bavaria expelled their Jews. In RUSSIA in 1881 Jews were expelled from 10 percent of the former area of the PALE OF SETTLEMENT. The POGROMS that occurred in Russia at the time were akin to expulsions, as thousands of Jews felt no option but flight. During World War II, vast numbers of Jews were pushed around the map in Europe between the Nazi-occupied countries both before and during the HOLOCAUST.

Further reading: John Edwards, *The Jews in Western Eupore, 1400–1600* (New York: Manchester University Press, 1995); Franz Kobler, ed., *A Treasury of Jewish Letters: Letters from the Famous and the Humble,* vol. 2 (Philadelphia: Jewish Publication Society of America, 1953); Yosef Hayim Yerushalmi, *Zakhor: Jewish History and Jewish Memory* (Seattle: University of Washington Press, 1996).

Ezekiel (sixth century B.C.E.) *biblical figure, prophet and mystic*

The prophet Ezekiel was active during the Babylonian attack on JERUSALEM and the subsequent exile to BABYLONIA after the destruction of the first TEMPLE in 586 B.C.E. Ezekiel preached and prophesized to the Jerusalemites about the impending fall of their holy city; his prophecies comprise the Book of Ezekiel, in the NEVI'IM section of the TANAKH, the Hebrew Bible.

Ezekiel was a member of the priestly house of Zadok. His language is sophisticated and riveting, full of visionary images while still informed by the priestly tradition of the TORAH. His main message was the sovereignty of God, who would punish the Jews for being sinful and rebellious (*see* SIN AND REPENTANCE).

The Book of Ezekiel begins with the image of a chariot leading God away from the sinful nation that would not listen to the prophets' warnings. The book ends with Ezekiel returning to Jerusalem and describing the horror and desolation of the city and the Temple.

While Ezekiel's warnings of destruction came true, he also reassured the people that God has promised to restore them to Jerusalem and rebuild the Temple, in keeping with his reputation for mercy. Ezekiel comforts the mourners with the image of the dry bones that come back to life and return to the land.

Ezekiel's rich otherworldly imagery plays a central role in subsequent Jewish mysticism. The mystical tradition of the KABBALAH is often traced back to this long-beloved book.

The imagery of God's chariot and of the dry bones are traditionally read during the festivals of PASSOVER and SHAVUOT. These holidays celebrate the promise of REDEMPTION and the restoration of God's law among the Jews.

Further reading: Norman K. Gottwald, *The Hebrew Bible: A Socio-Literary Introduction* (Philadelphia: Fortress Press, 1985); Moshe Greenberg, *Ezekiel 1–20* (New York: Anchor Bible Commentary, 1995); Moshe Greenberg, *Studies in the Bible and Jewish Thought* (Philadelphia: Jewish Publication Society, 1995); *Tanakh: The Holy Scriptures* (Philadelphia and Jerusalem: Jewish Publication Society, 1985).

Ezra (fifth century B.C.E.) *biblical figure, Jewish leader who helped rebuild Jerusalem*

Ezra, the chief character in the book bearing his name in the TANAKH, the Hebrew Bible, is credited with the reestablishment of Judaism in JERUSALEM in the 5th century B.C.E.

Ezra was the spiritual as well as political leader of the small Jewish community that had returned to Judea from exile in BABYLONIA. To stem a rising tide of ASSIMILATION to the surrounding pagan culture, he instituted a decree against INTERMARRIAGE. His greatest accomplishment, according to rabbinic tradition, was to restore the central place of the TORAH within ISRAELITE culture. Aware that the people were no longer familiar with the original HEBREW alphabet, Ezra ordained that the ancient Hebrew letters be replaced by the square ARAMAIC letters that are still used for Hebrew today. This allowed the people to reaccess their holy books.

Ezra fixed times for public readings of the Torah, settling on the morning of market days, Monday and Thursday, when the Jews would naturally gather, and the morning and afternoon of SHABBAT, the Sabbath, when Jews refrained from work and would have the time and leisure to learn. These times are still in effect today.

It was also Ezra, tradition says, who divided the Torah into 54 portions, to be read in a cycle over the course of a year. Many rabbis believe that Ezra also fixed certain Torah readings to be read at every public gathering. He is also credited with originating the SYNAGOGUE and Jewish prayer services outside the Temple precincts.

Further reading: Ismar Elbogen, *Jewish Liturgy: A Comprehensive History* (Philadelphia and Jerusalem: The Jewish Publication Society, 1993); Lawrence H. Schiffman, *From Text to Tradition: A History of Second Temple and Rabbinic Judaism* (Hoboken, N.J.: Ktav Publishing House, 1991); *Tanakh: The Holy Scriptures* (Philadelphia and Jerusalem: Jewish Publication Society, 1985).

F

Fackenheim, Emil (1916–2003) *post-Holocaust theologian/philosopher*

Born in Halle, GERMANY, in 1916, Emil Fackenheim studied progressive Judaism in Germany with Leo BAECK at the Hochschule für die WISSENSCHAFT DES JUDENTUMS (Academy of Jewish Studies) in Berlin. After KRISTALLNACHT in November of 1938, he was imprisoned in a CONCENTRATION CAMP. Released from the camp in March of 1939, Fackenheim immigrated to CANADA, becoming rabbi of the Reform Temple Anshe Sholom in Hamilton, Ontario, for five years (*see* REFORM JUDAISM), and then taking on his well-known role as professor of philosophy at the University of Toronto. Fackenheim eventually made ALIYAH to ISRAEL, becoming a fellow at the Institute of Contemporary Jewry at the HEBREW UNIVERSITY in JERUSALEM. He died in Jerusalem on February 19, 2003.

Fackenheim was a leading scholar of post-Holocaust Jewish theology and PHILOSOPHY. His life work was an attempt to help modern Jews understand the cataclysmic events of the HOLOCAUST, the murder of 6 million European Jews.

Fackenheim believed that Hegel was the greatest modern philosopher; when he began to develop his own theological response to the Holocaust, he drew on the Hegelian view of history, especially on the concept of myth. He argued that people need a "countermyth" to the Holocaust. For Fackenheim the Holocaust represents an extreme case of the modern desacralization of humanity. Jews need an equally powerful myth to counter this, and the best option rests with the experience of receiving the law at MOUNT SINAI.

Fackenheim notes that God gave 613 commandments at Mount Sinai, and he argues that the post-Holocaust world needs a new commandment, the 614th (*see* 614TH COMMANDMENT). This commandment is, "Do not give Hitler a posthumous victory by allowing Judaism to disappear." Judaism must survive and flourish in the modern world. For Fackenheim this is an existential crisis: the Holocaust indicates that evil is in the world. The only way for good to triumph is for Jews to assert their faith in God, especially in the face of this evil, and to live life fully.

The most telling symbol of embracing life is the State of Israel. Fackenheim asserts that the State of Israel is necessary, not just for the practical survival of the Jewish people, but as a visible symbol of life triumphing over death, of good triumphing over evil. In addition, the victims of the Holocaust must be remembered: "If we forget Judaism, the victims will have died in vain; if we forget the martyrs and what they stood for, their pain will be for naught; if we despair and give up the fight, then AUSCHWITZ will have the last word."

Further reading: Emil Fackenheim, *God's Presence in History: Jewish Affirmations and Philosophical Reflections* (New York: New York University Press, 1970); ———, *The Jewish Bible after the Holocaust: A Re-reading.* (Blooming: Indiana University Press, 1990); ———, *The Jewish Return into History: Reflections in the Age of Auschwitz and a New Jerusalem.* (New York: Schocken Books, 1978); ———, *To Mend the World: Foundations of Future Jewish Thought* (New York: Schocken Books, 1982); Peter J. Haas, *Morality After Auschwitz: The Radical Challenge of the Nazi Ethic* (Philadelphia: Fortress Press, 1988).

faith

The HEBREW word for faith is *emunah,* which is best understood as "trust." In Judaism, faith is understood not as intellectual assent or blind allegiance, but as living a life that trusts in God. The key verse is in Habakkuk (2:4): "But the righteous shall live by faith."

Biblical and rabbinic writers encouraged the Jews to maintain faith in God, even in the face of persecution, EXILE, and suffering. These writers presumed belief in the existence of God. It was only in the medieval period that Jewish writers began to present proofs of God's existence.

Within Judaism faith is transmitted through the community and family, through ritual practice and repetition of stories. The stories emphasize God's own faithfulness throughout history, and present examples of Jews who remained faithful even in the midst of great suffering and loss.

Recently the term *faith* has also been used in a more human context. In the Agudat Israel movement, an umbrella group for traditional followers of ORTHODOX JUDAISM, faith also connotes trust in certain contemporary rabbis as authoritative teachers of TORAH. In support of this view they point to the phrase "faith of the sages," found in the ETHICS OF THE FATHERS. Most other Jews read

the passage differently and do not understand it to imply that Jews should literally have "faith" in any human being.

Further reading: Samuel Huga Bergman and Alfred Jospe, *Faith and Reason: An Introduction to Modern Jewish Thought* (New York: Schocken Books, 1961); Louis Jacobs, *Principles of the Jewish Faith* (Northvale, N.J.: J. Aronson, 1964); Lawrence Kushner, *God Was in This Place and I, I Did Not Know: Finding Self, Spirituality and Ultimate Meaning* (Woodstock, Vt.: Jewish Lights Publishing, 1993).

family

In Judaism, the family is a crucial unit of religious and educational life. While attending SYNAGOGUE and receiving a formal Jewish education are important, traditionally much of Jewish prayer and education takes place in the home. So important is the family unit that even Jews unfamiliar with HEBREW will often use the word *mishpachah* (Hebrew for "family") in their ordinary speech.

Women have typically carried the primary responsibility for maintaining this central focus of Jewish life. It is in their purview to keep a kosher home (*see* KASHRUT), and prepare the home for SHABBAT (the Sabbath) and the many holidays. Traditionally, these practices were passed from mother to daughter within each family, though sons also learn a great deal in the process.

Some formal education occurs in the home setting too. TORAH portions are discussed during Sabbath meals; the PASSOVER SEDERS, which are also held in the home, are used as another opportunity to pass along Jewish knowledge and a sense of JEWISH IDENTITY.

One gets one's formal status as a Jew through one's mother and one's tribal lineage—*kohen* (*see* KOHANIM), LEVITE, or ordinary Jew—through one's father. One's Hebrew name includes the names of one's parents (e.g., "Abraham the son of Joseph," or "Abraham the son of Rachel," depending on the context). Children are seen as blessings from God.

Further reading: Gluckel, *The Memoirs of Gluckel of Hameln* (New York: Schocken Books, 1987); Michael Kaufman, *Love, Marriage, and Family in Jewish Law and Tradition* (Northvale, N.J.: Jason Aronson, 1992); Steven Carr Reuben, *Raising Jewish Children in a Contemporary World: The Modern Parent's Guide to Creating a Jewish Home* (Rocklin, Calif.: Prima Pub., 1992); Daniel B. Syme, *The Jewish Home: A Guide for Jewish Living* (New York: UAHC Press, 1988).

fast days

In the Jewish CALENDAR there are two major and five minor fast days. The two major fast days are YOM KIPPUR and TISHA B'AV. Yom Kippur is the only biblically prescribed fast; it falls on the 10th day of the month of Tishri, and is required as a day of atonement. Tisha B'av, the ninth day of the month of Av, is observed as a day of mourning for the destruction of the TEMPLES in ancient times and for other Jewish national calamities. These two major fast days include prohibitions against eating, drinking, washing, sex, and wearing leather; they last from sunset to sunset.

Minor fast days are more lenient; they last from sunrise to sunset and allow washing and the wearing of leather. Of the five minor fast days, three commemorate events related to the destruction of the Temple. The 10th of Tevet commemorates the day the siege began, the 17th of that month marks the day the city walls were breached, and the fast of Gedaliah on the third day of Tishri commemorates the death of Gedaliah, governor of Judea at the time.

The fast of ESTHER occurs on the 13th of Adar. According to the Book of Esther, she fasted three days before approaching the king on behalf of the Jews, and bid the Jews of the capital to fast as well in her support; the fast of Esther commemorates that event, and precedes the joyous holiday of PURIM. Finally, the fast of the firstborn occurs on the 14th of Nissan, the day before PASSOVER; first-born sons are expected to fast in gratitude for being spared from the 10th plague in EGYPT, though they may break the fast right after morn-ing prayers by participating in a communal meal with TORAH study.

Further reading: Irving Greenberg, *The Jewish Way: Living the Holidays* (New York: Touchstone, 1988); Naphtali Winter, ed., *Fasting and Fast Days* (Jerusalem: Keter Books, 1975).

fear of the eye (*marit ayin*)

Marit ayin (literally, "fear of the eye") is a legal principle that requires an observant Jew to refrain from any activity, even if permitted by HALAKHAH, Jewish Law, that might appear or imply to an observer that the person has done something forbidden.

An example of *marit ayin* would be walking into a nonkosher restaurant to use a bathroom. An observer who sees this might naturally assume the person was entering the restaurant to eat, and strict kosher laws (*see* KASHRUT) prohibit eating anywhere nonkosher food is served. This might encourage Jewish onlookers to disrespect Jewish law, or it might mislead them into thinking that the restaurant was in fact kosher. The principle of *marit ayin* is also designed to prevent non-Jewish observers from thinking that Jews are hypocritical in their practice of *halakhah*.

The many gradations of observance within ORTHODOX JUDAISM have led to a particular emphasis on the concept of *marit ayin*. Liberal Judaism tends to put less emphasis on halakhah, or interprets it more permissively; consequently those Jews who see themselves as liberal are less concerned about violating *marit ayin*. For example, many adherents of CONSERVATIVE JUDAISM consider it permissible to eat in nonkosher restaurants, as long as they avoid specifically nonkosher foods; they believe that an observer who saw them entering such a restaurant would have no reason to assume they would be eating nonkosher food there.

Further reading: Solomon B. Freehof, *A Treasury of Responsa* (Philadelphia: Jewish Publication Society, 1963); Blu Greenberg, *How to Run a Traditional Jewish Household* (New York: Simon and Schuster, 1983).

Feinstein, Dianne (b. 1933) *American politician*
Dianne Feinstein was born in San Francisco, California, in 1933. Although her mother was Catholic, and Feinstein attended Catholic school, her father, whose parents had emigrated from POLAND, sent her to a SUPPLEMENTARY SCHOOL to get a Jewish education, and she was confirmed at the age of 13 (it was not yet possible for girls to become a bat mitzvah in those days). Feinstein chose to identify as a Jewish woman, and she has been married to three Jewish men.

Feinstein graduated with a B.A. in history and political science from Stanford University in 1955 and entered San Francisco politics as a Coro Foundation public affairs intern. Feinstein has had a remarkable political career in California for a woman of her generation. She was appointed to the women's parole board at the age of 27. In 1969 she was elected to the San Francisco Board of Supervisors. In November 1978 she became mayor of San Francisco, calming the city after the assassination of Mayor George Moscone and Supervisor Harvey Milk by an angry former employee. She was subsequently elected to two four-year terms as mayor, and in 1987 was named the nation's "Most Effective Mayor" by *City and State Magazine.* In 1992 Feinstein was elected to the Senate for California, and she has been reelected to two full terms since then. Feinstein was the first woman on the San Francisco Board of Supervisors, the first woman mayor of San Francisco, the first woman elected to the Senate from California, and the first woman member of the Senate Judiciary Committee. Feinstein also holds honorary doctorate degrees from the University of Manila, Golden Gate University, and the Philippine Women's University.

In 1984 Feinstein became the first woman and the first Jew to be considered as a vice presidential candidate, when Walter Mondale was searching for a suitable ticket mate. As a Jewish woman in the public spotlight, Feinstein explains that Judaism "increased my sensitivity with respect to issues of discrimination and human rights in general."

Further reading: Maria Braden, *Women Politicians and the Media* (Lexington: University Press of Kentucky, 1996); Feinstein's official Web site: http://www.senate.gov/~feinstein/index.html; Frank P. Le Veness and Jane P. Sweeney, *Women Leaders in Contemporary U.S. Politics* (Boulder, Colo.: L. Rienner, 1987); Jerry Roberts, *Dianne Feinstein: Never Let Them See You Cry* (San Francisco: HarperCollins West, 1994); Elinor Slater and Robert Slater, *Great Jewish Women* (Middle Village, N.Y.: Jonathan David Publishers, 1994).

Feinstein, Moshe (1895–1986) *leading 20th-century Orthodox rabbinic authority*
Moshe Feinstein, affectionately called Reb Moshe, was born in Uzda, RUSSIA, a small village near Minsk. After studying in Lithuanian yeshivot (*see* YESHIVA), he was ordained as a RABBI at the age of 21. He immigrated to the UNITED STATES in 1937 when it became unsafe to remain. Feinstein was dean of Mesifta Tifereth Jerusalem in New York from 1938 to 1986. During that period the school became a leading yeshiva in the world of ORTHODOX JUDAISM.

Feinstein was known for seeking lenient interpretations of HALAKHAH in matters where individuals would suffer hardships, such as in cases of terminal illness. He also supported the use of artificial insemination even while his Orthodox peers did not, and he thought it acceptable to consider milk produced in the United States by ordinary commercial companies as kosher. He also contributed to Jewish law concerning issues that revolve around science, medicine, and technology.

On the other hand, in nonemergency situations Feinstein took a strict approach, such as forbidding Orthodox Jews to say "amen" to a prayer recited by a Reform rabbi (*see* REFORM JUDAISM). He is perhaps best known for his argument that marriages performed by Reform and most Conservative rabbis (*see* CONSERVATIVE JUDAISM) are not religiously valid, and thus do not need a religious DIVORCE if they are dissolved.

Feinstein served as president of the Union of Orthodox Rabbis of the United States of America and CANADA from 1968 to 1986. He is viewed as the most outstanding scholar of *halakhah* in the last 50 years, a leading TALMUD scholar and one of the most respected halakhic authorities in America. Feinstein was so beloved that approximately 60,000 Jews walked alongside his coffin in New York City when he died. His body was buried in ISRAEL, although he had never lived there.

Further reading: Shimon Finkelman, *Reb Moshe: The Life and Ideals of haGaon Rabbi Moshe Feinstein* (Brooklyn, N.Y.: Mesorah Publications, 1986); Bela M. Geffen, ed., *Celebration & Renewal; Rites of Passage in Judaism* (Philadelphia: Jewish Publication Society, 1993); Emanuel Rackman, "Halachic Progress: Rabbi Moshe Feinstein's Igrot Moshe on Even ha-Ezer," in *One Man's Judaism* (New York: Philosophical Library, 1970), 238–252.

Fiddler on the Roof

The musical *Fiddler on the Roof* premiered on Broadway in 1964. Based on the short stories of SHOLOM ALEICHEM, the musical examines the life of a Jewish milkman, Tevye, and his family in late-19th-century RUSSIA. As Tevye reacts to the unconventional marriages of three of his five daughters, he expresses the difficulties of adjusting traditional ways of life to the changing world around him. At the end of the musical, the entire village is forced to evacuate, and Tevye's family moves on to an uncertain future in America.

Fiddler on the Roof (later made into a hit movie) was written and produced by some of the leading figures in American theater in the 1960s: Jerry Bock, Sheldon Harnick, Joseph Stein, Hal Prince, and Jerome Robbins. The musical opened to immediate success, both with Jewish and non-Jewish audiences. Productions of *Fiddler on the Roof* continue all around the world to this day, and songs such as "Tradition," "If I Were a Rich Man," and "Sunrise, Sunset" have become Jewish classics.

Further reading: Sholom Aleichem, *Tevye the Dairyman and the Railroad Stories* (New York: Schocken Books, 1987); Richard Altman and Mervyn Kaufman, *The Making of a Musical: Fiddler on the Roof* (New York: Crown Publishers, 1971); Jerry Bock, *Fiddler on the Roof* [sound recording, original Broadway cast] (New York: RCA Red Seal, 1986); Joseph Stein, *Fiddler on the Roof,* libretto. Lyrics by Sheldon Harnick (New York: Crown Publishers, 1964).

Final Solution

The term *Final Solution* refers to the systematic plan by the German Nazis (*see* GERMANY; HOLOCAUST) to exterminate all Jews.

In September 1939 Reinhard Heydrich, the Third Reich chief of security, ordered all Polish Jews to be moved into GHETTOS in cities near major railways. In June 1941, after Germany invaded the Soviet Union, large-scale massacres of Jews were carried out by the EINSATZGRUPPEN, special forces under Heydrich's control. In January 1942, Heydrich convened a meeting of top leaders in Berlin, known as the WANNSEE CONFERENCE. This conference is considered a turning point in the development of the Final Solution.

At the Wannsee Conference, Heydrich laid out a systematic plan for the extermination of up to 11 million Jews, the entire Jewish population of Europe. This was simply a formalization and expansion of practices that were already in effect. At the time of the conference, a death camp (*see* CONCENTRATION AND DEATH CAMPS) was already operating at Chelmno in POLAND, and AUSCHWITZ, which had been established as a work camp, had already been equipped with gas chambers in the fall of 1941.

After the conference, however, the institutionalization of mass murder was taken to a new level. Heydrich called for a systematic worsening of ghetto conditions and an increase in the number of death camps. Belzec, Sobibor and Treblinka were set up for "Operation Reinhard," the mass extermination of Jews. From this time forward, Jews in ghettos were refused permission to work, and mass deportation from ghettos were carried out. By 1944 Jews were left only in the Lodz and

Kovno ghettos; the rest had been moved to camps or forced on long death marches toward the goal of their extermination.

Further reading: Götz Aly, *"Final Solution": Nazi Population Policy and the Murder of the European Jews.* Trans. Belinda Cooper and Allison Brown (New York: Oxford University Press, 1999); David Cesarani, ed., *The Final Solution: Origins and Implementation* (New York: Routledge, 1994); Gerald Reitlinger, *The Final Solution: The Attempt to Exterminate the Jews of Europe, 1939–1945* (London: Vallentine, Mitchel, 1953).

Finkelstein, Louis (1895–1991) *prominent Conservative rabbi, educator, and writer*

Louis Finkelstein was born in Cincinnati, Ohio. He graduated from the City College of New York, earned a Ph.D. from Columbia University in 1918, and was ordained as a Conservative Rabbi (*see* CONSERVATIVE JUDAISM) in 1919. Finkelstein taught TALMUD and theology at the JEWISH THEOLOGICAL SEMINARY OF AMERICA (JTS) beginning in 1920. He served as JTS president from 1940 to 1951 and chancellor from 1951 to 1972, when he retired.

Finkelstein led the seminary as a charismatic figure, skilled in both diplomacy and fundraising. He was a traditionalist, whose main passion was the study of Jewish texts. As his personal goals, he worked to ensure the continuation of Jewish scholarship, and to promote Jewish studies as part of the curriculum at mainstream universities. He achieved the latter goal, at least in part, when Louis Ginzberg, a Talmud scholar, received an honorary degree from Harvard University in 1936.

Finkelstein helped to strengthen the role of Judaism in modern society by showing the Jewish and American public that it was still a living tradition. In 1938 he founded the Institute for Religious and Social Studies, pioneering interfaith dialogue between Christians and Jews, and in 1938 he founded the Conference on Science, Religion and Philosophy. In 1944 he created a prize-winning radio show called *Eternal Light* that showcased the ethical teachings of real-life Judaism, bringing these ideas into millions of American homes.

A member of many Jewish religious and cultural organizations, Finkelstein was the author of countless articles and books, including popular as well as scholarly works on Jewish history and theology. He coedited the *Cambridge History of Judaism.* Some of his best-known works include *The Jews: Their History* and *The Jews: Their Religion and Culture.* The Louis Finkelstein Institute for Religious and Social Studies, established in 1938, reflects Finkelstein's legacy as a scholar of Judaism and of religion. Today the Finkelstein Institute works on interpreting issues of bioethics from a Jewish perspective.

Further reading: W. D. Davies and Louis Finkelstein, eds., *The Cambridge History of Judaism* (New York: Cambridge University Press, 1984); Louis Finkelstein, *The Jews: Their History* (New York: Schocken Books, 1970); Neil Gillman, *Conservative Judaism* (Springfield, N.J.: Behrman House, 1996); Michael Greenbaum, *Louis Finkelstein and the Conservative Movement: Conflict and Growth* (New York: Global Publications at SUNY Binghamton, 2001).

Five Disciples of Yochanan ben Zakkai

Yochanan BEN ZAKKAI was a disciple of the great sage HILLEL (first century B.C.E.), and the founder of the first great rabbinic academy at YAVNEH, called the SANHEDRIN. Tradition teaches that ben Zakkai had five outstanding disciples: Rabbi Eliezer ben Hyrcanus; Rabbi Joshua ben Hananiah; Rabbi Yosse ha-Cohen; Rabbi Simeon ben Nathaniel; and Rabbi Eliezer ben Erekh. These figures contributed significantly to the development of the rabbinic legal tradition. The disciples' title of RABBI, signifying their belonging to the Sanhedrin, marks the beginning of true rabbinic Judaism, when Jewish life and religion began to be defined by the traditions and rulings of leading rabbis. *Rabbi* was a title of respect that can be literally translated as "teacher," but the rabbis' primary role became the development and interpretation of HALAKHAH, Jewish law.

Further reading: Jacob Neusner, *A Life of Yohanan Ben Zakkai, Ca. 1–80 C.E.* (Leiden: E. J. Brill, 1970); Solomon Schechter, *Studies in Judaism: Second Series* (New York: Jewish Publication Society of America, 1908).

France

Individual Jews have lived in the geographic area that is now the republic of France since the first century C.E. However, it was not until the fifth century that a significant community appeared. Although the church produced anti-Jewish legislation (*see* ANTI-JUDAISM), it was somewhat ineffective, and the Jews were able to participate in the economy and even to pursue agriculture. In the sixth century a SYNAGOGUE was built on the Île de la Cité, in what is now Paris, and a Jewish community thrived there. By the 11th century the Jewish community was producing important Jewish scholarship. The most outstanding figure was RASHI, whose biblical commentary is often the first source consulted when studying TORAH, and whose frequent use of Old French words has made him an important linguistic source for students of that language.

The 11th century also marked the beginning of widespread persecution of the Jews in France. Massacres, forced conversions, and expulsions ravaged the French Jewish community between 1007 and 1394, by which time almost all Jews had been expelled from France, dismantling several major medieval centers of Jewish scholarship. The rabbis of France, who included the TOSAFOT, the Kabbalists (*see* KABBALAH), and the scholars of Provence, were scattered.

In the mid-16th century, CONVERSOS, or secret Jews, began to migrate to France from SPAIN and PORTUGAL, followed by Jews from eastern Europe beginning in the mid-17th century. By the time of the French Revolution there were approximately

40,000 Jews living in France, mostly ASHKENAZIM in Alsace-Lorraine and Paris and SEPHARDIM in the south of France. The first kosher inn in Paris opened in 1721 (*see* KASHRUT), and the first Parisian synagogue opened in 1788. In 1790 the Sephardic Jews became French citizens, followed by the Ashkenazim in 1791, marking the earliest EMANCIPATION of Jews in Europe. The law that

During an official visit to France, David Ben-Gurion (left), the first prime minister of Israel, meets with General Charles de Gaulle, president of France, in Paris at the Palais de l'Elysée. *(Fritz Cohen, Government Press Office, The State of Israel)*

granted Jews citizenship in 1791 also abolished the religious-legal autonomy that the Jewish communities had previously enjoyed. During the Reign of Terror from 1793 to 1794 the Jews suffered alongside others with ties to religious institutions. Synagogues and communal organizations were closed, and by the time they were reconstituted many French Jews had already taken advantage of an open society and begun the process of ACCOMMODATION and ASSIMILATION.

Napoleon Bonaparte revived the idea of Jewish autonomy in France. Napoleon believed that the emancipation of the Jews had not been successful and that the community needed to be regenerated. In 1806 he called together an Assembly of Jewish Notables, a committee of 112, to report on the compatibility of Jewish religious law and French civil law. He then organized a Sanhedrin (see NAPOLEON'S SANHEDRIN), consisting of 45 rabbis and 26 laymen, to codify the religious law as summarized by the Assembly of Jewish Notables. Two months later, having completed the task of writing the code, the Sanhedrin dispersed and the consistorial system took control. The consistory was responsible for monitoring the activities of the Jewish community, keeping track of the occupations and residences of Jews throughout France. These events were seen by many as a step backward in the process of emancipation.

In 1829 the French Ministry of Religions authorized the opening of a rabbinical school in Metz, a town that had historically housed the YESHIVA where most French RABBIS were trained before the French Revolution. In 1859, the rabbinical school relocated to Paris, where it continues to train rabbis today. By 1831 almost all anti-Jewish legislation had disappeared from France, and in 1846 the Jewish Oath, a special oath a Jew had to take when testifying in a Christian court against a Christian, was abolished by the Supreme Court of Appeals. Many Jews became prominent in the social, cultural, financial, and intellectual spheres, including actress Sarah Bernhardt, Isaac Cremieux in the Chamber of Deputies, the Rothschild and Pereires families in finance, the scholar Emil Durkheim, and the novelist Marcel Proust.

However, as the living conditions of Jews in France improved in the 19th century, ANTISEMITISM grew. The DAMASCUS AFFAIR, which occurred in Syria (then under French control), evoked hostility toward Jews in France. Communal leaders such as Adolphe Cremieux and the English Moses MONTEFIORE worked to balance the rising antisemitism by appealing to the French government, and by creating new organizations dedicated to the rights of Jews around the world, such as the ALLIANCE ISRAELITE UNIVERSELLE (1860). The second half of the century saw the emergence of antisemitic newspapers. In 1894 the DREYFUS AFFAIR, in which a French Jewish captain was charged with treason, brought French antisemitism to the forefront, though in the end Dreyfus was exonerated and his enemies defeated.

Since the late 18th century, two-thirds of French Jews have consistently lived in Paris. Several waves of Jewish immigrants arrived in France after 1881, in the wake of POGROMS in RUSSIA. Baron Edmond James de ROTHSCHILD, born in Paris, began to fund many settlements in PALESTINE as news of the pogroms in RUSSIA found its way to France. Over 25,000 Jews immigrated to France between 1881 and 1914, while many other Jewish migrants passed through France for other destinations. Antisemitism in France declined during World War I, when a patriotic spirit of unification prevailed. After the war, Jews from eastern Europe traveled through France, but did not stay; however, many Jews from Turkey and Greece did make Paris their home. In 1923 the Fédération des Sociétés Juives de France was created, uniting many Jewish groups under its aegis.

An estimated 300,000 Jews lived in France at the time of the German invasion of 1940. The Nazi FINAL SOLUTION, in concert with traditional French antisemitism, resulted in the deportation of an estimated 85,000–90,000 Jews during the HOLOCAUST. There were several CONCENTRATION CAMPS in France, such as Gurs, but most of the Jews were deported to death camps in Poland.

Perhaps 3,000 of these people survived the war. French Jews played a well-known and significant role in the resistance movements during the war, and despite some antisemitism, many French people played a positive role in helping Jews escape. Many children were successfully hidden on French farms. The church denounced deportations, and some Catholic and Protestant clergy were involved in rescue efforts.

Since World War II France has maintained the largest Jewish community in Europe, numbering between 550,000 and 600,000 by the 1970s. The community has become largely Sephardic, as it welcomed many North African and Middle Eastern Jews. The consistories created by Napoleon still manage some internal affairs of the French Jewish community, but without any of the restrictions that were originally imposed. In the contemporary world this organization is called the Consistoire Central Israelite de France et d'Algérie and represents mostly Orthodox Jews; it supervises kashrut standards and rabbinical training. There are some liberal synagogues that fall outside of the consistory's jurisdiction.

Most Jews in France are highly assimilated, and barely practice Judaism, although ORTHODOX JUDAISM has remained strong. There are a variety of Jewish publications and communal organizations, such as the Conseil Representatif des Institutions Juives de France, which coordinates 50 separate institutions. The Fonds Social Juif Unifié had its 40th anniversary in 1991, and it continues to organize social, educational, and cultural activities within the Jewish community, aiding in the absorption of new immigrants. The Alliance Israelite Universelle still plays an important cultural role in the French Jewish community, which is extraordinarily diverse and includes Jews from Turkey, Morocco, Tunisia, Algeria, EGYPT and Europe. In the 1970s and 1980s there was a significant increase in Jewish day schools and Jewish education in general in France.

Synagogues at Carpentras and Cavaillon, which date back hundreds of years, are considered national monuments. Another in Avignon did not survive, but was rebuilt in 1846. Generally, the Jewish community in France is divided along the lines of religion, culture, and whether or not one supports ISRAEL. France had close relations with Israel early in its history, and more recently has offered Paris as a meeting site for Israeli, Palestinian, other Arab, and European negotiators. However, since the SIX-DAY WAR in 1967 diplomatic relations with Israel have been more difficult.

Many French Jews have made ALIYAH to Israel. Antisemitism, in part based in the North African Muslim community, has become much more evident in recent years.

Further reading: Esther Benbassa, *The Jews of France: A History from Antiquity to the Present* (Princeton, N.J.: Princeton University Press, 1999); Paula E. Hyman, *The Jews of Modern France* (Berkeley: University of California Press, 1998); Michael R. Marrus and Robert O. Paxton, *Vichy France and the Jews* (New York: Basic Books, 1981); Renee Poznanski, "Reflections on Jewish Resistance and Jewish Resistants in France," *Jewish Social Studies* 2, 1 (1995); Emily Taitz, *The Jews of Medieval France: The Community of Champagne* (Westport, Conn.: Greenwood, 1994); Alan M. Tigay, ed., *The Jewish Traveler* (Northvale, N.J.: Jason Aronson, 1994).

Frank, Anne (1929–1945) *diarist and Holocaust victim*

Anne Frank is known around the world for her diary, which tells of her experiences hiding from the Nazis during the HOLOCAUST. Although her diary did survive, Anne died of typhus at the Bergen-Belsen CONCENTRATION CAMP.

Anne was born in Frankfurt, GERMANY, in 1929 to an assimilated Jewish family. When the Nazis came to power in 1933, her parents, Edith and Otto, understood the threat and fled to the NETHERLANDS, where the Frank family was safe in until 1940, when the Netherlands was defeated and occupied by Germany. Anti-Jewish decrees were passed that imposed restrictions on all Jews in Holland, and in 1942 many Jews were being captured and sent to slave camps, and then to the new death camps.

The Frank family, hoping to avoid deportation, hid for two years, beginning on July 6, 1942, in the annex of the building that housed Otto's business, along with several other Jews. Anne's diary recorded their experiences. In the beginning, she expressed a sense of adventure, but she soon focused on the inconveniences and hardships that hiding from the Nazis was placing on her and her family. Her diary describes her emotions, thoughts, and activities, providing a unique account of what it was like to hide from the Nazis during World War II. On August 4, 1944, the Frank family were discovered and arrested. They were sent to Auschwitz and then Bergen-Belsen, where Anne died weeks before the liberation in March of 1945. Of the Frank family, only Otto survived.

Anne Frank's diary was discovered and published by her father. *Anne Frank: The Diary of a Young Girl* has become a remarkable cultural phenomenon. It is read by many Jewish teens, serving as a lesson in the history of the Holocaust as well as an example of the indomitable spirit of Jews. The book is found on the reading lists of many schools. It was transformed into a successful play, and there have been several movie versions.

Many readers have been inspired by Anne Frank's ideals, as expressed in her own words. In her diary she writes: "That's the difficulty in these times: ideals, dreams, and cherished hopes rise within us, only to meet the horrible truth and be shattered. It's really a wonder that I haven't dropped all my ideals because they seem so absurd and impossible to carry out. Yet, I keep them, because in spite of everything I still believe that people are really good at heart."

Anne Frank's home in Holland has been turned into a museum, and a traveling exhibit has been created on her life. The exhibit includes 225 photographs that portray Anne's life and the horrors of Nazism. Some have said that Anne's diary is the most widely read book in the world after the Bible.

The *Diary of Anne Frank,* whose author is pictured here, is read by Jewish and non-Jewish teenagers around the world. The diary tells the poignant and true story of Anne and her family's years in hiding from the Nazis during World War II. Anne Frank died in a concentration camp weeks before the liberation in March of 1945. Her spirit lives on as those who read her words gain insight and hope for the future despite Anne's fate. *(Getty Images)*

Further reading: Anne Frank, *Anne Frank: The Diary of a Young Girl* (Bantam, 1993); Miep Gies, *Anne Frank Remembered* (New York: Simon & Schuster, 1988); Dick Van Galen Last and Rolf Wolfswinkel, *Anne Frank and After* (Amsterdam: Amsterdam University Press, 1996).

Frank, Leo (1884–1915) *victim of antisemitism in the southern United States*

Leo Frank was the only Jew ever to be killed by a lynch mob in the UNITED STATES. His death united the Jewish community to new efforts to fight ANTISEMITISM.

On April 27, 1913, 14-year-old Mary Phagan was found murdered in the basement of the pencil factory in which she worked. Leo Frank, her supervisor and a Jew, was quickly arrested for the crime. While certain circumstances made him an obvious suspect (he was one of the few in the factory the day of the murder, a Saturday), there was never any conclusive proof. Current evidence suggests that Phagan's murderer was Jim Conley, another employee at the factory. It is clear that local authorities were under pressure to arrest a suspect quickly, and when Frank was arrested an emotional frenzy developed around the case. Widespread jubilation spread throughout Atlanta when a guilty verdict was handed down in 1914. Pressure began to mount, for a speedy execution by some and for a new trial by others. Ultimately, Frank was dragged from his prison and lynched on the night of August 16/17, 1915. None of the men who lynched him were ever arrested or even identified.

Frank himself was born in Texas and graduated from Cornell University. He married the daughter of a wealthy Atlanta man, and he became a young leader in the local Jewish community. He seemed to exemplify the "ideal" American Jew: well-educated, professional, and affiliated with more liberal forms of Judaism. Leo Frank's arrest, public humiliation, trial, and lynching have often been understood as the eruption of latent antisemitism in the South. Some scholars have argued that Frank's particular troubles were as much the result of his northern origins and education, wealth, and social ungainliness as of antisemitism, but it is clear that the public attacks on Frank took on a strong and generalized antisemitic character. Frank was characterized as a "typical young libertine Jew" with a typically Jewish "ravenous appetite for . . . the girls of the uncircumcised."

Frank's appeals eventually attracted a national audience, most of whom viewed his conviction as a miscarriage of justice. Events surrounding Frank's accusation and death were a wake-up call to American Jews, particularly southern Jews, who had thought themselves safe from the kind of antisemitism that they knew was present in Europe. The case helped spur the creation of defense organizations like the ANTI-DEFAMATION LEAGUE. Historians have noted that Atlanta legal and political leaders were never overtly antisemitic; in fact, there seems to have been a desire to demonstrate they were not so. Even so, after Frank's trial and lynching, Atlanta Jews became markedly more hesitant to participate in public life.

Further reading: Leonard Dinnerstein, *The Frank Case* (New York: Columbia University Press, 1968); Albert S. Lindemann, "The Leo Frank Affair" in *The Jew Accused: Three Anti-Semitic Affairs (Dreyfus, Beilis, Frank) 1894–1915* (New York: Cambridge University Press, 1991); Steve Oney, *And the Dead Shall Rise: The Murder of Mary Phagan and the Lynching of Leo Frank* (New York: Pantheon Books, 2003).

Frankel, Zachariah (1801–1875) *German Jewish theologian*

Zachariah Frankel was born in Prague on September 30, 1801, and died in Breslau on February 13, 1875. He was the founder and leading thinker of the POSITIVE-HISTORICAL SCHOOL of Jewish thought. The school used a critical approach to Jewish scholarship while at the same time upholding the authority of tradition.

Frankel, on both his father's and mother's side of the family, was descended from great rabbinic scholars. He studied at a YESHIVA as a youth, and in 1825 went to Budapest to study at the university. After graduating, he secured a rabbinic position, and in 1836 became the chief RABBI of Dresden. By 1845 Frankel established his opposition to Reform when he walked out of the second Reform rabbinical conference, disagreeing with the removal of HEBREW from liturgy.

In 1859 Frankel published the *Darkhei HaMishnah* (The ways of the Mishnah), in which he introduced his theory of positive-historical Judaism. He presented immense textual support for his contention that Jewish law and the Jewish religion had always developed in response to changing historical conditions. While the divine origin of the TORAH may be true, human beings over time had taken charge of all Jewish legal development. The key to Judaism was commitment to Jewish law (*see* HALAKHAH), and the authority of that law had always rested on its faithful observance by Jewish communities over the generations.

Frankel believed that all human beings needed concrete symbols, and not just abstract ideas, though he never outlined his own personal theological position. Frankel's ideas are the fundamental philosophical foundation for CONSERVATIVE JUDAISM, which accepts that the community has always determined the shape of Jewish belief and practice in every generation.

Further reading: Neil Gillman, *Conservative Judaism: The New Century* (Springfield, N.J.: Behrman House, 1993); Michael A. Meyer, *Response to Modernity: A History of the Reform Movement in Judaism* (Oxford: Oxford University Press, 1988).

Freud, Sigmund (1856–1939) *founder of modern psychoanalysis*

Sigismund (Sigmund) Schlomo Freud was born on May 6, 1856, in Freiberg, Moravia. He was the oldest son of Jacob Freud with his third wife, Amalia. His family referred to him by the nickname of Sigi. He had seven younger brothers and sisters. His two half brothers, Emmanuel and Philipp, were approximately the same age as his mother, and he had a nephew near his own age. Freud's family life may have influenced his perspectives on family dynamics and his development of the theory of the Oedipus complex.

Jacob Freud was a financially modest Jewish wool merchant, who ultimately settled in Vienna (*see* AUSTRIA) in 1860. Sigmund remained in that city until 1938, when the Germans occupied Austria. He married Martha Bernays in 1886, and they had six children. In 1873 Freud began to study medicine at Vienna University, researching the mysteries of the central nervous system. Although he did encounter ANTISEMITISM at the university, he found his own niche there. Freud established a private practice that specialized in treating nervous disorders. In 1895 he copublished *Studies on Hysteria,* and he performed his first dream analysis on himself. From 1895–1900 Freud developed the basic concepts and methods of psychoanalysis, a term Freud coined to refer to the exploration or analysis of dreams and fantasies. He published his seminal essay "The Interpretation of Dreams" in 1899.

Many in the medical profession at that time did not welcome Freud's revolutionary ideas. Nevertheless, he was named a professor at the university. He founded the Viennese Association of Psychoanalysis, and cultivated a group of medical colleagues who worked with him and expanded his theories, including Carl Jung, Otto Rank, and Alfred Adler. Freud published many works, but they failed to attract much attention outside Austria until he visited the United States to lecture in 1909. The visit helped spark the psychoanalytic movement around the world, and the International Psychoanalytical Association (IPA) was founded in 1910. As psychoanalysis developed, Adler and Jung formed their own theoretical schools, placing significantly less emphasis on sexual/familial dynamics than Freud had.

Freud developed cancer of the jaw in 1923, but he continued working during his 16-year battle with the disease, which brought significant pain and 33 surgeries. Freud won the Goethe Prize for Literature in 1930, and in 1935 was elected an honorary Member of the British Royal Society of Medicine. When the Nazi regime in GERMANY annexed Austria in March of 1938, Freud fled Vienna and immigrated to ENGLAND with his family, at the insistence of friends. He died in London on September 23, 1939. His homes in Vienna and London have both become museums dedicated to his memory.

Freud was not a practicing Jew nor was he a member of Zionist organizations (*see* ZIONISM). However, he remained a member of the Jewish community, and kept up his membership in Vienna's B'NAI B'RITH Lodge; most of his colleagues were Jewish as well. In his last years,

Freud published *Moses and Monotheism,* his only major work that explicitly involved Judaism. In this work, he attempts to explain the distinct nature of the Jewish people, tracing their heritage back to Moses and EGYPT. He argues that the Jewish people remain filled with guilt until the present day because of their supposed murder of MOSES, their father (which is nowhere in the Bible account). His theories on Judaism and Moses were accepted neither by Jews nor non-Jews.

Freudian psychoanalysis has lost some prestige in recent decades. However, Freud's ideas about the unconscious and about the effects of family dynamics were enormously influential in 20th-century psychiatry, and are considered indispensable even today.

Further reading: David Bakan, *Sigmund Freud and the Jewish Mystical Tradition* (Princeton, N.J.: Van Nostrand, 1958); Sigmund Freud, *The Interpretation of Dreams* (New York: Avon, 1980); ———, *Moses and Monotheism* (New York: Vintage Books, 1967); Richard Wollheim, *Sigmund Freud* (Cambridge: Cambridge University Press, 1981).

Friedan, Betty (b. 1921) *feminist writer and leader*

Betty Friedan is recognized as the founder of the contemporary feminist movement. Her book, *The Feminine Mystique,* was a runaway best seller that jump-started the feminist movement and helped to revolutionize the lives of millions of woman.

Friedan was born on February 4, 1921, in Peoria, Illinois, as Betty Goldstein. She graduated with honors from Smith College in 1942, and afterwards settled in New York City. She married Carl Friedan in 1947; they were divorced in 1969. Friedan was a housewife, mother of three children, and freelance writer when she decided to mark her 15th college reunion by sending questionnaires to members of her class asking them to describe their lives since college. These surveys, combined with additional research, led to the book *The Feminine Mystique,* which was published

in 1963. The book was a best seller and Friedan became an instant celebrity.

Friedan maintained that many women did not feel fulfilled by their role as housewives and mothers. She criticized the prevailing culture, supported by education and the media, which directed women into lives segregated from men and from more fulfilling work.

Friedan cofounded the National Organization for Women (NOW) in 1966 and served as its first president for three years. She authored NOW's mission statement, demanding "full equality for women in the mainstream of American life."

Cofounder of the National Organization for Women (1966) and the founder of the contemporary feminist movement in the United States, Betty Friedan believes that the Jewish family is not threatened by feminism but will ultimately be strengthened by it. *(Library of Congress)*

Friedan's efforts led to NOW's support for an Equal Rights Amendment to the U.S. Constitution and the legalization of abortion. She traveled the country to preach on behalf of feminism. She welcomed younger women and encouraged them to share their more radical feminist ideas, though she always tried to keep a practical focus on the needs of average women.

During the late 1960s, Friedan taught nonfiction writing at the New School for Social Research and at New York University. Later, in 1988, she served as visiting professor at the University of Southern California's journalism school and at its Institute for the Study of Women and Men.

Friedan modified her feminist views in the 1980s and published *The Second Stage.* She began to argue that feminism should try not to polarize the sexes, but rather create a new system of equality that properly and equally addressed family issues. In 1993 she published *The Fountains of Age,* which addresses the "mystique of age."

Many of the feminist leaders of the 1960s in America were Jewish, including Betty Friedan; Gloria STEINEM, a founder of *Ms.* magazine; Bella Abzug, the first Jewish woman to serve on Capitol Hill; and Adrienne Rich, poet and theorist. Friedan was never an observant or religious Jew, but her encounters with antisemitism as a young girl increased her adult awareness of social injustice. Although she sees Judaism as a patriarchal system, she believes that feminism and its ideal of strengthening women do not threaten Judaism as a tradition. She stated in a *New York Times Magazine* article in 1984 that "Feminism is not a threat to the Jewish family. Family is basic to the survival of Jews. The liberation of women to full personhood will only help in the strengthening and evolution of the family." Betty Friedan was the only Jewish woman on *Life* magazine's list of the 100 most important Americans of the 20th century, published in the fall of 1990.

Further reading: Betty Friedan, *Life So Far: A Memoir* (New York: Simon & Schuster, 2001); Judith Hen-

nessee, *Betty Friedan: Her Life* (New York: Random House, 1999); Christine A. Lunardini, *Women's Rights* (Phoenix, Ariz.: Oryx Press, 1996); Judith Plaskow, *Standing Again at Sinai: Judaism from a Feminist Perspective* (San Francisco: HarperSanFrancisco, 1991).

Friedman, Thomas L. (b. 1953) *journalist and writer on the Middle East*

Thomas L. Friedman was born in Minneapolis, Minnesota, on July 20, 1953. He earned his B.A. in Mediterranean studies from Brandeis University, graduating with honors in 1975. During his university years he studied abroad both at the HEBREW UNIVERSITY of JERUSALEM and the American University in Cairo, pursuing a career in Middle East studies to compliment an early love of ISRAEL.

In 1978 Friedman obtained a master's degree in modern Middle East studies from Oxford. He took a journalist position with the London bureau of United Press International, and in 1979 was dispatched to Beirut. In 1981 Friedman joined the *New York Times* and after a brief period of journalist work in America, became their Beirut bureau chief in April 1982. At this time, Friedman returned to Beirut for several years.

After witnessing the Lebanon-Israel war (*see* LEBANON WAR), Friedman moved to Jerusalem and in June 1984 became the *New York Times's* Israel bureau chief until February 1988. In June 1989, he published *From Beirut to Jerusalem,* which became a best seller and won both the National Book Award for nonfiction and the Overseas Press Club Award for a foreign policy book. In *From Beirut to Jerusalem,* Friedman offers a straightforward eyewitness account of Lebanese and Israeli culture and politics. His balanced perspective makes this volume useful as a basic textbook for Middle East studies.

At the beginning of 1989 Friedman became the *New York Times's* chief diplomatic correspondent. At the conclusion of 1992 Friedman became the chief White House correspondent for the *New*

York Times. In 1995 Friedman became the *New York Times* foreign affairs columnist.

Friedman received the Pulitzer Prize for his writings on the Middle East in 1983, 1988, and 2002. He became a member of the Pulitzer Prize Board in 2005. Friedman continues to publish regularly in the *New York Times,* and his 2000 publication *The Lexus and the Olive Tree* made him a two-time winner of the Overseas Press Club Award. In April 2005, Friedman's latest book, *The World Is Flat: A Brief History of the Twenty-first Century,* was published.

Further reading: Thomas L. Friedman, *From Beirut to Jerusalem* (Garden City, N.Y.: Anchor, 1990); ———, *The Lexus and the Olive Tree: Understanding Globalization* (Garden City, N.Y.: Anchor Books/Doubleday, 2000); ———, *Longitudes and Attitudes: The World in the Age of Terrorism* (Garden City, N.Y.: Anchor, 2003).

G

galut *See* EXILE.

Galveston Plan

The Galveston Plan was a project to settle newly arriving Jewish immigrants in the U.S. interior, bypassing the densely populated urban areas where most Jews then lived. The plan was spearheaded by the prominent American financier and philanthropist Jacob SCHIFF, following its suggestion by President Theodore Roosevelt. Schiff and his supporters secured approval of a bill to establish an entry station for immigrants in Galveston, Texas. From 1907 to 1914 approximately 9,300 Jewish immigrants arrived via the port of Galveston.

Schiff wanted to rescue Jews from eastern European persecution, but also to divert them from the impoverished, ghettolike existence on the LOWER EAST SIDE of New York and other big cities in the East. He believed that settling Jews in communities where workers were needed would benefit the new immigrants immediately and have a positive overall economic effect. As long as most Jews entered via the eastern port cities, with their extensive and reassuring Jewish communities, they were unlikely to venture farther into the country, even though opportunities might exist for them there.

Between 1907–14, only a small number of Jews, approximately 9,300, was diverted to Galveston, and the overall plan was a failure. Conflict between the different Jewish agencies contributed to the failure. In addition, most Jewish immigrants wanted to be with family and friends who had arrived before them.

The Galveston Plan was not the only attempt to divert immigrants to the interior of the country. The INDUSTRIAL REMOVAL OFFICE also attempted to do so, providing opportunities for Jewish immigrants in Ohio and other midwestern states.

Further reading: Naomi Wiener Cohen, *Jacob H. Schiff* (Hanover, N.H.: Brandeis University Press, 1999); Joseph H. Udelson, *Dreamer of the Ghetto: The Life and Works of Israel Zangwill* (Tuscaloosa: University of Alabama Press, 1990); Howard M. Sachar, *A History of the Jews in America* (New York: Vintage Books, 1992).

Garden of Eden

The Garden of Eden is the earthly paradise created by God as a home for the first humans at the beginning of the TANAKH, the Hebrew Bible (Gn 2:8–3:22). The garden housed pleasing trees of all kinds, including the tree of life and tree of knowledge, and no human labor was necessary to provide food. Adam and Eve dwelt there until they were expelled for their disobedience. God then stationed the CHERUBIM at the entrance to the garden, along with a fiery sword, to guard against human entry. Over the centuries, many people have sought to find the Garden of Eden, but no one has been successful in that quest.

According to Jewish tradition, there is also a heavenly Garden of Eden, a paradise to which the souls of the righteous go after death. Once the MESSIAH comes, however, the entrance to the earthly Garden of Eden will be revealed and all will be able to enter.

Further reading: Gerard P. Luttikhuizen, ed., *Paradise Interpreted: Representations of Biblical Paradise in Judaism and Christianity* (Leiden and Boston: Brill, 1999); Raphael Posner, *The Creation According to the Midrash Rabbah: Rendered with Commentary by Wilfred Shuchat* (New York: Devora Publishing, 2002); *Tanakh: The Holy Scriptures* (Philadelphia and Jerusalem: Jewish Publication Society, 1985).

Gehinnom (Gehenna)

Gehinnom, or Gehenna in Yiddish, is a place of spiritual torment or purification. According to traditional Jewish thought (*see* TRADITIONAL JUDAISM), only a very few are ready to enter the GARDEN OF EDEN, or Paradise, upon death. The vast majority need some time to reflect upon their lives and repent for their sins. The period of time anyone spends in Gehinnom is not to exceed 12 months, about the same time relatives traditionally engage in MOURNING for the deceased. Some mystical texts state that we create demons with every sin we commit on earth (*see* SIN AND REPENTANCE), and these demons torment us after death in Gehinnom. After the time in Gehinnom has passed, the soul ascends to *OLAM HA-BAH*, the world to come, or, if the person was truly wicked, the soul is destroyed. Although many Jews contend that there is no Jewish equivalent to the Christian concept of hell, Gehinnom serves a similar purpose, albeit for a limited time.

Further reading: Abraham Cohen, *Everyman's Talmud: The Major Teachings of the Rabbinic Sages* (New York: Schocken Books, 1995); Moses Gaster, *Ma'aseh Book: Book of Jewish Tales and Legends*, vol. 1 (New York: Jewish Publication Society of America, 1934).

Geiger, Abraham (1810–1874) *a founder of German Reform Judaism*

Abraham Geiger was born in Frankfurt, GERMANY, on May 24, 1810, and he died in Berlin on October 23, 1874. His father was Rabbi Michael Lazarus Geiger, and his mother was Roeschen Wallau. Geiger is considered one of the most important of the founders of REFORM JUDAISM. He was a prolific author, historian, and teacher who helped develop the Jewish critical study of the Bible and other Jewish texts, a study that came to be called WISSENSCHAFT DES JUDENTUMS (the science of Judaism).

Geiger demonstrated genius at an early age, mastering Bible and TALMUD study while still a youth. He also learned Latin and Greek. At his BAR MITZVAH, he chose the unconventional practice of delivering his *DVAR TORAH*, or Torah teaching, in both German and Hebrew, which was considered extremely liberal.

Geiger's mastery of both traditional Jewish texts and secular studies transformed his religious views in the direction of liberal philosophy. From 1829 he studied Syriac and Arabic at the Universities of Heidelberg and Bonn, so as to improve his resources for the critical study of Jewish texts. On November 21, 1832, he was appointed as the rabbi for Wiesbaden. He became engaged to Emilie Oppenheim, but they did not marry until July 1, 1840. In Wiesbaden Geiger preached, taught, wrote, and introduced changes in the synagogue services, attempting to make them more like Christian liturgical forms.

In 1834, Geiger received his Ph.D. in philosophy from the University of Marburg. Geiger approached Judaism from a scientific perspective. He wanted complete critical freedom in dealing with the Jewish texts.

At Wiesbaden, Geiger gathered together other rabbis to pursue liberalization within Judaism; however, opposition from ORTHODOX JUDAISM forced him to resign his rabbinic position in 1838. Geiger relocated to a rabbinic position in Breslau. His liberalism appealed to the local non-Jewish government at the time; this was crucial, as the secular government's approval was needed for any rabbinic appointment. Geiger's new congregation followed their rabbi's liberal lead. They adopted his new prayer book, and supported his call for a "reform" of Judaism.

Geiger wanted his followers to embrace their German identity on equal footing with their Jewish identity. He noted that EMANCIPATION had resulted in high levels of ASSIMILATION among Jews, and he wished to stop the mass defections away from Judaism. His solution was to make Judaism a modern religion, appealing to the modern European Jew.

Geiger wanted to eliminate from Judaism any ritual that separated Jew from non-Jew. He was mainly concerned with upholding Jewish ethical laws; any ritual that did not support the ethical laws was not needed, and served only to separate the Jew from the modern non-Jew. Geiger's reforms included praying in German, reciting or singing prayers out loud in unison, abolition of the traditional cantillations, introduction of the organ as musical accompaniment, centralization of the sermon during the service, and delivering the sermon in German. Under Geiger's leadership Reform Jews rejected observance of the Jewish dietary laws (*see* KASHRUT), wearing a *KIPPAH* (head covering), wearing a *TALLIT* (prayer shawl), and putting on TEFILLIN (phylacteries). Within the liturgy Geiger removed all references to the return to Zion, the MESSIAH, the resurrection of the dead, or the restoration of the ancient sacrificial cult. Geiger personally opposed all prayer in HEBREW as well as ritual circumcision (*see* BRIT MILAH), but the Jews he led could not follow these doctrines, and Geiger did not pursue them.

Geiger established a school for the training of Reform rabbis, and he created the foundation for what became known as Classical Reform Judaism. His primary motivation was his fundamental belief that religious reform would allow Judaism to remain attractive to all modern Jews.

Further reading: Abraham Geiger and Max Wiener, *Abraham Geiger and Liberal Judaism: The Challenge of the Nineteenth Century* (Cincinnati, Ohio: Hebrew Union College Press, 1981); Robert Liberles, *Religious Conflict in Social Context: The Resurgence of Orthodox Judaism in Frankfurt Am Main, 1838–1877* (Westport, Conn.: Greenwood Press, 1985); Michael A. Meyer, *Response to Modernity: A History of the Reform Movement in Judaism* (New York and Oxford: Oxford University Press, 1988).

Gemara

The Hebrew word for "completion," *Gemara* is the term commonly applied to the commentary on the MISHNAH that appears in the TALMUD. The Gemara records the discussions of several generations of RABBIS as they analyzed and investigated the Mishnah, and reports the decisions they made on Jewish law, or *HALAKHAH*. The rabbis of the Gemara are referred to as the *AMORAIM*. The discussions in the Gemara constitute the basic foundation of RABBINIC LAW. The terms Talmud and Gemara are often used interchangeably, even though the Gemara is strictly speaking only one part of the Talmud.

Further reading: Isidore Epstein, ed., *Soncino Hebrew/English Babylonian Talmud* (Brooklyn, N.Y.: Soncino Press Ltd., 1990); Adin Steinsaltz, *The Essential Talmud* (New York: Basic Books, 1984); H. L. Strack and G. Stemberger, *Introduction to the Talmud and Midrash* (Minneapolis: Fortress Press, 1992); Jacob Neusner, *The Formation of the Babylonian Talmud: Studies in the Achievements of the Late Nineteenth and Twentieth Century Historical and Literary-Critical Research* (Leiden: E. J. Brill, 1970).

gematria

Gematria is a technique of textual interpretation that focuses on the numeric value of HEBREW letters.

Each letter of the Hebrew alphabet has a numerical value. Alef through yod have the values 1 through 10, yod through qof have the values 10 through 100, counting by 10s, and qof through tav have the values 100 through 400, counting by 100s. Consequently every word has a numerical equivalent, equal to the sum of the numerical values of each letter. For example, the Hebrew word for life, CHAI, has the numerical value 18. Therefore, it is a custom to give monetary gifts in multiples of 18 (36, 54, 72, 180), in the hope that the gift will bring long life to the donor or the recipient.

In this system, especially popular among mystical followers of the KABBALAH, relationships between words and concepts are established by noting similarities or mathematical relationships between their respective numerical values. The ancient rabbis used gematria to interpret the deeper meanings of texts, and mystics often associated the numerical values of letters to activities occurring on spiritual planes.

Further reading: Lewis Glinert, *The Joys of Hebrew* (New York: Oxford University Press, 1992); Louis Jacobs, *The Jewish Religion: A Companion* (Oxford: Oxford University Press, 1995); Gutman G. Locks, *The Spice of Torah—Gematria* (New York: Judaica Press, 1985); Howard Schwartz, *Reimagining the Bible: The Storytelling of the Rabbis* (Oxford: Oxford University Press, 1998).

gemilut chasadim

Gemilut chasadim technically translates as "love, grace, compassion, and kind deeds." In common discussion it is generally translated as "act of loving kindness." Whereas TZEDAKAH, righteous giving, refers to obligated giving from one's physical possessions, *gemilut chasadim* refers to giving of oneself. This can include donating time and energy to charitable activities, or simply performing acts of kindness.

The RABBIS of the TALMUD asserted that in three respects *gemilut chasadim* was superior to *tzedakah: Tzedakah* can be done only with one's

money, but *gemilut chasadim* can be done with one's person and one's money. *Tzedakah* can be given only to the poor, *gemilut chasadim* both to the rich and the poor. *Tzedakah* can be given to the living only whereas *gemilut chasadim* can be done both for the living and the dead (Talmud, Sukkah 49b). RASHI, the most-consulted biblical commentator, further explains *gemilut chasadim*: an act of *gemilut chasadim* can be "eulogizing the dead, rejoicing with a bride and groom, or accompanying a friend along the way." One can perform *gemilut chasadim* with one's money by "making a loan to another or lending your neighbor tools or livestock."

In Jewish Palestinian ARAMAIC, the phrase *gemilut chasadim* specifically referred to the burial of the dead and paying them last respects. In rabbinic HEBREW, *gemilut chasadim* refers to the whole range of pious acts that an individual can perform personally. Simeon the Just, in the Talmud, describes *gemilut chasadim* as one of the three pillars of Judaism along with TORAH and the TEMPLE service (Avot 1:2).

Further reading: Isidore Epstein, ed., *Soncino Hebrew/English Babylonian Talmud* (Brooklyn, N.Y.: Soncino Press Ltd., 1990); Lewis Glinert, *The Joys of Hebrew* (New York: Oxford University Press, 1993); Louis Jacobs, *The Book of Jewish Practice* (Springfield, N.J.: Behrman House Publishing, 1987).

genizah

Derived from the word meaning "to conceal," a *genizah* is a depository for unneeded books or other writings. HALAKHAH, Jewish law, teaches that no piece of writing containing the name of God may be destroyed, even if it has been damaged. Consequently, *genizahs* were established for damaged bibles, prayer books, ritual items, and any other paper or parchment that was no longer needed. When a *genizah* is full, it must be buried in a Jewish cemetery.

Ancient *genizahs* have proved to be valuable archives for scholars and historians. Perhaps the most famous collection is the Cairo Genizah, uncovered in 1890 and since moved to Cambridge, ENGLAND. The collection includes items from the 11th through 13th centuries, including rabbinical RESPONSA, poetry, treatises of legal teachings, philosophy, private letters, and contracts, many of them copies of important but otherwise unknown writings from still earlier periods. It opened a window on hundreds of years of Jewish and non-Jewish linguistic, literary, religious, and social history. The oldest item ever found in a *genizah* is a KETUBAH, or marriage contract, from the ninth century.

Further reading: Steven Fine, *Sacred Realm: The Emergence of the Synagogue in the Ancient World* (New York: Oxford University Press, 1996); Franz Kobler, *Treasury of Jewish Letters: Letters from the Famous and the Humble,* vol. 1 (New York: Farrar, Straus and Young, 1953); Lawrence H. Schiffman, *Reclaiming the Dead Sea Scrolls: The History of Judaism, the Background of Christianity, the Lost Library of Qumran* (New York: Jewish Publication Society, 1994).

genocide

Genocide is the attempt to partially or completely destroy a particular racial, religious, or national group. During World War II, the Third Reich embarked on a program of genocide by which they attempted to completely destroy European Jewry. Six million Jews, the majority of the European Jewish population and about one-third of all the Jews in the world, were ultimately murdered. This Nazi genocide has become known as the HOLOCAUST.

The Nazis also pursued genocide against Gypsies (Roma), and at least partial genocide against handicapped and homosexual Germans, Poles, Soviet prisoners of war, and other groups perceived by them as undesirable. There is evidence that had they won World War II, they would have pursued genocide against the Slavic masses of eastern Europe.

The Nazi agenda was to purify the so-called Aryan race of northern Europe. In the aftermath of the Nazi genocidal program, the UNITED NATIONS passed UN Resolution 260 in 1948, the "Convention on the Prevention and Punishment of the Crime of Genocide." The resolution recognized a history of genocide directed by one group toward another, and created the international law that criminalized anyone involved with actions related to genocidal behavior. Unfortunately, despite the convention, cases of genocide have continued to take place from time to time, as in the African nation of Rwanda in the 1990s.

Further reading: Doris Bergen, *War & Genocide: A Concise History of the Holocaust* (Lanham, Md.: Rowman & Littlefield Publishers, 2002); Frank Chalk and Kurt Jonassohn, *A History and Sociology of Genocide: Analyses and Case Studies* (New Haven, Conn.: Yale University Press, 1990).

Gentiles

In the Jewish context, a Gentile is any person who is not a member of the Jewish people or an adherent of Judaism. It is a translation for the Hebrew word *goy* (pl.: *goyim*), which literally means "nation," and popularly means "non-Jew"; the Hebrew word can have a pejorative connotation. According to traditional interpretations of HALAKHAH, Jewish law, Jews may have dealings with Gentiles, but there are restrictions on their interactions. In modern America, however, very few mainstream Jews restrict their interactions with non-Jews in any way, apart from religious participation in synagogues.

The State of Israel has coined the phrase "Righteous Gentile" to refer to non-Jews who took heroic and selfless risks to save Jewish lives during the HOLOCAUST. YAD VASHEM, the Holocaust Memorial in JERUSALEM, includes a grove of trees called the "Avenue of the Righteous," which honor these individuals and communities.

Further reading: Jacob Katz, *Exclusiveness and Tolerance: Studies in Jewish-Gentile Relations in Medieval and Modern Times* (New York: Oxford University Press,

1961); Morton Smith, *The Cambridge History of Judaism* (Cambridge: Cambridge University Press, 1999); Nechama Tec, *When Light Pierced the Darkness* (New York: Oxford University Press, 1986).

geonim (sing.: gaon)

The word *gaon* is Hebrew for "genius" or "great man." In Jewish history, the term *geonim* usually refers to the leading rabbis in the centuries after the completion of the TALMUD, though in common usage, any great religious or even secular scholar can be labeled a *gaon*.

Starting in the eighth century C.E., the leaders of the rabbinic academies in SURA and PUMBEDITA in Babylon were called *gaon*. These men were considered to be the most authoritative interpreters of the Talmud, although the post was usually transferred from father to son, or to the closest qualified relative, rather than according to merit. The most famous exception was the celebrated SAADIAH GAON, who earned his position as head of the yeshiva in Sura in the ninth century by his great stature as a scholar instead of inheriting the position. The *geonim* represented another stage in the long tradition of rabbinic interpreters, following the TANNAIM and AMORAIM.

The *geonim* exerted tremendous influence and authority within the DIASPORA and in Judea, and they oversaw the installation of the EXILARCH, the civil leader of the Babylonian Jewish community. They answered questions of HALAKHAH, Jewish law, posed by Jews throughout the world, often in the form of letters known as RESPONSA. They supervised the final redaction of the Babylonian Talmud, and their influence was crucial in establishing its authority over the Jerusalem Talmud. Saadia Gaon also wrote one of the earliest complete siddurim, or prayer books (see SIDDUR). The "period of the *geonim*" is usually reckoned as from the seventh through the 11th centuries. Other figures who appear later in Jewish history have been given that title to suggest spiritual authority, most prominently the Lithuanian Talmud scholar Elijah ben Solomon Zalman, the VILNA GAON, in the 18th century.

Further reading: Robert Brody, *The Geonim of Babylonia and the Shaping of Medieval Jewish Culture* (New Haven, Conn.: Yale University Press, 1988); Immanuel Etkes, *The Gaon of Vilna* (Berkeley: University of California Press, 2002); Franz Kobler, ed., *A Treasury of Jewish Letters: Letters from the Famous and the Humble,* vol. 1 (Philadelphia: The Jewish Publication Society of America, 1953); James Mann, *Response of the Babylonian Geonim As a Source of Jewish History* (Manchester, N.H.: Ayer Company Publishers, 1988); Solomon Schechter, *Aspects of Rabbinic Theology* (New York: Schocken Books, 1961).

Germany

The Jews in Germany have one of the longest and richest histories in all of European Jewry. Jews have lived in the German territories for almost 1,700 years, going back at least to the year 321 C.E., when a Jewish community in Cologne is mentioned in imperial Roman decrees. There were Jews at the court of Charlemagne in the ninth century. In the 10th century, the Jews in the German states looked to Palestine for religious leadership, and there is evidence of correspondence between the two communities. This was the origin of the liturgy and customs of the ASHKENAZIM, which took root in Germany and later spread to the lands to the east. Early German Jews participated in international trade with the East, and until the 11th century Jews were a respected component of the urban population. Many of the German Jews may have arrived there from Italy, following the trade routes.

At the end of the 10th century, there were Jewish communities in Mainz, Worms, and Regensburg. In the 11th century, Jews appear in Bamberg and Würzburg, and in the 13th century, there were Jewish communities in Breslau, Munich, and Vienna. As the social and political topography of the German states shifted, so too did the demographics and fate of the Jews who lived there. The city of Mainz became a center of TORAH learning in the 10th century, led by Gershom ben Judah, and the yeshivot of Mainz and Worms attracted

Torah scholars from all of Europe (*see* YESHIVA), including the well-known biblical commentator RASHI (1040–1105).

The rulers, whether secular or religious, who granted charters to Jewish communities were not always able to protect them from persecution. The First Crusade in 1096 brought violence, death, and destruction to the Jewish communities of Germany. The Jews of Mainz chose a martyr's death and coined a religious phrase to describe their death—*kiddush ha-shem,* the sanctification of God through martyrdom. The crusade seemed to bring with it permission for the common people to physically attack Jews, a practice that cropped up frequently in German lands throughout the Middle Ages. In addition to the violence, the Jews were usually denied the right to practice agriculture or crafts, and sometimes barred from trading as well. In the 12th and 13th centuries, the church began to enforce its laws barring Christians from charging interest on loans, which the church called usury. No longer allowed to practice any other livelihood, Jews began their long history of involvement in moneylending and pawnbroking. This only contributed to the evil image of German Jews, who were already considered to be rejected by God. Animosity toward Jews became chronic, and erupted frequently in physical violence throughout the Middle Ages. Nevertheless, the lack of any central authority, and the division of the country into many small principalities, meant that Jews were never expelled from the country as a whole.

During the 12th and 13th centuries a corpus of religious poetry, or *piyyutim,* and other religious literature was written by the Hasidei Ashkenaz, a Jewish movement that stressed piety in thought and deed, and developed the concept of *kiddush ha-shem.* By the 13th century the autonomous Jewish communities could usually boast a synagogue, a cemetery, a bathhouse, and a place for weddings and festivals. The Jews ruled and taxed their own communities, and published regulations, called *takkanot,* that described how Jews should live their lives. There were rules for how

much time to study Torah, how to protect family purity by regulating sexual relations, and how to observe SHABBAT, the Sabbath. Surviving until the modern period, this type of communal organization, called the KAHAL, satisfied the social and religious needs of the Jews; individual Jews had no more desire to leave the protection of the community than the outside world wanted them to do so.

By the 14th century the Jewish communities were well established; however, continued persecution and violence in that century and the next convinced many Jews to relocate to the east, to POLAND. Episodes of violence were accompanied by instances of BLOOD LIBEL beginning in 1235, in which Jews were accused of using the blood of Christians for rituals. Nevertheless, Jews of the 15th century were able to enter into trade and commerce. By the 16th century, COURT JEWS appeared in Germany, making the role of the Jew important once again to powerful rulers. Jews were invited into cities as readily as they were expelled, for their skills in trade, commerce, and moneylending.

Following the CHMIELNICKI MASSACRES of 1648, many Polish Jews sought refuge in Germany. There they incorporated their devotion toward KABBALAH, mysticism, and messianism (*see* MESSIAH) into the culture of German Jews. At the same time, the slowly modernizing governments of the small German states became more involved in the governance of Jewish life, decreasing the authority of the once-autonomous Jewish communities.

By the 18th century, the Jewish and non-Jewish worlds of Germany had begun to converge. Jews in the cities began to succumb to ASSIMILATION. Moses MENDELSSOHN, the father of the HASKALAH, or Jewish ENLIGHTENMENT, wrote his volume, entitled *Jerusalem,* suggesting that a Jew did not have to reject the modern world to remain Jewish. However, most wealthy Jews of this time did not take Mendelssohn's advice, instead choosing to assimilate completely, many converting to CHRISTIANITY.

In response to the huge rates of assimilation, many Jews began to focus on reforming Jewish practices and beliefs in an attempt to make Judaism more palatable to the modern mind. Abraham GEIGER and Samuel HOLDHEIM were two of the leaders of that movement. The first Reform synagogue was founded in Hamburg in 1817. REFORM JUDAISM was met by traditional Jews with the NEO-ORTHODOX MOVEMENT, which insisted on adherence to Jewish law even in a modern context; it was led by Samson Raphael HIRSCH. Alongside the rise of Reform and Neo-Orthodoxy, German Jews such as Zachariah FRANKEL suggested other modern variants of Jewish culture such as the critical and scientific study of Judaism, the POSITIVE-HISTORICAL SCHOOL and WISSENSCHAFT DES JUDENTUMS.

As the Jewish communities throughout the German states became more integrated within the non-Jewish world, the states themselves slowly followed the example of FRANCE in emancipating their Jews. In 1812 Prussia became the first German state to grant its Jews full rights as citizens, although many peasants did not approve this change in status. By 1870, when Germany had completely unified, Jews had achieved full citizenship everywhere in the country. Many Jews achieved high social status in Germany; incidents of ANTISEMITISM, which increased throughout the 19th and early 20th centuries, were dismissed as passing phenomena. By the 1920s the Jews had achieved prosperity and legal equality as German citizens.

This situation was totally reversed with the rise of Nazism in 1933. Jews lost all their rights with the Nuremberg Laws of 1935. In 1938 KRISTALLNACHT, the Night of Broken Glass, revived violence on a scale not seen for centuries, as scores of Jews were killed, hundreds of synagogues destroyed, and thousands of Jewish-owned businesses vandalized or destroyed. They were stripped of any university, government, or medical posts. Those who did not escape through emigration were starved and ultimately killed in Hitler's FINAL SOLUTION, the murder of 6 million Jews during the HOLOCAUST. Germany was declared completely free of Jews on May 19, 1938, although an estimated 19,000 remained there in hiding.

The effect of the Holocaust on German Jewry was devastating. Although most of the 6 million who perished were from eastern Europe, and the majority of Jews in Germany had time to escape between 1933 and 1939, the rich culture of German Jewry was destroyed. After the war, a small number of Jews came to Germany to join those who emerged from hiding, including some who returned to their cities and homes as well as displaced persons from other parts of Europe. Less than 5 percent of the pre–World War II community returned. In the 1950s many of the few remaining Jews in Germany immigrated to ISRAEL; by the 1960s the number of Jews in Germany hovered at 20,000, concentrated in West Berlin, Munich, Frankfurt, Düsseldorf, Hamburg, and Cologne. Very few lived in East Germany.

Until the late 1980s and the 1990s, the Jewish communities of Germany consisted mostly of the elderly. There were few communal organizations and only two Jewish schools. Intermarriage rates were very high. Oddly, however, the Jewish community of Germany became one of the wealthiest in the world because of reparations paid to Holocaust survivors and their descendents.

By the end of the 20th century, the Jewish community was revitalized by large numbers of immigrants from the former Soviet Union. By 1993, their numbers had reached 40,000. If one includes the nonaffiliated and the intermarried, the number of Jews in Germany is probably 100,000. The immigrants rekindled a vibrant Jewish communal life in Germany, opening kosher restaurants (see KASHRUT) and founding a variety of organizations. Religious life is primarily Reform or Conservative. Assimilation and intermarriage are still significant issues among contemporary German Jewry.

There is still antisemitism in Germany and many neo-Nazi groups exist. The German government, however, punishes hate crimes severely. In addition, the German government maintains good relations with the state of Israel, continues to send war reparations to many Israelis and encourages bilateral trade. There are many Holocaust memorials in Germany, including one in Berlin marking the spot where its 55,000 Jews were deported and another on the site of the old Jewish cemetery there.

Further reading: John Borneman and Jeffrey M. Peck, *The Return of German Jews and the Question of Identity* (Lincoln: University of Nebraska Press, 1995); Robert Chazan, *In the Year 1096: The First Crusade and the Jews* (Philadelphia: Jewish Publication Society, 1996); Ruth Gay, *The Jews of Germany: A Historical Portrait* (New Haven, Conn.: Yale University Press, 1994); Michael A. Meyer, *Response to Modernity: A History of the Reform Movement in Judaism* (New York and Oxford: Oxford University Press, 1988); W. E. Mosse, *The German-Jewish Economic Elite, 1820–1935: A Socio-Cultural Profile* (Oxford: Oxford University Press, 1989).

Gersonides (1288–1344) *medieval philosopher/ theologian*

Levi ben Gershom, known as Gersonides, was born in the year 1288 in Provence, FRANCE, a center for Jewish intellectual activity. Little is known about his life; although he produced many philosophical writings in HEBREW, he wrote little about himself. Scholars believe that Gersonides married, but are uncertain as to whether or not he had children.

Gersonides is considered the last of the Jewish Aristotelian thinkers. An authority on Jewish law, philosophy, and astronomy, Gersonides is best known for his work *Wars of the Lord,* in which he discusses Creation, divine providence, miracles, and the nature of the human soul.

Gersonides was criticized by his contemporaries for his attempts to reconcile religion and science in this work. For example, he taught that the world was created from eternal matter, not out of nothing. He did not believe that Jewish belief and rational thought were mutually exclusive. In fact, he explains many miracles as natural occurrences at providential moments: in the book of Joshua, the walls of Jericho fell because of the trampling of feet and the blasting of trumpets; the sun did not actually stop for Joshua—the battle

was over so quickly the sun did not have a chance to set. Gersonides also wrote a biblical commentary that explored the moral lessons that people can derive from the biblical narratives, thus making the stories relevant for the people of his time.

Further reading: Nahum N. Glatzer, *Essays in Jewish Thought* (n.p.: University of Alabama Press, 1978); Isaac Husik, "Levi Ben Gerson," in *A History of Mediaeval Jewish Philosophy* (New York: Meridian Books, 1958); Louis Jacobs, *The Jewish Religion: A Companion* (Oxford: Oxford University Press, 1995); *Tanakh: The Holy Scriptures* (Philadelphia and Jerusalem: Jewish Publication Society, 1985).

get (pl.: *gittin*)

A *get* is the official document that marks the rabbinic sanction of a DIVORCE. Rabbis in ORTHODOX and CONSERVATIVE JUDAISM, and some in the REFORM JUDAISM movement, require a *get* prior to performing a new marriage even after a civil divorce has been acquired. One tractate of the TALMUD, Gittin, directly addresses the subject of divorce and the correct legal procedures for writing and delivering the *get.*

Further reading: Isidore Epstein, ed., *Soncino Hebrew/English Babylonian Talmud* (Brooklyn, N.Y.: Soncino Press Ltd., 1990); Rela M. Geffen, *Celebration and Renewal: Rites of Passage in Judaism* (Philadelphia: Jewish Publication Society, 1993); M. Mielziner, *The Jewish Law of Marriage and Divorce in Ancient and Modern Times, and Its Relation to the Law of the State* (Buffalo, N.Y.: William S. Hein & Co., 1987); Shlomo Riskin, *Women and Jewish Divorce: The Rebellious Wife, the Agunah and the Right of Women to Initiate Divorce* (Hoboken, N.J.: Ktav Publishing, 2003).

ghetto

A ghetto was an urban community where Jews were forced to live by the secular authorities, usually surrounded by a wall. The word is Italian, though the original derivation is unclear.

Jews in many European countries were often forced to live in crowded walled neighborhoods in the Middle Ages. The practice became institutionalized in Italy by order of Pope Paul IV (1555). Jews were not allowed to leave their communities at night, and they were forced to wear identifying badges when they left the ghetto during the day.

The practice of segregating Jews in marginal neighborhoods quickly spread throughout Europe and continued in some places into the late 19th century. The Jewish ghettos offered some safety for Jews. Some even welcomed the seclusion that facilitated a large degree of self-rule.

The Nazis reinstituted the practice in POLAND during World War II, as a stage in the FINAL SOLUTION. These new ghettos were extremely crowded, squalid neighborhoods under strict and brutal surveillance, and were gradually depopulated by deportations to the death camps. Two of the most famous were the WARSAW GHETTO and the Lodz Ghetto, both of which saw failed but heroic uprisings against the Nazi authorities. The Warsaw Ghetto alone housed over 500,000 people, approximately one-third of Warsaw's population, but by winter 1943, only 60,000 Jews remained.

In modern times the term has been used to refer to voluntary communities of Jews. It is also used to refer to poor neighborhoods populated by any minority group, and in many communities the term continues to have negative connotations.

Further reading: Alan Adelson, ed., *The Diary of Dawid Sierakowiak: Five Notebooks from the Lodz Ghetto,* trans. Kamil Turowski (New York: Oxford University Press, 1996); Raya Cohen, "Against the Current: Hashomer Hatzair in the Warsaw Ghetto" in *Jewish Social Studies* 7 (2000); Jacob Katz, *Out of the Ghetto: The Social Background of Jewish Emancipation, 1770–1870* (Syracuse, N.Y.: Syracuse University Press, 1998).

Ginsberg, Allen (1926–1997) *American poet*

Allen Ginsberg was born in Newark, New Jersey, on June 3, 1926. He became one of America's most renowned poets.

Ginsberg was best known as a spokesman for the beatnik or hippie point of view. One masterwork, titled *Howl,* contains the famous opening line "I saw the best minds of my generation destroyed by madness." He wrote in an American idiom, but he traveled the world extensively, and his works eventually reflected a global consciousness. He became very interested in Eastern religions, and he ultimately became a Buddhist (*see* JUBU). Ginsberg's overall literary works are considered to be one of the great literary canons in American history.

Ginsberg energetically promoted his work, and also the works of colleagues. In 1973 he and poet Anne Waldman cofounded the Jack Kerouac School of Disembodied Poetics at the Naropa Institute in Boulder, Colorado.

Ginsberg often infused his literary works with Jewish imagery and YIDDISH expressions, though he primarily taught the values and beliefs of Buddhists, and to some extent, Hindus. He gave the posthumous biography of his mother, Naomi Ginsberg, the title *Kaddish,* the Jewish prayer for the dead. In the poem, one of his most celebrated, he chronicles his mother's tortured battles with mental illness.

Ginsberg died of liver cancer on April 5, 1997.

Further reading: Allen Ginsberg, *Howl and Other Poems* (San Francisco: City Lights Publishers, 1956); Allen Ginsberg, *Kaddish and Other Poems, 1958–1960* (San Francisco: City Lights Publishers, 1960); Jane Kramer, *Allen Ginsberg in America: With a New Introduction by the Author* (New York: Random House, 1969); Norman Podhoretz, "My War with Allen Ginsberg," *Commentary* 104, 2 (1997).

Ginsburg, Ruth Bader (b. 1933)
U.S. Supreme Court justice

Ginsburg was born on March 15, 1933, to Nathan and Cecelia Bader in a middle-class home in Brooklyn, New York. Ginsburg's early years were overshadowed by the HOLOCAUST, as World War II continued to rage and capture the attention of

Jews lucky enough to live in the UNITED STATES. After graduating from high school, she attended Cornell University, where she graduated with high honors in government. She then attended Harvard Law School, excelled in her studies, and served on the *Harvard Law Review.* She married while in school and transferred to Columbia University for her last year of study, achieving *Law Review* there as well.

After graduating from law school in 1960, Ginsburg was recommended to clerk for Supreme Court Justice Felix Frankfurter. Frankfurter acknowledged Ginsburg's qualifications, but refused to hire her because he was not ready to hire a woman. The incident deeply affected Ginsburg and motivated her to address issues of legal equality for women throughout her career.

Rebuffed by Frankfurter, Ginsburg instead clerked for District Judge Edmund L. Palmieri in New York and then joined the faculty of Rutgers University. To retain her faculty position she had to hide her pregnancy. Ginsburg was only the second woman on the school's faculty and among the first 20 women law professors in the entire country. In the early 1970s, Ginsburg became Columbia University's first tenured female professor.

Ginsburg excelled in her scholarship, but her major accomplishment was as the counsel to the American Civil Liberties Union (ACLU). In this position she founded and directed their Women's Rights Project. In a 1973 case Ginsburg successfully argued before the Supreme Court against a federal statute that gave more housing and medical benefits to men in the armed services than to women. She won five of the six cases she argued before the Supreme Court, ultimately demonstrating that equal protection under the constitution applied not just to race but also gender.

President Jimmy Carter appointed Ginsburg to the United States Court of Appeals. As a judge she ruled consistently in favor of laws defending equal rights, but she is still considered conservative in her legal scholarship. She believes and acts upon the legal principle that judges must interpret the laws and not create the laws. President Bill Clin-

Ruth Bader Ginsburg grew up in Brooklyn, New York, in the shadow of the Holocaust. She became an advocate of gender equality under the law and the second woman to be appointed a Supreme Court justice. *(The Supreme Court Historical Society)*

ton nominated Ginsburg to the Supreme Court. Although a Democratic president had nominated Ginsburg, her nomination was welcomed by many conservative Republicans, who saw her as a fair judge who would steer away from any ideological bias. On August 3, 1993, Ginsburg was confirmed by the Senate in a vote of 96 to 3, becoming the 107th Supreme Court justice, and its second female jurist.

As a Supreme Court justice, Ginsburg has continued to strongly back gender equality. In 1999, she won the American Bar Association's Thurgood

Marshall Award for her contributions to gender equality and civil rights. Ginsburg underwent surgery to treat colon cancer in September 1999 but recovered without complications. Ginsburg remains on the Court today and is considered to exemplify scholarly precision in her legal opinions.

Further reading: Hasia R. Diner and Beryl Lieff Benderly, *Her Works Praise Her: A History of Jewish Women in America from Colonial Times to the Present* (New York: Basic Books, 2003); Ruth Bader Ginsburg, "Affirmative Action as an International Human Rights Dialogue," *Brookings Review* 18, 1 (Winter 2000); *The Justices of the United States Supreme Court, Their Lives and Major Opinions*, vol. 5 (New York: Chelsea House, 1995).

Giving of the Torah

The Giving of the Torah, also known as the REVELATION, is one of three key moments in Jewish theology, along with CREATION and REDEMPTION.

According to the TANAKH, the Hebrew Bible, God gave the Torah to the ISRAELITES in the wilderness around MOUNT SINAI (Ex 19–20). God descended upon the mountain, which erupted with fire and smoke, and quaked amid thunder and lightning. God's voice was heard by the people of ISRAEL as the Ten Commandments (*see* DECALOGUE) were conveyed. The people, too terrified to continue, asked MOSES to receive the rest of the Torah directly from God and pass it along to them.

The ancient rabbis assigned a date to this event—the sixth day of the month of Sivan, and each year the moment is reenacted during the festival of SHAVUOT. The rabbis also related many stories about the event in the MIDRASH. Two of the best-known anecdotes are somewhat contradictory. In the first, God approaches other nations with the Torah, but each of them finds one of the commandments impossible to perform; only the people of Israel agree to all the commandments and thus are worthy of receiving the Torah. In the other story, God holds a large rock over the people until they agree to accept the law.

Traditional Judaism holds that the entire Torah was revealed to Moses at Mount Sinai, as was the Oral Law later elucidated by the rabbis in the TALMUD. However, most modern textual scholars dispute this. Since the 19th century, they have held to the Documentary Hypothesis theory, in which four different authors or editors had primary responsibility for shaping the Torah text we have today.

Further reading: Jacob Neusner, *Foundations of Judaism* (Atlanta, Ga.: Scholars Press, 1993); Michael D. Oppenheim, *What Does Revelation Mean for the Modern Jew?: Rosenzweig, Buber, Fackenheim* (Lewiston, N.Y.: Edwin Mellen Press, 1985); Norbert Max Samuelson, *Revelation and the God of Israel* (Cambridge and New York: Cambridge University Press, 2002); *Tanakh: The Holy Scriptures* (Philadelphia and Jerusalem: Jewish Publication Society, 1985).

Glueckel of Hameln (1645–1724) *German Jewish writer and businesswoman*

Glueckel was born in Hamburg in 1645 into a prosperous and prominent family. When she was 14 years old her family arranged for a marriage with Chayim of Hameln. Glueckel gave birth to 12 children, while assisting her husband in all business matters. When her husband died in 1689, she successfully took over his business. Depressed at the loss of her husband, Glueckel tried to deal with her melancholy by writing a memoir/diary of her life, in her native YIDDISH. She also wanted to provide a family history for her children and grandchildren. She began writing in 1691, completing the first five sections in 1699. She stopped writing upon her remarriage to banker Cerf Levy of Metz, though she resumed in 1715. Glueckel finished the last two sections of her memoirs in 1719.

The original manuscript is lost, but Glueckel's descendants preserved her words. In 1896 the diary was published by David Kaufmann in Yiddish; he included a German introduction. Translations later appeared in German, English, and

HEBREW. The book now has immense value to historians as the only Jewish document of its time written by a woman. It is also an important source of information on the Yiddish language of the time, and on daily life in Hamburg, Berlin, Amsterdam, and other European cities.

Glueckel had a poetic style, and demonstrated a firm grasp of Jewish religious texts. She was observant and enjoyed the *tchinot*, the traditional Yiddish prayers for women. She liked to include moral lessons in her writing. Most significantly, Glueckel's writings demonstrate that women as well as men have traditionally studied the Jewish sacred texts and were partners in their families' financial affairs.

Further reading: Glueckel of Hameln, *The Memoirs of Glueckel of Hameln* (New York: Schocken Books, 1977); Michele Klein, *A Time to Be Born: Customs and Folklore of Jewish Birth* (Philadelphia: Jewish Publication Society, 1998); Hilary L. Rubinstein, *The Jews in the Modern World: A History Since 1750* (New York: Arnold Publication, 2002).

God, names of

According to the RABBIS, seven names of God that appear in the TANAKH, the Hebrew Bible, require special care when a scribe is writing them: YHWH, Adonai, Ehyeh-Asher-Ehyeh, Adonai Tzevaot, El, Elohim, and El Shaddai.

The Hebrew Bible usually calls the deity by one of two Hebrew names: *Elohim* (usually translated by the English word "God") and *YHWH*, which is never pronounced as it is written but replaced with the word *Adonai* (usually translated as "Lord"), which also appears in the Hebrew Bible. *YHWH*, also called the tetragrammaton, is understood in Judaism to be God's proper name. In ancient times, it was pronounced only once a year by the HIGH PRIEST on YOM KIPPUR, the Day of Atonement. The pronunciation has since been lost, and Jews use the euphemism *Adonia*, meaning "my Lord," because of the traditional way *YHWH* is voweled. *YHWH* represents the consonants for the verb "to

be" or "exist," but vowels are needed to give it tense: "was," "is," or "will be." Since Jews do not know for certain the true vowels, this implies that God transcends tense and is eternal.

The phrase *Ehyeh-Asher-Ehyeh*, similarly contains the consonants of the verb to be and has been understood as meaning either "I am what I am" or "I will be what I will be." This is the response God gives in the book of EXODUS (3:14) when Moses asks God's name. Related to these is the term *Adonai Tzeva'ot* (*YHWH Tzeva'ot*), which is translated "Lord of Hosts" and refers to God's sovereignty over the angels in heaven (*see* MALAKHIM). *El Shaddai* is usually translated as "God Almighty"; *Shaddai* is the name of God that appears on MEZUZAHS.

Critical scholars maintain that the Hebrew Bible as we know it was created by merging two separate earlier traditions about God, the J, or "Yahwist," strand (*Jahwist* in German), and the E, or "Elohist," strand; the Yahwist uses *YHWH* (*Adonai*), the Elohist uses *Elohim*. *El* means "god," or "true God," depending on the context; *Elohim* is the "intensive plural" form of the word, and both terms appear in the Hebrew Bible, translated simply as "God" when referring to the Israelite deity. The plural form, which may have entered from a neighboring polytheistic culture, has always been understood in Judaism to refer to a singular God. Judaism entails a doctrine of radical monotheism, meaning there is only one God. There can be no trinity, duality, or other forms of God. However, the fact that God is referred to by different names in the Hebrew Bible (and *Elohim* is a plural word), may suggest a polytheistic origin. To avoid this implication, the ancient rabbis went to great lengths to account for different names of God that appear in the Hebrew Bible.

The traditions were placed side by side and redacted by an editor to create a unified text. Thus, the text often contains both names together, *Adonai* and *Elohim*, usually translated as "the Lord God." From a traditional Jewish perspective, the two names refer to one and the same God. The rabbis comment that the names denote different aspects of God. Elohim is the aspect of justice, while Adonai is the aspect of mercy. When the text wants to emphasize one aspect of God over another the appropriate designation is used, as in the case of Elohim meting out punishment.

A number of other terms appear in the Hebrew Bible that are understood to be names of God. Students of the KABBALAH, using mystical techniques of manipulating letters and numbers, count 72 names of God; Kabbalists believe that knowing these names can aid in all aspects of life.

It is considered blasphemy to utter God's personal names, and for followers of ORTHODOX JUDAISM, pronouncing any of the above names of God outside of PRAYER or TORAH reading is also blasphemy; such Jews instead refer to God as HaShem, meaning "the Name." Interestingly, this prohibition has crept into the practice of writing God's name in English. Many Jews will choose to write "G-d" instead of "God" to avoid blasphemy.

Further reading: Yehudah Berg, *The 72 names of God: Technology for the Soul* (Los Angeles: Kabbalah Centre, 2003); Herbert Chanan Brichto, *The Names of God: Poetic Readings in Biblical Beginnings* (New York: Oxford University Press, 1998); Peter Schafer, *The Hidden and Manifest God: Some Major Themes in Early Jewish Mysticism* (Albany: State University of New York Press, 1992); Richard Elliott Friedman, *Who Wrote the Bible?* (San Francisco: HarperSanFrancisco, 1987); Mark S. Smith, *The Origins of Biblical Monotheism: Israel's Polytheistic Background and the Ugaritic Texts* (Oxford and New York: Oxford University Press, 2001); *Tanakh: The Holy Scriptures* (Philadelphia and Jerusalem: Jewish Publication Society, 1985).

Gog and Magog

In a vision of the prophet EZEKIEL, Gog and Magog are peoples who will wage war against the Jews before the MESSIAH comes. Historically, various theologians and communities have tried to identify Gog and Magog with one of the parties in specific contemporary conflicts; this happened during both world wars. It is perhaps more help-

ful to understand the names as elements of Ezekiel's broader ESCHATOLOGY.

Further reading: Martin Goodman, *Jews in a Graeco-Roman World* (New York: Oxford University Press, 1998); Jacob Neusner, *The Theology of the Oral Torah: Revealing the Justice of God* (Montreal: McGill-Queens University Press, 1999).

Golden Calf

The Golden Calf was a statue representing a god that Aaron made at the demand of the ISRAELITES (Ex 32).

While MOSES is on MOUNT SINAI receiving the TORAH from GOD, the Israelites grow restless and anxious at his absence. They demand a tangible representation of God that they can worship. They bring their gold to AARON, who melts it down and creates a golden calf, the image of BAAL, a Caananite God (Ex 32). When Moses returns from the mountain and finds the Israelites practicing IDOLATRY, he smashes the tablets containing God's commandments and berates the people.

In Jewish tradition, the Golden Calf incident is frequently referred to as the epitome of sin. The Israelites were punished by a deadly plague and a decree that the entire generation would never enter the land of ISRAEL. Only the next generation, which had not participated in the incident, would be allowed to enter.

Some scholars interpret the Golden Calf story from the perspective of later Israelite political history. Throughout the book of Kings, the various monarchs are deemed good or bad based largely on their behavior regarding idolatry. The good kings centralize worship of the one God at the TEMPLE in JERUSALEM, while the bad kings allow worship at shrines outside Jerusalem and tolerate worship of Baal. One of the worst of these kings, Jeroboam, erects golden calves at Dan and Bethel. Thus, it is possible that the episode of the Golden Calf in the desert is a later polemic by the centralists who, the scholars say, wrote the book of Kings.

Further reading: Pier Cesare Bori, *The Golden Calf and the Origins of the Anti-Jewish Controversy* (Atlanta, Ga.: Scholars Press, 1990); Nahum M. Sarna, *Exploring Exodus: The Origins of Biblical Israel* (New York: Schocken Books, 1996); *Tanakh: The Holy Scriptures* (Philadelphia and Jerusalem: Jewish Publication Society, 1985).

golem

A golem can be described as the Jewish equivalent of the Frankenstein monster.

The word *golem* literally means "unformed matter"; it has come to refer to an artificial man created from earth. According to the lore of the KABBALAH, a highly trained Kabbalist can create a golem by shaping earth into human form and animating it by various methods: reciting secret names of God, or placing the name of God or other magical words under its tongue or on its forehead. There are many legends about sages who created golems, usually to act as servants, but then destroyed them when the golems' stupidity made them useless.

The most famous legend in the tradition concerns the golem created by Rabbi Judah Loew in Prague. After saving the Jewish community from a POGROM, the legend says, this golem was deanimated; it is said to be lying dormant in the attic of the Altneushul of Prague, the oldest standing synagogue in central Europe. Many novels, plays, and films have used this golem as a theme.

Further reading: Moshe Idel, *Golem: Jewish Magical and Mystical Traditions on the Artificial Anthropoid* (Albany: State University of New York Press, 1990); I. L. Peretz, "The Golem," in *A Treasury of Yiddish Stories,* eds. Eliezer Greenberg and Irving Howe (New York: Viking Press, 1954); David Wisniewski, *Golem* (New York: Clarion Books, 1996).

Gompers, Samuel (1850–1924) *American labor leader*

Samuel Gompers was born in London on January 27, 1850, to Solomon and Sarah Gompers, Dutch-Jewish immigrants to England. He attended a tuition-free Jewish school from age six to 10, but due to serious economic need in his family, left school and went to work. In 1863 he immigrated to New York, where he joined Local 15 of the Cigarmakers' International Union (CMIU) in 1864. In 1886 he was elected vice president of the CMIU; from that position he helped found the American Federation of Labor (AFL), an organization that united various trade unions across America. He served as AFL president almost non-stop from 1886 to 1924.

Samuel Gompers was a major force in the American labor movement, securing the availability of collective bargaining and participating in the foundation of the American Federation of Labor. Gompers received some Jewish schooling in England as a boy, but he had few Jewish loyalties beyond the belief in the idea of a Jewish homeland. *(Library of Congress)*

While Gompers subscribed early in life to Marxist ideology, he ultimately rejected the Socialist agenda. His primary belief was in simple trade unionism. His goal was to achieve collective bargaining agreements with management, and maintain decent relations between labor leaders, owners, and bankers. During World War I, Gompers actively supported President Woodrow Wilson, and he organized the War Committee on Labor. After the war, Wilson appointed him to the Commission on International Labor Legislation at the Versailles Peace Conference.

Over time, the AFL became a major political power, thanks largely to Gompers, who is considered a major historical figure in the American labor movement. In addition to his labor activism, he was committed to his family, having three sons and two daughters. When his first wife died in 1920, he married Grace Gleaves Neuscheler a year later. He published an autobiography in 1925, *Seventy Years of Life and Labor.* Though Gompers had few Jewish loyalties or concerns, he did support the idea of a Jewish homeland.

Further reading: Samuel Gompers, *An Autobiography: Seventy Years of Life and Labour* (New York: E. P. Dutton, 1925); Harold C. Livesay, *Samuel Gompers and Organized Labor in America* (Long Grove, Ill.: Waveland Press, 1993); Bernard Mandel, *Samuel Gompers: A Biography* (Yellow Springs, Ohio: Antioch Press, 1963).

Goshen

According to TANAKH, the Hebrew Bible, Goshen is the area of EGYPT where the ISRAELITES, children of Jacob (*see* PATRIARCHS), settled and multiplied. Generations later, when the Israelites became enslaved, they still lived there.

Goshen is sometimes referred to as the best part of Egypt. When God sent plagues to Egypt, they never affected Goshen.

Further reading: R. Hanbury Brown, *The Land of Goshen and the Exodus* (London: E. Stanford, 1899);

Nahum M. Sarna, *Exploring Exodus: The Origins of Biblical Israel* (New York: Schocken Books, 1996); *Tanakh: The Holy Scriptures* (Philadelphia and Jerusalem: Jewish Publication Society, 1985).

grace after meals *See* BIRKAT HA-MAZON.

Graetz, Heinrich (1817–1891) *Jewish historian*

German Jew Heinrich Graetz helped found the modern field of Jewish history.

As a young man, Graetz received a traditional Jewish education, while pursuing secular studies on his own. At an early age he was already struggling with the conflict between traditional dogma and critical knowledge.

At first, Graetz studied with Rabbi Samson Raphael HIRSCH, the founder of the NEO-ORTHODOX MOVEMENT. Hirsch himself was trying to balance modernity and tradition. Over time, the two men became estranged, as Hirsch rejected some of Graetz's critical historical approaches to the study of Judaism. Ultimately, Graetz came to the conclusion that Judaism had entered a new epoch, and was reaching a new level of self-awareness in the modern world.

As a young man, Graetz considered becoming an Orthodox Rabbi (*see* ORTHODOX JUDAISM), but he could not find a congregation—although he was a brilliant writer, he was considered a poor speaker. Instead he pursued an academic career, receiving his Ph.D. from Breslau University. There he found a new mentor in Zachariah FRANKEL, the founder of the Breslau School, which emphasized a historical approach to Judaism while maintaining an embrace of Jewish tradition. Graetz took a variety of teaching positions until he became a lecturer in Jewish history and Hebrew Bible at Frankel's YESHIVA in Breslau.

Graetz's scholarship was purely critical in method; he came to numerous nontraditional conclusions regarding the dating of biblical books. However, he never let his scholarship affect his

Orthodox ritual observance, and he strongly opposed REFORM JUDAISM.

Graetz's greatest work was his *History of the Jews*, which surveyed Jewish history from its earliest period to his own times. Presented in a systematic fashion, including detailed footnotes, his work became an instant historical classic.

One of Graetz's startling hypotheses was that the *ZOHAR* was not written in the second century by Rabbi Simeon ben Yohai, but instead authored by Moses de LEON in the 13th century. Graetz's hypothesis was later borne out by the research of Gershom SCHOLEM, and is now the commonly held scholarly view.

Further reading: Heinrich Graetz, *A History of the Jews* (Eugene, Oreg.: Wipf & Stock Publishers, 2002); ———, *Structure of Jewish History and Other Essays* (Hoboken, N.J.: Ktav Publishing, 1975); Leo Trepp, *Eternal Faith, Eternal People: A Journey into Judaism* (Englewood Cliffs, N.J.: Prentice Hall, 1962).

Gratz, Rebecca (1781–1869) *philanthropist and founder of Jewish Sunday schools*

Rebecca Gratz was born in Philadelphia in 1781 into a wealthy Jewish family that had been major supporters of the American Revolution. Gratz attended non-Jewish public schools, and acquired a wide knowledge of the secular world. She was considered by her contemporaries to be very beautiful and extremely gracious. She never married; family legend has it that she once loved a Gentile, but refused to marry outside of the Jewish religion.

Most important, she was selfless in her devotion to charitable causes. A devout Jew, her religious beliefs bolstered her dedication to assisting the needy, both in the Jewish and non-Jewish communities.

At the age of 20, she organized the Female Association for the Relief of Women and Children of Reduced Circumstances in Philadelphia. She also cofounded the Philadelphia Orphan Asylum in 1815 and served as the organization's

Rebecca Gratz was known for her grace and beauty, as well as for her contributions to charity and to Jewish education. It is said that Sir Walter Scott based the character Rebecca in *Ivanhoe* on Gratz. *(Library of Congress)*

secretary for more than 40 years. Addressing needs within the Jewish community, Gratz founded the Female Hebrew Benevolent Society in 1819. In 1855 she created the Jewish Foster Home and Orphan Asylum. A woman of tireless energy, Gratz managed her charitable efforts while raising the nine children of her sister, Rachel, who died in 1823.

Gratz was concerned about religious education for Jewish children. Imitating the Christian Sunday school model, she founded the Hebrew Sunday School Society of Philadelphia on March 4, 1818, her 37th birthday, with approximately 60 students. Gratz served as the school's president until 1864. The school welcomed all children and was tuition-free.

Rebecca Gratz is considered the greatest American Jewish woman of her era. She is said to have been the inspiration for the heroine Rebecca in Sir Walter Scott's *Ivanhoe*. She died in 1869 at the age of 88 and was buried in the Mikveh Israel Cemetery in Philadelphia.

Further reading: Dianne Ashton, *Rebecca Gratz: Women and Judaism in Antebellum America* (Detroit: Wayne State University Press, 1997); Salo W. Baron and Joseph L. Blau, *The Jews of the United States, 1790–1840: A Documentary History* (New York: Columbia University Press, 1963); Beryl Lieff Benderly and Hasia R. Diner, *Her Works Praise Her: A History of Jewish Women in America from Colonial Times to the Present* (New York: Basic Books, 2002).

Gratz College

Gratz College is the oldest nondenominational higher-education school of Jewish studies in North America. It was founded in 1895 as a Hebrew teacher's college through the joint efforts of Hyman Gratz, a member of Philadelphia's historic Gratz family, Sabato MORAIS, an important leader in CONSERVATIVE JUDAISM, and Gratz Mordecai, whose true aim had been to establish a Jewish university.

Originally, the school held classes inside the walls of Mikveh Israel Synagogue. Today, the college is located in Melrose Park just outside Philadelphia. At one time, Gratz served as the educational arm of the Philadelphia Federation, but it has since become a general college of Jewish studies. It offers programs in most aspects of Jewish communal life, Jewish education, Jewish studies, music, and communal service. At the heart of the institution is the desire to combine scholarship with service.

Gratz College offers an undergraduate degree in Jewish studies, but it does not offer general liberal arts classes, which undergraduates must pursue at other institutions. The college also offers extensive master's programs, as well as teaching certification in both secular and Jewish studies.

Adult learning is encouraged, and Gratz offers many opportunities for nondegree students. The school is accredited by the Middle States Association of Colleges and Schools.

Gratz College also houses a Jewish SUPPLEMENTARY SCHOOL at the high school level. Its Tuttleman Jewish Public Library includes the Holocaust Oral History Archive and the Schreiber Music Library, one of the most prestigious collections of Jewish music in the United States. The Tyson Music Department offers courses in Jewish music as well as events for the community.

Further reading: Moshe Davis, *The Emergence of Conservative Judaism: The Historical School in 19th Century America* (Philadelphia: Jewish Publication Society, 1963); Gratz College Web site URL: http://www.gratz.edu, accessed July 24, 2004; Irene Heskes, *Passport to Jewish Music: Its History, Traditions, and Culture* (Westport, Conn.: Greenwood Press, 1994).

Great Synagogue

Many SYNAGOGUES, often the largest in their cities, have been called the Great Synagogue. The most prominent today is the Great Synagogue of Jerusalem at 55 King George Street, built in 1982 adjacent to the headquarters of Israel's Chief Rabbinate. Leading into the marble-floored and chandelier-lined foyer, the synagogue's doors are designed to imitate the grand entrances to the first and second TEMPLES; inside the structure are two-story stained-glass windows. A collection of MEZUZAHs from around the world rests in the lobby. The CANTOR of the Great Synagogue, Naftali Herstik, leads a world-renowned choir that can be heard around the world via the Internet.

Great Synagogues can also be found in Sydney, Australia; London, ENGLAND; Budapest, HUNGARY; Bialystok, POLAND, and Vilna, Lithuania.

Further reading: Geoffrey Alderman, *Modern British Jewry* (Oxford: Oxford University Press, 1998); Israel

The Great Synagogue in Jerusalem is located at 55 King George Street. The grandeur of the building attempts to mimic the entrance to the Temple, and the inside of the Great Synagogue is as grand as the outside. Here, a Torah lies open on the reading table. Additional Torah scrolls sit in the Holy Ark below beautiful stained glass windows. *(Dave Bartruff/Corbis)*

Cohen, *Vilna* (Philadelphia: Jewish Publication Society, 1992); Simon Griver, *Insight Guide Jerusalem* (London: Insight Guides, 1998).

Greenberg, Hank (1911–1986) *U.S. baseball player*

Hank Greenberg was born on January 1, 1911, in New York City and died on September 4, 1986, in Beverly Hills, California. Along with Sandy Koufax, Hank Greenberg is arguably the best Jew ever to play professional baseball. If Koufax was the best Jewish pitcher, Hank Greenberg was the best batter.

From 1930 to 1947, Greenberg played first base and outfield, mostly for the Detroit Tigers, although his final season was with the Pittsburgh Pirates. Greenberg missed three seasons and parts of two others to fight in World War II. Had he played those years, he may have hit more than 500 home runs and reached 2,000 RBIs. Still, his 331 home runs, 1,276 RBIs and .313 lifetime batting average, in addition to his two Most Valuable Player awards, make Greenberg one of the best baseball players of all time.

Like Jackie Robinson, Hank Greenberg experienced discrimination from other players. Some believe ANTISEMITISM kept him from breaking Babe

Ruth's single-season home run record. In 1938, Greenberg hit 58 home runs, but it is said that he was intentionally walked during the last five games of the season. The walks may have been strategic, but some believe pitchers simply did not want to see a Jew break Ruth's record. Greenberg himself denied that he was a victim of anti-semitism. During the 1934 pennant race, Greenberg received a special rabbinic dispensation to play baseball on ROSH HASHANAH. He did not, however, play on YOM KIPPUR.

Further reading: Hank Greenberg, *Hank Greenberg: The Story of My Life* (New York: Times Books, 1989); Robert Slater, *Great Jews in Sports* (Middle Village, N.Y.: J. David Publishers, 1983).

Greenberg, Irving (b. 1933) and Blu

(b. 1936) *American Jewish writers and activists*

Rabbi Irving "Yitz" Greenberg is a prominent writer, educator, and communal leader within the Orthodox and general Jewish communities (*see* ORTHODOX JUDAISM). He was born in New York in 1933 to Rabbi Eliyahu Chayim Greenberg. As a rabbinical student Yitz was influenced by the teachings of the great Modern Orthodox rabbi Joseph B. SOLOVEITCHIK. He is also greatly influenced by his wife, Blu, a prominent Jewish feminist teacher and writer.

After ordination, Yitz served as rabbi for the Riverdale Jewish Center, and he became an associate professor of history at YESHIVA UNIVERSITY. He went on to found and chair the Department for Jewish Studies at City College of the City University of New York.

In 1974 Yitz cofounded, with Elie WIESEL and Rabbi Stephen Shaw, the National Jewish Resource Center, which in 1985 changed its name to CLAL—THE NATIONAL JEWISH CENTER FOR LEARNING AND LEADERSHIP. CLAL initially focused on strengthening Jewish life in the aftermath of the HOLOCAUST, and on the recreation of a Jewish state in ISRAEL. Yitz was CLAL president from its founding until 1997. Under his leadership, the organization became a pioneer in adult and leadership education in the Jewish community. It also spearheaded important intra-Jewish dialogue, as part of its mission to promote Jewish unity.

Yitz became a guiding force in helping to create the United States Holocaust Memorial Council and the Holocaust Memorial Museum. In 1997, he joined Michael Steinhardt in founding the Jewish Life Network/STEINHARDT FOUNDATION, which he continues to serves as president. Through philanthropic activism, this foundation is attempting to revitalize American Jewry.

Yitz has published numerous articles on Jewish thought and religion, including *The Jewish Way: Living the Holidays* (1988), a philosophy of Judaism based on an analysis of the Sabbath and holidays, and *Living in the Image of God: Jewish Teachings to Perfect the World* (1998).

Yitz and Blu Greenberg have worked together on many projects, such as accompanying a delegation to visit the Dalai Lama in India in 1990. The latter had invited a delegation to explain Judaism to him, in an attempt to learn how to maintain a community in exile. The results of that encounter are described in a book called *The Jew in the Lotus*, written by journalist Rodger Kamenetz.

Blu Greenberg is a widely published author and lecturer on the issues of feminism, Orthodoxy, and the Jewish family. Her books include *On Women and Judaism: A View from Tradition* (1981), *How to Run a Traditional Jewish Household* (1985), *Black Bread: Poems After the Holocaust* (1994), and a children's book called *King Solomon and the Queen of Sheba* (1998).

Since 1973, Blu has been active in the movement to bridge feminism and Orthodox Judaism. She chaired the first International Conference on Feminism and Orthodoxy in 1997, and the second in 1998. She is the cofounder and first president of the Jewish Orthodox Feminist Alliance and has served on the boards of many organizations.

Blu and Irving Greenberg have five children and 12 grandchildren.

Further reading: Shalom Freedman and Irving Greenberg, *Living in the Image of God: Jewish Teachings to Perfect the World: Conversations with Rabbi Irving Greenberg* (Northvale, N.J.: Jason Aronson, 1998); Blu Greenberg, *On Women and Judaism* (Philadelphia: Jewish Publication Society of America, 1981); ———, *How to Run a Traditional Jewish Household* (New York: Fireside, 1985); Irving Greenberg, *The Jewish Way: Living the Holidays* (New York: Touchstone/Simon & Schuster, 1993); Rodger Kamenetz, *The Jew in the Lotus: A Poet's Rediscovery of Jewish Identity in Buddhist India* (New York: HarperCollins, 1994).

grogger

A grogger is a noisemaker used to drown out Haman's name during the public reading of the book of ESTHER on PURIM.

During the holiday of Purim, Jews attend a SYNAGOGUE service to hear the reading of the MEGILLAH, or scroll, of the book of Esther. The book's villain is Haman, who tried to destroy the Jews; since he failed, the holiday of Purim is a festive, joyous, celebration of Jewish survival. It is considered meritorious to curse Haman, whom Jews have often seen as a stand-in for all the tyrants and antisemites in history.

One of the most popular rituals of the festival, especially for children, is to drown out Haman's name whenever it is pronounced. Congregants stamp their feet, clap their hands, shout, boo, and use groggers of various kinds for that purpose.

Further reading: Irving Greenberg, *The Jewish Way: Living the Holidays* (New York: Touchstone, 1988); Ronald H. Isaacs, *Every Person's Guide to Purim* (Northvale, N.J.: Jason Aronson, 2000).

Guggenheim family

Meyer Guggenheim (1828–1905) is recognized as the patriarch of the wealthy Jewish Guggenheim family. He immigrated to the UNITED STATES in 1847 and established a successful retail business. He later went into mining and expanded the family fortune. Successive generations have continued to pursue business while participating in national politics and philanthropy.

Daniel Guggenheim (1856–1930) and his wife established the Daniel and Florence Guggenheim Foundation, which supports aeronautical research. Harry Frank Guggenheim (1890–1971) served as ambassador to Cuba, and Solomon Guggenheim (1867–1941) served as a Colorado senator. Solomon Robert Guggenheim (1861–1949) established a foundation to encourage art appreciation, which in turn established the Solomon R. Guggenheim Museum for modern art in New York City in 1939, although it had a temporary residence on East 54th Street before Frank Lloyd Wright designed its current home on Fifth Avenue. The Guggenheim family continues to support the arts in a variety of ways. For example, the Peggy Guggenheim collection of 20th century art is a highly respected attraction in Venice, Italy.

Further reading: John Hagy Davis, *The Guggenheims: An American Epic* (New York: Morrow, 1978); Harvey

The Guggenheim Museum building was designed by Frank Lloyd Wright, and it initially opened in this location in 1959. Wright intended for his circular design to provide variety to New York's landscape and to reflect the uniqueness of the art pieces within. *(Morguefile)*

O'Connor, *The Guggenheims: The Making of an American Dynasty* (New York: Covici and Friede, 1937).

Gush Emunim (Bloc of the Faithful)

Established after the SIX-DAY WAR, Gush Emunim is an Israeli religious-political movement that supports Jewish settlement in the territories of JUDEA AND SAMARIA and Gaza. After the YOM KIPPUR WAR in 1973, Gush Emunim organized as a political party. It aimed to prevent the turnover to Arab states of any territory held by ISRAEL, and the annexation of those territories to Israel proper. The group was founded on the site of Kfar Etzion (*see* GUSH ETZION), a KIBBUTZ on the West Bank that had been seized by the Arabs during the ISRAELI WAR OF INDEPENDENCE and recovered by the Israelis during the SIX-DAY WAR.

The group is motivated by a combination of Jewish religious fundamentalism and secular ZIONISM. Its proponents claim that God has led Israel to take the West Bank (*see* JUDEA AND SAMARIA), which was part of the ISRAELITE kingdoms of the Bible and a key component of the Promised Land. They claim that it is possible to live in peace with Arab neighbors even if these lands are annexed.

Beginning as a faction of the National Religious Party (NRP), proponents of Gush Emunim include yeshiva graduates, rabbis, and teachers. Although they still have a connection to the NRP, they do not affiliate with any other Israeli political party. The party continues to oppose giving land for peace, and they stage demonstrations and rallies to promote their perspective favoring Jewish settlement in all areas of ERETZ YISRAEL.

Further reading: David Newman, ed., *The Impact of Gush Emunim: Politics and Settlement in the West Bank* (New York: St. Martin's Press, 1995); Ehud Sprinzak, *The Ascendance of Israel's Radical Right* (New York: Oxford University Press, 1991); ———, "Gush Emunim: The Tip of the Iceberg," *Jerusalem Quarterly* 21 (Fall 1981): 2847.

Gush Etzion (Etzion Bloc)

Gush Etzion was a bloc of Jewish agricultural communities located between JERUSALEM and Hebron in the days of the BRITISH MANDATE. They had been founded in part to secure a valuable strategic position to thwart a potential Arab attack against Jewish Jerusalem. By 1947, Gush Etzion consisted of four settlements: Kfar Etzion, created in 1943, Ein Tzurim, Masuot Yitzhak, and Revadim.

On January 14, 1947, some 1,000 Arabs, led by Abdul-Khadr Husseini, attacked the settlements. The 450 Jewish settlers were able to arrest the first attack, but they suffered high casualties and were in desperate need of reinforcements. The HAGANAH was able to send only 35 soldiers, led by Commander Danny Mass. The reinforcements were discovered, attacked, and massacred. A British patrol found their stripped and mutilated bodies the next day.

The following year, during the ISRAELI WAR OF INDEPENDENCE, Gush Etzion was again the target of Arab attack. In May 1948, the residents held off overwhelming Arab forces for three days, stopping their drive for Jerusalem. Ultimately, the attacking forces swamped the settlers and they surrendered; after the surrender Arab forces murdered 240 of the residents, taking the rest as prisoners. The settlement's buildings were completely destroyed.

The bravery of the settlers of Gush Etzion helped keep West Jerusalem within the State of Israel. However, following the massacre Israeli policy was changed: the ISRAEL DEFENSE FORCES are now charged to evacuate civilians in isolated outposts with little chance of withstanding attack.

During the SIX-DAY WAR 19 years later, Gush Etzion was recaptured by Israel. Israel rebuilt the original settlements and added new ones. Today, a 10-minute drive from Jerusalem, Gush Etzion is a collection of 15 communities with approximately 20,000 Israeli residents. In the debates within Israel about whether to dismantle settlements in the territories occupied in 1967, few politicians support the evacuation of Gush

Etzion, given its importance in terms of defense and historic symbolism.

Further reading: Chaim Herzog, *The Arab-Israeli Wars* (New York: Random House, 1982); Walter Laqueur, *A History of Zionism: From the French Revolution to the Establishment of the State of Israel* (New York: Schocken Books, 2003); Howard M. Sachar, *A History of Israel: From the Rise of Zionism to Our Time* (New York: Knopf, 1996); Shmuel Sandler, *The State of Israel, the Land of Israel: the Statist and Ethnonational Dimensions of Foreign Policy* (Westport, Conn.: Greenwood Press, 1993).

H

Habakkuk (seventh century B.C.E.) *biblical prophet*

Habakkuk was one of the 12 Minor Prophets in the TANAKH, the Hebrew Bible. He prophesied in JERUSALEM around 605–600 B.C.E. when the southern ISRAELITE kingdom was under siege by the empire of BABYLONIA. The prophet questions God about the suffering of Judea. God responds, criticizing the people's pride and infidelity. The book, probably crafted for liturgical use, describes a cosmic battle in which God demonstrates mastery of Creation by subduing the monsters of the sea.

Further reading: S. M. Lehrman, "Habakkuk: Introduction and Commentary," in A. Cohen, ed., *The Twelve Prophets* (London, Soncino Press, 1970); Bruce M. Metzger and Roland E. Murphy, "Habakkuk" in *The New Oxford Annotated Bible with the Apocrypha* (New York: Oxford University Press, 1991).

Hadassah

Hadassah is the Women's Zionist Organization in America (*see* ZIONISM). Its primary missions are to help ISRAEL meet health-care and other needs, ensure Jewish continuity, and actualize the power of Jewish women in American society. Hadassah believes that Israel is the historic homeland of the Jews and the primary vehicle for Jewish renaissance; it is dedicated to strengthening the ties between Jews in Israel and the UNITED STATES.

After a visit to PALESTINE in 1909, Henrietta SZOLD founded Hadassah in 1912 to ameliorate the poor living conditions she observed there. Over the years, the organization has carried out her mission by building several major hospitals in Israel, serving all sectors of the country's population, and by supporting education, youth institutions, and land development. Szold and the organization Hadassah are dedicated to "practical Zionism."

In the United States, the organization promotes Jewish education and Zionist youth programs such as Young Judaea (*see* ZIONIST YOUTH MOVEMENTS). Local chapters provide personal enrichment for members. The organization raises significant funds to support its mission. In 1981, its fund-raising in the Jewish community was second only to the United Jewish Appeal (*see* UNITED JEWISH COMMUNITIES).

The organization celebrates the American tradition of women's volunteer work, and it is operated by volunteers at the highest levels. Much of its work is carried out through subsidiary groups such as the Hadassah Medical Organization. It also works closely with other agencies such as the

Jewish National Fund and Youth Aliyah, and Hadassah Israel Education Services.

Hadassah publishes *Hadassah Magazine* monthly. Presently there are more than 300,000 members in North America.

Further reading: Mildred Efros, *The Story of Zionism* (New York: Education Department, Hadassah, 1952); Hadassah Web site URL: http://www.hadassah.org, accessed on July 24, 2004; Jules Harlow, et al, *Pray Tell: A Hadassah Guide to Jewish Prayer* (Woodstock, Vt.: Jewish Lights Publishing, 2003); Marlin Levin, *It Takes a Dream: The Story of Hadassah* (Jerusalem: Gefen Books, 2002).

haftarah (pl.: haftarot)

The *haftarah* is a brief passage from the NEVI'IM that is read following the TORAH reading during morning prayer at SYNAGOGUES on SHABBAT (the Sabbath day) and holidays. The term comes from a HEBREW root meaning "end" or "conclusion."

Historians are not certain when this practice originated, but its antiquity is documented by a reference in the Christian New Testament (Acts 13:15). Some scholars have suggested that the practice may have originated in a time of persecution, such as the reign of ANTIOCHUS, which prompted the MACCABEE revolt. When laws were passed prohibiting the public reading of the Torah, Jews substituted readings from the Prophets, choosing passages with themes that paralleled that week's intended Torah portion. When the Torah ban was lifted, say these scholars, the new custom of reading the *haftarah* was retained.

Another, more likely possibility is that the prophetic reading was introduced as a supplement to reinforce the lessons of the weekly Torah portion. This allowed for additional biblical study, beyond the five books of Moses.

The specific *haftarot* that are to be read on festivals are delineated in the TALMUD. However, the *haftarah* readings for ordinary Sabbaths were fixed during the Middle Ages. There are slight differences in readings between ASHKENAZIM and SEPHARDIM.

In any case, there is always a connection between a Torah portion and its accompanying *haftarah,* usually in the theme, although sometimes it is difficult for the layperson to discern. The *haftarah* is chanted with a different TROPE (cantillation melody) than the Torah portion. In modern times it is common for BAR/BAT MITZVAH children to chant from both the Torah and the *haftarah* as the ritual marker for becoming a "son or daughter of the commandments"; if only one is read, it is usually the *haftarah.*

Further reading: Rabbi Hyim Halevy Donin, *To Pray as a Jew: A Guide to the Prayer Book and the Synagogue Service* (New York: Basic Books, 1980); Elyse Goldstein, ed., *The Women's Haftarah Commentary: New Insights from Women Rabbis on the 54 Weekly Haftarah Portions, the 5 Megillot & Special Shabbatot* (Woodstock, Vt.: Jewish Lights Publishing, 2004); Abraham E. Milgram, *Jewish Worship* (Philadelphia: Jewish Publication Society, 1971); W. Gunther Plaut, et al., *The Haftarah Commentary* (New York: URJ Press, 1996).

Haganah

The Haganah was the underground military organization of the YISHUV, the Jewish community of PALESTINE. It was formed in June 1920, in response to Arab attacks against Jewish civilians and the tepid British military response. Modeled on an early settlement defense organization called Ha-Shamer, the Haganah eventually became a conventional military organization.

However, in its early years, during the BRITISH MANDATE, the group was a loose coalition of decentralized local defense militias in the large towns and agricultural settlements. In 1929, after a few hundred Jews were murdered, the Haganah tightened its organization.

By that time, almost all Jewish adults and youths in the rural settlements belonged to the Haganah, along with several thousand members in the cities. The Haganah set up formal training programs for soldiers and officers. It established secret weapon depots, smuggled in light weapons from Europe, and began to manufacture small arms, such as hand grenades. The Arab Revolt of 1936–39 provided opportunities for Haganah units to refine their military knowledge and capabilities. Though the British did not recognize the Haganah as legal, and often tried to restrict its activities, some British forces cooperated with the new "unofficial" Jewish army in restoring order.

In 1938, the British established special night squads under the command of Captain Orde Wingate. Haganah officers under his command learned how to maximize the use of surprise and mobility, which became the foundation of the group's tactical doctrine. Haganah units launched successful preemptive attacks against threatening Arab forces, and night squad leaders became the nucleus of the future Israeli officer corps. The Haganah was highly successful in protecting Jewish settlements against the growing Arab threat.

After 1939, British authorities abandoned their support for ZIONISM to win allies in the Arab world for their struggle against Nazi GERMANY. The Mandate sharply restricted Jewish immigration, just as millions of European Jews were falling under Nazi rule. The Haganah worked to facilitate illegal immigration. At the same time, many Haganah members enlisted in official Jewish brigades in support of the British war effort, and assisted British intelligence.

The war offered further opportunity for the Haganah to grow and mature. In 1941, the group created its first mobilized regiment, called the PALMACH. When World War II came to an end, and the British showed no desire to reverse their anti-Zionist policy, the Haganah formally organized their struggle against British rule over Palestine. The Haganah helped create organized Jewish resistance comprised of its own forces and the rival IRGUN ZEVA'I LE'UMI (Etzel), and Lohamei Herut Yisrael (Lehi).

The organization helped set up Jewish displaced-person camps in Europe and worked with HOLOCAUST survivors to prepare them for eventual immigration to Palestine. The Haganah ran illegal immigrant boats under very treacherous conditions. The stories of these illegal boats were brilliantly captured in Leon URIS's novel, *Exodus,* based on an actual Haganah incident (*see* EXODUS).

In anticipation of Arab attacks following the declaration of Israel's independence, the new State of Israel reconstituted the Haganah on May 26, 1948 to create the ISRAEL DEFENSE FORCES, Tzeva Haganah Le-Yisrael, or Tzahal, bringing several militias together to form a conventional military force.

Further reading: Ora Cummings, *The Exodus Affair: Holocaust Survivors and the Struggle for Palestine* (Syracuse, N.Y.: Syracuse University Press, 1998); Yaacov N. Goldstein, *From Fighters to Soldiers: How the Israeli Defense Forces Began* (Brighton, East Sussex, U.K.: Sussex Academic Press, 1998); Jon and David Kimche, *A Clash of Destinies: The Arab-Jewish War and the Founding of the State of Israel* (New York: Praeger, 1960); Walter Laqueur, *A History of Zionism: From the French Revolution to the Establishment of the State of Israel* (New York: Schocken Books, 2003).

Haggadah

The Haggadah (Hebrew for "telling" or "narration") is the book of prayers, stories, and songs that forms the order of service for the SEDER on PASSOVER. The rabbis composed the Haggadah over the centuries to ensure that the essential points of the story were conveyed to each new generation. The text includes quotations from the TORAH and the TALMUD, and other material from ancient times and the Middle Ages.

Though the Haggadah focuses on the events of the EXODUS, which was led by MOSES, the latter's name does not appear. This may represent a deliberate intent to emphasize that it was God who personally directed every detail.

A recurring theme in the Haggadah is the role of the younger generations. The historical narrative is preceded by four questions, traditionally asked by the youngest capable child. There is also a section explaining how to respond to different

The first printed Haggadah appeared in SPAIN near the end of the 15th century. The Haggadah, in a myriad of editions, is now the most widely printed Jewish book. In the 20th century many adaptations of the traditional Haggadah have been developed, including vegetarian, feminist, and even secular versions.

In a more general sense, the term *haggadah* can refer to any nonlegal rabbinic exposition (*see* AGGADAH).

Further reading: Nahum N. Glatzer, *The Schocken Passover Haggadah* (New York: Schocken Books, 1996 [1953]); *Passover Haggadah*, Deluxe Edition (N.p.: Maxwell House, 1984); Yosef Dov Sheinson, *A Survivors' Haggadah*, ed. Saul Touster (Philadelphia, Jewish Publication Society, 2000); Arthur Szyk, *The Haggadah*, ed. Cecil Roth (Jerusalem: Massadah & Alumoth, 1960).

Haifa

Like many sites in the state of ISRAEL, Haifa is a modern city with an ancient history. Today it is the country's major port, sitting at the edge of the Mediterranean Sea and crawling up the slopes of Mount Carmel. Atop the city is HAIFA UNIVERSITY, one of Israel's main institutions of higher learning. The TECHNION, Israel's technological institute, is also located in the city of Haifa.

It is said that ELIJAH the Prophet hid in a cave on Mount Carmel, known today as Elijah's Cave, to escape the wrath of King Ahab. The site is sacred to Jews, Christians, and Muslims. Jews of Middle Eastern descent observe TISHA B'AV by visiting Elijah's Cave to ask Elijah for his good blessings. The TALMUD also writes of an ancient Jewish community in the city.

During the Middle Ages, Haifa served as a shipping center, but all the Jewish residents were killed during the Crusades. Jews did not return to Haifa until the early 19th century, when North African Jews settled there, followed by European Jews in 1879. During the BRITISH MANDATE, Haifa was a gateway through which the HAGANAH smuggled new immigrants into the country.

The reading of the Haggadah takes place at a Passover seder, like the one in the background of this picture. The Haggadah read here has been written completely in Hebrew, although many are written in both Hebrew and English. *(Ya'acov Sa'ar, Government Press Office, The State of Israel)*

types of offspring—a wise son, a wicked son, a simple son, and a son too young to ask questions. The text provides answers tailored to each, highlighting that participants come to the seder from different spiritual places. The Haggadah includes several songs that have become known by almost all Jews, including "Dayeinu" or "It would have been enough," whose theme is that even one of God's many acts of mercy toward the Jews would have been sufficient to evoke their gratitude. The Haggadah traditionally closes with the song, "Leshana ha-Ba'ah be-Yerushalayim," which means "Next year in JERUSALEM."

Haifa serves as one of Israel's main industrial centers and is the country's third-largest city, with a population of 250,000. Haifa has always had a large Arab population, and it is a center of Israeli-Arab cooperation, which is encouraged through the Haifa University's Arab-Jewish Center. The city also hosts the world headquarters of the Bahai faith. Haifa is known as a blue-collar town, and it is the site of the founding of the HISTADRUT, Israel's labor union. Haifa is unique in being the only Israeli city where city buses run on the Sabbath (*see* SHABBAT); and it is known for its social and cultural atmosphere, enhanced by its theater, museums, orchestra, and zoos.

Further reading: C. A. Bayly and Tarazi Fawaz, eds. *Modernity and Culture: From the Mediterranean to the Indian Ocean* (New York: Columbia University Press, 2002); Alex Carmel, *Old Haifa* (London: I.B. Tauris, 2002).

Haifa University

Founded in 1963, Haifa University is located on top of Mount Carmel in the northern region of ISRAEL. The campus is situated in a splendid setting, boasting views of Haifa Bay, the forested Carmel National Park, and the mountains of the Galilee. The university was originally funded by the city of HAIFA and supported academically by the HEBREW UNIVERSITY in JERUSALEM.

Today the university hosts more than 12,000 students who have access to a curriculum of humanities, social sciences, law, science and science education, social welfare and health studies, education, and the graduate school of business. There is also an overseas student program, with students from around the world. Haifa University is a secular institution. Its mission is to combine first-rate higher education and service to the community at large.

The study of the KIBBUTZ is an important specialization at Haifa University, exploring the social and economic role that kibbutzim have played in the history of the state of Israel. The campus also hosts a Maritime Center, which focuses on the study of the strategic nature of water in Israel. The university has a research component, and it is the site of one of the first IBM research centers located outside the UNITED STATES. The university has an established program to study and foster cooperation between the Jewish and Arab populations of Israel and the Middle East. The Arab-Jewish Center, located on campus, provides opportunities for students to become involved with agricultural settlements, development towns, and Arab villages in the area. The university's Hecht Museum is the only archaeological museum on an Israeli university campus.

Further reading: Haifa University Web site URL: http://www.haifa.ac.il, accessed July 24, 2004.

halakhah

Halakhah is the HEBREW term that refers to the corpus of Jewish law. The word comes from a root meaning "to walk," and it is commonly understood by religious Jewish communities that *halakhah* is how the Jew walks upon God's intended path. There are several compilations of Jewish law. The most famous and most used of these CODES OF LAW are the *MISHNEH TORAH* of MAIMONIDES and Joseph CARO's *SHULCHAN ARUCKH.*

TRADITIONAL JUDAISM perceives all of *halakhah* as binding on all Jews. However, different laws have different degrees of stringency depending on their origin. Laws that are explicitly found in the text of the TORAH are called *d'raita* (Aramaic for "by Your light") and must be enforced strictly. For example, the fourth commandment, to observe SHABBAT, the Sabbath, is *d'raita* because it comes directly from the books of Exodus and Deuteronomy. In contrast, *d'rabbanan* laws ("by the rabbis") were laid down by the ancient RABBIS based on traditional interpretations of the Torah preserved in ancient oral traditions (thus the term ORAL LAW). Many *d'rabbanan* laws had the role of safeguarding the spirit of the Torah or WRITTEN LAW.

The bulk of the Jewish commandments come from laws prescribed in the rabbinic tradition. To continue with the above example: when the Torah forbids work on the Sabbath, the question arises, "what constitutes work?" The rabbis, noting that the ISRAELITES were commanded to suspend working on the TABERNACLE in the desert on Shabbat, specified 39 categories of work associated with the Tabernacle. By analogy, any activity that could fit into one of these categories constitutes forbidden work. For example, the priests routinely ground spices for incense; d'rabbanan (according to the rabbis), grinding of any ordinary spice is forbidden on the Sabbath as well.

A gezeira (decree) d'rabbanan is a rabbinic "fence" enacted to make it harder for people to inadvertently break a "true" law. For example, a gezeira forbids touching a pen during the Sabbath, for fear of forgetfully writing, which is a forbidden work. MINHAG, or religious custom, becomes its own legally binding agent. A common teaching is minhag k'mo halachah, "custom is like law." Although custom is not actually part of halakhah, and the rabbis recognize that it has changed with time and varies between communities, any custom commonly followed in a community is treated like law for people in that community. A universal example of minhag k'mo halachah is men covering their heads during worship. This activity is not in itself a law, but no traditional Jew would refrain from this custom.

Various Jewish movements disagree on the requirement to follow halakhah. For example, REFORM JUDAISM considers Jews to be bound by Jewish ethical laws, but not by the ritual laws, while CONSERVATIVE JUDAISM considers Jews to be bound to all of halakhah, but retains the option of reinterpreting the laws in the modern world. ORTHODOX JUDAISM considers Jews to be bound by all of halakhah—d'raita, d'rabbanan and gezeira. They also strive to follow the letter of the law as interpreted by previous generations of rabbis. Each movement's relationship with halakhah distinguishes it from the others, thus highlighting the central position that halakhah takes in all Jewish communities.

Halakhah extends to every aspect of life, providing guidance for all Jews when making ritual, ethical, and moral decisions. Whether a Jewish person rejects halakhah, takes on part of it, or attempts to follow every word as closely as possible, halakhah remains central to Judaism and Jewish life in all generations.

Further reading: Isaac Klein, *A Guide to Jewish Religious Practice* (New York: Jewish Theological Seminary of America, 1988); Joseph B. Soloveitchik, *Halakhic Man* (Philadelphia: Jewish Publication Society of America, 1983); Shnuer Zalman of Liadi, Eliyau Touger, and Uri Kaploun, *Shulchan Aruch: Code of Jewish Law* (Brooklyn, N.Y.: Kehot Publication Society, 2002).

Halevi, Yehudah (1075–1141) *medieval poet and philosopher*

Yehudah Halevi was born in Toledo, SPAIN, to a wealthy Jewish family. Uprooted by Christian invasion, as a young man Halevi traveled between many Jewish communities, writing his famous early love poems. He later returned to Toledo and became a physician. His poetry in this period reflects the turmoil between Christians, Muslims, and Jews, and his hopes for the coming of the MESSIAH. Halevi calls for a return to the Jewish homeland, the only place where he feels Jews will be safe. His poetry covers a myriad of topics, including love, friendship, religious devotion, hope, wisdom, and sorrow.

Halevi wrote prose as well as poetry. One of his most famous works was the *Kuzari*, originally written in Arabic. It is a fictional dialogue between the pagan king of the Kazars and a learned rabbi, who persuades the king to convert to Judaism over CHRISTIANITY or ISLAM as the most logical system of religious belief and action. The work served as a vehicle for Halevi to defend the ideas and beliefs of Judaism in the pluralistic culture of Spain.

Near the end of his life, Halevi decided to move to ISRAEL. He devoted many words and poems to explain his decision to family and friends, as he was leaving a life of comfort for an unpredictable and probably harsh existence in the land of Israel. Tradition has it that he died in EGYPT while waiting for a ship to take him from Alexandria. If Halevi actually managed to enter ERETZ YISRAEL, he probably died soon after. Yehudah Halevi is said to written more than 800 poems, as well as a number of prose works.

Further reading: Glenda Abramson, ed., *The Experienced Soul: Studies in Amichai* (Boulder, Colo.: Westview Press, 1997); Barbara Ellen Galli, *Franz Rosenzweig and Jehuda Halevi: Translating, Translations, and Translators* (Montreal: McGill-Queens University Press, 1995); Hans Lewy, Alexander Altmann, and Isaak Heinemann, eds. *Three Jewish Philosophers: Philo, Saadya Gaon, Jehuda Halevi* (New York: Atheneum, 1977).

halitzah

Halitzah literally means "taking away." It refers to the ancient ritual of removing a shoe, which was performed when an unwed man refused to honor his biblical obligation to marry his brother's childless widow. The custom of an unwed man marrying his dead brother's wife is called levirate marriage. It is laid down in Deuteronomy (25:7–9): "If the man does not want to marry his brother's widow, his brother's widow shall appear before the elders in the gate and declare, 'My husband's brother refuses to establish a name in Israel for his brother; he will not perform the duty of a levir.'" The elders of the town, after confirming the validity of the widow's statement, would place the widow before her brother-in-law in public, where she would remove his shoe, spit in his face, and declare, "Thus shall be done to the man who will not build up his brother's house!"

The biblical purpose of *halitzah* was to publicly shame the renegade brother in order to discourage such behavior. The RABBIS in practice removed the negative connotation of the ritual and made it a positive act, in which both man and woman are freed from a marriage they do not desire. They felt that while a levirate marriage had

merit in biblical times, it had less use in the medieval world. When faced with a situation requiring levirate marriage, they urged the parties to avail themselves of the ritual of *halitzah*.

In modern times, *halitzah* is still practiced with great solemnity. A BET DIN, a court of three rabbis, gathers the day prior and establishes a place for the act to take place. The widow fasts, and she and the levir appear before the *bet din*, where she recites the Torah's prescribed formula in HEBREW. A special shoe made of leather straps, constructed for each rabbinic court, is placed on the levir's right foot. He walks in it for a little while, and afterward the widow holds the levir's foot in her left hand, unties the shoe with her right hand, removes it, and casts it aside. She then spits in front of the levir and recites the Deuteronomic words. Immediately after the words are spoken, the *bet din* offers this prayer: "May it be God's will that the daughters of Israel will never have to resort to levirate marriage or *halitzah*."

The survival of *halitzah* among traditional Jews is a powerful illustration of how the rabbis over the centuries attempt to keep the letter of the law, yet alter the spirit so as to better fit the circumstances of their times.

Further reading: Hayim Donin, *To Be a Jew: A Guide to Jewish Observance in Contemporary Life* (New York: Basic Books, 1991); Ellen Frankel, *The Five Books of Miriam: A Woman's Commentary on the Torah* (San Francisco: HarperSanFrancisco, 1998).

Hallel

The Hallel is a set of psalms praising God that has been incorporated into the liturgy on festivals and new-moon days. It is recited on PASSOVER, SUKKOT, SH-MINI ATZERET, SIMCHAT TORAH, SHAVUOT, ROSH HODESH, CHANUKAH, and YOM HA'ATZMA'UT, Israel's Independence Day.

The psalms included in the Hallel recall the festivals as they were celebrated in the TEMPLE. They serve to remind worshippers, and remind God, of past redemptions and express faith in future redemption. A shorter version of Hallel that omits a few of the psalms is used during PASSOVER, because, the rabbis say, the deaths of the Egyptians take away from the pure joy of the festival.

Further reading: Adin Even-Israel, *A Guide to Jewish Prayer* (New York: Schocken Books, 2000); Rabbi Jules Harlow, ed., *Siddur Sim Shalom: A Prayerbook for Shabbat, Festivals, and Weekdays* (New York: Rabbinical Assembly, United Synagogue of America, 1989); Ronald H. Isaacs, *Every Person's Guide to Jewish Prayer* (Northvale, N.J.: Jason Aronson, 1997).

halutzim (pioneers)

The *halutzim* (Hebrew for "pioneers") were the Jews who came to PALESTINE in the first waves of Zionist immigration, especially those who worked in agricultural settlements.

There were five primary waves of immigration, or ALIYAH, between 1882 and 1939. The First Aliyah, covering the years 1882–1903, brought Jewish pioneers eager to escape persecution in RUSSIA. They had formed societies called HIBBAT ZION/HOVEVEI ZION (Lovers of Zion), and many of them aimed to found agricultural settlements.

Some 20,000 to 30,000 Jews made their way to Palestine in the years of the First Aliyah, and by 1900 they had founded 22 settlements. The death rate was high in the settlements, where conditions faced by the *halutzim* were extraordinarily difficult. Of those who came to Palestine, only 5,000 remained in Palestine, but in many ways they formed the foundation for the future Jewish state.

The Second Aliyah lasted from 1904–14. It brought mostly secular Jews who embraced a socialist-Zionist ideology. Among these pioneers was future leader David BEN-GURION. The *halutzim* of the Second Aliyah directly attacked the practical problems of colonization. They glorified physical labor, cooperation, and self-defense, and they developed the KIBBUTZ movement. Of the 40,000 *halutzim* who made their way to Palestine during these years, many left because the work

was too difficult. Nevertheless, by 1914 there were 50 Jewish agricultural settlements with a population of 15,000.

The Third Aliyah took place from 1919 to 1924. Close to 100,000 Jews arrived in that period. They continued the work of the earlier pioneers, draining the swamps, planting trees, and creating the necessary infrastructure for a thriving Jewish society in Palestine.

The era of the *halutzim* ended with the start of World War II, as the British closed Palestine to any further legal Jewish immigration. The early waves of *halutzim* made it possible for these others to follow. They also proved that it was possible to make the land bloom again and that there was hope for Jewish life in the land of Israel. Israel's Jewish population by 2004 had reached approximately 5.5 million.

Further reading: Walter Laqueur, *A History of Zionism: From the French Revolution to the Establishment of the State of Israel* (New York: Schocken Books, 2003); Howard M. Sachar, *A History of Israel: From the Rise of Zionism to Our Time* (New York: Alfred A. Knopf, 1996).

hamsa

A *hamsa* (Arabic for "five") is a hand-shaped amulet popular especially among Jews from Arab countries. It is said to provide magical protection against the EVIL EYE. The amulet is also commonly used by Muslim Arabs.

In the Jewish tradition, the *hamsa* is also referred to as the Hand of Miriam, the sister of MOSES, who tradition teaches helped sustain the ISRAELITES during their wanderings in the wilderness. *Hamsa*s containing magical words and names often appear in printed siddurim (*see* SIDDUR) and other sacred books used by Middle Eastern Jews, and are often framed and hung on the walls of SYNAGOGUES and homes for protection against evil spirits.

There is archaeological evidence that the use of a downward-pointing *hamsa* as a religious symbol may predate both Judaism and ISLAM. It may have referred to an ancient Middle Eastern goddess whose hand could ward off the evil eye.

Although most Jewish *hamsa* hands produced today are amulets designed to be worn, *hamsa* hands are also made in the form of ceramic wall plaques containing HEBREW prayers. Many religious Jews may regard the use of *hamsas* as purely superstitious, but they are not considered to be against HALAKHAH, or Jewish law. Today, even some nonbelieving Jews wear *hamsas* as jewelry, perhaps to display their Jewish identity.

Further reading: Steven M. Lowenstein, *The Jewish Cultural Tapestry: International Jewish Folk Traditions* (New York: Oxford University Press, 2002); Joshua Trachtenberg and Moshe Idel, *Jewish Magic and Superstition: A Study in Folk Religion* (Philadelphia: University of Pennsylvania Press, 2004).

hanukkiyah

A *hanukkiyah*, very often called a MENORAH, is a special eight-branched candelabra used specifically for the holiday of Chanukah. The word *menorah* (Hebrew for "lamp") technically refers to the seven-branched candelabra that was housed in the TEMPLE in JERUSALEM and contained the ETERNAL FLAME. Since the holiday of Chanukah lasts eight days, an eight-branched candelabra is used to light the eight candles of Chanukah, and traditional Jews refer to it as a *hanukkiyah*.

Further reading: Hersh Goldwurm and Meir Zlotowitz, *Chanukah, its History, Observance and Significance: A Presentation Based upon Talmudic and Traditional Sources* (Brooklyn, N.Y.: Mesorah Publications, 1989); Ronald H. Isaacs, *Every Person's Guide to Hanukkah* (Northvale, N.J.: Jason Aronson, 2000); Jeffrey A. O'Hare, *Hanukkah, Festival of Lights: Celebrate with Songs, Decorations, Food, Games, Prayers, and Traditions* (Honesdale, Pa.: Boyds Mills Press, 2000); Noam Zion and Barbara Spectre, *A Different Light: The Hanukkah Book of Celebration* (New York: Pitspopany Press, 2000).

Hasidism

Hasidism, or the Hasidic movement, began in eastern Europe in the mid-18th century. Its founder was Rabbi Israel BAAL SHEM TOV ("master of the good name").

The Baal Shem Tov was troubled by the void he sensed in the lives of many observant Jews, especially among the poor and less-educated majority. Though he wanted Jews to continue to observe Jewish law, he saw the need for a more emotional religious life that would allow Jews to connect with God.

The Baal Shem Tov was himself a Talmudic scholar, but he also embraced the KABBALAH, or Jewish Mysticism. His religious path, which

The *hamsa* is an amulet adopted from Middle Eastern culture. It has become a symbol of Jewish life, offering protection from evil spirits and spiritual good wishes for the home and synagogues. *(Mark Neyman Government Press Office, The State of Israel)*

became the core of Hasidism, included mystical study as well as other, less intellectual, vehicles for Jewish expression, such as music, dance, and stories. The early Hasidic legends emphasize emotion, and at times dismiss traditional ritual observance as a potential impediment to one's quest for God.

The Hasidic movement was often in conflict with the non-Hasidic Jews, known as the MITNAGDIM, which literally means "opponents." The primary clash was over issues of HALAKHAH, or Jewish law. The Mitnagdim believed that the Hasidim were careless in their observance of ritual law and cared more for mystical practices than they did for halakhah. The emotional exuberance of Hasidic worship, in contrast to the traditional worship of the Mitnagdim was also a source of conflict. The opponents of Hasidism also feared that the popular mysticism of the Hasidism might encourage messianic notions, creating a greater potential for a false messiah, as had happened in the previous century with SHABBATAI ZVI.

Within two generations, a large percentage of observant Jews in eastern Europe had become followers of Hasidism. They were the dominant group in much of present-day Poland, Hungary, and the Ukraine, and a considerable minority everywhere else in the region.

Over several generations Hasidic practices influenced the Mitnagdim; in addition, the Hasidic movement has moderated some of the practices that once distinguished them from their opponents. However, there still exists an intellectual, emotional, and customs gap between Hasidic and non-Hasidic ORTHODOX JUDAISM.

Most Hasidic Jews follow the spiritual and practical leadership of a rebbe, a charismatic RABBI who usually inherited the status from his father or other relative. Hasidic men wear distinctive clothing and hats, usually replicating the conservative black garb worn by their forefathers in eastern Europe; slight differences in clothing style allow those in the know to determine which rebbe another Hasid follows. Over the years, some of the dynastic lines have petered out, leaving major groups without recognized leaders.

Today there are approximately a dozen major Hasidic movements in the world. The largest movement is Lubavitch (see CHABAD), with approximately 100,000 followers, many of them BAAL TESHUVAHs (Jews who have become Orthodox). Other major groups include the Bianer, Bobov, Bostoner, Belzer, Breslov, Gerer, Gor, Munkacz, Puppa, Ribnitz, Satmar, and Vizhnitz. The names of these Hasidic groups come from the European towns in which their original rebbes lived.

Further reading: Martin Buber, *The Way of Man: According to the Teaching of Hasidism* (Secaucus, N.J.: Citadel Trade, 1995); Moshe Idel, *Hasidism: Between Ecstasy and Magic* (Albany: State University of New York Press, 1995); Gershom Scholem, *Major Trends in Jewish Mysticism* (New York: Schocken Books, 1995).

Haskalah

The Haskalah (from the Hebrew *sekhel*, "intellect") was the Jewish version of the European ENLIGHTENMENT; it began in the 1770s and continued for the next 100 years.

For several hundred years prior to the Haskalah, Jewish communities lived in isolation from the larger European society, following traditional ways unchallenged by the intellectual and political turmoil of the wider world. The writers of the Haskalah, called MASKILIM, wanted to integrate the Jewish people into European society, on the basis of legal equality and social emancipation. The movement wanted to replace traditional religion as the center of Jewish life with science and rational philosophy.

Proponents of the Haskalah, such as Moses MENDELSSOHN and Solomon Judah Rapaport, encouraged Jews to study European languages, philosophy, and science. They discouraged the use of YIDDISH, a Jewish language with both German and Hebrew elements, as a barrier to integration. They encouraged Jews to enter new occupations such as agriculture, crafts, arts and sciences. Traditional Jews opposed the Haskalah as a threat to their traditional way of life based on

HALAKHAH, Jewish law, and to their communities, till then safely insulated from the secular world.

The movement began in GERMANY and spread throughout Europe, although it stumbled in RUSSIA as the progress toward political emancipation was stalled by reactionary rulers. Proponents of the Haskalah believed one could be both Jewish and German, French, Dutch, or Russian. The Haskalah led to the development of REFORM JUDAISM, ZIONISM, WISSENSCHAFT DES JUDENTUMS, and the creation of Modern HEBREW literature.

Further reading: Shmuel Feiner, *Haskalah and History: The Emergence of a Modern Jewish Historical Consciousness* trans. Chaya Naor, and Sondra Silverton (Portland, Oreg.: Littman Library of Jewish Civilization, 2001); Jacob Katz, *Jewish Emancipation and Self-Emancipation* (Philadelphia: Jewish Publication Society, 1986); Michael A. Meyer, *Response to Modernity: A History of the Reform Movement in Judaism* (New York and Oxford: Oxford University Press, 1988).

"Hatikvah"

"Hatikvah" (Hebrew for "the hope") is the national anthem of the State of ISRAEL, and is popular among many Jews around the world as an expression of love for the Jewish people, ERETZ YISRAEL, and JERUSALEM.

"Hatikvah" was first popularized at the historic Zionist Congress in Basel, Switzerland, in 1897, where it was sung constantly. The lyrics had been written in 1877 or 1878 by Naphtali Herz Imber (1856–1909), an early settler in PALESTINE; the words were set by Samuel Cohen to the melody of a simple but haunting Czech folk song. The song was officially adopted as the national anthem of the Zionist movement during a subsequent conference at The Hague in 1907.

The text, as amended after Israeli independence in 1948, reads as follows: "As long as the Jewish spirit is yearning deep in the heart, / With eyes turned toward the East, looking toward Zion, / Then our hope—the two-thousand-year-old hope—will not be lost: / To be a free people in our land, / The land of Zion and Jerusalem."

Further reading: Peter Gradenwitz, *The Music of Israel: From the Biblical Era to Modern Times* (Portland, Oreg.: Amadeus Press, 1996); Irene Heskes, *Passport to Jewish Music: Its History, Traditions, and Culture* (Westport, Conn.: Greenwood Press, 1994); Hal Leonard, ed., *National Anthems from around the World: The Official National Anthems, Flags, and Anthem Histories from 56 Countries* (Milwaukee, Wisc.: Hal Leonard Publishing, 1996).

havdalah

Havdalah, which comes from a root meaning "to separate," is a ritual performed at the conclusion of SHABBAT (the Sabbath) and holidays, separating them from the mundane week.

Traditionally, one is supposed to experience the difference between sacred time and the profane with all one's senses. To that end, several ritual objects are included in the ceremony, each with its appropriate BRACHA, or blessing. A braided candle is lit in the darkness, and one puts one's hand up to it to feel the heat, using the senses of sight and touch. The participants sip wine to invoke taste, and sniff a spice-box to invoke smell; of course, all the blessings stimulate the sense of hearing. The ceremony concludes by praising God for making distinctions, such as those between holy and profane, light and dark, and the Sabbath (or holiday) and the rest of the week.

Further reading: Irving Greenberg, *The Jewish Way: Living the Holidays* (New York: Touchstone, 1988); Isidor Grunfeld, *The Sabbath: A Guide to Its Understanding and Observance* (Jerusalem and New York: Feldheim, 1981); Adin Steinsaltz, *Miracle of the Seventh Day: A Guide to the Spiritual Meaning, Significance, and Weekly Practice of the Jewish Sabbath* (San Francisco: Jossey-Bass Publishing, 2003).

Hebrew, Modern

In ISRAEL today the primary written and spoken language is Modern Hebrew. Modern Hebrew is based on the ancient Semitic language used in the TANAKH, the Hebrew Bible, the MISHNAH, and in many Jewish religious and literary creations of the Middle Ages.

Hebrew consists of 22 consonants, and it is written from right to left. Vowels appear as a series of dots and lines that are placed beneath, above, and inside the Hebrew letters. While Israelis do not use vowels in written texts, non-native Hebrew speakers find them to be a helpful learning aid.

BIBLICAL HEBREW had a relatively small vocabulary, with only two verb tenses, perfect and imperfect. Mishnaic and medieval Hebrew expanded the language, but only as a literary tool. Apart from the recitation of prayers, the language was rarely spoken.

Modern Hebrew emerged as a literary language in the 19th century during the period of the HASKALAH, when it began to be used for nonreligious purposes. Eliezer BEN YEHUDAH became the father of Modern Hebrew as a living language, making it his son's mother tongue. He wrote a 17-volume *Complete Dictionary of Ancient and Modern Hebrew,* that included many new words he coined himself, and founded the Hebrew Language Council in 1890, which became the standing Hebrew Language Academy in Israel today. Despite the new words and a somewhat altered grammar and syntax, any reasonably educated Hebrew speaker today can read and understand the Hebrew Bible and the Mishnah.

Some ultra-Orthodox Jews (*see* ORTHODOX JUDAISM) refuse to use Hebrew as an everyday language, as they consider it to be sacred. They speak YIDDISH or other languages in their daily life and reserve Hebrew for prayer and study. Most Jews, however, have accepted and study Modern Hebrew as the standard language for Jewish literacy and as the living language of Israel.

Further reading: Robert Alter, *Modern Hebrew Literature* (West Orange, N.J.: Behrman House, 1975); Joel M. Hoffman, *In the Beginning: A Short History of the Hebrew Language* (New York: New York University Press, 2004); Robert St. John, *Tongue of the Prophets: The Fascinating Biography of Eliezer Ben-Yehudah, the Father of Modern Hebrew* (Beverly Hills, Calif.: Wilshire Book Company, 1972).

Hebrew Immigrant Aid Society (HIAS)

When masses of poor Jewish immigrants began to arrive on the shores of the UNITED STATES in the late 19th century, a host of Jewish social service organizations emerged to care for their needs. Many of these agencies were funded and operated by prosperous members of the long-established German Jewish community.

The Hebrew Immigrant Aid Society (HIAS), by contrast, was founded and run by eastern European Jews for eastern European Jews. It was organized in 1902 as a *Landsmanschaft,* a self-help benevolent society for people from the same town in Europe (*see* LANDSMANSCHAFTEN). Its initial goal was to provide decent burials for Jews who died on ELLIS ISLAND, the immigrant processing center in New York harbor.

It soon became clear that the needs of the immigrants far surpassed burial societies. In response, HIAS grew into a huge organization that helped immigrants in every aspect of their lives, from finding shelter and jobs to reuniting families. On March 16, 1909, HIAS merged with another mutual aid society to create the Hebrew Immigrant Sheltering and Aid Society, but it kept the acronym HIAS. The group worked tirelessly during the crises of World War I and II, seeking relief for oppressed Jews abroad when immigration dried up during the wars.

In 1954, HIAS joined with other immigrant aid societies to become the United HIAS Service (UHS). UHS received funding from membership dues, donations, the United States government, and Jewish federations (*see* UNITED JEWISH COMMUNITIES) UHS is still an active federation-supported organization that continues to aid Jewish immigrants in the United States, such as those coming from Russia in the 1980s and 1990s, but also uses its expertise to help large numbers of non-Jews as well.

Further reading: J. J. Goldberg, *Jewish Power: Inside the American Jewish Establishment* (Reading, Mass.: Perseus Publishing, 1996); Howard M. Sachar, *A History of the Jews in America* (New York: Vintage Books, 1992); Mark Wischnitzer, *Visas to Freedom: The History of HIAS*

(Cleveland: World Publishing Co., 1956); UHS Archives at the YIVO Institute for Jewish Research in New York City.

Hebrew Union College–Jewish Institute of Religion

The oldest successful Jewish institute of higher learning in the Western Hemisphere, the Hebrew Union College–Jewish Institute of Religion serves as the rabbinical school for REFORM JUDAISM and an undergraduate and graduate school for Jewish studies. The university has four campuses, in New York, Cincinnati, Los Angeles, and JERUSALEM.

The school prides itself on academic excellence. It houses the Skirball Museum on its Los Angeles campus, and publishes a number of respected academic journals, such as the *Hebrew Union College Annual* and the *American Jewish Archives*. There is also an independent HUC Press. Programs in rabbinic studies, Jewish communal service, music, and education are supported by excellent libraries on each campus. The Klau Library and American Jewish Archives on the Cincinnati grounds hold impressive collections of Judaica.

Originally named Hebrew Union College (HUC), the school was founded in 1875 by Isaac Mayer WISE, a leader in the development of liberal American Judaism. Its purpose was to train rabbis to serve on American pulpits. Wise did not intend for the institution to be associated exclusively with the Reform movement, as his personal goal was to see a united Jewish community in America. The curriculum focused on the "classics" of Judaism, including the Babylonian and Palestinian TALMUDS, MIDRASH, CODES OF LAW, and TANAKH, the Hebrew Bible. However, Wise's worthy goal was torpedoed by a famous scandal that occurred at HUC's first ordination banquet in 1883. As the printed menu testified, shellfish was served, a particularly nonkosher food (*see* KASHRUT). The famous "*Trefa* [nonkosher] Banquet" provoked an exodus of many traditional rabbis, who went on to found American CONSERVATIVE JUDAISM.

In 1950 the Hebrew Union College merged with the Jewish Institute of Religion, founded in 1922 as

The Hebrew Union College has a campus in Jerusalem. Here an archaeology student from Los Angeles works on an ancient jar. The campus in Israel affords HUC's students a broader range of studies and different experiences than can be attained in the United States. *(Moshe Pridan Government Press Office, The State of Israel)*

an independent school. Study at the combined school aims at the impartial, scientific methods associated with German WISSENSCHAFT DES JUDENTUMS, the scientific study of Judaism. Although HUC-JIR remains a Reform institution, it has never laid down any clear dogma, leaving students and faculty free to struggle toward their own JEWISH IDENTITY. Since its inception, more than 2,000 rabbis have been trained to serve in American pulpits; a small program was recently begun at the Jerusalem campus to train Israeli Reform rabbis.

Further reading: Hebrew Union College Web site URL: http://www.huc.edu, accessed July 24, 2004; S.

E. Karff, ed., *Hebrew Union College–Jewish Institute of Religion at One Hundred Years* (Cincinnati: Hebrew Union College, 1976); Michael A. Meyer, *Response to Modernity: A History of the Reform Movement in Judaism* (New York and Oxford: Oxford University Press, 1988).

Hebrew University of Jerusalem

The Hebrew University is the oldest and most prominent higher education institution in the State of Israel.

The Hebrew University was founded as a university of the Jewish people. It was viewed as a primary component of the program of ZIONISM when the cornerstone was laid on Mount Scopus in JERUSALEM in 1918. Seven years later the dream became reality as the university opened with numerous prestigious figures in attendance, on the board, and on the faculty, including Lord Balfour, issuer of the BALFOUR DECLARATION, Albert EINSTEIN, Martin BUBER, Sigmund FREUD, Harry Sachar, and Felix M. Warburg.

On April 1, 1925, Chaim WEIZMANN, future first president of the modern state of ISRAEL and founding father of the University, spoke at the opening ceremony. He pointed out that "It seems at first sight paradoxical that in a land with so sparse a population, in a land where everything still remains to be done, in a land crying out for such simple things as ploughs, roads and harbors, we should be creating a center of spiritual and intellectual development. But it is no paradox for

The cornerstone of the Hebrew University was laid on Mount Scopus in Jerusalem in 1918. Lord Balfour declared the university open at this formal ceremony on April 1, 1925. *(Library of Congress)*

those who know the soul of the Jew." Weizmann noted that the Jewish thirst for knowledge would lead to success in the building of a nation.

The university had three research departments in its early years, including microbiology, chemistry, and Jewish studies. In 1933 it awarded its first master's degrees to 13 graduates, and boasted 141 students and 33 faculty members. Even before Israeli independence in 1948, the Hebrew University had become an established research and teaching institution, with departments in the humanities, science, medicine, education, and agriculture. The 1948 Israeli War of Independence cut the Mount Scopus campus off from the rest of the new state of Israel and alternate locations were found in Jerusalem: Givat Ram and Ein Kerem. By the time the 1967 SIX-DAY WAR resulted in repossession of Mount Scopus and the original campus, the school had more than 12,500 students.

The Mount Scopus campus was rebuilt, and it has been the main campus since 1981. Today the Hebrew University stands as a major world research institution, and is host to a multidisciplinary curriculum, which includes opportunities to study as an undergraduate, graduate, or overseas student. Its courses of study include science, medicine, dentistry, education, engineering, computer science, international studies, library science, nursing, nutrition, occupational therapy, pharmacy, public health, public policy, social work, and veterinary medicine. Almost 40 percent of Israeli civilian scientific research is done at the Hebrew University, contributing to the rise of Israel's technology sector.

The Hebrew University currently has 22,600 students enrolled in its programs and 1,200 tenured academic faculty. The university houses the Jewish National and University Library, founded in 1892 as a world center for the preservation of Jewish books; it holds the largest Hebraic and Judaic collection in the world. The campuses in Givat Ram and Ein Kerem still function as vital parts of the university.

Further reading: Norman Bentwich, *Hebrew University of Jerusalem, 1918–1960* (London, Weidenfeld, 1961);

Hebrew University Web site URL: http://www.huji.ac.il, accessed on July 25, 2004); Chaim Weizmann, *Trial and Error: The Autobiography of Chaim Weizmann* (Westport, Conn.: Greenwood Publishing, 1972).

Heine, Heinrich (1797–1856) *German-Jewish intellectual who converted to Christianity at least in name*

Heinrich Heine was a renowned German Romantic poet and essayist, who acknowledged his Jewish ancestry but converted to Christianity for practical reasons.

Born in Dusseldorf, GERMANY, on December 13, 1797, Heine died in his adopted city, Paris, on February 17, 1856. Heine's parents were Samson Heine and Betty von Geldern; his mother, who directed his education, embraced the ideas of the French Revolution and conveyed them to her son. Heinrich appears to have had little Jewish education as a youth; Napoleon's EMANCIPATION of the Jews afforded him the opportunity of complete ASSIMILATION into German culture.

Heine's romantic style reflects his youthful unrequited love for his cousin Amalie, whose father married her off to another for fear that Heinrich was unfit for business. Heine began to study law in 1819 and later settled in Berlin, where he published his first volume of poems. He came under the influence of enlightened German Jewish figures, and became part of a scholarly circle that supported the scientific study of Judaism, the WISSENSCHAFT DES JUDENTUMS. Heine's initial goal was to unite modern German culture with ancient Judaism.

However, Heine's ambitions in this regard were frustrated, as many of his like-minded Jewish colleagues converted to CHRISTIANITY. In order to become accepted by Prussian society, Heine abandoned his Jewish interests to focus on his imaginative writing. From 1822 to 1827 he produced a series of poems and travel sketches that made him the most popular German writer of the time. In 1825, he underwent baptism so as to become fully accepted into German society. He was somewhat contemptuous of his need to do this act, stating that he was being baptized—but not converting. Despite Heine's baptism, Jewish themes continued to appeared in his literary works.

Heine is considered one of the greatest of German lyric poets, and a leading revolutionary thinker who helped to popularize the ideals of the French Revolution. His anti-Prussian governmental satires caused him to leave Germany for France in self-imposed exile. His subsequent artistic life was colored by a combination of French and German culture.

Many of Heine's poems were set to music by Schumann, Schubert, Mendelssohn, Liszt, and others—his lyrics appear in more than 3,000 musical compositions. Most of Heine's literary works have been translated into English. Heine's poetry became so much a part of German identity that some poems continued to be published, with the author's name removed, under the antisemitic Nazi regime.

Further reading: Roger F. Cook, *A Companion to the Works of Heinrich Heine* (Buffalo, N.Y.: Camden House, 2002); Heinrich Heine, *Poetry and Prose* (New York: Continuum International Publishing Group, 1982); Philip Kossoff, *Valiant Heart: A Biography of Heinrich Heine* (New York: Cornwall Books, 1983).

Hellenism

Hellenism was a Greek-based cosmopolitan culture and viewpoint that arose after Alexander the Great (356–323 B.C.E.) united all the ancient civilized centers of the Middle East under his rule.

Alexander and his successors managed to spread Greek language and culture throughout their empire, especially among the upper classes. As a result, Jews came under pressure in this era to accommodate (*see* ACCOMMODATION) to Hellenistic practices and values, which often conflicted with Jewish laws and customs. Deep divisions developed not only between Jews and the occupying governments, but also between Jews themselves, as some Jews accused others of

abandoning faith in God and Jewish law by accommodating too freely to the Hellenistic influences around them; they in turn were accused of narrow-minded devotion to old-fashioned tribalistic practices. Although children are told that CHANUKAH commemorates a war between Jews and foreign oppressors, the struggle was in large part a civil war. One faction identified politically and culturally with the Seleucid rulers and wished to suppress traditional Judaism, while their more conservative opponents rejected Hellenism as heretical and offensive to God.

Further reading: Norman Bentwich, *Hellenism* (Philadelphia: Jewish Publication Society of America, 1920); Elias Bickerman, *The Jews in the Greek Age* (Cambridge and London: Harvard University Press, 1988); Louis H. Feldman, "How Much Hellenism in Jewish Palestine?" in *Hebrew Union College Annual* 57 (1986): 83–111.

herem

Herem, or excommunication, a punishment rarely used today, entails the expulsion of a Jew from all aspects of Jewish community life.

A BET DIN, or religious court, has the power to excommunicate an individual from the Jewish community. The threat of *herem* has historically been used to discourage practices that are considered antisocial such as promoting heretical ideas or refusing to grant a religious DIVORCE to an abandoned wife. Excommunication can involve a range of punishments, from relatively mild ostracism to full excommunication for the worst offenses, such as apostasy. *Herem* does not mean that the person ceases to be a Jew, but rather that he or she has been separated from the community.

Perhaps the most famous victim of *herem* was the philosopher Baruch SPINOZA, excommunicated from the Jewish community in the Netherlands in the mid-1650s for his atheistic views.

In earlier times, when most Jews lived in self-contained communities segregated from the wider world, *herem* could deprive an individual of livelihood and all human contact, and thus was a powerful tool to enforce obedience. In the contemporary setting, only rabbis in ultra-Orthodox communities would be able to use *herem* as an effective tool to regulate community life.

Further reading: Walter Jacob and Moshe Zemer, *Crime and Punishment in Jewish Law: Essays and Responsa* (Oxford, U.K.: Berghahn Books, 1999); Louis Jacobs, *A Tree of Life: Diversity, Flexibility, and Creativity in Jewish Law* (Oxford and New York: Oxford University Press, 1984).

heresy

Heresy is a teaching or act that directly contradicts a teaching of TORAH, not simply an untrue statement. Jewish individuals and movements have at times been branded as heretical, as have entire communities. For example, the KARAITES are considered heretics by mainstream Judaism because of their rejection of the ORAL LAW.

Further reading: Walter Jacob and Moshe Zemer, *Crime and Punishment in Jewish Law: Essays and Responsa* (Oxford, U.K.: Berghahn Books, 1999); Louis Jacobs, *A Tree of Life: Diversity, Flexibility, and Creativity in Jewish Law* (Oxford and New York: Oxford University Press, 1984).

hermeneutics

In the Jewish context the term *hermeneutics* refers primarily to the interpretation of the TORAH, especially using the rabbinic methods of PSHAT and DRASH. In the rabbinic period certain principles were developed to guide and circumscribe interpretation, most notably by Rabbi AKIBA, HILLEL, Rabbi Ishmael, and Rabbi Eliezer ben Yose ha-Gelili. These principles continue to be acknowledged today.

See also EXEGESIS.

Further reading: Louis Ginzberg, *Legends of the Bible* (Philadelphia: Jewish Publication Society of America,

1956); Moshe Greenberg, *Studies in the Bible and Jewish Thought* (Philadelphia: Jewish Publication Society, 1995); Bernard M. Levinson, *Deuteronomy and the Hermeneutics of Legal Innovation* (New York: Oxford University Press, 1997).

Herod (37–4 B.C.E.) *ancient Judean ruler*

Herod, often referred to as "Herod the Great," was born to the Idumean ruler Antipater and his Arabian wife, Cyprus. Antipater used his influence to have his 16-year-old son appointed governor of Galilee. As governor, Herod became popular with the SANHEDRIN, the local Jewish ruling body. Years later, after Antipater's death, Herod was appointed tetrarch of Galilee under Mark Antony. This appointment created dissatisfaction among the local Jews, who viewed Herod as racially impure through both his parents. Herod was briefly forced out of Galilee during a Jewish rebellion in 40 B.C.E.

Herod, however, convinced Mark Antony to restore him as ruler, or King in Judea (*see* JUDEA AND SAMARIA), where he reigned in the last years of the first century B.C.E. During his rule Herod initiated extensive building programs. In 20 B.C.E. he began to expand the second TEMPLE, including the Royal Portico. He also built a citadel, "Antonia," to guard the Temple. He rebuilt the walls of JERUSALEM and constructed several fortresses, including MASADA. Perhaps his most important contribution was the port at Caesarea, which was modeled on a Greek city plan.

Among Jews, however, Herod developed a reputation as a cruel and murderous ruler. He was notorious for murdering 45 members of the Sanhedrin as well as a high priest; he also murdered several of his own family members. The New Testament teaches that Herod had all boys in Bethlehem under the age of two murdered when court astrologers advised him that a king of the Jews had just been born (Mt 2:1–16). He limited the influence of the SADDUCEES, and he exacted excessive taxes from all his subjects. It is suspected that he ordered the fire that destroyed the monastery at Qumran in 8 B.C.E.

Herod died in 4 B.C.E., and sources suggest that it was a long and painful death. Upon his death Augustus divided Herod's kingdom among his three sons, Herod Antipas, Philip, and Archelaus. Herod was buried in Herodion, one of his fortresses whose ruins in the Judean desert can still be viewed today.

Further reading: F. J. Foakes-Jackson, *Josephus and the Jews: The Religion and History of the Jews as Explained by Flavius Josephus* (New York: R. R. Smith, 1930); Nikos Kokkinos, *The Herodian Dynasty: Origins, Role in Society and Eclipse* (Sheffield, England: Sheffield Academic Press, 1998); Norman H. Snaith, *The Jews from Cyrus to Herod* (New York: Abingdon Press, 1956); Solomon Zeitlin, *The Rise and Fall of the Judean State: A Political, Social and Religious History of the Second Commonwealth,* vol. 3 (Philadelphia: Jewish Publication Society of America, 1962).

Hertz, Joseph (1872–1946) *chief rabbi of the United Kingdom*

Joseph Herman Hertz was born in Slovakia and immigrated as a 12-year-old to the UNITED STATES, specifically the LOWER EAST SIDE in New York City. He received his doctorate from Columbia University, and was the first to graduate from the JEWISH THEOLOGICAL SEMINARY OF AMERICA as a rabbi. Hertz's scholarship and perspective on Jews and Judaism shows characteristics of Solomon SCHECHTER's desire to merge Jewish tradition with modern scholarship. His first rabbinic appointment was in Syracuse, New York, but he later took a pulpit in Johannesburg, SOUTH AFRICA, where he was very active in the struggle for human rights, standing in opposition to Boer discrimination.

After briefly serving as rabbi in a New York synagogue, Hertz became the chief rabbi for the United Hebrew Congregations of the British Empire in 1913. He remained in this position until his death in 1946. From this prominent position, Hertz set an example for English and world Jewry. He made his voice heard in the public square, taking a stand against RUSSIA's anti-Jewish

policy and speaking out against the rise of Nazism (*see* GERMANY) and Nazi sympathizers in ENGLAND. Hertz supported ZIONISM and his advocacy contributed to the publication of the BALFOUR DECLARATION. Yet Hertz became critical of British policies in PALESTINE, the result of which he had seen firsthand during visits to the area. On issues of religious doctrine and observance, Hertz stood against Liberal Judaism from his Modern Orthodox position.

While embracing modern scholarship, Hertz actively defended MODERN ORTHODOXY. Hertz wrote many books, but he is best-known for his translation and commentary of the TORAH and *haftarot* (*see* HAFTARAH). In his introduction to this work, Hertz wrote his defense for utilizing modern knowledge within biblical commentary: "Accept the truth from whatever source it comes." However, Hertz rejected the documentary hypothesis of multiple authorship of the Torah, calling the theory a "perversion of history and a desecration of religion." Thus, Hertz remained at the center of Jewish life and thought, criticized by both the Reform and Orthodox camps. In the United States, Hertz's *Pentateuch and Haftorahs* was the primary book utilized by Orthodox and Conservative synagogues (*see* CONSERVATIVE JUDAISM), until quite recently, when the Conservative movement published its own new commentary.

Further reading: Geoffrey Alderman, *Modern British Jewry* (Oxford: Oxford University Press, 1998); J. H. Hertz, *The Pentateuch and Haftorahs: Hebrew Text English Translation and Commentary* (London: Soncino Press, 1997); Harvey Warren Meirovich, *A Vindication of Judaism: The Polemics of the Hertz Pentateuch* (Philadelphia: Jewish Theological Seminary of America, 1997).

Herzl, Theodor (1860–1904) *Zionist leader and theoretician*

Theodor Herzl is recognized as the father of modern political ZIONISM. Born in Budapest in 1860, he was raised as a secular Jew by wealthy parents. At the age of 18 he moved with his family to

In 1896 Theodor Herzl wrote *The Jewish State,* which outlines his belief that the Jews needed their own homeland. Herzl spoke with many leaders in Britain, the Ottoman Empire, and Germany, seeking a political solution to the Jewish problem. He died in 1904, his dream unrealized, but his remains were flown to Israel after its independence was won in 1948. *(Government Press Office, The State of Israel)*

Vienna in AUSTRIA, and in 1884 received a doctorate of law from the University of Vienna. Herzl became a successful writer, publishing plays and working as a journalist. He served as the Paris correspondent for the influential Vienna newspaper, the *Neue Freie Presse.* Although Herzl was fluent in German and French, he had no fluency in Hebrew, Yiddish, or Russian—the languages of eastern European Jewry.

Herzl's experiences with ANTISEMITISM catalyzed him to establish the modern Zionist movement before he was aware of the Zionist ideals of prolific eastern European Jews such as Leon PINSKER or AHAD HA'AM. He experienced antisemitism as a student in Vienna, and also during his time in Paris as a journalist. In 1894 he wrote a drama, *The New Ghetto,* in which he describes the invisible ghetto walls of Europe, inpenetrable for even assimilated (*see* ASSIMILATION) and converted Jews. During the DREYFUS AFFAIR in 1894, in which a Jewish French officer was falsely convicted of treason, Herzl experienced shock as he heard mobs in Paris shouting, "Death to the Jews." He came to believe that Jews would have to seek a new refuge outside of Europe, a territorial solution characterized by Jewish sovereignty.

In 1896 Herzl published his essay *Der Judenstaat (The Jewish State),* which laid out the political Zionist agenda. It became an immediate international sensation and within months was translated into most of the languages of Europe. The publication of this seminal essay drew German-Jewish Zionist David Wolffsohn (1856–1914) to contact Herzl and meet with him. Wolffsohn had connections with HIBBAT ZION, an international group of Zionist organizations with local chapters in eastern Europe. Wolffsohn introduced Herzl to eastern European Zionist thinkers, providing a vital link between East and West.

In eastern Europe, many Jews embraced Herzl's Zionist call, some even calling the imposing, bearded Herzl "the Messiah" or "King." Together with Wolffsohn, Herzl convened the First Zionist Congress in Basel, Switzerland, on August 29, 1897, where delegates from around the world adopted the "Basel Program," which sought the establishment of a Jewish home in PALESTINE. The Zionist Organization became the political arm of the Jewish Zionists, and Herzl was elected its first president. From 1897 to 1902 he convened six Zionist Congresses, creating the Jewish National Fund to purchase and develop land in Palestine. A Zionist paper, *Die Welt,* was also published.

Herzl traveled extensively in pursuit of governmental support for the Zionist cause. Herzl's pleas for support from German and Turkish leaders failed. The only concrete proposal offered to Herzl was from Great Britain, which proposed UGANDA as a Jewish autonomous region. In 1903, following violent POGROMS in Kishiner, at the Sixth Zionist Congress Herzl proposed Britain's Uganda offer as a temporary solution for Jews in immediate, physical danger in Russia. Herzl's temporary solution was rejected by the Congress, although it was not formally rejected until the Seventh Zionist Congress of 1905.

Herzl died in Vienna, in 1904, a victim of pneumonia and a weak heart. It could almost be said that he died of a broken heart. But Herzl's workaholic habits probably brought him to his early grave. In 1949, Herzl's remains were brought to JERUSALEM and reinterred in Israel's national cemetery, named Mount Herzl in his honor.

Further reading: Theodor Herzl, *The Jewish State* (New York: Dover Publications, 1989); Jacques Kornberg, *Theodor Herzl: From Assimilation to Zionism* (Bloomington: Indiana University Press, 1993); Walter Laqueur, *A History of Zionism: From the French Revolution to the Establishment of the State of Israel* (New York: Schocken Books, 2003); Maurice C. Samuel, *Theodore Herzl* (Philadelphia: The Jewish Publication Society of America, 1941).

Herzog, Isaac (1888–1959) *chief rabbi in Palestine and Israel*

Born in Lomza, POLAND, Isaac Herzog was raised in Paris, FRANCE, and Leeds, ENGLAND, where his father served as an Orthodox rabbi. As a youth, Herzog studied on his own, completing his own study of the TALMUD by age 16. He received a formal education at London University, earning his doctorate in literature.

Herzog served as chief rabbi in Ireland early in his rabbinic career, and in 1937 he was named to succeed Rabbi Abraham Isaac KOOK as Ashkenazi (*see* ASHKENAZIM) chief rabbi of PALESTINE. When ISRAEL was established, he became the first Ashkenazi chief rabbi of the new state, in which post he greatly influenced religious life in Israel. Herzog's son, Chaim, born in 1918, would become the sixth president of Israel in 1983.

Further reading: Chaim Herzog, *Jewish Law Association Studies: The Halakhic Thought of R. Isaac Herzog: Jewish Law Association Papers and Proceedings* (Atlanta, Ga.: Scholars Press, 1991); Isaac Herzog, *The Main Institutions of Jewish Law* (London: The Soncino Press, 1936–1939); Moshe Sokol, *Engaging Modernity: Rabbinic Leaders and the Challenge of the Twentieth Century* (Northvale, N.J.: Jason Aronson, 1997).

Heschel, Abraham Joshua (1907–1972) *theologian*

Abraham Joshua Heschel was one of the most important Jewish theologians of the 20th century. Descended from Hasidic rabbis on both sides of his family (*see* HASIDISM), Heschel was born in Warsaw, POLAND, in 1907. His father was a well-respected rabbi, considered by some to be the reincarnation of the BAAL SHEM TOV, founder of the Hasidic movement. Heschel received a traditional YESHIVA education in TALMUD and rabbinics and was ordained as rabbi. His community in Warsaw saw in him the chance for a spiritual revival, but Heschel chose to leave to pursue secular studies at the University of Berlin. There he obtained a doctoral degree, producing a work on MAIMONIDES; he subsequently earned a second rabbinic ordination, this time from the more liberal Hochschule fur die WISSENSCHAFT DES JUDENTUMS.

In 1938 the Nazis rulers of GERMANY forced Heschel, and many other Polish-born Jews, to return to POLAND. A year later, he was invited to teach at the HEBREW UNION COLLEGE (HUC) in Cincinnati, an invitation that, as he later often said, saved his life; six weeks after he left Poland the Nazis invaded.

Heschel taught at HUC from 1940 to 1945. Learning that his family had been murdered in the HOLOCAUST, Heschel resolved to ensure that the legacy of eastern European Jewish tradition was preserved for both Jews and non-Jews. Heschel assumed the mission of maintaining continuity of Jewish tradition in the UNITED STATES. To that end, he wrote *The Earth Is the Lord's: The Inner World of the Jew in Eastern Europe,* his first English work; it was a popular success. In 1945 Heschel accepted an appointment to teach at the JEWISH THEOLOGI-CAL SEMINARY, where he found the emphasis on HALAKHAH, Jewish law, and on TALMUD study to be more in keeping with his traditional perspective than the liberal orientation of HUC. He taught at the seminary for 27 years until his death.

Heschel displayed a unique blend of classical training and modern thinking; he was a deeply observant man with a strong commitment to inter-religious cooperation. He lobbied for freedom for Soviet Jewry (*see* RUSSIA), marched for civil rights in Selma, Alabama, and opposed the war in Viet-nam. He participated in various official confer-ences and committees, such as the White House Conference on Children and Youth in 1960, the White House Conference on Aging in 1961, and the National Conference on Religion and Race in 1963. His spirituality has inspired Jews and non-Jews, and his presence in both communities sheds light on the viability of interfaith relations.

Heschel's books took the notion of "spiritual-ity" seriously, and he encouraged a quest for God. While he valued Jewish law and halakhic investi-gation, he also strove to bring a spiritual element to the American Jewish community. Among his books were *The Sabbath, God in Search of Man,* and *The Prophets.* In *The Sabbath,* Heschel tried to encourage modern individuals to consider con-temporary meanings of SHABBAT, and to recognize the value of living moments of sacred time.

Further reading: Abraham J. Heschel, *God in Search of Man* (New York: Noonday Press, 1976); Abraham J. Hes-chel, *The Prophets: An Introduction* (New York: Harper Torchbooks, 1962); ———, *The Sabbath* (New York: Noonday Press, 1975); Edward K. Kaplan and Samuel H. Dresner, *Abraham Joshua Heschel: Prophetic Witness* (New Haven, Conn.: Yale University Press, 1998).

Heschel, Susannah (b. 1957) *scholar/educator*

Daughter of Abraham Joshua HESCHEL, Susannah Heschel is a renowned scholar of Judaism in her own right. Heschel earned her doctorate degree at the University of Pennsylvania in 1989. Since that time she has authored or edited six books and dozens of articles, focusing on modern Jewish thought, feminist theology, and German Protes-tantism. Currently she is the Eli Black Associate Professor of Jewish Studies at Dartmouth College.

Heschel has taught at several major institu-tions including Princeton University, Southern Methodist University, Case Western Reserve Uni-versity, the University of Frankfurt, and Dart-mouth College. Her book *Abraham Geiger and the Jewish Jesus* won the 1998 National Jewish Book Award and the 2000 Abraham Geiger College Award. Heschel has become a popular speaker as well. She has spoken on Judaism as part of a panel on religion and the environment at the UN Earth Summit held in Rio de Janeiro in 1992, and she spoke on Judaism and population ethics at the UN Conference on Population and Development in Cairo in 1994.

Further reading: Susannah Heschel, *Abraham Geiger and the Jewish Jesus* (Chicago: University of Chicago Press, 1998); ———, ed., *On Being a Jewish Feminist: A Reader* (New York: Schocken Books, 1983).

Hibbat Zion/Hovevei Zion

Hibbat Zion (Love of Zion) was the first important Zionist organization in the modern world (*see* ZIONISM). It pioneered the theory and practice of Jewish agricultural settlement in ERETZ YISRAEL, the Land of Israel, sparked the First ALIYAH of immigration there, and helped spread the Zionist idea through its support chapters in several coun-tries. Local groups and their members were known as Hovevei Zion (Lovers of Zion).

Local Hovevei Zion societies sprang up across Europe and North America in the years 1883–84 as POGROMS terrorized the Jews of eastern Europe and tens of thousands of Jews were forced from their homes in the PALE OF SETTLEMENT in RUSSIA. During these early years of Zionist activity, it was still possible for different types of Jews to express themselves as a unified group. Hovevei Zion societies included Modern HEBREW writers, semi-assimilated students, MASKILIM (followers of the Jewish Enlightenment, or HASKALAH), and traditional adherents of ORTHODOX JUDAISM. They used the STAR OF DAVID as their emblem, enclosing the Hebrew word *ziyyon.*

The unity of the Jewish people was an important aspect of Hibbat Zion. The movement was inspired by Yehudah Lev PINSKER's pamphlet *Auto-Emancipation,* and its idea that Jews needed their own autonomous territory. Other Jewish leaders and writers of that era, such as Moshe Leib Lilienblum (1843–1910) and AHAD HA'AM (1856–1927), used the Hovevei Zion societies as sounding boards and dissemination points for their ideas.

Hibbat Zion took a practical approach to Zionism, calling on young Jewish men and women to settle in PALESTINE as HALUTZIM, or pioneers. These young people set up the first moshavot, or farm settlements, and dedicated their lives to transforming desolate land into fruitful farms and orchards. They played a major role in convincing world Jewry that a viable, autonomous Jewish homeland was not just a dream.

Further reading: Arthur Hertzberg, *The Zionist Idea: A Historical Analysis and Reader* (New York: Atheneum Publishers, 1959); Ehud Luz, *Parallels Meet: Religion and Nationalism in the Early Zionist Movement (1882–1904)* (Philadelphia: Jewish Publication Society, 1988); Yehuda Lev Pinsker, *"Auto-Emancipation"* (1882), trans. Dr. D. S. Blondheim (1916), posted at *Essential Texts of Zionism,* URL: http:// www.geocities.com/Vienna/6640/zion/essential.html, accessed July 25, 2004; David Vital, *The Origins of Zionism* (Oxford: Clarendon Press, 1975).

high priest *(kohein gadol)*

The high priest was the official charged with overseeing the sacrificial system in the TABERNACLE and later in the TEMPLE. In addition, he was responsible for entering the HOLY OF HOLIES one day a year, on YOM KIPPUR, to make atonement for the sins of the people.

The high priest was by law a descendant of AARON, MOSES' brother, from the tribe of Levi; the position and its elaborate duties were transferred from one generation to the next. The high priest held office until he died, and he was viewed by Jews and non-Jews alike as the leader of the Jewish community. As a result, he became an important political as well as religious figure. The Hasmoneans, descendants of the MACCABEES, established the best-known dynasty of high priests beginning in the second century C.E.

Further reading: John H. Hayes and Sara R. Mandell, *The Jewish People in Classical Antiquity: From Alexander to Bar Kochba* (Louisville, Ky.: Westminster/ John Knox Press, 1998); Clemens Thoma, "The High Priesthood in the Judgment of Josephus," in *Josephus, the Bible, and History* (Detroit: Wayne State University Press, 1989).

Hillel (first century B.C.E.) *rabbi/scholar*

Hillel is considered the leading teacher, or RABBI, of the first century B.C.E. Along with SHAMMAI, he is mentioned in Pirke Avot, ETHICS OF THE FATHERS, as the one of the two members of his generation who passed along the teachings of the ORAL LAW. He is also known as Hillel the Elder to distinguish him from another prominent rabbi of the same name who lived 300 years later.

It is difficult to reconstruct a biography of Hillel, because his teachings were oral and were only recorded centuries after his death. However, scholars believe he was born into a wealthy family, but rejected his family's financial aid and lived in poverty while studying in JERUSALEM. Perhaps as a result, Hillel never forgot to take into account the common person's situation when considering a judgment.

The best-known story about Hillel the Elder is recorded in the TALMUD (Shabbat 31a). In this legend, Hillel is asked by a non-Jew to teach him the TORAH while standing on one leg. Hillel, with patience and a smile, agrees. He then states the following: "That which is hateful to you, do not do to your neighbor. The rest is commentary. Now go and study."

Many theologians relate Hillel's words to the "Golden Rule" that Jesus preached. Jesus's words were in the form of a positive commandment, while Hillel's words were worded in the negative, but the message remains the same. The rabbis taught that the negative commandment of "do not do" is more easily performed, explaining that it is easier for people *not* to do certain things than to motivate themselves to do certain things.

Hillel is believed to have created a school of followers who become known as the "House of Hillel," or Bet Hillel. The MISHNAH and Talmud record many scholarly debates between the House of Hillel and the House of Shammai; most Jewish law follows the interpretation of Bet Hillel. Many assert that Hillel won the debate through his kindness and flexibility, and not necessarily because of his legal interpretations themselves.

Further reading: Yitzhak Buxbaum, *The Life and Teachings of Hillel* (Middle Village, N.Y.: Jason Aronson, 1994); Isadore Epstein, ed., *Soncino Hebrew/English Babylonian Talmud* (Brooklyn, N.Y.: Soncino Press, 1990); Joseph H. Hertz, ed., *Pirke Avot: Sayings of the Fathers* (Springfield, N.J.: Behrman House, 1986); Jeffrey L. Rubenstein, ed., *Rabbinic Stories (Classics of Western Spirituality)* (Ramsey, N.J.: Paulist Press, 2002); Adin Steinsaltz, *The Essential Talmud* (New York: Basic Books, 1976).

Hillel: The Foundation for Jewish Campus Life

Named for the ancient rabbi HILLEL, Hillel is an international organization that aims to meet the religious and community needs of Jewish students on college campuses. It was established in 1923 at the University of Illinois by B'NAI B'RITH, but today it is an independent organization. The organiza-

tion fosters Jewish community life on campuses by involving students in Jewish activities. Its mission is to get as many Jews as possible to "do Jewish" with other Jews. The organization is nondenominational and encourages each student to participate in whatever types of activities he or she chooses. Hillel's board of governors includes philanthropic Jewish leaders such as Edgar M. Bronfman (*see* BRONFMAN FOUNDATION) and Michael Steinhardt (*see* STEINHARDT FOUNDATION). Some campuses have a Hillel rabbi and regular worship services, but the group offers nonreligious cultural activities as well.

Further reading: Ruth Fredman Cernea and Jeff Rubin, *Hillel Guide to Jewish Life on Campus* (New York: Random House, 1999); Hillel Web site URL: http://www.hillel.org, accessed February 15, 2004.

Hirsch, Baron Maurice de (1831–1896)
philanthropic proponent of Jewish farm settlements
Born in 1831 to a wealthy German Jewish family, Maurice de Hirsch descended from Jewish bankers who associated closely with 19th-century European nobility, such as the Prince of Wales and the Austrian archduke Rudolph. Baron de Hirsch himself became a financier and generous benefactor, the first significant philanthropist who invested large sums of money in Jewish agricultural resettlement.

Grandson of Baron Jacob von Hirsch, the first Jewish estate owner in Bavaria, and son of Baron Joseph von Hirsch and Karoline Wertheimer, Maurice was, at his mother's insistence, given a solid HEBREW and religious education. Perhaps it is this grounding that led Hirsch to become so generous with his wealth and so focused on the plight of Jews less fortunate than he around the world.

Although Hirsch did go into banking with the firm Bischoffsheim & Goldschmidt in Brussels, marrying Clara, the daughter of the head of the firm, he made his own fortune through the Oriental Railway connecting Europe to Constantinople.

This project, in addition to his interests in sugar and copper, gained him a reputation as a great entrepreneur and industrialist, and gave him a net worth of $100 million by the year 1890.

While working on the Oriental Railway, Hirsch came into contact with Middle Eastern Jews and their difficult living conditions. He donated $200,000 to the ALLIANCE ISRAELITE UNIVERSELLE, an organization dedicated to improving the conditions of Jews around the world, especially in the Middle East. Hirsch's donation was earmarked for Jewish education and trade schools; he later set up a foundation with an annual income of $80,000. After learning from this experience, Hirsch established the Baron de Hirsch Foundation, which helped Jewish immigrants in the UNITED STATES and CANADA, and supported education for Jews in Galicia and Bukovina in eastern Europe.

But it was his Jewish Colonization Association (JCA) that drew most deeply on Hirsch's emotional and financial resources. He strongly believed that the Jews as a people could return to their ancient agricultural roots if given the proper support. The JCA helped Jews emigrate from RUSSIA to farming colonies in ARGENTINA and BRAZIL (and one smaller such colony in Saskatchewan, Canada).

In the long run, very few of these agricultural colonies succeeded, and most of the participants or their children eventually settled in nearby cities. Today, the JCA's funds are invested in agricultural projects in ISRAEL. Ironically, Hirsch never believed that the idea of a Jewish state in PALESTINE would succeed, and he refused to direct his beneficence in the direction of ZIONISM.

The benevolent activities of Hirsch and his wife, Clara, were vast, including major contributions to London hospitals. Hirsch himself maintained racehorses, and donated all of his race winnings to charity. Clara worked alongside her husband tirelessly to provide support for almshouses and soup kitchens, to distribute clothing to the needy, and to finance loan banks.

Maurice and Clara's only son, Lucien, died in 1887. Hirsch responded to words of sympathy with, "My son I have lost, but not my heir, humanity is my heir." After his death in 1896, his wife donated $15 million to charitable causes in New York, Galicia, Vienna, Budapest, and Paris. An additional $10 million was left for an endowment upon her death. Humanity was, indeed, the heir of Baron Maurice de Hirsch.

Further reading: Ismar Elbogen, *A Century of Jewish Life* (Philadelphia: Jewish Publication Society, 1946); Kurt Grunwald, *Turkenhirsch: A Study of Baron Maurice De Hirsch* (New Brunswick, N.J.: Transaction Publishing, 1966); Samuel James Lee, *A Century of Jewish Life* (Philadelphia: Jewish Publication Society of America, 1946).

Hirsch, Samson Raphael (1808–1888)
rabbi and founder of Neo-Orthodoxy

Born in 1808, Samson Raphael Hirsch was bought up in Hamburg, GERMANY. He attended secular schools, but obtained a traditional Jewish education from his family and rabbinic teachers. His father was an observant Jew, and his grandfather, Mendel Frankfurter, was the founder of the Talmud Torah, a Jewish religious school, in Hamburg.

Hirsch trained for the rabbinate with the express agenda of synthesizing traditional Judaism with modern Western culture. After ordination, he studied at the University of Bonn, joined by classmate Abraham GEIGER, who became the leader of the Reform movement (*see* REFORM JUDAISM). Hirsch studied classical languages, history and philosophy.

In 1830, Hirsch accepted the post of rabbi of Oldenburg and in 1846 he became the district rabbi of Moravia. In 1851 he assumed the post of rabbi of Frankfurt-am-Main. Upset by widespread ASSIMILATION in the Jewish community, he embarked on an initiative to build Jewish schools, encourage the practice of the MIKVAH (ritual bath), and ensure that kosher food was available (*see* KASHRUT).

In his pulpit, he copied many of the customs developed by the Reformers. He wore a clergy robe, utilized a male choir, delivered his sermons in German, and shaved off his beard. He emphasized the study of TANAKH, the Hebrew Bible, instead of TAL-MUD study. Despite these external adaptations, Hirsch was a defender of traditional Judaism. In 1836 he published the *Nineteen Letters of Ben Uziel,* an articulate defense of ORTHODOX JUDAISM, a term that only then began to be used. It was the first modern attempt to defend traditional Judaism against the claims of the new Reform movement, in sophisticated intellectual terms that assimilated Jews could understand. It was an effort that had not been needed in the past, when Jewish communities were isolated and somewhat autonomous. In 1838, Hirsch published *Choreb,* a rationalist explanation of the 613 Commandments (*see* MITZVAH). He then published a commentary to the TORAH.

Hirsch was both modern and traditional. He believed that the Jew could adhere to Jewish law and be part of the modern society. His followers became known as the NEO-ORTHODOX MOVEMENT. He completely rejected the Reformers' abrogation of the ritual laws in *HALAKHAH* and the historical approach to Judaism taught by Zachariah FRANKEL. He believed that the Torah was completely authored by GOD, and that Jewish law was dictated by God via oral tradition. His attitude was that the Jew could embrace any part of Western culture that did not conflict with the demands of Torah and Jewish law.

Hirsch became the direct opponent of Reform Judaism. In essence, he created the MODERN ORTHODOX movement, which embraces traditional Judaism but encourages its followers to fully interact with Western society. While traditional Judaism has existed throughout the centuries, a self-conscious Orthodox movement did not come into being until it was organized by Rabbi Samson Raphael Hirsch. The Jewish community Hirsch created in Frankfurt thrived until the Nazi takeover in Germany; most of its members emigrated, and recreated vibrant communities in the UNITED STATES and elsewhere that remain loyal to his teachings.

Further reading: Samson Raphael Hirsch, *Collected Writings of Rabbi Samson Raphael Hirsch,* 8 vols. (New York: Philip Feldheim, 1996); Michael A. Meyer, *Response to Modernity: A History of the Reform Movement in Judaism* (New York and Oxford: Oxford University Press, 1988); Noah H. Rosenbloom, *Tradition in an Age of Reform: The Religious Philosophy of Samson Raphael Hirsch* (Philadelphia: Jewish Publication Society, 1976).

Histadrut

The Histadrut, the General Federation of Labor in ISRAEL, is a combination labor union/social service agency that has also played a major economic role in Israeli life.

The Histadrut was founded in 1920, with a mission to establish autonomy for labor and fulfill the workers' needs. The organization served as a trade union, struggling to obtain better wages and conditions. The Histadrut also established an economic branch, Hevrat Ovdim, which created additional sources of employment. It set up factories that have, over the years, turned the organization into the leading economic force in Israel. Some of the economic systems that the Histadrut have built include: Bank HaPoalim, the Cooperative Center, the Koor Concern, the construction firm Solel Boneh, and the Tnuva food company. The Histadrut also established specific movements to serve working women and youth.

The Histadrut created Kupat Holim, the General Sick Fund, which takes care of the medical needs of more than 80 percent of the citizens of Israel. They set up savings and pension funds, a chain of senior citizens homes, and organizations to support pensioners, orphans, and widows. They have run a newspaper, theater, publishing company, and sports organization.

At the time of the establishment of the State of Israel, Histadrut represented approximately 35 percent of the entire adult working population; its network of institutions created much of the infrastructure for the new Israeli government. By 1994, the Histadrut had spun off many of its business endeavors; the "New Histadrut" has returned to its emphasis as a trade union, representing a confederation of 78 unions with more than 700,000 members.

Further reading: David Maisel, *The Founding Myths of Israel: Nationalism, Socialism, and the Making of the Jewish State* (Princeton, N.J.: Princeton University Press, 1998); Michael Shalev, *Labour and the Political Economy in Israel* (Oxford: Oxford University Press, 1992); Histadrut Web site URL: http://www.histadrut.org.il, accessed July 18, 2004.

Hitler, Adolf (1889–1945) *German leader who had millions of Jews killed*

Adolf Hitler was appointed chancellor in GERMANY in 1933. From that time until his death, he worked for the extermination of the Jewish people in Germany and throughout Europe.

Hitler was born in Braunau, AUSTRIA, along the Bavarian-German border, the son of an Austrian customs official. His early life involved a series of failures: he failed to gain admission to the Academy of Fine Arts in Vienna, he failed to escape conscription into the Austrian army, and then he failed the physical examination when he was caught. He became increasingly interested in the power of politics, and he developed masterful skills at political propaganda, while immersing himself in extreme nationalist and antisemitic literature.

Hitler became instrumental in the development of the Nazi, or National Socialist, Party in Germany. Though it took a number of years to develop, the party eventually was successful at tapping into the worries of Germans who had been hard hit by the Depression. In July 1932 the Nazis scored a major electoral success, and in 1933 Hitler was appointed chancellor by President Paul von Hindenburg.

Hitler's views on Jews were plainly stated in *Mein Kampf* (My struggle), written while he was in jail for political violence. In Hitler's view, Jews could never be converted, because Judaism was a racial designation. Jews were parasites who infiltrated the societies in which they lived, living off of the work of others. Hitler convinced fellow Germans that their only hope of reviving a vital German culture was to marginalize, then exile and exterminate the Jewish population. Hitler won support through a combination of intense patriotism based on the concept of Aryan superiority, promises of prosperity, denunciations of COMMUNISM, and ANTISEMITISM. Through a series of increasingly drastic measures, Hitler stripped Jews of their rights as citizens. He excluded them from most professions and stationed brutal guards outside Jewish-owned shops to scare away customers.

In 1935 the NUREMBERG LAWS deprived Jews of all basic rights of citizenship. Between 1941 and 1945 Hitler stepped up his efforts, working Jews to death in CONCENTRATION CAMPS and murdering millions of others in death camps in POLAND. Ultimately, approximately 6 million Jews died during the HOLOCAUST spearheaded by Hitler. In addition, many thousands of SYNAGOGUES, sacred texts, yeshivot (*see* YESHIVA), and ancient treasures were destroyed.

When it became clear that the Allied forces were about to defeat Germany, Hitler committed suicide in an underground bunker in Berlin. His final letter to the world emphasized his antisemitism, calling Jewry the "world-poisoner of all nations."

Further reading: Zygmunt Bauman, *Modernity and the Holocaust* (Ithaca, N.Y.: Cornell University Press, 1989); Alan Bullock, *Hitler: A Study in Tyranny* (New York, Harper & Row, 1962); Lucy Dawidowicz, *The War Against the Jews* (New York: Bantam Books, 1986); Ian Kershaw, *Hitler: Profiles in Power* (London: Pearson Education Limited, 1991).

Holdheim, Samuel (1806–1860) *rabbi/ scholar who helped found Reform Judaism*

Raised in POLAND, Samuel Holdheim received a traditional Jewish upbringing. At an early age he demonstrated his genius for the TALMUD, and later supplemented his Jewish education with general studies. As an adult, Holdheim joined Abraham GEIGER in laying the intellectual foundation for REFORM JUDAISM.

Holdheim asserted that historical Judaism had contained two primary elements: ethical MONOTHE-ISM and nationalistic identity as expressed through its rituals. He wanted to retain the universalist features of Judaism, while eliminating the particularism of the Jewish national identity so that the Jew could properly join modern society. Unlike Geiger and Zachariah FRANKEL, Holdheim did not find value in the scientific study of Judaism, WISSENSCHAFT DES JUDENTEMS. Instead, he interpreted the modern age as a completely new stage for JUDAISM, rather than a continuation of the old.

Holdheim was appointed rabbi of the province of Mecklenburg-Schwerin, an area whose government at the time was encouraging reform of the Jewish religion. He introduced slight reforms in the service upon his arrival in 1840, such as eliminating TROPE, the traditional melody, and reading the Torah without a chant. A year later, he founded a modern religious school. Holdheim attended three rabbinical conferences, Brunswick (1844), Frankfurt-am-Main (1845), and Breslau (1846), and at each he found himself to be on the radical left of Reform, wanting more vigorous and severe reforms than most of his colleagues.

In 1847 Holdheim became the rabbi of the Berlin Reform Temple, and introduced the most radical reforms, some of which were resisted by Geiger himself. He eliminated HEBREW from the worship services, and moved SHABBAT, the Sabbath, to Sundays. He also embraced INTERMARRIAGE. Holdheim's radical reforms were not widely accepted in Germany outside his own congregation, but his intellectual and anti-ritualist brand of Reform Judaism was exported to America, and for many years was the primary foundation of the American Reform Movement.

Further reading: Michael A. Meyer, *Response to Modernity: A History of the Reform Movement in Judaism* (New York and Oxford: Oxford University Press, 1988); Aaron M. Petuchowski and Elizabeth R. Petuchowski, eds., *Studies in Modern Theology and Prayer* (Philadelphia: Jewish Publication Society, 1998); W. Gunther Plaut, *The Rise of Reform Judaism* (New York: World Union for Progressive Judaism, 1963).

Holocaust (Shoah)

The Holocaust, called the Shoah in HEBREW, refers to the period from January 30, 1933, when Adolph HITLER became chancellor of GERMANY, until May 8, 1945, when Germany surrendered to the Allies.

Historically, the English word *holocaust* referred to a sacrificial offering that was completed burned to ashes; it seemed an appropriate term to describe the murder of 6 million Jews, many of whose bodies were burned completely in the death camp crematoriums. The Hebrew word *shoah* simply means "destruction" or "annihilation," a literal description of the fate of European Jewry during Hitler's reign of terror. The Holocaust ultimately culminated in the murder of approximately 6 million Jews, including 1.5 million children. This number represented one-third of the world's Jewish population. The Jews who perished in the Holocaust were not simply casualties of war. They were systematically annihilated, by what Hitler and the Nazi regime called the FINAL SOLUTION, or Endlosung.

Hitler and the Nazi regime embraced ANTISEMITISM as a means to create a scapegoat for all the woes of German society. Once Hitler was in complete control of Germany in 1934, his war against the Jews began in full. He promoted his racist version of antisemitism, building on long-standing religious and national prejudices. The Nazis contrasted their supposed "Aryan" super-race to the supposedly inferior Jewish race.

The Nazis enacted the NUREMBERG LAWS on September 15, 1935, which removed all legal rights from Jews and imposed severe discrimination. Because few countries were willing to accept Jewish refugees, the Jews of Germany and neighboring countries were trapped. On November 9, 1938, the Nazis organized an attack against German Jewry. This night became known as the Night of Broken Glass, or KRISTALLNACHT. Nazi thugs looted and destroyed Jewish homes and businesses and burned SYNAGOGUES. Many Jews were beaten and killed. Over 30,000 Jews were arrested and sent to CONCENTRATION CAMPS.

Germany invaded POLAND in September 1939 and World War II began. More than 10 percent of the Polish population was Jewish, numbering more than 3 million. Jews were forcibly deported from their homes to live in crowded GHETTOS, where they would be easy prey. Beginning in June 1941, Germany attacked the Soviet Union and the Final Solution began in earnest. Four mobile killing groups were formed, called EINSATZGRUPPEN, who moved just behind the advancing German lines. These units killed at least 1.5 million Jews.

On January 20, 1942, several leaders of the German government met at the WANNSEE CONFERENCE to organize an efficient system of mass murder for the Jews. By the spring of 1942, the Nazis had established six death camps in Poland: AUSCHWITZ, Belzec, Chelno, Maidanek, Sobibor, and Treblinka. They were all located near railway lines so that Jews could be transported easily. In each new country they conquered, the Nazis would identify the local Jews and mark them for deportation. Some escaped death through the altruistic actions of fellow countrymen, who are now called "Righteous Gentiles" (*see* YAD VASHEM); however, only in DENMARK did the country as a whole come together to protect their Jewish population.

The Holocaust is often seen as unique in world history. This is not to say that other peoples have not been murdered in mass numbers, or that the lives of the Jews who died in the Holocaust were more significant than others who died similarly horrific deaths. The uniqueness of the Holocaust is found in its systematic, assembly-line methods, and its unflinching goal of complete annihilation. Without the modern penchant for efficiency or the technological advances used in the killing, the Holocaust could not have occurred. The fact that Hitler and his men were able to use bureaucracy, science, and industry to systematically dehumanize and then murder millions of people, 6 million Jews and 5 million non-Jews, makes the Holo-

caust an event unique in world history, and the archetype of evil in the modern world.

Some argue that the event itself is testimony to the failure of the ENLIGHTENMENT, as it was the product of the most highly educated country in Europe. Others, such as Hannah ARENDT, note that those who actually performed the thousands of individual acts that made up the Holocaust were ordinary people bending to the political and social pressures that make us all human. If true, the very banal aspects of the Holocaust might serve as a warning that people must be vigilant in their efforts to lead moral and enlightened lives, and that they must never take goodness for granted, and that they must keep alive the memory of the Holocaust to prevent its happening again.

Further reading: Yehuda Bauer and Nili Keren, *A History of the Holocaust* (London: Franklin Watts, 2001); Zygmunt Bauman, *Modernity and the Holocaust* (Ithaca, N.Y.: Cornell University Press, 2001); Lucy S. Dawidowicz, *The War Against the Jews: 1933–1945* (New York: Bantam Books, 1975); Martin Gilbert, *A History of the Jews of Europe during the Second World War* (New York: Henry Holt, 1987); Joshua M. Greene and Shiva Kumar, eds., *Witness: Voices from the Holocaust* (New York: Free Press, 2000); David J. Hogan, ed., *The Holocaust Chronicle: A History in Words and Pictures* (Lincolnwood, Ill.: Publications International, Ltd., 2003).

Holocaust revisionists

Holocaust revisionists are individuals who deny that the HOLOCAUST ever happened or claim that it has been greatly exaggerated. They attempt to "disprove" the event, often with counterfeit evidence or poor historical analysis, while making much of the fact that documentary evidence about every last victim was sometimes lost in the chaos and destruction that prevailed as World War II came to a close.

Holocaust revisionists are often neo-fascists with political agendas who pretend to academic or expert authority. One Holocaust revisionist group is the Institute for Historical Review; among the significant figures in the movement are Arthur Butz, Ernst Zundel, and Fred Leuchter.

Holocaust scholar Deborah Lipstadt documented the falsehoods of Holocaust revisionism in her books *Beyond Belief* and *Denying the Holocaust: The Growing Assault on Truth and Memory.* The Holocaust revisionist David Irving sued Lipstadt for libel in England, after she identified and indicted him as a Holocaust denier in the latter's book. Irving attempted to label Lipstadt's charge as libelous because, he asserted, the Holocaust in fact did not occur. The British court formally rebuked Irving and Holocaust revisionism. The judge's 355-page verdict strongly challenged the legitimacy of Holocaust revisionism and labeled Holocaust deniers as "anti-Semitic crackpots."

Further reading: Alain Finkielkraut, *The Future of a Negation: Reflections on the Question of Genocide* (Lincoln: University of Nebraska Press, 1998); Deborah Lipstadt, *Beyond Belief* (New York: Free Press, 1993); ———, *Denying the Holocaust: The Growing Assault on Truth and Memory* (New York: Free Press, 1993); James Najarian, "Gnawing at History: The Rhetoric of Holocaust Denial" in *The Midwest Quarterly* 39, 1 (1987); Gill Seidel, *The Holocaust Denial: Antisemitism, Racism, and the New Right* (Leeds, U.K.: Beyond the Pale Collective, 1986).

Holy of Holies

The Holy of Holies was the innermost chamber of the TABERNACLE in the wilderness and the TEMPLE in JERUSALEM. It was believed that God's presence actually dwelt in this chamber, which housed the ARK of the Covenant. Only the HIGH PRIEST had access to the chamber, and even he was allowed in only once per year, on YOM KIPPUR, the Day of Atonement. On that day he would enter the Holy of Holies to perform an incense ritual that would atone for the sins of Israel; he would then emerge and pronounce, before the assembled people, the proper name of God, YHWH, the pronunciation of which is no longer known (*see* GOD, NAMES OF).

Most Jews believe that the Holy of Holies lies beneath the Dome of the Rock in Jerusalem. It was common practice for Muslims to build mosques on holy sites of other traditions, and thus this idea cannot be completely rejected.

Further reading: Menahem Haran, *Temples and Temple-Service in Ancient Israel: An Inquiry into Biblical Cult Phenomena and the Historical Setting of the Priestly School* (Winona Lake, Ind.: Eisenbrauns, 1985); Michael D. Swartz, *Place and Person in Ancient Judaism: Describing the Yom Kippur Sacrifice* (Ramat Gan, Israel: Department of Land of Israel Studies, Bar Ilan University, 2001); *Tanakh: The Holy Scriptures* (Philadelphia and Jerusalem: Jewish Publication Society, 1985).

holy places

There are numerous holy places in Judaism, consecrated by God's presence. The KOTEL, or Western Wall, on the site of the TEMPLE mount is currently the holiest spot accessible to Jews because it is the remnant of God's dwelling place. The holiest place of all, the Temple mount itself, is currently the site of two historic Muslim mosques, and is mostly off-limits to Jews, for two reasons. The Israeli authorities fear that Muslims might react violently against any organized Jewish presence, and some Jewish religious authorities argue that once on the mount, Jews might inadvertently step on the actual site of the Temple or the HOLY OF HOLIES, which might therefore be defiled.

The TANAKH contains many other stories of holy places. The PATRIARCHS marked sites where they had visions of God as holy by placing stones there and renaming the places, as in the case of Beth-El, "house of God." MOSES is told not to wear shoes at the site of the burning bush because it is holy ground. The PROPHETS criticize the kings and the people of ISRAEL for desecrating the holy places.

Besides the Kotel, the CAVE OF MACHPELAH and MOUNT SINAI are among the holiest of places. The cave of Machpelah is the burial site of the Patriarchs and MATRIARCHS, while Mount Sinai was the site of God's revelation of the TORAH to the people of Israel.

Finally, many people consider the burial places of famous rabbis holy. Both ASHKENAZIM and SEPHARDIM visit the gravesites of famous RABBIS, thus participating in a form of Jewish saint veneration.

Further reading: Ben Avraham Halevi, *A Modern Guide to the Jewish Holy Places* (Jerusalem: Posner, 1982); Seth Daniel Kunin, *God's Place in the World: Sacred Space and Sacred Place in Judaism* (London and New York: Cassell, 1998).

homiletics

Homiletics is the art of preaching. While preaching and public lectures on TORAH and RABBINIC LAW have always had a major role in Judaism, the rhetorical art of preaching has become a modern skill within Judaism.

With the advent of movements such as REFORM JUDAISM and the NEO-ORTHODOX MOVEMENT, RABBIS have been expected to preach at least once each week in the SYNAGOGUE in the non-Jewish language of the land, such as German or English. Pulpit rabbis, in addition to their pastoral duties, are expected to be capable preachers as well as teachers. Modern rabbinic seminaries have classes in homiletics, and many rabbis spend their entire careers honing their effective preaching skills.

There is no single methodological approach to Jewish preaching. One common suggestion of teachers of homiletics is to tell the congregation what you are preaching on, convey the lesson, and then tell them what you have told them. The threefold repetition of the theme makes it more likely that the sermon will be remembered (traditional Jews do not write on the Sabbath and so cannot take notes). Many rabbis enrich the message with quotations from sacred Jewish texts, topical references to issues of the day, and engaging stories, all designed to capture the interests of their congregation.

Further reading: Robert V. Friedenberg, *Hear O Israel: The History of American Jewish Preaching, 1654–1970*

(Tuscaloosa: University of Alabama Press, 1989); Marc Saperstein, *Jewish Preaching, 1200–1800: An Anthology* (New Haven, Conn.: Yale University Press, 1992).

homosexuality

Homosexuality among both men and women is prohibited in traditional Judaism. ORTHODOX JUDAISM reads the TORAH as specifically prohibiting homosexual conduct between males, and they read RABBINIC LAW as condemning homosexual acts by both men and women. Leviticus (19:22) declares (speaking to men): "You shall not lie with man, as with woman; it is an abomination," and (20:13) repeats: "If a man lie with mankind, as with womankind, both of them have committed abomination; they shall surely be put to death; their blood shall be upon them."

According to Orthodoxy the prohibition of homosexual behavior applies to both Jews and non-Jews, since sexual morality is considered to be one of the Noahide laws that apply to all of NOAH's descendants, namely the whole human race.

In REFORM JUDAISM today, homosexuality is seen not as a lifestyle choice subject to moral judgment, but as a biological predisposition. Reform writers have argued that the ancient prohibitions had in mind the kind of behavior in which one man asserts sexual power over another, and not consensual homosexual acts. The Reform movement ordains homosexual RABBIS, and many Reform rabbis perform same-sex marriages.

CONSERVATIVE JUDAISM has vigorously debated the issue of homosexuality, but still does not permit the ordination of gay rabbis who reveal their sexual orientation publicly. However, there are several known gay rabbis in the Rabbinical Assembly and they have not been forced to resign. Some Conservative rabbis, at their own discretion, perform commitment ceremonies between homosexuals who share the Jewish faith, and they have not been censured.

Orthodox Judaism maintains that homosexual acts are sinful, but does not condemn the person with a homosexual proclivity who remains celibate.

There are Orthodox rabbis who accept gay members of their congregations, and there are also Conservative and Reform Jews who reject homosexual behavior as immoral.

Further reading: Steven Greenberg, *Wrestling with God and Men: Homosexuality in the Jewish Tradition* (Madison: University of Wisconsin Press, 2004); Arthur Hertzberg, *Judaism: The Key Spiritual Writings of the Jewish Tradition* (New York: Simon & Schuster, 1991); Hayim Rapoport, *Judaism and Homosexuality: An Authentic Orthodox View* (Ilford, Essex, U.K.: Mitchell Vallentine & Company, 2004).

honoring parents

The honoring of parents is the fifth of the Ten Commandments, or DECALOGUE.

That Jews owe their parents honor is a fundamental teaching of Judaism. The ancient RABBIS explained that the fifth commandment served as a bridge between the first four, which deal with obligations toward God, and the last five, which deal with obligations toward other people. Parents are described by the rabbis as the bridge that connects God with humanity.

The TALMUD teaches that there exist three partners in giving birth: God, mother, and father. Parents represent God to the child, in both the act of CREATION and in their nurturing. The child therefore must respect the parents as one should respect God.

While parents have obligations they must perform on behalf of their children, children also have obligations toward their parents. Specifically, adult children are expected to take care of and provide for their elderly parents, as once their parents provided for them. The rabbis note that "love of parents" is not commanded, rather honor is commanded. The rabbis asserted that while the feeling of love cannot be commanded, when a parent and a child live up to their responsibilities to each other, love will be cultivated. However, even if children actively dislike their parents, they must still fulfill their obligations toward them.

While children are commanded to honor their parents, they may not commit a sin even if ordered by parents to do so. The parent is an extension of God to the child, but should the parent insist on un-Godly behavior, the child fulfills the mandate of God first.

Further reading: Arthur Hertzberg, *Judaism: The Key Spiritual Writings of the Jewish Tradition* (New York: Simon & Schuster, 1991); Moshe Lieber, *The Fifth Commandment: Honoring Parents* (Brooklyn, N.Y.: Mesorah Publications, Ltd., 1998); Chaim Potok, *Ethical Living for a Modern World: Jewish Insights* (New York: Jewish Theological Seminary of America, 1985).

Hoshanah Rabbah

Hoshanah Rabbah is the seventh day of SUKKOT. When the TEMPLE was still standing, it was a day of particular rejoicing. Participants would circle the Temple seven times, with seven TORAH scrolls, and with a lulav and etrog, symbols of the harvest, singing "Hoshanah," which means "Please help us O Lord." The Hoshanah was a prayer for rain; as it was repeated many times this day it became the "great Hoshanah" or Hoshanah Rabbah. On this day, when the festival season of the month of Tishri is drawing to a close, the decrees set into the BOOK OF LIFE on ROSH HASHANAH and sealed on YOM KIPPUR are thought to be finalized.

Further reading: Irving Greenberg, *The Jewish Way: Living the Holidays* (New York: Touchstone, 1988); Rabbi Jules Harlow, ed., "Hoshanot," in *Siddur Sim Shalom: A Prayerbook for Shabbat, Festivals, and Weekdays* (New York: Rabbinical Assembly, United Synagogue of America, 1989), 530–547; Ronald H. Isaacs, *Every Person's Guide to Sukkot, Shemini Atzeret, and Simchat Torah* (Northvale, N.J.: Jason Aronson, 2000).

hospitality

Hospitality is a major virtue in Judaism. The biblical story most connected to this virtue concerns

Abraham (*see* PATRIARCHS) and his hospitality toward the angels, or *MALAKHIM,* who visit him (Gn 18). Upon seeing three men standing near his tent, Abraham not only invites them to sit and rest, but hurries to serve them the best food and drink he has. As it turns out, the weary travelers are really messengers of God, and God rewards Abraham for his hospitality by granting him a son with Sarah (*see* MATRIARCHS). According to tradition, these same angels then traveled on to Sodom, where they were subjected to the extreme inhospitality that characterized that city (Gn 19). Abraham's hospitable actions are considered a model for all his descendants.

This ethic of hospitality shows up in later times as well. In medieval times, SYNAGOGUES served as rest houses for travelers, and in modern times it is traditional to invite visitors from synagogue home for a Sabbath (SHABBAT) meal. Also, at PASSOVER each family formally invites all who are hungry to enter and eat.

Further reading: Ronald H. Isaacs, *Legends of Biblical Heroes: A Sourcebook* (Northvale, N.J.: Jason Aronson, 2002); *Tanakh: The Holy Scriptures* (Philadelphia and Jerusalem: Jewish Publication Society, 1985); Meir Wikler, *Aishel: Stories of Contemporary Jewish Hospitality* (Spring Valley, N.Y.: Feldheim, 1994).

Humanistic Judaism

Established by Rabbi Sherwin T. Wine in 1963 in Detroit, Michigan, Humanistic Judaism is a non-theistic, human-centered movement that stresses human agency and rejects the idea of a higher, or supernatural, power that affects, guides or in any way controls human life, or did so at any time in history. Humanist Jews believe that only people determine the purpose and course of their lives; they have not only the power but also the responsibility to be the masters of their own lives. Since the movement does not believe in God, the liturgy of Humanist Judaism does not use any theistic language. Instead it sees Judaism as the historic, ethnic culture of the Jewish people.

Humanistic Judaism accepts intermarriage, defining as Jews those who identify with the history, culture, and future of the Jewish people. Thus, celebrations of holidays and life-cycle events are viewed as public demonstrations of a bond with the Jewish people at large. Humanistic Judaism stresses ethics, seeking the ethical core of Jewish history, literature, and culture, and emphasizes social action, community service, and social justice. Today, the movement has some 50 congregations in the UNITED STATES and CANADA and branches in ISRAEL, Europe, the former Soviet Union (*see* RUSSIA), Australia, and Latin America.

Further reading: Yaakov Malkin, *Secular Judaism: Faith, Values, and Spirituality* (London and Portland, Oreg.: Vallentine Mitchell, 2004); Society for Humanistic Judaism Web site URL: http://www.shj.org/, accessed July 30, 2004; Sherwin T. Wine, *Celebration: A Ceremonial and Philosophic Guide for Humanists and Humanistic Jews* (Buffalo, N.Y.: Prometheus Books, 1988); ———, *Humanistic Judaism* (Buffalo, N.Y.: Prometheus Books, 1978).

humility

The virtue of humility is considered within Judaism to be the hallmark of greatness. Rabbinic tradition states that humility was MOSES' greatest virtue. The Jewish definition of humility is a clear understanding of one's strengths and weaknesses; the humble person acts appropriately in response to this self-knowledge. To be humble does not disallow for greatness and in fact increases the potential for a greater character.

The TALMUD (Taanit 7a) states that only one with a humble heart is capable of listening to the word of God. However, the rabbis recognized the trait of false humility. The classic work on humility, *The Path of the Upright* by the CHAFETZ CHAIM, summarizes the standard rabbinic view on proper humility versus improper humility.

One legend of the Chafetz Chayim finds him traveling on a train opposite a man reading one of his books, who does not recognize him. He asks the man what he thinks of the book, and the man responds that it was written by the greatest rabbi ever. The rabbi protests that the writer of the book is not so great, but the reader insists, and in the end punches the rabbi in the nose for insulting "the great Chafetz Chayim." The rabbi laughs as he reveals his identity, and apologizes for the sin of "false humility."

A common Hasidic teaching on humility states that those who run away from fame are always looking over their shoulders to see if fame is following.

Further reading: Arthur Hertzberg, *Judaism: The Key Spiritual Writings of the Jewish Tradition* (New York: Simon & Schuster, 1991); George Robinson, *Essential Judaism: A Complete Guide to Beliefs, Customs & Rituals* (New York: Pocket Books, 2000).

humor

Jewish humor can be defined as humor that reflects particular aspects of Jewish life, created by Jews and largely intended to be appreciated by Jews. Jewish humor can be expressed in jokes, anecdotes, and witticisms and can cover a range of topics, including God, RABBIS, ANTISEMITISM, ASSIMILATION, FAMILY, self-deprecation, self-praise, professional success or failure, and guilt.

The TANAKH, or Hebrew Bible, contains a considerable amount of irony, satire, and laughter that can be interpreted as early Jewish humor. For example, when Sarah (*see* MATRIARCHS) was told that she would bear a child at the age of 90, she laughed (Gn 18:12); when the prediction came true, she wryly named her child Isaac, meaning "he shall laugh." Later in the biblical narrative, when JOSEPH's brothers throw him into a pit, they mock him sarcastically, saying: "We shall see what will become of his dreams" (Gn 37:20). References to jokes and laughter also appear occasionally in the TALMUD.

Each Jewish community's unique characteristics can alter the nature of the humor, whether the community is Ashkenazi (*see* ASHKENAZIM),

Sephardi (*see* SEPHARDIM), American, Russian, or Israeli. Many Jews have lived under oppressive regimes, where humor was used as an antidote to fear or depression, or as a covert method through which the Jewish community could express its feelings about the larger society or about its own failings.

The verbal nature of a good deal of Jewish humor lends itself to wordplay and interpretation, skills utilized often in the study of Torah. Thus both anxiety and logic are integral parts of much Jewish humor. The integration of different languages created much fodder for Jewish humorists—the interpolation of YIDDISH, HEBREW, and the vernacular of a larger society lent itself to many moments of laughter. Early 20th-century Jewish comedians (*see* BORSCHT BELT; ENTERTAINMENT; VAUDEVILLE) helped make Jewish humor part of contemporary mainstream humor in the United States, England, and other countries.

Further reading: Henry D. Spalding, *Encyclopedia of Jewish Humor: From Biblical Times to the Modern Age* (New York: Jonathan David Publishers, 1969); Joseph Telushkin, *Jewish Humor: What the Best Jewish Jokes Say About the Jews* (New York: William Morrow, 1992).

Hungary

Jews appeared in Hungary during Roman times, but the Jewish community did not grow steadily until the 11th century, when large numbers of immigrants came from the German states. As in many other European countries, the Jews in Hungary experienced good and bad times. At the end of the 11th century, the Jews were favored and protected by the king, but persecuted by the church. In 1349, the Jews were expelled after accusations of spreading the Black Plague. They were allowed back in 1364, and in the following year they were granted semiautonomous bodies to conduct their internal affairs.

By the beginning of the 15th century, conditions in Hungary were good for Jewish settlement and Jews began to settle in the city of Buda. However, by the end of that century conditions declined as the Jews suffered from BLOOD LIBEL, the claim that they were using Christian blood in ritual activities. Sixteen Jews were burned at the stake and riots followed in 1494. The financial situation of the Hungarian Jews deteriorated when King Ladislas VI canceled debts owed to Jews, and ANTI-JUDAISM grew. However, by 1526 the Ottoman Turks had conquered nearly the entire country, and Jews were granted freedom to practice Judaism and participate in trade.

By 1735 11,600 Jews lived in Hungary under the Hapsburg Empire, despite increased ANTI-SEMITISM. In the mid-18th century, Jews were required to pay "toleration taxes" and persecution was tolerated. The reign of Joseph II alleviated some of the harsh conditions of Jewish life in Hungary, and thus the Jewish population grew to 81,000 by 1787. Jews were granted increasing levels of civil rights in the 1830s and 1840s. After a short period of economic restrictions as punishment for participating in a failed revolution, the Jews of Hungary were allowed to become involved in commerce and to live in any Hungarian city. Full emancipation came in December 1867. Thereafter, the Jews participated in industry, the professions, politics, and economics. ANTISEMITISM grew, despite efforts by the government to control it.

Most Hungarian Jews were traditional. Many important yeshivot were built (*see* YESHIVA), and HASIDISM attracted many followers. Even a strict regard for traditional Judaism, however, could not keep the Jewish ENLIGHTENMENT, the HASKALAH, from affecting Hungarian Jews, and its influence was felt in the community in the 1830s. By 1870 there were three main divisions of Judaism in Hungary, including the Orthodox (*see* ORTHODOX JUDAISM), Neolog (moderate reform), and Status Quo Ante, or everyone else. ASSIMILATION and INTERMARRIAGE became common among Hungarian Jews, but so too did ZIONISM.

By 1910 there were close to 1 million Jews in Hungary, including more than half of the country's merchants. After World War I, in which close to 10,000 Jews died on the battlefield, communists

briefly seized power. Jews were active in the communist regime and Bela Kun, its leader, was Jewish. The overthrow of the communists in 1919 unleashed the White Terror; riots and violence resulted in the massacre of 3,000 Hungarian Jews. As the 1930s approached, the nationalistic regime imposed anti-Jewish laws, and antisemitism was widely promoted. Many Jews lost their livelihood and many converted to CHRISTIANITY.

During World War II, Hungary was an Axis power, allied with Nazi GERMANY. In 1941, the massacre of Hungarian Jewry began when 20,000 people were murdered by both Germans and Hungarians. Jewish property was confiscated and Jewish economic and cultural life was further restricted, but most Hungarian Jews remained physically unmolested. In 1943, Germany occupied Hungary after accusing its government of cooperating with the Allies and not deporting its Jewish population, though 63,000 Hungarian Jews had already lost their lives. Under direct Nazi rule, 400,000 more were herded in GHETTOS, and then deported to AUSCHWITZ, where almost all of them were eventually killed, either in the gas chambers or on death marches. The HAGANAH, the Jewish defense force in Palestine, tried to save Hungarian Jews by dropping paratroopers behind enemy lines; several were killed, including Hannah SENESCH, whose mother had remained in Hungary. Foreign diplomats Charles Lutz (1895–1975) and Raoul WALLENBERG (1912–1947?) saved many Jews through their heroic efforts, but a total of 565,000 Hungarian Jews died in the HOLOCAUST.

When World War II ended, Jews returned to Hungary, but their fate under Communist rule was not significantly better than it had been in the past. Before the Communists took power in Hungary, anti-Jewish legislation was abolished and war criminals were tried and imprisoned. Property, however, was not returned, and no war reparations came to the Jews of Hungary. The Jewish community had begun to rebuild when communism shut the door on the Western world, and expulsions from Hungarian cities resumed. By the 1970s only 60,000 Jews lived in Hungary, most in

Budapest. In 1989, the Communist regime collapsed, and restrictions upon the Jewish community of Hungary ended and relations with Israel began.

Antisemitism and assimilation are significant social problems for the Jews of Hungary today. The federation of Jewish communities organizes Jewish life, but many Hungarian Jews are not affiliated with any Jewish organization, institution, or denomination. There are also three Jewish day schools, a Jewish high school, Jewish youth groups, a couple of active Zionist organizations, Jewish newspapers, a community center, Jewish nursing homes, and successful kosher butchers (see KASHRUT). Jewish culture is alive as well; the country boasts a Jewish Museum and theater, dance, and music companies. Jewish religious leanings tend toward Reform and Conservative, and there are 20 synagogues in Budapest. Hungary's GREAT SYNAGOGUE survived the war and communism. Even so, only a small minority of Hungary's 100,000 Jews are involved in Jewish life.

Further reading: Charles Fenyvesi, *When Angels Fooled the World: Rescuers of Jews in Wartime Hungary* (Madison: University of Wisconsin Press, 2003); Maria M. Kovacs, *Liberal Professions and Illiberal Politics: Hungary from the Habsburgs to the Holocaust* (New York: Oxford University Press, 1994); Raphael Patai, *The Jews of Hungary: History, Culture, Psychology* (Detroit: Wayne State University Press, 1996).

I

Ibn Atar, Yehudah (1656–1733) and Chaim (1696–1743) *Kabbalistic rabbis*

The Ibn Atar family was one of the most famous Jewish families in Morocco. Two of its most eminent figures were the RABBIS and Kabbalists Yehudah Ibn Atar and Chaim Ibn Atar.

Yehudah is described in the book *Shem haGedolim,* by the 18th-century rabbi Chaim Yosef David Azulai, as a great rabbi who headed the rabbinic court in Fez and was particularly adept in performing miracles. In one legend recounted by Azulai, Yehudah survived untouched for 24 hours in a den full of hungry lions. Yehudah's tomb lies in the cemetery on the edge of the Jewish Quarter in Fez. As Yehudah Ibn Atar is considered a saint, many SEPHARDIM make an annual pilgrimage to his tomb, which overlooks a green and hilly view.

Chaim Ibn Atar was well known as the Ohr Ha-Chaim (Light of Life). He was born in Morocco in 1696 and died in JERUSALEM in 1743. Like Yehudah, he was a student and practitioner of the KABBALAH. Chaim Ibn Atar also fervently believed that the time of the MESSIAH was close at hand, and that it was his destiny to help usher in the MESSIANIC AGE. He made his way to ISRAEL, via Italy, and established a YESHIVA in Jerusalem. The BAAL SHEM TOV, founder of HASIDISM, was influ-

enced by the writings of Chaim Ibn Atar. The Hasidic movement modeled their notion of a tzadik, or righteous one, on Chaim's reputation as a saint.

Chaim Ibn Atar wrote on HALAKHAH, Jewish law, but his most important work was a mystical commentary on the TORAH entitled the *Ohr Ha-Chaim,* a pun on his own name; it was published in Venice in 1742. The book is still widely read by scholars and commentators. It has gone into many editions both as a separate work and as a commentary alongside the biblical text, and a number of subsequent rabbinic scholars have written commentaries on it.

Further reading: Louis Jacobs, *Holy Living: Saints and Saintliness in Judaism* (Northvale, N.J.: Jason Aronson, 1990).

Ibn Ezra, Abraham (1089–1164) *Spanish Jewish writer and biblical commentator*

Ibn Ezra's brilliant commentaries on the TANAKH, the Hebrew Bible, have been widely read for 900 years.

Abraham Ibn Ezra was born in SPAIN in 1089. There is evidence that he was friends with Yehudah HALEVI and may have been married to Halevi's daughter. It is thought that the death of one or more children and the conversion of another child to ISLAM prompted Ibn Ezra to become estranged from his surroundings and begin a life of wandering. During his travels through Italy, FRANCE, ENGLAND, and back to Spain looking for his prodigal son, he wrote exceptional works on astrology, HEBREW grammar, poetry, and science. Ibn Ezra's Hebrew grammar was the first in its era not written in Arabic, and it became an important textbook for Italian Jewry. He also introduced the decimal system to Jews living in the Christian world, who at that point were unaware of the mathematical principle.

Ibn Ezra's commentary on the Tanakh, the Hebrew Bible, is considered a classic. He concentrated on the PSHAT, the plain meaning of the text, examining in detail the grammar and literal sense. Many scholars believe that Ibn Ezra arrived at a version of the documentary hypothesis of biblical study, which was rediscovered by Christian scholars in the 19th century and is now the dominant approach to biblical criticism. According to that later theory, the TORAH was compiled from four different preexisting sources. Ibn Ezra's grammatical expertise enabled him to see evidence of editing. He took note of grammatical anomalies without actually discussing multiple authors, but perhaps he hinted at such a theory with his frequent aside that the "intelligent will understand." Often Ibn Ezra's work points at deeper meaning, and he valued the power of the human intellect to decipher meaning in the Torah, predating such ENLIGHTENMENT thought by centuries. Among Jewish students of Torah, only the great French biblical commentator RASHI surpasses Ibn Ezra in popularity.

In addition to his grammatical and pshat insights, Ibn Ezra provided philosophical commentaries on the Bible as well, Neoplatonic in tone and influenced by the views of the poet-philosopher Solomon Ibn Gabirol (c. 1021–1058). In turn, Ibn Ezra's theories on CREATION and the nature of God influenced the masters of KABBALAH. One of Ibn Ezra's best-known poems, "Nedod Hesir Oni," succinctly describes his life: "I resided in that place as a stranger, wrote books, and revealed the secrets of knowledge."

Further reading: Michael Friedländer, *Essays on the Writings of Abraham Ibn Ezra* (Yerushalayim: Mitshuf, 1963–64); Irene Lancaster, *Deconstructing the Bible: Abraham Ibn Ezra's Introduction to the Torah* (London: Routledgecurzon, 2002); Isadore Twersky, and Jay M. Harris, eds., *Rabbi Abraham Ibn Ezra: Studies in the Writings of a Twelfth-Century Jewish Polymath* (Cambridge: Harvard University Press, 1994).

idolatry

Judaism expressly forbids Jews to worship any deity other than the one true God. Any practice that involves worshipping another god is understood as idolatry. The worship of God alone and the prohibition of idolatry were so important that they took up more than 50 of the 613 commandments in the TORAH. It was a major theme of the prophets, too (*see* NEVI'IM); they warned repeatedly that God would not tolerate idolatry.

The original prohibition was clearly directed against ISRAELITE worship of the pagan gods of CANAAN. After CHRISTIANITY arose, the rabbis debated whether Christians were idolaters because of their worship of JESUS OF NAZARETH (the majority eventually said they were not); and after ISLAM appeared, they debated whether a Jew would be committing idolatry if he were forced to say "there is no God but Allah" (they concluded that the phrase was monotheistic and not idolatrous).

The Hebrew term for idolatry is *avodah zara* (meaning "strange or foreign worship").

Further reading: Jonathan Klawans, "Idolatry, Incest, and Impurity: Moral Defilement in Ancient Judaism," *Journal for the Study of Judaism in the Persian, Hellenistic and Roman Period* 29 (Winter 1998): 391–415; Jacob Neusner, *The Theology of the Oral Torah: Revealing the Justice of God* (Montreal: McGill-Queens University Press, 1999).

India

It is possible, as many local Jews claim, that the first Jews arrived in India between the second century B.C.E. and the early centuries of the Common Era. However, the earliest documented Jewish presence in India is far later. Copper inscriptions on coins possessed today by the White Jews in Cochin show that Jews lived in India in the late 10th or early 11th century. A Hebrew tombstone has also been found dated 1269.

Two main Jewish settlements, the Bene Israel and the Jews of Cochin, define Indian Jewish history. The Jews of Cochin are divided into three groups: the White Jews, the Black Jews, and the Freedmen. These three groups were kept separated by the rigid caste system of India until modern times. The Bene Israel group claims that their ancestors came to India in the second century B.C.E., though they were isolated from the rest of world Jewry for centuries. They did not maintain synagogues, but they did practice certain Jewish rituals through the years, including circumcision (BRIT MILAH), kosher food laws (KASHRUT), and the Sabbath (SHABBAT). The Bene Israel and the Jews of Cochin discovered one another in the 17th century. The Bene Israel have since been absorbed into the mainstream of modern JUDAISM, though they still remain a distinct community.

Parts of India were occupied in the colonial era by the Portuguese, the Dutch, and the British. The Jews suffered persecution only under the rule of the Portuguese, who introduced the Inquisition there in 1560. Jews prospered under Dutch rule, and were joined by other Jews immigrating from PALESTINE, Syria, and IRAQ. Other Jews came to India as agents of the East India Company under British rule, trading in diamonds and precious stones, but they did not remain in the country indefinitely.

In the second half of the 18th century a large Jewish community developed in Bombay. The first synagogue was established there in 1796 by the Bene Israel, who then translated many Jewish liturgical works into the vernacular. The Indian Jewish community was safe from Hitler's HOLO-CAUST, and many European Jews found safety in India during World War II.

While the Jews of India never lived through large-scale persecution, nationalistic fervor in the 20th century weakened their status in independent India, as they had not advocated independence—they had benefited from British rule. When the state of ISRAEL was born in 1948, a wave of Zionist fervor swept the Jews of India and many immigrated to Israel in 1949 and 1950. By 1968 the Jewish population in India had fallen to 15,000 from 26,000 in 1951. In 1970, 10,000 of these Jews lived in Bombay, and some of the 29 synagogues there still functioned. Jewish schools functioned in Bombay and Calcutta, but in the 1960s they admitted non-Jewish students. The Jewish community in India in the 1960s operated welfare agencies, including the Jewish Association of Calcutta, the Central Jewish Board, and the Zionist Association in Bombay; several periodicals dating back to the 1940s and 1950s still appear.

In the early 1970s a group of Indians living in northeast India began to practice Judaism. They believe that they are descended from the lost tribe of Manasseh (see TEN LOST TRIBES), and they discovered this after rejecting Christianity. The group calls itself Bnei Menashe, and they follow many Jewish practices, including circumcision on the eighth day, wearing a shawl that resembles a TALLIT, and honoring levirate marriage (see HALITZAH). The State of Israel has accepted the Bnei Menashe group as "safek Jews," meaning that they are welcome under the LAW OF RETURN, but since their ancestry is uncertain they must undergo ritual conversion. More than 300 of the Bnei Menashe have immigrated to Israel and more desire to do so, considering such a move as returning home.

By the mid-1990s the Indian Jewish community had a population of 6,000, most of whom lived in Bombay (Mumbai). A few Jews still live in Cochin. While there are no rabbis in India, there are three Jewish schools, a Council of Indian Jewry, and a Jewish Club, which sponsors social and cultural activities. India is unique in that there is little evidence of ANTISEMITISM or ASSIMILATION. The lack of assimilation can be attributed to the Indian caste system. In 1992, India and Israel established diplomatic relations, and El Al, the Israeli airline, routinely flies to India.

Further reading: Shirley Berry Isenberg, *India's Bene Israel: A Comprehensive Inquiry and Sourcebook* (Berkeley, Calif.: Judah Magnes Museum, 1989); Nathan Katz, *Who Are the Jews of India?* (Berkeley: University of California Press, 2000); J. B. Segal, *A History of the Jews of Cochin* (London: Vallentine Mitchell, 1993); Orpa Slapak, ed., *The Jews of India: A Story of Three Communities* (Lebanon, N.H.: University Press of New England, 2002).

Industrial Removal Office (IRO)

At the end of the 19th century and the beginning of the 20th, the LOWER EAST SIDE of New York City suffered from severe overcrowding and poor living conditions. In an attempt to alleviate the stress of this enormous number of Jewish immigrants in New York, the United Hebrew Charities, B'NAI B'RITH, the Baron de Hirsch Fund, and several other Jewish social welfare agencies established the Industrial Removal Office in 1901. Concerned that the United States government might close down immigration and appalled by the poor living conditions in the Lower East Side, the leaders of these agencies made an effort to move as many Jews as possible out of the Lower East Side and into the interior of the UNITED STATES.

Using the existing structure of B'nai B'rith lodges in many cities across the United States, the IRO enlisted the help of leaders in individual Jewish communities in the Midwest and the Far West. Knowing that once new immigrants became ensconced in the intricate Jewish community of the Lower East Side it would be difficult to convince them to move, IRO agents would meet them at the docks. There they would engage in conversation, speaking in YIDDISH, and describe employment opportunities in the western United States. Sometimes the IRO would provide transportation, and an agent in the appropriate city would meet

them when they arrived, arranging for housing and employment. Some of the cities that the immigrants arrived in included Champaign, Illinois; La Crosse, Wisconsin; Gary, Indiana; Cleveland, Ohio; St. Louis, Missouri; and Chicago, Illinois. The larger cities were more appealing to the immigrants because there were thriving Jewish communities already in place, but the smaller cities afforded the new immigrants some anonymity and a tighter, more supportive Jewish community once enough of them had arrived.

By 1914 the IRO had placed approximately 100,000 Jews in communities in the interior of the United States. The immigrants earned and saved more money than they would have been able to in the northeastern corridor, where most of the 2 million Jewish immigrants who came to the United States between 1881 and 1914 settled, and they were able to send for their wives and children sooner. In absolute terms the IRO was successful, yet it could not handle the vast number of immigrants who arrived.

Ultimately it was not possible for the IRO to divert a majority of new immigrants from already established northeastern communities. Immigrants wanted to be with their relatives, friends, and coreligionists, no matter how crowded the Lower East Side might have been. The moderate success of both the IRO and the GALVESTON PLAN, which diverted immigrant ships to a Texas port for debarkation, proved the importance of family and community among the Jewish people.

Further reading: Hasia R. Diner, *Lower East Side Memories: A Jewish Place in America* (Princeton, N.J., and Oxford: Princeton University Press, 2000); Howard M. Sachar, *A History of the Jews in America* (New York: Vintage Books, 1992).

intermarriage

The term *intermarriage* in the Jewish context refers to a Jew marrying a non-Jew who does not undergo conversion to Judaism. In the UNITED STATES today, surveys have found that about one out of every two Jews getting married in recent years has married a non-Jew; the rate has grown with each decade since the 1960s. This has sparked grave concern in the overall Jewish community, as it raises the fear of a crisis in Jewish continuity.

Biblical figures such as MOSES married non-Jewish women. However, the prophet EZRA, perceiving a danger that the small Jewish community that had returned to the land after the Babylonian exile might succumb to the surrounding idolatry, banned the practice and castigated the Jews who had married non-Jews.

It is neither surprising nor unusual that a small people such as the Jews might institutionalize negative feelings about intermarriage. Intermarriage invites exposure to non-Jewish religion and values; the ultimate purpose of Ezra and the rabbis who followed him was to keep the Jewish people together as a community.

The practice of intermarriage was rare prior to the EMANCIPATION of European Jewry in the 19th century. In the rare cases when it did occur, the person who chose that path was often excommunicated (see HEREM) from the Jewish community, even considered to be dead. After emancipation, the rights and freedoms afforded Jews in European countries made it easier for Jews to integrate into the greater culture, and to socialize with non-Jews to a far greater extent than had been possible; by the early 20th century, intermarriage had become quite common among urban Jews in central and western Europe.

In open societies around the world, intermarriage occurs frequently among Jews, and there is much discussion about its effect on ASSIMILATION and ACCOMMODATION to the surrounding non-Jewish culture. While many feel that intermarriage has led to higher rates of assimilation, thus resulting in the loss of a distinctive Jewish community, others argue that Jews find other ways to be Jewish together, such as living in the same neighborhoods and sharing professions, and that intermarried couples can participate in such communities.

In the contemporary world, ORTHODOX JUDAISM, REFORM JUDAISM, CONSERVATIVE JUDAISM, and RECONSTRUCTIONIST JUDAISM have responded in very different ways to the issue. While they all encourage the committed Jew to find a Jewish spouse, the Orthodox also insist on exclusively same-faith dating; one who marries a non-Jew is often alienated from the community, and even from the immediate family. The Conservatives also stress dating within the faith, but many Conservative rabbis actively promote outreach education to intermarried couples, with the hope of ultimately converting the non-Jewish partner or ensuring that the children are raised in the Jewish faith. Neither Orthodox nor Conservative rabbis will perform interfaith marriages. The Reconstructionist and Reform movements also promote outreach, but many rabbis from these movements will officiate at intermarriages, especially if there is a pledge by the couple to raise the children in the Jewish faith.

Further reading: Paul and Rachel Cowan, *Mixed Blessings: Overcoming the Stumbling Blocks in an Interfaith Marriage* (New York: Penguin Books, 1989); Gabrielle Glaser, *Strangers to the Tribe: Portraits of Interfaith Marriage* (New York: Houghton Mifflin Company, 1997); Ellen Jaffe McClain, *Embracing the Stranger: Intermarriage and the Future of the American Jewish Community* (New York: Basic Books, 1995).

Intifada

The Intifada (the word is Arabic for "shaking off") is the name given by Palestinian Arabs to the violent uprising against Israel that broke out in December 1987, died down after a few years, and resumed with renewed force in 2000. It can be viewed as the most recent violent phase in the long ARAB-ISRAELI CONFLICT that has persisted since the start of the BRITISH MANDATE after World War I.

In 1987, after 20 years of Israeli occupation of the West Bank and the Gaza Strip, Palestinians anxious for self-rule and disappointed with the failure of the PALESTINE LIBERATION ORGANIZATION

(PLO) to end the occupation, launched violent protests throughout the territories, beginning with rock-throwing, often involving minors. Israeli forces eventually suppressed the violence. In this phase of the Intifada, between the years 1987 and 1993, the number of Palestinian casualties far outweighed those of the Israelis. It is not possible to accurately report exact numbers, however, since sources do not agree. It is, however, important to note that in the early 1990s, hundreds of Palestinians were killed by other Palestinians in an uprising called the "intrafada" when they were accused of collaborating with Israel.

Relative peace prevailed in the 1990s, following the first Gulf War and a series of Israeli-Palestinian peace negotiations that culminated in the Oslo agreement of 1993, under which Israel handed over much of the land to the control of the PLO and the new Palestinian Authority. However, in 2000, in the midst of intensive negotiations toward a final peace settlement, the uprising was renewed. Palestinians dubbed this campaign the al-Aksa Intifada, as the first incident followed a visit by Israel's then-opposition leader Ariel SHARON to the Temple Mount in Jerusalem, site of the sacred al-Aksa Mosque.

Palestinians claimed that Sharon's visit sparked the uprising, together with disappointment at the results of the peace process. Israel claims that the uprising was deliberately provoked by Palestinian leader Yasser Arafat, either as a pressure tactic in the negotiations, or to avoid giving an answer to the Israeli-American peace offer, which Israel and America claim had acceded to almost all the Palestinian demands. In either case, rivalries between armed Palestinian factions have since complicated the struggle.

As a result of numerous suicide attacks against civilians within Israel, and intensive counterattacks by Israel against the violent factions, thousands of people had lost their lives, amid much destruction and political disarray in both the West Bank and Gaza. The fighting led to a three-year recession and unemployment in ISRAEL, which ended in 2004, as well as a near total collapse of

the Palestinian economy. During this period, peace negotiations ground to a halt.

In Arab and even some Western media, Israeli soldiers armed with machine guns are pictured fighting Palestinian children armed with rocks. The Israel Defense Forces (IDF) reports that in the first four years of the attacks more than 3,600 Molotov cocktails, 100 hand grenades, and 600 assaults with guns or explosives were used by the Palestinian fighters.

Further reading: Mitchell G. Bard, ed., *Myths and Facts: A Guide to the Arab-Israeli Conflict* (Chevy Chase, Md.: American-Israeli Cooperative Enterprise, 2001); Robert O. Freedman, ed., *The Middle East from the Iran-Contra Affair to the Intifada* (Syracuse, N.Y.: Syracuse University Press, 1991); Benny Morris, *Righteous Victims: A History of the Zionist-Arab Conflict, 1881–2001* (New York: Vintage Books, 2001); Don Peretz, *Intifada: The Palestinian Uprising* (Boulder, Colo.: Westview Press, 1990).

Iran

In 1935 the kingdom of PERSIA was renamed Iran. The country's Jewish community traces its origins to ancient times, as evidenced by the biblical book of ESTHER, which is believed to have taken place in the Persian capital.

Jews in Iran had been granted equal rights by the Constitution of 1906; by 1948 they numbered 95,000 souls, constituting the second-largest Jewish community in the Middle East, after the newly formed State of ISRAEL.

Although Iran voted against the PARTITION PLAN for PALESTINE in 1947 for the sake of Muslim solidarity, the country soon established trade and unofficial political ties with Israel. There was little to no violence against Jews in the decades after 1948, although some anti-Jewish leaflets were circulated. Jews had representation in the Iranian House of Representatives, although few Jews were judges or lawyers because even Jews preferred to be represented by Muslims. The Zionist movement was legal in Iran and it continued to encourage local Jews to make ALIYAH; some 20,000 did so, coming mostly from the poorer segments of the population. Others moved to the United States. The community steadily dwindled, reaching a population of 60,000 in 1968.

The Jewish population, which had been scattered in many regions, became more urban, with 72 percent living in cities by 1968. Literacy improved, as many Jews learned to read the Persian script; they had previously written and read Persian texts using a HEBREW script called Judeo-Persian. The Jews of Iran have consistently received help from various worldwide Jewish social service agencies such as the ALLIANCE ISRAELITE UNIVERSELLE, the AMERICAN JEWISH JOINT DISTRIBUTION COMMITTEE, and ORT, all of which financed schools, community organization, and hygienic improvements. An attempt in 1957 to create an Iranian Jewish social service agency failed.

Prior to 1948 most Jews living in Iran were observant, though a scarcity of rabbis and limited contact with other Jewish communities left many of them ignorant of Jewish rituals such as laying TEFILLIN. The newer generations are less observant and rates of INTERMARRIAGE have increased.

When Shah Mohammad Reza Pahlavi was overthrown and the Ayatollah Khomeini came to power in 1979, the Iranian government turned extremely hostile toward Israel, and life for Jews in Iran became oppressive. Iran no longer delivered oil to Israel, and the Israeli mission in Teheran was closed down. Yasser Arafat, the leader of the Palestine Liberation Organization, was welcomed in Teheran. Zionism was no longer legal, and many Jews in leadership positions were executed. The ayatollah encouraged bitter propaganda against Israel and Zionism. Though he made numerous disparaging and hostile comments about Jews, he promised to guarantee the safety and welfare of the Jews as long as they disengaged from Israel and Zionism. In 1982 and 1983 Iranian Jewish religious and lay leaders publicly protested Israel's invasion of Lebanon and what they called the oppression of the Palestinians, and called for the liberation of Jerusalem from Jewish hands.

Iranian Jews joined the national fight against the Iraqi invasion in the Iraq-Iran War of the 1980s; Israel reportedly supported Iran as well, viewing Saddam Hussein as the greater threat to stability in the Middle East.

After the death of the ayatollah, conditions for the Jews in Iran improved. Some became wealthy and friendly with the current strongmen. The Jewish community continued to publicize their support for the Islamic Revolution and their enmity for Israel and Zionism. Yet Jews continued to emigrate, most of them men, causing an increase in intermarriage as the remaining Jewish women married Muslim men.

By the 1990s the Jewish population had dropped to 25,000, most of whom lived in Teheran. There are three synagogues in Iran, and although strong rabbinic leadership does not exist, the Jews of Iran have begun to attend synagogue more often, seeking sanctuary and community. The Jewish cemetery was demolished in 1996. The school curriculum is Islamic, the Hebrew Bible is taught in Persian, and Jewish students are required to attend school on Saturday as the Jewish Sabbath is not recognized.

Further reading: Harvey E. Goldberg, ed., *Sephardi and Middle Eastern Jewries: History and Culture in the Modern Era* (Bloomington: Indiana University Press, 1996); Bernard Lewis, *The Jews of Islam* (Princeton, N.J.: Princeton University Press, 1987).

Iraq

Before the Muslim conquest of 634 C.E., the area now known as Iraq was called Mesopotamia or BABYLONIA, and Jews had lived there from the days of the first EXILE in the 6th century B.C.E. The new Arab rulers liberated Jews from religious persecution by the Zoroastrian rulers of PERSIA.

Under the rule of the Muslim caliphs of Baghdad, who had both religious and temporal authority, the Jews experienced a golden age of cultural and religious growth. Between the mid-seventh century and the mid-11th century they enjoyed semiautonomous communities headed by an EXI-LARCH or *NASI,* the political leader, and a *gaon,* the religious leader (*see* GEONIM), although there were periods of persecution during this time, as well. The rabbinic academies at SURA and PUMBEDITA thrived, and Jewish sages edited the final edition of the Babylonian TALMUD. The most famous rabbinic scholar in Iraq was SAADIA GAON, who headed the academy at Sura in the 10th century. The stability of the huge Muslim empire allowed for strong ties between the rabbinic academies of Iraq and Jewish communities in PERSIA, Syria, PALESTINE, EGYPT, North Africa, and SPAIN.

The quality of life in Iraq varied depending on the individual caliph's attitude; the Jews of Iraq experienced times of peace and freedom and times of persecution and discrimination. As a rule, they were able to participate in the community and economy of Iraq; some became physicians, writers, and even government officials. From time to time Jews were forced to wear distinguishing clothing, such as when in the 10th century Jewish physicians and tax collectors were required to wear yellow clothing with colored patches. In the 10th century, the position of exilarch was abolished and both Christians and Jews were severely persecuted. The office was later revived and continued until 1849, but the golden age had ended for the Jews of Iraq.

During the 11th and 12th centuries the Jews experienced a surge of messianic activity. Several false messiahs rose and fell. The rabbinic academies at Sura and Pumbedita disappeared after the 11th century, and the rabbinic Academy of Baghdad drew many students. Conditions improved for a while in the mid-12th century. There were 10 yeshivot (*see* YESHIVA) in Baghdad, which had the largest concentration of Jews. Communities also existed in Irbil, Baqsard, Raqqa, and Basra, which had 10,000 Jews and its own exilarch.

From the 13th through the 18th century, Iraq was ruled by a variety of peoples, including Turks and Mongols, who treated the Jews well at some points and poorly at others. As in Europe, many Jews acted as financiers, but they also held positions as physicians, historians, and craftsmen. In

1393, following the attack of Tamerlane, the Jews left Baghdad and did not return for almost a century. From the 16th to the 20th centuries the Iraqi Jewish community thrived, making major contributions to the culture of Judaism. They produced eminent and renowned rabbis, provided Jewish education to children and adults, and published a great deal of poetry.

The economic situation of the Jews was good for most of the 19th century. Jews had a large hand in the country's commerce, and influence in government circles. In 1908 the Ottoman Turkish government granted freedom of religion and equality to the Jews, several of whom served in Parliament. They traded in all goods, from textiles to medicines. From 1917 to 1932, under British influence, the Jews continued to prosper. They led in the country's commerce and banking, participated in government, and contributed to the financial security of Iraq. It is estimated that 125,000 Jews lived in Iraq in 1947, approximately 80,000 of them in Baghdad. The Jewish community supported Zionist groups and contributed funds to national educational and cultural activities. Organizations such as the Zionist Society of Mesopotamia (1921–29) and the Maccabi Sports Society flourished. Groups met to read Hebrew newspapers, and a Hebrew-Arabic weekly newspaper was even published in 1920.

These developments came to an abrupt halt in 1932, when Iraq became an independent nation. Jewish officials lost their jobs and discrimination increased. By 1941, encouraged by Nazi propaganda, riots broke out; Jews were tortured and murdered by mobs, property was looted, and synagogues were desecrated until the British intervened. In 1942 a Jewish underground developed in Iraq called The Babylonian Pioneer Movement. This organization encouraged Hebrew and Zionism, taught defense skills, and organized legal and illegal immigration to Palestine. In 1948 Jews were barred from emigrating. The emergence of ISRAEL on May 14, 1948, led to imprisonment, banishment from particular towns, and heavy fines. When martial law ended in December 1949, thousands of Jews escaped to IRAN. In 1950, Jews were allowed to leave if they gave up their Iraqi nationality, and the mass exodus to Israel began. Between 1948 and 1951, through both legal and illegal means and with the aid of the JEWISH AGENCY and the underground in Iraq, it is estimated that 123,500 Iraqi Jews settled in Israel. They left behind assets valued at $200 million, which were confiscated by Iraqi government officials.

Approximately 6,000 Jews remained in Iraq in 1952, but by 1968 there were only 2,500. Religious and educational institutions still existed, but the Jews of Iraq were severely persecuted. The wars between Israel and her Arab neighbors agitated the Iraqi population against the Jews, and in 1969 nine prominent Jews were hanged in a public square in Baghdad, having been accused of espionage. Iraq has been consistently more hostile toward Israel than most other Arab countries, even though the two countries share no border, and it systematically calls for the destruction of the state of Israel. In 1996, only 120 Jews remained in Iraq. One synagogue served their spiritual needs.

Further reading: David Kazzaz, *Mother of the Pound: Memoirs on the Life and History of the Iraqi Jews* (Brooklyn, N.Y.: Sepher Hermon Press, 2000); Nissim Rejwan, *The Jews of Iraq: 3,000 years of History and Culture* (Boulder, Colo.: Westview Press, 1985).

Irgun Zeva'i Leumi (Etzel)

The Irgun Zeva'i Leumi (National Military Organization), known by its HEBREW acronym Etzel, was founded in 1931 by a group of HAGANAH officers who disagreed with the Haganah's policy of self-defense against Arab violence. For the next several years Etzel units engaged in more aggressive military maneuvers against the perceived enemies of the Jews in PALESTINE.

In April 1937, after the outbreak of the Arab Revolt in a series of bloody riots, about half of Etzel's forces rejoined the Haganah in the name of Jewish military unity. The remainder of Etzel regrouped, enlisted new recruits, and officially embraced the platform of Revisionist Zionism as taught by the movement's leader, Ze'ev JABOTINSKY.

Etzel completely rejected Haganah's defensive policy of restraint, called *havlagah*, and sought opportunities to carry out armed reprisals against Arabs. Etzel's actions were condemned by both the JEWISH AGENCY and the British authorities. Many Etzel members were arrested by the British military government; one of them, Shlomo Ben Yosef, was hung for participating in a shooting on an Arab bus.

When the British issued the WHITE PAPER in May 1939, effectively abandoning the commitment of their Mandate to a Jewish national home (*see* BRITISH MANDATE), Etzel launched an underground military campaign against them. With the outbreak of World War II Etzel officially declared a truce with the British, and many members joined the British Army's Jewish Brigade. However, some Etzel members rejected the truce, and created the Lohamei Herut Yisrael or Lehi, Fighters for the Freedom of Israel, in order to continue the battle against both the British and the Arabs.

In 1943 Menachem BEGIN became the new head of Etzel, which resumed the war against the British military administration in Palestine, attacking any exposed British military installation they could find. The most famous attack occurred on October 31, 1946, when Etzel bombed the King David Hotel in Jerusalem, which was serving as the headquarters of the British administration. A warning to evacuate had come from Etzel, but even so, 91 people died, 17 of whom were Jewish.

Etzel's activities undermined sympathy for the Jews among the British public; on the other hand, they may have been the last straw that convinced Britain to abandon Palestine. After ISRAEL declared its independence, Etzel volunteered to integrate itself with the new ISRAEL DEFENSE FORCES, and by September 1948, the two groups had become one, unified to defend the infant State of Israel.

Further reading: David Ben-Gurion, *Rebirth and Destiny of Israel* (New York: Philosophical Library, 1954); Walter Laqueur, *A History of Zionism: From the French*

Revolution to the Establishment of the State of Israel (New York: Schocken Books, 2003); Howard M. Sachar, *A History of Israel: From the Rise of Zionism to Our Time* (New York: Random House, 1996).

Isaiah (c. 740–681 B.C.E.) *biblical prophet*

Isaiah was an ISRAELITE prophet (*see* NEVI'IM) who lived under the reigns of four kings of Judah: Uzziah, Yotham, Ahaz, and Hezekiah. He personally knew the major political leaders of JERUSALEM, and guided them through the serious social, political and military challenges they faced. While he himself was a member of the elite, he was a vocal spokesman on behalf of the common people. He railed against corruption within the leadership, demanding that they begin to dispense justice and protection to the weaker members of Israelite society, such as the poor, orphans, and widows.

Isaiah preached against reckless military endeavors aimed at the growing might of Assyria; he urged the leaders to place their trust in God and develop greater moral strength. He believed Assyria was God's instrument of punishing the Israelites for their behavior. If Israel repented and mended its ways, God would vanquish the enemy. When King Hezekiah implemented religious reforms to address Isaiah's outstanding concerns, the prophet declared that God would protect Hezekiah and the country. But, when Hezekiah formed military alliances with EGYPT and BABYLON, Isaiah came to believe the king did not have enough faith in God, and that Israel would be punished for this transgression.

Because Isaiah predicted severe punishments for Israel's sins, mainstream CHRISTIANITY has often used his sermons as support for its idea that God had supplanted the "original" COVENANT with the Jewish people in favor of a new covenant or testament with the Christian church. His prophesy of a MESSIANIC AGE in which a shoot will grow from the seed of Jesse became a key doctrine in Judaism, but it has been interpreted by most Christians as a reference to Jesus, said to be a descendant of Jesse's son King DAVID.

The medieval scholar Abraham IBN EZRA (1089–1164), as well as contemporary critical biblical scholarship, holds that the book of Isaiah contains the words of two different prophets. From chapter 40 on, the events described concern the destruction of the first TEMPLE and the Babylonian EXILE, which occurred a century after Isaiah lived. This latter part of the book of Isaiah is often referred to as Deutero-Isaiah, which was written, some scholars believe, by an "Isaianic School" that continued to teach in the moral tradition of the original Isaiah.

Isaiah has had an enormous influence on the values and practices of NORMATIVE JUDAISM. His words, "Holy, holy, holy is the Lord of Hosts, His presence fills all the earth" is the central line of the holiest prayer in Jewish liturgy, the Kedushah (*see* KEDUSHAH).

Further reading: Joseph Blenkinsopp, *Isaiah 1–39: A New Translation with Introduction and Commentary* (New York: Doubleday, 2000); ———, *Isaiah 40–55: A New Introduction and Commentary* (New York: Doubleday, 2002); ———, *Isaiah 56–66: A New Introduction and Commentary* (New York: Doubleday, 2003); Norman Gottwald, *The Hebrew Bible: A Socio-Literary Introduction* (Philadelphia: Fortress Press, 1985); *Tanakh: The Holy Scriptures* (Philadelphia and Jerusalem: The Jewish Publication Society, 1985).

Islam

Of all the world's religions, Islam is the closest theologically to Judaism, and the two share a common ancestry and many common practices as well. Both faiths espouse radical MONOTHEISM, a belief in one God who must not be depicted in any images. Both severely denounce IDOLATRY, mandate circumcision for males, and have strict dietary laws (*see* KASHRUT), prohibiting the consumption of pork and providing for special slaughtering procedures.

Both Islam and Judaism trace their ancestry to Abraham (*see* PATRIARCHS). According to the book of Genesis, Abraham had two sons, Ishmael and

Isaac. Ishmael became the progenitor of the Arabs, including Muhammad, and Isaac became the progenitor of the Jews. The two religions, in essence, are cousins and have often regarded themselves as such.

According to Jewish tradition, the COVENANT between God and Abraham was passed down through Isaac and Isaac's descendants, but according to Islam, Ishmael carried on the true religion, with Abraham's support. The God of Islam, Allah, is the same God as the God in the TANAKH, and the sacred scripture of Islam, the Qur'an, contains many of the same stories as the Tanakh, though often with slight variations. Muslims, however, see the Qur'an as a corrective to errors in the Tanakh and New Testament, whereas Jews see the Qur'an as a corruption of the Tanakh.

Over the centuries, there have been times of relative peace between Jews and Muslims, and times when the two have been bitter enemies. In Muhammad's time (570–632), there were battles between the newly founded Muslim community and Jewish Arabian tribes who refused to acknowledge Muhammad as God's greatest prophet. However, during the Golden Age in SPAIN, Jews held high-level positions and thrived under Muslim rule. In the present day, there are frequent clashes between Jews and Muslims, mostly revolving around the Arab-Israeli dispute (see ARAB-ISRAELI CONFLICT).

Further reading: John Bunzl, ed., *Islam, Judaism, and the Political Role of Religions in the Middle East* (Gainesville, Fla.: University Press of Florida, 2004); N. J. Dawood, trans., *The Koran* (New York: Penguin USA, 2000); Frederick Mathewson Denny, *An Introduction to Islam* (New York: Macmillan, 1994); F. E. Peters, *Islam, a Guide for Jews and Christians* (Princeton, N.J.: Princeton University Press, 2003).

Israel

Israel as a modern Jewish state came into being on May 14, 1948, issuing its declaration of independence in Tel Aviv. However, the notion of

ERETZ YISRAEL, the Land of Israel as the Jewish homeland, goes back to the beginnings of the Jewish people and has been a key element of Judaism ever since.

According to the TANAKH, the Hebrew Bible, God promised Abraham (see PATRIARCHS) the land of CANAAN (as the land was then called) as a birthright for himself and all his ISRAELITE descendants. When the Israelites escaped to freedom from EGYPT and received the TORAH, their sole aim was to make their way to the Promised Land.

After the Israelite conquest and a period of relative anarchy, when each of the 12 tribes governed its own lands, a Jewish kingdom was established and solidified under the heroic and pious King DAVID. When his son SOLOMON built the TEMPLE in JERUSALEM, the national religion was centralized, further unifying the country and lending additional sanctity to the land. Around the year 931 B.C.E., Solomon died and the kingdom split into two, Israel in the north and Judea in the south. In 722–721 the Assyrians destroyed the northern kingdom, dispersing the 10 northern tribes, who have since disappeared. During the eighth and seventh centuries B.C.E., the prophets helped to shape Israelite tradition by developing the concepts of MONOTHEISM and the ethical life (see NEVI'IM).

In the year 586 B.C.E. the Temple was destroyed by the armies of BABYLONIA, and the Israelites went into EXILE. When a remnant of the Jews returned to Judea 70 years later under the patronage of PERSIA, they were composed mostly of the tribe of Judah, with elements of the tribes of Benjamin and Levi, the latter constituting the priestly class.

In 332 B.C.E. Alexander the Great conquered Judea, which became a province of his Hellenistic empire. Alexander allowed the Jews to worship their God (and his name remains popular among Jewish men), but the country suffered from 125 years of war between his heirs, the Seleucids of Syria and the Ptolemys of Egypt. The Seleucids eventually won domination of the area, with Antiochus III taking power in 198 B.C.E. At first he allowed the Jews many freedoms, but after losing significant battles to the Romans, Antiochus became far less tolerant. His son ANTIOCHUS EPIPHANES launched a strict program to impose HELLENISM, outlawing the Sabbath (SHABBAT) and circumcision (BRIT MILAH), defiling the TEMPLE with an altar to Zeus, and allowing the sacrifice of pigs.

The Jewish community split in half and civil war ensued between those favoring some Hellenization and those who wanted to return to traditional JUDAISM. Ultimately, Seleucid extremism turned the community toward the more traditional proponents. Led by the MACCABEES, the Jews won independence and redeemed the Temple in 160 B.C.E. (as celebrated in the holiday of CHANUKAH). The Hasmonean dynasty ruled Judea until 40 B.C.E., when the Romans annexed the country to their expanding empire.

In 37 B.C.E. HEROD became governor of Judea. He began a massive building program, including the Temple itself, but his reputation for impiety made him unpopular with his Jewish subjects, and insurrections repeatedly broke out against the Romans. Ten years after Herod's death in 4 B.C.E. Judea came under direct Roman rule. In 66 C.E., a massive revolt broke out. Within four years the Roman general and later emperor, Titus, had destroyed the Temple; the last group of Jewish holdouts committed suicide at MASADA when it became clear that the Romans would prevail. The Romans renamed Judea PALESTINE, previously the name of the province on the southwest coast once inhabited by the Philistines.

After the Roman exile, Jewish sovereignty ended in Palestine, but Jews throughout the centuries made their way back to the Jewish homeland, and the dream of restoration of the Jewish state became a primary tenet in NORMATIVE JUDAISM. It was believed that God would eventually usher in a MESSIANIC ERA and restore the Jews to the land of Israel.

At the end of the 19th century, Theodor HERZL brought ZIONISM and its goal of creating an independent Jewish state in Palestine to the attention of the world. Zionism was largely a translation of the age-old longing for Zion (Jerusalem) into modern secular terms.

Zionism created a new form of Jewish identification that required no religious belief. Many adherents of ORTHODOX JUDAISM rejected the Zionist movement, because of its nonreligious character and its lack of faith in God's promised Messiah. Some followers of REFORM JUDAISM rejected the very idea of a Jewish nationality. However, most Jews soon embraced the idea of a return to Zion, especially in view of growing antisemitic persecution.

Jews began to trickle back to Palestine in the late 19th century, reinforcing the small, impoverished community of mostly religious Jews who already lived there. The trickle grew into a flood by the 1930s. In the spring of 1948, after 2,000 years of exile, Israel proclaimed its independence as a Jewish state. Its declaration of independence noted that the land was the birthplace of the Jewish people, and the cradle of its spiritual, religious, and political identity. The modern State of Israel declared a LAW OF RETURN, granting immediate citizenship to any Jew in the world who wished to return. The law defined Jewish status not according to religious belief, but by the same definition the Nazis had used: anyone with a Jewish grandparent (so that anyone who had been persecuted by the Nazis could find refuge in Israel).

While the UNITED NATIONS recognized the new Jewish state, the Arab countries refused to recognize its right to exist. Arab armies invaded, joined by local Arab irregulars. Facing heavy odds, the fledgling Jewish state held off all its opponents and wound up in control of the bulk of the former British Palestine; the Emirate of Transjordan annexed the territories on the west bank of the Jordan River (and changed its name to the Kingdom of Jordan), while Egypt took charge of the small Gaza strip.

An overwhelming Israeli military victory in the SIX-DAY WAR of 1967 gave Israel control of the remainder of pre-1948 Palestine as well as the Sinai Peninsula, which it returned to Egypt 12 years later in exchange for a peace treaty. When no further peace treaties emerged, Israel settled 250,000 Jews in the West Bank, which under the names JUDEA AND SAMARIA had constituted the heartland of the ancient Jewish kingdoms of Judah and Israel. Peace was signed with Jordan in 1994, after an interim peace agreement had been signed the previous year with representatives of the Palestinian Arabs under Yasser Arafat. The second INTIFADA, or uprising, launched in 2000 with spectacular suicide bombings, has stymied hopes for further progress toward a hoped-for comprehensive peace with all the Arab states.

While Israel fought for military security, it has had to deal with successive waves of ALIYAH or immigration. More than 2 million Jews from all over the world came to Israel, from displaced survivors of the European Holocaust to the majority of the ancient Jewish communities of the Arab and Muslim world. They have brought with them differences in religious attachment and ethnic or cultural loyalties, which has often led to internal strife.

Israel is a parliamentary democracy, with a multitude of political parties reflecting many different ideologies. In the religious realm, Israeli citizens are primarily divided between Orthodox and secular, although there are efforts to develop an Israeli REFORM and CONSERVATIVE JUDAISM. There is a degree of separation between religion and state, but in matters of MARRIAGE, DIVORCE, CONVERSION, burial, and religious supervision, Orthodoxy (alongside Christian and Muslim authorities) maintains a religious monopoly over Jews, supported by the state; Christian and Muslim authorities control the same functions for their respective communities. While Jews have the right to automatic Jewish citizenship, there are more than a million Arab-Israelis who are citizens as well.

In its first 50 years, Israel has developed a first-world economy. Agricultural settlements, including socialist communities called kibbutzim (*see* KIBBUTZ), turned swampland and desert into a green oasis. Basic industries, infrastructure, and tourism were built up in the early decades; more

recently, the high-tech and defense industries have been the engines for economic growth.

Further reading: Walter Laqueur, *A History of Zionism: From the French Revolution to the Establishment of the State of Israel* (New York: Schocken Books, 2003); Howard M. Sachar, *A History of Israel: From the Rise of Zionism to Our Time* (New York: Random House, 1996).

Israel Defense Forces (IDF)

The Israel Defense Forces (IDF) was created by the new state in 1948 based on the HAGANAH, the formerly underground military force. For the army of a small country, the IDF has a stellar military reputation, having successfully fought five major wars in defense of the Jewish state. The IDF's responsibilities also include a constant struggle against all forms of terrorism.

While the IDF's mission is to defend the Jewish state, it frankly reserves the right to take the offense if deemed necessary. In IDF doctrine, Israel is a tiny country with no margin of safety between being invaded and being overrun.

Israel has become a leader in military electronics and weapons development, often in cooperation with other countries including, at times, FRANCE, the UNITED STATES, CHINA, and INDIA. The greatest resource available to the IDF is its soldiers. There is a universal draft of men and women at age 18. Men serve a minimum of three years and women a minimum of two. Men remain in the reserves until the age of 51, although those who have served in combat may now complete their service at the age of 45. Orthodox women are exempted, though they are expected to perform some national service. Many ultra-Orthodox men receive repeated deferments to allow for TORAH study, which has caused intense debate and communal ill will. Career military men and women enjoy a high degree of social prestige.

There are three service branches within the IDF: air force, ground forces and navy. The IDF is headed by a chief of staff with the rank of lieutenant-general, who reports directly to the

An Israel Defense Forces naval unit stands at attention on the first anniversary of Israel's occupation of Eilat in 1967. *(Teddy Brauner, Government Press Office, The State of Israel)*

minister of defense, who is in turn appointed by Israel's prime minister. The IDF remains the most effective means to integrate the various Jewish ethnic groups, from Ethiopians to Russians, and to promote national cohesion. Among the non-Jewish population, the Druze and Circassian communities are also subject to the draft, and many bedouin serve on a volunteer basis. Non-Druze Arabs are exempt.

Israeli society and the IDF largely overlap, with civilian life often interrupted so reservists can answer the call to arms.

Further reading: Netanel Lorch and Carlos Lorch, *Shield of Zion: The Israel Defense Forces* (Charlottesville, Va.: Howell Press, 1992); Louis Williams, *The Israel*

Defense Forces: A People's Army (Lincoln, Nebr.: Authors Choice Press, 2000).

Israeli flag

The flag of the State of ISRAEL is white with two horizontal blue stripes near the top and bottom edges. A blue Shield of DAVID (in Hebrew, Magen David), often called a STAR OF DAVID, is centered between the two stripes.

The flag, designed by David Wolffsohn, second president of the Zionist Organization, resembles a *TALLIT,* or prayer shawl. The blue color represents the ancient dyed threads that were used in knotting the TZITZIT, the fringes on the corners of the tallit. It was originally adopted by the Zionist Organization as its official flag in 1933.

The Star of David had gained wide popularity among Jewish communities around the world as a symbol of Jewish identity, in the decades before it was adopted by Zionist organizations in the late 19th century. The star has no real religious signif- icance, and so could serve as a unifying, noncontroversial symbol for all types of Jews.

Further reading: Abraham J. Edelheit and Hershel Edelheit, *History of Zionism: A Handbook and Dictionary* (Boulder, Colo.: Westview Press, 2000); A. L. Frankl, "Juda's Farben," in *Ahnenbilder* (Leipzig, 1864); Handelman and

Israelis proudly carry these Israeli flags at the head of an Independence Day parade in Israel. The stripes and the Star of David in the center are blue, a color that was used to dye threads on tzitzit in ancient times. *(Hans Pinn, Government Press Office, The State of Israel)*

Lea Shamgar-Handelman, "Shaping Time: The Choice of the National Emblem of Israel," in Emiko Ohnuki-Tierny, ed., *Culture Through Time: Anthropological Approaches* (Stanford, Calif.: Stanford University Press, 1990); Gershom Sholem, "The Curious History of the Six Pointed Star: How the 'Magen David' became the Jewish Symbol," *Commentary* 8 (1949).

Israelites

The Israelites of the TANAKH, the Hebrew Bible, were the originators of Judaism and ancestors of the later Jewish people. Sometimes called Hebrews or the Children of Israel (Israel is the name given to Jacob as an adult by God), they claimed descent from Abraham, Isaac, and Jacob (*see* PATRIARCHS).

According to the Hebrew Bible, the Israelites entered into an eternal COVENANT with God, whose laws they pledged to observe in exchange for God's favor and possession of the land of Israel. Freed from slavery in EGYPT under the leadership of MOSES, the Israelites made their way to MOUNT SINAI to receive the TORAH. After 40 years of wandering in the wilderness they entered the promised land of Canaan, or ERETZ YISRAEL. The Hebrew Bible depicts the Israelites as far from perfect, perhaps all too human. They represent common people, with common issues.

The Israelites conquer the land, establish a monarchy, fight a civil war, and ultimately split into two kingdoms. After contending with many invaders and conquerors, the northern kingdom of Israel is ultimately destroyed by the Assyrians, and its people, 10 of the 12 Israelite tribes, disappeared from history. The southern kingdom of Judah survive (the word *Jew,* Hebrew *yehudi,* derives from its name). The Jews in the south suffer their own exile to BABYLONIA, after Judah is conquered and the TEMPLE in JERUSALEM is destroyed, but a remnant returns to rebuild the Temple. By now, of the original Israelites, only the tribe of Judah and a part of the tribes of Benjamin and Levi survive. In the year 70 C.E. the Romans destroy Jerusalem, and most of the Israelites remaining in the land are killed, enslaved, or exiled.

Jews today trace their spiritual ancestry to the Israelites; from the time of the Hebrew Bible to the present, the faith and practices have been passed down in an unbroken chain between the generations. However, as the Hebrew Bible itself makes clear, the Israelites were strengthened by many converts, individuals and groups. The LEVITE tribe still maintains its pure lineage, but every ethnic group in Europe, North Africa, and the Middle East, and some beyond, is represented in today's Jewish people.

Jews trace their religion back to the Israelites, but over the centuries of exile rabbinic Judaism has deviated tremendously from the ancient sacrificial religion, which was based on an agrarian economy. Rabbinic Judaism observes the Torah as interpreted by the rabbis in the tradition of the TALMUD, and it was developed specifically to unify an exiled people. While many regard CHRISTIANITY as a child of Judaism, some scholars consider it more like a twin. In their view, Christianity and rabbinic Judaism have the same mother, Israelite religion.

Further reading: Norman Gottwald, *The Hebrew Bible: A Socio-Literary Introduction* (Philadelphia: Fortress Press, 1985); *Tanakh: The Holy Scriptures* (Philadelphia and Jerusalem: Jewish Publication Society, 1985).

Israeli War of Independence

Within hours of the UNITED NATIONS'S approval of the PARTITION PLAN on November 29, 1947, Arab violence directed toward the Jews of PALESTINE commenced. The initial violence took the form of Arab riots, at first not unlike the Arab riots of previous years. The war itself would not end until the spring of 1949.

The 1948 Israeli War of Independence can be divided into two waves. The first wave was fought between the HAGANAH and Palestinian Arabs through methods of guerrilla warfare; it lasted from November 1947 until the middle of May

1948, when the British pulled out of the area. The second wave of the war was a conventional war, waged between the ISRAEL DEFENSE FORCES (IDF) and the armies of Syria, Jordan, EGYPT, Lebanon, and IRAQ.

Unlike the Jewish Haganah, which had been growing in strength and sophistication for many years, the Arab contingencies were poorly organized and poorly supplied, consisting of separate bands of Arabs that resisted Jewish force. These groups made their first major assault on January 9, 1948, when they attacked Jewish communities in northern Palestine. Approximately 1,000 Arabs participated in the attack, and the British forces turned over their military bases and weapons to these Arabs in February, claiming that they were overwhelmed by the numbers. The Jews lost control of most of the roads in Palestine and suffered high casualties. On May 4, 1948, the Arab Legion of Transjordan attacked GUSH ETZION, a Jewish settlement near JERUSALEM. Several hundred Jews were massacred, but the Haganah was able to safeguard Jerusalem and its Jewish residents. In the weeks leading up to Israel's Declaration of Independence, the Haganah managed to turn back the Arab forces, recapture the northern cities of Tiberius and HAIFA, and secure the road to Jerusalem.

On May 14, 1948, the British withdrew their last forces from Palestine, and the Haganah consolidated with smaller Jewish defense forces (*see* IRGUN) to become the IDF. Only at this point did the Israeli forces feel completely free to defend their territory, as the British presence had dictated a certain measure of restraint. Israel declared her independence, and the second phase of the Israeli War of Independence commenced. The armies of Syria, Jordan, Egypt, Lebanon, and Iraq attacked the tiny State of Israel, and the conventional war began.

An important step in defending the new Jewish state was the creation of a fledgling air force. For the first few days of independence, bombers from Egypt, Iraq, and Syria had total control of Israeli skies. TEL AVIV, the largest Jewish town, was routinely bombed. Under the command of Moddy Alon, Israel assembled a small squadron, and in a legendary military action, Alon shot down two bombers from the air and drove the rest back. Not only had Israel received equipment from abroad, but thousands of trained Jewish soldiers from abroad arrived to offer their physical support. Among these men were more than 300 American and Canadian soldiers with World War II experience; almost 200 of these soldiers were trained airmen. The new air force, equipped from Czechoslovakia and the United States with funds raised from Jews abroad, eventually helped stop the Egyptian advance from the south, although battles on all fronts raged on the ground.

On June 11 the "First Truce" was called, although it only lasted until July 8. A second truce lasted from July 19 to October 15. The Israeli War of Independence, however, did not officially end until April of 1949, when Israel and Syria signed the final Armistice Agreement. Israel had negotiated with all four surrounding Arab states individually, first Egypt, then Lebanon, followed by Jordan, and finally Syria. No agreement was ever made with Iraq.

Israel had acquired more land than had originally been assigned to the Jews in the partition plan that had been rejected by all Arab states and Palestinian Arab organizations. The United Nations tried to arrange a comprehensive peace settlement, using the original United Nations partition guidelines, but the Arabs refused to even recognize Israel's right to exist, and Israel refused to retreat to the old borders. Yet Israel had won the Israeli War of Independence, extending her borders and enhancing her military position. This left Israel better prepared for the major wars it would have to fight in the coming decades.

Further reading: Walter Laqueur, *A History of Zionism: From the French Revolution to the Establishment of the State of Israel* (New York: Schocken Books, 2003); Benny Morris, *Righteous Victims: A History of the Zionist-Arab Conflict, 1881–2001* (New York: Vintage Books, 2001); Howard M. Sachar, *A History of Israel:*

From the Rise of Zionism to Our Time (New York: Random House, 1996).

Isserles, Moses ben Israel (1525–1572)
rabbinic scholar and author of the Mapah

Born in Krakow, POLAND in 1525, Moses ben Israel Isserles stands in Jewish history as one of the greatest rabbinic scholars of eastern Europe. His work was instrumental in providing rabbinic direction to generations of Ashkenazic Jews (*see* ASHKENAZIM). He is usually known by the initials of his title and name: the Rema.

Isserles was born into a family of respected rabbinic scholars, and he married the daughter of the head of a YESHIVA in Lublin, although she died at the age of 20. After remarrying and returning to Krakow, Isserles started his own yeshiva. Not only was he a teacher and respected rabbinic scholar, but Isserles's halakhic (*see* HALAKHAH) opinions, opinions on Jewish law, were sought by other renowned rabbis of the time, such as Joseph CARO, author of the *SHULCHAN ARUKH,* one of the most significant Jewish code books in existence today. In fact, Isserles's most major work was his commentary on the *Shulchan Arukh. Shulchan Arukh* means "set table," and Isserles's commentary was called the *MAPAH,* or "Tablecloth."

Caro's rulings were based on Sephardic custom (*see* SEPHARDIM). Isserles adapted the work for an Ashkenazic readership. Isserles had been working on a code of laws of his own, but Caro's monumental work beat him to print, and he decided to adapt his manuscripts into a commentary on Caro's work. The combination of Caro and Isserles remains the primary Jewish code book still utilized today, in one edition or another, by Jews around the world. It is through Caro's and Isserles's work that numerous Jewish customs have been preserved.

While a great scholar of the TALMUD, from which he derived his law code, Isserles also studied secular subjects such as science, history, and philosophy. Many historians consider him a predecessor of the HASKALAH, or the Jewish ENLIGHTENMENT. Isserles died in 1572 and was buried in Krakow. His contribution to Jewish communal life, history, and literature was so significant that for generations before World War II many Jews would visit his gravesite annually.

Further reading: Byron L. Sherwin, *Sparks Amidst the Ashes: The Spiritual Legacy of Polish Jewry* (New York: Oxford University Press, 1997); Yaacov Dovid Shulman, *The Rema: The Story of Rabbi Moses ben Israel Isserles* (Lakewood, N.J.: CIS Publishers, 1991); Bernard D. Weinryb, *The Jews of Poland: A Social and Economic History of the Jewish Community in Poland from 1100–1800* (Philadelphia: Jewish Publication Society of America, 1973).

J

Jabotinsky, Ze'ev (1880–1940) *militant*
Zionist theorist and leader

Ze'ev (Vladimir) Jabotinsky was born on October 18, 1880, in Odessa, RUSSIA. Although Jabotinsky's father fared well economically in his position as a clerk and grain dealer, he died when Jabotinsky was six years old, leaving Jabotinsky's mother to support the family as the proprietress of a stationery store. He attended a secular gymnasium and excelled in his studies. After studying law in both Italy and Switzerland, he became a well-known Russian journalist, writing under the pseudonym Altalena. In 1903, a terrible POGROM occurred against the Jews of Kishinev, and this prompted Jabotinsky to become an active supporter of ZIONISM. He began to actively advocate on behalf of Russian Jews, and helped form self-defense units. Jabotinsky was a delegate at the Sixth Zionist Congress. His influence altered the character of Zionism from a dreamy nationalist movement to a movement driven by pride, resistance to oppression, militarism, and confidence. His personal charisma allowed him to rally people together, whether to fight with the British during World War I, organize a nascent youth movement, or defy the BRITISH MANDATE's authority, when necessary.

In 1914, while serving as a war correspondent, Jabotinsky met Joseph Trumpeldor in Alexandria; together they helped establish the Jewish Legion to fight with the British in World War I. Jabotinsky served as a lieutenant in the legion, and participated in military assaults to free PALESTINE from Turkish rule. Jabotinsky's military experience in the Jewish Legion served him well, and he became the head of the HAGANAH, the Jewish defense force in Palestine. During PASSOVER of 1920, he led the Haganah against Arab rioters in JERUSALEM. The local British government condemned the move, and Jabotinsky was sentenced to 15 years of hard labor. The sentence was met with great public outcry, and the British granted him amnesty.

In 1921, Jabotinsky cofounded the Keren Hayesod, or the Palestine Foundation Fund, and served as an executive of the Zionist Organization. Only two years later, in 1923, he created and headed the Zionist youth movement Betar (*see* ZIONIST YOUTH MOVEMENTS). His goal was to train youths in military knowledge and inculcate them with a Jewish nationalistic spirit. Jabotinsky's method for accomplishing this goal was twofold: He would teach the youths of Betar the Hebrew language and simultaneously train them in the art of self-defense and war. Through knowledge of Hebrew the youths would develop a self-confident Jewish culture that contrasted completely with the passivity of the ghetto Jew, and because of their military training, be able to defend Jewish territory and Judaism's right to flourish in a Jewish land.

After continual disagreements with fellow Zionist leaders, Jabotinsky created Hatzohar, the Union of Zionist Revisionists, which held its first conference in Paris on April 26, 1925. The primary mission of the revisionists was to establish a Jewish state without delay. Jabotinsky edited a Hebrew newspaper called *Doar Hayom* in 1928 and 1929, while living in Palestine, but his increasing political activity led him to leave Palestine in 1929 on a lecture tour, and the British government refused to let him back in. He continued leading the revisionists from outside Palestine. In 1935, when the Zionist Executive of the Zionist Organization again refused to adopt Hatzohar's mission to immediately establish a Jewish state, despite Jabotinsky's dire warnings of impending disaster for European Jews, he resigned from the Zionist Organization and founded the New Zionist Organization (NZO) to continue his work of creating a Jewish state.

In 1937 Jabotinsky created and commanded the Irgun Tzva'i Leumi (Etzel), which became the military division of the Zionist Revisionists in parallel to the political NZO. Betar continued its mission of educating youth and recruiting Jews to be smuggled into Palestine (after the British imposed sharp limitations on immigration). The Irgun, NZO, and Betar together managed to bring more than 40 ships to Palestine's shores, smuggling in tens of thousands of illegal immigrants. Jabotinsky maintained his political activism.

During 1939 and 1940, Jabotinsky was active in trying to set up a Jewish army to fight with the Allies against Nazi Germany, but on August 4, 1940, while in New York to encourage the United States to aid the war effort, he suffered a massive heart attack and died. Jabotinsky had requested to be buried in Palestine, but the British would not allow his body to be brought there. However, in 1964 he was brought by the Israeli government to be reburied near the grave of Theodor Herzl in Jerusalem.

Further reading: Jacob Abadi, *Israel's Leadership: From Utopia to Crisis* (Westport, Conn.: Greenwood Press, 1993); Vladimir Jabotinsky, *The Political and Social Philosophy of Ze'ev Jabotinsky* ed. Mordechai Sarig (London: Mitchell Vallentine, 1999); Shmuel Katz, *Lone Wolf: A Biography of Vladimir (Zeev) Jabotinsky* (New York: Barricade Books, Inc., 1996).

Jacob's Ladder

The Patriarch Jacob had a dream of a ladder ascending to heaven with angels moving up and down (Gn 28:12–22); the image of the ladder became an important symbol in the Jewish tradition.

According to the biblical story, Jacob tricks his father, Isaac, into giving him the blessing meant for his older brother, Esau (Gn 27). Once Esau discovers this, Jacob fears for his life and flees to his uncle Laban in Haran. Along the way, Jacob stops for the night and has his dream. In the dream, God renews the Covenant originally made with Jacob's grandfather Abraham and father, Isaac, and promises land and protection to Jacob and his descendants.

According to the rabbis, the story refers not only to Jacob but to the people of Israel; the angels represent various nations of the future, each of which will grow and decline in strength, while Israel endures. The Zohar provides more mystical commentaries on the story; in Kabbalah, Jacob's ladder is another name for the Sefirot, the hierarchy of emanations from God.

Further reading: David Curzon, *The View from Jacob's Ladder: One Hundred Midrashim* (Philadelphia: Jewish Publication Society, 1996); *Tanakh: The Holy Scriptures* (Philadelphia and Jerusalem: Jewish Publication Society, 1985).

Japan

The first Jews probably visited Japan in the 16th and 17th centuries, when Europeans were conducting limited trade with the Asian state. The first Jews to settle in the country arrived in the

1860s, mostly from POLAND, with some from EN-GLAND and the UNITED STATES. They established a burial society, a cemetery, and possibly a SYNA-GOGUE and a school.

Since the mid-19th century, Japan's few Jews have concentrated in Yokohama. A Jewish settlement existed in Nagasaki in the 19th century, but it did not endure, as Jews began to favor the port of Kobe instead. Later some Jews settled in Tokyo as well.

In the wake of the 1905 Russian Revolution and the 1917 BOLSHEVIK REVOLUTION many Jews fled Russia; some chose to settle in Japan, following advice from Jewish service organizations, such as the HEBREW IMMIGRANT AID SOCIETY. Some used Japan as a stopping-off point and later moved on to the UNITED STATES and Latin American countries such as BRAZIL and ARGENTINA, but some remained to reinforce the communities of Tokyo, Yokohama, and Kobe.

Antisemitism was unheard of in Japan until the 1920s; Japanese thought of the Jews as a variety of Christians. However, in the 1920s troops from Japan's Siberian Expedition (1918–22) brought back negative stories and images of Jews they had gleaned from antisemitic White Russians, connecting Jews with the BOLSHEVIK REVOLUTION.

As World War II approached, Japan entered into an alliance with Nazi Germany, and German antisemitic pamphlets were translated into Japanese. Yet ANTISEMITISM did not take root or affect the Jewish community in Japan. Some refugees from Nazi GERMANY and RUSSIA came to Japan in the early 1940s, but they did not remain for long. For example, in 1941 members of the Lithuanian Mir Yeshiva lived safely in Japan until they were transferred to the International Settlement at Shanghai.

These refugees arrived as part of the Fugu Plan, a program arranged by the Japanese that encouraged European Jews to settle in Japan's Manchurian puppet state called Manchukuo. Thousands of Jews were saved when Chiune Sugihara, a Japanese emissary in Lithuania, issued them visas. Only when the Japanese occupied

Shanghai did they feel compelled to gather its approximately 50,000 Jewish residents into internment camps for the duration of the war. The Jews living in Japanese cities remained safe.

From 1945–52, when the United States occupied Japan, the Jewish community grew, but its activities were mostly sponsored by Jewish military chaplains with U.S. forces. Japanese people became interested in Judaism, enough to establish the scholarly Japanese Association of Jewish Studies and publish a journal called *Studies on Jewish Life and Culture*. A few Japanese converted to Judaism, but most converts were women who married Jewish Americans and returned to the United States with their husbands. By 1970 the population of Jews in Japan was stable at approximately 1,000. These Jews occupied a niche in the economy of Japan, working in business and the professions. The number of Jews living in Japan remained at 1,000 in 1992, but the permanent community only numbers 200.

The Jewish community in Tokyo supports many of the same institutions one finds in many Jewish communities: a rabbi, a SYNAGOGUE, a religious SUPPLEMENTARY SCHOOL, a library, a restaurant, a MIKVAH (ritual bath), a burial society, and a Jewish community center. They also maintain membership in the World Jewish Congress, the Asia Pacific Jewish Association, and B'NAI B'RITH. Tokyo also boasts a CHABAD House, which opens its doors to all Jewish travelers. The city of Kobe also has an active Jewish community of 30 to 35 families, mostly SEPHARDIM.

Antisemitism is not a problem in Japan. Since most Japanese people know little about Jews and Judaism, the Japanese Jewish community works to combat the spread of negative European Jewish stereotypes. Several Christian religious sects, including the Makuya, the Christian Friends of Israel, the Tokyo Biblical Seminary, The Holy Jesus society, and the Association for the Propagation of the Gospel, probably together numbering around 50,000 members, offer support to ISRAEL based on their belief that the Jews must return to the land of Israel before the MESSIANIC AGE can arrive. In addition, Japan supports other interesting groups such as the Kibbutz Society, which is inspired by the moral and social values of the KIBBUTZ, sending, for example, three groups of Japanese youths to Israel each year in the late 1960s.

Relations between Israel and Japan are complex. Japan tends to be pro-Arab, but it has had friendly relations with Israel since 1952 and a positive trade relationship. However, because Japan gets 40 percent of its oil from Arab nations, it has had to join in the Arab boycott of Israel and so its trade with Israel has not reached its full potential.

Further reading: Isaiah Ben-Dasan, *The Japanese and the Jews* (Tokyo: Weatherhill, 1972); David G. Goodman and Masanori Miyazawa, *Jews in the Japanese Mind: The History and Uses of a Cultural Stereotype* (New York: Free Press, 1995); Abram Setsuzau, *From Tokyo to Jerusalem* (New York: B. Geis Associates, 1964); Marvin Tokayer and Mary Swartz, *The Fugu Plan: The Untold Story of the Japanese and the Jews* (New York: Weatherhill, 1996).

Jerusalem

The city of Jerusalem was the ancient capital of the Israelite kingdom and the center of its religious life from the days of King David; since that time, it has retained its central position as the focal point of Jewish prayer and the center of Jewish national identity. By extension, it has also become a holy city for CHRISTIANITY and ISLAM.

Scholars disagree as to the meaning of the name "Jerusalem" (Hebrew: *Yerushalayim*). Some believe it is based on the word *shalom,* or "peace;" they translate the name as "foundation of peace," "city of peace," or "city of the god of Peace." Others believe the city may have been named for the Assyrian god Shalem.

The Old City of Jerusalem, site of the ancient city, is surrounded on three sides by valleys, and hemmed in by a stone wall with eight main portals: Damascus Gate, Jaffa Gate, Mercy Gate, Herod's Gate, Dung Gate, Lion's Gate, New Gate, and Zion Gate. It is divided into four sections based on the religious affiliation of most of the residents: Christian, Jewish, Muslim, and Armenian. The Church of the Holy Sepulchre, the Dome of the Rock, and the KOTEL, or Western Wall, all represent holy sites for various religious traditions.

Jerusalem is the holiest place on earth for Jews. King DAVID unified ISRAEL by moving its capital to Jerusalem. Both the first and second TEMPLES were located there, the first built by David's son King SOLOMON. Because of the Temple, Jerusalem was the central point of the Jewish world and was the focus of pilgrimage in ancient and medieval times. It is considered the most efficacious place for prayer, and it is said that one always ascends (makes ALIYAH) to Jerusalem, not only because of its geographical location (one-half mile above sea level) but because it is spiritually elevated as well.

Many legends about Jerusalem exist. It is said that the AKEDAH (binding of Isaac) took place there. The city is said to be at the heart of the world, and was the foundation of CREATION. Legends even say its inhabitants never fell ill.

Jerusalem has been wracked by war for centuries. In 586 B.C.E., the Babylonians conquered the city and destroyed the first Temple. In 167 B.C.E., the Seleucid Greeks ravaged the second Temple and Jerusalem, which were then recaptured by the Maccabees. Finally, in 70 C.E., the second Temple was completely destroyed and the people of Jerusalem were butchered, enslaved, and exiled by the Romans. Only the walls of the Temple Mount, or platform, were left standing. Jerusalem remains the focal point of the Jewish desire to return to the Land of Israel. For example, in the TANAKH, Lamentations 2:13, a voice cries, "What can I compare or liken / To you, O Fair Jerusalem."

The site of the Temple, currently occupied by two historic Muslim mosques, is still consider the holiest Jewish site. Since Jews are not permitted to pray there to avoid offending Muslims, the Kotel (Hebrew for "wall"), the Western Wall of the Temple Mount, has remained the holiest accessible Jewish site. Prayers in synagogues worldwide contain the hope for a rebuilt Jerusalem. On PASSOVER, the SEDER ends with the phrase "next year in Jerusalem." According to Jewish lore, in Messianic times, Jerusalem will be a heavenly place capable of housing all nations.

Jerusalem was declared the capital of the new state of Israel in 1948, and the government moved there soon after. The president, prime minister, KNESSET (parliament), Supreme Court, and nearly all government departments of the state of Israel are located there. However, most foreign nations maintain their embassies in TEL AVIV, as they consider the final status of the city to be still in question.

Jerusalem today is a modern city covering a large area spreading out from the Old City in all directions. It houses more than 600,000 people, some two-thirds of them Jews, most of the rest Muslims.

Further reading: Lee I. Levine, ed., *Jerusalem: Its Sanctity and Centrality to Judaism, Christianity, and Islam* (New York: Continuum, 1999); Zev Vilnay, *Legends of Jerusalem* (Philadelphia: Jewish Publication Society of America, 1995 (1973); *Tanakh: The Holy Scriptures* (Philadelphia and Jerusalem: Jewish Publication Society, 1985).

Jerusalem Post

The *Jerusalem Post* is an English-language Israeli newspaper established in 1932; it was known as the *Palestine Post* prior to 1950. It is circulated six days a week in ISRAEL. It is not published on Saturdays, the Sabbath (*see* SHABBAT), or on Israeli national and religious holidays. The *Jerusalem Post* is circulated worldwide. It is a politically moderate newspaper, although it does lean somewhat to the right in its perspective. The *Jerusalem Post* generally gives support to the Israeli government, while at the same time offering criticism on economic and social policy. Another moderate newspaper in Israel, *Ha-Aretz,* literally "the land," publishes an English-language version. The *Jerusalem Post* maintains an Internet edition, a print edition, an

international edition, and a French-language edition. Its online archives date to 1989.

Further reading: Erwin Frenkel, *The Press and Politics in Israel: The Jerusalem Post from 1932 to the Present* (Westport, Conn: Greenwood Press, 1994); *Jerusalem Post* Web site URL: http://www.jpost.com, accessed July 29, 2004.

Jesus of Nazareth (c. 3 B.C.E.–30 C.E.)
founder of Christianity

Jesus of Nazareth is recognized as the founder of CHRISTIANITY; he is generally believed to have been born in Judea to a Jewish mother around 3 B.C.E. and crucified some 33 years later.

Jesus's followers, who were all originally Jews, believed that he was the MESSIAH (in Greek, "Christ"), the savior who was promised in prophesies of the TANAKH, the Hebrew Bible. Christianity eventually recognized him as part of the Holy Trinity along with God and the Holy Spirit. Christians believe his death on the cross acts as an atonement for human sin and that his bodily resurrection demonstrates his power over death.

Jews have never accepted these ideas. Some Jewish historians view Jesus as a teacher in the rabbinic tradition that was developing at that time. They point to similarities in some of his teachings to other contemporary rabbis, and interpret his statement: "not one dot, not one stroke, shall disappear from the Law until its purpose is accomplished" (Mt 5:18) as evidence that he supported HALAKHAH, or Jewish law, which all Christians later rejected. Others Jews view him as one of a number of false messiahs that arose in Judea in those times.

Throughout the centuries many Christian communities have persecuted Jews as "Christ killers." In the 20th century, the charge provided additional support for the HOLOCAUST. Jewish leaders have consistently denied that Jews were responsible for Jesus' crucifixion, claiming that he was killed by the Romans as a dangerous Jewish rebel. At the time of Jesus' death, they point out, capital punishment was entirely in the hands of the ruling Romans. In addition, they say, Jewish law forbade crucifixion because it involves torture, which is banned even for criminals.

Jesus continues to be a controversial figure in dialogues between Christians and Jews. In the last half of the 20th century, the Roman Catholic Church and most of the larger Protestant churches issued statements explicitly denying the charge that Jews were responsible for killing Jesus.

Further reading: E. P. Sanders, *Jesus and Judaism* (Philadelphia: Fortress Press, 1985); Geza Vermes, *Jesus the Jew: A Historian's Reading of the Gospels* (Philadelphia: Fortress Press, 1981); A. N. Wilson, *Jesus: A Life* (New York: Norton, 1992); Thomas Walker, *Jewish Views of Jesus* (New York, 1973).

Jethro (c. 14th century B.C.E.) *biblical figure, father-in-law of Moses*

According to the book of EXODUS (Ex 2–3) Jethro, also referred to as Reuel, was a priest of Midian who had seven daughters. When MOSES fled to Midian after killing an Egyptian taskmaster, he defended Jethro's daughters from a group of shepherds. Jethro invited Moses to stay with his family and later offered his daughter TZIPPORAH in marriage. Later, when Moses led the ISRAELITES to freedom, Jethro provided key advice on how to govern the people.

According to tales in the MIDRASH, Jethro had been an adviser to PHARAOH but fled Egypt himself to protest the decree that Israelite babies be cast into the Nile. Thus, Jewish history holds the character of Jethro in high esteem.

Further reading: Judith Reesa Baskin, *Pharaoh's Counsellors: Job, Jethro, and Balaam in Rabbinic and Patristic Tradition* (Chico, Calif.: Scholars Press, 1983); *Tanakh: The Holy Scriptures* (Philadelphia and Jerusalem: Jewish Publication Society, 1985).

Jew

The term *Jew* was first used as a reference to anyone who came from ERETZ YISRAEL (the Land of Israel) during the first EXILE in BABYLONIA. Prior to the exile these people were referred to as Bnei Yisrael, Children of Israel, emphasizing the lineage to the PATRIARCHS. Since those who remained and returned after the first Exile descended mostly from the tribe of JUDAH, whose territory had abutted JERUSALEM, they came to be known as Jews (Neh 1:2). During the time of the Greeks and Romans, and the second Exile beginning in 70 C.E., those whose ancestors came from Eretz Yisrael became known as *ioudaios*, or Jews.

Further reading: Moshe Greenberg, *Studies in the Bible and Jewish Thought* (Philadelphia: Jewish Publication Society, 1995); N. S. Hecht, *An Introduction to the History and Sources of Jewish Law* (New York: Oxford University Press, 1996).

Jewish Agency

In 1929 the government of the BRITISH MANDATE formed the Jewish Agency for PALESTINE so that Jews living there would have a channel through which to voice their concerns. Half of the members of the Jewish Agency lived in Palestine, but another half did not, a reality engineered by the Zionist Organization (*see* WORLD ZIONIST CONGRESS). The Zionist Organization and the Jewish Agency were closely linked in form and management. The Jewish Agency played a vital role in relations between the YISHUV, the Jewish settlement in Palestine, and world Jewry and between the yishuv and world political powers.

Before ISRAEL became a modern state, the Jewish Agency acted as its embryonic government. Its responsibilities included immigration, new immigrant absorption, economic development, educational and social services, and agricultural settlement. Outside Israel, the Jewish Agency took an active role in education, opportunities for investments in the yishuv, and youth activities. The Jewish Agency actively sought Jews who wanted to move to Israel and provided aid to Jews living in dangerous and violent areas. After the WHITE PAPER of 1939 was published restricting

Jewish immigration to Palestine, the Jewish Agency worked to support illegal immigration. In addition, it provided support from the yishuv to the Allies during World War II. The leaders of the Jewish Agency, such as Moshe SHARETT, were active in UNITED NATIONS discussions on Palestine and in the decision to implement the PARTITION PLAN in 1947.

After the creation of the State of Israel in 1948, the Jewish Agency ceded power to the new Israeli KNESSET, becoming a department within the government. In 1954 the Israeli government recognized the combined agencies of the Jewish Agency–World Zionist Organization as the representative of world Jewry, and gave the Agency responsibilities for immigration, absorption, agricultural settlement, external relations, youth aliyah, economics, and education and culture in the DIASPORA.

The Jewish Agency worked miracles, first aiding Jewish war refugees to escape Europe during the HOLOCAUST, and then helping the immigrants from displaced persons camps get to Israel and settle in after the war had ended. The Jewish Agency also helped absorb immigrants from Yemen (see OPERATION MAGIC CARPET), IRAQ, IRAN, and Turkey. In 1949, the Jewish Agency accommodated 239,000 immigrants, in 1950 169,000, and in 1951 another 174,000. The task was astronomical as most of the immigrants were shell-shocked and penniless. Ultimately the Jewish Agency acted as protector for any Jew who needed assistance around the world.

As mass immigration to Israel slowed, the Jewish Agency and the World Zionist Organization reorganized their departments and structures. The Jewish Agency focused on fund-raising outside Israel, such as in the UNITED STATES, and encouraged people to immigrate to Israel by providing Jewish education, information, cultural programs, and youth work that encouraged a positive relationship between Jews living in the DIASPORA and those in Israel. In Israel, the agency provided funds for immigrant absorption, land settlement, housing, social welfare, education, and child care for immigrants. Two-thirds of the budget for the Jewish Agency comes from funds raised in the United States by the United Jewish Appeal, the fund-raising arm of the UNITED JEWISH COMMUNITIES umbrella group.

Further reading: Daniel J. Elazar, "The Jewish Agency: Historic Role and Current Crisis," *Jerusalem Letter* 263 (October 15); Aviva Halamish, *The Exodus Affair: Holocaust Survivors and the Struggle for Palestine* (Syracuse, N.Y.: Syracuse University Press, 1998); Dan Horowitz and Moshe Lissak, *Origins of the Israeli Polity: Palestine under the Mandate* (Chicago: University of Chicago Press, 1978); Jewish Agency for Israel Web site URL: http://www.jafi.org.il.

Jewish Community Center Association

The Jewish Community Center Association is an umbrella organization uniting more than 350 Jewish community centers (JCCs), Young Men's and Young Women's Hebrew Associations (YMHA, YWHA), and camp sites throughout the UNITED STATES and CANADA.

Many Jewish communities build a central facility to serve as a social, cultural, educational, and recreational center for Jews in the area. Local Jews can cement their ties with one another, and have a central location to engage in sports, learn about Judaism, seek social services, and take their kids to camp. The Jewish Community Center Association provides resources to make the JCCs throughout North America as successful as possible.

The JCC movement began in 1854 to serve immigrants. As the needs of the Jewish communities change, so too do the services that JCCs provide. The Jewish Community Centers do not primarily serve the spiritual needs of the community, which are left to the various local SYNAGOGUES. The separation from religious polemics ensures that the centers remain open to all types of Jews.

Further reading: Jerome A. Chanes, Norman Linzer, and David J. Schnall, eds., *A Portrait of the American*

Jewish Community (Westport, Conn.: Praeger Publications, 1998); Daniel J. Elazar, *Community and Polity: The Organizational Dynamics of American Jewry* (Philadelphia: Jewish Publication Society, 1995); Jewish Community Center Associations Web site URL: http://www.jcca.org, accessed July 29, 2004.

Jewish Daily Forward

The *Jewish Daily Forward* was an American Jewish newspaper founded in 1897 as a YIDDISH daily. The paper was a strong voice in New York's immigrant community, supporting the trade unions and moderate, democratic socialism. Abraham Cahan, its dynamic founding editor, is credited with its many years of success. Cahan remained the editor of the *Forward* for half a century, until his death in 1950. The paper became the most important voice of the American Jewish immigrant and a permanent daily fixture in many Jewish households. The paper was a strong proponent of social justice, a necessary platform in a world of sweatshops and new immigrants.

In the early 1930s the *Forward* had a national daily circulation of 275,000, and it also boasted a Yiddish radio station. The paper has printed the voices of many Yiddish literary figures, such as Isaac Bashevis SINGER and Elie WIESEL. The *Forward* was also famous for editor Cahan's Bintel Brief, an advice column that reflected life on the LOWER EAST SIDE and the experiences of American Jewish immigrants.

As eastern European Jewish immigrants accommodated to American culture and language, the *Forward* lost its niche. When the Yiddish-speaking world dwindled, the editors were forced to make some difficult decisions. In 1983, the *Forward* began to publish weekly instead of daily, and it launched an English supplement. In 1990, the Forward Association remade the English-language *Forward* into a new weekly voice for world Jewry. It has become a source of information on Jewish news, opinion, and culture in the contemporary world. The *Forward* also focuses on young people in an attempt to appeal to the entire community.

In 1995 the *Forward* began to publish a Russian-language edition in New York. This edition has achieved success in the competitive market of Russian-language newspapers. Together the Yiddish, English, and Russian editions of the *Forward* continue the mission of the original *Jewish Daily Forward* in providing a voice for the American Jewish community.

Further reading: Irving Howe and Kenneth Libo, *How We Lived: A Documentary History of Immigrant Jews in America, 1880–1930* (New York: R. Marek, 1979); Jenna Weissman Joselit, *The Wonders of America: Reinventing Jewish Culture 1880–1950* (New York: Hill and Wang, 1994); Isaac Metzker, *The Bintel Brief: Sixty Years of Letters from the Lower East Side to the Jewish Daily Forward* (New York: Schocken Books, 1990).

Jewish day school movement

American Jews have historically supported the idea of public education and sent their children to public schools. In order to provide for their children's Jewish education, parents chose either to educate their children at home, which most American Jewish parents are not qualified to do, or send them to SUPPLEMENTARY SCHOOLS on weekday afternoons or Sundays. This prolonged the school day for children and infringed on after-school sports and other activities. The quality and professionalism of supplementary schools was, and continues to be, a challenge for the Jewish community.

By the 1960s, despite their reluctance to pull children away from public education, many parents in Jewish communities across the UNITED STATES had decided that the afternoon school option was inadequate. They wanted their children to receive a more complete Jewish education. Most parents did not want to send their children to a traditional YESHIVA, where the focus on TORAH and TALMUD study went beyond the desires of the average American Jewish family.

The Jewish day school was the solution to the problem. Jewish day schools now exist in many different varieties. Most adhere to one of the main synagogue movements, ORTHODOX, CONSERVATIVE, and REFORM JUDAISM, but many are nondenominational.

The day school offers bicultural education, teaching traditional academic subjects such as English, history, mathematics, and science as well as Jewish subjects such as Jewish history, rabbinics (TALMUD and Jewish law), TANAKH (the Hebrew Bible), and prayer, all within the regular school day. The day usually finishes a bit later than a traditional public school, but a child attending a Jewish day school has the opportunity to attend after-school activities and sports without interfering with his or her Jewish education. Some Jewish day schools split the day in half, having the students spend half the day on secular subjects and the other half on Jewish ones, while a newer trend is to integrate Jewish and secular studies throughout the day.

In 1935 there were 4,000 pupils attending Jewish day schools in the United States, all of which were located in New York City. By 1971 nearly 70,000 students were enrolled in schools in many cities. Orthodox Judaism runs the largest number of day schools, enrolling more than 100,000 students by 1980; any city with more than 5,000 Jews had at least one. Not all students attending Orthodox day schools came from Orthodox homes; rather, parents were choosing from what was available. This led to what some call cultural dissonance, where students learn rituals in school that their families do not practice at home. Yet the Jewish education the students received was solid, and it has been shown statistically that more Jewish day school students end up living Jewish lives than those without the benefit of that education.

Even so, some parents wanted a school that reflected their own Jewish values, and the non-Orthodox movements eventually responded. The Conservative movement has its own group of day schools named after Solomon SCHECHTER, the first president of the Jewish Theological Seminary and a key shaper of Conservative Judaism. In 1990 there were almost 70 Solomon Schechter schools in North America. The Reform movement also sponsors Jewish day schools, but they are far fewer in number. In 1981 there were only nine in existence. There are currently more than 80 non-denominational community Jewish day schools. They are characterized by pluralism, inclusivity, EGALITARIANISM, and independence. While denominational schools are affiliated with synagogue associations, many community schools are members of RAVSAK: The Jewish Community Day School Network.

All in all, some 200,000 children attended Jewish day schools in the United States in 2003, according to the Partnership for Excellence in Jewish Education.

Further reading: Daniel Judah Elazar, *Community and Polity: The Organizational Dynamics of American Jewry* (Philadelphia: Jewish Publication Society, 1999); Nachama Skolnik Moskowitz, ed., *The Ultimate Jewish Teacher's Handbook* (Denver, Colo.: A.R.E. Publishing Inc., 2003); Alvin I. Schiff, "Public Education and the Jewish School," *Journal of Jewish Communal Services* 6 (Summer 1985): 305–311; Edward S. Shapiro, *A Time for Healing: American Jewry since World War II* (Baltimore and London: Johns Hopkins University Press, 1992).

Jewish family services *See* ASSOCIATION OF JEWISH FAMILY AND CHILDREN'S AGENCIES.

Jewish identity

The question of Jewish identity in the modern world is complex, involving not just a person's religious beliefs and affiliation but also his or her cultural and national identity. As the modern world became more secular, so too did the Jews (*see* ACCOMODATION; ASSIMILATION; MODERNITY). ORTHODOX JUDAISM defines Jewish identity fairly simply: anyone who was born to a Jewish mother or who observes Jewish law (*HALAKHAH*) is Jewish. In this traditional realm, it is clear that a Jew is a person who participates in Jewish rituals and believes in the tenets of the Jewish tradition.

Yet many people in the modern world think of themselves as Jews even though they reject the binding nature of Jewish law, as has occurred in REFORM JUDAISM and RECONSTRUCTIONIST JUDAISM, and even if they do not affiliate with any Jewish religious movement at all. The issue becomes one of group identification and self-identification: how people perceive themselves, and how the family, school, and Jewish community impact the development of a person's identity as a child and into adulthood.

Orthodox and Conservative institutions only recognize a person as a Jew if he or she has a Jewish mother or has formally converted to Judaism. Reform Judaism considers a person a Jew even if only the father is Jewish and the person is raised as a Jew. This creates tensions between the movements regarding Jewish identity.

Some Jews will express their Jewish identity through participating in a Jewish community center, decorating their homes with Jewish religious or cultural artifacts, volunteering their time for Jewish causes or participating in the work of Jewish federations (*see* UNITED JEWISH COMMUNITIES), belonging to or attending a SYNAGOGUE, expressing their love for the State of ISRAEL and ZIONISM, or even simply by remaining connected to other Jewish people.

Mordecai KAPLAN, the founder of Reconstructionist Judaism, defined Judaism not as a religion, but as a civilization, with its own land, language, laws, sanctions, art, and social structure. Kaplan felt that religion was but one aspect of Jewish identity, and the Jew in the modern world seems to agree, finding myriad ways to be Jewish inside and outside of religious life.

Further reading: Calvin Goldscheider and Alan S. Zuckerman, *The Transformation of the Jews* (Chicago and London: The University of Chicago Press, 1984); Arthur Hertzberg, *Judaism: An Anthology of Key Spiritual Writings of the Jewish Tradition* (New York: Simon & Schuster, 1991); Edward S. Shapiro, *A Time for Healing: American Jewry since World War II* (Baltimore and London: Johns Hopkins University Press, 1992); Jonathan S. Woocher, *Sacred Survival: The Civil Religion of American Jews* (Bloomington: Indiana University Press, 1986).

Jewish Museum

The Jewish Museum in New York sits along prestigious Museum Mile of Fifth Avenue, thereby locating itself at the center of American and Jewish life.

In 2004, the museum celebrated its centennial year. In 1904, Judge Mayer Sulzberger (1843–1923) donated 26 Jewish art objects to the Jewish Theological Seminary, thus laying the foundation for the Jewish Museum.

The Jewish Museum is dedicated to an exploration of Jewish culture, past and present, through its collection of more than 28,000 paintings, sculptures, works on paper, photographs, archaeological artifacts, ceremonial objects, and broadcast media, and through visiting and special exhibits. Together the exhibits take the Jewish or non-Jewish visitor on a tour of Jewish life and an exploration of JEWISH IDENTITY. The museum was renovated and expanded in 1993 to make it possible to display more of its collection and to offer classrooms, an auditorium, and public amenities. The museum houses the most extensive collection of Jewish visual art in the Western Hemisphere.

Many institutions around the world, unrelated to the museum in New York, also use the name "the Jewish Museum," in English or other languages. Such museums can be found in London, ENGLAND; Florence, Italy; Budapest, HUNGARY; and Melbourne, Australia.

Further reading: Susan Tumarkin Goodman, *The Emergence of Jewish Artists in Nineteenth-Century Europe* (New York: Merrell in association with The Jewish Museum, New York, 2001); Grace Cohen Grossman, *Jewish Museums of the World* (Southport, Conn.: Hugh Lauter Levin Associates, 2003); Cecil Roth, *Jewish Art: An Illustrated History* (New York: McGraw-Hill, 1961).

Jewish Publication Society (JPS)

A Jewish Publication Society of America was originally founded by Isaac Leeser (1806–68) in 1845, but it did not survive past 1851. In 1888 the society was reborn, inspired by the needs of new immigrants and of the growing rabbinical schools and seminaries (*see* HEBREW UNION COLLEGE–JEWISH INSTITUTE OF RELIGION) in the UNITED STATES. The new JPS was founded by intellectual leaders such as Marcus Jastrow (1829–1903), Cyrus ADLER, and Henrietta SZOLD, and funded by German-Jewish American philanthropists such as Meyer Guggenheim (*see* GUGGENHEIM FAMILY) and Jacob SCHIFF. It aimed to produce books on Jewish history, religion, and thought, as well as material for Jewish religious instruction.

The nonprofit JPS is the oldest English-language publisher of Jewish books in the world. Its original intention to provide English-language books about Judaism to the children of Jewish immigrants in the UNITED STATES has widened; its educational mission is to enhance Jewish culture through the publication of exceptional secular and religious Jewish works.

JPS publications are circulated in the United States and abroad; they include biographies, histories, art books, holiday anthologies, books for young readers, religious and philosophical studies, and translations of scholarly and popular classics. The most famous of all JPS publications is its own English translation of the TANAKH (the Hebrew Bible). Recently JPS also published a new biblical commentary called *Etz Hayim: Torah and Commentary*. JPS is also responsible for publishing the *American Jewish Yearbook* on an annual basis. The JPS is supported by members and contributors. The society explains that dues and donations "support the publication of books that broaden and deepen the understanding of the Jewish heritage and advance Jewish scholarship."

Further reading: *The Jewish Publication Society of America Twenty-Fifth Anniversary* (Philadelphia: Jewish Publication Society of America, 1913); David L. Lieber, ed., *Etz Hayim: Torah and Commentary* (Philadelphia: Jewish Publication Society, 2000); Charles Madison, *Jewish Publishing in America* (New York: Sanhedrin Press, 1976); *Tanakh: The Holy Scriptures* (Philadelphia and Jerusalem: The Jewish Publication Society, 1985).

Jewish Reconstructionist Federation *See* RECONSTRUCTIONIST JUDAISM.

Jewish Renewal

Jewish Renewal is a nondenominational movement within Judaism that is committed to restoring the spiritual element to Judaism, which it believes is lacking for many people. Renewal draws upon HASIDISM in that it includes meditation, dancing, chanting, and mysticism among its practices. Yet unlike Hasidism, it encourages members from all branches of Judaism to bring what they believe to be formerly secret or hidden traditions into the mainstream. The movement sees its foundations as TORAH, KABBALAH, and other Jewish sources but is open to finding truths from introspection and communal discussion as well as from other faiths. In this way, like RECONSTRUCTIONIST JUDAISM, Jewish Renewal understands Judaism to be an evolving tradition with new and creative rituals and liturgies.

Jewish Renewal is a very recent development within Judaism. It traces its roots to two late 20th-century figures, Rabbi Schlomo Carlebach (1925–94) and Rabbi Zalman Schachter-Shalomi (b. 1924). These two rabbis were trained in the Hasidic movement but later left it to found their own communities and ordain their own students. Rabbi Zalman Schachter-Shalomi's original community, the B'nai Or Religious Fellowship, was the forerunner of the current organization ALEPH: Alliance for Jewish Renewal.

Renewal also stems from other 20th-century phenomena, particularly the CHAVURAH movement, process theology, and feminism. Because of its emphasis on spiritual experience, many understand Jewish Renewal to be a New Age form of Judaism. Others understand Renewal to be a fifth denomination within Judaism since it often has its own congregations and since the founding rabbis offer ordination. The movement itself, however, resists classification as New Age because of its grounding in Jewish concepts and traditions, and similarly resists classification as a new denomination because it offers no separate theological principles or interpretations of HALAKHAH, Jewish law. The movement prefers the term *trans-denominational* because it respects the diversity of Jewish expression, recognizes the historical importance of each denomination, and hopes to bring spiritual renewal to members of all denominations.

The two main Jewish concepts that Renewal emphasizes are TESHUVAH (repentance, return) and TIKKUN OLAM (repairing the world). *Teshuvah* is the term from which Renewal takes its name; it is most closely associated with the Days of Awe from ROSH HASHANAH through YOM KIPPUR. Understood as renewal, *teshuvah* suggests a perpetual return to faith, life, God, and spirituality. *Tikkun olam* denotes the mission of Jewish Renewal. The movement espouses a number of progressive activities that it considers a part of healing the world: these include empowering the disadvantaged, feminism, peace activism, gay rights activism, and environmental activism. However, these values do not take an explicitly political form within Jewish Renewal, but rather a personalized spiritual form that may or may not be expressed politically as well.

Further reading: Michael Lerner, *Jewish Renewal* (New York: G.P. Putnam's Sons, 1994); Zalman Schachter-Shalomi, *Paradigm Shift* (Northvale, N.J.: Jason Aronson, 1993); Arthur Waskow, *Godwrestling—Round 2* (Woodstock, Vt.: Jewish Lights, 1996); Shohama Wiener, ed., *The Fifty-Eighth Century: A Jewish Renewal Sourcebook* (Northvale, N.J.: Jason Aronson, 1996).

Jewish Theological Seminary of America

The Jewish Theological Seminary (JTS) was founded in 1886 by Rabbis SABATO MORAIS (1823–97) and H. Pereira Mendes (1852–1937), along with a group of prominent Sephardic lay leaders from congregations in New York and Philadelphia. The original mission of JTS was to preserve the knowledge and practice of historical Judaism in direct opposition to REFORM JUDAISM, which had become far too liberal and antiritual for many Jewish leaders. The first class of JTS was taught in 1887 and was composed of 10 students who gathered in the vestry of the Spanish-Portuguese Synagogue, New York City's oldest congregation.

JTS remained a small school, and in its first 15 years ordained only 15 rabbis. A new catalyst for growth came when Cyrus ADLER, who had been a private tutorial student of Morais, joined the Seminary's board of directors. While not wealthy himself, Adler helped to secure the support of some of America's wealthiest Jews. German-Jewish American philanthropists such as Louis MARSHALL (1856–1929) and Jacob SCHIFF (1847–1920), dedicated members of a Reform congregation, saw the rejuvenation of JTS as an opportunity to attract and Americanize the hordes of eastern European Jewish immigrants coming to American shores.

Together, intellectuals and financiers built JTS into a premier Jewish institution, and after raising more than a half million dollars, they secured the teaching services of the esteemed Jewish scholar Solomon SCHECHTER (1847–1915) from Oxford University. Schechter became JTS's new chancellor in March 1902. Modeling JTS after Zachariah FRANKEL's (1801–75) Beslau Jewish Theological Seminary, Schechter managed to secure JTS's reputation worldwide in his 13 years of leadership, and to create a significant endowment fund.

Over the decades, JTS has been the premier seminary in training and leading Jewish scholars and professionals within CONSERVATIVE JUDAISM. Today, it is considered a Jewish university with a world-class faculty and a diverse student body. It offers undergraduate, graduate, and professional degrees through five schools and offers continuing education for the Jewish community in the United States, ISRAEL, and around the world. JTS also operates a rabbinical school in Buenos Aires, ARGENTINA. In addition to its graduate, rabbinical, cantorial, Jewish education, and undergraduate schools, JTS runs a Jewish SUPPLEMENTARY SCHOOL on the high school level, a summer school, and five research institutes.

The JTS library is considered the greatest Jewish library outside of Israel, and possesses an extraordinary collection of rare Jewish books and manuscripts. It is affiliated with the JEWISH MUSEUM in New York and participates in a consortium with its prestigious academic neighbors—Columbia University, Barnard College, and Union Theological Seminary—creating a large and vibrant community of learning.

JTS is still considered the intellectual and religious center of Conservative Judaism, educating the movement's Jewish professionals and lay leadership, through both formal and informal programs.

Further reading: Neil Gillman, Conservative Judaism: The New Century (West Orange, N.J.: Behrman House Publishing, 1993); Jack Wertheimer, Tradition Renewed: A History of the Jewish Theological Seminary (New York: The Seminary, 1997).

Jewish youth groups

A variety of opportunities exist in the UNITED STATES for Jewish youth to socialize and learn about their heritage via Jewish youth groups. Children and teens of all ages can join a youth group associated with a SYNAGOGUE, community, or Zionist organization. These youth groups include Young Judaea, sponsored by the Zionist woman's organization HADASSAH (see ZIONIST YOUTH MOVEMENTS); United Synagogue Youth (USY), sponsored by CONSERVATIVE JUDAISM; the North American Federation of Temple Youth (NFTY), sponsored by the REFORM JUDAISM; the National Conference of Synagogue Youth (NCSY), sponsored by ORTHODOX JUDAISM; Noar Hadash, sponsored by RECONSTRUCTIONIST JUDAISM; and the B'nai B'rith Youth Organization (BBYO), sponsored by B'NAI B'RITH and independent Jewish

communities. Independent Jewish youth groups also exist. Most youth groups offer leadership opportunities to Jewish youth at the chapter, divisional, regional, and international levels. Members also have opportunities to attend conventions and summer programs, often in ISRAEL.

Further reading: Anita Diamant, Living a Jewish Life: Jewish Traditions, Customs and Values for Today's Families (New York: Harper Resource, 1996); Daniel J. Elazar, Community and Polity: The Organizational Dynamics of American Jewry (Philadelphia: Jewish Publication Society, 1995); Don Futterman, "How to Build Utopia in Only Minutes a Day in the Privacy of Your Own Home," Tikkun 8, 3 (May–June 1993): 33+.

Jews for Jesus

Jews for Jesus is a Christian evangelistic movement led and developed by Martin "Moishe" Rosen and incorporated as a nonprofit ministry in 1973. It aims at spreading the Christian gospel to Jews.

Jews for Jesus considers the evangelization of Jews to be its top priority. Unlike MESSIANIC JEWS, who maintain their own synagogues and community life as ethnically Jewish Christians, Jews for Jesus is primarily a gateway for Jews to become Christians and join other churches. Many of the members of Jews for Jesus are young Jewish adults who try to remain ethnically Jewish while maintaining their belief in JESUS OF NAZARETH as the MESSIAH.

The Jews for Jesus International Headquarters operates from San Francisco, California; its staff of more than 200 people works in 11 countries and 20 cities. The group values both the Old Testament and the New Testament, but they do not believe that Jewish law (HALAKHAH) is always relevant or binding. The group has centered its activity on college campuses and on city streets adjacent to urban Jewish communities, where it has become well known for passing out literature, attempting to attract Jews with a basic appeal that the Jewish heritage is not antithetical to a belief in

Jesus as the Messiah. Jews for Jesus have also established work in JERUSALEM. The group insists that it should have a place within the spectrum of other Jewish groups. However, the leadership of mainstream Judaism has persistently and adamantly rejected the idea that Judaism is compatible with a belief in Jesus as the Messiah. Jews for Jesus are not thus accepted as a part of NORMATIVE JUDAISM. They are not considered Jews for the purposes of the Israeli LAW OF RETURN.

Further reading: Juliene G. Lipson, *Jews for Jesus: An Anthropological Study* (New York: AMS Press, 1990); Ruth Tucker, *Not Ashamed: The Story of Jews for Jesus* (Sisters, Oreg.: Multnomah, 2000).

Job *biblical figure*

The book of Job appears in the KETUVIM, or Writings, part of the TANAKH, the Hebrew Bible. The book tells the story of Job, a righteous man who challenges God's justice for allowing a righteous man to suffer.

The book introduces Job as a good man who fulfills his responsibilities to family and community. As the story progresses, he suffers loss of livelihood and property, ill health, and finally the deaths of his wife and children. His friends try to convince him that his suffering must be a punishment for wickedness, but Job refuses to accept this explanation. Pushed by his friends to question why else God might allow these terrible things to happen to him, Job confronts God. Ultimately God speaks to Job from a whirlwind and tells him that he can possess only finite knowledge and cannot understand the divine plans for the universe. Job accepts this rebuke, and eventually is restored to health, prosperity and a new family.

The book of Job is considered to be a book of wisdom, defined by ancient Jews as the pursuit of knowledge to understand one's life and one's religion. The book of Job asks: "Where shall wisdom be found? . . . Man does not know the way to it. It is hidden from the eyes of all living things, God

understands the way to it" (Jb 28:12, 21, 23). The book thus reaffirms that wisdom comes as a divine gift.

The book of Job is unusual for the Bible in its radical questioning of conventional beliefs. The overall tone is individualistic and pessimistic, as the character Job probes the problems of justice and religion. It appears to reject the traditional Jewish perspective on suffering, which is that suffering is the result of wickedness.

However, while the book questions this biblical theology, it reaffirms that one must ultimately accept the will of God. As Job says, "Though He [God] slay me, yet will I trust in Him" (Jb 13:15). In modern times the book of Job has become a paradigm for some people to help them relate to the horrors of the HOLOCAUST. Ultimately, the one who suffered, Job, still trusts in God and God still trusts in Job.

Further reading: Robert Altar, *The Art of Biblical Poetry* (New York: Basic Books, 1985); Norman Gottwald, *The Hebrew Bible: A Socio-Literary Introduction* (Philadelphia: Fortress Press, 1985); Jon D. Levenson, *Creation and the Persistence of Evil* (San Francisco: HarperSanFranciso, 1988); Stephen Mitchell, *The Book of Job* (New York: Perennial, 1992); *Tanakh: The Holy Scriptures* (Philadelphia and Jerusalem: Jewish Publication Society, 1985).

Joseph *biblical figure*

The biblical story of Joseph and his brothers is the longest single-themed narrative in the book of Genesis, the first book of the TANAKH, the Hebrew Bible.

Joseph is the PATRIARCH Jacob's favorite son. His brothers harbor resentment toward him because of that favoritism. After he shares with them his dream that some day they will bow down before him, they decide to act. They sell him into slavery, and tell their father that he was killed by a wild animal; they present their brother's bloodied coat of many colors, a gift from Jacob, as proof.

Joseph is brought to EGYPT, where he successfully serves in Potiphar's home; when he rejects the advances of Potiphar's wife, on grounds of morality, she falsely accuses him of rape, and Joseph is imprisoned. While in prison, he correctly interprets the dreams of two fellow inmates, the former baker and butler of the PHARAOH. The butler is restored to service; when Pharaoh himself is troubled by dreams the butler tells him of Joseph, who is immediately summoned. Joseph easily interprets Pharaoh's dreams as omens of seven years of prosperity for Egypt followed by seven years of famine. Pharaoh is so impressed with Joseph that he places him in charge of food collection for distribution during the famine to come. Joseph marries an Egyptian priestess, Asenath, and they have two sons, Manasseh and Ephraim, whose descendants eventually become two of the ISRAELITE tribes.

During the famine, Joseph's brothers come to Egypt to buy food. Joseph recognizes them, accuses them of spying, and holds Simon as a hostage while the rest of the brothers return to Canaan to retrieve their youngest brother, Benjamin. When the brothers return to Egypt with Benjamin, Joseph continues to test them, falsely accusing Benjamin of stealing, and insisting that Benjamin must remain his slave. JUDAH begs Joseph to free Benjamin and offers himself as a replacement. Touched by this act of sibling protection and love, Joseph reveals himself to his brothers and forgives them for selling him into SLAVERY. Jacob learns that Joseph is still alive, and he and all his family come to relocate in Egypt, enjoying renewed prosperity.

The Joseph narrative is a biblical template teaching the lesson of Providence, the need to overcome family strife, and the potential for repentance or TESHUVAH. Traditional commentators perceive Joseph's ruse as a test of his brothers to see if they have changed. Joseph understood that God had decreed his fate at the hands of his brothers, but he wanted them to demonstrate that they understood their past sins, and would not repeat their mistakes.

Joseph is often seen as the paradigm of a Jew who succeeds in the wider Gentile society, without forgetting his family or his God.

Further reading: Norman Gottwald, *The Hebrew Bible: A Socio-Literary Introduction* (Philadelphia: Fortress Press, 1985); Ross Shepard Kraemer, *When Aseneth Met Joseph: A Late Antique Tale of the Biblical Patriarch and His Egyptian Wife, Reconsidered* (New York: Oxford University Press, 1998); David L. Lieber, ed., *Etz Hayim: Torah and Commentary* (Philadelphia: Jewish Publication Society, 2000); *Tanakh: The Holy Scriptures* (Philadelphia and Jerusalem: Jewish Publication Society, 1985).

Josephus (37–100 C.E.) *Jewish historian*

Josephus was a writer whose works on Jewish history of his own and previous eras have been invaluable sources for historians ever since.

Born a Jew in JERUSALEM, Joseph ben Matthias served as an officer in the uprising against the Roman occupation of Judea that began in 66 C.E. He is said to have somehow survived a suicide pact when he and some fellow soldiers were trapped in a cave by the Roman army. He was taken prisoner by Vespasian, who eventually adopted Josephus into his family. At this point he took the name Flavius Josephus. Josephus went on to assist TITUS, Vespasian's son.

Josephus became best known as a writer on Jewish life under Roman rule and on Jewish history. He tried to foster in his Roman readers an understanding of the Jewish people through his writings, which were sympathetic to both peoples. He has sometimes been characterized as a traitor because of his ongoing work with the Romans and because of his efforts to convince Jews in Jerusalem to surrender to Rome. Ultimately, his efforts at reconciliation between the two groups failed, and he witnessed the destruction of the city, including the second TEMPLE.

Josephus's writings include *The Jewish Wars* (78 C.E.), the only detailed description of the Great Revolt by a witness, and thus an important historical source. The text was originally written in ARAMAIC, and then translated into Greek and a number of other ancient languages. Later in his life he authored *Against Apion* and the *Antiquities* (93 C.E.).

Some editions of Josephus's writings include references to Jesus, including passages that suggest he himself may have converted to CHRISTIANITY. However, the majority of scholars now believe these references and passages were inserted later by Christian editors.

Further reading: Louis H. Feldman, *Josephus's Interpretation of the Bible* (Berkeley: University of California Press, 1998); Steve Mason, ed., *Flavius Josephus, Translation and Commentary* (Leiden: Brill, 2000); William Whiston, trans., *The Works of Josephus: Complete and Unabridged* (Grand Rapids, Mich.: Kregel Publications, 1960).

JUBU

The term *JUBU* is a popular designation for someone who is, in some fashion, both Jewish and Buddhist.

This can cover a variety of possibilities. An individual may have a Jewish family background, convert to Buddhism, and no longer participate in Jewish PRAYER and practices. Other people may feel both Jewish and Buddhist, belong to both communities and perform rites from each tradition. Others are practicing Jews who study Buddhism and accept some of its teachings or practices, such as meditation, without considering themselves Buddhist.

JUBUs have become an interesting phenomenon because of their relatively large numbers. Although Jews constitute less than 3 percent of the American population, there are estimates that as many as 30 percent of American converts to Buddhism are from Jewish backgrounds. A similar proportion of America's Buddhist studies scholars and a large number of America's most widely renowned Buddhist meditation teachers come from Jewish backgrounds.

Scholars are currently studying this phenomenon, whose causes are unclear. The most widespread hypothesis is that Judaism as experienced by American Jews today sometimes lacks the component of inner spirituality that earlier generations may have obtained from the KABBALAH or HASIDISM, driving some Jews to seek that spirituality elsewhere. Another reason may be that many Jewish Americans by now lack a solid grounding in NORMATIVE JUDAISM.

Further reading: Sylvia Boorstein, *That's Funny, You Don't Look Buddhist* (New York: HarperCollins, 1997); Roger Kamenetz, *The Jew and the Lotus* (New York, HarperCollins, 1994); Alan Lew and Sherril Jaffe, *One God Clapping* (Woodstock, Vt.: Jewish Lights, 2001); Judith Linzer, *Torah and Dharma* (Northvale, N.J.: Jason Aronson, 1996).

Judah *biblical figure*

Judah was one of the 12 sons of Jacob or Israel, according to Genesis, the first book of the TANAKH or Hebrew Bible. After the EXODUS, when the 12 tribes descended from Israel's sons entered Canaan, the tribe of Judah occupied the region just west of the Dead Sea, which ultimately included JERUSALEM.

As the tribal regions were consolidated, King DAVID, a descendant of Judah, became king of the united country (and the MESSIAH, a descendant of David, will be from the tribe of Judah as well, in Jewish tradition). When the country divided into two kingdoms, "Judah" was the term used to refer to the southern kingdom, which included the ancestral lands of that tribe; it eventually became the name for the entire land, whose inhabitants came to be called Judeans. This term is the source for the word *JEW*, which was eventually applied to any descendant of the Israelites, or anyone who adopted their religion.

Further reading: Martin Gilbert, *The Atlas of Jewish History* (New York: William Morrow, 1993); Edward F. Campbell, Jr., "A Land Divided: Judah and Israel from the Death of Solomon to the Fall of Samaria," in *Oxford History of the Biblical World* (New York: Oxford University Press, 1998): 272–319; Mordechai Cogan, "Judah Under Assyrian Hegemony: A Reexamination of Imperialism and Religion" in *Journal of Biblical Literature* 112 (Fall 1993): 403–414.

Judah Ha-Nasi (c. 135–220) *rabbi and political leader who compiled the Mishnah*

Judah Ha-Nasi (the Prince), also known simply as "the rabbi," was the political and spiritual leader of the Jews of his era. He is best known for compiling the final version of the MISHNAH, the oral traditions developed by the *TANNAIM,* and committing it to writing.

According to rabbinic sources Judah succeeded his father, Rabbi Shimon ben Gamiel II, as the head of the SANHEDRIN, the rabbinic government authorized by ROME to direct the internal affairs of the Jewish people. He is said to have developed a friendship with the Roman emperor Marcus Aurelius, which he used to improve the lot of the Jewish people. Although that story may be exaggerated, it is probably true that under Judah's leadership the Jews were able to diminish the level of conflict with Rome a half century after the destruction of the second TEMPLE.

Judah was reportedly wealthy, learned, and pious. Under his overall supervision, he and the members of the Sanhedrin redacted the Mishnah, which became the foundation for both the Babylonian and Palestinian TALMUDS.

Many of Judah's teachings are recorded in the Mishnah; they may have been placed there by other writers after his death. By his political and spiritual leadership, Judah Ha-Nasi played a crucial role in ensuring the survival of Judaism and of the Jewish people.

Further reading: Moshe and David Aberbach, *The Roman-Jewish Wars and Hebrew Cultural Nationalism* (New York: St. Martin's Press, 2000); David Weiss Halivni, *Revelation Restored: Divine Writ and Critical Responses* (Boulder, Colo.: Westview Press, 1997).

Judea and Samaria (West Bank)

Judea and Samaria are two small regions located to the west of the Jordan River, respectively situated to the south and north of the city of JERUSALEM. The names date back to the TANAKH, the Hebrew Bible. The book of Joshua first mentions Judea as the ISRAELITES are conquering the land of CANAAN; the area was assigned to the tribe of Judah, which gave it its name. Since that time, the district of Judea has stretched from Jerusalem south along the Judean mountain ridge and east to the Dead Sea. The area called Samaria stretches to the north of Jerusalem; it is named after the city that was the capital of the northern kingdom of ISRAEL. Samaria was first mentioned in 1 Kings.

Until recent times, the areas of Judea and Samaria were called by those names. During the ISRAELI WAR OF INDEPENDENCE in 1948, the Emirate of Transjordan seized the area; it proclaimed the new Kingdom of Jordan, combining the old emirate on the east bank of the Jordan and the newly conquered areas on the west bank. The area then became known as the West Bank, a name it kept even after it was captured by Israel in the SIX-DAY WAR of 1967 and after Jordan relinquished any claims there. Many maps designate the area as the "occupied territories," a reference to their disputed ownership.

Large parts of Judea and Samaria were turned over to Palestinian Arab rule after the 1993 Oslo Peace Accord, but many large Israeli settlements remain. Many religious and nationalist Israelis do not want to relinquish the area, which they consider the geographic and spiritual heartland of the biblical Promised Land. Other Israelis want to retain some sections for defense purposes, such as GUSH ETZION, which was instrumental in saving the Jews of Jerusalem during the Israeli War of Independence. They note that the western edge of Samaria lies only nine miles from the Mediterranean coast, where more than half of Israel's population lives and where Israel maintains a large portion of its industrial and economic infrastructure.

Further reading: Mitchell G. Bard, *Myths and Facts: A Guide to the Arab-Israeli Conflict* (Chevy Chase, Md.: American-Israeli Cooperative Enterprise, 2001); Daniel J. Elazar, *Judea, Samaria, and Gaza: Views on the Present and the Future* (Washington, D.C.: American Enterprise Institute, 1982); Norman Gottwald, *The Hebrew Bible: A Socio-Literary Introduction* (Philadelphia: Fortress Press, 1985).

Judenrat

The Judenräte were Jewish councils appointed by the Nazis (*see* GERMANY) in the Jewish communities and GHETTOS of German-occupied POLAND. They were ostensibly responsible for managing the affairs of the community, but their main role was to implement Nazi directives. SS leader Reinhard Heydrich (1904–42) signed a directive on September 21, 1939, establishing a Judenrat in every concentration of Jews in Nazi-occupied areas of Poland. The Nazis often chose well-known Jewish communal leaders to staff the councils.

The Judenräte experienced enormous internal stress, following Nazi orders (on pain of death or retaliation against civilians), while trying to protect and aid their communities. Some Judenrat members tried to resist the Nazis as much as possible. Others attempted to use their status to protect themselves and their families. Judenrat leaders often had to choose which Jews to save and which Jews to hand over to the Nazis, for almost certain death. Many leaders of the Judenräte tried to save the young and strong in the hope that they would survive World War II.

Today many Jews perceive the Judenräte as mistaken in their willingness to cooperate. While previous Jewish history had taught Jews to cooperate with the enemy in order to live for another day, the Nazis were determined to exterminate every Jew, and cooperation by the Judenräte may have done more harm than good. The subject has consumed many harrowing books of fiction and nonfiction.

Further reading: Yehuda Bauer, *A History of the Holocaust* (Danbury, Conn.: Franklin Watts, 1982); Lucy S. Dawidowicz, *The War Against the Jews: 1933–1945* (New York: Doubleday, 1991); Calel Perechodnik, *Am I a Murderer? Testament of a Jewish Ghetto Policeman* (Boulder, Colo.: Westview Press, 1996); Isaiah Trunk, *Judenrat: The Jewish Councils in Eastern Europe Under Nazi Occupation* (Lincoln: University of Nebraska, 1996).

justice

The term *justice* appears in a variety of contexts in Judaism. Most fundamentally, God's character includes perfect justice and as such he demands justice from his people. God's own justice is tempered by MERCY, and the ethical foundation of Judaism involves the tension between these two fundamental attributes of God.

One of the best-known prophetic passages, Amos 5:24, cries out, "Let justice roll down like waters, and righteousness like an ever-flowing stream." The prophets (*see* NEVI'IM) repeatedly chastise the people for setting justice aside in their commercial dealings and in their dealings with the poor. The importance of justice to the Jewish people is highlighted in the fifth book of the TANAKH, the Hebrew Bible. Deutoronomy 16:20 commands Jews: "Justice, justice shall you pursue," emphasizing that people should chase after justice, not merely follow it.

Justice is also one of the 10 SEFIROT, the emanations of God described in mystical literature. It is associated with the fifth *sefirah, gevurah* or *din,* which expresses God's stern judgment and punishment of sin.

Further reading: Ferdinand M. Isserman, *This Is Judaism* New York: (Willett, Clark & Company, 1944); Bruce M. Metzger and Roland E. Murphy, eds., *The Oxford Annotated Bible with the Apocrypha* (New York: Oxford University Press, 1994).

K

Kabbalah

Kabbalah is the mystical tradition within NORMA-TIVE JUDAISM. It relies on the sacred Jewish scriptures, like all of Judaism, but it uses an interpretive approach that treats the TORAH more as a symbolic text than as a historical narrative or a legal treatise.

Mystical thought can be traced back to the TANAKH, the Hebrew Bible. Ezekiel's discussion of the divine chariot and God's throne, for example, provided a rich source of mystical insights for many generations. Mystical thought and speculation developed alongside mainstream Judaism throughout the rabbinic period. Several of the RABBIS whose legal rulings are considered the most authoritative were devout mystics as well.

In fact, a common opinion was that Kabbalah should be practiced by only the most stable, learned scholars. A famous story from the TALMUD warns of the danger of engaging in mystical study. It claims that AKIVA, Ben Zoma, ELISHA BEN ABUYAH, and Assai all engaged in mysticism; Assai went mad, Ben Zoma died, Elisha ben Abuya became a heretic, and only Akiva "left in peace."

The most famous text of the Kabbalah is the ZOHAR, a 13th-century text probably written by MOSES DE LEÓN, but attributed by him to the ancient sage Shimon bar Yochai. The *Zohar* became the foundational text for Isaac LURIA in the 16th century, probably the best known and most influential mystic in the modern period.

Kabbalistic theology and cosmology were also influenced by neo-Platonic ideas developed late in antiquity and passed along by Christian medieval theologians. Basic elements of Kabbalistic theology include the characterization of God as the *Eyn Sof,* "without limit," and the elaboration on the *SEFIROT,* the 10 emanations from God that are objects of meditation for the mystics. Because of the complexity and spiritual danger involved, the medieval rabbis taught that only married men over 40 should engage in mystical study; only they might have the necessary spiritual and personal maturity.

The study of Kabbalah, as developed by Luria, is at the heart and soul of the Hasidic movement (*see* HASIDISM) that spread through eastern Europe starting in the 18th century. Hasidim tried to "reunite the sparks" that remained in the world after the Jews (and God's *Shekhina* or Presence) went into EXILE, to repair the world and bring redemption. Largely destroyed during the HOLO-CAUST, HASIDISM has undergone a major revival, especially in North America and ISRAEL. The largest Hasidic group is the Lubavitcher movement, based in Brooklyn, New York, with centers around the world.

Since the 1990s, the study of Kabbalah has also attained a new level of popularity among non-Jews and formerly secular Jews, due to several high-profile celebrities whose interest in the field became known. Hasidic leaders and other serious Kabbalistic scholars and practitioners continue their ancient practice of discouraging what they regard as the superficial and unorthodox study of mystical texts and practices.

Further reading: Daniel C. Matt, *The Essential Kabbalah: The Heart of Jewish Mysticism* (Edison, N.J.; Castle Books, 1997); Gershom Scholem, *Major Trends in Jewish Mysticism* (New York: Schocken Books, 1946); ———, *On the Kabbalah and Its Symbolism* (New York: Schocken Books, 1965).

Kabbalat Shabbat

The Kabbalat Shabbat ("Welcoming the Sabbath") ritual is a group of introductory PRAYERS that are added to the regular evening worship service on Friday night, as Shabbat arrives. Kabbalat Shabbat can also be translated as "Receiving the Sabbath." A common rabbinical teaching is that one can welcome without truly embracing, but with the Sabbath a Jew must do both.

The TALMUD records that the ancient RABBIS would make special preparations for the Sabbath, whether by preparing a special dish or wearing a specific robe. Prayers were created that detailed the arrival of the Shekhinah, God's Divine Presence. The Shekhinah is viewed as the feminine aspect of God, and during Kabbalat Shabbat God is seen as the Sabbath Bride. Eventually a set of prayers became the accepted ritual.

Because the welcoming of Shabbat with love is a commandment, or MITZVAH, for all Jews, there was a need to find a common religious expression for Kabbalat Shabbat. In the 16th century, the Jewish mystics of SAFED, an ancient and modern city in ISRAEL, developed a liturgy for Kabbalat Shabbat

that has become fixed and can be found in all traditional Jewish prayer books.

Around the year 1535, Solomon ben Moses HaLevi Alkabetz wrote the prayer L'KHA DODI, Come My Beloved. It became the climactic prayer of the ritual; it is sung after reciting Psalms 95 through 99 and Psalm 29—one psalm for each day of CREATION, and L'kha Dodi to honor the seventh day, when God rested. In addition to prayers, Alkabetz may have created the practice of visiting fields at sunset on Friday, just before the beginning of Shabbat; the intention of this custom was to welcome Shabbat by escorting the Sabbath Bride into the SYNAGOGUE.

Today, Jews turn toward the entrance of the synagogue and bow to remember the Safed mystics who actually went into the fields to welcome Shabbat. This physical act accompanies the last verse of L'kha Dodi: "Come in peace, crown of her husband, both in joy and gladness, among the faithful of a treasured nation, come, Bride, come, Bride."

Further reading: Ismar Elbogen and Raymond P. Scheindlin, *Jewish Liturgy: A Comprehensive History* (Philadelphia: Jewish Publication Society of America, 1993); Reuven Hammer, *Entering Jewish Prayer: A Guide to Personal Devotion and the Worship Service* (New York: Schocken Books, 1995).

Kaddish

The Kaddish, an ARAMAIC prayer praising God, is one of the most familiar features of every Jewish worship service. It is recited at the conclusion of every section of the liturgy.

There are five forms of the Kaddish. The Full Kaddish, or Kaddish Shalem, is recited at the end of the afternoon and evening recitations of the AMIDAH. The Half Kaddish is recited to mark lesser divisions of the service. The Rabbi's Kaddish, or Kaddish d'Rabbanan is recited after the study of any selection from the TANAKH, the Hebrew Bible, or TALMUD. The Mourner's Kaddish is recited toward the end of worship services by those in mourning or observing the YAHRZEIT, the anniversary of a loved one's death. The Burial Kaddish, or Great Kaddish, is recited by mourners at graveside during a funeral, and also at a celebration for completing a defined amount of religious study.

The prayer can be recited only in the presence of a MINYAN, a quorum of 10 Jews, and it is usually recited while standing. All forms of the Kaddish praise God and articulate the hope that God's presence will be established more strongly on earth. There is little in its text connecting it to mourning, but most Jews recognize the Kaddish primarily as the mourner's prayer.

The Kaddish was written in the first century C.E., when Aramaic was the everyday language of most Jews. It was developed for the Bet Midrash or House of Study (*see* SYNAGOGUE). After the Rabbi had taught his lesson, all would rise and praise God's name. The custom was first extended to rising and reciting Kaddish in memory of a rabbi, and soon this custom was again extended to rising for Kaddish to remember all loved ones. By the sixth century, Kaddish had become part of the fixed liturgy in synagogues.

The Talmud records many legends about the Kaddish and its value to the Jewish community. A well-known MIDRASH describes how Rabbi AKIVA BEN YOSEF (50 C.E.–132 C.E.) once discovered a departed man's spirit suffering in spiritual limbo. Akiva sought out the man's son and taught him to recite the words of Kaddish. These words, recited by the son, freed the father's spirit from torment and brought him eternal peace. A common Jewish tradition is that the recitation of Kaddish will shorten the period of God's judgment for a loved one's soul, sending the soul out of spiritual limbo and into eternal rest and peace. Jews in mourning for a mother, father, sibling, or child are required to say Kaddish every day for 11 months, although many modern Jews do not hold to this practice.

Further reading: Ismar Elbogen and Raymond P. Scheindlin, *Jewish Liturgy: A Comprehensive History* (Philadelphia: Jewish Publication Society of America, 1993); Reuven Hammer, *Entering Jewish Prayer: A Guide to Personal Devotion and the Worship Service* (New York: Schocken Books, 1995); Leon Wieseltier, *Kaddish* (New York: Vintage Books USA, 2000).

kahal, kehillah

Prior to modern times, Jews often lived in semi-autonomous communities within the wider host society. The organized Jewish community in the Western world during the medieval and early modern periods was called the *kahal* (eastern Europe) or the *kehillah* (central/western Europe). The leaders of these communities were responsible for collecting taxes for the government, but they also managed the community's religious, educational, charitable, and welfare services. They enforced Jewish law, or HALAKHAH, together with the rabbis, which helped bind the community together. They sometimes controlled their own municipalities and police forces.

The responsibilities of the *kahal* or *kehillah* were defined by biblical and Talmudic obligations as well as by the laws of the host society. As EMANCIPATION of the Jews trickled through Europe, many *kehillot* were abolished, though similar organizations still persist today in several central European countries, collecting taxes from Jews and maintaining religious and charitable institutions.

In 1908 New York's Jews attempted to set up a *kehillah* adapted to democracy and the new world that would serve to unify the American Jewish community, provide Jewish educational opportunities, fight crime, and supervise kosher food, or KASHRUT. Unable to succeed in the diverse American setting, the *kehillah* ceased operating in 1925, although some of the businesses and services it set up continued to serve the community independently. The model of the Jewish federation systems (*see* UNITED JEWISH COMMUNITIES) is loosely based on the idea of the *kahal* or *kehillah*.

Further reading: Israel Cohen, *Vilna* (Philadelphia: Jewish Publication Society, 1992); Arthur A. Goren, *New York Jews and the Quest for Community: The*

Kehillah Experiment, 1908–1922 (New York: Columbia University Press, 1979); Harry L. Lurie, *A Heritage Affirmed: The Jewish Federation Movement in America* (Philadelphia: Jewish Publication Society, 1961); Abraham A. Neuman, *The Jews in Spain: Their Social, Political and Cultural Life during the Middle Ages,* vol. 1 (Philadelphia; Jewish Publication Society, 1942).

Kahane, Meir (1932–1990) *rabbi and Israeli political figure*

Meir Kahane was an ordained rabbi whose militant political activity in New York and ISRAEL was extremely controversial within the Jewish world.

Kahane was born in Brooklyn, New York, on August 1, 1932. Perhaps because he was son of a Revisionist Zionist who had ties to Zionist leader Ze'ev JABOTINSKY, Kahane became active in Betar, a ZIONIST YOUTH MOVEMENT. Thus, he began his career as a right-wing Zionist leader as a child.

Kahane studied international law at New York University, and received rabbinical ordination from the prestigious Mir Yeshiva. He become editor of the *Jewish Press,* a weekly newspaper in New York. Kahane accepted a position as a pulpit rabbi and teacher, but in 1968, he founded the Jewish Defense League (JDL) in reaction to growing crime and a perceived ANTISEMITISM in the urban neighborhoods where many Jews lived. The symbol of the JDL was a STAR OF DAVID with a clenched fist, and the group came to be characterized by its slogan "Never again," and its efforts to link the image of the Jew to militant strength. Such an image reflected, Kahane's Revisionist outlook; he was determined to change the image of the Jew from that of weakness to one of strength. He used controversial methods in confronting the threat or existence of violence against the Jews. The JDL often found itself in confrontations with the African-American community (*see* BLACK-JEWISH RELATIONS), creating additional tensions between the two cultural groups who shared the same urban neighborhoods.

The JDL also focused on the plight of Jews who were suffering in the former Soviet Union (*see* RUS-SIA). The group was able to raise public awareness with effective slogans like "Never again," a reference to the HOLOCAUST, and Kahane's desire to protect Jews in danger won much sympathy in the Jewish community, but the majority of Jews, including other Jewish rights groups, believed he went too far and that his illegal tactics threatened violence. Kahane was convicted of possessing weapons without a license, planning to bomb the offices of Soviet organizations and the PALESTINE LIBERATION ORGANIZATION, and disturbing the peace, among other accusations.

After standing trial in the UNITED STATES and receiving a suspended prison sentence and a fine, Kahane and his family moved to Israel in 1971. He then founded the political party Kach, which advocated the complete annexation of all territories captured during the 1967 SIX-DAY WAR and the expulsion of all Arabs from Israel and the territories. Kahane preached a message of violence, and the more liberal Jewish leadership saw his attitude as reflecting a Jewish version of Hitler-like racism. The State of Israel charged him with sedition, but he was not convicted. He failed to win election to the KNESSET in 1976 and 1980, but he won a seat in 1984. Kahane's Kach party was growing in popularity when the Israeli government outlawed it in 1988, on the basis of a new law excluding any political party that incited racism. Two years later, Kahane was assassinated in New York City by an Egyptian militant. Although Kahane's assassin was acquitted on a technicality, he was later convicted of another crime related to the first World Trade Center bombing.

Kahane's views continue to influence the small extreme-right-wing political circles in Israel. In 1994 Israel and the United States declared the Kach party, and the new Kach Chai party created by Kahane's son Binyamin, to be terrorist groups. Several members had been responsible for attacks against Arabs and Jews who support the peace process.

Further reading: Raphael Cohen-Almagor, *The Boundaries of Liberty and Tolerance: The Struggle Against*

Kahanism in Israel (Gainesville, Fla.: University Press of Florida, 1994); Robert Friedman, *The False Prophet: Rabbi Meir Kahane: From FBI Informant to Knesset Member* (Chicago: Independent Publishers Group, 1990); Philippe Simonnot and Raphael Mergui, *Israel's Ayatollahs: Meir Kahane and the Far Right in Israel* (London and Atlantic Highlands, N.J.: Saqi Books, 1987).

Kaplan, Mordecai Menahem (1881–1983)
founder of Reconstructionism

Mordecai Menahem Kaplan was born in 1881 in the town of Svencionys, Lithuania. When he was eight years old his family immigrated to the UNITED STATES. Building upon his eastern European traditional Jewish education, Kaplan received further Jewish education at a SUPPLEMENTARY SCHOOL while attending public school. At Columbia University, he studied the Bible and religion using modern critical methods.

In 1902 Kaplan was ordained a rabbi after completing his studies at the JEWISH THEOLOGICAL SEMINARY (JTS). He served in a pulpit for seven years, and then in 1909 joined the faculty of JTS as dean of its Teachers Institute. He soon became a professor of HOMILETICS, MIDRASH, and PHILOSOPHY.

Kaplan was a significant presence on the JTS faculty for more than 50 years. A kind individual and a great scholar, he attracted many dedicated student followers. He was also an active leader in many Jewish communal efforts.

In 1917 Kaplan took on the additional job of a SYNAGOGUE rabbi. He wanted to try out his idea of using a Jewish community center approach to religion, Jewish culture, and everyday life, in an attempt to create what is now known as a synagogue-center. The synagogue-center was to provide both worship opportunities and programs for cultural activities such as sports, drama, and dance. Opposition from one segment of his congregation drove him from the pulpit, so in 1922 Kaplan and his supporters created the Society for the Advancement of Judaism. It became one of the preeminent congregations in New York and a national role model for other congregations over the decades.

Kaplan is credited with being the father of RECONSTRUCTIONIST JUDAISM. In 1934 his book, *Judaism as a Civilization,* called for a "reconstruction" of Jewish life, outlining his perspective of Judaism as a civilization, not only a religion. He and his followers created the journal *The Reconstructionist,* which became a major intellectual influence within liberal Judaism in the United States. Kaplan's Jewish Reconstructionist Foundation wrote new prayer books and created a Reconstructionist College in Philadelphia in 1968 to train rabbis and leaders for Reconstructionist congregations.

Kaplan's intention had not been to create a fourth American Jewish "denomination." He preached that Judaism was an eternally evolving religious civilization, but he cherished the tradition as well. He wanted to encourage adherents of CONSERVATIVE JUDAISM to critically study the TANAKH, the Hebrew Bible, and other sacred texts, such as the TALMUD, remain committed to ISRAEL, and observe Jewish law, or *HALAKHAH.* Like other Conservative Jews, he believed that Jewish law had to respond to the community's changing needs. His emphasis was on the community, on giving its members a voice in how they observed their Judaism.

Kaplan's emphasis on the community's role was completely at odds with ORTHODOX JUDAISM and its emphasis on the role of the rabbi. He was often ridiculed by Orthodox rabbis even though he was scrupulously observant of Jewish law in his own personal life. Kaplan's views on God were especially controversial. He believed that God was not a supernatural being, but rather a "transnatural" figure. Kaplan believed that God was the power that emerged from the actions of individuals on behalf of JUSTICE and MERCY. It was a force that transformed and transcended the individual elements to make the greater whole.

Kaplan's theology was seen as antitraditional, and rejected as heresy by Orthodox and many Conservative Jews. He rejected the notion that the Jews had been designated by a supernatural God as the CHOSEN PEOPLE. Instead, he believed that the Jews were a people who had chosen the idea of God, as manifested in their universal morality and particularistic rituals.

The Reconstructionist movement has remained quite small, but many Conservative rabbis and laypeople have come to accept many of Kaplan's ideas about God, community, and the way Jewish law should be determined.

Further reading: Neil Gillman, *Conservative Judaism: The New Century* (West Orange, N.J.: Behrman House Publishing, 1993); Neil Gillman, *Sacred Fragments: Recovering Theology for the Modern Jew* (Philadelphia: Jewish Publication Society, 1992); Jeffrey Gurock and Jacob J. Schacter, *A Modern Heretic and a Traditional Community: Mordecai M. Kaplan, Orthodoxy, and American Judaism* (New York: Columbia University Press, 1997); Mordecai M. Kaplan, *Judaism as a Civilization: Toward a Reconstruction of American Jewish Life* (Philadelphia: Jewish Publication Society, 1994).

kapparah

Kapparah is a ritual ceremony of atonement performed by many Jews on the day before YOM KIPPUR, the Day of Atonement.

The *kapparah* ceremony consists of waving a rooster (if one is male) or a hen (if one is female) over a person's head three times while reciting certain verses from Psalms, or TEHILLIM, and JOB. The person making atonement has the fowl slaughtered as a kind of sin offering or SACRIFICE, and given to the poor. Alternatively, the person can offer money to the poor in place of the fowl. The practice survives today only in ultra-Orthodox circles (see ORTHODOX JUDAISM), though many other Jews recall the ritual by giving charity to the poor just before Yom Kippur.

The word *kapparah* comes from the same root as Yom Kippur, and is the most common term in Jewish literature for the concept of atonement (see SIN AND REPENTENCE; *TESHUVAH*). The root meaning is to clean, scour, or erase, suggesting that atonement involves the complete cleansing or nullification of sin. The term has come to have a colloquial sense,

It is customary in many ultra-Orthodox Ashkenazic communities to swing a chicken around one's head as an act of atonement during the season of Yom Kippur, the Day of Atonement. Ultra-Orthodox children look on as a man from their community begins the ritual, which ends with the chicken going to feed the poor, either in kind or as a monetary contribution. *(Avi Ohayon, Government Press Office, The State of Israel)*

as when someone loses money and declares, "Let it be a *kapparah* for my sins." Rabbis and thinkers over the centuries have disagreed about the validity of the ceremony. While some—mainly SEPHARDIM—have claimed it to be a pagan practice that should be abolished, others—mainly ASHKENAZIM—have recognized it as a valid form of atonement.

Further reading: Philip Goodman, *The Yom Kippur Anthology* (Philadelphia and Jerusalem: Jewish Publication Society, 1992); Irving Greenberg, *The Jewish Way: Living the Holidays* (New York: Summit Books, 1988); Jacob Zallel Lauterbach, *Studies in Jewish Law, Custom, and Folklore* (New York: Ktav Publishing House, 1970).

Karaites

A sect that split from the Jewish community in the eighth century of the Common Era, the Karaites rejected the ORAL LAW and insisted on a literal interpretation of TORAH. For example, the Karaites observed SHAVUOT on a different day from mainstream Judaism, and they did not observe CHANUKAH at all because it was not prescribed in the Torah.

The Karaites emerged, according to a well-known medieval legend, due to a political dispute. The position of EXILARCH, political leader of the DIASPORA Jewish community, became open, and the community gave the post to Hananiah, the younger son of the former exilarch. When the elder son, Anan, rebelled in reaction, he was jailed and sentenced to death. Anan managed to convince the Muslim ruler that he was not, in fact, a rebel, but rather the leader of a new religious community. The Karaites reject this story, claiming instead that they are the only community that remains faithful to the original interpretation of the Torah.

In 19th-century RUSSIA, the Karaites were classified as a different religion, and so were spared the persecution inflicted on other Jews. Similarly, thousands of Karaites were spared from the HOLOCAUST when Jewish scholars agreed that they were not really Jews. Small communities of Karaites continue to exist to this day, including several in ISRAEL, Lithuania, CANADA, and the UNITED STATES. In Israel, they are ruled by their own independent rabbinic court system.

Further reading: "Karaite Korner Web site URL: http://www.karaite-korner.org/, accessed August 5, 2004. Jacob Mann, *Texts and Studies in Jewish History and Literature* (New York: Ktav Publishing House, 1972); Leon Nemoy, *Karaite Anthology* (New Haven: Yale University Press, 1952).

kashrut

Traditional Judaism contains a complex system of dietary laws that instruct Jews as to what foods they may eat, in what combinations, and at what times. These dietary laws are referred to as the laws of kashrut, or kosher, food.

The word *kosher* means ritually "fit." Food that is not kosher is called *treif,* which literally means "torn." This refers to the commandment, or MITZVAH, given to NOAH, and subsequently to all humankind, to avoid eating animals that have been killed (torn apart) by other animals.

The primary purpose of observing kashrut is to follow God's will, as stated in the TORAH and as interpreted by the RABBIS. Some Jews maintain that kashrut is at base a code of health and food safety; while there are in fact certain health advantages to kosher food and kosher butchering techniques, most rabbis insist that this is merely a tangential benefit. They maintain that the Torah specifies certain foods as permissible and others as forbidden, without any rationale apart from the fact that "God says so." This type of commandment falls under the category of *chukkim,* laws for which there is no obvious or rational reason. Religious or observant individuals show their fidelity to God by observing even the laws that have no inherent logic.

Nevertheless, the rabbis also preach that the ritual of regulating one's diet sensitizes religious individuals and helps lift them above their mere animal instincts. Whereas an animal will eat anything when hungry, religious Jews will restrain themselves, even when hungry, to eat only that which is permitted. The table then becomes an altar; just as food had to be ritually pure to be offered to God as a SACRIFICE in the TEMPLE, so should the altar in one's home be kept ritually pure.

Many modern rabbis have argued that the two most important commandments a modern Jew can observe today are kashrut and observing SHABBAT, the Sabbath. On Shabbat, one day a week is separated for holy purposes, and on weekdays, every meal and snack is consecrated through the ritual of kashrut.

The laws of kashrut are very broad, but there are basic categorical rules. Certain animals may not be eaten at all—their flesh, organs, eggs, or milk are forbidden. Forbidden land animals include any that do not possess a split hoof or do not chew their cud. Fish or seafood must have fins and scales to be kosher. Many bird species are excluded, mainly birds of prey.

As a result of these rules, all pork products are forbidden, as well as shellfish and any scavenger animal. Of the animals that may be eaten, birds and mammals must be alive and healthy before being butchered, and then must be killed in accordance with Jewish law, or *HALAKHAH*. The slaughterer, called a *shochet,* must pray before and after killing the animal; the animal is slaughtered with one quick slice across the trachea to avoid pain.

All blood, considered to contain the animal's spirit, must be drained from the meat or cooked out of it before it is eaten. Certain parts of even permitted animals may not be eaten. Best-known is the cut on the hindquarters that contains the sciatic nerve. This is not eaten as a reminder of the PATRIARCH Jacob's struggle with God, when he was crippled in that area of his leg. This forbidden section of beef is considered by gourmets to be the choice part and includes the filet mignon.

Meat, defined as the flesh of birds and mammals, cannot be eaten together with dairy foods. On three separate occasions, the Torah tells us not to "boil a kid in its mother's milk" (Ex 23:19 and 34:26; Dt 14:21). The rabbis interpreted these verses as prohibitions against eating meat and dairy together, and they later extended the prohibition to fowl. Fish, eggs, fruits, vegetables and grains are considered neutral, and can be eaten with either meat or dairy.

Utensils that are used for meat may not be used with dairy and vice versa, for fear that traces of the food may have adhered. Utensils that have come into contact with nonkosher food may not be used with kosher food, if the contact occurred while the food was hot or involved a spicy food.

Wine or other grape products made by non-Jews may not be consumed. The grape was the primary product of PALESTINE, and this was a form of economic protectionism. Also, it was a religious protection against potentially using wine that idolaters may have made with the intention of pouring libations to pagan gods.

An entire culture exists around the laws of kashrut. Many American Jews use YIDDISH terminology to describe the separation of milk and meat. They call meat "fleishig," dairy "milchig," and a food that is neither milk nor meat "pareve." Observant Jews keep separate sets of dishes, utensils, and pots and pans for meat and for milk. During the holiday of PASSOVER there are additional proscriptions against eating grains, and many observant families have two more sets of dishes, utensils, and pots to use for milk and meat during Passover.

Many prepared foods and products now carry a symbol, called a *hechsher,* which marks that food as kosher. The agency that grants the *hechsher* thus certifies that the product contains no nonkosher ingredient. The most widely known *hechsher* is the "OU," which appears as a circle with a U in it. Others include "half moon K," "circle K," and "star K." None of these agencies uses a simple K by itself, which cannot be copyrighted under UNITED STATES law; some manufacturers use a K as their own self-certification of kashrut, but most Orthodox Jews do not consider that adequate.

When a manufacturer or restaurant requests kosher certification, one of these agencies will send an expert known as a *MASHGIACH,* who is familiar with all the kosher laws and is also knowledgeable in the mechanics and chemistry of food production. The expert checks all the ingredients and observes the entire production process; reputable agencies will check periodically to ensure that nothing has changed.

Even foods that seem impossible to make nonkosher, such as orange juice, must have a certification, since there may be additives not listed on the label, or since nonkosher products, like grape juice, may be made on the same equipment.

In the contemporary world, the majority of Jews either do not keep the laws of kashrut or observe them only in part. REFORM JUDAISM does not consider them binding; the issue was a major bone of contention with CONSERVATIVE JUDAISM during the early years of the two movements.

It is not unusual for families to maintain a kosher home but eat nonkosher food outside the home. Some Jews choose only to refrain from pork and shellfish, but eat nonkosher beef and chicken. An observant Jew believes that one must keep kosher inside their home and outside to maintain the correct practice of *halakhah.*

Further reading: Esther Blau, Tzirrel Deitsch, and Cherna Light, *Spice and Spirit: The Complete Kosher Jewish Cookbook* (Brooklyn, N.Y.: Lubavitch Women's Cookbook Publications, 1990); Hayim Halevy Donin, *To Be a Jew: A Guide to Jewish Observance in Contemporary Life* (New York: Basic Books, 1972); Lise Stern, *How to Keep Kosher: A Comprehensive Guide to Understanding Jewish Dietary Laws* (New York: Morrow, 2004); *Tanakh: The Holy Scriptures* (Philadelphia and Jerusalem: Jewish Publication Society, 1985).

kavanah

Both the TANAKH, the Hebrew Bible, and the TALMUD explain that prayers and rituals should be performed with sincere devotion and conscious intent. This type of devotion is called *kavanah,* the Hebrew word for "direction."

The rabbis over the centuries warned that if Jews performed God's commandments, or mitzvot (*see* MITZVAH), without *kavanah,* as mere routine or habit, they might lose their effectiveness and might not be accepted by God. Individuals who did not cultivate *kavanah* in prayer and action were also more likely to stop observing these commandments.

The Talmud records a debate on the subject. There was a rabbinic consensus that the ideal was to possess *kavanah* in one's sacred actions, but disagreements remained as to whether a commandment counted with God if performed without intention. The debate continued in the medieval period. The 11th-century rabbi Bachya Ibn Paku-

dah taught that prayer without *kavanah* was like a body without a soul.

While *kavanah* is a term applicable to all God's commandments, the issue comes up most often in connection with prayers. Since PRAYER is a form of self-examination in the Jewish tradition, lack of intention may reduce, if not eliminate, its effectiveness. In Jewish tradition all prayers are recited in HEBREW, but because of the need for *kavanah,* Jews are obligated to study the prayers in their vernacular if their Hebrew is inadequate, so as to understand what they are reciting. In addition, Jewish liturgy was developed with an eye to focusing the worshippers on the actions they were taking or were going to take.

Further reading: Hayim Halevy Donin, *To Pray as a Jew: A Guide to the Prayer Book and the Synagogue Service* (New York: Basic Books, 1980); Ismar Elbogen and Raymond P. Scheindlin, *Jewish Liturgy: A Comprehensive History* (Philadelphia: Jewish Publication Society of America, 1993); Reuven Hammer, *Entering Jewish Prayer: A Guide to Personal Devotion and the Worship Service* (New York: Schocken Books, 1995).

kedushah

Kedushah is the HEBREW word for "holiness." Its root means "separate," and one makes something holy by separating it from the ordinary. Once separated from the mundane, an object may be used for a sacred purpose, or a person may participate in a sacred act.

Kedushah is a key concept in Judaism. It is emphasized in this teaching from Leviticus (19): "You shall be holy, for I, the Lord your God, am holy."

According to traditional Judaism, Jews are to achieve the state of *kedushah* by observing all of God's ritual and ethical commandments. Holiness is required of all of the Jewish people, and the holiness of ERETZ YISRAEL must be protected too. This is why Jews are referred to as the Holy People and ISRAEL as the Holy Land.

Because holiness is a prerequisite to be close to God, the RABBIS created a liturgical text to be recited during the prayer leader's twice-daily repetition of the AMIDAH prayer, to remind worshippers of the need to attain holiness in their lives. This text is called the Kedushah, and it is the third blessing of the opening section of the Amidah.

During the silent, individual reading of the Amidah, the worshipper simply acknowledges God's holiness. During the repetition, if there are 10 Jews present for a MINYAN, the congregation rises and recites, and the reader repeats, a series of prayers and biblical quotations that articulate the holiness and sacred nature of God. Highlighted is the prophet ISAIAH's vision of God surrounded by the angels declaring: "Holy, holy, holy is the Lord of Hosts, the whole world is filled with His glory." With each repetition of the word *holy*, the worshippers raise themselves on their toes, as if trying to get closer to the heavens. During the *Kedushah*, one is to stand upright with feet together, not engage in conversation, and not interrupt the prayer. On SHABBAT, the Sabbath, and holidays, many CANTORS sing the *Kedushah* to elaborate and moving melodies.

Further reading: Hayim Halevy Donin, *To Pray as a Jew: A Guide to the Prayer Book and the Synagogue Service* (New York: Basic Books, 1980); Ismar Elbogen and Raymond P. Scheindlin, *Jewish Liturgy: A Comprehensive History* (Philadelphia: Jewish Publication Society of America, 1993); Reuven Hammer, *Entering Jewish Prayer: A Guide to Personal Devotion and the Worship Service* (New York: Schocken Books, 1995).

kehillah See KAHAL.

ketubah (pl.: *ketubot*)
The *ketubah* is the Jewish wedding contract. It is the most ancient document still utilized by Jews, dating back several thousand years. No traditional Jewish MARRIAGE can occur without the signing of the *ketubah*.

The *ketubah* traditionally recorded the groom's financial obligations toward his bride. It is written in ARAMAIC, the vernacular of Jews in ancient times, and follows a precise legal formula as prescribed by the TALMUD. Over the centuries *ketubot* began to be treated as works of art. Many were written on fine parchment, with illuminated borders, beautiful calligraphy, and intricate designs throughout the document.

Today, the *ketubah* is purely symbolic for most people in terms of financial arrangements, but it is still signed with great solemnity prior to the wedding ceremony and read at the wedding canopy. If the bride has not been married before she is referred to as a *betulah* (maid, or virgin); if she has been married, she is referred to by the Aramaic word for woman.

Liberal Jews often find the ancient language of the *ketubah* to be offensive to their EGALITARIANISM, and many liberal rabbis will permit appropriate changes in the ancient legal formulas. More traditional rabbis will insist on the ancient language in the Aramaic original, but permit English interpretive translations to be included within the *ketubah*.

Further reading: Anita Diamant, *The New Jewish Wedding* (New York: Fireside, 2001); Lilly S. Routtenberg, *Jewish Wedding Book: A Practical Guide to the Tradition* (New York: Schocken Books, 1968); Shalom Sabar, *Ketubbah: The Art of the Jewish Marriage Contract* (New York: Rizzoli International Publications, 2001).

Ketuvim (Writings)
The Hebrew term *Tanakh* is an acronym standing for the three parts of the Jewish Bible: TORAH, NEVI'IM, and Ketuvim—Pentateuch, Prophets, and Writings.

Ketuvim consists of historical books, poetry, aphorisms, wisdom writing, apocalyptic writings, and liturgical scrolls, thus making this section of the Tanakh quite varied. It includes the following books: PSALMS, Proverbs, JOB, the Song of Songs, RUTH, LAMENTATIONS, Ecclesiastes, ESTHER, Daniel,

EZRA, NEHEMIAH, 1 Chronicles, and 2 Chronicles. Many of the themes included in the books in Ketuvim refer back to events and ideas found in the other two sections.

Of these volumes, scholars categorize 1 and 2 Chronicles, Ezra, and Nehemiah as late historical works; Psalms, Lamentations, and Song of Songs as poetry; and Ruth, Jonah, and Esther as short stories. Ketuvim also includes wisdom writings, which teach the reader how to deal with the expected and unexpected in life. Proverbs, Job, and Ecclesiastes fall into this category. Finally, Ketuvim includes one book of apocalyptic writings, about the end times. The Book of Daniel is the only real representative of apocalyptic literature in the Hebrew Bible, although some other books do contain apocalyptic passages.

According to Jewish tradition, King DAVID wrote the Psalms, and his son King SOLOMON wrote the Song of Songs, Proverbs, and Ecclesiastes. Meanwhile, five of these books are read liturgically: The Song of Songs on PASSOVER, Ruth on SHAVUOT, Lamentations on TISHA B'AV, Ecclesiastes on SUKKOT, and Esther on PURIM. These five books are called Megillot, or scrolls (see MEGILLAH).

Further reading: Frank S. Frick, *A Journey through the Hebrew Scriptures* (Fort Worth: Harcourt Brace College Publishers, 1995); Norman K. Gottwald, *The Hebrew Bible: A Socio-Literary Introduction* (Philadelphia: Fortress Press, 1985); *Tanakh: The Holy Scriptures* (Philadelphia and Jerusalem: Jewish Publication Society, 1985).

kibbutz (pl.: kibbutzim)

The kibbutz is a type of communal settlement created in PALESTINE before ISRAEL became an independent state. The founders of the early kibbutzim were dedicated to socialist principles. They aimed to meet all their members' economic and social needs, while serving as a strategic defense for the developing Jewish nation.

Initially, the kibbutzim were all agricultural settlements, and the work they did to drain swamps and irrigate desert land was instrumental in the economic survival of the new state of Israel. Members, called kibbutzniks, shared equally in all economic resources, according to their needs. The original kibbutzniks were primarily young Zionist *HALUTZIM*, or pioneers, dedicated to reclaiming the soil and making it fertile once again. The first generation achieved many of their goals in the face of multiple difficulties, helping to build up the infrastructure of the new state. Kibbutz members played a disproportionate role in the country's political and military leadership, and in elite units of the ISRAEL DEFENSE FORCES. Thus, the

Early kibbutzniks worked the land and raised livestock in order to make Eretz Yisrael bloom and thrive. This 17-year-old shepherd is from Kibbutz Givath. *(Eldan David, Government Press Office, The State of Israel)*

These children wait for Shabbat to arrive in a children's house on an Israeli kibbutz during the early 20th century. Most kibbutzim until contemporary times separated children and raised them in a children's house on the grounds of the kibbutz so that parents would be free to contribute to the success of the kibbutz. Today, children raised on a kibbutz live with their parents. *(Fritz Cohen, Government Press Office, The State of Israel)*

movement has played a larger role in the history of Israel than its numbers, always small, reflect.

With time the kibbutz movement has gradually abandoned its socialist orientation, and the movement as a whole has shrunk. Less than 3 percent of the Israeli population now lives on kibbutzim. Modern-day kibbutzniks are often allowed to work outside of the kibbutz, and keep a portion of their individual salaries for their own use. While the kibbutz continues to run in a participatory democratic fashion, the original communal living structures have largely disappeared. Whereas early in kibbutz history children were raised by the collective in housing separated from their parents, today individual families raise their own children, while taking advantage of communal support for day care and education.

In addition to farming, many kibbutzim today have factories and serve as resorts, providing guest houses and amenities. They use nonmember labor in their business enterprises, which would not have been allowed in the early days. The kibbutzim are primarily divided between secular and religious communities, most of the latter affiliated with ORTHODOX JUDAISM. There is one kibbutz associated with CONSERVATIVE JUDAISM and two associated with REFORM JUDAISM.

Further reading: Amia Lieblich, *Kibbitz Makom: Report from an Israeli Kibbutz* (New York: Pantheon Books,

1981); Henry Near, *The Kibbutz Movement: A History: Origins and Growth, 1909–1939* (Oxford: Oxford University Press, 1992); Eliezer Ben Rafael, *Crisis and Transformation: The Kibbutz at Century's End* (Albany: State University of New York Press, 1997).

kiddush cup

A kiddush cup is a special ornamental goblet used for sanctifying wine at the evening and midday meals on festivals and on SHABBAT, the Sabbath. The ancient RABBIS declared that holy time should be demarcated as separate from profane time and a blessing over wine is an appropriate way to mark that separation.

Traditionally, after the blessing is recited, the kiddush cup is either passed around for each person to sip, or poured into smaller glasses that are passed to everyone at the table. The kiddush cup also appears at weddings, when bride and groom each drink sanctified wine from the same cup.

The kiddush cup has become an ever-present symbol of Judaism. It must be large enough to hold the required minimum amount of wine (or grape juice), but otherwise can come in a variety of shapes and materials. It is frequently presented as a gift, often with an appropriate engraved dedication.

Further reading: Joyce Fischman, *Let's Learn about Jewish Symbols* (Northvale N.J.: Jason Aronson, 1992); Ellen Frankel and Betsy Platkin Teutsch, *The Encyclopedia of Jewish Symbols* (Northvale, N.J.: Jason Aronson, 1992).

kippah (pl.: *kippot;* yarmulke)

The traditional male skull cap is called a *kippah* in HEBREW or yarmulke in YIDDISH. The practice of covering the head as a sign of respect for God is recorded in the *Talmud* in several instances, but it is not a requirement of HALAKHAH, Jewish law. In the 12th century the custom became pervasive among Jewish men and boys, as RABBIS began to mandate that Jewish men could not study sacred texts, such as TANAKH or Talmud, or pronounce their prayers without covering their heads. As

time passed, the wearing of the *kippah* became an ingrained MINHAG, or custom, which is almost indistinguishable in practice from a law.

Today all traditional Jews will cover their heads for TORAH study or prayer, or when entering a holy place such as a SYNAGOGUE, *bet midrash* (study house), or cemetery. Many traditional Jews will also cover their heads during all hours they are awake. The kippah acts as a reminder that God exists above. Different styles of *kippot* might reflect the type of Jewish community one prefers to associate with. For example, a smooth, black *kippah* might identify a person as more traditional.

In liberal Judaism today, many women opt to wear a *kippah* during study and prayer. Ironically, men abandoned the *kippah* in the early days of classical liberal Judaism. Today many male and female worshippers in REFORM JUDAISM cover their heads for prayer. The Orthodox custom is for women to cover their heads after they are married or reach a certain age, as a sign of MODESTY. They will do so by wearing a wig, a hat, or a scarf.

Further reading: Hayim Halevy Donin, *To Pray as a Jew: A Guide to the Prayer Book and the Synagogue Service* (New York: Basic Books, 1980); Harold S. Kushner, *To Life!: A Celebration of Jewish Being and Thinking* (New York: Warner Books, 1994).

Kissinger, Henry (b. 1923) *American diplomat*

Born in Fuerth, GERMANY, Kissinger moved to the UNITED STATES in 1938 with his family. He became a naturalized United States citizen in 1943. Kissinger served in the Army from 1943 to 1946. Upon his return, he attended Harvard University, graduating summa cum laude in 1950, and winning his Ph.D. in 1954. From 1954 until 1969 Kissinger was a member of the faculty at Harvard University, but in 1952 he had already become director of the Harvard International Seminar. He received numerous awards for his scholarship in international relations, including a Guggenheim Fellowship (1965–66) and the Woodrow Wilson Prize (1958).

Kissinger's political career began in 1965 as a consultant to the Department of State (1965–68). From that time forward he worked in countless government positions, most notably as the first foreign-born secretary of state, under Presidents Richard Nixon and Gerald Ford (1973–77). He also served as assistant to the president for national security affairs (1969–75). In the 1980s Kissinger chaired the National Bipartisan Commission on Central America and served on the president's Foreign Intelligence Advisory Board.

Kissinger has drawn sharp criticism as well as high praise for his statesmanship. Critics point to his involvement in a number of covert United States activities, including secret bombings in Cambodia and Laos, the overthrow of Chilean president Salvador Allende, and the bloody Indonesian invasion of East Timor. Kissinger continues to be a highly controversial figure. When President George W. Bush selected him to head a government inquiry into the September 11, 2001, terrorist attacks, he stepped down after only a month amid a flurry of public criticism.

Kissinger has received numerous awards for his government work, including the Presidential Medal of Freedom (1977) and the Medal of Liberty (1986). Most significantly, he was awarded the Nobel Peace Price in 1973 for diplomatic efforts that ultimately led to a cease-fire in Vietnam.

Kissinger is also known for developing "shuttle diplomacy," involving numerous trips back and forth from ISRAEL to EGYPT to negotiate an interim peace agreement after the YOM KIPPUR WAR. Since leaving public office Kissinger has authored several books and taught on the faculty at Georgetown University. He is also chairman of Kissinger Associates, an international consulting group.

Further reading: Seyom Brown, *The Crises of Power: An Interpretation of United States Foreign Policy During the Kissinger Years* (New York: Columbia University Press, 1979); Robert D. Schulzinger, *Henry Kissinger: Doctor of Diplomacy* (New York: Columbia University Press, 1989).

Born in Germany, Henry Kissinger was a successful diplomat for the United States government. He was the first foreign-born secretary of state, serving under Presidents Richard Nixon and Gerald Ford. Kissinger developed "shuttle diplomacy," which led to a successful peace treaty between Israel and Egypt in 1979. *(Getty Images)*

kittel

A *kittel* (German for "smock") is a long white garment worn over one's clothes at certain Jewish prayer services and other occasions. It is considered a symbol of purity.

Traditional Jewish men often choose to be buried in a *kittel*. The TALMUD teaches that Rabban Gamaliel wanted to put an end to ostentatious behavior at burials. Though a wealthy man, he ordered that when he was buried he should simply be wrapped in an inexpensive white shroud. The Talmud encourages all Jews to do the same, so that they are equalized in death.

The *kittel* is worn on the night of SELICHOT, the Saturday midnight reading of penitential prayers prior to ROSH HASHANAH, and on Rosh HaShanah and YOM KIPPUR themselves. It is intended to be a reminder of one's mortality when facing God, and a spur toward attaining greater purity. Another customary reason for wearing a *kittel* is to remind oneself of the MALAKHIM, or angels, who are always clothed in white. At traditional Jewish weddings, the bridegroom often wears a *kittel*; some men wear *kittels* at PASSOVER SEDERS.

In many liberal synagogues of the CONSERVATIVE and REFORM JUDAISM movements, only clergy wear *kittels*. They do so during Rosh HaShanah and Yom Kippur services, and often when officiating at weddings.

Further reading: S. Y. Agnon, Maurice T. Galpert, Nahum Norbert Glatzer, *Days of Awe: A Treasury of Jewish Wisdom for Reflection, Repentance, and Renewal on the High Holy Days* (New York: Schocken Books, 1995); Irving Greenberg, *The Jewish Way: Living the Holidays* (New York: Simon & Schuster, 1993).

Knesset

The Knesset (HEBREW for "assembly") is the parliament of the State of ISRAEL. It consists of a single house with 120 members. The Knesset derived its name and the number of seats from the fifth century B.C.E. Great Assembly, or Knesset Ha-Gedolah, set up in JERUSALEM by EZRA and NEHEMIAH to govern the restored Jewish community.

The Knesset was established in 1949 and first gathered in TEL AVIV before moving to its current home in JERUSALEM the following year. The Knesset as a whole passes laws and chooses the government ministers who govern the land. Israel does not have a written constitution; Israeli law derives from five different sources: Ottoman jurisprudence, legislation passed by the British mandatory government, laws passed by the Knesset, British common law, and Jewish law as based in the TANAKH, the Hebrew Bible, and the TALMUD.

The 120 Knesset members are elected by proportional representation based on the number of votes each political party receives. No single party has ever achieved a majority of seats. After each election, the president of Israel asks one of the leading parties to assemble a coalition, which in turn appoints the prime minister and the rest of the cabinet.

The president of Israel is elected by the Knesset for a five-year term and may be reelected for an additional term. The president signs all laws, accepts the choice of foreign ambassadors and ministers, appoints ambassadors, ministers, judges, and the state comptroller. The president also has the power to pardon or commute prison sentences. Most of these powers are primarily symbolic; the Knesset usually chooses someone who has served the country and remained above party politics.

The prime minister and the cabinet exercise most of the Knesset's powers. However, unlike the president of the UNITED STATES, the prime minister cannot veto laws passed by the Knesset. The term for Knesset members is four years, though more often than not this is cut short by a call for early elections, usually when the government coalition loses its Knesset majority.

The Knesset system of government guarantees minority representation and, like all democratic parliamentary systems, ensures that the various political agendas of different constituencies all get some attention. However, the system can at times give a disproportionate degree of power to small political parties, which are needed to form coalitions of at least 61 Knesset members. Critics say, for example, that the smaller parties affiliated with ORTHODOX JUDAISM have often used this power to maintain their control over certain features of religious observance in Israel, and to receive special subsidies for religious education, programming, and institutions.

The Knesset is the Israeli parliament. Here, Golda Meir, at one time a member of the Knesset and at another the prime minister, sits by herself during proceedings in the Knesset. *(Moshe Milner, Government Press Office, The State of Israel)*

The two largest political parties in Israel have been LABOR on the left and LIKUD on the right. While the two blocs have at times formed national unity governments, each has primarily formed ruling coalitions with the smaller parties. Labor dominated every government until 1977, when Menachem BEGIN became the first Likud prime minister.

In the 1990s Israel experimented with direct election of the prime minister, but this proved ineffective, and the old system of voting for parties only was restored. Electoral reform has often been proposed in Israel, including the idea of dividing Israel into 120 districts. However, no agreement has yet been achieved in this area. Until such

reform takes place, the Knesset will most likely always require some form of coalition government.

The Knesset works through 12 standing committees: the House; Finance; Economics; Defense and Foreign Affairs; Interior and Environment; Immigration and Absorption; Education and Culture; Constitution, Law, and Justice; Labor and Social Affairs; Public Audit; War against Drug Affliction; and Advancing Status of Women Committees. The Knesset building, a dramatic modern structure, can be accessed by the public, and observers can sit in a gallery to witness parliament in session. The public areas are adorned by a collection of tapestries and mosaics depicting Jewish history, created by Marc CHAGALL.

Further reading: Ziva Amishai-Maisels, *Tapestries and Mosaics of Marc Chagall at the Knesset* (New York: Tudor Publishing, 1973); Gideon Doron and Don Peretz, *The Government and Politics of Israel* (Boulder, Colo.: Westview Press, 1997); Gregory S. Mahler, *The Knesset: Parliament in the Israeli Political System* (Cranbury, N.J.: Associated University Press, 1981); Itzhak Zamir and Allen Zysblat, *Public Law in Israel* (Oxford: Oxford University, 1996).

kohanim (sing.: kohen; cohanim, sing.: cohen)

The *Kohanim* constituted a subgroup of the tribe of Levi who were descended from AARON, the first HIGH PRIEST. They were responsible for the system of ritual SACRIFICE among the ISRAELITES and later in the TEMPLE in Jerusalem. The *kohanim* were assisted by the LEVITES, the remaining members of the tribe of Levi, who performed such functions as bearing water and singing hymns.

The *kohanim* had to carry out complex rites of purification and sacrifices of animals and grain on a daily basis; the fate of the nation depended on their scrupulous attention to detail. Since the destruction of the second Temple in 70 C.E., however, they have had little to do, although traditional Jews pray daily for the rebuilding of the Temple and the restoration of the sacrificial routine, which some believe will happen when the MESSIAH comes.

Since 1967 a small group of Jews, especially members of the Ateret Kohanim Yeshiva, located near the Temple Mount in the OLD CITY OF JERUSALEM, have been making practical preparations for this restoration. The YESHIVA trains young men of this lineage to carry out the sacrificial rituals, and prepares the clothing and implements that will be needed, according to the specifications of the TORAH and other ancient references.

After the destruction of the Temple, the power and prestige of *kohanim* diminished significantly in favor of the RABBIS; however, Jews continue to keep track of *kohen* lineage, passed down from father to son, to perform the few remaining priestly functions.

Kohanim are given the first ALIYAH on SHABBAT (the first opportunity to recite a BRACHA, or blessing, over the TORAH reading), which is considered an honor. They are also required to recite the priestly blessing over the congregation at certain times of the year. REFORM JUDAISM (and in some cases CONSERVATIVE JUDAISM) tends to reject these special privileges of the *kohanim* in favor of a principled equality among all Jews in the congregation.

The term *kohan* is the source of the common Jewish surname "Cohen," but not all Cohens are *kohanim* and not all *kohanim* are Cohens. "Katz" is also a common surname for *kohanim;* it is an acronym of *cohen tzedek* (righteous priest). Recent DNA research supports the claims of those who identify as *kohanim:* a study published in *Nature* in June 1997 shows that self-identified *kohanim* in three countries have common and otherwise rare elements in the Y chromosome, indicating that they have a common male ancestor, perhaps Aaron himself.

Further reading: N. S. Hecht, *An Introduction to the History and Sources of Jewish Law* (New York: Oxford University Press, 1996); John McHugh and Roland De Vaux, *Ancient Israel: Its Life and Institutions* (New York: McGraw-Hill, 1961); The Cohanim/DNA Connection at Aish.com http://www.aish.com for information about recent genetic studies.

Kol Nidre

Kol Nidre is the communal prayer said just before sunset at the start of the Day of Atonement, YOM KIPPUR. The dramatic prayer is usually attended by the largest number of worshippers of the year.

For the ceremony, TORAH scrolls are taken from the ARK and held by the leaders of the congregation, standing as a solemn court. The CANTOR asks permission from the heavenly and earthly courts to pray among sinners, and then chants the

Kol Nidre, which is a legal proclamation annulling vows. The idea is to prevent punishment because of vows one might have forgotten. Over the centuries there have been several versions of Kol Nidre; some versions annul the vows of the community from this Yom Kippur until the next, while others annul vows from the previous Yom Kippur to the present one.

Non-Jews have often raised the issue of whether Kol Nidre allows Jews to abandon their promises to other people, whether personal or business. Medieval Christians used the text to prove that Jews were untrustworthy. In order to address this issue, the GEONIM proclaimed that the annulment recited in the Kol Nidre only pertains to vows people make to God, not to those they make to other people.

Here is one translation of Kol Nidre: "All vows, renunciations, promises, obligations, and oaths, taken rashly, from this Day of Atonement till the next, may we attain it in peace, we regret them in advance. May we be absolved of them, may we be released from them, may they be null and void and of no effect. May they not be binding upon us. Such vows shall not be considered vows; such renunciations, no renunciations; and such oaths, no oaths. And may atonement be granted to the whole congregation of Israel and to the stranger who lives among them, for all have transgressed unwittingly. Forgive the sins of this people in accordance with Thy great mercy, as Thou hast continued to forgive them from the days of Egypt until now. As we have been promised: And the Lord said, I have forgiven, in accordance with Thy plea."

Further reading: Shmuel Yosef Agnon, *Days of Awe: Being a Treasury of Traditions, Legends, and Learned Commentaries Concerning Rosh ha-Shanah, Yom Kippur, and the Days Between, Culled from Three Hundred Volumes, Ancient and New* (New York: Schocken Books, 1965); Philip Goodman, *The Yom Kippur Anthology* (Philadelphia and Jerusalem: Jewish Publication Society, 1992); Irving Greenberg, *The Jewish Way: Living the Holidays* (New York: Summit Books, 1988).

Kook, Abraham Isaac Ha-Kohen
(1865–1935) *chief rabbi of Israel*

Rav (Rabbi) Abraham Isaac Ha-Kohen Kook was born in Griva, Latvia in 1865. Like his father before him, Kook entered the Volozhin YESHIVA at the age of 19, living and studying in the insular world of eastern European ORTHODOX JUDAISM. He excelled in his studies, and after his ordination at the age of 23, he became a pulpit rabbi.

While Kook was a religious man, he felt that religion shouldn't restrict, but rather open people up to possibility. At the beginning of the 20th century Kook began to publish articles in support of religious ZIONISM, advocating cooperation with the secular Zionists in working toward the creation of a Jewish state. Kook moved to PALESTINE in 1904, taking a rabbinic post. He served in a supervisory capacity to several secular Jewish agricultural settlements, attempting to influence them in a religious direction without overwhelming them with his personal orthodoxy.

Kook was a mystical and spiritual leader who aspired to bring God into daily life, infusing the world with the divine ideals of truth, justice, freedom, and peace. Kook avoided the polemics and politics often involved with religion and sought to locate the passionate core that had the potential to infuse life with moral and ethical perfection.

During World War I Kook spent time in Switzerland and ENGLAND, where he was active in helping to secure the BALFOUR DECLARATION, in which Britain embraced the concept of a Jewish state in Palestine. After the war, Kook returned to Palestine, becoming the chief rabbi of ISRAEL, even though there was yet to be a declared Jewish state.

While Rav Kook was scrupulously Orthodox in his own practices, he showed a unique accessibility to the non-Orthodox population as well. His teachings on HALAKHAH (Jewish law), PHILOSOPHY, and KABBALAH (mysticism) are still studied by secular and religious Jews in Israel and abroad. His stance that secular Zionism was a means to help bring the MESSIANIC AGE was highly controversial in pre-Israel Orthodoxy, but after the creation of the modern state of Israel, it was accepted by mainstream Orthodox groups. Rav Kook died in 1935; his life serves as a model for many Orthodox Jews today, showing how they can both live in the modern world and retain their religiosity.

Further reading: Abraham Isaac Kook, *Abraham Isaac Kook: The Lights of Penitence, the Moral Principles, Lights of Holiness, Essays, Letters, and Poems* (New York: Paulist Press, 1978); Ehud Luz, *Parallels Meet: Religion and Nationalism in the Early Zionist Movement (1882–1904)* (Philadelphia: Jewish Publication Society, 1988).

Kotel (Western Wall; Wailing Wall)

The Kotel (Hebrew Kotel Ha-Ma'arivi), or Western Wall, is located in the Jewish Quarter of the OLD CITY OF JERUSALEM. It is an exposed section of the massive ancient stone wall that surrounds the Temple Mount, the huge platform built by HEROD on which the second TEMPLE rested. For centuries, this small stretch of wall was the closest Jews could come to the site of the Temple and the HOLY OF HOLIES, the most sacred place in the world for Judaism. It is sometimes called the Wailing Wall, a name given by non-Jews when they saw Jews praying and sobbing there.

From 1948 to 1967 the Muslims controlled access to the Kotel, and they did not allow Jews to visit the site. On June 7, 1967, the third day of the SIX-DAY WAR, Israel gained control of JERUSALEM and the Kotel itself. Moshe DAYAN, the Israeli defense minister at the time, was one of the first to

Yitzhak Shamir places a note in the Kotel, also called the Western Wall. Many Jews place prayers and messages for God into the crevices of the wall as an expression of spirituality. The wall is located in the Jewish Quarter of the Old City of Jerusalem, and it was once part of the second Temple. *(Nati Harnik, Government Press Office, The State of Israel)*

reach the Kotel, and he placed a written prayer into the cracks of the wall, reigniting the tradition of inserting prayers into the stones. It is said that his prayer was for peace.

Locals pray at the wall daily, while others make pilgrimages there from around the world. It is traditional to write prayers down, fold them up, and place them within the cracks in the wall. It is believed that as God's dwelling place, one's prayers have their greatest efficacy at that point. In this age of technology, one can even e-mail or fax prayers to an office in Jerusalem where someone will take the prayer and place it in the Kotel. There is also a 24-hour Kotel videocam.

Though Israel has controlled the Temple Mount since 1967, it does not allow Jews to pray there, as it is the site of two ancient and historic mosques, and Jewish prayers might be considered provocative. Some zealous Jews want to rebuild the Temple at its original location, which is believed to be approximately where the Muslim Dome of the Rock now stands.

A second controversy concerns the right of women to pray at the wall. In traditional Judaism women and men pray in separate spaces so that they can fully concentrate on their prayers. The Kotel is divided into a men's section and a woman's section, but the woman's section is quite small and is located farther away from the Temple site. In addition, ultra-Orthodox Jews do not believe that women should lead people in prayer in a public place, or to read from the TORAH in public, and their policies have been enforced by the authorities in charge of the site. A group of women that calls itself "Women of the Wall" has formed to protest these policies; on occasion, their attempts to ignore the rules have been met with physical and verbal abuse from ultra-Orthodox men and youths.

Further reading: Michael B. Oren, *Six Days of War: June 1967 and the Making of the Modern Middle East* (Oxford and New York: Oxford University Press, 2002); Mandy Ross, *The Western Wall and Other Jewish Holy Places* (Chicago, Ill.: Raintree, 2003); Phyllis Chesler and Rivka

Haut, eds., *Women of the Wall: Claiming Sacred Ground at Judaism's Holy Site* (Woodstock, Vt.: Jewish Lights, 2003).

Kotsker Rebbe (1787–1859) *Hasidic master*

Rabbi Menachem Mendel was born in 1787 in Belgraj, near Lublin. His family was associated with the MITNAGDIM, who opposed HASIDISM, so it was not until he was married that he learned about the Hasidim through his father-in-law. After studying with various masters and especially Rabbi Simhah Bunem of Przysucha, he returned home to the area of Lublin, specifically the town of Kotsk. He settled down as the Reb of Kotsk, or alternatively, the Kotsker Rebbe.

The Przysucha branch of Hasidim emphasized intellectual ability, inwardness, and sincerity, and the Kotsker Rebbe continued in this vein. It is said he decried outward manifestations of piety. He had little patience for the ordinary Hasidim who would come to him requesting prayers on their behalf, and preferred to associate with a smaller circle of educated disciples who were sincere in their devotion and ready to sacrifice everything in order to seek God. These Kotsker Hasidim had such disdain for outward shows of piety that they would often sin in public but remain virtuous in private, as a reversal of the common human tendency to acting virtuously in public but sin in private. In this way they demonstrated an ideal of personal religiosity for its own sake.

The Kotsker Rebbe earned the epithet "the Seraph" because of his holy life and fiery temperament. He spent his last 20 years in seclusion, occasionally allowing a disciple to visit him, and occasionally leaving his isolation to burst into the SYNAGOGUE. When he did appear, it is said that his appearance was so awe-inspiring that some Hasidim even tried to jump out of the windows in terror.

The Kotsker Rebbe never composed any written works, but many of his sayings were recorded and passed down by his disciples, such as "Man must guard himself and his uniqueness and not imitate his fellow."

Further reading: Chaim Feinberg, *Leaping Souls: Rabbi Menachem Mendel and the Spirit of Kotzk* (Hoboken, N.J.: Ktav Publishing, 1993); Abraham Joshua Heschel, *A Passion for Truth* (Philadelphia: Jewish Publication Society, 1973); Simcha Raz, ed., *The Sayings of Menachem Mendel of Kotsk* (Northvale, N.J.: Jason Aronson, 1995); Ephraim Oratz, *And Nothing but the Truth: Insights, Stories, and Anecdotes of Menachem Mendl of Kotzk* (New York: Judaica Press, 1990).

Koufax, Sandy (b. 1935) *baseball player*

Sanford "Sandy" Koufax is considered to be one of the greatest pitchers in baseball history. A left-handed pitcher, he is often referred to as the "man with the golden arm." He established numerous records throughout his career with the Brooklyn and then Los Angeles Dodgers. In 1972 Koufax was elected into the Baseball Hall of Fame.

Koufax was born in Brooklyn, New York; after divorcing, his mother married attorney Irving Koufax, who both encouraged his stepson to pursue athletic interests and exposed both Sandy and his sister to YIDDISH theater.

Koufax, who was also a notable basketball player in high school, attended the University of Cincinnati on a basketball scholarship in 1953. However, he left school in 1954 to play baseball with the Brooklyn Dodgers. Koufax's first three years were erratic, as he learned to master his pitching craft. In 1961, Koufax broke out and had 18 wins, striking out 269 batters for a league record. In 1962, he suffered a blood clot that curtailed his effectiveness, and he won only 14 games. Amazingly, from 1963 to 1966 he won an unimaginable 97 games. In 1966, Koufax was awarded the Cy Young Award for excellence in pitching. He was the most effective pitcher in history for a four-year period, but he retired relatively young due to chronic pain in his pitching arm.

In 1965, when a World Series game fell on the important Jewish holiday of YOM KIPPUR, Koufax asked to be excused from the game. Weathering strong criticism, Koufax maintained that both his personal beliefs and his status as a Jewish role model would not let him violate the solemn day. To this day, young Jewish athletes are taught the "legend of Sandy Koufax," and many children refuse to play in sporting contests that violate their holy days, "just like Sandy did."

Further reading: Jane Leavy, *Sandy Koufax: A Lefty's Legacy* (New York: HarperCollins, 2002); Peter Levine, *Ellis Island to Ebbets Field: Sport and the American Jewish Experience* (Oxford: Oxford University Press, 1993).

Kristallnacht

Kristallnacht, the Night of Broken Glass, took place on November 9–10, 1938. It was a series of organized Nazi riots directed against the Jews of GERMANY and AUSTRIA. Essentially it was a POGROM. The aim was to terrorize the Jews, frighten away any sympathetic non-Jews, and accustom the German population to barbaric treatment of Jews.

Kristallnacht was the culmination of anti-Jewish actions by the Nazis that began with their rise to power in 1933. Fired up by antisemitic propaganda, organized mobs rampaged through the streets of every major town and city; about 100 Jews were murdered and many more injured, and over 1,000 synagogues were destroyed. More than 7,000 Jewish-owned businesses were ruined, and Jewish schools and cemeteries were vandalized. The Nazis rounded up some 30,000 Jews, many of them leaders of the Jewish community, and sent them to CONCENTRATION CAMPS.

The Nazis blamed the Jewish victims for the violence and held them financially responsible for the damages incurred by the riots. Therefore, they charged the Jews a levy of more than 1 billion German marks, and then sought to systematically eliminate the means for Jews to earn a living.

Kristallnacht is considered by historians to be the major turning point in Nazi actions against the Jews. It was the start of what would ultimately be the Nazi FINAL SOLUTION to exterminate European Jewry. Kristallnacht marks the official beginning of the HOLOCAUST.

Further reading: Lucy S. Dawidowicz, *The War Against the Jews: 1933–1945* (New York: Doubleday, 1991); Martin Gilbert, *A History of the Jews of Europe during the Second World War* (New York: Owl Books, 1987); Anthony Read and David Fisher, *Kristallnacht: The Nazi Night of Terror* (New York: Random House, Inc., 1990).

Kushner, Harold (b. 1935) *American rabbi and author*

Harold Kushner, a rabbi in the more progressive wing of CONSERVATIVE JUDAISM, has become a best-selling writer who articulates contemporary liberal Jewish theology.

Kushner was born and raised in Brooklyn, New York. He studied as an undergraduate at Columbia University, and won ordination from the JEWISH THEOLOGICAL SEMINARY. He is an active member in the Rabbinical Assembly, and served for many years as the pulpit rabbi for Temple Israel of Natick, Massachusetts, where he now holds the title of Rabbi Laureate.

Kushner is a well-known writer on Jewish topics. His most famous book, *When Bad Things Happen to Good People*, published in 1981, was eventually translated into 12 languages. The volume was inspired by Kushner's own pain when he learned that his toddler, Aaron, had a terminal disease and would not live past his teen years. Kushner has produced other spiritual writings intended to bring comfort and guidance to suffering people.

He has received six honorary degrees and numerous awards, including the Christopher Medal and the Yitzhak Rabin Award. In 1995, he was honored as one of 50 people who have made the world a better place in the past 50 years by the Christophers, a nonprofit organization that encourages people to make a positive impact on the world.

Kushner articulates modern Jewish liberal theology, and he has a significant following among both Jews and non-Jews. He understands God in a nontraditional manner; while God is all-good and all-knowing, God is not all-powerful and therefore cannot prevent bad things happening to good people. The challenge to those who experience bad times is to choose the appropriate response to their crisis—to reintroduce Godliness to the situation.

In addition to Kushner's essays on Judaism and philosophy, he is an accomplished rabbinic scholar who helped edit *Etz Hayim: A Torah Commentary*, the new official commentary for the Conservative movement. Kushner also serves on the board of directors for the Giving Back Fund, a nonprofit organization devoted to encouraging and facilitating the philanthropic efforts of professional athletes and entertainers.

Further reading: Harold S. Kushner, *To Life!: A Celebration of Jewish Being and Thinking* (New York: Warner Books, 1994); ———, *When Bad Things Happen to Good People* (New York: Avon Books, 1983).

L

Labor Party

The government of ISRAEL runs on a parliamentary system (*see* KNESSET), dominated by two major political parties, Labor and LIKUD. The Labor Party is one of Israel's oldest, with roots that long predate the establishment of the modern state of Israel. In 1968, the Mapai Party, established in the 1930s, merged with a reconstituted Ahdut Haavodah Party, established in 1954, and with the Labor Rafi Party, established in 1965, to create the contemporary political party called Labor. Until 1977, when Menachem BEGIN became prime minister, every prime minister of Israel since its birth in 1948 had come from the Labor Party. In 1984 Labor and Likud formed a Unity government and Likud prime minister Yitzchak SHAMIR and Labor prime minister Shimon PERES served together. Since that time, the two parties have alternated in power.

Labor stands left of center in Israeli politics; it is a social democratic party that continues the tradition of Labor ZIONISM. David BEN-GURION, Israel's first prime minister, came from this political group, which believed in the rights of working people and in social welfare. The movement was long identified with the Jewish socialist agricultural settlements in PALESTINE.

Labor is officially committed to maintaining a democracy, to supporting the economic well-being of Israeli citizens, to encouraging a free-market economy, to sustain the unity of the Jewish people by insisting upon the legitimacy of all types of Judaism, and to achieving lasting peace and security in the region based on a gradual implementation of the Oslo agreements. The Labor Party does not support new settlements or the expansion of existing ones in JUDEA AND SAMARIA (West Bank) or in Gaza, and it recognizes the Palestinian right to self-determination. At the same time, Labor also believes that Israel must have defensible borders and lasting security. The Labor Party also believes that government is responsible for insuring health, education, and social services for its citizens even in a privatizing free-market economy.

Prime ministers of the Labor Party have included David BEN-GURION (1948–54; 1955–63), Moshe SHARETT (1954–55), Levi ESHKOL (1963–69), Golda MEIR (1969–74), Yitzhak RABIN (1974–77; 1992–95), Shimon PERES (1984–86; 1995–96), and Ehud BARAK (1999–2001). The HISTADRUT, Israel's labor union, also emerged from the Labor Zionist movement.

Further reading: Gideon Doron and Don Peretz, *The Government and Politics of Israel* (Boulder, Colo.: Westview Press, 1997); Howard M. Sachar, *A History of Israel from the Rise of Zionism to Our Time* (New York: Alfred

A. Knopf, 1996); Michael Shalev, *Labour and the Political Economy in Israel* (Oxford: Oxford University Press, 1992); David M. Zohar, *Political Parties in Israel: The Evolution of Israeli Democracy* (New York and London: Praeger, 1974).

Ladino

Ladino is the Jewish-Spanish dialect spoken by many SEPHARDIM, the descendants of the Jews who were expelled from Spain in 1492. It is written in the HEBREW script. It is also called Judezmo, Spaniolit, and Judeo-Spanish.

Ladino was derived from 14th- and 15th-century Spanish, with some Hebrew admixture. After the EXPULSION in 1492, it was further influenced by the languages of the countries where Jews resettled. Today's Ladino has linguistic influences from Arabic, French, Italian, Portuguese, and Turkish. In fact, the name "Ladino" simply refers to its Latin roots, as opposed to Turkish. Ladino is considered the language of Sephardi culture as YIDDISH is considered the language of Ashkenazic culture (*see* ASHKENAZIM).

Collections of significant literary works written in Ladino exist, especially from the 16th and 17th centuries. In the 1740s a complete Ladino translation of the TANAKH, the Hebrew Bible, was published in Constantinople. The translation, edited by Abraham Assa, was popular among Ladino-speaking Jews well into the 19th century. There are many Ladino translations of prayer books (*see* SIDDUR), HAGGADAH, and rabbinic literary works.

Since the Nazis destroyed most Balkan Ladino-speaking communities during the HOLOCAUST, it is estimated that between 80,000 and 200,000 Jews speak Ladino today. Most of them live in ISRAEL and tend to be elderly.

Ladino is considered endangered. Since most of the survivors immigrated to Israel where the Hebrew language has prevailed, few of their children and grandchildren are actively learning the language. Ladino, like Yiddish for similar reasons, is in danger of becoming extinct as a spoken language.

Further reading: Esther Benbassa and Aron Rodrigue, *Sephardi Jewry: A History of the Judeo-Spanish Community, 14th to 20th Centuries* (Berkeley: University of California Press, 2000); Elli Kohen and Dahlia Kohen-Gorden, *Ladino-English, English-Ladino: Concise Encyclopedic Dictionary* (New York: Hippocrene Books, 2000); Sarah Abrevaya Stein, *Making Jews Modern: The Yiddish and Ladino Press in the Russian and Ottoman Empires* (Bloomington: Indiana University Press, 2003).

Lag b'Omer

Lag b'Omer is a joyous minor holiday in the spring, usually marked by outdoor activities.

The 49 days of counting the OMER between PASSOVER and SHAVUOT marked a joyous period in the agricultural society of biblical times, as farmers waited to offer the annual grain SACRIFICE, an amount called an *omer,* when the new grain could be eaten. However, in rabbinic times the *omer* period took on sad connotations. A plague, or perhaps an episode of persecution by the Romans, killed off a large number of Rabbi AKIVA BEN YOSEPH's students during that time of year; subsequent persecutions over the ages in the same time period led the rabbis to make the *omer* period a time of partial mourning, when celebrations were prohibited.

However, on the 33rd day of the *omer* the plague ended, and the day is celebrated as a break from mourning and sadness. (In the Hebrew letter-numeral system, the letters lamed and gimmel together total 33; they can be pronounced as the acronym *lag.*) Lag b'Omer also commemorates the death of Rabbi Simeon bar Yochai, a great Jewish scholar. The rabbi is credited with writing the *ZOHAR,* the greatest text in the KABBALAH, although modern scholars attribute it to MOSES DE LEÓN of the 13th century. In Israel many celebrate Lag b'Omer by visiting bar Yochai's gravesite for a day of dancing, feasting, and bonfires.

Jews celebrate Lag b'Omer with picnics and field games, because the rabbis and their students would study TORAH under the guise of hunting during times of persecution. Since haircuts are not permitted during the rest of the *omer*, it is also traditional to cut a three-year-old boy's hair for the first time on Lag b'Omer. Weddings and celebrations are also allowed. Today, many religious Jews return to normal life after Lag b'Omer, but traditionally the mourning did not end until all 49 days had passed.

Further reading: Larry Domnitch, *The Jewish Holidays: A Journey through History* (Northvale, N.J.: Jason Aronson, 2000); Irving Greenberg, *The Jewish Way: Living the Holiday* (New York: Summit Books, 1988).

lamedvovnik

In popular Jewish lore, the *lamedvovnik*s are the 36 anonymous saints who inhabit the world at any one time, without whom the world could not survive God's judgment. (In the Hebrew letter-numeral system, the letters lamed and vov together equal 36; -*nik* is a common Russian/Yiddish suffix.)

In the TALMUD, there is a legend that the world will never have less than 36 saints in each generation. The number 36 has several mystical meanings. It is twice 18, the numeric value of CHAI. The word *chai* means "life," and double chai suggests double life. Thirty-six was also the number needed for a majority in the rabbinic SANHEDRIN, which was comprised of 70 sages.

The Talmud never identifies the *lamedvovnik*s other than to say they are saintly, righteous men who do not necessarily have a relationship with one another. In the 18th century, legends began to surface about hidden *lamedvovnik*s living among the common people. Stories were told of their magical powers, which could protect the Jews against violent enemies. Such stories have been elaborated among Hasidim ever since (*see* HASIDISM). Andre Schwartz-Bart's novel *The Last of the Just* (1960) was based upon the *lamedvovnik* legends.

Further reading: Richard Kieckhefer and George D. Bond, *Sainthood: Its Manifestations in World Religions* (Berkeley: University of California Press, 1990); Andre

Schwarz-Bart, *The Last of the Just: A Novel* (New York: Overlook Press, 2000).

Lamentations

The biblical book of Lamentations is a collection of dirges, or funeral poems, that mourn the destruction of JERUSALEM and the first TEMPLE. It is called Eicha in HEBREW, after the first word: "How lonely sits the city once full of people." Lamentations is read on TISHA B'AV, the ninth of Av, which is the day set aside to commemorate the destruction of the two Temples and other great tragedies in Jewish history. According to Jewish tradition, the book was written by the prophet Jeremiah (*see* NEVI'IM).

Lamentations presents an unrelieved series of horrifying descriptions of Jerusalem under siege by the Babylonians (*see* BABYLONIA) and of the city's ultimate destruction. Jerusalem has fallen into chaos, with children crying for food and comfort and residents resorting to cannibalism. The writer blames all the destruction on the sins of the Jewish people. Their immorality and lack of ethical behavior caused God to bring such terrible punishments. At the conclusion of the book, the author lays out the only path to Jewish renewal and restoration of Jerusalem. Repentance alone will bring redemption: "Turn us to you, O Lord, and we will return. Renew our days as of old."

Further reading: Jacob Neusner, *Israel After Calamity: The Book of Lamentation* (Harrisburg, Pa.: Morehouse Publishing Company, 1995); *Tanakh: The Holy Scriptures* (Philadelphia and Jerusalem: Jewish Publication Society, 1985).

Landsmanschaften

Jewish immigrants in America in the 19th and early 20th centuries formed thousands of *Landsmanschaften* (sing.: *Landsmanschaft*), informal clubs of people who came from the same village, town, or city in the country from which they had emigrated. The purpose of the group was largely social: to speak the native tongue, reminisce, and offer mutual support. They often collected money to help each other in time of need, providing the means to bury a member or manage insurance benefits for WIDOWS AND ORPHANS.

Many *Landsmanschaften* grew to have thousands of members. Some developed complex networks of social services, while others acted as guilds for certain business interests or crafts. These included the Brisker Painters and Tile Workers Society, the Lemberg Bakers Relief Society, the Piatara-Neamets Businessmen's Benevolent Association, and the Minsker Realty Company. Between 1864 and 1923 almost every community from which Jews immigrated to the UNITED STATES was represented by a *Landsmanschaft*. In 1914 there were 2,000 registered in New York alone. Almost half of all Jewish immigrants were members at some time during their immigrant years. The *Landsmanschaften* were instrumental in creating a bridge between the old world and the new.

Further reading: Daniel J. Elazar, *Community and Polity: The Organizational Dynamics of American Jewry* (Philadelphia: Jewish Publication Society, 1976); Howard M. Sachar, *A History of the Jews in America* (New York: Vintage Books, 1992); Daniel Soyer, "Traditions of Grass-Roots Organization and Leadership: The Continuity of Landsmanschaften in New York," *American Jewish History* 76 (September 1986): 25–39.

Lantos, Tom (b. 1928) *American congressman*

Tom Lantos was elected to Congress from California in 1980 and has served for well over 20 years. As of 2005, Lantos was serving his 13th term in the House of Representatives. Born in Budapest, HUNGARY, on February 1, 1928, Lantos was 16 when Nazi GERMANY occupied Hungary. Lantos was active as a member of the anti-Nazi underground, and he was sent to a forced labor camp in northern Budapest. He managed to escape from the forced labor camp, and like many Hungarian Jews, was saved by the great Swedish humanitar-

ian Raoul WALLENBERG. Lantos's story was one of several depicted in Steven Spielberg's Academy Award–winning documentary about the HOLOCAUST in Hungary entitled *The Last Days*.

After the Holocaust, Lantos immigrated to America, and in the summer of 1950, he married his childhood sweetheart Annette Tillemann; they had two daughters. Lantos received his B.A. and M.A. in economics at the University of Washington and his Ph.D. from the University of California at Berkeley. He taught economics at San Francisco State University for three decades, during which time he was also active in public affairs.

In 1980 Lantos became the only Holocaust survivor ever to be elected to the U.S. Congress. He has never forgotten his personal history. He and his wife were instrumental in securing honorary U.S. citizenship for Wallenberg in 1981, in the hope that he was still alive in RUSSIA and would be released. Lantos is also the founder and cochairman of the bipartisan Congressional Human Rights Caucus.

Further reading: Samantha Power, *"A Problem from Hell": America and the Age of Genocide* (New York: Perennial, 2003); Kinue Tokudome, *Courage to Remember: Interviews on the Holocaust* (St. Paul, Minn.: Paragon House, 1999).

lashon hara

Lashon hara, literally "evil tongue" or "evil speech," is the Hebrew term for "gossip," which is considered a very serious sin in Judaism.

The ancient RABBIS claimed that *lashon hara* was as bad as IDOLATRY, murder, and adultery. The divine punishments for *lashon hara* were said to include leprosy and a strong temptation to commit the very sins the gossiper attributed to others. Even saying good things about someone else is prohibited, since it encourages the listener to say or think, "Oh, he's not so great." It is only permissible to speak about another person if it is absolutely necessary or if the person discussed is present.

Further reading: Moshe Goldberger, *A Review Guide to the Laws of Proper Speech Based on Sefer Chofetz Chayim* (Brooklyn, N.Y.: Eichler, 1986); Ze'ev Grinvald, *Taharas Halashon: A Guide to the Laws of Lashon Hara and Rechilus* (Jerusalem and New York: Feldheim, 1994).

Law of Return

In 1950 the Israeli government drafted and passed the Law of Return, which grants automatic citizenship to any Jew who "returns" to reside in the land of ISRAEL, with the exception of those who are involved in activities that threaten the Jewish people or who are dangers to public health or the security of the state. In 1970 the law was amended to include a definition of a Jew: anyone born of a Jewish mother or who has converted to Judaism, and who does not profess to be a member of a religion other than Judaism. Under the Law of Return, any child, grandchild, or spouse of a Jew is granted automatic citizenship status as well.

Further reading: Yoram Hazony, *The Jewish State: The Struggle for Israel's Soul* (New York: Basic Books, 2000); Walter Laqueur, *The Israel-Arab Reader: A Documentary History of the Middle East Conflict* (New York: Penguin Books, 2001); Nissim Rejwan, *Israel in Search of Identity: Reading the Formative Years* (Gainesville: University Press of Florida, 1999).

Lazarus, Emma (1849–1887) *poet and writer*

Born on July 22, 1849, Emma Lazarus was the fourth of seven children of Esther Nathan Lazarus and Moses Lazarus. Her father was a successful sugar merchant and a descendant of the original Sephardic settlers in New York (*see* SEPHARDIM). Lazarus was raised in luxury and privately educated in literature, music, French, German, Italian, and science. Her family was active in Shearith Israel, the oldest congregation in New York City. As a young woman, Lazarus showed a keen interest in writing, and in 1866 her father had her first book of poems printed. Subsequently she was introduced to Ralph Waldo Emerson, who mentored her for the next 16 years, until his death.

Lazarus published many significant works, including a volume of translations entitled the *Poems and Ballads of Heinrich HEINE*. She also wrote on Jewish topics, urging her fellow Jews to advocate on behalf of European Jewry and to supporting immigration to PALESTINE. Lazarus learned HEBREW and was active in supporting world Jewry. She continually balanced her American literary identity with her Jewish activism, galvanized by the Russian POGROMS during the 1880s.

In 1883, Lazarus was asked to write a poem for a literary auction to raise funds to build the pedestal for the Statue of Liberty. Her poem, "The New Colossus," was published, and in 1903 was inscribed on a bronze tablet and displayed inside the pedestal of the Statue of Liberty. The words have been inscribed in the hearts and souls of millions of Americans: "Give me your tired, your poor, / Your huddled masses yearning to breathe free . . . I lift my lamp beside the golden door."

Further reading: Martin A. Cohen and Abraham J. Peck, eds., *Sephardim in the Americas: Studies in Culture and History* (Tuscaloosa: University of Alabama Press, 1993); Emma Lazarus, *Emma Lazarus: Selected Poems* (New York: Library of America, 2005); Diane Lichtenstein, *Writing Their Nations: The Tradition of Nineteenth-Century American Jewish Woman Writers* (Bloomington: Indiana University Press, 1992); Bette Roth Young, *Emma Lazarus in Her World: Life and Letters* (Philadelphia: Jewish Publication Society, 1997).

Lebanon War

The State of ISRAEL invaded Lebanon in 1982, igniting what became the most hotly debated military episode in the country's history.

This action was a response to the buildup of Palestinian bases in southern Lebanon in the years since the SIX-DAY WAR (1967), from where they repeatedly shelled towns in northern Israel and launched land and sea attacks against civilian Israeli targets. The PALESTINE LIBERATION ORGANIZATION

(PLO) had taken over the area after thousands of its armed fighters were expelled from Jordan.

The PLO set up its operational center in Lebanon, and maintained an estimated 18,000 troops in bases throughout the country, reinforced with recruits from other nations such as Libya, Iraq, India, Sri Lanka, Chad and Mozambique. They were armed with mortars, rockets, antiaircraft equipment, tanks, and surface-to-air missiles from Syria. The Israeli government felt an invasion was justified both to curtail the attacks and remove a growing threat. The June 6, 1982, invasion was called Operation Peace for Galilee, and its main objective was to remove the PLO and its arms from Lebanon.

In 1976 Lebanese leaders had complained in the UNITED NATIONS General Assembly that the PLO was destroying their country, and PLO aggression and violence toward Lebanese citizens was widely reported. Still, once the war began and escalated, the Israeli army was accused in the international media of unnecessary attacks in civilian areas. Unfortunately, the PLO routinely located its southern Lebanon artillery positions in village centers, leaving the Israelis no safe options. As the Israelis approached Beirut, the PLO dispersed its positions within the civilian population of West Berlin, making civilian casualties inevitable. Nevertheless, total civilian losses from Israeli actions were far below the toll inflicted by years of civil war and Syrian intervention.

By May 31, 1985, Israel had successfully negotiated the removal of PLO bases from Lebanon. However, many Palestinian and other Arab terrorist groups, including Hezbollah, continued to operate from Lebanon, and small-scale fighting continued for many years. Syrian troops replaced Israeli troops as they withdrew, and they allowed terrorist groups to set up camp in the areas they controlled. Israeli troops patrolled a small strip of territory across Lebanon's borders until 2000, when they were suddenly removed by Prime Minister Ehud BARAK.

The Lebanon War was the most controversial and divisive war in Israel's history. Many Israelis did not believe that the Israeli army should have remained there as long as it did. Prime Minister Menachem BEGIN was forced to resign, and the new coalition government that took over in 1984 decided to withdraw from most of Lebanon. The effects of a war that did not have the support of all of Israel's citizens had a lasting effect on the Israeli psyche. In the summer of 2006, Israel invaded Lebanon to remove the threat of the terrorist organization Hezbollah. Again, the war was controversial, not only leaving many Lebanese homeless and in refugee status, but ending with accusations that Israel did not properly prepare its troops for the war under the leadership of Ehud Olmert.

Further reading: A. J. Abraham, *The Lebanon War* (Westport, Conn.: Greenwood Press, 1996); Yaron Ezrahi, *Rubber Bullets: Power and Conscience in Modern Israel* (New York: Farrar, Straus and Giroux, 1997); Thomas L. Friedman, *From Beirut to Jerusalem* (New York: Doubleday, 1989); Howard M. Sachar, *A History of Israel from the Rise of Zionism to Our Time* (New York: Alfred A Knopf, 1996).

Leeser, Isaac (1806–1868) *American Orthodox rabbi*

Isaac Leeser was one of the leading American rabbis of the 19th century. He established the first American publication in the HEBREW language, a periodical called *The Occident,* in 1843, and published numerous Jewish textbooks for children. He initiated the first Jewish college, Maimonides, in Philadelphia. His English translation of the TANAKH, the Hebrew Bible was the commonly accepted Jewish translation in the UNITED STATES for more than 50 years, until the JEWISH PUBLICATION SOCIETY published its translation in 1917.

Leeser was born in Westphalia, Prussia, GERMANY, on December 12, 1806. In 1824 he immigrated to America.

In 1825, Philadelphia's prestigious congregation Mikveh Israel offered him its pulpit. In Philadelphia, Leeser founded Maimonides

College, the first Jewish Publication Society, the first Hebrew high school (with Rebecca GRATZ in 1849), and the first Jewish representative and defense organization, the Board of Delegates of American Israelites (1859). Leeser was a leader in the Sephardic community, and he published the first English translation of the Sephardi prayer book in 1848 (*see* SEPHARDIM).

Although Leeser was not a Reformer, and he worked to lessen the impact of REFORM JUDAISM on the community, he introduced the first regularly scheduled English sermon into the synagogue service. He was also instrumental in posting Jewish chaplains in the American military under President Lincoln. During his 46-year career Leeser was the most productive American Jewish writer, and he significantly contributed to the structure of the American Jewish community in his time. Leeser, however, considered himself primarily an educator, a fact highlighted by his early publication of his translation and writing of children's Jewish education materials, such as J. Johlson's *Instruction in the Mosaic Religion* (1830), and his own *The Hebrew Reader* (1838).

Further reading: Robert V. Friedenberg, *Hear O Israel; The History of American Jewish Preaching, 1654–1970* (Tuscaloosa: University of Alabama Press, 1989); Bertram Wallace Korn, *American Jewry and the Civil War* (Philadelphia: Jewish Publication Society, 1951); Lance J. Sussman, *Isaac Leeser and the Making of American Judaism* (Detroit, Mich.: Wayne State University Press, 1995).

Leibowitz, Nechama (1905–1997) *Israeli scholar/educator*

Nechama Leibowitz was a renowned scholar and teacher of the TANAKH, the Hebrew Bible. Born in 1905 in Riga, Latvia, and educated in Berlin, Leibowitz moved to PALESTINE in 1930. For many years she taught at the Mizrachi Women Teachers Seminary at TEL AVIV UNIVERSITY, among other schools. In 1942 she began to provide questions about the weekly TORAH portion to encourage the regular study of Torah. Leibowitz became known for her insightful questions and her pages were, and still are, quite popular.

Leibowitz was commonly known as Nechama to her students. In her own eyes, she was a teacher rather than a scholar. She sought to teach not only the biblical text, but love of Torah study as well. Her approach to Bible study was through active questioning of the text. For many years, Leibowitz, in her "pages," simply asked questions, only publishing answers many years later. Leibowitz was interested in both traditional and modern biblical commentaries and in exploring the literary, psychological, and religious meanings of the text.

The Leibowitz "pages" have been translated into many languages and published in book form. Leibowitz is recognized as one of the leading popular teachers of the Torah in the 20th century, and as a role model in ORTHODOX JUDAISM for women scholars and teachers. Leibowitz was awarded the Israel Prize for Education in 1956, and died in Jerusalem in 1997.

Further reading: Leah Abramowitz, *Tales of Nechama: Impressions of the Life and Teachings of Nehama Leibowitz* (Jerusalem: Gefen Publishing House, 2003); Blu Greenberg, *On Women and Judaism: A View from Tradition* (Philadelphia: Jewish Publication Society, 1998); Nehama Leibowitz, *Studies in Bereshit* (Jerusalem: World Zionist Organization, 1981).

Leibowitz, Yeshayahu (1903–1994) *Israeli scholar/educator*

Yeshayahu Leibowitz was born in Riga, Latvia, and, like his scholarly sister Nechama LEIBOWITZ, was educated in GERMANY and Switzerland. He studied both philosophy and chemistry at Berlin University, but received his Ph.D. in philosophy. In addition, Leibowitz attended Basel University, earning a medical degree there in 1934. One year later, in 1935, he immigrated to PALESTINE. Leibowitz joined the faculty of HEBREW UNIVERSITY and taught chemistry, history, physiology, and the philosophy of science. He penned many articles and books on scientific and Jewish topics. In the early 1950s, Leibowitz served as editor for several volumes of the *Encyclopedia Hebraica,* also called the "Hebrew Encyclopedia."

Leibowitz was an outspoken individual, creating great antagonism among supporters of ORTHODOX JUDAISM in ISRAEL, especially supporters of religious ZIONISM. When the government sought to award him the Israel Prize in 1992, there was significant political controversy when Prime Minister Yitzhak RABIN refused to attend the ceremony if Leibowitz was honored there. Leibowitz declined his award. He died two year later in JERUSALEM.

Leibowitz strongly believed that Judaism's sole focus should be on HALAKHAH, or Jewish law, and not be distracted by the needs of the state; the Jew's obligation to observe God's commandments, or mitzvot (*see* MITZVAH), was the end in itself, and did not provide any earthly benefit for the observer. However, Leibowitz believed that the RABBIS must renew their deliberations on Jewish law, more properly applying *halakhah* to the needs of the modern world. He advocated the complete separation of religion and state in Israel so that religions and secular spheres could focus on appropriate goals. He did not believe that religion should ever be the government's business.

Leibowitz also antagonized the political right by calling for Israel to withdraw from all the Arab territories captured after the SIX-DAY WAR, urging Israelis to refuse to serve in Arab territories, and labeling his opponents "Judeo-fascists" and "Judeo-Nazis." He ridiculed CONSERVATIVE and REFORM JUDAISM, and denounced as "idolatrous" many customs of HASIDISM and of Israel's SEPHARDIM. Leibowitz led the charge against any type of governmental corruption, and he made political enemies in many camps.

Yeshayahu Leibowitz was an anomaly in Israel. Personally observant, he maintained an uncommon combination of traditional theology and politically left-wing views.

Further reading: Yeshayahu Leibowitz and Eliezer Goldman, *Judaism, Human Values, and the Jewish State*

(Cambridge, Mass.: Harvard University Press, 1992); Adam Zachary Newton, *The Fence and the Neighbor: Emmanuel Levinas, Yeshayahu Leibowitz, and Israel Among the Nations* (Albany: State University of New York Press, 2000).

lesbianism

Traditionally, lesbianism has been discouraged in Judaism, although not to the same degree as male HOMOSEXUALITY, which involves "spilling seed," a specific prohibition in the TORAH (Lv 18:2–3). While lesbianism is not specifically prohibited, it was severely frowned on by the ancient RABBIS, and some contemporary rabbis have interpreted MIDRASH in a way that would prohibit lesbianism.

Currently, feminist movements within Judaism portray lesbianism in a more positive light, arguing that not only is it not prohibited, but that it can be a means of overcoming some of the traditional misogyny within the tradition.

Further reading: Christie Balka and Andy Rose, eds., *Twice Blessed: On Being Lesbian, Gay and Jewish* (Boston: Beacon Press, 1991); Evelyn Torton Beck, ed.: *Nice Jewish Girls: A Lesbian Anthology* (Boston: Beacon Press, 1989); *Tanakh: The Holy Scriptures* (Philadelphia and Jerusalem: Jewish Publication Society, 1985).

Levi, Asser (d. 1681) *American colonial leader*

One of the first Jewish settlers in the American colonies, Asser Levi came to the Dutch colony of New Amsterdam in 1654 (*see* NETHERLANDS, THE). He was among the small group of Jews who had fled the Portuguese Inquisition in BRAZIL. Governor Peter STUYVESANT tried to expel this destitute group, but Levi successfully petitioned the authorities in Holland to allow the group to stay in New Amsterdam. However, Stuyvesant imposed severe restrictions on their activity. He permitted their practice of Judaism, but forbade them to build a SYNAGOGUE, seek assistance from the citizenry or government, or engage in the fur or any retail trade.

Levi fought Stuyvesant's prohibition against the Jews' serving in the militia, and he won the right to participate in the citizens' guards in November 1655. Levi continued to battle the prohibitions against the Jews and eventually won the right to carry on a trade in New Amsterdam. He built a prosperous real estate business and opened a kosher butcher shop. Levi became one of the most prominent New Yorkers of the 17th century.

Levi helped to secure the principles of equality under the law for the first time in America. He helped to create the precedent that would result in the future open-door policy for immigrants to the UNITED STATES.

Further reading: Edwin G. Burrows, *Gotham: A History of New York City to 1898* (New York: Oxford University Press, 1998); Jeffrey S. Gurock, ed., *American Jewish History*, vol. 1, *The Colonial and Early National Periods, 1654–1840* (New York: Routledge, 1997); Russell Shorto, *The Island at the Center of the World: The Epic Story of Dutch Manhattan, the Forgotten Colony That Shaped America* (New York: Doubleday, 2004).

Leviathan

Leviathan is a sea monster mentioned in passing in the TANAKH, the Hebrew Bible. While Psalm 74 indicates that God long ago crushed Leviathan, Isaiah 27 indicates that the slaying will take place in a future age. Jewish tradition accounts for this discrepancy by claiming that there were two such beasts, one male and one female. According to legend, God slew the female so the two would not be able to reproduce and destroy the world; it is even said that Adam and Eve had garments made from her skin. The male, however, will be slain in messianic (*see* MESSIAH) times. At that time, it is said, the righteous in heaven will feast on his flesh. God is also seen in Psalms "sporting" with Leviathan, suggesting God's dominance over the creature, but also God's willingness to allow the creature to live.

The idea of the conquest of a giant sea monster as part of the CREATION of the world has a remark-able parallel in the Enuma Elish, a Mesopotamian creation myth in which the god Marduk slays the female sea monster Tiamat. Thus it is quite possible that the legend entered Judaism from Mesopotamian culture.

Further reading: Arthur Hertzberg, ed., *Judaism: The Classic Introduction to One of the Great Religions of the Modern World* (New York: Simon and Schuster, 1991); David Wolfers, *Deep Things Out of Darkness: The Book of Job: Essays and a New English Translation* (Grand Rapids, Mich.: Wm. B. Eerdmans, 1995); Leo W. Schwarz, *Enduring Ideas in the Jewish Heritage: A Discussion Guide for Youth and Adults Based on the Feat of Leviathan* (New York and Toronto: Rinehart, 1956); Psalms 104:26 in *Tanakh: The Holy Scriptures* (Philadelphia and Jerusalem: Jewish Publication Society, 1985).

Lévi-Strauss, Claude (b. 1908) *theoretical anthropologist*

Born in Brussels in 1908, Claude Lévi-Strauss was raised in a French Jewish intellectual family and was the grandson of a RABBI. Nevertheless, he was a self-described "unbeliever" from a young age. He graduated from the Sorbonne in 1932 with degrees in philosophy and law, but rejected these disciplines in favor of anthropology, which would allow him to study more diverse cultures; the philosophy curriculum at that time was limited to Western thought.

In 1934 Lévi-Strauss accepted a position as a visiting professor at the University of São Paulo in BRAZIL, where he conducted his first ethnographic fieldwork. He was drafted into the French army and returned to FRANCE in 1939, but because he was Jewish, he fled to the UNITED STATES when the Germans occupied France in 1941. Along with many other European intellectual refugees, Lévi-Strauss taught at the New School for Social Research in New York from 1942 to 1945. He returned to France in 1947 and was awarded his doctoral degree in ethnology from the Sorbonne in 1948.

Lévi-Strauss was particularly interested in marriage customs. His dissertation, which was also published as his first book, was *The Elementary Structures of Kinship,* in which he argued that kinship patterns are based on alliances made by exchanging women. His method of analyzing cultures based on specific patterns of relationships that work as units of culture became known as structural anthropology, and his fame derives from his role as the founder of this branch of anthropology.

Since structural anthropology views all cultures as working according to patterns or codes, it inherently rejects the idea of the superiority of any one culture. Lévi-Strauss was a student of Emile Durkheim, another French Jewish intellectual anthropologist who argued that modern Western civilization, including Judaism and CHRISTIANITY, was more evolved than other more primitive cultures. While this evolutionary idea was prevalent at the time, and while Lévi-Strauss's own secular Judaism revealed rationalistic modernist tendencies, Lévi-Strauss's work in fact challenged such notions. His rejection of Western superiority was a distinct factor in his popularity.

Lévi-Strauss served as a chairperson at the École des Hautes Études in Paris, France from 1950 to 1959, after which he assumed a post as chair of social anthropology at the Collège de France, which he held until 1982. He filled a number of other academic posts until his retirement. As recently as 2003, he received the Meister-Eckhart Prize in philosophy. Some of his most important works include *Tristes Tropiques, Structural Anthropology, The Raw and the Cooked,* and *Mythologiques.*

Further reading: John Murray Cuddihy, *The Ordeal of Civility: Freud, Marx, Lévi-Strauss and the Jewish Struggle with Modernity* (Boston: Beacon Press, 1987); Edmund Leach, *Claude Levi-Strauss* (Chicago: University of Chicago Press, 1989); Claude Lévi-Strauss, *The Raw and the Cooked* (Chicago: University of Chicago Press, 1990); ———, *Structural Anthropology* (Chicago: University of Chicago Press, 1983); ———, *Tristes Tropiques* (New York: Penguin, 1992).

Levites

The Levites, descendants of Levi, the third son of Jacob, were the tribe set aside for priestly service. They were divided into two groups: the KOHANIM or priests, including MOSES and AARON, who were assigned the specific responsibility of offering SACRIFICES, and the ordinary Levites.

Under the biblical COVENANT, the Levites were the only tribe not assigned a specific territory or agricultural land, although they were given cities in which to live. They were to be supported by the rest of the community via regular offerings and taxes. In exchange, the Levites were responsible for maintaining the required ritual practices for the community. In contemporary times, the first ALIYAH in a SHABBAT (Sabbath) or holiday service is reserved for a *kohen,* and the second for an ordinary Levite. In addition, the Levites wash the hands of the *kohanim* before the latter recite the priestly blessing on major festivals.

Further reading: Gary Knoppers, "Hierodules, Priests, or Janitors: The Levites in Chronicles and the History of the Israelite Priesthood" in *Journal of Biblical Literature* 118 (Spring 1999), 49–72; J. H. Hertz, "The Book of Leviticus" in *The Pentateuch and Haftorahs* (London, 1960), 554–9; Gordon J. Wenham, *The Book of Leviticus* (London, 1979).

Levi Yitzchak of Berditchev (1740–1810)
Hasidic rabbi

Levi Yitzchak of Berditchev was a disciple of DOV BAER, the Maggid of Mezritch. He became one of the most important leaders in the third generation of HASIDISM. He succeeded in bringing the movement to POLAND, and served as the leader in the debates and power struggles between the Hasidim and their opponents, the MITNAGDIM.

Levi Yitzchak stressed the primary role of joy in one's life, the need to cling to God, and the role that fervent PRAYER could play in elevating the spirit. In order to teach a new model for Jewish prayer, he traveled with his followers and introduced his Hasidic style wherever they went.

Many of Levi Yitzchak's sermons were collected in the book *Kedushat Levi*. He preached that one must always try to find the good in other people. He is also known for his emphasis on the need for humility before God. For the last 25 years of his life he served as RABBI of Berditchev, and became known as: "The Berditchever."

Levi Yitzchak died in Berditchev in 1810 and, although no named tombstone was placed on his grave, everyone knew that it was the Berditchever who was buried there. A pilgrimage to his gravesite is still made by the Berditchever followers today.

Further reading: Samuel H. Dresner, *World of a Hasidic Master: Levi Yitzhak of Berditchev* (Northvale, N.J.: Jason Aronson, 1994); Gershom Scholem, *Major Trends in Jewish Mysticism* (New York: Schocken Books, 1995); Adin Steinsaltz, *Opening the Tanya: Discovering the Moral and Mystical Teachings of a Classic Work of Kabbalah* (San Francisco: Jossey-Bass, 2003).

Lieberman, Joseph (b. 1942) *U.S. senator*

Joseph Isador Lieberman was born in Stamford, Connecticut, on February 24, 1942. Raised in a traditional Jewish home, Lieberman became the first adherent of ORTHODOX JUDAISM to become a UNITED STATES senator. In 2000, Lieberman was chosen by the Democratic presidential nominee Al Gore to be his running mate. Unlike Al Smith in 1928, who endured enormous bigotry in his bid for the presidency because of his Catholic faith, Lieberman received little negative press because of his commitment to Orthodox Judaism. Rather, his traditional family values that were linked to his Orthodoxy seemed to serve him well in the polls. Lieberman became the first Jew to be on a major political party's presidential ticket. He publicly announced his loyalty to the United States when discussing Middle Eastern politics to reassure voters.

Lieberman completed his undergraduate studies at Yale University in 1964, and graduated from Yale law school three years later. He served as a Connecticut state senator from 1975 to 1981 and in 1982 was elected Connecticut's attorney general. In 1988 he was elected to the U.S. Senate, where he still serves.

As a United States senator, Lieberman became a prominent leader of the moderate wing of the Democratic Party. Known for his traditional family values, he was praised by both Democrats and Republicans for publicly rebuking his own party's president, Bill Clinton, in 1988, for his immoral conduct in the Monica Lewinsky scandal. Al Gore's choice of Lieberman as a running mate was viewed as an attempt to distance himself from the immoral image of Clinton, for whom he served as vice president.

Lieberman and Gore received the majority of the popular vote in the 2000 election, but after the controversial vote count in Florida was settled by the U.S. Supreme Court, they lost the election in the electoral college. In 2003, Lieberman declared his candidacy for president, but after poor returns in the early primaries, he withdrew from the race.

Further reading: J. J. Goldberg, *Jewish Power: Inside the American Jewish Establishment* (Reading, Mass.: Addison Wesley, 1996); Joseph I. Lieberman and Hadassah Lieberman, *An Amazing Adventure: Joe and Hadassah's Personal Notes on the 2000 Campaign* (New York: Simon & Schuster, 2003); ———, *Joseph Lieberman Is a Pious Liberal and Other Observations* (Brooklyn, N.Y.: Ish Yemini Press, 2003).

Lieberman, Saul (1898–1983) *Talmud scholar and Conservative leader*

Saul Lieberman is considered to have been one of the great students of TALMUD of the 20th century. He was born in Belarus in 1898. He studied first at the Slobodka YESHIVA, and then at universities in Kiev and FRANCE. In 1928 he became a professor of Talmud at the HEBREW UNIVERSITY in JERUSALEM, and then dean of the Harry Fischel Institute for Talmudic Research.

In 1940 he left the Hebrew University to join the faculty of the JEWISH THEOLOGICAL SEMINARY

(JTS) in New York. There he additionally served as dean of the rabbinical school and as rector. Lieberman was a member of many major academic organizations, including the American Academy of Arts and Sciences, the Academy for the Hebrew Language, the Academy for Jewish Research, and the Israeli Academy of Science and Humanities. In 1971, Lieberman received the Israel Prize for Jewish Studies.

Lieberman combined a thorough knowledge of the classical Greek and Roman period with his immense mastery of rabbinic texts. He was thus able to gain significant insight into the cultural and social phenomena that lay behind the Jewish literature of the period.

Lieberman's particular area of interest was the Palestinian, or Jerusalem Talmud. He devoted the majority of his academic study to the TOSEFTA, a collection of rabbinic teachings from the period of the MISHNAH that were not included in the Mishnah itself, but that formed the literary foundation for the Jerusalem Talmud. Lieberman's greatest scholarly contribution was in this field of study, called the Tosefta Ki-Feshuta, but he had an even greater impact through his 40 years of leadership in CONSERVATIVE JUDAISM.

Today, Lieberman is commonly known by many contemporary Conservative Jews through his "Lieberman Clause," found in most Conservative *ketubot* (wedding contracts; *see* KETUBAH). It is a legal formula to prevent the wife from ever becoming an AGUNAH. According to this clause, if the marriage dissolves and the husband refuses to give the wife a GET, or Jewish divorce, both parties are obligated to appear before a rabbinic court authorized by the JTS and abide by its decision. In almost every case, the court would order the husband to issue a *get*. The newly divorced woman could then remarry, which, according to HALAKHAH, or Jewish law, would be forbidden without a *get*.

The Lieberman clause was accepted by the great Modern Orthodox rabbi, Joseph SOLOVEITCHIK, but rabbis in the more extreme circles of ORTHODOX JUDAISM have refused to recognize its validity.

Further reading: Anita Diamant, *The New Jewish Wedding, Revised* (New York: Fireside, 2001); Saul Lieberman and Meir Lubetski, *Saul Lieberman, 1898–1983, Talmudic Scholar* (Lewiston, N.Y.: Edwin Mellen Press, 2002); Saul Lieberman, *Greek in Jewish Palestine* (New York: Jewish Theological Seminary of America, 1994).

life cycle

The basic events in the Jewish life cycle are birth, circumcision/naming, coming-of-age, MARRIAGE, and death (*see* MOURNING). Each of these events is commemorated in Jewish ritual.

When a Jewish boy is born, he traditionally undergoes a ceremony known as a BRIT MILAH. This is a ritual circumcision performed by a mohel when the infant is eight days old. If he is a first-born son, an additional ceremony is performed when the boy is 31 days old, called *PIDYON HA-BEN*. Since all first things belong to God, the first-born son must be consecrated to God as well; he is ransomed back in the ceremony, usually for five silver shekels (or dollars). A boy is given his name at the *brit*, but a special naming ceremony for girls has become popular, usually occurring at a SYNAGOGUE service, during the parents' ALIYAH. It is a custom, or MINHAG, among ASHKENAZIM to name a child after a deceased relative, but among SEPHARDIM it is permitted to name the child after someone living.

The coming-of-age ceremony is called a bar mitzvah for boys and a bat mitzvah for girls (*see* BAR/BAT MITZVAH). At the age of 13 for boys, and 12 or 13 for girls, the child formally enters the community of adults, and is bound to uphold the commandments. The ceremony generally includes reading from the TORAH and/or the HAFTARAH during a SHABBAT (Sabbath) synagogue service. In ORTHODOX JUDAISM, however, the bat mitzvah girl often delivers a DVAR TORAH at home or at synagogue on a Sunday. In REFORM and CONSERVATIVE JUDAISM, teenagers often observe a second coming-of-age ceremony known as CONFIRMATION, which was adopted from Christian culture. It marks the completion of a series of courses in Jewish studies, usually at age 16 or 18.

The next event in the Jewish life cycle is marriage, commemorated with a Jewish wedding. A Jewish wedding has a number of requirements, such as a veil for the bride, a CHUPPAH, or canopy, to stand under, the circling of the groom by the bride seven times, a blessing over wine drunk together, the recitation of seven blessings, the exchange of rings, and the breaking of a glass.

Finally, there are many rituals to commemorate death. Funeral requirements are extensive and include a swift funeral, a burial underground, and clothing the deceased in a simple shroud. Because death is seen as an impurity, many things cannot be said or done in the presence of the body. KOHANIM, those descended from the priestly class, may not come into contact with the body, and anyone else who does must wash afterwards. The mourners sit SHIVA for seven days after the burial, sitting on low stools or the floor; they do not wear leather shoes, shave or cut their hair, wear cosmetics, work, or do anything for comfort or pleasure, such as bathe, have sex, put on fresh clothing, or study TORAH. Mourners wear the clothes that they tore at the time of the funeral and cover their mirrors to avoid the mundane activities associated with vanity. Visitors bring food and hold worship services in which the mourner can say KADDISH, the prayer for the dead, as long as a MINYAN of 10 Jews past the age of bar or bat mitzvah is present. For 30 days the mourner may not celebrate in any way or partake in amusements, and should attend services each day for a year in order to say Kaddish.

Further reading: Hayim Halevy Donin, *To Be a Jew: A Guide to Jewish Observance in Contemporary Life* (New York: Basic Books, 1972); Harvey E. Goldberg, *Jewish Passages: Cycles of Jewish Life* (Berkeley: University of California Press, 2003); Ronald H. Isaacs, *Rites of Passage: A Guide to the Jewish Life Cycle* (Hoboken, N.J.: Ktav Publishing House, 1992).

Likud

The government of ISRAEL runs on a parliamentary system (*see* KNESSET), dominated by two large political parties, LABOR and Likud. Likud is Hebrew for "gathering-in," and the party is structured as a coalition of smaller parties that maintain their individual identities. The party was formed for the 1973 election by three parties—the Free Center, Laam, and Gahal. Since its inception, Likud has either controlled the Knesset as part of the ruling coalition or acted as the leading opposition party. In 1988 two more parties merged with Likud—Herut and the Liberal Party.

Likud is considered to be Israel's more rightwing party, mostly on issues of security and foreign affairs. In the past, Likud encouraged settlements in the occupied territory of the West Bank (*see* JUDEA AND SAMARIA) and in Gaza. Currently the Likud Party does not support new settlements, but it does allow expansion of established settlements. On the other hand, the first Likud government under Prime Minister Menachem BEGIN returned the entire Sinai peninsula to Egypt in exchange for a peace settlement, and the current Likud government under Prime Minister Ariel SHARON has announced plans to withdraw from all settlements in Gaza and several settlements in the West Bank.

Likud historically opposes socialism and supports privatization of government-owned enterprises. It also supports parallel reforms in public health, education, and social service.

Likud prime ministers include Begin (1977–83), Yitzhak SHAMIR (1983–84; 1986–92), Benjamin NETANYAHU (1996–99), and Sharon (2001–present).

Further reading: Gideon Doron and Don Peretz, *The Government and Politics of Israel* (Boulder, Colo.: Westview Press, 1997); Howard R. Penniman, ed., *Israel at the Polls: The Knesset Elections of 1977* (Washington, D.C.: American Enterprise Institute, 1979); David M. Zohar, *Political Parties in Israel: The Evolution of Israeli Democracy* (New York and London: Praeger, 1974).

Lilith (Lillith) *legendary figure*

Lilith does not appear in the TANAKH, the Hebrew Bible, but the ancient rabbis claim she was the first companion of Adam. There are two separate accounts of the CREATION in Genesis, one in which God creates male and female together, and one in which woman is created out of man's body. Jewish tradition holds that the first of these two women was Lilith, but that she was fiercely independent and was banished from the GARDEN OF EDEN so that a second, more submissive wife, Eve, could be produced.

Tradition depicts Lilith as bitter and vengeful because of her plight. In the Middle Ages Jews believed she became the demon queen of the evil SAMAEL; she was said to enter homes to mate with men sleeping alone, steal children, and harm newborn infants. Various inscriptions, incantations, and amulets were used to protect children from Lilith.

Feminist Jews have recently given a more positive slant to the story of Lilith. They see her as a role model for the strong independent woman. She has even been honored by having a feminist journal named after her, LILITH MAGAZINE.

Further reading: Doris B. Gold and Lisa Stein, comps., *From the Wise Women of Israel: Folklore and Memoirs* (New York: Biblio Press, 1993); Naomi M. Hyman, *Biblical Women in the Midrash: A Sourcebook* (Northvale, N.J.: Jason Aronson, 1997); Joy Kogawa, *A Song of Lilith* (Vancouver, B.C.: Laurel Glen, 2001).

Lilith magazine

Lilith magazine is named after the character of LILITH in the MIDRASH, which describes her as the biblical Adam's first wife. According the magazine's editors, they chose the name based on Lilith's status as Adam's equal. Published since 1976, the magazine is subtitled *The Independent Jewish Women's Magazine* and is not sponsored by any other Jewish or non-Jewish institution. *Lilith* is a nonprofit magazine dedicated to illustrating the lives of Jewish women, providing investigative reports about issues important to Jewish women, explaining new rituals and celebrations, reporting first-person accounts from historical and contemporary perspectives, and providing reviews of

entertainment, fiction, poetry, art, and photography. Contributors to *Lilith* magazine have included Cynthia OZICK, Letty Cottin Pogrebin, Nessa Rappoport, Blu GREENBERG, and others. *Lilith* also publishes the work of new writers. *Lilith* magazine is published in New York City.

Further reading: Joy Kogawa, *A Song of Lilith* (Vancouver, B.C.: Laurel Glen, 2001); *Lilith: The Independent Jewish Woman's Magazine* (New York: Lilith Publications, Inc., 1997–2002); Steven P. Schneider, "Poetry, Midrash and Feminism," in *Tikkun* 16, no. 4 (July 2001): 61; Howard Schwartz, *Reimagining the Bible: The Storytelling of the Rabbis* (New York: Oxford University Press, 1998).

Lion of Judah

Lion imagery appears throughout the TANAKH, the Hebrew Bible, and the TALMUD. In Genesis (49), JUDAH, one of Jacob's 12 sons, is likened to a lion. The text refers to his leadership qualities and his ability to command obedience. Lions were used to depict the tribe of Judah and were possibly used as a symbol of the Davidic kings, as King DAVID was himself a descendant of Judah. The rabbinic text ETHICS OF THE FATHERS states that a man should have the boldness of a lion.

The lion of the tribe of Judah has been a common symbol in Jewish art since classical antiquity, often depicted on a shield as a gold lion. Today it is used to symbolize a level of women's charitable gifts in the federation culture in the UNITED STATES (*see* UNITED JEWISH COMMUNITIES).

Further reading: Cecil Roth, *Jewish Art: An Illustrated History* (New York: McGraw-Hill, 1961); *Tanakh: The Holy Scriptures* (Philadelphia and Jerusalem: Jewish Publication Society, 1985).

Lipstadt, Deborah (b. 1947) *rabbi and noted historian*

Deborah Lipstadt is the director of the Rabbi Donald A. Tam Institute for Jewish Studies at Emory

University and the Dorot Professor of Modern Jewish and HOLOCAUST Studies. She received her B.A. from City College of New York and her M.A. and Ph.D. from Brandeis University. Lipstadt has taught in several universities, including the University of California at Los Angeles, Occidental College, and Emory University.

Lipstadt is best known for the controversy surrounding her book *Denying the Holocaust* (1993), which has been characterized as the first full-length study of HOLOCAUST REVISIONISTS. The book attracted international attention and received the 1994 Jewish Book Honor Award. It also sparked a lawsuit initiated by one of the Holocaust deniers profiled in her book, who accused Lipstadt of libel based on his belief that her claims of the Holocaust were untrue. The case was resolved in 2000 in Lipstadt's favor.

Lipstadt has served as a consultant for the UNITED STATES HOLOCAUST MEMORIAL MUSEUM and on President Clinton's Holocaust Memorial Council. She also consults with government agencies on steps to take when confronted with Holocaust denial. Lipstadt has served as well on a variety of education committees such as the Konrad Adenauer Foundation's Jewish-German exchange program, and she has worked with the German government to explore ways of teaching Jewish history and the Holocaust in GERMANY.

Lipstadt has lectured around the UNITED STATES and in countries such as ENGLAND, GERMANY, Switzerland, CANADA, Australia, New Zealand, and ISRAEL. She has appeared in on CNN, CBS's *60 Minutes*, NBC's *Today Show*, ABC's *Good Morning America*, National Public Radio's *Fresh Air*, and PBS's *Charlie Rose Show*. Lipstadt has also contributed newspaper columns to the *Los Angeles Times, Washington Post, Cleveland Plain Dealer, Atlanta Constitution, Baltimore Sun, New York Times, Time, Newsweek,* and *New York Newsday*.

However, Lipstadt refuses to appear on a televised interview if a Holocaust denier has also been invited to speak. She believes that Holocaust deniers should not be given the forums they seek in an attempt to establish their legitimacy. Lip-

stadt is also the author of *Beyond Belief: The American Press and the Coming of the Holocaust* (1986).

Further reading: Edward Alexander, "False Witness: The Irving-Lipstadt Trial and the *New Yorker*" in *Judaism* 50, no. 4 (Fall 2001): 453–456; Deborah Lipstadt, *Beyond Belief: The American Press and the Coming of the Holocaust* (New York: Free Press, 1986); ———, *Denying the Holocaust: The Growing Assault on Truth and Memory* (New York: Maxwell Macmillan International, 1993).

Lithuania *See* POLAND; VILNA GAON.

L'kha Dodi

The prayer L'kha Dodi was composed in Safed, PALESTINE, in the early 16th century by the mystic and RABBI Shlomo Ha-Levi Alkabetz. Alkabetz was part of a circle of masters of the KABBALAH, Jewish mysticism, that included Rabbis Moses CORDOVERO, Joseph CARO, and Isaac LURIA. The lyrics of L'kha Dodi constitute an acrostic of the author's name.

L'kha Dodi was adopted by Jews everywhere as the climactic prayer of the KABBALAT SHABBAT liturgy, which aims to prepare the worshippers to receive the Sabbath (*see* SHABBAT) in the tradition of the ancient rabbis. The Talmud states that Rabbi Chanina would wrap himself in his cloak and say, "Come, let us go and greet the Shabbat Queen" and Rabbi Yannai would don his robe and say, "Enter O bride! Enter, O bride!"

The hymn's refrain is, "L'kha dodi likrat kallah penei shabbat n'kabaalah," which translates, "Come out my Beloved, the Bride to meet; the inner light of Shabbat, let us greet." The refrain reminds the worshipper of the days when the mystics would go out to the fields on the Sabbath eve, welcome the metaphoric Sabbath bride, escort her to the SYNAGOGUE, and recite their Sabbath prayers.

The Sabbath bride is a common motif in Kabbalistic literature, where the Sabbath is commonly associated with the Shekhinah (the aspect of God that dwells among the people), the tangible feminine presence of God. The mystics perceived Shabbat as the time of mystical union between God's male and female aspects, and between the Jewish people and God. The custom remains for worshippers to rise and face the entrance of the synagogue as they recite the concluding stanza of L'kha Dodi, "Come my Bride, Come my Bride," bowing to welcome the Divine Presence into their midst.

Further reading: Ismar Elbogen and Raymond P. Scheindlin, *Jewish Liturgy: A Comprehensive History* (Philadelphia: Jewish Publication Society of America, 1993); Reuven Hammer, *Entering Jewish Prayer: A Guide to Personal Devotion and the Worship Service* (New York: Schocken Books, 1995).

Lord *See* GOD, NAMES OF.

Lower East Side

During the last few decades of the 19th century and the first few decades of the 20th, the Lower East Side of New York City became both a haven and a hell for hundreds of thousands of Jewish immigrants. Living near immigrants of other religions and nationalities, eastern European Jews crowded into frequently run-down TENEMENTS or apartment buildings. Seven or eight people often lived in three-room apartments. Many immigrants did "piecework" at home, which meant that the limited space was crowded with the supplies needed to produce clothing and fabric. Pushcarts filled with aromatic foods from abroad lined the streets, and people shopped among them for groceries and other necessary supplies. Burdened with a far larger population than it could accommodate, the Lower East Side was choked with garbage and waste. Sanitation was poor and the air polluted with the products of a growing industrial city.

Yet in spite of its poor living conditions, the Lower East Side also contained a rich medley of Jewish culture, a combination of the new and the old. Jewish cultural and religious life flourished when the people lived in close proximity, and many Jewish immigrants headed for the Lower East Side for the community feeling and opportunity it held. The streets were often filled with loud discussions and arguments about politics, religion, family, and America.

The established German-Jewish community tried to draw immigrants away from the Lower East Side, through the GALVESTON PLAN and the INDUSTRIAL REMOVAL OFFICE, but they had little success. YIDDISH was the mother tongue of the majority of the Jewish immigrants who inhabited the Lower East Side, and a lively Yiddish theater and press was locally available (*see* ENTERTAINMENT; *JEWISH DAILY FORWARD*). Hundreds of SYNAGOGUES were built, often named after the towns from which the members came. To supplement the synagogues, *LANDSMANSCHAFTEN* emerged, providing social services and camaraderie for those hailing from the same European town.

Many contemporary American Jews see the story of the Lower East Side as part of their collective memory, whether or not their direct ancestors ever lived there. Today the Lower East Side still boasts kosher restaurants and Jewish stores, offering ritual items and foods that are difficult to find elsewhere. Yet, most Jewish residents left the Lower East Side in the 1950s, as they gained middle-class status and succeeded in living the American dream. Newer groups of immigrants, especially from Puerto Rico and China, replaced them in the tenements and storefronts, leaving a mostly elderly Jewish community. However, in recent years the Jewish population has seen a resurgence, with Orthodox families taking advantage of large apartments, and young Jews attracted by the gentrification of downtown Manhattan.

The history of the Jews in America can be experienced at the Lower East Side Tenement Museum or on the Onion Tour, a guided walk among the remaining landmarks of the original neighborhood where Jewish immigrants settled and became Americans.

These men gather outside the local post office on the Lower East Side. It was often quite hot in the tenements on the Lower East Side and only windows provided needed ventilation. *(Library of Congress)*

Further reading: Hasia R. Diner, *Lower East Side Memories: A Jewish Place in America* (Princeton and Oxford: Princeton University Press, 2000); Irving Howe, *World of Our Fathers: Immigrant Jews of New York, 1881 to Present* (New York: Schocken Books, 1989); Isaac Metzker, *The Bintel Brief: Sixty Years of Letters from the Lower East Side to the Jewish Daily Forward* (New York: Schocken Books, 1990); Ronald

Sanders, *The Downtown Jews: Portraits of an Immigrant Generation* (New York: Dover Publications, 1987).

Luria, Isaac (1534–1572) *Hasidic rabbi and master of Kabbalah*

Isaac Luria, also known as the Ari or lion, was born in JERUSALEM to parents from GERMANY. He grew up in EGYPT and studied rabbinic literature and Jewish law. Though he was always devoted to study, he earned his living through commerce.

When he was 21, Luria devoted himself to studying the ZOHAR, the central book of the KABBALAH, and other mystical texts. He apparently believed that ELIJAH the Prophet spoke to him often, and he made attempts to speak only in HEBREW. Luria is rumored to have meditated on the mystical text the *Zohar* for seven years.

In 1569, Luria moved to the land of ISRAEL on instruction from Elijah the Prophet. He studied with the Kabbalist Moses CORDOVERO of SAFED until Cordovero's death in 1570, and with other Kabbalists in the town, and began teaching there himself. Luria never wrote down his theories; his disciples put them to paper only after his death.

Luria taught that to create the universe, an omnipresent God had to withdraw himself (*tzimtzum*), thus making space for the CREATION. After the initial withdrawal, light flowed from God and formed 10 SEFIROT, vessels of light. God's pure light was so powerful that it shattered the vessels, and chaos ensued. Over a series of contractions and expansions, Creation came to be composed of broken vessels and light, resulting in an ongoing struggle between good and evil. Human beings have a role to play in this chaos by recapturing the divine sparks that have been scattered throughout the world, thus uniting the earthly and divine realms.

Luria's system provided a spiritual explanation for the EXILE, and a purpose for Jewry in the DIASPORA. Jews were to gather the sparks of divine light through the performance of good deeds, wherever they lived. Every human action gained cosmic significance and would ultimately repair the world (TIKKUN OLAM) and usher in the MESSIANIC AGE.

Further reading: Lawrence Fine, "Maggidic Revelation in the Teachings of Isaac Luria," in *Mystics, Philosophers, and Politicians* (Durham, N.C.: Duke University Press, 1982), 141–157; Ronit Meroz, "Faithful Transmission versus Innovation: Luria and His Disciples" in *Gershom Scholem's Major Trends in Jewish Mysticism 50 Years After* (Tubingen: Mohr, 1993), 257–274; Gershom Scholem, *Major Trends in Jewish Mysticism* (New York: Schocken Books, 1974 [1946]; Isaiah Tishby, *The Doctrine of Evil in Lurianic Kabbalah* (London: Kegan Paul International, Ltd., 2005).

Luzzatto, Moses Hayyim (1707–1747) *eighteenth-century Italian mystic*

Both a rabbinic scholar and a mystic, Moses Hayyim Luzzatto was born in Padua, Italy, to a well-established Jewish family. As a child he received a traditional Jewish education, focusing his study on TANAKH (the Hebrew Bible) and TALMUD. However, he was also taught literature, classics, and secular culture.

Even at a young age Luzzatto built a reputation as a great scholar of both Jewish and secular works. At age 20 he began to concentrate on KABBALAH. He claimed to have heard the voice of the *maggid*, the divine messenger who is supposed to reveal the heavenly secrets to humanity, and continued to get many messages from him over the years. He passed the messages on to fellow mystics who studied at the university in Padua. Luzzatto's messages were often hints about the coming of the MESSIAH. He taught that if he and his followers pursued their studies properly, they could help bring final redemption to the world. They applied the term *tikkun*, which means "repair," to their mystical efforts (*see* TIKKUN OLAM).

Luzzatto came to believe that he was a reincarnation of MOSES of the book of EXODUS. Luzzatto's mystical messages and messianic fervor alarmed the majority of RABBIS in Venice, who feared a revival of the false messianism that had been preached by SHABBATAI ZVI in the previous century. Luzzatto confessed that he was influenced by the writings of Nathan of Gaza, Shabbatai Zvi's "prophet." The rabbis ordered him to stop teaching the Kabbalah, and he withstood years of persecution.

In 1731, Luzzatto relocated to Amsterdam in the NETHERLANDS, where he continued to write on the Kabbalah, but did not teach. In 1743 he took his family to Acco in PALESTINE. He and his family died from the plague three years later. Luzzatto's legacy includes significant Kabbalistic writings and ethical treatises, still commonly studied in yeshivot (*see* YESHIVA) today. His most significant work is titled *The Path of the Upright,* a volume of devotional literature. This text is often used by followers of the Musar movement (*see* SALANTER). In this work, Luzzatto discusses ethics and different levels of saintliness and its connection to study and learning.

Further reading: Yirmeyahu Bindman, *Rabbi Moshe Chaim Luzzatto: His Life and Works* (Northvale, N.J.: Jason Aronson, 1995); Moses Hayyim Luzzatto, *The Path of the Upright: Mesillat Yesharim* (Northvale, N.J.: Jason Aronson, 1995).

M

Ma'ariv

Established in 1948 by Azriel Carlebach, the HEBREW-language *Ma'ariv* has the second-largest circulation of any daily newspaper in ISRAEL. It appears every afternoon from Sunday through Friday. Today it is owned by the Nimrodi family and reflects the opinions and viewpoint of the Israeli consensus. With the growth of the World Wide Web, *Ma'ariv* has established two Internet editions, in Hebrew and, since 2002, in English. The English edition can be found online at http://www.maarivenglish.com/.

Further reading: Yoram Hazony, *The Jewish State: The Struggle for Israel's Soul* (New York: Basic Books, 2000); Yoav Peled and Gershon Shafir, eds., *The New Israel: Peacemaking and Liberalization* (Boulder, Colo.: Westview Press, 2000).

The Israeli newspaper *Ma'ariv* has been in circulation since 1948, the same year the State of Israel was born. This paper's headline reports news of the funeral of the ashes of 200,000 Jews murdered during the Holocaust. *(Hans Pinn, Government Press Office, The State of Israel)*

Maccabees

The name *Maccabee* means "hammer"; it came to be used by the family who in 165 C.E. led the revolt against ANTIOCHUS EPIPHANES, whose religious persecution culminated in the desecration of the TEMPLE. The Maccabee leader, the priest Mattathias, was killed early on, but his son Judah continued the revolt, and fighters under his leadership recaptured JERUSALEM and rededicated the Temple. Their revolt and the rededication are commemorated in the festival of CHANUKAH. Legend has it that there was only enough oil for the Temple lamp for one night, but miraculously the lamp burned for eight nights. The oil lamp is a minor miracle, but the larger miracle was the Jewish success against the Seleucid forces.

The story of the Maccabee revolt is recorded in the books of Maccabees in the APOCRYPHA. The revolt was against Antiochus Epiphanes, but also against those Jews who were willing to accommodate to practices of HELLENISM.

Further reading: E. J. Bickerman, *The Maccabees: An Account of Their History from the Beginnings to the Fall of the House of the Hasmoneans,* trans. Moses Hadas (New York: Schocken Books, 1947); Shaye J. D. Cohen, *From the Maccabees to the Mishnah* (Philadelphia: Westminster Press, 1987).

Machzor

A Machzor is a special prayerbook used for the festivals of ROSH HASHANAH and YOM KIPPUR. It contains particular prayers that are chanted only on these occasions, such as KOL NIDRE, confessions, and petitions for a good year. It also contains prayers accompanying the blowing of the SHOFAR. In addition, some of the regular prayers are amended to include extra lines that convey the sentiments and themes of Rosh HaShanah and Yom Kippur—confession, repentance, and hope for the upcoming year.

Further reading: Jeffrey M. Cohen, *Prayer and Penitence: A Commentary on the High Holy Day Machzor* (Northvale, N.J.: J. Aronson, 1994); Sidney Greenberg and Jonathan D. Levine, eds., *Mahzor Hadash: The New Mahzor for Rosh HaShanah and Yom Kippur* (Bridgeort, Conn.: Prayer Book Press, 1994); Nossen Scherman and Meir Zlotowitz, eds., *The Complete ArtScroll Machzor: Rosh Hashanah: Nusach Ashkenaz* (Brooklyn, N.Y.: Mesorah Publications, 1985).

Magnes, Judah (1877–1948) *educator and Zionist leader*

Judah Magnes was born in San Francisco, California, in 1877. However, he spent a major part of his life in New York, where he cofounded AMERICAN JEWISH COMMITTEE in 1906. Magnes was also an influence in the founding of the Society for the Advancement of Judaism, the American Civil Liberties Union, and the AMERICAN JEWISH JOINT DISTRIBUTION COMMITTEE. Magnes created and served as president of the *kehillah* (*see* KAHAL/KEHILLAH) of New York City from 1908 until 1922. The *kehillah* represented an attempt to unify the Jews of New York City as they had been previously in Europe. Since early 20th century Jews were often involved in the American labor movement, the *kehillah* also became involved in mediation and labor issues to represent its constituency. Under Magnes's leadership, the *kehillah* was instrumental in bringing together the two culturally distinct constituencies of German and eastern European Jews.

Magnes was ordained as a Reform rabbi in 1900 at the Hebrew Union College in Cincinnati, but he advocated a Reform embrace of tradition, uncommon for most American Reform rabbis of the time. Also unlike most Reform rabbis, he was an ardent Zionist (*see* ZIONISM), a follower of the Zionist philosophy of AHAD HA'AM. Magnes was inspired to embrace Zionism after a trip to eastern Europe. In addition, he raised funds for the Self-Defense Association, which purchased weapons for Jewish self-defense groups in RUSSIA after the 1903 Kizhinev POGROMS. He made ALIYAH to PALESTINE in 1922. There he became an active leader in creating the HEBREW UNIVERSITY, which he served as chancellor and then president.

Magnes tried to foster cooperation between Palestinian Jews and Arabs, and he hoped to use the Hebrew University as a means to achieve success in this endeavor. Magnes believed Palestine should be a binational state for Jews and Arabs. In 1925 he cofounded Brit Shalom, the Covenant of Peace, to help foster this binational goal. The group failed to attract significant support in either the Jewish or Arab world, but Magnes continued to argue in defense of a binational solution even after the violent Arab uprisings of 1929.

Magnes used his leadership skills to foster Jewish community in both the United States and Palestine. In the U.S. he worked to establish organizations instrumental in the well-being of American Jews and in Palestine he remained committed to pacifist ideals in a violent atmosphere until his death in 1948.

Further reading: Norman Bentwich, *For Zion's Sake: A Biography of Judah L. Magnes, First Chancellor and First President of the Hebrew University of Jerusalem* (Philadelphia: Jewish Publication Society, 1954); William M. Brinner and Moses Rischin, *Like All the Nations?: The Life and Legacy of Judah L. Magnes* (Albany: State University of New York Press, 1987); Judah Magnes and Martin Buber, *Arab-Jewish Unity: Testimony before the Anglo-American Inquiry Commission for the Ihud (Union) Association* (Westport, Conn.: Hyperion Press, 1976).

Maharal of Prague (1525–1609) *rabbi and mystic*

Rabbi Judah Loew Ben Bezalel, commonly known as the Maharal of Prague or as Der Hohe, the Eminent, was born in 1525 in POLAND, the fourth son of a distinguished family of RABBIS. For 20 years, from 1553 to 1573, he served as the chief rabbi of Moravia, before settling in Prague, where he died in 1609. Rabbi Loew was the recognized leader of Ashkenazi Jewry (*see* ASHKENAZIM), much admired for his rabbinic and mystical learning. He was asked to adjudicate questions on matters of HALAKHAH, Jewish law, by rabbis from all over Europe. His approach and ideas influenced the philosophies of the VILNA GAON, HASIDISM, and the Musar movement (*see* SALANTER, ISRAEL).

A prolific writer, Loew contributed to most branches of Jewish thought. His expositions of Jewish ethics are some of the most important writings in this field. Loew was a master of KABBALAH, and his writings tried to explain Kabbalistic ideas without using its technical jargon. Combining Kabbalah and ethics, Loew believed that there is an unbreakable connection between the moral and the metaphysical realms. He developed an entirely new approach to AGGADAH, devoting more space to its interpretation than any other rabbi. Education was also among Loew's many pursuits, and he was an innovator in this field as well. According to the established tradition of the time, boys began their education with the TALMUD at a very early age and learned other subjects at fixed ages. Loew argued that children should be taught each subject of the curriculum in accordance with their maturity and intellectual ability and not their chronological age.

For all his learning and writings, the Maharal is best known to later generations as the hero of the legend of the GOLEM. A golem is a clump of clay made into human form and brought to life by the magical and correct use of the ineffable name of God, the TETRAGRAMMATON (*see* GOD, NAMES OF). The four letters YHWH were believed to be the original source of life; hence one who knew how to use them correctly could also create life. According to the legend, the Maharal created the golem to protect the Jews of Prague from threatening Christian mobs following a BLOOD LIBEL accusation. For months the golem, who was mighty in strength and supernatural in prescience, guarded the GHETTO. Eventually, however, he threatened innocent lives and the Maharal was forced to remove the ineffable name of God and thus render the golem a lifeless lump of clay once more. One story about the golem suggests that it still guards the synagogue, one of the few left standing in central Europe after the HOLOCAUST. In 1917 a statue of the Maharal was erected near the Prague city hall.

Further reading: Ben Zion Bokser, *The Maharal: The Mystical Philosophy of Rabbi Judah Loew of Prague* (Northvale, N.J.: Jason Aronson, 1994); Bedrich Thieberger, *The Great Rabbi Loew of Prague: His Life and Work and the Legend of the Golem* (London: East and West Library, 1954).

Mailer, Norman (b. 1923) *American writer*

Norman Mailer is a prolific novelist, short-story writer, poet, essayist, playwright, and screenwriter. He has tried every genre and narrative form and even invented some himself.

Mailer was born in Long Branch, New Jersey, in 1923 but raised in Brooklyn, New York, graduating from Boys High School in 1939. Mailer received a Jewish education as a child, attending

Jewish schools and becoming a BAR MITZVAH. However, he distanced himself from Jewish life at college until he discovered Martin BUBER and his tales of HASIDISM, which sparked his interest in Jewish MYSTICISM. Even so, Mailer's Jewish background appears in his novels only in the occasional Jewish character. His expression of Jewishness remains minimal. Some argue that Mailer's writings are permeated with ideas of masculinity and femininity as expressed in Jewish mysticism and the KABBALAH.

Mailer graduated from Harvard University in 1943 with a B.S. in engineering. His first short story appeared in 1941 while he was still in college. In 1944 Mailer was drafted into the army and he served as a rifleman in the South Pacific. His experiences served as the basis for his first book, *The Naked and The Dead* (1948), one of the most significant novels to emerge from World War II. After a stint in Hollywood as a screenwriter, Mailer published two more novels, *Barbary Shore* (1951), about the cold war, and *The Deer Park* (1955), about Hollywood and artistic integrity. Neither achieved the critical acclaim or popularity of his first novel. In 1959 he published *Advertisements for Myself,* in which short stories, essays and parts of novels are linked with an autobiographical commentary, designed as a therapeutic self-evaluation and serving as a brilliant study of a talented writer growing up in the postwar period. Its huge influence on a generation also seeking to achieve creativity and self-realization gave Mailer a new audience and set the stage for the 1960s.

Between 1962 and 1972, Mailer published 17 books, including five that were nominated for the National Book Award in four different categories. All in all, he has won almost every major literary award except for the Nobel Prize. He introduced a new kind of journalism with *The Armies of the Night* (1968), for which he won the Pulitzer Prize. It is an account of the 1967 peace march on Washington, D.C., written in a poetic, witty style combining factual analysis with the intimacy of a memoir and the perceptive density of a novel. Mailer also reported on seven political conventions—six Democratic and one Republican—for *Esquire* magazine.

Mailer won his second Pulitzer for the critically acclaimed 1979 best seller, *The Executioner's Song,* a 1,000-page "true-life novel" that chronicled the life and death of Utah murderer Gary Gilmore. His latest best seller was *Harlot's Ghost* (1996). So far, he has written some 40 books and contributed to at least 75 different magazines and journals. In 1955 he cofounded, with Dan Wolf and Ed Fancher, the alternative weekly newspaper *The Village Voice,* which he also named.

Mailer has been married six times; in 1969 he ran unsuccessfully for the office of New York City mayor. Today, he lives in Provincetown, Massachusetts.

Further reading: Harold Bloom and Perry King, eds., *Norman Mailer* (New York: Chelsea House, 1986); Louis Harap, *In the Mainstream: The Jewish Presence in Twentieth-Century American Literature, 1950s–1980s* (New York: Greenwood Press, 1987); Norman Mailer, *The Armies of the Night, History as a Novel, the Novel as History* (New York: New American Library, 1968); ———, *The Naked and the Dead* (New York: Henry Holt & Company, 1998).

Maimonides (Moses ben Maimon; Rambam) (1135–1204) *influential medieval rabbi and thinker; author of* Mishneh Torah

Historians and philosophers of Judaism consider Maimonides to be one of the greatest Jewish thinkers in history, if not the greatest. Rabbi Moses ben (son of) Maimon is known by Jews as the RAMBAM, an acronym of his name, and by scholars generally as Maimonides, Greek for "son of Maimon."

Maimonides was born in Córdoba, SPAIN, in the year 1135. He was said to be a descendant of JUDAH HA-NASI, the man known to have compiled the MISHNAH, and through him to King DAVID. Whether or not this genealogy can be proven, scholars do know that he was born to a family of scholars. In fact, Maimon, Maimonides' father, was a known Talmudist, mathematician, and astronomer.

By the time of Maimonides' birth, the city of Córdoba had become the world center of Jewish life and culture. Like the cities of SURA and PUMBE-DITA in BABYLONIA before it, Córdoba was esteemed by Jews around the world for Jewish learning and authority. TALMUD and Bible scholarship flourished there under Moorish rule, as did the study of Jewish literature, philosophy, and spirituality, which could be easily supplemented by science, mathematics, and secular learning. However, in the year 1148, when Maimonides was 13 years old, the city fell to a fanatic Muslim tribe that did not tolerate the arts and sciences, as had the previous Muslim rulers. Córdoba was no longer safe for Jews, and Maimonides fled with his family.

For 12 years Maimonides experienced life as a wandering Jew, as his family moved around Spain with few possessions and little financial security. Luckily, he had what today would be called a photographic memory, retaining every book he had ever read. He wrote his first works during these years, producing a treatise on logic and some Talmudic commentary.

The family finally settled in Fez, Morocco, in the year 1160, although the city was ruled by the same fanatical sect that had destroyed Jewish life in Córdoba. Despite persecution, Maimonides was able to train in the fields of theology and medicine. Some surmise that the family must have converted to Islam in a nominal sense, but this has never been widely accepted by scholars. In fact, in 1165, Maimonides published his *Letter Concerning Apostasy*. The letter reassured Jews pretending to be Muslims that they were still considered Jews by the Jewish community. He wrote it in Arabic, risking exposure to the Muslim rulers, in order to reach the entire Jewish community, for whom Arabic was the most common language. Unfortunately, the letter made it necessary for Maimonides and his family to flee once again. They left Fez by boat in the year 1165 and headed for PALESTINE, ERETZ YISRAEL.

The family did not find Palestine hospitable either, and Maimondies was especially distressed by its lack of rabbinic scholars or schools. Maimonides was 30 years old at this time, and he searched for a place to settle, frustrated by the severe persecution that Jews were experiencing in Christian lands around the world and the pseudo-Judaism that had become necessary in Muslim lands. He finally settled in EGYPT, which had become a haven for Jewish life despite the biblical history of Jewish slavery there. Under the rule of the Fatimid dynasty, Jews were not only allowed to live, but were given freedom to develop Jewish life and religious culture. They were also allowed to own possessions and to establish institutions such as schools. The Jewish community flourished, even having their own representation in the courts. Egypt had once again become the center of Jewish cultural life, as it had been in the Hellenistic era, and Moses Maimonides settled there to fulfill his own potential as a leader in Jewish life.

Maimonides lived in Alexandria for a few years, but then moved to Fostat, near the new capital Cairo, presumably because it would be easier for his family to continue their trade in precious stones from there. Maimonides himself became a physician, acting as the personal doctor to the vizier of the land, maintaining a busy private practice, writing commentary on the TANAKH, the Hebrew Bible, and the Talmud without letup, and providing legal and spiritual leadership to the Jewish community in Egypt and around the world.

In his correspondence, Maimonides answered many questions of Jewish law (*HALAKHAH*) posed by Jews from other communities around the world, and he contributed to science, astronomy, and medicine. Some scholars say that Maimonides held the office of nagid, or leader, of the Jewish community in Egypt, and it is a known fact that his descendants did so. He took clear stands on many issues. He insisted that men should not earn money through Talmud study, thus making obsolete the then-common practice of being paid to study. Maimonides was the most prominent Jewish thinker to maintain a consistently rational point of view; he rejected apocalyptic descriptions of the MESSIANIC AGE in favor of a more natural transition to a peaceful world, and he explained miracles in natural terms.

The body of work that Maimonides produced is vast. His most important works include the MISHNEH TORAH (1178), the first commentary to codify *halakhah* in a logical system; THE GUIDE TO THE PERPLEXED (1185–90), which attempted to reconcile Judaism and Aristotelian thought; and the THIRTEEN PRINCIPLES OF FAITH, a treatise outlining Maimonides' interpretation of the basic theological beliefs of Judaism. These 13 principles are recalled in Jewish liturgy by the popular prayer known as Yigdal. The prayerbook *Sim Shalom* summarizes the principles as follows: "God is eternal; God is one, unique, with neither body nor form; only God is to be worshiped; God alone created and creates all things; the words of the prophets are true; Moses was the greatest prophet; the source of the Torah is divine; the Torah is immutable; God knows our deeds and thoughts; God rewards and punishes; the messiah will come; God, ever loving, will resurrect the dead." It would not be an overstatement to claim that Maimonides is the most influential Jewish thinker in postbiblical history.

Further reading: Rabbi Jules Harlow, ed., *Siddur Sim Shalom: A Prayerbook for Shabbat, Festivals, and Weekdays* (New York: Rabbinical Assembly, United Synagogue of America, 1989); Moses Maimonides, *Ethical Writings of Maimonides,* trans. Raymond L. Weiss with Charles E. Butterworth (New York: Dover Publications, 1975); ———, *The Guide to the Perplexed,* trans. M. Friedlander (New York: Dover Publications, 1956); ———, *Mishne Torah, Hilchot Yesodei Hatorah: The Laws, Which Are the Foundations of the Torah,* Mishne Torah Series (New York: Moznaim Publishing, 1989); Jacob S. Minkin, *The World of Moses Maimonides: With Selections from His Writings* (New York: T. Yoseloff, 1957); Kenneth Seeskin, *Searching for a Distant God: The Legacy of Maimonides* (New York: Oxford University Press, 2000).

malakhim

Traditionally translated as "angels," the Hebrew word *malakhim* that appears in biblical texts refers specifically to messenger beings. Some streams of Judaism teach that *malakhim* are sent to help people make the right choices during their lives. They are said to be present among the "children of God" who stand before the divine judgment on ROSH HASHANAH.

Further reading: Lewis Glinert, *The Joys of Hebrew* (Oxford: Oxford University Press, 1992); Morris B. Margolies, *A Gathering of Angels: Angels in Jewish Life and Literature* (Northvale, N.J.: Jason Aronson, 2000).

Malamud, Bernard (1914–1986) *American writer*

Bernard Malamud was born in Brooklyn, New York, graduating from the City College of New York in 1936 and earning a master's degree from Columbia University in 1942. A novelist and short story writer, he taught in various universities.

Malamud's first novel, *The Natural* (1952), tells of the brief glory and final ruin of Roy Hobbs, a baseball player. His next work was *The Assistant* (1957), in which a hold-up man becomes a poor Jewish grocer's assistant, inheriting the man's store and with it his honesty, morality, and righteousness and eventually becoming a Jew himself.

Malamud's special talent is for the fable and the symbolic tale. A running theme in his work is the idea of REDEMPTION in a squalid world illuminated by extraordinary bursts of love. In his work, he often uses the Jew as a metaphor for humankind and explores Jewish tradition and its stress on the nobility of the humble man. Malamud's *The Fixer* (1966), for which he won the Pulitzer Prize, is a fictionalized retelling of the Mendel Beilis BLOOD LIBEL case; it explores the tension between Jewish group solidarity and the solitary individual Jew. Two of Malamud's finest short stories are "The Magic Barrel" (1958) and "The Jewbird."

Further reading: Alan Cheuse, *Listening to the Page: Adventures in Reading and Writing* (New York: Columbia University Press, 2001); Bernard Malamud, *The Assistant:*

A Novel (New York: Farrar, Straus and Giroux, 2003); ———, *The Complete Stories* (New York: Farrar, Straus and Giroux, 1997).

Malbim (Meir Lev Ben Yechiel Michael)
(1809–1879) *rabbi and biblical commentator*

Meir Lev ben Yechiel Michael, known by the acronym of his name, the Malbim, was born in a small town in the district of Volhynia, RUSSIA, in 1809 to a family of RABBIS. His father died while he was a small child and he studied with his stepfather, also a rabbi. He showed talent early, and in Warsaw, where he went at age 13 to continue his studies, he became known as the prodigy from Volhynia. The Malbim spent much of his life wandering, serving as rabbi in various towns of eastern Europe. His longest appointment was in the city of Kempen, where he was chief rabbi from 1845 to 1860.

The Malbim is best known for his commentary to the TANAKH, the Hebrew Bible. In it he emphasized the unity and agreement of the Torah, or the WRITTEN LAW, and the rabbinic works, or the ORAL LAW. He also tried to show that the AGGADAH is based on the literal meaning of the biblical text. A special feature of the Malbim's approach to biblical commentary is the principle that each word has a special meaning even if it is a synonym of another word in the verse. That is, every word has its own special significance and none are superfluous. Synonyms are used not to enliven and vary the text but to transmit specific meanings. The first biblical commentary that the Malbim published was to the book of ESTHER in 1845. By 1876 he had published commentaries to all the other books of the Bible.

The Malbim's approach to the Bible and aggadah conflicted with the philosophy of the growing movement of REFORM JUDAISM, which viewed the aggadah as allegorical in nature. The conflict came to a head in Bucharest in 1860, where the Malbim as chief rabbi clashed with the German-speaking segment of the Jewish community who wanted to introduce elements of Reform practice that he vehemently opposed. As a result

of various intrigues and allegations he was imprisoned by the secular authorities. Released thanks to the intercession of Moses MONTEFIORE, the Malbim left for Constantinople. He subsequently traveled to FRANCE, POLAND, and Russia. In 1870 he assumed the rabbinical office in Moghilev, Russia. But here too he came into conflict with some segments of the Jewish community and was consequently expelled from the city by the Russian governor. The Malbim died in Kiev in 1879 on his way to yet another rabbinic post.

Further reading: David Weiss Halivni, *Peshat and Derash: Plain and Applied Meaning in Rabbinic Exegesis* (New York: Oxford University Press, 1991); Shmuel Kurtz, trans., *Malbim on Ruth* (New York: Philipp Feldheim, 1999); Jonathan Taub, trans., *The Malbim Esther* (New York: Feldheim Pub., 1998).

Mamet, David (b. 1947) *playwright and writer of screenplays*

David Mamet is a playwright, screenplay writer, and film director. Born in Flossmoor, Illinois, near Chicago, in 1947, Mamet grew up in a broken home, becoming very close to his sister. He studied at Goddard College in Vermont and at the Neighborhood Playhouse School of Theater in New York City before becoming an actor there.

Mamet has written more than 25 plays or films, including the play *Speed the Plow* (1987) and the film *The Postman Always Rings Twice* (1981). In 1984 he was awarded the Pulitzer Prize in drama for his play *Glengarry Glen Ross,* which was eventually made into a movie. Mamet's screenplays also include *About Last Night . . ., The Untouchables, Wag the Dog,* and *The Spanish Prisoner.* Mamet's movie *Homicide* is about an underground Zionist group that fights ANTISEMITISM and terrorism.

Mamet's style includes clipped dialogue that often conveys his image of a modern world lacking in emotion and spirituality. His characters are often male, and he portrays macho attitudes in a fresh and provocative voice. In addition to his writing and directing, Mamet has taught at Goddard College, New York University, and the Yale Drama School. He has received many awards, including the Joseph Jefferson Award (1974), the Obie Award (1976, 1983), the New York Drama Critics Circle Award (1977, 1984), the Outer Circle Award (1978), the Society of West End Theatre Award (1983), the Pulitzer Prize (1984), the Dramatists Guild Hall-Warriner Award (1984), the American Academy Award (1986), and the Tony Award (1987). Though Mamet's Jewish roots do not appear frequently in his work, he visited ISRAEL in December of 2002 as a guest of the JERUSALEM Film Festival. He penned an article for the *Forward* demonstrating a connection to his fellow Jews and expressing a deep respect for those Israelis who live with terrorism each day. As expressed in the movie *Homicide,* Mamet has an underground reputation for supporting the ideas of Jewish militants.

Further reading: Leslie Kane, ed. *David Mamet's Glengarry Glen Ross: Text and Performance,* Studies in Modern Drama, vol. 8 (New York: Garland Publishing, 1996); David Mamet, *True and False: Heresy and Common Sense for the Actor* (New York: Pantheon Books, 1997); David Mamet, " 'If I Forget Thee, Jerusalem': The Power of Blunt Nostalgia," in *Forward* (December 27, 2002).

mamzer

A *mamzer* is the child of an adulterous or incestuous relationship. The TORAH (Dt 23:3) forbids such a person from entering the congregation of the Lord. In rabbinic times this was interpreted to mean that a *mamzer* may not marry a Jew, apart from another *mamzer.* A *mamzer* was considered to be in the lowest class of Jewish society, along with slaves.

The RABBIS found significant issues surrounding the treatment of the *mamzer,* as the child seems to be punished for the actions of others. Consequently, there have been attempts to provide legal means to avoid designating someone as a *mamzer.* REFORM JUDAISM has rejected the concept of *mamzerut,* and many rabbis in CONSERVATIVE and ORTHODOX JUDAISM follow the tradition of devising legal strategies to avoid identifying someone as a *mamzer.*

Further reading: Hayim Halevy Donin, *To Be a Jew: A Guide to Jewish Observance in Contemporary Life* (New York: Basic Books, 1972); Louis Jacobs, "The Problem of the Mamzer," in *A Tree of Life: Diversity, Flexibility, and Creativity in Jewish Law* (New York: Oxford University Press, 1984), 257–275; Daniel B. Sinclair, "Assisted Reproduction in Jewish Law" in *Fordham Urban Law Journal* 30 (2002).

manna

Manna was one of the foods provided miraculously for the ISRAELITES during their wandering in the wilderness.

The book of EXODUS in the TANAKH, the Hebrew Bible, reports that the Israelites, after being freed from SLAVERY in EGYPT, began to worry and complain to MOSES that they would not find sufficient food to eat in the wilderness, where they would wander until they could enter and conquer the land of CANAAN. God therefore supplied them with manna.

Exodus describes manna as a fine, flaky substance that would be found on the ground each morning, which MOSES declared to be bread from God. Each weekday the Israelites would gather manna to eat; twice as much would fall on Fridays, so the Israelites could gather double portions and not have to gather on SHABBAT, the Sabbath. The rabbis claimed manna had the taste of anything a person desired, but neither they nor modern scholars have been able to determine exactly what the substance was, though various plant products and other natural substances have been proposed as the source.

Further reading: David Frankel, *The Murmuring Stories of the Priestly School: A Retrieval of Ancient Sacerdotal Lore* (Leiden and Boston: Brill, 2002); H. Freedman and Maurice Simon, eds., *Soncino Midrash Rabbah* (CD-ROM), 3rd ed. (New York: Soncino Press, 1983); *Tanakh: The Holy Scriptures* (Philadelphia and Jerusalem: Jewish Publication Society, 1985).

Mapah

The *Mapah* (Hebrew for "tablecloth") is a widely used commentary on the SHULCHAN ARUKH (Hebrew for "prepared table"), the 16th-century guide that became the universal reference on HALAKHAH, or Jewish law.

The *Mapah* was written by Rabbi Moses (Moshe) ISSERLES. Isserles (1525–72) was born to a well-to-do family in Kraków, POLAND, where he later founded a YESHIVA. Recognized from an early age as an authority on *halakhah,* he is sometimes considered the "MAIMONIDES of Polish Jewry." In his rulings, Isserles stressed the importance of local custom, MINHAG, holding that it has the force of law. It should be noted that he did not uphold every custom indiscriminately. Where it seemed to him to be absurd, Isserles ruled the custom unacceptable. Isserles was a great codifier, writing an extensive compendium of law entitled *Darkhe Moshe,* or *The Ways of Moses,* which contained criticisms of the *Bet Joseph* of Joseph CARO.

When Caro's *Shulchan Arukh* was published in 1565, Isserles felt that Caro's "table" was not sufficiently "prepared" and so he provided it with a "tablecloth." The *Mapah* is both a criticism and a supplement to the *Shulchan Arukh.* Whereas Caro, being a Sephardi, ignored Ashkenazi practice, the *Mapah* stresses Ashkenazi rites and customs (*see* ASHKENAZIM; SEPHARDIM). The *Mapah* was first published in a 1571 Cracow edition of the *Shulchan Arukh* as insertions in different type within Caro's text. It is these insertions that made the *Shulchan Arukh* widely accepted among the Ashkenazim, resulting in its becoming the singularly most influential CODE OF LAW to this day. When Ashkenazim speak of the *Shulchan Arukh,* they understand by it both Caro's text and the *Mapah,* and when there is a conflict between the two, the *Mapah* is taken as the authority.

Further reading: Boaz Cohen, "The Shulhan Aruk as a Guide to Religious Practice Today," in *Law and Tradition in Judaism* (New York: Ktav Publishing House, 1959), 62–99; N. S. Hecht, *An Introduction to the History and Sources of Jewish Law* (Oxford: Oxford University Press, 1996); Schneur Zalman of Liadi and Eliyahu Touger, trans., *Shulchan Aruch: Code of Jewish Law,* vol. 1 (Brooklyn, N.Y.: Merkos L'Inyonei Chinuch, 2002); Isadore Twersky, "The Shulhan 'Aruk: Enduring Code of Jewish Law" in *Studies in Jewish Law and Philosophy* (New York: Ktav Publishing House, 1982), 130–47.

Marranos *See* CONVERSOS.

marriage

Because of the MITZVAH (commandment) in traditional Judaism to reproduce, marriage is considered obligatory.

The ideal age for marriage has varied over the ages. The Babylonian TALMUD advocated early marriage, at age 16 to 20 for a man, before he has completed his studies. The Jerusalem Talmud argued for the opposite, explaining that a man should marry only after he has finished his studies. Since consent of both the bride and the groom is required, a marriage cannot take place with a girl who is younger than 12 years and one day and a boy who is younger than 13, the ages of consent set by the Talmudic RABBIS; but the rabbis always advocated for an older age than that. In the Middle Ages the trend was for early marriage despite staunch rabbinic opposition. The people wanted to make sure their children were married as soon as possible due to fears of expulsions, unpredictable Christian rulers who sometimes issued prohibitions on Jewish marriage, and fears of property confiscation.

There are two stages to marriage that in earlier times were separated by up to 12 months. They are called *erusin* or *kiddushin* (betrothal) and *nissuin* (marriage). In betrothal, the man gives the woman an object of value, in the presence of witnesses, and recites, "You are hereby betrothed unto me in accordance with the law of Moses and Israel." A betrothal may be broken and the marriage called off only with a *GET,* a formal divorce decree. In marriage, the *KETUBAH,* or marriage contract, is signed by two witnesses and publicly read out; the bride and groom stand together under the

CHUPPAH, or wedding canopy, and the SHEVA BRA-CHOT (Seven Benedictions) are recited. The couple then retires for a short time to a private room, called the *yichud* (together) room, and a celebratory meal is held.

The modern marriage ceremony combines *erusin* and *kiddushin*. Its basic elements have the couple stand under the chuppah, where the groom places a gold ring without a stone on the bride's finger and recites the betrothal formula. The *ketubah* that had been earlier signed is then read out and the Sheva Brachot are recited. It is also customary for the groom at this point to break a glass with his foot; this is customarily explained as a reminder of the destruction of the TEMPLE. In Orthodox communities (*see* ORTHODOX JUDAISM), it is customary to hold a marriage feast on each day of the week following the ceremony and recite the Sheva Brachot each time. Some Conservative Jews hold one such feast the day following the marriage ceremony.

Today, arranged marriage is still practiced in the ultra-Orthodox and Hasidic communities (*see* HASIDISM), where matchmakers are often used. The parties may see each other only once or twice before the ceremony, but both bride and groom must approve the match.

Further reading: Anita Diamant, *The New Jewish Wedding* (New York: Simon & Schuster, 1985); David C. Gross and Esther R. Gross, *Under the Wedding Canopy: Love and Marriage in Judaism* (New York: Hippocrene Books, 1996); Isaac Klein, *A Guide to Jewish Religious Practice* (New York: Jewish Theological Seminary of America, 1988).

Marshall, Louis (1856–1929) *American lawyer and community leader*

Louis M. Marshall was born in Syracuse, New York, in 1856 to German-Jewish immigrants. In 1894 he began his law career specializing in constitutional and corporate law. Many of the numerous cases he argued before the UNITED STATES Supreme Court were of major constitutional significance. He was even at one time seriously considered for appoint-ment to the Supreme Court. Marshall was heavily involved in the American Jewish community, but not to the exclusion of non-Jewish causes. He championed the rights of everyone, believing that if one group or minority is discriminated against, no one is safe from discrimination. He was active in the National Association for the Advancement of Colored People (NAACP), fighting significant legal battles on behalf of African Americans. In 1920 he also defended five socialist New York state assemblymen who were refused their seats in the legislature during the Red Scare then sweeping the country following the BOLSHEVIK REVOLUTION.

Early on, Marshall became involved in the Jewish community, acting as spokesman both within the United States and abroad. He worked to protect the interests of both the settled German-Jewish community and the new immigrants from eastern Europe. In 1906 he cofounded the AMERICAN JEWISH COMMITTEE (AJC), whose presidency he held from 1912 until his death in 1929. He played a leading role in its successful campaign to abrogate the Russo-American Treaty of 1832. RUSSIA repeatedly violated the first article of this commerce treaty by discriminating against American citizens of Jewish faith, going so far as to refuse to grant visas to Jewish naturalized American citizens who were born in Russia. Marshall and the AJC believed that by ignoring these violations and failing to protect its citizens, the U.S. government was itself in violation of the U.S. Constitution, by differentiating among its citizens and discriminating against some on the basis of religion.

During World War I, Marshall was president of the American Jewish Relief Committee, and in 1914 was one of the organizers of the AMERICAN JEWISH JOINT DISTRIBUTION COMMITTEE. Following the war, he was a member of the Jewish delegation to the Paris Peace Conference, where he helped secure minority rights guarantees in the treaties that established the new states in central and eastern Europe.

Marshall took on many causes. In 1913 he participated in the legal defense of Leo FRANK, a Jewish factory manager who was wrongly convicted of murder in Georgia and eventually lynched. He was instrumental in the campaign to delay the imposition of progressively harsher restrictions on immigration. In 1922, his intervention helped reverse Harvard University's announced intention to impose a quota system for the admission of Jewish students. One cause in which Marshall failed was his attempt to block the American publication of the fraudulent PROTOCOLS OF THE ELDERS OF ZION, a book that contributed to ANTISEMITISM all over the world. In 1920, the *Dearborn* (Michigan) *Independent,* a newspaper owned by Henry Ford, began publishing a series of articles based on the *Protocols* entitled "The International Jew." In 1927, however, after lawsuits brought by individuals libeled in the articles, including Marshall himself, Ford agreed to cease his attacks and to sign a formal apology to the Jews, prepared by Marshall.

Marshall, like many adherents of REFORM JUDAISM in his day, was not a Zionist, but he supported the BALFOUR DECLARATION and acknowledged PALESTINE as a Jewish spiritual center and refuge, especially after the United States severely limited immigration in the early 1920s. He prepared an agreement with Chaim WEIZMANN that paved the way for the participation of non-Zionists like himself in the JEWISH AGENCY, which bought and developed land in Palestine. Marshall's lasting contribution to the American Jewish community is immeasurable.

Further reading: Neil Baldwin, *Henry Ford and the Jews: The Mass Production of Hate* (New York: Public Affairs, 2001); Salo Baron, *Steeled by Adversity: Essays and Addresses on American Jewish Life* (Philadelphia: Jewish Publication Society of America, 1971); Louis Marshall, *Louis Marshall: Champion of Liberty, Selected Papers and Addresses,* ed. Charles Reznikoff (Philadelphia: Jewish Publication Society of America, 1957).

Marx, Karl (1818–1883) *radical philosopher and political leader*

Karl Marx was born on May 5, 1818, in Trier, Prussia, in GERMANY, and died on March 14, 1883, in London, ENGLAND. Marx was born into a Jewish family with rabbi ancestors on both sides, but he converted to Lutheranism in 1824.

Marx pursued history and philosophy and was influenced by Ludwig Feuerbach and G. W. F. Hegel. In 1844, he published an essay entitled "On the Jewish Question." In the essay, Marx criticizes Protestant culture for its treatment of the Jews but is equally critical of the Jews for demanding EMANCIPATION yet wanting to keep their separate culture, which he derided as money-oriented. Since Marx's ideas largely claim that differences cause suffering, his ultimate solution is the abolition of religion altogether. His ideas continued to solidify in this regard as he later criticized religion in general for serving as the opiate of the masses.

Karl Marx is best known as the founder of communism, from his publication of *The Communist Manifesto* with Friedrich Engels in 1848. Here Marx argues that economic systems will evolve past capitalism into socialism and will eventually settle into the ideal system of communism. This German philosopher of Jewish origin became an icon who was long revered by millions of people in Communist countries around the world.

Further reading: Dennis K. Fischman, *Political Discourse in Exile: Karl Marx and the Jewish Question* (Amherst: University of Massachusetts Press, 1991); Karl Marx and Friedrich Engels, *The Communist Manifesto* (New York: Signet Classics, 1998); Robert C. Tucker, *The Marx-Engels Reader* (New York: Norton, 1978).

Marx Brothers *American entertainers*

The Marx Brothers are considered to be one of the iconic American comedy acts, on a par with the Three Stooges and Laurel and Hardy. There were five brothers in all: Leonard, better known as Chico (1887–1961); Adolph, or Harpo (1888–1964); Julius, or Groucho, perhaps the best known of the brothers (1890–1977); Milton, or Gummo (1892–1977); and Herbert, or Zeppo (1901–79). They were born in New York City to poor Jewish immigrants from GERMANY and Alsace, FRANCE. Their mother Minnie's parents were entertainers, and her brother was one-half of a successful comedy duo. Minnie encouraged her sons to go into ENTERTAINMENT. Groucho was the first to start performing as a child, usually appearing on stage as a singer. He was successively joined by his brothers and, eventually, even by his mother in various VAUDEVILLE acts. By 1924, the act was successful enough to take the Marx Brothers to Broadway and ENGLAND.

As Hollywood moved to talking pictures, the brothers transitioned to film. In 1929, they released their first movie, *Cocoanuts*, which, like their next few films, was based on their stage productions. In all, the Marx Brothers made 13 films between 1929 and 1949. Some of the most famous ones are *Animal Crackers* (1930), *Duck Soup* (1933), *Night at the Opera* (1935), and *A Day at the Races* (1937). Their humor is characterized by slapstick, sight gags, puns, and wisecracks. The confident flamboyance of the Marx Brothers' acts exhibited a subversion of power in society. On stage, the brothers acted in ways that the Jews of eastern Europe could only dream of. Drawing upon Jewish life on the LOWER EAST SIDE of New York, the Marx Brothers used details from daily experience for comic material; for example, a Jewish straight man appears in their acts.

Though all five brothers were part of the act at one point or another, Gummo was the first to leave, to become an agent. Zeppo left soon after *Duck Soup*. From 1935 only Groucho, Chico, and Harpo appeared as the Marx Brothers. In the 1950s, Groucho hosted the long-running hit television show *You Bet Your Life*. The brothers were inducted into the Motion Picture Hall of Fame in 1977. Their stage personalities were broadly based on their actual traits. Harpo's trademark was that he never talked, and Groucho, who sported glasses, a big mustache, and a cigar, was the wisecrack artist. One of his famous quips is "I don't want to belong to any club that will accept me as a member."

Further reading: Lawrence J. Epstein, *The Haunted Smile: The Story of Jewish Comedians in America* (New

Four of the five Marx Brothers are pictured here. As a team, the Marx Brothers performed on stage and in movies for three decades, spanning the 1920s, the 1930s, and the 1940s. Through slapstick, sight gags, puns, and wisecracks, the Marx Brothers were able to provide satiric entertainment for Jews and non-Jews alike. *(Library of Congress)*

York: Public Affairs, 2001); Wes D. Gehring, *The Marx Brothers: A Bio-Bibliography* (New York: Greenwood, 1987); Simon Louvish, *Monkey Business: The Lives and Legends of the Marx Brothers* (New York: St. Martin's Griffin, 2001).

Masada

Masada (Hebrew for "stronghold") is a naturally formed citadel located among the stony hills near the DEAD SEA. HEROD the Great used it during his own military struggles, then transformed it into a heavily defended palace. It is best known as the

Herod the Great turned Masada, a natural landmass, into a fortress and palace when he ruled Judea. Masada was also the site of the Zealots' last stand after the Temple was destroyed in the year 70 C.E. In contemporary times, tourists visit Masada, climb its walls, and learn about its history. *(Courtesy Embassy of Israel, Washington D.C.)*

place where ZEALOT fighters took their last stand against ROME in 73–74 C.E. Ultimately these warriors committed suicide, turning swords upon themselves and their families rather than be taken into slavery. Masada has come to symbolize faithfulness and self-sacrifice in the face of persecution.

Further reading: Shaye J. D. Cohen, *From the Maccabees to the Mishnah* (Philadelphia: Westminster Press, 1987);

Herschel Shanks, "Questioning Masada," in *Biblical Archaeology Review* 24 (November–December 1998): 30–53.

mashgiach

The word *mashgiach* means supervisor in HEBREW. A *mashgiach* is an overseer appointed to supervise the observance of KASHRUT, or Jewish dietary laws, in the preparation of food in public establishments. Kosher restaurants, institutional cafeterias, and manufacturers of prepared kosher foods hire a *mashgiach* who is either permanently on the premises or has free access to come and inspect the kitchen at random and unannounced. Though not required to be a RABBI, the *mashgiach* often is one, since the job requires full knowledge of all the intricacies and rationales of kashrut.

Further reading: Solomon Poll, *The Hasidic Community of Williamsburg* (New York: Free Press of Glencoe, 1962); Star-K Web site URL: http://www.star-k.org/kashrus/kk-issues-mashgiach.htm, accessed on August 8, 2004.

mashiach See MESSIAH.

maskilim

The *maskilim* were the leaders and followers of the HASKALAH, the Jewish ENLIGHTENMENT movement of the 18th and 19th centuries. Moses MENDELSSOHN was one of the most prominent examples. The *maskilim* were interested in reconciling Judaism with modern Western Enlightenment thought and bringing Jews into the broader community as fully integrated citizens. They encouraged secular education, including non-Jewish languages and philosophy, and they often advocated changes in liturgy to reflect a modern sensibility. They were opposed by traditional Jews, who feared that the changes encouraged by the *maskilim* would lead to the gradual ASSIMILATION of Jews.

Further reading: Moses Mendelssohn, *Jerusalem*, trans. Allan Arkush (Hanover, N. H., and London: University Press of New England, 1983); Michael Meyer, *The Origins of the Modern Jew: Jewish Identity and European Culture in Germany, 1749–1824*; Arthur Hertzberg, "Modernity and Judaism," in Stanley Wagner and Allen Breck, eds., *Great Confrontations in Jewish History* (Denver, Colo.: University of Denver Dept. of History, 1977).

Masorti movement

Founded in 1979, the Masorti movement is the HEBREW name for the movement of CONSERVATIVE JUDAISM in ISRAEL. Masorti, whose name means "traditional" in Hebrew, combines a commitment to Jewish tradition and HALAKHAH (Jewish law) with an openness to the modern world. Like the Conservative movement in the UNITED STATES, the Masorti movement believes that *halakhah* must evolve with the times. The movement has approximately 50,000 adherents and some 50 synagogues. It also includes a KIBBUTZ, a MOSHAV, a youth movement, a student organization, a rabbinical seminary, preschool programs, and educational centers for adults.

One of the central activities of the Masorti movement in Israel is legal advocacy and lobbying for Jewish religious choice. Since there is no separation of religion and state in Israel, Jewish lifecycle events such as MARRIAGE, DIVORCE, burial and CONVERSION are administered by the state-run rabbinical establishment. This establishment is controlled by adherents of ORTHODOX JUDAISM who refuse to recognize non-Orthodox RABBIS or the legal validity of their divorces or conversions. Masorti lawyers and activists promote the religious rights of Masorti Jews before the Israeli parliament (*see* KNESSET), government ministries, municipalities and the Supreme Court, arguing for changes in law and filing precedent-setting lawsuits.

Further reading: David Golinkin, *Insight Israel: The View from Schechter* (Jerusalem: Leshon Limudim Ltd., 2003); Masorti Web site URL: http://www.masorti.org, accessed July 31, 2004; John S. Ruskay and David M. Szonyi, *Deepening a Commitment: Zionism and the Conservative/Masorti Movement: Papers from a Conference of Conservativ/Masorti Movement Leadership* (New York: Jewish Theological Seminary of America, 1990).

Matriarchs (Sarah, Rebecca, Leah, Rachel)

The four Matriarchs, the female ancestors of the Jewish people, were Sarah, Rebecca, Rachel, and Leah. Biblical narratives identify these four women as the wives of the three PATRIARCHS. Sarah married Abraham, Rebecca married Isaac, and both Rachel and Leah married Jacob.

According to Genesis, Sarai accompanies Abram when he obeys God's order to leave his home and go to a land God will show him. Initially, Sarai is unable to bear children, and she gives Abram her handmaid Hagar as a concubine. Hagar bears Ishmael (later honored by ISLAM as Abraham's legitimate heir). Even though Sarai has no children and Abram does have a son through Hagar, God repeats his covenantal promise to Abram and Sarai and changes their names to Abraham and Sarah as a formal representation of their relationship with God.

When the two hear prophecies that 90-year-old Sarah will indeed bear a son, the elderly pair both laugh. When Sarah's son is born after all, he is named Yitzhak (Isaac), meaning "he will laugh" in HEBREW, an eternal reminder of his parents' joyous amusement. Through Isaac, Sarah is included in God's covenantal promise to Abraham to make a great nation from the pair's descendants.

When Isaac is born, Sarah casts out Hagar and Ishmael. Rabbinic tradition justifies this act by explaining that Ishmael was a bad influence. However, Sarah's action is perceived by many Jewish commentators as inappropriate, and they suggest that the near sacrifice of Isaac, the AKEDAH, served to punish Sarah for exiling Hagar and Ishmael from their home.

Sarah dies at the age of 127 in Hebron, and Abraham purchases the burial site called the CAVE OF MACHPELAH for her; all the Patriarchs and Matriarchs but Rachel will eventually be buried there. After burying Sarah, Abraham sends his servant Eliezer to find a wife for Isaac. The servant travels to the city of Nahor, the land of Abraham's kin, and he prays to God to direct him to the woman destined for Isaac. Eliezer discovers Rebecca, the daughter of Bethuel, Abraham's nephew, at the city's well; her kind words and deeds are a sign to him that she is God's choice, After a familial negotiation, it is agreed that Rebecca will return with Abraham's servant to become Isaac's wife.

After Rebecca and Isaac are married, she gives birth to twin sons, Esau and Jacob. Rebecca favors Jacob over Esau, truly the first born, as the more spiritually appropriate heir to God's covenant with Abraham and Isaac. Rebecca and Jacob conspire to trick Isaac into giving Jacob, the younger twin, the spiritual blessing that will make him the vehicle of God's covenant.

Rebecca never sees her beloved son Jacob again, perhaps in punishment for her deceit. Rebecca and Jacob fear that Esau will seek retribution, so Jacob flees from home, not to return until after Rebecca's death. In the town of Haran, Jacob meets Rachel and Leah, sisters of his maternal uncle Laban. It is there that Laban tricks Jacob, as Jacob had tricked his own father. Jacob loves Rachel, the younger daughter, and he agrees to work seven years for his uncle in order to marry his bride of choice. After his labor is complete, Laban substitutes the veiled Leah at the wedding, at which women literally had no voice. Jacob agrees to work an additional seven years in order to marry Rachel as well.

Leah bears four sons, but Rachel is initially barren. She gives Jacob her maid Bilha, who bears two additional sons, and Leah provides her maid Zilpah, who bears two sons and one daughter. Finally Rachel conceives and bears Joseph. Later Rachel will bear one more son, Benjamin, but die in the process.

Rachel is the only matriarch not buried in the tomb of the patriarchs and matriarchs. According to the MIDRASH, rabbinic legend, this is because Jacob foresaw that the Jews would pass by Bethlehem, Rachel's burial place, when the Babylonians exiled them. As they passed by, Rachel would plead to God on their behalf. This MIDRASH is one of many that portray the matriarchs as women who can act as agents of change, not merely as one-dimensional figures of womanly virtue. Women, and men, still stream to Rachel's tomb to pray for her to intercede in personal problems.

While the Bible is primarily male-centered, women do play a meaningful role. Modern Jewish thinkers reemphasize the role of biblical women such as Sarah, Rebecca, Leah, and Rachel to counterbalance the patriarchical nature of the TORAH for contemporary readers. Many Liberal Jews have adapted the liturgy in the Jewish prayer book to recognize the role of the matriarchs, especially in the crucial formula "God of Abraham, God of Isaac, and God of Jacob, to which they append some version of "God of Sarah, Rebecca, Rachel and Leah."

Further reading: Alice Ogden Bellis, *Helpmates, Harlots, and Heroes: Women's Stories in the Hebrew Bible* (Louisville, Ky.: Westminster/John Knox Press, 1994); Katheryn Pfisterer Darr, *Far More Precious Than Jewels* (Louisville, Ky.: Westminster Press, 1991); Anita Diamant, *The Red Tent* (New York: Picador, U.S.A., 1998) (fiction); Norman K. Gottwald, *The Hebrew Bible: A Socio-Literary Introduction* (Philadelphia: Fortress Press, 1985); H. Freedman, and Maurice Simon, eds., *Soncino Midrash Rabbah* (CD-ROM), 3rd ed. (Soncino Press, 1983); *Tanakh: The Holy Scriptures* (Philadelphia and Jerusalem: The Jewish Publication Society, 1985).

matzah

Matzah is a type of flat, unleavened bread eaten during PASSOVER. According to Jewish tradition, it symbolizes the affliction of SLAVERY. It also reminds Jews of the speed with which the ISRAELITES had to flee EGYPT: according to the book of EXODUS, after the first nine plagues in Egypt, PHARAOH agreed to free the Israelite slaves, but soon changed his mind. Thus, after the 10th plague, the Israelites fled quickly while they had the chance, without having time to allow their bread to rise.

Later, the rabbis created restrictions on exactly how matzah should be prepared. According to *HALAKHAH* (Jewish law), matzah is a simple mixture of flour and water that must be mixed, kneaded and fully baked within 18 minutes.

Pre-Israelite nomadic tribes also had a spring ritual in which they ate unleavened bread, and the inhabitants of CANAAN had a harvest festival in which they offered unleavened bread, so it is pos-sible that the practice of eating matzah actually entered into Judaism from one of these neighboring communities.

Further reading: Larry Domnitch, *The Jewish Holidays: A Journey through History* (Northvale, N.J.: Jason Aronson, 2000); Irving Greenberg, *The Jewish Way: Living the Holidays* (New York: Summit Books, 1988); Moshe Lieber, *The Pesach Haggadah Anthology: The Living Exodus: with Commentary and Anecdotes from Talmudic and Rabbinical Literature* (Brooklyn, N.Y.: Mesorah, 1997).

mazel tov

Mazel tov, which literally means a "good astrological sign," and by extension "good luck," is a phrase used to express congratulations. While it is especially appropriate for *simcha*s (happy occasions) such as weddings and BAR/BAT MITZVAHS, it is also used for more minor occurrences and often for someone who has just made a purchase, such as a new home.

Further reading: Lewis Glinert, *The Joys of Hebrew* (New York: Oxford University Press, 1992); Jackie Mason, *How to Talk Jewish* (New York: St. Martin's Press, 1991).

Mazon

Founded in 1985 by Leonard Fine, Mazon, which takes its name from the HEBREW word for food, is a national nonprofit agency that provides food and grants to hungry people regardless of religion or ethnic origin. Since its founding, Mazon has distributed more than $30 million to hunger relief organizations, food banks, and advocacy groups that seek long-term solutions to the issue of hunger in the UNITED STATES, ISRAEL, and countries worldwide. In addition to soliciting direct contributions, Mazon partners with SYNAGOGUES. Congregants of partner synagogues are encouraged to donate 3 percent of the cost of their LIFE CYCLE celebrations, as well as to donate before festivals such as ROSH HASHANAH and PASSOVER. Mazon's national headquarters are in Los Angeles, California.

Further reading: Mazon Web site URL: www.mazon. org, accessed July 31, 2004.

Mea Shearim

One of the first neighborhoods built outside the walls of the Old City of JERUSALEM, Mea Shearim was established in 1873 in response to overcrowding in the ancient Jewish Quarter. The HEBREW name, which means "100 measures" is derived from the verse the TANAKH, the Hebrew Bible, "Isaac sowed in that land and reaped in the same year a hundredfold" (Gn 26:12).

Today the neighborhood is characterized by its time-capsule atmosphere that evokes an 18th- or 19th-century eastern European Jewish GHETTO. The neighborhood is settled by ultra-Orthodox (*see* ORTHODOX JUDAISM) and Hasidic Jews (*see* HASIDISM), who interpret HALAKHAH, or Jewish law, in the strictest way. Some 5,000 of them belong to the extreme Neturei Karta sect, which denies the legitimacy of the State of ISRAEL, believing that no Jewish sovereign state of any kind can exist before the MESSIAH comes. The men in Mea Shearim wear long black coats and, on SHABBAT (the Sabbath) and festivals, round, fur-covered hats called *shtreimels;* they sport long PAYIS (sidecurls). Certain of the Hasidim wear long white stockings and knicker-like pants. The women all wear long-sleeved shirts and skirts, and those who are married cover their shaved heads with *SHEITELS,* or wigs. On SHABBAT, barricades block traffic from driving through; on occasion, secular people drive through anyway, and on other occasions, residents throw stones at cars driving on nearby streets, which brings the residents in conflict with secular Israelis.

Further reading: Samuel Heilman, *The Gate Behind the Wall: A Pilgrimage to Jerusalem* (New York: Summit Books, 1984); Daniel Meijers, *Ascetic Hasidism in Jerusalem* (New York: E. J. Brill, 1992); Vanessa L. Ochs, *Words on Fire: One Woman's Journey into the Sacred* (Boulder, Colo.: Westview Press, 1999); Rita James Simon, *Continuity and Change: A Study of Two Ethnic Communities in Israel* (New York: Cambridge University Press, 1978).

mechitza

The partition separating men and women in SYNAGOGUES that adhere to TRADITIONAL JUDAISM is called the *mechitza*.

The actual partition may be physical and made of cloth or wood running down the middle of the synagogue or separating the front from the back, or it may just mean that women sit on a balcony above the main sanctuary or in another room. The physical partition may be from floor to ceiling or it may be only a couple of feet high. The exact nature of the partition varies from synagogue to synagogue depending upon the strictness with which the congregation or its rabbi interprets HALAKHAH, Jewish law. One justification for the *mechitza* is that it enables men to concentrate on their prayers without distraction; the TALMUD typically considers men to need help in controlling their sexual urges.

Excavations of synagogues from the first centuries before and after the Common Era have not clarified when the *mechitza* first appeared. The TALMUD attributes its origins to the architecture of the TEMPLE, and equates the women's section of the synagogue to certain Temple areas. According to tradition, the Temple's outside courtyard allowed for the mixing of men and women, Jews and non-Jews. The next inner courtyard was for Jewish men and women. Only priests (who were all men) could enter the Temple itself and only the HIGH PRIEST entered the HOLY OF HOLIES. The Talmud records that at some point a balcony was erected in the Jewish courtyard separating men and women during religious celebrations, to control inappropriate behavior that had broken out.

In the years following World War II, many synagogues in the UNITED STATES, especially those of CONSERVATIVE JUDAISM, removed the *mechitza*. On the other hand, many MODERN ORTHODOX congregations in those years reintroduced the *mechitza*, which had fallen into disuse as an earlier generation of immigrants tried to Americanize (*see* AMERICANIZATION). Today, all but one or two Conservative synagogues have mixed seating, and the *mechitza* has become a defining feature of ORTHODOX JUDAISM in its many forms around the world.

Further reading: Beryl Lieff Benderly and Hasia R. Diner, *Her Works Praise Her: A History of Jewish Women in America from Colonial Times to the Present* (New York: Basic Books, 2002); Jeffrey S. Gurock, *A Modern Heretic and a Traditional Community: Mordecai M. Kaplan, Orthodoxy, and American Judaism* (New York: Columbia University Press, 1997); Baruch Litvin, *The Sanctity of the Synagogue: The Case for Mechitzah-Separation Between Men and Women in the Synagogue—Based on Jewish Law, History, and Philosophy* (Hoboken, N.J.: Ktav Publishers, 1987).

Megillah (pl.: Megillot)

The term *Megillot* (Hebrew for "scrolls") commonly refers to five books in KETUVIM (Writings), the third section of the TANAKH (Hebrew Bible), that are typically still written as scrolls and read in the SYNAGOGUE on certain festivals or Sabbaths.

The five Megillot are the books of ESTHER, RUTH, LAMENTATIONS, SONG OF SONGS, and Ecclesiastes. Ecclesiastes (in Hebrew, Kohelet) is read by ASHKENAZIM on SHABBAT (the Sabbath) during SUKKOT; the book of Esther is read in all Jewish communities on PURIM, which commemorates the events it relates; SONG OF SONGS is read in Ashkenazi communities on Shabbat during PASSOVER, and by many SEPHARDIM every Friday afternoon and at the end of the Passover SEDER; the book of Ruth is read on the holiday of SHAVUOT, either before the morning TORAH reading or the night before. Lamentations (in Hebrew, Eikha) is read on TISHA B'AV (the Ninth of Av), which commemorates the destruction of the two TEMPLES.

Further reading: Robert Alter and Frank Kermode, *The Literary Guide to the Bible* (Cambridge, Mass.: Harvard University Press, 1987); Norman K. Gottwald, *The Hebrew Bible: A Socio-Literary Introduction* (Philadelphia: Fortress Press, 1985).

Meir, Golda (1898–1978) *Israeli prime minister*

Golda Meir, one of the founding figures of the State of ISRAEL, was the first woman prime minister in world history and the first woman ruler in known history to gain power on her own, unaided by birth or marriage. Her chosen family name, Meir, means "to burn brightly."

Meir was a leader of Labor ZIONISM and the LABOR PARTY of Israel, an effective diplomat, and the country's fourth prime minister. Born Golda Mabovitch in Kiev, UKRAINE, in 1898, Meir immigrated to the UNITED STATES when she was eight years old. Raised in Milwaukee, Wisconsin, she joined a ZIONIST YOUTH MOVEMENT called Poalei Zion or Workers of Zion. Meir married Morris Myerson, and, in 1921, immigrated to PALESTINE.

In 1924, Meir began to hold a series of positions as an official of the HISTADRUT labor federation, and she soon became a member of its inner circle. By 1948, Meir had demonstrated such dedication and leadership potential that she was one

American-raised Golda Meir was Israel's fourth prime minister. She was a member of the State of Israel's founding generation. She was the world's first woman prime minister, and Meir led with authority, passion, and a tough demeanor. *(Library of Congress)*

of the people who signed the document declaring Israel's status as a sovereign nation. She played a part in internal labor Zionist politics and in diplomatic efforts abroad. In June 1948, she was appointed Israel's first ambassador to the Soviet Union (see RUSSIA), and was elected a member of the KNESSET the following year. Meir served as minister of labor until 1956, and as minister of foreign affairs for the next 10 years, winning many friends for Israel and inspiring Jews and women everywhere with her tough yet humane public personality.

Upon the death of Prime Minister Levi ESHKOL in 1969, Golda Meir became his successor. As a consequence of the devastating Arab surprise attack and the subsequent YOM KIPPUR WAR in 1973, Meir resigned from office in 1974. She quit only after turning near-defeat into victory and rebuilding the country's security and self-confidence. Meir withdrew from public life and began to write her memoirs, but was present in the Knesset to greet Egyptian president Anwar SADAT on his historic visit to JERUSALEM in November 1977.

Golda Meir died in December 1978 at the age of 80. She is considered one of the greatest Jewish woman role models. Her life has been popularly depicted in books, film, television and, most recently, in the 2003 hit Broadway play "Golda's Balcony."

Further reading: Jacob Abadi, *Israel's Leadership: From Utopia to Crisis* (Westport, Conn.: Greenwood Press, 1993); Peter R. Beckman and Francine D'Amico, *Women in World Politics: An Introduction* (Westport, Conn.: Bergin & Garvey, 1995); Golda Meir, *My Life* (New York: Putnam, 1975).

Meiri, Menachem ben Solomon
(1249–1316) *medieval rabbi and scholar*

Born in 1249 in Provence, Menachem ben Solomon Meiri grew up as a member of one of the most distinguished families in the region. Few details of his life are known to us and many are only conjectures. He may have earned his living as a moneylender. What we do have is his vast literary production, most of which remained in manuscript form until the 20th century.

Many of his works, which include expositions on TALMUD and HALAKHAH (Jewish law), biblical exegesis, and writings on customs, ethics, and philosophy, are exceptionally long. Meiri's magnum opus was the massive *Beit Ha-Bechira,* which he wrote from 1287 to 1300. The work, which follows the order of the MISHNAH and is arranged in a manner similar to the Talmud, is a digest of rabbinic commentaries on the GEMARA, elucidating the arguments and the laws derived from them. Meiri used all the literature available to him, including the Jerusalem Talmud, making the *Beit Ha-Bechira* a comprehensive survey of halakhic exposition up to his own time. Meiri's writing style is characterized by clarity and directness of thought.

Meiri participated in the late-13th-century controversy among the rabbis of SPAIN and Provence over the study of philosophy and the philosophical works of MAIMONIDES. He argued against banning such study or excommunicating any man who read philosophical works in his youth. He endorsed freedom of thought for the scholars of each country and freedom from intervention by outside scholars.

One of Meiri's innovations was determining that Christians are not idolaters even though they believe in the Trinity and use graven images in their worship. The Talmud puts many restrictions on the interactions between Jews and idol-worshippers. By removing Christians from this category (though he did not do the same regarding Muslims), Meiri significantly eased commercial and social interaction between Jews and their Christian neighbors.

Further reading: Yecheskel Folger, *Tractate Kiddushin According to Meiri: Translation of Classic Commentary to Tractate Kiddushin* (New York: Philipp Feldheim, 1989); Jacob Katz, *The "Shabbes Goy": A Study in Halakhic Flexibility* (Philadelphia: Jewish Publication Society, 1989).

Mendelssohn, Moses (1729–1786)
philosopher and founder of the Haskalah

Moses Mendelssohn was born in Dessau, GERMANY, in 1729 to a family of modest means. He received a Jewish education from the town's rabbi, David Fraenkel. He followed Fraenkel to Berlin when the latter took the post of rabbi there, studying Jewish texts in his YESHIVA. While in Berlin, Mendelssohn also studied secular subjects, including mathematics, logic, physics, and languages. He eventually began writing essays in the German language, a practice not common among Jews in Europe during this time period. Most Jews spoke and wrote in their own vernacular, YIDDISH. In 1750 Mendelssohn established himself as a teacher with Isaac Bernhard, owner of a silk factory, and in turn picked up skills as a merchant that he used to support himself throughout his adult life.

Moses Mendelssohn is often credited with ushering in the modern age of Judaism. He translated the TORAH (Pentateuch) into German as part of his broader efforts to reform Judaism. His work *Jerusalem* (1783) was the first extended attempt by a Jewish thinker to reconcile Jewish beliefs with the modern thought of the ENLIGHTENMENT. It advocated freedom of worship and the separation of religion and state, and argued that Jews had a responsibility to bring God's values to the attention of all humankind. Mendelssohn also worked for the reform of Jewish education, and he helped found a Jewish free school in Berlin in 1781, which combined secular and traditional religious curricula.

Mendelssohn was hailed by some as a brilliant thinker, but criticized just as vehemently by others for encouraging ASSIMILATION and therefore endangering Judaism. Although Mendelssohn remained loyal to TRADITIONAL JUDAISM, four of his six children converted to CHRISTIANITY. He is considered the most influential thinker of the HASKALAH, the Jewish enlightenment. Mendelssohn is also known for being the grandfather of the composer Felix Mendelssohn.

Further reading: Alexander Altmann, *Moses Mendelssohn: A Biographical Study* (London and Port- land, Oreg.: Littman Library of Jewish Civilization, 1998); Moses Mendelssohn, *Jerusalem* (Hanover, N.H.: University Press of New England, 1983); Michael A. Meyer, *Response to Modernity: A History of the Reform Movement in Judaism* (New York and Oxford: Oxford University Press, 1988); W. E. Mosse, *The German-Jewish Economic Elite, 1820–1935: A Socio-Cultural Profile* (Oxford: Oxford University Press, 1989).

Mengele, Joseph (1911–1979) *Nazi criminal*

One of the most notorious of the Nazi criminals (*see* HOLOCAUST), Joseph Mengele came from a family of well-to-do Bavarian industrialists. He held doctorates in anthropology and medicine. He joined the Nazi Party in 1937 and the SS the next year. After being wounded on the Russian front, Mengele was assigned in 1943 as a medical officer to the Gypsy (Rom) section at the Auschwitz-Birkenau complex (*see* AUSCHWITZ; CONCENTRATION AND DEATH CAMPS). In August 1944 he became chief medical officer of the main infirmary at Birkenau.

During his 21-month stay at Auschwitz, Mengele excelled in cruelty and sadism. He acquired the nickname Angel of Death for his role in selections. When trains arrived with new inmates, Mengele was the one who decided who was sent directly to the gas chambers and who could live a while longer.

Mengele was also involved in some of the most gruesome medical experiments ever devised. His special interest was twins, most of whom, if they survived the actual experiment, were then murdered and dissected. With the Allies approaching Auschwitz, Mengele fled to another camp sometime in January 1945. He was briefly held in a prison camp near Munich but was released; the American Army did not realize he was a member of the SS, as he was holding fake identification documents and did not have SS tatoos.

After hiding out in GERMANY, Mengele escaped to ARGENTINA in 1949. One of the most hunted of the Nazi criminals, he moved around South American countries before finally settling in BRAZIL. It is believed that he died in 1979 from a stroke suffered while swimming. In 1985 the body in the grave attributed to him was exhumed and positively identified.

Further reading: Lucette Matalon Lagnado and Sheila Cohn Dekel, *Children of the Flames: Dr. Josef Mengele and the Untold Story of the Twins of Auschwitz* (New York: Penguin Books, 1992); Guenter Lewy, *The Nazi Persecution of the Gypsies* (New York: Oxford University Press, 2000); Robert Jay Lifton, *The Nazi Doctors: Medical Killing and the Psychology of Genocide* (New York: Basic Books, 2000); Miklos Nyiszli, *Auschwitz: A Doctor's Eyewitness Account* (New York: Arcade Publishing, 1993).

menorah

The Menorah (Hebrew lamp) was the seven-branched candelabra housed in the TEMPLE in JERUSALEM that was kept lit at all times. It had a long straight stem in the center and three curved branches on each side. The image of the Menorah became one of the most common symbols of Judaism; it is found in most ancient and modern SYNAGOGUES and was inscribed on Jewish gravestones dating back to ancient times. *HALAKHAH* (Jewish law) forbids replicating the Menorah, but synagogues recall the sacred lamp with pictures and with an ETERNAL LIGHT over the Torah ARK.

Most Jews have a kind of menorah in their homes that is traditionally called a *HANUKKIYAH* (though most American Jews call it a menorah). It is used during CHANUKAH, which commemorates the second century B.C.E. revolt of the MACCABEES against the Seleucid Greeks and the subsequent rededication of the desecrated Temple. The Maccabees needed to relight the Menorah and keep it burning, yet, the legend goes, they could find only enough oil for one day. Miraculously, the oil kept burning for eight days, until more sanctified oil could be found. In commemoration Jews light a nine-branched candelabra on Chanukah, with the four branches on each side representing the eight days.

Further reading: Rachel Hachlili, *The Menorah, The Ancient Seven-Armed Candelabrum: Origin, Form, and*

This larger-than-life menorah stands outside the Israeli Knesset (Parliament). Unlike a *hanukkiyah,* a menorah has seven branches. This menorah is decorated with relief panels that portray different moments and figures in Jewish history. *(Courtesy Bernard Reich)*

Significance (Leiden and Boston: Brill, 2001); Yael Israeli, *In the Light of the Menorah: Story of a Symbol* (Jerusalem: The Israel Museum, and Philadelphia: Jewish Publication Society, 1999).

menschlikeit

The YIDDISH word for "man" is *mensch*. However, in Jewish culture when someone is called a mensch it means that he or she is a decent, capable person who can be trusted to do the right thing. By extension, *menschlikeit* is the quality shown by a mensch—responsible, ethical behavior. Phrases often heard in the Jewish community (and sometimes among non-Jewish Americans) include "be a mensch" (do the right thing), or "he's a real mensch" (he's one helluva guy).

Further reading: Robin Gorman Newman, *How to Meet a Mensch in New York: A Decent Responsible Person Even Your Mother Would Love* (New York: City and Company, 1994); Shelley Rosenberg, *Raising a Mensch* (Philadelphia: Jewish Publication Society of America, 2003).

mercy

According to Jewish tradition, God has two main aspects, that of JUSTICE and that of mercy. In fact, according to the rabbis the reason God has two names in the TANAKH (the Hebrew Bible) is that one name—Elohim (in English, "God")—is the aspect of justice and the other—YHWH (in English, "Lord")—is the aspect of mercy (*see* GOD, NAMES OF).

God's justice is responsible for the punishment of sin, but confession and acts of repentance can bring mercy to the fore. The book of Jonah is an excellent example of this: God, through the prophet Jonah, threatens the city of Nineveh with destruction, but when its king proclaims a fast and the city repents, God forgives them and they survive.

It is thus no accident that the book of Jonah is read on YOM KIPPUR, the Day of Atonement, when Jews confess and repent and are confident that God's mercy will overcome God's sense of justice. In fact, on ROSH HASHANAH, the Jewish new year, which begins the 10 Days of Awe that end with Yom Kippur, it is said that when the SHOFAR blows, up in heaven God moves from the throne of justice to the throne of mercy.

Further reading: Max Arzt, *Justice and Mercy: Commentary on the Liturgy of the New Year and the Day of Atonement* (New York: Holt, Rinehart and Winston, 1963); Abraham Cohen, *Everyman's Talmud: The Major Teachings of the Rabbinic Sages* (New York: Schocken Books,

1995); Louis E. Kaplan, *Gates of Mercy: A Guide to the Synagogue Services of the High Holy Days* (New York: Sepher-Hermon Press, 1979).

Merkabah

The Merkabah (Hebrew for "chariot") is the stream of Jewish MYSTICISM inaugurated in Ezekiel (1), in which the prophet describes his vision of God's divine chariot.

Each scholar and mystic of this school aimed to become the "Merkabah rider," the one freed from this bodily existence to ascend to Paradise. The Merkabah tradition involved intense prayer, TORAH study, MEDITATION, and fasting. Experiences of mystics in this tradition are recorded in the *hekhalot* (Hebrew for "heavenly courts") literature from the seventh to the 11th centuries C.E.

Further reading: Joseph Dan, "The Concept of History in Hekhalot and Merkabah Literature," in *Studies in Jewish History* (New York: Praeger Publishers, 1989): 47–48; C. R. A. Morray-Jones, "Transformational Mysticism in the Apocalyptic-Merkabah Tradition," in *Journal of Jewish Studies* 43 (Spring 1992): 131; Gershom Scholem, *Major Trends in Jewish Mysticism* (New York: Schocken Books, 1946).

Messiah

The English word *messiah* is the anglicized form of the Hebrew *mashiach,* "anointed one." Scholars differ as to when the concept of a Messiah developed in Judaism, but it is clear that by the end of the prophetic period some of the fundamental details of the idea were already in place.

Jewish tradition affirms the following general things about the Messiah: he will be a man of flesh and blood descended from King DAVID (who was anointed like all kings); he will appear in a time of great crisis to save the Jews; he will gain sovereignty over the land of ISRAEL, gather in the Jewish EXILES from the four corners of the earth, and restore them to full observance of TORAH law; and he will help establish God's Kingdom on earth, a

MESSIANIC AGE of peace (Is 11:6–9), when the whole world will acknowledge the God of ISRAEL as the one true God (Is 2:3).

Because the term has become widely associated with JESUS OF NAZARETH, many Jews simply use the word *mashiach* rather than the anglicized term. Some RABBIS have said that the Messiah will come when all Jews observe a single SHABBAT (Sabbath day) properly, when a generation arises that is totally innocent, or when the world has become so evil it cannot persist another day, but no such idea has attracted any rabbinic consensus.

The rabbis did not spend too much time discussing the Messiah, preferring to concentrate on how Jews should live and worship God in the here and now. In fact, the first-century Rabbi Yochanan BEN ZAKKAI is quoted as saying that should you happen to be holding a sapling in your hand when they tell you that the Messiah has arrived, first plant the sapling and then go out and greet the Messiah. Yet the belief in a Messiah is a fundamental principle of Judaism. It is reiterated in daily liturgy and is one of the Thirteen Articles of Faith formulated by MAIMONIDES. This article states "I believe with complete faith in the coming of the Messiah and, though he may tarry, each day I wait for him."

In the course of Jewish history several claimed Messiahs have attracted wide support from rabbis and laypeople, including Shimon BAR-KOKHBA, Jesus of Nazareth, and SHABBATAI ZVI. Few of them are regarded favorably in Jewish tradition; as a result, some Jews have speculated that the Messiah will not be an individual person. REFORM JUDAISM and other modern streams and thinkers, such as Mordecai KAPLAN, do not believe that the Messiah is a real person but rather a symbol of the ideas of redemption, universal peace, and a more perfect human world. They look forward to a Messianic Age that will be ushered in by the actions of the Jewish people themselves. In contrast, the CHABAD Lubavitch Hasidim have placed an increasing emphasis on the imminence of the Messiah's arrival; their cars carry bumper stickers that declare "We want Mashiach now." One faction of the movement believes that the last Lubavitch leader, Rabbi Menachem SCHNEERSON, is the Messiah himself.

Further reading: Gershom Scholem, *The Messianic Idea in Judaism and Other Essays on Jewish Spirituality* (New York: Schocken Books, 1995); Abba Hillel Silver, *A History of Messianic Speculation in Israel* (Whitefish, Mont.: Kessinger Publishing Company, 2003); *Tanakh: The Holy Scriptures* (Philadelphia and Jerusalem: Jewish Publication Society, 1985).

Messianic Age

The term *Messianic Age* refers to the Kingdom of God on earth that will arise after the coming of the MESSIAH. The RABBIS have proposed many different theories and speculations about the nature of this age.

Over the centuries two general schools of thought developed. One held that the Messianic Age will be much like our own, except that peace will prevail, and the Jews will return from EXILE under a Davidic king (*see* DAVID), and rebuild the TEMPLE. The other school held that in addition to all of the above, the age will be an unprecedented time of wonders. The two schools are best exemplified in their interpretation of Isaiah's vision (11:6) of the wolf dwelling with the lamb and the calf with the young lion. MAIMONIDES, adherent of the first, more rationalistic, school, believed that Isaiah's language is a metaphor for an age in which there shall be neither famine nor war, jealousy nor strife. Everyone will live in comfort, their only preoccupation being to know God. NACHMANIDES, follower of the second school, asserted that Isaiah's vision is literal, that in the Messianic Age even wild animals will become sweet-tempered.

Today, these two school are challenged by yet another. Followers of ORTHODOX JUDAISM and many adherents of CONSERVATIVE JUDAISM accept either Maimonides' or Nachmanides' view, while those in the camps of REFORM and RECONSTRUCTIONIST JUDAISM tend to believe that the Messianic Age will simply be one of peace and justice, without any ingathering of Jews, Davidic monarchy, or Temple.

Further reading: Matt Goldish and Richard H. Popkin, *Millenarianism and Messianism in Early Modern European Culture: Jewish Messianism in the Early Modern World* (Dordrecht, Netherlands: Kluwer Academic Publishers, 2001); Martin Sicker, *Judaism, Nationalism and the Land of Israel* (Boulder, Colo.: Westview Press, 1992); Leo Trepp, *Eternal Faith, Eternal People: A Journey into Judaism* (Englewood Cliffs, N.J.: Prentice Hall, 1962).

Messianic Jews

Messianic Jews are often people from Jewish ethnic or religious family backgrounds who have accepted the basic Christian message that JESUS OF NAZARETH was the Messiah promised by the prophets (*see* NEVI'IM) of the TANAKH, the Hebrew Bible. They have created "Messianic Jewish" congregations that retain some elements of Jewish ritual and custom, and they consider themselves to still be Jews.

The movement comprises many streams, with about 200 congregations in the United States claiming some 100,000 adherents. The two largest denominations are the Messianic Jewish Alliance of North America and the Union of Messianic Jewish Congregations. JEWS FOR JESUS, whose evangelistic activities have made them widely known, do not maintain congregations of their own, but send converts to become members of existing Christian churches.

The various Messianic Jewish groups differ from each other in their mixture of Jewish and Christian traditions and sources. All believe in Jesus, though they refer to him by what they believe was his Hebrew name, Yeshua. All subscribe to the concept of original sin. All accept the New Testament as part of the Holy Scripture. Many hold their services on Saturday instead of Sunday, either because they see it as part of their JEWISH IDENTITY or because they believe that its observance is obligatory for Jews, even those who believe in Jesus. Most also celebrate the Jewish

festivals such as PASSOVER and even CHANUKAH; the most extreme of the Messianic Jews do not celebrate Christian holidays such as Easter and Christmas. Many also observe the Jewish dietary laws of KASHRUT. They usually call their places of worship congregations or SYNAGOGUES rather than churches. They display MENORAHS and STARS OF DAVID and wear *KIPPAH* (head covering) and *TALLIT* (prayer shawl).

All mainstream Jewish denominations, from ORTHODOX to REFORM and RECONSTRUCTIONIST, hold that Messianic Jews are not practicing Judaism. There are a few dissenting voices but their views have failed to win acceptance. All forms of Messianic Judaism in the contemporary world are considered to fall outside of NORMATIVE JUDAISM.

The most basic reason for the universal Jewish denial of the Messianic claims made on Jesus' behalf is that he did not fulfill any of the achievements prophesied for the MESSIAH and MESSIANIC AGE. He did not end Jewish EXILE, restore Jewish sovereignty, revive the Davidic monarchy, rebuild the TEMPLE, or bring peace and justice to the world. Over the centuries, a number of other Jews, apart from Jesus, have been considered to be the Messiah by large numbers of followers, such as Shimon BAR-KOKHBA in the second century C.E. and SHABBATAI ZVI in the 17th century. All eventually proved themselves to be false messiahs and lost almost all of their followers when they failed to fulfill the Messianic prophesies before their death.

The concept of original sin is also considered utterly alien to Jewish concepts of free will and reward and punishment.

Further reading: David A. Rausch, *Messianic Judaism: Its History, Theology, and Polity* (New York: Edwin Mellen Press, 1982); Francine K. Samuelson, "Messianic Judaism: Church, Denomination, Sect, or Cult?" in *Journal of Ecumenical Studies* 37, no. 2 (2000): 161; Trude Weiss-Rosmarin, *Judaism and Christianity: The Differences* (New York: Jonathan David Publishers, 1965).

mezuzah

The word *mezuzah* literally means "doorpost"; it commonly refers to the miniature parchment scroll and decorative scroll holder that are affixed to the right side of doorposts in Jewish homes, businesses, and institutions. The mezuzah scroll contains a handwritten text of the first two paragraphs of the SHEMA prayer, which proclaims, "Hear O Israel! The Lord is our God, the Lord is One."

According to the book of Deuteronomy (6:4–9), these words should be recited when one lies down and rises up, they should be bound on one's arm and upon one's forehead, and they should be inscribed on the doorposts of one's house and upon one's gates. Evening and morning prayer services fulfill the commandment to say the Shema when one lies down and rises up; laying TEFILLIN fulfills the requirement to bind the words on one's arm and forehead; and placing a mezuzah at the entrance to one's home fulfills the MITZVAH (commandment) to inscribe the words on one's doorposts. According to Jewish tradition, a mezuzah protects the home and the people who live inside it. In addition, seeing the mezuzah each day reminds a person not to sin.

Further reading: Marc-Alain Ouaknin, *Symbols of Judaism* (Paris: Editions Assouline, 1995); Belle Rosenbaum, *Upon Thy Doorposts: The Law, The Lore, The Love of Mezuzot: A Personal Collection* (Hackensack, N.J.: Tangent Graphics, 1995); Zeev Rothschild, *The World of Tefillin and Mezuzos* (Lakewood, N.J.: CIS:STAM Gemilas Chessed Fund Publications, 1987).

A mezuzah holds a parchment inside that declares the Jewish belief in one God. It is found affixed to the doorposts of Jewish homes, institutions, and businesses. The case is often decorative, and many artists and schoolchildren use it as a canvas for expressions of Jewish life and belief. *(Ya'acov Sa'ar, Government Press Office, The State of Israel)*

midrash

In addition to compiling the MISHNAH and the TALMUD, the ancient RABBIS also wrote midrash, a rich literature of stories and textual interpretations that were eventually collected into various compilations. The most famous of these are the Rabbah compilations, such as Genesis Rabbah, Exodus Rabbah and so on, which comment on particular books of the TANAKH.

The word *midrash* comes from the Hebrew root that means to "investigate" or "inquire." Midrash are line-by-line interpretations called exegetical midrash, which provide deeper interpretations of a text. There is also homiletical midrash, which often take the form of sermons and end with a particular quotation, often for liturgical purposes. A good example of homiletical midrash is the compilation Pesikta de Rav Kahana.

Midrash can also be categorized by another twofold distinction, halakhic midrash (midrash HALAKHAH) and aggadic midrash (midrash AGGADAH). Halakhic midrash draw lessons from the text about Jewish law, while aggadic midrash are generally stories that give further background about biblical characters or draw ethical lessons from their behavior.

Further reading: Jacob Neusner, *The Midrash: An Introduction* (Northvale, N.J.: J. Aronson, 1994, 1990; H. L. Strack and G. Stemberger, *Introduction to the Talmud and Midrash* (Minneapolis: Fortress Press, 1992); H. Freedman and Maurice Simon, eds., *Soncino Midrash Rabbah* (CD-ROM), 3rd ed. (Brooklyn, N.Y.: Soncino Press, 1983).

mikvah (pl.: *mikvahot*)

A *mikvah* is a ritual bath used for purification. According to HALAKHAH (Jewish law), men, women, and even certain inanimate objects have to be immersed in a ritual bath on certain occasions.

A *mikvah* has to contain at least 120 gallons of running water and be deep enough to cover the body of a person of average size. The water filling the *mikvah* has to come from a natural spring or a river. *Halakhah* states that every Jewish community must have a *mikvah*; it is even permitted to sell a SYNAGOGUE to help pay for building one.

Traditionally Jewish women immersed themselves in a *mikvah* following menstruation or childbirth (*see* TAHARAT HA-MISHPACHA). Today, this practice is widely observed in ORTHODOX and occasionally in CONSERVATIVE JUDAISM, but REFORM JUDAISM has abandoned it altogether. Some men (especially Hasidim; *see* HASIDISM) also immerse in the *mikvah*, often before SHABBAT (the Sabbath) or festivals or after seminal emissions, but more as a MINHAG (custom) than by law.

Dishes and pots may be immersed in the *mikvah* as the final step in koshering a kitchen (*see* KASHRUT). Immersion in the *mikvah* is also the final step in the CONVERSION process to Judaism and is the origin for the Christian baptism ceremony. Numerous *mikvahot* have been found in archaeological excavations throughout ISRAEL, some dating from before the Common Era, and in the Near East and Europe—everywhere Jews once lived.

Further reading: Hayim Halevy Donin, *To Be a Jew: A Guide to Jewish Observance in Contemporary Life* (New York: Basic Books, 1972); Aryeh Kaplan, *Waters of Eden: An Exploration of the Concept of Mikvah: Renewal and Rebirth* (New York: National Conference of Synagogue Youth of the Union of Orthodox Jewish Congregations of America, 1976); Vanessa L. Ochs, *Words on Fire: One Woman's Journey into the Sacred* (Boulder, Colo.: Westview Press, 1999); Rivkah Slonim, *Total Immersion: A Mikvah Anthology* (Northvale, N.J.: Jason Aronson, 1996).

Miller, Arthur (1915–2005) *American playwright*

Arthur Miller was born in Manhattan in 1915 to Jewish immigrant parents. He came of age during the Depression which, together with his own father's disastrous business failure, had a lasting effect on him. When he was 13 the family moved to Brooklyn. After graduating from high school, Miller worked at a number of blue-collar jobs to save money for college. In 1934 he enrolled in the University of Michigan, where he studied journalism. During this time he also began to write plays and radio scripts which gained him prizes and a living. He even worked briefly with the Federal Theater Project established under the New Deal. During World War II, Miller worked as a fitter in the Brooklyn Navy Yard and helped produce an army training film.

His first performed play, *The Man Who Has All the Luck* (1944), opened to horrible reviews. Its major themes, however, have recurred in Miller's subsequent works: the insecure relationships between a man's honor, his work, and his family, and the nature of business ethics and personal ethics under capitalism. In 1945, Miller published his first novel, *Focus,* which deals with ANTISEMITISM in American cities. After the publication of *Focus,* Miller included fewer Jewish characters for fear of catalyzing antisemitic behavior himself. Yet, throughout Miller's texts is the examination of what it takes to survive, a theme pervasive in Jewish history, whether as a response to violence or to economic failure.

Miller's first play to be performed on Broadway was also his first success. *All My Sons*, opened in 1947, dealt with a manufacturer who sells faulty parts to the military during World War II in an attempt to save his business. Two years later Miller returned to the themes of desperation and paternal responsibility in perhaps his most famous and most successful play, *Death of a Salesman* (1949). Winning both a Pulitzer Prize and a Drama Critics Circle Award, it ran for more than 700 performances and was quickly translated into over a dozen languages. Neither work has openly Jewish characters or themes, yet Harold Bloom, an American writer, claims that both *Death of a Salesman* and *All My Sons* reflect the pain inherent in collective Jewish memory.

In 1953 with the emergence of McCarthyism, Miller wrote *The Crucible,* the third of his most

Playwright Arthur Miller sits over his typewriter. Some of his plays depict Jewish characters, but most do not, as Miller was sensitive to accidentally drawing negative attention to the Jewish community. *(Library of Congress)*

famous plays. Though set in 17th-century Massachusetts during the Salem witch trials, it was intended to be an indictment of the current McCarthy investigations of communist influence, which Miller considered to be Salem-like "witch hunts." Three years later, Miller himself was called before the House Committee on Un-American Activities and convicted of contempt of Congress when he refused to answer questions about Communist Party members he may have known.

During the 1960s and 1970s Miller published very little of note. In 1960 he wrote the script for the movie *The Misfits,* which was filmed by John Huston and starred Marilyn Monroe, to whom he was briefly married. In 1968 he published a collection of short stories *I Don't Need You Any More*. During this time, Miller was also involved in the anti–Vietnam War movement. His career saw a resurgence in the early 1990s with the production of *The Ride Down Mount Morgan* and *The Last Yankee,* which returned to the themes of success and failure, moral equivocations, and betrayals of faith in public and family situations. Arthur Miller remains one of the most highly regarded and widely performed American playwrights. Throughout his life, Miller exhibited extraordinary insight into the psychology of desperation and matchlessly investigated guilt, responsibility, and the conflict between self and society. He died February 10, 2005, of heart failure, at the age of 89.

Further reading: Harold Bloom, ed., *Arthur Miller* (New York: Chelsea House, 1987); Martin Gottfried, *Arthur Miller: His Life and Work* (Cambridge, Mass.: Da Capo Press, 2003); Arthur Miller, *Focus* (New York: Penguin Books, 2001); ———, *Timebends: A Life* (New York: Penguin Books, 1995).

minhag

In addition to observing HALAKHAH, the laws and commandments handed down in the TORAH and TALMUD, traditional Jews strictly adhere to other ritual practices and customs that emerged out of centuries of communal tradition that followed the

Talmudic era. These customs are known as *min-hag*. In fact, the Talmud itself recognizes local custom as authoritative. During the Middle Ages, a variety of local customs emerged, but eventually even customs themselves were codified when Ashkenazi rabbi Jacob Levi Molin composed a book of *minhagim* in 1427.

The most pronounced differences in customs are found between ASHKENAZIM and SEPHARDIM. There are slight differences in the order and wording of many prayers, varying customs in naming children, and different dietary restrictions in observing PASSOVER. For example, Sephardic Jews eat corn, beans, and rice during Passover, while Ashkenazic Jews are not permitted to do so. A custom adopted by both communities is the wearing of a KIPPAH, or head covering. This custom is widely followed by Jewish men even though it is not demanded by Jewish law.

Further reading: Lucien Gubbay and Abraham Levy, *The Jewish Book of Why and What: A Guide to Jewish Tradition, Custom, Practice, and Belief* (New York: Shapolsky Publishers, 1989); Harvey Lutske, *The Book of Jewish Customs* (Northvale, N.J.: J. Aronson, 1995); Aharon Verthaim, *Law and Custom in Hasidism* (Hoboken, N.J.: Ktav Publishers, 1992).

minyan

A minyan is a quorum or minimum number of worshippers needed for Jewish communal prayer. It consists of at least 10 Jews above the age of BAR/BAT MITZVAH. Within liberal Judaism, girls of at least bat mitzvah age and women are counted, while ORTHODOX JUDAISM counts only males in the minyan. Any number of Jews can recite most prayers in unison, but a minyan is needed to recite certain key prayers, or to read from the TORAH, a central feature of many services.

Though the word *minyan* comes from a HEBREW root connected to counting, the word itself does not appear in the TANAKH (Hebrew Bible). The RABBIS created the concept based on biblical notions of community and assembly.

They considered all prayer to be important, but they believed communal prayer was superior. The number 10 was chosen as the minimum number for a minyan because the Bible seemed to define a group as having at least 10 components: There are Ten Commandments (*see* DECALOGUE), 10 brothers of JOSEPH who sold him into SLAVERY, 10 spies who gave a bad report (Nm 14:27), 10 righteous ones for whose sake God would have spared Sodom and Gomorrah (Gn 18:32), and 10 Days of Awe between ROSH HASHANAH and YOM KIPPUR.

The TALMUD states what prayers may not be recited or rituals observed without a minyan. These include the SHEMA, taking the Torah from the ARK, the Priestly Blessing, the Torah or HAFTARAH readings, KADDISH, KEDUSHAH, and God's name in the opening of BIRKAT HA-MAZON. The rabbis later added additional prayers which cannot be recited without a minyan, including the call to worship in the morning and evening services, and the repetition of the AMIDAH.

Further reading: Ismar Elbogen and Raymond P. Scheindlin, *Jewish Liturgy: A Comprehensive History* (Philadelphia: Jewish Publication Society of America, 1993); Reuven Hammer, *Entering Jewish Prayer: A Guide to Personal Devotion and the Worship Service* (New York: Schocken Books, 1995).

Miriam (c. 13th century B.C.E.) *biblical figure, sister of Moses*

Miriam is the elder sister of MOSES in the TORAH, and one of the most well-developed heroines and leaders in the TANAKH and MIDRASH. She plays an impressive role in rabbinic literature; in contemporary times she is viewed as a Jewish feminist role model.

The Torah reports that it was Miriam who saved Moses from certain death at the hands of PHARAOH by placing him in a waterproof basket and floating him down the Nile. She keeps her eye on the baby until she sees Pharaoh's daughter pulling him from the water. She rushes to the princess, and offers to find a Hebrew wet-nurse for the baby. The wet-nurse she finds is in fact her own and Moses' mother Yocheved.

After the ISRAELITES are freed and experience the miracle of the Sea of Reeds, Miriam has her own prophetic experience with God and leads the Israelite women in their own song celebrating their new freedom. Later in the Torah, she appears to commit a sin in speaking ill of Moses' wife and is stricken with leprosy. Moses prays on her behalf, and God heals her. Miriam dies in the desert towards the end of the Israelites' wanderings, and soon thereafter a plague strikes the Israelites with the sudden absence of water.

There are many stories in the midrash tradition that fill in the details about Miriam's identity and why she merited being Moses' sister and a leader of Israel. One midrash suggests that it was Miriam and her mother who were the Hebrew midwives who refused to carry out Pharaoh's orders to kill the newborn Israelite males. According to this story Miriam was the midwife Puah; the name can mean cooing, and the tale suggests that Miriam will coo baby Moses in the future. Yocheved was Shiphra, which can mean shapely, because she will get pregnant and give birth to Moses. By their refusal to obey Pharaoh's orders, they merit becoming mother and sister to Moses.

Another midrash explains that Miriam is responsible for her mother's getting pregnant. The Jewish men had separated from their wives so as not to sire babies that Pharaoh would only kill. Miriam tells her father, Amram, "You are worse than Pharaoh. Pharaoh decrees only against the male children, you have decreed against all children." Amram returned to his wife and as a result Moses was conceived.

Just as she complained to her father, Miriam later complained to Moses, accusing him of being a poor husband. She is afflicted by leprosy, which, according to the midrash, was a punishment for Moses, making him understand that he should listen to his sister when it comes to family harmony. Many rabbis, uncomfortable with this positive portrayal of a women leader, prefer to say that

Miriam's leprosy was punishment for the women's sin of gossip; they accuse her of complaining about Moses' non-Israelite wife.

A common midrash explains that it was through the merit of Miriam that water was provided to the Israelites during their wanderings in the desert. When she died, the water disappeared, which explains the sudden water crisis that occurs in the Torah soon after her death. This midrash inspired a custom that has emerged among modern liberal Jews; a cup called the Miriam's cup is placed on the SEDER table at PASSOVER, filled with water, as a reminder of the great feminine hero of the story of EXODUS. Miriam's cup is also a reminder of a Talmudic teaching that the righteousness of women assured redemption from Egypt.

While there is no traditional blessing said over Miriam's cup, feminist liturgy writers have suggested the following statement: "This is the Cup of Miriam, the cup of living waters. Let us remember the Exodus from Egypt. These are the living waters, God's gift to Miriam, which gave new life to Israel as we struggled with ourselves in the wilderness. Blessed are You God, Who brings us from the narrows into the wilderness, sustains us with endless possibilities, and enables us to reach a new place."

Further reading: Penina V. Adelman, *Miriam's Well: Rituals for Jewish Women Around the Year* (New York: Biblio Press, 1996); Rita J. Burns, *Has the Lord Indeed Spoken Only Through Moses?: A Study of the Biblical Portrait of Miriam* (Atlanta, Ga.: Scholars Press, 1987); Fran Manushkin and Bob Dacey, *Miriam's Cup: A Passover Story* (New York: Scholastic, 1998); William E. Phipps, *Assertive Biblical Women* (Westport, Conn.: Greenwood Press, 1992).

Mi Sheberakh

A Mi Shebreakh is a prayer recited for a particular recipient during SYNAGOGUE services, wishing him or her good health and welfare. It may be recited over a person who has just completed the act of being called to the TORAH (*see* ALIYAH), or it may be said on behalf of people who are ill, calling on God to grant them a speedy recovery. The text of the blessing varies depending on the occasion, such as for a mother and her newborn child, a couple soon to be married, or a bar/bat mitzvah child.

The Mi Sheberakh for a person called to the Torah can be translated as, "May He who blessed our ancestors, Abraham, Isaac, and Jacob, Sarah, Rebecca, Rachel, and Leah, bless [name of person and father's name] who has come for an aliyah with reverence for God and respect for the Torah. May the Holy One bless him/her and his/her family and prosper all his/her deeds, together with our fellow Jews everywhere. And let us say: Amen." When a Mi Sheberakh is said over a sick person, or a list of persons in the community who are ill, it reads something like this: "May He who blessed our ancestors, Abraham, Isaac, and Jacob, Sarah, Rebecca, Rachel, and Leah, bless and heal [enter name of person and *mother*'s name]. May the Holy One in mercy strengthen him/her and heal him/her soon, body and soul, together with others who suffer illness. And let us say: Amen." In modern American synagogues, the Mi Sheberakh is often recited or sung in English as well as in HEBREW to ensure that everyone present can hear its always relevant and deeply moving content.

Further reading: Hayim Halevy Donin, *To Pray as a Jew: A Guide to the Prayer Book and the Synagogue Service* (New York: Basic Books, 1980); Jules Harlow, *Siddur Sim Shalom: A Prayerbook for Shabbat, Festivals, and Weekdays* (New York: Rabbinical Assembly, United Synagogue of America, 1989); Abraham Milgram, *Jewish Worship* (Philadelphia: Jewish Publication Society of America, 1971).

Mishkan

The Mishkan, or Tabernacle, was the portable temple that the ISRAELITES built during their wanderings in the desert after their liberation from EGYPT. The TORAH reports that God gave MOSES detailed instructions for the Tabernacle, which was built to be dismantled and reassembled.

The term derives from a root meaning to dwell or abide, suggesting that the Tabernacle was the vessel through which God abided with his people. God's presence was said to abide in the innermost sanctum of the Tabernacle, near the ARK of the COVENANT.

The Mishkan was dedicated with elaborate ceremonies, also dictated by God, including many sacrifices performed by AARON, the HIGH PRIEST, and his family. After the Israelites entered the Promised Land, the Mishkan was placed at Shiloh, where it stayed throughout the period of the Judges until King DAVID had it brought to JERUSALEM. His son SOLOMON built the first TEMPLE, thus replacing the Mishkan forever.

Further reading: Samuel James Andrews, "The Worship of the Tabernacle Compared with that of the Second Temple," in *Journal of the Society of Biblical Literature and Exegesis* 6 (June 1986): 56–68; Umberto Cassuto, "The Tabernacle and its Service," in *A Commentary on the Book of Exodus,* trans. Israel Abrahams (Jerusalem: Magnes Press, Hebrew University, 1967), 319–485; Nahum M. Sarna, "The Tabernacle," in *The JPS Commentary: Exodus* (Philadelphia: Jewish Publications Society, 1991): 155–237.

mishloach manot

Mishloach manot, also known as *shaloch manos,* is the practice of giving gifts during the festival of PURIM.

According to the book of ESTHER, Jews give gifts on the 14th of Adar to celebrate their defeat of Haman and his genocidal plot. It is said that another reason for the custom is to show the unity and devotion of the Jewish people toward one another. Haman had justified his murderous plans by charges that the Jews of PERSIA were a divided and scattered people. Giving gifts at Purim proves that there was no truth to Haman's charge.

The rabbis noticed that the use of the plural "gifts" was unclear: it could refer to multiple gifts to one person, or one gift each to multiple recipients. To avoid ambiguity, the rabbis maintained that one should give at least two types of items to at least two individuals. Most people like to give two different types of food so that the receiver has the opportunity to say two *brachot* (blessings; *see* BRACHA). Over time, the practice has evolved into giving large baskets of treats, especially hamantaschen, a cookie shaped like Haman's three-cornered hat.

Further reading: Irving Greenberg, *The Jewish Way: Living the Holidays* (New York and London: Simon and Schuster, 1988); Ronald H. Isaacs, *Every Person's Guide to Purim* (Northvale, N.J.: J. Aronson, 2000); *Tanakh: The Holy Scriptures* (Philadelphia and Jerusalem: Jewish Publication Society, 1985).

Mishnah

Mishnah literally translates as "repeated study" or oral instruction. The term refers to a major work of Jewish law compiled from oral traditions by JUDAH HA-NASI (the Prince) around the year 220 C.E., and committed to writing to ensure that the tradition would not be lost in those difficult times, Intended as a comprehensive summary of Jewish law, it became the first layer of the TALMUD, the huge collection of rabbinic literature written over the following centuries.

The Mishnah, written in a clear, simple Hebrew still accessible today, contains both HALAKHAH (Jewish law), derived from interpretations of the TANAKH, the Hebrew Bible, and AGGADAH, materials such as legends and parables. In its legal aspects, it is a systemized collection of both the ORAL LAW believed by some to have been handed to Moses at the same time he received the TORAH, and the civil and political laws of Judaism (*see* TORAH MI-SINAI). The legal traditions of the Mishnah go back at least as far as 450 B.C.E., a period when all material was transmitted orally.

The Mishnah is arranged in six orders with 63 tractates, each divided into chapters. The end result is a vast compilation of Jewish law based upon 1,000 years of oral traditions. The six orders are as follows: (1) Zera'im, "Seeds," with 11 trac-

tates, which deals with daily prayer and laws about agriculture—everything from technical issues to taxation; (2) Mo'ed, "Festival," with 12 tractates describing ceremonies, rituals, observances and prohibitions for the Sabbath, festivals, fast days and other occasions; (3) Nashim, "Women," with seven tractates, which treats issues of married life, divorce, and other topics of the family and home; (4) Nezikin, "Damages," with 10 tractates, which deals with criminal law, the court system, and punishment; (5) Kodashim, "Holy Things," with 11 tractates, concerning the TEMPLE in JERUSALEM and its rituals; and (6) Tohorot, "Purifications," with 12 tractates, which discuss ritual purity of everything from food to persons.

The Mishnah is the primary source of the Oral Law embraced by rabbinic Judaism. Further interpretations and discussions of its contents led to the evolution of two collections called the GEMARA. One was developed by the scholars of PALESTINE, the other emerged in the yeshivas of BABYLONIA, the great community that originally developed during the EXILE following the destruction of the first Temple. Each collection of Mishnah and Gemara was called a Talmud. The Babylonian Talmud has been the legally authoritative commentary for NORMATIVE JUDAISM ever since.

Further reading: Shaye J. D. Cohen, *From the Maccabees to the Mishnah* (Philadelphia: Westminster Press, 1987); Jacob Neusner, *The Classics of Judaism: A Textbook and Reader* (Louisville, Ky.: Westminster John Knox Press, 1995); Jacob Neusner, trans., *The Mishnah: A New Translation* (New Haven, Conn.: Yale University Press, 1991); H. L. Strack and G. Stemberger, *Introduction to the Talmud and Midrash* (Minneapolis: Fortress Press, 1992).

Mishneh Torah

MAIMONIDES' masterwork was his *Mishneh Torah*. It was the first comprehensive code of Jewish law (*see* HALAKHAH) ever published (*see* CODES OF LAW). It was also written in Hebrew, though Maimonides also wrote in Arabic. It seemed as if Maimonides wanted to free ordinary Jews from spending time on TALMUD study; all they needed was to study the TORAH and his code. His intention was to free up time to pursue the study of philosophy.

The *Mishneh Torah* was not well received by most RABBIS of his time, who thought Maimonides' approach was arrogant. They opposed his goal of having Jews cease intensive Talmudic study, and criticized him for not including the sources for his legal rulings. In addition, it was felt that offering Talmudic rulings without details decreased the flexibility of *halakhah,* Jewish law.

Because of historic rabbinic objection, rabbis are not supposed to rule from the *Mishneh Torah* in matters of Jewish law. However, after Maimonides' code became well established in the Jewish world, others built upon his literary foundation. Two centuries later Jacob ben Asher compiled his own code, the *Arbaah Turim* (Four Rows), which became the basis for Joseph CARO's code of Jewish law, the *SHULCHAN ARUKH,* the most common source used by rabbis in answering Jewish legal questions.

Further reading: Philip Birnbaum, *Mishneh Torah: Maimonides Code of Law and Ethics* (New York: Hebrew Publishing Co, 1970); Maimonides, *Mishne Torah, Hilchot Yesodei Hatorah: The Laws, Which Are the Foundations of the Torah* (New York: Moznaim Publishing, 1989).

mishpachah See FAMILY.

Mitnagdim

When HASIDISM emerged in the mid-18th century, its emphasis on mysticism and simple piety as sources of authority was directly opposed by the Mitnagdim (Hebrew for "opponents"). The Mitnagdim were traditional Jews, mostly Lithuanian, and they emphasized scholarship, TORAH study, and Jewish law (*see* HALAKHAH) above all else. Mitnagdim looked to the head of the YESHIVA, called the rosh yeshiva, as their authoritative source, while Hasidim preferred to follow and revere saintly or "wonder-working" rabbis.

The VILNA GAON (1720–97), leader of the Mitnagdim, was appalled by the Hasidic tendency to adjust the times of prayer (which are traditionally determined by sunrise, sunset, and other objective means) whenever emotions took over, to venerate men who were not Torah scholars but spiritual leaders, and to emphasize the idea that God is everywhere, which verged on pantheism for the Vilna Gaon.

In the 18th century, the differences between the Mitnagdim and the Hasidim seemed unbridgeable. Families were devastated if a child shifted from one community to the other, and the Vilna Gaon forbade intermarriage and business relationships. However, EMANCIPATION and the Jewish Enlightenment, the HASKALAH, changed the face of Judaism so radically that the chasm between the Mitnagdim and Hasidim has narrowed considerably in the modern world.

Further reading: Lucy S. Dawidowicz, *The Golden Tradition: Jewish Life and Thought in Eastern Europe* (Syracuse, N.Y.: Syracuse University Press, 1996); Samuel Heilman, *Defenders of the Faith: Inside Ultra-Orthodox Jewry* (New York: Schocken Books, 1992); Jacob Katz, *Tradition and Crisis: Jewish Society at the End of the Middle Ages* (New York: Free Press of Glencoe, 1961).

mitzvah (pl.: mitzvot)

The word *mitzvah* means "commandment." Jewish tradition holds that there are 613 of them in the TORAH. According to MIDRASH, 365 of these mitzvot are positive, meaning one is commanded to do something, such as HONORING PARENTS; 248 others are negative, meaning one is commanded not to do something, such as not to steal. This numerical division was based upon the midrash that 365 reminds people to observe the commandments every day of the year, and 248 was the number of bones the rabbis believed existed within the human body, metaphorically representing that everybody should observe the commandments of God "with every bone in their body."

While 613 mitzvot is the common metaphor to represent the collective commandments of God, rabbinic Judaism actually evolved thousands of commandments. Some are clearly articulated in the Bible, while others call for greater interpretation. A law that is clear in the Bible is said to be *d'raita,* Aramaic for "in the Torah." A law that derives from rabbinical interpretation is called *d'rabbanan,* which means "from the rabbis." The number 613 is important because the numeric value of the Hebrew letters that form the word Torah equals 611; in addition there are two commandments that precede the giving of the Torah: "I am the Lord, your God," and "You shall have no other gods before Me." The most well-known and accepted list of 613 Commandments was written by Moses MAIMONIDES as an introduction to his MISHNEH TORAH.

Another way to group mitzvot is that some are considered to be between humans and God, such as prohibitions against idolatry or dietary restrictions (*see* KASHRUT), while others are considered to be between humans, such as prohibitions against stealing or lying. While rabbinic Judaism posited that there are 613 Commandments from God, the rabbis extended the term *mitzvah* to any law or custom that Jews should observe.

Upon reaching formal adulthood, at the age of 13, a male becomes a bar mitzvah, or son of the commandments. After that point he is officially bound to uphold them. While some Jews see a bat mitzvah, or daughter of the commandments, in the same way, traditional ORTHODOX JUDAISM holds that women are not bound to uphold all the mitzvot (*see* BAR/BAT MITZVAH). Some mitzvot, such as dietary restrictions, are universal for both men and women. However, while women have some extra mitzvot concerning menstruation, many mitzvot, such as those regarding prayer times, are not binding on women because they are time-bound mitzvot, dependent on the time of day. Women are considered to have so many domestic responsibilities that could demand their attention at any moment, such as crying children, that they are excused from most time-bound mitzvot, such as the regular thrice-daily prayer liturgies. An exception is lighting the SHABBAT candles, which must be done before the Sabbath begins on Friday evenings.

According to Jewish tradition, one cannot be harmed while performing a mitzvah, and according to the mystical stream of Judaism known as KABBALAH, each mitzvah performed helps to repair the world (*see* TIKKUN OLAM). In contemporary times, the word *mitzvah* carries a second meaning; colloquially, a mitzvah is a good deed.

Further reading: Abraham Chill, *The Mitzvot: The Commandments and their Rationale* (Jerusalem: Keter Publishing House, and New York: Lambda Publishers, 2000); Dan Cohn-Sherbok, *Judaism: History, Belief, and Practice* (London and New York: Routledge, 2003); Elliot Dorff, *Mitzvah Means Commandment* (New York: United Synagogue Youth, 1989).

Mizrachi movement

The Mizrachi movement is the largest worldwide religious Zionist movement. Its name is derived from the Hebrew acronym "Merkaz Rukhani," or spiritual center. Though its roots can be traced back to the middle of the 19th century, Mizrachi was founded in 1902 in Vilna, RUSSIA, by Rabbi Yitzchak Yaacov Reines (1839–1915) in response to the decision of the Fifth Zionist Congress to develop official educational and cultural programs.

Many Orthodox RABBIS (*see* ORTHODOX JUDAISM) opposed ZIONISM in both its political and cultural forms as a heresy that replaced the belief in a MESSIAH who would bring about a miraculous ingathering of the Jews from EXILE with a reliance on human interference with God's plan of redemption. They totally rejected the concept of a nonreligious Jewish identity, and they feared that the predominantly secular movement would seduce young Jews from religious observance.

Some rabbis and other religious Jews, on the other hand, saw Zionist activism as a fulfillment of the commandment, or MITZVAH, to settle in the land of ISRAEL, and of the commandment to save lives, since it promised a refuge for Jews wherever they were persecuted. This group fully supported

Theodor HERZL's enterprise of political Zionism; in their zeal to save lives, some Mizrachi members even supported his UGANDA plan.

Unlike Herzl, however, religious Zionists saw religion as an indispensable part of Jewish identity and of life in the land of Israel, especially in a future sovereign Jewish state. They could not accept the secular cultural program that the Fifth Zionist Congress had launched, so they organized the Mizrachi movement. Mizrachi was the first official Zionist political party; it saw its role as spreading Zionism among religious Jews and Judaism among secular Zionists. Its motto was and remains "The People of Israel in the Land of Israel living according to the Torah of Israel." It reflects Mizrachi's view of Zionism as an instrument for realizing religious objectives, especially through the greater opportunities a Jewish society dwelling on its own soil would provide for observing commandments.

In 1921, a workers' movement, Hapoel Hamizrachi, split off to organize and unify religious HALUTZIM and to establish kibbutzim and moshavim (see KIBBUTZ, MOSHAV) under the slogan "Torah and Labor" They were able to observe the ancient agricultural commandments that are only applicable to ERETZ YISRAEL, the Land of Israel.

Consistent with its emphasis on national religious education, Mizrachi established a network of schools that became the basis of the Israeli State Religious School System, and a publishing house. In 1955 it founded BAR-ILAN UNIVERSITY. From the founding of the State of Israel both Mizrachi and Hapoel Hamizrachi were active in its politics, helping to set up the ministry of religion. In 1956 the two merged to form the NATIONAL RELIGIOUS PARTY. Today the World Mizrachi Movement is active in 37 countries. It sponsors a youth movement, Bnei Akiva (see ZIONIST YOUTH MOVEMENTS), founded in 1929, and two women's organizations.

Further reading: Ehud Luz, *Parallels Meet: Religion and Nationalism in the Early Zionist Movement (1882–1904)* (Philadelphia: Jewish Publication Society, 1988); Mizrachi Web site URL: http://www.mizrachi.org, accessed August 6, 2004; Yosef Salmon, "Tradition and Nationalism," in *Essential Papers on Zionism,* ed. Jehuda Reinharz and Anita Shapira (New York: New York University Press, 1996).

Mizrahi, Isaac (b. 1961) *fashion designer and entertainer*

Born on October 16, 1961, in Brooklyn, New York, Isaac Mizrahi received a JEWISH DAY SCHOOL education in his early years. He attended the High School of Performing Arts as an acting major and went on to study fashion at Parsons School of Design. Mizrahi is an internationally acclaimed fashion designer known for his luxurious clothes and shoes and his outgoing personality, and has been active in theater, movies, and television.

Mizrahi appears in a documentary called *Unzipped,* for which he and friend Douglas Keeve received a special Council of Fashion Designers of America (CFDA) Award, for bringing the fashion world into the theater. Mizrahi has also participated in costume design for movies and dance, and in 2002 he received the Drama Desk Award. He has been awarded the CFDA Designer of the Year three times. Mizrahi has hosted his own television show, focusing on the worlds of fashion and entertainment, and has starred in his own one-man show on Broadway called *Les Mizrahi.* He ran his own clothing business from 1987 to 1998, but later restricted his designs to shoes, coats, and fine jewelry. He has written a series of comic books entitled *The Adventures of Sandee the Supermodel.* In 2003 Mizrahi introduced a low-priced line of clothing at Target stores throughout the United States, acting on his belief that fashion can be relevant for ordinary people.

Further reading: Isaac Mizrahi, *Isaac Mizrahi Presents the Adventures of Sandee the Supermodel* (New York: Simon & Schuster, 1997).

Moabites

The Moabites were a people living to the east of ancient ISRAEL, often cited in the Hebrew Bible (*see*

TANAKH) in a negative light. The most important Moabite, however, was RUTH, heroine of the biblical book of Ruth. Ruth the Moabite is often considered the first real convert to Judaism (*see* CONVERSION). After converting and marrying a Jew, she gave birth to Obed, the grandfather of King DAVID and eventual progenitor of the hoped-for MESSIAH.

Further reading: Alfred J. Hoerth, Gerald L. Mattingly, and Edwin M. Yamauchi, eds., *Peoples of the Old Testament World* (Grand Rapids, Mich.: Baker Books, 1998, 1994); A. H. Van Zyl, *The Moabites* (Leiden: E. J. Brill, 1960); *Tanakh: The Holy Scriptures* (Philadelphia and Jerusalem: Jewish Publication Society, 1985).

Modern Hebrew *See* HEBREW, MODERN.

modernity

Modernity is a value system that began to prevail during the ENLIGHTENMENT. It privileges rationality and efficiency over emotion and tradition; the industrial revolution can be seen as one of its products.

The onset of modernity has had a dramatic effect on Judaism. While the Hasidic communities (*see* HASIDISM) have remained largely immune to its effects, REFORM JUDAISM, CONSERVATIVE JUDAISM, RECONSTRUCTIONIST JUDAISM, and the MODERN ORTHODOX MOVEMENT are all to a degree the products of modern points of view. For example, traditional interpretations of the Bible seem outmoded to many people in modern times, so the Reform movement encourages individual interpretation. These movements are all aware in different ways of the need to change certain customs or practices to survive in the modern world.

Further reading: Michael A. Meyer, *Judaism within Modernity: Essays on Jewish History and Religion* (Detroit, Mich.: Wayne State University Press, 2001); Marc Lee Raphael, ed., *What Is Modern about the Modern*

Jewish Experience? (Williamsburg, Va.: Department of Religion, College of William and Mary, 1997).

Modern Orthodox movement

Modern Orthodoxy is a movement within ORTHODOX JUDAISM that emphasizes the compatibility between traditional Judaism and modern life. Those who adhere to Modern Orthodoxy believe that Jewish law, HALAKHAH, should be lived on a daily basis, although their interpretation of *halakhah* and MINHAG, or custom, is more flexible than that of more traditional Orthodox Jews.

German rabbis Azriel Hildesheimer (1820–99) and Samson Raphael HIRSCH (1808–88) first developed the idea of being observant Jews in the world rather than relying on the cultural protection of isolated communities. It was a very fruitful concept; and Modern Orthodoxy became a dynamic, successful movement in Germany, and then, in the 20th century, in the UNITED STATES, where it dominated the Orthodox world, and in ISRAEL.

More recently, according to sociologist Jack Wertheimer, the movement has lost some of its dominance, as many mainstream Orthodox Jews have become more traditional or right-wing. For example, the Young Israel movement, at one time the vanguard of Modern Orthodoxy, no longer accepts SYNAGOGUES that do not have a MECHITZA, a partition between men and women. YESHIVA UNIVERSITY, the rabbinical seminary once most identified with Modern Orthodoxy, has also shifted to a more traditional stance concerning the appropriate way to live a Jewish life in the modern world.

Further reading: David Ellenson, *Rabbi Esriel Hildesheimer and the Creation of a Modern Jewish Orthodoxy* (Tuscaloosa: University of Alabama Press, 1990); Samson Raphael Hirsch, *Collected Writings of Rabbi Samson Raphael Hirsch*, 8 vols. (New York: Philip Feldheim, 1996); Jacob Neusner, *Sectors of American Judaism: Reform, Orthodoxy, Conservatism, and Reconstructionism* (New York: Ktav Publishing, 1975); Jack Wertheimer, *A People Divided: Judaism in Contemporary America* (New York: Basic Books, 1993).

modesty

Traditional Judaism teaches the concept of *tzniut,* or modesty in dress and behavior. *Tzniut* also implies privacy, restraint, decency, and chasteness. In the contemporary world, these issues are most significant for those who are part of an Orthodox community (*see* ORTHODOX JUDAISM), and even then the levels of modesty vary greatly between communities. Although Orthodox men are also expected to respect modesty laws, it is emphasized more in the lives of women and how they relate to men. Modesty laws also apply to the bedroom of a married couple.

Women are often expected to cover their elbows, their collarbone, and their knees in public. Some women even insist on covering their toes with stockings at all times, but in ISRAEL this custom is more flexible. Married women are required to cover their hair; some use a drab kerchief, others a modern wig and/or stylish hat. Modesty laws are meant to protect the sanctity of marriage and sexual relations, and not to restrain or punish women. They are often justified as necessary to keep men from licentious thoughts. Women are often discouraged from speaking and singing in the company of men, although this restriction is much less observed in MODERN ORTHODOX circles.

Further reading: Blu Greenberg, *On Women and Judaism: A View from Tradition* (Philadelphia: Jewish Publication Society, 1998); Samuel Heilman, *Defenders of the Faith: Inside Ultra-Orthodox Jewry* (New York: Schocken Books, 1992); Judith Plaskow, *Standing Again at Sinai: Judaism from a Feminist Perspective* (New York: Harper-SanFrancisco, 1991).

Moment

Moment magazine is an independent, bimonthly journal that covers cultural, political, and religious issues in the Jewish world. The writer Elie WIESEL and community activist Leonard Fein founded the magazine in May 1975. The name was taken from a Warsaw YIDDISH daily newspaper that was destroyed during the HOLOCAUST.

As the magazine is not sponsored by any other Jewish or non-Jewish institution, it has been free to develop its own personality and style. It has covered topics such as Jewish parenting, adultery, yoga in Israel, and the Israeli-Palestinian peace process. *Moment* is the largest independent Jewish magazine in America, with 65,000 subscribers, including CANADA and ISRAEL. According to the *Moment* magazine Web site its mission is "to present all responsible sides of the difficult issues that divide us, confident that our readers will have the judgment and intelligence to make up their own minds. As our flag states, we are committed to an open conversation on Jewish politics, culture, and religion." Headquarters for *Moment* magazine are in Washington, D.C.

Further reading: Leonard Fein, *Jewish Possibilities: The Best of Moment Magazine* (Northvale, N.J.: Jason Aronson, 1987); *Moment* Web site URL: http://www.momentmag.com, accessed August 5, 2004.

monotheism

Judaism, like CHRISTIANITY and ISLAM, is characterized as a monotheistic tradition; that is, a community that believes in a single God. In the biblical era of the ISRAELITES, monotheism may have been less pure. The Israelites asserted the superiority of the God of Abraham, Isaac, and Jacob (*see* PATRIARCHS) over other gods in language that seems to imply that the other gods did in fact exist. It is in the second TEMPLE period that the concept of monotheism clearly took hold. In the face of strong influences from HELLENISM and ROMAN civilization that encouraged worship of multiple gods or some form of SYNCRETISM, mainstream Judaism maintained its commitment to the God of the Patriarchs. In the post-EXILE period, when prophecy came to an end, God became increasingly distant, and the Jewish conception of God became increasingly abstract.

Further reading: Michael Mach, "Concepts of Jewish Monotheism During the Hellenistic Period," in *Jewish*

Roots of Christological Monotheism (Leiden: E. J. Brill, 1999); L. E. Goodman, *God of Abraham* (New York: Oxford University Press, 1996).

Montefiore, Moses (1784–1885)
businessman, philanthropist, and Jewish activist

Sir Moses Montefiore was born in Livorno, Italy, to a Sephardic Jewish family (*see* SEPHARDIM) but was brought up in London, ENGLAND. First apprenticed to a firm of grocers and tea merchants, he went into a brokerage partnership with his brother, establishing a fine reputation. In 1812, upon his marriage, he became Nathan Mayer Rothschild's brother-in-law and stockbroker. This business collaboration proved very successful, allowing him to amass a nice fortune and retire at age 40. He devoted the rest of his long life to philanthropy, and community and civic affairs.

Montefiore became famous throughout the Jewish world for his mission to the Ottoman sultan following the DAMASCUS AFFAIR to plead on behalf of that city's Jewish community. He interceded personally on behalf of many Jewish communities around the world, wherever their rights were compromised or their safety threatened. He met with world leaders, traveling twice to RUSSIA, in 1846 and 1872, to meet with two different czars in an attempt to alleviate conditions for the country's Jews. He met with the sultan of Morocco in 1863, traveled to ROMANIA in 1867, and was granted an interview with the shah of PERSIA. Montefiore also helped individual Jews. He unsuccessfully interceded in 1858 on behalf of the Italian Mortara family, whose young son was kidnapped by their Christian maid and secretly baptized. The Vatican took custody of the boy to raise him as a Christian and refused to return him to his Jewish parents.

Montefiore traveled to PALESTINE seven times. His first trip, in 1827, profoundly influenced him toward greater observance and piety. The poor among the Jewish community in Palestine became Montefiore's favorite cause. He responded to every call for help due to hunger, earthquake, plunder or pestilence, as well as to the general needs of individuals and institutions. He bought the land on which the first Jewish neighborhood outside the city walls of JERUSALEM was built in 1865. The neighborhood was later named Yemin Moshe in his honor. Montefiore also worked to organize the first agricultural Jewish settlements in Palestine by buying land and providing financial assistance.

Montefiore was sheriff of London from 1837–38 and was the first English Jew to be knighted, receiving a baronetcy in 1846. With one brief interruption, he was the president of the Board of British Jews from 1838 till 1874, in which capacity he strenuously opposed REFORM JUDAISM. Montefiore was a giant both physically—he was 6 foot 3 inches tall—and figuratively. His name became synonymous with beneficence, and he helped establish the philanthropic predominance of western European Jewry in the 19th century.

Further reading: Geoffrey Alderman, *Modern British Jewry* (Oxford: Oxford University Press, 1998); Myrtle Franklin, *Sir Moses Montefiore, 1784–1885* (London: A. Blond, 1984); Sonia Lipman and V. D. Lipman, eds. *The Century of Moses Montefiore* (Oxford and New York: Oxford University Press, 1985).

Morais, Sabato (1823–1897) *founder of the Jewish Theological Seminary and leader of early Conservative Judaism*

Born in Leghorn, Italy in 1823, Sabato Morais immigrated to the UNITED STATES in 1851. Prior to his immigration, he had studied with Jewish teachers in his home community and attended the rabbinical seminaries of Rome and London. At age 22 he became an assistant rabbi at the Sephardic Bevis Marks SYNAGOGUE in London, and director of the congregation's orphan school the following year. During his five years in ENGLAND, he established a friendship with the English Jewish leader Moses MONTEFIORE.

After immigrating to the United States in 1851, Morais followed Isaac LEESER as rabbi in the Mikveh Israel Congregation in Philadephia, working to unite the SEPHARDIM and ASHKENAZIM among his congregants. He remained rabbi there until his death in 1897.

Morais became active in the growing movement of CONSERVATIVE JUDAISM, helping to found the JEWISH THEOLOGICAL SEMINARY (JTS) and serving as its first president from 1887 until his death.

Morais had earlier participated in the growing movement of REFORM JUDAISM. He considered himself a reformer, but he believed in gradual and moderate change. After the publication of the radical PITTSBURGH PLATFORM of Reform in 1885, Morais came to believe that an institution was needed to train Conservative rabbis, in parallel to Isaac Mayer WISE's Reform-oriented Hebrew Union College (see HEBREW UNION COLLEGE–JEWISH INSTITUTE OF RELIGION). Morais commuted to New York once a week from Philadelphia to manage all aspects of JTS, including curriculum, administration, financing, staff, and students.

Morais loved Jewish music and had a particular interest in Sephardic studies. He became involved in the revival of the Hebrew language, writing prose and poetry in Modern HEBREW. He also translated the book of Jeremiah for the JEWISH PUBLICATION SOCIETY and wrote a commentary on the book of ESTHER. Morais pursued interests apart from Jewish life as well, speaking out against slavery and supporting the Union during the Civil War. Morais was the first Jew to receive an honorary doctorate from the University of Pennsylvania.

Further reading: Moshe Davis, *The Emergence of Conservative Judaism: The Historical School in 19th-Century America* (Philadelphia: Jewish Publication Society, 1963); Neil Gillman, *Conservative Judaism: The New Century* (West Orange, N.J.: Behrman House, 1993); Sabato Morais, *A Thanksgiving Sermon Delivered before the Congregation Mikve Israel of Philadelphia, at their Synagogue in Seventh Street on Thursday, November 26, 5624–1863, the National Thanksgiving Day* (Philadelphia: Collins, 1863).

Moses (c. 13th century B.C.E.) *prophet, lawgiver, and leader of the Israelites*

Moses is considered by Jews to be the greatest human figure in the TANAKH and in Jewish history, as leader, lawgiver, and prophet.

Moses was the leader who took the ISRAELITES out of SLAVERY in EGYPT. He faced down the awesome PHARAOH on their behalf, and following God's orders led them out of slavery and into freedom. For 40 years in the wilderness, he held together an undisciplined group of former slaves and molded them into a cohesive nation ready to assume its historic task.

Moses was the lawgiver who brought the Israelites the Ten Commandments (DECALOGUE) and wrote down the TORAH, also known as the Five Books of Moses. Traditional Judaism teaches that the Torah was dictated by God to Moses, word for word. In addition to the WRITTEN LAW, God provided an oral interpretation of the law to Moses (see ORAL LAW), who subsequently transmitted it to future generations. Although only the most observant and religious Jews believe that the Torah literally came from the mouth of Moses, all Jewish communities see Moses as the figure who brought law to the Israelites. Jews call Moses Moshe Rabbeinu, Moses our Teacher. His faith is central to Judaism, and the language of God's commandments is understood by traditional Jews as obligatory because "*Torah tziva lanu Moshe*" (God's law was commanded to us by Moses).

Moses is considered the prophet par excellence, with the greatest ability to perceive God's presence. He was the only human who saw God "face to face," without the intervention of a messenger or dream.

Within the Hebrew Bible there is scant biographical data. As an infant, Moses was placed in a basket by his sister, MIRIAM, who cast the basket into the Nile to evade Pharaoh's soldiers, who had orders to kill all newborn Israelite males. The basket is recovered by Pharaoh's daughter, who names the baby Moses, literally "drawn out" of the river. Through Miriam's intervention, his own mother becomes his wet nurse.

Moses, MIDRASH says, is raised as an Egyptian prince, yet as a young man he is angered when he sees an Egyptian overseer beating a Jewish slave. In righteous indignation he kills the overseer, and must flee Egypt to avoid punishment. Moses reaches Midian, where he marries TZIPPORAH, daughter of the Midianite priest JETHRO. As Jethro's shepherd, Moses is called to God's holy mountain, where he finds a "burning bush that is not consumed" (Ex 3:2). God speaks from the bush, telling Moses to return to Egypt and demand of Pharaoh that he free the Hebrews. With the help of his brother Aaron, Moses acts as God's agent and calls forth TEN PLAGUES that finally convince Pharaoh to agree.

This narrative, described in the book of EXODUS, is retold annually in every Jewish home at the SEDER ritual during the festival of PASSOVER. Because Moses is so central to Jewish life, the rabbis were concerned that Jews might deify him. Therefore, the traditional Passover liturgy in the HAGGADAH excludes any mention of Moses. Biblical and rabbinic literature indicates that it would be a sin to deify Moses, for while he was the greatest of men, he was still only a man, chosen as an agent by God.

After escaping from Egypt and defeating the pursuing Egyptians, Moses leads the Israelites through 40 years of wandering in the wilderness and brings them to the Promised Land. Along the way he conveys God's laws to them and organizes them into a powerful nation. More than three books of the Tanakh, the Hebrew Bible, are devoted to this phase of his life.

The legend of Moses has moved countless generations, and inspired numerous books and, in the 20th century, movies. Among the most widely seen depictions of Moses were Cecil B. DeMille's *Ten Commandments,* and Dreamworks' animated *Prince of Egypt.*

Further reading: Hayyim Nahman Bialik, et al., eds., *The Book of Legends Sefer Ha-Aggadah: Legends from the Talmud and Midrash* (New York: Schocken Books, 1992); Louis Ginzberg, *Legends of the Bible* (Philadelphia: Jewish Publication Society of America, 1956); *Tanakh: The New JPS Translation According to the Traditional Hebrew Text* (Philadelphia, New York, Jerusalem: Jewish Publication Society, 1985).

Moses de León (1240–1305) *medieval mystic and author of the* Zohar

Moses ben Shemtov de León lived his life in Muslim-ruled SPAIN from 1240 to 1305. Nothing is known about his formative years. He acquired knowledge of philosophy, and was familiar with the works of Moses MAIMONIDES, but his focus was always the KABBALAH, Jewish mysticism. He wanted to curb the rationalistic trends within Jewish scholarship in favor of mystical insights into TORAH and the Jewish religion.

Toward the late 1270s Moses de León was disseminating mystical essays, but rather than claim authorship he attributed them to ancient rabbinic sages, apparently to lend them greater credibility. By 1286 Moses de León had created the literary foundation for the ZOHAR, the most important book in the Kabbalah and the foundation for all subsequent Kabbalistic writings, the *Midrash ha-Ne'elam,* or "Mystical Midrash." He assigned authorship of both works to the second-century sage Rabbi Shimon bar Yochai. However, apart from some scholars within ORTHODOX JUDAISM, most people today recognize Moses de León as the author of the *Zohar.*

One interesting facet of Moses de León's writing is his concept of a marital relationship between the Jewish people and God. He also contributed to the limited amount of Jewish literature on the feminine aspects of God, especially the Shekhinah, or divine spirit, sometimes viewed as a female dimension of God.

Further reading: Karen Armstrong, *A History of God: The 4,000-Year Quest of Judaism, Christianity and Islam* (New York: Ballantine Books, 1994); Steven T. Katz, ed., *Mysticism and Language* (New York: Oxford University Press, 1992); Gershom Scholem, *Origins of the Kabbalah* (Princeton, N.J.: Princeton University, 1987); Moses ben Shem Tov, ed., *R. Moses De Leon's Sefer Shekel ha-kodesh* (Los Angeles: Hotsaat Keruv, 1996).

moshav (pl.: moshavim)

A cooperative agricultural village in Israel is called a moshav. In contrast to a KIBBUTZ, each family owns its individual plot of land, which they cultivate as they wish. The residents of the moshav cooperate in purchasing equipment and selling produce. Certain facilities and sometimes livestock are also owned in common. The first moshav, Be'er Yakov, was established in 1907. The moshav was very popular during the Third ALIYAH, when some of the largest moshavim, such as Nahalal, were established.

Further reading: Y. Azmon, et al. *Moshava, Kibbutz, and Moshav: Patterns of Jewish Rural Settlement and Development in Palestine* (Ithaca, N.Y.: Cornell University Press, 1969); Gideon M. Kressel, Susan Lees, and Moshe Schwartz, eds., *Rural Cooperatives in Socialist Utopia: Thirty Years of Moshav Development in Israel* (Westport, Conn.: Praeger Publishers, 1995).

Mossad

Ha-Mossad Le-Modi'in Uletafkidim Meyukhadim, the Institution for Intelligence and Special Tasks, commonly known as the Mossad, is the Israeli secret intelligence agency, roughly equivalent to the American CIA. Its operations are focused outside ISRAEL. The Mossad was established in 1951 and has had 10 directors. Only the last two have been publicly identified when they assumed the office.

The Mossad has carried out some stunning and daring operations, which have helped build its mystique, but it has also been involved in several spectacular debacles. Its successes include obtaining a copy of Khrushchev's secret speech in 1956 denouncing Stalin, capturing Adolf EICHMANN, aiding the successful rescue of hostages held at ENTEBBE airport in UGANDA in 1977, and planting a spy in the inner circle of Syrian leaders in the early 1960s. Its failures include the killing of an innocent Arab waiter in Lillehammer, Norway, mistaken for

one of the terrorists responsible for the massacre of Israeli athletes at the 1972 Munich Olympics, and getting caught in Jordan in 1997 while trying to assassinate a leader of the Hamas terrorist group.

Further reading: Aviva Halamish, *The Exodus Affair: Holocaust Survivors and the Struggle for Palestine* (Syracuse, N.Y.: Syracuse University Press, 1998); Mossad Web site URL: http://www.mossad.gov.il, accessed August 6, 2004; Jeffrey T. Richelson, *A Century of Spies: Intelligence in the Twentieth Century* (New York: Oxford University Press, 1995); Gordon Thomas, *Gideon's Spies: The Secret History of the Mossad,* updated ed. (New York: St. Martin's Griffin, 2000).

Mount of Olives

The Mount of Olives in JERUSALEM was the traditional site for the SACRIFICE of the RED HEIFER. Bridges and gates had to be built between the Mount of Olives and the TEMPLE on the opposite hill so that the *kohen* (*see* KOHANIM) burning the Red Heifer could be clearly seen. During the second Temple period the Mount of Olives served as the site for lighting bonfires to announce the new moon. MIDRASH teaches that at the end of days Ezekiel will blow his trumpet and raise the dead, beginning with those buried on the Mount of Olives. Because of this midrash, many Jews have been buried on the slopes of the Mount of Olives, where a large Jewish cemetery is still in use.

The Mount of Olives is also an important site for CHRISTIANITY. It is said to be the place where JESUS OF NAZARETH wept over Jerusalem, where he prophesied the destruction of the Temple, and where he gave his final blessing to the disciples before ascending to heaven. There has been a church on the site since the fourth century of the Common Era.

Further reading: John B. Curtis, "An Investigation of the Mount of Olives in the Judaeo-Christian Tradition," in *Hebrew Union College Annual* 28 (1957): 137–180; Louis Ginzberg, *Legends of the Jews* (Philadelphia: Jewish Publication Society, 2003); Gershom Gorenberg, *The End of Days: Fundamentalism and the Struggle for the*

Gebel Musa, or Mount Moses, is theorized to be the biblical Mount Sinai, where the Israelites received the law from God. It is located in the Sinai desert. *(Moshe Pridan, Government Press Office, The State of Israel)*

Temple Mount (Oxford: Oxford University Press, 2002); Julian Morgenstern, "The Cultic Setting of the 'Enthronement Psalms,'" in *Hebrew Union College Annual* 35 (1964): 1–42.

Mount Sinai

Mount Sinai, also known as Horeb, is one of the most sacred places in Judaism, since it is considered to be the place where God contacted MOSES through the BURNING BUSH, as well as the place where God revealed the TORAH to Moses and to the ISRAELITES. According to MIDRASH, Mount Sinai was chosen because it was the smallest mountain in the area. God wanted to emphasize humility and show that no corner of Creation is too small for God's attention.

The exact location of Mount Sinai is unknown, and Jewish tradition holds that it is purposefully hidden. However, one mountain in the Sinai desert, known as Gebel Musa (Mount Moses) has become the site of pilgrimages and currently houses St. Catherine's monastery, which was built in the sixth century.

Further reading: Louis Ginzberg, *Legends of the Bible* (Philadelphia: Jewish Publication Society of America, 1956); Norman K. Gottwald, *The Hebrew Bible: A Socio-Literary Introduction* (Philadelphia: Fortress Press, 1985); *Tanakh: The New JPS Translation According to the Traditional Hebrew Text* (Philadelphia, New York, Jerusalem: Jewish Publication Society, 1985).

Mount Sinai Hospital

One of the oldest and largest voluntary teaching hospitals in the UNITED STATES, Mount Sinai Hospital is located in New York City, straddling the

Upper East Side and Harlem. The hospital was founded in 1852 as the Jews' Hospital by German Jewish Americans who felt the need for a Jewish hospital to treat Jewish patients and offer free medical care to needy immigrants. The Jews' Hospital became known as one of the most successful benevolent institutions in New York in the last half of the 19th century. In 1866 the hospital changed its name to Mount Sinai Hospital, in commemoration of the biblical MOUNT SINAI.

As immigrants began to undergo AMERICAN-IZATION, the need for a special hospital for Jewish patients declined. Another need emerged; in the 1920s Mount Sinai, like other Jewish hospitals throughout the United States, used its facilities to train Jewish doctors who could not easily get internships, residencies, and appointments at non-Jewish institutions because of discrimination. When such discrimination declined in the 1950s, the excellent medical care available at Mount Sinai and similar institutions came to be regarded as a Jewish-sponsored service to the greater community.

Mount Sinai Hospital is known for its treatment of prolonged illness, research, and teaching. It has maintained a reputation of excellence in clinical care, education, and scientific research in most aspects of medicine. The hospital has a medical staff of almost 1,800, representing all faiths and many national origins. The state-of-the-art facilities include the Guggenheim Pavilion, which is designed to use natural light and space to create an atmosphere of positive energy and promote good health. Mount Sinai Hospital opened its own medical school in 1968 and named it the Mount Sinai School of Medicine.

Further reading: Arthur H. Aufses, Jr., and Barbara J. Niss, *This House of Noble Deeds: The Mount Sinai Hospital, 1852–2002* (New York: New York University Press, 2002); Joseph Hirsh, *The First Hundred Years of the Mount Sinai Hospital of New York, 1852–1952* (New York: Random House, 1952); Mount Sinai Hospital Web site URL: http://www.mountsinai.org, accessed August 4, 2004.

mourning

Judaism provides mourners with a series of powerful rituals that guide them through several phases and gradually help them adjust to the new reality.

When a spouse, parent, child, or sibling dies, a Jew begins the process of mourning by tearing his or her clothes above the heart to represent grief and to acknowledge God's will in the death of their loved one. The usually brief period from the time of death until the body of the deceased is buried is called *aninut.* During this time, the relatives must ensure that the body is properly cleansed and guarded, and they are not required to perform any MITZVAH (commandment) that requires them to do something, such as put on TEFILLIN or say prayers. Burial must take place as soon as possible, preferably within a day or two.

After the body is buried, the mourners enter into the period of SHIVA, which generally lasts seven days. Family and friends gather in the deceased's home; the mourners sit on low stools, and are encouraged to remember their loved ones among family and friends, although they are not forced to do so and can remain silent. Mirrors are covered to discourage vanity, and prayer services are held at the home so that the bereaved can recite the Mourner's KADDISH, the prayer for the dead.

Shiva is followed by a 30-day mourning period called *sheloshim* (Hebrew for 30), where family members are prohibited from attending parties and celebrations, cutting their hair, or listening to music. When a parent has passed away, the children observe an additional 11 months of mourning called *avelut.* They recite Kaddish every day for 11 months.

Every year thereafter the survivors observe the anniversary of their loved one's death by lighting a candle that burns for 24 hours. This is called YAHRZEIT (YIDDISH for "anniversary"). Deceased loved ones are also remembered during memorial SYNAGOGUE services called YIZKOR on the holidays of YOM KIPPUR, SHEMINI ATZERET, PASSOVER, and SHAVUOT.

Further reading: Hayim Halevy Donin, *To Be a Jew: A Guide to Jewish Observance in Contemporary Life* (New York: Basic Books, 1972); Maurice Lamm, *The Jewish Way in Death and Mourning* (New York: Jonathan David Publishers, 2000); Jack Riemer, *Wrestling With the Angel: Jewish Insights on Death and Mourning* (New York: Schocken Books, 1995); Leon Wieseltier, *Kaddish* (New York: Vintage Books USA, 2000).

Muhammad (571–632) *leader, founder, and prophet of Islam*

Prophet and founder of ISLAM, Muhammad was born in the year 571 C.E. Little is known of his childhood, other than that his father died before he was born. As a young man, Muhammad became financially secure after working as steward for and then marrying a rich widow perhaps 15 years his senior. Only Fatima, one of Muhammad and Khadija's six children, produced a lasting line of descendants. Muhammad did not take any other wives while Khadija lived, and she provided him with important moral support as he began his life as a prophet.

Muhammad had a practice of meditating in a cave outside Mecca, and from the year 610 began hearing messages from the archangel Gabriel. It is considered possible that Muhammad was exposed to Jewish and Christian traditions, practices, and Bible stories, as both religions had large followings in the region. However, Islamic tradition holds that Muhammad heard his message directly from God; his prophetic utterances were later collected into the Qur'an, a large part of which consists of familiar stories from the Hebrew Bible (*see* TANAKH) and MIDRASH.

Arabic-speaking Jews and Christians followed the religious and political leadership of their coreligionists in the major centers of the Byzantine and Persian Empires. Other, pagan Arabs living in the area of Mecca and Medina, while influenced by monotheistic ideas and traditions, were apparently willing to consider their own autonomous national religion. Muhammad preached to his friends and established a small community, emphasizing God's goodness, power, and final judgment, and calling on his followers to show humility, generosity, and respect for the poor and weak, and to worship God.

Nevertheless, the inhabitants of Mecca were not at first ready to accept Muhammad. In the year 620, a group of people from Medina asked Muhammad to help them mediate a dispute. Muhammad and his followers left Mecca and before long took power in Medina. By 622 most of the clans of Medina accepted Muhammad as a prophet, and they began to study his teachings. Muhammad acted as both religious leader and mediator of disputes. Collections of narratives about Muhammad's life, called hadith, are still studied today to provide insight for Muslims on how to live their own daily lives.

The Jewish tribes rejected Muhammad as a prophet, beginning a history of polemics that continues into the modern day. Once the dominant power in the area, the tribes had lost much of their power; they were defeated and either killed off or exiled, although a few Jewish communities who did not participate in hostile activities were left alone. It was at this time that Muhammad moved further away from Jewish practices, for example, by facing Mecca rather than Jerusalem to pray.

In the year 630 Muhammad traveled to Mecca with 10,000 men, and the city submitted without significant resistance. Soon after, Muhammad led a victorious battle against 20,000 Bedouin, proving his position as the most powerful leader in Arabia. Arabic tribes all over the area followed Muhammad and became Muslims, driving toward the north to conquer other lands. Muhammad led a pilgrimage, called the hajj, to Mecca in 632 but died after returning to Medina. He had made little provision for an heir, and many lasting Muslim divisions have resulted from conflict over the legitimate political and religious succession.

Further reading: Norman Stillman, *The Jews of Arab Lands* (Philadelphia: Jewish Publication Society of America, 1979); William Montgomery Watt, *Muhammad: Prophet and Statesman* (Oxford: Oxford University Press, 1974).

muktzeh

Muktzeh is the HEBREW term used to refer to objects that must not be handled or even touched on the Sabbath (*see* SHABBAT) and festivals.

The rabbis believed that to honor the Sabbath and festivals, one must not simply cease work but also withdraw from weekday activities. That is the best way, the TALMUD asserts, to achieve the mood of holiness one strives for on those days. The concept of *muktzeh* is one of the tools the rabbis devised to accomplish this task.

There are several categories of objects that are defined as *muktzeh*. They include objects whose sole use is in activities expressly forbidden on the Sabbath and the festivals, such as money; useless objects such as broken things; religious objects that cannot be used on these days such as the SHOFAR and the TEFILLIN; and objects that by themselves are not forbidden but may contain things that are, such as a purse that may contain money. One of the reasons for labeling an object as *muktzeh*, untouchable, is to remove the temptation to break the Shabbat by using it.

Further reading: Isaac Klein, *A Guide to Jewish Religious Practice* (New York: Jewish Theological Seminary of America, 1988); Adin Steinstaltz, *The Essential Talmud* (New York: Basic Books, 1976).

Museum of Jewish Heritage

Since 1946 Jewish leaders in New York have considered how best to memorialize the HOLOCAUST in New York City, which has one of the largest Jewish populations in the world. However, local politics complicated the proceedings, and it was not until the 1990s that a Holocaust museum was built. Opening in 1997, the Museum of Jewish Heritage is dedicated to the study of Jewish life before, during, and after the Holocaust. It is unique in its approach, as it focuses not only on the atrocities that occurred during World War II, but gives significant attention to the rich Jewish communities that were lost during the war.

The museum sits in Manhattan's Battery Park City. The building has six sides, symbolizing both the six points of the STAR OF DAVID and the 6 million Jews lost during the Holocaust. The positive symbol of the star represents the museum's mission to educate Jews about their European heritage. The museum teaches its lessons using first-person narratives and multimedia. It is organized around the three themes of "Jewish Life a Century Ago," "The War Against the Jews," and "Jewish Renewal." The museum seeks to provide hope for the future while encouraging attention to the past.

Further reading: Museum of Jewish Heritage Web site URL: http://www.mjhnyc.org, accessed on July 25, 2004; Rochelle G. Saidel, *Never Too Late to Remember: The Politics behind New York City's Holocaust Museum* (New York: Holmes & Meier, 1996).

Museum of Tolerance

The Museum of Tolerance opened in 1993 in Los Angeles, California. The museum Web site explains that it "focuses on two central themes through unique interactive exhibits: the dynamics of racism and prejudice in America and the history of the Holocaust." Museum exhibits include the Tolerance Center, which focuses on contemporary issues associated with intolerance; a HOLOCAUST section, with an interactive component, artifacts and documents, and special exhibitions related to the themes of tolerance and nonviolence. The museum is the educational arm of the Simon Wiesenthal Center, and it offers numerous educational resources for teachers and schools.

Further reading: Museum of Tolerance Web site at www.wiesenthal.com/mot/, accessed February 20, 2005; Jon Wiener, "The Other Holocaust Museum" in *Tikkun* 10 (May–June 1995): 22–23, 82–84; Oren Baruch Stier, "Virtual Memories: Mediating the Holocaust at the Simon Wiesenthal Center's Beit Hashoah—Museum of Tolerance," in *Journal of the American Academy of Religion* 64 (Winter 1996): 831–851.

Muslim-Jewish relations

The prophet MUHAMMAD was born in 570 C.E. and died in 632 C.E. He created a new religion, ISLAM, which unified the Arab tribes in the Arabian Peninsula and started them on a path of conquest and conversion. They brought an Arabic form of MONOTHEISM to vast territories, from INDIA and Central Asia in the East to Morocco and SPAIN in the West, all in about 150 years. In the early years of Islam, most of the Jews in the world lived in the lands where Islam grew. The Jews were often able to participate in the economic and cultural growth that Islam brought in its wake, though at other times they were threatened with violence and religious persecution.

In 622 Muhammad traveled to Medina to spread the message of Islam. When the many Jews there refused to convert, violence broke out, and the Muslims eventually expelled and killed most Jewish men, and seized the women and children. Despite this unfortunate beginning, violence has not always defined the relationship between Jews and Muslims.

Islam holds that Jews and Christians are "People of the Book," who merit protected status as compared with idolators. This status, called *dhimmi,* extended to those Jews and Christians who accepted their second-class role and who acknowledged the "superiority" of the Muslims. As *dhimmi,* both Jews and Christians were allowed to practice their religious traditions. A yearly poll tax on the *dhimmi* symbolized their submissive standing; additional regulations governing their lives were added over the course of years. These rules excluded Jews from public office and the armed services, and forbade them from riding horses or camels and from building SYNAGOGUES higher than mosques. Jewish oaths were unacceptable in Muslim courts, and Jews could not offer testimony against Muslims. In some communities Jews had to wear distinctive clothing; in ninth-century Baghdad, the yellow badge first made its appearance as a distinguishing sign for Jews.

Because the rules governing Jews as *dhimmi* were enforced differently by various Muslim rulers, in many instances Jews were appointed to high public office. In addition, many Muslim leaders did not seriously discriminate against the Jews, allowing a rich Jewish culture to develop, especially at the peak of Muslim power and glory. During the High Middle Ages from 850 to 1250, Jewish culture flourished. The Babylonian TALMUD was developed to become the foundation of Judaism in the DIASPORA; the SYNAGOGUE as an institution was solidified and Jewish PRAYER adopted much the form it has today; Jewish theology was systematized, Jewish law (*see* HALAKHAH) was codified, and the HEBREW language was studied. The Jews of Muslim Spain enjoyed prosperity and political influence throughout the 11th and 12th centuries. This period is often remembered as the golden age of Spain in Jewish history.

However, after around 1250, the quality of life for the Jews in the Muslim world began a steady decline, lasting until around 1800. Even during periods of tolerance for Jews, sporadic violence and heavy discrimination often appeared. Cooperation between Muslims and *dhimmi* was based on an unequal relationship. When the Jews became too secure, violence often erupted (*see* ANTI-JUDAISM). In the eighth century in Morocco whole Jewish communities were murdered, and in 1066 in Granada, Spain, an angry Muslim mob razed the Jewish quarter and massacred its 5,000 Jews. Joseph Ha-Nagid, the Jewish vizier of Granada, was crucified after Muslim preachers railed against too much Jewish political power. In 1465, Muslims in Fez and throughout Morocco killed thousands. Times of tolerance were laced with times of violence, not unlike the experiences of Jews in Christian-ruled areas in the Middle Ages (*see* CHRISTIAN-JEWISH RELATIONS).

In the 19th century, European influences spread to the Muslim East, and local Jews, like Christians, were eager to adopt Western culture and values. However, Westernization had mixed effects for Jews in the Muslim world, as it altered their position in Muslim society. A conflict developed between the modern values of many Jewish communities and the traditional values of the wider Muslim society. In the 20th century, Arab and Jewish nationalism (*see* ZIONISM) came into direct conflict as Jews began to settle in PALESTINE and worked toward creating a national homeland in the biblical territory of ERETZ YISRAEL. In the 1940s anti-Jewish riots took place in Iraq, Libya, Egypt, Syria, and Yemen, prompting their very ancient Jewish communities to emigrate. Today few Jews live in Muslim-controlled countries, although significant communities still remain in Iran and Morocco.

The current tense relationship between Jews and Muslims around the world revolves largely around the ARAB-ISRAELI CONFLICT. Although Israel achieved peace with two of its neighbors and maintains good relations with several Muslim countries such as Turkey, nearly all Muslims have come to support the political position of the Palestinian Arabs. The Palestinian Arab INTIFADA has succeeded in evoking intense emotions against Israel in many Muslim countries. The common religious roots and often positive relationship between Jews and Muslims in the High Middle Ages has been eclipsed by strong emotions and rhetoric on both sides.

In this climate, some Jewish organizations have redoubled their efforts to try to work toward interreligious understanding. For example, the AMERICAN JEWISH COMMITTEE has made efforts to meet with Muslim leaders around the world, and to encourage dialogue between Jewish and Muslim communities in the United States. The committee condemns any scapegoating of Muslim people as a backlash against terrorist attacks and atrocities by Muslim extremists.

Further reading: Bernard Lewis, *The Jews of Islam* (Princeton, N.J.: Princeton University Press, 1984); Ronald L. Nettler and Suha Taji-Farouki, *Muslim-Jewish Encounters: Intellectual Traditions and Modern Politics* (Amsterdam, the Netherlands: Harwood Academic Publishers, 1998); Norman Stillman, *The Jews of Arab Lands* (Philadelphia: Jewish Publication Society of America, 1979); Bat Ye'or, *The Dhimmi* (Rutherford, N.J.: Fairleigh Dickinson University Press, 1985).

mysticism

Judaism has always included a stream of mysticism, dedicated to a symbolic and esoteric study of TORAH rather than a historical, narrative, or legal approach. Jewish mystics emphasize an immediate, individual experience of God. Their goal is not merely intellectual understanding of Torah and practical performance of mitzvot (*see* MITZVAH), but also a personal spiritual transformation through the unmediated experience of God that results from mystical practice. Historian Gershom SCHOLEM has argued convincingly that mystical streams have always developed alongside mainstream Judaism, often provoking major transformations within the tradition. Perhaps the most influential mystical schools or movements were MERKABAH mysticism, HASIDISM, and the KABBALAH of Isaac LURIA. Like all Jewish piety, mysticism emphasizes prayer and the performance of mitzvot, but it puts more than the usual emphasis on fasting (*see* FAST DAYS), personal piety, and various spiritual practices like meditation in combination with close study of the Torah.

Further reading: Karl E. Grözinger, "Types of Jewish Mysticism and Their Relation to Theology and Philosophy," in *Experience et écriture mystiques dans les religions du livre* (Leiden: E. J. Brill, 2000), 15–23; Daniel C. Matt, comp., *The Essential Kabbalah: The Heart of Jewish Mysticism* (San Francisco: HarperSanFrancisco, 1996); Gershom Scholem, *Major Trends in Jewish Mysticism* (New York: Schocken Books, 1946); ———, *On the Kabbalah and Its Symbolism* (New York: Schocken Books, 1965).

N

Nachmanides (Moses ben Nachman; Ramban) (1194–1270) *medieval rabbi, scholar, and defender of Judaism*

Nachmanides was one of the greatest TORAH commentators, who excelled in mystical insights, yet was able to defend Talmudic law against Christian opponents with razor-sharp logic. Rabbi Moses ben (son of) Nachman is known by Jews as the RAMBAN, an acronym of his name, and by scholars generally as Nachmanides, Greek for "son of Nachman."

Nachmanides was born in Gerona, SPAIN, in the year 1194. He was a scholar of the TALMUD, teacher of HALAKHAH, or Jewish law, and student of MYSTICISM. He was influenced not only by Spanish Jewish learning, but by that of the Jews of FRANCE, who inspired his interest to mystical issues and the KABBALAH. Unlike MAIMONIDES, who lived under Muslim rule, Nachmanides lived later, in Christian Spain. Like Maimonides, he became a known rabbinic scholar in his teenage years, later studied and practiced medicine, and gained a scope of expertise that was broad and deep.

In those years, there were Jewish factions that supported the naturalist and rationalist teachings of Maimonides, and others that did not. Though Nachmanides did not completely agree with all of Maimonides' views, his tendency to revere his predecessors led him to mediate between the two schools. His authority was widely accepted among Jews, and even the Christian rulers of the land recognized his expertise in matters of religious thought.

It was common in the Middle Ages for Christians to stage public DISPUTATIONS with Jewish scholars in order to discredit Jewish religious beliefs. Although in France the debates were set up to favor the Christians, and the Jewish defendants often were not able to speak freely, in Spain Nachmanides managed to gain a more level playing field when he was asked to participate in such a debate by King James I of Spain in 1263. Nachmanides is said to have told the king that he would participate only if he was allowed to speak freely, and the king granted his request. The event became known as the Barcelona Disputation.

Nachmanides' opponent in the debate was a convert from Judaism named Pablo Christiani. Christiani was well versed in rabbinic literature and skilled in writing polemics. He knew Judaism well, and he had already spent a good part of his life trying to persuade the Jews that they should see the truth of Christianity as he had. His method was somewhat unique. Christiani used the Talmud itself as a proof text to support the belief that JESUS OF NAZARETH was the MESSIAH promised by the prophets. Christians had used a similar technique for years by reinterpreting the TANAKH, the Hebrew Bible, but using rabbinic literature that came after the life of Jesus provided new possibilities for argument. Nachmanides was aware of Christiani's technique, and he prepared well for the debate.

The importance of the Barcelona Disputation reached far beyond disagreements between Christians and Jews, and actually impacted the Jewish approach to the Talmud. During the debate, Nachmanides used an argument not heard before by most of his Jewish brethren. He argued that Christiani was trying to prove a truth using AGGADAH, material in the Talmud usually viewed as metaphoric as opposed to the legal material, which is called halakhah. Nachmanides took a huge risk in that he implied there were sections of the Talmud that did not serve as an absolute authority for Jews.

Scholars today possess two versions of the Barcelona Disputation, one written by Nachmanides himself and the other by the Christians. The debate itself ended when the Franciscans asked to stop the discussion after four days, an action that leads historians to believe that Nachmanides proved his points well. King James acknowledged the abilities of Nachmanides and is said to have provided him with some monetary compensation following the debate. Even though Nachmanides had gained permission to speak freely at the disputation, and the two extant sources report that he did indeed do so, his life was threatened by this success and he was forced to flee Spain in 1267.

Leaving his family behind, Nachmanides settled in PALESTINE. He was elderly by this time, and he felt the pain of leaving his children behind in Spain. Even so, Nachmanides clearly valued living in ERETZ YISRAEL, the Land of ISRAEL. He now wrote explicitly that Jews should aspire to live in Israel, and that commandments fulfilled while living there held more power than the same commandments fulfilled in exile. Nachmanides visited JERUSALEM but settled in Acre, where he left a written record of the impoverished and devastated condition of the land at that time. He died there three years later.

Among Nachmanides' great contributions to Jewish thought was a commentary on the Five Books of Moses. It was a vehicle to express many of his views on Judaism, including his disagreement with Maimonides on the nature of miracles. Nachmanides valued the belief in the supernatural, while Maimonides tended to explain biblical miracles in naturalistic terms. Nachmanides believed that Judaism depended upon the belief in CREATION out of nothing, the OMNISCIENCE of God, and Divine Providence. Nachmanides is well known for his penchant toward the mystical realms of Jewish knowledge, but he also wrote extensively on Jewish law. Among his specialties were the laws of excommunication (see HEREM), the examination of butchered animals (see KASHRUT), the laws of MOURNING and burial, ESCHATOLOGY (the ultimate purpose and destiny of life), the holiness of MARRIAGE, and the MESSIANIC AGE.

Further reading: Charles B. Chavel, *Ramban: His Life and Teachings* (New York: Philipp Feldheim, 1960); Charles Chavel, trans., *Ramban (Nachmanides): Commentary on the Torah,* 5 vols. (New York: Shiloh Publishing House, 1974); Jane S. Gerber, *The Jews of Spain: A History of the Sephardic Experience* (New York: Free Press, 1992); Avivah Gottlieb Zornberg, *Genesis: The Beginning of Desire* (Philadelphia: Jewish Publication Society, 1995).

Naomi *biblical figure*

Naomi is one of the main characters in the book of RUTH, which is found in KETUVIM, the third section of the Hebrew Bible, or TANAKH. She is the wife of Elimelekh from the tribe of JUDAH; together with him and their two sons, Makhlon and Khilion, she leaves Bethlehem for Moab during a famine in the period of the Judges. Ten years later, after her husband and both her sons have died without any children, Naomi decides to return to ISRAEL. She complains that her name should have been Mara, which means bitterness, instead of Naomi, which means sweetness, because of the losses she has suffered. Her Moabite daughter-in-law, Ruth, insists on accompanying her. Back in Bethlehem, Naomi is instrumental in arranging Ruth's marriage to her kinsman, Boaz, thus making her the forebear of King DAVID.

Further reading: Norman K. Gottwald, *The Hebrew Bible: A Socio-Literary Introduction* (Philadelphia: Fortress Press, 1985); Cristiano Grottanelli, *Kings & Prophets: Monarchic Power, Inspired Leadership, & Sacred Text in Biblical Narrative* (New York: Oxford University Press, 1999); William E. Phipps, *Assertive Biblical Women* (Westport, Conn.: Greenwood Press, 1992); *Tanakh: The New JPS Translation According to the Traditional Hebrew Text* (Philadelphia: Jewish Publication Society, 1985).

Napoleon's Sanhedrin

Midway through his reign Napoleon Bonaparte convened what he called the Sanhedrin, a body of 26 French Jewish lay leaders and 45 RABBIS, for the express purpose of confirming the decisions already reached by his Assembly of Jewish Notables (*see* FRANCE). It met in Paris from February 9 through March 9, 1807. With its 71 members and its very name harking back to the beginnings of rabbinic Judaism, the body was meant to evoke the Great Sanhedrin that was active during the Roman period (*see* ROME) as the supreme religious and juridical authority of the Jews. The revival of the Sanhedrin by Napoleon was part of his plan to "regenerate" the Jews and was intended to evoke awe and gratitude toward the French emperor.

The Assembly of Jewish Notables, 112 lay leaders and rabbis, had met in Paris the previous summer to respond to 12 questions posed by Napoleon. The questions dealt with Jewish law, the relationship of Jews and Judaism to Christians and to the French state, and the position of Judaism on USURY. When convening the Sanhedrin, Napoleon repeated the questions and added the answers he expected to receive, includ-

ing a recommendation of mixed marriages "for the protection and propriety of the Jewish people." The Sanhedrin was also supposed to consider "methods which might end or contain the Jews' evil ways," primarily their business dealings and moneylending. The Sanhedrin was expected to act as a rubber stamp, not to debate or discuss the issues. Everything about it was arranged in advance, including what prayers to say and when and how the men should cover their heads.

Despite all these restrictions, the Sanhedrin succeeded in standing its ground, at least to a degree. It prescribed adherence to the civil code but only so far as it did not conflict with HALAKHAH, or Jewish law. Thus, it refused to recommend or even accept INTERMARRIAGE, openly replying that such unions were frowned upon on religious grounds.

Following the meeting of the Sanhedrin, Napoleon issued three decrees that, in effect, put the Jews on probation until they could prove themselves worthy of the citizenship that they had been granted nearly 17 years earlier, and of the benefits of citizenship that were now being partially withdrawn. Napoleon's Sanhedrin never convened again.

Further reading: Frances Malino, *The Sephardic Jews of Bordeaux: Assimilation and Emancipation in Revolutionary and Napoleonic France* (Tuscaloosa: University of Alabama Press, 2004); Howard Sachar, *The Course of Modern Jewish History* (New York: Vintage Books USA, 1990); Simon Schwarzfuchs, *Napoleon, the Jews, and the Sanhedrin* (London: Routledge and Kegan Paul, 1979).

nasi

The word *nasi* literally means "prince" in HEBREW. The *nasi* was the patriarch, or president, of the SANHEDRIN in PALESTINE under the Romans (*see* ROME). The exact origins of the office are obscure. There is evidence that before the destruction of the TEMPLE the *nasi* was also the HIGH PRIEST, unless there were two Sanhedrins, one religious and one political in function. The title was already used by Yochanan BEN ZAKKAI and his successors at YAVNEH soon after the Temple's destruction. BAR-KOKHBA, in 132 C.E., also assumed the title on the coins he minted during his revolt.

By the middle of the second century, the *nasi* was recognized by the Roman authorities as the supreme representative and leader of the Jewish people and by the Jews as their spiritual and religious authority. It became a hereditary office passing down from father to son among the descendants of HILLEL, who himself claimed descent from King DAVID. Perhaps the greatest man to hold the title was JUDAH HA-NASI, compiler of the MISHNAH. A towering, scholarly figure, he maintained a practically royal court at Tiberias, supported by funds collected from all over the DIASPORA. Several of the *nasis* were not only learned in TORAH and the ORAL LAW but also in secular Greek subjects, and corresponded with non-Jewish scholars.

The office was abolished by the Romans, together with the Sanhedrin, around 425 C.E. The title was later revived in some areas, such as SPAIN, to designate the lay leaders of the community; it ultimately became a mere surname.

Further reading: Marvin Goodman, *State and Society in Roman Galilee A.D. 132–212* (Totowa, N.J.: Rowman & Allanheld, 1983); Lee Levine, "The Jewish Patriarchate (Nasi) in 3rd Century Palestine," in *Aufstieg und Niedergang der romischen Welt,* part 2, vol. 19.2, ed. Wolfgang Haase and Hildegard Temporini (Berlin and New York: Walter de Guyter, 1979), pp. 649–688; Adin Steinsaltz, *The Essential Talmud* (New York: Basic Books, 1976); Solomon Zeitlin, *The Rise and Fall of the Judaean State: A Political, Social and Religious History of the Second Commonwealth,* vol. 3 (Philadelphia: Jewish Publication Society of America, 1962).

National Conference of Synagogue Youth *See* JEWISH YOUTH GROUPS.

National Jewish Center for Learning and Leadership *See* CLAL–THE NATIONAL JEWISH CENTER FOR LEARNING AND LEADERSHIP.

National Religious Party (NRP; Mafdal)

The National Religious Party (usually called by its HEBREW acronym, Mafdal) was formed in 1956 by the merger of MIZRACHI, Hapoel Hamizrachi, and several smaller factions, in an attempt to unite the entire religious Zionist camp (*see* ZIONISM). The party, or its predecessor Mizrachi, participated in every single government coalition from the founding of the State of ISRAEL in 1948 until 1992. Until that year it always headed the ministry of religious affairs and/or the ministry of interior. In 1996 Mafdal joined Ehud BARAK's government but left when Barak proposed territorial concessions in JERUSALEM. In 2003, the party joined the government of Ariel SHARON.

Though it recognizes and accepts that Israel is a secular state, the NRP's stated goal is to make Israeli law consistent with HALAKHAH, Jewish law. It founded and developed the state-run religious school system, helped establish the religious courts that have sole jurisdiction over matters of family law and personal status among the Jewish citizens of Israel, and ensured the exclusive use of kosher food (*see* KASHRUT) in the army and government facilities.

Members of the NRP were among the founders of GUSH EMUNIM in 1974, and the party has since strongly supported Jewish settlement in the West Bank (*see* JUDEA AND SAMARIA) and Gaza. Though its views on national security and settlements moderated for a period following the 1982 LEBANON WAR, the party has since returned to its militant posture. NRP's platform opposes the creation of a Palestinian state west of the Jordan River, any division of Jerusalem or surrender of Israeli sovereignty over any part of the city, and any peace treaty based on the "land for peace" model. Instead it calls for limited Palestinian self-rule. From the beginning NRP opposed the Oslo Peace Accords, accepting them only as a fait accompli. The party sees the al-Aksa INTIFADA as a vindication of its position.

For years, NRP was the largest, most important, and best organized of the religious parties, typically polling at least 10 percent of the vote and winning 12–15 seats in the KNESSET. With the 1981 election, however, it lost ground to other religious parties, never to fully win it back. Thus, for example, in the 2001 and 2003 elections, it won only five seats in the Knesset. Many of its supporters live in religious settlements in the West Bank and Gaza. Since April 2002, NRP has been led by Brigadier General (ret.) Effi Eitam.

Further reading: Alan Arian, *The Second Republic: Politics in Israel* (Chatham, N.J.: Chatham House, 1998); Howard R. Penniman, ed., *Israel at the Polls: The Knesset Elections of 1977* (Washington, D.C.: American Enterprise Institute, 1979); Mafdal Web site URL: http://www.mafdal.org.il, accessed August 8, 2004; Howard M. Sachar, *A History of Israel from the Rise of Zionism to Our Time* (New York: Alfred A. Knopf, 1996).

Nehemiah (5th century B.C.E.) *prophet and political leader*

Nehemiah is known as the man who rebuilt the walls of JERUSALEM (Neh 2:17), and who helped restore a stable Jewish community following the return from the EXILE in BABYLONIA.

The only source of information about Nehemiah is the book in the TANAKH, or Hebrew Bible, that bears his name. He was cupbearer to Artaxerxes, ruler of the Persian Empire (*see* PERSIA) and won permission from him to return to Jerusalem to rebuild its walls and assist the returning exiles 70 years after the destruction of the first TEMPLE in 586 B.C.E.

After the walls were rebuilt, Nehemiah implemented political and religious reforms. He restored lands to their original owners, who had lost them to their wealthy creditors. He reinstituted the TORAH laws, stressing full observance of the Sabbath (*see* SHABBAT). He also created a formal taxation system to maintain the Temple in Jerusalem. Nehemiah is also known for discouraging intermarriage between Judeans and members of other nations.

Jewish tradition perceives Nehemiah as one of the primary leaders who helped restore the character of the Jewish people and religion. His reforms, together with the charismatic leadership of EZRA, brought effective Jewish sovereignty back to the land of Israel.

Further reading: Robert Alter and Frank Kermode, eds., *The Literary Guide to the Bible* (Cambridge, Mass.: Harvard University Press, 1987); Norman K. Gottwald, *The Hebrew Bible: A Socio-Literary Introduction* (Philadelphia: Fortress Press, 1985); *Tanakh: The New JPS Translation According to the Traditional Hebrew Text* (Philadelphia, New York, Jerusalem: Jewish Publication Society, 1985).

Neo-Orthodox movement

Neo-Orthodoxy was the first attempt by a traditional Jewish group to combat the rise of REFORM JUDAISM in the mid-19th century.

The founder and first leader of the new movement was Rabbi Samson Raphael HIRSCH. Hirsch advocated a new style of Jewish living that combined full observance of HALAKHAH, Jewish law, in the home and synagogue, with full participation in the modern economic and cultural life of the wider society. The Neo-Orthodox movement was thus the ideological forerunner of MODERN ORTHODOXY, and Hirsch proposed the idea of TORAH in Derekh Eretz, Torah with the way of the land, as its central philosophy.

Unlike other more traditional RABBIS, for example, Hirsch believed that secular and professional education could be compatible with Jewish life. The Neo-Orthodox community he built in Frankfurt consisted of German-speaking Jews who looked and comported themselves like good German citizens, and practiced a complete range of occupations from business to skilled trades to the professions. He even permitted his followers to study and adopt many of the ideas of the ENLIGHTENMENT. Many Orthodox rabbis, especially in POLAND and RUSSIA, who were spending time and energy fighting off the "heresies" of the HASKALAH in their communities, responded to Hirsch's approach with trepidation, preferring to keep their flocks protected within insulated religious Jewish communities.

Hirsch believed in the divine origin of Jewish law. Unlike the Reformers, he did not believe that a Jew could choose which laws to observe and which not to observe. To help modern people, Hirsch explained the law and approached it from a rational viewpoint. In the end, however, the final justification for the law was that it was from God.

However modern he might be, Hirsch was a strong political opponent of REFORM JUDAISM, and worked to separate his congregations from Reform-dominated *kehillah* (*see* KAHAL/KEHILLAH) in the German cities. Neo-Orthodoxy welcomed the embrace of secular life and knowledge, but insisted that when Torah law came into conflict with modernity, then TORAH always took priority. That continues to be the position of today's Modern Orthodox movement.

Further reading: Samson Raphael Hirsch, *Collected Writings of Rabbi Samson Raphael Hirsch*, 8 vols. (New York: Philip Feldheim, 1996); Robert Liberles, *Religious Conflict in Social Context: The Resurgence of Orthodox Judaism in Frankfurt Am Main, 1838–1877* (Westport, Conn.: Greenwood Press, 1985); Noah H. Rosenbloom, *Tradition in an Age of Reform: The Religious Philosophy of Samson Raphael Hirsch* (Philadelphia: Jewish Publication Society of America, 1976).

Netanyahu, Benjamin (b. 1949) *Israeli prime minister and politician*

Benjamin Netanyahu is renowned as a soldier, diplomat, and the ninth prime minister of the State of ISRAEL. Born in TEL AVIV in 1949, he grew up in JERUSALEM but spent his adolescent years in the UNITED STATES, where his father, a noted historian, taught Jewish history. Netanyahu returned to Israel in 1967 to fulfill his military obligations, volunteering for an elite commando unit of the ISRAEL DEFENSE FORCES and participating in a num-

ber of daring operations. Netanyahu also succeeded in the academic world, earning degrees in architecture and management from the Massachusetts Institute of Technology.

Netanhayu was much affected by the death of his eldest brother Yonatan, who had fallen while commanding the 1976 ENTEBBE rescue operation, which freed Israeli and Jewish passengers of an Air France airliner held hostage in UGANDA. Netanyahu initiated and organized two international conferences on ways to combat international terrorism, in Jerusalem in 1979 and in Washington in 1984.

In 1982, Netanyahu joined Israel's diplomatic mission in the United States, and two years later was appointed ambassador to the UNITED NATIONS. He proved an articulate speaker, forceful debater, and media-oriented diplomat. In 1988 Netanyahu was elected to the KNESSET. He served as minister of foreign affairs for four years, which were marked by the INTIFADA and the 1991 Gulf War, when his persuasive words and charisma won much sympathy for Israel as its cities were being attacked by Iraqi missiles.

In 1996, in the first direct election of an Israeli prime minister, Benjamin Netanyahu defeated the incumbent Labor Party candidate Shimon PERES, and became the ninth prime minister of the State of Israel, serving until 1999. After the election of Ariel SHARON in 2001, Netanyahu was appointed finance minister in 2003. He is expected to push through a large degree of economic liberalization and privatization of the formerly quasi-socialist Israel economy after requesting and receiving expanded powers from Prime Minister Sharon.

Further reading: Ben Caspit and Ilan Kfir, *Netanyahu: The Road to Power* (New York: Birch Lane, 1998); Robert O. Freedman, ed., *The Middle East and the Peace Process: The Impact of the Oslo Accords* (Gainesville: University Press of Florida, 1998); Adam Garfinkle, *Politics and Society in Modern Israel* (Armonk, N.Y.: M. E. Sharpe, 2000); Benjamin Netanyahu, *A Durable Peace: Israel and Its Place Among the Nations* (New York: Warner Books, 2000).

Netherlands, the

It is possible that Jews came to the Netherlands during the Roman conquest, as they did to other European countries, though there is little evidence of their presence. A 12th-century Jewish community is well documented. The Jews in the Netherlands in the Middle Ages, like their European neighbors, lived from one episode of persecution to another. During the Black Plague in 1349 and 1350, rioters murdered almost the entire population of the Jews of the Netherlands, who were accused of spreading the disease. Though Jewish numbers were small, there is significant evidence of ANTI-JUDAISM in the literature and poetry of the period.

In the 16th century, Jews again appeared, as Portuguese Jewish merchants found refuge in the Netherlands. Amsterdam had become the center of world trade, and many CONVERSOS, secret Jews, found their way there after the EXPULSION from SPAIN in 1492. Some Protestant authorities in the Netherlands wanted to oppress the Jews, but Christians involved in trade disagreed. Some cities allowed Jews to reside within their boundaries, and some did not. The Jews were not citizens, and their rights were limited, but Jews were generally able to find a livelihood in the Netherlands.

By 1635 a group of ASHKENAZIM from central and eastern Europe had also settled in the Netherlands, forming their own community. As in much of Europe, the Jews were allowed to establish a semiautonomous governing body, called the KAHAL.

Although Jewish history in the Netherlands resembles that of other European countries in some ways, there are also significant differences. The SEPHARDIM integrated into society as early as the 17th century, 200 years before the rest of European Jewry was able to do so. They were not restricted to moneylending and pawnbroking. They entered the medical profession and became important components of the shipping and trading industry; they succeeded in tobacco, sugar, printing, and diamonds.

This economic integration afforded Holland's Sephardic Jews some freedom in society. The Ashkenazim, however, did not become professionally successful; they continued to speak YIDDISH and live in their insulated communities. They did not contribute in any significant way to the history of the Netherlands, nor did they leave their mark on Jewish history, producing none of their own rabbis or any important literature or thought. Even so, life in the Netherlands was safer for them than it was in many other parts of Europe.

The Jews in the Netherlands experienced a number of schisms. There were vast differences between Sephardim and Ashkenazim. Within the Ashkenazic community there was a further division between those of German and Polish descent. In the mid-1600s, the community suffered from the impact of the false messiah SHABBATAI ZVI. The community was also home to several famous Jewish heretics, specifically Baruch SPINOZA (1632–77) and Uriel da Costa (1585–1640).

The Dutch ascendancy in world trade and shipping declined by the mid 18th century, and along with it, so did the gap between the Ashkenazic and Sephardic populations. By the close of the 18th century the two communities were equally poor, with 54 percent dependent on charity. Some Jews worked to gain EMANCIPATION, or full citizenship, while others rejected it when it was granted in 1796 by Napoleon Bonaparte's French puppet government. Even after emancipation the Jews did not regain their economic prosperity until after Holland became an independent country in 1814, when they once again became active in industry, succeeding in the trades of cotton and diamonds.

In that era King William I disbanded the kehillah, forced Jewish children to attend secular schools, and banned the use of Yiddish. The Dutch MASKILIM, proponents of the HASKALAH, or Jewish Enlightenment, welcomed these changes. Jews soon reentered the professions, becoming doctors and lawyers. As they became involved in secular society, the traditionalist character of

Holland's Jews shifted toward liberalism. The Jewish population declined as a result of low birth rates, INTERMARRIAGE, and CONVERSION. High rates of ASSIMILATION made it difficult for ZIONISM to take hold.

Some 140,000 Jews lived in the Netherlands by 1933. Jewish refugees from GERMANY swelled this number to around 170,000 by 1940. Almost none of the country's Jews were able to escape Hitler's advancing HOLOCAUST. In the summer of 1943, the occupying Nazis deported most of Holland's Jews to the death camps AUSCHWITZ and Sobibor, although some, like the family of Anne FRANK, found hiding places within the country. After the war, 40,000 Jews remained in Holland, but they were highly assimilated, and the population decreased in the 1950s due to low birth rates and emigration. Life in Holland for the Jews was good, non-Jews were friendly, and war reparations made the Jewish community wealthy. However, little remained of traditional Judaism.

In contemporary times, the number of Jews in Amsterdam hovers between 25,000 and 30,000. Perhaps surprisingly, they have become more observant, in part thanks to the influence of CHABAD, a Hasidic movement dedicated to outreach among nonreligious Jews. Relations between Holland and ISRAEL have been mostly positive; the country voted in favor of the UNITED NATIONS partition plan in 1947 and has defended Israel there and in the European Union. In recent years, the media has been accused of bias in favor of the Palestinian cause and against Israel.

Amsterdam is home to several restored synagogues, a MIKVAH (ritual bath), a Holocaust memorial, and the Anne Frank House. The Hague boasts several museums housed in homes in which Spinoza once lived, run by the Spinoza Society, as well as Spinoza's grave. In death Spinoza was reclaimed by the Jewish people when the Israel Spinoza Society placed the Hebrew word *amcha,* meaning "your people" on his gravesite. The Hague also boasts an active Jewish community with a community center and several synagogues.

Further reading: Jozeph Michman, *The History of Dutch Jewry during the Emancipation Period, 1787–1815: Gothic Turrets on a Corinthian Building* (Amsterdam: Amsterdam University Press, 1995); Nechama Tec, *When Light Pierced the Darkness: Christian Rescue of Jews in Nazi-Occupied Poland* (New York: Oxford University Press, 1986); Alan Tigay, *The Jewish Traveler* (Northvale, N.J.: Jason Aronson, Inc., 1994); Geoffery Wigoder, *Jewish Art and Civilization* (New York: Walker and Co., 1972).

netillat yadayim

The HEBREW term *netillat yedayim* refers to the act of ritually washing one's hands prior to eating bread. The TALMUD mandates this practice to cleanse the hands from any ritual impurity that may have been picked up, and to imitate the act of washing as practiced by the priests in the ancient TEMPLE prior to performing SACRIFICES.

Hands were considered potentially impure because they are always very active and often come into contact with ritually unfit objects. If the hands are not washed, then the ritual impurity would be passed along to the food, which is unacceptable in Jewish tradition. Eating requires prayers both before and after (*see* BRACHA, BIRKAT HA-MAZON), in imitation of the offerings of the priests in the Temple.

The act of *netillat yadayim* is intended to focus one's attention on the proper attitude toward eating, and to induce gratitude for God's bounty. From the time one recites the blessing over *netillat yadayim* until pronouncing the blessing over the bread, the individual must remain silent and avoid distraction from his or her solemn purpose.

Many scholars have speculated that the ancient RABBIS understood basic hygiene in the modern sense, that cleanliness helps prevent disease. The practice of *netillat yadayim* ensured that individuals cleaned their hands before eating, a vital measure at a time when even cultivated people ate primarily with their fingers and hands. NACHMANIDES taught that anyone who touched dirt must clean their hands. Washing of hands also paralleled the rabbinic doctrine requiring ritual immersion in a bath, or the MIKVAH. Both intend to remove ritual impurity with water. Unlike the *mikvah*, however, running water is not directly used; instead, one hand pours water from a vessel onto the other, the vessel is switched to the other hand, and the process is repeated.

Further reading: Hayim Halevy Donin, *To Be a Jew: A Guide to Jewish Observance in Contemporary Life* (New York: Basic Books, 1991); Hyam Maccoby, *Ritual and Morality: The Ritual Purity System and Its Place in Judaism* (Cambridge: Cambridge University Press, 1999).

Neusner, Jacob (b. 1932) *scholar of Judaism*

Jacob Neusner is one of the best-known academic scholars of Judaism in the current era. A graduate of Harvard College, the JEWISH THEOLOGICAL SEMINARY, and Columbia University, Neusner has been a prolific writer for decades. He has authored countless books, articles, and lectures, and he has founded and edited several book series, including *Classics of Judaism, Studies in Judaism,* and *The Encyclopedia of Judaism, Supplements 1, 2,* and *3.* Certain concerns dominate his research. First, he has attempted to make the history and methods of rabbinic literature (*see* MIDRASH; RABBI; TALMUD) accessible to a broad audience, including non-Jews. In addition, he has argued for a true religious-studies approach to Jewish sacred texts, arguing that these works were edited over time, and need to be studied with that editorial process in mind.

Further reading: Jacob Neusner, *Handbook of Rabbinic Theology: Language, System, Structure* (Boston: Brill Academic Publishers, 2002); ———, *The Halakhah: Historical and Religious Perspectives* (Leiden: Brill, 2002); ———, Alan J. Avery-Peck, and William Scott Green, eds. *Encyclopedia of Judaism.* Supplement (New York: Continuum International Publishing Group, 2002); John C. Poirier, "Jacob Neusner, the Mishnah, and Ventriloquism" in *Jewish Quarterly Review* 87, no. 1–2 (July–October 1996): 61–78.

Nevi'im

Nevi'im is the designation for one of the three sections of the TANAKH, the Hebrew Bible, the others being TORAH and KETUVIM.

Nevi'im means "prophets," though the first several books in the series can be characterized as historical—Joshua, Judges, 1 and 2 Samuel and 1 and 2 Kings. However, many famous and important prophets figure prominently in these narratives as well, including DEBORAH, Samuel, Nathan, and ELIJAH.

The rest of Nevi'im is divided into three major prophets—ISAIAH, Jeremiah, and EZEKIEL, and 12 minor (in length) prophets, whose briefer outputs are combined in one book—Hosea, Joel, Amos, Obadiah, Jonah, Micah, Nahum, HABAKKUK, Zephaniah, Haggai, Zechariah, and Malachi.

Hebrew prophets did not necessarily tell the future. Rather, their role was to receive communications from God and pass the messages along to the rulers and the people. Generally, the prophets criticized rulers and the people, often for idolatry and religious faithlessness, and often for corruption and social injustice. As an example of the latter, Isaiah tells the people that performing sacrifices and observing fasts is highly offensive to God if the people doing them pursue profit during the Sabbath and oppress the poor and WIDOWS AND ORPHANS.

Still, the prophets did sometimes predict the future. God would often send them to tell the people to repent; the prophets would then predict punishment from God if the warnings were not heeded. The story of Jonah is a good example. God tells the prophet Jonah to go to Nineveh and prophesize the people's demise *if they did not repent.* Jonah is reluctant to obey because, as he later complains to God, he knew Nineveh would repent and God in his mercy would forgive them, making him look like a false prophet. God eventually forces Jonah to obey. The relationship between God and prophet has fascinated Jews and Christians ever since, especially since so many of the prophets suffered ridicule, harassment, and persecution in their lifetimes.

Further reading: Frank S. Frick, *A Journey through the Hebrew Scriptures* (Fort Worth, Tex.: Harcourt Brace College Publishers, 1995); Abraham J. Heschel, *The Prophets: An Introduction* (New York: Harper Torchbooks, 1962); *Tanakh: The New JPS Translation According to the Traditional Hebrew Text* (Philadelphia, New York, Jerusalem: Jewish Publication Society, 1985).

New Israel Fund

The New Israel Fund was founded in 1979 in San Francisco as an alternative to the United Jewish Appeal–Jewish Federation system (*see* UNITED JEWISH COMMUNITIES). It is a nonprofit fund-raising group that supports social change via grassroots organizations in ISRAEL, working in the areas of human and civil rights, bridging of social and economic gaps, and religious tolerance and pluralism. Since its founding, it has distributed more than $120 million to more than 700 nongovernmental organizations. Though these organizations are not officially associated with any specific party in Israel, they tend to be on the left of the political spectrum, as do most of the contributors in the United States. The fund does not support groups that work with any Jews residing beyond the Green Line, the cease-fire line that prevailed between the end of the ISRAELI WAR OF INDEPENDENCE in 1949 and the SIX-DAY WAR in 1967.

Further reading: Michael M. Laskier, "Israeli Activism American-Style: Civil Liberties, Environmental, and Peace Organizations as Pressure Groups for Social Change," *Israel Studies* 5, no. 1 (2000): 131; Cathryn S. Mango, *The New Pythian Voices: Women Building Capital in NGO's in the Middle East* (New York: Routledge, 2002); New Israel Fund Web site URL: www.nif.org, accessed August 10, 2004.

New Testament

When the early Christians codified their own canon of sacred texts, they incorporated all the books of the TANAKH, the Hebrew bible, which had become fixed before that time. CHRISTIANITY refers to the Tanakh as the "Old Testament." Christians also incorporated books and letters written by the first followers of JESUS OF NAZARETH, which they called collectively the "New Testament." In this context, the word *testament* means "COVENANT"; Christians believed that God had ended the old covenant with the Jews in favor of a new covenant with the followers of Jesus.

The New Testament, written in Greek (although some claim the Greek is a translation from original Aramaic or Hebrew), includes four accounts of Jesus' life, called Gospels, an account of the history of the early church, entitled Acts, and letters to communities and individuals discussing aspects of Christian doctrine and practice. The final book, Revelation, is an apocalyptic work describing the end times yet to come.

The works included in the New Testament were probably written between 70 C.E. and 100 C.E., but there was certainly some later editing, based on oral traditions or other manuscripts, that shaped the texts we have today. PAUL, formerly Saul of Tarsus, a Jewish convert and zealous missionary for the new faith, authored more of the material than any of the other named authors, and he is often called the first Christian theologian. In his letters he formulates fundamental Christian doctrines, and attempts to explain the relationship between God's covenant with the Jews and the new covenant established through Jesus.

The New Testament canon was not closed until the fourth century of the Common Era, and even then controversy continued. A number of works, including what have become known as the Gnostic Gospels, were not included in the canon because they presented a history or theology of Jesus that differed from the canonical works.

Further reading: Craig A. Evans, "Faith and Polemic: the New Testament and First Century Judaism," in *Anti-Semitism and Early Christianity* (Minneapolis: Fortress Press, 1993), 1–17; Bruce M. Metzer and Roland E. Murphy, *The Oxford Annotated Bible with the Apocryphal/Deuterocanonical Books* (New York: Oxford University Press, 1994).

Nimoy, Leonard (b. 1931) *television and movie personality*

Leonard Nimoy was born on March 26, 1931, in Boston, Massachusetts. His parents were Jewish immigrants from RUSSIA. Nimoy grew up in a family and community that observed ORTHODOX JUDAISM; he sang in his SYNAGOGUE's choir and was active in the Jewish youth group BBYO (*see* JEWISH YOUTH GROUPS). He spoke YIDDISH at home, and was very familiar with Jewish literature.

At a young age Nimoy took an interest in acting. He entered Boston University on a drama scholarship, but left school soon after beginning his studies to pursue his career in California. Nimoy had occasionally appeared in both television and movies when in 1965 he was introduced to Gene Roddenberry, who was developing a script for a new science fiction series that would forever change Nimoy's life. Nimoy would be cast as Spock for the television show *Star Trek,* which premiered on September 8, 1966. Spock was a half-"Vulcan," half-human character who struggled to balance his Vulcan logic with his human emotions. Nimoy himself came up with Spock's signature hand sign, an exact copy of the sign made by KOHANIM during the PRIESTLY BLESSING in synagogues on major festivals. *Star Trek* concluded its series run in 1969, but Nimoy found himself typecast as the popular Spock, a role which he continued to play in the many *Star Trek* movie sequels. He became a minor cult figure.

Nimoy did manage to garner two interesting Jewish roles. He played the overshadowed husband, Morris Meyerson, to Ingrid Bergman's GOLDA MEIR in the 1982 TV biography *A Woman Called Golda.* Then, in 1991, he won admiration in the Jewish community for portraying Mel Mermelstein in the TV docudrama *Never Forget.* Mermelstein successfully sued the Institute for Historical Review, which claimed the HOLOCAUST never happened. Nimoy was moved by the Mermelstein story, and he has used the film in outreach to various organizations in order to help educate people about the Holocaust.

Nimoy has also pursued a second career in photography. In 2000 he published a controversial photo collection entitled *Shekhina,* which is the feminine name for God's divine presence. The photos included erotic scenes of women, often wearing traditional male ritual items, such as tefillin and *tallit.* The nudity outraged traditional Jewish groups, but some liberal Jewish groups saw his work as an attempt to embrace a Jewish feminist theology. Nimoy has consistently articulated that the controversial photos are part of his journey to reattach himself to his Jewish roots. The book includes quotes placed beside Nimoy's nudes, from famous rabbis and the TANAKH, the Hebrew Bible.

Further reading: Sonia Levitin, "A Conversation with Leonard Nimoy: The Vulcan Is a Real Jew," *Reform Judaism* (Spring 1998); Leonard Nimoy, *I Am Not Spock* (Milbrae, Calif.: Celestial Arts, 1975); ———, *I Am Spock* (New York: Hyperion, 1995); ——— and Donald Kuspit, *Shekhina* (New York: Umbrage, 2002).

Noah *biblical figure*

The biblical progenitor of all living humans, Noah is described in Genesis (6:9), the first book of the TANAKH, as "a righteous man; he was blameless in his age." Unfortunately, the rest of humanity is described as evil, and God determines to wipe them out in a universal flood. God commands Noah to build an ARK and gather in his family and seven pairs of all ritually clean animals, and one pair of all the unclean animals, found on earth.

The flood lasts for 40 days, destroying all things that live on land and in the air, apart from the remnant saved on Noah's ark (Gn 7:6–23). When the flood is over, Noah and his family repopulate the earth. God promises Noah that he will not destroy the earth again, and he enters a COVENANT that is symbolized by the RAINBOW (Gn 9:8–17). This covenant obliged Noah's descendants to obey the Noahide laws. These seven laws are understood by Judaism as being binding upon all of humanity. They prohibit idolatry, blasphemy, murder, adultery and incest, stealing, and eating flesh torn from a living animal. The final law insists that humanity create just courts of law.

According to rabbinic teaching, a non-Jew who observes these laws will have a place in OLAM HA-BAH, the world to come.

After fulfilling his mission, Noah becomes drunk and this leads to improper behavior (Gn 9:20–23). Modern rabbis often utilize Noah's drunkenness as an illustration of how alcohol and drugs can lead good people to bad choices.

Further reading: Hayyim Nahman Bialik, et al., eds., *The Book of Legends Sefer Ha-Aggadah: Legends from the Talmud and Midrash* (New York: Schocken Books, 1992); Louis Ginzberg, *Legends of the Bible* (Philadelphia: Jewish Publication Society of America, 1956); Louis Jacobs, *The Jewish Religion: A Companion* (New York: Oxford University Press, 1995); David Novak, *The Image of the Non-Jew in Judaism: An Historical and Constructive Study of the Noahide Laws* (New York: E. Mellen Press, 1983); *Tanakh: The New JPS Translation According to the Traditional Hebrew Text* (Philadelphia, New York, Jerusalem: Jewish Publication Society, 1985).

Noahide laws   *See* NOAH.

Noar Hadash
Noar Hadash is the youth programming network for the Jewish Reconstructionist Federation (*see* RECONSTRUCTIONIST JUDAISM).

See also JEWISH YOUTH GROUPS.

Normative Judaism
Normative Judaism is a term commonly used today by rabbis, Jewish groups, and even sociologists. The term implies that there is a common norm or standard for Jewish beliefs, practices, or identity. It is difficult to define such a norm, due to the serious divergences among the modern Jewish religious streams. It is often easier to say what is *not* normative, rather than what is.

To complicate matters, mainstream Jewish movements and groups often refer to their own practices as normative and reject other groups as aberrations. However, the rejection is often theoretical and not really practiced. For example ORTHODOX JUDAISM rejects both CONSERVATIVE and REFORM JUDAISM as invalid, yet Orthodox individuals and synagogues often join together with other Jews in communal activism, not questioning the validity of their Jewishness while working on a particular program or project. Normative Judaism is based on God, TORAH, and ISRAEL.

When discussing God, both observant and liberal Jews recognize that the Hebrew Bible (the TANAKH) describes the ISRAELITES as embracing a belief in One God who commanded certain things. The Israelites accepted the COVENANT that taught Jews ethical MONOTHEISM. Biblical theology presented a God of many different attributes. This theology was further developed by the PHARISEES, the ancient RABBIS, from whom Normative Judaism is derived. Rabbinic Judaism taught that the One God was the God of CREATION, Nature, REVELATION, History, Truth, Love, etc. Rabbinic theology was diverse, but also definitive. There is a God, and that God is One. Atheism and agnosticism are relatively modern inventions. While the pre-Enlightenment rabbis viewed God in multiple ways, each time with different attributes, they consistently acknowledged that it was not as important to agree about the various attributes of God as it was to embrace God's commandments.

Rabbinic Judaism demands actions. The normative Jew is one who lives the life of Jewish beliefs, not necessarily subscribing to the common rabbinic theology. The prophet Jeremiah condemns the Israelites for forsaking God and the Torah, but a sixth-century MIDRASH rebukes Jeremiah, saying that God wishes, "If only they had forsaken me and kept my Torah." The Jew is required to have *emunah,* or trust in God, not necessarily to affirm God. Living the commandments (*see* MITZVAH) and observing Jewish tradition and customs commonly define the normative Jew, although the levels to which a Jew follows those customs and laws varies greatly.

Moses MAIMONIDES contradicted the common Jewish position that accepting specific dogma is not required of the Jew, and extracted his *Thirteen Principles of Faith*. He further asserted that these 13 principles were essential to one's JEWISH IDEN-TITY. However, with the exception of Orthodox Judaism, today's world Jewry often feels free to reject specific dogmas.

Liberal Judaism, and for that matter, nonreligious cultural Jews, perceive certain practices, customs, and learning as sufficient to define one's Jewishness. Ironically, the more traditional Jewish movements, Orthodox and Conservative, actually embrace the broadest notion of "who is a Jew." They simply define it on biological terms. According to traditional rabbinic Judaism, if your mother was Jewish, than you are Jewish, regardless of your beliefs or actions. The more liberal movement, Reform, modified the traditional teaching. If either parent is Jewish, or you are raised as a Jew, then you are also Jewish. If one parent is not Jewish, and you are not raised as a Jew, then you are not Jewish. By the dogma of the Orthodox and Conservative, one who can factually declare "my mother is Jewish" is counted as a Jew. In the Reform world, this is not necessarily true.

The fact that one is a Jew does not necessarily make one a good Jew. The movements, or specific communities, will have their own criteria of what defines a good follower of laws and customs. However, often the "bad Jew" is still commonly considered part of the Jewish collective.

Israel can denote a tie to the land itself, but also can simply be one's identity as a Jew and a member of a broader Jewish community. Jacob, one of the Jewish PATRIARCHS, was renamed Israel by God in the Torah. Jews and Israelites are called the children of Israel, and so the concept of Israel means more than a geographical location. The connection to the Jewish people can come from traditional Jewish beliefs and practices, modified beliefs and practices, or simply the articulation "I am a Jew and I will participate as a Jew." Jewish identity can be chosen as a religious expression of identity, or as a cultural expression of identity. One can be a Jew by belonging to something Jewish. It could be a synagogue, community center, or any Jewish institution or activity. A common identity pull for modern Jews is the new State of Israel. For many Jews, ZIONISM defines their Jewishness.

From the traditional rabbinic perspective, the ideal normative Jew would be equally and strongly committed to God, Torah and Israel. However, the individual Jew could gravitate to one or two points more than the other.

One can safely say that a person or group ceases to fall into the category of Normative Judaism when all three points are rejected or when the Jewish community rejects the theology, philosophy, and practices of the nonnormative group. Such groups would include JEWS FOR JESUS, MESSIANIC JEWS, and some JUBUS, or Jewish Buddhists. A person will also fall outside the category of Normative Judaism if he or she actively chooses a different religious or cultural identity. Jews who completely reject Israel and Zionism also would be considered nonnormative, as they would fall outside the consensus of Orthodox, Conservative, Reform, and Reconstructionist Jewish communities.

Further reading: Jacob Neusner, *Early Rabbinic Judaism: Historical Studies in Religion, Literature and Art* (Leiden, the Netherlands: E. J. Brill, 1975); Jacob Neusner, ed., *Normative Judaism* (New York: Garland Publishing, 1990).

North American Federation of Temple Youth (NFTY)

The North American Federation of Temple Youth, commonly referred to by the acronym NFTY (pronounced "nifty"), is the youth group for REFORM JUDAISM.

See also JEWISH YOUTH GROUPS.

Nudel, Ida (b. 1931) *Soviet refusenik*

Ida Nudel was born in 1931 in Crimea, in the Soviet Union (*see* RUSSIA), to a poor Jewish family. By the time she was three years old, the family had moved to Moscow, and she grew up like all other Soviet children. During World War II,

Nudel's father was killed fighting near Stalingrad, and her mother's parents, siblings, nephews, and nieces were murdered by the Nazis (*see* HOLO-CAUST) near Simferopol, Crimea. In 1954, Nudel graduated from the university and began working as an economist for a construction firm in Moscow. Though she had faced ANTISEMITISM throughout her life, it was her young nephew's experiences in 1968 that convinced her that the only option for Jews in the Soviet Union was immigration to ISRAEL.

In 1971, Nudel applied for an exit visa to Israel and was refused on the grounds that she might know state secrets. For the next 16 years, she was constantly harassed by the Soviet author-ities and the KGB. She was fired from successive jobs, accused of spying, arrested several times, and in 1978 tried and convicted of "malicious hooliganism" for hanging a sign from her balcony that read "KGB give me a visa to Israel," and sen-tenced to four years in exile in a remote Siberian village. Upon the completion of her exile, Nudel was not allowed to return to her home in Moscow until the summer of 1986. In October 1987 she was finally granted a visa and was flown to Israel, where she has lived ever since.

From the very beginning of her ordeal, Nudel became an active REFUSENIK. She organized and par-ticipated in demonstrations, protests, and hunger strikes on behalf of fellow refuseniks and "prison-ers of Zion" (refuseniks who were in jails and prison camps). She became a lifeline and moral support for the prisoners and their families, writ-ing regularly to them, complaining on their behalf to the Soviet authorities, collecting and passing information about their condition and treatment to activists in the Western world, and helping those who were released. Her indefatigable efforts earned her the nickname of "Guardian Angel" of the prisoners of Zion.

Since the early 1990s, Nudel has developed and successfully maintained an organization called Mother to Mother. A nonprofit organiza-tion, it has provided after-school activities for as many as 4,000 poor Russian immigrant children.

Nudel has saved these children from crime and drugs and hopes to help them become an inte-grated part of Israeli society.

Further reading: Ida Nudel, *A Hand in the Darkness: The Autobiography of a Refusenik* (New York: Warner Books, 1990); Dina Siegel, *The Great Immigration: Russian Jews in Israel* (Providence, R.I.: Berghahn Books, 1998).

Nuremberg Laws

On September 15, 1935, the Nazis published the Nuremberg Laws, officially excluding Jews from German citizenship and severely limiting their rights within German society. The new laws also defined whom the Nazis considered legally to be a Jew: anyone who had at least one maternal or paternal Jewish grandparent. The Nazis claimed the laws were needed to protect "German Blood and German Honor." The Nuremberg Laws became the cornerstone for further action against the Jews, ultimately evolving into the HOLOCAUST.

The Nuremberg Laws forbade all marriages between Jews and non-Jewish Germans and demanded that the latter annul their marriages with Jews through special new procedures. They also forbade any sexual relations between a Jew and a non-Jewish German. Jews were forbidden to hire non-Jewish women as household employ-ees. Jews were forbidden to raise the flag of the Reich, but instead were encouraged to raise a flag that represented the Jewish nation. A Jew could neither vote nor hold public office—all current Jewish officials were forced to retire by the end of the year. In addition, the Nuremberg Laws rescinded German citizenship for Jews. Any Jew or non-Jew who violated the Nuremberg Laws was subject to prosecution and a sentence of hard labor. The Nazis set up a Reich minister of the interior, as a deputy führer, to enforce the Nuremberg Laws.

Further reading: Yehuda Bauer, *A History of the Holo-caust* (Danbury, Conn.: Franklin Watts, 2001); Lucy S.

Dawidowicz, *The War Against the Jews: 1933–1945* (New York: Doubleday, 1991); Marion A. Kaplan, *Between Dignity and Despair: Jewish Life in Nazi Germany* (New York: Oxford University Press, 1998); Karl A. Schleunes, ed., *Legislating the Holocaust: The Bernard Loesener Memoirs and Supporting Documents* (Boulder, Colo.: Westview Press, 2001).

Nuremberg Trials

After the May 1945 military defeat of the Nazi government in GERMANY, the victorious Allied nations, FRANCE, ENGLAND, the UNITED STATES, and the Soviet Union (*see* RUSSIA), determined to bring Nazi war criminals to justice. Between November 1945 and August 1946 the allied authorities held a series of widely publicized trials of top Nazi officials at the Palace of Justice in Nuremberg, Germany. The location was chosen because of its connection to the NUREMBERG LAWS, which had institutionalized and catalyzed the Nazis' war against the Jews.

The Nuremberg Trials took place under the auspices of the International Military Tribunal (IMT) and consisted of prosecutors and judges from the four allied nations. Sentenced to death by hanging were Martin Bormann, Hans Frank, Wilhelm Frick, Hermann Göring, Alfred Jodl, Ernst Kaltenbrunner, Wilhelm Keitel, Joachim von Ribbentrop, Alfred Rosenberg, Fritz Sauckel, Artur Seyss-Inquart, and Julius Streciher. Sentenced to life imprisonment were Walter Funk, Rudolph Hess, and Erich Raeder. Lesser prison sentences went to Albert Speer, Constantin von Neurath, Karl Doenitz, and Baldur Shirach. Three were acquitted: Hans Fritzsche, Franz von Papen, and Hjalmar Schacht. The judges also declared that three Nazi organizations—the Gestapo-Sicherheitsdienst (SD), the leadership corps of the Nazi Party, and the Schutzstaffel (SS)—were criminal organizations.

The IMT held as its goal lawful judgment of those who planned, organized, or commanded others to commit war crimes. The IMT finished its work and handed down its verdicts on October 1, 1946. Those sentenced to death were hanged at Spandau Prison in Berlin on October 6, 1946, and those given prison sentences were incarcerated there. Those acquitted were placed in a "denazification" program.

More Allied trials of Nazi war criminals followed the first major trials under the auspices of the IMT, but all were held before American tribunals. These trials prosecuted second- and third-ranking Nazi officials, including commanders of the EINSATZGRUPPEN; administrators of CONCENTRATION CAMPS; army field commanders and staff officers; officials in the justice, interior, and foreign ministries; physicians and public health officials; the SS leadership; and senior administrators of industrial concerns that used concentration camp laborers.

Further reading: Eugene Davidson, *The Trial of the Germans: An Account of the Twenty-Two Defendants Before the International Military Tribunal at Nuremberg* (Columbia: University of Missouri Press, 1997); Michael R. Marrus, *The Nuremberg War Crimes Trial 1945–46: A Documentary History* (Boston, Mass.: Bedford Books, 1997); Alan S. Rosenbaum, *Prosecuting Nazi War Criminals* (Boulder, Colo.: Westview Press, 1993).

ohr la-goyim

Judaism imposes a heavy responsibility on the Jewish people to act as *ohr la-goyim,* "a light unto the nations." They are to be an eternal witness of ethical MONOTHEISM before all the peoples of the world. This role was part of the COVENANT that the PATRIARCHS made with GOD, which was confirmed by the entire people when they accepted the TORAH at MOUNT SINAI.

In Genesis 12:2–3, God tells Abraham: "I will make you into a great nation. . . . Through you all the communities of the earth shall be blessed." Isaiah 42:6 (*see* NEVI'IM) reaffirms God's intentions: "I, the Lord, have called you in righteousness, and will hold your hand and keep you. And I will establish you as a covenant of the people, for a light unto the nations." Isaiah 60:2–3 continues: "For behold, darkness shall cover the earth, and a thick darkness the nations. But God will shine upon you. Nations shall then go by your light and kings by your radiant illumination."

Religious Jews are expected to observe the will of God not only for themselves, but also as an example for others. The historical role of the Jews was to bring ethical monotheism to the world, and in Western and Islamic civilization the mission was successful. To be a "light unto the nations" requires that Jews treat all human beings as created in the image of God. To be a "light" is to indi-vidually and collectively live up to one's religious, ethical, and social responsibilities.

The image of light, as a manifestation of God, is a powerful symbol in Jewish ritual. The Sabbath and holiday CANDLES, the *HANUKKIYAH,* the ETERNAL LIGHT, all remind Jews of their role as God's light unto the nations.

Many early-20th-century Zionists hoped that the future Jewish state would embody the concept of *ohr la-goyim,* by its high-minded behavior toward its own citizens and its neighbors. However, in the 1950s that hope was gradually abandoned. The new state of Israel was faced with often violent hostility from its neighbors, and did not feel it could maintain a prophetic stance, especially when it was regularly condemned for simply protecting its borders and citizens against aggression. Nevertheless, the state and the ISRAEL DEFENSE FORCES insist that wherever possible they try to enforce the highest standards, even exposing soldiers to added risks in order to avoid civilian casualties.

The concept of *ohr la-goyim* has been easier to follow, and thus more successful, in the world of American Jewish social service organizations. It has provided a theological foundation for Jewish social work in the modern world. As the 19th century drew to a close, the American Jewish community began to build up a vast infrastructure of social service agencies and programs that have touched the Jewish and the non-Jewish communities. The concept of *ohr la-goyim* encourages Jewish agencies to provide programs in non-Jewish inner city neighborhoods and other needy areas in the UNITED STATES without compromising the Jewish nature of the agencies or their programs.

On the political front, the obligation to be a "light unto the nations" has had an important impact as well. It has propelled Jews to become involved in issues of church-state separation, equality of opportunity in education, employment, and housing, medical care for the aged, rehabilitation, and other civil and social issues in the contemporary world.

Further reading: Charles Liebman, "The Idea of 'Or L'goyim' in Israeli Reality," *Gesher* 81, no. 4 (December 1974): 88–93; Sherry Rosen, "Jewish Family Service: The Oldest and Newest Chair at the Jewish Communal Table," in *Journal of Jewish Communal Service* (Winter/Spring 1996/97): 103–115; Shmuel Sandler, *The State of Israel, the Land of Israel: The Statist and Ethnonational Dimensions of Foreign Policy* (Westport, Conn.: Greenwood Press, 1993); *Tanakh: The New JPS Translation According to the Traditional Hebrew Text* (Philadelphia, New York, Jerusalem: Jewish Publication Society, 1985).

olam ha-bah

In Jewish tradition the SOUL, after death and a period of repentance (*see* SIN AND REPENTANCE), is said to move on to *olam ha-bah,* the world to come. This is a place of spiritual reward, and the texts compare its joys to sexual pleasure and to a perfect Sabbath (*see* SHABBAT). It is a place of spiritual perfection with no sin, no suffering, and no separation from GOD.

Traditional Judaism tends to focus on life in this world, rather than in the life to come, so there is comparatively little teaching on the afterlife in Judaism. It is clear, however, that Judaism teaches that there is a life after this one, one in which the righteous will be united with God and their loved ones, while the unrighteous will be punished.

Further reading: Neil Gillman, *The Death of Death: Resurrection and Immortality in Jewish Thought* (Jewish Lights Publishers, 1997); Simcha Paull Raphael, *Jewish Views of the Afterlife* (Northvale, N.J.: Jason Aronson, 2002).

Old City of Jerusalem

The section of JERUSALEM that includes its most ancient sites—such as the KOTEL, modern Judaism's most sacred site—is called the Old City. It is traditionally divided into four quarters: Jewish,

The Old City of Jerusalem is constructed largely of stone, today called Jerusalem stone, such as that which constitutes the Kotel, or Western Wall, pictured here. The Kotel is Judaism's holiest site, which Jews again gained access to after Jerusalem was reunited under Israeli rule in 1967. *(Courtesy Bernard Reich)*

Christian (*see* CHRISTIANITY), Muslim (*see* ISLAM), and Armenian. At the end of the ISRAELI WAR OF INDEPENDENCE in 1949, Jerusalem was divided into two sections. The New City was under Jewish control, while the Old City was under Jordanian control. Israelis were denied access to their holy sites under Jordanian control. As a result of the 1967 SIX-DAY WAR, Israel gained control of the Old City, and Jews moved back into the historic Jewish Quarter. Since then Jews have had access to the Kotel.

Further reading: Meir Ben-Dov, *Historical Atlas of Jerusalem* (New York: Continuum, 2002); Martin Gilbert, *The Atlas of Jewish History* (New York: William Morrow and Company, 1993), 111; *Jerusalem* (Jerusalem: Israel Pocket Library, 1973); F. E. Peters, *Jerusalem* (Princeton, N.J.: Princeton University Press, 1984).

omer, counting of the

Omer means a "sheaf of grain." In biblical times, an *omer* of new barley—the first crop to be harvested in the spring—was offered at the TEMPLE in JERUSALEM on the second day of PASSOVER, the first harvest festival of the year. Until this offering was made it was forbidden to eat from the barley harvest. Each day from then until SHAVUOT 49 days later, an *omer* of barley was brought and waved. This period of the year became known as the counting of the *omer* (in Hebrew, *sefirat ha-omer*). It lasts 49 days and in ancient times marked the passage from the barley harvest to the wheat harvest. This was a joyful period, moving from one joyous holiday to the next.

These seven weeks also serve as a reminder of the countdown between the ISRAELITES' liberation from bondage in EGYPT (commemorated on Passover) to the day they received the TORAH at MOUNT SINAI (commemorated on Shavuot). The countdown expresses the eagerness of the Jew to receive the Torah. However, the rabbinic Jew is also to recall during this period the terrible massacres and plagues that occurred in Jewish history, which the rabbis commonly assert occurred in the spring. During *sefirat ha-omer*, Jews recall the martyrdom of Rabbi AKIVA BEN YOSEPH and his students, and the many martyrs who died during the Crusades.

Thus, one acts as a mourner during the counting of the *omer*. Jews may not marry during this time period, with a few exceptions, nor should they attend joyful celebrations. They are not even supposed to get their hair cut. The exception to this is the 33rd day of the *omer*, known as LAG B'OMER. On this day a plague supposedly ended, and Jews commemorate with dancing, singing, celebration, and, often, picnics—it is a traditional field day. It recalls how the Rabbi Akiba and his students would play field games when the Romans would approach them, so as to hide the secret that they were gathering together to study the Torah.

ASHKENAZIM mourn from the second day of Passover until Lag b'Omer. SEPHARDIM observe from the beginning of the new month of Iyar until Shavuot. Both groups have a tradition of studying Pirkei Avot, the ETHICS OF THE FATHERS, during the *omer*. It is a summary of the ethical teachings of the ancient rabbis.

Further reading: Larry Domnitch, *The Jewish Holidays: A Journey through History* (Northvale, N.J.: Jason Aronson, 2000); Hayim Halevy Donin, *To Pray as a Jew: A Guide to the Prayer Book and the Synagogue Service* (New York: Basic Books, 1980); Irving Greenberg, *The Jewish Way: Living the Holidays* (New York: Summit Books, 1988).

omnipotent

God is traditionally said to be omnipotent, capable of doing anything. This attribute has generated some theological issues, particularly related to the problem of suffering (*see* THEODICY): If all-powerful, why does God allow suffering to continue? Various theologians have debated this issue, but the only thing on which they agree is that God's omnipotence cannot be set aside as a fundamental attribute. Both CHRISTIANITY and ISLAM share the concept of omnipotence with Judaism.

Further reading: Samuel S. Cohon, *Jewish Theology: A Historical and Systematic Interpretation of Judaism and Its Foundations* (Assen: Van Gorcum, 1971); Louis Jacobs, *A Jewish Theology* (New York: Behrman House, 1973); Kaufmann Kohler, *Jewish Theology Systematically and Historically Considered* (New York: Ktav Publishing, 1968); Arthur Marmorstein, *The Old Rabbinic Doctrine of God* (reprint, London: Oxford University Press, 1968).

omniscient

God is said to be omniscient or all-knowing. Nothing escapes divine awareness. This attribute, along with being OMNIPOTENT and omnipresent (being everywhere), is what distinguished the God of the PATRIARCHS from the localized gods of CANAAN in the biblical period, and the Greek and ROMAN gods in the late second TEMPLE and early rabbinic periods. CHRISTIANITY and ISLAM also believe that God is omniscient.

The theme of God's omniscience is especially prominent in the liturgy of Yom Kippur, the Day of Atonement. God is aware of all sins, the worshippers are reminded, even those that people do without thinking, and even those they forget.

Further reading: Samuel S. Cohon, *Jewish Theology: A Historical and Systematic Interpretation of Judaism and Its Foundations* (Assen: Van Gorcum, 1971); Louis Jacobs, *A Jewish Theology* (New York: Behrman House, 1973); Kaufmann Kohler, *Jewish Theology Systematically and Historically Considered* (New York: Ktav Publishing, 1968); Arthur Marmorstein, *The Old Rabbinic Doctrine of God* (reprint, London: Oxford University Press, 1968).

Onkelos (second century C.E.) *translator of Hebrew Bible to Aramaic*

Onkelos, according to rabbinic tradition, was a late-first-century Palestinian proselyte, whose translation of the TANAKH, the Hebrew Bible, is still used as an authoritative resource by traditional Jews. There are two translations of the Hebrew Bible, one into Greek and the other into Aramaic, that are attributed to two different proselytes, or converts of the time period. One is Onkelos and the other is Aquila and they are often conflated, even by scholars, because the texts are quite similar and Talmudic references to them confusing.

The Talmud describes Onkelos as a nephew of the Roman emperor Titus (*see* ROME). After Onkelos discovers the truth of Judaism he converts and becomes a disciple of the RABBIS. Outraged at the news, Titus sends a brigade of soldiers to bring him back to ROME. However, when Onkelos engages the Roman soldiers in discussion, he convinces him of the truth of TORAH, and they themselves convert to Judaism. Titus then sends another brigade, with the same result. Titus then sends a third brigade, instructing them not to listen to Onkelos. However, as the soldiers lead him away, Onkelos places his hand on the MEZUZAH and asks: "What is that?" The soldiers respond: "You tell us." Onkelos patiently explains: "Normally, a human king sits inside and his servants stand outside and guard him. But, the Holy One Blessed be He, His servants are inside and He guards them from outside." These words are enough to convert the third brigade. Titus, having learned his lesson, decides to send no more soldiers.

Onkelos created the first Targum, or translation of the Torah into ARAMAIC. One can often find his Targum printed in small type in the margins of a Hebrew Bible. Every translation is in effect an interpretation; scholars consider Onkelos's Targum to be an authoritative reflection of how the rabbis of his day understood difficult or obscure passages in the Hebrew original. Onkelos, like the editors in the DEUTERONOMIC HISTORY tradition several hundred years before, avoids all anthropomorphic descriptions of God. Onkelos's work was widely respected by Jewish scholars of his time, and his translation became almost as authoritative a text as the Hebrew Bible itself. It was also popular among the masses of Jews, since it was written in the Aramaic vernacular and many Jews were illiterate in Hebrew. When the Torah was read in public in those days, each Hebrew verse was followed by the Onkelos translation.

According to the Babylonian TALMUD, Onkelos delivered his Targum orally in Palestine. Most scholars believe that the written version of Targum Onkelos had become fixed by the third century C.E. He also translated the NEVI'IM, the Prophets.

Further reading: J. W. Etheridge, *Targums of Onkelos and Jonathan Ben Uzziel on the Pentateuch with the Fragments of the Jerusalem Targum from the Chaldee* (Hoboken, N.J.: Ktav Publishing House, 1969); Max Kedushin, *The Rabbinic Mind* (New York: Jewish Theological Seminary of America, 1952); Moses Maimonides, *The Guide for the Perplexed* (New York: Dover Publications, 1956); Alexander Sperber, *The Pentateuch According to Targum Onkelos 1959, the Former Prophets According to Targum Jonathan 1959, the Latter Prophets according to Targum: Based on Old Manuscripts and Printed Texts* (Leiden and New York: Brill Academic Publishers, 1992).

Operation Magic Carpet

After the creation of the State of ISRAEL in 1948, attacks against the ancient Jewish community of Yemen intensified. Fearing for their lives, the new Israeli government arranged to airlift almost the entire Yemenite Jewish community to Israel, to join a substantial Yemenite community that had arrived in the country starting in the 1880s. This successful operation, carried out between June 1949 and September 1950, was called Operation Magic Carpet; it saved approximately 50,000 Jewish Yemenite lives. Many of those brought to Israel were children. The cost of the operation was for more than Israel's entire budget, but saving the lives of fellow Jews was priceless to the young state.

All told there were approximately 380 flights. American and British planes were used to airlift the Jews from Aden, a British colony south of the kingdom of Yemen. The flights were extremely dangerous; Magic Carpet was kept secret and not announced until the operation had concluded.

Operation Magic Carpet missions routinely took 16 to 20 hours to complete. The most com-

mon airplanes used were the C-46 or DC-4. The planes would take off from Asmara in Eritrea in the morning and fly to Aden to pick up their passengers and refuel. They would then fly over the Red Sea and the Gulf of Aqaba, landing at the airport in TEL AVIV. The planes would then need to immediately depart for Cyprus for the night because they could not remain in Israel for fear of Arab bombers. The logistics were difficult. Fuel was scarce, and the desert sand wreaked havoc on the airplanes' engines. Planes were shot at, but during all the missions not a single life was lost.

The Yemenite Jews knew very little about the modern world. However, their reluctance to board airplanes was overcome when one of the rescuers quoted the biblical verse that God would return the Jews to their Holy Land on the "wings of eagles." To these new immigrants to Israel, the airplanes were indeed a miracle.

Further reading: Howard M. Sachar, *A History of Israel: From the Rise of Zionism to Our Time* (New York: Alfred A. Knopf, 1996); Michael A. Weingarten, *Changing Health and Changing Culture: The Yemenite Jews in Israel* (Westport, Conn.: Praeger Publication, 1992).

Oral Law (Oral Torah)

Traditionally Judaism's sacred literature is all referred to as TORAH, often translated as law. This law is then categorized as either WRITTEN LAW or Oral Law. The Written Law is the Bible itself. Oral Law refers to the vast rabbinic literature that is based on interpretation of the Written Law.

Oral Law includes the MISHNAH, the TOSEFTA, the two TALMUDS, and the various books of MIDRASH. Oral Law is said to have been transmitted from MOSES to Joshua, from Joshua to the ISRAELITE elders, from the elders to the prophets, from the prophets to the leaders of the Great Assembly, and from the Great Assembly to the RABBIS. Thus rabbinic tradition traces its interpretive roots all the way back to Moses, making the rabbis the only authoritative interpreters within the community.

Until the final redaction of the Mishnah around the year 220 C.E. and of the Talmud around the year 550, all these interpretations of the Hebrew Bible, or TANAKH, together with all the rules concerning the customs and rituals of Jewish life in general, were entrusted to memory alone. This body of rabbinic literature is still called the Oral Law, in commemoration of its status from the days of Moses to the later rabbis. The midrashim that are part of the Oral Law provide color and depth to the written legal tradition. The Written Law has been perceived as the body of Judaism, but the Oral Law has been perceived as its soul (*see AGGADAH*).

Further reading: David Weiss Halivni, *Revelation Restored: Divine Writ and Critical Responses* (Boulder, Colo.: Westview Press, 1997); N. S. Hecht, *An Introduction to the History and Sources of Jewish Law* (Oxford: Oxford University Press, 1996); Adin Steinsaltz, *The Essential Talmud* (New York: Basic Books, 1976); Ephraim E. Urbach, *The Sages: Their Concepts and Beliefs*, trans. Israel Abrahams (reprint, Cambridge, Mass.: Harvard University Press, 1987).

ORT (Society for Trades and Agricultural Labor)

ORT is one of the largest nonprofit nongovernmental education and training organizations in the world; it is registered as an NGO with the UNITED NATIONS. It works to provide impoverished communities and individuals with the educational and vocational skills they need to become self-sufficient. Annually, ORT teaches and trains more than 250,000 students in more than 50 countries.

The name ORT is an acronym of the Russian Obshchstvo Remeslenogo i zemledelschskogo Truda, meaning "Society for Trades and Agricultural Labor." It was the brainchild of Nikolai Bakst (1842–1904), a Jewish writer and physiology professor, and Samuel Poliakov (1836–88), a Jewish railroad magnate and philanthropist. Together with Baron Horace de Gunzburg (1833–1909), one of the foremost leaders of the Russian Jewish community at the time, they petitioned Czar Alexan-der II (1818–81) for permission to establish a Jewish charitable fund. They argued that a society to spread and teach handicrafts, manual trades, and agricultural labor needed to be established in order to improve the condition of the Jews in the PALE OF SETTLEMENT and to raise them from their crushing poverty. On March 22, 1880, the Russian minister of interior granted the charter authorizing collection of money for this purpose. Over the next 20 years, ORT raised more than 1 million rubles and trained more than 25,000 Jews in 350 towns throughout the Russian Empire.

During and after World War I, ORT expanded its activities worldwide, establishing a network of vocational schools and cooperative workshops. After 1918, the Russian ORT was funded for the most part by the AMERICAN JEWISH JOINT DISTRIBUTION COMMITTEE (AJJDC), but it was eventually shut down by Stalin.

In 1921 the World ORT Union was born. The following year, the American ORT Federation was established in the UNITED STATES, and in the late 1940s it became a membership organization, agreeing not to fund-raise on its own as long as the United Jewish Appeal (*see* UNITED JEWISH COMMUNITIES) and the AJJDC agreed to provide funds for its programs. Today, it operates in Europe, ISRAEL, North and South America, SOUTH AFRICA, INDIA, and, after an absence of 52 years brought on by Stalin's purges, RUSSIA and other countries of the former Soviet Union, training both Jewish and non-Jewish students.

Further reading: Jack Rader, *By the Skill of Their Hands: The Story of ORT* (Geneva: World ORT Union, 1970); ORT Web site URL: www.ort.org, accessed August 8, 2004; http://archive.ort.org/files/d02/d02a002/index.htm, accessed August 8, 2004; Leon Shapiro, *The History of ORT: A Jewish Movement for Social Change* (New York: Schocken Books, 1980).

Orthodox Judaism

Orthodox Judaism, or Orthodoxy, is the theology, ideology, customs, and social patterns of those

Jews who strictly follow traditional Jewish law, or HALAKHAH. The belief system of Orthodox Judaism rests on the idea that TORAH in its entirety was handed down from GOD to MOSES at MOUNT SINAI, a concept called TORAH MI-SINAI. The majority of Jews who consider themselves Orthodox accept divine authorship of both the ORAL LAW and the WRITTEN LAW. Thus, all Jewish law is a direct or indirect result of revelation from God, and Jews are obligated to live by that law, as interpreted by the RABBIS and collected in authoritative CODES OF LAW such as the SHULCHAN ARUKH.

Orthodox Judaism can be distinguished from what may be called traditional Judaism by its self-awareness. Orthodox Jews are aware of the modern world and are conscious that they have chosen a way of life that faces many challenges in an environment full of abundant consumer goods and services, secular education, and pluralistic worldviews. Although Orthodox Judaism does not acknowledge that there are legitimate forms of Jewish life outside the authoritative rabbinic tradition, it is conscious of itself as a denomination among other Jewish denominations. Orthodox Jews openly reject the ideology of REFORM JUDAISM; they often disagree with the interpretations of Jewish law found in CONSERVATIVE JUDAISM, and with the nontraditional theology often taught by Conservative Rabbis.

A self-conscious Orthodox movement took shape in the first quarter of the 19th century in HUNGARY, and reappeared toward the middle of that century in GERMANY. The word *orthodox* is derived from the Greek term *orth doxa*, which can be translated as "right doctrine." It was not until the rise of Reform Judaism in the 19th century that it became necessary for more traditional Jews to define themselves with such a label.

The history of Orthodox Judaism begins with a rabbi named HATAM SOFER (1762–1839), who resisted the modern world through a program of neotraditionalism that rejected all change and adaptation on the grounds that new things are forbidden by Torah. In order to reinforce this idea, neotraditionalists deemed that all Jewish laws were equal in weight and scope, in theory making it difficult for reformers to identify more important and less important laws in order to preserve the more important and adapt the less important. Neotraditionalists also deemed that the old, autonomous Jewish communities (*see* KAHAL, KEHILLAH) that existed before EMANCIPATION were vital to the survival of Judaism; they thus rejected emancipation and the inclusion of Jews in larger society. In Germany, Orthodoxy appeared to be a more adaptable tradition. Samson Raphael HIRSCH (1808–88) developed the NEO-ORTHODOXY MOVEMENT from the viewpoint that traditional Judaism could be compatible with the modern world and with emancipation.

In eastern Europe, traditional Judaism did not transform itself into Orthodox Judaism in a significant, organized way in the 19th century, because the forces of emancipation and the ENLIGHTENMENT entered eastern Europe much later. Thus, traditional Jewry in eastern Europe did not possess an awareness of itself as one type of Judaism among many. Modern ideas trickled into eastern Europe and some Jews did follow the path of ASSIMILATION, but not at the same rate as in central Europe; Reform Judaism was almost nonexistent in the East.

However, some movements did form in eastern Europe beyond the attempt to strengthen Torah study by establishing yeshivot (*see* YESHIVA). One such was the Musar Movement, which focused on ethics (*see* SALANTER, ISRAEL). Finally, in 1912 German Orthodox leaders established Agudat Israel, an organization that united Orthodoxy in central and eastern Europe and provided eastern European Jews with the language and tools they needed to contend with the threatening Jewish and non-Jewish forces they could no longer ignore.

Orthodox Judaism is far from homogeneous, as can be seen in the complex of different organizations that organize social and political life within Orthodoxy. In the contemporary world, the two largest streams are the ultra-Orthodox or Haredim (the fearful, or God-fearers), and the MODERN ORTHODOX. The Haredim do not call themselves ultra-Orthodox; sometimes they prefer the simple term *Yidn,* a Yiddish word for Jews.

The Haredim include all the different groups within HASIDISM, plus the non-Hasidic yeshiva world. These "yeshivish" Jews are similar to the Hasidic community in that they reject modern life as much as possible; however, they follow the traditions of the European MITNAGDIM, the opponents of the Hasidim. The Haredim believe that all of life should ideally consist solely of dedication to Torah in daily life, practice, study, and prayer. In principle, modern distractions from Torah are unacceptable and to be rejected, although there has been some relaxation among Israeli Haredim, in part as a result of the Internet.

Modern Orthodox Jews also believe that one must adhere scrupulously to traditional Jewish law, but unlike the Haredim, they do not believe that participation in the modern world and observance of Jewish law are mutually exclusive. Within the Orthodox world, the majority belongs to the Modern Orthodox camp, although the Haredi minority may be growing. According to sociologist Jack Wertheimer, many modern Orthodox Jews today prefer the term *Centrist Orthodoxy,* as they have become progressively more strict in their observance, moving toward the right on the spectrum of Jewish groups and farther away from progressive forms of Judaism.

There are Modern Orthodox seminaries, the best-known being YESHIVA UNIVERSITY in New York. The largest grouping of organized Orthodox rabbis is found under the umbrella of the Orthodox Union, centered in North America but providing outreach to Jews all over the world. Orthodox Judaism in the United States includes synagogue communities that are generally smaller than those of Conservative and Reform Judaism. Synagogues that have less than 250 families, like most in the Orthodox world, tend to engender closer communities, thus offering a more tight-knit social world to its members. Many children in Orthodox homes attend Jewish day schools (*see* the JEWISH DAY SCHOOL MOVEMENT). Extensive religious school systems from kindergarten to college

have helped the Orthodox community navigate the tension between modernity and traditional Judaism, though the schools emphasize tradition over innovation. Since most Haredi men attend a yeshiva, the majority achieve ordination as rabbis. In the ultra-Orthodox community, this is simply the title given to those who have completed traditional Talmudic (*see* TALMUD) study over a long period of time. Most Haredi rabbis do not attend the kind of graduate or professional classes and programs that Modern Orthodox rabbis do.

Two of the most important Orthodox leaders in the contemporary period were Moshe FEINSTEIN (1895–1986), an outstanding adjudicator of Jewish law, and Joseph SOLOVEITCHIK (1903–93), one of the greatest Talmudic authorities of contemporary times. Soloveitchik was known for his ability to navigate the intricate paths where the modern world and Jewish life intersect. Perhaps the most famous Haredi leader was Menachem SCHNEERSON (1902–94), who remains influential even after his death, as the CHABAD movement he led continues to work to bring secular Jews back into the fold of Orthodoxy, using nonjudgmental outreach and providing easy access to traditional Judaism.

While Orthodoxy is commonly defined as modern or ultra, there are also distinctions between ASHKENAZIM and SEPHARDIM. Most Sephardic families identify themselves as Orthodox, even though only a minority are strictly observant. Even among Ashkenazim, there are many who belong to and attend Orthodox synagogues, yet do not live according to the Orthodox standard. Each community determines how much they will accept such non-practicing, but affiliated, Orthodox Jews.

Further reading: Samuel Heilman, *Defenders of the Faith: Inside Ultra-Orthodox Jewry* (New York: Schocken Books, 1992); Charles S. Liebman, "Orthodoxy in American Jewish Life," *American Jewish Year Book* 66 (1965): 21–97; Charles S. Liebman and Eliezer Don-Yehiya, *Civil Religion in Israel: Judaism and Political Culture in the Jewish State* (Berkeley: University of California Press, 1983); Jack Wertheimer, *A People*

Divided: Judaism in Contemporary America (New York: Basic Books, 1993).

Orthodox Union   See ORTHODOX JUDAISM.

Oz, Amos   (b. 1939)   *Israeli writer*

Amos Oz was born in 1939 in JERUSALEM, ISRAEL, and moved to a KIBBUTZ at the age of 15. After army service, he studied philosophy and literature at the HEBREW UNIVERSITY in Jerusalem. Oz writes short stories and novels for children and for adults, as well as nonfiction articles and books. His work has been translated into more than 30 languages and has garnered him worldwide renown. Over the years, Oz has won many prizes and awards, including the French Prix Femina (1992) and the Israel Prize for Literature (1998), Israel's most prestigious prize. He has also been a visiting fellow at Oxford University and a writer-in-residence at Colorado College.

Oz's first novels were *Elsewhere Perhaps* (1966), set in a kibbutz, and *My Michael* (1968), set in Jerusalem, locations that recur in his work, standing in for Israeli society at large. He writes about the splits and strains in contemporary Israeli life, and pleads for dialogue between different groups of Israelis. Oz also writes about ANTISEMITISM and the HOLOCAUST, themes treated in *Unto Death* (1978) and *Touch the Water, Touch the Wind* (1974). His style is richly atmospheric, often incorporating elements of fantasy; his language is poetic.

A leading figure in the Israeli PEACE NOW movement since 1977, Oz is strongly identified with the political left. His political views can be found in the collection of articles *In the Land of Israel* (1993). Today, Oz lives in the southern town of Arad and teaches literature at Ben Gurion University of the Negev. His most recent work is *A Story of Love and Darkness* (2003), based on his parents' courtship.

Further reading: Avraham Balaban, *Between God and Beast: An Examination of Amos Oz's Prose* (University Park: Pennsylvania State University Press, 1993); Heim Chertok, *We Are All Close: Conversations with Israeli Writers* (New York: Fordham University Press, 1989); ———, *The Hill of Evil Counsel: Three Stories* (London: Chatto & Windus, 1978); ———, *Panther in the Basement* (New York: Harcourt Brace, 1997).

Ozick, Cynthia   (b. 1928)   *American writer*

Cynthia Ozick, one of the major living American writers today, was born in Manhattan, New York City, in 1928, the second child of Lithuanian Jewish immigrants. Her family moved to the Bronx, where her parents ran a pharmacy. At age five and a half, Ozick was enrolled in a heder, or Jewish religious school. The rabbi at first tried to send her home, saying that girls do not have to study, but her grandmother insisted and Ozick remained in the school. In public school and her neighborhood, Ozick encountered a great deal of ANTISEMITISM. Stones were thrown at her and she was called a "Christ-killer."

A quiet child by nature, she was a bookworm who excelled in academics. After Hunter College High School, Ozick attended New York University and then Ohio State University, where she received a master's degree in English literature for a thesis on Henry James's late novels. It was at this time that she decided to become a writer. Her first forays were unsuccessful attempts at novels on which she worked for years but never finished. Ozick's true talents, however, lay in short stories that she has published in such magazines as COMMENTARY and the *New Yorker,* and for which she has won numerous awards. Three of Ozick's stories won first prize in the O. Henry competition and five have been chosen for the yearly anthologies *Best American Short Stories.* Among the various awards Ozick has won are the Guggenheim and the National Endowment for the Arts Fellowships.

During the years Ozick was working on her unfinished novels, she studied Jewish history and tradition, mastering many of its texts. Themes from Jewish history, culture and religion permeate her writing. One of her best stories is *The Shawl,* first published in 1980 in the *New Yorker*, which deals with the HOLOCAUST. Nine years later she expanded it into a novella and added a sequel. In many of her works, Ozick explores the question of what it means to be Jewish, especially in America and after the Holocaust. Ozick's writing style is often demanding but her language is distinguished by virtuosic, unexpected metaphors.

Ozick has returned to the novel form, with great success, publishing *The Messiah of Stockholm* in 1987 and *The Puttermesser Papers* in 1997. In addition to fiction, she has also published several collections of essays and reviews that range over Western literature and questions of writing.

Further reading: Amy S. Gottfried, *Historical Nightmares and Imaginative Violence in American Women's Writings* (Westport, Conn.: Greenwood Press, 1998); Louis Harap, *In the Mainstream: The Jewish Presence in Twentieth-Century American Literature, 1950s–1980s* (New York: Greenwood Press, 1987); Cynthia Ozick and Elaine M. Kauvar, *A Cynthia Ozick Reader* (Bloomington: Indiana University Press, 1996); Cynthia Ozick, *Metaphor & Memory: Essays* (New York: Vintage Books USA, 1991).

P

Pale of Settlement

The area in the Russian Empire where Jews were permitted to live was called the Pale of Settlement. The foundation for the Pale was laid in a 1791 decree by Catherine the Great following the partitions of POLAND, which brought large numbers of Jews into RUSSIA for the first time.

Catherine's decree barred Jewish merchants from operating freely outside the newly annexed territories. It was issued in response to protests by Moscow merchants who complained of an influx of Jewish competition. A 1794 decree further defined where Jews could trade and settle. Subsequent decrees defined and redefined the borders of the Pale, which eventually covered parts or all of 17 provinces in what is today the UKRAINE, Lithuania, Belorussia, Latvia, POLAND, and Moldova. Most of these were areas of traditional Jewish settlement that Russia acquired through power struggles with Prussia, the Austro-Hungarian Empire (*see* AUSTRIA; HUNGARY) and the Ottoman Empire. Even within the various provinces of the Pale, different regulations were applied. Thus in some provinces, no new Jewish residents were allowed nor new Jewish settlements permitted, while in others Jews were forbidden from living within 33 miles of the border. The basis of Jewish life in the Pale was the SHTETL, the isolated and cohesive small towns populated mostly by Jews.

ALEXANDER II (1818–81) relaxed some of the rules. First, big businessmen, members of the first merchants' guild, were permitted to reside outside the Pale. Then certain skilled artisans, ex-soldiers and their children, university graduates and members of the liberal professions were granted the same right. However, in reaction to Alexander's assassination, his successor Alexander III promulgated the most restrictive settlement laws of all, in May 1882. They prohibited all Jews from living in villages and rural areas of the Pale and forbade them from owning or managing real estate there. All these restrictions severely hampered the economic development of the Jewish community. Confined within tight borders, most Jews lived in harsh inescapable poverty. The Pale was effectively abolished in August 1915 during World War I, when the government opened the interior of Russia, except for capital cities, to Jewish settlement. The Pale was legally abolished following the February Revolution of 1917 that overthrew the czar.

Further reading: S. Ansky, *The Enemy at His Pleasure: A Journey through the Jewish Pale of Settlement During World War II* (New York: Owl Books, 2004); Chester G. Cohen, *Shtetl Finder: Jewish Communities in the 19th and*

20th Centuries in the Pale of Settlement of Russia and Poland, and in Lithuania, Latvia, Galicia, and Bukovina, with Names of Residents (Bowie, Md.: Heritage Books, 1989); S. M. Dubnow, *History of the Jews in Russia and Poland: From the Earliest Times until the Present Day* (Philadelphia: Jewish Publication Society, 1916).

Palestine

Palestine is one of the names used to describe the territory in the Middle East between modern-day Syria and modern-day EGYPT. Other well-known names for this area, or parts of this area, are CANAAN, JUDEA, and ISRAEL.

Scholars speculate that when ROME defeated the Jewish revolt led by BAR-KOKHBA in 132 C.E., they renamed the country and its capital as a way to suppress Jewish national identity. JERUSALEM was named Aelius Hadrianus, and Judea was named Palaestina, most likely after the Philistines, a people who no longer existed. Most Jews left the area and moved to Babylonian cities and later migrated around the world. Still, the Jews probably remained a majority of the devastated population, concentrated largely in the Galilee. They did not prosper economically; nevertheless they flourished culturally, and managed to produce some of the key texts of Judaism, including the MISHNAH and MIDRASH.

Rome converted to CHRISTIANITY under Constantine, and by the fourth century C.E. Christians dominated Palestine. In the seventh century, Muslim Arabs conquered the land; from then until the 20th century, various Muslim rulers held political control, apart from 150 years of crusader rule. The Muslims ruling Palestine allowed Jews and Christians to practice their traditions for the most part (*see* MUSLIM-JEWISH RELATIONS), but much of the population was converted to ISLAM.

The Christian-Muslim fighting during the Crusades, which lasted from the end of the 11th century to the end of the 13th, left the land devastated. Even after, crusaders continued to raid the coast of Palestine; in defense, the Muslim rulers evacuated the area of settlers and destroyed the land along the coast, leading to depopulation and poverty for hundreds of years.

By the mid-13th century most of the population of Palestine was of Arab origin and spoke Arabic, though Jews began arriving again in the 14th century, some fleeing persecution in SPAIN. In 1517 Palestine was conquered by the Ottoman Empire, and the Turkish sultan invited Jews to settle there. Three hundred years later, however, many Arabs and Jews fled Palestine when Napoleon (*see* FRANCE) entered the area; furthermore, Egyptian and Ottoman rulers did not administer the land well. By the 1880s there were 400,000 inhabitants living in Palestine; 50,000 of them Jews, many of them immigrants motivated by ZIONISM. Though Turkish authorities began to limit Jewish immigration, Jews continued to arrive. By 1914 the population had reached 700,000, perhaps 100,000 of them Jews. Under the Turks, the land was part of the vilayet of Beirut, and further divided into several administrative districts. Palestine did not exist as a separate political entity, except in the mind of its Jews and Christians, who regarded it as ERETZ YISRAEL or the Holy Land, respectively.

During World War I, the Ottoman Empire allied itself with GERMANY and Austria-Hungary (*see* AUSTRIA; HUNGARY), and many Jews (who often had Russian nationality) fled from Palestine. When the war ended, ENGLAND and France determined to divide the lands of the Middle East between them into colonies and protectorates. It is possible that Britain promised the same land to two different entities; the Arabs thought that Britain would help them establish Arab independence in the Middle East and France felt that they were promised the regions of Syria and Lebanon. Arab leaders claim that Palestine was included in the land that the British promised them, but in 1917 Britain issued the BALFOUR DECLARATION supporting the establishment of a Jewish homeland in Palestine. The Arabs did not want to live under Jewish rule and they opposed the idea of a Jewish national home in Palestine in debates at the League of Nations (*see* UNITED NATIONS). Nevertheless, the league created the BRITISH MANDATE for Palestine for just that purpose. In 1922, the British removed all the lands east of the Jordan River from the Mandate, some 80 percent of the original territory, creating a protectorate that later became today's Kingdom of Jordan.

Conflict between Jews and Arabs over the remaining territory became inevitable as European nations cut up the Middle East, granting some independence to certain lands and none to others. In 1929, the JEWISH AGENCY, formerly run by the Zionist Organization, expanded to govern the YISHUV, the Jewish community in Palestine. The British had tried to establish governing bodies composed of both Jews and Arabs, but the Arabs were not amenable and these entities never came to be. Arab riots broke out several times during the Mandate years, while the Jews created their own force, the HAGANAH, to defend the yishuv. As World War II approached in Europe and conditions for Jews declined, Arab pressures eventually resulted in the British publication of the WHITE PAPER (1939), which limited Jewish immigration to Palestine to 15,000 Jews per year for five years. Illegal Jewish immigration continued.

After World War II, when it became clear that many of the 6 million Jews murdered by Germany in the HOLOCAUST might have lived if there were a place of refuge for the Jews, the issue of establishing a Jewish state came to the forefront. On November 29, 1947, UN Resolution GA 181 approved the PARTITION PLAN, dividing the Palestine Mandate, consisting of less than 11,000 square miles, into two states, one with an Arab majority, the other with a Jewish majority, each made up of three separated enclaves that resembled a jigsaw puzzle. About 650,000 Jews lived in Palestine, almost all in the sectors assigned to them, along with 1.2 million Arabs. Jerusalem was to be an international city. The Arab countries and local Arab leaders rejected the plan and when the modern state of Israel declared its independence in 1948 the ISRAELI WAR OF INDEPENDENCE ensued.

Further reading: Michael Avi-Yonah, *The Jews under Roman and Byzantine Rule: A Political History of Palestine from the Bar Kokhba War to the Arab Conquest* (New York:

Schocken Books, 1985); Moshe Gil, *A History of Palestine, 634–1099* (New York: Cambridge University Press, 1997); J. C. Hurewitz, *The Struggle for Palestine* (New York: W. W. Norton, 1950); Robert L. Wilken, *The Land Called Holy: Palestine in Christian History and Thought* (New Haven, Conn.: Yale University Press, 1994).

Palestine Liberation Organization (PLO)

During the ISRAELI WAR OF INDEPENDENCE in 1948, several hundred thousand Arabs in PALESTINE fled the new Jewish state with the encouragement of the other Arab nations. Two Arab countries, Jordan and EGYPT, occupied the remaining lands where, according to the UNITED NATIONS, an Arab Palestinian state was supposed to be established. Most of the lands were annexed to the kingdom of Jordan and the rest was under Egyptian military rule. A host of paramilitary groups arose in the 1950s, drawing support from the refugees and their supporters in the Arab countries, dedicated to liberating the rest of the old BRITISH MANDATE of Palestine from Jewish rule.

In 1964 several of these groups jointly created an umbrella group called the Palestine Liberation Organization (PLO). The cofounder of the PLO, Yasser Arafat, was the head of the largest and best financed of the founding groups, called al-Fatah. In 1968, Arafat became the general chairman of the PLO. The PLO articulated a primary goal: to destroy the Jewish state of ISRAEL and replace it with an Arab Palestinian state, thus allowing the return of the refugees who had been dispossessed in 1948. Winning political and military support from several Arab governments and especially from the Soviet Union and several of its satellite countries, they increased the tempo of military incursions.

After Israel won the SIX-DAY WAR in 1967, all the remaining territories of the former British Mandate, namely the Gaza Strip and the West Bank (*see* JUDEA AND SAMARIA) came under Israeli military control, as did the Sinai Peninsula and the Golan Heights. As a result of Israel's occupation of these territories, the PLO intensified its attacks against Israel. The PLO utilized Jordan as its primary base to plan and execute terrorist operations. However, in September 1970, the PLO was expelled by the Jordanian government and they moved their operations to Lebanon (*see* LEBANON WAR).

Beginning in the 1970s the PLO became one of the most notorious terrorist groups in the world. They hijacked airplanes, assassinated Jordan's prime minister, and murdered 11 Israeli athletes at the Olympic Games in Munich in 1972. While their terrorist activities were considered repugnant by civilized nations, they drew renewed world attention to the Palestinian refugee plight.

After the 1973 YOM KIPPUR WAR, the Arab League recognized the PLO as the sole legitimate representative of the Arab Palestinians and formally endorsed the PLO's mission to establish an Arab Palestinian state in Israel. The United Nations granted the PLO "observer" status in the General Assembly and other UN organizations. In 1976, the PLO became a full member of the Arab League.

Because the PLO insisted on continuing to utilize terrorism as a means to achieve its goals, Israel refused to negotiate with it. Israel attempted to discuss peace with other independent Palestinian leaders, especially during its successful peace negotiations with Egypt in 1977–79; several local leaders who responded to the call were assassinated by the PLO. The UNITED STATES, while maintaining communication with the PLO, refused to recognize it until it renounced terrorism.

Increased PLO violence targeting Israel resulted in the Israeli invasion of Lebanon in 1982. Israel's intention was to physically drive the PLO out of Lebanon, freeing northern Israel from repeated attacks. They succeeded in that Arafat and the PLO offices had to flee to Tunisia. They failed in that Lebanon became highly unstable, and the violence toward Israel only increased. In 1987, the PLO directed its first INTIFADA, or general uprising against Israel. They coordinated attacks against Israel and popularized the use of children in their overt battles with Israeli soldiers.

The PLO created a "government-in-exile" that was recognized by approximately 70 countries.

The PLO's governing body, the Palestine National Council, appointed Arafat as president for the theoretical new state of Palestine. The PLO, in theory, accepted UN resolutions that called for negotiations between Israel and the Palestinians to secure a peace, condemned terrorism, and recognized the existence of the modern state of Israel.

On September 13, 1993, Israel and the PLO signed the Oslo Accord, in which Israel agreed to an arrangement for interim self-government for the Palestinians, operated by the PLO. The PLO renounced terrorism as a tool and transformed itself into the governing Palestinian Authority. Arafat and other former PLO leaders set up their base of operations in the West Bank. Unfortunately, the PLO never removed from its covenant the clause calling for the destruction of Israel, as it had pledged to do. Under Arafat's leadership, the PALESTINIAN AUTHORITY (PA) launched a full-scale Intifada in 2000, during final stage U.S.-Israel-Palestinian peace talks. In 2004, peace negotiations were stalled. However, with Arafat's death in November 2004, the subsequent election of Mahmoud Abbas as president of the PA, and Israeli prime minister Ariel Sharon's plan to pull out of Gaza, peace may again become a possibility.

Further reading: Neil C. Livingston and David Halevy, *Inside the PLO: Covert Units, Secret Funds, and the War against Israel and the United States* (New York: Morrow, 1990); David Makovsky, *Making Peace with the PLO: The Rabin Government's Road to the Oslo Accord* (Boulder, Colo.: Westview Press, 1996); Barry Rubin, *Revolution Until Victory? The Politics and History of the PLO* (Cambridge, Mass.: Harvard University Press, 1994); Harris O. Schoenberg, *A Mandate for Terror: The United Nations and the PLO* (New York: Shapolsky Publishers, 1989).

Palestinian Authority (PA)

The Oslo Accord and the subsequent 1993 Israeli-Palestinian Declaration of Principles (DOP) provided for a two-phase pullout of Israeli military presence in the large Arab population centers in the West Bank (*see* JUDEA AND SAMARIA) and Gaza

Strip. During this time there was to be a transfer of power to an elected Palestinian governing body called the Palestinian Authority (PA).

On May 4, 1994, ISRAEL transferred the Gaza Strip and the Jericho area to the PA, and Yasser Arafat returned there, assuming hands-on control. Over the years, additional West Bank areas were transferred to PA control. The second phase of permanent transfer is supposed to come with a final agreement, which is to remedy the outstanding Israeli/Palestinian issues on borders, JERUSALEM, refugees, security, Israeli settlements, intercommunal relations and cooperation with other Arab neighbors.

The PA was given the responsibility for combating terrorism and coordinating security with Israel. On January 20, 1996, Palestinian Arabs elected an 88-member legislative council and elected Yasser Arafat as the president of the PA. Arafat won 88 percent of the vote; consistent with past practices, he used violence as a means to reduce or eliminate internal Palestinian opposition.

Arafat ultimately rejected a proposed final agreement, offered by President Clinton and Prime Minister Ehud BARAK, which would have permanently turned over nearly all the West Bank and Gaza to the PA, as well as half of Jerusalem, which would have become the PA capital. After Arafat's rejection, cooperation between Israel and the PA became increasingly strained. Arafat directly and indirectly cooperated with a second INTIFADA against Israel, which included intentional violence directed at civilians. In 2003, UNITED STATES president George W. Bush asserted that Arafat's acceptance of terrorism and long-time corruption made him unfit to lead. The president, like Israel, refused to deal directly with Arafat, although contacts were maintained with other PA officials.

In November 2004 Arafat died in a Paris hospital. In January 2005 Mahmoud Abbas was elected to succeed Arafat as PA president. In January 2006, the militant and Islamist organization Hamas won the Palestinian Authority elections, forcing the creation of a unity government with their main opposition, Fatah. In June 2007, Hamas staged a coup in the Gaza Strip, establishing military dominance in that area and ending the unity government. Currently, the PA controls the West Bank and Hamas controls the Gaza Strip, splitting the Palestinians in two politically as well as geographically.

Further reading: Anthony H. Cordesman, *Perilous Prospects: The Peace Process and the Arab-Israeli Military Balance* (Boulder, Colo.: Westview Press, 1996); Arlene Kushner, *Disclosed: Inside the Palestinian Authority and the PLO* (Douglas, Mich.: Pavilion Press, 2004); Barry M. Rubin, *The Transformation of Palestinian Politics: From Revolution to State-Building* (Cambridge, Mass.: Harvard University Press, 1999).

Palmach

On May 19, 1941, the HAGANAH, the Jewish underground military organization that had been established under the BRITISH MANDATE in 1920, created an elite military strike force called the Palmach (from the HEBREW *pelugot mahaz,* "assault companies"). The Palmach companies were assigned the task of defending the Jews living in PALESTINE from GERMANY, whose North African army was threatening Egypt from the West. The Palmach also participated in dropping parachutists into occupied Europe during the war and assisted Jews trying to immigrate to Palestine.

Three units were established to protect the Galilee. The Palmach led preemptive attacks into Lebanon and Syria, then under control of Vichy France. Palmach members commonly dressed in Arab guise and many were fluent in Arabic. When they entered Arab territory, their usual aim was to sabotage Arab military capacity and gather information about the enemy.

The Palmach eventually grew to 12 companies, with many new members trained on kibbutzim around the country (*see* KIBBUTZ). It served as the core of the developing Israeli army. Many top Israeli military and political leaders started out in its ranks. These included Yigal Alon (1918–80), Haim Bar-Lev (1924–94), Moshe DAYAN, Yitzhak RABIN, Uzi Narkiss (1925–97), and Ezer Weizman (b. 1924). Prime Minister David BEN-GURION dissolved the Palmach on November 7, 1948, along with other pre-independence militias. Its structure and soldiers were merged into the evolving ISRAEL DEFENSE FORCES (IDF).

Further reading: Reuven Gal, *A Portrait of the Israeli Soldier* (Westport, Conn.: Greenwood Press, 1986); Walter Laqueur, *A History of Zionism: From the French Revolution to the Establishment of the State of Israel* (New York: Schocken Books, 2003); Howard M. Sachar, *A History of Israel: From the Rise of Zionism to Our Time* (New York: Alfred A. Knopf, 1996); Martin Van Creveld, *The Sword and the Olive: A Critical History of the Israeli Defense Force* (New York: Public Affairs, 1998).

parsha (pl.: *parshiyot*)

The TORAH (the Five Books of MOSES) is divided into 54 portions, or *parshiyot*, roughly 10 for each book. Jewish tradition teaches that EZRA the Scribe made the divisions in the fifth century B.C.E. He decreed that the *parshiyot* were to be read in public in sequence, one (or sometimes two) per week. The readings were to be held on Monday and Thursday mornings, which were the market days in Ezra's time, and Sabbath mornings and afternoons (*see* SHABBAT). The Saturday afternoon reading began the new PARSHAT HA-SHAVUA, or weekly Torah portion.

The practice continues to this day. The entire Torah is thus read in SYNAGOGUES in a yearly cycle beginning on SIMCHAT TORAH. Relevant Torah *parshiyot* are also assigned for each of the Jewish holidays, such as YOM KIPPUR, ROSH HASHANAH, CHANUKAH, and PASSOVER. There is also a special *parsha* read on the first day of each month, which is called ROSH HODESH. Many modern congregations do a triennial reading of the Torah, reading one-third of each *parsha* each week and completing the entire reading over a period of three years. Some weeks double portions are read because the Jewish calendar is based on a lunar-solar CALENDAR and adjustments are necessary to keep the calendar synchronized with the seasons of the year.

Each of the *parshiyot* has its own name, always taken from a word or phrase within its first verse. RABBIS and often congregants will comment on and discuss the portion before, during or after it is read in SYNAGOGUE. Many rabbis hold a weekly *parashat ha-shavua* class during the week. Both Jewish day schools (*see* JEWISH DAY SCHOOL MOVEMENT) and SUPPLEMENTARY SCHOOLS often use the format of *parshat ha-shavua* to teach Torah to young children and teens.

There are many Web sites with links dedicated to the weekly *parsha*, providing a large number of sermons and lessons each week from many different points of view. The straightforward format provides Jews with approachable bits of TORAH to use in their own study, no matter their level of Jewish knowledge.

The portions are Book of Genesis (Bereshit): Bereshit (1:1–6:8), Noach (6:9–11:32), Lekh-L'kha (12:1–17:27), Vayera (18:1–22:24), Haye Sarah (23:1–25:18), Toldot (25:19–28:9), Vayetze (28:10–32:3), Vayishlah (32:4–36:43), Vayeshev (37:1–40:23), Miketz (41:1–44:17), Vayigash (44:18–47:27), Vayehi (47:28–50:26); Book of Exodus (Shemot): Shemot (1:1–6:1), Vaera (6:2–9:35), Bo (10:1–13:16), Beshalah (13:17–17:16), Yitro (18:1–20:23), Mishpatim (21:1–24:18), Terumah (25:1–27:19), Tetzaveh (27:20–30:10), Ki Tissa (30:11–34:35), Vayakhel (35:1–38:20), Pekudei (38:21–40:38); Book of Leviticus (Vayikra): Vayikra (1:1–5:26), Tzav (6:1–8:36), Shemini (9:1–11:47), Tazria (12:1–13:59), Metzora (14:1–15:33), Ahare Mot (16:1–18:30), Kedoshim (19:1–20:27), Emor (21:1–24:23), Behar (25:1–26:2), Behukotai (26:3–27:34); Book of Numbers (Bamidbar): Bamidbar (1:1–4:20), Naso (4:21–7:89), B'ha'alotekha (8:1–12:16), Shelah (13:1–15:41), Korah (16:1–18:32), Hukkat (19:1–22:1), Balak (22:2–25:9), Pinhas (25:10–30:1), Mattot (30:2–32:42), Mase (33:1–36:13); Book of Deuteronomy (Devarim): Devarim (1:1–3:22), Vaet'hanan (3:23–7:11), Ekev (7:12–11:25), Reeh (11:26–16:17), Shoftim (16:18–21:9), Ki Tetze (21:10–25:19), Ki Tavo (26:1–29:8), Nitzavim (29:9–30:20), Vayelekh (31:1–30), Haazinu (32:1–52), V'zot HaBrakha (33:1–34:12).

Further reading: Jewish Theological Seminary Parashat ha Shavuoh Web site URL: http://www.jtsa.edu/community/

parashah/index.shtml, accessed on August 14, 2004; Mordechai Kamenetsky, *Parsha Parables* (New York: Philip Feldheim, 1997); Stuart Kelman and Joel Lurie Grishaver, *Learn Torah With . . . 1994–1995 Torah Annual: A Collection of the Year's Best Torah* (Los Angeles: Alef Design Group, 1996); Nehama Leibowitz, *Studies in Bamidbar* (Jerusalem: World Zionist Organization, 1981); ———, *Studies in Bereshit* (Jerusalem: World Zionist Organization, 1981); ———, *Studies in Devarim* (Jerusalem: World Zionist Organization, 1981); ———, *Studies in Shemot* (Jerusalem: World Zionist Organization, 1981); ———, *Studies in Vayikra* (Jerusalem: World Zionist Organization, 1981); Ohr Somoyach International Web site URL: http://ohr.edu, accessed on August 14, 2004; *Tanakh: The Holy Scriptures* (Philadelphia and Jerusalem: Jewish Publication Society, 1985).

Partition Plan

At the end of World War II, the British were in a political bind over the future of the PALESTINE Mandate. After the Nazi HOLOCAUST, in which six million European Jews were killed, large segments of world public opinion were pressuring them to fulfill their Mandatory obligation of creating a Jewish state in Palestine. However, Arab countries wanted the British to stop Jewish immigration to Palestine entirely. Unable to square their moral obligation to help the Jews acquire a modern homeland with the economic and political price they might pay in the Arab world, the British turned the entire issue over to the UNITED NATIONS in February of 1947.

By November of that same year, the United Nations resolved to partition Palestine into two separate states, one Jewish and the other Arab. The resolution also directed British troops to leave Palestine by August 1948.

The Partition Plan was accepted by the Palestinian Jewish leadership only grudgingly, because it offered less land than would be needed to settle Jewish refugees. However, the Arabs rejected the plan entirely. They warned that if the Jews declared their state, they would immediately launch a military attack.

The Partition Plan granted the Jews most of the coastal plain of Palestine, with the exception of Jaffa, near TEL AVIV. Additionally, they were to take possession of the Huleh and Yizrael valleys in Northern Palestine and the Negev Desert in the south. All other lands were to be in Arab control. Under the plan, JERUSALEM was to be an international city.

The Partition Plan was never really implemented, as fighting between Arabs and Jews broke out immediately. When Israel's independence was declared the surrounding Arab countries attacked escalating the fighting to conventional warfare (*see* ISRAELI WAR OF INDEPENDENCE). In the fighting, Israel captured additional territory beyond what had been assigned, including the Western Galilee and a corridor to West Jerusalem. Today, some Arab nations have called for an Israeli withdrawal to the original 1947 lines, but no political faction in Israel will consider such a move, as the Jewish population of Israel has increased more than eightfold since 1947.

Further reading: J. C. Hurewitz, *The Struggle for Palestine* (New York: W. W. Norton, 1950); Barry Rubin, *The Arab States and the Palestine Conflict* (New York: Syracuse University Press, 1981); Howard M. Sachar, *A History of Israel: From the Rise of Zionism to Our Time* (New York: Alfred A. Knopf, 1996); Avi Shlaim, *The Politics of Partition: King Abdullah, the Zionists, and Palestine, 1921–1951* (New York: Oxford University, 1998); Herman L. Weisman, *The Future of Palestine: An Examination of the Partition Plan* (New York: Lincoln Printing Company, 1937).

passion play

CHRISTIANITY gives great theological significance to the events of the "Passion" of JESUS OF NAZARETH. These are the stories about Jesus' trial, suffering, crucifixion, and resurrection. Within the Gospels of the Christian New Testament are four different accounts of the Passion and in each story Jews participate in different ways.

It became common in Christian communities to dramatically portray the "Passion of Christ" in plays, most famously in the town of Oberammergau, GERMANY, starting in 1634. These passion plays often were performed in the period just before Easter, when Christians focused on the terrible events of the Passion. Since the New Testament included polemics against the Jews, a common motif of the plays was to portray the Jews as killing Jesus. Over the centuries, the charge of deicide has led to much violence directed against the Jews (*see* POGROM). Holy Week, the week prior to Easter, often witnessed the worst massacres. Passion plays were often deliberately used to incite violence against Jews.

In 1965 the Roman Catholic Church, at the Second Vatican Council, took steps to formally remove the charge of deicide against the Jews. The church issued the *Nostra Aetate,* a document that condemned such charges as well as all other forms of ANTISEMITISM. Soon after, mainstream Protestant churches followed the Catholic Church's precedent.

Since 1965, many passion plays have focused on the life of Christ, and the theological meaning of his death, and have usually avoided polemics against the Jews. In 1988, the U.S. Catholic Bishops Committee for Ecumenical and Interreligious Affairs drew up specific criteria for dramatizations of the Passion. They stressed that passion plays must avoid caricatures of Jews and must not falsely accuse the Jews of killing Jesus. Catholics were instructed to portray Jews accurately and with sensitivity.

In 2004, Mel Gibson, a popular Hollywood actor and producer, released a film that represented his interpretation of the Passion of Christ. The movie was extremely controversial within both the Christian and Jewish communities. Gibson's interpretation was pre-1965, and he himself rejects Vatican II teachings. The movie portrayed Jewish villains as indirectly, if not directly, responsible for the killing of Jesus, while showing the Roman authorities as mere tools of Jewish hatred. Gibson's portrayal of Jesus' death was extremely graphic and disturbing. The movie was repudiated by many mainstream Catholic and Protestant groups and roundly condemned by the Jewish community. However, the film was a significant commercial success. Many Christians in the UNITED STATES who saw the film said they were inspired by how Jesus died for their sins; most said the Jewish component seemed insignificant. Others simply reiterated that the deicide charge was accurate and should be portrayed.

While the Gibson movie of the passion play was highly controversial and created the potential for renewed antisemitism, it had the ironic result of further strengthening ties between Christians and Jews who were strongly committed to interfaith dialogue. Throughout the United States churches and synagogues sponsored interfaith discussion groups, and these resulted in furthering the significant ties created between Christians and Jews since 1965.

Further reading: Kathleen E. Corley, ed., *Jesus and Mel Gibson's The Passion of the Christ* (London and New York: Continuum International Publishing Group, 2004); Saul S. Friedman, *The Oberammergau Passion Play: A Lance against Civilization* (Carbondale: Southern Illinois University Press, 1984); Eric Lane and Ian Brenson, ed., *The Complete Text in English of the Oberammergau Passion Play: With an Introduction by Eric Lane & Ian Brenson* (London: Dedalus, 1984).

Passover (Pesach)

Passover, or Pesach in Hebrew, which commemorates the EXODUS of the ISRAELITES from Egyptian SLAVERY, is perhaps the most celebrated holiday of the Jewish year. While SYNAGOGUE attendance is higher on ROSH HASHANAH and YOM KIPPUR, the main Passover ritual, the SEDER, takes place in the home. Even Jews who never attend synagogue are likely to attend a Passover seder at the home of family or friends, or hold one of their own.

The seder takes place at a dinner table, since certain ritual foods must be consumed and a festive meal is at the heart of the evening's program. The liturgy and instructions are detailed in the HAGGADAH, an ancient prayer book that is handed out to everyone, which includes a full telling of the Exodus story in song, narration, and quotes from the Bible and the TALMUD.

The event is a time for families to come together, recall their heritage, reinscribe their Jewish identities, and break bread, albeit unleavened bread (*see* MATZAH), together. Passover begins on the 15th day of the month of Nissan, and lasts seven days in the land of ISRAEL and eight in the DIASPORA. For that whole time Jews may not eat CHAMETZ, or leavening, including any products made with grain (wheat, rye, oat, spelt, barley) and yeast. ASHKENAZIM also refrain from eating *kitniyot,* which include rice, corn, and beans.

The book of Exodus itself describes the first Passover celebration in EGYPT, which was commanded by God through MOSES. While the last of the TEN PLAGUES—the death of the first-born—was taking place, each Israelite family sacrificed a lamb and daubed its blood on their doorpost so that the plague would "pass over" their home. The English name Passover derives from this event. The various symbolic foods eating at the seder recall other aspects of the story. Bitter herbs, saltwater, unleavened bread, and *charoset,* a mortarlike mixture containing fruit and wine, represent the afflictions of slavery, while a bone on the table symbolizes the sacrificed lamb. The unleavened bread also symbolizes the speed with which the Israelites had to flee Egypt. Other elements such as green vegetables and eggs suggest the coming of spring and freedom. The combination of rituals and stories instill a sense of Jewish history and identity in each participant.

In biblical times, Passover was one of three annual PILGRIMAGE FESTIVALS. Israelites would make a pilgrimage to JERUSALEM, offer sacrifices, and bring the first products of their harvests as offerings in the TEMPLE. After the destruction of the Temple, Passover became a much more homebound festival as described above.

It is possible that a number of the rituals of Passover entered into Jewish tradition from neighboring communities in ancient times. The nomadic shepherds of the region engaged in a spring festival in which they ate unleavened bread together with lamb. The people of CANAAN also had a seven-day spring harvest festival which involved unleavened bread. Finally, pagan spring rites often include eggs and green vegetables.

Further reading: Larry Domnitch, *The Jewish Holidays: A Journey through History* (Northvale, N.J.: Jason Aronson, 2000); Irving Greenberg, *The Jewish Way: Living the Holidays* (New York: Summit Books, 1988); Moshe Lieber, ed., *The Pesach Haggadah Anthology: The Living Exodus: With Commentary and Anecdotes from Talmudic and Rabbinical Literature* (Brooklyn, N.Y.: Mesorah, 1997).

Patriarchs (Abraham, Isaac, Jacob)

Abraham, Isaac, and Jacob are identified by the Jewish faith as the Patriarchs, or Avot (Hebrew for "fathers"). Their stories are told in Genesis, the first book of the TORAH (the Five Books of MOSES). They are considered to be the physical and spiritual ancestors of the Jewish people and of Judaism.

Abraham, born with the name Abram, was the son of Terach, an idol maker by trade, according to an often-quoted MIDRASH. This midrash tells that even as a child Abram questioned his father's religion and occupation and sought to discover the true God. His search is rewarded, as God calls upon him, telling him to leave his home and his family and go to a new land, and promising to make of him a great nation (Gn 12). Abram obeys God's command, thus inaugurating the COVENANT (in Hebrew, *brit*) between God and the Jewish people.

Abraham leaves his homeland with his wife Sarai (*see* MATRIARCHS). Together they journey to the land of CANAAN, later to be known as the Land of ISRAEL, or the Promised Land. In Canaan, Abram and Sarai have difficulty conceiving a child; Sarai offers her handmaid Hagar, who bears Abram's first son, Ishmael (revered by Muslims as the progenitor of the Arabs). God renews the covenant with Abram and with Sarai's future offspring, changing their names to Abraham and Sarah (Gn 17). When Sarah ultimately gives birth to Isaac, Hagar and Ishmael are sent away, and God makes clear that Abraham's covenant will continue through Sarah's son, Isaac, rather than Ishmael.

Isaac and Abraham are the central players in the narrative of the AKEDAH, or the Binding of Isaac. Abraham is commanded by God to offer his son Isaac as a human sacrifice. According to rabbinic literature, this trial was a test of Abraham's faith. Would he take the only son he had fathered with his wife, Sarah, and sacrifice him to God? This divine command tested Isaac's faith, as well. Midrashic literature reports that Isaac was aware of Abraham's intentions yet did not resist. After Isaac's binding on the altar, at the last moment God sends an angel (*see* MALAKHIM) to stop the sacrifice. Abraham and Isaac had both shown their willingness to make the ultimate sacrifice, even when it meant giving up the expected rewards of the covenant. The willingness to sacrifice one's life for God later became a paradigm for Jewish faith during times of extreme persecution and hardship.

Isaac marries Rebecca, who bears him twin sons, Jacob and Esau. These twin brothers are at odds with each other from the time of conception, struggling, according to the biblical narrative, within Rebecca's womb. There are many midrashic stories about Jacob's machinations in his successful pursuit of his brother's birthright and blessing as first-born. The midrash tends to excuse Jacob, thanks to his genuine understanding and appreciation of the worth of the birthright and blessing. In rabbinic literature, Esau becomes a paradigmatic symbol of all peoples, empires, and nations who mistreat the Jewish people.

Rebecca and Jacob trick an old and blind Isaac into giving Jacob the blessing of the first-born intended for Esau. Esau, upon hearing of the trick, is furious, and Jacob has to flee. The biblical narrative then demonstrates how the "trickster" is tricked. Jacob is deceived into marrying the wrong woman, and later deceived into believing his favorite son Joseph had died. The common rab-

binic interpretation teaches that through these events Jacob is taught that his spiritual legacy must come with honesty and correct moral behavior.

Jacob, in the process of spiritual growth, has a physical struggle with God. Injured in this struggle, Jacob's name is changed to Yisrael, or Israel, translated "the one who struggles with God." The struggle itself becomes the spiritual marker by which the Jews identify themselves. The Torah most often refers to the ISRAELITES as Bnei Yisrael, the Children of Israel. They are the spiritual ancestors of the modern Jewish people. The RABBIS taught that the Israelites descended from the best that was within Jacob. Thus, the spiritual charge of the Israelites, and then of the Jewish people, was to be like Jacob/Israel—to struggle with God and, in the end, observe the moral and ethical mandates by their own choice.

The first blessing of the thrice-daily AMIDAH prayer (also known as Shmonei Esrei, or the Eighteen Benedictions) begins with the words "Blessed are You, our Lord, our God and the God of our fathers, God of Abraham, God of Isaac, God of Jacob." Thus, still today the descendants of Abraham, Isaac, and Jacob call out in prayer the centrality of these men to their own theological identity, recognizing that even with their faults, there have been men on earth worthy of emulation. Together, the characteristics, situations, and choices made by each forefather provide guidelines that are timeless for all people. Their very flaws allow the reader or worshipper to relate to these paradigms, thus ensuring that the lessons taught by these particular men remain dynamic for all generations.

Further reading: H. Freedman and Maurice Simon, eds., *Soncino Midrash Rabbah* (CD-ROM), 3rd ed. (Brooklyn, N.Y.: Soncino Press, 1983); Norman K. Gottwald, *The Hebrew Bible: A Socio-Literary Introduction* (Philadelphia: Fortress Press, 1985); David L. Lieber, ed., *Etz Hayim: Torah and Commentary* (Philadelphia: Jewish Publication Society, 2001); *Tanakh: The New JPS Translation According to the Traditional Hebrew Text* (Philadelphia, New York, Jerusalem: Jewish Publication Society, 1985).

Paul (Saul of Tarsus) (8 C.E.–65 C.E.)

Paul, a convert from Judaism to CHRISTIANITY, was the first and most important theologian of Christianity. Some have even characterized him as the founder of Christianity rather than JESUS OF NAZARETH—he helped found the earliest churches, developed the fundamentals of Christian theology in his letters, and brought GENTILES into the fold of the largely Jewish sect that Jesus had left behind. The bulk of the material in Acts, the fifth book of the NEW TESTAMENT, describes Paul's work.

Paul was born as Saul to a Jewish family in Tarsus, where he was raised. The New Testament describes him as well-educated in the tradition of the PHARISEES and in the best of Greek and ROMAN thought. The book of Acts indicates that he was trained at the feet of Gamliel, the NASI or president of the Academy of HILLEL. Saul originally was intent on destroying the sect that had developed around Jesus. He traveled around persecuting Christians, even overseeing their first martyrdom (Acts 7:54–8:1).

On the road to Damascus, Saul was confronted with a vision of the risen Jesus, and from that moment on became a zealous Christian missionary and teacher, using his Roman name, Paul. Traditionally Paul is said to have made three missionary journeys, during which he established churches in Asia Minor and Macedonia, Europe, Greece, and PALESTINE. He was imprisoned in ROME, and the bulk of his letters are said to have been written while he was in jail. Most of the New Testament letters or "epistles" are traditionally attributed to him, although academic scholars dispute some of these attributions.

Paul contributed a theological foundation to the fledgling Christianity. Drawing on his own interpretation of TORAH and the Prophets (*see* NEVI'IM), as well as on Platonic concepts, Paul planted the seeds of doctrinal positions that continue to be at the heart of Christianity today: Jesus as fully human and fully divine; Jesus as MESSIAH; the atonement for human sin by Jesus's death on the cross; the bodily resurrection of Jesus; the coming day of judgment; the supersession of the old covenant with the Jews by a new covenant open to Jew and Gentile alike; and salvation through faith alone.

Tradition teaches that Paul died a martyr's death in 65 C.E. His writings continue to have great theological and liturgical significance among Christians. Virtually every major Christian theologian has been influenced by his thought and writings.

Further reading: Hyam Maccoby, *The Mythmaker: Paul and the Invention of Christianity* (New York: Harper-Collins, 1989); Richard Rubenstein, *My Brother Paul* (New York: Harper & Row, 1972); E. P. Saunders, *Paul and Palestinian Judaism: A Comparison of Patterns of Religion* (Philadelphia: Fortress Press, 1983); Alan Segal, *Paul the Convert* (New Haven, Conn.: Yale University Press, 1992).

payis

Payis (from the Hebrew *payot*, or "edges") are the uncut earlocks of hair grown by many religious Jewish men just to the front of the ears. In Leviticus 19:27, the TORAH commands men not to round off the hair at the edge of their head. The early RABBIS interpreted "edge" to refer to the hair between the ears and the hairless portion of one's face.

Moses MAIMONIDES further clarified this rabbinic interpretation in his *MISHNEH TORAH*, ruling that one must leave a minimum of 40 hairs. However, he continued, a Jew may remove the hair with scissors, as the prohibition applies only to total removal with a razor. The *SHULCHAN ARUKH* expands the definition by stating that Jews are forbidden to shave where the skull is joined to the jawbone.

The commandment seems to have been a safeguard against idolatry. The rabbis assert that it was customary for pagan priests to shave the corners of their heads, and therefore the Torah prohibited this custom. The prohibition was applied only to men. In premodern Jewish communities in both Europe and the Middle East, most Jewish men bore the distinctive *payis*. Since EMANCIPATION, when many Jews have tried to blend in with the general population, only ultra-Orthodox Jewish men (*see* ORTHODOX JUDAISM) have continued the custom of growing *payis* and displaying them prominently. Modern Orthodox Jews will cut their hair with scissors or with electric razors, which generally have a scissors action, but not with manual razors. In one interpretation, electric razors, like scissors, are unlikely to cut a vital vein, while razors may, which is why God prohibited them. The prohibition of shaving the "edges" of male facial hair was also the reason traditional Jews grew beards.

Further reading: Philip Birnbaum, *Mishneh Torah: Maimonides Code of Law and Ethics* (New York: Hebrew Publishing, 1970); *Tanakh: The New JPS Translation According to the Traditional Hebrew Text* (Philadelphia, New York, Jerusalem: Jewish Publication Society, 1985).

Peace Now (Shalom Achshav)

One of the largest grassroots movements in the history of the State of Israel is Peace Now, or Shalom Achshav. It was founded in March 1978 by 348 Israeli reserve commanders, officers, and combat soldiers of the ISRAEL DEFENSE FORCES. They had come to believe that only a politically negotiated solution could bring about an Israeli-Palestinian peace agreement and peace with neighboring Arab countries.

Peace Now actively attempts to create dialogue between Israeli Jews and Arabs. The organization takes credit for helping to foster the peace treaties signed with EGYPT and later Jordan, and for the beginning of real negotiations with the PALESTINE LIBERATION ORGANIZATION.

Peace Now asserts that the only way to secure a permanent peace is by withdrawing troops and settlements from the West Bank (*see* JUDEA AND SAMARIA) and the Gaza Strip. They urge the creation of a Palestinian state that would then negotiate a peace and security treaty whereby JERUSALEM would become the capital city for both the Jews and the Arabs. Peace Now also believes

Israel should withdraw from the Golan Heights and seek a peace treaty with Syria.

Peace Now is considered to be well on the left side of Israel's political bell curve, with most of their political activists affiliated with the left wing of the Israeli LABOR Party. A group called Americans for Peace Now was founded in 1981 to support the activities of Peace Now in Israel.

Further reading: Joel Beinin and Zachary Lockman, eds., *Intifada: The Palestinian Uprising Against Israeli Occupation* (Boston, Mass.: South End Press, 1989); Benjamin Gidron, Stanley Nider Katz, and Yeheskel Hasenfeld, *Mobilizing for Peace: Conflict Resolution in Northern Ireland/Palesine, and South Africa* (Oxford and New York: Oxford University Press, 2002); Michael M. Laskier, "Israeli Activism American-Style: Civil Liberties, Environmental, and Peace Organizations as Pressure Groups for Social Change, 1970s–1990s," *Israel Studies* 5, no. 1 (2000): 150; Frederick A. Lazin and Gregory S. Mahler, eds., *Israel in the Nineties: Development and Conflict* (Gainesville: University Press of Florida, 1996).

peoplehood

Jews have commonly referred to themselves as Am Yisrael, the people of Israel, for centuries. By contrast, they rarely use the phrase Dat Israel, the religion of Israel. This highlights one unusual trait of the Jewish heritage, the tendency of Jews to emphasize their adherence to a culture and a people, and not just a strictly religious group. Jewish peoplehood is based on a common ancestry and history, on rituals and beliefs, and on an attachment to the land of ISRAEL (*see* ZIONISM).

The initial source for the idea of Jewish peoplehood is the COVENANT that GOD made with Abraham (*see* PATRIARCHS) and his descendents. Later, God applies the covenant to MOSES and the Jewish people as a whole at MOUNT SINAI. From this time forward the ISRAELITES and their descendants, the JEWS, would identify with each other as having common ancestry and a common story. Whether one believes that the "story" is fully historical or largely metaphorical is irrelevant, for all

Jews refer back to the families and personalities in the TANAKH, the Hebrew Bible, as their point of departure.

Traditional Judaism determines a new child's identification as a Jew through biology. If the child's mother is Jewish, that person is considered to be Jewish in both ORTHODOX JUDAISM and CONSERVATIVE JUDAISM. REFORM JUDAISM, however, considers a child Jewish if either parent is a Jew, and the child is raised as a Jew.

However, from the very beginning it was considered possible for a non-Jew to join the Jewish people, whatever his or her ancestry. Today, the way to become part of the Jewish people without having been born to a Jewish mother (or parent) is to undergo formal CONVERSION. Once the conversion process is completed, it is considered irrevocable. The convert permanently becomes a member of the Jewish people, even adopting the forefather Abraham (see PATRIARCHS) and the foremother Sarah (see MATRIARCHS) as symbolic parents.

The sense of Jewish peoplehood is so strong in Judaism that many Jews consider themselves a people that happen to have a religion. It is for this reason that Jews can vary so much in personal theology and observance; for many, it is their peoplehood that defines their Jewish identity. For example, when Jews observe PASSOVER, they view the EXODUS story as "their story." The Jew states *avadim hayyinu*, "we were slaves." The Exodus story is understood by religious Jews as both a religious narrative and a national narrative. The nonreligious Jew will accept the national implications as part of their Jewish national heritage.

Because peoplehood is so central to Judaism, many Jews choose to live in communities that can support a vibrant Jewish life. Jews seek out other Jews, whom they identify with. Jewish communities create institutions that will support the continuity of the Jewish people, such as SYNAGOGUES, educational institutions (see JEWISH DAY SCHOOL MOVEMENT; SUPPLEMENTARY SCHOOLS), Jewish social services (see ASSOCIATION OF JEWISH FAMILY AND CHILDREN'S SERVICES), Jewish philanthropies (see UNITED JEWISH COMMUNITIES), camps (see JEWISH YOUTH GROUPS, ZIONIST YOUTH GROUPS), and Jewish community centers (see JEWISH COMMUNITY CENTER ASSOCIATION).

Jewish community organization has been a hallmark of Jewish continuity. From the time of the first EXILE (586 B.C.E.), Jewish communities created semiautonomous governing bodies, which often insulated them from the surrounding cultures (see KAHAL, KEHILLAH; SHTETL). When the ENLIGHTENMENT values of individualism and EMANCIPATION spread throughout Europe, these semiautonomous local communities all but disappeared, except among the ultra-Orthodox (see ORTHODOX JUDAISM).

According to traditional Jewish texts, Jews have a divine obligation to fully embrace the Jewish people. Many Jews today have developed their JEWISH IDENTITY, regardless of religious perspective and practices, through their involvement in a Jewish community, thus showing the power of Am Yisrael. The common slogan of the committed Jew is "The People of Israel will live forever," and the Jew who cares for his or her people actively integrates in Jewish communal life.

Further reading: Arthur Hertzberg, *Judaism: The Classic Introduction to One of the Great Religions of the Modern World* (New York: Simon & Schuster, 1991); Michael A. Meyer, *Jewish Identity in the Modern World* (Seattle: University of Washington Press, 1990); Jacob Neusner, *Judaism in the Secular Age: Essays on Fellowship, Community and Freedom* (London: Valentine, Mitchell, 1970); Jonathan S. Woocher, *Sacred Survival: The Civil Religion of American Jews* (Bloomington and Indianapolis: Indiana University Press, 1986).

Peres, Shimon (b. 1923) *prime minister of Israel*
Shimon Peres has been a key public servant of the State of ISRAEL since its early days; he became its eighth prime minister in 1984.

Born in Wolozyn, POLAND in 1923, he immigrated to PALESTINE with his family at the age of 11. He grew up in TEL AVIV and studied at the Ben Shemen Agricultural School at Ben Shemen. Peres spent several years living on kibbutzim (see

KIBBUTZ), and he was one of the founders of Kibbutz Alumot. He was involved in a ZIONIST YOUTH MOVEMENT, and, as was the case with many early Zionist leaders, Peres became one of the founders of the LABOR PARTY. He has helped steer the party toward his position of support for the peace process with Israel's Arab neighbors and Palestinians. Peres was active in creating peace with the Palestinians, Jordan, and Lebanon.

Shimon Peres was closely associated with the development of Israel's defense capabilities. In the late 1940s he joined the HAGANAH and was assigned responsibility for recruitment and weapons. During and after the ISRAELI WAR OF INDEPENDENCE, he served as head of naval services, and he later headed the defense ministry's delegation to the UNITED STATES. Peres is also known for founding Israel's defense industries.

In 1959 Peres was elected to the KNESSET and has been a member ever since. He has served in numerous ministerial positions, most notably as minister of defense and foreign minister. Peres first briefly served as acting prime minister following the resignation of Prime Minister Yitzchak RABIN in 1977.

Peres later served as prime minister in his own right, in two nonconsecutive terms. His first tenure was from 1984 to 1986 in the National Unity government. While working with Yitzchak Rabin in the mid-1990s, Peres received the Nobel Peace Prize when Arafat, Rabin, and Peres signed the Oslo Accords, agreeing on a peace plan for Israel and the Palestinians. His second term began in the wake of the assassination of Yitzhak Rabin on November 4, 1995. At that time he served for seven months, until the general elections of May 1996. During this trying period, Peres strove to maintain the momentum in the peace process, despite a wave of terrorist attacks by Palestinian suicide bombers against Israeli civilians.

In 1996, Peres founded the Peres Center for Peace, continuing his commitment to finding peace for the Middle East. Despite his advanced years, Peres remained an important player in the

Labor Party and in Israeli political life in the early 21st century. He is the author of articles, essays, and books, such as *David's Sling* (1970); *Entebbe Diary* (1991), and *The New Middle East* (1993).

Further reading: Bill Clinton, "Partners in Peace," *Presidents and Prime Ministers* 5, no. 1 (January–February 1996): 11; Adam Garfinkle, *Politics and Society in Modern Israel* (Armonk, N.Y.: M. E. Sharpe, 2000); Matti Golan, *Shimon Peres: A Biography* (New York: St. Martin's Press, 1982); Shimon Peres and Robert Littell, *For the Future of Israel* (Baltimore, Md.: Johns Hopkins University Press, 1998).

Perlman, Yitzhak (b. 1945) *master violinist*

Born in TEL AVIV, ISRAEL, Yitzhak Perlman was crippled by polio at the age of four. He began playing the violin shortly after that and gave his first public performance at the age of nine. Studying at the Shulamit High School in Tel Aviv, he completed his initial training at the Academy of Music in Tel Aviv. He came to New York in the 1950s and studied violin at the Juilliard School under Ivan Galamian and Dorothy DeLay Galamian. He soon was propelled into the international arena with an appearance on *The Ed Sullivan Show* in 1958.

Perlman debuted professionally at Carnegie Hall and won the prestigious Leventritt Competition prize in 1964. This led to a burgeoning worldwide career. Since then, Perlman has appeared with every major orchestra and in recitals and festivals throughout the world. He has been honored with four Emmy Awards. Perlman's recordings regularly appear on the best-seller charts and have won 15 Grammy Awards. He toured Israel in 1965 and created a master class in violin at the Meadowbrook Festival in 1970.

Recently Perlman has also appeared on the conductor's podium and through this medium he is further delighting his audiences. On television, he has entertained and enlightened millions of viewers of all ages. Numerous publications and institutions have paid tribute to him for the unique place he occupies in the artistic and humanitarian fabric of our times. Perlman has become one of the most sought-after violin soloists. He has performed and recorded classical, modern, and folk music, and he is one of the best-known musicians around the world.

One of Perlman's proudest achievements was his collaboration with film score composer John Williams in Steven SPIELBERG's Academy Award–winning film *Schindler's List,* for which he performed the violin solos. His presence on stage, on camera, and in personal appearances of all kinds speaks eloquently on behalf of the disabled. Perlman's devotion to their cause is an integral part of his life.

Further reading: Perlman recordings: *Concertos from My Childhood* (Angel, 1999); *Holiday Tradition* (Angel, 1998); *In the Fiddler's House* (Angel, 1995); *Tradition: Popular Jewish Melodies* (Angel Recordings, 1987); Bernard D. Sherman, *Inside Early Music: Conversations with Performers* (New York: Oxford University Press, 1997).

Persia

The beginnings of the Jewish community in Persia are shrouded in ancient history. Tradition ascribes its origins to the forced deportations from the kingdom of ISRAEL by one of its conquerors, either Tiglath-pileser III (d. 727 B.C.E.), Sargon II (d. 705 B.C.E.), or Sennacherib (d. 681 B.C.E.). At the latest, it dates from Nebuchadnezzar's destruction of the TEMPLE in JERUSALEM in 586 B.C.E. and the exile of Jews from Judea (*see* JUDEA AND SAMARIA) to Mesopotamia. In 538 B.C.E. CYRUS the Great founded the Persian Empire, inaugurating several centuries of peace and tolerance toward the Jewish community in Persia and Judea. Jewish historical memory looks favorably on this period, as evidenced by the biblical books of EZRA and NEHEMIAH. This was also the only time that Israel and the entire DIASPORA were under one ruler. The links that were forged between the various Jewish centers remained strong for millennia.

It is certain that at least from the fourth century B.C.E. Jews lived in considerable numbers in Persia itself. Scholars have determined that under the Parthian Empire, which lasted from 249 B.C.E. to 226, the Jewish community continued to grow, was well-organized, and enjoyed considerable autonomy. The Persian Jewish community is mentioned by PHILO JUDAEUS OF ALEXANDRIA and by JOSEPHUS. The Book of Tobit from the APOCRYPHA, dating from approximately 200 B.C.E., illustrates the family life, faith, and popular religion of Persian Jewry at the time. Although scholars have no proof that the events of the book of ESTHER actually took place, it is considered plausible that the story of Esther, Mordecai, and Haman might have occurred in Persia sometime in the second century B.C.E.

Persia regained its independence in 226 C.E. under the Sassanid Dynasty (226–642 C.E.). The Jewish population grew and spread throughout the region. Communities existed in cities such as Nehardea, Hamadan (Ecbatana), Susa, and Shiraz. There was also a sizable Jewish immigration from the Roman Empire (*see* ROME). As in BABYLONIA, political authority within the Jewish community was vested in the EXILARCH, whose office can be definitively traced to the second century C.E. He was appointed by the king and held an honored place in the king's council. Religious authority, on the other hand, lay with the famous rabbinic academies in SURA and PUMBEDITA in neighboring Babylonia that were beginning to flourish at the time.

Nevertheless, Jews suffered intermittent oppression and persecution under the Zoroastrian Sassanids. Yezdegerd II (438–57 C.E.) tried to suppress Jewish observance. Even more severe persecution followed in 468 under Firuz (459–86 C.E.). Under Kavdah I (485–531 C.E.) the oppression reached such a point that the Jews, led by the Exilarch Mar Zutra II, revolted and succeeded in establishing an independent state that lasted seven years. It was eventually suppressed and Mar Zutra was crucified in 520 C.E.

In 642 Muslim Arabs conquered Persia and made it part of the Eastern Caliphate, with its seat in Baghdad. Though the Jews were designated as *dhimmis* (see MUSLIM-JEWISH RELATIONS) and relegated to second-class citizenship, they generally experienced a more tolerant atmosphere than they had under the Sassanids. The community continued to be organized around the Exilarch and the GEONIM, the heads of the rabbinic academies.

During this time Persian Jewry became a cradle of sectarian movements and a birthplace of false messiahs. This paralleled the religious and social development in Persian Muslim society. One of the first sectarian movements about which we have some basic information revolved around the figure of Abu Isa (d. 705), a tailor who proclaimed himself to be a messiah. He acknowledged Jesus and Mohammed as prophets and ordered changes in the Jewish calendar, ritual and prayer. Abu Isa had a considerable following, especially among the Jews of Isfahan and, though he was executed by the Muslim authorities, his adherents continued to revere him, possibly into the 10th century. Another false messiah, from the ninth century, is remembered only through the refutation of his claims by SAADIA GAON.

False messiahs continued to appear in Persia over the centuries, most notably David Alroy in the 12th century. The most important, far-reaching, and lasting sectarian movement to appear in Persia was Karaism (see KARAITES), which originated sometime in the eighth century and is still practiced today. Its most distinguished founders and leaders hailed from Persia and it spread quickly throughout its provinces.

Mongol rule (13th–15th centuries) brought a general improvement in the status of the Persian Jews. All religions were put on equal footing and the dhimmi status of non-Muslims was abolished. Jews participated in the affairs of the state, some rising to the highest levels of government. This was also the time when Judeo-Persian literature flourished and reached its peak.

In 1502 the Safavid dynasty restored Persian independence. The Safavids, who adhered to the Shi'ite branch of ISLAM, were known for their intolerance. Their rule marked the low point for the Jews of Persia, who suffered worse treatment than their fellow Jews in any other Muslim land. There was some relief under Shah Abbas I (d. 1629) but widespread persecution resumed under his successors. The second half of the 17th century saw forced conversions and imprisonment of those who refused to convert. Under Nadir Shah (1736–47), a Jewish community was allowed to settle in the new capital of Meshed. However, upon his death oppression and persecution were renewed.

Jews were forced to wear a special badge and headgear, and their oaths were not accepted in the courts. A Jew who converted to Islam was entitled to take his or her family's entire inheritance, at the expense of any Jewish heirs. Forcible conversions of individuals and whole communities occurred in many provinces. The trend peaked in 1838 when the entire Jewish community of Meshed was forcibly converted to Islam. Like their counterparts in PORTUGAL (see CONVERSOS), many of these converts and their descendants retained a secret allegiance to Judaism into the 20th century, when they were finally allowed to return to Judaism. Despite all this persecution, and the isolation of Persian Jews from Jewish communities outside of Persia, they managed to keep up a fairly vigorous intellectual and cultural life.

Reports of the sad fate of the Persian Jews, exacerbated by a famine in 1871, reached the West through European Christian missionaries. Moses MONTEFIORE and Adolphe Cremieux of the ALLIANCE ISRAELITE UNIVERSELLE were among the Jewish community leaders who tried unsuccessfully to intervene on their behalf. In 1873 when Nasr-ed-Din Shah traveled through Europe, Jewish representatives in each city through which he passed presented him with appeals. Though he pledged to alleviate the situation, upon his return to Persia he did not keep his promises. Conditions did improve temporarily under his successor, thanks to a constitutional movement. However, the movement was short-lived and its reforms were reversed in 1909. During World War I, American Jewry became involved in attempts to alleviate the plight of Persian Jews.

In the face of this unrelenting discrimination and persecution, many Persian Jews made their way to PALESTINE in the course of the 19th century. When modern ZIONISM was founded toward the end of the century it spread quickly in Persia.

The Pahlavi Dynasty, established in 1925, broke the power of the Shi'ite clergy and embarked on policies of secularization and westernization. With these changes, Jews finally achieved EMANCIPATION and began to participate fully in the economic and cultural life of the country. In 1935 the empire of Persia came to be known as the nation of IRAN.

Further reading: S. D. Goitein, *Jews and Arabs: Their Contacts through the Ages* (New York: Schocken Books, 1974); Bernard Lewis, *The Jews of Islam* (Princeton, N.J.: Princeton University Press, 1984); Michael Shterenshis, *Tamerlane and the Jews* (London and New York: Routledge/Curzon, 2002); Norman A. Stillman, *The Jews of Arab Lands: A History and Source Book* (Philadelphia: Jewish Publication Society of America, 1979).

pharaoh

In biblical times, the pharaoh was the ruler of EGYPT. According to the book of Genesis in the TANAKH, the Hebrew Bible, JOSEPH, whose brothers sold him into SLAVERY in Egypt, eventually becomes top adviser to the ruling pharaoh, who gratefully treats the ISRAELITES well. The book of EXODUS records that a later pharaoh, concerned that the numerous Israelites might pose a danger to the Egyptians, enslaves them and orders all their newborn males to be killed. One such baby, MOSES, is spared by Pharaoh's daughter and raised in Pharaoh's household.

As a young man Moses kills an Egyptian who was beating an Israelite and has to flee the country. In exile, he is told by God to return and demand that the pharaoh free the Israelites. Through Moses and his brother AARON, God sends TEN PLAGUES upon the Egyptians; only after the 10th plague—

the death of the first-born—does Pharaoh finally relent. Even then, he sends his armies to pursue the fleeing Israelites, but his troops are drowned in the Sea of Reeds.

Pharaoh's stubbornness has posed a problem for Jewish theology. Exodus explicitly states that God hardened Pharaoh's heart. In other words, God caused Pharaoh to stubbornly refuse to free the Jews, in order to prove to the Egyptians just how powerful the God of Israel was. Traditionally, Jews have responded to this demonstration of power with increased faith and trust in God as their protector. Many commentators, on the other hand, have said that God's actions present moral issues requiring analysis and new interpretations.

Further reading: Louis Ginzberg, *Legends of the Bible* (Philadelphia: Jewish Publication Society of America, 1956); Moshe Lieber, ed., *The Pesach Haggadah Anthology: The Living Exodus: with Commentary and Anecdotes from Talmudic and Rabbinical Literature* (Brooklyn, N.Y.: Mesorah, 1997); *Tanakh: The New JPS Translation According to the Traditional Hebrew Text* (Philadelphia, New York, Jerusalem: Jewish Publication Society, 1985).

Pharisees

The Pharisees, whose reputation has suffered over the centuries due to a few unfavorable references in the Christian NEW TESTAMENT, were historically the faction of Jewish leaders and scholars who stood for the interests and beliefs of the Jewish masses, and stressed the ethical and compassionate elements of Jewish law. Some historians believe that the teachings of JESUS OF NAZARETH as recorded in the Gospels show him to have been a Pharisee himself, and that the anti-Pharisee references are later additions.

The Pharisees were one of the three mainstream factions of Judaism in PALESTINE in the late second TEMPLE period (150 B.C.E.–70 C.E.). The other two were the SADDUCEES, who represented the priestly caste and the aristocracy, and the ESSENES, an ascetic sect that separated itself from the rest of the community.

The Hebrew word for Pharisees, *perushim,* literally means "separate." The name probably refers to their strict separation of pure from impure foods, and their practice of separating themselves from the table of those who did not make such distinctions. They began as one of many small factions, but eventually drew wide support.

Most scholars identify the Pharisees as the forerunners of rabbinic Judaism (*see* RABBI, RABBINIC LAW). Rabbinic literature identifies them as the group of sages and rabbis who began to pull together the sacred Jewish written and oral laws after the destruction of the second Temple. They are described as coming from the middle and lower classes, less Hellenized in their culture (*see* HELLENISM), and more devoted to their people's ancient culture. They accepted as valid all the nonbiblical laws and customs passed down orally through the generations and practiced by the ordinary masses of Jews.

According to the Roman-Jewish first-century C.E. historian JOSEPHUS, the Pharisees taught the dogma that souls were immortal and would live on after death, and that one's deeds would bring reward and punishment in the afterlife. These teachings contradicted the teachings of the Sadducees, who believed that the present life was the only life.

Many modern RABBIS find value in historian Louis FINKELSTEIN's theory, which stresses socioeconomic reasons for the eventual victory of the Pharisees over the Sadducees in their struggle for control over the Jewish community. These rabbis stress that the Pharisees, seen as the founders of rabbinic Judaism, taught that all Jews must be mindful of the interests of the common people.

The New Testament depicts the Pharisees as concerned only with rituals at the expense of the spirit of the law. Judaism rejects this notion of the Pharisees, and firmly teaches that the Pharisees were concerned with the full yoke of God's commandments (*see* MITZVAH), in the spiritual, ritual, and ethical realms.

Further reading: Louis Finkelstein, *Akiba: Scholar, Saint and Martyr* (Northvale, N.J.: Jason Aronson Press,

1990); Lawrence H. Schiffman, *From Text to Tradition: A History of Second Temple and Rabbinic Judaism* (Hoboken, N.J.: Ktav Publishing House, 1991); Julius Wellhausen, *The Pharisees and the Sadducees: An Examination of Internal Jewish History* (Macon, Ga.: Mercer University Press, 2001).

Philo Judaeus of Alexandria

(20 B.C.E.–50 C.E.) *Jewish Hellenistic philosopher*

A Platonist philosopher from Alexandria, PHILO is considered the most influential Jewish thinker of his day. Scholars have no information on Philo's ancestry, but they do know that he was born to a wealthy and prominent family in Alexandria and served as a community leader, particularly during the reign of Roman emperor Gaius Caligula.

Philo received an excellent education in Greek philosophy and literature (*see* HELLENISM). He studied many schools of thought, including the Platonists, Aristotelians, Neo-Pythagoreans, Cynics, and Stoics. He was a multifaceted man with interests in every topic and arena that presented itself in Alexandria's vast collection of books and vibrant daily life. He studied mathematics, science, metaphysics, and philosophy, while busying himself with socializing, banquets, theater, and athletics, including boxing and chariot racing.

As a result, Philo's legacy mixes Alexandrian culture with high-level intellectual analysis of the events, history, and philosophy of his time. He wrote extensively on many subjects, with the overall aim of synthesizing Greek philosophy with the revealed religion of his people, the Jews.

Philo's works are traditionally divided into studies of biblical texts, philosophical treatises, and historical-apologetic writings. Among the apologetic writings is a defense of the Jews' refusal to accept the emperor Gaius as a deity; he reminded the Roman authorities that the Jews were particularly good citizens, who brought profit to the empire.

Scholars differ as to whether Philo's works were more Jewish or Greek. There is no doubt that he was well-schooled in Greek philosophy, but he also knew TORAH well, although some claim that he showed little if any knowledge of the ORAL LAW. Much of Philo's writings, however, can be seen as his own kind of MIDRASH or interpretation of the TANAKH, the Hebrew Bible. There is no doubt that he himself identified as a Jew, as he spent a considerable amount of time writing apologetics and even visiting Gaius Caligula to defend his community. Yet he was also rooted in the cosmopolitan culture of Alexandria itself, not unlike many modern American Jews who are both American and Jewish simultaneously. Philo is best known for a series of volumes about the history, commandments, and ethics of Judaism; yet his concept of the *logos*, the word, is thought to have influenced the NEW TESTAMENT authors Paul and John.

Further reading: Erwin R. Goodenough, *An Introduction to Philo Judus* (New Haven, Conn.: Yale University Press, 1940); Matthew J. Martin, "Philo's Interest in the Synagogue" in *Ancient Near Eastern Studies* 37 (2000): 215–223; Philo, *On the Creation of the Cosmos According to Moses,* trans. David T. Runia (Leiden: E. J. Brill, 2001); David T. Runia, *Philo of Alexandria: An Annotated Bibliography, 1987–1996,* in collaboration with the International Philo Project (Leiden: E. J. Brill, 2000); Matthew B. Schwartz, "Greek and Jew: Philo and the Alexandrian Riots of 38–41 C.E.," in *Judaism* 49, no. 2 (Spring 2000): 206–216.

philosophy

Philosophy is an intellectual discipline that includes logic, ethics, aesthetics, metaphysics, and epistemology. In other words, it investigates the nature of reality, the ways in which one can obtain accurate knowledge, while it also explains, compares, and creates systems of values.

Philosophy and Judaism have at times been intertwined. The TANAKH, the Hebrew Bible, has been interpreted to provide answers to philosophical questions. Conversely, a number of Jewish thinkers have used insights from philosophy to better understand the God of ISRAEL, reality, and the best way to live one's life. Such philosophers drew upon Jewish thought but were also influenced by Greek and Arabic philosophy. In particular, Jewish philosophers have drawn upon Plato, Aristotle, medieval Muslim philosophers, and Enlightenment European philosophers.

Perhaps the best-known Jewish philosopher is Moses MAIMONIDES (1135–1204), who composed the 13 articles of Jewish faith. Maimonides wrote treatises on God, knowledge, ethics, and Jewish law; he proclaimed the unlimited nature of God, and celebrated intelligence—especially spiritual intelligence or knowledge of God—as the highest virtue. Like the Muslim and Christian philosophers of his time, Maimonides held that one could not describe God with words; any attributes you could list would only make God appear limited, more human and less transcendent. One can only say *that* God is, not *what* God is.

Jewish philosophers have continued to contribute to the field. Some of the most prominent have been Baruch SPINOZA (1632–77), Moses MENDELSSOHN (1729–86), Martin BUBER (1878–1965), Abraham Joshua HESCHEL (1907–72), and Emmanuel Levinas (1906–95). Spinoza's fame derives from his inquiries into the nature of God, the Bible, and ethics. He was excommunicated by the Jewish community of Amsterdam for describing God as the mechanism of nature and the universe—a belief amounting to pantheism—and for claiming that the Bible was a metaphorical and allegorical work about God rather than the literal truth. Mendelssohn, although he created proofs of the immortal soul and the existence of a personal God, became better known for his social and political philosophy. Bucking the popular views of the time, Mendelssohn argued that one could be both Jewish and modern, while he also argued for the separation of church and state, freedom of religion, and the granting of full civil rights to Jews. Buber connected Jewish mysticism with philosophy by developing an ethic of what he called the I-Thou relationship, in which one has in a true dialogue and opens up completely to God. Similarly, Heschel combined mysticism and ethics with a love of the prophets to develop insights into the nature of religious experience and to become an activist in pursuit of social justice. Levinas also focused on ethics, combining Jewish and continental philosophy of infinite responsibility to the "other," a responsibility that precedes our very being.

Further reading: Dan Cohn-Sherbok, *Medieval Jewish Philosophy: An Introduction* (Richmond, Surrey: Curzon, 1996); Emil Fackenheim, *Jewish Philosophers and Jewish Philosophy* ed. Michael L. Morgan (Bloomington: Indiana University Press, 1996); Daniel H. Frank, Oliver Leaman, and Charles H. Manekin, eds., *The Jewish Philosophy Reader* (New York: Routledge, 2000); Ronald Isaacs, *Every Person's Guide to Jewish Philosophy and Philosophers* (Northvale, N.J.: Aronson, 1999); Moses Maimonides, *The Guide for the Perplexed,* ed. Julius Guttmann (Indianapolis: Hackett Publishing, 1995); Naomi Pasachoff, *Jewish History in 100 Nutshells* (Northvale, N.J.: Aronson, 1995).

pidyon ha-ben

Pidyon ha-ben is a traditional Jewish ceremony in which a first-born son is "redeemed" by his parents from a *kohen,* or priest (*see* KOHANIM). The fundamental purpose of *pidyon ha-ben* is to recognize God's role in the child's life and to make a commitment to raise the child in the Jewish faith.

The tradition has its roots in the Hebrew Bible (*see* TORAH). When the first-born sons of the Egyptians were killed in the last of the TEN PLAGUES, the first-born of the ISRAELITES were spared. God commands the Israelites that they must "redeem every first-born male among your children," when they dwell in the land of Yisrael as a reminder of God's mercy upon them in Egypt (Ex 13:13).

Numbers 18:16 fixes the ceremony on the 31st day of the boy's life, and sets a redemption payment of five shekels, to be consigned to the Temple's *kohanim.* Because this was perceived as a potential financial burden, the RABBIS interpreted the requirement with leniency. Only the first child conceived and born could be considered a first-

born male. If the mother had earlier had a miscarriage or given birth to a daughter, then the first-born male category did not apply. Also, if a mother gave birth through caesarean section, *pidyon ha-ben* was not required.

A common custom that developed in the medieval period was to place the five silver coins on a silver tray, whose manufacture and design became a Jewish art form. Often a community would collectively own the silver tray used by all local Jewish families when a *pidyon ha-ben* was required. The custom was to place the baby on the silver tray, then replace him with the coins.

Today, some liberal Jews, in a bow to EGALITARIANISM, practice a *pidyon ha-bat,* whereby they symbolically redeem a first-born daughter. Other liberal Jews will observe the *pidyon ha-ben* even with a caesarean birth or after a previous miscarriage, as the five silver dollars are no longer considered a financial hardship. They find meaning in the symbolic value of being first-born. Unlike the BRIT MILAH, or ritual circumcision, the *pidyon ha-ben* is postponed for SHABBAT (the Sabbath) or a festival.

Many modern Jews use special *pidyon ha-ben* coins produced by the Israeli Mint. They will then buy back the coins from the *kohen* as a keepsake, in exchange for donations to TZEDAKAH, or charity. Some people put sugar on the boy's body, as a prayer for a sweet life; others use garlic, to keep away evil spirits. Others drape the child in their jewelry, as a symbol of preciousness.

Further reading: Anita Diamant, *Living a Jewish Life: Jewish Traditions, Customs and Values for Today's Families* (New York: HarperPerennial, 1996); Hayim Halevy Donin, *To Be a Jew: A Guide to Jewish Observance in Contemporary Life* (New York: Basic Books, 1972); Abraham E. Millgram, *Jewish Worship* (Philadelphia: Jewish Publication Society, 1971).

pilgrimage festivals

With the exception of ROSH HASHANAH and YOM KIPPUR, the most important Jewish holidays are the three pilgrimage festivals of PASSOVER, SHAVUOT, and SUKKOT. When the ancient TEMPLE was still standing any Jew who could was expected to make a pilgrimage to JERUSALEM to make a sacrifice for each of these holidays. In cases of economic hardship, the RABBIS allowed each community to send an appointed delegate to Jerusalem, carrying with him the money for sacrifices raised by the community. A special liturgy was recited in Jerusalem by the Jews who made the pilgrimage.

The pilgrimage festivals are prescribed in the TANAKH or Hebrew Bible. They combine elements of agricultural harvest festivals with commemorations of Jewish historical events. Deuteronomy 16:16 commands the ISRAELITES: "Three times a year shall all your men appear before the Lord your God in the place that God will choose; on the festivals of Passover, Shavuot, and Sukkot. They shall not appear empty handed. Each shall bring his own gift, appropriate to the blessing which the Lord your God has given you." The Bible only commanded men, as women were not treated as religious equals.

Passover, or Pesach, in HEBREW, celebrates the beginning of the new planting season after the winter rains in ISRAEL. It also commemorates the EXODUS of the Israelites from EGYPT. The Tanakh mentions Shavuot only as an agricultural celebration; it falls exactly seven weeks after Passover, thus placing it at the time of the late spring harvest. The rabbis added a historical aspect: Shavuot was a commemoration of the Israelites receiving the TORAH at MOUNT SINAI, exactly seven weeks after their Exodus from Egypt. Sukkot commemorates the 40 years that the Israelites spent in the wilderness after receiving the Torah, when they had to rely on God alone for food and protection. Sukkot also represents the last harvest festival before the onset of the winter rains.

When the second Temple was destroyed by the Romans in 70 C.E. the observance of the pilgrimage festivals had to refocus on local worship, and on rituals such as the Passover SEDER and the *sukkahs* or temporary homes built on Sukkot.

Since there is no longer a Temple, Jews need not make a pilgrimage to Jerusalem. However, Jews throughout the centuries have traveled to Israel during these major festivals, so as to symbolically experience the pilgrimage. The pilgrimage festivals have become peak tourist seasons in the modern State of Israel, when religious Jews flood Jerusalem's hotels and synagogues and flock to the KOTEL, the Western Wall.

Further reading: Irving Greenberg, *The Jewish Way: Living the Holidays* (New York: Simon & Schuster, 1993); Michael Strassfeld, *Jewish Holidays: A Guide and Commentary* (New York: Harper & Row, 1985).

Pinsker, Yehudah Lev (Leon Pinsker)
(1821–1891) *Zionist thinker*

Yehudan Lev Pinsker's 1882 book entitled *Auto-Emancipation* had a profound impact on eastern European Jews, giving impetus to the development of ZIONISM at the end of the 19th century.

In response to the growing and increasingly violent ANTISEMITISM of his era, Pinsker proposed that the Jewish people, who were living dispersed throughout the world, should free themselves from their plight by creating, supporting, and living in their own territorial homeland. On a more theoretical level, Pinsker argued that Jews needed to stop depending on external forces to protect them and better their situation, and begin to look at how they as a people could influence their own future. They needed most of all to abandon their traditional mindset of helplessness and homelessness.

Pinsker provided a "territorial solution" to the problem of antisemitism and the Jews' lack of a homeland. He felt that nationhood would restore the Jewish people's dignity, which had been lost before the 19th century.

Pinsker's hoped-for audience, the western European Jews who might be able to fund his ideas, paid little attention to him. However, the eastern European Jewish movement called Hovevei Zion (*see* HIBBAT ZION) that arose around 1883 explicitly adopted his idea that the regeneration of the Jewish people in the modern world could occur only through mass evacuation of Europe and resettlement in a territorial Jewish homeland.

Further reading: Arthur Hertzberg, *The Zionist Idea: A Historical Analysis and Reader* (New York: Atheneum Publishers, 1959); Ehud Luz, *Parallels Meet: Religion and Nationalism in the Early Zionist Movement (1882–1904)* (Philadelphia, New York, and Jerusalem: Jewish Publication Society, 1988); David Vital, *The Origins of Zionism* (Oxford: Clarendon Press, 1975.

Pittsburgh Platform

The Pittsburgh Platform of 1885 was a document drawn up by American Reform RABBIS that sharply defined REFORM JUDAISM in contrast to all other Jewish points of view. The platform came to be known as the definition of classical Reform Judaism in the UNITED STATES.

All rabbis in the United States who were interested in reform, progress, and united action for American Judaism were invited to attend a conference in Pittsburgh, Pennsylvania, on November 16–19, 1885. The organizers felt the need to define Reform Judaism in a positive manner, explaining what it was, instead of the prior approach of defining Reform by what it was not, TRADITIONAL JUDAISM. In the final document drafted at the conference, the rabbis detailed all their positions regarding Jewish traditions and rituals. It was a radical alteration of Jewish beliefs and practices with the goal of conforming to the modern world. Rabbi Isaac Mayer WISE presided at the assembly.

The Pittsburgh Platform recognized the godliness of humanity and the divine weight of morality. They described the Hebrew Bible (*see* TANAKH) as inspiring for its religious and moral instruction, but declared that it reflected the primitive ideas of its own age. They accepted the binding nature of its moral and ethical laws, but rejected any ritual that did not in their view embrace the ideas of modern civilization.

The platform explicitly rejected the Jewish dietary laws (*see* KASHRUT). It rejected the traditional Jewish desire to return to PALESTINE, and discarded the idea of restoring a sovereign Jewish state. The assembly saw CHRISTIANITY and ISLAM as the religious children of Judaism, sharing in its mission to teach moral truth. It also called for complete social justice for all of humanity.

Over the decades, many of the principles outlined in the Pittsburgh Platform of 1885 have been revised in line with more traditional perspectives. In 1999, the Reform movement issued a new Pittsburgh Platform. Rabbi Richard Levy, a leader of the more traditionally-minded wing of Reform Judaism, outlined a platform that called for the observance of kashrut and MIKVAH, the Jewish ritual bath. Levy's recommendations were not developed in full to placate those who still adhered to classic Reform and remained largely antiritual in ideology and theology.

The new Pittsburgh Platform suggests that Reform Jews study HEBREW and TORAH, observe SHABBAT, and recognize the importance of mitzvot (*see* MITZVAH), the sacred obligations laid down in the Torah or by the rabbis. The Reform traditionalists believed the new platform was a move back to a greater embrace of Jewish tradition. The classicists saw it as a renewed legitimization of any and all Reform Jewish practices, highlighting unity in the face of change.

The New Pittsburgh Platform of 1999 laid down a set of principles, yet acknowledged the diversity of Reform Jewish beliefs and practices. It invited Reform Jews to engage in a serious dialogue with the sources of Jewish tradition, and use their knowledge to choose rituals that would help them obtain holiness. It also took a strong stance in support of ZIONISM and the Jewish state, a concept that had been completely rejected by the original Pittsburgh Platform of 1885.

Further reading: Walter Jacob, ed., *The Pittsburgh Platform in Retrospect: The Changing World of Reform Judaism* (Pittsburgh: Rodef Shalom Congregation Press, 1985); Dana Evan Kaplan, *Contemporary Debates in American Reform Judaism: Conflicting Visions* (New York: Routledge, 2000); Michael A. Meyer, *Response to*

Modernity: A History of the Reform Movement in Judaism (New York and Oxford: Oxford University Press, 1988).

pluralism

In the religious context, pluralism is a situation in which multiple religious communities coexist within a single city or society. The term is generally used when these religious communities coexist peacefully, respecting one another's views while each maintaining its own distinctive beliefs and practices.

Diana Eck at Harvard University has attracted wide attention recently for her work on pluralism, which she distinguishes from exclusivism and inclusivism. According to Eck, exclusivism teaches that only one religious tradition is true or valid. Inclusivism teaches that all religions are valid, but does not allow for distinctive commitments to a single tradition. Pluralism maintains a balance between respect for other traditions while participating actively within one's own community. Eck refers to pluralism as a "symphony of difference," in which distinctive views and voices are the building blocks of a rich society.

Jewish thought does not oppose the idea of pluralism, as much Jewish theology sees the responsibilities of the Jew as different from those of the non-Jew. The Jew must observe 613 commandments (*see* MITZVAH), while the non-Jew is responsible for the seven Noahide laws found in Genesis (*see* NOAH). Thus, Judaism sees the paths to God of Jewish and non-Jewish individuals differently, but most Jewish thought does not deny non-Jews access to God. The Pluralism Project, which was established by Eck at Harvard University, supports the study of pluralism in metropolitan areas of the United States, with particular attention to Asian and South Asian immigrant communities.

Further reading: Diana L. Eck, *Encountering God: From Bozeman to Banares* (New York: Beacon Press, 1995); ———, *A New Religious America* (San Francisco: HarperSanFrancisco, 2001); ———, "A New Religious America: Managing Religious Diversity in a Democracy: Challenges and Prospects for the 21st Century," keynote address at MAAS International Conference on Religious Pluralism in Democratic Societies, Kuala Lumpur, Malaysia, August 20–21, 2002, at URL www.usembassymalaysia.org.my/eck.html; Paul Morris, "Judaism and Pluralism," in *Religious Pluralism and Unbelief* (London: Routledge, 1990), 179–201.

pogrom

The term *pogrom* is derived from the Russian word meaning "to wreak havoc." It was used to describe an organized attack or massacre, often with government support, against any non-Russian ethnic group. By extension, it has come to mean any organized violent attack against an ethnic minority at any time or place, especially against Jews.

The term was most often used in connection with the anti-Jewish pogroms in RUSSIA of the period 1881 to 1921. There were three waves of such attacks, in 1881–84, 1903–06, and 1917–21. These attacks resulted in increasingly major destruction of property, theft, rape, and murder.

Violence against Jews had been a frequent occurrence in czarist Russia. Often pogroms occurred during times of national and social upheaval, creating widespread anxiety and uncertainty. The violence was often government-sanctioned.

Most Russian Jews were forced to live in urban communities within the PALE OF SETTLEMENT, subject to many unfavorable decrees by the czars, and easily targeted for attacks. In 1881, when Czar Alexander II was assassinated, a rumor began that Jews had been behind the crime. Pogroms broke out in more than 30 towns in the Ukraine, the most serious in Kiev. Later in the year, on Christmas Day, the Jews of Warsaw (which was within Russia) were attacked. On Easter Sunday the next year Jews were attacked in Balta. The year 1883 brought more pogroms. From 1900 to 1906 there were hundreds of pogroms. In 1903 in Kishinev 45 Jews were killed and hundreds injured. In 1905 in Odessa some 300 were murdered and thousands wounded. The pogroms that followed the Russian Revolution of 1917 were the most severe. Jews were harassed, attacked, and murdered by peasants and soldiers from both the Red Army and the White Army. Between 1917 and 1921 the death toll reached 60,000 lives. The Jews of eastern Europe had suffered through approximately 1,200 pogroms.

As the Russian pogroms continued, thousands of Jews fled Russia for the UNITED STATES. In immigrant studies, violence such as pogroms are considered "push" factors for immigration, and the Russian pogroms certainly "pushed" many Jews to seek lives elsewhere. From 1880 to 1925, the American Jewish population grew from approximately 300,000 to 4.5 million. In addition, many eastern European Jews began to look toward PALESTINE as a refuge against the continued pogroms.

Further reading: Paul R. Brass, *Riots and Pogroms* (New York: New York University Press, 1996); S. M. Dubnow, *History of the Jews in Russia and Poland: From the Earliest Times until the Present Day,* 3 vols. (Philadelphia: Jewish Publication Society, 1916); John Doyle Klier and Shlomo Lambroza, eds., *Pogroms: Anti-Jewish Violence in Modern Russian History* (Cambridge and New York: Cambridge University Press, 2004).

Poland

According to some legends, Jews have lived in Poland since the ninth century, but little is known about the earliest Jewish settlers, either their numbers or where they came from.

History and archaeology show no definite evidence of Jewish communities before the middle of the 12th century. This evidence indicates that the early immigrants came from Bohemia, GERMANY, AUSTRIA, the Crimea, and possibly Italy, at the invitation of the Polish rulers. The Tatar invasions of the middle of the 13th century had devastated the country; to restore the economy, the rulers encouraged immigration from the more developed West, mainly Germany. Among the immigrants who were welcomed were Jews. Even more Jewish immigrants reached Poland during the 15th cen-

tury, a time of frequent persecution and expulsions from many cities and regions in Germany, Austria, and Bohemia.

The first extant charter of protection, or privilege, dates from 1264 and was granted to the Jewish community by Bolesław the Pious (1221–79), grand duke of Poland. King Casimir the Great (1310–70) reconfirmed the charter in 1334 and later extended it to vast territories he acquired in Belorussia. In 1388, when Lithuania was joined to Poland, Władysław II Jagiełło (1351–1434) reconfirmed and extended the charter yet again. These charters regulated the legal conditions of the Jewish community in the Polish lands, their relationship to the king, their economic opportunities and permitted professions, and any judicial suits that might arise between Jews and Christians. The charter also provided safeguards for Jewish life, property, and freedom of trade. These charters were renewed and reconfirmed by successive Polish kings including the last, Stanisław Augustus (1835–1908).

Despite these protections, the second half of the 14th century and the 15th century saw attacks on Jews and their property and expulsions from various towns. The motivation for these attacks varied, including economic competition with non-Jewish burghers, anti-Jewish agitation by itinerant preachers (*see* ANTI-JUDAISM), BLOOD LIBELS, and accusations of spreading the Black Death, charges that occurred elsewhere in Europe as well.

Nevertheless, the overall situation was positive, and the Jewish population grew and spread throughout the Polish lands. Both Polish Jews and those abroad viewed life in Poland as more secure and generally better than life elsewhere in Europe. Jews were taxed at the same rate as non-Jews, unlike in most other countries; they were not confined to GHETTOS; and they enjoyed great economic opportunity from the unusual variety of opportunities open to them, including diverse trades and crafts, managing nobles' estates, owning land, moneylending, and banking. By the 16th century, Polish kings used Jews as their bankers, and Jews occupied key positions in the economic and political life of the country.

By the middle of the 16th century, more than 50 percent of world Jewry lived in the Polish-Lithuanian state. They enjoyed autonomy, with each community governed by a body called the KAHAL. There were regional councils, which in turn were answerable to the Council of the Four Lands. The network of councils oversaw the allocation and collection of taxes, appointed community rabbis, adjudicated disputes between individual Jews and Jewish communities, regulated commerce and interaction with non-Jews, and adopted rulings regarding political, educational, spiritual and charitable matters affecting the Jews of Poland and Lithuania. TORAH study flourished. Yeshivot, or Jewish religious schools (see YESHIVA), were established, and questions of Jewish law were no longer sent to Germany or Bohemia, as there were now local scholars of stature (see MAPAH). Poland was acquiring a reputation as a center of Jewish learning in its own right.

Though anti-Jewish attacks and incidents did occur in various cities throughout the 16th and 17th centuries, the single most traumatic episode in the life of Polish Jewry (which also left its mark on the historical memory of all European Jews) was the CHMIELNICKI MASSACRES that took place in 1648 and 1649. Some 20–25 percent of the total Jewish population of Poland and Lithuania were killed. Of the survivors, many fled westward. Until this time, a steady stream of Jewish immigrants had moved into Poland, but after the Chmielnicki uprisings this trend ceased and even reversed.

As Polish Jewry was still recovering from the devastation of the Chmielnicki Massacres, many of the survivors fell under the sway of the Sabbatean movement. SHABBATAI ZVI (1626–76) proclaimed himself Messiah in 1666 and quickly gained a worldwide following among Jews. He and his followers were excommunicated by rabbis, and when he converted to Islam and later died, most accepted that he was a false messiah. However, secret followers, especially in Poland,

awaited his return for years. Almost 100 years later another false messiah, Jacob Frank, created a smaller but still powerful stir. The 18th century saw the rise of HASIDISM, a Jewish spiritual movement, and later, its opposition, the MITNAGDIM.

With the three successive partitions of Poland in 1772, 1793 and 1795 the Jewish population ended up under Russian (see RUSSIA), Austro-Hungarian (see HUNGARY), or Prussian rule. The severely truncated Polish state was itself under Russian control. Though ANTISEMITISM grew in the 19th century, Jews participated in large numbers in the liberal professions and trade. The HASKALAH, the Jewish ENLIGHTENMENT, and ASSIMILATION were among the new forces influencing the intellectual and cultural life. Jews took part in the Polish revolts against Russia in 1830 and again in 1863 and suffered the consequences of Russian repression. By the end of the century, ZIONISM and socialism (see BUND) predominated, while immigration to Europe, the UNITED STATES, and PALESTINE grew significantly.

Following World War I, Poland regained its independence and some of the territories it lost in the partitions. Lithuania became an independent state. The Treaty of Versailles recognized Polish Jews as a minority whose rights the Polish government pledged to protect—with mixed results. Jews did enjoy a very active political life that included parties from the socialist Bund to the nationalist Zionists to the ultra-Orthodox Agudath Israel (see ORTHODOX JUDAISM). These parties all sponsored schools and a vibrant press and cultural life. Yet as the post–World War I economic situation began to seriously deteriorate, Jews were pushed out of trades, handicrafts, and industry. Emigration continued to grow, with almost 400,000 people leaving during the interwar period. On the eve of the German invasion of Poland on September 1, 1939, there were still more than 3 million Jews in Poland. By the time Germany surrendered to the Allies on May 7, 1945, more than 85 percent had been annihilated in the gas chambers, ghettos, and CONCENTRATION AND DEATH CAMPS (see HOLOCAUST).

Following World War II, those survivors who did not leave Poland for Palestine or the United States tried to rebuild their lives with the help of the AMERICAN JEWISH JOINT DISTRIBUTION COMMITTEE and ORT. However, antisemitism was rampant in postwar Communist Poland, and pogroms prompted a wave of emigration. By 1948, there were only 100,000 Jews left in Poland. This number was further halved in 1958–59 through immigration to Israel. The last mass emigration took place following the SIX-DAY WAR in 1967, when the Polish government broke off diplomatic relations with Israel and closed down all Jewish cultural institutions. Relations between Israel and Poland were not restored until 1990, after the Communist rule in Poland ended. Today there are about 8,000 Jews left in Poland, many of them elderly, living mainly in Warsaw, Kraków, and Lodz. Religious and cultural life has returned with the help of American Jewish foundations and organizations. Among the much larger population of Poles with some Jewish ancestry, there has been a small revival of interest in their heritage.

Further reading: Yisrael Gutman, et al., eds., *The Jews of Poland between Two World Wars* (Hanover, N.H.: Brandeis University Press, 1989); M. J. Rosman, *The Lords' Jews: Magnate-Jewish Relations in the Polish-Lithuanian Commonwealth during the 18th Century* (Cambridge, Mass.: Harvard University Press, 1990); Bernard D. Weinryb, *The Jews of Poland: A Social and Economic History of the Jewish Community in Poland from 1100–1800* (Philadelphia: Jewish Publication Society, 1973).

Pollard, Jonathan Jay (b. 1954) *convicted spy*

Jonathan Jay Pollard is an extremely controversial figure within American Jewry. In November 1985, while serving as a UNITED STATES Navy intelligence analyst, he was arrested by the FBI; he was eventually charged with and convicted of selling classified documents to ISRAEL.

Pollard received a sentence of life imprisonment, and his wife, Anne, received a five-year sentence for aiding him in this act of treason. Pollard,

who was raised in South Bend, Indiana, and attended both Tufts University and Stanford University before taking his post in Washington, D.C., came from a family of Zionists (*see* ZIONISM). During his trial, he claimed that he had contacted an Israeli agent to supply information because he felt that the United States was holding back intelligence that could be vital to Israel's security.

Israel was embarrassed by Pollard's espionage against its strongest ally and apologized to the United States. Israel claimed that his activities had been unauthorized, and that the country followed a firm policy not to spy on the United States. Working with United States intelligence, Israel managed to prove that Pollard had not worked for any of the major Israeli intelligence groups, but rather for a small unit of Israelis who, it said, had chosen to keep the chief Israeli intelligence offices out of the loop.

At his trial Pollard said he had provided Israel with secret documents on Soviet arms shipments to Arab countries, including chemical weapons. He also passed along materials on Libya's air defenses and Pakistan's nuclear bomb program.

Pollard's guilt is unambiguous. His actions shamed many American Jews, who believed this one individual was creating an impression that American Jews had a dual loyalty between the United States and Israel. However, some Jews have asserted that Pollard's life sentence was unfair. He received the most severe sentence of any individual ever convicted of selling secrets to American allies. Some Jewish groups have pointed out that Pollard received a prison sentence more severe than many who spied for the Soviet Union (*see* RUSSIA).

In 1998 Israeli prime minister Benjamin NETANYAHU granted Pollard Israeli citizenship and asked the United States to grant him clemency. Over the years, many Jewish groups have asked for clemency or a presidential pardon for him. President Clinton gave serious thought to providing a pardon, but American intelligence agencies have consistently and strongly opposed such a presidential act. Supporters of Pollard's release have also included Yitzhak RABIN, Ariel SHARON,

Elie WIESEL, Congressman Anthony Weiner, and law professors Alan DERSHOWITZ, Charles Ogletree, and Michael Tigar. In addition, many rabbis and Jewish leaders have asked for Pollard's release, if not a pardon. His release is strongly opposed by many as well, including significant numbers of senior intelligence officers who are Jewish. Senator Joseph LIEBERMAN, the first Jew on a major presidential ticket, has joined a significant number of American Jews with strong pro-Israel views who believe that Pollard's betrayal of America hurt the American-Israeli friendship, and that he does not deserve leniency. Many Jews believe Pollard betrayed America for the money he received from his Israeli contacts.

Further reading: David Biale, "The Case of Jonathan Pollard: Ten Years Later," *Tikkun* 12, no. 3 (May–June 1997): 41; Wolf Blitzer, *Territory of Lies: The Exclusive Story of Jonathan Jay Pollard: The American Who Spied on His Country for Israel and How He Was Betrayed* (New York: Harper & Row, 1989); Mark Shaw, *Miscarriage of Justice: The Jonathan Pollard Story* (St. Paul, Minn.: Paragon House, 2001).

Portugal

Jews may have first arrived in Portugal during the time of the Romans (*see* ROME), who conquered the area in the first century C.E. The first historical records pointing to a Jewish presence date back to the fifth century when the Visigoths ruled the area. More certainly arrived from North Africa with the Moors in the eighth century. When the Christian Reconquista established the Portuguese state in 1139 there were already Jewish communities in Lisbon, Baja, and Santarem.

Little is known of Jewish life in Portugal in the 12th century. As in neighboring Spanish kingdoms, some Jews served as tax collectors for the crown and even reached positions of prominence as royal advisers and physicians. In his law code, Afonso III (r. 1248–79) reorganized the Jewish community with a chief rabbi at its head. Except for one anti-Jewish riot in Lisbon in 1373 (*see*

ANTI-JUDAISM), life was tranquil for Jews in Portugal in the 13th and 14th centuries. The Jewish population numbered about 200,000, or about 20 percent of population, and was active in the economic life of the state. More Jews arrived from SPAIN following the 1391 riots and wave of attacks.

Under the influence of anti-Jewish agitation by itinerant preachers in Portugal that same year, João I (r. 1385–1432) ordered the Jews to wear special clothing and obey a curfew. His successor, Duarte (r. 1433–38) forbade Jews from employing Christian domestics. Many of these restrictions were repealed by Afonso V (r. 1438–81). During this time Jews participated in Portugal's Age of Discovery. Some helped finance voyages; some, like Abraham Zucato and IBN ATAR (1656–1733), contributed to the mathematics and cartography that were essential for navigational science; some even traveled themselves.

When King Ferdinand of Aragon and Queen Isabella of Castile and León expelled all the Jews from their dominions in 1492, many of the exiles were allowed into Portugal upon payment of a poll tax. Even so, many of the refugees were detained and sold into slavery. In 1493, João II (r. 1481–95) ordered the separation of Jewish children from their parents, sending 700 of them to the newly discovered island of São Tomé off the west coast of Africa. He also exiled many other Jews to Cape Verde. In 1496, to secure the hand of the Spanish infanta in marriage, Manoel I (r. 1495–1521) ordered the expulsion of the Jews from Portugal. When they arrived in Lisbon's port to leave, he had them forcibly baptized instead.

This act created a large number of CONVERSOS, or Crypto-Jews. Some of the newly converted embraced their new religion. However, many more, though outwardly acting as Christians, continued to practice Judaism in secret. When they could, they left Portugal for other countries where they returned openly to Judaism. In 1540, to fight the Judaizing of these new Christians, the Inquisition was introduced. Many Conversos were tortured and executed, while many more continued to flee to places like Amsterdam, London, and

New York, where Portuguese synagogues were established. The phenomenon of Conversos survived into the 20th century in remote villages, though the secret Jewish practices had dwindled due to centuries of isolation and attrition.

In the beginning of the 19th century, to improve Portugal's deteriorating economic condition, João VI invited Jews to return. Some, mainly from Gibraltar and North Africa, responded positively. Official recognition of the Jewish community was not granted, however, until 1892. When a synagogue was built in Lisbon, it still could not face the street. Following a revolution in 1910, full freedom of worship was finally established. The Jewish community, nevertheless, remained very small and anti-Jewish feelings continued to prevail in the general populace.

During the HOLOCAUST, the murder of 6 million Jews during World War II, Portugal served as a transit point for Jews fleeing the Nazis. Most of the visas granted to these refugees were given on the condition that their holders not remain in Portugal but continue on their journey. Portuguese diplomat Aristides de Sousa Mendes defied his government's orders and issued hundreds of visas to Jews fleeing FRANCE. His act saved many and he was later recognized at YAD VASHEM, the Holocaust memorial in ISRAEL, as a "Righteous Gentile."

The small Jewish community of Portugal was further decreased in number following the revolution of 1974 and the ensuing unrest. Today there are about 600 Jews living in Portugal, with the largest community in Lisbon, which is served by two synagogues—one for SEPHARDIM and the other for ASHKENAZIM.

Further reading: Yitzhak Baer, *A History of the Jews in Christian Spain* (Philadelphia: Jewish Publication Society, 1992); Eduardo Mayone Dias, *Portugal's Secret Jews* (Rumford, R.I.: Peregrinacao Publications, 1999); David M. Gitlitz, *Secrecy and Deceit: The Religion of the Crypto-Jews* (Philadelphia: Jewish Publication Society, 1996); David Raphael, ed., *The Expulsion 1492 Chronicles: An Anthology of Medieval Chronicles Relating to the Expulsion of the Jews from Spain and Portugal* (North Hollywood, Calif.: Carmi House Press, 1992).

Positive-Historical School

When REFORM JUDAISM was still in its early stages in Germany, one of its leaders, Zachariah FRANKEL (1801–75), decided that the Reformers were too radical in their approach and too quick in applying reforms. Frankel advocated that reform should be introduced gradually and carefully, with an overriding concern for the integrity of Jewish tradition and the unity of Jews. He began to develop what would become a precursor of CONSERVATIVE JUDAISM when, in the year 1843, he first expressed his ideas of a positive and historical approach to Judaism.

The movement that he inspired came to be known as the Positive-Historical School of Judaism. Frankel labeled as "positive" all those elements of Judaism that stood outside history and had to be accepted through faith, such as revelation at Sinai (*see* MOUNT SINAI, TORAH MI-SINAI), Jewish law (*see* HALAKHAH), and TORAH, the Five Books of MOSES. On the historical side, Frankel tried to demonstrate how the interpretation of Torah and Jewish law had developed in a dynamic fashion; it had kept its integrity over the generations, but had changed to adapt to changing times.

Frankel argued that the ancient rabbis had transformed Judaism from a sacrificial cult to rabbinic Judaism without sacrificing a sense of continuity and without disturbing the framework of Jewish law. The rabbis had also created a structure and method that enabled future generations to approach the law from their own perspectives. Modern rabbis, cognizant of the historical and positive aspects of Judaism, should be able to do the same in a gradual, almost imperceptible fashion.

Thus, the Positive-Historical School of Judaism came to embody an embrace of both the positive elements of the faith that stood outside history, and its historical development in line with the collective will of the people. It could be achieved only through the scholarly study of Judaism (*see* WIS-SENSCHAFT DES JUDENTUMS) combined with attention to continuity, tradition, and the collective will of the people, holding in tension faith and scholarship, revelation and tradition.

Frankel's hope to maintain the unity of the Jewish people while instituting reform, however, was not to be fulfilled in Germany. Orthodox leaders such as Samson Raphael HIRSCH (1808–88) claimed that Positive-Historical Judaism lacked Jewish faith despite its emphasis on retaining Jewish law. On the other hand, having studied at Frankel's Breslau Seminary, Rabbi Alexander Kohut (1842–94) brought his approach to the United States, helping Solomon SCHECHTER (1847–1915) and Sabato MORAIS (1823–97) institute its ideology at the JEWISH THEOLOGICAL SEMINARY at New York, thus creating American CONSERVATIVE JUDAISM.

Further reading: Moshe Davis, *The Emergence of Conservative Judaism: The Historical School in 19th-Century America* (Philadelphia: Jewish Publication Society, 1963); Neil Gillman, *Conservative Judaism: The New Century* (West Orange, N.J.: Behrman House, Inc., 1993); Michael A. Meyer, *Response to Modernity: A History of the Reform Movement in Judaism* (New York and Oxford: Oxford University Press, 1988); Mordecai Waxman, ed., *Tradition and Change* (New York: Burning Bush Press, 1958).

Potok, Chaim (1929–2002) *American Jewish novelist*

Born in the Bronx, New York, in 1929, Chaim Potok was the eldest of four children in his family. He was named Herman Harold Potok by his Polish immigrant parents, both of whom had strong ties to the Hasidic world (*see* HASIDISM). Potok was raised in an environment steeped in ORTHODOX JUDAISM, attending YESHIVA and receiving a solid education in Jewish texts.

Potok knew as a teenager that he wanted to be a writer, even though his Orthodox parents, friends, and teachers criticized such work as a waste of time. Those around him did not see any way to reconcile the world of fiction with that of Orthodox Judaism. Potok himself struggled with the problem, eventually becoming involved with CONSERVATIVE JUDAISM, which was more open to new ideas and modern ways of living. Having completed his B.A. cum laude in English literature from YESHIVA UNIVERSITY in 1950, Potok was ordained a Conservative RABBI in 1954 at the JEWISH THEOLOGICAL SEMINARY in New York. Potok also received an M.A. in Hebrew Literature from the Seminary. He earned his Ph.D. from the University of Pennsylvania in 1965.

Potok continued to pursue his dream of writing, and in 1967 published his most famous novel, *The Chosen.* The story juxtaposed the mid-20th-century worlds of Hasidic Jewry and secular Jewish life, using the story of a friendship between two boys, one from each world. It was an eye-opener for the Jewish and non-Jewish communities, presenting a picture of ultra-Orthodox (*see* ORTHODOX JUDAISM) Judaism that had not previously been seen, or at least noticed, by the public.

Apart from his work as a writer, Potok served as a combat chaplain in Korea, as a teacher at the UNIVERSITY OF JUDAISM in Los Angeles, as editor of *Conservative Judaism,* and as editor in chief of the JEWISH PUBLICATION SOCIETY. Other fiction achievements include *The Promise* (1969), *My Name Is Asher Lev* (1990), and *In the Beginning* (1975). He also penned nonfiction works, including *Wanderings: Chaim Potok's History of the Jews* (1978), and *The Gates of November* (1996), the story of a Jewish family in the Soviet Union. Potok's writings were successful with both Jewish and non-Jewish audiences.

Further reading: Louis Harap, *In the Mainstream: The Jewish Presence in Twentieth-Century American Literature, 1950's–1980's* (New York: Greenwood Press, 1987); Chaim Potok, *The Chosen* (Greenwich, Conn.: Fawcett Crest Book, 1967); ———, *In the Beginning* (New York: Knopf, 1975); ———, *My Name Is Asher Lev* (New York, Knopf, 1972).

Prager, Dennis (b. 1948) *Jewish talk-show host and author*

Dennis Prager is a well-respected Jewish talk-show host and author, who has often interpreted TRADITIONAL JUDAISM for a wider audience. His best-known books are *The Nine Questions People Ask About Judaism, Why the Jews? The Reason for Antisemitism, Think a Second Time,* and *Happiness Is a Serious Problem.*

Prager was born on August 2, 1948, to MODERN ORTHODOX parents. As a youth, he attended the co-ed day school Yeshiva of Flatbush in Brooklyn, New York. There, in the 10th grade, he met Joseph Telushkin. They became close friends, authoring two books together. Prager attended Brooklyn College and graduated with a double major in anthropology and history. From 1970–72, he attended the Middle East and Russian Institutes at the Columbia University School of International Affairs. Prager also studied international history, comparative religion, and Arabic at the University of Leeds.

Prager tired of academia, and left graduate school. He decided to write an introduction to Judaism with his friend Joseph Telushkin. *The Nine Questions People Ask About Judaism,* published by Simon & Schuster in 1976, became a best seller, popular in all the major American Jewish movements. The book was intended for the nonobservant Jew, and asked and attempted to answer the following questions: (1) Can one doubt God's existence and still be a good Jew? (2) Why do we need organized religion and Jewish law? Isn't it enough to be a good person? (3) If Judaism is supposed to make people better, how do you account for unethical religious Jews and for ethical people who are not religious? (4) How does Judaism differ from Christianity, Marxism and humanism? (5) What is the Jewish role in the world? (6) Is there a difference between anti-Zionism and antisemitism? (7) Why are so many young Jews alienated from Judaism and the Jewish people? (8) Why shouldn't I intermarry? Doesn't Judaism believe in universal brotherhood? (9) How do I start practicing Judaism? Unlike

Telushkin, who became an Orthodox rabbi, Prager abandoned his Orthodoxy as an adult, although he continues to maintain many traditional Jewish practices.

In April 1976, Shlomo Bardin, the founder and director of the Brandeis Institute, invited Prager to succeed him as the director, and Prager hired Telushkin as education director. Prager remained at the institute until September 1983. During his tenure he succeeded in influencing many young Jews and built up a cadre of "Prager followers."

In 1981, Prager married Janice Goldstein, and in 1983 they had their son, David. In 1982, KABC hired Prager to host a talk show on religion every Sunday night. Prager hosted the show for more than 10 years. In 1983, Prager and Telushkin published their second book: *Why the Jews? The Reason for Antisemitism.* Later that year Prager became the Monday-Thursday talk show host for KABC, but he refused to work on Friday night, the beginning of SHABBAT (the Sabbath). He also wrote a syndicated column for newspapers across the country. In 1985 Prager launched his own quarterly journal, *Ultimate Issues,* which became the *Prager Perspective* in 1996.

In August 1986 his wife initiated a divorce, and he lost his daily talk show. A year of intense therapy had a significant impact on his book *Happiness Is a Serious Problem.* In October 1986, President Reagan appointed Prager as a U.S. delegate to the Vienna Review Conference on the Helsinki Accords. His weekly religion show slowly expanded, eventually becoming a five-hour broadcast on Sunday nights. Prager married Francine Stone, and together they had a daughter, Anya.

In 1992, Prager became active in the Stephen S. Wise Reform synagogue. Although socially conservative, he has become an active teacher in liberal Judaism. He frequently teaches at the University of Judaism, where his evening continuing education classes regularly draw hundreds.

In 1994 Prager hosted a nationally syndicated TV talk show for one year. In 2000 Prager switched his show to KRLA, which is owned by a conservative Christian group. Prager often serves as scholar in residence at synagogues throughout the United States, and he is considered one of the leading socially conservative Jewish political spokesmen.

Further reading: Dennis Prager, *Happiness Is a Serious Problem: A Human Nature Repair Manual* (New York: ReganBooks, 1998); ———, "TV and Me: What My TV Talk Show Taught Me," *The American Enterprise* 8, no. 5 (September–October 1997); Dennis Prager and Joseph Telushkin, *The Nine Questions People Ask about Judaism* (New York: Simon and Schuster, 1981); Prager's Web site URL: http://www.dennisprager.com, accessed August 15, 2004.

prayer

After the destruction of the TEMPLE in JERUSALEM in 70 C.E., prayer replaced SACRIFICE as the means by which Jews could commune with God. The rabbis of that era asserted that while prayer had accompanied the sacrifices in the time of the TEMPLE, the primary focus was on the sacrifices, not the words recited. However, with the Temple's destruction, one's words replaced sacrifice. In fact, they were to be considered a superior means by which to connect with God.

The MISHNAH, the earliest rabbinic legal code, provides a general outline of the prescribed liturgy that was to substitute for sacrifices. There was to be a recitation of the SHEMA, the statement of belief in one God (*see* MONOTHEISM) who taught the distinction between right and wrong, accompanied by blessings that spoke of God's power in nature, law, and history. In addition there were to be public readings from the TORAH, and recitation of "The Prayer," usually called the AMIDAH, which consisted of 18 blessings.

The TALMUD expanded and clarified these requirements, adding to the number and length of the prayers. However, it was the *GEONIM*, the post-Talmudic sages, who ultimately created the first prayer books.

The Talmudic and medieval periods saw an immense literary effort to create Jewish liturgical poems, called *piyyutim,* that were intended to enhance the daily and holiday liturgy. The Kabbalists or Jewish mystics (*see* KABBALAH) also created many prayers, which were added into common Jewish worship. The Hasidic movement (*see* HASIDISM) contributed its own fervor for prayer; perhaps its greatest contribution was an expanded repertoire of dynamic melodies for use in public prayer.

Traditionally, Jewish males are required to recite prescribed prayers morning, afternoon, and evening, on a daily basis, preferably in a communal setting as part of a MINYAN of 10 or more Jewish men (*see* EGALITARIANISM). If a minyan is not available or convenient they may pray on their own.

Each service has a name based on the time of day it is recited. The morning service is called Shacharit (dawn), the afternoon service is called Mincha (gift, a reference to the afternoon offering in the Temple), and the evening service is called Maariv (evening). Women are also obligated to pray daily, but they are not restricted to specific times of the day. In more liberal Jewish settings, women are counted in the minyan, and women do take on the obligations of men. Liberal Jews engage in Jewish worship, but usually only when they attend SYNAGOGUE.

The structure of the prayer service is similar in most synagogues, as it is dictated largely by the SIDDUR, or prayer book. The first section in the siddur is usually the Birchot HaShachar, or blessings of the morning, a collection of blessings and psalms. It includes initial meditations that were originally meant to be recited at home upon waking, but were later moved to the morning service itself, and a series of *brachot,* or blessings (*see* BRACHA) that affirm God's role in providing for all the needs of humanity. The next section of the siddur is called Pesukei D'Zimra, verses of song (mostly from the Book of Psalms).

After these introductory prayers, the core of Shacharit is recited. It begins with the prayer leader calling out: "Praise the Lord who is blessed," to which the congregation responds:

"Praised be the Lord, who is blessed, forever and ever." This leads into the main elements of the service—the Shema, with its surrounding *bera-chot,* blessings that proclaim the God of Nature, Revelation, and History, and the Amidah.

On every Shabbat and festival the morning service includes a liturgical unit surrounding the public Torah reading. The morning service during non-festival weekdays always concludes with the mourner's KADDISH, followed by a hymn praising God. On Sabbath and festivals an additional service called *amusaf* is added. It is meant as a recollection of the extra sacrifice offered on those days in the Temple. On festivals, a special collection of Psalms called the HALLEL is also added.

The afternoon and evening services have no introductory prayers. They begin with an antiphonal response, Ashrei in the afternoon, and Barchu in the evening. Both services have an Amidah, but only the evening service includes the Shema.

All Jews pray for different reasons. There is the desire to communicate with God and ask for God's support. There is the desire to focus on the blessings of life, and develop a greater appreciation for all of God's gifts. Most Jewish prayers fall within one of the three categories of petition, thanksgiving, or praise.

A fundamental understanding of prayer can be found in the Hebrew word meaning "to pray," *lehitpalel,* which is a reflexive verb as opposed to an active verb. Prayer is something one does to oneself first, before moving outward. It is thus a form of self-examination. When praying, you are evaluating yourself, your beliefs, and your actions. In a communal setting, prayer is both the evaluation of the individual and the community. Because many Jews are not fully literate in Hebrew today (not unlike in the past), a cantor or public prayer leader is often used in synagogues to lead the worshipers in their prayers. Anyone who can not read or understand the Hebrew can answer Amen to the prayer leader's words, thus affirming that the words recited are "true" in the ears of the listener.

Further reading: Ismar Elbogen, *Jewish Liturgy: A Comprehensive History* (Philadelphia: Jewish Publication Society of America, 1993); Reuven Hammer, *Entering Jewish Prayer: A Guide to Personal Devotion and the Worship Service* (New York: Schocken Books, 1995); Lawrence A. Hoffman, *Beyond the Text: A Holistic Approach to Liturgy* (Bloomington and Indianapolis: Indiana University Press, 1987); Adin Steinsaltz, *A Guide to Jewish Prayer* (New York: Schocken Books, 2002).

Priesand, Sally (b. 1946) *first woman ordained as a rabbi*

Sally Priesand was the first woman to be ordained a RABBI in the United States. Priesand was born in 1946, the first year of the baby boom, in Cleveland, Ohio. Her father was an engineer and her mother a homemaker. Priesand's family, in her youth, was affiliated with a nonegalitarian (*see* EGALITARIANISM) SYNAGOGUE affiliated with CONSERVATIVE JUDAISM, but when Priesand was in junior high school her family moved and joined Beth Israel, a synagogue affiliated with REFORM JUDAISM. There Priesand was introduced to gender inclusivity in Jewish rituals, and she became very active in the temple's youth group (*see* JEWISH YOUTH GROUPS). Priesand routinely delivered the sermon at the temple's youth service, and she won a temple sisterhood scholarship to a Reform movement summer camp (*see* JEWISH CAMPS). There, she began to think about the possibility of becoming a rabbi. She prepared by studying for confirmation, graduating from Hebrew High School, and becoming a religious school teacher (*see* SUPPLEMENTARY SCHOOLS).

Priesand earned a B.A. at the University of Cincinnati, and then an M.A. from Hebrew Union College (*see* HEBREW UNION COLLEGE–JEWISH INSTITUTE OF RELIGION) in Cincinnati. In 1972 Priesand was ordained a Reform rabbi, the first woman ever to be ordained a rabbi in the UNITED STATES. She assumed the pulpit at Temple Beth El in Elizabeth, New Jersey, and in 1981 became rabbi of the Monmouth Reform Temple in Tinton Falls, New Jersey. Priesand is active in civic and religious organiza-

These men have covered their heads to recite the priestly blessing at the Western Wall in Jerusalem during the festival of Sukkot. *(Moshe Milner, Government Press Office, The State of Israel)*

tions, and in 1975 published her book *Judaism and the New Woman.*

Priesand ushered in a new era of religious opportunity for Jewish women, many of whom have since become rabbis and cantors in the Reform and Conservative Jewish movements. Upon the 25th anniversary of her ordination, Hebrew Union College established the Rabbi Sally J. Priesand Visiting Professorship of Jewish Women's Studies. In addition, Priesand was awarded an honorary doctorate of divinity by the Hebrew Union College–Jewish Institute of Religion for her 25 years of service to the Jewish community.

Further reading: Hasia R. Diner and Beryl Lieff Benderly, *Her Works Praise Her: A History of Jewish Women in America from Colonial Times to the Present* (New York: Basic

Books, 2002); Pamela Susan Nadell, *Women Who Would Be Rabbis: A History of Women's Ordination, 1889–1985* (Boston: Beacon Press, 1998); Sally Priesand, *Judaism and the New Woman* (New York: Behrman House, 1975).

priest *See* KOHANIM.

priestly blessing

Traditionally the priestly blessing is performed during festival days by all the KOHANIM in the congregation, with the assistance of the LEVITES, as prescribed in Numbers 6:22–27 (*see* TORAH). The blessing was first introduced through AARON, whom God commanded to bestow his blessing upon the ISRAELITES.

Today, the *kohanim*, who are understood to be merely the instruments through which God will transmit the blessing, stand before the ARK of the Covenant on the bima facing the congregation. They cover their heads with prayer shawls and then recite a benediction. Then they raise their hands and hold their fingers so as to form "windows," suggesting that God is sending his blessing through the openings symbolized by the hands. The reader then recites the blessing, with the *kohanim* chanting verbatim after them. The blessing is three lines long: "The Lord bless you and keep you. The Lord make His face to shine upon you and be gracious unto you. The Lord lift up His countenance upon you and give you peace." These words imply that blessings come from God and that peace is valued in God's eyes. In addition, because the blessing is said in a communal setting, its recitation reinforces the power and importance of community.

REFORM JUDAISM and many synagogues affiliated with CONSERVATIVE JUDAISM no longer include the priestly blessing, as they believe it to violate their ideas of equality among Jews; the *kohanim* acquire their position through parentage alone, and are all males.

Some parents recite the same prayer for their children before a SHABBAT meal at home, but it is technically not a priestly blessing unless it is performed by a *kohen* in the SYNAGOGUE.

Further reading: Avie Gold, *Bircas Kohanim: The Priestly Blessing* (Brooklyn, N.Y.: Mesorah Publications, 1986); Nehama Leibowitz, "The Priestly Blessing," in *Studies in Bamidbar (Numbers)* (Jerusalem: World Zionist Organization, 1980), 60–67; Jacob Milgrom, "The Priestly Blessing," in *The JPS Torah Commentary: Numbers*, ed. Sarna, Nahum M. (Philadelphia: Jewish Publication Society, 1990), 360–362; *Tanakh: The New JPS Translation According to the Traditional Hebrew Text* (Philadelphia, New York, Jerusalem: Jewish Publication Society, 1985).

prime minister   *See* KNESSET.

prophecy

In Judaism, prophecy is not merely telling the future. Rather, a prophet is someone who is called by God to deliver a message to the Jewish people, generally warning them against faithlessness, corruption or injustice. The prophets often condemn the people, or their rulers, for worshipping idols, for failing to trust in God in the face of danger, for oppressing the poor or the weak, for violating ritual laws like the Sabbath, or for hypocrisy in fulfilling the letter of the law while ignoring the spirit. They warn of the suffering that awaits the nation if it does not change its ways, but they also often predict future salvation, which suffering and repentance will eventual bring. Many of the prophetic writings date to periods of immense crisis, especially the years in the eighth century B.C.E. before the Assyrian invasion, and those of the sixth century B.C.E. before the conquest by the Babylonians (*see* BABYLONIA).

The period of prophecy began during the era of the Judges and continued throughout the time of the ancient kingdom of ISRAEL. There were three major prophets—EZEKIEL, ISAIAH, and Jeremiah— and 12 minor prophets, all of whose writings are recorded in the section of the TANAKH known as NEVI'IM, or Prophets. Besides the three major and 12 minor prophets, there are many other prophets and prophetesses mentioned throughout the Tanakh. The rabbis count 48 prophets and seven prophetesses in all. After the destruction of the TEMPLE, the rabbis discerned that the period of prophecy was over and that God would no longer communicate to the Jewish people via prophets.

The 19th-century HASKALAH, or Jewish ENLIGHTENMENT, brought a new interest in the prophets, and some of their ideas and themes influenced REFORM JUDAISM. Such reform movements often focused on prophetic utterances that seem to reduce the importance of external rituals in favor of an increased importance for individual virtue and social ethics. Some people have even referred to modern reformers and philosophers, such as Moses MENDELSSOHN (1729–86) and Abraham Joshua HESCHEL (1907–72) as prophets, though neither of them professed to speak in the name of God, as all the earlier prophets did.

Further reading: David Arthur, *A Smooth Stone: Biblical Prophecy in Historical Perspective* (Lanham, Md., University Press of America, 2001); Joseph Blenkinsopp, *A History of Prophecy in Ancient Israel* (Louisville, Ky.: Westminster John Knox Press, 1996); Norman Podhoretz, *The Prophets: Who They Were, What They Are* (New York, Free Press, 2002); Michael Shire, ed., *The Jewish Prophet: Visionary Words from Moses and Miriam to Henrietta Szold and A. J. Heschel* (Woodstock, Vt.: Jewish Lights, 2001); *Tanakh: The Holy Scriptures* (Philadelphia and Jerusalem: The Jewish Publication Society, 1985).

Protocols of the Elders of Zion

The most notorious and insidious antisemitic (*see* ANTISEMITISM) piece of writing in modern history is *The Protocols of the Elders of Zion*. It was composed by a Russian secret service agent in FRANCE sometime around 1894 or 1895. Its 24 sections purport to be a secret plan by Jewish leaders from around the world to attain world domination.

The apparent inspiration and basis for the *Protocols* was an 1864 French satire by Maurice Jolly entitled *Dialogues in Hell Between Machiavelli and Montesquieu*, which made absolutely no mention of Jews but was an attack on the political ambitions of Emperor Napoleon III.

The manuscript of the *Protocols* was brought to RUSSIA sometime in 1895 and published privately in 1897. Following the unsuccessful Revolution of 1905, the *Protocols* were publicly published by the mystic priest Sergius Nilus, who claimed that they were secretly read at the First Zionist Congress (*see* ZIONISM) held in Basel in 1897. A variant text was published in 1906 and attributed to the Masonic conspiracy. Nilus's text proved to be the more popular and was used extensively during the civil war that followed the Bolshevik Revolution of 1917 to incite anti-Jewish POGROMS. In 1919 the *Protocols* were introduced to

western Europe by Russian émigrés and quickly translated into many languages. They were exposed as an obvious forgery and a plagiarism of Jolly's work by Lucien Wolf in 1920, and the following year by *London Times* correspondent Philip Grave, and once again in the UNITED STATES in a pamphlet written by Norman Bernstein; yet they continued to circulate widely and were translated into more and more languages.

In the United States the *Protocols* first appeared in a series of articles entitled the "International Jew" published between 1920 and 1922 in the *Dearborn Independent,* the newspaper of automobile mogul Henry Ford. In 1927, following a libel suit and a Jewish boycott of Ford products, Henry Ford publicly apologized for the articles (*see* MARSHALL, LOUIS). The Nazis used the *Protocols* extensively in their antisemitic propaganda. Adolf HITLER cited them to justify his anti-Jewish legislation and his suppression of all opposition to the Third Reich, which he attributed to the Jewish conspiracy.

The *Protocols* are still widely circulated around the world. They have been translated into Japanese and circulated in Japan, where a book citing them became a best seller; they have been published in Latin American countries; in 1987 a book released in the Soviet Union quoted many of the canards of the *Protocols.* Today they are also popular among U.S. right-wing extremists such as the Ku Klux Klan and the Aryan Nations. Since 1965 the *Protocols* have been a favorite source of anti-Israel and anti-Zionist propaganda by Arab and Muslim groups. Numerous books quoting or relying on them have been published in Arabic. In Iran the *Protocols* themselves were published by the government as recently as 1994 and 1999. Arab leaders and representatives have also referred to them as genuine in public speeches, as the Jordanian delegate to the UNITED NATIONS did in 1980.

Further reading: Neil Baldwin, *Henry Ford and the Jews: The Mass Production of Hate* (New York: Public Affairs, 2001); Norman Cohn, *Warrant for Genocide: The Myth* of the Jewish World Conspiracy and the Protocols of the Elders of Zion (London: Serif, 1967); Binjamin W. Segel, A Lie and a Libel: The History of the Protocols of the Elders of Zion (Lincoln: University of Nebraska Press, 1995).

Psalms See Tehillim.

pshat

Pshat is a method of reading the Tanakh (the Hebrew Bible) that aims only to discover the plain meaning of the text itself. It is the first of four levels of meaning of a biblical text traditionally analyzed in the study of Torah.

A pshat approach tries to discern the historical and factual content of a passage, using grammar and linguistics where appropriate. When a person approaches a text to discern its meaning, pshat is often the first place to begin, followed by drash (hermeneutical), remez (allegorical), and sod (mystical) levels of meaning.

For example, when one reads the first three words of the Tanakh, "In the beginning," the method of pshat simply says, this is the beginning of the story, and moves on. In drash, on the other hand, one may ask, "why is the text pointing out the obvious?" and come up with a host of messages that the words might be conveying.

Further reading: David Weiss Halivni, Peshat and Derash: Plain and Applied Meaning in Rabbinic Exegesis (New York: Oxford University Press, 1991); Solomon Schechter, Aspects of Rabbinic Theology (New York: Schocken Books, 1961); Adin Steinsaltz, The Talmud: The Steinsaltz Edition (New York: Random House, 1989).

Pumbedita

The rabbinic academies of Babylonia were established in the third century of the Common Era near the Euphrates River, after the exile of the Jews from the land of Israel following the destruction of the second Temple by the Romans. Pumbedita and Sura became the two main academies. R. Judah bar Ezekiel founded the academy at Pumbedita and served as its first head. The academy continued to function well into the 10th century C.E., when it moved to Baghdad.

In the ninth century C.E., Abbaye, head of the Pumbedita academy, sent the Babylonian Talmud and its commentaries to Jewish scholars in Spain, thus encouraging the spread of the Babylonian rabbinic tradition. The last heads of the academy at Pumbedita were Rav Sherira Gaon and his son, Rav Hai Gaon.

Further reading: Louis Jacobs, Theology in the Responsa (London and Boston: Routledge and Kegan Paul, 1975); Norman A. Stillman, The Jews of Arab Lands: A History and Source Book (Philadelphia: Jewish Publication Society of America, 1979); H. L. Strack and G. Stemberger, Introduction to the Talmud and Midrash (Minneapolis: Fortress Press, 1992).

Purim

The festival of Purim occurs annually on the 14th day of the month of Adar. It celebrates the rescue from annihilation of the Jews of ancient Persia, as recorded in the biblical book of Esther.

The book recounts how the wicked vizier Haman condemns all the Jews of King Ahasuerus's vast kingdom to death, simply because Mordechai the Jew would not bow down before him. Haman casts a lottery, or pur, to determine the date of the Jews' destruction, and chooses the 13th of Adar. Unbeknownst to either Haman or the king, the king's wife, Queen Esther, is a Jew. Esther pleads with the king to save her life and the lives of her people, at which point Haman is put to death, and the king issues a decree allowing Jews to defend themselves forcefully if anyone rises up against them. The Jews defeat their attackers on the 13th of Adar and celebrate on the 14th. Scholars agree that such an event may have taken place in Persia, but there is no evidence for it outside the book of Esther.

This child is dressed up for the holiday of Purim. Israelis dress in costume to celebrate Purim, and it is fun to walk around on that day to see the variety of festive outfits. *(Einat Anker, Government Press Office, The State of Israel)*

On Purim, Jews read the MEGILLAH (scroll of) Esther in SYNAGOGUES and celebrate avidly. They give gifts of food and charity, known as MISHLOACH MANOT, dress in costumes, get drunk, and put on satirical plays known as *Purimspiels*. The holiday is a favorite of children, since in addition to putting on costumes and plays, they often attend carnivals and are encouraged to use GROGGERS, or noisemakers, to drown out Haman's name as the tale is read. The Purim Megillah is often referred to simply as "the Megillah," but it is only one of five of such scrolls in the TANAKH.

Purim was also a favorite Jewish holiday in the Middle Ages. In a stressful time of expulsions and persecution, Purim served as a reminder that Jews have always survived such episodes in the past. Moreover, the *Purimspiels* allowed the Jews to convey their political fears in a lighthearted manner, and the general merriment of the festival allowed them to release some of the tension such fears engendered. If a particular community or family survived a dangerous situation, they could institute a special Purim, such as the Purim of Las Bombas in PORTUGAL in the 16th century. The original holiday is also observed, but the community or family, and their descendants, also celebrates their special Purim to commemorate their day of deliverance from danger.

Further reading: Philip Goodman, *The Purim Anthology* (Philadelphia: Jewish Publication Society, 1988); Irving Greenberg, *The Jewish Way: Living the Holidays* (New York: Summit Books, 1998); Ronald H. Isaacs, *Every Person's Guide to Purim* (Northvale, N.J.: Aronson, 2000); Chanoch Landesman and Dovid Landesman, eds., *As the Rabbis Taught: Studies in the Aggados of the Talmud: Tractate Megillah* (Northvale, N.J.: Aronson, 1996); *Tanakh: The Holy Scriptures* (Philadelphia and Jerusalem: Jewish Publication Society, 1985).

Qumran *See* DEAD SEA SCROLLS.

Rabbenu Tam (1100–1171) *prominent Talmud commentator*

Jacob Ben Meir, known as Rabbenu Tam ("our teacher, the perfect one"), is best known for his work as a commentator on the TALMUD. He was born and raised in Ramerupt, FRANCE, and was the grandson of RASHI and the brother of RASHBAM. Rabbenu Tam was probably the greatest of the Tosafists (*see* TOSAFOT), the first important generation of Talmud commentators after Rashi.

Almost every page of the standard edition of the Talmud includes comments by Tam on its outer edges. He is considered to be one of the greatest Talmudic scholars of all time. One sage commented on Rabbenu's brilliance, stating "he had the heart of a lion, and one cannot know whether he really intended to interpret in this way or merely wanted to display his brilliance." Tam established a YESHIVA in Ramerupt, and he was well known throughout European Jewry. His best-known work is the *Sefer ha-Yashar,* a compilation of HALAKHAH, Jewish law.

Tam is also noted for a disagreement he had with his grandfather, RASHI, regarding the order of the TEFILLIN. As a result, some Jews today wear two pairs of tefillin, those according to Rashi's instructions and those according to Tam's instructions.

Further reading: Solomon B. Freehof, *A Treasury of Responsa* (Philadelphia: Jewish Publication Society, 1963); Jacob Katz, *Exclusiveness and Tolerance: Studies in Jewish-Gentile Relations in Medieval and Modern Times* (Oxford: Oxford University Press, 1961); Adin Steinsaltz, *The Essential Talmud* (New York: Basic Books, 1976); Shmuel Teich, *The Rishonim: Biographical Sketches of the Prominent Early Rabbinic Sages and Leaders from the Tenth–Fifth Centuries,* edited by Hersh Goldwurm (Brooklyn, N.Y.: Messcrah Publishing, 1982).

rabbi

A rabbi in the Jewish tradition is a scholar and a teacher. He or she is not a priest, and has no more special authority to perform RITUALS than any other Jew. In many SYNAGOGUES, rabbis do not even lead worship services. Their main function is to teach Jewish law and custom and provide leadership to the community.

In HEBREW, the root letters of the word are RV, meaning "great" or "distinguished," a reference to the level of Jewish learning a rabbi is supposed to have achieved. The root is augmented with the first person possessive suffix to create the title rabbi, which thus means "my master."

The term *rabbi* is not used in the TANAKH, the Hebrew Bible. It first appeared in written form in the MISHNAH, the early rabbinic law collection redacted in the year 220 C.E., and it did not appear in a text as a general title until the Talmudic period, after 500 C.E. However, Jewish leaders who lived at the end of the first century of the Common Era, following the destruction of the second Temple, were given the title rabban by those who wrote down the Mishnah (220) and the GEMARA (550). Thus, the word was used to designate someone distinguished for his learning and authoritative in his teaching of Jewish law (*see* HALAKHAH), and who, at times, acted as spiritual head of a community. Jewish communities in different eras and countries have used derivatives of the word such as *rebbe, rav, rab,* and *rabban*; the latter was used for the president of the SANHEDRIN, the ancient Jewish court of law and the ancient sages of the first century. In order of title prestige, rabban holds more authority than rabbi, which holds more authority than the title rav.

The chief role of the rabbi has long been to instruct the community in matters of Jewish law. As rabbinic academies and yeshivot (*see* YESHIVA) were created to train Jewish scholars, it became the practice to grant ordination, or SEMIKHA, to those students who completed a certain level of learning in the CODES OF LAW and RESPONSA (legal rulings issued in response to queries). Once a man received semikha, he might be embraced by a community and his opinions on Jewish law followed by the people in that community.

In modern times there are many Orthodox men (*see* ORTHODOX JUDAISM) who have received semikha and are thus entitled to be called rabbis, but who choose other careers. In contrast, most liberal Jews who choose rabbinical training do so as a career choice. Liberal rabbinic education does not resemble a traditional yeshiva environment. Students engage in traditional text study but also undertake formal academic work on the graduate level, as well as course work in pastoral care. In CONSERVATIVE JUDAISM and REFORM JUDAISM, rabbinic training requires a minimum of five years of graduate school. Yet, even many liberal rabbis choose a nonpulpit rabbinic career. A pulpit rabbi must teach, preach, and minister to the congregants' needs, often at times of personal crisis. The time demands on pulpit rabbis are immense; many rabbis choose to take teaching, counseling, or administrative positions instead.

Orthodoxy only ordains men, though in recent years several women have been certified by the Chief Rabbinate of ISRAEL as halakhic advisers to women, and others have been accepted there as pleaders in rabbinical courts on divorce issues. Liberal Jewish movements ordain both men and women and accept both in all rabbinic roles. The first woman to become a rabbi, Sally PRIESAND, was ordained by the Reform movement in the UNITED STATES in 1972. The first Conservative woman rabbi was ordained in 1985. While there is no clear HALAKHAH, or Jewish law, forbidding a woman to be a rabbi, there were many issues regarding a woman's ability to lead a congregation (*see* MODESTY) and her obligations to follow time-bound commandments (*see* MITZVAH). These issues have been addressed and overcome by the Reform and Conservative movements, but every sector in the Orthodox world has so far retained the tradition of ordaining only men.

A congregation does not need a rabbi for rituals to be performed or worship conducted. However, nearly all congregations feel the need for a rabbi so as to access the wealth of rabbinic knowledge, and to have a full-time teacher, preacher, and adviser. Most congregations hire rabbis and provide multiyear contracts, which are typically renewed for additional periods, and occasionally for life. In Orthodox and Conservative synagogues, the rabbi generally retains control of all matters of Jewish law.

Judaism as practiced in the modern world is not the sacrificial tradition of the ancient ISRAELITES as depicted in the Bible. It is the creation of the ancient rabbis; thus the common designation Rabbinic Judaism. After the destruction of the second TEMPLE in JERUSALEM in 70 C.E., rabbinic Judaism began to take shape. It was developed and tweaked by centuries of study, thought, and discussion by the early rabbis. The role of the rabbi continues to develop as history progresses. In the contemporary world rabbis who accept pulpit positions in synagogues often take on new roles, offering counseling, comfort, and spiritual leadership to their congregants.

Further reading: Neil Gillman, *Conservative Judaism: The New Century* (West Orange, N.J.: Behrman House, 1993); Jacob Neusner, "Phenomenon of the Rabbi in Late Antiquity" in *Numen* 16 (April 1969): 1–20; Lawrence H. Schiffman, *From Text to Tradition: A History of Second Temple and Rabbinic Judaism* (Hoboken, N.J.: Ktav Publishing House, 1991); Howard Schwartz, *Reimagining the Bible: The Storytelling of the Rabbis* (New York: Oxford University Press, 1988).

Rabbi Akiva *See* AKIVA BEN YOSEPH.

Rabbinical Assembly *See* CONSERVATIVE JUDAISM.

rabbinic law

The term *rabbinic law* refers to that part of HALAKHAH (Jewish law) that was formulated by the ancient rabbis themselves, and not based on explicit commandments (*see* MITZVAH) in the TORAH, the Five Books of Moses. The rabbis developed these laws for one of two reasons. First, many laws were designed as auxiliary rulings meant to keep people from inadvertently violating any Torah commandments. ETHICS OF THE FATHERS refers to this as putting a "fence around the Torah." Torah prohibitions were expanded to make doubly certain that violations would not occur. Second, many rabbinic laws seek to find loopholes in the law to make life easier, rather than more difficult. For example, though Jews are prohibited from making fire on SHABBAT, they are permitted to reheat food on an already hot surface, like a hotplate, and they can preprogram electric lights to turn on for Sabbath afternoons.

Rabbinic law is not on the same level as biblical law; thus, violations of rabbinic law are not punished as seriously. Nevertheless, it is still considered authoritative for the community; in fact, the rabbis reshaped Judaism in such a way that it is difficult for any but the scholar to differentiate between biblical and rabbinic law. Scholars refer to rabbinic law as *d'rabbanan,* literally "from the rabbis," and biblical or Torah law as *d'raita,* "from the Torah."

The rabbis believed that biblical law was more important than rabbinic law; nevertheless, while they would never overrule a biblical prohibition, they were willing to forbid that which the TANAKH, the Hebrew Bible, permits. For example, they long ago prohibited polygamy, which is clearly accepted in the Torah. There are several examples in which the rabbis created a *takanah,* an amendment to the Bible, which did bypass a biblical prohibition. The best-known ancient case was the *prosbul,* an innovation devised by HILLEL that allowed people to reestablish claim debts after the SABBATICAL YEAR, even though the Bible orders them to be canceled.

Modern-day Jews are considered to be rabbinic Jews because their Jewish lives revolve mostly around rabbinical interpretations of laws, narratives, and customs. Modern rabbis continue to make legal interpretations of *halakhah* for their communities. There were some Jews, however, who rejected the rabbinic way of life. The KARAITES, a sect that emerged in the ninth century, rejected rabbinic law and based their code of law on a more literal interpretation of the Torah. Their strict interpretation often left them eating cold food and sitting in the dark on SHABBAT.

Further reading: Alexander Guttman, "Foundations of Rabbinic Judaism" in *Hebrew Union College Annual* 23 (1950–1951), 453–473; Jacob Katz, "Rabbinical Authority and Authorization in the Middle Ages" in *Studies in Medieval Jewish History and Literature* (Cambridge, Mass.: Harvard University Press, 1979), 41–56; Jacob Neusner, "Phenomenon of the Rabbi in Late Antiquity" in *Numen* 16 (April 1969), 1–20; John D. Rayner, *Jewish Religious Law: A Progressive Perspective* (New York: Berghahn Books, 1998); H. L. Strack and G. Stemberger, *Introduction to the Talmud and Midrash* (Minneapolis: Fortress Press, 1992).

Rabin, Yitzhak (1922–1995) *Israeli military and political leader*

Yitzhak Rabin, ISRAEL DEFENSE FORCE (IDF) chief of staff, diplomat, and the fifth prime minister of the State of ISRAEL, was born in JERUSALEM in 1922, the son of an ardently labor Zionist family. He was an early member of the PALMACH, the elite strike force of the HAGANAH.

Rabin distinguished himself as a military leader early on, both within the Palmach and then the IDF. Rising to the rank of major general at the age of 32, Rabin established the IDF training doctrine and the leadership style that became known by the command "follow me." In 1962 he was appointed chief of the general staff and promoted to the rank of lieutenant general. He developed the IDF fighting doctrine, based on movement and surprise, that was employed during the 1967 SIX-DAY WAR, resulting in a famous military victory.

With his retirement from the military in 1968, Rabin was appointed ambassador to the UNITED STATES. During his five years in Washington he strove to consolidate bilateral ties, and he played a major role in promoting strategic cooperation with the United States, which led to massive American military aid to Israel.

Rabin returned to Israel in 1973 and was elected to the KNESSET. Following the 1973 YOM KIPPUR WAR, Rabin became the first native-born prime minister, serving for four years. He continued to serve in the Knesset, and was minister of defense for six years (1984–90) in two national unity governments.

Rabin's second term as prime minister was marked by two historic events—the Oslo Accords with the Palestinians and the Treaty of Peace with Jordan. Working closely with Shimon PERES, the foreign minister and his longtime rival, Rabin masterminded negotiations on the Declaration of Principles signed with the PALESTINE LIBERATION ORGANIZATION at the White House in September 1993. This won Rabin, Peres, and Arafat the 1994 Nobel Peace Prize.

On November 4, 1995, as Rabin was leaving a mass rally for peace held under the slogan "Yes to Peace, No to Violence," a Jewish right-wing extremist assassinated him. Rabin was mourned as a champion of peace and a symbol of hope for Israelis and people around the world.

Further reading: Gideon Doron and Don Peretz, *The Government and Politics of Israel* (Boulder, Colo.: Westview Press, 1997); Robert O. Freedman, ed., *Israel under Rabin* (Boulder, Colo.: Westview Press, 1995); David Makovsky, *Making Peace with the PLO: The Rabin Government's Road to the Oslo Accord* (Boulder, Colo.: Westview Press, 1996); Yoram Peri, "The Media and Collective Memory of Yitzhak Rabin's Remembrance," *Journal of Communication* 49, no. 3 (1999); Yitzhak Rabin, *The Rabin Memoirs* (Boston: Little, Brown, 1979).

Yitzhak Rabin (third from left), shown here with Shimon Peres (left), was Israel's fifth prime minister. He was awarded the Nobel Peace Prize in 1994, and he represented hope for those who live in the political and violent Middle East. He was tragically assassinated by a Jewish extremist who did not agree with his plans and actions to negotiate land for peace between Israelis and Palestinian Arabs. This photo was taken minutes before Rabin's assassination at a peace rally in Tel Aviv on November 4, 1995. *(Courtesy Embassy of Israel, Washington D.C.)*

rainbow

In Judaism, the rainbow is a symbol of the promise God made to NOAH, vowing never again to destroy the world with a flood (Gn 7–9). The pledge is incorporated in the COVENANT God makes with Noah, which according to Jewish tradition was the first covenant God made with a human being, and which according to Judaism is still in effect for all people in the world.

Although the Bible does not list people's obligations in this covenant, Jewish tradition holds that they include the seven Noahide Laws. God's obligation is the vow never to destroy CREATION again, and as the symbol and reminder of this covenant, God places a bow among the clouds. Anytime a rainbow appears after a storm, it is a reminder that God remembers his promise and will refrain from flooding the earth.

In scholarly terms, this story is an excellent example of an etiological myth, or a story that explains the reason for a natural phenomenon, such as thunder or snow or, in this case, a rainbow.

Further reading: Yirmeyahu Bindman, *The Seven Colors of the Rainbow: Torah Ethics for Non-Jews* (San José, Calif.: Resource Publications, 1995); Jacob Neusner, *Genesis Rabbah: The Judaic Commentary to the Book of Genesis* (Atlanta: Scholars Press, 1985); David Novak, *The Image of the Non-Jew in Judaism: An Historical and Constructive Study of the Noahide Laws* (New York: E. Mellen Press, 1983); *Tanakh: The Holy Scriptures* (Philadelphia and Jerusalem: Jewish Publication Society, 1985).

Rapoport, Solomon (1790–1867) *rabbi and pioneer Jewish historian*

Solomon Judah Loeb Rapoport was born in Lemberg in POLAND in 1790. From a young age, while supporting himself through various business activities, he studied the TALMUD, science, and Western languages, developing excellent skills in critical inquiry and writing. In addition to publishing poetry and translations, he wrote extensively on Jewish subjects. His first such article, in 1824, discussed the independent Jewish tribes of Arabia and Abyssinia. His 1829 article on SAADIA GAON brought him into the public eye, and he continued to publish articles about medieval Jewish sages. His notoriety came from his use of historical-critical methods to examine the lives of these sages, along the lines of the new WISSENSCHAFT DES JUDENTUMS movement, which used scientific methods in the study of Judaism.

Rapoport was rejected for a rabbinical post in Berlin due to his lack of fluency in German, and for another post in Italy due to his lack of formal academic credentials. He finally won a post as rabbi of Tarnopol in 1837, and three years later became the rabbi of Prague.

Ironically, the Jews of Prague hired Rapoport as their new rabbi in part because of his secular learning and daring historical analysis; the HASKALAH, the Jewish ENLIGHTENMENT, had made inroads in Prague and the community wanted a more modern rabbi. Yet Rapoport was ardently opposed to REFORM JUDAISM. Despite his use of historical-critical methods of scholarship, he was a traditional Orthodox rabbi (*see* ORTHODOX JUDAISM). The combination of his modern attitude toward scholarship and his conservative attitude toward Jewish practice placed Rapoport in an unusual position within the Jewish community of his time—he was criticized by Orthodox rabbis and Hasidim (*see* HASIDISM) on the right and by Reform Jews and radical scholars on the left.

One of Rapoport's most ambitious academic goals was to compose an encyclopedia of Judaism, but he only managed to complete a small portion of it, never getting beyond the letter alef, the first letter of the HEBREW alphabet. He died in Prague in 1867.

Further reading: Isaac Barzilay, *Shlomo Yehudah Rapoport, 1790–1867, and his Contemporaries: Some Aspects of Jewish Scholarship of the Nineteenth Century* (Israel: Massada Press, 1969); Nathan Stern, *The Jewish Historico-Critical School of the Nineteenth Century* (New York: Arno Press, 1973).

Rashbam (Rabbi Shmuel ben Meir)
(1085–1174) *Bible commentator*

Rabbi Shmuel ben Meir is known among Jews by the acronym of his title and name, Rashbam. Born in Ramerupt, France to RASHI's learned daughter Yochebed, Rashbam studied with his famous grandfather in Troyes, FRANCE.

Rashi once told the boy that he wished he had placed more emphasis on the PSHAT, or plain meaning of the text in his commentaries. Taking his cue from that statement, Rashbam made that his life work. He also studied the DRASH, or interpretations of other rabbis. Rashbam sometimes contradicted the interpretations that were used to create HALAKHAH (Jewish law), based on his own understanding of the plain meaning of the TORAH text. Nevertheless, in such cases Rashbam defended halakhah based on a deeper drashic meaning. Rashbam's Torah commentaries became standard alongside those of Rashi and NACHMANIDES.

In his earliest work, Rashbam used an aggadic approach (*see* AGGADAH) to EXEGESIS, interpreting SONG OF SONGS as an allegory of the love between God and ISRAEL, showing Israel in both happy and sad times. After this early work, however, Rashbam concentrated mainly on the literal interpretation of scripture.

As a biblical exegete, Rashbam had the following five goals: to harmonize his comments with the exegesis of his time; to simplify exegesis; to preserve traditional interpretations when they agreed with the literal sense; to show connections between seemingly disconnected passages in the text; and to defend Judaism.

One of Rashbam's most famous unconventional interpretations of the TANAKH, the Hebrew Bible, concerns Genesis 1:5, which in his understanding shows that days begin at dawn. This is in direct contradiction to Jewish custom, by which days begin at sunset. Rashbam was also revolutionary in his commentary on Ecclesiastes, both for his claim that the phrase "vanity of vanities" was added by a later editor and for his willingness to interpret pessimistic and doubting passages according to their literal meaning.

Further reading: Benjamin J. Gelles, "Samuel ben Meir—Rashbam," in his *Reshat and Derash in the Exegeis of Rashi* (Leiden: Brill, 1981); David Weiss Halivni, *Peshat and Derash: Plain and Applied Meaning in Rabbinic Exegesis* (New York: Oxford University Press, 1991); Sara Japhet and Robert B. Salters, eds., *The Commentary of R. Samuel ben Meir, Rashbam, on Qoheleth* (Leiden: E. J. Brill, 1985); Jane Dammen McAuliffe, Barry D. Walfish, and Joseph W. Goering, eds., *With Reverence for the Word: Medieval Scriptural Exegesis in Judaism, Christianity, and Islam* (Oxford: Oxford University Press, 2003).

Rashi (1040–1105) *preeminent commentator on the Bible and Talmud*

Rashi is an acronym for Rabbi Shlomo ben Yitzchak. He is considered by many to be the greatest rabbinic commentator on both the TANAKH, the Hebrew Bible, and the TALMUD. Rashi lived most of his life in his birthplace, the northern French city of Troyes, although he spent time as a youth in Mayence, GERMANY. There he studied with rabbinic scholars, and these teachers often appear in his commentaries.

After returning from his studies in Germany, Rashi began supporting himself as a winemaker using vineyards that he owned; it was to remain his lifelong business. However, his real vocation was teaching and writing. Rashi is popular among both beginners and advanced students, as his commentaries guide readers through both simple and complicated material. Regardless of difficulty level, however, Rashi's commentaries are among the most comprehensive ever composed. In his commentaries on GEMARA, Rashi stops to translate many ARAMAIC terms, using this as an opportunity to better explain the concepts under discussion. His frequent translations into Old French words have made his commentaries a valuable source for linguists.

Rashi's commentary on the TORAH, the Five Books of Moses, combines a summary of traditional commentaries such as MIDRASH, the teachings of his own teachers, and his own personal insights. His primary intention was to teach the PSHAT, or the plain meaning of the text. The most important question a student of Rashi might have is What was Rashi's problem? By asking this question, a student is able to explore both the biblical text and Rashi's commentary on it.

Rashi was quickly accepted as a master authority, but his influence was enhanced in the early 16th century, when printers began publishing the corpus of Jewish sacred texts. The first printed editions of the Talmud and the Bible contained Rashi's commentary, printed in a special "Rashi script" to distinguish it from the Bible text. For many traditional Jews, the Rashi commentary seems almost an integral part of the original text.

Rashi was still alive when the Crusades began. He does not explicitly refer to these events, though life became very dangerous for the Jews of northern Europe. However, scholars have interpreted Rashi's comments on the very first verse of the Bible as a subtle rebuke to the crusaders and their goal of conquering the Holy Land for themselves. He poses the question of why the Torah begins with the story of CREATION; his answer: to remind all human beings that God owns the land, and that people do not. As the owner, God gives the land to whomever he chooses. In the case of the Holy Land, the Bible will soon show that God gave it to the Jews.

Rashi had only daughters, but tradition has it that they were scholars in their own right and even used TEFILLIN like their male counterparts. They married scholars, and bore two sons who carried on their grandfather's scholarly tradition, RASHBAM and RABBENU TAM. Rashi's grandsons and disciples formed a group called the *Baalei Tosafot*, "Those who extended." This group continued Rashi's tradition of explaining the *pshat* of biblical and rabbinic texts. Together, Rashi and the TOSAFOT are placed as the primary commentaries on any page of Talmud, and no Gemara is studied without their input.

Further reading: Avigdor Bonchek, *What's Bothering Rashi?—Bereishis (What's Bothering Rashi Series)* (New York: Philipp Feldheim, 1997); Rashi, *Rashi: Commentaries on the Pentateuch* (New York: Norton, 1970); Esra Shereshevsky, *Rashi: The Man and His World* (Northvale, N.J.: Jason Aronson, 1996); M. Rosenbaum and A. M. Silbermann, eds., *The Pentateuch with Rashi*, 5 vols. (New York: Feldheim, 1973).

Reb of Kotsk *See* KOTSKER REBBE.

Reconstructionist Judaism

Unlike REFORM, CONSERVATIVE, and ORTHODOX JUDAISM, Reconstructionist Judaism is an American-born Jewish denomination; it arose and took root in the hearts and minds of American Jews.

Mordecai KAPLAN is known as the father of Reconstructionist Judaism, although he did not originally intend for the movement to separate itself from Conservative Judaism. As a member of the faculty at the JEWISH THEOLOGICAL SEMINARY beginning in 1909, Kaplan sought to develop his ideas that Judaism was not only a religion, but also a civilization, complete with its own language, land, music, art, folkways, and culture. When the Orthodox congregation he led rejected his leadership, he and his supporters founded a synagogue, which they called the Society for the Advancement of Judaism (SAJ), in New York City in 1922. The synagogue helped work through Kaplan's ideas, offering social gatherings, worship services, and education. The SAJ remains a vibrant community today.

Between the years 1920 and 1940 Kaplan and colleague Ira Eisenstein, assistant rabbi at the SAJ, developed the Reconstructionist movement. Kaplan's greatest work was published in 1934: *Judaism as a Civilization: Toward a Reconstruction of American-Jewish Life*. In 1935, the first issue of the magazine *Reconstructionist*, was published, and in 1940 the Jewish Reconstructionist Foundation was founded to support its publication. By 1955, congregations practicing the ideals of Reconstructionist Judaism felt the need to create an umbrella organization, which they called the Reconstructionist Fellowship of Congregations. The name of this organization went through several changes; since 1995 it has been known as the Jewish Reconstructionist Federation (JRF). The Reconstructionist Rabbinical College was established in 1967, completing the transition of the movement into a full-fledged Jewish denomination. Although movements usually take on a life of their own, as did the Reconstructionist movement, Kaplan is known to have felt that it had become too liberal.

Reconstructionist Judaism centers on the idea of an active and involved Jewish community that studies Jewish traditions to make informed decisions about which rituals and customs are meaningful in their modern lives. Because of this, rituals, customs, and even the format of the SIDDUR, or prayer book, differs greatly from one Reconstructionist congregation to another. The Jewish Reconstructionist Federation offers aid to groups attempting to define themselves, but each group is free to make its own decisions.

Some of the tenets of Reconstructionism have changed over time, such as Kaplan's original view of God. He did not accept a personal God, but rather saw God as the ability of humans to become self-fulfilled. Many Reconstructionist Jews, however, maintain a theistic view of a personal God open to relationships with individuals.

Because Reconstructionist Judaism emphasizes the evolving nature of Judaism, as Jews adapt its rituals and customs to their own lives in the modern world, Reconstructionism values personal autonomy, the individual's right to choose, over Jewish law (see HALAKHAH) and theology. Kaplan saw Jewish laws as folkways, rather than binding rules, thus opening up the possibility for change. However, classic Reconstructionist Judaism tends to lean more toward tradition than does Reform, especially the classic Reform of Europe in the 19th century, as Reconstructionism encourages individuals and communities to maintain Jewish laws and traditions unless there is a specific reason to reject them.

Also unlike Reform Judaism, Reconstructionist Judaism views decisions about laws and traditions to be a communal effort, not an individual one. Although this is difficult to enforce in any practical way, especially because of the congregation-based structure of the movement, the principle shows the importance of Jewish community in the worldview of Reconstructionism. As a result, Reconstructionist Judaism encourages the use of Hebrew in the prayer service, the wearing of *kippot*, or yarmulkes (see KIPPAH), TALLIT, and TEFILLIN during prayer, and observance of Jewish holidays. One might find several Reconstructionist synagogues that value the tradition of KASHRUT, kosher laws, as well. In addition, the denomination supports traditional rabbinic methods of study, alongside modern scholarly tools and the methods of critical text study.

Theologically, Reconstructionism explains that Judaism grew out of the social and historical experiences of the Jewish people (see PEOPLEHOOD). It does not insist upon a belief in a supernatural God, divine intervention, Jews as the CHOSEN PEOPLE, revelation, or the binding nature of any of its tenets. These statements are generalities; any Reconstructionist group may accept these ideas or reject them. Zionism receives support from Reconstructionist Judaism, and the modern state of Israel plays a central role in its ideology, as the Jewish civilization posited by the movement needs a common land or territory. Reconstructionist Judaism also encourages its members to choose to be active in activities that support social justice. In their efforts to revitalize and reconstruct Judaism, participation in social action can become an important component of an individual's and a community's search for meaning and a fulfilling life.

Reconstructionist Judaism is an egalitarian tradition, ordaining women and members of marginal groups such as homosexuals, and including them in every aspect of Jewish life. About half of Reconstructionist rabbis will officiate at an INTERMARRIAGE, but they are free not to do so. Reconstructionist Judaism identifies a Jew as someone with either a Jewish mother or a Jewish father who is raised Jewish, as does Reform Judaism. Reconstructionist Judaism is the smallest Jewish denomination, but it pioneered many innovations that other denominations have adopted, and it has adopted some ideas from other Jewish movements, such as the concept of the CHAVURAH.

One of the great innovations of Reconstructionism was the synagogue center. Kaplan encouraged the development of such centers, which offered worship as well as cultural activities, including gymnasiums and sports. Many synagogue centers sprang up in the 1970s in Conservative Judaism.

Today, the Jewish Reconstructionist Federation includes 103 affiliated organizations with 16,000 families; it continues to grow throughout the UNITED STATES. The denomination maintains the Reconstructionist Rabbinical College in Pennsylvania and the Reconstructionist Rabbinical Assembly. The denomination also maintains a youth movement called Noar Hadash (see JEWISH YOUTH GROUPS) and the Reconstructionist Press.

Further reading: Rebecca T. Alpert and Jacob J. Staub, *Exploring Judaism: A Reconstructionist Approach* (Elkins Park, Pa.: Reconstructionist Press, 1988); Jeffrey S. Gurock and Jacob J. Schacter, *A Modern Heretic and a Traditional Community* (New York: Columbia University Press, 1997); Mordecai M. Kaplan, *Judaism as a Civilization: Toward a Reconstruction of American-Jewish Life* (Philadelphia and Jerusalem: Jewish Publication Society, 1994); Jacob Neusner, *Sectors of American Judaism: Reform, Orthodoxy, Conservatism, and Reconstructionism* (New York: Ktav Publishing House, 1975).

redemption

Along with CREATION and REVELATION, redemption is one of three key terms in the Jewish view of universal history. Creation refers to the beginning of the universe and revelation refers to God's giving of the TORAH at Mount Sinai; redemption will come at the end of time.

According to Jewish tradition, God will send a MESSIAH to inaugurate the redemption. There will be an ensuing battle between good and evil, and when the battle is over, there will be an ingathering of the exiles, meaning all Jews will return to ISRAEL. The remaining nations will enter the outer circles of Israel as well, and there will be a resurrection of the dead and a day of judgment. The righteous ones who pass through the day will live happily and peacefully in this world-to-come or MESSIANIC AGE. According to the rabbis, if every Jew keeps the Sabbath (see SHABBAT) for two consecutive Sabbaths, the redemption will occur.

In addition, Jewish history includes individual or national redemption events, most notably the EXODUS from EGYPT. God's actions in the Exodus demonstrate redemptive power, which will be magnified in the final redemption.

There is some debate among Jewish theologians about whether the sovereign state of Israel is a step toward or away from the Messianic Age. While some argue that it is a first step in the ingathering of exiles, ultra-Orthodox (see ORTHODOX JUDAISM) Jews refuse to recognize the current state of Israel because they feel that only God can reestablish Israel, and the event will only happen at the time of redemption. They also believe that it is prohibited to try to purposefully hurry the coming of the Messiah.

The hope for redemption is a central part of Jewish liturgy and practice, and it is said that the Sabbath is a foretaste of the Messianic Age. Such faith in the promise of redemption is probably a major factor in the survival of the Jews over thousands of years.

Further reading: Dan Cohn-Sherbok, *The Jewish Messiah* (Edinburgh: T & T Clark, 1997); Abraham Joshua Heschel, *The Sabbath: Its Meaning for Modern Man* (New York: Noonday Press, 1996); Jacob Neusner, *Foundations of Judaism* (Atlanta: Scholars Press, 1993); Raphael Patai, ed., *The Messiah Texts* (Detroit: Wayne State University Press, 1988); Gershom Scholem, *The Messianic Idea in Judaism and Other Essays on Jewish Spirituality* (New York: Schocken Books, 1995).

Red Heifer

The TORAH (Five Books of Moses) provides some elaborate laws and procedures to ensure ritual purity for individuals. God tells Moses in Numbers (19:1–22) how to slaughter and burn a Red Heifer and use its ashes for purification. When the TEMPLE stood, the heifer would be slaughtered and burned according to the law, and its ashes would be mixed with water to purify anyone who had touched a corpse. It was considered vital to purify priests before they entered the Temple so that it would not be defiled.

The Red Heifer had to be completely red in color, without even one hair of a different color. No such completely red heifer has been found in modern times. Jews committed to rebuilding the Temple in JERUSALEM have been working in cooperation with American conservative Christian cattlemen to breed a red heifer. Thus, the Red Heifer has generated an unlikely cooperation between the two modern communities.

Further reading: John Mchugh and Roland De Vaux, *Ancient Israel: Its Life and Institutions* (Grand Rapids, Mich.: W.B. Eerdmans Publishing, 1997); Red Heifer Web site URL: http://templeinstitute.org/current-events/RedHeifer/, accessed August 16, 2004; *Tanakh: The Holy Scriptures* (Philadelphia and Jerusalem: Jewish Publication Society, 1985).

Reform Judaism

The oldest of modern Jewish denominations, Reform Judaism has played a vital role in the modern history of the Jewish people. After more than a millennium of Jewish life centered on HALAKHAH, or Jewish law, certain Jewish community leaders began to argue that comprehensive changes in both the ideology and the practice of Judaism were needed in the modern world.

Moses MENDELSSOHN (1729–86), the first ENLIGHTENMENT Jewish thinker, published *Jerusalem* in 1783. Encouraged by the promise of EMANCIPATION, full rights as citizens, for Jews in Europe, Mendelssohn offered *Jerusalem* as proof that it was possible for a Jew to be true to both Judaism and MODERNITY. He was the first in a powerful movement of Jews wishing to reform Judaism and achieve a place in European society for Jews as individuals and as a religious group. These modern thinkers were called *MASKILIM,* and they supported the Jewish Enlightenment, called the HASKALAH.

Mendelssohn's work was published in the 18th century, but it was not until the 19th century that Reform Judaism began to grow from the roots he had planted. The early Jewish leaders who supported Reform, such as Samuel HOLDHEIM (1806–60) and Abraham GEIGER (1810–74), aimed to attract Jews who had begun to leave the Jewish community for a secular or Christian life, by adapting the Jewish prayer service and SYNAGOGUE rituals to Western ideals, values, and esthetics. These leaders, many of them rabbis who had received both a Jewish and a secular education, began by instituting polite decorum in the synagogue, where worshippers were accustomed to behaving as if they were at home. The rabbis donned vestments like their Protestant colleagues, gave sermons in formal German (instead of the Yiddish dialect), and developed prayer books (*see* SIDDUR) that were shorter and included translations in the vernacular. They encouraged their congregants to pray in the vernacular too, and some even brought in organs for live instrumental music on the Sabbath (*see* SHABBAT), which was unprecedented in Jewish worship since the TEMPLE was destroyed in the year 70 C.E. The Hamburg Temple in GERMANY was the first Reform congregation; its very name revealed its new ideology.

Using the name *Temple* represented a major ideological break from traditional Judaism because it denied the long-held Jewish dream that the Messiah would come to bring the Jews back to JERUSALEM and rebuild the Temple. The reformers saw this break as essential to their quest for emancipation and rights as citizens of the European nation states; otherwise, their loyalty to their adopted European countries would be in question and the possibility of emancipation made tenuous. These leaders wanted their national loyalty to be clear to other Jews and to their non-Jewish neighbors.

In addition to the rejection of a personal Messiah, the reformers denied the divine authorship of the TORAH (*see* TORAH MI-SINAI) and TALMUD. They considered themselves bound only by those Jewish laws, or *halakhah,* that concerned ethics. Reform emphasized the Prophetic tradition and social justice, which contributed to the movement's long involvement in social justice and social action. They renounced ZIONISM as a legitimate pursuit of modern Jews for the same reasons that they rejected a personal Messiah and a return to ERETZ YISRAEL.

Ultimately, this meant that those who believed in the authenticity of Reform Judaism no longer had an obligation to adhere to Jewish rituals such as circumcision (*see* BRIT MILAH) and dietary laws (*see* KASHRUT), although classic Reformers expected Jews as individuals to examine their religious practices and choose which ones they considered binding, and not simply to abandon Jewish rituals out of laziness or ignorance. In order to develop new perspectives on Jewish ideology and theology, the reformers took advantage of modern scientific methods to examine Judaism, its literature, its history, and its rituals. Subjecting rabbinic texts such as the TANAKH and the Talmud to modern literary criticism (*see* WISSENSCHAFT DES JUDENTUMS) brought Jewish study into the modern world, but offended traditional Jews and their leaders. Because of this, the Conservative and Orthodox movements arose to provide their own counterpoints to reform—respectively, the POSITIVE-HISTORICAL SCHOOL and the NEO-ORTHODOX MOVEMENT. The new movements stood in defense of what they saw as traditional, authentic Judaism.

To solidify the new Reform movement, work out its tenets, and add to its legitimacy, rabbis who favored reform convened in Germany three times in the 1840s, in Brunswick (1844), Frankfurt (1845), and Breslau (1846). However, Reform soon provoked the rise of a strong Orthodox opposition, and the various German governments began to discourage Reform by the end of the 1840s. The center of the Reform movement crossed the Atlantic and took root in American soil. Significant numbers of German Jews immigrated to the UNITED STATES in the 1830s and 1840s. These immigrants tended to be more liberal than those who stayed behind. Eventually, these products of early Reform Judaism in Europe helped found American Reform, which became one of the largest Jewish movements in American history.

American Reform ideology solidified, and sometimes changed, via the platforms published by its leaders over the course of more than 100 years. The first platform was issued in Philadelphia in 1869, the second in Pittsburgh in 1885 (*see* PITTSBURGH PLATFORM), the third in Columbus in 1937, and the fourth in San Francisco in 1976. In addition, a revised Pittsburgh Platform was published by the Reform movement in 1999. The original 1855 Pittsburgh document was the most radical; it sought to lay down a clear ideology rather than remaining vague, as Reform leader Isaac Mayer WISE (1819–1900) had encouraged in a desire to maintain Jewish unity.

The Pittsburgh Platform established the tenets of Reform Judaism that would be supported by most Reform Jews until the Columbus Platform was passed more than 50 years later. It proclaimed Judaism to be a tolerant, universal belief system grounded in freedom; it was a religion, and not a nation, and it did not conflict with science. The movement upheld respect for Jewish law, but viewed only its ethical laws as binding; ritual laws, such as those that dictated one's diet, purity, and dress, were optional. The platform also rejected Jewish belief in resurrection, heaven and hell, and gave up any expectation that the Jews would return to PALESTINE and restore Jewish sovereignty there. On a positive note, the platform described Judaism as a belief system committed to social justice and the historical identity of the Jewish people as a group searching for truth.

By 1937, when the Columbus Platform, also called the Guiding Principles of Reform Judaism, was written, the face of Reform Judaism had begun to change. The movement now encouraged the observance of Jewish holidays, home rituals, more frequent synagogue attendance, the use of the Hebrew language, and a love of the land of Israel. Reform did not suggest that all Jews should return to Israel, but it recognized the centrality of the land and encouraged a cultural and spiritual ZIONISM. Like Reconstructionist Judaism, Reform still rejected the concept of the CHOSEN PEOPLE; unlike Reconstructionism, it insisted that Judaism was a religion, not a civilization, and that a God exists who transcends time and space.

The San Francisco Platform reiterated the broad beliefs of Reform, but treaded softly to maintain unity in the Reform community, which now included many descendants of more traditional eastern European Jews. Following the HOLOCAUST, Israel's birth, and the SIX-DAY WAR in Israel, the San Francisco Platform made a strong case for supporting the modern State of Israel.

In the contemporary world, Reform Judaism believes in the autonomy of individuals in choosing their own path of Jewish expression, that the Jewish people is dedicated to the improvement of the world (*see TIKKUN OLAM*), that Reform Jews are part of a historical tradition embodied in Torah and rabbinic literature, that the principles of pluralism are important, and that all Jews are obligated to study the traditions, history, and mitzvot (*see MITZVAH*) that link them together.

The institutions that supported the growth of Reform Judaism in the United States include the Union of American Hebrew Congregations, established in 1873, the Hebrew Union College (*see HEBREW UNION COLLEGE–JEWISH INSTITUTE OF RELIGION*), established in 1875, the Central Conference of American Rabbis (CCAR), established in 1889, the Religious Action Center (for social and political activity), the North American Federation of Temple Youth (NFTY; *see JEWISH YOUTH GROUPS*), the UAHC Press, a well-established publisher of Jewish thought and teaching materials, and *Reform Judaism* magazine.

In recent years, the name of the Reform movement's umbrella organization has changed to Union of Reform Judaism (URJ), which represents Reform congregations in North America, and the name of the press to URJ Press. The URJ includes

This Reform synagogue stands in London, England. Liberal synagogues in England are also known to use the descriptor *Progressive*. *(Courtesy J. Gordon Melton)*

900 congregations and more than 1.5 million adherents. Although Reform Judaism is strongest in the United States, there are Reform congregations around the world, represented by the World Union for Progressive Judaism, founded in 1926.

Further reading: Moses Mendelssohn, *Jerusalem* (Hanover, N.H., and London: University Press of New England, 1983); Michael A. Meyer, *Response to Modernity: A History of the Reform Movement in Judaism* (New York and Oxford: Oxford University Press, 1988); Jacob Neusner, *Sectors of American Judaism: Reform, Orthodoxy, Conservatism, and Reconstructionism* (New York: Ktav Publishing House, 1975); W. Gunther Plaut,

The Rise of Reform Judaism (New York: World Union for Progressive Judaism, 1963).

refuseniks

Refuseniks were Soviet Jews (*see* RUSSIA) who were not allowed to leave the country and immigrate to ISRAEL. In Russian, they are known as *otkaznik*, and the HEBREW term is *mesuravim*.

Many Soviet Jews applied for exit visas to leave the Soviet Union for Israel after Israel's victory in the SIX-DAY WAR in 1967. A few were granted permission, but most were turned down. The KGB, the Soviet secret service, was in charge of all exit visas; the common excuse it gave for rejection was that the refuseniks knew critical information that could damage Soviet national security if they left the country.

The Soviet Union probably feared a brain drain and also did not want foreigners or Soviet citizens to know that many people preferred to live in the West. They hoped that punishing the refuseniks would deter others from applying for exit visas.

Even though they could not leave the country, the refuseniks and often their entire families were forced out of their jobs, which exposed them to the charge of being social parasites, a serious crime in the Soviet Union. Some of them were arrested. Most Western nations limit immigration, but Israel grants automatic citizenship for any Jews who wish to immigrate, so all the refuseniks had a legitimate destination if allowed to leave.

In 1976, the Helsinki Watch Group for human rights was created. One of the founders, Natan SHARANSKY, himself a refusenik, became a leading spokesman for the movement. He was subsequently arrested and subjected to harsh imprisonment.

In the 1970s and 1980s, the refusenik movement grew stronger in the Soviet Union. In addition to the routine discrimination that Soviet Jews faced, the Soviet economy was falling apart and Jews were desperate to leave. Many Soviet Jews had economic motives for leaving, but many others wanted to live openly as Jews and practice Judaism freely, rights that were denied in the Soviet Union.

American Jewry eventually became heavily involved in the refusenik movement. The high point of Jewish activism was a rally of 250,000 people in Washington, D.C., in December 1987, following the prisoner exchange that freed Sharansky.

When Mikhail Gorbachev instituted glasnost and perestroika, Jews were finally allowed to immigrate to Israel freely, if they so chose. Hundreds of thousands took advantage of the new opportunities that Israel presents. Some Soviet Jews also immigrated to the United States, and when the Soviet Union dissolved, many more Jews immigrated to Israel and the United States, as well.

In an ironic use of the term, a small group of Israeli soldiers have called themselves refuseniks to describe their refusal to serve in Israeli occupied territories, including the Golan Heights, the West Bank (*see* JUDEA AND SAMARIA), and the Gaza Strip. The Israeli government and most Israelis have criticized these refuseniks; some call them unpatriotic; others say they threaten democracy by refusing to obey the democratically elected government.

Surprisingly, these refuseniks have also been criticized by progressive Israelis, who claim that if soldiers who oppose Israel's presence there refuse to be stationed in the territories, then only soldiers who support the policy will end up in the territories, which they fear might exacerbate the problem. They also note that right-wing soldiers may refuse to evacuate settlements if they are called upon to do so. In February 2004, 26 Israeli soldiers were prosecuted for their refusal to serve in the occupied territories. It is estimated that there are several thousand Israeli soldier refuseniks. The term, while popular among left-wing Israelis, is considered disrespectful to the many Jews who suffered as refuseniks in the former Soviet Union.

Further reading: Mark Azbel, *Refusenik: Trapped in the Soviet Union* (New York: Paragon House, 1987); Robert O. Freedman, ed., *Soviet Jewry in the 1980s: The Politics* of *Anti-Semitism and Emigration and the Dynamics of Resettlement* (Durham, N.C.: Duke University Press, 1989); Ida Nudel, *A Hand in the Darkness: The Autobiography of a Refusenik* (New York: Warner Books, 1990); Natan Sharansky, *Fear No Evil: The Classic Memoir of One Man's Triumph Over a Police State* (New York: Vintage Books, 1989).

reincarnation

The concept of reincarnation is not mentioned in either the TANAKH, the Hebrew Bible, or the TALMUD. The topic is not often discussed within the circles of NORMATIVE JUDAISM.

However, SAADIA GAON wrote in the ninth century that he had met Jews who believed that a dead person's soul may indeed move into another body. He surmised that those Jews were looking for an explanation for the suffering of innocents, and finding comfort in the idea that an innocent child's death releases the soul to find another body.

Certain Jewish mystical schools believe that souls are not just resurrected, but reincarnated multiple times. They believe the righteous are reborn to participate in TIKKUN OLAM, the reparation of the world. Some schools teach that everyone will be reborn; others teach that only a few will merit that fate. The concept of reincarnation is also used to explain the traditional teaching that every Jewish person in history was present when the COVENANT was made with God at MOUNT SINAI. In this view, each of the individuals present at that moment continues to be reborn.

Further reading: Louis Jacobs, "Immortality," in *Religion and the Individual: A Jewish Perspective* (Cambridge and New York: Cambridge University Press, 1992), 94–112; W. Hirsch, *Rabbinic Psychology: Beliefs about the Soul in Rabbinic Literature of the Talmudic Period* (London: E. Goldston, 1947); J. Ross, *The Jewish Conception of Immortality and the Life Hereafter* (Belfast, News-letter, 1948); Gershom Scholem, "Gilgul," in *Kabbalah* (Jerusalem: Keter Publishing House, 1974), 344–50.

Renewal Movement *See* JEWISH RENEWAL.

reparations

The term *reparations* usually refers to compensation paid to victims following a war by the country that inflicted the damage, as for example the reparations paid by GERMANY to the victorious Allies following World War I.

In the Jewish context, the term usually refers to HOLOCAUST reparations, compensation given to Holocaust survivors or to victims' families by various governments and corporations involved in the atrocities.

Shortly after the end of World War II and the establishment of the State of ISRAEL, the Israeli government argued that West Germany owed money to Israel on behalf of the 500,000 Holocaust survivors absorbed by the State of Israel. West Germany agreed to a reparations agreement in 1952 out of a desire to atone for Germany's actions and to win acceptance from other Western countries. The agreement stipulated that Germany provide $715 million in goods and services to the state of Israel as compensation for taking in survivors; $110 million toward programs to finance the relief, rehabilitation, and resettlement of Jewish Holocaust survivors around the world, and direct reparations to selected individuals over a 12-year period.

The issue was controversial among Jews. Many spoke out against the plan, arguing that the Germans could never atone for their actions by paying money; others thought it made sense that the money needed to rehabilitate the survivors should come from the German government. The original agreement was continued and expanded over time, eventually resulting in payments of billions of dollars and aiding Jewish communities in 39 countries.

In the 1990s, agencies working on behalf of Jewish Holocaust survivors began investigating Swiss banks (*see* SWITZERLAND) to determine the disposition of certain Holocaust-related accounts. Some of the accounts had been opened by Jews who later died in the Holocaust, and others belonged to Nazis who deposited money stolen from Holocaust victims. Other agencies began to pressure individual German companies to make reparations for their use of forced labor during the Holocaust. These companies include Deutsche Bank, Siemens, BMW, Volkswagen, Ford, and Opel. In 1999, the German government established a fund to help Holocaust survivors with money contributed by those companies. Similar funds were set up by the Swiss and the Hungarians (*see* HUNGARY).

Further reading: Benjamin Ferencz, *Less Than Slaves: Jewish Forced Labor and the Quest for Compensation* (Bloomington: Indiana University Press, 2002); Menachem Rosensaft and Joana Rosensaft, *A Measure of Justice: The Early History of German-Jewish Reparations* (New York: Leo Baeck Institute, 2003); Ronald Zweig, *German Reparations and the Jewish World* (London: Frank Cass, 2001).

Resnick, Judith (1949–1986) *pioneering woman astronaut*

Judith Resnik was born on April 5, 1949, in Akron, Ohio. Defying the social norms of her time, she was one of the first female astronauts and was the first Jew to go into space. Tragically, she died during the crash of the space shuttle *Challenger* on January 28, 1986, at the age of 36.

Resnick went to public schools and graduated from high school in 1966. She received a bachelor of science degree in electrical engineering from Carnegie-Mellon University in 1970, and a doctorate in electrical engineering from the University of Maryland in 1977. After finishing her doctoral degree, Resnick first worked for RCA, the National Institutes of Health, and Xerox before NASA selected her as an astronaut candidate in 1978. She completed her training in 1979, and served in a number of capacities. In 1984, Resnik went on her first trip into space as a mission specialist on the maiden voyage of the space shuttle *Discovery*. On the mission, Resnik logged 144 hours and 57 minutes in space.

Although Resnik was brought up as a Jew and became a bat mitzvah (*see* BAR/BAT MITZVAH), as an adult she was not an observant Jew. Also, she wanted to be thought of as an astronaut, rather than a "Jewish astronaut" or a "female astronaut."

On January 28, 1986, millions watched Resnik on television as she boarded the space shuttle *Challenger*, smiling and waving. The *Challenger* was launched from the Kennedy Space Center at 11:38 A.M., but in a horrible tragedy, Resnik and the rest of the seven-member crew died at 11:39 when the shuttle exploded seconds after it was launched. Far more media attention than usual had surrounded this shuttle mission, since it included the first civilian in space, teacher Christa McAuliffe. After the tragic explosion, most of the media attention centered on McAuliffe, overshadowing the heroic and tragic deaths of the other crew members such as Judith Resnik.

Further reading: Joanne Bernstein, *Judith Resnik, Challenger Astronaut* (New York: Lodestar Books, 1990); Seymour Brody, *Jewish Heroes and Heroines of America: 150 True Stories of American Jewish Heroism* (Hollywood, Fla.: Lifetime Books, 1996).

responsa (sing.: responsum)

A responsum is a written rabbinic answer to a question of HALAKHAH, or Jewish law. Responsa literature has been in existence from the era of the GEONIM (seventh to 11th centuries) to the present. There are well over a thousand printed collections of responsa, many of which had great influence on Jewish CODES OF LAW.

A responsum offers a rabbinical opinion on a contemporary legal issue, usually in response to a practical question. It uses proof texts from sacred literature, previous legal precedents, and the customs of the community involved, and it presents the reasoning used to arrive at the decision, so that readers will feel compelled to follow the rabbinic guidance.

Orthodox rabbis (*see* ORTHODOX JUDAISM) are still writing and following responsa. In the Conservative movement (*see* CONSERVATIVE JUDAISM), the Law Committee will write responsa to guide other Conservative rabbis when making their decisions as to what would be most proper for their community. The Reform movement also writes responsa, but they are considered advisory, and not authoritative to each Reform Jew.

Further reading: Avraham Finkel, *Responsa Anthology* (Northvale, N.J.: Jason Aronson, 1990); Solomon Bennett Freehof, *The Responsa Literature and A Treasury of Responsa* (Hoboken, N.J.: Ktav Publishing, 1973); N. S. Hecht, *An Introduction to the History and Sources of Jewish Law* (Oxford: Oxford University Press, 1996); Walter Jacob and Moshe Zemer, eds., *Crime and Punishment in Jewish Law* (New York: Berghahn Books, 1999).

resurrection

Resurrection is the belief that the physical bodies of the departed will revive to full life at some time in the future. Jews have expressed different views on this subject over the centuries. According to the historian JOSEPHUS, the SADDUCEES rejected the idea of a bodily resurrection, while the PHARISEES accepted it. RAMBAM included the notion of resurrection in his Thirteen Principles of Faith. Tradition teaches that only the righteous will be resurrected when the MESSIANIC AGE begins; the wicked will not.

The first explicit reference to resurrection appears in the book of Daniel, but Ezekiel had earlier prophesized about God "lift[ing] you out of the graves, O My People, and bring[ing] you to the Land of Israel. . . . I will put my breath into you and you shall live again, and I will set you upon your own soil" (Ezekiel 37). Jewish tradition teaches that resurrection may be part of the end times; according to some views, all those buried on the Mount of Olives in JERUSALEM will rise first. However, most schools within Judaism do not spend much time discussing these concepts; instead, they usually emphasize the issues and rewards of life in the here and now.

Further reading: Abraham Cohen, *Everyman's Talmud: The Major Teachings of the Rabbinic Sages* (reprint, New York: Schocken Books, 1995), 346–390; W. Hirsch, *Rabbinic Psychology: Beliefs about the Soul in Rabbinic Literature of the Talmudic Period* (London: E. Goldston, 1947); Louis Jacobs, "Immortality," in *Religion and the Individual: A Jewish Perspective* (Cambridge and New York: Cambridge University Press, 1992), 94–112; J. Ross, *The Jewish Conception of Immortality and the Life Hereafter* (Belfast, News-letter, 1948).

revelation

Judaism traditionally teaches that God has interacted with the CHOSEN PEOPLE throughout history by means of direct revelation; in other words, God, law, and the divine plan are revealed to people living on earth.

In the beginning of Jewish history God singled out Abraham and the other PATRIARCHS, and spoke to them. God later spoke to MOSES, and still later the prophets (*see* NEVI'IM) were granted revelations as well.

The TORAH, both Written and Oral, is all considered to be revealed truth, and God continues to use it as the main tool of revelation. The Torah was revealed through Moses and the succeeding generations of prophets, and interpreted by the ancient RABBIS. Consequently, everything that Jews know about God they know because God chose to disclose it directly.

As the single most important revelation, the Torah records God's activity throughout human history, particularly in relationship to the Jews. It illuminates God's character. Finally, it teaches how Jews should behave as individuals and as God's community in the world.

Further reading: Samuel S. Cohon, "Revelation: Traditional View," and "A Modern View," in *Jewish Theology* (New York: Behrman House, 1974); Isidore Epstein, "The Relation of Revelation to Reason," and "Revelation and Prophecy," in *The Faith of Judaism* (London: Soncino Press, 1954); Louis Jacobs, "Torah as Divine Revelation" in *God Torah Israel: Traditionalism without Fundamentalism* (Cincinnati, Ohio: Hebrew Union College Press, 1990).

reward and punishment

A system of reward and punishment is central to Judaism. According to the book of Deuteronomy (*see* TORAH), the system works on the level of the nation. If the Jews obey the commandments of the Torah, they will be blessed with wealth, numbers, and success. If they disobey they will be cursed, fall ill, experience calamities, be impoverished and fail to succeed.

Jews have usually understood this system to apply on an individual level too. The holidays of ROSH HASHANAH and YOM KIPPUR, and the days of awe in between emphasize this process. Individual Jews atone for their individual sins at this time and ask to be inscribed individually for a good year. The TANAKH also suggests that rewards and punishment will extend to an individual's descendants, up to the fourth generation for punishments, and up to the thousandth generation for rewards.

However, Jewish tradition has generally understood the system of reward and punishment to apply collectively. That is the fundamental idea behind DEUTERONOMIC HISTORY, as expressed in several books of the Tanakh. Because the people collectively entered into a COVENANT with God at MOUNT SINAI, the people are punished collectively and exiled for sins, and they are rewarded collectively as well. The biblical history of the ISRAELITE kings is written from this point of view; when the king and people are faithful, the kingdom is prosperous and successful, but when the king and people become unfaithful, they are open to calamities and to defeat in battle. Even in the liturgy of Rosh HaShanah and Yom Kippur, this collective aspect of the system of reward and punishment survives, as the confession is recited in the plural and in a community setting.

The HOLOCAUST has raised serious problems for Jewish theology regarding this system of collective reward and punishment. While some hold that the system remains intact and that the Holocaust was in part divine retribution for the sin of ASSIMILATION, such a view seems callous to many other Jews. Many cannot conceive of any sin that would warrant such massive and inhumane retribution, and can only see the Holocaust as a refutation of Deuteronomic history and proof of the impossibility of any system of reward and punishment.

Further reading: Shmuel Boteach, *Wrestling with the Divine: A Jewish Response to Suffering* (Northvale, N.J.: Aronson, 1995); Dan Cohn-Sherbok, *Holocaust Theology: A Reader* (Exeter: University of Exeter Press, 2002); Terence Fretheim, Lloyd R. Bailey, and Victor P. Furnish, eds., *Deuteronomic History* (Nashville, Tenn.: Abington Press, 1983); Jacob Neusner, *The Theology of the Oral Torah: Revealing the Justice of God* (Montreal: McGill-Queen's University Press, 1999).

Romania

There has been a Jewish population in Romania for millennia, as Jews probably arrived with the Roman legions as early as the second century C.E. Large communities arose in 1367 composed of Jews expelled from HUNGARY, and more Jewish refugees arrived from SPAIN in the 16th century, mainly settling in the principality of Walachia. Even more Jews came after the CHMIELNICKI MASSACRES of 1648–49. In the 18th century rulers of the principality of Moldavia granted special charters to attract Jews; the charters exempted them from taxes, and provided land for SYNAGOGUES, ritual baths (*see* MIKVAH), and cemeteries. They were also given the right to be represented on councils. Jews were encouraged to set up commercial centers, called burgs, and many worked as craftsmen, such as furriers, tailors, bootmakers, tinsmiths, and watchmakers.

Romanian Jews were not immune to ANTISEMITISM, however. Some anti-Jewish feelings resulted from commercial competition (*see* ANTIJUDAISM); in 1579 one ruler of Moldavia expelled the Jews because of the perceived risk to other merchants. In 1640, the Greek Orthodox Church in Moldavia denounced Jews as heretics and forbade relations with them as a matter of law. Anti-Jewish riots occasionally occurred, often around Easter.

Times grew worse for the Jews in the 19th century as Romania fought to become independent from the Ottoman Empire. As rebellion broke out in 1821, Greek volunteers crossed into Moldavia and plundered and massacred Jews. From 1819 to 1856 Moldavia and Walachia were under the control of RUSSIA, and Russian antisemitism spread to those areas. Laws were passed to mimic the antisemitic laws in Russia, forbidding Jews to settle in villages, lease lands, or establish factories. Jews were denied citizenship and often exploited by corrupt administrators; the authorities were even given permission to expel any Jews they deemed not useful to the country. Another Romanian revolt, this time against the Russians, ensued in 1848. Jews were recruited to participate in the revolt and some did, but the revolt was put down.

The second half of the 19th century brought ups and downs for the Jews of Romania. The 1856 peace treaty ending the Crimean War left the area under Ottoman suzerainty but granted local autonomy in some areas; freedom of religion was granted, at least in theory. When Moldavia and Walachia were united in 1859 under Alexandry Ioan Cuza, who was not unfriendly to the Jews, some 3 percent of the resulting population was Jewish. In 1864 Jews achieved suffrage in local councils as well as other political rights. However, new leadership emerged in 1866 and a new constitution was adopted that restricted citizenship to Christians, and many Jews were persecuted and expelled starting in 1867. ENGLAND, FRANCE, HOLLAND, and GERMANY protested the treatment of Romanian Jews, but the Romanian government insisted that the "Jewish problem" was an internal one.

The great powers made civil rights for Jews a condition of Romanian independence, which was formalized in 1878 at the Congress of Berlin. Romania ignored the condition and proceeded with its antisemitic policies. The European powers eventually relented, which led to a worsening of the situation of Jews in Romania. Jews were no longer considered subjects of Romania but foreigners, and they were prohibited from working as lawyers, teachers, chemists, stockbrokers, or in government occupations including officers, rail-

way workers, state hospital workers, or sellers of such goods as tobacco, alcohol, or salt. Individual Jews advocating EMANCIPATION were expelled, while all Jews were denied public education starting in 1893. Officially antisemitic parties were established and rose to power.

In the early 20th century, the Jews of Romania began to organize. They set up their own schools and founded a political organization to fight antisemitism and advocate emancipation. The community suffered from some internal struggles over the issue of ASSIMILATION.

World War I brought large new territories to Romania, including Bessarabia and Transylvania. Romanian Jews had cause for optimism, because both provinces had large populations of Jews who had been citizens of Russia and Hungary, respectively; in addition, the international peace conference in Paris called for civil rights for minorities, including Jews. Naturalization of Jews was provided for in the Romanian constitution of 1923, but in practice there were numerous procedural restrictions for Jews and many occupations remained closed.

Antisemitism continued to increase through the 1920s and 1930s, with demonstrations and violent outbreaks. Murderers of Jews were sometimes acquitted and synagogues were occasionally burned. After Adolf HITLER's rise to power in 1933, relations between Germany and Romania grew close. Romania complied with German trade agreements that stipulated the removal of Jews from industry. Romanian political parties copied Nazi antisemitic platforms, and Jews gradually lost most of their rights and all but one member of parliament. In 1940, as a result of the German-Soviet pact, Romania was forced to transfer territories to the Soviet Union; as the Romanian troops retreated they massacred many Jews and threw Jewish travelers off moving trains.

During World War II, Romania tried to ward off German conquest by making various concessions to Germany. The country became in effect a satellite of Nazi Germany. Jewish citizenship was revoked, Jewish-owned shops and property were confiscated, and Jewish business owners were tortured until they transferred their assets to the government. In 1941, a bloody POGROM took place in Bucharest in which Jewish homes were looted, shops burned, and synagogues vandalized or destroyed; about 120 Jews were rounded up and murdered.

The Romanian army joined Germany in the war against the Soviet Union in the summer of 1941. During their advance into Soviet provinces, soldiers massacred Jews or deported them, only to have them killed or sent back. Half of the 320,000 Jews living in Bessarabia, Bukovina, and the Dorohoi districts were murdered during the first few months of the war, up to September 1, 1941. As in other countries, Romanian Jews were moved into GHETTOS and CONCENTRATION CAMPS, where they were easy prey for bloody incursions by soldiers, and from which they were often deported or sent into forced labor. Discriminatory economic practices also continued, leaving Jews impoverished, with no occupations but with high taxation. Overall, of the prewar Jewish population of Romania, 43 percent, or 264,900, were murdered or died from epidemics, famine, or exposure. Almost 80 percent of the remaining population was left jobless and destitute.

In 1944 Romania switched sides and joined the Allies. After the war the country came under Soviet influence and a Communist government was installed. Religion was curbed, but not completely suppressed. Romanian Jews were permitted to immigrate to ISRAEL. This policy led to a steady decrease in the number of Romanian Jews. A large number emigrated between 1945 and 1947, fleeing the terror that had been instilled by the HOLOCAUST. Among those who remained, Zionist (see ZIONISM) organizations received more and more resistance from the Communist government, and were eventually dismantled, but Jewish religious and educational organizations were allowed to operate. It is estimated that less than 15,000 Jews remain in Romania, and the number continues to dwindle due to emigration despite the decrease in antisemitism.

Further reading: Randolph Braham, *The Tragedy of Romanian Jewry* (New York: Columbia University Press, 1994); Dinu C. Giurescu, *Romania in the Second World War: 1939–1945* (New York: Columbia University Press, 2000); Charles Hoffman, *Gray Dawn: Jews of Eastern Europe in the Post-Communist Era* (New York: HarperCollins, 1992); Carol Iancu, *Jews in Romania 1866–1919: From Exclusion to Emancipation* (New York: Columbia University Press, 2000).

Rome

Ancient Rome, and the Roman Empire, was the predominant foreign overseer of the Jewish people during its reign. The Roman Empire reached its apex in the second century, when it controlled Africa, Asia, Europe, and the Near East. Rome maintained its rule in Judea until the seventh century. While there were brief periods in which Jews and Judaism prospered under Roman control, the majority of ancient Jewish texts perceive Rome as the epitome of evil. The common rabbinic MIDRASH asserts that all the Romans descended from Esau, the PATRIARCH Jacob's twin brother, who is known in rabbinic texts (*see* TORAH, TALMUD) for his murderous, idolatrous, and licentious behavior.

Jews came to live in the Roman DIASPORA as early as the second century B.C.E. The history of the Jewish community of ancient Rome is known in both Greek and Latin historical records, and additional information can be found in the Talmud. One significant text written on Roman Jewry was recorded by PHILO JUDAEUS OF ALEXANDRIA. Philo visited Rome in 40 C.E., and he details how the Jews of Rome lived, and how the Roman emperor Augustus had protected the Jews. Augustus had permitted the Jews to send tithes to their TEMPLE in JERUSALEM, granted Jews Roman citizenship, permitted them to study Jewish law (*see* HALAKHAH), and allowed them to observe their SHABBAT, or the Sabbath. Philo portrayed a positive climate for the Roman Jews, but there are other primary documents that portray that the Jews were not treated well in the Rome of this era.

These documents report that Jews were denied access to cleaner water supplies, religiously persecuted or ridiculed, and impoverished.

While approximately 40,000 Jews lived in Rome itself in the beginning of the first century, those who remained in the Jewish homeland in the Roman province of Judea were severely oppressed at the same time. Rome heavily taxed the local Jewish residents, and a growing anti-Jewish (see ANTI-JUDAISM) religious sentiment developed. This oppression of the Judean Jews culminated in a Jewish revolt against Rome in the year 66. The Roman retaliation was swift and overwhelming. The Jewish revolt, called the Great Revolt, was defeated, and the Temple of Jerusalem was destroyed in the year 70.

One of the few holdouts against Rome took place at MASADA, a fortress built by Herod years earlier in the desert, but the Roman siege ultimately resulted in the suicide of the Jewish residents in the year 73 when it became clear that the Roman soldiers would breach the gates. While under Roman rule, Jewish communities were established in some of the Roman provinces, including Asia Minor and Egypt, but some of these communities revolted in the early second century, and they too were quickly defeated.

The final major Jewish revolt against Rome, the Bar Kokhba Revolt, (see BAR-KOKHBA, SHIMON), occurred from 132–135. Rome had forbidden common Jewish practices such as teaching the TORAH, circumcision (see BRIT MILAH), and observing the Sabbath. They also transformed Jerusalem into a pagan city and renamed it Aelius Hadrianus, after the Roman emperor Hadrian who initiated the hateful Hadrianic persecution of the Jews. The Bar Kokhba rebellion was motivated by a Jewish messianic fervor, but after little more than three years, the rebellion was completely defeated, and thousands upon thousands of Jews had been slaughtered. With the Jewish population decimated or exiled, Jews became a minority in Judea. Hadrian desired to completely eliminate the Jewish character of Judea, so he changed the name of the province of Judea to Palaestina (see PALES-TINE), the name of the now nonexistent Philistines, who had once ruled over the land.

Roman occupation was brutal, and it was responsible for the persecution of many non-Roman groups in Palestine. Another victim of Rome in the early first century had been the Jew JESUS OF NAZARETH. The Roman Pontius Pilate had Jesus crucified because he was considered a religious and political agitator. The early Jewish-Christians and Gentile-Christians, like the Jews, were also heavily persecuted by Rome. However, the Gentile influx into CHRISTIANITY over the centuries ultimately resulted in the Roman Empire becoming a Christian empire in 315. The once-oppressed Christians kept in place the Roman anti-Jewish legislation of the past centuries, helping to cement the second-class status of the Jews and Judaism throughout the world until the Napoleonic EMANCIPATION in the late 18th century. Roman rule extended over Palestine until the beginning of the seventh century, when Palestine came under Muslim control.

While Jerusalem was decimated by Rome in the year 70, and the Jewish Temple cultic system was obliterated, the Romans did permit the Jews to establish a cooperative Jewish rabbinic government at YAVNEH, initially under the leadership of Yochanan BEN ZAKKAI. The Roman permission for the establishment of Yavneh saved the Jews, and permitted the full development of rabbinic Judaism. The sages of Yavneh developed a full religious system to substitute for the former Temple cultic practices. Under the pharisaic (see PHAR-ISEES) rabbinic leadership, the Jews continued their religious scholarship and leadership. Ultimately, under Roman law, rabbinic authority became primary in the Jewish life. Oral rabbinic tradition was recorded in the MISHNAH, and the creation of the TALMUD would soon comprise a fully portable constitution for the Jews to carry wherever exile would bring them.

Further reading: Leonard Victor Rutgers, "Roman Policy toward the Jews: Expulsions from the City of Rome During the First Century," in *Judaism and Christianity in*

First-Century Rome (Grand Rapids, Mich.: Eerdmans, 1998); Lawrence H. Schiffman, *From Text to Tradition: A History of Second Temple and Rabbinic Judaism* (Hoboken, N.J.: Ktav Publishing House, 1991); Marcel Simon; *Versus Israel: A Study of the Relations between Christians and Jews in the Roman Empire* (Oxford and New York: Littman Library by Oxford University Press, 1986).

Rosenzweig, Franz (1886–1929) *philosopher and theologian*

Franz Rosenzweig was born in Kessel, GERMANY, in 1886 into a wealthy and assimilated Jewish family that had little connection to Jewish life. He received hardly any Jewish education, yet he earned a doctorate in philosophy in 1912 with a doctoral thesis on the political and historical theory of Hegel.

Thus, Rosenzweig was well versed in philosophy and history, including the history of religion. He accepted the view of the broader German culture that CHRISTIANITY was the greatest religion, representing the end of a long process of religious evolution. At one point Rosenzweig even considered converting to Christianity, as had his cousin.

Then, in 1913, Rosenzweig had an intense religious experience on YOM KIPPUR in an Orthodox SYNAGOGUE (*see* ORTHODOX JUDAISM) in Berlin. After that point, his respect for Judaism soared, though he did not abandon his positive attitude toward Christianity. He reconciled his admiration for both religions by constructing a new theology: all people except Jews had to go through Jesus to reach God the Father, but Jews had their own direct relationship to that same God, which preceded the birth of Jesus. In this respect, Rosenzweig understood both Judaism and Christianity to be authentic religions.

After his religious experience, Rosenzweig immersed himself in Jewish studies, working to combine his existentialist philosophy with his new devotion to Judaism. While serving in the German army in World War I, he worked out his new theological perspective on postcards he would send home. These notes ended up as part of

Rosenzweig's main work, *The Star of Redemption.* Rosenzweig's philosophy as set out in the *Star of Redemption* begins with a person knowing the actions of God and humanity, moves to a discussion of revelation as a miracle of faith, and ends with the explanation that truth is only significant when it is proved to be truth. Rosenzweig explains, "Truth is no longer what is true, but becomes that which has been proved to be true."

Rosenzweig graphically represents his theory, using the image of the six-pointed STAR OF DAVID. The complete star stood for the relationships between God and humans. The three points of the downward triangle represent God relating to the world through CREATION, REVELATION, and REDEMPTION, while the three points of the upward triangle represent humans, the world, and God, showing that humans relate to God via their relationship to the world.

Rosenzweig's understanding of Creation, revelation, and redemption was existentialist as well. Creation begins the relationship between God and humans, and the Torah acts as revelation as the individual finds meaning in the world through the experience of Torah. Similarly, redemption for Rosenzweig was not a collective salvation at the end of time but an individual redemption as the individual finds fulfillment and purpose in this life.

In 1920, Rosenzweig established a center in Berlin where Jewish teachers could lecture on Jewish topics to help other German Jews find their own authentic form of Judaism. Rosenzweig felt that in learning with others he could authenticate his philosophy that the meaning of life is found in dialogue and tension, not in an often sought-after essence of being. He founded his school to live up to his own beliefs, and he called it Das Freie Jüdische Lehrhaus, or the Free Jewish House of Teaching. The Lehrhaus was open to anyone who wanted to learn, Jew or non-Jew.

Rosenweig died a young man on December 10, 1929 from paralysis caused by amyotrophic lateral sclerosis (ALS), from which he suffered for at least the last eight years of his life. Even so, he continued to lecture and put his thoughts down in letters. He and Martin BUBER produced in these years a translation into German of the TANAKH, or Hebrew Bible. After Rosenzweig's death the Lehrhaus continued until 1930, and in 1933 Buber reopened the school.

Further reading: Nahum N. Glatzer, *Franz Rosenzweig: His Life and Thought* (Philadelphia: Jewish Publication Society of America, 1953); Julius Guttmann, *The Philosophy of Judaism: The History of Jewish Philosophy from Biblical Times to Franz Rosenzweig* (Northvale, N.J.: Aronson, 1988); Franz Rosenzweig, *God, Man, and World: Lectures and Essays* (Syracuse, N.Y.: Syracuse University Press, 1998); ———, *The Star of Redemption* (Notre Dame, Ind.: Notre Dame University Press, 1985); Fritz A. Rothschild, ed., *Jewish Perspectives on Christianity: Leo Baeck, Martin Buber, Franz Rosenzweig, Will Herberg, and Abraham J. Heschel* (New York: Continuum, 1996).

Rosh HaShanah

Literally, Rosh HaShanah means the "head" of the year. It falls on the first day of the Hebrew month of Tishri. Despite the fact that the Hebrew Bible refers to Tishri as the seventh month of the Jewish CALENDAR, the first of Tishri has been celebrated since ancient times as the Jewish New Year. According to Jewish tradition, the date is the anniversary of CREATION, so Rosh HaShanah is the birthday of the world.

The only requirements for Rosh HaShanah in the TORAH are that it is a day of rest, that the priests offer special SACRIFICES, and that it is commemorated with trumpet blasts. The second requirement can no longer be fulfilled since there is no TEMPLE. Blowing the SHOFAR, or ram's horn, fulfills the third requirement. The rabbis assigned the story of the AKEDAH, the binding of Isaac (see PATRIARCHS), as the Torah portion to be read in synagogue on Rosh HaShanah, perhaps because of the ram whose horn was caught in the thicket that Abraham sacrificed in place of his son.

The Torah portion is also significant in that it testifies to Abraham's FAITH as a paradigm of the merits of the Patriarchs. On Rosh Hashanah, Jews ask God to take the merits of their ancestors into account when judging their own lives; the day has come to be seen as a trial or judgment day. According to Jewish tradition, God writes down each Jew's fate in the coming year on Rosh HaShanah and seals the decree on YOM KIPPUR. On these two holidays and the Days of Awe in between, Jews pray, repent their sins, and engage in acts of charity to try to ensure a good fate. For this reason, it has become customary on Rosh HaShanah to eat apples dipped in honey and to use sweet round challahs for the blessing over bread. The sweetness reinforces the hope for a sweet year ahead, and the round shape represents the cycle of the entire new year ahead.

Further reading: Shmuel Yosef Agnon, *Days of Awe* (New York: Schocken Books, 1965); Irving Greenberg, *The Jewish Way: Living the Holidays* (New York: Touchstone, 1988); Jacob Neusner, ed., *Tractate Moed Qatan* (Atlanta: Scholars Press, 1992).

Rosh Hodesh

Rosh Hodesh literally means the head of the month; it is a minor festival celebrating each new moon, which is always the first day of the Jewish month. The book of Numbers (see TORAH), prescribes special sacrifices and trumpet blasts on Rosh Hodesh. Other books of the TANAKH tell of joyful celebrations, festive meals, and family gatherings on that day. While the book of Amos indicates it may have been a day of rest at one time, the rabbis permit work on Rosh Hodesh, though they mention a tradition of women abstaining from work. Some traditional Jewish women still refrain from sewing and other household tasks on the day.

With the destruction of the TEMPLE and the elimination of sacrifices, Rosh Hodesh became a minor festival. While some kabbalists (see KABBALAH) emphasized the importance of Rosh Hodesh, and a few extra prayers are recited on new moon days, the festival largely fell into disregard until feminists reclaimed it in the 1970s. At the present time, Rosh Hodesh has become a women's festival, in which groups of women come together to feast, celebrate, and usually engage in discussions with a religious theme.

The female connection to the moon is well evidenced cross-culturally and probably stems from the correlation between the cycle of the moon and women's menstrual cycles. One medieval Jewish source, Or Zaaruah, makes this connection as well. Feminists have further connected Rosh Hodesh and feminist ideals to the kabbalistic idea that in the MESSIANIC AGE the moon will be restored to its original size, equal to the sun. The feminist interpretation is that at the time when the moon is restored to its original status, women too will be restored to theirs.

Further reading: Susan Berrin, ed., *Celebrating the New Moon: A Rosh Chodesh Anthology* (Northvale, N.J.: Aronson, 1996); Irving Greenberg, *The Jewish Way: Living the Holidays* (New York: Touchstone, 1988); Elizabeth Koltun, ed., *The Jewish Woman: New Perspectives* (New York: Schocken Books, 1976); Judith Solomon, *The Rosh Hodesh Table: Foods at the New Moon: Jewish Women's Monthly Festivals* (New York: Biblio Press, 1995).

Roth, Aaron (1894–1944) *rabbi and Hasidic leader*

Aaron Roth was born in Ungvar, HUNGARY. He studied TALMUD, the great compilation of Jewish literature, under various Hasidic masters (*see* HASIDISM). Thanks to his intellectual abilities and sincere piety, Roth was eventually recognized as a mystical teacher and a Hasidic master himself. His case was unusual, since in his day only sons or sons-in-law of Hasidic rebbes became leader of Hasidic communities. Generally, such successions were made on a hereditary basis, but an exception was made in Roth's case, and he was able to establish his own Hasidic community.

Roth became known as Reb Arele. He gained two circles of disciples, one in Beregovo, Ukraine,

and one in JERUSALEM. His followers, known as the Reb Arelich Hasidim, were noted for their intense piety and their extreme opposition to ZIONISM. The Reb Arelich Hasidim divided into two branches after Roth's death, one of which followed his son, and the other his son-in-law.

Unlike many Hasidic masters who transmitted their ideas orally or through notes written down by disciples, Roth composed a number of works. His main work, *Shomer Emunim* (Guardian of faith) stresses the supreme value of simple, uncomplicated faith. It contains a famous section titled "Agitation of the Soul," in which Roth provides his own personal mystical testimony. He also wrote *Shulchan HaTahor* (The pure table), which focuses on eating as an act of divine worship. In other works, Roth encourages his followers to practice both asceticism and ecstatic prayer.

One of the most famous stories about Aaron Roth recounts how lighting a HANUKKIYAH miraculously saved his life. Reb Arele was severely ill and on his deathbed, but it was the first night of Chanukah, so his students brought him a *hanukkiyah* to light. He could barely hold the candle that lights the others and barely whisper the first blessing, but as he lit the candle his body and voice grew stronger. By the end of the night he was dancing, and he went on to live for many more years.

Further reading: Yitzhak Buxbaum, *Jewish Tales of Mystic Joy* (Indianapolis: Jossey-Bass, 2002); Dan Cohn-Sherbok and Lavinia Cohn-Sherbok, *Jewish and Christian Mysticism* (New York: Continuum, 1994); Louis Jacobs ed., *The Shocken Book of Jewish Mystical Testimonies* (New York: Schocken Books, 1997); Mindy Ribner, *Kabbalah Month by Month* (Indianapolis: Jossey-Bass, 2002); Rabbi Zalman Schachter Shalomi ed., *Wrapped in a Holy Flame: Teachings and Tales of the Hasidic Masters* (Indianapolis: Jossey-Bass, 2003).

Roth, Henry (1906–1995) *novelist of immigrant life*

Henry Roth was born in 1906 in Tysmenica, Galicia, Austria-Hungary (*see* AUSTRIA; HUNGARY) but moved to New York City in 1907 with his mother to join his father. Raised first in Brooklyn, then on the LOWER EAST SIDE, and then in Harlem, Roth eventually attended the City College of New York, where he began his writing career. His fame derives from his best-known novel, *Call It Sleep*, originally published in 1934. Because of the Depression, the publisher went bankrupt and the book went out of print despite critical acclaim. It became immensely popular upon reissue in the 1960s, when it sold more than a million copies and was heralded as a classic of Jewish-American literature.

Call It Sleep is the story of a young Jewish immigrant, David Shearl, living in New York City just prior to World War I, whose father cannot hold a job and becomes abusive, while his mother tries to protect him. The novel has been praised for its use of interior monologue and idiomatic language. It provides a window into the life of Jewish immigrants on the Lower East Side in the early 20th century through vivid descriptions of all facets of life, including antisemitic encounters (*see* ANTI-SEMITISM) and through the accurate use of broken English, Yiddish phrases, and even the dialects of an Irish policeman and Italian street sweeper.

After publishing *Call It Sleep* in 1934, Roth continued to write but did not publish another novel for decades. He worked at various jobs including metal grinder and poultry farmer, married in 1939, and became active in the Communist Party through the 1940s. In the 1960s after the reissue of *Call It Sleep*, Roth took a position at the University of New Mexico. In 1987 Roth published a collection of short stories, and in 1994 he published his second novel, *Mercy of a Rude Stream*, the story of another Jewish immigrant in New York in the 1920s, Ira Stigman. Stigman's story continues in *Driving Rock on the Hudson*, published a year later in 1995. Critics have found many parallels between Roth's own life and Ira Stigman's, but Roth noted that while there are parallels, the novels are not autobiographical. The third volume in the set, *From Bondage*, was published posthumously in 1996, after Roth's death in 1995.

Further reading: Daniel S. Burt, *The Novel 100: A Ranking of the Greatest Novels of All Time* (New York: Checkmark Books, 2004); Milton Hindus ed., *The Jewish East Side, 1881–1924* (New Brunswick, N.J.: Transaction Publishers, 1996); Henry Roth, *Call It Sleep* (San Francisco: Arion Press, 1995).

Roth, Philip (b. 1933) *novelist*

Philip Roth was born in Newark, New Jersey, in 1933. Scenes from his northeastern Jewish childhood often appeared in his first novels and short stories. He graduated from Bucknell College and received a master's degree in English from the University of Chicago in 1955, but he abandoned his doctoral studies in 1959 to write film reviews for the *New Republic*.

Roth's name became known to both the Jewish and non-Jewish worlds that same year when he published his first work, *Goodbye Columbus*, five short stories and the title novella, which satirized the life of a suburban middle-class Jewish family; it won a National Book Award. It popularized the figure of the Jewish American Princess and shed a less than flattering light on Jewish life in America.

In 1969 Roth published *Portnoy's Complaint*, which became a number-one best seller. It was met with widespread criticism for its graphic sex scenes and its negative portrait of the Jewish mother. Unlike other American Jewish writers, Roth does not hesitate to show Jewish American life warts and all; he uses his canvas to express feelings of frustration about life in general. In his later work, Roth explores ideas of Jewish identity, building upon his earlier portraits of Jewish life.

Roth has not been universally embraced in the Jewish community, because of the criticisms he seems to level in his novels at American Jewish family and community life. Yet he remains popular with readers and many critics. He has taught writing in many venues, such as the State University of Iowa, Princeton University, the State University of New York, and the University of Pennsylvania. In 1988, Roth became a Distinguished Professor at Hunter College in New York.

Novelist Philip Roth often uses imagery associated with American Jewish life in his stories and novels. Despite his critical approach to the Jewish community, Roth's works are popular among both Jews and non-Jews. *(Library of Congress)*

Roth's career has been peppered by many awards. These include: a Guggenheim fellowship (1959), the National Book Award (1960, 1995), a Rockefeller fellowship (1966), the National Book Critics Circle award (1988, 1992), the PEN/Faulkner Award (1993, 2000), National Medal of Arts at the White House (1988), and the Gold Medal in fiction (2001, the highest award one can receive from the American Academy of Arts and Letters). Roth recently published his latest controversial, novel, *The Plot Against America: A Novel* (2004), that imagines life in America had Charles A. Lindbergh, a Nazi sympathizer, defeated Franklin Delano Roosevelt in the 1940 presidential election.

Further reading: Alan Cooper, *Philip Roth and the Jews* (Albany: State University of New York Press, 1996); Steven Milowitz, *Philip Roth Considered: The Controversial Universe of the American Writer* (New York: Garland Publishing, 2000); Philip Roth, *Goodbye, Columbus, and Five Short Stories* (Boston: Houghton Mifflin, 1959); ———, *Portnoy's Complaint* (New York: Random House, 1969); Jeffrey Rubin-Dorsky, "Philip Roth and the American Jewish Identity," in *American Literary History*, Vol. 13, Issue 1: 79 (2001).

Rothschild, Edmond James de
(1845–1934) *art collector and philanthropist*
Baron Edmond James de Rothschild was born in Paris in 1845 into a wealthy family of bankers, but he chose to devote his own life to art and culture. A noted philanthropist, he used his family fortune to establish institutes for sciences and fine arts. He eventually curtailed his art acquisitions to use his financial resources to help Jews settle in the land of ISRAEL.

Rothschild first became involved in agricultural settlement activity in Israel after the POGROMS in RUSSIA in the 1880s. He helped a number of failing settlements of Russian Jewish immigrants, such as one called Rishon L'Zion that desperately needed a water well. Eventually, he purchased large amounts of land. Although Rothschild continued to live in Paris, he traveled to the land of Israel many times, mostly to tour young settlements. His support of such settlements earned him the nicknames "Father of the YISHUV," "Builder of Modern ERETZ YISRAEL," and "Hanadiv" (The Benefactor).

After World War I and the BALFOUR DECLARATION (which, incidentally, was addressed to the British Jewish leader Lord Lionel Walter Rothschild, one of Edmond's relatives), Edmond became an active Zionist (*see* ZIONISM). However, his support for industrialization and concern for Arab neighborhoods sometimes led to disagreements with other Zionist leaders. In 1924, Rothschild established PICA, the Palestinian Jewish Colonization Association, which acquired more than 125,000 acres of land. In addition, he established various industrial facilities. His work in the land of Israel was continued from 1924 by his son James. It is estimated that overall Edmond Rothschild contributed more than $50 million to the support of at least 30 Jewish settlements in the land of Israel, and another half million towards research and development of electricity in the land of Israel.

Edmond Rothschild died in Paris in 1934. In 1954 his remains were moved to Israel, where a state funeral was held at which Prime Minister David BEN-GURION delivered the eulogy.

Further reading: Ran Aharonson, *Rothschild and the Early Jewish Colonization* (Lanham, Md.: Rowman and Littlefield, 2000); Edmund de Rothschild, *Edmund de Rothschild, a Gilt-Edged Life: A Memoir* (London: Murray, 1998); Simon Schama, *Two Rothschilds and the Land of Israel* (London: Collins, 1978).

Rubenstein, Richard L. (b. 1924) *theologian*

HOLOCAUST theologian Richard L. Rubenstein was born in New York in 1924. He studied at both City College of New York and HEBREW UNION COLLEGE (HUC) before receiving his B.A. from the University of Cincinnati in 1946. He then began his rabbinical training at HUC, the seminary of REFORM JUDAISM, but he found his studies there to be unfulfilling. He transferred to the Conservative JEWISH THEOLOGICAL SEMINARY OF AMERICA in New York, earning a master's in hebrew literature in 1952 and eventually achieving ordination there.

Rubenstein served as a rabbi with Temple Beth Emunah in Brockton, Massachusetts, from 1952 to 1954 and Temple Israel in Natick, Massachusetts, from 1954 to 1956. He then took positions as assistant director of the B'NAI B'RITH HILLEL Foundation and chaplain to Jewish students at Harvard University, Radcliffe, and Wellesley from 1956–58. He earned a master's of theology at Harvard University Divinity School

in 1955 and a doctorate in the history and philosophy of religion in 1960. He served as director of Hillel and chaplain to Jewish students at the University of Pittsburgh, Carnegie-Mellon University, and Duquesne University from 1958 to 1970.

Rubenstein has taught at a number of institutions, including the Albert Schweitzer College in Churwalden, Switzerland, the University of Pittsburgh, Florida State University at Tallahassee, and the University of Bridgeport (Connecticut), which he also served as president and chairman of the board of trustees. He has taught courses on French existentialism, 20th-century European literature, religion and society, Freud, Hegel, modern Judaism, and the Holocaust. He has served on the steering committee and been a Fellow of the Aegis Trust, a public-policy organization in the United Kingdom dedicated to the prevention of genocide. In addition, Rubenstein was director and member of the executive committee of the U.K.-based Beth Shalom-Holocaust Memorial Centre. He also currently participates as a member of the board of trustees of the United Way of Eastern Fairfield County (Connecticut) and the Greater Bridgeport Public Educational Fund.

Rubenstein is most noted for his 1966 publication *After Auschwitz*, the first sustained theological response to the Holocaust. Rubenstein argued that the traditional Jewish belief in a benevolent God and the concept of the COVENANT between God and the people of ISRAEL had failed the Jewish people. For Rubenstein, such a God could not possibly allow the Holocaust to happen. The fact that the Holocaust did happen leads Rubenstein to argue that this God did not exist. He writes, "I do not believe that a theistic God is necessary for Jewish religious life . . . I have suggested that Judaism is the way in which we share the decisive times and crises of life through the traditions of our inherited community. The need for that sharing is not diminished in the time of the death of God." Consequently, Rubenstein called for a "Death of God" theology.

At the same time Rubenstein argued that Judaism could and should support a vital community without maintaining a belief in God. He encouraged Jews to focus on their cultural heritage and religious traditions, including their rejection of the Christian view of reality that has dominated the world for centuries.

Many readers found Rubenstein's response to the Holocaust unsatisfactory if not blasphemous, but Rubenstein offered a way for Jews to express their anger and horror, and he set the agenda for Holocaust theologies to come. In a second edition of his work that appeared in 1992, he tempered his original views. He now included ideas of a God of Nature and a God of History, while still rejecting a transcendent God that is OMNIPOTENT and capable of controlling human actions.

Rubenstein remains an active scholar and leader in the academic field of philosophy and religion, remaining on the University of Bridgeport faculty and serving as director of its Center for Holocaust and Genocide Studies. His work is studied by others, and he is the subject of several books, including *(God) After Auschwitz* by Zachary Braiterman of Syracuse University and *Beyond Auschwitz: Post-Holocaust Thought in America* by Michael Morgan. In 1990 his work was the subject of a panel discussion at the Annual Meeting of the American Academy of Religion in New Orleans, at which he provided a response to the presenters.

In addition to *After Auschwitz*, Rubenstein has published: *The Cunning of History* (1975), *The Age of Triage* (1983); *Approaches to Auschwitz* (1986), coauthored with John K. Roth, *The Religious Imagination* (1968), and *My Brother Paul* (1972), a psychoanalytic study of Paul of Tarsus.

Further reading: Zachary Braiterman, *(God) After Auschwitz* (Princeton, N.J.: Princeton University Press, 1999); Peter Haas, *Morality after Auschwitz: The Radical Challenge of the Nazi Ethic* (Philadelphia: Fortress Press, 1998); Michael Morgan, *Beyond Auschwitz: Post-Holocaust Thought in America* (Oxford and New York: Oxford University Press, 2001); Richard Rubenstein, *After Auschwitz:* *History, Theology, and Contemporary Judaism* (Baltimore: Johns Hopkins University Press, 1992); ———, *After Auschwitz: Radical Theology and Contemporary Judaism* (Indianapolis: Bobbs-Merrill, 1966).

Russia

Some legends and traditions report that Israel's TEN LOST TRIBES may have arrived in the region of Russia as far back as the first EXILE around 721 B.C.E., but there is no physical evidence to back this up. There is evidence of Jews living in the region in Hellenistic times (*see* HELLENISM), in Greek colonies on the Black Sea. However, Russia's recorded Jewish history begins in the seventh century of the Common Era, when Jews leaving Greece, BABYLONIA, PERSIA, and the Middle East migrated past the Caucasus Mountains and onto the shores of the Black Sea. These communities maintained a connection to the Babylonian academies (*see* PUMBEDITA; SURA). During the early Middle Ages traveling Jewish merchants were known to pass through Slavonic and Khazar (a kingdom in eastern Europe between the seventh and 10th centuries) lands on their way to CHINA and INDIA. Sometime around 740 C.E. a unique event in Jewish history transpired—the conversion to Judaism of the Khazar kingdom, or at least its ruling elite. Scholars believe the kingdom had been influenced by the presence of strong Jewish settlements in the area. Scholars still debate how much Khazar Jews contributed to the large Jewish populations that later emerged in eastern Europe.

The first clear evidence of permanent Jewish settlement in Russia itself was in Kiev, in the Rus principality, dating from 1018. Under Grand Duke Svyatopolk II (1093–1113) Jews enjoyed complete liberty of trade and commerce. In the 12th century their fortunes fluctuated depending on the ruler. The fate of this community is not clear, but sometime in the 13th century, before or around the time of the Mongol invasion, they disappeared from the historical record. Under Mongol rule from the 13th to the 15th centuries, other Jewish settlements in Russia enjoyed good contacts with those in the Crimea; both rabbinic Judaism and the KARAITE sect continued to develop. With the rise of Moscow, Jews appeared there as merchants, doctors, and diplomats. However, under the Judeophobic influence of the Byzantine Church, Muscovite grand dukes began to restrict Jewish presence. This policy escalated under Czar Ivan IV (Ivan the Terrible) who, after occupying the Polish town of Pskov in 1563, ordered its Jews to convert to Christianity; those who refused were drowned in the nearby river. Successive czars and czarinas frequently expelled Jews who made their way to Moscow or other Russian territories under their control.

Russia acquired a historically unprecedented number of Jews as a result of three successive partitions of Poland-Lithuania in 1772, 1791 and 1793. The largest number, more than 500,000, came under Russian rule in the 1791 partition. It was at this time that the PALE OF SETTLEMENT was created as an attempt to deal with an alien population that had been traditionally feared and despised by Russians. In 1812 the borders of the Pale were finalized. Despite many expulsions from different areas during different periods, some Jews managed to remain outside the Pale, because of their importance to commerce. However, the Jews of the Pale, suffering from economic restrictions and additional tax burdens, were impoverished. It was during the 18th century that the Hasidic movement (see HASIDISM) developed in Russia; the conflict between the scholarly MITNAGDIM and the mystical and emotional Hasidim played out largely in Russia and Lithuania (see VILNA GAON). The two groups would eventually find common ground against Jewish reformers (see REFORM JUDAISM), but the HASKALAH (Jewish Enlightenment) and EMANCIPATION came to eastern Europe later than it did to western Europe.

In the 19th century, the Jewish community in Russia was to experience new terrors, starting with the rule of Czar Nicholas I (r. 1825–55). In his quest to destroy Jewish life, Nicholas conscripted Jewish boys for 25 years of military service at the age of 12, kidnapping many of them. Those who were left behind found themselves randomly expelled from their villages and towns. Morale was low in the Jewish communities, although some Jews avoided conscription and persecution by developing government-encouraged agricultural settlements in southern Russia and the Pale of Settlement. In the 1840s, the Russian government established schools meant to forcibly assimilate (see ASSIMILATION) Jewish children; Jews were prohibited from growing side curls (see PAYIS) and wearing traditional Jewish attire.

Relief arrived for Russian Jews when Czar ALEXANDER II (r. 1855–81) took the throne. Alexander did not actively persecute the Jews; his government still aimed at Jewish assimilation, but through a more benign policy of Russian secondary education and an easing of settlement restrictions outside the Pale. Jews were encouraged to speak Russian instead of YIDDISH. Those who did assimilated more quickly into Russian culture. As the Jews began to prosper, they became more visible in Russian society, and anti-Jewish feelings (see ANTI-JUDAISM; ANTI-SEMITISM) increased. Talk of emancipating the jews began at this time, which triggered an antisemitic backlash.

Under Alexander II, the Jewish population in Russia doubled, reaching 5 million. Jews diversified their occupations, entering construction, banking, academia, and the liberal professions. The promise of emancipation and the easing of residence rules led to increased urbanization, as their new professions enabled many Jews to move into cities where they had been previously banned.

Eventually, the ideals of modernization found in the Enlightenment and the Haskalah reached the Jews of Russia. For many Russian Jews who sought to become part of the general Russian culture, ZIONISM, Yiddish literature, and Jewish socialist movements (see BUND) presented options that were not religious but still Jewish in character. A strong Jewish press developed in all of the three languages of Russian Jews—Hebrew, Yiddish, and Russian. The MASKILIM, leaders of the Haskalah, encouraged fellow Jews to learn Russian, as had the Russian government in earlier years. The widespread assimilation into Russian culture was a strong argument for emancipation, as the Jews had "proved" themselves capable of acculturation and were making positive contributions to Russian civilization.

In 1881 disaster once again struck the Jews of Russia. Alexander II was assassinated by revolutionaries trying to spark mass rebellion among the peasants. This provoked a severe general repression throughout Russia as the government cracked down on revolutionaries and freethinkers. Waves of POGROMS swept through Jewish communities as the Jews were blamed for the assassination. These events, combined with anti-Jewish statements by Russian intellectuals, shocked the assimilated *maskilim* out of their hopes for emancipation and integration anywhere within Russia's borders. Persecution and discrimination against Jews rose once again at every level, from government to the people. Jewish rights to own land, settle in villages and attend Russian schools were curtailed. The reign of Czar Nicholas II (r. 1894–1918) brought further violence. Pogroms were organized and encouraged by the government, the *PROTOCOLS OF THE ELDERS OF ZION* was published, and antisemitic propaganda flourished. Zionism and emigration to the West rose among Jews, as many sought a means to escape the brutal terror aimed at them. In the 30-year period before World War I, more than 1 million Jews emigrated from Russia, most heading to the UNITED STATES. Despite the poor living conditions of most Jews in Russia during this period, Hebrew and Yiddish literature mushroomed. Great Jewish writers such as AHAD HA'AM, Chaim Nachman BIALIK, and SHOLOM ALEICHEM produced their compositions during this time of upheaval.

Many of those Jews who remained in Russia managed to participate in the Russian economy and culture, and large numbers fought in World War I. But even in this capacity many were accused of treason; the Jews were expelled from Lithuania and Courland in June of 1915. Following the overthrow of the czar in early 1917, the provisional government abolished all the restrictions on the Jews of Russia; the Pale was abolished, and Jews were granted all the rights of citizenship. The revolution held great promise for the Jews. They formed their own parties, including socialist ones, fully supporting and participating in the change in government. When Russia descended into civil war between the years 1917 and 1921, pogroms resumed as the White Russian armies accused Jews of supporting the Bolsheviks and of destroying Russia.

By the time the Soviet borders were defined in 1921, only 2.5 million Jews remained within them. A large majority ended up in the independent states of Lithuania, POLAND, and ROMANIA. Under the revolutionary Soviet regime, Jewish communities were dissolved, property confiscated, and yeshivot, the Jewish schools (*see* YESHIVA), were closed. Yiddish culture continued to develop, but its ties to Hebrew were severed as the Yiddish alphabet and spelling were "reformed." Assimilation of Jews into Russian culture continued successfully as Jewish children attended Russian schools, stopped speaking Yiddish, and intermarried. Although repression of distinctly Jewish culture was eased during World War II, it resumed with great ferocity after the war; those who wanted to remain distinctly Jewish were persecuted, sent to jail, exiled to the gulag, or executed. Jewish books and ritual objects were ruled illegal; eventually, new ones had to be smuggled into the country.

Those Jews who continued to practice Judaism, or continue the traditions of Yiddish or Hebrew culture, had to do so behind closed doors and lived dangerously. Many sought to leave the country; but emigration in general from the Soviet Union was forbidden for many years. Later, when limited immigration was allowed for the purpose of "reunification of families," many Jews were still denied permission to leave because the government claimed they would threaten national security. These Jews were called REFUSENIKS, and their cause was taken up in the Western world, especially in Israel and the United States. In 1965 there were only 65 synagogues standing in the Soviet Union even though one of the world's largest Jewish communities resided within its borders (the population had expanded after the war as new territories were added).

Since the fall of the Soviet Union, conditions have improved for Jews living in Russia and the other independent former Soviet republics such as Ukraine. Hundreds of thousands immigrated to ISRAEL and the United States when that became possible. Today, the population is shrinking, although emigration has slowed; a Jewish revitalization effort has begun in recent years. By 2003, Russian Jewry boasted 17 Jewish day schools, 11 preschools, 81 SUPPLEMENTARY SCHOOLS, and four Jewish universities. Synagogues with rabbis stand in most towns, and world Jewish movements have begun to educate Russian Jewry. Many foreign groups have a presence in Russia's Jewish community, including CHABAD, Orthodox (see ORTHODOX JUDAISM), Progressive (see REFORM JUDAISM), and Masorti (see CONSERVATIVE JUDAISM). Nevertheless, due to decades of religious suppression, most Russian Jews view their heritage from an ethnic-cultural perspective, rather than a religious one. It is difficult to pin down the number of Jews still in Russia, but estimates hover between 400,000 and 700,000.

Further reading: Salo Wittmayer Baron, *The Russian Jew Under Tsars and Soviets* (New York: Schocken Books, 1987); S. M. Dubnow, *History of the Jews in Russia and Poland: From the Earliest Times until the Present Day* (Philadelphia: Jewish Publication Society, 1916); Louis Greenberg, *The Jews in Russia: The Struggle for Emancipation* (New York: Schocken Books, 1976); Benjamin Nathans, *Beyond the Pale: The Jewish Encounter with Late Imperial Russia* (Berkeley: University of California Press, 2002).

Ruth   *biblical figure and model of conversion*
The Book of Ruth is found in KETUVIM (Writings), the third section of the TANAKH, the Hebrew Bible.

The book takes its name from one of its two primary characters, Ruth. She and her mother-in-law, NAOMI, are the two heroines of the story.

When Naomi, living in the foreign land of Moab, loses her husband and two sons, she determines to return to her homeland of CANAAN. Ruth, one of her daughters-in-law, insists on remaining at her side; her loyalty is the main theme of the story. Ruth's declaration to Naomi became a commonly used liturgical phrase uttered by a convert during the CONVERSION ritual. She says: "Do not urge me to leave you, to turn back and not follow you. For wherever you go, I will go; wherever you lodge, I will lodge; your people shall be my people, and your God my God" (Ru 1:16). Upon returning with Naomi to the land of Canaan, Ruth marries wisely and becomes, with the birth of her son, the direct ancestor of King DAVID, and thus, ultimately, of the future MESSIAH.

Ruth's determination to remain with Naomi, and to adopt her native land and religion, became the model for Jewish conversion. It also serves as a model for Jews by birth of how they can choose to embrace their spiritual heritage. The book of Ruth is read on the holiday of SHAVUOT, which celebrates God's gift of the TORAH to the ISRAELITES at MOUNT SINAI, in effect making them the first "converts" to Judaism.

Further reading: Alice Ogden Bellis, *Helpmates, Harlots, and Heroes: Women's Stories in the Hebrew Bible* (Louisville, Ky.: Westminster/John Knox Press, 1994); Katheryn Pfisterer Darr, *Far More Precious Than Jewels* (Louisville, Ky.: Westminster Press, 1991); Danna Nolan Fewell and David Miller Gunn, *Compromising Redemption: Relating Characters in the Book of Ruth* (Louisville, Ky.: Westminster John Knox Press, 1991); *Tanakh: The New JPS Translation According to the Traditional Hebrew Text* (Philadelphia, New York, Jerusalem: Jewish Publication Society, 1985).

S

Saadia Gaon (882–942 C.E.) *philosopher, legalist, and head of rabbinic academy in Sura*

Saadia Gaon was the most famous and influential figure in the era of the GEONIM, the rabbis who made the Babylonian TALMUD the supreme authority for all Jews. He was instrumental in establishing the legal and liturgical tradition of the SEPHARDIM, and was also the first and one of the greatest medieval Jewish philosophers.

Saadia was head of the famous rabbinic academy in SURA, BABYLONIA, in the ninth century of the Common Era (the term *gaon* was his title), although unlike other Babylonian *geonim*, he was born in EGYPT. Only after studying in the yeshivot of ERETZ YISRAEL did he take the position that the Babylonian academies, Sura and PUMBEDITA, were the superior authorities for RABBINIC LAW. In 928 he was called to head the Babylonian academy at Sura. Saadia was a great scholar and a strong personality, known for his protracted dispute with the EXILARCH, the secular ruler of the Jews of Babylonia. He also entered the intellectual fray against the KARAITES.

Saadia's philosophy argues that humans have three sources through which they can pursue God: 1) the WRITTEN LAW, (2) the ORAL LAW, and (3) the intellect. His position that the intellect is a viable tool for acquiring knowledge of higher things was novel in the 10th century, and his works become seminal. He also spoke out against asceticism; he argued that humans were not meant to ignore their needs and passions, but to channel them toward intellectual achievements, not to abuse each other or the natural world.

Saadia is best known for his *Book of Beliefs and Opinions*, a systematic explanation of Judaism that utilized rational thought and was influenced by both Greek and Arab philosophy. The volume lays out Saadia's philosophical approach to Jewish beliefs; it also outlines the controversies and debates that occupied Jewish intellectual circles in Baghdad in the first half of the 10th century. Saadia also produced an Arabic translation of the Bible and a uniform prayer book that was adopted by Jews living throughout the Arab world.

Further reading: Hars Lewy, ed. *Three Jewish Philosophers: Philo, Saadya Gaon, Jehuda Halevi* (New York: Atheneum, 1969); Arthur Hyman, *Eschatological Thames in Medieval Jewish Philosophy* (Milwaukee: Marguette University Press, 2002); Henry Malter, *Life and Works of Sa'adiah Gaon; Saadiah Gaon: The Book of Beliefs and Opinions*, trans. Samuel Rosenblatt (New Haven, Conn.: Yale University Press, 1948).

Sabbatical Year

The TORAH commands that every seven years the land (in ERETZ YISRAEL) must be permitted to lay fallow: "For six years you shall sow your land and gather in its yield, but the seventh year you shall let it rest and lie fallow, so that the poor of your people may eat" (Ex 23:10–11). The produce of the land was left for the poor to gather during this year. In addition, debts were to be cancelled (Dt 15:1–5).

The Sabbatical Year (*shmita*) is only one of many practices ordained in the Torah meant to help the poor. In fact, the rabbis eventually created a loophole in the law called a *prosbul*, which allowed the people to reclaim debts after the Sabbatical Year (*see* RABBINIC LAW) because people became less likely to loan money as the Sabbatical Year approached. After the destruction of the second TEMPLE and the imposition of foreign rule and taxes, it became increasingly difficult to observe the laws regarding the Sabbatical Year and the rabbis became more lenient, allowing at least some farming to take place.

Further reading: Calum Carmichael, "The Sabbatical/ Jubilee Cycle and the Seven-Year Famine in Egypt" in *Biblica* 80, no. 2 (1999): 224–239; Roland De Vaux, *Ancient Israel: Its Life and Institutions* (Livonia, Mich.: Dove Booksellers, 1997); Solomon B. Freehof, *A Treasury of Responsa* (Philadelphia: Jewish Publication Society, 1963); Ehud Luz, *Parallels Meet: Religion and Nationalism in the Early Zionist Movement (1882–1904)* (Philadelphia: Jewish Publication Society, 1988).

sacred space

Examples of sacred space have changed throughout Jewish history. The most longstanding example of sacred space is ERETZ YISRAEL itself, the Promised Land, whose sacred status can be traced back to the promise made to Abraham (*see* PATRIARCHS). When the ISRAELITES were wandering in the desert before entering the Promised Land after the EXODUS, they constructed a sacred Tabernacle (*see* MISHKAN), in which God's presence dwelt.

Eventually this dwelling was established more permanently in the TEMPLE in JERUSALEM. With the destruction of the first and second Temples in Jerusalem, in 586 B.C.E. and again in 70 C.E., the Jews have had to find sacred space in other forms. The two most important are the SYNAGOGUE and the home.

Many Jewish religious practices are centered on the home, rather than the synagogue; the home—particularly the table—is a central feature of most festivals and celebrations. The table is seen as a stand-in for the sacrificial altar at the ancient Temple. Various rituals around the table, including readings from TORAH, recountings of Jewish history, songs, and food, replace the ancient SACRIFICEs. With the establishment of the State of ISRAEL, Judaism enjoys both the global sacred space of the Promised Land and the localized spaces of the home and synagogue.

Further reading: Haviva Pedaya, "The Divinity as Place and Time and the Holy Place in Jewish Mysticism," in *Sacred Space,* trans. Jonathan Chipman (New York: New York University Press, 1998), 84–111; Lawrence Schiffman, *From Text to Tradition: A History of Second Temple and Rabbinic Judaism* (Hoboken, N.J.: Ktav Publishing House, 1991).

sacred time

In Judaism the paradigm for sacred time is the Sabbath (*see* SHABBAT). The seventh day commemorates the completion of CREATION, when God rested from creative work. It also provides a period of rest and release from worldly concerns and troubles. Finally, it prefigures the coming MESSIANIC AGE, in which there will be no suffering or pain or separation from God. Abraham Joshua HESCHEL's *The Sabbath* is a landmark treatment of the concept of the Sabbath as the model for all other sacred time. He argues that Judaism in the DIASPORA world is a community centered on sacred time rather than SACRED SPACE. Shabbat lifts Jews out of historical time into cosmic time, connecting them with God.

Further reading: Abraham Joshua Heschel, *A Passion for Truth* (New York: Farrar, Straus and Giroux, 1973); ———, *The Sabbath: Its Meaning for Modern Man* (New York: Farrar, Straus and Giroux, 1951); Haviva Pedaya, "The Divinity as Place and Time and the Holy Place in Jewish Mysticism" in *Sacred Space,* trans. Jonathan Chipman (New York: New York University Press, 1998), 84–111.

sacrifice

Jewish traditions of sacrifice can be dated as far back as Abraham (*see* PATRIARCHS). The Patriarchs offered animal sacrifices on specially built altars throughout the land of CANAAN. As the ISRAELITES were preparing to enter ERETZ YISRAEL, God established a COVENANT with them that involved elaborate offerings of animals and grain.

Other ancient Near Eastern communities also offered sacrifices, but the Israelites were required to give sacrifice only to the God of Abraham, Isaac, and Jacob. The rituals were performed by *KOHANIM,* members of the tribe of Levi who were set apart for this service. Sacrifices were performed for several reasons: to atone for sins (*see* SIN AND REPENTANCE), to generate purification, and to offer praise and thanksgiving. The elaborate sacrificial system required regular daily, monthly, and annual sacrifices, as well as sacrifices for particular occasions and festivals.

In the days before the TEMPLE was built in Jerusalem, sacrifices were performed in the Tabernacle as well as other locations across the land. When DAVID became king, he made JERUSALEM the religious, civil, and political center of his kingdom, and he commanded that sacrifices be performed only in the Temple there. This later created tensions for those living in the northern kingdom, who found it difficult to travel to Jerusalem for festivals. For centuries afterwards, certain communities continued to offer sacrifices in Samaria (*see* JUDEA AND SAMARIA), challenging Jerusalem's authority. Records indicate that sacrifices were performed in the far reaches of the northern kingdom and even among Jews in EGYPT.

Both times the Temple was destroyed—first in 586 B.C.E. and then in 70 C.E.—Jewish theology was challenged by the inability to carry out the sacrifices commanded in the Bible. After the first exile the Temple was eventually rebuilt under EZRA and NEHEMIAH, but after 70 C.E. the sacrificial system ceased altogether. The roots of rabbinic tradition were already in place in the first century of the Common Era, and TORAH study and prayer came to be seen as replacements for the Temple's sacrificial system.

In the modern period, many Jewish theologians have argued that sacrifice had always been intended as a temporary practice. They explain that the sacrificial system was designed to keep the relatively primitive Israelites focused on their God but is unnecessary now. The term "sacrifice" for most Jews is now a metaphor for commitment to God or the community, expressed in Torah study, prayer, and mitzvot (*see* MITZVAH). Some groups disagree, and work toward a rebuilding of the Temple and the reinstitution of the sacrificial system. Tradition teaches that when the MESSIAH returns, the Temple will be rebuilt and sacrifice will once again be offered.

Further reading: H. C. Brichto, "On Slaughter and Sacrifice, Blood and Atonement," *Hebrew Union College Annual* 47 (1976): 19–56; Howard Eilberg-Schwartz, *The Savage in Judaism* (Bloomington: Indiana University Press, 1990); Jacob Milgrom, *Leviticus 1–16,* Anchor Bible Series. (New York: Doubleday, 1991); ———, "Sacrifice and Offerings, OT" in *The Interpreter's Dictionary of the Bible,* supplemental volume (Nashville, Tenn.: Abingdon, 1976).

Sadat, Anwar (1918–1981) *president of Egypt who made peace with Israel*

Anwar Sadat was Egypt's president from 1970 to 1981. A lifelong enemy of ISRAEL, he determined several years after the YOM KIPPUR WAR to negotiate peace with Israel. His lasting legacy is peace between Israel and Egypt. Oddly, Sadat was influenced by men as disparate as Mohandas Gandhi, who advocated peace under all circumstances, and Adolf HITLER, who engineered World War II.

Sadat was born in 1918 into a family of 13 children in the town of Mit Abul Kom, about 40 miles north of Cairo. He attended a British/Egyptian military school, where he made friends with the future Egyptian president Gamal Abdel Nasser. Nasser, Sadat, and other nationalists plotted to overthrow the British colonial power and the monarchy and create an independent Egypt. When they succeeded in 1952, Sadat remained in Nasser's inner circle. In 1956 Egypt nationalized the Suez Canal, provoking an attack by Israel, FRANCE, and Britain. UNITED STATES intervention

Egyptian president Anwar Sadat negotiated peace between Israel and Egypt, reaching a peaceful solution between the two nations in 1979. Sadat won the Nobel Peace Prize for his efforts. *(Ya'acov Sa'ar, Government Press Office, The State of Israel)*

forced the British and French to withdraw from the canal and Israel to withdraw from the Sinai Peninsula. By 1967, Nasser prepared to launch a new Arab war against Israel, but Israel preempted the attack, destroying the Egyptian Air Force before the planes could leave the ground. During the SIX-DAY WAR, Israel recaptured the Sinai, rendering the canal inoperable. Humilated, Nasser died several years later, and Sadat became president in 1970.

After initiating another military strike against Israel on Yom Kippur of 1973, Sadat successfully occupied parts of the Sinai desert, but the Israelis were able to repel the invasion, cross the canal, and threaten Egyptian cities. In defeat, Sadat courageously sought a new route to regaining the Sinai for Egypt. He decided to seek peace with Israel.

Sadat traveled to Israel in 1977 and addressed the Israeli governing body, the KNESSET, in JERUSALEM. While there, he met with Israeli prime minister Menachem BEGIN, and they met again at Camp David (*see* CAMP DAVID ACCORDS) in the UNITED STATES, where they concluded a historic peace treaty in 1979. That year Sadat and Begin jointly won the Nobel Peace Prize. After signing the peace accords, Sadat was the target of militant Arab nationalists who opposed the existence of Israel. He was assassinated in 1981.

Further reading: Anwar Sadat, *Anwar El Sadat: In Search of Identity: An Autobiography* (New York: Harper-Collins, 1978); Kenneth W. Stein, *Heroic Diplomacy: Sadat, Kissinger, Carter, Begin, and the Quest* (New York: Routledge, 1999).

Sadducees

The Sadducees, or *tzaddukim* in HEBREW, were one of the three primary sects of Judaism during the late second-TEMPLE period (150 B.C.E.–70 C.E.). The PHARISEES and the ESSENES were the other two sects.

Modern scholarship asserts that the Sadducees perceived themselves as descendants of Zadok, the priest who served King DAVID. Ezekiel, chapter 44, declares that "only the sons of Zadok will be worthy to serve in the Temple." The Temple priests in JERUSALEM were indeed prominent among the Sadducees. They constituted the Jewish aristocracy, deriving their power from the tax revenues that were earmarked for the many animal and grain SACRIFICES. The Sadducees were the most Hellenized sector of the population (see HELLENISM); their way of life was highly influenced by their surrounding culture, in this case, Greek and Roman, and they were criticized by the other sects for that reason.

The early rabbinic sages, whose voices we hear in the MISHNAH, and the Roman Jewish historian JOSEPHUS, record the differences in legal interpretation between the Sadducees and the Pharisees. While the Sadducees emphasized the present life over any possible afterlife, the Pharisees preached life after death, reward and punishment, and immortality as essential components of Jewish theology and culture. The Sadducees also did not accept the orally transmitted laws and customs by which the Pharisees—and their followers—lived their daily lives.

The Sadducees disappeared when the second Temple was destroyed in the year 70 C.E., and Pharisaic Judaism became the preeminent Jewish sect. Without the Temple as a site to offer sacrifice, the Sadducees became obsolete.

Further reading: Louis Finkelstein, *Akiba: Scholar, Saint and Martyr* (Northvale, N.J.: Jason Aronson Press, 1990); Lawrence H. Schiffman, *From Text to Tradition: A History of Second Temple and Rabbinic Judaism* (Hoboken, N.J.: Ktav Publishing House, 1991); Julius Wellhausen, *The Pharisees and the Sadducees: An Examination of Internal Jewish History* (Macon, Ga.: Mercer University Press, 2001).

Safed

Safed, a principal town in the Galilee in the north of ISRAEL, rests on a mountain 2,780 feet above sea level 30 miles east of Acre and 25 miles north of Tiberias. Its history reaches back at least 2,000 years, with varying Jewish, Muslim, Christian, and pagan inhabitants. Today, the population is approximately 21,200.

Safed has been under the control of many powers. In 66 C.E., JOSEPHUS fortified the city against the Romans. After the destruction of the second TEMPLE, it became a haven for priestly families. During the Crusades, the city changed hands several times. After the EXPULSION from SPAIN in 1492, a sizable Jewish population developed there. In the late 1490s the Jews who lived there traded in spices, cheese, oil, vegetables, and fruit.

Safed soon became the home of several important religious leaders. This group included Joseph CARO, author of the *SHULCHAN ARUKH*, the most revered of the Jewish CODES OF LAW, and the master of KABBALAH mysticism, Isaac LURIA.

The first printing press in the Middle East was built in Safed in 1563 by two Ashkenazi brothers (see ASHKENAZIM). During the centuries when the town flourished as a center for scholars and mystics, it was supported through TZEDAKAH, or charity, by large European Jewish communities. Only at the end of the 19th century did Rabbi M. Taubenhaus found a weaving shop to provide economic resources to the inhabitants.

The changes in population over time have left Safed with many thousands of inhabitants—and as few as 300. On September 28, 1918, the town was occupied by British forces. On May 10–11, 1948, days before Israel declared independence, Jewish forces took over the entire city, expelling non-Jewish inhabitants. Since Israel's independence, Safed has grown from 7,900 people to more than 20,000. The economy is based on a mixture of tourism, recreation, and industry. The industry consists of metal factories, textile weaving and apparel, food products, tobacco and diamond polishing. The town is home to a picturesque artists' quarter with many galleries; it has long been considered a colorful part of the tapestry of culture that comprises the State of Israel.

Further reading: Joseph Dan, *Jewish Intellectual History in the Middle Ages* (Westport, Conn.: Paulist Press,

1984); Lawrence Fine, *Safed Spirituality: Rules of Mystical Piety, the Beginning of Wisdom* (New York: Paulist Press, 1984); Yisrael Shalem and Phyllis Shalem, *Guide to Safed* (Brooklyn, N.Y.: Lambda Publishers, 1991); Norman Stillman, *The Jews of Arab Lands: A History and Source Book* (Philadelphia: Jewish Publication Society of America, 1979).

St. Louis, SS

After KRISTALLNACHT, the massive November 1938 Nazi POGROM against the Jews of GERMANY, German Jews who had hesitated to leave Germany when Adolf HITLER first rose to power were now anxious to leave the country. However, that goal became ever more difficult. Jews needed to obtain valid visas and needed enough money to travel. Many countries, including the UNITED STATES, retained strict limits on the number of Jews they were willing to accept, and German Jews felt the Nazi trap closing in upon them.

Several hundred Jews managed to book passage on the SS *St. Louis,* armed with valid tourist visas for Cuba, where they hoped to remain until they could enter the United States. They paid exorbitant fares, money obtained through great effort, often with the help of relatives who lived outside of Germany. Some of the passengers had already been incarcerated for periods of time in the Dachau concentration camp (*see* CONCENTRATION AND DEATH CAMPS). Many had to leave their families behind, hoping to send for them once they had relocated.

On May 13, 1939, the SS *St. Louis* set sail for Cuba. While it was at sea, Cuba passed a law drawing a distinction between tourists and refugees; the latter were required to post $500 bonds as a guarantee that they would not become wards of the Cuban state. The tourist visas held by the *St. Louis* passengers thus became invalid. When the ship approached Cuba, it was ordered to anchor off the coast.

The ship was held in limbo, as Joseph Goebbels, the Nazi propaganda minister, determined to use the episode to stir up world ANTI-SEMITISM. His agents spread rumors in Havana that the Jews on board were all criminals. The Cuban government began to see these refugees as a threat to their society. Negotiations began with the president of Cuba, but he would not allow the Jews to enter the country.

As the world became aware of the plight of the SS *St. Louis,* Nazi propaganda stressed the theme that no country wanted to take in the Jews. American Jewish leaders tried to negotiate with the Cuban government on behalf of the refugees, but the Cuban government refused to enter negotiations unless the ship left Cuban waters. They were given a deadline of June 2 to depart voluntarily or be ejected by the Cuban navy.

After failing to meet the Cuban government's suggested blackmail payments, the SS *St. Louis* headed toward the Florida coastline in the hope that the United States would grant entry. But the United States refused. On June 6, the Cuban government closed down all negotiations. The ship, with only a two-week supply of food and water, was forced to begin its journey back to Europe.

The American Jewish leadership was able to negotiate with some European countries to take in approximately 750 of the 937 refugees. The rest were returned to Germany to face the horrors of the HOLOCAUST. Many of those who received refugee status in other European countries would again face the Nazi threat as the Germans conquered their countries of refuge early in World War II.

Further reading: John Mendelsohn, *Jewish Emigration: The S.S. St. Louis Affair and Other Cases* (New York: Garland Publishing, 1982); Gordon Thomas and Max Morgan-Witts, *Voyage of the Damned* (London: Hodder and Stoughton, 1974).

Salanter, Israel (1810–1883) *scholar and ethicist*

Israel Salanter was born in 1810 in Zhagare, Lithuania. His father, whose surname was Lipkin, was a prominent rabbi who wrote a gloss of the

TALMUD and rabbinic literature, which he called *Ben Aryeh.* Israel became known as Salanter after his teacher Rabbi Zundel of Salant, whom he met when he was 12 years old after enrolling in the YESHIVA of Zevi Hirsch Broida in the town of Salant. From Zundel, Salanter learned the ethical principles that would underlay his Musar movement.

After completing his early studies, Salanter became a preacher in a yeshiva in Vilna, the center of Lithuanian Jewish scholarship. He rose to head the yeshiva. After a short while he formed his own yeshiva in Vilna, where his teachings sparked a movement known as Musar. The movement stressed the importance of moral behavior based on the study of traditional ethical literature.

Salanter never became an ordained RABBI, but he set a strong example of religious leadership. During a cholera epidemic in Vilna he was in the middle of dangerous relief activities. He ordered his community to take every measure possible to protect life, even on the Sabbath (*see* SHABBAT) and holidays. In fact, during the epidemic, Salanter ordered his community to eat on Yom Kippur, the most holy fast day, to keep up their strength. He led by example and ate publicly.

Soon after 1848, Salanter moved to Kovno, Lithuania, where he founded a Musar yeshiva with 150 students, many of whom became great rabbis in their own right. Salanter organized his yeshiva in a progressive fashion; he made sure that his students had suitable accommodation and that they were neatly dressed and clean.

In 1857, Salanter made a move to Memel, which was nearby but across the border in GERMANY. He became a German citizen, adopted the German fashion of dress and taught in German, rather than Yiddish. but he also kept in contact with his old students through letters. In 1880 he moved to FRANCE, where he spent two years teaching and strengthening the Jewish community there.

As a revolutionary thinker, Salanter supported the translation of the Talmud into European lan-guages, and proposed a Hebrew-Aramaic dictionary to help further its study. Salanter had sons who became prominent in their own right: Aryeh Leib Horowitz was an author, Isaac Lipkin was a rabbi, and Yom Tov Lipkin was a scientist.

Further reading: Immanuel Etkes, *Rabbi Israel Salanter and the Mussar Movement: Seeking the Torah of Truth* (Philadelphia: Jewish Publication Society, 1993); Hillel Goldberg, *Israel Salanter, Text, Structure, Idea* (New York: Ktav Publishing House, 1982).

Salem *See* JERUSALEM.

Salk, Jonas (1914–1995) *scientist who developed polio vaccine*

Jonas Edward Salk was born October 28, 1914, in New York City and died June 23, 1995. He is best known for his work as an epidemiologist and discoverer of the Salk Poliomyelitis Vaccine. Polio was a crippling disease that has since been nearly eradicated.

Salk was the son of Jewish immigrants from eastern Europe. He was the first member of his family to complete college, at City College of New York. At first intent on studying law, he became intrigued by medical science and became a doctor. He finished medical school in 1939, receiving his degree from the College of Medicine at New York University. Many public health experts at the time feared that a flu epidemic might follow the war, as it had in 1919 after World War I, killing millions. Salk became a member of the U.S. Army Influenza Commission.

While attending the University of Michigan as a research fellow, Salk met Dr. Thomas Francis, Jr., who was working on the development of an influenza vaccine. Inspired by his example, Salk moved to the University of Pittsburgh's school of medicine, where he became professor of bacteriology in 1949, professor of preventative medicine in 1954, and in 1957, professor of experimental medicine.

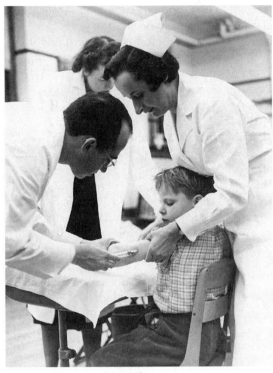

Jonas Salk developed the polio vaccine, which practically eradicated the disease from the earth. Here he inoculates a boy with the vaccine, assisted by two nurses. *(Library of Congress)*

Salk theorized that he could make a polio vaccine that would prevent infection by injecting a killed virus into the human body. In 1955 his work brought results, and he was credited with creating the vaccine. He had no desire to profit personally from the discovery and refused to take patents out on the vaccine. The tragedy of polio was eradicated in most of the world. Salk was awarded the Presidential Citation and the Congressional Medal for Distinguished Achievement. In 1994, he was listed as one of the 100 most influential Jews of all time.

In 1963, Salk formed the Jonas Salk Institute for Biological Studies in La Jolla, California. He published several books, *Man Unfolding* (1972), *The Survival of the Wisest* (1973), *World Population*

and Human Values: A New Reality (1981), and *Anatomy of Reality* (1983). Salk's last years were devoted to the study of AIDS.

Further reading: Kathryn Black, *In the Shadow of Polio: A Personal and Social History* (Reading, Mass.: Perseus Publishing, 1996); Bruno Latour and Steve Woolgar, *Laboratory Life: The Construction of Scientific Facts,* with an introduction by Jonas Salk (Princeton, N.J.: Princeton University Press, 1986); Micheal B. A. Oldstone, *Viruses, Plagues and History* (Oxford: Oxford University Press, 2000); Jonas Salk and Jonathan Salk, *World Population and Human Values: A New Reality* (New York: Harper & Row, 1981).

Samael

Samael (poison of God) is the king of the demons in Jewish tradition, and is responsible for evil. He is often equated with SATAN. In fact, some understand the word *Satan,* which means "prosecutor" or "accuser," to be merely a description of Samael's function, while Samael is his proper name.

According to Jewish tradition, Samael opposes the angel Michael in heaven; while Michael defends Israel's actions to God, Samael consistently acts as Israel's accuser. Samael tempts people to sin; when they do so, his power increases. Legend holds that it was Samael who sent the serpent to the GARDEN OF EDEN to tempt Eve.

Further reading: Ileene Smith Sobel, *Moses and the Angels* (New York: Delacorte Press, 1999); Ronald H. Isaacs, *Ascending Jacob's Ladder: Jewish Views of Angels, Demons, and Evil Spirits* (Northvale, N.J.: Aronson, 1998).

Samaritans

The Samaritans are a religious-ethnic community related to the Jews; they are few in number today but were once the dominant group in Samaria (*see* JUDEA AND SAMARIA). They apparently descend from settlers who were brought to Samaria by the ASSYRIANS after they conquered the Northern Kingdom of ISRAEL in 722 B.C.E. The Samaritans themselves claim they are among the true descendants of the biblical ISRAELITES; they say that the TORAH was changed to obscure the evidence. After centuries of controversy, the chief rabbi of Jerusalem in 1842 told the Muslims who had charged that the Samaritans were atheists that the Samaritans did indeed believe in the truth of the Torah, the Five Books of Moses. In modern Israel, the Samaritans are considered Jews under the LAW OF RETURN, permitting them citizenship in Israel even though they do not maintain traditional practices.

The central holy site for Samaritans is Mount Gerizim in Samaria; they still practice sacrifices there. The Samaritans claim that only the Torah is sacred, rejecting NEVI'IM (Prophets) and KETUVIM (Writings). They also reject RABBINIC LAW. Their Torah differs somewhat from the traditional Jewish manuscript as well. For example, in the Samaritan list of the DECALOGUE, the 10th commandment requires them to build an altar to God on Mount Gerizim. The Samaritan festival calendar also differs from the Jewish calendar. Small communities of Samaritans continue to live in Israel to the present day.

Further reading: R. J. Coggina, *Samaritans and Jews* (London: Blackwell, 1975); James B. Montgomery, *The Samaritans, The Earliest Jewish Sect: Their History, Theology and Literature* (New York: Ktav Publishing, 1968).

Sanhedrin

The Sanhedrin (Greek for "sitting in council") was an ancient council of rabbis that for several hundred years acted as the highest religious authority within Judaism. It was led by a NASI (prince) and an *av bet din* (father of the court). It traditionally had 70 members, each of whom had to be ordained as a rabbi and reside in Judea (*see* JUDEA AND SAMARIA).

The Sanhedrin had powers to punish offenders, and theoretically could even impose capital punishment; however, a court that used capital punishment even once in 70 years was considered a "bloody" court. Under the Hasmonean Dynasty (second to first century B.C.E.), the Sanhedrin also developed tremendous political influence, but under HEROD its political power faded and it was restricted to religious issues.

After the destruction of the second TEMPLE, the Sanhedrin was recognized as the supreme representative authority over Jews both in Judea and in the DIASPORA. This body supervised the completion of the biblical canon, created a system for ordaining rabbis, and developed the basic daily prayer liturgy still in use by Jews today. After the Shimon BAR-KOKHBA revolt between 132 and 135 C.E., the Sanhedrin relocated from Sepphoris in the Lower Galilee to Usha and eventually settled in Tiberias. The Sanhedrin was dissolved when the Romans abolished the office of the *nasi* in the beginning of the fifth century.

In the modern era, Napoleon established a Jewish council he called the Sanhedrin (*see* FRANCE; NAPOLEON'S SANHEDRIN). In its brief existence, it pledged loyalty to him, and agreed to void any Jewish practices that would conflict with French citizenship.

Further reading: Michael S. Berger, *Rabbinic Authority* (New York: Oxford University Press, 1998); Shaye J. D. Cohen, *From the Maccabees to the Mishnah* (Philadelphia: Westminster Press, 1987); Sidney B. Hoenig, *The Great Sanhedrin* (New York: 1953); Hugo Mantel, *Studies in the History of the Sanhedrin* (Cambridge, Mass.: 1961).

Sarna, Jonathan (b. 1955) *historian*

Dr. Jonathan Daniel Sarna is the Joseph H. and Belle R. Braun Professor of American Jewish history at Brandeis University. He was born in Philadelphia and raised in New York City and Boston. He studied at Brandeis University, the Boston Hebrew College, and Merkaz HaRav Kook in JERUSALEM, and obtained his doctorate from Yale University in 1979. His field encompasses American Jewish history from the colonial period to the present. His studies emphasize social, cultural, and religious history.

From 1979 until 1990, Sarna taught at HEBREW UNION COLLEGE–JEWISH INSTITUTE OF RELIGION in

Cincinnati. He rose to the position of professor of American Jewish history and director of the Center for the Study of the American Jewish Experience. In 1990 he returned to Brandeis to take his current position.

Sarna has published many volumes, including *People Walk on Their Heads,* a volume dealing with Jewish immigrant life in New York; *Jacksonian Jew,* a biography of Mordecai Noah; and *The Jews of Boston,* an illustrated history of that community, co-authored by Ellen Smith.

Besides being a teacher, author, public speaker, and department chair, Sarna holds many other positions. He was the chief historian for Celebrate 350, the 2004 national celebration of the 350th anniversary of American Jewish life. He chairs the Academic Advisory and Editorial Board of the Jacob Rader Marcus Center of the American Jewish Archives in Cincinnati and is the consulting historian to the National Museum of American Jewish History in Philadelphia. Sarna also reviews Jewish books for the *Boston Globe* newspaper.

Sarna has written, edited, or coedited more than 20 books. He is a public speaker on several topics related to American Jewish history, such as George Washington's correspondence with the Jews of Newport and the Americanization of matzah. Most recently Sarna completed an interpretive history of American Judaism titled *American Judaism: A History,* published by Yale University Press. He is married to Professor Ruth Langer, also a scholar of Jewish studies, and they have two children, Aaron and Leah.

Further reading: Jonathan D. Sarna, *American Judaism: A History* (New Haven, Conn.: Yale University Press, 2004); ———, *The American Jewish Experience* (New York: Holmes & Meier, 1997).

Satan

Satan, meaning "prosecutor" or "accuser," appears in the TANAKH in the book of JOB as a heavenly prosecutor; he wagers with God that Job will not pass real tests of piety. The accusation that Job is not as pious as he seems is typical for the Satan portrayal in the Tanakh, whose job is to report Israel's sins to God. In fact, according to Jewish tradition, one reason the SHOFAR is blown on ROSH HASHANAH is to drown out the accusations that Satan presents to God at that time. Satan also appears elsewhere in the Tanakh, for example, in Zechariah, Tehillim (Psalms), and Chronicles.

Over time, legends about Satan developed, the most popular of which was that he had started a battle among the angels (*see* MALAKHIM) in Heaven by refusing to show respect for Adam, the first man. He and his followers were expelled from heaven. Satan became known as SAMAEL, a demon king who tempts people to sin (*see* SIN AND REDEMPTION). He thus was responsible for Eve's temptation and for tempting the ISRAELITES to build the golden calf. He eventually became the personification of wickedness, and it is believed he can take any form to tempt people to give in to their evil inclinations.

Further reading: Peggy Lynne Day, *An Adversary in Heaven: SATAN in the Hebrew Bible* (Atlanta: Scholars Press, 1988); Ronald H. Isaacs, *Ascending Jacob's Ladder: Jewish Views of Angels, Demons, and Evil Spirits* (Northvale, N.J.: Aronson, 1998); *Tanakh: The Holy Scriptures* (Philadelphia and Jerusalem: Jewish Publication Society, 1985); David Wolfers, *Deep Things out of Darkness: The Book of Job: Essays and a New English Translation* (Grand Rapids, Mich.: Wm. B. Eerdmans, 1995).

Saul (11th century B.C.E.) *first Israelite king*

The book of Samuel reports that the ISRAELITES desired a king so that they could be more like their neighboring countries. The Prophet Samuel, after consulting with God, anoints Saul, the people's choice, as the first king of ISRAEL. Saul's victories in battles against the Ammonites, Philistines, and Amalekites (*see* AMALEK) make him very popular, but the Bible eventually concludes that the people were unwise to choose him. His only qualification for the job that the TANAKH, the Hebrew Bible, cites is that he was a head taller than all other Israelites and very handsome. When God later instructs

Samuel to anoint DAVID as king in place of Saul, God explains that David was chosen for what is in his heart and not for his appearance.

Saul at first befriends David, but eventually he becomes jealous of the youth's might and popularity. David flees, and Saul tries to have him pursued and killed. Saul ends up a tragic figure, paranoid, desperate, and humiliated. At that point, his army suffers a big defeat by the Philistines, and the king falls on his own sword in despair.

The story of Saul is known mainly from 1 Samuel. Scholars hypothesize that the author of Deuteronomy (often termed "D") wrote that book and others in the Tanakh from the ideological perspective of DEUTERONOMIC HISTORY. Saul's life is portrayed as a moral lesson: his fate is determined by God, who works through history to reward the faithful and punish the disobedient (see REWARD AND PUNISHMENT). From this view, Saul makes two fatal mistakes: he sacrifices when he is not supposed to, and when God tells him to destroy everything in a particular town, Saul allows his troops to keep some of the booty. For these sins, God's presence abandons Saul in favor of David. Nevertheless, Jewish tradition maintains a positive view of Saul as a great military leader and a good first king.

Modern historians have since questioned whether Saul was a king at all. Some view him as a transitional figure, bridging the era of dispersed Israelite agricultural settlements as described in the book of Judges, and the centralized monarchies of David and Solomon. They surmise that internal economic pressures and external military forces caused a shift in Israelite culture, enabling Saul to become an exalted judge who took control beyond his localized community. His character represents a new type between the temporary military champions of judges and the later dynastic kings.

Further reading: Diana Vikander Edelman, *King Saul in the Historiography of Judah* (Sheffield, England: JSOT Press, 1991); Margaret Nutting Ralph, *Discovering Old Testament origins: The Books of Genesis, Exodus, and Samuel* (New York: Paulist Press, 1992); Naomi Pasachoff, *Jewish History in 100 Nutshells* (Northvale, N.J.: Aronson, 1995); John A. Sanford, *King Saul, the Tragic Hero: A Study in Individuation* (New York: Paulist Press, 1985); *Tanakh: The Holy Scriptures* (Philadelphia and Jerusalem: Jewish Publication Society, 1985).

Schechter, Solomon (1847–1915) *scholar and educator*

Solomon Schechter was born in Fascani, ROMANIA. His father was a *shochet,* a kosher slaughterer, affiliated with the CHABAD branch of HASIDISM. During his youth, Schechter received a traditional Jewish education, but in his twenties he determined to attend a more modern rabbinical college in Vienna. There he was exposed to Meir Friedmann, a critical scholar of the TALMUD.

Schechter later studied at both the Berlin School for the Science of Judaism (see WISSENSCHAFT DES JUDENTUM) and the University of Berlin. In Berlin, he struck up a relationship with fellow student Claude Montefiore, and returned with him to England as his tutor. Schechter engrossed himself in English literature, and developed an elegant English writing style, thanks in part to his wife and editor, the former Mathilde Roth.

In 1892, Schechter was appointed reader in rabbinics at Cambridge University, and seven years later he became a professor of Hebrew at University College in London. Schechter achieved Jewish scholarly fame for his critical work on the *Fathers, According to Rabbi Nathan,* which was published in 1887.

The high point of his scholarly career was his role in uncovering and studying the Cairo GENIZAH, a vast store of ancient sacred texts and documents that had been squirreled away in the city's Ben Ezra synagogue. Schechter facilitated the transportation of more than 100,000 textual fragments to Cambridge. Among his Genizah finds was the original Hebrew version of the APOCRYPHA book of Ben Sira. This discovery is considered one of the greatest of its kind.

Schechter was recruited by the JEWISH THEO-LOGICAL SEMINARY OF AMERICA in New York City to become its president. He served in this capacity from 1902 until his death in 1915, helping to create a new and vibrant form of CONSERVATIVE JUDAISM in America. Schechter's embrace of the teachings of Zachariah FRANKEL—POSITIVE-HISTORICAL JUDAISM—made Frankel's view of Judaism a lived reality. Schechter advocated for a proper balance between tradition and MODERNITY, unlike the Orthodox (see ORTHODOX JUDAISM), who Schechter believed failed to properly appreci-ate critical knowledge, and the Reform (see REFORM JUDAISM), who turned their back on TRADI-TIONAL JUDAISM.

Schechter's emphasis was on what he called "Catholic Israel." This term meant that the collective that was the Jewish people was the source of authority for all of Jewish law (see HALAKHAH). When the community embraced a consensus in belief and practice, that is what becomes binding for the time. Schechter is considered one of the great modern Jewish theologians, and in essence he became the father of American Conservative Judaism.

Further reading: Azriel Eisenberg, *Fill a Blank Page: A Biography of Solomon Schechter* (New York: United Synagogue Book Service, 1980); Neil Gillman, *Conservative Judaism: The New Century* (West Orange, N.J.: Behrman House, 1993); Solomon Schechter, *Aspects of Rabbinic Theology: With a New Introduction by Neil Gillman, Including the Original Preface of 1909 and the Introduction by Louis Finkelstein* (Woodstock, Vt.: Jewish Lights Publishing, 1999).

Serving as president of the Jewish Theological Seminary from 1902 until 1915, Solomon Schechter was instrumental in rejuvenating Conservative Judaism for contemporary Jewry. He is also well known for his discovery of the Cairo Genizah. *(Courtesy of the Library of Jewish Theological Seminary of America)*

Schiff, Jacob (1847–1920) *American Jewish philanthropist*

Jacob Schiff was born on January 10, 1847, in Frankfurt, GERMANY, to Clara and Moses Schiff. He received both a secular and a religious education at the local Jewish parochial school. At age 18, Schiff left Germany for the UNITED STATES. He found work at a brokerage firm in New York. In 1875, Schiff married Theresa Loeb, the daughter of Solomon Loeb, a major Jewish banker, and he joined his father-in-law's bank, Kuhn, Loeb and Company. Schiff was a brilliant financier. He recognized the impact railroads would have on industry and invested in them. Ten years later, he became president of the bank, in recognition of his great banking acumen. Jacob Schiff had become extraordinarily wealthy; he would use his funds to help the penniless eastern European Jewish immigrants who were arriving in droves in the United States.

Schiff did not believe in differentiating between Jewish and non-Jewish causes at the beginning of his philanthropic career, but as he witnessed the great need of arriving Jewish immigrants from eastern Europe, he focused on the needs of the Jewish community. Although an adherent of REFORM JUDAISM, Schiff maintained many Jewish traditions in his own life, as did the new immigrants, and he harbored a deep concern for his fellow Jews. He collaborated in establishing both HEBREW UNION COLLEGE and the JEWISH THEOLOGICAL SEMINARY. He was one of the primary supporters of the JEWISH PUBLICATION SOCIETY, funding a new translation into English of the Hebrew Bible (see TANAKH). Schiff also endowed the Jewish Division of the New York Public Library.

In addition to supporting intellectual causes, Schiff became one of the major Jewish contributors in support of resettling eastern European Jews in America. He understood the range of their needs, and funded settlement houses, Young Men's Hebrew Associations, clinics, and free-loan societies. Schiff was not merely a financial benefactor, however. He visited the people to whom he extended help; he spent his Sunday mornings speaking to the patients at the Montefiore Home for Chronic Invalids.

Schiff accomplished more for Jews than just donating money. He had the ear of President Theodore Roosevelt, thanks to his expertise on railroad matters, and he appealed to Roosevelt on behalf of Jews in countries such as ROMANIA, where they suffered constant persecution and violent attacks.

Schiff had a holistic view of the immigrant situation; he understood the pressure on city life that so many poor Jewish immigrants brought to the United States, on social, cultural, and economic levels. Therefore, he worked to bring as many immigrants as he could into the Midwest and southern regions of the United States, where their prospects for employment and success seemed higher. Though his work in this regard was not as successful as he had hoped, the GALVESTON PLAN and the INDUSTRIAL REMOVAL OFFICE kept thousands of Jewish immigrants away from the congested, unsanitary conditions of the LOWER EAST SIDE.

In addition to his generous donations in support of his fellow Jews and Jewish causes, Schiff also assisted the larger American population; he actively supported hospitals, museums, and universities. He died on September 25, 1920, in New York City.

Further reading: Cyrus Adler, *Jacob H. Schiff: His Life and Letters* (Grosse Pointe, Mich.: Scholarly Press, 1968); Naomi W. Cohen, *Jacob H. Schiff: A Study in American Jewish Leadership* (Waltham, Mass.: Brandeis University Press, 1999); Howard M. Sachar, *A History of the Jews in America* (New York: Vintage Books, 1992).

Schindler, Oskar (1908–1974) *Austrian businessman who aided Jews*

Born in Zeittau, AUSTRIA, on April 28, 1908, Oskar Schindler grew up in a privileged family. He was raised a Catholic, but he enjoyed his vices, especially women, gambling, and alcohol. Although he married Emilie at 19, he was notorious for keeping mistresses. Because of his carefree lifestyle, he lost the family business and subsequently became a salesman.

When World War II broke out, Schindler seized an opportunity to profit. He relocated to POLAND and became active in the black market. He developed profitable friendships with both the criminal world and the Gestapo leadership. He parlayed these connections into securing a factory, in which he was given Jews to serve as slave labor. The business was very profitable; but sometime during his work as overseer of the factory, he came to care greatly for his Jewish factory workers.

As the HOLOCAUST, and the imminent destruction of European Jewry, reached a crescendo, Schindler recognized the impending horror. He decided to utilize all his funds to secure the lives of his Jewish workers. Using his own financial resources and his connections, Schindler increased the number of Jewish workers in his factory, ultimately saving approximately 1,200 Jewish lives.

Schindler wrote a list of his factory workers, and, perhaps in the most successful venture of his life, saved the people whose names were printed on it. Not only did Schindler save the lives of the people who worked for him, but he cared for them, procuring food and insuring their physical safety.

Schindler fled to ARGENTINA after the war, fearing he would be prosecuted as a war criminal despite his actions on behalf of his workers. In 1958 he returned to GERMANY. In the early 1960s, Schindler was honored at Israel's Holocaust Museum, YAD VASHEM, and proclaimed a Righteous Gentile. He was invited to plant a tree on the Avenue of the Righteous at the museum. He was recognized both by ISRAEL and Germany as being that rare exception of the individual who risked his own life to save Jews. Today there are more than 6,000 descendants of the Jews Schindler saved living in Europe, the UNITED STATES, and Israel. Schindler died in Hildesheim, Germany, in 1974.

Thomas Keneally's best-selling book *Schindler's List* was transformed by Steven SPIELBERG into one of the great movies of cinematic history; educating a whole new generation of moviegoers on the horrors of the Holocaust. The film received the Academy Award for Best Picture in 1993.

Further reading: Thomas Fensch, ed., *Oskar Schindler and His List: The Man, the Book, the Film, the Holocaust and Its Survivors* (Forest Dale, Vt.: P.S. Eriksson, 1995); Thomas Keneally, *Schindler's List* (New York: Touchstone, 1993); Samuel P. Oliner and Pearl M. Oliner, *The Altruistic Personality: Rescuers of Jews in Nazi Germany* (New York: Free Press, 1988).

Schneerson, Menachem Mendel
(1902–1994) *influential Hasidic leader*

Menachem Mendel Schneerson was one of the most influential rabbis of the modern era. Though he always remained ultra-Orthodox (*see* ORTHODOX JUDAISM), his knowledge of science and of the modern world and his charismatic leadership helped him attract large numbers of secular and unaffiliated Jews to Orthodox Judaism.

Schneerson was born on April 18, 1902, in the town of Nikolayev in the Ukraine. His father, Rabbi Levi Yitzchock Schneerson, was an established scholar. His mother, Channa, came from a wealthy rabbinic family. Schneerson was the oldest of three boys. In 1907 the family relocated to Yakaterinoslav so that his father could become the town's chief RABBI.

Schneerson exhibited genius at a young age, and his parents pulled him from school so that he could be privately tutored. Considered a TORAH prodigy from a young age, at age 21 he was introduced to his cousin Rabbi Yosef Schneersohn, then the rebbe or leader of the Lubavitcher Hasidim (*see* HASIDISM). He quickly entered the rebbe's inner circle of CHABAD leaders. In 1928, he married the rebbe's second eldest daughter, Chaya Mushka, in Warsaw. The newlyweds relocated to Berlin, and Schneerson pursued secular studies at the University of Berlin. When the Nazis came to power in 1933, Schneerson and his wife left for Paris, where he studied at the Sorbonne. In addition to his secular studies, Schneerson maintained his religious study and vigorously pursued his practice of prayer and meditation. His father-in-law began to increasingly rely on him, and Schneerson took on the major role of preparing all Lubavitch publications.

With the Nazi occupation of France, Schneerson and his wife fled to Brooklyn, New York, and his father-in-law appointed him the chief in charge of Lubavitch's worldwide educational network and successful publishing house. When his father-in-law passed away in 1950, Schneerson became the seventh Lubavitcher Rebbe. Schneerson oversaw the Chabad-Lubavitch movement's continued growth and determined to raise its public profile. He especially increased the sect's outreach to nonobservant Jews. He set up a system of emissaries whom he dispatched around the world. In smaller Jewish communities, these Chabad rabbis helped to revitalize Jewish life. Schneerson's leadership influenced the establishment of education and outreach centers as well as social services in many communities.

Because Schneerson was the first Lubavitcher rebbe who was not a son of the previous rebbe, thus breaking a string of successions, there were many who came to believe that he would be the last rebbe before the MESSIANIC AGE, which they believed was imminent. Many Lubavitch followers came to believe that the rebbe was the MESSIAH himself. Schneerson neither affirmed nor denied this messianic claim. When he died childless in 1994, at the age of 91, no rebbe was named to replace him. The Lubavitch have suffered an institutional split over the matter of Schneerson's messianic status. Nevertheless, the movement has continued to be a major Jewish institutional force, with emissaries all over the world. It is estimated that their annual operating budget exceeds $1 billion.

While there are approximately 200,000 Lubavitcher Jews, there are many other Jews from all strands of life who participate in Chabad programming and financially support the movement. While there are many detractors of Chabad, all agree that Schneerson was a charismatic figure who made an indelible impression upon modern Jewry. The Lubavitcher movement continues to grow, with influence well beyond the Orthodox world. After Schneerson's death, the U.S. Congress awarded him the Congressional Gold Medal by a unanimous vote.

Further reading: Sue Fishkoff, *The Rebbe's Army: Inside the World of Chabad-Lubavitch* (New York: Schocken Books, 2003); Menachem Mendel Schneerson, *Bringing Heaven Down to Earth: Meditations and Everyday Wisdom from the Teachings of the Rebbe, Menachem Schneerson*, comp. Tzvi Freeman (Holbrook, Mass.: Adams Media Corp., 1999).

Scholem, Gershom (1897–1982) *historian of Jewish mysticism*

Gershom Scholem was born in GERMANY in 1897. Although Scholem's family can be described as assimilated (*see* ASSIMILATION), he joined the Zionist (*see* ZIONISM) movement while he was in college and then proceeded to steep himself in a study of Jewish history, philosophy, and culture. Scholem began as a student of philosophy and mathematics, but he eventually became interested in languages as well, which brought him to study Jewish MYSTICISM, or KABBALAH, through his doctoral thesis, which was a translation of the *Sefer Ha-Bahir*, a Kabbalistic text. Scholem was part of a Jewish intellectual group in Germany during World War I that included Chaim Nachman BIALIK (1873–1934), Shuel Yosef Agnon (1888–1970), and Zalman Shazar (1889–1974); they all came to admire and study the philosophies of eastern European Jews.

Scholem became the head of the department of Hebrew and Judaism at the National Library in Israel in 1923. Later he became a lecturer and a professor of Jewish mysticism. Scholem is best known as a historian of Jewish mysticism. In 1933, Scholem became the first professor of Jewish mysticism at the Hebrew University. In addition to teaching at the Hebrew University, Scholem published widely.

His book *Major Trends in Jewish Mysticism* (1946) argued that mystical traditions are not an aberration in Judaism. Rather, they are part of a dynamic dialectic with mainstream Judaism that propels the tradition forward to innovation from generation to generation. Scholem argues that mysticism's interaction with mainstream Judaism is what keeps the tradition alive and vibrant. As a result of Scholem's efforts, Jewish mysticism has become a serious and respected field of study within Jewish studies.

Scholem was also known for his efforts as a Zionist. He was awarded the Israel Prize in 1958, and he served as president of the Israel Academy of Sciences and Humanities.

Further reading: Joseph Dan, ed. *Studies in Jewish Thought* (New York: Praeger, 1989); Daniel C. Matt, *The Essential Kabbalah: The Heart of Jewish Mysticism* (New York: HarperSanFrancisco, 1995); Gershom Scholem, *Major Trends in Jewish Mysticism* (New York: Schocken Books, 1946); ———, *On the Kabbalah and Its Symbolism* (New York: Schocken Books, 1965).

Schulweis, Harold (b. 1925) *conservative rabbi*

Rabbi Harold M. Schulweis, the senior rabbi of Congregation Valley Beth Shalom (VBS) in Encino, California, has been a major source of innovation in the American Jewish community and specifically in the United Synagogue of Conservative Judaism (*see* CONSERVATIVE JUDAISM).

Upon completion of a B.A. at Yeshiva College in 1945, Schulweiss attended New York University, earning a master's degree in philosophy, and the JEWISH THEOLOGICAL SEMINARY IN AMERICA, winning a master's degree in Hebrew literature in 1950. From 1952 through 1970, Schulweis was the rabbi of Temple Beth Abraham in Oakland, California. He assumed his current position at Valley Beth Shalom in 1970.

Throughout his career he has taught at many universities; he has been adjunct professor of Jewish contemporary civilization at the UNIVERSITY OF JUDAISM, lecturer in Jewish theology at HEBREW UNION COLLEGE, instructor of philosophy at City College of New York, and faculty member of B'NAI B'RITH Adult Education Commission.

Schulweis's notable achievement lies in his creation of the synagogue CHAVURAH, a small worship and study group within a larger SYNAGOGUE community. The *chavurah* can be a means to address the individual tastes and needs of participants. Sometimes a chavurah will form independent of a synagogue, as an antiestablishment gesture.

The idea has grown in popularity, aided by Schulweis's writings on how to create a *chavurah*. Schulweis has also been instrumental in initiating many other programs, including MAZON, the Jewish Response to Hunger; the Family Empowerment Program; the Para-Rabbinic Program; the VBS Counseling Center; and the Jewish Foundation for Rescuers.

Schulweis is the author of several books, most recently *In God's Mirror, Passages in Poetry,* and *For Those Who Can't Believe.* He has received a number of honors and awards throughout his career, including honorary doctorates of humane letters from the Jewish Theological Seminary, Hebrew Union College, and the University of Judaism. He is the recipient of the Maurice Eisendrath Bearer of Light Award of the Union of American Hebrew Congregations. Also, he has been awarded the Martin BUBER Award of the American Friends of Hebrew University. Schulweis has also earned the Crown of the Good Name Award of the Reconstructionist Rabbinical College (*see* RECONSTRUCTIONIST JUDAISM).

Further reading: Harold M. Schulweis, *Evil and the Morality of God* (Cincinnati: Hebrew Union College Press, 1984); ———, *For Those Who Can't Believe: Overcoming the Obstacles to Faith* (New York: HarperCollins, 1994); Valley Beth Shalom Web site URL: http://www.vbs.org/, accessed August 18, 2004.

secularism

Secularism is a way of life that excludes religious observance or relegates it to a minor role.

It may seem odd to call someone a secular Jew, since Judaism is usually perceived as a religion. Nevertheless, a large number of Jews are secular Jews, which demonstrates that Judaism is more than a religion; it is also an ethnicity or nationality. According to the ancient RABBIS, a person is Jewish if he or she has a Jewish mother. Thus, it is possible for a person to be Jewish yet not participate in any Jewish holidays, ceremonies or rituals and not believe in the TORAH or even God. Such a person may nevertheless have a connection to a Jewish community or to Jewish history or culture, or may have a personal connection to the state of Israel. In these ways, the person can have a JEWISH IDENTITY without being religiously Jewish. Thus, secularism and Judaism are not necessarily opposites. In fact, some estimate that up to 80 percent of modern Israelis (*see* ISRAEL) are secular Jews, although many of them observe religious festivals and other practices as "customs."

Over the past hundred years, people of many religions became increasingly secular, though the trend may have reversed more recently as new ways to be religious develop. Since the EMANCIPATION of the Jews in Europe, Jews have been confronted with both ENLIGHTENMENT philosophy and a pluralistic society, which create a dynamic of both assimilation and secularization. This has created a concern in the Jewish community that without the religious elements of Judaism, Jews will intermarry more and more, and the existence of Judaism itself will be threatened.

Further reading: Alan M. Dershowitz, *The Vanishing American Jew: In Search of Jewish Identity for the Next Century* (New York: Simon and Schuster, 1997); Gerhard Falk, *American Judaism in Transition: The Secularization of a Religious Community* (Lanham, Md.: University Press of America, 1995); Arthur Hertzberg, *The Fate of Zionism: A Secular Future for Israel and Palestine* (New York: HarperSanFrancisco, 2003); Charles S. Liebman, ed., *Religious and Secular: Conflict and Accommodation between Jews in Israel* (Jerusalem: Kter Publishing House, 1990).

seder

The seder (Hebrew for "order") is a ritual meal and ceremony performed in Jewish homes on the first night (or first two nights) of PASSOVER. It follows a specific order of 15 steps as laid down in the HAGGADAH (Hebrew for "telling"), the Passover prayerbook.

The steps of the seder are *kadesh*, the recitation of the kiddush over wine; *urchatz*, the washing of hands; *karpas*, the eating of a vegetable dipped in saltwater; *yachatz*, the breaking of the middle of three MATZAHS; *maggid*, the recitation of the story of the EXODUS; *rachtzah*, the washing of the hands a second time; *motze*, the blessing over bread; *matzah*, the blessing over unleavened bread; *marror*, the eating of the bitter herbs; *korech*, the eating of the sandwich of matzah and bitter herbs; *shulkhan orech*, the eating of the festive meal; *tzafun*, the eating of the AFIKOMEN; *barech*, the recitation of the BIRKAT HA-MAZON, or grace after meals; *hallel*, the recitation of psalms of praise; and *nirtzah*, the conclusion of the seder.

The seder is generally observed outside of ISRAEL on the first two nights of Passover and in Israel for the first night only. Most of the time is devoted to telling the story of the Exodus, eating a large family meal, and informal discussions on Passover and related topics. Blessings and RITUALS in the order listed above pepper the ceremony, which can last into the small hours of the morning for some.

A seder plate sits on the table, holding a variety of ritual foods and symbols that are used during the seder, such as bitter herbs, representing the hardships of SLAVERY, and a shank bone, representing the ancient ritual of SACRIFICE. Seder plates have become an expression of Jewish art; they can be quite elaborate and beautiful or very simple in style.

The seder is a very ancient practice. The TORAH, or the Five Books of Moses, commands parents to inform their children about their deliverance from slavery in EGYPT: "And you shall tell your son in that day, saying: It is because of that which God did for me when I came forth out of Egypt." (Ex 13:8). To fulfill this commandment, the ancient RABBIS of the MISHNAH designed the seder, with its prescribed ritual structure.

Over the centuries, there have been a few additions and variations to the original seder. Two contemporary additions stand out. It is now a tradition in some liberal Jewish homes to add a "Miriam's cup" to the seder table, representing the biblical personality of MIRIAM and her connection to life-giving water. A feminist tradition has developed that involves placing an orange on the seder plate to remember marginalized Jews such as women and homosexuals while telling the story of freedom from slavery. An orange is an odd object to have on a seder plate, and thus it well represents marginalized people.

The seder begins with the recitation of the kiddush, the sanctification of the festival, over a cup of wine (*see* KIDDUSH CUP). This is followed by a reading out loud of the Exodus story, by a leader or by all participants in turn. One eats the bitter herbs, so as to remember the bitterness of slavery,

This table is set for the Passover seder. The seder plate sits in the center of the table and there is plenty of wine for all to drink the ceremonial four cups of wine during the storytelling and the meal. *(Ziv Korean, Government Press Office, The State of Israel)*

and the haroset, which looks like the mortar the slaves once were forced to use in their labor, but tastes sweet, and is thus a reminder of the sweetness of God's liberation of the Israelite slaves. Matzah, unleavened bread, is eaten as a reminder that the Israelites had to flee quickly from Egypt, before the bread had time to rise, and as a reminder of their poverty and affliction. Four cups of wine are drunk, each a reminder of God's biblical promise for REDEMPTION. The participants sing psalms of HALLEL, or thanksgiving, as well as other traditional Passover songs. The participants invite the prophet ELIJAH, who has his own cup of wine on each seder table. The seder ends with the words "Next year in JERUSALEM."

The seder was designed to be a timeless liturgy. It describes the defeat of evil by good, and its lessons can be applied to any era. When the rabbis of the Mishnah composed the seder, they most likely had in mind not just the Egyptians, but also the Romans, who were brutally occupying PALESTINE. The seder was designed so that Romans would not understand the political critique, but the Jews would understand the message. The rabbis imitated the mode of the Greek symposium for their seder service. Like the Greeks, the celebrants drank four cups of wine and reclined comfortably around the table; even the word *afikomen*, the final food of the evening, derives from the Greek word for "dessert."

The Egyptians were the explicit enemy; since Egyptians were also traditional enemies of the Romans, Roman authorities would have perceived the seder as a acceptable ritual. It imitated Greek forms, and criticized an ancient Roman enemy. They would not discern that in fact the Romans were being subtly criticized and identified with the Egyptians, and that the rabbis hoped that God would eventually secure their defeat and once more liberate the Jews, this time from Roman persecution and repression.

The seder includes clever textual hints pointing to Rome as the intended address for divine rebuke. For example, in the beginning of the telling of the Exodus story, it calls Laban an Aramean who was worse than the Egyptian Pharaoh in his persecutions of Jacob. This is an absurd statement and the average Jew in ancient times would have known Laban as the Roman who was worse than Pharaoh. However, when Rome ceased to be the chief enemy of the Jews, the Haggadah's symbolic design remained relevant in the face of all evil enemies and those who would try to suppress freedom. In the contemporary world, many seders reflect general struggles for freedom and encourage those who still struggle such as women and survivors of the HOLOCAUST.

The seder was also designed to be pedagogically efficient. Ritual questions are asked as pointers and attention-grabbers for children. Tradition dictates that the youngest child capable should read the four questions at the seder table, with their refrain *Mah Nishtanah,* "Why is this night different from all other nights?"

In the contemporary world, the Passover seder is the most widely attended ritual among American Jews. Perhaps the family orientation, the ease of performing a ritual at home, or merely the food itself draws modern Jews into retelling a central story of their common heritage.

Further reading: Baruch M. Bokser, *The Origins of the Seder* (Berkeley: University of California Press, 1986); Nahum N. Glatzer, *The Schocken Passover Haggadah* (New York: Schocken Books, 1996 [1953]); Irving

Greenberg, *The Jewish Way: Living the Holidays* (New York: Simon & Schuster, 1988); Philip Goodman, *The Passover Anthology* (Philadelphia: Jewish Publication Society of America, 1993); *Passover Haggadah,* Deluxe Edition, Maxwell House, 1984.

Sefer Yetsirah

The *Sefer Yetsirah* ("Book of Creation" or "Book of Formation") is the oldest HEBREW-language text of Jewish MYSTICISM extant today. It was probably written between the third and sixth centuries of the Common Era. Gershom SCHOLEM associates it with MERKABAH mystical literature and with theories of magic. In its brief 1,600 words, it focuses on issues of cosmology, exploring the elements of the world as expressed in the 10 primordial numbers and the letters of the Hebrew alphabet. Each letter has secret meaning on three levels: the level of man, the level of celestial objects, and the level of time. The 13th-century Kabbalist Abraham ben Samuel Abulafia (1240–c. 1291) once wrote that the *Sefer Yetsirah* and MAIMONIDES' *Guide to the Perplexed* represented the only correct explications of Kabbalism, and he made a close study of the text himself.

Further reading: Daniel C. Matt, *The Essential Kabbalah: The Heart of Jewish Mysticism* (San Francisco: HarperSanFrancisco, 1995); Gershom Scholem, *Major Trends in Jewish Mysticism* (New York: Schocken Books, 1946); ———, *On the Kabbalah and Its Symbolism* (New York: Schocken Books, 1965).

sefirat ha'omer See OMER, COUNTING OF.

sefirot

In the Jewish mystical tradition, the 10 *sefirot* (from *safar,* "to count") are the emanations of God that were generated during the CREATION of the world. These emanations are direct expressions of God's attributes; they became the foundation of everything in CREATION.

The *sefirot* manifest the potencies of God. They are *kether elyon* (supreme crown); *hokhmah* (wisdom); *binah* (intelligence); *hesed* (mercy); *gevurah* or *din* (power or judgment); *rahamim* (compassion); *netsah* (lasting endurance); *hod* (majesty); *yesod* (foundation); and *malkuth* (kingdom). The *Bahir,* a Kabbalistic text, says "All the divine powers form a succession of layers and are like a tree." All of the created world comes from and is sustained by the *sefirot.* Much of mystical literature is devoted to understanding the nature and workings of the *sefirot* in Creation, in human life, in the generation of evil, and in the eventual triumph of good in God's Creation.

Further reading: Daniel C. Matt, *The Essential Kabbalah* (Edison, N.J.: Castle Books, 1995); Gershom Scholem, *Major Trends in Jewish Mysticism* (New York: Schocken Books, 1946); Gershom Scholem, *On the Kabbalah and Its Symbolism* (New York: Schocken Books, 1965).

Seinfeld, Jerry (b. 1954) *comedian*

Jerry Seinfeld was born April 29, 1954, in Brooklyn, New York. He graduated with a B.A. in theater and communication in 1976 from Queens College of the City University of New York, and later became a stand-up comedian. He regularly appeared on the *Tonight Show* and on *Late Night with David Letterman* until he ended up with his own television series, the hit show *Seinfeld,* which aired from 1988 to 1998.

While the topic of Judaism does not specifically come up in many episodes, Seinfeld's parents are portrayed as stereotypically Jewish characters and the show is imbued with a sense of New York Jewish culture; the *Seinfeld* show was able to popularize New York Jewish culture for a national audience.

Seinfeld's persona does not follow the typical Jewish comedy style laden with manic, burlesque humor. Instead, he chose a more low-key, laid-back type of comedy, marking him as a pioneer in contemporary Jewish humor. He has received many awards, including American Comedy: Funniest Male Stand-Up Comic (1988), American Comedy: Funniest Actor in a TV Series, *Seinfeld* (1992); Emmy: Outstanding Comedy Series, *Seinfeld* (1993); Golden Globe: Best Actor in a TV Series (comedy or musical), *Seinfeld* (1993); and several other awards for his hit television series.

Further reading: Vincent Brook, *Something Ain't Kosher Here: The Rise of the "Jewish" Sitcom* (New Brunswick, N.J.: Rutgers University Press, 2003); Jerry Oppenheimer, *Seinfeld: The Making of an American Icon* (New York: HarperCollins, 2002); Jerry Seinfeld, *SeinLanguage* (New York: Bantam Books, 1995); David Zurawik, *The Jews of Prime Time* (Hanover, N.H.: Brandeis University Press, 2003).

selichot

Selichot are the penitential prayers (asking forgiveness) recited during the High Holiday period, beginning before Rosh HaShanah and ending with Yom Kippur; they are also recited on all fast days. Some of the *selichot* were written as early as the first century, but the majority of them were composed by Hebrew poets of the 12th and 13th centuries, many from Spain. The main subjects of the *selichot* prayers are martyrdom, suffering (*see* theodicy), the destruction of the Temple, sin (*see* sin and repentance), confession, and God's mercy and forgiveness.

The term *selichot* also refers to the traditional service that takes place at midnight on the Saturday preceding Rosh HaShanah, which primarily consists of the selichot penitential prayers. The *selichot* service also emphasizes the recitation of "The Thirteen Attributes of God," also recited on Rosh HaShanah and Yom Kippur. The 13 attributes are taken from a verse in Torah that describes an ever-loving, compassionate, forgiving God.

Further reading: Irving Greenberg, *The Jewish Way: Living the Holidays* (New York: Simon & Schuster, 1993); Abraham Millgram, *Jewish Worship* (Philadelphia: Jewish Theological Seminary, 1971); Michael Strassfeld, *Jewish Holidays: A Guide and Commentary* (New York: HarperResource, 1993).

semikha

Semikha is the transmission of rabbinic authority (*see* RABBI); in other words, the ordination of a new rabbi. A person who "has *semikha*" is a recognized rabbi.

The term was also used in the days of the TEMPLE in JERUSALEM; it described the the priests' practice of resting their hands on an animal sin offering. The priests thus symbolically transferred sins to the animal about to be sacrificed. In a modern setting, semikha is equivalent to rabbinic ordination.

The first form of formal Jewish transmission of authority occurred when MOSES transferred significant portions of his authority to 70 elders at the urging of his father-in-law, Jethro. When the PHARISEES came to dominate what would become rabbinic Judaism, they implemented the ceremony of *semikha,* by which the master teacher laid his hands on the disciple and authorized him to become a rabbi. When the SANHEDRIN ceased to exist, the form and power of *semikha* changed as well. *Semikha* became the acknowledgement by a formal Jewish body that a student had satisfactorily completed his sacred textual study and was qualified to interpret Jewish law.

There have been cases where recognized Jewish scholars did not hold *semikha,* even though they were thought of as rabbis. One notable case was the CHAFETZ CHAYIM (1838–1933), a world-renowned authority who never formally received *semikha.* When the Gentile Polish authorities would not give him an official passport because he was not a "recognized" rabbi, he had to arrange for a telegraphed *semikha* from colleagues who were authorized to grant it.

Within the Orthodox rabbinate today (*see* ORTHODOX JUDAISM), the title "rabbi" is bestowed upon learned individuals who complete their studies in a satisfactory manner. Different levels of *semikha* can be granted. The first level is *yorei yorei,* which means "he shall teach." Most Orthodox rabbis possess this level of *semikha.* However, a higher level of *semikha* exists called *yadin yadin,* which means "he shall judge." These are rabbis especially qualified to sit on a *BET DIN,* a rabbinic court.

In the ultra-Orthodox world, *semikha* can be obtained without any modern education. In the MODERN ORTHODOX world, most yeshivot (*see* YESHIVA), schools of Jewish learning, require at least a university undergraduate education before granting *semikha,* although there are exceptions. Women cannot receive *semikha* in the Orthodox world. The Conservative (*see* CONSERVATIVE JUDAISM) movement will ordain men and women, and do not refer to their rabbinical ordination as *semikha.* They believe the term to be historically distinct from the needs of a modern-day rabbi's education, which includes traditional and critical study of sacred texts as well as significant exposure to graduate studies in numerous fields. The Reform movement (*see* REFORM JUDAISM) ordains both men and women and does not require traditional levels of textual study. Orthodoxy does not accept the rabbinic status of Conservative and Reform rabbis.

Further reading: Jacob Barnai, *The Jews in Palestine in the Eighteenth Century* (Tuscaloosa: University of Alabama Press, 1992); Basil Herring, *The Rabbinate As Calling and Vocation: Models of Rabbinic Leadership* (Northvale, N.J.: Jason Aronson, 1991); Jacob Neusner, *American Judaism: Adventure in Modernity* (Englewood Cliffs, N.J.: Prentice Hall, 1972); ———, "Phenomenon of the Rabbi in Late Antiquity," in *Numen* 16 (April 1969): 1–20; Chaim Potok, *Wanderings: Chaim Potok's History of the Jews* (New York: Fawcett Books, 1990).

Senesh, Hannah (Hannah Szenes)
(1921–1944) *heroic Israeli fighter*

Hannah Senesh was born in Budapest, HUNGARY, in 1921. She was the daughter of an author and journalist, and at a young age demonstrated her love of writing. Beginning at the age of 13 until her death at the hands of the Nazis (*see* HOLOCAUST), she kept a diary that provided unique insights into her thoughts and the challenges of the era.

Senesh's family were assimilated (*see* ASSIMILATION) Hungarian Jews, but when ANTISEMITISM in

Budapest began to grow stronger, she became involved with Zionist (*see* ZIONISM) youth activities and left for PALESTINE at the age of 18. She studied at an agricultural school and prepared for KIBBUTZ life. At Kibbutz Sdot Yam she wrote poetry and a play about kibbutz life.

Joining the British army in 1943, Senesh underwent military training in EGYPT, and then volunteered to parachute into Nazi-occupied Europe. Her responsibilities included organizing and facilitating connections with anti-Nazi resistance fighters, with the ultimate goal of reaching her hometown of Budapest.

Senesh parachuted in March 1944 into Yugoslavia. Her first three months were spent with local resistance fighters, and she managed to help besieged Jewish communities. On June 7, 1944, as the Nazis were accelerating their deportation of Hungarian Jews to the death camps (*see* CONCENTRATION AND DEATH CAMPS), Senesh tried to enter Hungary. As she left on her mission, she handed a comrade her famous poem, "Blessed is the Match." She was captured almost immediately and severely tortured over several months of interrogations. Senesh refused to give up any information, even when the life of her mother was threatened. She was placed on trial in October of 1944 and offered a blistering condemnation of the Nazis and Hungarian collaborators. She was executed on November 7, 1944, refusing a blindfold before the firing squad.

In 1950, Senesh's remains were reinterred at the Har Herzl military cemetery in JERUSALEM. Her diary and other literary works were published after her death in both English and Hebrew, and many of her poems have been set to music. She has been the subject of artistic works and a popular play written by Aharon Megged. Senesh exemplified a young woman who found courage and hope in the bleakest circumstances.

Through her brief but noteworthy life, Hannah Senesh became a symbol of idealism and self-sacrifice. Her poems, made famous in part because of her unfortunate death, reveal a woman imbued with hope in the face of adverse circumstances.

Senesh's poetry is well known in Israeli culture. She exemplified the famous flame of her poem:

> Blessed is the match consumed in kindling flame.
> Blessed is the flame that burns in the heart's secret places.
> Blessed is the heart with strength to stop its beating for honor's sake
> Blessed is the match consumed in kindling flame.

Further reading: Howard M. Sachar, *The Course of Modern Jewish History* (New York: Vintage Books, 1990); Maxine R. Schur, *Hannah Szenes* (Philadelphia: Jewish Publication Society of America, 1998); Hannah Szenes, *Hannah Senesh: Her Life and Diary* (New York: Schocken Books, 1972).

Sephardim

Two major religious-cultural groupings emerged within Judaism in the Middle Ages. One group is the ASHKENAZIM, and the other is the Sephardim.

The term *Sephardim* comes from the place-name Sephard in the TANAKH, or Hebrew Bible, referring to a land where Jews were exiled (*see* EXILE) after the destruction of the first TEMPLE in JERUSALEM. The term *Sephardim* was first used by the Jews who lived in SPAIN and PORTUGAL before the expulsion in 1492. After the Jewish EXPULSION from Spain in 1492, the Sephardim resettled in the Balkans, EGYPT, Italy, the Netherlands, North Africa, PALESTINE, Syria, and throughout the Turkish empire. *Sephardim* was initially applied only to those Jews who were descendants of the Jews of Spain and Portugal, but the term is commonly applied today to all Jews who are not Ashkenazim. Another term applied to this group of Jews is *mizrachim*, which directly translates as "easterners."

Sephardi Jews spoke LADINO, which was a blend of Spanish and HEBREW. Much of the religious scholarship of the Sephardim was written in either Hebrew or Arabic, as Arabs occupied Spain during much of the time that the Jews prospered there. Sephardic culture is distinguished from Ashkenazic mostly in the details of religious practices. Many Sephardic traditions can be traced back to the Jewish community of BABYLONIA in the early Middle Ages; at that time, Mesopotamia and Spain were under common Muslim rule.

Sephardic culture was highly influenced by the interaction with Muslim Arabs. Sephardi Jews commonly spoke Arabic, and thus had access to Arab achievements in mathematics, medicine, poetry, and philosophy. Sephardim also developed their own unique methods of studying the Tanakh, they pioneered the study of KABBALAH, and they started the process of codifying Jewish law (*see* CODES OF LAW). When Joseph CARO penned the most often-used code, the *SHULCHAN ARUKH*, he followed Sephardic

customs and interpretations of law. It was necessary for Moses ISSERLES to add the *MAPAH* to address many issues important to the Ashkenazim.

Sephardic SYNAGOGUES often differ from those of Ashkenazim in that the bima, or raised platform from where the services are led, is located in the center of the space rather than at the front. Another well-known difference between the two groups concerns PASSOVER customs. While Sephardim are permitted to eat a category of food called *kitniyot*, which includes corn, rice, and beans, during Passover, Ashkenazim are prohibited from doing so. In addition, Ashkenazim often make *charoset,* a dish for Passover, with apples, while Sephardim use dates. This reflects the fruits most readily available in the original regions of each group.

This modern Sephardic synagogue is located in Los Angeles, California. *(Courtesy J. Gordon Melton)*

Further reading: Daniel J. Elazar, *The Other Jews: The Sephardim Today* (New York: Basic Books, 1989); Stephen Sharot, *Judaism: A Sociology* (New York: Holmes & Meier Publishers, 1976); Yedida K. Stillman and Norman A. Stillman, *From Iberia to Diaspora: Studies in Sephardic History and Culture* (Leiden, Netherlands: Brill, 1999); H. J. Zimmels, *Ashkenazim and Sephardim, Their Relation, Differences, and Problems as Related in the Rabbinical Responsa* (London: Marla, 1976).

Septuagint

The Septuagint is a Greek translation of the Hebrew Bible, the TANAKH, produced by Jews in Alexandria, EGYPT, in the third century B.C.E., and sponsored by the ruler Ptolemy II. Tradition has it that 70 Jewish scholars were involved in the translation, hence the name of the text. Tradition also states that while each scholar translated the Hebrew Bible in complete isolation, when the 70 translations were compared, not a single difference was found. This fanciful legend was intended to underscore the reliability of the translation.

While the Septuagint itself is no longer popularly read, it serves both religious and secular scholars as a check on the accuracy of other versions of the Bible, and as a way to learn how the work was understood in ancient times.

Further reading: Sidney Jellicoe, *Studies into the Septuagint: Origins, Recensions, and Interpretations* (New York: Ktav Publishing House, 1974); Adrian Schenker, *The Earliest Text of the Hebrew Bible: The Relationship between the Masoretic Text and the Hebrew Base of the Septuagint Reconsidered* (Atlanta, Ga.: Society of Biblical Literature, 2003).

shaatnez

The TORAH, the Five Books of MOSES, has several commandments, or mitzvot (*see* MITZVAH), against mixing certain substances together. Included is a prohibition against mixing wool and linen in the same piece of clothing. Deuteronomy 22:11 declares: "You shall not wear combined fibers, wool and linen together." In HEBREW, this forbidden mixture is called *shaatnez*. The word is an acronym for the Hebrew words "combed, spun and woven," and it refers to the stages in processing a fabric. Observant traditional Jews observe the commandment of *shaatnez* by checking manufacturer labels on the clothes or by sending their clothes to a *shaatnez* laboratory for inspection.

The law of *shaatnez* is the classical rabbinic example of a *hok* (pl.: *hukkim*), a divine law that does not seem to humans to have any self-evident purpose. Another example of the category would be the prohibition against eating pork. The ancient RABBIS distinguished *hukkim* from another category of laws called *mishpatim*, which any one could derive from common sense, such as "do not murder" or "do not steal." The *hukkim*, by contrast, test the individual's willingness to observe the will of God by the very fact that they are not intrinsically logical. *Mishpatim* create universal humanism, but *hukkim* create Judaism, according to traditional rabbinic thought.

While the ancient rabbis assert no intrinsic logic to *hukkim*, they still frequently attempt to provide metaphoric lessons from these laws. One suggestion that explains *shaatnez* is that since only human beings wear clothes, *shaatnez* reminds the Jews that unlike animals, all their actions should be kosher (*see* KASHRUT), or ritually proper in the eyes of God. Another interpretation is that mixing wool and linen upsets the metaphysical fabric of the universe. God created different species that work together and those that do not. Following the law of *shaatnez* teaches that people must learn to respect the orderliness to God's creations.

Further reading: Blu Greenberg, *How to Run a Traditional Jewish Household* (New York: Feldheim, 1989); Dovid Loebenstain, *Guide to Shatnez* (New York: Feldheim, 1989).

Shabbat

Shabbat is the HEBREW term for Sabbath. Jewish law (*see* HALAKHAH) stipulates that from sunset on

Friday night until nightfall on Saturday, Jews are supposed to "remember and observe" the Shabbat. According to the Book of Genesis (*see* TANAKH), God created the world on the first six days and rested on the seventh (*see* CREATION). God therefore declared in the Ten Commandments (*see* DECALOGUE) that one should recall that God rested and remember and observe the Sabbath by resting as well.

The general rabbinic notion is that "observing" the Sabbath refers to the laws concerning prohibited activity on Shabbat, but "remembering" the Sabbath refers to the positive acts you perform. Positive Sabbath obligations include worshipping God, studying sacred texts, sharing Sabbath meals with family and friends, and celebrating with song.

Shabbat is considered the sign of the eternal COVENANT between the Jewish people (*see* PEOPLEHOOD) and God. After the destruction of the second TEMPLE by the Romans, Jewish communal life and worship often centered on the Sabbath; it still does among those who observe Jewish law.

Shabbat represents the ultimate separation of the sacred and mundane in Jewish life. God marked the seventh day from the previous six, and Jews reenact this each week, separating the holy day of rest from others. Prohibiting certain actions on the Sabbath not only defines the day of rest, but it allows for personal introspection and private time because one is not allowed to work on that day.

The Torah specifically commands that no work should be performed on the Sabbath, by Jews, their animals, their employees, or strangers who live among them. The ancient rabbis defined work through 39 categories of activity, each of which has subcategories. While there are numerous traditional prohibitions for Jews on the Sabbath, such as writing, spending money, and driving, all Sabbath prohibitions are set aside if a human life is at stake. Therefore emergency professionals can work, if necessary, on Shabbat; many Orthodox Jewish doctors, for example, are on call during Shabbat, and many carry pagers with the approval of their rabbis.

There are many different Shabbat laws and customs; Jews differ in their observances, but few would deny that the Sabbath is one of the primary foundations of the Jewish religion. Many Jews who no longer observe many the Jewish laws still attend SYNAGOGUE for Shabbat services. The great cultural Zionist leader AHAD HA'AM caught the meaning of Shabbat in Jewish civilization when he declared: "More than the Jewish people has preserved Shabbat, Shabbat has preserved the Jewish people."

Further reading: Irving Greenberg, *The Jewish Way: Living the Holidays* (New York: Simon & Schuster, 1988); Abraham Joshua Heschel, *The Sabbath: Its Meaning for Modern Man* (New York: Farrar, Straus and Giroux, 1994); Ron Wolfson, *The Shabbat Seder* (Woodstock, Vt.: Jewish Lights Publishing, 1995).

Shabbatai Zvi (1626–1676) *false messiah*

Shabbatai Zvi was a Turkish Jew born in Smyrna in 1626. He exhibited early promise in the study of TALMUD, and he became a student and teacher of KABBALAH, often speaking about his own mystical experiences. Shabbatai had a charismatic personality; he was either loved or hated by everyone he met.

While living in JERUSALEM, Shabbatai met Nathan of Gaza, who proclaimed him to be the MESSIAH. With his strong personality and the fervor of MYSTICISM around him, Shabbatai embraced the role. Thousands of Jews followed him, believing that he would liberate them from Turkish rule. Even Jews living in cities far away, such as Venice, Livorno, and Amsterdam, participated in the messianic fervor. Many followers became antinomians, believing that the coming of the Messiah meant that Jewish law should be abandoned or even deliberately violated.

In the year 1666, the sultan of Turkey threatened Shabbatai with two choices: either convert to ISLAM or be tortured to death. Shabbatai converted to Islam and took the name Mehemet Effendi.

Shabbatai's conversion shook the Jewish world, which had experienced what they considered to be false messiahs in the past, including JESUS OF NAZARETH and Shimon BAR-KOKHBA. Nathan continued to argue that Shabbatai was the Messiah after his conversion. Some scholars see the people's desire for a Messiah to have been a larger factor in Shabbatai's popularity than the endorsement of Nathan of Gaza. The Jews were eager for a Messiah because of the horrific persecutions of their time, particularly the CHMIELNICKI MASSACRES. In any case, Shabbatai's conversion to Islam devastated thousands of followers. Gershom SCHOLEM argues that the movement and the subsequent disappointment catalyzed the global Jewish community, eventually sparking the Zionist movement (see ZIONISM). Others have made connections between Shabbatai's less legalistic mystical movement and HASIDISM and REFORM JUDAISM, which both emerged a century later.

Further reading: Abraham J. Karp, *From the Ends of the Earth: Judaic Treasures of the Library of Congress* (Washington, D.C.: Library of Congress, 1991); Gershom Scholem, *Sabbatai Sevi: The Mystical Messiah 1626–1676* (London: Routledge & K. Paul, 1973); Hayim Greenberg, "Shabbetai Zevi—The Messiah as Apostate," in *The Inner Eye: Selected Essays*, ed. Schlomo Katz, vol. 2, 84–98.

shalom bayit

Shalom bayit (Hebrew for "peace in the home") is considered a goal of every Jewish family. Jewish tradition states that every home is supposed to imitate in some way the holiness that existed in the TEMPLE in JERUSALEM. The common gathering place of the family, at the kitchen table, is often referred to as a "little altar." Rituals are performed at the family dinner table to imitate cultic practices of the Temple, such as placing salt on the challah, and ritually washing one's hands (see NETILLAT YADAYIM), like the ancient priests.

The concept of *shalom bayit* begins with marriage and is found in the text of the seventh marriage blessing (see SHEVA BRACHOT): "love and

unity, peace and companionship." The RABBIS believed that no home could be holy if there was family disharmony. Beginning with the early rabbinic period (around 10 to 220 C.E.), they forbade husbands from acting in a manner that would make their wives dread their presence. Husbands were told to be respectful to their wives, even to honor them more than themselves.

The commandment to love your neighbor as yourself was specifically applied to the members of one's own family. Keeping peace in the family, by rabbinic tradition, even allowed for the telling of white lies, to avoid hurting someone's feelings and causing unnecessary friction. The ancient rabbis believed that peace could never be secured in a community, nation, or world until it was firmly established in the home.

The general framework of *shalom bayit* remains a powerful lesson for husband, wife, children, and all those who share one roof. In contemporary times, some rabbis have used the concept in their opposition to any and all forms of domestic violence.

Further reading: Eugene Borowitz and Frances Weinman Schwartz, *The Jewish Moral Virtues* (Philadelphia: Jewish Publication Society, 1999); Don S. Browning, et al., *Religion, Feminism and the Family* (Louisville, Ky.: Westminster John Knox Press, 1996); Anita Diamant, *Living a Jewish Life* (New York: HarperResource, 1996); Hayim Halevy Donin, *To Be a Jew: A Guide to Jewish Observance in Contemporary Life* (New York: Basic Books, 1972).

Shamir, Yitzhak (b. 1915) *Israeli independence fighter and political leader*

Yitzhak Shamir, underground leader, spymaster, and parliamentarian, was the seventh prime minister (see KNESSET) of the State of ISRAEL. He was born Yitzhak Yzernitzky in Ruzinoy, POLAND, in 1915. At the age of 14 he joined the Betar youth movement, and in 1935 he moved to PALESTINE.

In 1937, opposing the mainstream Zionist (see ZIONISM) policy of restraint vis-à-vis the British,

Shamir joined the IRGUN ZEVA'I LEUMI (Etzel), the Revisionist underground organization. In 1940 he became a member of the smaller, more militant faction led by Avraham Stern, called the Stern Gang or Lechi. Shamir was arrested twice by the British during and after World War II, escaping both times. He commanded the Lechi until it was disbanded following the establishment of the State of Israel.

Shamir joined Israel's security services in the mid-1950s and held senior positions in the MOSSAD. In 1970 he joined Menachem BEGIN's opposition Herut party and became a member of its governing body. In 1973 he was elected a member of Knesset for the LIKUD, a right-wing party that wanted Jews to settle all of the West Bank and make few, if any, concessions to Israel's Arab neighbors or to the Palestinians. Shamir remained a member of the Knesset for 23 years, often serving as a minister with various portfolios.

Following the resignation of Menachem Begin in October 1983, Yitzhak Shamir became prime minister until the general elections in the fall of 1984. During this year, Shamir concentrated on economic matters as the economy was suffering from hyperinflation, while also nurturing closer strategic ties with the UNITED STATES.

Indecisive results in the 1984 general elections led to the formation of a National Unity Government based on a rotation agreement between Shamir and Labor leader Shimon PERES. Thus, Shamir served for seven years as prime minister, first from 1983–84, and then from 1986–92. First, he served as the head of the Likud Party (1983–84), and then as head of a narrow coalition government (1986–92). During Shamir's time as prime minister, he made possible Operation Solomon, the rescue by air of thousands of Ethiopian Jews (see ETHIOPIA).

Further reading: Arnold Blumberg, *The History of Israel* (Westport, Conn.: Greenwood Press, 1998); Asher Cohen and Bernard Susser, *Israel and the Politics of Jewish Identity: The Secular-Religious Impasse* (Baltimore: Johns Hopkins University Press, 2000); Adam Garfin-kle, *Politics and Society in Modern Israel* (Armonk, N.Y.: M. E. Sharpe, 2000); Howard M. Sachar, *A History of Israel From the Rise of Zionism to Our Time* (New York: Alfred A. Knopf, 1996).

Shammai (first century B.C.E.) *ancient sage*

Shammai and his friend and rival HILLEL were the preeminent teachers of Jewish law in the first century B.C.E. Though renowned as a scholar, Shammai was often disliked for lacking human qualities, especially when compared with Hillel. The Talmudic tractate, *Shabbat* 31a, taught the following: "Be as humble as Hillel, and never as rude as Shammai."

An irony within rabbinic literature is that Shammai is quoted as teaching: "Welcome cheerfully every human being" (*Ethics of the Fathers* 1:15) even though he was not known for his hospitality toward others. Shammai, like Hillel, had a school of disciples who followed his teachings. They were known as Bet Shammai, or the House of Shammai. Whereas the House of Hillel was known to be liberal in its interpretation of Jewish law (*see* HALAKHAH), the House of Shammai was known for strictly following the letter of the law.

Further reading: Isadore Epstein, ed., *Soncino Hebrew/English Babylonian Talmud.* 30 Volumes (London: Soncino Press, 1990); Joseph H. Hertz, ed., *Pirke Aboth: Sayings of the Fathers* (West Orange, N.J.: Behrman House, 1986); Jeffrey L. Rubenstein, ed., *Rabbinic Stories* (New York: Paulist Press, 2002); Adin Steinsaltz, *The Essential Talmud* (New York: Basic Books, 1976).

Sharansky, Natan (Anatoly Sharansky) (b. 1948) *human rights activist and Israeli political leader*

Natan (Anatoly) Sharansky was born in the Ukraine in 1948. Growing up in an assimilated Jewish family under Soviet rule, Sharansky's childhood lacked the influences of traditional Judaism, although he grew up knowing he was Jewish and understanding that this could be dangerous. He graduated from the Moscow Physics Technological Institute with a degree in mathematics and became a computer science specialist in the early years of computer technology. After struggling with the nature of Soviet politics and culture, Sharansky began to read the underground articles of top scientist Andre Sakharov. When Sharansky became Sakharov's English interpreter, he also joined the human rights movement in the Soviet Union (see RUSSIA). After a time, he developed into one of the major spokesmen for Jewish rights in the Soviet Union, becoming a rallying force for the worldwide effort to allow Soviet Jews to immigrate to ISRAEL. Sharansky developed his Jewish identity, first becoming a Zionist (see ZIONISM) and then finding spiritual interest in Judaism.

In 1973, Sharansky applied for an exit visa to Israel. The Soviet government refused his application on "security" grounds because of a job he had held previously. He continued to participate in REFUSENIK activities until he was arrested in 1977. In 1978, Sharansky was sentenced to 13 years of imprisonment for presumably spying for the UNITED STATES. Ironically, this sentence made it possible to include Sharansky in a Soviet-U.S. prisoner swap years later, leading to his release from the gulag in 1986. Sharansky remained a prisoner of the Soviet regime for nine years, enduring more than 400 days in special "torture cells" and spending more than 200 days on hunger strikes; Sharansky continued his struggle from prison.

After gaining his freedom Sharansky wrote his memoirs, *Fear No Evil*, in which he brought to life for the reader the immense challenges and hardships he faced. While he was to the world a symbol for human rights and the plight of the Soviet Jews, he had to struggle daily to maintain his sanity. He refused to be broken by the Soviets. He survived countless hours of confinement by meditating on biblical passages and playing chess in his mind to keep himself intellectually stimulated.

Leading the cause to free Sharansky was his wife, Avital. She had immigrated to Israel shortly after their wedding, hoping that he would soon follow. They would not be reunited for 12 years,

until February 11, 1986, when Sharansky finally arrived in Israel. He was granted immediate citizenship as Natan Sharansky. Sharansky, with his new free status, continued to fight on behalf of the Soviet Jews who were still trapped behind the Iron Curtain, and he also became a strong advocate for the new Soviet immigrants in Israel. He and his wife have two daughters.

In 1995 Sharansky created a new political party, Yisrael Ba'Aliya, which was dedicated to helping immigrants' professional, economic and social acculturation. In the 1996 elections his political party won seven KNESSET seats, and Sharansky was named minister of industry and trade, a position he held until June 1999. He then became minister of the interior for one year, and in March 2001 was appointed minister of housing and construction and deputy prime minister. In 2003, Sharansky became minister of Jerusalem affairs. He is also a contributing editor to the *JERUSALEM POST*.

Further reading: Robert O. Freedman, ed., *Soviet Jewry in the 1980s: The Politics of Anti-Semitism and Emigration and the Dynamics of Resettlement* (Durham, N.C.: Duke University Press, 1989); Natan Sharansky, *The Case for Democracy* (New York: Public Affairs, 2004); ———, *Fear No Evil: The Classic Memoir of One Man's Triumph Over a Police State* (New York: Vintage Books, 1989).

Sharett, Moshe (1894–1965) *Israeli political leader*

Moshe Sharett was a Zionist leader (see ZIONISM) who became the first foreign minister, and the second prime minister, of the independent State of ISRAEL.

Sharett was born Moshe Shertok in Kherson, Ukraine, in 1894 and arrived with his family in PALESTINE at the age of 12. His family was among the founders of what became the city of TEL AVIV. They had moved to Jaffa after living in an Arab village. Sharett learned to speak Arabic during this time, making it possible for him to serve as an Arab affairs and land purchase agent after the end of World War I.

In 1920 Sharett joined the socialist Ahdut Ha'avoda, which later became Mapai, the leading party in the YISHUV, the Jewish community in Palestine. He was able to spend several years studying at the London School of Economics before his 1925 appointment as deputy editor of *Davar*, the daily paper of the HISTADRUT, the General Federation of Labor, and editor of *Davar's* English language weekly. In 1931 he joined the political section of the JEWISH AGENCY, the "almost-government" of the Jews in Palestine.

From 1933 until the establishment of the State of Israel in 1948, Sharett served as head of the political section of the Jewish Agency, a role second only to that of David BEN-GURION. He was the chief negotiator and spokesman of the yishuv, to the BRITISH MANDATE authorities, and an important architect of Zionist policy. He supported Ben-Gurion's strategy of organized mass "illegal" immigration in defiance of British policy, and played a major role in mobilizing international support for the November 1947 UNITED NATIONS vote on the PARTITION PLAN, and for the admission of Israel into the United Nations.

Moshe Sharett was one of the signers of Israel's Declaration of Independence, and served as Israel's first minister of foreign affairs from 1948 until 1956. In 1953, when Ben-Gurion retired to Kibbutz Sde Boker, Moshe Sharett became prime minister, and retained his foreign affairs portfolio. Following a rift with the still politically active Ben-Gurion, Sharett resigned his office in 1956 and left political life.

Further reading: Adam Garfinkle, *Politics and Society in Modern Israel* (Armonk, N.Y.: M. E. Sharpe, 2000); Howard M. Sachar, *A History of Israel: From the Rise of Zionism to Our Time* (New York: Alfred A. Knopf, 1993); Gabriel Sheffer, *Moshe Sharett: Biography of a Political Moderate* (Oxford: Oxford University Press, 1996).

Sharon, Ariel (b. 1928) *Israeli military and political leader*

Born Ariel Scheinerman in PALESTINE in 1928, Ariel Sharon joined the HAGANAH, the Jewish military force in British Mandatory Palestine, at the young age of 14. After Israel declared her independence, Sharon served in the ISRAEL DEFENSE FORCE (IDF) for more than 25 years, retiring as a major general. During the 1948 Israeli War of Independence, Sharon was wounded in his position as platoon commander; however, by 1951, he had become an intelligence officer. After controversy surrounded Sharon's service in the 1956 Suez War, he attended law school at Tel Aviv University. Yet he remained active in the Israeli military, and became a military hero during the 1967 SIX-DAY WAR. Although Sharon resigned from the Israel Defense Forces in 1972, he was recalled when the 1973 YOM KIPPUR WAR broke out. Leading the crossing of the Suez Canal, Sharon participated in the success of the campaign and a victory for Israel.

Ariel Sharon was elected to the KNESSET in December 1973, where he supported the eventual Egypt-Israel peace treaty; he was in charge of removing Israeli settlers from the Sinai. In 1981 he was appointed defense minister. That year he brought about the first strategic cooperation agreement with the UNITED STATES; he eventually widened defense ties between Israel and many nations. He also helped bring thousands of Jews from Ethiopia through Sudan in an attempt to save their lives.

Sharon was defense minister during the LEBANON WAR in 1982, which brought about the destruction of the PALESTINE LIBERATION ORGANIZATION terrorist infrastructure in that country. His political position was weakened, however, when an Israeli commission found him indirectly responsible for the massacre of civilians in Beirut.

Serving in various ministerial capacities, Sharon eventually became prime minister in 2001, leading the LIKUD PARTY, the more right-wing faction of the Israeli parliament. He succeeded in taming the second Palestinian INTIFADA through three years of relentless military, police, and intelligence efforts. Sharon is known for his strong leadership in the face of terrorism, and many see his choices as brutal and possibly detrimental to the peace process. However, in 2004 he proposed a unilateral Israeli withdrawal from Gaza and from some West Bank settlements. Israel completed its unilateral withdrawal from the Gaza Strip in August 2005. Several months later, Sharon resigned from the Likud Party to form the new centrist party Kadima. In January 2006, Sharon suffered a severe stroke, which left him in a coma. The Kadima Party won the March 2006 election under the leadership of Ehud Olmert.

Further reading: David Chanoff and Ariel Sharon, *Warrior: An Autobiography* (New York: Simon & Schuster, 2001); Martin Van Creveld, *The Sword and the Olive: A Critical History of the Israeli Defense Force* (New York: Public Affairs, 1998); Gideon Doron and Don Peretz, *The Government and Politics of Israel* (Boulder, Colo.: Westview Press, 1997).

Shatner, William (b. 1931) *actor*

William Shatner was born on March 22, 1931 in Montreal, Quebec, CANADA. He earned a bachelor of commerce degree from McGill University. Refusing to join his Jewish parents' garment business, Shatner instead chose to pursue acting. Shatner is best known for playing Captain James T. Kirk in the popular television series *Star Trek*. Shatner went on to act in and direct Star Trek motion pictures and is still active in television and film.

Further reading: Dennis William Hauck, *William Shatner: a Bio-Bibliography* (Westport, Conn.: Greenwood Press, 1994); William Shatner, *Get a Life!* (New York: Pocket Books, 1999); William Shatner, Sondra Marshak, and Myrna Culbreath, *Shatner: Where No Man: The Authorized Biography of William Shatner* (New York: Grosset and Dunlap, 1979).

Shavuot

Shavuot (Hebrew for "weeks") is an important Jewish spring festival; its name derives from the fact that the counting of the OMER lasts for seven weeks from PASSOVER to Shavuot.

In biblical times, Shavuot was one of three annual PILGRIMAGE FESTIVALS to JERUSALEM, along with PASSOVER and SUKKOT. ISRAELITES would come to Jerusalem from all over ISRAEL and the DIASPORA to offer sacrifices and bring the first fruits of their crops. Shavuot marked the wheat harvest, so people would bring wheat to offer at the TEMPLE. Unlike the other two pilgrimage festivals, Shavuot lasted only one day and did not have many requirements attached to it beyond pilgrimage and SACRIFICE.

After the destruction of the Temple, the festival of Shavuot seemed to be superfluous; the TANAKH gives no historic meaning to Shavuot. The rabbis found several historic meanings in the oral tradition (*see* ORAL LAW). They said that the sixth of Sivan (on which Sukkot falls) was the actual date on which the TORAH was revealed on MOUNT SINAI. The festival came to be called "the time of the giving of our Torah."

The rabbis kept the festival alive; they assigned the book of RUTH to be read that day in SYNAGOGUES, since an important part of the book takes place in wheat fields. Also, Ruth is considered a convert (*see* CONVERSION), who took on the COVENANT voluntarily as did the Israelites at Mount Sinai. Moreover, Ruth is the great-grandmother of DAVID, who was known for his love of Torah study.

The festival of Shavuot is celebrated by staying up all night to study Torah, by reciting the Ten Commandments (*see* DECALOGUE), and by holding mock wedding ceremonies symbolic of the marriage between God and the Israelites at Mount Sinai. It is also traditional to feast on dairy foods and triangular-shaped foods.

Further reading: Philip Goodman, *The Shavuot Anthology* (Philadelphia and Jerusalem: Jewish Publication Society, 1974); Irving Greenberg, *The Jewish Way: Living the Holidays* (New York: Touchstone, 1988); Ronald H. Isaacs, *Every Person's Guide to Shavuot* (Northvale, N.J.: Aronson, 1999).

sheitel

Sheitel is the Yiddish word for "wig," which is often worn by Orthodox (*see* ORTHODOX JUDAISM) women. Traditional Jewish law (*see* HALAKHAH) maintains that married women should always cover their heads as an act of MODESTY. Some women utilize scarves or hats, but many use *sheitels*. Many *sheitels* are obviously wigs; however, some modern Orthodox Jews choose to wear *sheitels* made of human hair that look quite authentic. There is some debate in more traditional communities about whether it is appropriate for observant woman to wear wigs that look natural and attractive.

Clothing has a powerful history in Judaism. The ancient rabbis taught that the ISRAELITE practice of wearing distinctive dress in EGYPT, so as to remain separate from society, was one of the reasons God decided they were worthy of being redeemed from bondage. In many cultures Jews continued to wear distinctive dress for the same reason. For women, the motive of wearing distinctive clothing was bolstered by their requirement of modesty; covering their hair was considered an act of modesty.

Further reading: Hasia R. Diner, *Her Works Praise Her: A History of Jewish Women in America from Colonial Times to the Present* (New York: Basic Books, 2002); Frida Kerner Furman, *Facing the Mirror: Older Women and Beauty Shop Culture* (New York: Routledge, 1997); George Robinson, *Essential Judaism* (New York: Atria, 2001).

shekel

The shekel was a unit of weight used for payments in gold and silver in the TANAKH, the Hebrew Bible. The term is recorded in the book of Genesis, when Abraham negotiated the purchase of a field worth 400 shekels of silver. The Tanakh later stipulated the number of shekels Israelites had to pay in taxes.

In pre-exilic Judaism, half-shekels and quarter-shekels are mentioned. The TEMPLE tax was determined according to the "shekel of the sanctuary,"

The shekel is the name of the currency used in the modern State of Israel. Unlike American money, the shekel bills are quite colorful. *(Avi Ohayon, Government Press Office, The State of Israel)*

which was most likely the standard weight of coinage kept in the Temple. The shekel was both the unit of coinage, and a specific weight. The pieces of metal that served for currency were either multiples or fractions of the standard shekel.

The early Zionists (*see* ZIONISM) revived the term when they named the certificate of membership in the Zionist Organization the "Zionist Shekel." The Zionists were imitating the Hebrew

Bible's collection of shekels as a means to both tax the population and take a proper census of the people. The Zionist Organization allowed any Jew 18 years old or more to purchase a Zionist Shekel. This entitled the owner to vote in the organization's elections. The sale of shekels, or *shekalim,* funded Zionist activities.

Today, the shekel is the unit of currency of the State of Israel.

Further reading: Roland De Vaux, *Ancient Israel: Its Life and Institutions* (New York: McGraw-Hill, 1961); Frederic William Madden, *History of Jewish Coinage of the Money in the Old and New Testament* (West Orange, N.J.: Ktav Publishing, 1967).

Shema

The Shema (Hebrew for "hear") prayer is considered the core statement of Jewish belief. It consists of three passages from the TORAH: Deuteronomy 6:4–9; Deuteronomy 11:13–21; and Numbers 15:37–41. It is recited in the morning and the evening prayers. Many observe the custom of reciting the Shema before going to sleep at night, and traditionally it is supposed to be recited on one's deathbed.

The prayer is named for the first word of its first verse: *Shema Yisrael Adonai Eloheinu Adonai Echad*—"Hear O Israel, the Lord our God, the Lord is one." This first line declares the Jewish belief in MONOTHEISM. God is a single unit. The following passages teach the key lessons of ethical monotheism, a belief in one God who teaches the difference between right and wrong. It also teaches that God is the power of nature and is involved in the events of human history.

The Shema commands the individual to acknowledge the oneness of God and the commanding voice of the ethical God. The worshipper is told to meditate on this lesson when you "rise up in the morning, and lay down at night." One is also obligated to teach this message to Jewish children diligently. The Shema presents a biblical theology that teaches that if one properly observes the will of God, rewards will follow, but if not, punishment is assured. Many liberal Jews perceive this biblical theology as metaphoric.

The entire Shema prayer is intended to remind Jews of their need to obey God's commandments to live the will of God. It self-referentially tells Jews to write down its words and place them inside MEZUZAHS on their doorposts, and inside TEFILLIN, small boxes which are tied to a Jew's forehead and arm during morning prayers. In addition, the prayer commands one to wear fringes on a four-cornered garment as a reminder of God's commandments (*see* MITZVAH) and of the liberation of the Jews from their Egyptian bondage. The *TALLIT,* or prayer shawl, and TZITZIT, its fringes, were created to observe this commandment.

When reciting the first verse of the Shema it is traditional to cover one's eyes, for various reasons. One practical reason is to achieve a state of deep concentration. A MIDRASH suggests that if you close your eyes, angels will descend at that moment and join you in your prayers.

In the Torah scroll itself the word *echad* ("one") is written with an elongated dalet, the last letter. The reason is that this letter could easily be confused with the similar-looking letter reish. If one reads the word ending in an "r" sound as opposed to the correct "d" sound, one would be declaring that God is "another" rather than "one." Thus, the oral tradition is to emphatically pronounce the ending of the word *echad.* Once the scribe elongated the last letter of *echad,* he also made larger the last letter of the word *Shema* itself, which is an ayin. The scribe's logic was that the ayin, put together with the letter daled, spells the word *Aid,* which translates to mean "witness." In other words, when one recites the Shema, one performs the act of witnessing God.

Two names for GOD are mentioned in the Shema. YHWH, the TETRAGRAMMATON, is considered the personal name of God for the Jews. The name itself is not pronounced; tradition dictates that one instead pronounces the word *Adonai* (Hebrew for "my master"). *Eloheinu* is the generic name of God for all peoples.

The second sentence of Shema is often quoted: "You shall love the Lord your God with all your heart and with all your soul and with all your might." One must not only observe the will of God, but also develop a loving relationship with God. This text leads to the concept of KAVANAH, which is the devotion the Jew should show in observing God's commandments. While reading the Shema, as an act of love one kisses the tzitzit every time it is mentioned.

Further reading: Ismar Elbogen, *Jewish Liturgy: A Comprehensive History* (Philadelphia: Jewish Publication Society of America, 1993); Reuven Hammer, *Entering Jewish Prayer: A Guide to Personal Devotion and the Worship Service* (New York: Schocken Books, 1995); Jules Harlow, *The Shema and Its Blessings* (West Orange, N.J.: Behrman House Publishing, 1996).

Shemini Atzeret

The book of Leviticus in the TORAH commands Jews to celebrate the festival of SUKKOT for seven days; the eighth day is to be a sacred occasion with a solemn gathering. The first and eighth days are to be days of rest. The eighth day came to be known as Shemini Atzeret, *shemini* meaning "eighth" and *atzeret* meaning "assembly." The congregation comes together to pray but without the ritual accoutrements of Sukkot.

The Torah left the meaning of this day unclear, but MIDRASH provides many possible explanations. Some consider it an encore. Since Sukkot is the last of the three great pilgrimage festivals, God grows sad that there will be no more pilgrimage for several months, so he mandates an extra day to be together. Others say that just as Shavuot is a one-day holiday that is the culmination of PASSOVER, just so Shemini Atzeret is the one-day festival that is the culmination of Sukkot; it must take place right away, however, since the rainy season is about to begin and will make pilgrimage impossible.

In ISRAEL, Shemini Atzeret has developed into the holiday of SIMCHAT TORAH, and the two are observed on the same day. In the DIASPORA, Simchat Torah comes the following day, in effect the ninth day of the fall festival.

Further reading: Irving Greenberg, *The Jewish Way: Living the Holidays* (New York: Touchstone, 1988); Ronald H. Isaacs, *Every Person's Guide to Sukkot, Shemini Atzeret, and Simchat Torah* (Northvale, N.J.: Aronson, 2000).

Sheol

Sheol is the closest biblical equivalent to the later concept of Hell. The book of Numbers in the TANAKH, the Hebrew Bible, states the Sheol is a region that is "dark and deep," the place where humans descend after their death. The books of Ecclesiastes and JOB both state that Sheol is the place where all the dead go. In fact some have interpreted Sheol as oblivion itself, where all dead meet the same fate of nothingness. Sheol may simply be the place where the ancient ISRAELITES imagined all spirits reside together. Rabbinic interpretation later imagined that Sheol is the netherworld, a place where the souls that were cut off from God live eternally in limbo.

The Hebrew Bible itself has no direct teachings on the afterlife, or on the concepts of Heaven and Hell. However, rabbinic dogma has suggested that there is an OLAM HA-BA, a world to come. While *olam ha-ba* is often described as being like paradise in the Garden of Eden, Jewish tradition describes GEHINNOM as the location where one would go to be judged before being allowed to enter *olam ha-ba*. The truly wicked souls that did not embrace the will of God were placed in eternal limbo in Sheol. An example of a soul believed to be eternally trapped in Sheol was PHARAOH, who refused to accept the will of God and free the Israelite slaves by his own free will.

Further reading: Hayim Shoys, *The Lifetime of a Jew throughout the Ages of Jewish History* (Cincinnati, Ohio: UAHC, 1950); Rifat Sonsino and Daniel B. Syme, *What Happens After I Die?: Jewish Views of Life after Death* (New York: UAHC Press, 1990).

Sheva Brachot

The Sheva Brachot (Hebrew for "seven blessings") are recited near the end of the Jewish wedding ceremony and are the last "blessings" recited by the wedding officiate, usually a RABBI or CANTOR. During the recitation of the Sheva Brachot, a cup of wine is held by the individual reciting the blessings. Upon the conclusion of the blessings, both bride and groom drink from the cup.

The Sheva Brachot meditate upon the themes of CREATION, joy, and bride and groom. The blessings, with the exception of the last one, do not focus on love. Marriage was perceived by the rabbis as connecting with the proper "state of nature," man and woman being together like Adam and Eve. By joining together as husband and wife, the couple was continuing God's process of Creation.

The traditional custom is to recite the Sheva Brachot not only at the wedding, but at the festive meal following the wedding, as the conclusion of the BIRKAT HA-MAZON, or grace after meals. Two cups of wine are held, one for Birkat Ha-Mazon and one for the Sheva Brachot. At the conclusion of both sets of blessings, the two cups of wine are poured into one cup, which the bride and groom share.

Traditionally, the Sheva Brachot are also recited after Birkat Ha-Mazon for the first seven nights that the bride and groom are married, as long as there is present at the table at least one person who was not present at any of the previous recitations. On Shabbat, the blessings are recited even if everyone has been present before, because the Sabbath itself is considered a new person. In Orthodox (see ORTHODOX JUDAISM) circles, the bride and groom are treated to seven meals on the seven nights following the wedding, one for each of the Sheva Brachot.

The text of the Sheva Brachot liturgy is as follows: (1) Praised are You, O Lord our God, King of the Universe, Creator of the fruit of the vine. (2) Praised are You, O Lord our God, King of the Universe, Who created all things for Your glory. (3) Praised are You, O Lord our God, King of the Universe, Creator of man. (4) Praised are You, O Lord our God, King of the Universe, Who created man and woman in Your image, fashioning woman from man as his mate, that together they might perpetuate life. Praised are You, O Lord, Creator of man. (5) May Zion rejoice as her children are restored to her in joy. Praised are You, O Lord, Who causes Zion to rejoice at her children's return. (6) Grant perfect joy to these loving companions, as You did to the first man and woman in the Garden of Eden. Praised are You, O Lord, who grants the joy of bride and groom. (7) Praised are You, O Lord our God, King of the Universe, who created joy and gladness, bride and groom, mirth, song, delight and rejoicing, love and harmony, peace and companionship. O Lord our God, may there ever be heard in the cities of Judah and in the streets of Jerusalem voices of joy and gladness, voices of bride and groom, the jubilant voices of those joined in marriage under the bridal canopy, the voices of young people feasting and singing. Praised are You, O Lord, Who causes the groom to rejoice with his bride.

Further reading: Anita Diamant, *The New Jewish Wedding, Revised* (New York: Simon & Schuster, 2001); Ronald H. Isaacs, *The Bride and Groom Handbook* (West Orange, N.J.: Behrman House Publishing, 1989).

shiva (siva)

Shiva (Hebrew for "sitting") is a seven-day mourning period that follows the burial of a loved one. Although it is obligatory only for a parent, spouse, sibling, or child of the deceased, other close relatives often assume the obligation as well.

During the period of shiva the mourner is supposed to remain at home, or the designated shiva home, and refrain from all work, concerns for vanity, or sexual relations. If the family of the deceased is in desperate economic circumstances, its members are permitted to return to work after three days of MOURNING. The traditional mourner sits without shoes, either on the floor or a low stool. It is a MITZVAH for friends to visit those sitting shiva, and to bring them food so that they do not have to bother with cooking.

It is usual for friends to make visits to the mourners' home to offer prayers and condolences. During the time sitting shiva, *minyanim*, worship services with a quorum present (*see* MINYAN), are led at the shiva house. Local synagogues usually assure the presence of a minyan. At these *minyanim*, the mourner has the opportunity to recite the mourner's KADDISH.

When visiting a shiva home, you are to refrain from greeting the one in mourning, until spoken to by the mourner. This is so as not to infringe on the mourner's contemplations. The mourner is under no obligation to speak to the shiva visitor. However, if he or she does not feel up to speaking, the shiva visitor upon preparing to leave the shiva home recites the traditional words: "May you be comforted amongst the mourners of Zion." At this point, a mourner will most likely engage in a brief acknowledgement to the visitor, even if they do not feel up to it.

Most mourners do not refrain from speaking and express gratitude that a shiva visitor has come to pay respects. The logic of the laws of mourning was to ensure that the one in mourning would not perform the normal duties of being a host. Instead, they are to be encouraged to struggle with their grief, yet also realize that the world continues while they are in mourning.

On SHABBAT, the individuals are to leave their shiva homes and attend a congregational service. This is to make the one in mourning realize that the Sabbath takes precedence over one's personal loss. If shiva is interrupted by a major festival observance, then the shiva period ends with the beginning of the festival. On the seventh day of sitting shiva, one must only sit in the morning. Then the mourners leave their homes and walk around their block, so as to physically mark their return to daily life.

Further reading: Anita Diamant, *Saying Kaddish: How to Comfort the Dying, Bury the Dead, and Mourn as a Jew*

(New York: Schocken Books, 1998); Hayim Halevy Donin, *To Be a Jew: A Guide to Jewish Observance in Contemporary Life* (New York: Basic Books, 1972); Blu Greenberg, *How to Run a Traditional Jewish Household* (New York: Fireside, 1985); Maurice Lamm, *The Jewish Way in Death and Mourning* (Middle Village, N.Y.: Jonathan David Publishers, 2000).

Shoah *See* HOLOCAUST.

shofar

The shofar is traditionally a ram's horn, although it can be the horn of any kosher animal with the exception of a bull. The TORAH commands that on the first day of the seventh month, the ISRAELITES should observe a day of rest, and that this sacred occasion should be commemorated with loud blasts. The book of Numbers (*see* TORAH) further expands on this commandment, saying it shall be a day when the "horn" is sounded. Jews have customarily also blown the shofar to celebrate the monthly new moon (*see* ROSH HODESH), but the commandment only applied to the seventh month's new moon, which is the celebration of the Jewish New Year, ROSH HASHANAH.

From a biblical perspective, the blowing of the shofar on the Jewish New Year was most likely a celebratory technique utilized to embrace God with joy, as evidenced by the Psalmist (*see* TEHILLIM) who wrote that it is with trumpets and the blast of the horn that one raises a shout before the Lord. However, the common MIDRASH provides a different explanation for why the shofar is blown on Rosh HaShanah: when God instructed Abraham (*see* PATRIARCHS) to SACRIFICE his son Isaac, and then stayed his hand from doing so, a ram whose horn was caught in a nearby thicket was offered in the boy's place. The ram's horn blown on Rosh HaShanah reminds God of Abraham's willingness to obey, no matter the circumstances. Therefore, when God is judging Abraham's children, the Jews, God should remember the merit of the Patriarch's actions of faith. Tradition also

This man blows the shofar, traditionally the horn of a ram or kosher animal, before Yom Kippur. A shofar can be a simple horn, like the one shown here, or one that is long with many turns and curls. *(Fritz Cohen, Government Press Office, The State of Israel)*

states that the shofar blasts drown out Satan's accusations against the Jews.

It is a common theme of RABBIS to refer to the shofar as a spiritual alarm; a blast to awaken sinners, so that they will properly repent. The ancient rabbis outline the specific blessings that one reads prior to the blasts of the shofar and what type of sounds should be made. Two blessings are recited by the *baal tekiah*, the master blower of the shofar. A blessing is recited for the hearing of the shofar and another in celebration of the new and joyous occasion. Traditionally only one person blows the shofar, while all others listen to the blasts.

The Torah mentions two different sounds. The *tekiah* is one long blast, and the *teruah* is a shorter blast. The ancient rabbis were uncertain as to what the *teruah* sound was supposed to be, so they created two types of short blasts. They are the *shevarim*, three broken sounds resembling moaning, and the *teruah*, which is a series of nine very short blasts. The blowing of the shofar on Rosh HaShanah follows a prescribed pattern. There are three sets of blasts, each consisting of three repetitions of three notes, each set different from the other. At the conclusion of all the sets, a *tekiah gedola*, a very long note, is played out.

Traditional Jews sound the shofar every weekday morning during the month of Elul, which directly precedes Rosh HaShanah. The final shofar blast of the season comes at the very end of YOM KIPPUR, the Day of Atonement, and is a sign that the fast and spiritual work has been completed.

Further reading: Philip Goodman, *The Rosh HaShanah Anthology* (Philadelphia: Jewish Publication Society, 1992); Irving Greenberg, *The Jewish Way: Living the Holidays* (New York: Simon & Schuster, 1993); Adin Steinsaltz, *A Guide to Jewish Prayer* (New York: Schocken Books, 2002); Michael Strassfeld, *Jewish Holidays: A Guide and Commentary* (New York: HarperResource, 1993).

Sholom Aleichem (1859–1916) *Yiddish writer*

Originally named Solomon J. Rabinowitz, Sholom Aleichem (the name means "peace be with you," a popular greeting) was born in Pereyaslev, Ukraine. After serving as a rabbi for a number of years, he became a writer, at first in HEBREW and Russian, and then in YIDDISH, which was undergoing a literary revival. He worked as a playwright and is best known for dozens of satiric but sympathetic volumes of novels, stories, and plays about Russian Jewish life in the late 19th century.

Sholom Aleichem adopted his pen name to conceal his identity from his father, who would have preferred that he write in Hebrew, rather than in parochial Yiddish. Sholom Aleichem became perhaps the most popular Yiddish writer in eastern Europe and the Americas, among both critics and a mass audience. After the POGROMS of 1905, Sholom Aleichem traveled to many cities, not settling permanently in any. With the outbreak of World War I he relocated to Denmark with his family, and then settled in New York until his death in 1916.

Many of Sholom Aleichem's works were translated into English, and a number of stories were adapted for the stage. The Broadway musical and movie *FIDDLER ON THE ROOF* was based on his tragicomic stories about Tevye, a long-suffering but pious Russian Jewish dairyman. Sholom Aleichem died in New York City.

Further reading: Sholom Aleichem, *From the Fair: The Autobiography of Sholom Aleichem,* trans. Curt Leviant (New York: Viking, 1985); ———, *Tevye and the Dairyman and The Railroad Stories,* trans. Hillel Halkin (New York: Schocken Books, 1987); Adrianne Onderdonk Dudden and Louis Falstein, *The Man Who Loved Laughter: The Story of Sholom Aleichem* (New York: Jewish Publication Society of America, 1968); Maurice Samuel, *The World of Sholom Aleichem* (New York: Random House, 1943, 1981).

shtetl

Shtetl is a Yiddish word for town or small city. A shtetl was an eastern European town with a large, cohesive Jewish community whose life revolved around Judaism and Jewish culture. Every shtetl had a market, a SYNAGOGUE, other communal buildings, and homes. The shtetl comprised well-to-do and poor Jews, and often had few resident non-Jews. A shtetl could have fewer than 1,000 inhabitants or more than 20,000. By extension, the term can sometimes be used in a derogatory fashion to imply small-town or parochial attitudes.

In the Middle Ages, Jews were not allowed to own land or even, in most cases, to rent agricultural land. The shtetl developed as smaller towns invited Jews to settle and offered them protection. Jews often established their own small towns to serve the nobility with their skills; they were able to follow a protected communal life ruled by Jewish law (*see* HALAKHAH) and insular customs and rituals.

Famous Jewish writers and artists who came from shtetls include SHOLOM ALEICHEM and Marc CHAGALL. In their art, they portrayed life in the shtetl, eventually for a world audience. The well-known play *FIDDLER ON THE ROOF* molds Sholom Aleichem's stories into a dramatic portrait of life in the shtetl. According to the play, being humane and being Jewish were the factors that guided life.

Usually there was a certain amount of economic and social stratification in the shetl, though the majority of residents were always poor. The community was strong and there was not much privacy. The values of the community dictated how life would be led in the shtetl.

The synagogue was the place where Jews gathered together to pursue learning, prayer, or social activities. In the marketplace, the Jews acted as middlemen, used by the nobility and scorned by peasants. The market was a bridge between Jews from the shtetl and non-Jews from the outside. It was also the scene of conflicts between individual Jews.

During the 19th century persecution and violence (*see* ANTISEMITISM) aimed at the shtetls forced many residents from their homes. Many Jews moved to large cities where they lived in specific Jewish areas instead of in their own town, or emigrated to the West. In the 20th century, the brutal effects of Soviet communism destroyed shtetl culture in Russia, while the Nazi HOLOCAUST wiped out the entire Jewish population of the remaining shtetls in the rest of eastern Europe. Non-Jews took over whatever Jewish homes had not been destroyed.

Further reading: Sholom Aleichem, *Tevye and the Dairyman and The Railroad Stories* (New York: Schocken Books, 1987); Yaffa Eliach, *There Once Was a World: A Nine-Hundred Year Chronicle of the Shtetl of Eishyshok* (Boston: Little, Brown, 1998); Elizabeth Herzog, Margaret Mead, and Mark Zborowski, *Life Is with People: The Culture of the Shtetl* (New York: Schocken Books, 1962).

shuckling

Shuckling is the distinctive Ashkenazic (*see* ASHKENAZIM) Jewish custom of rhythmic swaying, usually up and down, sometimes side to side, while davening (reciting prayers). The practice sometimes appears during Talmud study as well.

Tradition suggests numerous reasons for this practice. One is that swaying aids concentration. The BAAL SHEM TOV wrote that the act of swaying in prayer is like the individual attempting to extricate himself from raging waters. The ones swaying are attempting to rid themselves of the impurities clinging to them, so as to throw out all the extraneous thoughts distracting them from their concentration on his prayers. It can be viewed as a Jewish meditation technique.

The great biblical commentator RASHI is cited to support the custom of swaying, as inspired by the notion that every worshipper should shudder when facing the might of the Lord. Others have suggested that the custom of swaying to and fro arose in the days before printing presses, when there were not enough prayer books. Shuckling developed as a means to periodically look into one's neighbor's prayer book.

Some modern rabbis speculate that the swaying motion helps create a high akin to the high a jogger feels after a strong workout. Others have posited it as a device to keep people fully awake during prayer.

Further reading: B. S. Jacobson, *Meditation on Siddur* (Tel Aviv: Sinai, 1966); Aryeh Kaplan, *Call to the Infinite* (Brooklyn, N.Y.: Moznaim Publishing, 1986).

Shulchan Arukh

The *Shulchan Arukh* is the 16th-century legal code written by Joseph CARO (1488–1575), which has since become the most authoritative of all Jewish CODES OF LAW. Before it was written, the body of Jewish law, HALAKHAH, was embedded within the complex, often cryptic debates of the TALMUD, and was accessible only to very learned Jews, mostly RABBIS. There was a need for a reference volume that ordinary people could use to look up by topic any law in question. The *Shulchan Arukh* was Caro's answer to this need.

The *Shulchan Arukh* consists of brief paragraphs that state a particular *halakhah*, or Jewish law, an explanation, and an example of its use. Caro wrote the *Shulchan Arukh* as a compressed commentary on his longer work, *Beth Joseph*, finishing it in 1554 while living in SAFED.

The phrase *shulchan arukh* means "prepared table" or "arranged table." In writing this code, Caro followed the practices and customs of Spanish Jews, or SEPHARDIM. Moses ISSERLES (1525–72), feeling that the text was slanted toward Sephardic opinions, prepared a supplement to it called MAPAH ("tablecloth") to make it more acceptable to ASHKENAZIM. Thus, the Jewish community now finds itself with the set table, along with the tablecloth, accessible and ready to use. Both Caro's *Shulchan*

Arukh and Isserles's *Mapah* are most often found bound together in one volume. It has become the standard legal code for ORTHODOX JUDAISM.

Further reading: Boaz Cohen, "The Shulhan Aruk as a Guide to Religious Practice Today," in *Law and Tradition in Judaism* (New York: Klav Publishing House, 1959), 62–99; Isadore Twersky, "The Shulhan 'Aruk: Enduring Code of Jewish Law" in *Studies in Jewish Law and Philosophy* (New York: Klav Publishing House, 1982), 130–47.

Shylock

The character Shylock appears in William Shakespeare's play *The Merchant of Venice*. Shylock is a Jewish moneylender who insists that Antonio, a non-Jew, pay for an overdue loan with a pound of flesh. While the payment is never exacted in the play, the ugly image of this character has been used to defame Jews for centuries since.

The caricature of the cruel moneylender persists even to this day. It is important to note that Shakespeare had probably never met a Jew, since they had been expelled from ENGLAND in 1290, and that there is no historical record of any Jewish moneylender ever requesting flesh in response to an overdue loan. However, the court decision to absolve a non-Jew from paying back a loan to a Jewish lender, and the decision to punish the creditor instead, have all too many precedents in medieval Europe.

Further reading: Bernard Glassman, *Antisemitic Stereotypes Without Jews: Images of the Jews in England, 1290–1700;* (Detroit: Wayne State University Press, 1975); William Shakespeare, *The Merchant of Venice: Texts and Contexts*, ed. M. Lindsay Kaplan (Boston: St. Martin's, 2002).

siddur (pl.: siddurim)

The siddur (from the Hebrew root *SDR*, meaning "order") is the Jewish PRAYER book. It presents all the prayers to be recited at the various daily and Sabbath (*see* SHABBAT) worship services, in their proper order according to the tradition of the community that printed it.

Prior to the period of the GEONIM, prayers were either known by heart, or recorded in rare scrolls, accessible to very few individuals. In the ninth century the first siddur, or prayer book, emerged, compiled by SAADIA GAON. The text was soon expanded by the *gaon* rabbi Amram. In that early medieval period, the prayer book was still a fluid work that encouraged individual expression during prayer. Over the centuries it continued to evolve, but the creation of the printing press brought in mass production, which rather quickly locked in particular manuscripts as the standards for specific Jewish communities. In addition to the weekday and Shabbat siddurim, special prayer books were created for ROSH HASHANAH and YOM KIPPUR. Such a prayer book is called a MACHZOR (Hebrew for "cycle").

The siddur consists of collections of passages from various books of TANAKH, the Hebrew Bible, other material drawn from the TALMUD, and special prayers and hymns composed by individual writers and poets over the centuries. The formal structure and the wording for certain blessings are specified in the Talmud.

Historically, rabbis have created their own versions of siddurim, building upon works that preceded them. The siddur grew longer, as new prayers were added, and a few old ones removed. The first person to attempt to modernize the siddur and the Machzor was Wolf Heidenheim (1757–1832), who removed almost all vestiges of Lurianic (*see* LURIA, ISAAC) MYSTICISM. The first significant changes appeared in 1818 when a synagogue called the Neue Israelitische Templeverein in Hamburg decided to modernize the liturgical service and publish a prayer book that included only the liturgy for Sabbath and festivals. The congregation recited many of the fixed prayers in German. Reference to the restoration of the TEMPLE and SACRIFICE were replaced by a petition to accept prayer instead of sacrifice, and texts that looked toward the MESSIANIC AGE were altered. These

changes reflected some of the themes of EMANCIPA-
TION, as Jews believed that it might be harder to
win citizenship in their countries of residence if
they wanted to become a Jewish nation once
again.

In 1854, reformer and historian Abraham
GEIGER (1810–74) published a Reform prayer
book that retained the Hebrew language but short-
ened the prayers and omitted liturgical poems. His
German "translations" were really renderings of
the spirit of the prayers into well-crafted German.
Geiger removed negative references to non-Jews,
eliminated prayers for the restoration of sacrifice
and the Jewish state, and softened the idea of the
CHOSEN PEOPLE.

In the UNITED STATES, Isaac Mayer WISE
(1819–1900), father of American REFORM JUDAISM,
published *Minhag America: The American Rite* in
1857. Wise's goal was to unify American Judaism
rather than introduce radical reform; though his
new prayer book dropped the second day of Rosh
HaShanah and eliminated some outdated language, it preserved the majority of HEBREW
prayers and followed the lead of classic reformers
such as Abraham Geiger. Wise's *Minhag America*
was considered by other reformers to be too traditional, and David EINHORN (1809–79) produced
a more radical version of his own in 1858 called
*The Daily Offering: Prayer Book for Israelite
Reform Congregations.* In 1896, the Reform movement produced its siddur, which was based on
Einhorn's work rather than Wise's. The book was
called *The Union Prayer Book for Jewish Worship,*
and it remained in use by hundreds of Reform
synagogues until its revision, *The Gates of Prayer,*
appeared in 1975.

Conservative Judaism also produces its own
siddurim; the latest is called Sim Shalom,
although other prayer books are used in many
Conservative synagogues, such as Siddur
Hadash. Unlike Reform prayer books, the Conservative siddur retains the *musaf* (additional)
service on the Sabbath, which recalls the sacrifices in the TEMPLE. The Conservative prayer
book retains mention of the sacrifice and the

Temple, but does so in the past tense, unlike the
traditional siddur, which calls for their restoration. Many American Jews who adhere to
ORTHODOX JUDAISM long used a siddur edited by
Philip Birnbaum and published in 1949, called
Daily Prayer Book: Ha-Siddur Ha-Shalem; it has
recently been replaced in many congregations in
the English-speaking world by a siddur published by the Artscroll company. Artscroll siddurim are often used by learning synagogues
because of their extensive notes and explanations; earlier Orthodox siddurim assumed that
worshippers were familiar with synagogue ritual
and omitted instructions.

A huge variety of siddurim have been published in the past 200 years, in many different languages. The significance of the Reform prayer
book remains central because of the radical
changes it brought to the siddur and the prayer
service itself. Overall, the main characteristics of
Reform prayer include the abridgment of traditional prayers, the use of the local vernacular language, elimination of images of angels, reduction
of particularism or chosenness, and the reduction
or elimination of the traditional Jewish desire to
return to the sacrificial rite and hope for the Messianic Age; there is also a greater amount of variety and choice, so that the service may vary from
week to week. Other Jewish movements such as
Conservative Judaism, the JEWISH RENEWAL movement, and RECONSTRUCTIONIST JUDAISM have either
copied these changes or maintained more traditional elements of the siddur.

Further reading: Ismar Elbogen, *Jewish Liturgy: A Comprehensive History* (Philadelphia: Jewish Publication
Society of America, 1993); Jules Harlow, *Siddur Sim
Shalom* (New York: Rabbinical Assembly and the United
Synagogue of America, 1989); Jakob Petuchowski,
Prayerbook Reform in Europe (New York: World Union
for Progressive Judaism, 1968); N. Scherman, *The Complete Artscroll Siddur* (Brooklyn, N.Y.: Mesorah Publications, 1989); Chaim Stern, *Gates of Prayer: The New
Union of Prayer* (Cincinnati, Ohio: Central Conference
of American Rabbis, 1975).

Siegel, Danny (b. 1944) *American writer and lecturer*

Danny Siegel is a noted American Jewish author, lecturer, and poet. He grew up in Virginia, but earned a bachelor of science degree in comparative literature from Columbia University's School of General Studies, and bachelor's and master's degrees of Hebrew literature from the JEWISH THEOLOGICAL SEMINARY OF AMERICA. Siegel has spoken in more than 500 North American Jewish communities. His topics are primarily TZEDAKAH, loosely translated as charity, GEMILUT CHASADIM, acts of loving kindness, and Jewish values, although he is often asked to share selections from his poetry. He has published 29 books on these subjects, as well as educational materials to teach children the value of *tzedakah*. In 1993, Siegel won the Covenant award as an exceptional Jewish educator. He is also well known for his own charitable work, in particular the Ziv Tzedakah Fund.

Siegel helped to popularize the concept of "microphilanthropy." This is the notion that small acts of giving and small-scale charitable organizations can have a huge impact on the betterment of society. In 1981, Siegel began the Ziv Tzedakah Fund. His organization is dedicated to the collection and distribution of funds for supporting little-known *tzedakah* projects and for teaching the values of *tzedakah* to communities throughout CANADA, ISRAEL, and the UNITED STATES. The organization has raised and distributed more than $6.7 million and operates with an overhead of less than 9 percent, remarkably low for an American charity.

Further reading: Danny Siegel, *Gym Shoes and Irises: Personalized Tzedakah* (Spring Valley, N.Y.: Town House Press, 1982); Danny Siegel and Naomi Eisenberger, *Mitzvah Magic: What Kids Can Do to Change the World* (Minneapolis: Kar-Ben Publishers, 2002); Danny Siegel, *Tell Me A Mitzvah: Little and Big Ways to Repair the World* (Rockville, Md.: Kar-Ben Copies, 1993); ———, *Where Heaven and Earth Touch: An Anthology of Midrash and Halachah* (Northvale, N.J.: J. Aronson, 1989).

Simchat Bat

Simchat Bat (Hebrew "joy of a daughter") is a contemporary LIFE CYCLE event that celebrates the birth and the HEBREW naming of a Jewish baby girl. The new ritual emerged within liberal Judaism beginning in the 1970s. There was a desire to create a home ritual that would have equal solemnity with the BRIT MILAH, the covenantal (*see* COVENANT) circumcision and naming ceremony for a boy.

While Simchat Bat ceremonies are a modern liberal practice, traditional Judaism has its own long-standing customs on welcoming daughters into the covenant with God and giving them Hebrew names. The TANAKH, the Hebrew Bible, explains names for both men and women. When the TEMPLE still stood in JERUSALEM, thanksgiving sacrifices were required after the birth of a child of either gender. The TALMUD reports that in ancient ISRAEL it was customary to plant a cypress tree when a girl was born. Over the centuries, new customs emerged among both ASHKENAZIM and SEPHARDIM, to celebrate the birth of a daughter.

A common traditional custom is for the father to go to the SYNAGOGUE at the first opportunity after the birth, and receive an ALIYAH when the Torah was read. After reciting the Torah blessing, a MI SHEBERACH prayer for healing is said for his wife, and the daughter's Hebrew name is announced. The custom is commonly observed in both Orthodox (*see* ORTHODOX JUDAISM) and liberal Jewish synagogues. In egalitarian (*see* EGALITARIANISM) synagogues, both the father and mother receive the aliyah.

The first known published ritual for a Simchat Bat was created by the Reform movement (*see* REFORM JUDAISM) in 1973. Since then, many different versions have been created, with a variety of blessings, readings, and terminology. Two other common names for these ceremonies are Brit Bat, a daughter's covenant, or simply a baby-naming ceremony. Since the mid-1980s, all liberal Jewish movements have published their own suggested Simchat Bat ceremonies in their rabbinic manuals, but it is not uncommon for a couple to build their own ceremony.

Further reading: Debra Nussbaum Cohen and Sandy Eisenberg Sasso, *Celebrating Your New Jewish Daughter* (Woodstock, Vt.: Jewish Lights Publishing, 2001); Douglas Weber and Jessica Brodsky Weber, *The Jewish Baby Handbook: A Guide for Expectant Parents* (West Orange, N.J.: Behrman House Publishing, 1990).

Simchat Torah

Simchat Torah (Hebrew for "joy in the TORAH") is a one-day festival that occurs at the end of SUKKOT. In ISRAEL, SHEMINI ATZERET and Simchat Torah occur on the same day, the eighth day of Sukkot, while in the DIASPORA Shemini Atzeret takes place on the eighth day of Sukkot, and Simchat Torah takes place the following day.

During the year, a different portion of the Torah is read in the SYNAGOGUE each SHABBAT, or Sabbath, so that a congregation reads through the whole scroll once per year. On Simchat Torah the congregation reaches the end of the scroll, ceremoniously rolls the scroll back, and begins anew. The congregation bestows a special honor on two members: one is the *hattan Torah*, literally "groom of the Torah," who receives the ALIYAH for the last portion of the scroll. The other is the *hattan bereshit*, literally "groom of the beginning," who receives the aliyah for reading the first passage in the Torah.

Simchat Torah is an extremely joyous holiday. Congregations take the Torah out into the streets, dance with it, and kiss it. Children parade around as candy is thrown to them. A custom in some congregations in contemporary America is to unroll the entire Torah scroll, having the congregation hold it gingerly so that all can see the beauty that is Torah.

Further reading: Philip Goodman, *The Sukkot/Simhat Torah Anthology* (Philadelphia: Jewish Publication Society, 1988); Irving Greenberg, *The Jewish Way: Living the*

Holidays (New York: Touchstone, 1988); Ronald H. Isaacs, *Every Person's Guide to Sukkot, Shemini Atzeret, and Simchat Torah* (Northvale, N.J.: Aronson, 2000).

sin and repentance

In Jewish theology, there is no forgiveness for sin without repentance. The term for sin (*averah*) connotes transgression of God's law. The term for repentance (*teshuvah*) means "turn," thus turning away from sin back to God.

According to the ancient RABBIS, human beings experience temptation but are free to choose good or evil. Whenever an individual genuinely repents from evil, forgiveness is assured. One can repent and ask for forgiveness at any time, but each year a season is set aside where those acts are specially emphasized. During the days from ROSH HASHANAH to YOM KIPPUR, also called the Ten Days of Penitence or Days of Awe, individuals are particularly encouraged to confess their sins and ask for forgiveness. Tradition holds that repentance during this period may win a reprieve for any punishment that God had decreed for the sins in the new year.

Further reading: Abraham Cohen, *Everyman's Talmud: The Major Teachings of the Rabbinic Sages* (New York: Schocken Books, 1995), 95–110; Louis Jacobs, *Jewish Theology* (London: Darton, Longman and Todd, 1973).

Singer, Isaac Bashevis (1904–1991) *Nobel Prize–winning Yiddish writer*

Isaac Bashevis Singer was born in 1904 in Leoncin, POLAND. Singer's brother was a noted novelist named I. Singer, and so when Singer himself began to write he took on the name Bashevis (based on his mother's name, Bathsheva) to distinguish himself from his brother. Isaac was a novelist, critic, and journalist, writing primarily in YIDDISH, and collaborating in his English translations. Singer's writings are a bridge to a world lost when 6 million Jews were murdered during the HOLOCAUST of World War II.

In his formative years, Singer grew up in Warsaw, Poland. His father was a RABBI who held a Jewish court of law called a BET DIN in his home. Singer studied in a YESHIVA, a traditional Jewish school. Uniquely, Singer's yeshiva in Bilgoraj, Poland, also taught Modern Hebrew and secular topics. While working for a Yiddish-language newspaper in Warsaw, Singer began to write fiction.

After immigrating to the United States in 1935, Singer worked for the JEWISH DAILY FORWARD, a prominent Jewish newspaper; it began to publish his fiction in a serialized format. Many of Singer's Yiddish stories were translated into English and appeared in COMMENTARY, the New Yorker, and other magazines. His unique point of view combines respect for religious and cultural tradition with a sophisticated knowledge of human psychology and Jewish social realities.

Singer's fictional works fall into three groups: realistic novels and stories that stress character, short romances, and short stories with often magical and mystical themes. From 1953 to 1955, he published The Manor in the Forward. The story is a family chronicle of late 19th-century Polish Jewish life. He later wrote The Estate. Singer is known for short story collections such as "Gimpel the Fool and Other Stories," "Spinoza of Market Street," and "Short Friday."

Singer is considered to be the most significant writer of Yiddish imaginative prose. His writings were rooted in Jewish tradition; however, he used the technique of comparing and contrasting to create an imaginative and entertaining body of literature that highlights the differences between one's present life and the past. Often his tales mesh tragedy and comedy to highlight human angst. Singer was awarded the Nobel Prize in literature in 1978, the first ever awarded for Yiddish literature. He received an honorary doctorate from the Hebrew University in Jerusalem in 1975. Singer, one of the most prolific writers of Yiddish literature, passed away in 1991.

Further reading: Marcia Allentuck, ed., *The Achievement of Isaac Bashevis Singer* (Carbondale: Southern Illinois University Press, 1969); Grace Lee Farrell, *From Exile to Redemption: The Fiction of Isaac Bashevis Singer* (Carbondale: Southern Illinois University Press, 1987); Isaac Bashevis Singer, *The Collected Stories of Isaac Bashevis Singer* (New York: Farrar, Straus, and Giroux, 1983); ———, *Shadows on the Hudson* (New York: Plume, 1999).

Six-Day War

In 1967, the State of ISRAEL won its most significant military victory in the aptly named Six-Day War.

Since the creation of the Jewish state in 1948, the Arab nations surrounding it had refused to recognize its right to exist. Especially vocal was President Nasser of EGYPT. He clearly articulated to his fellow Arab rulers, and in speeches to masses of Egyptians, that the only solution to the problems with the State of Israel was her complete annihilation.

Egypt threatened Israel from the south, while the Syrians in the north used the Golan Heights to routinely shell Israeli communities. In the two years prior to 1967, Syria's attacks became more frequent, and Nasser's threats more ominous. In addition, those years saw a dramatic increase in terrorist attacks across Israel's borders.

On April 7, 1967, Israel struck back in retaliation against the Syrians, shooting down six Syrian fighters. Beginning on Israel's Independence Day, May 15, 1967, Egypt, in close coordination with Syria, began to move troops into position to attack Israel. Egypt advised the UNITED NATIONS to pull out its peacekeeping forces that were in the Sinai Desert. On May 18, 1967, Egypt announced that with the United Nations withdrawal from the Sinai, it was going to solve the problem of Israel's existence once and for all. Syria echoed the direct threat to Israel.

On May 22, Egyptian forces sent into Sinai blockaded all Israeli shipping headed for Eilat. The blockade cut off Israeli supply routes to Asia, and the majority of its oil supply imported from Iran. The Egyptian blockade was declared illegal by the UNITED STATES, but American leadership was unable to reverse it.

Nasser communicated Egypt's willingness to fight the final war with Israel, and on May 30, arranged for King Hussein of Jordan to join his nation and Syria in a defense pact against Israel. In addition Lebanon joined in the direct threat to Israel, making all border nations of the Jewish state part of the impending military action. Other Arab nations joined in the rhetoric against Israel, stating their willingness to join in the battle against the Jewish state. On June 4, Iraq formerly joined the Egyptian, Jordanian, Lebanese, and Syrian military alliance.

Arab military forces gathered more than a quarter of a million soldiers, supported by more than 2,000 tanks and 700 aircraft. Israel, which had stood on full military alert for three weeks, a crushing economic burden, believed it had no choice but to launch a preemptive attack. Waiting to be attacked would have severely limited Israel's military response options, as the Jewish state itself had a limited geographic area. Many Israelis point to the experience of the YOM KIPPUR WAR six years later, when Israel suffered massive casualties after it decided not to preempt an apparent Arab attack, as proving the wisdom of the preemptive attack in 1967.

On June 5, Israeli planes attacked Egypt, where half of the threatening Egyptian military forces had been amassed. The United States declared a state of neutrality, and both the United States and FRANCE ordered a weapons embargo against Israel. However, the Soviet Union (see RUSSIA) fully armed the Arab nations, and Algeria, Iraq, Kuwait, and Saudi Arabia sent reinforcements to Egypt, Jordan, and Syria.

Israel pleaded with Jordan not to enter the hostilities, and refrained at first from hostilities on Jordanian land. However, King Hussein ordered the shelling of West JERUSALEM on June 5. The Jordanian involvement caused more than 325,000 Palestinian Arabs to flee the West Bank (see JUDEA AND SAMARIA), going across the Jordan River, where they believed greater safety existed. While most Palestinians fled of their own accord, some Palestinians were told by fellow Arabs that they needed to be temporarily resettled.

In just six days of battle, the ISRAEL DEFENSE FORCES managed to break through all the Arab enemy lines. They were within easy reach of Amman, Cairo, and Damascus. The United States led negotiations for a cease-fire, which came on June 10. Syria had lost the Golan Heights, Jordan lost all of the West Bank, including East Jerusalem, and Egypt had lost Sinai and the Gaza Strip. Israel, a country of 8,000 square miles, now controlled an area exceeding 26,000 square miles. Israel's unification of Jerusalem, and capture of the Old City and the KOTEL was wildly celebrated; the day became a national holiday called YOM YERUSHALAYIM (Jerusalem Day). In addition, the danger to the Israeli people during the Six-Day War catalyzed activity around the Jewish world, in the form of empathy and donations, to save the state of Israel from destruction.

With the occupation of these new territories, Israel also was placed in the position of directly ruling over more than 750,000 Arab Palestinians. The lands conquered by Israel raised the possibility of land-for-peace treaties. Egypt reached its agreement in 1979, with the CAMP DAVID ACCORDS, and Jordan also has signed a peace treaty. However, there is still no treaty in place with Syria, with Syrian-controlled Lebanon, or with the Palestinian people. Though large parts of the West Bank and the Gaza Strip were formally transferred to Palestinian control in the 1990s, Israel still retains ultimate military control there.

Further reading: Eric Hammel, *Six Days in June: How Israel Won the 1967 Arab-Israeli War* (New York: Scribner's, 1992); Chaim Herzog, *The Arab-Israeli Wars* (New York: Vintage Press, 1983); Michael Oren, *Six Days of War* (New York: Oxford University Press, 2002); Howard M. Sachar, *A History of Israel: From the Rise of Zionism to Our Time* (New York: Alfred A. Knopf, 1996).

614th Commandment

Emil L. FACKENHEIM, a HOLOCAUST theologian, coined the idea of a new commandment mandating that Jews survive so that Adolf HITLER's wish to exterminate all Jews can never come true. Traditional Judaism identifies 613 commandments from God in the TORAH that Jews are supposed to follow. Fackenheim called his new law the 614th Commandment.

The 614th Commandment states that "the authentic Jew of today is forbidden to hand Hitler yet another, posthumous victory." In other words, Fackenheim derives the 614th Commandment from what he calls the "Commanding Voice of AUSCHWITZ." He postulates that there were those in the concentration camps who heard the "Commanding Voice of God" even if none heard a redeeming voice. The voice that some heard commanded the Jews to survive or to strive to die as human beings rather than as the living dead that the Nazis sought to create. That voice continues to be heard among modern Jews today.

Fackenheim suggests that the existence of Jews today shows that many are living as though they have heard this commanding voice of God. He claims that individuals can choose to remain Jews only with the faith that a second Holocaust will not happen; only through faith in the commanding voice at Auschwitz can Jews today know that their trust in Judaism is not unfounded, that their children and grandchildren can hope for a future. Finally, Fackenheim sees the Holocaust and the idea of the 614th Commandment as appealing to both observant and nonobservant Jews, bridging the gap between religious and secular world Jewry.

Further reading: Elliot N. Dorff and Louis E. Newman, eds., *Contemporary Jewish Theology: A Reader* (New York: Oxford University Press, 1999); Emil L. Fackenheim, *The Jewish Return into History: Reflections in the Age of Auschwitz and a New Jerusalem* (New York: Schocken Books, 1978).

slavery

Slavery is an important concept in Judaism, thanks to the period of ISRAELITE slavery in EGYPT. The liberation from slavery remains a key historic moment in Jewish memory and is crucial for understanding JEWISH IDENTITY. Each year Jews reenact their journey from slavery to freedom in the PASSOVER SEDER; through various symbols the seder attempts to create the feelings of slavery and redemption. It is also a MITZVAH, or commandment, to remind oneself of slavery in EGYPT each day. For this reason, Jews today believe their history and scriptures force them to fight for the oppressed and avoid oppressing others.

It is ironic, therefore, that the TORAH permits slavery, although it provides ample opportunities for redemption and prohibits permanent slavery for Jews. In other words, the Torah states that Jews can have non-Jewish slaves but not Jewish slaves. Many attribute this to the fact that slavery was an accepted reality at the time. And for its time, the laws in the books of Exodus, Leviticus, and Deuteronomy regarding slaves were more lenient than in neighboring societies; for example, the Sabbath (*see* SHABBAT) laws stipulate that one must provide a day of rest for one's slaves.

The permission to own slaves led not only to Jewish slaveholders, but also Jewish slave traders throughout the Middle Ages and into the early modern period—though they never controlled more than a small fraction of the business. In America, Jews were active in the abolitionist movement, but at the same time, there were Jewish slaveholders in the South, as well as Jews who held prominent positions in the Confederate government.

In modern times, Jews prefer to focus on their own history of being slaves, rather than on biblical law allowing slavery or on Jewish slave owners and slave traders. For example, there have been initiatives such as the Passover Project in 2002, a joint effort by the Religious Action Committee of REFORM JUDAISM and the American Anti-Slavery Group to bring attention to and ultimately abolish slavery in Sudan.

Further reading: Maurianne Adams and John Bracey, eds., *Strangers & Neighbors: Relations between Blacks & Jews in the United States* (Amherst: University of Massachusetts Press, 1999); Gregory Chirichigno, *Debt Slav-*

ery in Israel and the Ancient Near East (Sheffield: JSOT Press, 1993); Eli Faber, *Jews, Slaves, and the Slave Trade: Setting the Record Straight* (New York: New York University Press, 1998); David Goldenberg, *The Curse of Ham: Race and Slavery in Early Judaism, Christianity, and Islam* (Princeton, N.J.: Princeton University Press, 2003); Anthony Phillips, *Essays on Biblical Law* (New York: Sheffield Academic Press, 2002); *Tanakh: The Holy Scriptures* (Philadelphia and Jerusalem: Jewish Publication Society, 1985).

Sodom and Gomorrah

According to the book of Genesis (*see* TORAH), the people of the two Dead Sea cities of Sodom and Gomorrah were so wicked, that an outcry rose up from them to God.

God sends two angels (*see* MALAKHIM) disguised as visitors to see whether the sins of Sodom and Gomorrah are as great as reported. Abraham (*see* PATRIARCHS) is informed of the plan to destroy the towns. He pleads with God for MERCY to overcome JUSTICE; he asks God to save the cities if 50 righteous people can be found there, and God agrees. Abraham reduces the number to 45, 40, 30, 20, and finally 10. God agrees.

When the angels reach Sodom, Abraham's nephew Lot offers them shelter and shows them hospitality, but the townspeople gather around and insist that Lot turn over the strangers so that they can sexually assault them. It is from this passage that the word *sodomy* derives. Lot protects the visitors, who then reveal themselves as angels who have now decided to destroy the town (as they have seen no righteous people there). They advise Lot to take his family and leave quickly; Lot's sons-in-law refuse, but Lot, his wife, and two daughters escape. God rains sulfurous fire upon Sodom and Gomorrah, annihilating the cities and destroying all life there, including vegetation. Disobeying orders not to look back, Lot's wife is turned into a pillar of salt.

The ancient RABBIS enumerated Sodom and Gomorrah's sins. For example, they report that the town authorities actually punished people if they performed good deeds. The story thus demonstrates God's aspect of justice, though the willingness to spare the whole town because of 10 innocent people also shows the aspect of mercy.

The debate about the meaning of the story of Sodom and Gomorrah continues today. Some point to this narrative as an argument against HOMOSEXUALITY, especially since the townspeople reject Lot's offer of his daughter in place of the male visitors. Others argue that the key sins are general viciousness, violence, and a lack of hospitality, rather than homosexual acts per se.

Further reading: Steven Greenberg, *Wrestling with God and Men* (Madison: University of Wisconsin Press, 2004); Jacob Neusner, *Genesis Rabbah: the Judaic Commentary to the Book of Genesis: a New American Translation* (Atlanta, Ga.: Scholars Press, 1985); *Tanakh: The Holy Scriptures* (Philadelphia and Jerusalem: Jewish Publication Society, 1985); Donald Wold, *Out of Order: Homosexuality in the Bible and the Ancient Near East* (Grand Rapids, Mich.: Baker Books, 1998).

sofer (pl.: sofrim)

A *sofer* is a religious scribe. Over the centuries the word has had a variety of connotations. The original term applied to the *sofrim*, or scribes who meticulously copied sacred scrolls to provide copies for Jewish communities. The term also came to be a title for a recognized scholar. In the ancient monarchy of Judea the scribe held the highest political office after the king himself. In the book of EZRA, Ezra is described as the scribe for the law of the God of heaven. In the book of Ecclesiastes, a scribe is one who is literate and occupied with studying the law.

In the MISHNAH, the first compilation of Jewish law, or *HALAKHAH,* the phrase "words of the scribe" signified post-biblical legislation. In rabbinic sources, the scribe came to be recognized as someone who had mastered the craft of copying the words of TORAH, the Five Books of MOSES, and preserving sacred texts. The TALMUD, the commentary on the Mishnah, contains a tractate dedicated to the subject of *sofrim,* and it details how sacred documents are to be copied.

Scribes today write the sacred scrolls by hand with special kosher materials. *Sofrim* also write out the miniature scrolls needed for a MEZUZAH, which is put on the doorpost of a Jewish home, and for TEFILLIN, leather boxes wrapped around a person's arm and head during prayer. According to Jewish law the *sofer* must be a fully observant Jew. He must also be able to write so that even the youngest child is able to read the letters.

The *sofer* writes on parchment made from the skins of a kosher animal (see KASHRUT), and utilizes special natural ink and quills. If one letter is detected to be imperfect, the scroll becomes *pasul,* ritually unfit, and must be corrected before it can be used. If a correction is not possible due to major damage, the scroll must be buried. Any Torah read in a synagogue must be handwritten, but scribes often write scrolls of the Megillot (see MEGILLAH) and other sacred works as artistic products for collectors or especially pious individuals; some synagogues use scrolls written by *sofrim* for the public readings of NEVI'IM, or Prophets.

A *sofer* who is writing a Torah usually needs approximately a year to complete the task. The price for one Torah is approximately $25,000. In the Orthodox (see ORTHODOX JUDAISM) world only men can be *sofrim.* Liberal Judaism permits women to serve as *sofrim* as well.

Further reading: Solomon Poll, *The Hasidic Community of Williamsburg* (New York: Free Press of Glencoe, 1962); Eric Ray, *Sofer* (Los Angeles: Torah Aura Productions, 1998).

Sofer, Moses (Hatam Sofer) (1762–1839)
influential rabbi and legal scholar

Moses Sofer, born in Frankfurt, GERMANY, in 1762, was a RABBI, communal leader, and authority in Jewish law (HALAKHAH). He was known for his advocacy of a strict interpretation of Jewish law; he is credited with laying the groundwork for the Orthodox fight against changing tradition (see ORTHODOX JUDAISM).

Sofer made a dramatic statement when he declared "anything new is forbidden from the Torah." He followed his teacher Nathan Adler when Adler left Frankfurt. He served as rabbi of Dresnitz and Mattersdorf, and in 1806 was appointed rabbi of Pressburg, Moravia, where he became the unquestioned leader of the Orthodox Jewish community of HUNGARY.

During Sofer's life, the ideas of the ENLIGHTENMENT (the equality of individuals) and EMANCIPATION (the granting of full citizenship to the Jews) spread through the western European Jewish community. Gradually, Jews were granted more rights than they had experienced during the Middle Ages; and many of them chose to leave their communities and mingle with non-Jews. Many reforms in Jewish tradition followed, as the Jews who went out into general society no longer felt that the Judaism of their fathers worked in the modern world (see MODERNITY).

Sofer believed that there was an inner perfection in the way of life that his ancestors lived. He believed so strongly in the traditional lifestyle that he encouraged a complete separation from modernity, allowing the minimum contact necessary for work or survival. To him and his followers, modernity itself was anti-Jewish. To spread his point of view, he founded the largest YESHIVA (Jewish religious school) in Europe, and wrote books on Jewish law, commentaries, letters, poems, and a diary. Sofer lent his support to the Jewish settlement of PALESTINE in the 19th century, reinforcing his deep religious belief in the 2,000-year-old Jewish desire to return to ERETZ YISRAEL.

After Sofer's death in 1839 his family began to publish his work, which had a tremendous impact on Orthodoxy. Among these was a voluminous collection of RESPONSA (answers to Jewish legal questions), called Chidushai Teshuvot Moshe Sofer. This work is known by an acronym *Hatam Sofer;* Sofer himself became known by the name of the work, and is referred to as the Hatam Sofer.

Sofer's children became leaders in many of the largest and most prominent Jewish communities of Europe. His son Abraham Samuel Benjamin Wolf succeeded him as head of the yeshiva before his death. Simeon, his second son, became rabbi of Krakow, POLAND. Sofer's son-in-law became a prominent Orthodox rabbi in Vienna, AUSTRIA.

Further reading: Solomon B. Freehof, *A Treasury of Responsa* (Philadelphia: Jewish Publication Society, 1963); Yaakov Dovld Shulman, *The Chasam Sofer: The Story of Rabbi Moshe Sofer* (New York: CIS Publishers, 1992); Yosef Stern, ed., *Hatam Sofer = Chasam Sofer: Commentary on the Torah* (Brooklyn, N.Y.: Mesorah Publications, 1996).

Solomon (r. c. 965–925 B.C.E.) *last king of the united Israelite monarchy*

Solomon was the son of King DAVID and Bathsheba. He succeeded David as king of ISRAEL, ruling from approximately 965 to 925 B.C.E. Because of David's sins, the privilege of building the TEMPLE in JERUSALEM fell instead to Solomon.

In Jewish tradition, Solomon is best known for his wisdom. In the book of Kings, God gives him a choice of wisdom, fortune or fame; he chooses wisdom. Pleased by Solomon's choice, God grants him all three. The book further illustrates his wisdom in the famous story of two women who each claim to be the mother of a baby. Solomon orders the child to be split in two—the true mother is the one who willingly gives up the child rather than see it hurt.

Rabbinic literature abounds in legends of Solomon's wisdom; on the other hand, the RABBIS concluded that his wisdom made him feel invulnerable, which was his downfall in the end. The early years of Solomon's reign constituted a golden age for Israel. While he did not expand the kingdom beyond David's borders, he solidified the state politically and ushered in a period of prosperity. Then, like Saul and David before him, he fell out of favor with God because of a particular sin—in his case, idolatry. According to the book of Kings,

Solomon married hundreds of foreign women, largely for diplomatic reasons, and he allowed them to build altars to their foreign gods. The punishment was dissension in the kingdom, which ultimately broke into two lesser kingdoms—Israel and JUDAH—just after Solomon's death.

Jewish tradition attributes three books in the TANAKH, the Hebrew Bible, to Solomon: SONG OF SONGS, Proverbs, and Ecclesiastes. Song of Songs represents the love and hope of Solomon's youth, PROVERBS represents his wisdom in middle age, and ECCLESIASTES represents the philosophical reflections of his last years. However, modern textual criticism disputes his authorship of all three works.

Secular scholarship disagrees with the biblical analysis of Solomon in some respects, but agrees on many of the facts. Historians depict Solomon as politically calculating. He probably did marry foreign princesses to form alliances; he also reorganized the kingdom administratively to reduce the old tribal identities in favor of a national identity. Building the Temple further unified the kingdom by providing a true religio-political center. However, Solomon's building projects, including the Temple, a palace, and numerous defensive fortifications, forced him to increase taxes and introduce forced labor around the country. While the book of Kings includes most of these facts, there is a theological overlay that conforms to the themes of DEUTERONOMIC HISTORY, the idea that God moves history in accordance with divine aims. Thus, God decides which king will build the Temple; times of prosperity are due to a righteous king who wins God's favor; and the breakdown of the unified kingdom is due to Solomon's sins.

Further reading: Lowell K. Handy, ed., *The Age of Solomon: Scholarship at the Turn of the Millennium* (New York: Brill, 1997); Ronald Isaacs, *Legends of Biblical Heroes: A Sourcebook* (Northvale, N.J.: Aronson, 2002); Naomi Pasachoff, *Jewish History in 100 Nutshells* (Northvale, N.J.: Aronson, 1995); *Tanakh: The Holy Scriptures* (Philadelphia and Jerusalem: Jewish Publication Society, 1985).

Soloveitchik, Joseph (1903–1993)
preeminent Modern Orthodox leader

Joseph Soloveitchik was born in Pruzhany, POLAND, in 1903. His family lineage boasted many great Lithuanian RABBIS, including his maternal grandfather, Rabbi Eliyahu Feinstein of Pruzhany, and his paternal grandfather, Rabbi Haym Soloveitchik, of Brisk. Soloveitchik was educated in a traditional YESHIVA, Jewish religious school, and with special private tutors. He was recognized at a young age as a TALMUD prodigy. He married his wife Tonya and together they moved to Berlin, GERMANY, where he earned a doctorate at the University of Berlin in 1931.

Soloveitchik immigrated to America in 1932, where he became the chief rabbi of Boston, which remained Soloveitchik's primary home until his death. In 1937, he established the Maimonides School in Boston, the first Jewish day school in the greater New England area (*see* JEWISH DAY SCHOOL MOVEMENT). He served as chief rabbi until 1941, when he accepted the post of professor of Talmud at the Rabbi Isaac Elchanan Theological Seminary of YESHIVA UNIVERSITY in New York, succeeding his father as Rosh Yeshiva or head of the school. He also served as a professor of Jewish philosophy at the Yeshiva University's Bernard Revel Graduate School. Soloveitchik commuted weekly to New York for a two-and-a-half-day period, during which time he delivered three lengthy daily Talmudic discourses. In 1952 he also began to teach Talmud at Congregation Moriah in Manhattan, attracting thousands of Jewish laymen from the tristate area.

Soloveitchik ushered in a new era of MODERN ORTHODOXY. He was an immensely accomplished scholar in both secular and religious fields. Modern Orthodox Jews looked to his rabbinic leadership for both the proper interpretation of HALAKHAH, Jewish law, and general guidelines for dealing with the religious and political issues of Jewish life in MODERNITY. Soloveitchik's leadership helped ensure the continued growth of Modern Orthodoxy independent from activists in the ultra-Orthodox movement.

Soloveitchik ordained more than 2,000 rabbis during his 45 years at Yeshiva University. He was commonly referred to as "the Rav," the rabbi. He is considered by most to be the preeminent Talmudic scholar of the second half of the 20th century. Soloveitchik balanced tradition and science, and although religiously observant, he asserted that modern Orthodox Jews must work and cooperate on communal issues with their Jewish brothers and sisters who were not Orthodox. He also advocated the teaching of Talmud to women, helping to introduce the study of Talmud at Yeshiva University's women's school, STERN COLLEGE.

Soloveitchik was an ardent supporter of religious ZIONISM; Menachem BEGIN, after his election as prime minister of ISRAEL in 1977, reportedly offered Soloveitchik the post of chief rabbi of Israel. Soloveitchik's literary works, and his lectures to his students, continue to influence Jewish scholars and thinkers today.

Further reading: Aaron Rakeffet-Rothkoff, *The Rav: The World of Rabbi Joseph B. Soloveitchik* (Hobokwn, N.J.: Ktav, 1999); Joseph B. Soloveitchik, *Halakhic Man* (Philadelphia: Jewish Publication Society, 1984); Joseph B. Soloveitchik, *The Lonely Man of Faith* (Northvale, N.J.: Jason Aronson, 1997); Joseph B. Soloveitchik and Abraham R. Besdin, *Reflections of the Rav: Lessons in Jewish Thought* (Hoboken, N.J.: Ktav, 1992).

Song of Songs

Song of Songs, sometimes called the Song of Solomon, is one of the more controversial books in the TANAKH. There is no mention of God, and the text reads more like secular love poetry than religious scripture. In fact, much of it probably originated in ancient secular wedding songs.

Jewish tradition attributes the work to King SOLOMON, although modern biblical scholars estimate that the work was written after the time of Solomon. Regardless of when it was composed, the Song of Songs represents the hope and love of Solomon's youth, while Proverbs represents the wisdom of his middle age, and ECCLESIASTES represents the philosophy that comes with old age.

Rabbi AKIVA BEN YOSEPH declared the work to be the holiest book in the Tanakh; the rabbis understood the text as an allegory for the love between God and the people of ISRAEL. The story begins with the love that develops between the two during the EXODUS from EGYPT and the marriage at MOUNT SINAI, symbolized by the COVENANT. Song of Songs goes on to describe unfaithful episodes within a system of everlasting love, akin to the people of Israel's sins against God within the context of everlasting love and a promise of redemption.

The rabbis chose to include Song of Songs as the liturgical reading in the SYNAGOGUE during the festival of PASSOVER because of the metaphor of the love between God and Israel that is so pure at the time of the Exodus; a mention in the text of PHARAOH's chariot; and a considerable amount of nature imagery that fits nicely with the springtime aspects of Passover.

Christians have also debated the meaning of Song of Songs. While some wanted to delete it from the canon, others view the love song as an allegory of the relationship between JESUS OF NAZARETH and the church.

Further reading: Jacob Neusner, *Song of Songs Rabbah* (Atlanta: Scholars Press, 1997); Jacob Neusner, *Israel's Love Affair with God* (Valley Forge, Pa.: Trinity Press International, 1993); *Tanakh: The Holy Scriptures* (Philadelphia and Jerusalem: Jewish Publication Society, 1985); Meir Zlotowitz, ed., *Shir haShirim: Song of Songs: An Allegorical Translation Based upon Rashi with a Commentary Anthologized from Talmudic, Midrashic and Rabbinic Sources* (New York: Mesorah, 1977).

soul

According to Jewish tradition, each person has a spiritual essence or soul. In the post-biblical period, that essence came to be seen as an eternal spirit.

The TANAKH or Hebrew Bible contains three words often translated as soul: *nefesh, neshama,*

and *ruach*. In some contexts, they are better translated as person or spirit. In any case, the soul was seen as inseparable from the body. There are hints that after death the soul might descend to SHEOL, the underworld, but this is not a clear or central theme in biblical literature.

During the Hellenistic period (*see* HELLENISM), the RABBIS were exposed to the Greek notion that the soul exists independent of the body. They accepted the idea, which became normative in the rabbinic tradition. The soul came to be understood as created in heaven and placed in the body at birth. Students of Kabbalah, Jewish mysticism, further developed these ideas. The rabbis came to believe that when the body dies, the soul goes to GEHINNOM, where it faces divine judgment for up to a year before entering OLAM HA-BA, or paradise; once there, the soul's proximity to God's essence depends on the judgment in Gehinnom.

In contemporary times ORTHODOX JUDAISM continues to teach the traditional rabbinic idea that the soul is independent from the body and eternal. Within liberal Judaism, some accept the traditional view; others treat the soul as a metaphoric concept, and still others completely reject the idea that the body and spirit are anything other than the totality of self while alive in this world.

Further reading: Abraham Joshua Heschel, *God in Search of Man: A Philosophy of Judaism* (New York: Farrar, Strauss, and Giroux, 1976); Woolf Hirsch, *Rabbinic Psychology: Beliefs about the Soul in Rabbinic Literature of the Talmudic Period* (London: E. Goldston, 1947); Rifat Sonsino, *What Happens After I Die? Jewish Views of Life After Death* (New York: UAHC Press, 1990).

South Africa

The earliest evidence of Jews in South Africa dates back to Jewish cartographers and scientists from PORTUGAL who assisted Vasco da Gama in his 1497 discovery of the Cape of Good Hope. In 1652 Jewish names appear on settlement lists, but these people may have been Jewish converts to Protestantism, as the Dutch East India Company required its settlers to be Protestants. It was not until the early 19th century that a Jewish community grew in South Africa. In 1803, the Dutch introduced complete religious tolerance in South Africa and when the British took over in 1806 they continued the policy. This allowed Jews to settle openly. They founded the first Jewish congregation in a private home in 1841, and built the first SYNAGOGUE, called Tikvat Israel, Hope of Israel, in 1849. It still stands in Cape Town today.

The Jews who came to South Africa in the mid-19th century were attracted by the growing economy. They helped set up the economic infrastructure, including trading stations, business centers, and a credit system. They developed shipping, fishing, sugar enterprises, trading, wineries, and the clothing and steel industries. When diamonds and gold were discovered in South Africa, the Jews became involved in mining and distribution. More Jewish immigrants arrived on the shores of South Africa from America, Australia, and eastern Europe. The largest contingent came from Lithuania in the late 19th century, the first large community of eastern European Jews. Most of the new immigrants settled in urban centers such as Johannesburg. In 1880 the Jewish population numbered approximately 4,000 Jews, and by 1890 it had increased to 10,000, and by 1904 it reached 38,000.

From 1910 to 1960, approximately 30,000 Jews immigrated to South Africa. Those who arrived prior to 1890 had included many English and German Jews, but after that year the immigrants came mostly from eastern Europe. The South African government imposed immigration quotas and restrictions in the 1920s and 1930s, and by the end of World War II, only a few hundred Jews were arriving each year.

The Jews of South Africa have enjoyed a relatively open society, with only occasional evidence of ANTISEMITISM. The Jews experienced equality within the white community, with equality and privileges in all spheres of economic, social, and cultural life. During the 1930s, Nazi sympathies spread somewhat in South Africa, but by 1948 the government removed any institutional vestiges of discrimination against Jews. South Africa has generally been supportive of the modern state of ISRAEL, although Israel's position against apartheid was not well received. Although the Jewish community in South Africa did not stand officially against apartheid, many whites who did were Jewish and they formed two organizations in 1985 to oppose apartheid: Jews for Justice and Jews for Social Justice. These groups supported the antiapartheid position of Helen Suzman (b. 1917), a Jewish woman who served as a member of South Africa's parliament.

As soon as large numbers of Jews arrived in the country, they began to set up synagogues, Jewish education systems, philanthropic societies, and burial societies. By the end of the 19th century, the eastern European immigrants had established many LANDSMANSCHAFTEN, or fraternal organizations based on town of origin; academies for the study of rabbinic literature (see MIDRASH; MISHNAH; TALMUD); Zionist organizations (see ZIONISM); and Jewish sports clubs. Examples of these organizations include the Hebrew Order of David, the Zionist and Young Israel Societies, the Union of Jewish Women, and B'NAI B'RITH Lodges.

By the 1980s, Jewish communal life included the United Communal Fund, which worked to raise money for services in South Africa as well as in Israel. In 1912, the South African Jewish Board of Deputies was founded; by 1969 it boasted 330 member organizations. The Board of Deputies acted as the voice of the South African Jewish community, and it worked to prevent discrimination and defamation against Jews. It also supported agencies that provided relief to the needy, especially to war refugees during the World War II era.

Some 80 percent of South Africa's synagoguegoers are affiliated with ORTHODOX JUDAISM. The other 20 percent are Reform or Progressive Jews (see REFORM JUDAISM). Conservative Judaism is not represented in South Africa. Orthodox synagogues fall under the umbrella organization called the Union of Orthodox Synagogues, and Reform or Progressive synagogues are held together by the South African Union for Progressive Judaism. Many Jewish children in South Africa attend Jewish day schools (*see* JEWISH DAY SCHOOL MOVEMENT). CHABAD Lubavitch has a branch in South Africa, and the *BAAL TESHUVAH* movement, Jews who become more traditional by choice, is growing. It is estimated that in 1970 there were almost 118,000 Jews living in South Africa. However, in 1991, only 59,000 chose to identify their religious preference on the census form. Demographers believe that there are between 104,500 and 107,500 Jews living in South Africa today, the large majority in Johannesburg and the next largest group in Cape Town.

Further reading: Daniel J. Elazar and Peter Medding, *Jewish Communities in Frontier Societies—Argentina, Australia, and South Africa* (New York: Holmes & Meier, 1983); Louis Herrman, *A History of the Jews in South Africa, from the Earliest Times to 1895* (Westport, Conn.: Greenwood Press, 1975); Naomi Musiker, *The Jews of South Africa: An Illustrated History to 1953, with an Epilogue to 1975* (Johannesburg: Scarecrow, 2001); Gideon Shimoni, *Community and Conscience: The Jews in Apartheid South Africa* (Hanover, N.H.: University Press of New England, 2003).

Soviet Jewry   *See* REFUSENIKS; RUSSIA.

Spain

The history of the Jews in Spain is critical to any discussion of Judaism and world Jewry. The Jews of Spain had a rich history stretching across some 1,000 years, under both Muslim and Christian rulers. Their experiences varied from periods of extraordinary intellectual and religious freedom and economic prosperity to times of severe discrimination, persecution, and expulsion.

The earliest Jews probably arrived in Spain, specifically in Granada, under the Roman Empire (*see* ROME). The oldest physical evidence of a Jewish presence is a third century C.E. tombstone inscription.

Between the sixth century and the early eighth century, significant Jewish communities lived under Visigoth rule. The Visigoths became Christian (*see* CHRISTIANITY) in the year 587. Over the next century the Jews experienced forced conversion and expulsion, and also at times tolerance. Some Spanish kings tried to forcibly convert the Jews to Christianity while others wanted the Jews to convert according to their own hearts. Some Jews converted and then returned to Judaism when a more tolerant king rose to power; still others left Spain only to return when a more tolerant king emerged.

The fourth Council of Toledo in the year 633 accepted the church doctrine that the Jews were not to be baptized by force. However, King Erwig (680–687) convened the 12th Council of Toledo to get permission to force baptism on the Jews; but he failed to get full support from the church or from his nobles, who depended upon the economic service of the Jews. Erwig's successor, Egica (687–702), took a different approach, offering financial benefits to converts and ensuring the impoverishment of those who remained Jewish. Egica then accused these Jews of treasonously supporting a Muslim invasion, and he enslaved those who did not escape. Thus, when the Muslims finally did invade in the year 711, there were no openly practicing Jews left.

As the Muslims entered various areas of Spain, they sought out those Jews who were hiding their religious beliefs, bringing them out into the open. The Jews offered military help in the already conquered territories, and administered the areas for the new rulers. This occurred in Córdoba, Granada, Toledo, and Seville. For a time, the Jews were the favored minority, trusted by the Muslims. Many who had left for the safety of North Africa returned, and the Jewish population of Spain increased once again.

However, once the Muslims gained firm control, they imposed heavy taxes on both Jews and Christians, although Jews did enjoy some prosperity and religious freedom. For example, under Umayyad rule (eighth–11th centuries) Jews prospered in the Muslim courts as physicians and financial advisers, and also contributed to agriculture and crafts.

Leaders of the growing Jewish communities maintained correspondence with the Jews of BABYLONIA (*see GEONIM*) at the other end of the Muslim world. Jewish culture and literature flourished. Muslim aesthetics were adopted, showing up for example in religious poetry called *piyyutim*. Muslim philosophy and science were also adopted and developed by many Jews during this time, breaking the monopoly of France and Germany on European Jewish thought and practice. Much of the time Jews spent under Muslim rule in Spain was safe and prosperous.

The 10th and 11th centuries were considered to be a Jewish golden age in Spain, where Jews flourished in literature, religion, scholarship, business, and even government service. Two figures, Hasdai the Nasi and Samuel the Nagid, represent the inroads Jews made in government. Among notable cultural and religious figures among the SEPHARDIM, as the Jews from the Iberian Peninsula were called, were Yehudah HALEVI, Moses MAIMONIDES, and Isaac ABRAVANEL.

As the Umayyids declined in the 11th century, Jewish life resumed its back and forth motion between prosperity and poverty, religious persecution and freedom, under the dynasties of the Almoravids and the Almohads. Some Jews left for Christian territories, others became secret Jews (*see* CONVERSOS).

Christians worked to regain rule over Spain from the moment the Muslims arrived. At the beginning of the 11th century they began to take back significant territory. The Jews sometimes benefited from the struggle between Christians and Muslims, which diverted those groups' attention away from the Jews and reduced persecution. However, by the beginning of the 12th century, the Christian powers had once again instituted policies of economic, social, and cultural discrimination and persecution toward Jews who refused to convert. Forced DISPUTATIONS, or debates,

between RABBIS and priests took place; in the 13th century, the Jewish scholar NACHMONIDES was forced to flee Spain after winning one such disputation. These debates were not fair, and they put the Jews in a dangerous position of defending their faith to those who would punish them for such a public display of faith in Judaism and its texts.

By the end of the 14th century, the Jews of Christian Spain were suffering periodic persecution and violence, intensified by the Spanish Inquisition. Some 700 Conversos, outward converts who secretly practiced Judaism, were burned at the stake in Seville; as many as 30,000 were killed throughout Spain. In 1492, Jews were completely expelled from Spain by Isabella and Ferdinand, who considered them a threat to the unity of the country. As the Spanish Jews migrated around the world, they brought Sephardic culture with them, and it became one of the defining Jewish cultures in the modern period.

Jews did not return to Spain until the late 19th century, and even then they were only allowed entry as individuals rather than as communities. Western ideas of emancipation, enlightenment, and religious reform did not become prevalent among Spanish Jews until the early 20th century, as Sephardic Jewry was heavily influenced by the traditions of eastern Judaism. The 1492 edict of expulsion was not repealed until the late date of 1968, but ideas of religious tolerance appeared in the country as early as 1868; full citizenship and equality was granted to all minorities in 1966. In 1924 Sephardic Jews living abroad were allowed to claim Spanish nationality and were invited to return to Spain. For these Jews, Spain provided a haven from the Nazi terror (*see* HOLOCAUST). In addition to protecting Jewish nationals, Spain allowed many refugees to pass through to other destinations, numbering up to 20,000. Even so, Spain deported many Jewish refugees, although at the end of the war the country did extend protection to 2,750 Hungarian Jews who were not Spanish nationals, in a successful effort to save their lives.

After World War II, the Jewish community in Spain developed cultural and religious institutions such as synagogues, schools, community centers, summer camps, a Council of Jewish Communities (1963), and a monthly newsletter. Universities began encouraging the study of the Hebrew language, Jewish history, and Jewish literature. Although Spain has not formally recognized Israel as a nation, relations between the two countries are fairly cordial, and trade ties exist. After the death of General Franco in the 1970s, conditions for Jews in Spain improved even more. In 1991 the first step toward the Oslo Accords, an attempt to bring an end to the ARAB-ISRAELI CONFLICT, took place at the Madrid Peace Conference.

In 1992 Spain celebrated the 500th anniversary of Columbus's discovery of the new world. Before the celebration, Spain officially revoked the 1492 Edict of Expulsion against the Jews. This act publicly proclaimed Spain's welcome and openness. In the mid-1990s 14,000 Jews lived in Spain, mostly in Madrid and Barcelona. Most, including Jews from Turkey, Morocco, and the Balkans, have Sephardic origins, but there are also some who derive from eastern Europe.

Further reading: Eliyahu Ashtor, *The Jews of Moslem Spain* (Philadelphia: Jewish Publication Society, 1992); Yitzhak Baer, *A History of the Jews in Christian Spain* (Philadelphia: Jewish Publication Society, 1992); Jane S. Gerber, *The Jews of Spain: A History of the Sephardic Experience* (New York and London: Free Press, 1992); Raymond P. Scheindlin, *Wine, Women and Death: Medieval Hebrew Poems on the Good Life* (Philadelphia: Jewish Publication Society, 1986).

Spiegelman, Art (b. 1948) *cartoonist and social commentator*

Art Spiegelman was born in Stockholm, SWEDEN, to parents who survived the HOLOCAUST, and was brought to the UNITED STATES when he was three years old. Growing up in New York, Spiegelman attended Harper College and the State University

of New York at Binghamton. Though Spiegelman did not formally complete a degree, he eventually received an honorary doctorate of letters from SUNY Binghamton, in June 1995.

Spiegelman began his career working for Topps Gum Co. in 1966, creating candy and gum wrappers, including the "Garbage Pail Kids." He moved on to drawings and cartoons for the *New York Times,* the *Village Voice,* and *Playboy,* and became an art teacher at the School of Visual Arts. In 1979 he and his wife cofounded *Raw* magazine, an avante-garde collection of comics.

Spiegelman is best known for his graphic novel *Maus.* This novel in two volumes, published in 1986 and 1991, depicts his father's experiences in the Holocaust and his own struggles as the child of Holocaust survivors. The main characters are all depicted as animals throughout the books: Jews as mice, Germans as cats, Americans as dogs, and French as pigs. Spiegelman's black-and-white graphic format has an unsettling effect on the reader, and the power of his work was recognized with a special Pulitzer Prize in 1992. He has been awarded a Guggenheim Fellowship and a nomination for the National Book Critics Circle award in recognition for both volumes of *Maus. Maus* has been published in 20 languages.

Further reading: Sara R. Horowitz, *Voicing the Void: Muteness and Memory in Holocaust Fiction* (Albany: State University of New York Press, 1997); Ed Richardson, "The Tale of Maus: A Cartoonist Confronts the Holocaust," in *Sojourners* 18 (May 1989); Art Spiegelman, *Maus: A Survivor's Tale* (New York: Pantheon Books; 1986) and *Maus II: And Here My Troubles Began* (New York: Pantheon Books, 1991).

Spielberg, Steven (b. 1946) *American film director*

Steven Spielberg was born on December 18, 1946, in Cincinnati, Ohio. He became the most commercially successful Hollywood filmmaker in history, directing major blockbusters such as *Jaws, Raiders of the Lost Ark, E.T.,* and *Jurassic Park.*

Spielberg felt ashamed of his Jewish heritage as a teenager, partially because of antisemitic attacks he experienced in high school (*see* ANTISEMITISM), when other students teased and even beat him. Spielberg later rediscovered his religious and historical heritage as a Jew, and he has contributed significantly to the Jewish community. Spielberg credits much of the renewal of his interest in Judaism to the interest of his family, including his wife, actress Kate Capshaw, who underwent CONVERSION to Judaism in 1993.

In particular, Spielberg has had an important impact on documenting the HOLOCAUST. His Hollywood epic, *Schindler's List,* uses the story of Oskar SCHINDLER to depict the horror and brutality of the Holocaust. While researching and directing the film, Spielberg came face to face with the geography and reality of the Holocaust: the filming took him to AUSCHWITZ and Birkenau, for example. Since working on *Schindler's List,* Spielberg has launched a massive project to assemble a video archive of survivor testimonies via the Survivors of the Shoah Visual History Foundation. Many of these videos are shown regularly as part of an exhibit at the Holocaust museum in Washington, D.C.

Further reading: Steven Spielberg, *The Last Days* (New York: St. Martin's Press, 1999); Philip M. Taylor, *Steven Spielberg: The Man, His Movies, and Their Meaning* (New York: Continuum, 1999).

Spinoza, Baruch (1632–1677) *philosopher*

Baruch (Benedictus) Spinoza was born in 1632 in Amsterdam, the NETHERLANDS, to a Sephardic Jewish family (*see* SEPHARDIM). His innovative ideas on religion and philosophy earned him widespread notoriety, and he was excommunicated (*see* HEREM) from the Amsterdam Jewish community on July 27, 1656. He was also condemned by Christians. Nevertheless, he influenced many later philosophers.

Spinoza was excommunicated for denying that the TORAH was literally true and given by God (*see* TORAH MI-SINAI) and that the soul is immortal. Spinoza rejected the idea of a personal God. He believed that God or nature is the force that sustains the universe; consequently everything in it is an aspect of God. The religious concept of God should not be accepted on faith without scrutiny.

Ironically, Spinoza's father had fled from PORTUGAL to find religious tolerance in the Netherlands. His excommunication typified the struggle between those who wanted to protect religion from scrutiny by other disciplines and those who were willing to use all tools available to uncover what they thought to be the truth. After his excommunication, during which he was cursed and anathematized, Spinoza studied at the University of Leiden.

Spinoza taught that human happiness comes from direct knowledge. Any belief that derives from direct knowledge cannot be questioned. For Spinoza, knowledge was the key to freedom and blessedness. A good society, in his political theory, was one that allowed rational people to think freely and achieve true knowledge. Spinoza was a pioneer in philosophy whose writings are studied in the present day.

In a time when religion was unquestioned, and bloody wars were still being fought over religious beliefs, Spinoza created a critique of revealed religion. He felt that nature and God acted in ways that could be understood; he would not accept any idea by authority or faith alone. Spinoza was one of the first modern scholars to look at the TANAKH, the Hebrew Bible, critically. Living 100 years before Moses MENDELSSOHN published *Jerusalem,* an attempt to reconcile the modern world with Judaism, Spinoza's philosophy was ahead of its time.

Among the great works that Spinoza left to the world were *Tractatus Theologico-Politicus* and *Ethics.* After his death Spinoza's other writings were published, including an opera, a Hebrew grammar, and letters. In his lifetime, Spinoza was able to make a living as a lens maker and with support from patrons. He died from consumption in 1677.

Further reading: Henry Allison, *Benedict de Spinoza: An Introduction* (New Haven, Conn.: Yale University Press,

1987); Steven Nadler, *Spinoza: A Life* (Cambridge and New York: Cambridge University Press, 1999); Steven B. Smith, *Spinoza, Liberalism and the Question of Jewish Identity* (New Haven, Conn.: Yale University Press, 1997); Baruch Spinoza, *The Collected Writings of Spinoza* (Princeton, N.J.: Princeton University Press, 1985).

Spitz, Mark (b. 1950) *Olympic swimming champion*

Mark Spitz, born February 10, 1950, in Modesto, California, remains the greatest Olympic swimmer of all time. He began swimming as a small boy while living in Hawaii, and he swam in college at Indiana University. In the 1972 Olympics in Munich, GERMANY, he won seven gold medals, all with world-record times. Spitz was forced to leave the games soon after earning his medals, for his own safety, after Arab terrorists murdered eleven Israeli Olympic team members.

In 1965 and 1969 Spitz competed in the international Maccabiah Games in Israel, winning 10 gold medals. He was named World Swimmer of the Year in 1967, 1971, and 1972. After a two-decade hiatus, he attempted to return to the Olympics, but did not qualify. All told, between 1968 and 1972, Spitz won nine Olympic gold medals, one silver, and one bronze; five Pan-American golds; 31 National U.S. Amateur Athletic Union titles; and eight U.S. National Collegiate Athletic Association Championships. During those years, he logged 33 world records.

Further reading: P. H. Mullen, Jr., *Gold in the Water: The True Story of Ordinary Men and Their Extraordinary Dream of Olympic Glory* (New York: Thomas Dunne Books, 2001); Mark Spitz, *Seven Golds: Mark Spitz Own Story* (New York: Bantam Dell, 1987).

Star of David

The Star of David, or Magen David (Hebrew for "shield of David"), is a conventional symbol of Judaism and the Jewish people, consisting of two overlapping triangles that form a six-pointed star.

Archaeological evidence of the symbol dates as far back as a third-century SYNAGOGUE at Capernaum in ISRAEL, but the star did not come into popular use until many centuries later.

Beginning in the 13th century the term *Magen David* appears in the literature of the KABBALAH. It also appears in a Jewish context in Prague in the 17th century. In the 19th century it came to be used by the HIBBAT ZION movement, and was formally adopted by the Second Zionist (*see* ZIONISM) Congress in 1897 as its symbol. It now appears on the official flag of the State of Israel (*see* ISRAELI FLAG).

Scholars are unsure about the meaning or origin of the star. Since the symbol is sometimes called the Shield of David, prominent rabbi Moshe FEINSTEIN suggested that it had been used by King David to signify that God shielded him in war. This theory has no current scholarship to support it, and the mystical meaning of the Star of David is open to interpretation. The Kabbalah describes the two triangles as representing the dichotomies inherent in humanity: good versus evil, spiritual versus physical, etc. The two triangles may also

This six-pointed star is a Star of David, or Magen David. Its meaning and origin are unclear, which make it a perfect symbol for unifying Jews around the world. Often one finds symbols such as the Star of David embroidered on a *tallit* (prayer shawl) bag, such as this one. The Hebrew word *tallit* is embroidered in the center of the star. *(Getty Images)*

represent the reciprocal relationship between the Jewish people and God.

The Star of David was used by modern anti-semites, especially the Nazis, as a badge to mark Jews for discrimination. The modern state of Israel purposely put the star on its flag as a rebuke to those who attempted to demean the Jews with their own symbols. However, the Zionist Organization had adopted the star as its symbol, mostly because its lack of significance left little to create division. Thus the Star of David has become a universal symbol of all streams of Judaism.

Further reading: Asher Eder, *The Star of David: An Ancient Symbol of Integration* (Jerusalem: R. Mass, 1987); Morris N. Kertzer, *What Is a Jew?* (New York: Touchstone, 1996); Charles Panati, *Sacred Origins of Profound Things* (New York: Penguin Books, 1996).

Stein, Edith (St. Theresa Benedicta of the Cross) (1891–1942) *Catholic theologian of Jewish birth, saint*

Edith Stein was born on October 12, 1891, to Jewish parents in Breslau, GERMANY. In her autobiography, Stein explains that although her family did not participate in any organized religion, her mother did mark the Sabbath (*see* SHABBAT) and Jewish festivals. Stein sought her own religious path, becoming interested in Spanish mysticism and the Catholic Church. She pursued philology and philosophy at the Universities of Breslau and Göttingen, and earned her doctorate in philosophy from the University of Freiburg, where she worked with Edmund Husserl, the famous founder of phenomenology. Despite her qualifications, she was denied various teaching positions both as a woman and as a Jew, even though she herself did not identify herself as Jewish.

Stein's pursuit of "truth" led her to the Catholic Church, and she was baptized on New Year's Day, 1922. Her conversion to CHRISTIANITY eventually led her to pursue the solitude and contemplation of Carmel, and she became a nun in the Carmelite order. Her new name was Teresia

Benedicta ac Cruce (Teresa Benedicta of the Cross). By 1935, Stein realized that her presence in the monastery at Cologne-Lindenthal was dangerous for her fellow Catholics, and she asked to be transferred to a safer country. She crossed over into the NETHERLANDS and spent her last years in the Carmel of Echt, writing her last work, *The Science of the Cross.*

In 1942, when the Dutch authorities refused to hand the local Jews over to the Nazis, the Germans gathered together all of the Catholics they could find of Jewish descent. Stein and her sister Rosa were arrested that summer and transported by cattle train to AUSCHWITZ, where on August 9 they were murdered in the gas chambers.

In recognition of her suffering, Edith Stein was beatified by Pope John Paul II in 1987 and canonized as a martyr-saint on October 11, 1998. In the 1980s, a Carmelite monastery was established near Auschwitz, largely in her memory. Some have viewed these efforts as an attempt to draw attention away from the mostly Jewish nature of the HOLOCAUST. Abraham H. Foxman, national director of the ANTI-DEFAMATION LEAGUE at the time of Stein's canonization, wrote, "The presence of the nuns [in the newly founded Carmelite monastery] was a way of conveying the idea that Auschwitz was a place of true Christian martyrdom. While there is no doubt that many Christians died in Auschwitz, especially Polish priests, nevertheless the main industry of that CONCENTRATION CAMP was the extermination of the Jewish people. The monastery diminished this reality."

Controversy continues to swirl around Stein. Critics point out that Stein was killed because she had "Jewish blood" in her veins, despite her religious conversion. She serves as an example of the Nazi view that Jewishness was a racial identity that could not be changed by conversion.

Further reading: Abraham Foxman and Rabbi Leon Kleniclei, "The Canonization of Edith Stein: An Unnecessary Problem," at URL: www.adl.org/opinion/edith_stein.asp; Mary Gordon, "Saint Edith?" in *Tikkun* 14, no. 2 (March–April 1999): 17–20; Eleanor Michael,

"Saints and Nazi Skeletons," in *History Today* 48, no. 10 (Oct 1998): 4–5; Edith Stein, *Life in a Jewish Family: 1891–1916* (Washington, D.C.: I.C.S, 1986).

Steinberg, Milton (1903–1950) *American rabbi and writer*

Milton Steinberg was born on November 24, 1903, in Rochester, New York. His father, Samuel, had studied in the Volozhin YESHIVA, a Jewish religious school, but after immigrating to the UNITED STATES he embraced a more flexible level of Jewish observance by which he and his wife Fannie raised their children. Steinberg was an avid reader as a youth, and he excelled at school. He was part of a group of boys who were privately tutored in their Hebrew education at the Leopold Street Synagogue.

Steinberg's family moved to Manhattan when he was 15 years old. He attended De Witt Clinton High School, and had the honor of addressing the class as valedictorian. At age 17 he entered the City College of New York, majoring in Greek and Latin classics, and graduating first in his class. He won academic prizes in Greek, history, philosophy, and Latin.

Steinberg continued to pursue Jewish studies on his own. He took a BIBLICAL HEBREW class at Anshei Chesed synagogue, where he also became a part-time teacher. There he met his wife, Edith Alpert, who he married after being ordained a RABBI from the JEWISH THEOLOGICAL SEMINARY in the late 1920s. At the seminary he became president of the student body and graduated with many awards. He was highly influenced by his teacher, Rabbi Mordecai KAPLAN, the founder of RECONSTRUCTIONIST JUDAISM.

Following graduation from the seminary, Steinberg became rabbi of a Conservative (*see* CONSERVATIVE JUDAISM) SYNAGOGUE in Indianapolis, serving there for five years. In 1933 he assumed the pulpit of the then small congregation of the Park Avenue Synagogue in New York City. Steinberg introduced an informal tone, preferring to be addressed by congregants by his first name. He was an eloquent writer and speaker on such topics as God, faith, and reason.

Steinberg's primary interest was in Kaplan's "reconstruction" of Judaism. He became a founding staffer, editor, and writer for *The Reconstructionist* magazine. He also helped edit the Reconstructionist Sabbath (*see* SHABBAT) Prayer Book. Steinberg, unlike Kaplan, believed in God as a conscious, moral Creator of the universe, whose power was limited by the free will of humanity. Steinberg was pushing Reconstructionist Judaism into metaphysical realms, but his tragic death at a young age prevented him from a systematic definition of his religious thinking.

In 1934, Steinberg's first book, *The Making of the Modern Jew,* began to outline how the modern Jew should stand in both the world of tradition and MODERNITY. In 1945 he published *A Partisan Guide to the Jewish Problem,* which explored the issues Jews faced with the conclusion of World War II. Steinberg's best-selling book was his *Basic Judaism,* written for nonscholarly Jews and non-Jews. His historical novel, *As a Driven Leaf,* tells the story of the second-century rabbi Elisha BEN ABUYAH, who seeks a rational faith and in the end becomes a heretic. The popular novel ultimately reaffirms Steinberg's belief that one must properly balance reason and faith.

Steinberg was rejected for a military chaplaincy during World War II because of physical problems. In December 1943, while on a speaking tour of army camps for the Jewish Welfare Board, he suffered a heart attack in Brounwood, Texas. After weeks of recuperating indoors, he was finally permitted to go outside. His sermon: "To Hold with Open Arms," details his feelings about illness and immersing himself into the world once again. It is considered one of the great modern rabbinic sermons. In 1946, JTS awarded Steinberg an honorary doctorate, citing his immense contributions to American Jewish life. Steinberg died at the age of 46 on March 17, 1950.

Further reading: Louis Kaplan, "On the Fiftieth Yahrheit of Milton Steinberg," *Judaism* (Winter 2001);

Simon Noveck, *Portrait of a Rabbi* (New York: Ktav Publishing House, 1978); Milton Steinberg, *As A Driven Leaf* (New York and Indianapolis: Bobbs-Merrill Company, 1939); Milton Steinberg, *Basic Judaism* (New York: Harcourt, Brace & World, 1947); ———, *A Partisan Guide to the Jewish Problem* (New York and Indianapolis: Bobbs-Merrill Company, 1945).

Steinem, Gloria (b. 1934) *American feminist activist and writer*

Gloria Steinem was born on March 25, 1934, in Toledo, Ohio. After her parents divorced, Steinem lived with and helped take care of her chronically depressed mother. She won a scholarship to Smith College, graduating Phi Beta Kappa in 1956, followed by a graduate fellowship for two years of study in India. While attending the Universities of Delhi and Calcutta she became active with a nonviolent protest group called the Radical Humanists. Her activism in India was the beginning of a lifelong interest in social and political issues.

In 1960, Steinem began a career as a writer and journalist in New York City. She earned fame by publishing an article in 1963 titled "I Was a Playboy Bunny," in which she wrote about her undercover job as a waitress for a New York Playboy Club. She condemned the club for exploiting the women, who suffered poor wages and working conditions.

In 1968, Steinem became contributing editor to the newly created *New York* magazine. Through her column she became a strong advocate for the new feminist movement. She would rise to become one of the movement's most prominent American spokespeople. In 1971 she helped create the National Women's Political Caucus. The following year she became one of the founding editors of the feminist magazine *Ms.*, serving in the position for the next 15 years, after which she continued as a columnist and consulting editor for the magazine.

In 1983, Steinem published her first book, *Outrageous Acts and Everyday Rebellions.* In 1986 she published a biography of Marilyn Monroe. In

Born to a Jewish father, Gloria Steinem became one of the leaders of the feminist movement in the United States in the 1970s. *(Library of Congress)*

1992, she wrote *Revolution from Within;* in 1994, *Moving Beyond Words.* Steinem is still considered one of the great feminist leaders in the world today.

Gloria Steinem's father was Jewish, but she was not raised as a Jew, although she did grow up with a certain amount of "Jewish Pride." Therefore, by the standards of all the major American Jewish denominations, Steinem might not be considered to be Jewish. However, many American Jews, and America as a whole, thinks of Steinem as part of the Jewish community. For example, the Seattle Jewish Federation's Women's Division in 2002 invited Steinem to be their keynote speaker on the topic of what it means to be a Jewish woman and how to live as one. In addition, Steinem was included in the September 2004 City University of New York program CUNY Celebrates 350, celebrating the history of the Jews in America.

Further reading: Beryl Lieff Benderly and Hasia R. Diner, *Her Works Praise Her: A History of Jewish Women in America from Colonial Times to the Present* (New York: Basic Books, 2002); Carolyn G. Heilbrun, *The Education of a Woman: The Life of Gloria Steinem* (New York: Ballantine Books, 1996); Gloria Steinem, *Outrageous Acts and Everyday Rebellions* (New York: Owl Books, 1995).

Steinhardt Foundation

Michael Steinhardt is considered one the most successful money managers in Wall Street history, building an enormously successful financial record for more than 30 years. In 1995, he stunned the financial world by closing his investment firm to devote full time and his immense resources to assisting philanthropic causes in the Jewish world. The Steinhardt Foundation has become one of the most important sources of Jewish philanthropy in the contemporary world.

Beneficiaries of the Steinhardt Foundation have included the Israel Museum and B'NAI B'RITH HILLEL, which was enhanced by the Steinhardt Jewish Campus Service Corps. The Steinhardt Foundation created the Jewish Life Network (JLN), whose stated mission is to "revitalize Jewish identity through educational, religious and cultural initiatives that reach out to all Jews, with an emphasis on those who are on the margins of Jewish life." Among its best-known initiatives are PEJE, Makor, and Birthright Israel. PEJE, an acronym for Partnership for Excellence in Jewish Education, is devoted to strengthening Jewish day schools, while Makor is an organization that helps to build a sense of Jewish community among Jews between the ages of 20 and 50.

Finally, Birthright Israel seeks to send young adults aged 18 to 26 to ISRAEL free of charge. The trips are reserved for those who have never visited Israel, as Birthright Israel believes that such a visit is a Jew's birthright.

Further reading: Michael Steinhardt, *No Bull: My Life In and Out of the Markets* (New York: Wiley, 2001); Jewish Life Web site URL: http://www.jewishlife.org/, accessed August 18, 2004.

Stern, Isaac (1920–2001) *world-renowned violinist*

Isaac Stern was born in Kreminiecz, RUSSIA, in 1920, but came to the UNITED STATES when he was 10 months old, as his parents were fleeing the BOLSHEVIK REVOLUTION in RUSSIA. Stern was raised in San Francisco, California. He began to play the violin at the age of eight and made his orchestral debut in 1936 with the San Francisco Symphony. At the age of 22 he appeared for the first time at Carnegie Hall. Stern is considered the greatest violinist of his time.

Stern was strongly connected to his Jewish roots, especially the modern state of ISRAEL. After the SIX-DAY WAR in 1967, he performed the movie soundtrack for *FIDDLER ON THE ROOF* with the Israel Philharmonic at Mount Scopus in JERUSALEM. He served as chairman of the board for the American-Israel Cultural Foundation and chairman and founder of the Jerusalem Music Centre. In 1991, during the Gulf War, Stern traveled to Israel to play a concert in support of the Jewish nation, which was undergoing missile attacks from IRAQ. He traveled from the United States to perform a concert while wearing a gas mask. This was a major boost to Israeli morale.

Stern was the first recipient of the Albert Schweitzer Music Award, and in 1984 President Reagan presented him with the Kennedy Center Honors Award. He also won the Grammy Lifetime Achievement Award and Israel's Wolf Prize for service to humanity. In 1991, he received the

National Medal of the Arts from President George H. W. Bush, who in 1992 also awarded him the Presidential Medal of Freedom. He was a founding member of the National Endowment for the arts and held honorary degrees from many institutions, including Howard University, the Hebrew University in Jerusalem, The Juilliard School, Tel Aviv University, and Yale University.

At the age of 81, Stern died on September 23, 2001. He was survived by three children and five grandchildren.

Further reading: Irving Kolodin, *The New Guide to Recorded Music* (Garden City, N.Y.: Doubleday, 1950); Isaac Stern and Chaim Potok, *My First 79 Years: Isaac Stern* (New York: Da Capo Press, 2001); Isaac Stern, *Brahms: Concerto for Violin/Double* (CBS/Epic/WTG Records, Audio CD Edition, 2002).

Stern College

Stern College is the college of arts and sciences for women at YESHIVA UNIVERSITY. It was established in 1954 through a major gift by Max Stern, the honorary chairman of the university's board of trustees.

Stern College is a unique Orthodox institution, emblematic of the MODERN ORTHODOX MOVEMENT embraced by Yeshiva University. It offers training in careers, professions, and continued graduate study. The women students are also trained to hold significant leadership responsibilities and fully participate in the modern world while maintaining Modern Orthodox values.

Stern College is located at Yeshiva University's New York City Midtown Center in the Murray Hill section of Manhattan. The college has on average 900 students per academic year. It offers academic majors in 19 arts and sciences disciplines, all leading to a bachelor of arts degree. It also awards an associate in arts degree in HEBREW language, literature, and culture. In addition, combined and joint degree programs are offered in several other disciplines, including engineering, dentistry, optometry, podiatry, Jewish studies, social work, nursing, and psychology, in conjunction with other Yeshiva University graduate schools and other leading universities.

Further reading: Samuel G. Freedman, *Jew vs. Jew: The Struggle for the Soul of American Jewry* (New York: Simon & Schuster, 2001); Stern College Web site URL: http://www.yu.edu/stern/, accessed August 18, 2004.

streimel (shtreiml)

A *streimel* is a round, flat fur hat often worn by Hasidic men (*see* HASIDISM) on the Sabbath (*see* SHABBAT) and festivals.

Over the centuries, Jews often adapted forms of dress that would keep them distinctive from non-Jews and help them remain separated from the prevailing non-Jewish culture. Hasidic men today often utilize centuries-old European dress for that purpose. Ironically, the *streimel* was a type of fur hat worn by Polish nobility (*see* POLAND) during the rise of the Hasidic movement. Most of the traditional Sabbath and festival clothing worn by Hasidic men dates back to the 18th and 19th centuries. Ultraconservative clothing among Hasidim, as among the Amish of Pennsylvania, can be seen as a rejection of modernity.

Further reading: Etan Diamond, *And I Will Dwell in Their Midst: Orthodox Jews in Suburbia* (Chapel Hill: University of North Carolina Press, 2000); Zalman Schachter Shalomi, *Wrapped in a Holy Flame: Teachings and Tales of the Hasidic Masters* (San Francisco, Calif.: Jossey-Bass, 2003).

Streisand, Barbra (b. 1942) *American singer, actress, and filmmaker*

Barbra Streisand was born on April 24, 1942, in Brooklyn, New York. After graduating from high school she moved to Manhattan to pursue an acting career. She began by singing in New York nightclubs, and in 1961 she appeared on *The Tonight Show*. In 1962, she debuted in the Broadway musical *I Can Get It for You Wholesale,* and she was subsequently nominated for a Tony Award. Streisand's Broadway success resulted in a record contract with Columbia Records, and by 1963 she was the top-selling woman singer in America. She would move on to major star success on Broadway, records and in the movies.

In 1983, Streisand directed and starred in *Yentl,* a film based on an Isaac Bashevis SINGER story about a Jewish girl who poses as a boy in order to study the TALMUD, sacred Jewish literature. The movie received mixed reviews, but Streisand proudly and publicly embraced her Judaism. Streisand is also a liberal political activist. She has vocally and financially supported the Democratic Party, as well as the causes of women's rights, gay rights, and environmentalism.

Streisand was married to actor Elliott Gould from 1963 to 1971, and they have a son, Jason. In 1998, Streisand married actor James Brolin. Streisand has publicly supported Jewish causes and created the Streisand Cultural Center at the B'NAI B'RITH HILLEL branch at the University of California at Los Angeles.

Further reading: Randall Riese, *Her Name Is Barbra: An Intimate Portrait of the Real Barbra Streisand* (Secaucus, N.J.: Carol Publishing, 1993); Ethlie Ann Vare, ed., *Diva: Barbra Streisand and the Making of a Superstar* (New York: Boulevard Books, 1996).

Stuyvesant, Peter (1592?–1672) *colonial Dutch administrator of New Netherland*

Peter Stuyvesant was the Dutch director-general for New Netherland (later New York State). In 1647 he arrived in the small colony of New Amsterdam (later New York City) where he established his autocratic rule. Stuyvesant was intolerant of perceived religious dissenters, like the Quakers and the Jews.

In September 1654, 23 Jews who had fled the Portuguese Inquisition in BRAZIL sailed into New Amsterdam harbor seeking refuge. Stuyvesant firmly barred them from landing, thus becoming

the first documented antisemite (*see* ANTISEMITISM) in American history. He referred to the Jews as enemies and blasphemers who should not be allowed to infect the colony.

Stuyvesant asked his superiors in the Dutch West India Company to let him expel the Jews. The Jews themselves, led by the dynamic Asser LEVI, appealed to the company, and sought support from their fellow Jews living in the NETHERLANDS. Levi and the Jews eventually prevailed, and they went on to found the first Jewish community in North America. However, they had to promise not to become a financial burden, and to take sole responsibility for each other. (Stuyvesant tried to keep Jews from civic leadership roles, but Levi was able on several occasions to get the Dutch company to overrule his orders.) The Jews accepted this obligation and settled in New Amsterdam. The pledge that the Jews made in exchange for the right to settle came to be known as the Stuyvesant Promise. New York City became home to many Jewish social service organizations that did not accept government funding until the 1930s, when the severity of the Great Depression made it impossible for any social welfare organization to survive without government aid.

Further reading: Edwin G. Burrows, *Gotham: A History of New York City to 1898* (New York and Oxford: Oxford University Press, 1998); David G. Dalin, "Judaism's War on Poverty," *Policy Review,* No. 85 (1997): 28; Russell Shorto, *The Island at the Center of the World: The Epic Story of Dutch Manhattan, the Forgotten Colony That Shaped America* (New York: Doubleday, 2004).

suffering servant

ISAIAH 53 contains a passage that refers to a "suffering servant." The identity of the servant has generated centuries of debate. Christians (*see* CHRISTIANITY) view the passage as a prophecy of JESUS OF NAZARETH; they point to verse 5 in particular as a reference to Jesus's torture and crucifixion. Christians link the suffering servant with the MESSIAH figure and argue that Jesus combines the two.

Jews traditionally view the suffering servant as distinct from the Messiah. The servant, they believe, is the people of ISRAEL, who suffer as a community around the world. Some interpreters have also argued that the servant is the prophet Isaiah himself, who suffers on behalf of the people. Academic scholars place this passage in the "Second Isaiah" material, and argue that the image of the servant reflects the suffering of Judeans in EXILE and in the ravaged city of JERUSALEM.

Further reading: C. G. Montefiore and H. Loewe, eds. and trans., "Suffering Servant," in *A Rabbinic Anthology* (London: Macmillan, 1938); Christian E. Hauer and William A. Young, *An Introduction to the Bible: A Journey into Three Worlds*, 4th ed. (Upper Saddle River, N.J.: Prentice Hall, 1998), 143–144; Christopher R. Noth, *The Suffering Servant in Deutero-Isaiah: An Historical and Critical Study* (London: Oxford University Press, 1956); *Tanakh: The Holy Scriptures* (Philadelphia and Jerusalem: Jewish Publication Society, 1985).

Sukkot

Sukkot is the Hebrew word for "huts" or "booths"; the holiday of Sukkot is thus often called in English the Festival of Booths. It is an ancient Jewish harvest and pilgrimage festival that commemorates the wanderings of the ISRAELITES in the wilderness before entering the PROMISED LAND.

Sukkot is celebrated each year on the 15th day of Tishri, the seventh Jewish month. According to the TANAKH, the Hebrew Bible, the festival lasts seven days, but an eighth day of solemn assembly, known as SHEMINI ATZERET, occurs at its conclusion. In the DIASPORA, a ninth day is celebrated as SIMCHAT TORAH.

The Tanakh stipulates numerous requirements for the festival of Sukkot. Jews must dwell in booths for seven days to commemorate the way they lived in the wilderness. There should be complete rest and no work on the first and eighth days. A palm frond and fragrant branches, together

called a *lulav*, and a citron, called an *etrog*, are ritually shaken before God in individual prayer and communal processions. It is a requirement to rejoice on Sukkot, possibly because it coincides with the grape harvest, suggesting an abundance of wine. It also marks the end of the period of judgment; by Sukkot, one has passed through the trials of ROSH HASHANAH and YOM KIPPUR and has come through unscathed. The book of Numbers also provides a set number of animals of various types as SACRIFICES on each day of the festival.

During the holiday of Sukkot, the *lulav* and *etrog* are shaken in a ritual nod to the four corners of the earth. Here a man stands in front of the Kotel, or Western Wall, during the holiday, ready to perform the ritual with a *lulav* made of a palm frond and fragrant branches. *(Moshe Milner, Government Press Office, The State of Israel)*

In biblical times, Sukkot was one of three main PILGRIMAGE FESTIVALS, the other two being PASSOVER and SHAVUOT. On each of these festivals, ISRAELITES would travel to the TEMPLE in JERUSALEM to offer the fruits of their harvest. On Passover they offered barley, on Shavuot wheat, and on Sukkot fruit. The connection between Sukkot and the fruit harvest may provide an added explanation for the booths (sukkahs), since farmers would often set up temporary dwellings in their fields during the harvest, also called *sukkot*.

After the destruction of the Temple, it became traditional to dwell in sukkahs built at home. Religious Jews eat all their meals in their sukkahs for the duration of the holiday, and many sleep there as well. The ancient RABBIS stipulated specific measurements and requirements for the sukkah, to ensure that it is a temporary structure. For example, one must be able to see the stars through the roof, and the sukkah may not have four complete walls. The roof of the sukkah is usually made up of fallen leaves and tree branches, called *s'chach*, which allows one to see the stars.

The sukkah developed theological meanings over time; the temporary nature of the sukkah places one under the protection of God, and its permeable walls and roof connect one directly to God's Creation. The rabbis dictated that the book of Ecclesiastes be read in the SYNAGOGUE on Sukkot due to its references to rejoicing, nature, and impermanence.

Further reading: Philip Goodman, *The Sukkot/Simhat Torah Anthology* (Philadelphia: Jewish Publication Society, 1988); Irving Greenberg, *The Jewish Way: Living the Holidays* (New York: Touchstone, 1988); Ronald H. Isaacs, *Every Person's Guide to Sukkot, Shemini Atzeret, and Simchat Torah* (Northvale, N.J.: Aronson, 2000); Jeffrey L. Rubenstein, *The History of Sukkot in the Second Temple and Rabbinic Periods* (Atlanta: Scholars Press, 1995).

summer camps, Jewish

A variety of Jewish summer camps operate in the UNITED STATES, offering different levels of Jewish education in a vacation setting, mostly for children and youth. Many Jewish community centers offer day camps, but Jewish educators consider the overnight camp to be the ideal, as campers can be immersed in Jewish life among other Jews the entire time. A few organizations offer family camps, such as the one found at the Brandeis-Bardin Institute in California.

Jewish educators and clergy consider the Jewish camp experience to be an important booster for those who attend afternoon SUPPLEMENTARY SCHOOLS, which are usually limited by severe time restraints. On the other hand, many parents who send their children to Jewish summer camps also send them to Jewish day schools (*see* JEWISH DAY SCHOOL MOVEMENT) as well. While most Jewish children do not attend Jewish summer camp, it is considered to be a positive, Jewish experience for those who do, helping to create Jewish memories that will stay with them into their adult lives.

The Catskill Mountains of New York and the Poconos of Pennsylvania are host to a plethora of Jewish summer camps, many of them oriented toward one of the main religious movements—ORTHODOX, REFORM, and CONSERVATIVE JUDAISM. Reform maintains the Union for Reform Judaism camps, while the Conservative movement has a network of camps under the name Ramah at locations throughout the UNITED STATES. There are also hundreds of nondenominational summer camps, summer youth programs, and camps sponsored by nonreligious Jewish institutions. HADASSAH operates Camp Young Judaea, for example, which promotes ZIONISM as well as general Jewish values and rituals.

Whether a Jewish camp teaches a specific ideology or general Jewish life skills, the opportunity for children to experience Jewish life and socialize with other Jewish children in a concentrated period of time is considered priceless by Jewish educators. Such positive Jewish experiences can help a child develop a strong JEWISH IDENTITY, which is difficult in a pluralistic society that exposes children to many competing influences during the school year.

Further reading: Anita Diamant, *How to Be a Jewish Parent: A Practical Handbook for Family Life* (New York: Schocken Books, 2000); Amy L. Sales and Leonard Sales, *How Goodly Are Thy Tents: Summer Camps As Jewish Socializing Experiences* (Hanover, N.H.: University Press of New England, 2004).

supplementary school

Supplementary schools provide formal after-school religious instruction to American Jewish children who attend public or non-Jewish private schools during the day. While some Jewish parents choose to send their children to a Jewish day school (*see* JEWISH DAY SCHOOL MOVEMENT), many prefer public schools. When it became clear, as early as the beginning of the 19th century, that most Jewish parents were not capable of imparting a Jewish education to their children at home, SYN-AGOGUES and communities set up what are now called Hebrew schools, religious schools, or supplementary schools to provide that education.

Most supplementary schools are run by synagogues, but others, called community schools, provide for the children of several synagogues in a given community. It is estimated that close to 75 percent of Jewish children who receive any kind of formal Jewish education do so in supplementary schools.

Rebecca GRATZ (1781–1869) created the first serious Jewish supplementary school in 1818 in Philadelphia. Her first effort failed, but she tried again, using the Christian Sunday school model. She created the Hebrew Sunday School Society of Philadelphia, and served as its president until 1864. The school welcomed all children, and was tuition free.

In the UNITED STATES most synagogues offer formal supplementary schools for families who are members. Many Jewish families join synagogues primarily to send their children to the supplementary school. Most children attend until the age of their BAR/BAT MITZVAH, usually 12 or 13. A few institutions offer a supplementary Hebrew high school, mostly in large Jewish communities such as Boston and New York.

The content and form of instruction depends largely on the number of hours parents are willing to have their children spend. Other after-school activities such as sports often interfere with the time available. Most schools strive to teach Hebrew literacy and language, SIDDUR (prayer book) skills, holiday observances, customs, Jewish history, and about Israel. Many schools require that children attend services on the Sabbath (*see* SHABBAT) a certain number of times each year.

The mission of these supplementary schools is to teach Jewish children the joys of being Jewish and imbue within them a desire to live a Jewish life, but the limited time and commitment from families often stymies this mission. Students often spend most of their limited time in acquiring basic prayer-book skills and Hebrew literacy, because these are the subjects parents feel are necessary for their child's bar or bat mitzvah.

Many Jewish educators and rabbis have tried to find new, energizing formats for supplementary schools. Many synagogues have instituted family education programs so that families can learn together and parents can model learning behavior for their children. Most Jewish educators who work in supplementary school settings admit that the part-time school cannot come close to providing the Jewish education and JEWISH IDENTITY one finds in a day school setting.

Further reading: Barry Chazan, "Education in the Synagogue: The Transformation of the Supplementary School," in *The American Synagogue: A Sanctuary Transformed* edited by Jack Wertheimer (Hanover, N.H.: University Press of New England, 1987); Burton I. Cohen, *Case Studies in Jewish School Management: Applying Educational Theory to School Practice* (West Orange, N.J.: Behrman House, Inc., 1992); Alexander M. Dushkin and Uriah Z. Engelman, *Jewish Education in the United States* (New York: American Association for Jewish Education, 1959); Joseph Reimer, *Succeeding at Jewish*

Education: How One Synagogue Made It Work (Philadelphia: Jewish Publication Society, 1997).

Sura

Sura was one of the two leading centers of Talmudic study in BABYLONIA, along with PUMBEDITA. The academy at Sura was founded in the year 219 C.E. by Rav Abba Arika, who had been trained in PALESTINE. Sura rivaled the Palestinian Talmudic centers, and it was at Sura that the Babylonian TALMUD was compiled in the sixth and seventh centuries C.E. The academy survived for over 700 years. In the ninth century, SAADIA GAON (882–942) was the head of the rabbinic academy at Sura.

Further reading: Lawrence Schiffman, *From Text to Tradition: A History of Second Temple and Rabbinic Judaism* (Hoboken, N.J.: Ktav Publishing House, 1991); Adin Steinsaltz, *The Essential Talmud,* trans. Chaya Galai (New York: BasicBooks, 1976).

swastika

The swastika was adopted as the emblem for the Nazi Party of GERMANY in 1920. It is a hated symbol to Jews, as it represents those who tried to exterminate the Jewish people during the HOLOCAUST.

The swastika is an ancient geometric symbol found at various archaeological sites in different parts of the world. It has appeared in many cultures around the world, including CHINA, ENGLAND, GERMANY, Greece, and INDIA. The name is derived from the Sanskrit word *svastika,* or "well-being." Before 1920, the swastika symbol was commonly used on mundane items, such as cigar labels, business emblems, and poker chips. During World War I an orange swastika on a red field was the shoulder patch for the American 45th Division.

Adolf HITLER had the Nazi party adopt the emblem, which he believed to be of ancient "Aryan" origin. It was placed on armbands, flags, posters, and bunting. Hitler posited an ancient Aryan race as ancestors of the German people and the source of their racial "purity." Some German ultra-nationalists had begun to use the swastika in the mid-19th century. Due to its Nazi associations, the symbol is never used today (except by neo-Nazi groups).

Further reading: Steven Heller and Jeff Roth, *The Swastika: Symbol Beyond Redemption?* (New York: Allworth Press, 2000); Malcolm Quinn, *The Swastika* (New York: Routledge, 1995).

sweatshop

A sweatshop is a factory or shop where people work under harsh conditions, with inadequate ventilation and few safety precautions. In the 19th and early 20th centuries small and then large sweatshops became common in the UNITED STATES. When between 1880 and 1924 more than 2 million poor Jewish immigrants came to the country, many found employment in such sweatshops, especially in the garment industry. The conditions of these sweatshops affected the lives of hundreds of thousands of Jewish immigrants, some of whom were instrumental in changing labor conditions in the United States.

Many Jews initially lived in TENEMENT quarters with small sweatshops in residential apartments, which kept workers divided and unable to unionize. However, by the start of the 20th century women's clothing became one of the largest consumer-goods industries in the country, and larger, more efficient factories were needed in order to compete. These factories were still accurately referred to as sweatshops. The larger number of employees made it easier for labor leaders to unionize the garment industry. Eventually these unions, mostly led by Jews, helped create pressure for reform in the United States, resulting in laws that made sweatshops illegal.

At the forefront of this struggle were activists of the International Ladies Garment Workers Union (ILGWU). Following the major catastrophe of the TRIANGLE FIRE in New York City on March 25, 1911, the ILGWU, joined by its union cohorts, brought immediate pressure to bear for better working conditions for sweatshop workers and better fire inspections. Jewish labor leaders such as David Dubinsky and Samuel Gompers were instrumental in changing the nature of factory work in the United States.

Further reading: Daniel E. Bender and Richard A. Greenwald, eds., *Sweatshop USA* (New York: Routledge, 2003); Hasia R. Diner, *Lower East Side: A Jewish Place in America* (Princeton and Oxford: Princeton University Press, 2000); David von Drehle, *Triangle: The Fire That Changed America* (New York: Atlantic Monthly Press, 2003).

synagogue

A synagogue is a Jewish house of worship. In Hebrew the common term is *bet knesset* ("house of assembly") or *bet tefillah* ("house of prayer"). The synagogue is often referred to by many American Jews by the Yiddish word *shul*. In liberal Judaism, the term often used is *temple*. The word *synagogue* itself is from the Greek, meaning "place of assembly."

Synagogues have served three main functions throughout the course of Jewish history: worship, study, and gathering place. A scholarly debate has long been waged around the origin of the synagogue. Some trace the institution back to the sixth century B.C.E. These scholars believe that during the first Exile in Babylonia, the synagogue became the central place for Jews to gather to pray and hear readings from the Torah. There is no textual evidence for the existence of a synagogue until the third century B.C.E., when a Greek document from Alexandria in Egypt referred to prayer houses. Archeologists have uncovered a first century B.C.E. building on the Aegean island of Delos that bears Greek inscriptions including the words "highest God" and "prayer house," both terms later used in synagogues.

The oldest known synagogue in Israel dates from the first century C.E.; an inscription was found in Jerusalem that revealed the existence of the synagogue and mentioned some of its functions,

This synagogue stands in Nashville, Tennessee. Synagogues have a variety of architectural styles and this one displays a Star of David on its front. *(Courtesy J. Gordon Melton)*

including reading of the law, teaching the commandments, and serving as a guest house. The New Testament treats synagogues as simply gathering places for Jews. Over the centuries synagogues have become formal buildings, primarily for worship and study. The Talmud states that a synagogue built by a Jewish community should never be sold unless it has to raise money to save a Jewish life, for such was the holiness of the constructed building.

The synagogue serves as a gathering place for Jews to this day. It is common to find in the synagogue an ark, or sacred cabinet, with at least two Torah scrolls, located on the bima, a raised dais. Traditionally the ark is set in a location so that the worshippers face East, the direction of Jerusalem, the site of the ancient TEMPLE. Above the ark is the *ner tamid* (ETERNAL LIGHT). Most synagogues have at least one RABBI, and many also have a CANTOR to lead services. The modern synagogue is utilized for prayer, study, communal programming, and educational programs. Most modern synagogues house SUPPLEMENTARY SCHOOLS, as well.

In the 1970s and 1980s it was common for some American synagogues to build synagogue centers (*see* KAPLAN, MORDECAI; RECONSTRUCTIONIST JUDAISM), which included space for a variety of community activities, such as sports and art programs. Many of the synagogue centers housed complete gymnasiums and cultural centers.

When building a synagogue, congregations will usually aim for pleasing architecture and design, but ostentation is often frowned upon. A common form of Jewish art for synagogues has been stained glass windows, but they do not show human forms, to avoid creating "graven images," prohibited by HALAKHAH, Jewish law.

Further reading: Steven Fine, ed., *Sacred Realm: The Emergence of the Synagogue in the Ancient World* (New York: Oxford University Press, 1996); Neil Folberg and Yom Tov Assis, *And I Shall Dwell Among Them: Historic Synagogues of the World* (New York: Aperture, 1995); Martin Goodman, ed., *Jews in a Graeco-Roman World* (Oxford: Oxford University Press, 1998); Jack Wertheimer, ed., *The American Synagogue: A Sanctuary Transformed* (Hanover, N.H., and London: University Press of New England, 1987).

synagogue centers *See* RECONSTRUCTIONIST JUDAISM; SYNAGOGUE.

syncretism

Syncretism refers to the blending of two or more religious traditions by a group or culture. It was a particular threat to Judaism in the biblical period, when the ISRAELITES occupied lands inhabited by peoples who worshipped foreign gods. Commandments discouraging idolatrous practices or marrying foreign wives were designed to head off syncretism. Biblical accounts of purification drives after the first EXILE suggest that syncretism had been a problem during the Jews' stay in BABYLONIA as well. Such problems continued through the Hellenistic (*see* HELLENISM) and Roman (*see* ROME) periods, sparking conflicts within Jewish communities about accommodating the cultures of occupying powers.

Further reading: Janet Liebman Jacobs, *Hidden Heritage: The Legacy of the Crypto-Jews* (Berkeley: University of California Press, 2002); Jon D. Levenson, "The Problem with Salad Bowl Religion," in *First Things* 78 (Dec. 1997): 10–12; JoAnn Scurlock, "One Hundred Sixty-Seven B.C.E.: Hellenism or Reform?" in *Journal for the Study of Judaism* 31, no. 2 (2000): 125–161.

Szold, Henrietta (1860–1945) *publisher, editor, Zionist leader, and founder of Hadassah*

Henrietta Szold was born in 1860, in Baltimore, Maryland. Her father, Benjamin, was a RABBI, who taught his daughter HEBREW and German and exposed her to the study of Jewish texts. As a teenager, Szold's language abilities allowed her to find work as a translator and editor. She pursued teaching and wrote for many Jewish journals.

In 1888, Szold became the only woman among the 10 members of the JEWISH PUBLICATION SOCIETY'S (JPS) publication committee. Szold worked with Cyrus ADLER (1863–1940) on the first JPS publication, *Outlines of Jewish History*. She edited and translated Heinrich GRAETZ'S voluminous *History of the Jews* from German to English. Five years after serving on the committee she took the position of executive secretary, a job she would hold for almost 20 years. She was a major contributor to the editing, translating, and publishing of some of the greatest American Jewish literary works. In addition, Szold filled in significant role in the production of the first American Jewish yearbook. She remained its sole editor from 1904 to 1908.

But Szold's influence did not end with publishing. She was one of the first great leaders of American ZIONISM. In 1898, she became the only woman member of the executive committee of the Federation of American Zionists. After she visited PALESTINE in 1909, her Zionist fervor became even stronger. She founded HADASSAH, a Zionist organization for women; under her direct leadership it soon became the largest and strongest American Zionist group. Hadassah implemented support systems for both education and health in PALESTINE. The organization made great efforts to settle new immigrants in Palestine as well.

In 1920 Szold made ALIYAH, that is, she went to live permanently in ERETZ YISRAEL. There she took charge of Hadassah's medical programs. Szold spent the last 25 years of her life dedicated to helping the Jews and Arabs of Palestine. Her tireless labors on behalf of the Jews, and especially the youth of Palestine, earned her the title "mother of the YISHUV" (the Jewish community in Palestine). Szold died in 1945, three years before the new Jewish state of Israel was born. The Hadassah hospitals she created remain among the best hospitals in Israel.

Further reading: Nachum Tim Gidal, *Henrietta Szold: A Documentation in Photos and Text* (Jerusalem and New York: Gefen Publishing, 1997); Alexander L. Levin, ed., *Henrietta Szold and Youth Aliyah: Family Letters, 1934–1944* (New York: Herzl Press, 1986); Marvin Lowenthal, *Henrietta Szold: Life and Letters* (Westport, Conn.: Greenwood Press, 1975).

A Zionist leader and founder of Hadassah, Henrietta Szold led women to establish hospitals and educational institutions in Palestine in the early 20th century. *(Library of Congress)*

T

Tabernacle *See* MISHKAN.

taharat ha-mishpacha

HALAKHAH (Jewish law) regulates the days of the month when a husband and wife may be physically intimate, using the laws of family purity, or *taharat ha-mishpacha*. The RABBIS prohibited all physical intimacy (even nonsexual) during the five or so days of menstruation and for the week after the conclusion of the cycle, known as the "clean days." These laws were based upon precepts in the Book of Leviticus (*see* TORAH), barring a menstruating woman from having sexual relations with her husband.

In rabbinic literature, a woman who is menstruating is referred to as a *niddah*. One tractate of the TALMUD is dedicated to the laws of *niddah*. Over the centuries, ultra-Orthodox Judaism (*see* ORTHODOX JUDAISM) has extended the prohibitions of *taharat ha-mishpacha* to include any form of physical contact between a woman who is *niddah* and her husband. Ultra-Orthodox couples will refrain from sharing a bed during these 12 days. At the conclusion of the prohibited period of time, the woman will go to a MIKVAH, the Jewish ritual bath, and immerse herself undressed, so as to ritually purify her body. She recites a blessing to

God, acknowledging the commandment to fulfill ritual immersion. Traditionally, a woman will also go to the *mikvah* prior to her wedding and after childbirth.

Different reasons are offered for the laws of *taharat ha-mishpacha*. Many believe they were designed to make the woman sexually available to her husband only during ovulation, thus increasing the potential for procreation. Others believe it was a rabbinic device to keep a marriage sexually fresh and healthy and encourage fidelity. Clearly, the basic intention is to imbue the realm of human sexuality with holiness.

Many in the Orthodox tradition scrupulously observe the laws of *taharat ha-mishpacha*. The overall laws are generally not observed within liberal Judaism, with the possible exception of actual abstinence from sexual intercourse during the woman's menstruation period.

Further reading: David Biale, *Eros and the Jews: From Biblical Israel to Contemporary America* (New York: Basic Books, 1992); Hayim Halevy Donin, *To Be A Jew: A Guide to Jewish Observance in Contemporary Life* (New York: Basic Books, 1972); Blu Greenberg, *On Women & Judaism* (Philadelphia: Jewish Publication Society, 1998); Judith Hauptman, *Rereading the Rabbis: A Woman's Voice* (Boulder, Colo.: Westview Press, 1998).

tallit (pl.: *tallitot*)

The Hebrew word *tallit* originally meant "cloak," but it long ago became limited to the four-cornered prayer shawl worn during prayer. Traditionally only men are required to don a *tallit,* but recently women in egalitarian (*see* EGALITARIANISM) congregations have begun to wear them as well, while in some Reform (*see* REFORM JUDAISM) congregations the men choose not to wear them. In some Orthodox communities (*see* ORTHODOX JUDAISM) only married men wear a *tallit;* in German and Sephardi Orthodox communities, however, all boys who have had a bar mitzvah (*see* BAR/BAT MITZVAH) wear a *tallit.* While one generally wears a *tallit* over one's shoulders, some choose to place it over their heads to express awe in the presence of God.

A special blessing is said as one puts on a *tallit;* the prayer is often embroidered onto a band at the top called an *atarah.* A *tallit* includes fringes known as TZITZIT, to fulfill the commandment to put fringes on one's garment so as to remember the commandments (*see* MITZVAH). Observant Jewish men often wear a smaller *tallit* under their shirts, a vest with tzitzit, so as to keep God's commandments in mind all day.

It is traditional to wrap a Jew in a *tallit* for burial, but in that case, the fringes of one corner are cut off. Some Jewish communities, mostly Sephardic, use a *tallit* at wedding ceremonies as well; it serves the function of a CHUPPAH, or canopy.

Further reading: Hayim Halevy Donin, *To Be A Jew: A Guide to Jewish Observance in Contemporary Life* (New York: Basic Books, 1972); Sholom Gross, *Tzitzis Laws: Critical Laws and Observations* (Brooklyn, N.Y.: Mosad Brochas Tova, 1981); Aharon Verthaim, *Law and Custom in Hasidism* (Hoboken, N.J.: Ktav, 1992).

Talmud

Second only to the Hebrew Bible (*see* TANAKH), the Talmud (Hebrew for "study" or "learning") is the most important sacred text in TRADITIONAL JUDAISM. It is a vast, multivolume compilation of legal, ethical, and allegorical discussions and debates conducted by the ancient RABBIS over a period of several hundred years. As such, it is a historical record of the founding generations of rabbinic Judaism (*see* RABBI; RABBINIC LAW), and the basic source of Jewish law as still observed by Orthodox Jews.

There are actually two versions of the Talmud. One is known as the Babylonian Talmud (Bavli), and the other is known as either the Palestinian or Jerusalem Talmud (Yerushalmi). The names reflect their origins; although they share a great deal of material, the Bavli largely represents the work of the great academies of BABYLONIA, while the Yerushalmi reflects the discussions at the academies at various cities in PALESTINE. The Babylonian Talmud was finalized around 500 C.E., approximately 100 years after the JERUSALEM Talmud. The Babylonian commentaries were more expansive and comprehensive, and this became the authoritative Talmud within rabbinic Judaism.

Both Talmuds depend on the MISHNAH as their foundation text. The Mishnah is the collection of teachings of the TANNAIM, the rabbis who studied and taught in Palestine around the first two centuries of the Common Era (the Tannaitic period); it was compiled and published in 220 C.E.; the full text of the Mishnah is included in every edition of the Talmud for easy reference. The GEMARA, the other major section of the Talmud, consists of commentary and elaboration on the Mishnah; it is attributed to the AMORAIM, the rabbis who lived during the third to the fifth centuries (the Amoraic Period). These commentaries were originally made orally, carefully memorized by scribes, and redacted, or edited, into a written version in the middle of the sixth century. In common parlance, the terms *Gemara* and *Talmud* are used interchangeably.

Traditional Judaism teaches that God's revelation to the Jews included both the TORAH, the WRITTEN LAW said to be recorded by MOSES at MOUNT SINAI, and the "ORAL LAW," which also came from God and explained how to interpret the Written Law. The Oral Law was passed down through the generations but eventually had to be written down in digest form as the Mishnah. The rabbis of the Gemara also cited many ancient oral traditions that were not included in the Mishnah. The entire Talmud is thus considered to be the Oral Law.

Over the centuries, certain post-Talmudic rabbinic commentaries were found to be useful in the study of Talmud. Today, Talmud scholars frequently use the medieval commentaries of RASHI, TOSAFOT, and RAMBAM to elucidate their reading of the texts; many of these commentaries are included in the standard editions of the Talmud. A modern commentary widely used today was written by Israeli scholar Adin STEINSALTZ and his students.

The Talmud is divided in the same manner as the Mishnah, with six sections, and 63 tractates, each one primarily devoted to a different topic. The style of the Talmud is unique. It records the free-association discussions of the ancient rabbis, or sages, of many time periods. Part of the genius of the Talmud is that individuals who did not live in the same era often appear in the same discussion. In addition, even though a tractate is nominally about one subject, other material is often covered because of the fluid nature of discussion. Because of this, the Talmud contains cross-references, not unlike the links on a modern-day Web page.

In recent times, many observant Jews around the world participate in a program called *daf yomi*, or "daily page." They study one full page of Talmud every day—the same page around the world. The practice began in 1923 under the leadership of the Rav of Lublin, Rabbi Meir Shapiro, who believed that the Jewish people could be united in their daily study of a page of Talmud.

Further reading: Max Kedushin, *The Rabbinic Mind* (Binghamton: Global Publications at SUNY Binghamton, 2001/1972); David Kraemer, *The Mind of the Talmud: An Intellectual History of the Bavli* (New York and Oxford: Oxford University Press, 1990); Jacob Neusner, *Sources and Traditions: Types of Compositions in the Talmud of Babylonia* (Atlanta, Ga.: Scholars Press, 1992); Jacob Neusner, trans., *The Talmud of Babylonia* (Lanham, Md.: University Press of America, 1985).

This child sits and studies a page of Talmud in a yeshiva, a school for Jewish learning. *(Moshe Milner, Government Press Office, The State of Israel)*

Tanakh

Tanakh is an acronym for TORAH, NEVI'IM (Prophets), and KETUVIM (Writings). Combined, these three collections of canonical books make up the Tanakh, sometimes referred to as the Hebrew Bible or the Written Torah. In Christian communities, this body of works is referred to as the Old Testament.

tannaim (sing.: *tanna*)

Tannaim (Hebrew for "repeaters" or "reciters") were the Jewish sages from the Tannaitic period (10 C.E.–220 C.E.), which followed the death of HILLEL and lasted until the editing of the MISHNAH.

The *tannaim*, whose opinions, thoughts, and ideas are recorded in the Mishnah, are distinguished from the later AMORAIM, whose works appear in the GEMARA, the commentary on the Mishnah.

The *tannaim* were primarily scholars and teachers. Among their major literary achievements in addition to the Mishnah were the TOSEFTA, and the halakhic (legal) MIDRASH (*see* HALAKHAH). These works are together recognized to be the primary authoritative interpretations of the ORAL LAW.

Three of the best-known *tannaim* were Rabbi AKIVA, Rabbi Meir, and Rabbi JUDAH HA-NASI. The term RABBI was originally utilized in application only to the *tannaim*.

Further reading: Alfred J. Kolatch, *Masters of the Talmud: Their Lives and Views* (Middle Village, N.Y.: Jonathan David Publishers, 2002); Richard Lee Kalmin, *Sages, Stories, Authors and Editors in Rabbinic Babylonia* (Atlanta, Ga.: Scholar's Press, 1994); Adin Steinsaltz, *The Essential Talmud* (New York: Basic Books, 1976); H. L. Strack and G. Stemberger, *Introduction to the Talmud and Midrash* (Minneapolis: Fortress Press, 1992).

Tashlich

After the Mincha, or afternoon service, on ROSH HASHANAH, it is customary for Jews to perform the ceremony of Tashlich (Hebrew for "to throw"). People throw scraps of bread representing their sins from the past year into the nearest body of water. Generally a group will gather together near the SYNAGOGUE and walk together to the closest river, lake, or ocean. Like the scapegoat ceremony of ancient times, this ritual sends sins away so that one can be unburdened and start off the year with a clean slate. While tossing the crumbs into the water to be carried away, Jews recite prayers asking God to forgive and forget their sins. The tashlich practice has bothered many rabbis over the centuries because of its superstitious aspects and because of the possibility that this kind of social gathering could lead to new sins such as LASHON HARA, gossip. Neverthe-less, it has remained popular across the spectrum of Jewish religious communities.

Further reading: Shmuel Yosef Agnon, *Days of Awe* (New York: Schocken Books, 1965); Irving Greenberg, *The Jewish Way: Living the Holidays* (New York: Touchstone, 1988).

Technion

The Technion, or the ISRAEL Institute of Technology, in HAIFA, is the leading engineering and technology school in the country.

The school was initially planned to open in 1912 with the support of Jews from overseas. However, a dispute broke out between the majority of financial backers, who wanted German to be the language of instruction, and a vocal minority who insisted on HEBREW, which delayed the opening. The school was further delayed by the start of World War I. After the war, Hebrew officially became the language of instruction.

The Technion finally opened in 1924 in midtown Haifa. In 1953, the growing school relocated to a larger site in Haifa on Mt. Carmel. It now has approximately 12,000 students and more than 600 faculty members. The majority of Israeli-educated scientists and engineers are graduates of the Technion.

Over the years, the Technion has excelled in developing and promoting new technologies. Its leadership has helped create the highest concentration of high-tech start-up companies anywhere in the world outside of California's Silicon Valley. Some 54 percent of Israel's industrial exports, and 26 percent of all exports, come from the high-tech industry.

The Technion faculty itself can boast many outstanding scientific achievements, such as developing a conductive wire one-thousandth the thickness of a human hair; creating a new class of materials called quasiperiodic crystals; assisting with the successful development of the Israeli space program; devising the Lempel/Ziv algorithm, which has become the world standard for data compression; providing genetic proof that all Jews belonging to the *kohen* (priestly) (*see* KOHANIM) lineage are descendants of the first biblical high priest, AARON; discovering the crucial role of the enzyme "ubiquitin" in the process of protein cell degradation; developing an alternative low-cost method for electricity production and water desalination; discovering how to create "super-iron" batteries, and developing Rasagaline, a new drug against Parkinson's disease.

In 2004, Professors Avram Hershko and Aaron Ciechanover, both faculty at the Technion, won the Nobel Prize in chemistry. Their research on ubiquitin and protein cell degradation earned them the prize.

Further reading: Carl Alpert, *Technion: The Story of Israel's Institute of Technology* (New York: American Technion Society, 1982); Technion Web site URL: http://www.technion.ac.il/, accessed August 20, 2004.

tefillin

Both *Exodus* and Deuteronomy (*see* TORAH) command Jews to bind God's commandments (*see* MITZVAH) "as a sign upon your hands and let them be a reminder between your eyes." To enable Jews to fulfill this commandment, the RABBIS invented tefillin, or phylacteries. These are small boxes containing biblical verses on tiny parchment scrolls; the attached leather straps can be bound around one's arm and forehead.

The wearing of tefillin is perceived within rabbinic tradition to be one of the three signs of the Jew's COVENANT with God; the others are BRIT MILAH, ritual circumcision of males at eight days old, and the SHABBAT, or Sabbath. Tefillin are traditionally worn by men, but in liberal Judaism, some women have embraced the custom.

Within the black boxes are four passages from the TORAH known together as the Kriat SHEMA. The handwritten scroll is the same as the one that is inserted in a MEZUZAH, which Jews place on their doorposts. The passages speak of the Jewish embrace of ethical MONOTHEISM, the belief in a God

who rules over nature, supplies humans with laws, and acts through history.

Initially the custom was to wear the tefillin all day, but over the centuries the custom arose to wear it only during morning prayers. On the Sabbath and festivals tefillin are not worn, since the act of celebrating those days constitutes the sign of the covenant in itself.

After binding on the tefillin, the worshipper takes the arm strap and forms the HEBREW word *Shaddai*, one of God's names, on his or her hand. The tradition also calls for wearing the tefillin on one's weaker arm, signifying that embracing God

An eastern European immigrant sails to Haifa from Cyprus. He prays with *tallit* and tefillin. The tefillin are black leather straps wrapped around the man's head and arm. *(Government Press Office, The State of Israel)*

strengthens the pious one. After binding the arm tefillin, one recites a blessing for the commandment to wrap oneself with the tefillin. After binding the forehead tefillin, one recites a blessing for the commandment to sanctify oneself by wearing the tefillin. When writing Shaddai on the hand, the Jew recites two verses from the book of Hosea, which state that the individual is betrothed to God in faith.

Further reading: Aryeh Kaplan, *Tefillin* (New York: Union of Orthodox Jewish Congregations of American, 1993); Abraham E. Milgram, *Jewish Worship* (Philadelphia: Jewish Publication Society, 1971); Moshe Chanina Neiman, *Tefillin: An Illustrated Guide* (New York: Philipp Feldheim, 1995); *Tanakh: The Holy Scriptures* (Philadelphia and Jerusalem: Jewish Publication Society, 1985).

Tehillim (Psalms)

The Book of Tehillim, or Psalms, is a collection of 150 songs; it is in KETUVIM, the Writings or third section of the Hebrew Bible, the TANAKH. The book is divided into five sections, beginning at Psalms 1, 42, 78, 90 and 107. At the conclusion of each section of tehillim a special prayer of thanksgiving is presented. The themes of Tehillim vary. There are songs that teach moral lessons, praise and thank God, honor festivals, celebrate ISRAELITE history, and exalt certain individuals who played significant roles in prior Jewish history.

According to rabbinic tradition (*see* RABBI), Tehillim was compiled by King DAVID; he wrote most of the songs himself, but included some by other authors, including MOSES. Tradition also states that the Levites, the servants in the TEMPLE, sang a psalm for every day of the week and for Shabbat and festivals. The main proof text for David's authorship is 2 Samuel 23:1, which calls David the "sweet singer in Israel."

Modern biblical scholarship has rejected the Davidic authorship of most of the songs. Critical scholars note that some psalms describe events that took place long after David's death. The dating of most individual songs is difficult; they may range from the early Israelite times to the post-biblical period of the MACCABEES.

From a religious Jew's perspective, the dating is not relevant to the poetic expressiveness and relevance of the tehillim. The psalms are commonly used by religious Jews, especially women, to articulate their spiritual and emotional feelings. Certain psalms are assigned to daily, Sabbath, and holiday services (*see* PRAYER). Appropriate psalms are studied during MOURNING or when VISITING THE SICK, *bikur cholim* in Hebrew. In addition, quotations from Psalms appear in many prayers found throughout the traditional SIDDUR, or prayer book. Jews have developed a rich variety of melodies for various psalms; however, the most ancient cantillations (*see* TROPE) are no longer known.

Further reading: Eli Cashdan, *The Book of Psalms: Sefer Tehillim* (London: Minerva Press, Ltd., 1997); S. E. Gillingham, *The Poems and Psalms of the Hebrew Bible* (Oxford and New York: Oxford University Press, 1994); Norman Gottwald, *The Hebrew Bible: A Socio-Literary Introduction* (Philadelphia: Fortress Press, 1985); *Tanakh: The Holy Scriptures* (Philadelphia and Jerusalem: Jewish Publication Society, 1985).

Tel Aviv

Tel Aviv was ISRAEL's first modern city. It was founded by 60 Jewish families in 1909 on sand dunes near the ancient city of Jaffa on the Mediterranean coast. The founders originally called it Ahuzat Bayit, but a year later they changed the name to Tel Aviv (Hebrew for "hill of spring"), a name that appears in the book of Ezekiel 3:15.

Many of the initial residents were expelled by the Turks during World War I, but Jews returned when the British took over PALESTINE after the war. The population of Tel Aviv grew with immigration, and with Jews who began to leave Jaffa because of Arab violence. In the period right before the ISRAELI WAR OF INDEPENDENCE, Tel Aviv was routinely shelled by Arab troops, but Jewish soldiers secured the city, and two days later Israel's Declaration of Independence was signed at the home of Tel Aviv mayor Meir Dizengoff.

Tel Aviv served as the temporary capital of Israel until West JERUSALEM was secured in 1949; it still houses the headquarters of the Israel Defense Forces. Because the 1947 PARTITION PLAN of the UNITED NATIONS marked Jerusalem as an "international city," most countries in the world have not recognized Jerusalem as the capital of Israel and maintain their official diplomatic headquarters in Tel Aviv. Even so, it is Jerusalem, not Tel Aviv, that is the capital of Israel.

Presently, Tel Aviv is the second-largest city in Israel, after Jerusalem, with a population of more than 360,000 residents. The metropolitan area is the country's largest, with well over 1 million people. It is Israel's main business center, and its primary cultural center for museums and the arts. The Israeli Stock Exchange is located in Tel Aviv, and the Diamond Exchange operates in Ramat Gan, adjacent to Tel Aviv. Tel Aviv also houses Tel Aviv University.

The social, retail, and dining center of Tel Aviv is called Dizengoff, after the city's first mayor. Like modern American cities, Tel Aviv has expanded with suburban sprawl, including the settlements of Bnei Brak, Petach Tikvah, Ramat Aviv, Ramat Gan, and Savyon. For the younger Israelis, Tel Aviv is the primary location for the social scene, and it is also a major tourist hot spot because of its beaches, luxury hotels, and night life.

Further reading: Iris Graicer and Izhak Schnell, "Rejuvenation of Population in Tel-Aviv Inner City," in *The Geographical Journal* 160, no. 2 (1994): 185; Nahum Gutman, *Path of the Orange Peels: Adventures in the Early Days of Tel Aviv* (New York: Dodd, Mead, 1979); Mark LeVine, *Overthrowing Geography: Jaffa, Tel Aviv, and the Struggle for Palestine, 1880–1948* (Berkeley and Los Angeles: University of California Press, 2004); Joachim Schlor, *Tel Aviv* (London: Reaktion Books, 1999).

Temple

Construction on the first Temple (Beit ha-Mikdash), built by King SOLOMON, was begun in JERUSALEM in approximately 965 B.C.E. It became the central religious, civil, and social institution in Judaism until its destruction in 586 B.C.E. Solomon's father, King DAVID, had wanted to build the Temple, according to the TANAKH, the Hebrew Bible, but God forbade him from doing so because there was blood on his hands. (David had sent Uriah into danger on the front lines of war to ensure Uriah's death so that David could marry Bathsheba, Uriah's wife.)

Solomon's Temple included three main areas: the outer court, the inner court, and the HOLY OF HOLIES (Kodesh Kodashim). Sacrificial rituals (*see* SACRIFICE) were performed in the inner and outer court; the Holy of Holies contained the ARK of the COVENANT, and was not entered by anyone except the HIGH PRIEST, and then only on YOM KIPPUR, the Day of Atonement. The Temple was a magnificent structure for its time, 180 feet long, 90 feet wide, and 50 feet high, made of the finest cedar and stone available. Unfortunately, this monument was built at a huge cost. Solomon levied exorbitant taxes to pay for the project, and drafted thousands of laborers.

The first Temple was destroyed by the Babylonians (*see* BABYLONIA) in 586 C.E., but the exiles were permitted to build a second Temple when they returned approximately 50 years later. King HEROD expanded the second Temple, adding features including the royal portico. The Romans destroyed this Temple while suppressing a massive Jewish uprising in the late 60s C.E. The ninth of Av, TISHA B'AV, commemorates the destruction of the second Temple. All that survives of the Temple is the Temple Mount, the vast terrace built by Herod to accommodate the expanded complex; the Western or Wailing Wall (in Hebrew, KOTEL), a section of the terrace's retaining wall, is considered the holiest site where Jews can pray.

When the Muslims (*see* ISLAM) took control of Jerusalem, they built mosques on the Temple Mount. As a result, the site has become the focus of an ongoing conflict, as both Muslims and Jews vie for access to and control of their holy sites. To this day, Orthodox Jews (*see* ORTHODOX JUDAISM) pray daily for the restoration of the Temple. Small groups of radical Jews are working to prepare service vessels and priestly garments for a restored Temple.

Further reading: Menahem Haran, *Temples and Temple-Service in Ancient Israel* (Oxford: Oxford University Press, 1978); Baruch A. Levine, *In the Presence of the Lord* (Leiden: Brill, 1974); Jacob Neusner, trans., *The Mishnah: A New Translation* (New Haven, Conn.: Yale University Press, 1991); Lawrence H. Schiffman, *From Text to Tradition: A History of Second Temple and Rabbinic Judaism* (Hoboken, N.J.: Ktav Publishing House, 1991).

Ten Commandments *See* DECALOGUE.

tenement

In the modern Jewish context, the word *tenement* evokes the crowded apartments jammed into clusters of apartment buildings where most Jewish immigrants to the UNITED STATES lived in the late 19th and early 20th centuries. These homes often failed minimum standards of comfort, sanitation, and safety. Jewish tenement neighborhoods were found in all the large East Coast cities, most notably on the LOWER EAST SIDE of Manhattan.

Although the closely packed Jewish immigrants could form tight, supportive communities, the living conditions were poor and often dangerous. SWEATSHOP work in the garment industry was a common vocation for tenement residents, often performed in the tenements themselves. Jewish tenement history is preserved in the Lower East Side Tenement Museum in New York City. It has documented the mass Jewish immigrant experience, and the daily struggles to persevere in the tenement community. These experiences and struggles are a large part of American Jewish consciousness, even among those whose ancestors did not reside there.

Further reading: Hasia R. Diner, *Lower East Side Memories: A Jewish Place in America* (Princeton and Oxford: Princeton University Press, 2000); Irving Howe, *World of Our Fathers: Immigrant Jews of New York, 1881 to Present* (New York: Schocken Books, 1989); Irving Howe and Kenneth Libo, *How We Lived: A Documentary History of Immigrant Jews in America, 1880–1930* (New York: R. Marek, 1979).

Ten Lost Tribes

According to TANAKH (the Hebrew Bible), after King SOLOMON died his kingdom split into two; the northern kingdom, called ISRAEL, covered the lands previously settled by 10 of the 12 tribes of ISRAELITES. When the Assyrians destroyed the northern kingdom in 722 B.C.E., they either annihilated or exiled the local population, as was the Assyrian practice. History has lost track of these 10 tribes. They may have assimilated into other groups, but a large body of folklore has developed around the idea that they survived, and that their descendants are still alive today. For example, some argue that the Jews of ETHIOPIA are descended from the tribe of Dan; others say that various population groups in Asia (*see* CHINA; INDIA; JAPAN) are descended from other lost tribes. Since no one knows the true fate of the 10 lost tribes, modern Jews are assumed to be descendants of the two remaining tribes, Levi (*see* LEVITES) and JUDAH.

Further reading: "Lost Tribes of Israel" (videorecording). (South Burlington, Vt.: WBGH/Boston Video) 2000; Simcha Shtull-Trauring, *Letters from Beyond the Sambatyon: The Myth of the Ten Lost Tribes* (New York: Maxima, 1997); *Tanakh: The Holy Scriptures* (Philadelphia and Jerusalem: Jewish Publication Society, 1985).

Ten Martyrs

Ten great rabbis of the Tannaitic period are said to have died as martyrs under the Romans, in the first several centuries of the Common Era, including AKIVA, Ishmael, and Raban Simeon ben Gamaliel. Poetic descriptions of the martyrs' deaths are included in the liturgy for the Ninth of Av (TISHA B'AV) and YOM KIPPUR. According to tradition, the Roman emperor claimed he was executing the 10 scholars to atone for the sin of JOSEPH's 10 brothers, who sold him into slavery. Scholars doubt the veracity of most of the legends of the 10 martyrs; several of the rabbis did not actually live at the same time. The legend serves primarily as a lesson about Jewish courage in the face of suffering throughout the ages.

Further reading: Abraham Halkin and David Hartman, "The Epistle on Martyrdom," in their *Crisis and Leadership: Epistles of Maimonides* (Philadelphia: Jewish Publication Society of America, 1985); George Foot Moore, *Judaism in the First Centuries of the Christian Era, the Age of the Tannaim* (New York: Schocken Books, 1971).

Ten Plagues

According to the book of EXODUS, GOD sent MOSES to plead with PHARAOH for the liberation of the ISRAELITES from slavery. When Pharaoh refused, God loosed 10 plagues upon the Egyptians. After each plague, Pharaoh would relent, only to recant and refuse once more. Only after the 10th and final plague did Pharaoh release the Israelites. Even then he recanted and sent his army after them; the troops perished in the Sea of Reeds.

The first plague turned the water in EGYPT to blood, the second was a plague of frogs, and the third was a plague of lice. After these came swarms of insects, a disease that plagued livestock, and then boils. The seventh plague was hail, the eighth locusts, and the ninth darkness. Finally the 10th plague came, the death of every first-born male among the Egyptians and their animals. The plagues did not affect GOSHEN, the area of Egypt that the Israelites inhabited.

The plagues were an awesome demonstration of God's power. The TANAKH, the Hebrew Bible, relates that God actually hardened Pharaoh's heart after each plague, presumably to have the opportunity to demonstrate immense power, and thus instill great faith in the Israelites. Many theologians have struggled with the ethical ramifications of this strategy.

Part of the PASSOVER SEDER includes a recitation of the 10 plagues. As they recite each plague, participants spill a drop of wine from their cups, a symbol that the cup of joy cannot be full, because the Egyptians who suffered from the plagues were also God's creatures.

Further reading: Moshe Lieber, *The Pesach Haggadah Anthology: The Living Exodus: With Commentary and Anecdotes from Talmudic and Rabbinical Literature* (Brooklyn, N.Y.: Mesorah, 1997); *Tanakh: The Holy Scriptures* (Philadelphia and Jerusalem: Jewish Publication Society, 1985).

Terezín (Terezienstadt)

Terezín, now in the Czech Republic, was a Jewish GHETTO and CONCENTRATION CAMP used by the Nazis (*see* GERMANY; HOLOCAUST) to deceive public opinion into thinking that the Germans were treating the Jews decently. Most of the 200,000 Jews who were sent there were eventually killed.

Many Czech and German Jews were forced to relocate in Terezín, including some notable Jewish scholars, artists, and leaders whose disappearance the world might have noticed. The Nazis created a "model ghetto," with relatively mild conditions, to ward off any world pressure about the treatment of the Jews. In fact, thousands died of hunger and disease, and tens of thousands were later shipped to the death camps.

More than 97,000 of the Czech Jews sent to Terezín died, 15,000 of them children; only 132 children are known to have survived the Terezín ghetto. The Nazis allowed the Red Cross to visit Terezín once; they created a false front for the ghetto, with an illusion of prosperity, hiding most of the true living conditions. The Red Cross representatives failed to see past what the Nazis showed them, and issued an incorrect report that the Jews of Terezín were treated well.

Terezín functioned both as ghetto and a concentration camp. For many Jews, Terezín was merely a short station on the way to those camps. However, some of the longer-term residents had a greater chance of survival than those in the death camps proper. The many musicians in Terezín organized musical recitals to help them escape the daily horror of the ghetto. Many Jewish artists created artworks that depicted life in Terezín; some of the Terezín children were also encouraged to pursue their own art. Some historians consider this kind of artistic expression to be a form of passive, or spiritual, resistance. More than 6,000 drawings were hidden, and recovered at the conclusion of the war. The children's art of Terezín remains a powerful reminder of the Nazi horrors directed toward the Jews. Most of the child artists themselves were murdered.

Further reading: Thelma Gruenbaum, *Nesarim: Child Survivors of Terezin* (London and Portland, Ore.: Vallentine Mitchell, 2004); Richard Ives and Doris Rauch, eds., *Theresienstadt: Hitler's Gift to the Jews* (Chapel Hill, N.C.: University of North Carolina Press, 1991); Marie Rut Krizkova, et al., *We Are Children Just the Same: Bedem, the Secret Magazine by the Boys of Terezin* (Philadelphia: Jewish Publication Society of America, 1995); Hana Volavkova, *I Never Saw Another Butterfly: Children's Drawings and Poems from Terezin Concentration Camp, 1942–1944* (New York: Schocken Books, 1994).

teshuvah

Teshuvah (Hebrew for "return") means the act of repentance. It is a central theme of the Days of Awe, the 10 days in between ROSH HASHANAH and YOM KIPPUR, when repentance, prayer, and charity can mitigate one's deserved punishments for the upcoming year and ensure a good year.

According to the philosopher MAIMONIDES, drawing on rabbinic traditions, repentance is not complete until one has another opportunity to sin in the same way and resists. Traditionally, when one person sins against another, the act of *teshuvah* comprises three steps: first, one must acknowledge that one has done something wrong; second, one must ask the person who was wronged for forgiveness (but can ask God if that person refuses to forgive after having been asked three times); and third, one must not do the act again.

Further reading: Shmuel Yosef Agnon, *Days of Awe* (New York: Schocken Books, 1965); Moshe Braun, *The Jewish Holy Days: Their Spiritual Significance* (Northvale, N.J.: Aronson, 1996); Irving Greenberg, *The Jewish Way: Living the Holidays* (New York: Touchstone, 1988); Leonard S. Kravitz and Kerry M. Olitzky eds., *The Journey of the Soul: Traditional Sources on Teshuvah* (Northvale, N.J.: Aronson, 1995).

Tetragrammaton

The Tetragrammaton is the four-letter name of God—YHWH—that appears more than 6,000 times in the TANAKH, the Hebrew Bible (*see* GOD, NAMES OF). It is the name God uses in the Book of Exodus (3:15) in answer to MOSES' query.

Biblical manuscripts lack vocalization (vowels) for any words, including names. The vowels are always supplied by the reader based on oral traditions. However, in the case of the Tetragrammaton neither the vowels nor the consonants are ever pronounced; instead, the reader uses the euphemism *Adonai* (Hebrew for "my Lord").

In rabbinic literature the Tetragrammaton is known as "the Name." Some Christians (*see* CHRISTIANITY), developed the tradition of vocalizing the Tetragrammaton as "Yahweh" or "Jehovah," but this has never been an acceptable practice in Judaism. Out of respect, some Jews will write the English word "G-d," omitting the vowel as in the original Hebrew manuscripts.

Further reading: George Foot Moore, *Judaism in the First Centuries of the Christian Era, the Age of the Tannaim* (New York: Schochen Books, 1971); Moses Maimonides, *The Guide for the Perplexed* (New York: Dover Publications, 1956).

theodicy

Theodicy is a discipline within theology that concerns itself with suffering. Its basic question is, if God is all-good and all-powerful, why do evil and suffering exist? While the traditions of CHRISTIANITY and ISLAM often focus on evil as the work of a devil or of demonic forces, Jews focus their response almost entirely on the concept of free will.

In Jewish thought, each individual is endowed with YETZER HA-TOV/YETZER HA-RAH, good and bad inclinations. While one should always follow one's good inclination, people are often tempted by the urge to sin. Thus, evil can be attributed to human motives.

Suffering has other rationales in Jewish thought. According to DEUTERONOMIC HISTORY, Jews are punished when they ignore God's commandments; in this case, suffering is inflicted as a punishment from God. As reflected in the book of the prophet ISAIAH, there is a strand in Jewish thought that sees Jewish suffering as a SACRIFICE for the rest of the world; the idea is that the Jews take upon themselves the sins and punishments of other nations, much in the way that Christians believe that Jesus Christ (*see* JESUS OF NAZARETH) takes upon himself their sins and punishments. Finally, another Jewish response to suffering is humility, as most clearly expressed in the book of JOB. One should not be so arrogant as to presume to question God about such matters.

The HOLOCAUST raised issues of theodicy and problems for theology in general. The massive suffering of the Jews through no apparent fault of their own suggests a lack of meaning to many observers. Some Jews who are strict adherents of Deuteronomic history believe European Jews were punished for the sin of ASSIMILATION. Others continue to see Jews as the sacrificial lamb for the whole world, while others simply point out that God cannot be questioned. However, new theologies have emerged in response to the Holocaust, ranging from the denial of God's existence to a belief in a new phase of the COVENANT in which God has become more distant, to a strident questioning of God's motives, most beautifully articulated by the Nobel laureate Elie WIESEL.

Further reading: Shmuel Boteach, *Wrestling with the Divine: A Jewish Response to Suffering* (Northvale, N.J.: Aronson, 1995); Dan Cohn-Sherbok, *Holocaust Theology: A Reader* (Exeter, U.K.: University of Exeter Press, 2002); Albert H. Friedlander, ed., *Out of the Whirlwind* (New York: UAHC Press, 1999); Alan Mintz, *Hurban: Responses to Catastrophe in Hebrew Literature* (New York: Columbia University Press, 1984); Jacob Neusner, *The Theology of the Oral Torah: Revealing the Justice of God* (Montreal: McGill-Queen's University Press, 1999); Jacob Neusner, ed., *Judaism Transcends Catastrophe: God, Torah, and Israel Beyond the Holocaust* (Macon, Ga.: Mercer University Press, 1996).

tichel

According to traditional Jewish laws of modesty, married women are required to cover their heads. Many women in eastern Europe wore *tichel*s (Yiddish for "kerchiefs"), a square cloth used as the head covering. Today many ultra-Orthodox (*see* ORTHODOX JUDAISM) women still use the traditional *tichel*, while others wear a full scarf, a SHEITEL (wig), and/or a hat to fulfill their need for modesty.

Further reading: Hasia R. Diner, *Her Works Praise Her: A History of Jewish Women in America from Colonial Times to the Present* (New York: Basic Books, 2002); Frida Kerner Furman, *Facing the Mirror: Older Women and Beauty Shop Culture* (New York: Routledge, 1997); George Robinson, *Essential Judaism* (New York: Atria, 2001).

tikkun olam

In the contemporary setting, the term *tikkun olam* (Hebrew for "world repair") usually means social or political action. It derives from classical rabbinic literature (*see* RABBI). The MISHNAH, Judaism's first book of laws, applied the term to the Jew's role in protecting those who are powerless.

In the KABBALAH, as interpreted by the 16th-century mystic Isaac LURIA, *tikkun olam* plays a key theological role. In this system, God created the physical universe by contracting to make room for matter. Some of God's "light" remained in the world, however, retained in special vessels. These vessels became broken, and while most of the divine light returned to God, some shards remained in the world. These broken shards were what the Kabbalist understood as evil. The mystic's role is to restore God's light back to its divine source, but sin saps the ability to accomplish this goal. To perform the mystical act of *tikkun olam*, the mystic must gather the shards of light, through pious religious acts or mitzvot (*see* MITZ-VAH). These acts separate that which is holy from that which is profane and help restore CREATION to its intended state.

The term became popular among Jewish social activists beginning in the 1950s. These activists generally do not assign a mystical purpose to their actions; their use of the term is more in line with the Mishnah's understanding. In 1986, Rabbi Michael Lerner (*see* JEWISH RENEWAL), a left-wing Jewish American activist, founded a magazine entitled *Tikkun,* thus appropriating the ancient Jewish concept to the liberal political agenda that he and his fellow activists believe can help "repair the world." *Tikkun* magazine has resulted in a larger *tikkun* initiative, as a vehicle for pursuing its political, religious, and social agenda.

JEWISH YOUTH GROUPS and SYNAGOGUES have also frequently used the term to encourage children, teens, and families to practice social action, acts of kindness, and good deeds.

Further reading: Michael Lerner, *The Politics of Meaning: Restoring Hope and Possibility in an Age of Cynicism* (Reading, Mass.: Addison Wesley, 1997); David Shatz, *Tikkun Olam: Social Responsibility in Jewish Thought and Law* (Northvale, N.J.: Jason Aronson, 1997); Tikkun Web site URL: http://www.tikkun.org, accessed August 20, 2004.

Tisha B'Av

Tisha B'Av, the ninth day of the month of Av, is one of two major fast days in Judaism, the other being YOM KIPPUR. It commemorates the destruction of the second TEMPLE in JERUSALEM by the Romans in 70 C.E.; in Jewish tradition, the first Temple was destroyed on the same calendar date in 586 B.C.E. The day is spent in mourning; as with Yom Kippur, Jews are barred from celebrating, eating, drinking, bathing, and sex on this day. This fast lasts from sundown to sundown. The SYNAGOGUE service for Tisha B'Av centers on the mournful book of LAMENTATIONS, after which other prayers of mourning are recited, as well as stories about other tragic events in Jewish history, including the

Tisha B'Av is a day of mourning and fasting in the Jewish tradition. This man prays and remembers the catastrophes that have befallen the Jewish people throughout history, such as the destruction of the second Temple in 70 C.E. *(Ya'acov Sa'ar, Government Press Office, The State of Israel)*

EXPULSION from SPAIN and the HOLOCAUST. It is also traditional to sit uncomfortably on the floor to accentuate the suffering of the day.

Further reading: Chanoch Gebhard and Dovid Landesman, eds., *As the Rabbis Taught: Studies in the Aggados of the Talmud: a Tishah b'Av Reader* (Northvale, N.J.: Aronson, 1996); Irving Greenberg, *The Jewish Way: Living the Holidays* (New York: Touchstone, 1988); Naomi Pasachoff, *Jewish History in 100 Nutshells* (Northvale, N.J.: Aronson, 1995); Abraham Rosenfeld, trans., *Tisha b'Av Compendium: Including Kinot for the Ninth of Av, Prayers for the Evening, Morning, and Afternoon Services, Reading of the Law and the Blessing of the New Moon according to the Ashkenazic Rite: Also Two Elegies on the York Massacres and a Special Elegy in Memory of our Six Million Martyrs Who Perished during the Nazi Regime* (New York: Judaica Press, 1983).

tithing

Tithing is a biblical principle by which the ISRAELITES set aside a portion of their produce for certain disadvantaged groups as an offering to God. The major tithing was 10 percent of one's produce.

Jewish tradition included several categories of tithing. In the book of Numbers (*see* TORAH), a tithing of one's produce was to be given to the LEVITES in the TEMPLE, after a portion was set aside for the *KOHANIM* (priests). In Leviticus and Deuteronomy a portion of the first tithe needed to be offered and subsequently consumed by the owner himself after making a pilgrimage (*see* PILGRIMAGE FESTIVALS) to JERUSALEM.

As Judaism developed away from its agricultural roots, and the Temple sacrificial cult ceased to function, the practice of tithing became less central. The MISHNAH dedicated one of its six orders or sections to agricultural laws, reflecting the agricultural roots of the Israelite culture and the centrality of the Temple cult and the tithing process; however, the later Babylonian TALMUD does not include a GEMARA for that order.

In contemporary Judaism the concept of tithing is applied to one's personal income, and the obligation to provide money to support the poor with the MITZVAH of TZEDAKAH. The minimum amount that a person should give in support of the poor is considered to be 10 percent, in keeping with the primary tithing of ancient Israel.

Further reading: Martin S. Jaffee, *Mishnah's Theology of Tithing: A Study of Tractate Maaserot* (Chico, Calif.: Scholars Press, 1981); R. T. Kendall, *Tithing* (London: Zondervan Publishing Company, 1983); Jacob Neusner, trans., *The Mishnah: A New Translation* (New Haven, Conn.: Yale University, 1991).

Titus (39/41 C.E.–81 C.E.) *Roman general and emperor*

Titus was the son of Vespasian, the Roman emperor who conquered JERUSALEM. Titus served with his father in quashing the rebellion of the Jews against ROME; he is deemed responsible for actually destroying the second TEMPLE in Jerusalem.

Some historians maintain that Titus urged his reluctant troops to sack the Temple; others say he tried to avoid destroying it. In any case, the rabbis condemn him for his part in the crime. Rabbinic legends say he defiled the TORAH, pierced the veil of the ARK of the COVENANT, and had sexual relation with prostitutes there. Another tale has a mosquito flying into his ear after the destruction of the Temple; the mosquito buzzed in his head for the rest of his life, driving him mad. Whether these legends are true or metaphorical, they reveal the contempt and hatred with which the rabbis viewed Titus.

Further reading: Josephus, *The Jewish War*, ed. G. R. Williamson (n.p.: Harmondsworth, Middlesex, Baltimore, Md.: Penguin Book, 1959); Daniel Friedenberg, "Early Jewish History in Italy" in *Judaism* 49, no. 1 (Winter 2000): 3–14.

Torah

The Torah (Hebrew for "teaching") refers to the sacred scripture of the Jewish people as well as the scroll it is written on, their most identifiable

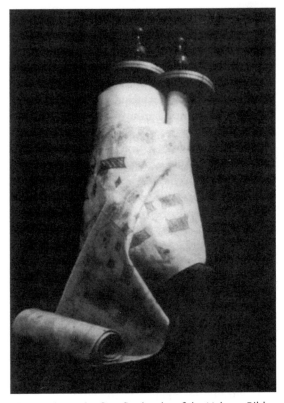

The Torah, or the first five books of the Hebrew Bible, is used in the form of a scroll in synagogues and prayer services. During services, a reader reads the Torah from the scroll itself, which has no vowels or punctuation. The words are written by hand onto animal skin parchment. *(Courtesy of the Image Bank)*

physical symbol. The word has several meanings. Strictly speaking, it refers to the Pentateuch, the five books of MOSES (Genesis, Exodus, Leviticus, Numbers, and Deuteronomy). The entire text is said to have been dictated to Moses on MOUNT SINAI; these are the books contained in the Torah scroll that Jews read aloud in SYNAGOGUEs on the Sabbath and festivals.

Critical Bible scholarship of the past two centuries suggests a different source for these five books. The Documentary Hypothesis maintains that they were compiled from four different sources, which are labeled J, E, P, and D. The book of Deuteronomy is ascribed entirely to D, while the other four books contain lines interspersed from the three other sources. J is believed to be the earliest source, from the southern kingdom of JUDAH around the 10th century B.C.E. E is slightly later and from the northern kingdom of ISRAEL, while P represents a priestly (*see* HIGH PRIEST) redaction of a combined text of J-E, that reflects the interests and values of the KOHANIM and LEVITES.

The Torah scroll is considered holy and is treated as such in the synagogue. It is carried in procession and kissed by worshippers as it passes. Penitence must be made if it is dropped or damaged. It is considered an honor to be called up to the Torah to say a blessing or to read the weekly PARSHA (portion). The Torah even has its own holiday, SIMCHAT TORAH (literally "joy in the Torah"), when the final chapters are read, the scroll is rewound, and the annual cycle of readings is begun from the start. Congregants dance around the synagogue—and often into the streets—carrying all the congregation's Torah scrolls.

A wider meaning of the word *Torah* is the entire corpus of scripture, both the written Torah (*see* WRITTEN LAW), which is equivalent to the whole TANAKH, or Hebrew Bible, and the oral Torah (*see* ORAL LAW), which includes the TALMUD and all the other interpretations of the written Torah. According to Jewish tradition, God revealed these interpretations to Moses on Mount Sinai as well, and Moses passed these teachings orally to the next generation. These teachings were finally written down from 200–900 C.E. in the form of the MISHNAH, the two Talmuds, and various MIDRASH.

More abstractly, Torah means all Jewish law, or all the religious and ethical principles of Judaism. Jews say that any act of kindness or any act of obedience to God's will is an act done in accordance with Torah. The rabbis even claimed that the world rests on Torah and that God created the universe using Torah as the blueprint. Many Jews will refer to any Jewish concept as Torah, universalizing the concept beyond a book or a scroll. There is a famous rabbinic quote: "Turn it, turn it, for all is in it." This quote refers to the totality of Torah and reminds the reader that everything in life can be found in Torah, in one form or another.

Further reading: Nathan T. Lopes Cardozo, *The Written and Oral Torah: A Comprehensive Introduction* (Northvale, N.J.: Aronson, 1997); Norman Cohen, *The Way into Torah* (Woodstock, Vt.: Jewish Lights, 2000); Richard Elliott Friedman, *Who Wrote the Bible?* (San Francisco: HarperSan Francisco, 1997); Shmuel Rubenstein, *The Sefer Torah* (New York: Sefer Torah Project, 1976); *Tanakh: The Holy Scriptures* (Philadelphia and Jerusalem: Jewish Publication Society, 1985).

Torah mi-Sinai

The term *Torah mi-Sinai* literally means "Torah is from Sinai." This term is laden with ideological meaning. It reflects the traditional doctrine of the divine origin of both the WRITTEN LAW and the ORAL LAW. Jewish traditionalists believe that God dictated to MOSES, word for word, syllable by syllable, letter by letter, the five books of Moses, or the TORAH. The idea is that the written Torah that Moses received at MOUNT SINAI has remained unchanged up to the present day. This concept is also encapsulated by the phrase *Torah min ha-Shamayim,* meaning "Torah is from heaven."

According to this point of view, God gave Moses the oral Torah on Sinai to explain the written Torah. Moses transmitted the oral law exactly to the Elders, who kept passing it along through the leaders of the various generations, until it was received by the authorized transmitters of the Oral Law, the RABBIS of the MISHNAH and TALMUD. Moses MAIMONIDES, in his brief summary of Jewish dogma, the Thirteen Principles of Faith, asserts that the dogma of Torah mi-Sinai is one of the central beliefs of Judaism. In the Orthodox (*see* ORTHODOX JUDAISM) tradition the theology of Torah mi-Sinai is axiomatic. Liberal Judaism encompasses various theological understandings of this doctrine; some liberal Jews reject it entirely.

Further reading: David Ellenson, *Rabbi Esriel Hildesheimer and the Creation of a Modern Jewish Orthodoxy* (Tuscaloosa: University of Alabama Press, 1990); Neil Gillman, *Sacred Fragments: Recovering Theology for the Modern Jew* (Philadelphia: Jewish Publication Society of America, 1992); Irene Lancaster, *Deconstructing the Bible: Abaraham Ibn Ezra's Introduction to the Torah* (London and New York: RoutledgeCurzon, 2002).

Tosafot

The Tosafot (Hebrew for "additions" or "supplements") is a collection of commentaries commonly printed in the margin of every page of the TALMUD. It is located opposite the commentary of RASHI, the 11th-century French Torah commentator. Like Rashi's commentary, it is printed in a cursive HEBREW typeface known as Rashi script.

The Tosafists, the rabbis whose names are attributed in the commentary, were a group of TORAH scholars, most of whom were Rashi's grandsons and great-grandsons. Some of the Tosafists were students in Rashi's academy. They were ASHKENAZIM who lived during the 12th, 13th, and 14th centuries in Christian Europe during the time of the Crusades. The Tosafists usually limited their commentary to matters in which they disagreed with Rashi, or to specific Talmudic themes they wished to explore in greater depth than Rashi had. For example, the Tosafists discussed HALAKHAH, Jewish law, more often than did Rashi.

Two of the most prominent Tosafists were Rabbi Jacob ben Meir, also known as RABBENU TAM, who lived from 1100 to 1171, and Rabbi Samuel ben Meir, also known as the RASHBAM, who lived from 1080–1158. These brothers were Rashi's grandsons.

Further reading: David Weiss Halivni, *Peshat and Derash: Plain and Applied Meaning in Rabbinic Exegesis* (New York: Oxford University Press, 1991); Meiri, Menahem Ben Solomon, *Tosafot Yeshanim Al Massekheth Yebomoth* (Jerusalem: Klivland: Mekhon Ofek, 1991, 1992); Emily Taitz, *The Jews of Medieval France: The*

Community of Champagne (Westport, Conn.: Greenwood Publishing, 1994).

Tosefta

When JUDAH HA-NASI edited the MISHNAH, the first Jewish law code, he chose to include only a portion of the available rabbinic material. The Tosefta was the first written collection of excluded material; it appeared soon after the completion of the Mishnah in the early third century C.E. Thus, the Tosefta consists of teachings of the TANNAIM that thematically paralleled and supplemented the Mishnah.

The Tosefta, mirroring the Mishnah, has six orders with the same names as those found in the Mishnah. Some of the paragraphs in the Tosefta, called *baraitot* (*see* BARAITA), are alternative versions of mishnaic paragraphs; they are often cited in the GEMARA as instructive extra-mishnaic sources. Other portions of the Tosefta supplement the Mishnah or provide greater insight into a Mishnah topic. The Tosefta often cites a passage of the Mishnah and then adds an appropriate proof text to that passage. The format of the Tosefta, a dialogue with the Mishnah, created the template for future commentary on the Mishnah, most notably, the GEMARA, the most authoritative such commentary.

Further reading: Harry Fox, Tirzah Meacham, and Diane Kriger, *Introducing Tosefta: Textual, Intratextual, and Intertextual Studies* (Hoboken, N.J.: Ktav Publishing House, 1999); Jacob Neusner, *The Tosefta* (Atlanta, Ga.: Scholar's Press, 1981).

traditional Judaism

There is no Jewish denomination that calls itself "traditional Judaism," but there are many traditional Jews. A desire to follow the same path as one's parents, grandparents, and those who came before them encapsulates what it means to be a traditional Jew. While innovation connotes the new, tradition champions the old; the proponents of traditional Judaism, for example, value the insights of the past over those of today's Jews. They want to pass down the rituals and customs they believe defined life for Jews since the distant past (*see* TORAH MI-SINAI).

Perhaps this is the key to the authenticity of both traditional Judaism and its opposite, liberal or progressive Judaism. Since it is not always possible to truly know what our recent or not so recent ancestors did in a given situation, both the traditional Jew and the liberal Jew must make a decision. Traditional Jews choose to follow as closely as possible the actions they believe their ancestors took, though they are aware that they too must interpret Jewish law (HALAKHAH) and custom for their own circumstances. Liberal, or progressive, Jews are more open to innovation, trusting the modern belief in logic and critical thinking.

These days, Orthodox Jews, even ultra-Orthodox Jews, recognize that even when they follow to the letter the path of their forebears they are exercising a choice that the contemporary world offers them. Traditional Jews before the advent of the ENLIGHTENMENT and EMANCIPATION had no such choice; they were constrained by the SHTETL or GHETTO walls, cushioned by Jewish institutions and conventions that controlled every aspect of life, and denied access to the non-Jewish world and its choices. It is no longer possible for any Westerner to remain ignorant of the outside world, thus making traditional Judaism one choice among many.

ORTHODOX JUDAISM today defines itself as "traditional Judaism," while CONSERVATIVE JUDAISM defines itself as a movement that balances tradition with change. The Conservative movement asserts that historical Judaism has always developed through a dialogue between tradition and change; therefore, even their boldest changes do not break completely from the past, and they thus remain traditional. Both movements claim to authentically embrace traditional Judaism. The right wing of the Conservative movement, especially the splinter group that formed in 1985, the Union for Traditional Judaism, strictly adheres to traditional Judaism in theology, ideology, and sociology, though perhaps not to the letter as do the Orthodox.

Most Reform (*see* REFORM JUDAISM) and Reconstructionist (*see* RECONSTRUCTIONIST JUDAISM) Jews accept that they are not traditional Jews, although they believe that their progressive Judaism is more authentic for modern times. Reform and Reconstructionist Judaisms deliberately choose the new over the old and innovation over tradition.

Further reading: Lucy S. Dawidowitz, *The Golden Tradition: Jewish Life and Thought in Eastern Europe* (Syracuse, N.Y.: Syracuse University Press, 1996); Emanuel S. Goldsmith and Raphael Patai, *Events and Movements in Modern Judaism* (New York: Paragon House, 1995); Samuel Heilman, *Defenders of the Faith: Inside Ultra-Orthodox Jewry* (New York: Schocken Books, 1992).

Triangle Fire

The Triangle Fire or the Triangle Shirtwaist Fire was one of America's greatest and most consequential industrial tragedies. On March 25, 1911, a fire swept through the Asch building of the Triangle Shirtwaist Company at 23-29 Washington Place in Manhattan. The factory was a SWEATSHOP where mostly female workers suffered poor working conditions and poor pay. There were inadequate safety procedures in place, no fire escapes, and the management followed a practice of locking exits to prevent workers from taking breaks.

The fire that broke out killed 146 workers, many of whom were Jewish. The factory's owners were indicted on charges of manslaughter, but a jury acquitted them, which only exacerbated popular outrage over the incident. The Triangle Fire galvanized unionism among women workers,

After the horrific Triangle Shirtwaist Company fire in 1911, a funeral procession for the victims makes its way down the street. One hundred forty-six workers, many of them Jewish, died trapped in the building as it burned. *(Library of Congress)*

particularly in the International Ladies Garment Workers Union, and led to major reforms to improve working conditions, especially regarding safety. The Triangle Fire remained a rallying call in the American Jewish labor movement for many years to come.

Further reading: David von Drehle, *Triangle: The Fire That Changed America* (New York: Atlantic Monthly Press, 2003); Leon Stein and William Greider, *The Triangle Fire* (Ithaca, N.Y.: Cornell University Press, 2001).

trope

One of the key elements of SYNAGOGUE ritual is the public reading from the TORAH and other books of the TANAKH, the Hebrew Bible. To be more precise, these texts are chanted, according to a special set of musical notes or symbols called trope or cantillation. The term *trope* can refer to the symbols themselves, or to the style in which they are interpreted.

The trope does not appear on the handwritten TORAH scroll, but the assignment of notes for each word was fixed long ago and is accepted by Jewish communities around the world; the trope now appears in nearly every Jewish printed Bible. There are nuances between communities as to how the individual notes should be interpreted melodically. The symbols that signify the trope for the Hebrew text were introduced at the end of the 10th century of the Common Era.

The same set of symbols is used for all readings, but they are interpreted somewhat differently depending on the text being read. One style is used to chant Torah, another to chant HAFTARAH and Prophets (*see* NEVI'IM), and one each for the books of ESTHER, LAMENTATIONS, SONG OF SONGS, RUTH, and Ecclesiastes. In addition, there are different tropes used to chant Torah and *haftarah* on the holidays such as ROSH HASHANAH and YOM KIPPUR; furthermore, certain key passages of the Torah have tropes of their own, such as the Ten Commandments (*see* DECALOGUE) or the Song of the Sea.

The Jewish practice of cantillation serves two distinct purposes. It gives instructions for how to read and sing a text, and it clarifies the grammatical structure of the underlying Hebrew text. Hebrew was originally written without punctuation marks or vowels, but the written texts were accompanied by ancient oral traditions about how they should be read; eventually this tradition was recorded via the trope or written cantillation marks, which show where sentences and clauses begin and end, what words should be stressed within a sentence, and what syllables should be stressed within a word.

Since for many Jews Hebrew is a language of books and not part of their vernacular, cantillation enables the proper reading or singing of the text even if the reader lacks comprehension. BAR/BAT MITZVAH students often study cantillation signs in order to read from the Torah or *haftarah* at their bar/bat mitzvah service. Because most Jews are not able to chant Torah and *haftarah* beyond their bar/bat mitzvahs, a rabbi, cantor, or a well-trained layperson, often called Ba'al Korei, usually do the actual reading.

Further reading: Irene Heskes, *Passport to Jewish Music: Its History, Traditions, and Culture* (Westport, Conn.: Greenwood Publications, 1994); Marshall Portnoy and Josee Wolff, *The Art of Torah Cantillation: A Step-by-Step Guide to Chanting Torah* (New York: UAHC Press, 2000); ———, *The Art of Cantillation, Volume 2: A Step-by-Step Guide to Chanting Haftarah and M'gillot* (New York: UAHC Press, 2000).

Trotsky, Leon (1879–1949) *Russian revolutionary leader*

Leon Trotsky was born Lev Davidovich Bronstein in Yanovka, Ukraine. He was the son of a Jewish farmer, David Bronstein. His father purchased land in the town of Bobrinets and over time increased his landholdings greatly. His mother, Anna, had received an education, and she regularly read books to her eight children, encouraging them to get a proper education. Trotsky attended a Jewish primary school and afterward

A disciple of Karl Marx, Leon Trotsky became a leader of the Communist Party until Joseph Stalin exiled him and then had him assassinated in 1940. *(Library of Congress)*

studied at the state school in Odessa. He was a very good student, who especially loved mathematics.

Trotsky became an ardent disciple of Karl MARX in his youth. In 1896 Trotsky joined the Social Democrats, a political party, and two years later was arrested as a Marxist and exiled to Siberia. Four years later he escaped and reached ENGLAND by means of a forged passport that used the name of a jailer in Odessa's prison, Trotsky. In London Trotsky met Lenin and other Russian revolutionary leaders. In 1903 Trotsky broke from Lenin's group of Bolsheviks and became a leader of the Menshevik wing of the Social Democratic Party. His primary concern had been that Leninist theory would result in a one-man dictatorship.

In 1905 Trotsky organized the first revolutionary Soviet (council) in St. Petersburg and was appointed its president. The revolutionary attempt was defeated, and he was again exiled to Siberia,

from which he once again escaped. Trotsky subsequently became a journalist in Vienna, and the editor of the newspaper *Pravda* (Truth). During World War I he moved to Zurich, SWITZERLAND, and then to GERMANY. There he was briefly imprisoned for opposing the war.

During World War I Trotsky led the Mensheviks, denouncing Russia's involvement in the war. In 1915 he moved to Paris, continuing to work as a journalist, but he was expelled from France for his pacifist writings. After briefly residing in New York, he returned to RUSSIA in 1917, rejoining the Bolsheviks in St. Petersburg and establishing the magazine *Vperied* (Forward). Trotsky was arrested by Kerensky's provisional government, but after his release, he played a major role in the BOLSHEVIK REVOLUTION. From 1919 to 1927 he was a member of Politburo, and from 1918 to 1925 he was also the commissar for war and created the Red Army. The Red Army grew from 800,000 to 3 million, and fought on 16 fronts simultaneously.

After Lenin's death, Stalin and Trotsky both aspired to be his successor. Lenin had rejected Stalin as his successor, but nevertheless Stalin won the struggle. Under his rule Trotsky's influence declined, and he was removed from his post as the commissar for war. In 1929 Stalin expelled Trotsky from the Soviet Union, to become the sole leader of the Communist Party. Trotsky lived in Turkey, FRANCE, Norway, and then Mexico, where Stalin had him assassinated in 1940 with the help of local Communists.

Further reading: Ronald Segal, *Leon Trotsky: A Biography* (New York: Pantheon Books, 1979); Leon Trotsky, *The Basic Writings of Trotsky* (New York: Schocken Books, 1976); Leon Trotsky, *My Life* (New York: Pathfinder Press, 1970).

Truman, Harry S. (1884–1972)
U.S. president

When Harry S. Truman succeeded President Roosevelt as president of the UNITED STATES in 1945, he expressed strong sympathies for the plight of the Jews, in the aftermath of the HOLOCAUST, and embraced the principles enshrined in the BALFOUR DECLARATION that there should be a Jewish state in PALESTINE. However, Truman's Departments of War and State were concerned that if the president actively interceded on behalf of the Jews, the Soviet-Arab relationship would be strengthened, and Arab oil producers might restrict shipments to the United States. Nevertheless, when the UNITED NATIONS proposed the PARTITION PLAN for Palestine in 1947, Truman instructed the State Department to support it.

At midnight TEL AVIV time on May 14, 1948, the provisional government of Israel proclaimed a new state of Israel; 11 minutes later President Truman

U.S. president Harry Truman recognized the infant state of Israel after it declared its independence in 1948. *(Library of Congress)*

recognized that government as the de facto authority of the Jewish state. That Truman ultimately supported the creation of the Jewish state is commonly attributed to the influence of his close Jewish childhood friend and former business partner, Eddie Jacobson. Truman had become weary of the Jewish Zionist (*see* ZIONISM) lobbyists and, in frustration, had refused to meet with Zionist leader Chaim WEIZMANN (1874–1952). Jacobson understood his friend's frustration with the heavy lobbying efforts, but reminded him that a just cause should not suffer because its leaders are insufferable. Truman listened to his friend's advice and ultimately met with the Zionist leaders, paving the way for U.S. support for the creation of the State of ISRAEL.

Further reading: Michael T. Benson, *Harry S. Truman and the Founding of Israel* (Westport, Conn.: Praeger Publishers, 1997); David McCullough, *Truman* (New York: Simon & Schuster, 1993).

Tu B'Shevat

Tu B'Shevat, the 15th day of the month of Shevat, is a minor holiday in Judaism. The ancient RABBIS considered the date to mark the new year for trees, since by then rainfall has ended in ISRAEL. Traditionally, Jews celebrate by eating fruits, especially those grown in ERETZ YISRAEL; and in modern times, many Jews also plant trees on that day. Some communities also read passages from the TALMUD and the *ZOHAR* that relate to plants and agriculture. There is no biblical reference to Tu B'Shevat; it probably derives from an ancient festival marking a change of seasons.

In modern times, many Jewish communities have developed a new ritual to celebrate the holiday, which they call a Tu B'Shevat Seder, named after the SEDER on PASSOVER. Like the Passover ritual, participants eat various foods in a certain order, accompanied by the appropriate blessing. The first Tu B'Shevat Seder took place among followers of the KABBALAH in SAFED in the 16th century. It included four cups of wine, some white and some red, and many different types of fruit.

Tu B'Shevat seders are popular with schoolchildren, reminding them to celebrate trees and reinforcing the value of trees. These seders often focus on the three categories of fruit: (1) fruits that can be completely eaten, like grapes and apples, (2) fruits whose outer layer is thrown away while the inside is eaten, such as oranges and walnuts, and (3) fruits whose inner layer is inedible, such as olives, dates, and plums. Eating different kinds of fruits has esoteric Kabbalistic meaning; the wide variety of fruits eaten can also represent the abundance that the land of Israel possesses during the celebration of the New Year for trees.

Further reading: Ari Elon, Naomi Mara Hyman, Arthur Waskow eds., *Trees, Earth, and Torah: A Tu B'Shvat Anthology* (Philadelphia: Jewish Publication Society, 1999); Karen L. Fox, *Seasons for Celebration* (New York: Putnam, 1992); Irving Greenberg, *The Jewish Way: Living the Holidays* (New York: Touchstone, 1988).

tzaddik (pl.: *tzaddikim*)

A *tzaddik* (Hebrew for "righteous one") is a kind of saint or holy person. In the Hasidic community many religious leaders are considered *tzaddikim* by their followers, in keeping with the example of the founder of the movement, the BAAL SHEM TOV (*see* HASIDISM). Among Hasidic Jews, the *tzaddik* is traditionally called "rebbe." A *tzaddik* is not only a master of TORAH and a community civil leader, but also a role model in his own spiritual life. The most famous *tzaddikim* are known for their goodness as much as their learning. Usually the role of *tzaddik* is handed down from father to son.

The TALMUD teaches that the world must always contain 36 *tzaddikim*, called LAMEDVOVNIKS; if their numbers should diminish, the world will perish; in that tradition, the *tzaddik* may be an unknown, hidden individual. In common parlance, the term *tzaddik* (or *tzaddeket* for women) has come to connote any individual who is particularly righteous, or selflessly performs good deeds.

Further reading: Samuel H. Dresner, *The Zaddik: The Doctrine of the Zaddik According to the Writings of Rabbi Yaakov Yosef of Polnoy* (Northvale, N.J.: J. Aronson, 1994); Louis Jacobs, "The Prayers of the Zaddik," in *Hasidic Prayer* (Washington, D.C.: The Littman Library of Jewish Civilization, 1993): 126–139; Simcha Raz, *A Tzaddik in Our Time: The Life of Rabbi Aryeh Levin* (Jerusalem and New York: Feldheim Publishers, 1976); Gershom Scholem, *Major Trends in Jewish Mysticism* (New York: Schocken Books, 1974).

tzedakah

Tzedakah literally means an act of righteousness or justice; in common parlance, it means "charity."

Deuteronomy, the last book of the TORAH, the Five Books of Moses, states *"Tzedek, tzedek tirdof,"* which means, "justice, justice shall you pursue." This commandment to pursue justice has been interpreted as a commandment to act in ways that make the world a fairer place, or to do *tzedakah*. Thus, *tzedakah* is not selfless giving, but commanded righteousness. In other words, it is the duty of every Jewish person to give, both of time and worldly goods. In modern usage, *Tzedakah* is often fulfilled by giving money in support of others who are less fortunate. A common theme throughout TANAKH, the Hebrew Bible, is the command that Jews take care of those who are needy, often symbolized as the widow, the orphan, the stranger, and the aged (*see* WIDOWS AND ORPHANS).

The MISHNAH, the first Jewish law book, laid down parameters for individuals and communities to follow in helping the needy. Individuals were to assess themselves a progressive tax ranging from 10 to 20 percent of their annual income (*see* TITHING). In some Jewish communities throughout history, the assessment was made by the RABBIS, formally taking on the nature of a progressive income tax. In the contemporary world, even though the government taxes individuals for social needs, the obligation to provide *tzedakah* remains intact. The traditional Jew should still donate a minimum of 10 percent of personal income for charitable purposes.

A common liturgical refrain on the High Holidays (*see* ROSH HASHANAH; YOM KIPPUR) is that *tzedakah,* repentance (*see* SIN AND REPENTANCE), and PRAYER are the means through which human beings can set aside any negative judgment by God. Many homes include a TZEDAKAH BOX, so that all change left in one's pockets at the end of the day can be set aside for charitable purposes.

The commandment for providing *tzedakah* became well established in Judaism, and in the Middle Ages Jews began to establish formal philanthropic institutions to more efficiently assist those in need. In the 19th and 20th centuries Jews participated heavily in developing such institutions, both Jewish and for the wider community (*see* SCHIFF, JACOB; UNITED JEWISH COMMUNITIES). The rabbis wanted the entire Jewish community to participate in the commandment (*see* MITZVAH) of *tzedakah,* especially by means of the highest form of giving: when the donor and recipient are anonymous. Moses MAIMONIDES had stated that there were eight levels of *tzedakah.* The lowest form is one who gave grudgingly, the highest, one who enabled others to support themselves in the future.

Further reading: Beryl Lieff Benderly, and Hasia R. Diner, *Her Works Praise Her: A History of Jewish Women in America from Colonial Times to the Present* (New York: Basic Books, 2002); Hayim Halevy Donin, *To Be A Jew: A Guide to Jewish Observance in Contemporary Life* (New York: Basic Books, 1972); Avrohom Chaim Feuer, *The Tzedakah Treasury* (Brooklyn, N.Y.: Mesorah Publications Ltd., 2000); Arthur Hertzberg, ed., *Judaism: The Classic Introduction to One of the Great Religions of the Modern World* (New York: Simon & Schuster, 1991).

tzedakah box (*pushke*)

A fundamental commandment, or MITZVAH, in Judaism is to give TZEDAKAH, in the sense of donating work or money to charity. In order to encourage the regular practice of *tzedakah,* it became a tradition in Jewish homes to display a *tzedakah* box (*pushke* in YIDDISH) in a prominent place. The *tzedakah* box was also used to teach children the mitzvah of charitable giving. A tradition developed to give children money each week just prior to SHABBAT, so that they could drop it in the *tzedakah* box. In addition, many synagogues display *tzedakah* boxes, so that people who come to worship, study, and celebrate can also fulfill the precept of charitable righteousness. In addition, it has become a custom to place *tzedakah* boxes in a house of MOURNING, where people are sitting SHIVA, as a collection device for a bereaved family in need.

In the contemporary Jewish world a *tzedakah* box remains a common ritual object in the home. It represents the traditional Jewish practice of giving liberally of time and money and encourages philanthropic efforts. It has also become an object of artistic creativity, serving the dual purpose of beautifying the home and adding glory to the MITZVAH itself. The boxes can take any form, from elaborately carved wood or silver to used coffee cans decorated by children.

For a hundred years or more, perhaps the most common *tzedakah* box was the "blue box," the ubiquitous symbol of the Jewish National Fund (JNF) that was found in almost any Jewish home that supported ZIONISM. Money collected through the JNF blue box supported the purchase and development of land in ERETZ YISRAEL. When the JNF was established in 1901, a bank clerk by the name of Haim Kleinman from Nadvorna, Galicia, placed a blue box marked Keren Le'umit, which means "National Fund," in his office. He suggested that such a box be placed in every Jewish home and that everyone contribute to the newly created national fund at every possible opportunity. JNF began to produce the first official blue boxes in 1904, and the financial impact was immediate. The blue box became an expression of the deep bond between DIASPORA Jews and the land of Israel. In the 1930s it was estimated that more than 1 million JNF blue boxes were to be found in Jewish homes. Today the blue box remains popular, commonly distributed to children in Jewish day schools (*see* JEWISH DAY SCHOOL

MOVEMENT), and SUPPLEMENTARY SCHOOLS. Old blue boxes have become treasured family heirlooms.

Further reading: Anita Diamant, *Living a Jewish Life: Jewish Traditions, Customs, and Values for Today's Families* (New York: HarperResource, 1996); Teresa Odendahl, *Charity Begins at Home: Generosity and Self-Interest Among the Philanthropic Elite* (New York: Basic Books, 1990); Howard M. Sachar, *A History of Israel: From the Rise of Zionism to Our Time* (New York: Alfred A. Knopf, 1996).

Tzipporah (c. 13th century B.C.E.) *biblical figure*

Tzipporah was MOSES' wife. According to EXODUS, Moses flees from EGYPT to Midian after killing an Egyptian taskmaster who was beating a HEBREW slave. In Midian he encounters Jethro's daughters, whom he protects from shepherds who are trying to drive them from a well. In reward, Jethro gives his daughter Tzipporah to Moses as his wife. Later, when God or an angel seeks to kill Moses, Tzipporah saves his life by circumcising their son, a job he had apparently neglected.

Further reading: Ilana Pardes, *Countertraditions in the Bible: A Feminist Approach* (Cambridge, Mass: Harvard University Press, 1992); *Tanakh: The Holy Scriptures* (Philadelphia and Jerusalem: Jewish Publication Society, 1985).

tzitzit

Tzitzit (Hebrew for "fringes") are the batches of string that hang from each of the four corners of the TALLIT, or prayer shawl. The laws pertaining to tzitzit are cited in the TORAH, the Five Books of MOSES. The text reads, "And you shall see [the tzitzit] and remember all the commandments of the Lord, and observe them" (Nm 15:39).

The fringes were in danger of falling into disuse when people no longer wore garments with four corners. To prevent the MITZVAH from becoming lost, Jews in the Middle Ages created a four-cornered prayer shawl known as a *tallit*, to which tzitzit were affixed.

Since the tzitzit are worn as a visual reminder of the commandments, it was considered most appropriate to wear them during daylight. Hence, tzitzit is a time-bound commandment. The *tallit*, according to RABBINIC LAW, is worn during the morning prayers. It is worn at night only once during the year, at the KOL NIDRE service, which begins YOM KIPPUR, the Day of Atonement. At Kol Nidre, due to the holiness of the time, the prayer shawl with its tzitzit is worn. Since tzitzit and *tallit* are time-bound obligations, women are exempt, since time-bound obligations can interfere with the woman's traditional role of attending to home and children.

Thus, traditionally, the *tallit* is worn by men only, and in Orthodox (*see* ORTHODOX JUDAISM) SYNAGOGUES today, this is generally the case. However, in Conservative (*see* CONSERVATIVE JUDAISM), Reform (*see* REFORM JUDAISM), and Reconstructionist (*see* RECONSTRUCTIONIST JUDAISM) synagogues, many women wear colorful *tallitot* and participate in such customs as kissing the tzitzit when it is mentioned during the SHEMA prayer, touching the tzitzit to the Torah scroll during its procession, and raising and kissing the tzitzit when the open Torah scroll is held up so that everyone can see the writing.

Some worshippers cover their heads with the *tallit* during prayers for complete concentration, in imitation of the priests in the ancient TEMPLE. The priests believed they were in God's presence; since the Hebrew Bible states that no human can see God and live (Ex 33:20), they shielded their eyes. Thus, the tzitzit beckons the eyes and reminds us to remember, yet the *tallit*, when placed on the head, veils our vision of God's presence. The practice teaches that both presence of mind and humility are necessary when approaching God.

Very traditional Jews, generally Orthodox, also wear an undergarment called a *tallit katan* (Hebrew for "small *tallit*") or *arba kanfot* (Hebrew for "four corners"). This is a four-cornered white garment worn all day underneath clothing like a T-shirt. The wearer often leaves the tzitzit hanging out for visibility. Tying tzitzit is an art form. A hole is made in each corner of the *tallit*. Through each hole, four strands are inserted: three short strands and one long strand. These strands are then tied and wound together in a pattern dictated by Jewish law. When done correctly, the tzitzit will have 7-8-11-13 winds between the double knots. One interpretation for these numbers is that each set of windings corresponds to one of the four letters in God's name. Another interpretation employs GEMATRIA, Jewish numerology, and the numbers of knots and winds correspond to meaningful references to God. Another common interpretation is that the gematria value of the word *tzitzit* is 600, and when you add the eight strands plus the five knots, you have the total of 613, which, according to tradition, is how many commandments (*see* MITZVAH) are in the Torah.

The Torah also commanded that tzitzit contain a thread of *techelet* (blue). The reason for this is found in the Talmud: "Blue is like the sea. The Sea is like the sky, and the sky is like the Throne of the Lord." *Techelet* was a sky-blue wool, and the dye for this color came from an animal called the *chilazone*. Over the centuries, the exact identity of the *chilazone* was forgotten, and the obligatory "strand of *techelet*" became a mitzvah Jews are now unable to fulfill. In memory of this dye, some Jews have the custom to place a blue stripe on the Tallit garment itself. Others place a black stripe, in mourning for the lost mitzvah of *techelet*. In recent years, some observant Jews have once again chosen to add a blue string in the knots of the tzitzit.

Further reading: Hayim Halevy Donin, *To Be a Jew: A Guide to Jewish Observance in Contemporary Life* (New York: Basic Books, 1972); Isaac Klein, *A Guide to Jewish Religious Practice* (New York: Jewish Theological Seminary of America; distributed by Ktav Publishing House, 1979); Abraham E. Millgram, *Jewish Worship* (Philadelphia: Jewish Publication Society, 1971).

U

Uganda

Theodor Herzl (1860–1904) was the first to bring the East African country of Uganda to the attention of the world's Jews. In pursuit of the Zionist (*see* Zionism) aim of creating a homeland for the Jewish people, Herzl met with British government officials in 1903; they proposed Uganda, at the time one of their colonies, as a Jewish autonomous region in place of Palestine. At the Sixth Zionist Congress in 1903 Herzl formally proposed that Uganda become a temporary refuge for Jews, as a desperate response to the threatening situation of Russian Jewry in 1903. The proposal was highly controversial and nearly led to a split in the Zionist movement. It was finally rejected at the Seventh Zionist Congress in 1905. It should be noted that although in this "Uganda Controversy," the principles called the British East African country "Uganda" the territory suggested was actually what is today Kenya.

Uganda again came to the attention of world Jewry in 1976, when on June 27 German radical terrorists hijacked an Air France plane and forced it to land in Uganda. They demanded that Israel release 53 convicted terrorists, on pain of death for the hostages. The hijackers freed the French crew and non-Jewish passengers, keeping as hostages 105 Jewish passengers. The Israeli government felt that negotiations were untenable; instead, they organized a surprise military attack led by Lt. Col. Yonatan Netanyahu, the brother of future prime minister Benjamin Netanyahu. On July 4 soldiers caught the terrorists by surprise and freed all the hostages, killing the eight terrorists in the process. The only Jewish casualty was the Israeli Commander Netanyahu. The Uganda mission in Entebbe was one of Israel's greatest military achievements, and boosted Israeli morale at a time of international isolation.

In eastern Uganda today there are 500 black Ugandans who practice Judaism. Their community converted to Judaism in the 1920s, when their leader, Semei Kakungulu, was leading a resistance against European colonialists and missionaries. Kakungulu had become friends with a European Jewish trader, who taught him and his followers Judaism. From 1920 until 1992, approximately 15 Jews from outside Uganda visited Kakungulu's small Jewish community.

In 1992, Julia Chamovitz and Matthew Meyer visited what has become known as the Abuyudaya Jews. Subsequently it has been arranged to send more Jewish visitors and two rabbis. The Abuyudaya Jews asked for assistance to rebuild their synagogue, and were provided with a Torah scroll in 1995.

Further reading: James R. Ross, *Fragile Branches: Travels through the Jewish Diaspora* (New York: Riverhead Books, 2000); Howard M. Sachar, *A History of Israel: From the Rise of Zionism to Our Time* (New York: Alfred A. Knopf, 1996); Richard Sobol and Jeffrey A. Summit, *Abayudaya: The Jews of Uganda* (New York: Abbeville Press, 2002).

Ugaritic

Ugaritic was the ancient language most similar to HEBREW. It is an important link between the TANAKH, the Hebrew Bible, and other ancient Near Eastern texts and culture. Many Ugaritic and Hebrew words are identical; when a Hebrew word is unclear, a Ugaritic text can sometimes help scholars come up with a proper translation.

Ugaritic texts have also yielded interesting new information about ancient ISRAEL. The language was first discovered in 1928, when archaeologists located the ancient city of Ugarit in current-day Syria; they uncovered numerous clay tablets bearing a variety of inscriptions. The tablets shed light on the religion of ancient CANAAN, the culture among which the ISRAELITES lived.

Further reading: Peter Craigie, *Ugarit and the Old Testament* (Grand Rapids, Mich.: Eerdmans Publishing, 1983); Frank Cross, *Canaanite Myth and Hebrew Epic: Essays in the History of the Religion of Israel* (Cambridge, Mass.: Harvard University Press, 1997).

Union for Reform Judaism *See* REFORM JUDAISM.

Union of American Hebrew Congregations *See* REFORM JUDAISM.

Union of Orthodox Rabbis of the United States *See* ORTHODOX JUDAISM.

United Jewish Appeal *See* UNITED JEWISH COMMUNITIES.

United Jewish Communities

The United Jewish Communities is a nondenominational philanthropic Jewish organization that serves 155 member federations and 400 independent Jewish communities in North America. Combining two historical organizations, the Council of Jewish Federations and the United Jewish Appeal, the relatively new United Jewish Communities strives to reflect a focus on social justice, humanitarianism, and caring that is inherent among Jews of all ideologies.

By 1860, 44 Jewish charitable and benevolent groups were registered in New York, and others existed in other states as well. Each of these early groups focused on one particular goal, such as providing food to the needy or offering insurance to cover burial costs. But by the end of the 19th century, with the influx of millions of eastern European Jews to the UNITED STATES, the Jewish community found that these smaller agencies and associations were not strong enough to provide for the needs of a growing immigrant population. In fact, there were so many different groups that the people in the Jewish community began to tire of the many volunteers who came to their doors asking for donations. The solution to the problem was found in an organizational structure called a federation. The leaders of the Boston Jewish community decided to bring all willing Jewish charitable organizations in their city under one single organizational umbrella. The Federated Jewish Charities of Boston was created in 1895 and the Jewish community in Cincinnati, Ohio federated in 1896. Today there are close to 200 Jewish federations across the United States.

The federation idea emerged from European ideas of Jewish communal responsibility as evidenced by the KAHAL or *kehillah*, the autonomous Jewish communities that arose in the Middle Ages. However, many characteristics of federations, such as independence and democracy, were distinctly American. Jewish federations were successful in the United States because of their commitment to religious pluralism and the individual nature of their member agencies. This meant that

Jews who believed in different interpretations of Judaism could work together to achieve a common goal: caring for the welfare of the American Jewish people. As a result Jewish social welfare activities have not taken place in SYNAGOGUES for the most part, but in the federation system, which makes it easier for those who adhere to different Jewish ideologies to work together.

Tensions between synagogues and federations exist in some communities and in others the two work closely together. REFORM JUDAISM has historically integrated a platform of social welfare and social justice into synagogue life. But many American Jews are not comfortable in synagogues of any denomination; instead, their participation in the federation system and in campaigns for the United Jewish Appeal has shaped their JEWISH IDENTITY. Volunteerism is a particularly American phenomenon, and American Jews have found that volunteering their time and money in Jewish social welfare has been a way to express themselves as Jews.

Federations operate under the principle that all social service agencies within one city or Jewish community should maintain their independence, while at the same time use one another as resources for information and fund-raising. On a yearly basis each federation met to allocate funds among the member agencies. As the number of federations grew, it became clear that they needed to share information and perhaps develop a unified voice. In 1932 the National Council of Jewish Federations and Welfare Funds (NCJFWF) united the Jewish federations across the country. In 1935 the organization changed its name to the Council of Jewish Federations and Welfare Funds (CJFWF), and in 1979 the name became the Council of Jewish Federations (CJF). This national forum provided information for individual federations about the kinds of programs that had been successful in other places, and provided a national voice for all members. The General Assembly meets annually to present new ideas and experiences and to distribute materials. As the years passed, the CJFWF developed different foci, including the coordination of large city federations, representing federations to the U.S. Congress, improving services for the aged, Jewish education across the country, helping federations to attain federal grants, and responding to the needs of Jews overseas in Europe, PALESTINE, and ISRAEL.

In 1939, inspired by the needs of Jews settling in PALESTINE and catalyzed by violence between Arabs and Jews there, the United Jewish Appeal (UJA) was born as a national campaign to raise funds for the United Israel Appeal, the American Jewish Joint Distribution Committee, and the New York Association for New Americans. Since then, the United Jewish Appeal has been the largest beneficiary of federation funds. Differences often emerge within federations as to how much funding should apply toward Israel and other Jews abroad and how much should remain local. While the United Jewish Appeal raised unprecedented amounts of money during and after the SIX-DAY WAR in 1967, in the past few decades many federations have channeled their allocations more toward domestic issues such as Jewish education and care for an aging Jewish community. Some larger federations contribute programs to non-Jewish communities, as well, universalizing their charitable traditions (*see* OHR LA-GOYIM).

Although there has always been a symbiotic relationship between the United Jewish Appeal and the local federations, represented by the Council of Jewish Federations, tensions have existed between the two groups. In 1999, the United Jewish Appeal and the Council of Jewish Federations merged to become the United Jewish Communities. The relationship is still new and the effects of both organizations operating under the same umbrella are yet to be seen.

Further reading: Philip Bernstein, *To Dwell in Unity: The Jewish Federation Movement in America since 1960* (Philadelphia: The Jewish Publication Society of America, 1983); Harry L. Lurie, *A Heritage Affirmed: The Jewish Federation Movement in America* (Philadelphia: Jewish Publication Society of America, 1961); Marc Lee

Raphael, ed., *Understanding American Jewish Philanthropy* (New York: Ktav Publishing, 1979); Jonathan S. Woocher, *Sacred Survival: The Civil Religion of American Jews* (Bloomington and Indianapolis: Indiana University Press, 1986); United Jewish Communities Web site URL: http://www.ujc.org, accessed August 29, 2004.

United Nations (UN)

In a terrible irony, the United Nations, which was responsible for legitimizing the creation of the modern state of ISRAEL, has become universally distrusted by Israel and much of world Jewry.

In February 1947, ENGLAND turned to the United Nations to resolve the struggle for national status between the Jews and Arabs of its BRITISH MANDATE for PALESTINE. The UN established a Special Commission on Palestine. The committee members concluded that the conflicting national aspirations of the two nations were irreconcilable. They recommended that two separate states be established, Jewish and Arab, to be joined in an economic union. Jerusalem was to remain an international city.

The Jews living in Palestine were not happy with their land allotment, but they formally accepted the proposal (*see* PARTITION PLAN). The Arabs rejected it completely, threatening war if the Jews should declare their own state. On November 29, 1947 the UN General Assembly approved the UN Partition Plan by the required two-thirds vote, thereby authorizing the Jews of Palestine to declare their state, which they did in TEL AVIV on May 15, 1948, just after the last British troops withdrew.

Since 1948, in the decades of conflict between Israel and the Arabs, the United Nations has come to be seen by Israel and world Jewry as biased against the Israeli side. Israel is the only nation that is not allowed a rotating seat on the United Nations Security Council, or most other UN bodies. Whereas the United Nations General Assembly rarely calls emergency special sessions in regard to any other issue, they are frequently called for the express purpose of condemning Israel.

From the perspective of many Jews and the State of Israel, the many Arab nations have used the UN to isolate Israel from the world. The General Assembly has proposed numerous anti-Israel statements, such as UN Resolution 3379, which was passed in 1975 and explicitly called Zionism a form of racism. The General Assembly has created two Special Committees and two "special units" in the Secretariat devoted solely to Israeli practices, at the cost of millions of dollars per year. These groups generate anti-Israeli and anti-Zionist propaganda, which is distributed throughout the world. Since the Oslo Accords were signed in 1993, Israel has continued to be brutalized by Palestinian terrorist attacks striking civilian targets, yet the UN continues to pass numerous resolutions condemning Israel's perceived aggression, without condemning attacks that have struck Israeli civilians.

At the UN Commission on Human Rights in 1991, the Syrian ambassador to the UN was allowed to insert the false BLOOD LIBEL against the Jews dating from the infamous DAMASCUS AFFAIR of the 1840s into the official records of the world organization. On March 11, 1997, again at the commission, the Palestinian representative was allowed to charge Israel with injecting Palestinian children with the HIV virus. The UN refuses to stop these types of false, incendiary charges. If it was not for the leadership of the UNITED STATES, the UN would certainly go further in its anti-Israel measures.

The United Nations is considered by many Jews as an incubator for ANTISEMITISM in the world. Despite its fine work in some other areas of the world, the organization fails miserably to reach any semblance of a balanced perspective on the ARAB-ISRAELI CONFLICT. As a result the UN has little credibility with Israel, which has not used its services for any of its peace talks with Arab states. Many Jews have debated whether the good the UN may accomplish in other areas still justifies retaining such a blatantly unfair organization.

Further reading: Mitchell Bard, *Myths and Facts: A Guide to the Arab-Israeli Conflict* (Chevy Chase, Md.:

American-Israeli Cooperative Enterprise, 2002); Avi Beker, *The United Nations and Israel: From Recognition to Reprehension* (New York: Simon & Schuster, 1988); U.S. House Committee on International Relations, *The Treatment of Israel by the United Nations: Hearing Before the Committee on International Relations*, 106th Congress, 1st sess., July 14, 1999 (U.S. Government Printing Office, Supt. of Docs., Congressional Sales Office, 1999).

United States

The year 2004 marked the 350th anniversary of the Jews on American soil. There the Jews found new life and new methods of expressing their Jewish heritage and beliefs. Although not completely devoid of ANTISEMITISM and discrimination, the experience of the Jews in the United States has been uniquely positive.

Successive waves of Jewish immigration have defined the development of the American Jewish community, and the organizations and institutions developed in the United States have, in turn, breathed new life into Judaism itself. Today, the American Jewish community stands as one of two main centers of Jewish life in the world, sharing the spotlight with the modern state of ISRAEL.

In 1654 the first Jews arrived on what would one day become United States soil. They were Dutch subjects, fleeing Portuguese (*see* PORTUGAL) rule in BRAZIL. Although Peter STUYVESANT (1592–1672), the Dutch administrator of the colony of New Netherland, did not want to allow them to remain, he was forced to do so by his superiors. Even so, by the 1660s this first Jewish colony in America had all but disappeared. However, the community was revitalized by the English (*see* ENGLAND) when they took over New Amsterdam and changed its name to New York. Six East Coast towns soon became home to Jewish communities: Montreal, Quebec; Newport, Rhode Island; New York; Philadelphia; Charleston, South Carolina; and Savannah, Georgia. In the year 1700 there were at least 200 Jews in the New World, and by 1776 there were about 2,500.

Up until 1720, the Jews in the New World were predominantly SEPHARDIM from Spain and Portugal, and even when some ASHKENAZIM arrived they adopted the Sephardic rites and rituals. At first the Jews were not allowed to be salespeople or craftsmen, but English rule loosened such restrictions and the history of American Jews as salesmen and entrepreneurs begun. A few incidents of anti-Jewish (*see* ANTI-JUDAISM) desecration or graffiti occurred in the colonies, but there was very little violence. The community established charitable giving, schools, and synagogues, but there were no rabbis in the New World until 1840 and the Jewish population remained small. The first Sephardic community dwindled because of ASSIMILATION and INTERMARRIAGE, but they still maintained a strong sense of kinship with world Jewry. By 1820 the Jews had achieved status in professions such as law, medicine, engineering, education, and journalism. There were about 6,000 Jews in the United States.

It was new Ashkenazic immigrants from central Europe, mostly Germany, who revitalized the American Jewish community as they arrived in large numbers after 1840. In 1840, there were 15,000 Jews in America, 20 years later, in 1860 there were 150,000. The new immigrants brought along ideas of religious reform (*see* REFORM JUDAISM), establishing Reform congregations and benevolent organizations. These Jews settled farther inland than the first Sephardic wave of immigrants, populating the towns of Albany, Syracuse, Rochester, and Buffalo in New York State; Cleveland and Cincinnati in Ohio; then Chicago, Detroit, Milwaukee, and even northern California. They worked hard to fit into American society and achieved their goals, beginning as peddlers and becoming successful businessmen. Few became professionals. There was no significant legal inequality in the United States for the Jews, and many achieved acceptance.

As the 19th century waned, however, the established German Jews were hit hard by the arrival of more than 2 million impoverished eastern European Jewish immigrants fleeing antisemitic violence in their countries of origin. The eastern European Jews did not fit the modern, sophisticated profile that the Germans had worked for decades to achieve in the American milieu. They were traditional in religious practice, little educated in modern ways, and needy. They massed in New York's LOWER EAST SIDE, creating congestion and drawing the attention of non-Jews. To ameliorate their condition, the settled German-Jewish community set up extensive social service organizations and settlement projects such as the Hebrew Immigrant Aid Society, the Hebrew Orphan Asylum, the GALVESTON PLAN, and the INDUSTRIAL REMOVAL OFFICE. In a unique move, German-Jewish leaders, who were themselves mostly Reform, funded the revitalization of the JEWISH THEOLOGICAL SEMINARY to buttress CONSERVATIVE JUDAISM; they saw the need to provide a more traditional synagogue that the new immigrants would find more comfortable than they did the established Reform congregations.

The eastern European Jews began to arrive en masse to the United States after the assassination of Czar ALEXANDER II (1818–81), and the flow of immigrants did not abate until 1923, with the implementation of severe federal restrictions. These Jews set up vibrant communities with social services and YIDDISH culture, which provided a bridge between immigrants and native-born American Jews. Many of the immigrants brought socialist ideas with them, and this translated into heavy involvement and leadership in the American labor movement. Like the German Jews before them, the eastern European immigrants worked as peddlers, eventually finding success in business. As decades passed, the gap between the German Jews and the eastern European Jews grew smaller, and the strong network of Jewish leaders came together to do what they could to help the Jews who remained in Europe during World War II and the HOLOCAUST. Though many Reform Jews did not support ZIONISM in its early years, this changed as the fate of the 6 million became clear. Even more support for ISRAEL flowed from the American Jewish community after the SIX-DAY WAR, when Israel's survival was uncertain.

After World War II, American Jews migrated to the southern and western United States. In unprecedented numbers they left the East Coast and the Midwest and found new homes and communities in Florida, Texas, and California. Soldiers returning from the war realized that there were opportunities they had not yet seen, and their eyes had been opened to the possibilities by travel. In the second half of the 20th century, Jews moved into the law and medical professions in large numbers. They were the children of peddlers and entrepreneurs, who had gained access to the American university system and took advantage of it.

Despite some incidences of antisemitism, such as Henry Ford's publication of the *PROTOCOLS OF THE ELDERS OF ZION,* the Leo FRANK lynching, and anti-immigration quotas, the United States has offered the Jews an unprecedented opportunity to live openly as Jews. Some have chosen to remain in more traditional venues, such as in Orthodox (*see* ORTHODOX JUDAISM) communities, others have chosen to participate in new American Jewish movements such as RECONSTRUCTIONIST JUDAISM and JEWISH RENEWAL, and still others have chosen to express themselves as Jews only via volunteer work or even simply by choosing Jewish friends and occupations with high concentrations of Jews. JEWISH IDENTITY, assimilation, and ACCOMMODATION are important discussions among the American Jewish leadership and the American Jewish community. The conversation continues to galvanize the community to fund Jewish education and programs that bring Jews together socially and intellectually.

As the 350th anniversary of the first Jewish community on the North American continent passes, American Jews celebrate their place in American society. Jews have found successful careers as businesspeople, entertainers (*see* ENTERTAINMENT), professionals, athletes, and politicians. They have provided for their own welfare and for the welfare of needy non-Jewish communities. The American Jewish experience continues to be full of surprises and developments as it enters a new century and continues to find new ways to ensure its survival.

Further reading: Daniel J. Elazar, *Community and Polity: The Organizational Dynamics of American Jewry,* *updated edition* (Philadelphia: Jewish Publication Society, 1995); Samuel G. Freedman, *Jew vs. Jew: The Struggle for the Soul of American Jewry* (New York: Simon and Schuster, 2001); Deborah Dash Moore, *To the Golden Cities: Pursuing the American Jewish Dream in Miami and L.A.* (New York: Free Press, 1994); Howard M. Sachar, *A History of the Jews in America* (New York: Vintage Books, 1992); Jack Wertheimer, *A People Divided: Judaism in Contemporary America* (Hanover, N.H.: University Press of New England, 1997).

United States Holocaust Memorial Museum

Several important memorials were long ago established to honor Jews who were tortured and murdered during the HOLOCAUST under Adolf HITLER. In the UNITED STATES, Jewish activists and others worked for years to build an institution in the nation's capital, Washington, D.C., to serve both as a memorial and as a Holocaust museum. Finally, the Holocaust Museum was chartered by a unanimous act of Congress in 1980; it opened its doors to the public in 1993.

In its mission statement, the museum pledges "to broaden public understanding of the history of the Holocaust through multifaceted programs," including permanent and temporary exhibitions, preservation of documents and artifacts, commemorations of the Day of Remembrance (*see* YOM HA-SHOAH), and the distribution of educational materials. An extensive Web site and impressive archive collection make it one of the premier sites for Holocaust research in the world. The unusual architecture of the building and its exhibit design evoke strong emotional reactions from the thousands of visitors who come to the museum daily.

Some controversy has surrounded the Holocaust Museum. It was built near the Mall, an indication that America sees the Holocaust as part of its own national past. The allocation of such a prominent site has prompted other communities to request similar recognition of their own suffering. It should be noted that the museum allocates prominent space to honor and remember non-Jewish victims of the Nazis as well.

Further reading: James Ingo Freed, "The United States Holocaust Memorial Museum: What Can It Be?" (Washington, D.C., U.S. Holocaust Memorial Council, 1990); United States Holocaust Memorial Museum Web site URL: http://www.ushmm.org; James E. Young and James B. Young, *The Texture of Memory: Holocaust Memorials and Their Meaning* (New Haven, Conn.: Yale University Press, 1994).

United Synagogue of America *See* CONSERVATIVE JUDAISM.

United Synagogue of Conservative Judaism *See* CONSERVATIVE JUDAISM.

United Synagogue Youth *See* JEWISH YOUTH GROUPS.

University of Judaism (UJ)

The University of Judaism (UJ) was founded in 1947 in Los Angeles, California. Its original home was the Sinai Temple, and it was housed in many different locations in Los Angeles up until 1979, when it moved into its permanent home at its Bel Air campus.

Under its first director, Dr. Simon Greenberg, and first president, Dr. David Lieber, the UJ became a successful Jewish university and local resource center. It is now led by its second president, Dr. Robert Wexler. The University of Judaism is dedicated to the pursuit of secular and religious studies, providing undergraduate, graduate, and rabbinical degrees. It also has an extensive continuing education program.

Once affiliated with the JEWISH THEOLOGICAL SEMINARY, its rabbinical school in 1996 became an independent institution. The UJ is formally recognized by CONSERVATIVE JUDAISM as a legitimate training ground for Jewish educators and Conservative RABBIS.

Further reading: Anita Diamant, *Living a Jewish Life: Jewish Traditions, Customs, and Values for Today's Families* (New York: HarperResource, 1991); University of Judaism Web site URL: www.uj.edu, accessed August 25, 2004.

Uris, Leon (1924–2003) *American novelist*

Leon Uris was born in Baltimore, Maryland. His parents were Anna, who was born in America, and William Uris, an immigrant from POLAND. Uris attended schools in Maryland and Virginia, though he never graduated from high school. He joined the UNITED STATES Marine Corps at the age of 17 and served in the South Pacific and New Zealand during World War II.

In 1950, Uris turned to writing as a full-time vocation. After covering the 1956 Suez War in Israel as a war correspondent, Uris researched and wrote his novel *Exodus,* published in 1958. It was a huge international success. This work of historical fiction was inspired by the story of the *Exodus,* a famous ship that tried to smuggle HOLOCAUST survivors past the British blockade into PALESTINE (*see* EXODUS). The novel dramatically narrated the prehistory of the modern state of ISRAEL, while capturing the inhumane treatment suffered by the Jews of Europe in the 19th and 20th centuries. The wildly successful novel won masses of supporters all over the world for Israel among ordinary Jews as well as among its huge non-Jewish readership. Smuggled copies are said to have helped spark a renewal of Jewish identity in the old Soviet Union. The book was turned into a movie starring Paul Newman.

Although he wrote popular works on non-Jewish themes such as *Trinity,* about Ireland, Uris continued to specialize in themes related to Israel and the Holocaust. His novel *Mila 18* caught the essence of the WARSAW GHETTO struggle, while *QB VII* retold the story of the despicable medical experiments done to Jews during the Holocaust. Uris also wrote *JERUSALEM: A SONG OF SONGS, THE HAJ,* and *MITLA PASS,* all on Jewish topics.

Further reading: Kathleen Shine Cain, *Leon Uris* (Westport, Conn.: Greenwood Press, 1998); Leon Uris, *Exodus* (New York: Bantam Books, 1983); ———, *Mila 18* (New York: Bantam Books, 1983).

ushpizin

Ushpizin is an Aramaic term that means "guests." Jewish tradition teaches that on SUKKOT one should invite *ushpizin* to one's sukkah, the temporary dwelling erected for the holiday, to share in the festive celebration. Hospitality is considered a key MITZVAH, or commandment, and was considered perhaps the greatest trait of Abraham and Sarah (*see* MATRIARCHS; PATRIARCHS).

The mystical students of the KABBALAH of the 16th century had the custom of inviting a different biblical "guest" to sit among the living guests in the sukkah on each of the seven nights of the holiday. The guests were Abraham, Isaac, Jacob, JOSEPH, MOSES, AARON, and DAVID. Many Jews hang pictures of these characters on their sukkah walls. A special blessing is read to welcome the *ushpizin*.

The mitzvah of *ushpizin* was meant as a reminder that one should always invite the poor to join in celebration and festive meals. The mystical tradition taught that the historical spirits of the *ushpizin* would not enter the sukkah unless the poor were welcome as well. SEPHARDIM set a special chair for the evening's guest and put sacred books on it, so that the guest could teach those who are gathered. It was customary to give any leftover food to the poor, calling it the portion uneaten by the *ushpizin*. Others invited a needy person to sit in for the biblical guest.

Liberal Jews have developed a custom to also invite seven female guests: Sarah, Rachel, Rebecca, Leah, MIRIAM, Abigail, and ESTHER.

Further reading: Philip Goodman, *The Sukkot and Simhat Torah Anthology* (Philadelphia: Jewish Publication Society, 1988); George Robinson, *Essential Judaism: A Complete Guide to Beliefs, Customs, & Rituals* (New York: Atria, 2001).

USSR *See* RUSSIA.

usury

In modern countries, the term *usury* is defined as charging an excessive rate of interest on a loan. But for most of history, the term, and its equivalents in other Western languages, simply meant charging interest on a loan.

Two passages in the TANAKH (the Hebrew Bible), Exodus 22:24 and Deuteronomy 23:20–1, specifically bar usury between Jews. Lending money was meant to be a charitable act to help someone out in difficult times, rather than an opportunity for profit. The rabbis expanded upon the prohibition, so that the lender could not benefit in any way (not just monetarily) from offering a loan. In the 16th century a "dispensation for commerce" (*hetter iska*) was developed, an arrangement in which half of the money invested in a commercial venture was considered a loan and half was considered a deposit. The practice of using a *hetter iska* document continues today among many observant Jews.

In practical terms, non-Jews are not bound by the prohibitions or protections of Jewish law; as a result, Jewish law allows Jews to borrow from and lend to non-Jews, including Christians. CHRISTIANITY imposed similar limits among Christians, which meant that moneylending as a business in the Middle Ages was often transacted between members of the two different communities.

Further reading: J. David Bleich, "Hetter Iska," in *Contemporary Halakhic Problems* (New York: Ktav, 1983): ii.376–384; Hillel Gamoran, "The Talmudic Law of Mortgates in View of the Prohibition against Lending on Interest" in *Hebrew Union College Annual* 52 (1981): 153–162; Benjamin C. Ravid, "Moneylending in the Seventeenth Century: Jewish Vernacular Apologetics," in *Jewish Thought in the Seventeenth Century* (Cambridge, Mass.: Harvard University Press, 1987): 257–283.

V

vaudeville

Vaudeville, the "theater of the people," was at one time the preeminent form of American popular ENTERTAINMENT. It had a significant impact on the American stage, movies, and television. Many of the great vaudeville entertainers were Jews.

The height of the vaudeville era began in October 1881 when the "father of vaudeville," Tony Pastor, opened his theater in New York. A typical vaudeville show would include a string of different types of acts, including comedy sketches, vocalists, dramatists, and circus-style performances. Ethnic and racial humor was widely used, helping to create multicultural awareness among Americans.

Jewish comics who first came onto the national scene through vaudeville included the MARX BROTHERS, Jack Benny, Eddy Cantor, George Burns, Fanny Brice, and Milton Berle. The singer Sophie Tucker became famous in vaudeville; she familiarized audiences with YIDDISH with her famous performances of *My Yiddishe Mama*.

Further reading: Paul Buhle, *From the Lower East Side to Hollywood: Jews in American Popular Culture* (New York: Verso Books, 2004); Lawrence J. Epstein, *The Haunted Smile: The Story of Jewish Comedians in America* (New York: Public Affairs, 2001); Neal Gabler, *An Empire of Their Own: How the Jews Invented Hollywood* (New York: Crown Publishers, 1988).

Vienna *See* AUSTRIA.

Vilna Gaon (Elijah ben Solomon Zalman) (1720–1797) *Lithuanian scholar and opponent of Hasidism*

Elijah ben Solomon Zalman, also known as the Vilna Gaon, was the foremost scholar and RABBI of Lithuanian Jews and perhaps all ASHKENAZIM in the 18th century. The title *gaon* (Hebrew for genius; *see* GEONIM) had been bestowed on many revered rabbis in medieval BABYLONIA, and the Vilna Gaon was perceived as possessing genius. The Vilna Gaon is considered the spiritual forefather of today's non-Hasidic YESHIVA system. He was based in Vilna, one of the great Jewish centers of the early modern period.

The Vilna Gaon was a great Talmudic scholar, who also studied the KABBALAH. He had a solid mastery of astronomy, grammar, mathematics, and music. His approach to TALMUD study was to search for the PSHAT, the plain, literal sense intended by the ancient rabbis. He believed that secular fields of study could help in teasing out this simple meaning. However, the study of TORAH and TALMUD was the Vilna Gaon's main purpose, and he devoted most of his waking hours to this practice. The Vilna Gaon was scrupulous in his observance of both the ethical and ritual laws. He was known for his benevolence and ethical actions as much as for his scholarship. Indeed, he would halt his Torah study to meet with a person or family in need.

After the BAAL SHEM TOV's disciples began to attract followers in the later 18th century, the Vilna Gaon became a staunch opponent of HASIDISM; he soon emerged as leader of all the opponents, who were called MITNAGDIM. He believed that the Hasidim were taking liberties in their observance of Jewish law (see HALAKHAH), and were substituting dangerous emotionalism for the traditional intellectual study of sacred texts. He also was concerned that they were moving too far away from the traditional Jewish style of prayer.

Most of the Vilna Gaon's teachings were recorded by his students, one of whom was Rabbi Chaim of Volozhin, the founder of the Volozhiner Yeshiva, which is considered the precursor for all non-Hasidic yeshivot of today. The Vilna Gaon's greatest scholarly contribution was his correction of scribal mistakes that had crept into sacred texts, especially the Talmud. His breadth of knowledge enabled him to recognize errors and correct them, so as to clarify the original intended meaning of the text.

Further reading: Immanuel Etkes and Yaacov Jeffrey Green, *The Gaon of Vilna: The Man and His Image* (Berkeley: Unversity of California Press, 2002); Betzalel Landau and Yonason Rosenblum, *The Vilna Gaon: The Life and Teachings of Rabbi Eliyahu, the Gaon of Vilna* (Brooklyn, N.Y.: Mesorah Publications, 1994).

visiting the sick (*bikur cholim*)

The HEBREW term for visiting the sick is *bikur cholim;* it is an important MITZVAH, or commandment, for all Jews. While RABBIS often visit the sick in their communities, especially pulpit rabbis,

many SYNAGOGUES have created committees or societies of laypeople whose sole purpose is to visit the sick. Early *bikur cholim* societies helped lead to the development of private hospitals sponsored by the Jewish community.

If a close relative or family member becomes seriously ill, it is permitted by Jewish law (see HALAKHAH) to violate the Sabbath (see SHABBAT) restrictions against traveling in order to visit the sick person. One famous MIDRASH (illustrative rabbinic teaching) holds that a person who visits the sick relieves the patient of one 60th of his or her suffering. There are many rabbinic guidelines for visiting the sick, designed to respect their feelings, encourage optimism and a sense of control, and enhance their dignity.

Another classic midrash portrays God as the model for *bikur cholim*. In Genesis 18 (see TORAH), God appears before Abraham (see PATRIARCHS) shortly after his circumcision, or BRIT MILAH; the midrash interprets the visit as God's way of paying Abraham a sick call. The specific Talmudic reference is in Tractate Sotah: "The Holy Blessed One visited the sick, as it is written, 'Adonai appeared to him [Abraham] by the terebinths of Mamre,' and so you must also visit the sick." Elsewhere the Talmud promises that "He who visits the sick will be spared the punishments of the next world."

The tradition of offering a prayer on behalf of the sick is well established. MOSES' prayer for his sister MIRIAM is the shortest in the Bible: "O Lord, please heal her" (Nm 12:13). The prayer for healing known as the MI SHEBERAKH is commonly recited in synagogues. One of the blessings in the AMIDAH, the central prayer in every Jewish worship service, is for healing of the sick.

Further reading: Bradley Shavit Artson, *It's a Mitzvah!: Step-by-Step to Jewish Living* (New York: Behrman House Publishing, 1995); Eugene B. Borowitz and Frances Weinman Schwartz, *The Jewish Moral Virtues* (Philadelphia: Jewish Publication Society, 1999); H. Freedman and Maurice Simon, eds., *Soncino Midrash Rabbah* (CD-ROM), 3rd ed. (Brooklyn, N.Y.: Soncino Press, 1983).

VOWS

According to the Book of Numbers (*see* TORAH), any vow made by swearing an oath using any of the names of GOD must be fulfilled. To do otherwise is to take the name of the God in vain, a violation of the Ten Commandments (*see* DECALOGUE), and a sin punishable by death. Any vow entails making a promise to God. The RABBIS did not consider a vow to be formal unless it was articulated out loud; promises to God that people make in their minds alone are not considered binding.

The rabbis of the TALMUD debated whether it was appropriate to take any vows at all, given that they could lead to the violation of a serious commandment (*see* MITZVAH). Ultimately they left it up to the individual, but provided strict warnings and laws regarding vows, primarily covered in the section of the Talmud titled Nedarim (Hebrew for "vows"). They also gave themselves the power to annul a vow made without direct intent, through a specific legal procedure. The legal formula for the KOL NIDRE prayer, recited at the beginning of YOM KIPPUR, was designed to protect Jews if they made unintentional vows to God, by invalidating such vows on a yearly basis.

Traditional Jews will state, when making promises to one another, that they do so *bli neder,* "without a vow." While it is their intention to keep their promise, they want it understood that they are not making a formal vow. Honesty is highly valued in the Jewish religion, and the reluctance of traditional Jews to take a formal vow is nothing more than showing great respect for the name of God. Despite all the literature devoted to annulling vows, promises that are ethical should always be kept and legal contracts between people are binding. Kol Nidre only applies to vows taken between a person and God, not between two people.

Further reading: Isidore Epstein, ed., "Tractate Nedarim" in *Soncino Hebrew/English Babylonian Talmud* (Brooklyn, N.Y.: Soncino Press Ltd., 1990); Stuart Weinberg Gershon, *Kol Nidrei: Its Origin, Development & Significance* (Northvale, N.J.: Jason Aronson, 1994); Jacob Neusner, *The Talmud of Babylonia: An Academic Commentary: Bavli Tractate Nedarim* (Atlanta, Ga.: Scholars Press, 1994).

W

Wallenberg, Raoul (1912–1947?) *Swedish diplomat who saved thousands of Jews*

Raoul Wallenberg is considered to have been the most effective of all the "Righteous Gentiles" (*see* YAD VASHEM), non-Jews who saved Jewish lives during the HOLOCAUST. He saved more than 100,000 Jews in HUNGARY from certain death at the hands of the Nazis.

Wallenberg was born in Sweden on August 4, 1912. His family belonged to the prestigious Wallenberg clan, which for generations had produced leaders in business and politics. His education was supervised by his grandfather Gustav Wallenberg, and he was groomed to enter the family's banking business. However, his own interests focused on architecture and trade. After serving in the military he studied architecture at the University of Michigan in the UNITED STATES, and graduated with honors in the field. He worked as an architect in SOUTH AFRICA, but after a short while, agreed to a job arranged by his grandfather at a Dutch bank in the port city of HAIFA in PALESTINE. There he was exposed to many Jews who had escaped Nazi GERMANY, and he was deeply affected by the Nazi persecution of the Jews. Wallenberg also was aware that his great-grandmother's father had been Jewish.

In 1936, Wallenberg returned from Haifa to Sweden to engage in business. He joined the company of a Hungarian Jew, Koloman Lauer, as a director, and became involved with the Hungarian food trade. Wallenberg spoke several European languages, and was able to travel freely throughout Europe, a great asset to Lauer's company. Quickly, Lauer made Wallenberg a joint owner and the international director for the company. Wallenberg traveled extensively in Nazi-occupied FRANCE, as well as Germany, and saw the Nazi threat firsthand. He also traveled to Hungary and became friendly with the Lauer family.

Hungarian Jewish nationals had been protected from the worst of the Holocaust until 1944, when the Germans began accelerating their roundup of Jews throughout the country for deportation to the death camps. The Jews of Budapest desperately sought assistance from neutral countries in the form of travel visas to flee to their lands. Sweden at first provided only 700 such lifesaving documents.

When the United States established the War Refugee Board, Wallenberg became the Swedish representative for the board in Hungary. When he arrived in Hungary in July 1944, 400,000 Hungarian Jews, mostly from the countryside, had already been shipped to the camps (*see* CONCENTRATION AND DEATH CAMPS). Approximately 230,000 Budapest Jews remained alive. Wallenberg jumped into his responsibilities with astonishing eagerness, refusing to be bogged down by bureaucracy or even legalities. He used bribery and threats to help secure the assistance of Hungarian officials. He devised a Swedish "protective pass," knowing the Nazis tended to respect official-looking documents. The document itself had no legal value, but the Nazis did in fact accept these papers, which were created with the approval of the Hungarian Foreign Ministry. Wallenberg initially won permission to provide only 1,500 of them, but he secured another 1,000 by threatening the ministry, and eventually received a total of 4,500 passes. He organized the forgery of another 9,000 passes. In addition, he hired hundreds of Jews, who were protected from Nazi deportations as his employees.

In August 1944, the Hungarian head of state Miklós Horthy dismissed his pro-Nazi prime minister and the situation for the Jews began to improve. Wallenberg began to close down his operation as the Soviet Union's troops rapidly approached Hungary. On October 15 Horthy publicly appealed for peace with the Soviet Union. The Nazis immediately seized him and took control of Hungary, putting the Jews in imminent danger once again.

Wallenberg tried to continue his operations to save the Jews, but direct Nazi rule made things much more difficult. He created Swedish safe houses, offering refuge for about 15,000 Jews. He also helped convince other neutral representatives in Hungary to start issuing protective passes for Jews. As the Nazis faced imminent defeat, they accelerated their war against the Jews. Wallenberg began issuing scaled-down one-page "protective passes" that he personally signed. Even this simple document managed to stop Nazis from seizing many groups of Jews. When the Nazis began their infamous death marches, Wallenberg personally went to offer food to the starving Jews, and he brazenly pulled those who held his passes out of the line.

When the Soviet Union occupied Hungary, only 120,000 Hungarian Jews remained alive; most of them owed their lives to Wallenberg. Wal-lenberg was arrested by the Soviet army as a suspected Western agent, and he disappeared into the Soviet prison system. The Russians claim that he died on July 17, 1947; however, prisoner testimony indicates that he was still alive in the Soviet prison system in the 1950s. One of Wallenberg's survivors, Tom Lantos, became a U.S. congressman. He initiated a process that made Wallenberg an honorary citizen of the United States in 1981. One can visit the Raoul Wallenberg Institute of Human Rights and Humanitarian Law at the Lund University in Sweden, an institute that promotes the study of human rights and humanitarian laws in honor of Wallenberg's good works in Hungary during World War II.

Further reading: John Bierman, *Righteous Gentile: The Story of Raoul Wallenberg, Missing Hero of the Holocaust* (London and New York: Penguin Books, 1995); Tom Streissguth, *Raoul Wallenberg: Swedish Diplomat and Humanitarian* (New York: Rosen Publishing, 2001).

wandering in the desert

According to the book of Exodus in the Torah, the Israelites reached Mount Sinai, where they received the Torah, only several weeks after leaving Egypt. From there they were supposed to cross the desert into the land of Canaan, the Promised Land. However, 10 of the 12 spies sent by Moses into the land of Israel on a scouting mission reported that the land was rich and fertile, but the Canaanites who dwelled there were giants. The negative report of the 10 prompted God to realize that the generation of Israelites raised in slavery would never have the correct mentality to enter and take possession of their land.

The next generation, born in freedom, would not have to depend on false idols and would be worthy of entering the land of Israel. Thus, the Israelites were "punished," condemned to wander in the wilderness for 40 years until a new generation of Israelites grew up with no slave mentality, hardened by the wilderness, knowing nothing but freedom.

The Israelite wanderings in the desert for 40 years are detailed in the book of Numbers. Wherever they wandered, they took with them the Tabernacle (*see* MISHKAN) and the Tent of Meeting so that they could properly worship God. However, according to the book of Numbers, the generation that wandered through the desert was unfaithful. Throughout their wanderings, they would complain, rebel against Moses, and question God. Sometimes they even suggested that they had been better off under SLAVERY in Egypt. Sometimes Moses had to plead with God to allow them to live at all.

Further reading: Jacob Neusner, *Sifre to Numbers: An American Translation and Explanation* (Atlanta: Scholars Press, 1986); Nahum M. Sarna, *Exploring Exodus: The Origins of Biblical Israel* (New York: Schocken Books, 1996); *Tanakh: The Holy Scriptures* (Philadelphia and Jerusalem: Jewish Publication Society, 1985).

wandering Jew

The Christian legend of the wandering Jew dates back to medieval times. According to the legend, a Jew (usually named Ahasuerus) had refused to let JESUS OF NAZARETH rest while he was carrying his cross; in punishment Jesus condemned the Jew to wander the earth until his own second coming. The legend was often used to justify anti-Jewish (*see* ANTI-JUDAISM) persecution, such as the numerous EXPULSIONS of those years.

Interestingly, most Jews remain unaware of this particular legend. They usually understand the term *wandering Jew* as a positive, or at least a neutral, historical metaphor for the ancient Hebrews as a nomadic people and for the later Jews as wanderers through the DIASPORA.

Further reading: George Kumler Anderson, *The Legend of the Wandering Jew* (Hanover, N.H.: University Press of New England, 1991); Frank Felsenstein, *Antisemitic Stereotypes: A Paradigm of Otherness in English Popular Culture, 1660–1830* (Baltimore: Johns Hopkins University Press, 1995); Galit Hasan-Rokem and Alan Dundes, eds., *The Wandering Jew: Essays in the Interpretation of a*

Christian Legend (Bloomington: Indiana University Press, 1986); Nadia Grosser Nagarajan, *Jewish Tales from Eastern Europe* (Northvale, N.J.: Jason Aronson, c1999).

Wannsee Conference

At a conference of high-level Nazi leaders at the Wannsee Villa in southwest Berlin (*see* GERMANY) on January 20, 1942, the FINAL SOLUTION to the "Jewish problem" was officially endorsed. Only the extermination of all European Jews, the conference decided, could permanently cleanse Nazi-controlled Europe. This was a turning point; until then, the Nazis had been inconsistent in handling the Jews under their control. All were targeted for persecution, and more than a million were already massacred, but there had been no general policy on how to deal with the Jews in the various occupied countries.

Attending the meeting were the operational architects for the Final Solution, Reinhard Heydrich and Adolf EICHMANN. Most of those who joined these leaders were highly educated officials representing the key departments of the Third Reich. The American television cable network HBO aired a dramatized documentary of the Wannsee Conference called *Conspiracy* in 2001. The film opens with a mundane scene of servants preparing a luncheon for the Nazis, juxtaposing the normalcy of their actions with the horrifying official plans for genocide.

Further reading: Yehuda Bauer with the assistance of Nili Keren, *A History of the Holocaust* (New York: Franklin Watts, 2001); Lucy S. Dawidowicz, *The War Against the Jews: 1933–1945* (New York: Doubleday, 1991); Mark Roseman, *The Wannsee Conference and the Final Solution: A Reconsideration* (New York: Metropolitan Books, 2002).

Warsaw Ghetto

The Warsaw Ghetto was the largest GHETTO, a walled Jewish community, established by the Nazis to contain Jews. Plans for the ghetto began

This group stands in solidarity on the anniversary of the Warsaw Ghetto uprising. They are all survivors of the Warsaw Ghetto and the Nazi concentration camps. The Warsaw Ghetto uprising represents one of the few instances that Jews were able to put up armed resistance against the Nazis during World War II and the Holocaust. *(Fritz Cohen, Government Press Office, The State of Israel)*

right after GERMANY conquered POLAND in September 1939. The goal was to isolate the Jews from the non-Jewish population. At first, however, the JUDENRAT, or Jewish Council of Warsaw under

Adam Czerniakow, managed to convince the Nazis to delay their plans for the ghetto. They argued that the Jews could be a valuable labor force for the Nazi war machine (Czerniakow eventually committed suicide rather than participate in the deportation of thousands of Jews to their deaths).

The Nazis delayed only until October 16, 1940, when the order to create the ghetto was issued. About 380,000 Jews, who made up 30 percent of the Warsaw population, were forced to move into an area covering less than 2.5 percent of the city. The ghetto was closed off from the rest of the world on November 16, 1940. Over the next 18 months, thousands of Jews from other cities and villages were moved in as well.

The ghetto was plagued by starvation and disease. Beginning on July 22, 1942, the Nazis began mass deportations of ghetto inhabitants to the death camp (*see* CONCENTRATION AND DEATH CAMPS) Treblinka. Over a 52-day period, approximately 300,000 Jews were transported to their deaths under the ruse that they were being shipped to a more hospitable location. Less than 60,000 Jews remained in the ghetto, and, in an ironic twist of Nazi cruelty, their living conditions improved without the excessive crowding that had overwhelmed living conditions.

Upon learning of the true fate of the deported Jews, approximately 500 of the remaining Jews organized a resistance group, led by Mordechai Anielewicz. Another group of 250 organized their own fighting unit. They had almost no weapons, but they now fully understood the Nazi intent to exterminate the Jews and prepared to battle until death. A few more small weapons were procured, with the limited assistance of the Polish resistance, and the Jews made their own home-made explosives. The Warsaw Ghetto fighters' preparations for resistance were complete when the next round of Nazi deportations arrived. On April 19, 1943, they received information regarding the final deportation. Sending those unable to fight into hiding, the 750 resistance fighters ambushed the Nazis when the German troops entered the ghetto. The German soldiers, taken by surprise, suffered casualties and were forced to withdraw from the ghetto. They returned better prepared but again were forced out of the ghetto. The German commander decided to burn the ghetto to the ground, building by build-

ing, but the Jewish resistance held out for 27 days against overwhelming odds.

On May 8, the resistance headquarters on 18 Mila Street was finally captured. Only a few of the resistance fighters escaped, through the Warsaw sewers. Around 300 Germans died in the resistance revolt, and approximately 7,000 Jews were killed, with another 7,000 Jews ultimately deported to Treblinka.

The fate of the Warsaw Ghetto uprising was known before it began, but it has become a lasting symbol to the Jews of resistance to evil. It has a historical importance similar to MASADA, the last stronghold of Jewish zealots who resisted the Romans, committing suicide when capture was unavoidable. In his historical novel *Mila 18,* Leon URIS captured the intensity of the struggle in the Warsaw Ghetto for a broad group of readers, just as John Hersey did for an earlier generation with his best-selling novel *The Wall.*

Further reading: Ulrich Keller, *The Warsaw Ghetto in Photographs: 206 Views Made in 1941* (New York: Dover Publications, 1984); Dan Kurzman, *The Bravest Battle: The Twenty-Eight Days of the Warsaw Ghetto Uprising* (New York: Da Capo Press, 1993); Charles G. Roland, *Courage under Siege: Starvation, Disease, and Death* (New York: Oxford University Press, 1992); Simhah Rotem and Barbara Harshay, *Memoirs of a Warsaw Ghetto Fighter: Critical Essays* (New Haven, Conn.: Yale University Press, 2001).

Weizmann, Chaim (1874–1952) *Zionist leader and first president of Israel*

Chaim Weizmann was born in Motol, RUSSIA, in the PALE OF SETTLEMENT, in 1847. He was one of 15 children, and until the age of 11 he received a traditional Jewish education. However, he then attended school in the nearby town of Pinsk, continuing his education in the secular realm. In 1899 Weizmann earned his doctorate in chemistry from the University of Freiburg in Switzerland. Then, he taught chemistry at the University of Geneva and the University of Manchester. In 1910, he became a British subject (*see* ENGLAND), and during World

War I served as director of the British military laboratories. He succeeded in developing a synthetic acetone that could be used in the production of TNT explosives and was a critical help to the Allies in the war against GERMANY.

Weizmann was the British leader for the Zionist (*see* ZIONISM) movement, and in 1917 helped convince Lord Balfour to issue the BALFOUR DECLARATION offering British support for the goal of a Jewish national home in PALESTINE. He was a highly visible leader in the overall diplomatic

Chaim Weizmann was Israel's first president from 1949 to 1952. Weizmann was a scientist and diplomat with great influence in the British government during the British Mandate over Palestine. His skills in diplomacy proved instrumental in the development of the Zionist movement and the creation of the State of Israel. *(Courtesy Embassy of Israel, Washington, D.C.)*

effort to obtain international support for the Zionist cause. In 1919, Weizmann met with the future king of Iraq, signing an agreement for cordial relations between Jews and Arabs in the Middle East. A year later, he became the leader of the world Zionist movement, serving as president of the World Zionist Organization (*see* WORLD ZIONIST CONGRESS) from 1920–31 and from 1935–46.

As Zionist leader, Weizmann helped lead the efforts to resettle Jews in Palestine. In 1921 he played an instrumental role in the creation of the HEBREW UNIVERSITY in JERUSALEM, which opened in 1925. He also helped found a scientific institute bearing his name in Rehovot. During World War II, he once again served as scientific adviser to the British military, working on the development of a synthetic rubber and high-octane gasoline to better supply Allied troops. After the war, Weizmann lobbied President HARRY S. TRUMAN to secure UNITED STATES support for the creation of the Jewish state. When Israel was born in 1948, Weizmann served as its first president, lending his stature in Israel's early years. Four years after the creation of the modern State of Israel, Weizmann passed away on November 9, 1952.

Further reading: Jehuda Reinharz, *Chaim Weizmann: The Making of a Statesman* (Oxford: Oxford University Press, 1993); ———, *Chaim Weizmann: The Making of a Zionist Leader* (Oxford: Oxford University Press, 1985); Chaim Weizmann, *Trial and Error: The Autobiography of Chaim Weizmann* (Westport, Conn.: Greenwood Publishing, 1972).

West Bank *See* JUDEA AND SAMARIA.

Western Wall *See* KOTEL.

Wexner Foundation

Leslie Wexner, owner of the clothing company Limited Brands, created the Wexner Foundation to support his philanthropic interests in 1984.

Following his own business model, he decided to target a certain niche, in this case, the development of Jewish leadership. Wexner began the work of the foundation with a donation of $500 million to support advanced graduate work in the fields of Jewish scholarship and rabbinics.

The foundation set up three different leadership initiatives, all aimed at revitalizing Jewish life and helping communities to strengthen Jewish continuity. The Wexner Graduate Fellowship Program identifies and supports high-caliber graduate students training for careers in the rabbinate, the cantorate, Jewish education, Jewish communal leadership, or Jewish studies. More than 250 individuals have participated in this program. The Wexner Israel Fellowship Program is cosponsored by the Harvard University John F. Kennedy School of Government. The program annually brings as many as 10 Israeli public officials to Harvard for a yearlong master's in public administration program, joined with intensive leadership development institutes. Over 135 Israeli officials have participated so far. The Wexner Heritage Foundation operates as a separate foundation, and focuses on volunteer leaders in the North American Jewish community, training them in an intensive two-year study program. More than 1,300 individuals have participated in the program.

Further reading: Howard M. Sachar, *A History of the Jews in America* (New York: Vintage Books, 1992); Werner Foundation Web site URL: http://www.wexner-foundation.org, accessed August 25, 2004.

White Paper

A White Paper is a type of British government document issued after an investigation of a specific event by a commission. The British government issued White Papers on PALESTINE in 1922 and 1930, but the White Paper of 1939 was by far the most significant in the pre-history of the modern state of ISRAEL.

The 1939 document essentially overturned the British government policy of supporting a Jewish homeland in Palestine, as established in the BALFOUR DECLARATION of 1917. The White Paper was issued in response to Arab concerns about the growing Jewish community. It called for the creation of a unified Palestinian state, and severely limited Jewish immigration to Palestine and the right of Jews to purchase land in the country.

In the context of the Nazi onslaught against the Jews of Europe (*see* GERMANY; HOLOCAUST), the 1939 White Paper led to a dramatic increase of Jewish illegal immigration to Palestine, directed by the HAGANAH, the Jewish community's fighting force. They smuggled as many Jews as possible into Palestine from the sea. The British resisted these efforts; by curtailing immigration, they closed the last option available to European Jews, and turned Europe into an inescapable death trap for the Jews.

Further reading: Michael J. Cohen, *The Rise of Israel: Implementing the White Paper, 1939–1941* (New York: Garland Publishing, 1987); Abraham J. Edelheit, *The Yishuv in the Shadow of the Holocaust: Zionist Politics and Rescue Aliya, 1933–1939* (Boulder, Colo.: Westview Press, 1996); Kenneth W. Stein, *The Land Question in Palestine, 1917–1939* (Chapel Hill: University of North Carolina, 1984).

widows and orphans

Judaism is grounded on a belief in ethical MONOTHEISM. The TANAKH, the Hebrew Bible and rabbinic literature (*see* MIDRASH; TALMUD) teach the fundamental notion that belief in God entails ethical behavior.

First and foremost, Judaism aims to protect those most in need of protection. The historical and theological background for this orientation is the common heritage of ISRAELITE slavery in EGYPT. God redeemed the Israelites from bondage, saving them in their time of greatest need. A repeated theme in Jewish literature and lore is God's concern for the widow and the orphan, as symbols for the weak and defenseless; the religious individual is commanded to behave in the image of God and meet that concern.

The prophets Jeremiah and Zachariah (*see* NEVI'IM) warn that one should not oppress the orphan and widow (Jer 22:3 and Zec 7:10). The author of the Psalms (*see* TEHILLIM) indicates that God takes time to watch over the orphan and the widow (Psalms 146:9). The book of Job relates that God protects the orphan because there is no one else to help, and brings blessing to the widow (Job 29:12–13).

The book of Deuteronomy contains the command of TITHING crops to support the orphan and the widow, who should be able to eat to their satisfaction (Dt 14:22, 29). If one fulfills this commandment (*see* MITZVAH), God promises divine reward (Dt 24:19). Tithing for the widow and orphan is also required when harvesting fruit (Dt 24:20–21).

In biblical times, orphans, widows, and strangers were seen as the key categories of powerless people among the Israelites. Today, the powerless are all those in need of help. Jews have created specific organizations to support widows and orphans, but Jewish philanthropy is extended to help all those who are in need (*see* TSEDAKAH; UNITED JEWISH COMMUNITIES). Rabbinic commentary explains that God stands before the individual Jew, as he or she stands before the orphan, widow, or stranger.

The sage HILLEL, as recorded in the MISHNAH, codifies the ethical responsibility of the Jew: "If I am not for myself, who will be for me? And if I am only for myself, what am I?" (Avot 1:14). The Jew must answer both questions, and act accordingly.

Further reading: David Biale, *Cultures of the Jews: A New History* (New York: Schocken Books, 2002); Harry L. Lurie, *A Heritage Affirmed* (Philadelphia: Jewish Publication Society of America, 1961); *Tanakh: The Holy Scriptures* (Philadelphia and Jerusalem: Jewish Publication Society, 1985).

Wiesel, Elie (b. 1928) *Nobel Peace Prize winner, writer on the Holocaust and Jewish themes*

Born in Sighet, Transylvania, now in ROMANIA, Elie Wiesel spent has childhood in an Orthodox Jewish

A Holocaust survivor, Elie Wiesel spreads a message of remembrance and hope in the human spirit. He is a dynamic speaker and author, and he received the Nobel Prize in 1986. *(Dan Porges, Government Press Office, The State of Israel)*

home and received a Jewish education. His world, however, turned upside down when he was imprisoned in a NAZI CONCENTRATION CAMP at the age of 15. Wiesel spent time in AUSCHWITZ and Buchenwald, where his mother and younger sister died. Wiesel's two older sisters survived, but his father died in Buchenwald just before the liberation in April 1945. The death march from Auschwitz to Buchenwald, which Wiesel and his father endured, became the subject of Wiesel's first novel, *Night*.

After the war, Wiesel lived in FRANCE and studied at the Sorbonne. In the 1950s, he was a correspondent for Israeli, American, and French newspapers. He became a UNITED STATES citizen in 1963. Wiesel's prolific writings focus on the importance of remembering the HOLOCAUST. His more than 40 published works of fiction and non-fiction include *Night* and *The Trial of God,* both of which examine Jewish sufferings experienced in concentration camps and POGROMS and the theological questions these experiences raise.

Wiesel is probably the best-known theorist on the Holocaust in the world. Drawing heavily on the Jewish mystical tradition, Wiesel argues that human beings are unique in CREATION in that they contain both earthly and divine elements. They alone can bridge the gap between Creation and the divine realm. They do this by performing mitzvot (*see* MITZVAH). People create holiness through their actions, and if they generate enough holiness, evil can be overcome. The significant means of generating holiness is through the spoken and written word. Words are powerful because they prompt memory, and memory is powerful because it prompts good intentions and actions. Wiesel says that "memory will save humanity" (Nobel Prize lecture, 1986).

In 1978, Wiesel was appointed by President Jimmy Carter as chairman of the President's Commission on the Holocaust; in 1980 he was the founding chairman of the United States Holocaust Memorial Council. Wiesel has received more than 100 honorary degrees from institutions of higher learning. He has taught at many universities, including City University of New York, Yale University, and Boston University, where he is the Andrew W. Mellon Professor in the Humanities and a member of both the Department of Religion and the Department of Philosophy. Wiesel's awards include the Presidential Medal of Freedom, the U.S. Congressional Gold Medal and the Medal of Liberty Award, and the rank of Grand-Croix in the French Legion of Honor. In 1986 he received the Nobel Peace Prize. The full text of his speech can be found on the Web site of The Elie Wiesel Foundation for Humanity, established that year.

Wiesel does not ignore the pain of the Holocaust, but he does not allow humanity to reject God

because of the suffering. He points to JOB as the role model for all who suffer, but he also calls on humanity to speak out against suffering and evil.

Further reading: Peter J. Haas, *Morality After Auschwitz: The Radical Challenge of the Nazi Ethic* (Philadelphia: Fortress Press, 1988); Elie Wiesel, *Dimensions of the Holocaust: Lectures at Northwestern University* (Evanston, Ill.: Northwestern University Press, 1990); ———, *Night; Dawn; Day* (Northvale, N.J.: Jason Aronson, 1985); ———, *Ethics and Memory* (New York: W. de Gruyter, 1997).

Wiesenthal Center

The Simon Wiesenthal Center, established in 1977, is an international Jewish human rights center. It is named after a HOLOCAUST survivor who became famous as a "Nazi hunter." Wiesenthal wanted to make sure that the Nazis did not get away with the evil they perpetrated. In the spirit of Wiesenthal's concern for justice, the center's mission is to preserve "the memory of the Holocaust by fostering tolerance and understanding through community involvement, educational outreach, and social action." The center, based in Los Angeles, has offices worldwide and is registered as a nongovernmental organization (NGO) both with the UNITED NATIONS and UNESCO. The center sponsors educational programs and social action efforts, particularly regarding discrimination, racism, terrorism, and genocide. The MUSEUM OF TOLERANCE in Los Angeles is an arm of the Simon Wiesenthal Center.

Further reading: "Virtual Memories: Mediating the Holocaust at the Simon Wiesenthal Center's Beit Hashoah—Museum of Tolerance," in *Journal of the American Academy of Religion* 64 (Winter 1996): 831–851; Wiesenthal Center Web site URL: http://www.wiesenthal.com.

wisdom literature

The KETUVIM, or sacred writings section of the TANAKH, the Hebrew Bible, contains several works of wisdom literature, including Psalms, Proverbs, JOB, SONG OF SONGS, and Ecclesiastes. They are called "wisdom literature" because they transmit wise instruction about life, usually focused on the importance of learning and a temperate lifestyle. This kind of wisdom is more than intellectual knowledge; it is the kind of learning one gains through life experience and the study of human nature. All of these texts are included in the Christian Bible (*see* CHRISTIANITY) as well.

Further reading: Abraham Cohen, *Proverbs* (London, 1952); Norman K. Gottwald, *The Hebrew Bible: A Socio-Literary Introduction* (Philadelphia: Fortress Press, 1985); Daniel J. Harrington, "Two Early Approaches to Wisdom: Sirach and Qumran Sapiential Work A," in *Journal for the Study of Pseudepigrapha* 16 (July 1997): 25–38; *Tanakh: The Holy Scriptures* (Philadelphia and Jerusalem: Jewish Publication Society, 1985).

Wise, Isaac Mayer (1819–1900) *leader of American Reform Judaism*

Isaac Mayer Wise was born on March 29, 1819, in Steingrub, Bohemia. He was the oldest son of Leo and Regina Weiss. His father taught him until the age of nine; showing early genius, he was sent for more intensive study with his grandfather, who was a doctor. After his grandfather's death Wise attended several traditional Jewish schools, and then pursued a formal education at the University of Prague and then the University of Vienna. In 1842, Wise was ordained a RABBI, and in 1844 he married Therese Bloch. Together they had 10 children.

In 1846, the Wise family immigrated to America in search of greater religious freedom. Wise took a pulpit in Albany, New York, serving there for four years and introducing many reforms to the standard worship services. He added choral singing, allowed men and women to sit together, and replaced the bar mitzvah (*see* BAR/BAT MITZVAH) ceremony with a confirmation service. Wise's reforms were ill-received by many in the congregation, and his position as rabbi was terminated. A group of congregants broke away and formed a new congregation with Wise as their leader. Four years later Wise and his family moved to Cincinnati, Ohio, so that he could become the pulpit rabbi for the Reform congregation Beth Eichim (*see* REFORM JUDAISM), where he remained until his death.

Wise emerged as a national leader among reform-minded American rabbis, organizing a union that brought 34 Reform congregations together in 1873. The organization became known as the Union of American Hebrew Congregations (UAHC), today known by the name Union of

In the 19th century, Isaac Mayer Wise attempted to unify the American Jewish community. Despite his dreams of unity, Wise's efforts eventually became the cornerstone for the development of Reform Judaism in the United States. He was the founder and first president of the Hebrew Union College, established in 1875. *(Library of Congress)*

Reform Judaism. The UAHC was the beginning of the American Reform movement. In 1875, Wise had the union establish the Hebrew Union College (*see* HEBREW UNION COLLEGE–JEWISH INSTITUTE OF RELIGION), the first Jewish seminary in the UNITED STATES. Wise served as president and as a teacher on the faculty. The college was originally intended to unify all American rabbis (*see* ORTHODOX JUDAISM), but at its first ordination ceremony in 1883, the school chose to serve nonkosher food (*see* KASHRUT). The traditionalists left the college in anger, and eventually formed their own school, the JEWISH THEOLOGICAL SEMINARY. In 1889, Wise established the Central Conference of American Rabbis. The rabbis adopted a standard prayer book to be used at their Reform synagogues. They called it the *Union Prayer Book for Jewish Worship* and based it on a previous prayer book written by David EINHORN (1809–79), a more radical reformer.

Wise's main goal was to maintain the unity of the American Jewish community, and he wrote a prayer book in 1857 called *Minhag America* that he thought would appeal to all groups. The prayer book was too traditional for reformers and too liberal for traditionalists. Although Wise did not achieve his dream of a unified American Jewish community, he made a lasting impression on Jewish life as the primary architect of American Reform Judaism.

Further reading: Howard M. Sachar, *A History of the Jews in America* (New York: Vintage Books, 1992); Sefton D. Temkin, *Creating American Reform Judaism: The Life and Times of Isaac Mayer Wise* (Portland, Oreg.: Littman Library of Jewish Civilization, 1998); Sefton D. Temkin, *Isaac Mayer Wise: Shaping American Judaism* (Oxford and New York: Oxford University Press, 1991); Isaac Mayer Wise, *Reminiscences* (New York: Arno Press, 1973).

Wise, Stephen S. (1847–1949) *American rabbi and Jewish activist*

Stephen Wise was born in Budapest, HUNGARY, in 1874. When he was a young child his family immigrated to New York, where his father, who was a RABBI, had taken a new pulpit. It was in New York that Wise received his secular and Jewish education. He was ordained a rabbi at the JEWISH THEOLOGICAL SEMINARY in 1893, and he married Louise Waterman in 1900. Together they had two children, James and Justine. Wise became a Reform rabbi (*see* REFORM JUDAISM).

In 1907, Wise founded the Free Synagogue in New York City, serving as its rabbi until his death. He became very active in social causes. In 1909, he was a cofounder of the National Association for the Advancement of Colored People. After the 1911 TRIANGLE FIRE, Wise fought strongly against SWEATSHOPS and unsafe factories. Wise's interest in social action reflected the general tendencies of Reform leaders of the era, but unlike most Reform rabbis he was an ardent Zionist (*see* ZIONISM). In 1898, he attended the Second Zionist Congress, and joined their General Actions Committee. Over time, Wise became frustrated with the established Zionist organization, and in 1914, he joined Louis BRANDEIS to develop a new American Zionist movement.

In 1916, Wise became the chairman of the Provisional Executive Committee for General Zionist Affairs, and he successfully convinced President Woodrow Wilson to support the BALFOUR DECLARATION. In 1925, Wise became chairman for the United Eretz Yisrael Appeal, and he lobbied within Reform Judaism to obtain support for the American Zionist Movement. When Hitler rose to power, Wise publicly denounced the rise of Nazism (*see* GERMANY; HOLOCAUST). He cofounded the World Jewish Congress specifically to combat Nazism, and he lobbied President Roosevelt to fight Nazism and support a Jewish state in PALESTINE. During World War II, Wise cochaired the American Zionist Emergency Council. In 1945, he became the representative of the JEWISH AGENCY at the UNITED NATIONS Conference in San Francisco, and in 1946 he testified before the Anglo-American Commission in support of the Jewish state. After a very long and productive life, Stephen Wise died in New York in 1949.

Further reading: Melvin I. Urofsky, *A Voice that Spoke for Justics: The Life and Times of Stephen S. Wise* (Albany: State University of New York Press, 1981); Carl H. Voss, *Stephen S. Wise: Servant of the People* (Philadelphia: Jewish Publication Society, 1969); Stephen S. Wise, *As I See It* (New York: Jewish Opinion Publishing, 1944).

wise men of Chelm

The phrase "wise men of Chelm" is drenched in irony. In Jewish folklore, the inhabitants of Chelm, a town in POLAND, are the brunt of endless jokes; they are always depicted as fools. The current American equivalent would be "blond jokes." Especially foolish are the so-called wise men of Chelm, the town's rabbis who propose naïve or illogical solutions to every problems. For example, one such wise man of Chelm proposed solving the town's poverty problem by having the poor drink cream instead of milk and having the rich drink milk instead of cream. When asked how to accomplish this he replied that the town should start calling milk cream and calling cream milk.

One particular story about the people of Chelm is popular in sermons for the High Holiday (*see* ROSH HASHANAH; YOM KIPPUR), as it relates to the blowing of the SHOFAR. Once a wise man of Chelm traveled to a big city. That night a fire broke out; horns were sounded, people awoke, and everyone pitched in with buckets of water to end the fire. So the wise man went back to Chelm and told his neighbors about the great way they have of putting out fires in the city: they blow horns. The next time a fire broke out in Chelm, all the people blew horns, and the city burned down. The spiritual point of the story is that the horn— or shofar—is a call to action, but that without individual action, the call accomplishes nothing.

Further reading: Francine Prose, *The Angel's Mistake: Stories of Chelm* (New York: Greenwillow Books, 1997); Steve Sanfield, *The Feather Merchants & Other Tales of the Fools of Chelm* (New York: Beech Tree Books, 1993); Solomon Simon, *The Wise Men of Helm and Their Merry Tales* (West Orange, N.J.: Behrman House, 1995); Isaac Bashevis Singer, *Shlemiel and Other Fools of Chelm* (Boston: Houghton Mifflin, 1993).

Wissenschaft des Judentums

Wissenschaft des Judentums is German for the "Science of Judaism." It refers to a particular approach to the study of Judaism and Jewish history that was developed in the 19th century in Europe, following the ENLIGHTENMENT and the rise of REFORM JUDAISM. German Jewish scholars used Wissenschaft des Judentums to analyze Judaism, Jewish texts, and the origin and development of Jewish traditions from the perspective of secular academic disciplines such as history, literary criticism, and philology. The Wissenschaft scholars wanted to place Jewish culture on an equal footing with Western European culture, and restore a sense of pride to the Jewish community. The movement was an important component of the HASKALAH, the Jewish Enlightenment, and of Reform Judaism.

In their work to reestablish intellectual respectability for Jewish scholarship, the Wissenschaft scholars often ignored matters of contemporary religious relevance. Wissenschaft des Judentums's pioneering scholar was Leopold ZUNZ (1794–1886). He was joined by other Jewish scholar of the time, including Abraham GEIGER, Zachariah FRANKEL, and Solomon RAPOPORT. Zunz's POSITIVE-HISTORICAL SCHOOL of Judaism was eventually embraced at the JEWISH THEOLOGICAL SEMINARY (JTS) in New York City, which applied it to the study of the Hebrew Bible, the TANAKH, and TALMUD. Generations of JTS scholars have carried on the Wissenschaft approach to Jewish scholarship. However, as they are affiliated with the chief rabbinical school for CONSERVATIVE JUDAISM, many JTS scholars have explored the contemporary religious relevance of their scholarly findings.

Further reading: David Ellenson, *Rabbi Esriel Hildesheimer and the Creation of a Modern Jewish Orthodoxy* (Tuscaloosa: University of Alabama Press, 1990); Albert H. Friedlander and Walter Homolka, *Jewish Iden-*

tity in Modern Times: Leo Baeck and German Protestantism (Providence, R.I.: Berghahn Books, 1995); Michael A. Meyer, *Response to Modernity: A History of the Reform Movement in Judaism* (New York and Oxford: Oxford University Press, 1988); Nathan Stern, *The Jewish Historico-Critical School of the Nineteenth Century* (New York: Arno Press, 1973).

Workmen's Circle

The Workmen's Circle (in YIDDISH, Arbeiter Ring) is a fraternal organization founded in 1892 in the UNITED STATES. It became a national order in 1900. It aimed to be a social and cultural fraternal order for labor-oriented Jews. It provided members with mutual aid, offered health and death benefits, and was dedicated to raising the educational levels of its members. In the early 20th century, the Workmen's Circle was the largest organization of its kind. Over the decades, its membership has shrunk and it has lost much of its socialist political agenda, surviving as a fraternal insurance society and a supporter of Yiddish-language culture.

The Workmen's Circle always showed strong sympathies for the labor and socialist movements around the world. It maintained significant ties with Jewish labor unions, the Yiddish labor press, and the Socialist Party. The Circle hoped to ferment positive social change in America. Many radicals belonged to the Workmen's Circle, as it gave them a safe place to share their ideas. Initially, the Workmen's Circle insisted that all its members belong to a union.

The organization was at first unsympathetic to religion. However, it was committed to Yiddish culture and established many Jewish resources, including book publishing, adult education classes, singing and drama clubs, Yiddish schools, and camps for children.

Further reading: Paul Buhle and David P. Shuldiner, *Of Moses and Marx: Folk Ideology and Folk History in the Jewish Labor Movement* (Westport, Conn.: Bergin & Garvey, 1999); Irving Howe, *World of Our Fathers: The Journey of the East European Jews to America and the Life*

They Found and Made (New York: Random House, 1997); Howard M. Sachar, *A History of the Jews in America* (New York: Vintage Books, 1993).

World Zionist Congress

The First Zionist Congress was organized by Theodor HERZL. It gathered in Basel, SWITZERLAND, on August 29, 1897, and laid the groundwork for the modern political Zionist movement. It created the Zionist Organization (which in 1960 was renamed the World Zionist Organization), adopted official policy and elected leaders for the Zionist General Council and the Zionist Executive, which was charged with carrying out the congress's policies.

The Zionist Congress remained the most important governing institution in the Zionist Organization. It continued to meet every other year in different European cities from 1897 until 1946, with an interruption during World War II.

The goal of the Congress was to facilitate the creation of a new Jewish state in PALESTINE, and to provide assistance for Palestine's Jewish settlers. The Zionist Congress lost its primary purpose after the modern state of ISRAEL declared independence in 1948. However, the World Zionist Organization still calls periodic meetings of the World Zionist Congress every four years, to maintain ties between Israel and DIASPORA supporters.

Further reading: Michael Berkowitz, *Zionist Culture and West European Jewry before the First World War* (Chapel Hill: University of North Carolina Press, 1996); William Hare, *The Struggle for the Holy Land: Arabs, Jews, and the Emergence of Israel* (Lanham, Md.: Madison Books, 1995); Howard M. Sachar, *A History of Israel: From the Rise of Zionism to Our Time* (New York: Alfred A. Knopf, 1996).

Wouk, Herman (b. 1915) *American novelist*

Herman Wouk was born in New York City in 1915. His parents, Abraham Isaac Wouk and Esther Levine, were both Russian-Jewish immigrants. His father rose from immigrant poverty to become a successful businessman. Wouk attended Townsend Harris High School and Columbia University, majoring in comparative literature and philosophy. At Columbia, he wrote for the college humor journal and authored several variety shows that caught the attention of the entertainment business. Wouk got a job offer to write for radio, and eventually became a scriptwriter. He was soon one of the highest-paid writers in the ENTERTAINMENT field.

When World War II broke out, Wouk joined the Department of the Treasury and produced radio shows to promote government bonds. After the attack on Pearl Harbor, Wouk joined the UNITED STATES Navy and was commissioned an officer. He served on the *Zane,* a destroyer-minesweeper. During his three years in the military he began work on his first novel. After his discharge, he published several books. One of them, *Slattery's Hurricane,* was filmed in 1949; he coauthored the screenplay. In 1951, Wouk published *The Caine Mutiny.* It won the Pulitzer Prize, and became one of the best-selling English-language novels in the 20th century. *The Caine Mutiny* was transformed into a stage drama, a television production, and an immensely successful movie starring Humphrey Bogart. Wouk continued to write, becoming one of the most successful authors of his era. He also taught at YESHIVA UNIVERSITY in 1958, and was a scholar-in-residence at the Aspen Institute in Colorado in 1973–74.

Judaism was a major theme in many of Wouk's novels. *Marjorie Morningstar* dealt with a young Jewish American woman's efforts to find a place for herself and her religion in the modern world. A later novel, *Inside, Outside,* was a social comedy about Jewish-American life. Wouk's novels *The*

Winds of War and *War and Remembrance* captured the history of World War II and the horror of the HOLOCAUST. Each was transformed into a large-scale television miniseries, helping to educate millions of Americans about these subjects. Wouk's novels *The Hope* and the sequel *The Glory* captured the early history of the modern state of ISRAEL. In 1959, Wouk published a perennially popular nonfiction work entitled *This Is My God,* presenting his personal perspective on Judaism, which approximated a Modern Orthodox perspective.

Further reading: Louis Harap, *In the Mainstream: The Jewish Presence in Twentieth-Century American Literature, 1950s–1980s* (New York: Greenwood Press, 1987); Herman Wouk, *Marjorie Morningstar* (Garden City, N.Y.: Doubleday, 1955); ——, *This Is My God* (Garden City, N.Y.: Doubleday, 1959); ——, *The Winds of War* (London: Collins, 1971).

Written Law (Written Torah)

The Written Law refers to the material found in the TANAKH, the Hebrew Bible. This includes the Pentateuch (the first five books of the Bible) traditionally said to have been handed down by MOSES. It also includes the prophetic material (*see* NEVI'IM) and the other sacred writings (*see* KETU-VIM). The Written Torah was codified early in the Common Era, and it is understood to be God's direct REVELATION to his people.

Further reading: Adin Steinsaltz, *The Essential Talmud* (New York: BasicBooks, 1976); Ephraim E. Urbach, *The Sages: Their Concepts and Beliefs,* trans. Israel Abrahams (reprint, Cambridge, Mass.: Harvard University Press, 1987).

Y

Yad VaShem

Yad VaShem is Israel's national HOLOCAUST museum and memorial. The name (Hebrew for "hand and name") comes from the book of ISAIAH (56:5), where it is a metaphor for a monument or lasting good name. Established by the KNESSET in 1953, the mission of Yad VaShem: The Holocaust Martyrs' and Heroes' Remembrance Authority is to document the history of the Jewish people through the Holocaust period, and teach the legacy of the Holocaust for all future generations. The institution maintains archives, a library, a school, and museums. Currently, Yad VaShem has documented 3.2 million names of Holocaust victims. The effort represents the Jewish desire to see each victim as an individual, rather than simply one of millions. Yad Vashem also maintains a tree-lined "Avenue of the Righteous among the Nations," honoring non-Jews who saved Jewish lives during the Holocaust while risking or losing their own. Some 19,700 individuals have been documented as meeting the criteria of a Righteous Gentile.

Yad VaShem is located at Har Hazikaron, the Mount of Remembrance, in JERUSALEM. Its site adjoins Har Herzl, Israel's military cemetery. It is a vast complex, consisting of tree-studded walkways leading to museums, exhibits, archives, monuments, sculptures, and memorials. One of its most powerful exhibits is the Children's Memorial, which has the appearance of a hollowed-out underground cavern. It consists of memorial candles, reflected infinitely in a dark and somber space. The candles are a tribute to the approximately 1.5 million Jewish children who were murdered during the Holocaust.

Further reading: Chana Byers Abells, *Authority, Jerusalem, Israel* (New York: Greenwillow Books, 1986); Nechama Tec, *When Light Pierced the Darkness: Christian Rescue of Jews in Nazi-Occupied Poland* (New York: Oxford University Press, 1986); *Yad Vashem Studies on the European Jewish Catastrophe and Resistance, a periodical* (Jerusalem: Yad Vashem, 1963–74).

yahrzeit

Yahrzeit is the anniversary of a person's death. Traditionally, a child, spouse, or parent observes *yahrzeit* each year for a deceased loved one, on the day the person died according to the Hebrew calendar. On that day mourners light a *yahrzeit* or memorial candle that burns for 24 hours and recite the Jewish memorial prayer, El Malei Rachamim. In addition, they attend a MINYAN, a prayer gathering of at least 10 Jews, so that they can recite the

Mourner's KADDISH. Most SYNAGOGUES read aloud the names of those whose *yahrzeits* occurred that day or week, preceding the recitation of the Mourner's Kaddish.

Yahrzeit candles are lit just before YOM KIPPUR, SHEMINI ATZERET, and the second days of PASSOVER and SHAVUOT. These are holidays when the YIZKOR, or memorial service, is conducted. The tradition of the *yahrzeit* candle is connected to the teaching of Proverbs: "The candle of God is the soul of Man."

Further reading: Anita Diamant, *Saying Kaddish: How to Comfort the Dying, Bury the Dead, and Mourn as a Jew* (New York: Schocken Books, 1999); Irving Greenberg, *The Jewish Way: Living the Holidays* (New York: Simon & Schuster, 1988); Maurice Lamm, *The Jewish Way in Death and Mourning* (New York: Jonathan David Publishers, Inc., 2000).

yarmulke *See* KIPPAH.

Yavneh

According to legend, Yochanan BEN ZAKKAI was smuggled out of JERUSALEM in a coffin by his disciples just before the Romans sacked the city, and brought before the Roman general Vespasian. Yochanan informed Vespasian that he would become emperor; if the prediction came true, Yochanan asked that Vespasian grant him the village of Yavneh as a safe haven for Jewish scholars. Vespasian agreed, and when he became emperor he fulfilled his promise.

Whether the legend is true, it is known that Yochanan established an academy of learning at Yavneh that became the foremost Palestinian academy. This academy, which eventually moved to Tiberias in the second century, contributed significantly to the formulation of RABBINIC LAW and literature, eventually including the MISHNAH and the Palestinian TALMUD. Scholars in the academy included Rabbi Eliezer ben Hyrcanus, Joshua ben Hanina, Ishmael ben Elisha, and the Rabbi AKIVA BEN YOSEPH (50–132 C.E.).

Further reading: C. H. Montefiore and H. Loewe, *A Rabbinic Anthology* (New York: Schocken Books, 1974); Solomon Schechter, *Aspects of Rabbinic Theology* (New York: Schocken, 1961); H. L. Strack and G. Stemberger, *Introduction to the Talmud and Midrash* (Minneapolis: Fortress Press, 1992).

yellow star

As the persecution of the Jews worsened in Nazi GERMANY, the government demanded that all Jews wear a yellow star, often with the word *Jude* in the center, on their clothing. The purpose of publicly identifying Jews was to further isolate them from non-Jews and invite harassment and persecution from bigots and thugs. Almost every Jew who came under the rule of the Nazis was forced to wear a six-pointed STAR OF DAVID anytime they appeared in the public domain. These stars were yellow and sometimes blue; they were often called *Judenstern* by the Nazis and *Davidstern* by Jews. The emblem was commonly found on an armband or pinned to a shirt, blouse, or coat. In some areas the badge had to be sewn onto every garment worn in public, even wedding dresses. In the concentration camps, (*see* CONCENTRATION AND DEATH CAMPS) all prisoners were forced to wear triangular badges that identified them by their category. Yellow triangle badges were used exclusively to label the Jews.

The Nazis were not the only governing body to impose dress regulations on the Jews. In fact, the first evidence of such a distinguishing mark or article of clothing appeared under Muslim rule in the eighth century. Christians (*see* CHRISTIANITY) were also required to wear distinctive signs on their clothing as a sign of their *dhimmi* status (*see* MUSLIM-JEWISH RELATIONS).

Distinctive clothing or badges for Jews appeared in Christendom as early as the beginning of the 13th century. As the centuries passed such badges were used in ENGLAND, FRANCE, SPAIN, Italy, and GERMANY. By the 16th century the badge was no longer generally imposed, and as political EMANCIPATION spread throughout Europe the practice was discarded.

These Holocaust survivors attend a ceremony on Holocaust Memorial Day, Yom ha-Shoah, at Yad VaShem in Jerusalem. They wear the yellow star that European Jews were forced to wear at all times during the Nazi persecutions and the Holocaust. *(Avi Ohayon, Government Press Office, The State of Israel)*

After the German occupation of Poland in 1939, the wearing of the yellow star was imposed once again upon the Jews. Since the Holocaust, the symbol of the yellow star has been eternally connected with Nazi Germany and the murders of 6 million European Jews in the HOLOCAUST.

Further reading: Ada June Friedman, and Philip Friedman, eds., *Roads to Extinction: Essays on the Holocaust* (New York: Conference on Jewish Social Studies, 1980); Marion A. Kaplan, *Between Dignity and Despair: Jewish Life in Nazi Germany* (New York: Oxford University Press, 1998); Gerhard Schoenberner, *The Yellow Star: The Persecution of the Jews in Europe, 1933–1945* (London: Corgi, 1969).

yeshiva (pl.: yeshivot)

A yeshiva is a traditional Jewish school. Today the term is sometimes applied to any day school (*see* JEWISH DAY SCHOOL MOVEMENT) with a traditional or Orthodox orientation. Traditionally, however, a yeshiva is a rabbinical academy devoted to the study of the Hebrew Bible, the Tanakh, TALMUD, and other rabbinic literature (*see* MIDRASH; MISHNAH). The yeshiva as an institution is a direct academic continuation of the rabbinic academies of PALESTINE and BABYLONIA that flourished during the Talmudic (first to eighth centuries C.E.) and Geonic (8th to 11th centuries) eras (*see* GEONIM). In the contemporary world, many yeshivot offer secular studies as well as traditional Jewish study.

Most yeshivot are Orthodox (*see* ORTHODOX JUDAISM) institutions, although there are several affiliated with liberal Judaism.

The Mishnah, the first Jewish law compilation, states that in every Jewish community the number of students should total at least three times the number of RABBIS on the town's rabbinical court. Some have asserted that this is the origin of the yeshiva. The Talmud further explains that every Jewish adult male should pursue full-time TORAH study two months every year.

Rabbi Chaim of Volozhin, a student of the VILNA GAON, created the modern yeshiva with his establishment of the Volozhin Yeshiva in 1800. The rabbi gathered a large number of students and standardized an intellectual curriculum for the study of Torah and Talmud. The Russian government closed this prestigious yeshiva in 1892 when it refused to introduce secular subjects into the curriculum. By this time many other yeshivot had been opened in imitation of Volozhin. Most of the non-Hasidic (*see* HASIDISM) yeshivot today follow the Volozhin academic model.

Further reading: Lucy S. Dawidowicz, *The Golden Tradition: Jewish Life and Thought in Eastern Europe* (Syracuse, N.Y.: Syracuse University Press, 1996); David Ellenson, *Rabbi Esriel Hildesheimer and the Creation of a Modern Jewish Orthodoxy* (Tuscaloosa: University of Alabama Press, 1990); Rita James Simon, *Continuity and Change: A Study of Two Ethnic Communities in Israel* (New York: Cambridge University Press, 1978).

These men study at a yeshiva in Israel. A yeshiva is a school dedicated to the study of Jewish texts, such as the Tanakh and the Talmud. Often these texts are studied in pairs. *(Moshe Milner, Government Press Office, The State of Israel)*

Yeshiva University

Yeshiva University in New York City began as Yeshiva Eitz Chaim in 1886 on New York's LOWER EAST SIDE. In 1896, the Rabbi Isaac Elchanan Theological Seminary (RIETS) was founded there, and in 1897 the New York State Board of Regents chartered Rabbi Elchanan's school. In 1915, the two schools merged; Dr. Bernard Revel served as president from 1915 until his death in 1940. Under Revel's leadership the school grew dramatically. In 1929, the institution moved to its Wilf Campus in Manhattan's Washington Heights. The study of the liberal arts was introduced in 1928 when Yeshiva College was established. In 1935, the first graduate curriculum in Jewish studies was introduced.

In 1943, Dr. Samuel Belkin became president, and he ushered in a new era of expansion. The school obtained official university status in 1945 from the New York State Board of Regents. Programs were introduced to support general and professional studies, research, and special projects to benefit different constituencies. A college of liberal arts and sciences was created for women (*see* STERN COLLEGE), in addition to graduate schools for medicine, law, social work and psychology. In 1976, Dr. Norman Lamm was elected president following Dr. Belkin's death. He expanded undergraduate study opportunities, introduced a new undergraduate school of business, and broadened the offerings within the graduate and professional schools. In 2003, Richard M. Joel became the next Yeshiva University president.

The stated mission of Yeshiva University is to serve as the flagship of Torah Umadda, the synthesis of Jewish learning and general human knowledge. Yeshiva University has become the greatest university within the centrist world of MODERN ORTHODOXY (*see* ORTHODOX JUDAISM). The University's undergraduate schools and divisions include Yeshiva College, Stern College for Women, and the Sy Syms School of Business. The graduate and affiliated schools include: Albert Einstein College of Medicine, Benjamin N. Cardozo School of Law, Wurzweiler School of Social Work, Ferkauf Graduate School of Psychology, Azrieli Graduate School of Jewish Education and Administration, Bernard Revel Graduate School of Jewish Studies, and the Rabbi Isaac Elchanan Theological Seminary. The university conducts academic and scientific research, issues publications, and sponsors service and outreach projects. It also supports the Yeshiva University Museum, an institution dedicated to providing exhibits and educational activities that chronicle Jewish life through art, architecture, culture and history.

Yeshiva University has approximately 7,000 students, 40 percent of them undergraduates. Students come from the UNITED STATES and around the world. The faculty consists of approximately 5,000 full-time and part-time staff. Yeshiva University also runs a university program in ISRAEL for men and women.

Further reading: Victor B. Geller, *Orthodoxy Awakens: The Belkin Era and Yeshiva University* (Jerusalem: Urim Publications, 2003); Jeffrey S. Gurock, *The Men and Women of Yeshiva: Higher Education Orthodoxy, and American Judaism* (New York: Columbia University Press, 1988).

yetzer ha-tov/yetzer ha-rah

In rabbinic literature (*see* AGGADAH; RABBINIC LAW) human beings are understood to be born morally neutral, possessing both a good inclination, called the *yetzer ha-tov,* and a bad inclination, called the *yetzer ha-rah.* The two inclinations are both necessary; they work in tension with one another keep a human being motivated but also properly walking on God's path by observing HALAKHAH, Jewish law.

The *yetzer ha-rah,* often translated as evil inclination, might better be described as the personal impetus that drives someone to fulfill a certain desire, whether it be pleasure, security, or material acquisition. The rabbis believed such a drive in a person is necessary, but must be mitigated by the *yetzer ha-tov,* which will rein in the urge and sanctify the desire, thus resulting in the forming of marriages, ethical businesses, and productive contributions to society.

In a famous rabbinic legend, the rabbis capture and imprison the *yetzer ha-rah,* hoping to eliminate evil. However, soon men stopped marrying, people did not want to work, and society began to fall apart. They released the *yetzer ha-rah,* and all of society's normative functions were restored. The legend emphasizes the rabbis' point, and to some extent, prefigures Freud's much-later psychological theory of ego, id, and superego.

The medieval French commentator par excellence, RASHI, notes that the inclinations of *yetzer ha-tov* and *yetzer ha-rah* come into battle especially during adolescence. The adolescent must learn to navigate between right and wrong. The familiar sexual awakening and rebelliousness of adolescents is apparently not a new, modern phenomenon.

Further reading: Hayyim Nahman Bialik, Yehoshua Hana Ravnitzky, and William G. Braude, *The Book of Legends Sefer Ha-Aggadah: Legends from the Talmud and Midrash* (New York: Schocken Books, 1992); Eugene B. Borowitz, *Renewing the Covenant: A Theology for the Postmodern Jew* (Philadelphia: Jewish Publication Society, 1991); Wendy Mogel, *The Blessing of a Skinned Knee: Using Jewish Teachings to Raise Self-Reliant Children* (New York: Penguin Books, 2001).

Yiddish

A language spoken by eastern European Jews, Yiddish is a composite of several languages, influenced by the various countries where those Jews lived. Linguistically it is a dialect of German with a heavy admixture of HEBREW words and a substantial contribution from several Slavic tongues. The word *Yiddish* literally means "Jewish," and many Jews use the words interchangeably, referring to the "Jewish language" and using Yiddish as an adjective for anything Jewish.

Yiddish uses Hebrew letters and is written from right to left. The Hebrew (and occasional ARAMAIC) words are spelled exactly as they are in Hebrew texts, even if they are pronounced differently in spoken Yiddish; the German, Polish, Russian, Romanian, Ukrainian, Slovene, and English words are spelled phonetically. The vocabulary of Yiddish is about 20 percent Hebrew and 75 percent German, with the remaining 5 percent borrowed from the aforementioned eastern European languages. While Hebrew is considered the sacred language, Yiddish has always been known as the people's tongue. Hebrew was used in the SYNAGOGUE, and Yiddish spoken in the home. The dominant language of the resident country was used for communication with the larger population, when it occurred.

Yiddish is a language rich in character, HUMOR, sarcasm, and psychology. It reflects the necessity of Jews to use humor to cope with the oppression they experienced as outsiders throughout Jewish history. The subtleties of character evinced by the multiple variations of words referring to personality types show that Jews studied people with such scrutiny in order to know them and anticipate their behaviors. Yiddish, like English, borrows from many languages and makes the words its own. It also shows an uncanny ability to infiltrate other languages and impact them. As Jewish immigrants from eastern Europe flooded into the UNITED STATES at the end of the 19th century, they brought Yiddish with them, establishing Yiddish newspapers and Yiddish theater. Yiddish terminology also influenced the comedy of VAUDEVILLE and the ENTERTAINMENT industry. Yiddish suffixes (for instance, *-nik* as in beatnik) and vocabulary (*bagel*) entered and influenced English.

Yiddish inflection, emphasis, and semantic inversion has influenced English as well, for example, "This I need!" when the issue in question is the last thing you might need. One of the most appealing and humorous features of Yiddish is its use of graphic and clinical words, such as *kishka,* which means "intestines" or a sausage-like food, to describe emotional feelings and situations: "That remark struck me in my kishkas!"

Many ultra-Orthodox Jews (*see* ORTHODOX JUDAISM), even in ISRAEL, continue to speak Yiddish in their daily lives; they maintain a lively press and publishing industry. Outside their communities, however, Yiddish has nearly disappeared among contemporary Jews. While Yiddish may fade from usage, its influence has taken root in other languages, striving to endure like the Jewish people themselves.

Further reading: Leo Rosten, *The New Joys of Yiddish, Completely Updated* (New York: Crown Publishers, 2001); Howard M. Sachar, *A History of the Jews in America* (New York: Vintage Books, 1993); Uriel Weinreich, *Modern English-Yiddish Dictionary* (New York: Schocken Books, 1987); Miriam Weinstein, *Yiddish: A Nation of Words* (New York: Ballantine Books, 2001).

yishuv

Before the modern state of ISRAEL was born as a political entity in 1948, Jewish settlers in PALESTINE were collectively called the yishuv, the word for "settlement" in HEBREW. The term was initially used to refer to the first wave of Jewish immigration to Palestine in the last two decades of the 19th century (*see* ALIYAH). At this time there were approximately 78,000 Jews living in the area called Palestine. The term *yishuv* continued to refer to Jewish settlers in Palestine until the creation of the State of ISRAEL in 1948. By this time 700,000 Jews lived in the country. Some scholars and historians refer to Jews who lived in Palestine under Ottoman rule before 1918 as the Old Yishuv and the newer Jewish immigrants to Palestine after 1922, during the time of the BRITISH MANDATE, as the New Yishuv.

The government of the yishuv was embryonic in many respects. Although it developed several paramilitary groups, such as the HAGANAH, it did not have a police force. The population of the yishuv was a minority among a large Arab majority, and the yishuv depended heavily on financial and political support from outside itself, specifically Jews living in the DIASPORA.

Further reading: Abraham J. Edelheit, *The Yishuv in the Shadow of the Holocaust: Zionist Politics and Rescue*

Aliya, 1933–1939 (Boulder, Colo.: Westview Press, 1996); S. N. Eisenstadt, *The Transformation of Israeli Society: An Essay in Interpretation* (Boulder, Colo.: Westview Press, 1985); Jeff Halper, *Between Redemption and Revival: The Jewish Yishuv of Jerusalem in the Nineteenth Century* (Boulder, Colo.: Westview Press, 1991); Dan Horowitz and Moshe Lissak, *Origins of the Israeli Polity: Palestine under the Mandate* (Chicago: University of Chicago Press, 1978).

Yizkor

Yizkor literally translates as "remember." It is the formal name for a memorial service held on YOM KIPPUR and the three PILGRIMAGE FESTIVALS: SUKKOT, PASSOVER, and SHAVUOT. During the service individuals recall with love and affection deceased relatives and pray for their souls to enjoy eternal rest.

Traditionally, Jews are obligated to observe Yizkor if they have lost a parent, spouse or child. Those who are not within this category, by traditional custom, consider it bad luck to stay in the SYNAGOGUE during this service. However, in recent years, many congregations encourage everyone to stay in the sanctuary to say prayers for the deceased in general and for the 6 million Jews who were murdered during the HOLOCAUST.

Further reading: Shmuel Yosef Agnon, *Days of Awe* (New York: Schocken Books, 1965); Irving Greenberg, *The Jewish Way: Living the Holidays* (New York: Touchstone, 1988).

Yom ha-Atzma'ut

Yom ha-Atzma'ut is the State of ISRAEL's Independence Day. The country declared its independence on the fifth day of the month of Iyar, 5708, or May 14, 1948. A war immediately broke out with the neighboring Arab states (*see* ISRAELI WAR OF INDEPENDENCE), which did not recognize Israel's right to exist, but the Israelis won the war and have celebrated their independence ever since.

The importance of this event to Judaism cannot be underestimated. The establishment of a sovereign Jewish state in the biblical Promised Land ended 2,000 years of EXILE and 50 years of Zionist (*see* ZIONISM) activism. It also created physical and mental security for Jews unknown in the past 2,000 years. Jews would never again have to fear expulsion or persecution. Given the horrors of the HOLOCAUST, which ended just a few years before, such security was more important than it had ever been.

Practices and rituals for celebrating Yom ha-Atzma'ut arose organically. Some observe memorials for fallen soldiers, while others organize military parades, and still others hold torchlight parades on Mount Herzl, the gravesite of Theodor HERZL (1860–1904), the founder of Zionism. It is also common to run races around Israel, have fireworks, and bonk people on the head with harmless toy hammers.

Eventually, the holiday split into two: YOM HA-ZIKARON was established as a memorial day for fallen soldiers; it is held one day before Yom ha-Atzma'ut, which could now become a day of unalloyed celebration.

Further reading: Joseph Heller, *The Birth of Israel* (Gainesville: University Press of Florida, 2000); Uri Milstein, *History of the War of Independence* (Lanham, Md.: University Press of America, 1996).

Yom ha-Shoah

Yom ha-Shoah is a memorial day for the HOLOCAUST. In its inception, there was considerable debate about choosing an appropriate day for the commemoration, as well as whether such a holiday should even exist. In the end, the 27th day of Nissan was chosen because it marks the beginning of the WARSAW GHETTO uprising. In 1951, the Israeli KNESSET declared the day to be Yom ha-Shoah, and in 1959 the commemoration was passed as a law. Because the holiday is still so young, a liturgy is still being developed, and there are many options for readings and prayers. All ISRAEL observes a moment of silence, and candles are usually lit and names of victims are read all

day long at public forums. The day has also become a time of remembering the horrors of the Holocaust through testimonials of survivors and documentary film showings.

Further reading: Irving Greenberg, *The Jewish Way: Living the Holidays* (New York: Touchstone, 1988); Megilat Ha-Shoah: *The Shoah Scroll: A Holocaust Liturgy* (Jerusalem: Schechter Institute, 2003).

Yom ha-Zikaron

Yom ha-Zikaron is a memorial day for Israeli soldiers who have died in battle. It is connected with YOM HA-ATZMA'UT, Israel's Independence Day, and is commemorated on the preceding day. Yom ha-Zikaron began spontaneously. In the country's early years many people used Yom ha-Atzma'ut to commemorate the loss of loved ones; then it was decided to make the day of remembrance a formal holiday. All Israel observes a moment of silence, memorial candles are lit, and flags fly at half-mast. Because Israel's wars have all been so recent, the day has a strong emotional impact; and many Israelis find it challenging to move immediately from intense sorrow to the intense joy that follows on Yom ha-Atzma'ut.

Further reading: Irving Greenberg, *The Jewish Way: Living the Holidays* (New York: Touchstone, 1988); Esther Raizen, trans., *No Rattling of Sabers: An Anthology of Israeli War Poetry* (Austin: Center for Middle Eastern Studies, University of Texas, 1995).

Yom Kippur (Day of Atonement)

Yom Kippur falls annually on the 10th of Tishri, marking the end of the Days of Awe that follow ROSH HASHANAH. According to tradition, God seals the book of life on this day, confirming each person's fate for the following year. The day is commemorated with fasting and prayers, including the mourning prayer known as YIZKOR.

In biblical times, Yom Kippur was the one day of the year on which the HIGH PRIEST of the

ISRAELITES would enter into the inner sanctum of the TEMPLE, known as the HOLY OF HOLIES; he would then emerge and call out the true name of God, and the people would prostrate themselves in awe.

A number of SACRIFICES were performed for this occasion in order to purify both the physical Temple and the people of ISRAEL. To purify the Temple, the high priest offered a sacrifice and sprinkled the blood in specific ways. To purify the people of Israel, two goats were brought forth. On one would be placed all the sins of the Israelites; this goat would be sent into the wilderness to AZAZEL (the meaning of Azazel is unknown; it may have been either a demon or the wilderness itself). The other goat would be sacrificed as a sin-offering on behalf of the people of Israel.

After the destruction of the Temple, when sacrifices could no longer be performed, the ancient RABBIS passed laws to strengthen Yom Kippur as a day of self-denial and atonement. They mandated the following prohibitions: there is to be no eating, drinking, washing, wearing of cosmetics, or sex, and leather shoes are also prohibited. Work is prohibited as well, as Yom Kippur is deemed the "Sabbath of Sabbaths" (*see* SHABBAT).

Today, the day is filled with prayers and repentance, including repeated recitations of the ritual confession, called *vidui;* if the soul is chastened, one is able to start a new year with a clean slate. For most Jews Yom Kippur is the holiest day of the year; for those who attend SYNAGOGUE only once per year, the day they attend is almost always Yom Kippur.

Further reading: Shmuel Yosef Agnon, *Days of Awe: Being a Treasury of Traditions, Legends and Learned Commentaries Concerning Rosh ha-Shanah, Yom Kippur and the Days Between, Culled from Three Hundred Volumes, Ancient and New* (New York: Schocken Books, 1965); Philip Goodman, *The Yom Kippur Anthology* (Philadelphia and Jerusalem: Jewish Publication Society of America, 1971); Irving Greenberg, *The Jewish Way: Living the Holidays* (New York: Touchstone, 1988).

Yom Kippur War

The YOM KIPPUR War began on October 6, 1973, and concluded after approximately three weeks of combat. The war was fought between ISRAEL on one side and EGYPT and Syria on the other. Israel was supported with supplies by the UNITED STATES, and Egypt and Syria received financial aid and troops from other Arab nations and supplies from the Soviet Union (*see* RUSSIA).

The president of Egypt, Anwar SADAT, who succeeded Gamal Nasser in 1970, was considered a more moderate Arab leader, but he ultimately decided to fight Israel to win back Egyptian territory that had been lost in the 1967 SIX-DAY WAR, and, some historians speculate, to redeem Egyptian honor and self-esteem. He arranged a military coalition with Syria and planned the attack on Israel, which they called Operation Badr ("full moon"). They launched their surprise attack against Israel on the holiest day of its year, Yom Kippur. Syria attacked in the Golan Heights, and Egypt attacked in the Sinai and at the Suez Canal. The initial attack caught the Israelis by surprise, and the Israeli Army suffered many casualties.

Israel quickly called up its reserve soldiers, and during the next three weeks of combat managed to push Egypt and Syria back beyond the 1967 lines. Israel was supported in its efforts by an emergency airlift mission, by which the United States sent weapons and ammunition for Israel. A total of 2,688 Israeli soldiers died in the Yom Kippur War, several thousand were wounded, and 295 were taken prisoner by the Arab forces. Israel lost 114 warplanes during the conflict. The surprise attack was humiliating for the Israeli political and military leadership, and world Jewry was horrified. Although it is forbidden to write on Yom Kippur, many RABBIS set aside the prohibition to encourage worshippers to purchase Israel government bonds while attending SYNAGOGUES on Yom Kippur. The Jewish legal justification for this act was the principle of *pekuach nefesh,* the permission to break nearly any Jewish law in an emergency in order to preserve life.

After the Yom Kippur War concluded, the former Israeli war hero, Defense Minister Moshe Dayan, was forced to resign. Prime Minister Golda Meir resigned as well, considering herself responsible. While Israel won the war, the state suddenly appeared vulnerable, as both Egypt and Syria claimed partial success in their military endeavors. U.S. secretary of state Henry Kissinger launched his famous "shuttle diplomacy" and Israel agreed to return some of the territory it had captured in the war. Kissinger hoped to broker a comprehensive peace agreement with Soviet cooperation, but this proved unobtainable.

Despite Egypt's partial success, Sadat decided that regaining Egyptian land through war was not a viable option. A few years later, through the Camp David accords, he won back all occupied Egyptian land through a peace treaty with Israel.

Further reading: Walter J. Boyne, *The Two O'Clock War and the Airlift that Saved Israel* (New York: Thomas Dunne Books, 2002); Abraham Rabinovich, *The Yom Kippur War: The Epic Encounter that Transformed the Middle East* (New York: Schocken Books, 2004); Howard M. Sachar, *A History of Israel: From the Rise of Zionism to Our Time* (New York: Alfred A. Knopf, 1996).

Yom Yerushalayim

At the conclusion of the Israeli War of Independence in 1949, East Jerusalem was still under Arab control, and Jews could not gain access to the Kotel or Western Wall, the holiest site in Judaism. In the Six-Day War of 1967, however, Israel gained control of all of Jerusalem. The country commemorates that event in the holiday of Yom Yerushalayim (Jerusalem Day). The holiday is not universally observed by Jews outside Israel, but its character is joyous wherever it is marked. Many Jews recite the Hallel psalms in synagogues along with other special prayers. Hikes to and through Jerusalem have become a common way to celebrate.

Further reading: Irving Greenberg, *The Jewish Way: Living the Holidays* (New York: Touchstone, 1988); Reuven Hammer, ed., *The Jerusalem Anthology: A Literary Guide* (Philadelphia: Jewish Publication Society, 1995).

Z

Zangwill, Israel (1864–1926) *author and Zionist*

Israel Zangwill was born in 1864 in London, the eldest son of poor Jewish immigrants from RUSSIA. After graduating from London University he worked as a schoolteacher at the Jews' Free School and began making his name as a writer. His first fiction, the 1888 novel *The Premier and the Painter,* did not do very well. After leaving teaching, Zangwill turned to journalism and founded the humorous paper *Ariel,* in which he published his own short stories. In 1892, Zangwill published his best-known and most successful work, *Children of the Ghetto,* a partly autobiographical novel that described life in the Jewish East End of London. The book was later turned into a play that was performed in both ENGLAND and the UNITED STATES to great acclaim. It was followed by *Ghetto Tragedies* (1893), *Ghetto Comedies,* and *The King of the Schnorrers* (1894).

Zangwill's best work was always on Jewish themes, which he treated with humor and sympathy. He never achieved the same success with works on non-Jewish themes. A prolific writer, Zangwill also wrote plays, such as *The Melting Pot* (1914), and nonfiction, such as *Dreamers of the Ghetto* (1898), a series of biographical studies, and *Voice of Jerusalem,* essays on Jewish themes.

Zangwill was an early supporter of ZIONISM. In the early 1890s he joined the Order of Ancient Maccabeans, an English Zionist society established in 1891, with which he visited PALESTINE in 1897. On his first visit to London in 1895, Theodor HERZL deeply impressed Zangwill, who introduced him to leading people and became his enthusiastic supporter. Zangwill attended the First Zionist Congress (*see* WORLD ZIONIST CONGRESS) in Basel in 1897, as well as the next six congresses.

In 1905 when Herzl's UGANDA plan was rejected by the Seventh Zionist Congress, Zangwill founded the Jewish Territorial Organization (JTO), which held that priority should be given to finding the most suitable territory for a Jewish homeland wherever that may be, even outside PALESTINE. Its platform rejected any Jewish historical rights to Palestine. Zangwill remained JTO's president until it was dissolved. JTO looked at and sent investigative expeditions to many places around the world, from CANADA, Mexico, and Texas to British East Africa, Australia, Angola, Cyrenaica in Libya, and IRAQ. JTO, however, never commanded the credibility and support enjoyed by the Zionist Organization, due both to its utter lack of success and its failure to acknowledge the emotional attachment that Jews have had to Palestine over the millennia. With the BALFOUR

Declaration of 1917, JTO fell into decline and was officially disbanded in 1925.

Zangwill never opposed Zionist efforts in Palestine. In a series of articles written during World War I, he did criticize the Zionist Organization for ignoring the fact that Palestine was not empty. His solution, however, was radical—he advocated a mutually agreed upon population transfer whereby Jews would move to Palestine and Arabs would move to Arabia, leading to the establishment of two states side by side. Zangwill was also active in the English suffragette movement and in the pacifist movement. He died in 1926.

Further reading: Caroline Miles Hill, *The World's Great Religious Poetry* (New York: Macmillan, 1923); Maurice Simon, ed., *Speeches, Articles, and Letters of Israel Zangwill* (Westport, Conn.: Hyperion Press, 1976); Joseph H. Udelson, *Dreamer of the Ghetto: The Life and Works of Israel Zangwill* (Tuscaloosa: University of Alabama Press, 1990).

Zealots

Our main source for information on the Zealots is Josephus, the first century C.E. Jewish/Roman historian. There may have been several groups in that era with the same name, and scholars have disagreed as to whether or not they were related.

Historians know of one extreme Jewish sect formed in 6 C.E. which rebelled against the Romans over their demand for a census. Their slogan was, "there is no king but God," and they attacked both Romans and any Jews who cooperated with them. This revolt was suppressed and their leader was executed. Perhaps an offshoot of this group were the Sicarii, named after the daggers they carried hidden in their clothes, which they used to assassinate their opponents.

When the Jewish revolt against Rome broke out in 66 C.E. the Zealots were not included by the other factions in the revolutionary council. A group of them fled to Herod's fortress atop Masada and spent the next seven years there, until they killed themselves when Roman invasion was imminent. The rest remained in Jerusalem where they fought the Romans and their opponents among the Jews. When the final siege of the city began in 70 C.E., they gained control of the Temple, killed the High Priest and elected a replacement from among their priestly followers.

In recent years, scholars have argued that the Zealots who were active during the revolt against Rome in 66–73 C.E. were neither the same group nor the descendants of those who opposed the Roman census in 6 C.E.; the Sicarii, they say, were not an offshoot of those Zealots but a separate and older sect. This school of thought holds that the later Zealot group was formed sometime in the winter of 67–68 C.E., after the revolt began, and consisted for the most part of peasants who fled to Jerusalem as the Romans swept southward from Galilee. They were equally hostile to the Jewish aristocrats and the rich, the upper priesthood of the Temple, and the Roman rulers. They were a small but highly militant and effective group that played an important part in the defense of Jerusalem and formed various alliances with and against other revolutionary groups. They did gain control of the Temple and remove the High Priest, replacing him with one of their own.

Further reading: Shaye Cohen, *From the Maccabees to the Mishnah* (Philadelphia: Westminster Press, 1987); William Reuben Farmer, *Maccabees, Zealots, and Josephus: An Inquiry into Jewish Nationalism in the Greco-Roman Period* (Westport, Conn.: Greenwood Press, 1973); Martin Hengel, *The Zealots: Investigations into the Jewish Freedom Movement in the Period from Herod I until 70 A.D.* (Edinburgh: T. & T. Clark, 1989); Morton Smith, "Zealots and Sicarii, Their Origins and Relations," in *Harvard Theological Review* 64 (1971): 1–19.

Zelophehad *See* Daughters of Zelophehad.

Zionism

Zionism is a Jewish nationalist movement born in the late 19th century, a period of rising nationalistic feelings throughout the world. Its founders believed in a Jewish return to a permanent, independent homeland in ERETZ YISRAEL. This return was seen as the only solution to the poor living conditions and shaky political situations in which Jews in the DIASPORA often found themselves.

Zionist theory understands Jewish identity as national rather than cultural or religious, and thus does not endorse the prospect of successful Jewish ASSIMILATION, or integration, into other nations and cultures. Zionism became the vehicle through which Jews around the world reemphasized the concept of the Jewish people as an autonomous political entity living in their own homeland, as they had before the destruction of the TEMPLE in the first century of the Common Era.

Jews living in western and eastern European countries had different perspectives on the nascent Zionist movement. Western European Jews lived in an ENLIGHTENMENT atmosphere, where ideas of equality and liberty pervaded general society, and where, therefore, nationalistic aspirations toward another land were unwanted. Eastern European Jews had little reason to trust in the benevolence of the peoples among whom they lived, and were more willing to imagine leaving their homes for Palestine. They also saw the example of rising nationalist thought among the minority peoples of Russia and Austria-Hungary, and adapted it to create a new kind of Jewish identity in the modern world.

Some eastern European Jews embraced Zionism as a secular vehicle to express their Jewish feelings. Eastern European Jews had a tradition of communal orientation, which secular Jews did not necessarily want to abandon. But they looked for a movement that would stress HEBREW language and literature and promote the cultural, rather than the religious, aspects of Jewish civilization.

However, a large percentage of eastern European Jews were religious; they wanted Judaism to keep a central place in the Zionist movement. When it became clear that the organized Zionist movement would emphasize cultural, economic, and social issues, many religious Zionists with-

drew their support, for fear that the movement would lack authentic Jewish characteristics.

A vast spectrum of different trends and factions arose from the very start of the the movement. They included revolutionary Zionism, socialist Zionism, political Zionism, religious Zionism, messianic Zionism, and cultural Zionism.

Theodor HERZL's idea of "messianic" and political Zionism asserted that the existence of a Jewish homeland would enable the Jews to become like all the other peoples of the world. He also believed that the state would be achieved through the agency of a benevolent liberalism, nationalism, or socialism. This belief lost much of its power after the shocking antisemitic spectacle at the DREYFUS AFFAIR in 1894.

AHAD HA'AM, an eastern European Jewish thinker, supported the idea of cultural Zionism. Unlike Herzl, he believed that Jews would never be accepted by other peoples as equals; he agreed with Herzl that Jews needed an autonomous Jewish homeland, but thought it would not look like other independent states. His cultural Zionism emphasized the development of Hebrew language, Jewish literature, art, music, history, and philosophy. Ahad Ha'am's Jewish homeland would be a Jewish cultural center that could explore these aspects of Jewish life in the modern world.

Religious Zionism insisted that Jewish law, HALAKHAH, must be at the core of any autonomous Jewish state. All the rituals, laws, and customs determined by the rabbis would govern the lives of the Jews who would live in the proposed homeland.

Socialist Zionism insisted that the new Jewish homeland be organized around socialist principles, rather than religious ones. This Zionist faction saw revolutionary change as the only way through which the Jewish people could positively alter their condition and place in the world.

The Zionist movement was born as an option for the Jewish people in a historical time period that embraced nationalistic sentiment. For some it represented the only hope of saving Jews from their increasingly dangerous life in Europe in the generations leading up to World War II. For others it became a way to retain their Jewish identity without sacrificing their ability to live in the modern, secular world. Yet in the end, the passions it evoked reflected the millennia-old desire of Jews to live safely in their own ancient homeland.

American Jews have shown varying degrees of commitment to the Zionist project. Prior to World War II, the REFORM MOVEMENT did not endorse the movement at all, and some rabbis were explicitly hostile to its aims. Their theology had no room for an actual return to the land of ISRAEL. The concept of ERETZ YISRAEL served only a metaphorical purpose, representing the desire for a messianic, utopian age for humankind. However, after the war, the Reform movement altered its opinion of Zionism and the need for the State of Israel in the face of the great dangers the world clearly still posed to Jews everywhere.

Zionism has often been criticized as a racist movement. In 1975 the UNITED NATIONS passed a resolution equating Zionism with racism. However, most Jews see Zionism as a simple attempt to win a place for Jews similar to that of hundreds of other peoples with states of their own. The existence of the State of Israel, a result of the Zionist movement's efforts, is meant to ensure the safety of all Jews living inside and outside the Land of Israel, protecting them from the ravages of racism. A Jewish state does not of necessity threaten the rights of any other individual or group, including non-Jews within the country.

Zionism remains extraordinarily relevant to present-day Jewish communities around the world. Israel remains the central focus and symbol of the unity of the Jewish people. The success of Israel has restored the pride and creativity of the Jewish people, and the country has become a center of Jewish cultural life. Finally, Israel continues to serve as a safe haven for Jewish refugees, and as a vocal advocate for Jewish issues in the world at large.

Further reading: Arthur Hertzberg, *The Zionist Idea: A Historical Analysis and Reader* (New York: Atheneum Publishers, 1959); Ehud Luz, *Parallels Meet: Religion and Nationalism in the Early Zionist Movement (1882–1904)* (Philadelphia, New York, and Jerusalem: Jewish Publication Society, 1988); Judah Leib (Leon) Pinsker, *Auto-Emancipation,* trans. Dr. D. S. Blondheim, in *Essential Texts of Zionism,* The Zionist Library, URL: http://www.geocities.com/Vienna/6640/zion/essential.html; David Vital, *The Origins of Zionism* (Oxford, U.K.: Clarendon Press, 1975).

Zionist youth movements

Historically, youth movements were a key component of the Zionist enterprise. Many of the great leaders of ZIONISM and, later, of the State of ISRAEL were first inspired and motivated during their activism in youth groups. Most of these movements were created in eastern Europe at the start of the 20th century. Their mission was to recreate a Jewish homeland for the Jews in PALESTINE. Today, such groups continue to cultivate the dream of Zionist revival in culture, education, and politics, and give Jewish teenagers the opportunity to live their ideals.

The early Zionist youth groups were critical of Jewish society. They wanted to leave behind the urban occupational structure of DIASPORA Jews and return to a more rural way of life. The largest and oldest of the major groups was Hashomer Hatza'ir. It promoted a socialist ideology that heavily influenced the politics and economics of the State of Israel. The major Israeli political LABOR PARTY grew out of this youth group (*see* KNESSET). Hashomer Hatza'ir in the Diaspora developed an educational ideology that combined scouting, personal living, and socialism to teach the skills needed to successfully make ALIYAH. Success was measured by the decision to move to Palestine and join a collective community, such as a KIBBUTZ.

The group was founded in POLAND in 1913. Its members first arrived in Palestine with the Third Aliyah of 1919–23. Over the years they founded many kibbutzim. During World War II, Hashomer Hatza'ir continued to operate underground in Nazi-occupied areas, principally in Poland, and it members were among the leaders of the ghetto uprisings. Mordechai Anielewicz, leader of the WARSAW GHETTO uprising, was a member of Hashomer Hatza'ir. In 1946, Hashomer Hatza'ir formed a political party which in 1948 became Mapam, the major faction in the Labor Party confederation. Hashomer Hatza'ir still functions as a youth movement in towns, villages, and kibbutzim in Israel, as well as in some Diaspora communities.

A second major Zionist youth movement was Betar, an acronym standing for the initials of Brit Yosef Trumpeldor. Trumpeldor (1880–1920) had died defending a Jewish settlement from Arab attack in 1920, and the group was named the Covenant of Yosef Trumpeldor in his memory. This youth movement reflected the Revisionist Zionist ideology of Ze'ev JABOTINSKY. Betar created the Herut movement in 1923, which became the nucleus for the LIKUD political party in modern Israel. The ideology of Betar was to establish a Jewish state in all of the territory of Palestine, and bring home all of world Jewry. It was a nonsocialist youth group, but it did preach the need for a just society, and imbued members with a pioneering spirit, along with military training for self-defense. Betar members also established settlements in Palestine and assisted with organizing the secret Jewish immigration to Palestine prior to World War II.

Bnei Akiva was the first religious Zionist youth movement. It was founded in JERUSALEM in 1929 with a philosophy of blending MODERN Orthodox with Zionist pioneering. In 1947 the movement's first kibbutz, Sa'ad, was founded in the northern Negev. Bnei Akiva members established kibbutzim and moshavim (*see* MOSHAV) throughout the country over the subsequent decades. In Israel today, Bnei Akiva is the youth group for the National Religious Party (NRP). The movement has some 70,000 members in Israel as well as 45,000 in Diaspora communities around the world.

Hatzofim is the Israeli Hebrew Scout Federation, founded in 1919 in Palestine. It was created to comply with the views of Robert Baden-Powell, Baron of Getwell, the founder of world scouting. The group teaches allegiance to Jewish spiritual values and culture, and personal fulfillment of Zionist ideals. Many early scouts grew up to join the HAGANAH, the Jewish self-defense organization, and established several kibbutzim. The movement is still affiliated with the World Organization of Scout Movements.

Young Judaea is the oldest Jewish youth movement in the United States. It was founded in 1909 by the Zionist Organization of America. It promotes the Zionist idea, encourages Jewish youth in their spiritual and physical development, and fosters Jewish culture and identity. The movement, operating in conjunction with American afternoon SUPPLEMENTARY SCHOOLS, was the largest youth movement in American Jewry for many years. In World War I, some of its members joined the Jewish regiments. From 1924 Young Judaea developed a cooperative relationship with Hatzofim, the Scouts organization in Palestine. In 1967, it accepted the patronage of HADASSAH, the Women's Zionist Organization of America. Today Young Judaea continues to run successful Zionist summer camps and youth groups throughout the United States.

Further reading: Abraham J. Edelheit, *The Yishuv in the Shadow of the Holocaust: Zionist Politics and Rescue Aliya, 1933–1939* (Boulder, Colo.: Westview Press, 1996); Young Judaea Web site URL: http://www.youngjudaea.org/, accessed June 16, 2004.

Zohar

Sefer ha-Zohar (Hebrew for "Book of Splendor") is one of the canonical texts of the KABBALAH, the Jewish mystical tradition. Though traditionally ascribed to Shimon Bar Yochai, a second-century scholar of the MISHNAH in PALESTINE, it was almost certainly written sometime before 1286 C.E. by MOSES DE LEÓN, a Jewish mystic who lived in Guadalajara, Castile. It is written in an artificial Aramaic that is a blend of the styles and language of the Babylonian TALMUD, rabbinic commentary, and the ONKELOS translation of the Bible.

The *Zohar* encompasses in its five volumes a multitude of different literary genres, including short midrashim (explanatory stories; *see* MID-RASH), homilies, short discourses, narrative, and parables. The main part of the *Zohar* is a biblical commentary or midrash, covering verses from the weekly TORAH portion (*see* PARSHA) through Numbers 29 and an additional three portions from Deuteronomy, the SONG OF SONGS, the book of RUTH, and LAMENTATIONS. The number of verses that are interpreted differs in each case, and the discussion often digresses to other subjects. In other sections MOSES explains to Shimon Bar Yochai the mystical meanings and reasons behind the commandments, and Bar Yochai discusses with his disciples and colleagues the mysteries of the Torah while they are on a journey to the Galilee.

By the 14th century the *Zohar* had secured a firm place in Kabbalistic literature. Its influence was solidified after the 1492 EXPULSION from SPAIN; it was the foundation for all the works of the later Kabbalists. The *Zohar* also made an impact on Judaism in general and on popular beliefs and customs.

Further reading: Arthur Green, *A Guide to the Zohar* (Stanford, Calif.: Stanford University Press, 2004); Daniel C. Matt, *The Zohar: Translation and Commentary* (Stanford, Calif.: Stanford University Press, 2004); Gershom Scholem, *Major Trends in Jewish Mysticism,* Chs. 5–6 (New York: Schocken Books, 1961); ———, *The Zohar: The Book of Splendor: Basic Readings from the Kabbalah* (New York: Schocken Books, 1995).

Zoroastrianism

Zoroastrianism was founded by the Iranian prophet Zarathustra in the sixth century B.C.E. It later became the official religion of the Persian Empire; thus, in the period of the AMORAIM, from approximately 219 C.E. until 500 C.E. the Jews of BABYLONIA were forced to contend with the religion. Judaism rejected the dualism at the core of Zoroastrianism, which posited a cosmic struggle between Ormuzd and Ahriman, the classic fight between good and evil. The ancient RABBIS saw this as a challenge to MONOTHEISM, which they viewed

as fundamental to Jewish thought. Some have argued that this dualism presented a more serious challenge to monotheism than polytheism ever had, because it addressed the problem of good and evil in the world, a problem that Judaism has wrestled with since its inception. Zoroastrianism is thought by some scholars to have had an impact on Jewish conceptions of the final judgment, in which the righteous shall be separated from the wicked.

Further reading: Mary Boyce, *Zoroastrians: Their Religious Beliefs and Practices* (New York: Routledge, 2001); George Foot Moore, *Judaism in the First Centuries of the Christian Era, the Age of the Tannaim* (New York: Schocken Books, 1971).

Zunz, Leopold (1794–1886) *scholar and founder of modern Jewish studies*

Born in 1794 in GERMANY, Zunz was orphaned early and at age seven was sent to a Jewish boarding school in Wolfenbuettel in the Duchy of Brunswick. Its curriculum was very traditional, concentrating solely on the study of TALMUD. The German language was taught only three hours a week and mathematics only one hour. Zunz learned German from the Bible translation of Moses MENDELSSOHN, which was taught on Thursdays and Fridays. It was the only German book he read until he was 11 years old. When he was 14 the curriculum of the school was modernized by a new principal and more secular subjects were introduced. By the time Zunz graduated, he was well prepared for Gymnasium (classics-oriented high school) and university. In 1821 he received a doctorate from the University of Halle for a dissertation he wrote in Latin on a work of a 13th-century RABBI.

Zunz is considered the chief founder and pioneer of WISSENSCHAFT DES JUDENTUMS, the scientific study of Judaism and its texts. In 1818 he published an essay that outlined a program for Jewish scholarship. On November 7, 1819, together with six friends, he founded the Society for the Culture and Science of the Jews, whose aim was "to work for the improvement of the situation of the Jews in the German federated states." The society published a journal, of which he was the editor, called *Periodical for the Science of Judaism,* which appeared for one year. In the first volume of the journal, Zunz published a study on the life of the medieval scholar RASHI, the first scientific biography in Jewish studies ever published. In this first volume, he also wrote a study on Jewish statistics. Though it grew in membership, the society, in which Zunz served as a vice president, disbanded in May 1824. Zunz was the only member who maintained his commitment to Jewish studies throughout his life.

In 1832 Zunz published his monumental study of the history of the Jewish sermon, which established his fame and reputation. The results of his research into AGGADAH and MIDRASH are still considered fundamental. Zunz was a prodigious scholar who published numerous works on a wide range of Jewish subjects, some of which are still influencing modern scholarship. These include a survey of Jewish names from biblical times that he wrote at the request of the Berlin Jewish community, a history of Jewish geographic literature, a history of Jewish liturgy, three books on medieval *piyyutim* (hymns) and their authors, and Bible studies.

Though his life was devoted to Jewish scholarship, Zunz refused to support the establishment of an independent institution for Jewish studies, which he feared might sever the emerging discipline from general academic and cultural life.

Zunz also refused to convert to CHRISTIANITY, which closed the doors to an academic career in any German university. To support himself, he worked variously as preacher in a Reform SYNAGOGUE (*see* REFORM JUDAISM), for which purpose he obtained a Reform ordination; editor of a Berlin newspaper; headmaster of a Jewish primary school; and finally, director of the Berlin Jewish Teacher's Seminary.

Zunz was an early, passionate supporter of the Reform movement. He expressed hostility to the dominance of Talmudic Judaism in Jewish life and called for its overthrow. Over the years, however, he moderated his views and distanced himself from Reform, ending up midway between Reform and ORTHODOX JUDAISM. Thus, for example, he advocated the retention of certain rituals like the wearing of TEFILLIN and circumcision (*see* BRIT MILAH), which the radical Reformers opposed.

Further reading: Salo W. Baron and Arthur Hertzberg, *History and Jewish Historians: Essays and Addresses* (Philadelphia: Jewish Publication Society of America, 1964); Michael A. Meyer, *Response to Modernity: A History of the Reform Movement in Judaism* (New York and Oxford: Oxford University Press, 1988); Solomon Schechter, *Studies in Judaism: Third Series* (Philadelphia: Jewish Publication Society of America, 1924); Nathan Stern, *The Jewish Historico-Critical School of the Nineteenth Century* (New York: Arno Press, 1973); Luitpold Wallach, *Liberty and Letters: The Thoughts of Leopold Zunz* (London: Published for the Institute by the East and West Library, 1959).

BIBLIOGRAPHY

Abrahams, Israel. *Jewish Life in the Middle Ages.* Philadelphia and Jerusalem: The Jewish Publication Society, 1993.

Ackerman, Walter. *Out of Our People's Past.* New York: The United Synagogue Commission on Jewish Education, 1977.

Adler, Morris. *The World of the Talmud.* New York: Schocken Books, 1963.

Alter, Robert. *The Art of Biblical Narrative.* New York: Basic Books, 1981.

Alter, Robert. *Modern Hebrew Literature.* New York: Behrman House, 1975.

Amsel, Nahum. *The Jewish Encyclopedia of Moral and Ethical Issues.* Northvale, N.J.: Jason Aronson, 1996.

Ariel, David. *The Mystic Quest: An Introduction to Jewish Mysticism.* New York: Schocken Books, 1988.

Bard, Mitchell G. *The Complete Idiot's Guide to Middle East Conflict.* Indianapolis, Ind.: Alpha Books, 2003.

Barnavi, Eli. *A Historical Atlas of the Jewish People: From the Time of the Patriarchs to the Present.* New York: Schocken Books, 2003.

Baron, Salo W. *Great Ages and Ideas of the Jewish People.* New York: Modern Library, 1983.

Baron, Salo W., and Joseph L. Blau. *The Jews of the United States, 1790–1840: A Documentary History.* New York: Columbia University Press, 1963.

Baron, Salo W., et al. *Economic History of the Jews.* New York: Schocken Books, 1975.

Bauer, Yehuda, and Nili Keren. *A History of the Holocaust.* New York: Franklin Watts, 2002.

Beinart, Haim. *Atlas of Medieval Jewish History.* New York: Simon & Schuster, 1992.

Ben-Sasson, H. H., ed. *A History of the Jewish People.* Cambridge, Mass.: Harvard University Press, 1976.

Blech, Benjamin. *The Complete Idiot's Guide to Jewish History and Culture.* Indianapolis, Ind.: Alpha Books, 2004.

Bial, Morrison Daniel. *Liberal Judaism at Home: The Practices of Modern Reform Judaism.* New York: UAHC Press, 1971.

Biale, Rachel. *Women and Jewish Law: An Exploration of Women's Issues in Halakhic Sources.* New York: Schocken Books, 1984.

Bialik, Hayyim Nachman, and Y.H. Rawnitzky, *Book of Legends: Sefer Ha-Aggadah: Legends from the Talmud and Midrash.* New York: Schocken Books, 1992.

Birmingham, Stephen. *Our Crowd: The Great Jewish Families of New York.* Syracuse, N.Y.: Syracuse University Press, 1996.

Birnbaum, Philip. *A Book of Jewish Concepts.* New York: Hebrew Publishing Company, 1964.

Blady, Ken, and Steven Kaplan. *Jewish Communities in Exotic Places.* Northvale, N.J.: Jason Aronson, 2000.

Blech, Benjamin. *The Complete Idiot's Guide to Jewish History and Culture.* New York: Alpha Books, 1999.

————. *Understanding Judaism: The Basics of Deed and Creed.* Northvale, N.J.: J. Aronson, 1991.

Bloom, Harold, ed. *Jewish Women Fiction Writers.* Philadelphia: Chelsea House, 1998.

Bonchek, Avigdor. *Studying the Torah: A Guide to In-Depth Interpretation.* Northvale, N.J.: Jason Aronson, 1996.

Borowitz, Eugene B. *Understanding Judaism.* New York: Union of American Hebrew Congregations, 1979.

Borowitz, Eugene, and Frances Weinman. *The Jewish Moral Virtues.* Philadelphia: Jewish Publication Society, 1999.

Braiterman, Zachary. *(God) After Auschwitz: Tradition and Change in Post-Holocaust Jewish Thought.* Princeton, N.J.: Princeton University Press, 1998.

Brenner, Frederic. *Diaspora: Homelands in Exile.* New York: HarperCollins Publishers, 2003.

Bridger, David. *The New Jewish Encyclopedia.* Springfield, N.J.: Behrman House Publishing, 1976.

Bright, John. *A History of Israel.* Louisville, Ky.: Westminster J. Knox Press, 2000.

Brody, Seymour. *Jewish Heroes & Heroines of America: 150 True Stories of American Jewish Heroism.* Hollywood, Fla.: Lifetime Books, 1996.

Buber, Martin, and Franz Rosenzweig. *Scripture and Translation.* Translated by Lawrence Rosenwald and Everett Fox. Bloomington: Indiana University Press, 1994.

Buxbaum, Yitzhak. *Jewish Spiritual Practices.* Northvale, N.J.: Jason Aronson, 1990.

Cahill, Thomas. *The Gifts of the Jews: How a Tribe of Desert Nomads Changed the Way Everyone Thinks and Feels.* New York: Nan A. Talese, 1998.

Chazan, Robert. *Church, State, and Jews in the Middle Ages.* New York: Behrman House, 1980.

Cohen, Arthur A., and Paul Mendes-Flohr. *Contemporary Jewish Thought.* New York: Free Press, 1987.

Cohen, Israel. *Vilna.* Philadelphia: Jewish Publication Society, 1992.

Cohn-Sherbok, Dan. *Fifty Key Jewish Thinkers.* London and New York: Routledge, 1997.

Cohn-Sherbok, Lavinia and Dan. *A Short History of Judaism.* Oxford: Oneworld, 1994.

————. *Short Introduction to Judaism.* Oxford: Oneworld, 1997.

Comay, Joan, and Lavinia Cohn-Sherbok, *Who's Who in Jewish History after the Period of the Old Testament.* New York: Oxford University Press, 1995 (1974).

Dan, Joseph. *The Ancient Jewish Mysticism.* Translated by Shmuel Himelstein. Tel Aviv: MOD Books, 1993.

————. *Jewish Mysticism.* Vol. 1, *Late Antiquity.* Northvale, N.J.: Jason Aronson, 1996.

————. *Jewish Mysticism.* Vol. 2, *The Middle Ages.* Northvale, N.J.: Jason Aronson, 1996.

Daryl, Mark Erickson, Joseph E. Goldberg, Stephen H. Gotowicki, Bernard Reich, and Sanford R. Silverburg, eds. *An Historical Encyclopedia of the Arab-Israeli Conflict.* Westport, Conn.: Greenwood Press, 1996.

Davidman, Lynn, and Shelly Tenenbaum, eds. *Feminist Perspectives on Jewish Studies.* New Haven and London: Yale University Press, 1994.

Dawidowicz, Lucy. *The Golden Tradition: Jewish Life and Thought in Eastern Europe.* Syracuse, N.Y.: Syracuse University Press, 1996.

————. *A Holocaust Reader.* New York: Behrman House Publishing, 1976.

De Lange, Nicholas. *The Illustrated History of the Jewish People.* New York, San Diego, and London: Harcourt Brace, 1997.

Diamant, Anita, with Howard Cooper. *Living a Jewish Life.* New York: HarperCollins, 1991.

Dimont, Max I. *Jews, God, and History.* New York: Signet Books, 1994.

Diner, Hasia R. *A Time for Gathering: The Second Migration, 1820–1880.* Baltimore and London: Johns Hopkins University Press, 1992.

Dobkowski, Michael N. *Jewish American Voluntary Organizations.* Westport, Conn.: Greenwood Press, 1986.

Dosick, Wayne. *Living Judaism: The Complete Guide to Jewish Belief, Tradition and Practice.* San Francisco: HarperCollins, 1994.

Epstein, Isidore, ed. *Soncino Hebrew/English Babylonian Talmud.* New York: Soncino Press, 1990.

Faber, Eli. *A Time for Planting: The First Migration, 1654–1820.* Baltimore and London: Johns Hopkins University Press, 1992.

Feingold, Henry L. *A Time for Searching: Entering the Mainstream, 1920–1945.* Baltimore and London: Johns Hopkins University Press, 1992.

Feldman, Louis H. *Jew and Gentile in the Ancient World: Attitudes and Interactions from Alexander to Justinian.* Princeton, N.J.: Princeton University Press, 1993.

Fishman, David. *Russia's First Modern Jews: The Jews of Shklov.* New York: New York University Press, 1995.

Fishman, Sylvia Barack. *A Breath of Life: Feminism in the American Jewish Community.* New York: Free Press, 1993.

Freedman, David Noel. *The Unity of the Hebrew Bible.* Ann Arbor: University of Michigan Press, 1991.

Friedland, Roger, and Richard Hecht. *To Rule Jerusalem.* Berkeley: University of California Press, 2000.

Friedman, Richard E. *Who Wrote the Bible?* San Francisco: HarperSanFrancisco, 1997.

Frankel, Ellen, and Betsy Platkin Teutsch. *The Encyclopedia of Jewish Symbols.* Northvale, N.J.: Jason Aronson, 1992.

Frymer-Kensky, Tikva, and David Novak, Peter Ochs, David Fox Sandmel, and Michael Signer, eds. *Christianity in Jewish Terms.* Boulder, Colo.: Westview Press, 2000.

Gates to Jewish Virtual Heritage. URL: http://www.jewishgates.com. Accessed on October 30, 2004.

Gilbert, Martin. *The Atlas of Jewish History.* New York: William Morrow, 1992.

———. *The Holocaust: A History of the Jews of Europe During the Second World War.* New York: Holt, Rinehart, and Winston, 1985.

———. *Israel: A History.* New York: William Morrow, 1998.

———. *The Routledge Atlas of the Arab-Israeli Conflict: The Complete History of the Struggle and the Efforts to Resolve It.* New York: Routledge, 2002.

Gilman, Sander L., and Jack Zipes, eds. *Yale Companion to Jewish Writing and Thought in German Culture, 1096–1996.* New Haven, Conn.: Yale University Press, 1997.

Ginzberg, Louis. *Legends of the Bible.* New York: Simon and Schuster, 1956.

———. *Legends of the Jews.* Philadelphia: Jewish Publication Society, 2003.

Glatzer, Nahum. *Hammer on the Rock: A Midrash Anthology.* New York: Schocken Books, 1962.

Glatzer, Nahum N. *The Judaic Tradition.* New York: Behrman House, 1969.

Goldberg, David J. *To the Promised Land: A History of Zionist Thought.* New York: Penguin Books, 1996.

Goldberg, Harvey E. *The Life of Judaism.* Berkeley: University of California Press, 2001.

Golding, Martin P. *Jewish Law and Legal Theory.* New York: New York University Press, 1993.

Goldsmith, Emanuel S. *Modern Yiddish Culture: The Story of the Yiddish Language Movement.* New York: Fordham University Press, 1997.

Goldwater, Raymond, ed. *Jewish Philosophy and Philosophers.* London: Hillel Foundation, 1962.

Goldwurm, Hersh, ed. and Shmuel Teich, *The Rishonim: Biographical Sketches of the Prominent Early Rabbinic Sages and Leaders from the Tenth–Fifteenth Centuries.* Brooklyn, N.Y.: Mesorah Publications, 1982.

Goodman, Martin, ed. *The Oxford Handbook of Jewish Studies.* Oxford: Oxford University Press, 2002.

Goodman, Philip. *Rejoice in Thy Festival: A Treasury of Wisdom, Wit and Humor for the Sabbath and Jewish Holidays.* New York: Bloch Publishing, 1956.

Gottwald, Norman K. *The Hebrew Bible: A Socio-Literary Introduction.* Philadelphia: Fortress Press, 1987.

Graetz, Heinrich. *A History of the Jews.* Eugene, Ore.: Wipf & Stock Publishers, 2002.

Green, Arthur. *Jewish Spirituality from the Bible through the Middle Ages.* New York: Crossroad, 1994.

———. *Jewish Spirituality from the Sixteenth-Century Revival to the Present.* New York: Crossroad, 1997.

Greenberg, Irving. *The Jewish Way: Living the Holidays.* New York: Touchstone, 1993.

Gribetz, Judah. *The Timetables of Jewish History: A Chronology of the Most Important People and Events in Jewish History.* New York: Simon & Schuster, 1993.

Gutstein, Linda. *History of the Jews in America.* Secaucus, N.J.: Chartwell Books, 1988.

Hartman, David. *Conflicting Visions: Spiritual Possibilities of Modern Israel.* New York: Schocken Books, 1990.

Hertzberg, Arthur. *The Zionist Idea: A Historical Analysis and Reader.* Philadelphia: Jewish Publication Society of America, 1997.

Herzog, Chaim. *The Arab-Israeli Wars: War and Peace in the Middle East.* New York: Vintage Books, 1984.

Heschel, Susannah, ed. *On Being a Jewish Feminist*. New York: Schocken Books, 1995.

Hilberg, Raul. *The Destruction of the European Jews*. New Haven, Conn.: Yale University Press, 2003.

Holtz, Barry W. *Back to the Sources: Reading the Classic Jewish Texts*. New York: Simon & Schuster, 1986.

Howe, Irving. *World of Our Fathers*. New York: Schocken Books, 1989.

Husik, Jacob. *A History of Medieval Jewish Philosophy*. New York: Jewish Publication Society, 1930.

Hyman, Paule E., and Deborah Dash Moore, eds. *Jewish Women in America*. 2 vols. New York and London, Routledge, 1997.

Idel, Moshe. *Kabbalah: New Perspectives*. New Haven, Conn.: Yale University Press, 1988.

Isaacs, Ronald H. *The Jewish Bible Almanac*. Northvale, N.J.: Jason Aronson, 1997.

———. *Mitzvot: A Sourcebook for the 613 Commandments*. Northvale, N.J.: Jason Aronson, 1996.

Jacobs, Louis. *The Book of Jewish Belief*. New York: Behrman House Publishing, 1984.

———. *The Book of Jewish Practice*. New York: Behrman House Publishing, 1987.

———. *Hasidic Prayer*. New York: Schocken Books, 1973.

———. *The Jewish Religion: A Companion*. Oxford: Oxford University Press, 1995.

Jewish Encyclopedia, The. New York and London: Funk and Wagnalls, 1925.

Jewish Learning.com. The Personal Gateway to Jewish Exploration. URL: http://www.myjewishlearning.com. Accessed October 30, 2004.

Jewish Virtual Library. URL: http://www.us-israel.org. Accessed October 30, 2004.

Johnson, Paul M. *A History of the Jews*. New York: Perennial, 1988.

Kalmin, Richard. *Sages, Stories, Authors and Editors in Rabbinic Babylon*. Providence, R.I.: Brown University Press, 1994.

Kandel, Peter, ed. *Gates of the Seasons: A Guide to the Jewish Year*. New York: Central Conference of American Rabbis, 1983.

Kantor, Mattis. *The Jewish Time Line Encyclopedia*. Northvale, N.J.: Jason Aronson, 1992.

Kaplan, Aryeh. *Jewish Meditation*. New York: Schocken Books, 1985.

Katz, Michael and Gershon Schwartz. *Swimming in the Sea of Talmud*. Philadelphia: Jewish Publication Society, 1997.

Katz, Mordechai. *Menucha v'Simcha: A Guide to the Basic Laws of Shabbos and Yom Tov*. Spring Valley, N.Y.: Feldheim Publishers, 1982.

Katz, Steven T. *Jewish Philosophers*. New York: Bloch Publishing Co., 1975.

———. *Post-Holocaust Dialogues: Critical Studies in Modern Jewish Thought*. New York: New York University Press, 1983.

Kaufman, Michael. *The Woman in Jewish Law and Tradition*. Northvale, N.J.: Jason Aronson, Inc., 1993.

Kellner, Menachem Marc, ed. *Contemporary Jewish Ethics*. New York: Sanhedrin Press, 1988.

Klein, Isaac. *A Guide to Jewish Religious Practice*. New York: Jewish Theological Seminary of America, 1979.

Kolatch, Alfred J. *Jewish Book of Why*. Middle Village, N.Y.: Jonathan David, 1995.

———. *The Second Jewish Book of Why*. Middle Village, N.Y.: Jonathan David, 1995.

Kolatch, Alfred J. *Who's Who in the Talmud*. New York: Jonathan David, 1964.

Laqueur, Walter. *A History of Zionism: From the French Revolution to the Establishment of the State of Israel*. New York: Schocken Books, 2003.

Laqueur, Walter, and Judith Tydor Baumel. *The Holocaust Encyclopedia*. New Haven, Conn.: Yale University Press, 2001.

Laqueur, Walter, and Barry Rubin, eds. *The Israel-Arab Reader: A Documentary History of the Middle East Conflict*. New York: Penguin Books, 2001.

Levenson, Jon D. *Sinai and Zion: An Entry into the Jewish Bible*. New York: HarperCollins, 1985.

Levinas, Emmanuel. *Difficult Freedom: Essays on Judaism*. Translated by Sean Hand. Baltimore, Md.: Johns Hopkins University Press, 1990.

Levitan, Tina. *The Laureates: Jewish Winners of the Nobel Prize*. New York: Twayne Publishers, 1960.

Lewis, Bernard. *The Jews of Islam*. Princeton, N.J.: Princeton University Press, 1984.

Lyman, Darryl. *Great Jews in Music*. Middle Village, N.Y.: J. David Publishers, 1986.

———. *Great Jews on Stage and Screen*. Middle Village, N.Y.: Jonathan David, 1994.

Maccoby, Haym. *Revolution in Judaea: Jesus and the Jewish Resistance.* New York: Taplinger Publishing, 1980.

Marcus, Jacob Rader. *The Jew in the Medieval World: A Source Book: 315–1791.* Cincinnati: Hebrew Union College Press, 1990.

———. *Memoirs of American Jews, 1775–1865.* Philadelphia: Jewish Publication Society of America, 1955.

Margolies, Morris B. *Twenty Twenty: Jewish Visionaries Through Two Thousand Years.* Northvale, N.J. and Jerusalem: Jason Aronson, 2000.

Martin, Bernard. *Great 20th Century Jewish Philosophers: Shestov, Rosenzweig, Buber.* New York: Macmillan, 1970.

Mendes-Flohr, Paul, and Jehuda Reinharz, eds. *The Jew in the Modern World: A Documentary History.* 2nd ed. Oxford: Oxford University Press, 1995.

Meyer, Michael A. *Ideas of Jewish History.* Detroit: Wayne State University Press, 1987.

———. *The Origins of the Modern Jew: Jewish Identity and European Culture in Germany, 1749–1824.* Detroit: Wayne State University Press, 1967.

Mihaly, Eugene. *A Song to Creation: A Dialogue with Text.* Cincinnati: Hebrew Union College Press, 1975.

Moore, George Foot. *Judaism in the First Centuries of the Christian Era, the Age of the Tannaim.* New York: Schocken Books, 1971.

Morris, Benny. *Righteous Victims: A History of the Zionist-Arab Conflict, 1881–2001.* New York: Vintage Books, 2001.

Neusner, Jacob. *Ancient Israel After Catastrophe: The Religious Worldview of the Mishnah.* Charlottesville: University Press of Virginia, 1983.

———. *Invitation to the Talmud: A Teaching Book.* New York: Harper and Row, rev. ed., 1984.

———. *The Midrash: An Introduction.* Northvale, N.J.: Jason Aronson, 1990.

———. *The Mishnah: A New Translation.* New Haven and London: Yale University Press, 1988.

———. *A Short History of Judaism: Three Meals, Three Epochs.* Minneapolis: Fortress Press, 1992.

Noveck, Simon, ed. *Great Jewish Thinkers of the Twentieth Century.* Washington, D.C.: B'nai B'rith Department of Adult Jewish Education, 1963.

———. *Great Jewish Personalities in Ancient and Medieval Times.* New York: Farrar, Straus and Cudahy, 1959.

Nulman, Macy. *The Encyclopedia of Jewish Prayer: Ashkenazic and Sephardic Rites.* Northvale, N.J.: Jason Aronson, 1993.

Olitsky, Kerry M., and Ronald H. Isaacs. *A Glossary of Jewish Life.* Northvale, N.J.: Jason Aronson, 1996.

Oppenheim, Michael. *Mutual Upholding: Fashioning Jewish Philosophy through Letters.* New York: Peter Lang, 1992.

Posner, Raphael, Uri Kaploun, and Shalom Cohen, eds. *Jewish Liturgy: Prayer and Synagogue Service through the Ages.* New York: Leon Amiel, 1975.

Prager, Dennis, and Joseph Telushkin. *The Nine Questions People Ask about Judaism.* New York: Simon & Schuster, 1981.

———. *Why the Jews?: The Reason for Anti-Semitism.* New York: Simon & Schuster, 2003.

Rabinowicz, Tzvi M., ed. *The Encyclopedia of Hasidism.* Northvale, N.J.: Jason Aronson, 1996.

Raphael, Chaim. *Festival Days: A History of Jewish Celebrations.* New York: Grove Weidenfeld, 1991.

Raphael, Marc Lee. *Judaism in America.* New York: Columbia University Press, 2003.

Robinson, George. *Essential Judaism: A Complete Guide to Beliefs, Customs, and Rituals.* New York: Pocket Books, 2000.

Rosenberg, Shalom. *Good and Evil in Jewish Thought.* Translated by John Glucker. Tel Aviv: MOD Books, 1989.

Roth, Cecil and Geoffrey Wigoder, eds. *Encyclopaedia Judaica.* Jerusalem: Keter Publishing House, 1972.

———. *Encyclopedia Judaica.* CD-ROM ed., Version 1.0. Shaker Heights, Ohio: Judaica Multimedia, 1997.

Roth, Norman. *Medieval Jewish Civilization: An Encyclopedia.* London and New York: Routledge, 2002.

Sachar, Howard M. *The Course of Modern Jewish History: The Classic History of the Jewish People, from the Eighteenth Century to the Present Day.* New York: Vintage Books, 1990.

Sachar, Howard M. *A History of Israel from the Rise of Zionism to Our Time.* New York: Alfred A. Knopf, 1996.

———. *A History of the Jews in America.* New York: Vintage Books, 1993.

Scheindlin, Raymond P. *A Short History of the Jewish People: From Legendary Times to Modern Statehood.* Oxford and New York: Oxford University Press, 1998.

Schneerson, Menachem M. *Timeless Patterns in Time: Chassidic Insights into the Cycle of the Jewish Year.* Adapted by Eliyahu Touger, translated by Uri Kaploun. 2 vols. Brooklyn, N.Y.: Kehot Publication Society, 1994.

Scholem, Gershom. *Kabbalah.* New York: Meridian Books, 1974.

———. *On the Mystical Shape of the Godhead: Basic Concepts in the Kabbalah.* Translated by Joachim Neugroschel. New York: Schocken Books, 1991.

———. *On the Possibility of Jewish Mysticism in Our Time and Other Essays.* Edited by Avraham Shapira, translated by Jonathan Chipman. Philadelphia: Jewish Publication Society, 1997.

Schwartz, Howard. *Reimagining the Bible: The Storytelling of the Rabbis.* Oxford: Oxford University Press, 1998.

Segev, Tom. *One Palestine Complete: Jews and Arabs under the British Mandate.* New York: Henry Holt, 2000.

Seltzer, Robert M., ed., *Judaism: A People and its History.* New York: Macmillan, 1989.

Shapiro, Edward S. *A Time for Healing: American Jewry since World War II.* Baltimore and London: Johns Hopkins University Press, 1992.

Sherman, Moshe D. *Orthodox Judaism in America: A Biographical Dictionary and Sourcebook.* Westport, Conn.: Greenwood Press, 1996.

Shimoni, Gideon. *The Zionist Ideology.* Hanover, N.H.: Brandeis University Press/University Press of New England, 1995.

Siegel, Richard, Michael Strassfeld, and Sharon Strassfeld. *The First Jewish Catalog: A Do-It-Yourself Kit.* Philadelphia: Jewish Publication Society of America, 1973.

Slater, Elinor, and Robert Slater. *Great Jewish Men.* Middle Village, N.Y.: Jonathan David, 1998.

———. *Great Jewish Women.* Middle Village, N.Y.: Jonathan David, 1994.

———. *Great Moments in Jewish History.* Middle Village, N.Y.: Jonathan David, 1998.

Slater, Robert. *Great Jews in Sports.* Middle Village, N.Y. : J. David, 1983.

Snyder, Louis L. *Encyclopedia of the Third Reich.* New York: Marlowe, 1997.

Sokoloff, Naomi B., Anne Lapidus Lerner, and Anita Norich. *Gender and Text in Modern Hebrew and Yiddish Literature.* New York and Jerusalem: Jewish Theological Seminary of America, 1992.

Soncino, Rifat, and Daniel B. Syme. *What Happens After I Die: Jewish Views of Life After Death.* New York: UAHC Press, 1990.

Sorin, Gerald. *A Time for Building: The Third Migration, 1880–1920.* Baltimore and London: Johns Hopkins University Press, 1992.

Spector, Shmuel, and Geoffrey Wigoder, eds. *The Encyclopedia of Jewish Life: Before and During the Holocaust.* New York: New York University Press, 2001.

Steinberg, Avraham, and Fred Rosner. *Encyclopedia of Jewish Medical Ethics: A Compilation of Jewish Medical Law on All Topics of Medical Interest.* New York: Feldheim, 2003.

Steinberg, Milton. *Basic Judaism.* Northvale, N.J.: J. Aronson, 1987.

Steinsaltz, Adin. *The Essential Talmud.* New York: Basic Books, 1976.

———. *The Talmud: A Reference Guide.* New York: Random House, 1989.

Strack, H. L., and G. Stemberger. *Introduction to the Talmud and Midrash.* Minneapolis: Fortress, Press, 1992.

Strassfeld, Michael and Sharon Strassfeld. *The Second Jewish Catalog: Sources and Resources.* Philadelphia: Jewish Publication Society of America, 1976.

———. *The Third Jewish Catalog: Creating Community: With a Cumulative Index to All 3 Indexes.* Philadelphia: Jewish Publication Society of America, 1980.

Syme, Daniel B., and Cindy Frenkel Kanter, *100 Essential Books for Jewish Readers.* Secaucus, N.J.: Carol Publishing Group, 1998.

Taitz, Emily. *JPS Guide to Jewish Women.* Philadelphia: Jewish Publication Society, 2003.

Tanakh: The Holy Scriptures. Philadelphia, New York, and Jerusalem: Jewish Publication Society, 1985.

Tcherikover, Victor. *Hellenistic Civilization and the Jews.* New York: Atheneum, 1975.

Telushkin, Joseph. *Biblical Literacy: The Most Important People, Events, and Ideas of the Hebrew Bible.* New York: William Morrow, 1997.

———. *The Book of Jewish Values: A Day-by-Day Guide to Ethical Living.* New York: Bell Tower, 2000.

———. *Jewish Literacy: The Most Important Things to Know About the Jewish Religion, Its People, and Its History.* New York: William Morrow, 1991.

———. *Jewish Wisdom: Ethical, Spiritual, and Historical Lessons from the Great Works and Thinkers.* New York: William Morrow, 1994.

Terry, Michael, ed. *Reader's Guide to Judaism.* Chicago and London: Fitzroy Dearborn, 2000.

Visotzky, Burton. *Reading the Book: Making the Bible a Timeless Text.* New York: Schocken Books, 1996.

Waskow, Arthur. *Seasons of Our Joy: A Handbook of Jewish Festivals.* New York: Summit Books, 1982.

Waxman, Meyer. *A History of Jewish Literature.* New York: T. Yoseloff, 1960.

Weiner, Herbert. *9½ Mystics: The Kabbala Today.* New York: Holt, Rinehart, and Winston, 1969.

Weisbard, Phyllis Holman, and David Schonberg, eds. *Jewish Law: Bibliography of Sources and Scholarship in English.* Littleton, Colo.: F. B. Rothman, 1989.

Weiss, Saul. *Insights: A Talmudic Treasury.* New York: Philipp Feldheim, Inc., 1996.

Werblowsky, R. J. Zwi, and Geoffrey Wigoder. *The Oxford Dictionary of the Jewish Religion.* New York: Oxford University Press, 1997.

Wigoder, Geoffrey. *The Holocaust.* 4 vols. Danbury, Conn.: Grolier Educational, 1997.

———. *The New Standard Jewish Encyclopedia.* New York: Facts On File, 1992.

———. *Dictionary of Jewish Biography.* New York: Simon and Schuster, 1991.

———. *Encyclopedic Dictionary of Judaica.* New York and Paris: Keter Publishing House Jerusalem, 1974.

———. *The New Encyclopedia of Zionism and Israel.* Madison, N.J.: Fairleigh Dickinson University Press, 1994.

Wigoder, Geoffrey, and R. J. Zwi Werblowsky, eds. *The Encyclopedia of the Jewish Religion.* New York: Adama Books, 1986.

Wistrich, Robert S. *Antisemitism: The Longest Hatred.* New York: Pantheon Books, 1991.

Wistrich, Robert S. *Who's Who in Nazi Germany.* London and New York: Routledge, 1995.

INDEX